HARVARD ORIENTAL SERIES

Edited by MICHAEL WITZEL

VOLUME FIFTY-TWO

ŚAUNAKĪYĀ CATURĀDHYĀYIKĀ

A Prātiśākhya of the Śaunakīya Atharvaveda

With
the commentaries

Caturādhyāyībhāṣya, Bhārgava-Bhāskara-Vṛtti
and
Pañcasandhi

**Critically edited,
translated & annotated**

by

Madhav M. Deshpande

PUBLISHED BY THE DEPARTMENT
OF SANSKRIT AND INDIAN STUDIES,
HARVARD UNIVERSITY

DISTRIBUTED BY
HARVARD UNIVERSITY PRESS
CAMBRIDGE, MASSACHUSETTS
AND LONDON, ENGLAND

1997

Printed in the United States of America

For information write to Editor, Harvard Oriental Series,
Department of Sanskrit and Indian Studies,
2 Divinity Avenue, Cambridge MA 02138, USA
phone: 617-495 3295; email: witzel@fas.harvard.edu

Library of Congress Cataloguing in Publication Data

Vedas. Prātiśākhya.

Śaunakīyā Caturādhyāyikā. *A Prātiśākhya of the Śaunakīya Atharvaveda* with the commentaries Caturādhyāyībhāṣya, Bhārgava-Bhāskara-Vṛtti and Pañcasandhi / critically edited, translated & annotated by Madhav M. Deshpande

(Harvard Oriental Series; v. 52)
ISBN 0-674-78987-3

I. Deshpande, Madhav M., 1946- II. Title
III. Series: Harvard Oriental Series; 52

CIP

Dedicated
with
affection
to
my
loving twin daughters
Manjushree & Madhushree

Preface

In her Foreword to Tatyana Elizarenkova's fascinating work *Language and Style of the Vedic Ṛṣis* (SUNY Press, 1993), Wendy Doniger makes an interesting distinction between "the modern, trendy, obscure" disciplines such as semiotics, and "the ancient, dusty, arcane discipline of Vedic philology." By this yardstick, the present work proudly fits within the latter type. This work simultaneously continues and criticizes the work of the great American Sanskritist, W.D. Whitney, who published the first edition of this text with the title Atharvaveda-Prātiśākhya in 1862, and Surya Kanta, who produced the magnificent edition of a different Atharva-Prātiśākhya in 1939. It is the result of my own research that spans more than two decades. During this period, many trendy varieties of linguistics came to pass. Fortunately perhaps, I have been more interested in the history of both modern and ancient linguistic theory, than in becoming an ardent follower of any one of the transient theories. I have used my knowledge of modern phonetics and phonology to elucidate the ancient theories of the Prātiśākhyas so that they can be made comprehensible to a modern reader. However, here my approach has been primarily textual and historical, rather than theoretical.

It was in 1974 while reading the Śaunakīyā Caturādhyāyikā with my student James Bare at the University of Michigan that I detected a number of faulty readings and made a note of possible emendations. That very same year, during a visit to Pune in search of manuscripts, I found half a dozen manuscripts of this text at the Bhandarkar Oriental Research Institute and the Vaidika Samshodhana Mandala. To my delight, these manuscripts supported many of my emendations to Whitney's text. This led me to think about preparing a critical edition of this text.

The critical edition, however, could not be properly undertaken without gaining access to many more manuscripts of this text which were known to exist in different libraries around the world. In the year 1979, several more manuscripts became available to me. These came from the Staatsbibliothek Prussischer Kulturbesitz of Berlin, the library of the University of Tübingen, the Asiatic Society of Calcutta, and the Scindia Oriental Institute of Ujjain. In 1980, I found a manuscript in Banaras at the home of an Atharvaveda reciter, Pandit Narayan Shastri Ratate. Twelve years later, several important manuscripts were obtained in 1992 from the library of the Sampurnananda Sanskrit University in Banaras. In the summer of 1995, I found three rare manuscripts of the Kramapāṭha and the Jaṭāpāṭha of the Śaunakīya Atharvaveda at the Bhandarkar Oriental Research Institute, Pune, which significantly assisted my interpretation of this text. In the midst of my other research, my work on this project continued on and off from 1974. I thank all the institutions that supported my research during this long period:

1974, U.S. Department of Education, through the Center for South and Southeast Asian Studies, University of Michigan.

1976, Rackham Graduate School Faculty Research Grant, University of Michigan.

1979-80, Rackham Graduate School Faculty Research Grant, University of Michigan.

1990, College of Literature, Science, and the Arts, Faculty Research Grant, University of Michigan.

1992-93, American Institute of Indian Studies, the National Endowment for the Humanities, and the Office of the Vice-President for Research, the University of Michigan.

Numerous people have helped me throughout this long period in many different ways. I would like to specifically thank the following individuals who helped me in acquiring manuscripts:

Dr. Dieter George and Dr. Hartmut-Ortwin Feistel, Staatsbibliothek Prussischer Kulturbesitz in Berlin.

Dr. N.B. Marathe of the Central Reference Library, Calcutta, (currently at the Bhandarkar Oriental Research Institute, Pune).

Dr. Amalendu De, the Asiatic Society, Calcutta.

Dr. K. Gruessner, Library of the University of Tübingen.

Dr. V. Venkatachalam, Director, Scindia Oriental Institute, Ujjain.

Pandit Narayan Shastri Ratate, Durga Ghat, Banaras.

Dr. B.N. Misra, Librarian, Sampurnananda Sanskrit University, Banaras.

Dr. T.N. Dharmadhikari, Vaidika Samshodhana Mandala, Pune.

Dr. R.N. Dandekar, Bhandarkar Oriental Research Institute, Pune.

A major part of this work was carried out at the Bhandarkar Oriental Research Institute during my various research visits, but most intensively during 1992-93, and the summer of 1995. Besides the excellent manuscript collection of this institute, my daily conversations with Dr. R.N. Dandekar, Dr. M.A. Mehendale, Dr. A.M. Ghatage, and Dr. G.B. Palsule were most exciting. Many knotty problems of this text and its interpretation were solved during our afternoon tea. I thank all these scholars, and especially Dr. Dandekar, who introduced me to the mysteries of the Śaunakīya Atharvaveda at the University of Poona, when I was studying for my Master's degree in Sanskrit in the years 1966-68. In the U.S., my most sincere thanks go to Professor George Cardona. In spite of his own heavy commitments, Cardona has gone through this entire work and made numerous suggestions for improvement. At home in Ann Arbor, my colleague Professor John C. Catford, Professor (Emeritus) of Phonetics, University of Michigan, took a keen interest in this work. He read my translations with great interest and made suggestions to make them comprehensible to non-Sanskritist linguists. I must also thank Professor Michael Witzel, the editor of the series, for making numerous helpful suggestions. Finally I wish to thank my wife Shubhangi and my daughters Madhushree and Manjushree who have tolerated my eccentricities while I was lost in deep communication with my manuscripts and my computer.

I dedicate this work to my two lovely daughters, Madhushree and Manjushree, who have brought immense joy to me and my wife. The book is typeset using Nagari and Roman diacritics fonts which I developed over the past several years. These fonts are named after my daughters. The Nagari font is titled Madhushree and the Roman diacritics font is titled Manjushree. During the long time it has taken to finish this project, I have learned a great deal about the history of the grammatical traditions in ancient India, and I hope that this book will spur further interest in this 'ancient, dusty, and arcane,' but highly important, branch of Vedic philology. While much of this work criticizes the views of Whitney and Surya Kanta, I wish to express my great indebtedness to these two predecessors. The more I read and analyzed their contributions, the more respect I have developed for their wisdom and industry. I close this preface with a special salutation to them: *namo bhavadbhyām pathikr̥dbhyām r̥ṣibhyām.*

May 16, 1997

Madhav M. Deshpande
Ann Arbor, Michigan

Contents

Preface

Introduction

1. Critical Edition of the *Śaunakīyā Caturādhyāyikā* 1-4
2. Description of the Manuscripts 4-9
3. New Features of the Critical Edition of the *CA* 9-31
4. General Features of the Ancient Indian Phonetics 31-47
5. Phonetics vs Phonology in Indian Grammatical Tradition 47-59
6. Pāṇinian Impact on the Tradition of the *CA* 59-80
7. The AV Prātiśākhyas and the ŚAV Text-Transmission 80-95

Śaunakīyā Caturādhyāyika

Adhyāya 1, Pāda 1 97-166
Adhyāya 1, Pāda 2 167-200
Adhyāya 1, Pāda 3 201-240
Adhyāya 1, Pāda 4 241-262
Adhyāya 2, Pāda 1 263-304
Adhyāya 2, Pāda 2 305-325
Adhyāya 2, Pāda 3 326-347
Adhyāya 2, Pāda 4 348-373
Adhyāya 3, Pāda 1 374-393
Adhyāya 3, Pāda 2 394-421
Adhyāya 3, Pāda 3 422-450
Adhyāya 3, Pāda 4 451-477
Adhyāya 4, Pāda 1 478-545
Adhyāya 4, Pāda 2 546-571
Adhyāya 4, Pāda 3 572-606
Adhyāya 4, Pāda 4 607-630

***Pañcasandhi* of Kṛṣṇadāsa**	631-687
Bibliography & Abbreviations	689-705
Sūtra Index	707-728
Index of Sanskrit Terms	729-775
Index of Texts and Authors	777-815

INTRODUCTION

1. Critical Edition of the *Śaunakīyā Caturādhyāyikā*

1.1. William Dwight Whitney, the great American Sanskritist, published the first edition of the Śaunakīyā Caturādhyāyikā in the journal of the American Oriental Society in 1862. This edition was based exclusively on a single manuscript of this text which Whitney found in Berlin. Whitney fully realized that this manuscript (= Chambers 143) was in bad shape, and attempted to find more manuscripts in European and Indian libraries. Having failed in his search for more manuscripts, and having realized the importance of this text for the study of the Śaunakīya-Atharvaveda, which he and Roth had edited and published from Berlin in 1856, Whitney decided to edit and publish this text. In the introduction to his edition, Whitney makes the following comments about his lone manuscript source (Whitney 1862: iv):

> Most unfortunately, considering the extreme rarity of the work, the manuscript is a very poor one. Not only is it everywhere excessively incorrect, often beyond the possibility of successful emendation; it is also defective, exhibiting lacunae at several points. Some may be of opinion, then, that the publication of the Prātiśākhya upon its authority alone is premature, and should not have been undertaken.

Emphasizing the "faintness of the hope that additional manuscripts would later be obtainable" (Whitney 1862: iv) and "the peculiar interest of this class of works," (ibid.) Whitney published his excellent edition in 1862, with a translation and notes based on the commentary in the Berlin manuscript. From this lone poor manuscript, Whitney could only salvage the text of the Śaunakīyā Caturādhyāyikā. He extensively used and cited the commentary in that manuscript, though due to the poor condition of the manuscript, he did not publish the complete text of this commentary. Considering the odds against Whitney, one must admit that he produced a masterly edition which has been widely used by scholars since its publication.

1.2. The Berlin manuscript did not call the text by the title Atharvaveda Prātiśākhya. However, Whitney argued (1862: iii):

> The treatise was first brought to light, and its character determined, by Roth. It was recognized by him as being what is indicated by our title, a Prātiśākhya to a text of the Atharvaveda. That it has any inherent right to be called *the* Prātiśākhya to *the* Atharvaveda is not, of course, claimed for it; but, considering the extreme improbability that any other like phonetic treatise, belonging to any other schools of that Veda, will ever be brought to light, the title of Atharvaveda Prātiśākhya finds a sufficient justification in its convenience, and in its analogy with the names given to the other kindred treatises by their respective editors.

Whitney's text has been widely used under the name of the Atharvaveda-Prātiśākhya. The above paragraph from Whitney needs to be read carefully, and one should note that he nowhere asserted that this text is *the Prātiśākhya of the Atharva-Veda,* an accusation hurled at him unjustly by Surya Kanta (*APR, Introduction,* p. 31): "Whitney turns an APr into the APr." Whitney never made such a claim.

Whitney's modest claim that the Śaunakīyā Caturādhyāyikā belongs to the class of Prātiśākhyas was indeed not outlandish. Support for the same conclusion comes from an important source. Uvaṭa in his introductory comments on the RPR quotes CA (1.1.2-3: एवमिहेति च, विभाषाप्राप्तं सामान्ये) and introduces it as (M.D. Shastri's edition, Vol. II, p. 23): तथा चाथर्वणप्रातिशाख्ये 'so it is said in the Prātiśākhya of the Atharvaveda.' The second likely traditional source of information is the commentary Chāyā by Vaidyanātha Pāyaguṇḍe on Nāgeśabhaṭṭa's Uddyota. In his MB on P.1.1.10 (नाज्झलौ), Patañjali quotes a sequence of rules from some text, and they look very similar to CA (1.1.29-32). Ramadeva Tripathi (1977: 141) ascribes to Pāyaguṇḍe's Chāyā a remark that these rules are cited from the Śaunaka Prātiśākhya. I have not been able to trace this remark to citations of Chāyā in the Nirnaya Sagara edition of the MB. However, I find a remark स्पृष्टमित्यादीनि चत्वारि शौनकप्रातिशाख्यसूत्राणि बोध्यानि, Nirnaya Sagara Edition of the MB, Vol.I., Bombay, 1917, edited by Pt. Shivadatta Kuddala, p. 228. This comment is followed by the abbreviation *dā.* This abbreviation indicates that the comment belongs to the editor, rather than to Vaidyanātha's Chāyā. It is possible that the learned editor was familiar with Whitney's edition of the CA, which called it the Atharva-Veda-Prātiśākhya. In any case, one can at least say that a traditional Pandit did not see anything wrong in calling this text a Śaunaka Prātiśākhya.

This is also supported by the Ātharvaṇa-Pariśiṣṭa (= Atharva-Vidhāna) included in the *Śikṣāsaṃgraha* (p. 479). It refers to a Śaunakīya-Prātiśākhya and to the Māṇḍūkī-Śikṣā :

प्रातिशाख्यं शौनकीयं स्वरवर्णविभागजम् ॥ ५cd ॥
शिक्षा प्रकल्पिता सम्यङ्मण्डूकेन महर्षिणा ।
शिष्याणामुपदेशार्थं सम्यगुच्चारणाय वै ॥ ६ ॥

From the description of the Śaunakīya-Prātiśākhya as *svara-varṇa-vibhāgajam,* one can be certain that the Pariśiṣṭa is referring to the CA.

1.3. The subsequent scholarship on the Atharvaveda has happily disproved Whitney's earlier bleak expectations. In 1880, Whitney himself published "Collation of the Second Manuscript of the Atharvaveda Prātiśākhya" in the tenth volume of the *Journal of the American Oriental Society.* Albrecht Weber was instrumental in drawing Whitney's attention to this manuscript which was purchased by Georg Bühler for the Government of Bombay. This second manuscript collated by Whitney is now deposited at the Bhandarkar Oriental Research Institute (# 11/1870-71). Whitney duly notes that this second manuscript gives the title of the work simply as Caturādhyāyikā throughout. It also calls itself Caturādhyāyī-Vyākaraṇa in some places. Whitney, however, still insists on calling this text Atharvaveda-Prātiśākhya.

1.4. In 1923, Vishva Bandhu Shastri published a different treatise from Lahore under the name Atharva-Prātiśākhya. This edition is based on six different manuscripts. Referring to Whitney's earlier statements, Vishva Bandhu Shastri pointed out that many new manuscripts of the Śaunakīyā Caturādhyāyikā had also been found and preserved and that "a new and revised edition of the Caturādhyāyikā has thus become a matter of necessity" (*Atharva-Prātiśākhya,* edited by V. B. Shastri, p. 12). However, Vishva Bandhu Shastri seems to have been unaware of Whitney's collation of the second manuscript, and he did not undertake the task of preparing this new revised edition of the Caturādhyāyikā.

In 1937, Surya Kanta Shastri prepared a critical edition of this other Atharvaveda-Prātiśākhya for his Ph.D. at Oxford, and this text has been published from Lahore in 1939. This text includes Vishva Bandhu's text as one of the versions, and is obviously different from the Caturādhyāyikā. In fact, several manuscripts which contain this Atharvaveda-Prātiśākhya also contain the text of the Śaunakīyā Caturādhyāyikā. Thus, the labors of Vishva Bandhu Shastri and Surya Kanta Shastri have conclusively proved the existence of two separate texts, i.e. the Śaunakīyā Caturādhyāyikā and Atharvaveda-Prātiśākhya, and that the text that Whitney then called the Atharvaveda-Prātiśākhya must now be called simply the Śaunakīyā Caturādhyāyikā.

1.5. The existence of other manuscripts of Caturādhyāyikā became known to the world of scholarship since Weber noticed in 1863 a second manuscript in the *Literarisches Central-Blatt* (No. 29). This was just one year after Whitney published his edition. Later, more manuscripts of the Caturādhyāyikā were noticed by Vishva Bandhu Shastri and Surya Kanta Shastri. Additionally, in 1937, the curator of the Scindia Oriental Institute, Ujjain, Sadashiv L. Katre, discovered a manuscript titled Kautsa-Vyākaraṇa, which is identical with the Śaunakīyā Caturādhyāyikā. He published a detailed notice of this manuscript and its comparison with Whitney's text (Katre 1938-39). However, Katre does not show any awareness of the existence of the other manuscripts of the Śaunakīyā Caturādhyāyikā which were noticed by Vishva Bandhu Shastri and Surya Kanta Shastri.

I have myself been interested in this text for many years and have located several new manuscripts of the Śaunakīyā Caturādhyāyikā. The library of the Vaidika Saṃsodhana Maṇḍaḷa, Pune, has three manuscripts of this text, two of which bear the title Kautsa-Vyākaraṇa. These two manuscripts also contain commentaries on this text by Bhārgava Bhāskara and Kr̥ṣṇadāsa, and in an article published in 1976, I have discussed some points connected with these manuscripts. In the course of my personal search for more manuscripts of this text at Banaras in December 1979, I located a manuscript of the Śaunakīyā Caturādhyāyikā with a Maharashtrian Brahmin reciter of the Atharvaveda, Shri Narayan Shastri Ratate, and with his kind permission was able to obtain a Xerox copy of the same. A further significant discovery is that of a manuscript at the Asiatic Society, Calcutta, which contains the same commentary as in the Berlin manuscript used by Whitney, and that this manuscript, though incomplete, is in a much better shape. This is a great help in editing the text of this commentary.

2. Description of the Manuscripts

2.1. Below, I shall briefly describe all the manuscripts which are utilized in the preparation of this critical edition:

A. *Caturādhyāyikā.* Bhandarkar Oriental Research Institute, Pune. No. 1/1873-74. Devanagari. Complete. Folios: 12-21, 10" x 5 1/2". From Bikaner. ± 1700 A.D. The entire manuscript contains Pañcapaṭalikā, Dantyoṣṭhyavidhi, Kālātītaprāyaścitta, Caturādhyāyikā and Atharvaprātiśākhya. There is no information about who copied this manuscript, when and where, because there is no usual elaborate colophon at the end of the bundle. Since the manuscript ends with the second Prapāṭhaka of the Atharva-Prātiśākhya, most likely there are several missing folios.

B. *Caturādhyāyikā.* Bhandarkar Oriental Research Institute, Pune. No. 179/ 1880-81, 408. Devanagari. Complete. Folios: 56-66, 9 1/2" x 4". From Anahilapurapattana (= Patan in Gujarat). The date given is Saṃvat 1717 (= 1659 A.D.) and the colophon provides a precise day: संवत् १७१७ वर्षे भाद्रपदमासे कृष्णपक्षे ११ रविवासरे अद्ये श्रीअनहलपुरपत्तनमध्ये वास्तव्यं आभ्यन्तरनागरज्ञातीयपञ्चोलीसोमजीसुतबृहस्पतिजीपठनार्थम्. The entire manuscript contains Māṇḍūkīśikṣā, Jyotiṣam, Mahāśāntiḥ, Pañcapaṭalikā, Dantyoṣṭhyavidhi, Kālātītaprāyaścitta, Caturādhyāyikā, Atharvaprātiśākhya, and Chandaściti. The manuscript makes irregular use of the Pṛṣṭhamātrās and the Avagraha. The manuscript comes from the Pañcoli family of Patan. The first 27 folios are in a different hand and are utterly damaged, which perhaps indicates a different age for the two parts of the manuscripts.

C. *Caturādhyāyikā.* Bhandarkar Oriental Research Institute, Pune. No. 2/1884-86. Devanagari. Incomplete. Folios: 1-8, Folios 4a and 5b are missing. Also missing is the first page of the text. 9 3/8" x 4 1/4". From Anahilapurapattana. ± 1700 A.D. The colophon says: पञ्चुलीईश्वरसुतनीलकण्ठपठनार्थम्. It comes from the Pañcoli family from Patan. This manuscript is closely related to P below. See information on P below.

D. *Caturādhyāyikā.* Bhandarkar Oriental Research Institute, Pune. Nos: 178(vii)/ 1880-81 and 87/1880-81, #405 and #407. Folios were scattered in these two bundles, and I have now put them together and they are kept in the bundle 178(vii)/1880-81. The second bundle now contains only the text of the Kauśikagṛhyasūtra. Devanagari. Incomplete. Folios 58-69, Folio 63b missing, 10 1/2" x 4 3/4". From Anahilapurapattana. 1695 A.D. The manuscript contains the following texts: Māṇḍūkīśikṣā, Jyotiṣa, Mahāśānti, Pañcapaṭalikā, Dantyoṣṭhyavidhi, Kālātītaprāyaścitta, Caturādhyāyikā, Atharvaprātiśākhya, and Chandaściti. It shows occasional use of the Pṛṣṭhamātrās. This manuscript is also related to Roth's Bikaner manuscript (transcript at Tübingen). The colophon reads: संवत् १७५३ वर्षे चैत्रशुदि २ रवौ अद्य श्रीअनहीलपुरपत्तने वास्तव्यं आभ्यन्तरज्ञातीयतुलापुरश(?)ब्रह्माण्डमहीमहादानादिअतिरुद्रकर्ताहिताग्नीपञ्चकृत्वचातुर्मास्ययाजित्रिपाठिश्रीअनन्तजीसुतव्रजभूशणेन श्रीसाम्बसदाशिवार्पणबुद्ध्या लिखापितमिदं परोपकाराय.

E. *Caturādhyāyikā.* Bhandarkar Oriental Research Institute, Pune. No. 11/1870-71, #403. Devanagari. Complete. Folios: 1-13, 8 1/2" x 4 1/8". From Kaṇvālaya in Gujarat. 1660 A.D. Colophon: संवत् १७१८ कार्तिकशुदि ११ बुध. This manuscript is written by: पञ्चोलीनागजित्सूनुना कण्वालयनिवासिना

भवदेवेन इदं ग्रन्थं लिखितम्. This manuscript makes occasional use of the Avagraha, but does not use Pr̥ṣṭhamātrās. Importantly, it lists 180 as the measure of the text (*granthasaṃkhyā*). It was this manuscript which was transcribed for Whitney who published the "Collation of the Second Manuscript of the Atharvaveda-Prātiśākhya" (1880). The cover page of the manuscript calls it Caturādhyāyikāvyākaraṇam and as a matter of fact it is closely related with mss. F which also calls itself Caturādhyāyī-Vyākaraṇa.

F. *Caturādhyāyī-Vyākaraṇa.* Gore collection, Vaidika Saṃśodhana Maṇḍala, Pune. No. 4177. Devanagari. Complete. Folios 1-12, 9 1/2" x 4 1/2". From Mahuli near Satara. 1819 A.D. The colophon says that the manuscript was copied by a certain Raghunāthātmajamārtaṇḍabhaṭṭa. The date is specified as: शके १७४३ वृषानामाब्दे संवत् १८७७ नन्दननामाब्दे दक्षिणायने हेमर्तौ मार्गशीर्षशुक्लद्वितीया. It also mentions 180 as the measure of the work (*granthasaṃkhyā,* 180x32 = number of syllables?). The manuscript came from the Gore family, originally belonging to Mahuli near Satara. This family was in charge of the Atharvavedic priestcraft for the king of Satara. Later the family moved to Sangli. The manuscript occasionally uses the Avagraha, but does not use Pr̥ṣṭhamātrās.

G. *Kautsavyākaraṇasya Caturādhyāyātmakasya Bhārgavabhāskarīyavr̥ttiḥ.* Gore collection, Vaidika Saṃśodhana Maṇḍala, Pune. No. 4178. Devanagari. Incomplete. Folios: 1-24, 7.9" x 4.2". From Sangli, Maharashtra. ± 1700 A.D. This manuscript contains a commentary by Bhārgava Bhāskara. An important feature of this manuscript is that in contrast with all other manuscripts it gives three numbers for each rule, i.e. numbers for the Adhyāya, Pāda, and Sūtra. It occasionally uses the Avagraha, but does not make use of the Pr̥ṣṭhamātrā. In its incomplete state, it covers rules 1.1.10 to 1.4.8, or Whitney 1.8 to 1.99.

H. *Caturādhyāyī-Bhāṣya.* Staatsbibliothek Preussischer Kulturbesitz, Berlin. Chambers 143. Complete. Folios: 1-77, 8 1/4 " x 3 3/4". From North India. Saṃvat 1714 (= 1656 A.D.) This is the manuscript used by Whitney for his edition. In this manuscript of the commentary, there is a general pattern as follows. First a Sūtra is stated. Then it is explained and analyzed in the commentary. Then the Sūtra is again repeated at the end of the commentary. These three readings of the Sūtra are respectively labeled Ha, Hc, and Hb.

I. *Kautsa-Vyākaraṇa.* Oriental Institute, Ujjain. No. 3576. Devanāgarī. Complete. Folios: 1-12. 11 1/4" x 6". Belonged to Bāḷaśāstrī Garde from Gwalior. ± 1700 A.D. A detailed notice of this manuscript was published by S.L. Katre (1938-39) who informs us that "a few years ago, however, a considerable portion of his collection was actually emersed into a well by the last surviving lady of this line, possibly in a fit of despair, but, thanks to the timely intervention of some authorities of Gwalior State, the remnant could be rescued and deposited at the Oriental Manuscript Library of Ujjain maintained by the state."

J. *Caturādhyāyikā*. Personal property of Late Pt. Narayan Shastri Ratate, Durga Ghat, Banaras. Devanagari. Complete. Folios: 1-5, 11" x 5". From Banaras. ± 1700 A.D. The colophon says: श्रीमती गङ्गादेवी वरदा भवतु. I have a Xerox copy of this manuscript in my personal collection.

K. *Kautsavyākaraṇe Pañcasandhiḥ*. With a commentary by Kr̥ṣṇadāsa. Gore collection, Vaidika Saṃśodhana Maṇḍala, Pune. No. 4179. Devanagari. Incomplete. Folios: 1-36, 7 4/5" x 4 1/5". 1862 A.D. This manuscript was copied by Ātmārām Tivāḍi in: संवत् १९२०, शक १७८५ कार्तिकमासे शुक्लपक्षे तिथौ पञ्चम्यां रविवासरे. It occasionally uses the Avagraha, but does not use Pr̥ṣṭhamātrās.

L. *Caturādhyāyikā*. Universitätsbibliothek, Tübingen, Germany. An incomplete transcript of a Bikaner manuscript made by Roth. The original could not be traced. The original manuscript contained the following texts: Prāyaścitta, Māṇḍūkīśikṣā, Jyotiṣa, Mahāśānti, Pañcapaṭalikā, Dantyoṣṭhyavidhi, Kālātītaprāyaścitta, Caturādhyāyikā, Prātiśākhyamūla-sūtra, Chandaściti, and Nivitpraiṣādhyāyapuroruk. This manuscript generally belongs together with the manuscripts B and D which come from Patan in Gujarat.

M. *Caturādhyāyī*. Asiatic Society, Calcutta. No. 7852. Devanagari. Complete. Folios: 35b-43b, 4 1/4" x 9 1/2". Unknown origin. 1613 A.D. The date is specified as संवत् १६७१ वर्षे ज्येष्ठवदि ११. This manuscript uses occasional Pr̥ṣṭhamātrās and the Avagraha. The manuscript also contains the text of the Atharva-Prātiśākhya.

N. *Caturadhyāyī-Bhāṣya*. Asiatic Society, Calcutta. No. 1272. Devanagari. Incomplete. Folios: 1-61a, 63b-64a, 101. 8 3/4" x 4 1/4". Unknown origin. 1624 A.D. The colophon reads: संवत् १६८२ वर्षे पुरुषोत्तममासे कृष्णपक्षे त्रयोदशीमन्दवासरे लिखितमिदम्. This commentary is identical with the commentary found in the manuscript H from Berlin used by Whitney. Like the manuscript H, N also repeats each Sūtra three times, and these three readings are labeled Na, Nc, and Nb, respectively.

O. *Kautsavyākaraṇe Caturādhyāyikā*. Sarasvati Bhavana Library, Sampurnananda Sanskrit Vishvavidyalaya, Banaras. No. 2086. Devanagari. Complete. Folios 1-10. 8 3/4" x 4". No indication of place or date in the colophon. Approximately a hundred and fifty years old. Does not make use of Pṛṣṭhamātrās. The first and the last folios have a stamp in English showing that the last owner was Mr. S.B. Vaidya of Durgaghat, Banaras, an Atharvavedin Brahmin.

P. *Caturādhyāyī.* Sarasvati Bhavana Library, Sampurnanda Sanskrit Vishvavidyalaya. Banaras. No. 2074. Devanagari. Complete. 10 1/4" x 4 1/5". Folios 1-27. Caturādhyāyikā extends from folio 19 to 25. The ms. contains Māṇḍūkīśikṣā, Jyotiṣam, Chandaściti, Pañcapaṭalikā, Dantyoṣṭhyavidhi, Kāltītaprāyaścittam, Caturādhyāyikā, and Atharva-Prātiśākhya. It is a relatively old ms., and it makes occasional use of Pṛṣṭhamātrās. On folio 13, it gives the date of copying as संवत् १६८५ वर्षे मागशरवदि ५ गुरौ लिखितम्. However, on folio 27, at the end of the manu-script, a different hand adds संवत् १६३४ वर्षे आश्वनशुदि १५ दिने पंचोलि श्री इश्वर लक्षणग्रंथ भणे छे पंचोलि श्री गोविन्दजी कनेर (?) भणे छे. It looks like the ms. belonged to the Pañcolī family of Gujarat. The original ms. probably goes back to Saṃvat 1685, and that it was supplemented and corrected by another hand in Saṃvat 1734. The same person, Śrī Īśvara Pañcolī, is referred to in the ms. C above, and both the manuscripts probably belong to the same family. It is clear that the same hand has added corrections to both of these manuscripts.

2.2. I propose the following genealogy for these manuscripts.

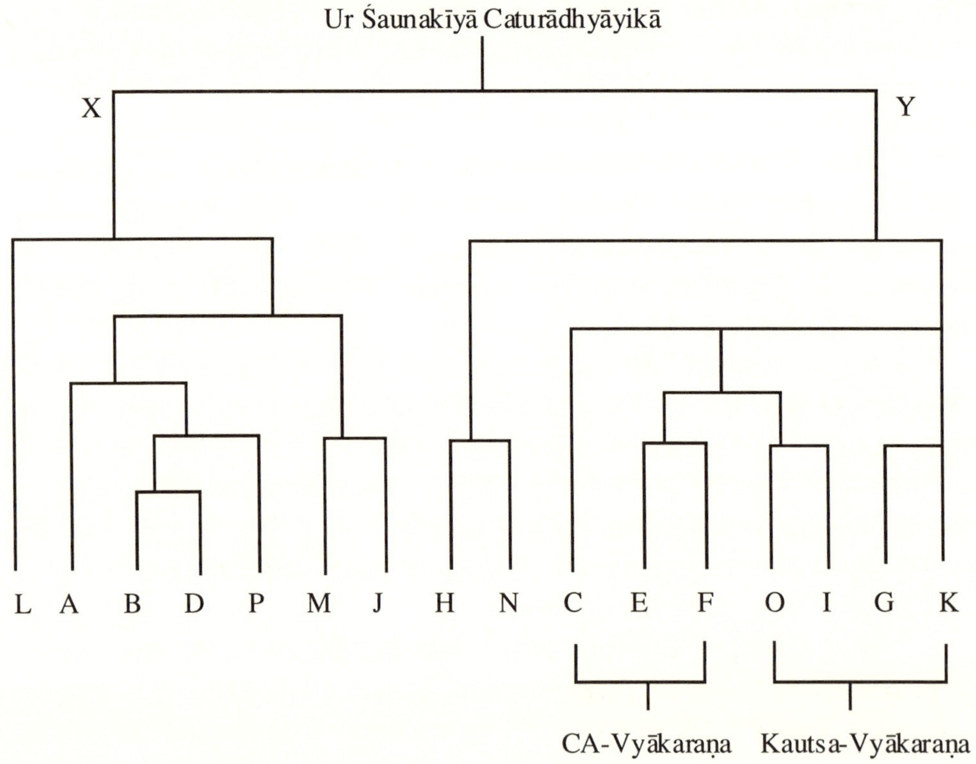

2.3. Taking into account the significant shared errors and other shared deviant features, the following groups of manuscripts seem to have strong relationships. The number given in the bracket stands for the shared errors and other shared deviant features noted in this edition: A-B-D (47), A-B (44), A-B-D-M-J (16), A-B-D-M (11), A-B-D-J (4), A-B-L (4), B-D (21), C-E-F (6), C-E-F-I (5), C-H-N (4), E-F (27), E-F-H (4), E-F-I (28), F-I (4), H-N (42). It is not necessary to record information about groups of manuscripts which share one or two errors. The above chart takes into account this information. Some of these relationships are particularly complex. For example, consider the relationship between A, B, and D. All three share 47 common deviations, and hence must go back to a common source. However, A and B share 44 common deviations which are different from the 21 common deviations shared by B and D. This must mean that the source of A and B must be slightly different from the source of B and D. In my opinion, the only way to resolve this situation is to suggest that the manuscript B used multiple sources. One of its sources was shared in common with A. However, another source for B was shared in common with D. The manuscripts O and P became available to me after all other manuscripts were already collated and the basic relationships were determined. I have shown their appropriate relationships in the diagram above, though I have not given counts of shared deviant features.

This stemma should be viewed only as a convenient grouping of the manuscript material. One must keep in mind the possibility and the probability that the persons copying and correcting the manuscripts used various sources, and this accounts for the erratic readings, which violate the otherwise plausible linkages between the manuscripts. Thus, while the manuscripts B, C, D, and P, all derive from Anahilapurapattana (= Patan in Gujarat), the manuscript C seems to share closer links with the manuscript E from Kaṇvālaya in Gujarat and F from Maharashtra. One may also note that the mss. C, E, and F contain only the text of the CA, while the mss. in the X group contain other texts besides the CA, and they usually contain the same set of texts. As a general observation, it is interesting to note all the manuscripts seem to derive from the Western regions ranging from Rajasthan to Maharashtra, and that the regions of Southern and Eastern India are not represented in these available manuscripts.

3. New Features of the Critical Edition

3.1. Here I shall briefly indicate some of the important gains which are already evident from the manuscript material now available to us. Whitney had divided his text only into four Adhyāyas. He knew that each Adhyāya had four Pādas, but his manuscript was not clear on these divisions. Hence, he could not subdivide each Adhyāya into Pādas. The manuscript material now available settles this issue once and for all. Below I have given the colophons occurring at the end of the first Pāda of the first Adhyāya as found in the various manuscripts.

A, B, M, P	प्रथमः पादः ।
C	इति चतुराध्यायिकायां प्रथमस्याध्यायस्य प्रथमः पादः ।
D	इति प्रथमः पादः ।
E, F	प्रथमस्य प्रथमः पादः ।
G	इत्यथर्ववेदाङ्गकौत्सव्याकरणे प्रथमाध्यायस्य प्रथमपादस्य भार्गवभास्करीयवृत्तिः परिपूर्णा ।
H, N	चतुराध्यायिकायां प्रथमस्याध्यायस्य प्रथमः पादः । सूत्र ४१ । एकचत्वाशिंत् ।
I	४१ इत्यथर्ववेदे कौत्सव्याकरणे प्रथमस्याध्यायस्य प्रथमः पादः ।
J	इति प्रथमाध्यायस्य प्रथमः पादः ।
O	१ ।। ४१ ।। इत्यथर्ववेदे कौत्सव्याकरणे चतुराध्यायिकस्य प्रथमः पादः ।।

Since all of these colophons occur at the same juncture, we can now be completely certain where the Pādas end, and we can now subdivide the text properly.

3.2. Several prose and metrical passages found in the Berlin manuscript were relegated by Whitney to the commentary. He did not consider them to be part of the text of the CA. Several of these passages are found in almost all the manuscripts which give only the text of the Sūtras of the CA. This helps us assign these passages to the text of the CA, rather than to the text of the commentary. For instance, Whitney (1.105) reads as follows:

> खष्वखा३ इ खैमखा इ मध्ये तदुरि । इदं भूया३ इदा३मिति । ऊर्ध्वो नु सृष्टा३स्तिर्यङ्नु सृष्टा३ः सर्वा दिशः पुरुष आ बभूवाँ३ । पराञ्चमोदनं प्राशीः प्रत्यञ्चामिति । त्वमोदनं प्राशीस्त्वामोदना३ इति । वशेया३मवशेति । यत्तदासी३दिदं नु ता३दिति । इति प्लुतानि ।

Whitney includes this long passage in the Berlin manuscript in the text of the *Caturādhyāyikā*, but stops abruptly, while the passage actually continues further in that manuscript:

किमर्थः परिपाठः । इत उत्तरम् अधिकम् । एतावत् स्वार्थोऽपि । बहुविधा-स्त्रिविधाः प्लुतयो भवन्ति । स्वरपरा अभिनिष्ठानपरा व्यञ्जनपरास्तासां याः समानाक्षरपरास्ता इतावप्लुतवद्भवन्ति । इतावप्लुतवद्भवन्ति ।

The entire passage with some minor variations is now supported by the manuscripts A, B, D, E, F, H, I, J, M, N, O and P and it is most certainly a part of the text of the CA. There are many such passages. On the other hand, many passages which are ascribed to the commentary by Whitney are not found in any of the manuscripts of the CA, and hence we know that they indeed do not form a part of the CA.

3.3. The new manuscripts help us detect rules which are missing in Whitney's edition and in the Berlin manuscript. For instance:

After Whitney (3.28), the manuscripts A, B, D, E, F, I, J, M, N, O and P have the rules छकारश्च (or °स्य) and पिप्पल्यादिषु पूर्वात्.

After Whitney (3.80), the manuscripts A, B, C, D, E, F, I, J, M, O and P have the rules नसश्च, धातुस्थादयकारात्, उरु, ब्रह्मण्वत्यादीनाम् and निपातस्य (or °श्च) स्वः.

After Whitney (3.86), the manuscripts A, B, C, D, E, F, I, J, M, O and P have the rule नभेः.

After Whitney (4.93), the manuscripts A, B, C, D, E, F, I, J, M, O and P have the rule इंग्यवच्च.

After Whitney (4.107), the manuscripts A, B, C, D, E, F, I, J, M, O and P have the rule संहितादार्ढ्यार्थम्.

Many of these rules were noticed by Whitney himself in his "Collation of the Second Manuscript" in 1880, and were again noticed by S.L. Katre (1938-39: 384). Now with the help of the substantially increased manuscript evidence, we can be more certain about the text of these rules.

3.4. The manuscripts occasionally offer a different splitting of rules from what has been offered by Whitney. For instance, consider the three rules given by Whitney:

Whitney (1.14): समानयमेऽक्षरमुच्चैरुदात्तम् ।
Whitney (1.15): नीचैरनुदात्तम् ।

Whitney (1.16): आक्षिप्तं स्वरितम् ।

Now, all the manuscripts we have give just one continuous rule as:

समानयमेऽक्षरमुच्चैरुदात्तं नीचैरनुदात्तमाक्षिप्तं स्वरितम् ।

The manuscript G in fact provides a single number (i.e. 1.1.16) for this rule.

3.5. In some cases, the manuscripts help us discard some of Whitney's emendations. Consider the following examples:

Whitney (1.19): कण्ठ्यानाम् अधरकण्ठः. Against the reading of the Berlin manuscript, i.e. °*kaṇṭhyaḥ*, Whitney emended the text to °*kaṇṭhaḥ*. Now the Berlin manuscript stands supported by all manuscripts, except I which supports Whitney's emendation. However, I believe it is most likely that this widely shared reading is an error going back to the archetype.

Whitney (1.25): ओष्ठ्यानामधरौष्ठम्. This goes against the reading of the Berlin manuscript, i.e. °*auṣṭhyam*. The Berlin reading is supported by all manuscripts, except I which supports Whitney's emendation. However, I believe it is most likely that this widely shared reading is an error going back to the archetype.

Whitney (1.82): आर्त्वी इवादिष्विवादितिः परः. Berlin reads °*ditiparaḥ*. This is supported by all the manuscripts.

3.6. In several cases, the manuscripts now available support Whitney's expectations. Consider the following rules:

Whitney (1.66): लकारस्य रेफः पादमंगुलिमित्येवमादीनाम्. Whitney says on this rule: "We should have expected here *pādam-aṃgurim* ..." Whitney's expectation is supported by all the available manuscripts, including a reading in the Berlin manuscript, i.e. H.

Whitney (2.92): स्यासहिसिचीनामकारव्यवायेऽपि. The Berlin text is severely mutilated, and the above text is Whitney's own conjecture, which is now fully supported by the manuscripts C, D, E, F, I, J, M, N, O and P.

Whitney (3.29): [न] विसर्जनीयः. There is no support for *na* in the Berlin manuscript, and this is Whitney's conjecture. It is now supported by the manuscripts A, B, D, E, F, I, J, M, N, O and P.

3.7. I hope I have sufficiently illustrated the new features of the present critical edition of the CA alias Kautsa-Vyākaraṇa, and the extent to which it replaces Whitney's pioneering work. It is hoped that this critical edition of the CA will open up new dimensions for the study of the Atharvaveda and its ancillary literature. As indicated above, the new manuscript material leads to a wholly new numbering for the rules of the CA. Most of the manuscripts do not provide any numbering whatsoever. However, there are several manuscripts which do provide numbering of the rules in different ways. For instance, manuscript G provides a continuous numbering for all rules. It gives the number of the Adhyāya, the Pāda, and the Sūtra. Manuscript I provides numbering within each Pāda, mostly for rules 10, 20, etc. The mss. H and N provide cumulative numbers for the Pādas and Adhyāyas. The ms. O also provides, in its colophons, totals for the rules in each Pāda. The numbers provided in these different mss. do not always agree with each other, but tell us something about the different textual traditions, some of which included more material than others. Sometimes we find that a given tradition of transmission split a rule into two, or joined two rules into one. Such changes obviously affected the counting of rules in the text. Below, I have provided a complete numbering of the CA rules found in this edition, along with the corresponding numbers in Whitney's edition, and the numbers found in different manuscripts:

3.8. This edition presents not only the revised text of the CA, but a fairly complete text of the commentary Caturādhyāyībhāṣya (= CAB) based on two manuscripts. It further offers partial texts of the commentaries Vṛtti by Bhārgava-Bhāskara and a reworking of the CA rules with a commentary called Pañcasandhi by Kṛṣṇadāsa, along the lines of Bhaṭṭojī Dīkṣita's Sidhānta-Kaumudī and Anubhūtisvarūpācārya's Sārasvata-Vyākaraṇa. Both of these commentaries are edited here on the basis of single manuscripts preserved at the Vaidika Saṃśodhana Maṇḍaḷa at Pune. The three commentaries are discussed in some detail later in this introduction in the context of the successive degrees of Pāṇinian influence. We know nothing about the authors of these commentaries, beside their names. For the Caturādhyāyībhāṣya, we do not even know the name of its author. In general terms, one may say that the Caturādhyāyībhāṣya belongs to a period closer to the Kāśikāvṛtti on Pāṇini, while the other two commentaries seem to follow Bhaṭṭojī Dīkṣita's Siddhāntakaumudī. The Caturādhyāyībhāṣya is also very closely linked to the tradition as represented by the Atharva-Prātiśākhya edited by Surya Kanta. In several hundred cases, the CAB cites the first few examples from a long list of examples fully listed under the rules of the APR. In my notes on the CA, I have fully indicated this relationship. On the other hand, the commentaries of Bhārgava-Bhāskara and Kṛṣṇadāsa are completely unaware of the existence of the CAB or the APR, and explain the rules of the CA more on the basis of the parallel rules of Pāṇini. Even here, one notices that the commentary of Bhārgava-Bhāskara shows full familiarity with the text of the Śaunakīya AV, while Kṛṣṇadāsa hardly ever cites examples from the AV. The Caturādhyāyībhāṣya is closely familiar with an ancient Śikṣā which is in part also contained in the AV Pariśiṣṭa called Varṇapaṭala, but is not familiar with either the Māṇḍūkīśikṣā or the versified Pāṇinīyaśikṣā. In contrast with this, the latter two commentaries show no awareness of the ancient Śikṣā cited by the CAB. On the other hand, they show direct familiarity with the Māṇḍūkīśikṣā and the versified Pāṇinīyaśikṣā. Thus, the present edition provides means to understand the changing nature of the CA tradition from a period going close to that of Pāṇini to a period coming close to that of Bhaṭṭojī Dīkṣita. During this long period, the text of the CA underwent successive interpretations at the hands of commentators who were gradually more and more influenced by the tradition of the Pāṇinian commentaries. It is hoped that more manuscripts of these commentaries will come to light in the future and a more complete account of this tradition can be eventually put together. However, I am delighted to present the available materials in this edition. I have been engaged in collecting and interpreting these materials almost since 1975 when I first noticed the manuscripts available in Pune at the Bhandarkar Oriental Research Institute and at the Vaidika Saṃśodhana Maṇḍal. Now I have made use of almost every known manuscript (and also some not listed in Aithal 1991) in preparing this edition which marks a substantial advance over the edition prepared so valiantly by Whitney in 1862 on the basis of a single manuscript.

3.9. The new numbering for the CA

Adhyāya 1, Pāda 1

CA	Whitney	Mss.
1.1.1.	missing	G: 1.1.1.
1.1.2.	1.1.	
1.1.3.	1.2.	
1.1.4.	1.2.	
1.1.5.	1.3.	
1.1.6.	1.4.	
1.1.7.	1.5.	
1.1.8.	1.6.	
1.1.9.	1.7.	
1.1.10.	1.8.	G: 1.1.10.; I: 1.10.
1.1.11.	1.9.	G: 1.1.11.
1.1.12.	1.10.	
1.1.13.	1.11.	G: 1.1.13.
1.1.14.	1.12.	G: 1.1.14.
1.1.15.	1.13.	G: 1.1.15.
1.1.16.	1.14-16.	G: 1.1.16.
1.1.17.	1.17.	G: 1.1.17.
1.1.18.	1.18.	G: 1.1.18.
1.1.19.	1.19.	G: 1.1.19.
1.1.20.	1.20.	G: 1.1.20.; I: 1.20.
1.1.21.	1.21.	G: 1.1.21.
1.1.22.	1.22.	G: 1.1.22.
1.1.23.	1.23.	G: 1.1.23.
1.1.24.	1.24.	G: 1.1.24.
1.1.25.	1.25.	G: 1.1.25.
1.1.26.	1.26.	G: 1.1.26.
1.1.27.	1.27.	G: 1.1.27.
1.1.28.	1.28.	G: 1.1.28.
1.1.29.	1.29.	G: 1.1.29.
1.1.30.	1.30.	G: 1.1.30.; I: 1.30.
1.1.31.	1.31.	G: 1.1.31.
1.1.32.	1.32.	G: 1.1.32.
1.1.33.	1.33.	G: 1.1.33.

1.1.34.	1.34.	G: 1.1.34.
1.1.35.	1.35.	G: 1.1.35.
1.1.36.	1.36.	G: 1.1.36.
1.1.37.	1.37.	G: 1.1.37.
1.1.38.	1.38.	G: 1.1.38.
1.1.39.	1.39.	G: 1.1.39.
1.1.40.	1.40.	G: 1.1.40.; I: 1.40.
1.1.41.	1.41.	G: 1.1.41.

Colophons: H, N: 41; I: 41; O: 41.

Adhyāya 1, Pāda 2

CA	Whitney	Mss.
1.2.1.	1.42.	G: 1.2.1.
1.2.2.	1.43.	G: 1.2.2.
1.2.3.	1.43.	G: 1.2.3.
1.2.4.	1.44.	G: 1.2.4.
1.2.5.	1.45.	G: 1.2.5.
1.2.6.	1.46.	G: 1.2.6.
1.2.7.	1.47.	G: 1.2.7.
1.2.8.	1.48.	G: 1.2.8.
1.2.9.	1.49.	G: 1.2.9.
1.2.10.	1.50.	G: 1.2.10.; I: 10.
1.2.11.	1.51.	G: 1.2.11.
1.2.12.	1.52.	G: 1.2.12.
1.2.13.	1.53.	G: 1.2.13.
1.2.14.	1.54.	G: 1.2.14.
1.2.15.	1.55.	G: 1.2.15.
1.2.16.	1.56.	G: 1.2.16.
1.2.17.	1.57.	G: 1.2.17.
1.2.18.	1.58.	G: 1.2.18.
1.2.19.	1.59.	G: 1.2.19.
1.2.20.	1.60.	G: 1.2.20.
1.2.21.	1.61.	G: 1.2.21.
1.2.22.	1.62.	G: 1.2.22.; I: 21.

Colophons: H, N: 62 rules in the first two Pādas; O: 21 (for this Pāda, agrees with I).

Adhyāya 1, Pāda 3.

CA	**Whitney**	**Mss.**
1.3.1.	1.63.	G: 1.3.1.
1.3.2.	1.64.	G: 1.3.2.
1.3.3.	1.65.	G: 1.3.3.
1.3.4.	1.66.	G: 1.3.4.
1.3.5.	1.67.	G: 1.3.5.
1.3.6.	1.68.	G: 1.3.6.
1.3.7.	1.69.	G: 1.3.7.
1.3.8.	1.70.	G: 1.3.8.
1.3.9.	1.71.	G: 1.3.9.
1.3.10.	1.72.	G: 1.3.10.
1.3.11.	1.73.	G: 1.3.10.; I: 16(?)
1.3.12.	1.74.	G: 1.3.11.
1.3.13.	1.75.	G: 1.3.12.
1.3.14.	1.76.	G: 1.3.13.
1.3.15.	1.77.	G: 1.3.14.
1.3.16.	1.78.	G: 1.3.15.
1.3.17.	1.79.	G: 1.3.16.
1.3.18.	1.80.	G: 1.3.17.
1.3.19.	1.81.	G: 1.3.18.
1.3.20.	1.82.	G: 1.3.19.; I: 20.
1.3.21.	1.83.	G: 1.3.20.
1.3.22.	1.84.	G: 1.3.21.
1.3.23.	1.85.	G: 1.3.22.
1.3.24.	1.86.	G: 1.3.23.
1.3.25.	1.87.	G: 1.3.24.
1.3.26.	1.88.	G: 1.3.25.
1.3.27.	1.89.	G: 1.3.27.
1.3.28.	1.90.	G: 1.3.26.
1.3.29.	1.91.	G: 1.3.28., I: 29.

Colophons: H, N: 91 (cumulative); O: 29 (matches with the number in I).

Adhyāya 1, Pāda 4.

CA	Whitney	Mss.
1.4.1.	1.92.	G: 1.4.1.
1.4.2.	1.93.	G: 1.4.2.
1.4.3.	1.94.	
1.4.4.	1.95.	
1.4.5.	1.96.	
1.4.6.	1.97.	
1.4.7.	1.98.	G: 1.4.7.
1.4.8.	1.99.	G: 1.4.8.
1.4.9.	1.100.	
1.4.10.	1.101.	
1.4.11.	1.102.	
1.4.12.	1.103.	
1.4.13.	1.104.	
1.4.14.	1.105.	

Colophons: C: 103 (cumulative); H, N: 13 (for this Pāda); I: 110 (cumulative); O: 19 (for this Pāda). While the figures given in C, H, and N are close, though not identical, with the numbers in our edition, the numbers given in O and I are somewhat problematic. It is not clear for instance, how O arrives at the number 19 for the rules in this Pāda. The text found in I and O does not offer any additional rules.

Adhyāya 2, Pāda 1.

CA	Whitney	Mss.
2.1.1.	2.1.	
2.1.2.	2.2.	
2.1.3.	2.3.	
2.1.4.	2.4.	
2.1.5.	2.5.	
2.1.6.	2.6.	
2.1.7.	2.7.	
2.1.8.	2.8.	
2.1.9.	2.9.	I: 10.

2.1.10.	2.10.	
2.1.11.	2.11.	
2.1.12.	2.12.	
2.1.13.	2.13.	
2.1.14.	2.14.	
2.1.15.	2.15.	
2.1.16.	2.16.	
2.1.17.	2.17.	
2.1.18.	2.18.	
2.1.19.	2.19.	
2.1.20.	2.20.	
2.1.21.	2.21.	I: 20.
2.1.22.	2.22.	
2.1.23.	2.23.	
2.1.24.	2.24.	
2.1.25.	2.25.	
2.1.26.	2.26.	
2.1.27.	2.27.	
2.1.28.	2.28.	
2.1.29.	2.29.	
2.1.30.	2.30.	
2.1.31.	2.31.	
2.1.32.	2.32.	
2.1.33.	2.33.	
2.1.34.	2.34.	
2.1.35.	2.35.	
2.1.36.	2.36.	
2.1.37.	2.37.	
2.1.38.	2.38.	
2.1.39.	2.39.	I: 39.

Colophons: O: 39 (agrees with the final count in I).

Adhyāya 2, Pāda 2.

CA	**Whitney**	**Mss.**
2.2.1.	2.40.	
2.2.2.	2.41.	

2.2.3.	2.42.	
2.2.4.	2.43.	
2.2.5.	2.44.	
2.2.6.	2.45.	
2.2.7.	2.46.	
2.2.8.	2.47.	
2.2.9.	2.48.	
2.2.10.	2.49.	I: 10.
2.2.11.	2.50.	
2.2.12.	2.51.	
2.2.13.	2.52.	
2.2.14.	2.53.	
2.2.15.	2.54.	
2.2.16.	2.55.	
2.2.17.	2.56.	
2.2.18.	2.57.	
2.2.19.	2.58.	
2.2.20.	2.59.	I: 20.

Colophons: H, N: 59 (cumulative for this Adhyāya); O: 20 (agrees with the count in I).

Adhyāya 2, Pāda 3.

CA	**Whitney**	**Mss.**
2.3.1.	2.60.	
2.3.2.	2.61.	
2.3.3.	2.62.	
2.3.4.	2.63.	
2.3.5.	2.64.	
2.3.6.	2.65.	
2.3.7.	2.66.	
2.3.8.	2.67.	
2.3.9.	2.68.	
2.3.10.	2.69.	
2.3.11.	2.70.	
2.3.12.	2.71.	
2.3.13.	2.72.	

2.3.14.	2.73.	
2.3.15.	2.74.	
2.3.16.	2.75.	
2.3.17.	2.76.	
2.3.18.	2.77.	
2.3.19.	2.78.	
2.3.20.	2.79.	
2.3.21.	2.80.	I: 21.

Colophons: H, N: 80 (cumulative for this Adhyāya); O: 21 (for this Pāda, agrees with the count in I).

Adhyāya 2, Pāda 4.

CA	Whitney	Mss.
2.4.1.	2.81.	
2.4.2.	2.82.	
2.4.3.	2.83.	
2.4.4.	2.84.	
2.4.5.	2.85.	
2.4.6.	2.86.	
2.4.7.	2.87.	
2.4.8.	2.88.	
2.4.9.	2.89.	
2.4.10.	2.90.	I: 10.
2.4.11.	2.91.	
2.4.12.	2.92.	
2.4.13.	2.93.	
2.4.14.	2.94.	
2.4.15.	2.95.	
2.4.16.	2.96.	
2.4.17.	2.97.	
2.4.18.	2.98.	
2.4.19.	2.99.	
2.4.20.	2.100.	I: 20.
2.4.21.	2.101.	
2.4.22.	2.102.	
2.4.23.	2.103.	

2.4.24.	2.104.	
2.4.25.	2.105.	
2.4.26.	2.106.	
2.4.27.	2.107.	I: 26.

Colophons: H, N: 106 (cumulative for this Adhyāya); I: 107 (cumulative for this Adhyāya), 217 (cumulative for the first two Adhyāyas); O: 37 (error for 27?).

Adhyāya 3, Pāda 1.

CA	**Whitney**	**Mss.**
3.1.1.	3.1.	
3.1.2.	3.2.	
3.1.3.	3.3.	
3.1.4.	3.4.	
3.1.5.	3.5.	
3.1.6.	3.6.	
3.1.7.	3.7.	
3.1.8.	3.8.	
3.1.9.	3.9.	
3.1.10.	3.10.	
3.1.11.	3.11.	I: 11.
3.1.12.	3.12.	
3.1.13.	3.13.	
3.1.14.	3.14.	
3.1.15.	3.15.	
3.1.16.	3.16.	
3.1.17.	3.17.	
3.1.18.	3.18.	
3.1.19.	3.19.	
3.1.20.	3.20.	
3.1.21.	3.21.	
3.1.22.	3.22.	
3.1.23.	3.23.	
3.1.24.	3.24.	
3.1.25.	3.25.	

Colophons: O: 25.

Adhyāya 3, Pāda 2.

CA	**Whitney**	**Mss.**
3.2.1.	3.26.	
3.2.2.	3.27.	
3.2.3.	3.28.	
3.2.4.	missing	
3.2.5.	missing	
3.2.6.	3.29.	
3.2.7.	3.30.	
3.2.8.	3.31.	
3.2.9.	3.32.	
3.2.10.	3.33.	I: 10.
3.2.11.	3.34.	I: 11.
3.2.12.	3.35.	
3.2.13.	3.36.	
3.2.14.	3.37.	
3.2.15.	3.38.	
3.2.16.	3.39.	
3.2.17.	3.40.	
3.2.18.	3.41.	
3.2.19.	3.42.	
3.2.20.	3.43.	
3.2.21.	3.44.	
3.2.22.	3.45.	
3.2.23.	3.46.	
3.2.24.	3.47.	
3.2.25.	3.48.	
3.2.26.	3.49.	
3.2.27.	3.50.	
3.2.28.	3.51.	
3.2.29.	3.52.	
3.2.30.	3.53.	
3.2.31.	3.54.	I: 31.

Colophons: O: 31 (agrees with the count in I).

Adhyāya 3, Pāda 3.

CA	Whitney	Mss.
3.3.1.	commentary	
3.3.2.	commentary	
3.3.3.	commentary	
3.3.4.	commentary	
3.3.5.	commentary	
3.3.6.	3.55.	
3.3.7.	3.56.	
3.3.8.	3.57.	
3.3.9.	3.58.	
3.3.10.	3.59.	
3.3.11.	3.60.	
3.3.12.	3.61.	
3.3.13.	3.62.	
3.3.14.	3.63.	
3.3.15.	3.64.	
3.3.16.	3.65.	
3.3.17.	3.66.	
3.3.18.	3.67.	
3.3.19.	3.68.	
3.3.20.	3.69.	
3.3.21.	3.70.	
3.3.22.	3.71.	
3.3.23.	3.72.	
3.3.24.	3.73.	
3.3.25.	3.74.	
3.3.26.	commentary	
3.3.27.	commentary	
3.3.28.	commentary	
3.3.29.	commentary	
3.3.30.	commentary	
3.3.31.	commentary	
3.3.32.	commentary	
3.3.33.	commentary	
3.3.34.	commentary	
3.3.35.	commentary	

Colophons: O: 40. Where are the five additional rules? Possibly the first four verses and the fifth rule are each counted as being two Sūtras.

Adhyāya 3, Pāda 4.

CA	**Whitney**	**Mss.**
3.4.1.	3.75.	
3.4.2.	3.76.	
3.4.3.	3.77.	
3.4.4.	3.78.	
3.4.5.	3.79.	
3.4.6.	3.80.	
3.4.7.	missing	
3.4.8.	missing	
3.4.9.	missing	
3.4.10.	missing	I: 10.
3.4.11.	missing	
3.4.12.	3.81.	
3.4.13.	3.82.	
3.4.14.	3.83.	
3.4.15.	3.84.	
3.4.16.	3.85.	
3.4.17.	3.86.	
3.4.18.	missing	
3.4.19.	3.87.	
3.4.20.	3.88.	
3.4.21.	3.89.	
3.4.22.	3.90.	
3.4.23.	3.91.	
3.4.24.	3.92.	
3.4.25.	3.93.	
3.4.26.	3.94.	
3.4.27.	3.95.	
3.4.28.	3.96.	I: 29.

Colophons: H: 105 (cumulative for this Adhyāya); I: 125 (cumulative for this Adhyāya); O: 29 (identical with the count in I). The difference of twenty rules in the counting for this Adhyāya in the mss. H and I can be explained only on the assumption that H considered certain passages as belonging to the commentary. This refers in all likelihood to CA 3.3.1-5 and CA 3.3.26-35. In our count, these are 15 rules, which Whitney relegated to the commentary. However, as the colophon in O on Adhyāya 3, Pāda 3 shows, some traditions counted 40 rules in this Pāda, instead of our 35. There is a strong possibility that the verses in CA 3.3.1-4, and the prose in CA 3.3.5, were counted as having two rules each. This accounts for 20 rules. It is clear that the ms H of the CAB contains all these passages and yet does not count them as Sūtras. On the other hand, the ms. I gives 125 as the total number of rules in this Adhyāya, indicating that it includes these passages as part of the text. This is also supported by the ms. O.

Adhyāya 4, Pāda 1.

CA	**Whitney**	**Mss.**
4.1.1.	commentary	
4.1.2.	commentary	
4.1.3.	commentary	
4.1.4.	commentary	
4.1.5.	commentary	
4.1.6.	commentary	
4.1.7.	commentary	
4.1.8.	commentary	
4.1.9.	commentary	
4.1.10.	commentary	
4.1.11.	commentary	
4.1.12.	commentary	
4.1.13.	commentary	
4.1.14.	commentary	
4.1.15.	commentary	
4.1.16.	commentary	
4.1.17.	commentary	
4.1.18.	commentary	
4.1.19.	commentary	
4.1.20.	commentary	
4.1.21.	commentary	
4.1.22.	commentary	
4.1.23.	4.1.	
4.1.24.	4.2.	

4.1.25.	4.3.	
4.1.26.	4.4.	
4.1.27.	4.5.	
4.1.28.	4.6.	
4.1.29.	4.7.	I: 48.
4.1.30.	4.8.	I: 49.
4.1.31.	4.9.	I: 50.
4.1.32.	4.10.	
4.1.33.	4.11.	
4.1.34.	4.12.	
4.1.35.	4.13.	
4.1.36.	4.14.	
4.1.37.	4.15.	
4.1.38.	4.16.	
4.1.39.	4.17.	
4.1.40.	4.18.	
4.1.41.	4.19.	I: 60.
4.1.42.	4.20.	
4.1.43.	4.21.	
4.1.44.	4.22.	
4.1.45.	4.23.	
4.1.46.	4.24.	
4.1.47.	4.25.	
4.1.48.	4.26.	
4.1.49.	4.27.	
4.1.50.	4.28.	
4.1.51.	4.29.	I: two rules 70, 71.
4.1.52.	4.30.	
4.1.53.	4.31.	
4.1.54.	4.32.	
4.1.55.	4.33.	
4.1.56.	4.34.	
4.1.57.	4.35.	
4.1.58.	4.36.	
4.1.59.	4.37.	
4.1.60.	4.38.	I: 80.
4.1.61.	4.39.	
4.1.62.	4.40.	
4.1.63.	4.41.	

4.1.64.	4.42.
4.1.65.	4.43.
4.1.66.	4.44.
4.1.67.	4.45.
4.1.68.	4.46.

Colophons: H: 47. This agrees with Whitney's exclusion of CA 4.1.1-22 as belonging to the commentary and not to the text of the CA. On the other hand I gives 98 as the number of rules in this Pāda, while O gives 99 as the number of the same rules. Our number is 68. How do we account for this difference? We can only suggest that the passages in CA 4.1.1-22 were differently sliced into separate sūtras by the traditions represented by I and O. While the manuscript H physically contains these passages, it does not count them among the Sūtras of the CA. We have no way of knowing how exactly these passages were subdivided.

Adhyāya 4, Pāda 2.

CA	**Whitney**	**Mss.**
4.2.1.	4.47.	
4.2.2.	4.48.	
4.2.3.	4.49.	
4.2.4.	4.50.	
4.2.5.	4.51.	
4.2.6.	4.52.	
4.2.7.	4.53.	
4.2.8.	4.54.	
4.2.9.	4.55.	
4.2.10.	4.56.	
4.2.11.	4.57.	
4.2.12.	4.58.	
4.2.13.	4.59.	
4.2.14.	4.60.	
4.2.15.	4.61.	
4.2.16.	4.62.	
4.2.17.	4.63.	
4.2.18.	4.64.	
4.2.19.	4.65.	

4.2.20.	4.66.	
4.2.21.	4.67.	
4.2.22.	4.68.	
4.2.23.	4.69.	
4.2.24.	4.70.	
4.2.25.	4.71.	
4.2.26.	4.72.	I: 29

Colophons: O: 29. This agrees with I. Where are the three additional rules?

Adhyāya 4, Pāda 3.

CA	Whitney	Mss.
4.3.1.	4.73.	
4.3.2.	4.74.	
4.3.3.	4.75.	
4.3.4.	4.76.	
4.3.5.	4.77.	
4.3.6.	4.78.	
4.3.7.	4.79.	
4.3.8.	4.80.	
4.3.9.	4.81.	
4.3.10.	4.82.	I: 10.
4.3.11.	4.83.	
4.3.12.	4.84.	
4.3.13.	4.85.	
4.3.14.	4.86.	
4.3.15.	4.87.	
4.3.16.	4.88.	
4.3.17.	4.89.	
4.3.18.	4.90.	
4.3.19.	4.91.	
4.3.20.	4.92.	
4.3.21.	4.93.	
4.3.22.	missing	
4.3.23.	4.94.	
4.3.24.	4.95.	
4.3.25.	4.96.	

4.3.26.	4.97.	
4.3.27.	4.98.	
4.3.28.	4.99.	
4.3.29.	4.100.	I: 30.

Colophons: H: 102 (cumulative for this Adhyāya); I, O: 30 (for this Pāda).

Adhyāya 4, Pāda 4.

CA	Whitney	Mss.
4.4.1.	4.101.	
4.4.2.	4.102.	
4.4.3.	4.103.	
4.4.4.	4.104.	
4.4.5.	4.105.	
4.4.6.	4.106.	
4.4.7.	4.107.	
4.4.8.	missing	
4.4.9.	4.108.	
4.4.10.	4.109.	I: 10.
4.4.11.	4.110.	
4.4.12.	4.111.	
4.4.13.	4.112.	
4.4.14.	4.113.	
4.4.15.	4.114.	
4.4.16.	4.115.	
4.4.17.	4.116.	
4.4.18.	4.117.	
4.4.19.	4.118.	I: 20.
4.4.20.	4.119.	
4.4.21.	4.120.	
4.4.22.	4.121.	
4.4.23.	4.122.	
4.4.24.	4.123.	
4.4.25.	4.124.	
4.4.26.	4.125.	
4.4.27.	4.126.	I: 26.

Colophons: F: 580 (total for all Adhyāyas); G: 174 (for this Adhyāya); I: 27 (for this Pāda), 174 (for this Adhyāya), 516 (total for all Adhyāyas); O: 27 (for this Pāda). Our total for all the rules of the CA is 483, while Whitney's total comes to 435. The difference is accounted for by Whitney's exclusion of certain passages which he thought belonged to the commentary rather than to the text of the CA. The figure 516 found in the ms. I as the total for all the rules is explainable by supposing that this counting resulted because of primarily the included verses being represented as each containing at least two Sūtras, if not more. There are actually no extra passages as such. The figure 580 found in the ms. F as the total of all rules could possibly accounted for if we assume that each of the included verses is equivalent to four Sūtras. Such a calculation comes close to this figure. Again, we must note that the ms. F does not actually have any extra passages as such.

4. General Features of the Ancient Indian Phonetics[1]

4.1. Ancient Indian Phonetics

4.1.1. The tradition of phonetic analysis and description of Sanskrit in ancient India developed as one of the traditional tools used for the preservation and propagation of the Vedas, the religious scriptures of the ancient Hindus and it eventually came to be incorporated in a vastly developed tradition of Sanskrit grammar. While the Vedic literature was originally composed by individual Vedic priests and was orally maintained by generations of Vedic priestly families, eventually the Vedic texts came to be collected and edited into organized volumes, and systematic efforts were made to preserve both the texts themselves as well as the understanding of the meaning and the ritual application of these texts. The results of this organized effort have survived in the form of manuals of various kinds pertaining to various Vedic schools. Among these manuals, many deal with topics of linguistic interest, i.e. phonetics (*Śikṣā*), metrics (*Chandas*), etymology (*Nirukta*), and grammar (*Vyākaraṇa*).

The treatises on phonetics, generally divided into two types called Śikṣās and Prātiśākhyas, deal with specific Vedic texts and their recitation, rather than dealing with Sanskrit or Vedic language as such. This makes the

[1] This section of the Introduction is a revised and expanded version of my article "Ancient Indian Phonetics" which appeared in *The Encyclopedia of Language and Linguistics*, Volume 6, Pergamon Press, Oxford, 1994. I am grateful to the publisher for granting me permission to incorporate this revised version here.

phonetic manuals very special in some sense. The observations contained in the phonetic manuals are of a non-generalized, highly specific nature, and thus they provide for us a microscopically detailed picture of the sounds of Sanskrit as used in specific oral scriptural traditions. They contain a highly developed set of analytical tools and terminology which has won the admiration of Western linguists and Sanskritists ever since the discovery of Sanskrit by the West (cf. Whitney 1884, Allen 1953: 3ff).

4.2. Origins of Sanskrit Phonetics

4.2.1. The various Vedic texts were produced in different regions of India, beginning with about 1500 B.C. in the Northwestern corner, and the texts produced in one region were carried orally into other areas. During this movement, there was social and linguistic contact and convergence with peoples who were historically of non-Indo-European backgrounds, e.g. Dravidians, Tibeto-Burmans, and Austro-Asiatics. As a result of this contact and convergence, the Indo-Aryan dialects continuously went on changing and slowly a gap began to develop between the language of the preserved ancient scriptures and the language of the contemporary colloquial usage. This gap began to affect both the phonetic form of the orally preserved scriptural texts as well as their comprehension. A realization of this gap and its perceived negative impact on the preserved scriptural texts is indeed the starting point of the development of the analytical efforts reflected in the manuals left to us by the Vedic schools. On the phonetic side, it is quite clear that the same text was pronounced with slight differences eventually leading to doubts as to the exact wording. Emergence of sounds such as the retroflex consonants within the Indo-Aryan dialects was a gradual process leading to more or less retroflexed versions of the same Vedic text. The accents of ancient Vedic dialects were preserved as musical pitch variation in the recitation of Vedic texts, but these were no longer used in the colloquial contemporary dialects. Thus, it became increasingly difficult to naturally pronounce the Vedic texts with proper accents. The late Vedic texts (e.g. Śatapatha-Brāhmaṇa 1.6.3.8-10) narrate an interesting story about how a demon named Tvaṣṭṛ mispronounced a ritual expression and achieved disastrous results. The demon wished to have a son who would slay god Indra. Thus, he should have asked for a son who would be *indraśatrú* 'Indra's slayer.' However, being an ignorant demon, he mispronounced this expression as *índraśatru* which gave him a son who was killed by Indra. The version of this story in the Śatapatha Brāhmaṇa says that the demon actually should have said: *indrasya śatrur vardhasva.* This has been interpreted by scholars like Johannes Bronkhorst to suggest that using the proper accents for compounds had already become so difficult by this time, that the text asks that the compound be broken down to a phrase to avoid the confusion once for all. This story has been cited by phoneticians and grammarians to indicate why it is so important to learn how to properly pronounce the Vedic scriptures.

4.2.2. The pre-scientific phase of Sanskrit phonetics is already manifest in the earliest Vedic literature. The terms *akṣara* 'letter, sound, syllable' and *pada* 'metrical foot,' [and 'word' in some contexts] go back to the different phases of the Vedic literature. Thieme (1985) has presented an important conjecture concerning the beginnings of Sanskrit phonetics. Thieme translates the first verse of the Śaunakīya-Atharvaveda as follows:

> ये त्रि॑ष॒प्ताः प॑रि॒यन्ति॒ विश्वा॑ रू॒पाणि॒ बिभ्र॑तः ।
> वा॒चस्पति॒र्बला॑ ते॒षां त॒न्वो॑ अ॒द्य द॑धातु मे ॥ (शौ.अ.वे. १.१.१)
> "The thrice seven that go around, wearing all the shapes -- let the Lord of Speech put their powers into my body's parts today."

After detailed argumentation, Thieme concludes that this verse refers to twenty-one sounds of Sanskrit as distinctly conceived by the earliest Vedic thinkers and he lists them as follows:

a i u r̥ e o ai au	8 vowels
y r l v	4 semi-vowels
k c ṭ t p	5 occlusives
ś ṣ s h	4 spirants

Thieme (1985: 563) argues that "the sacred number 'thrice seven' could indeed be taken as the number of the abstract forms (*ākr̥ti-*), of the types, the kinds (*varṇa-*) of sounds of the sacred language." Such a listing, if indeed this is what is intended by the verse, would indicate that certain phonetic features were perhaps understood more clearly by this time than others, and that the number twenty-one, in all likelihood, is a reflection of this early pre-scientific phase, rather than an explicit representation of the "types" of Sanskrit sounds as found in the later developed texts on Sanskrit phonetics. Perhaps, the distinctions between the different points of articulation were implicitly understood, while the distinctions of quantity, voicing, aspiration, etc. were not arrived at.

4.2.3. However, there is one major difficulty in accepting Thieme's interpretation. It is not clear that all the classes of sounds listed by him in order to arrive at the number twenty-one were definitely recognized by the ancient phoneticians in India. We find several phonetic categories mentioned explicitly in late Vedic texts like the Aitareya-Āraṇyaka (2.2.4):

> तद्वा इदं बृहतीसहस्रं सम्पन्नम् । तस्य यानि व्यञ्जनानि तच्छरीरं, यो घोषः स आत्मा, य ऊष्माणः स प्राणः ।
>
> "Thus, this [collection of] a thousand *bṛhatī* verses comes into existence. Of that collection, the consonants (*vyañjana*) are the body, the voice (*ghoṣa* = vowels) is its soul, and the spirants (*ūṣman*) are its vital breath."

In the Chāndogya-Upaniṣad (2.22.5), vowels (*svara*) are distinguished explicitly from consonants (*vyañjana*), and among the consonants, a distinction is made between stops, i.e. *sparśa* 'contact sounds,' and spirants, i.e. *ūṣman* 'aspiration sounds':

> सर्वे स्वरा घोषवन्तो बलवन्तो वक्तव्याः ... सर्व ऊष्माणोऽग्रस्ता अनिरस्ता विवृता वक्तव्याः ... सर्वे स्पर्शा लेशेनानभिहिता वक्तव्याः ।
>
> "All vowels (*svara*) should be pronounced with resonance (*ghoṣa*) and force. ... All spirants (*ūṣman*) should be pronounced open, and not constricted or spitted out. ... All stops (*sparśa* = contact sounds) should be pronounced slightly incomplete."

4.2.4. While these terms seem to have been well established by the period of the Āraṇyakas, such is indeed not the case with the category of *antaḥsthā*. The Aitareya-Āraṇyaka (3.2.1) tells us that the specific category of semi-vowels (*antasthā* / *antaḥsthā*) was newly proposed by the scholar Hrasva Māṇḍūkeya, but that it was as yet not recognized by the author of the Aitareya-Āraṇyaka.

> तस्यैतस्यात्मनः प्राण ऊष्मरूपमस्थीनि स्पर्शरूपं मज्जानः स्वररूपं मांसं लोहितमित्येतदन्यच्चतुर्थमन्त(:)स्थारूपमिति ह स्माह ह्रस्वो माण्डूकेयः । त्रयं त्वेव न एतत्प्रोक्तम् ।
>
> "Of this self, the breath is like the spirants (*ūṣman*), the bones the mutes (*sparśa*), the marrow the vowels (*svara*), and flesh and blood the fourth part, the semi-vowels (*antasthā*). So says

Hrasva Māṇḍūkeya. **However, only three elements have been taught to us.**"

We know from other evidence (Deshpande 1979: 261) that the scholarly tradition of Hrasva Māṇḍūkeya came from the Northeastern region of Magadha, and that it is an innovative tradition, which among other things admitted more retroflexion into the oral text of the Ṛgveda, and that its views were contested by others. If indeed the above statement of the Aitareya-Āraṇyaka can be interpreted as an indication that the category of *antaḥsthā* was a relatively late category, this then raises serious doubts concerning Paul Thieme's interpretation of the first verse of the Śaunakīya-Atharvaveda as referring to twenty-one types of Sanskrit sounds including the four *antaḥsthā* sounds. If the inference based on the Aitareya-Āraṇyaka is correct, it would seem more likely that in a much more ancient period, such as the composition of the AV hymns, the vowels and the semi-vowels were not analytically distinguished from each other. Since the semi-vowels are not covered by either the term *sparśa* or *ūṣman* appearing in the Āraṇyaka literature, the non-distinction of semi-vowels from vowels is perhaps the strongest possibility for the earlier period. If vowels and semi-vowels were not yet clearly distinguished at this early period of the composition of the Saṃhitās, we may need to reconsider our understanding of the early form of the Saṃhitās as conceived by the pre-Āraṇyaka traditions. I am simply mentioning this subject here. I shall deal with it exhaustively on another occasion.

4.3. Emergence of Formal Phonetic Analysis

4.3.1. Sometime around 700 B.C., a standardized ordered alphabet of Sanskrit called *akṣarasamāmnāya* had come into existence. By this process, I am referring to an ordered presentation or grouping of Sanskrit sounds, with no necessary connection with any form of writing. This standardization was necessitated, among other things, by an increasing diglossic gap between the language of the orally preserved Vedic texts and the contemporary Sanskrit, as well as the vernacular languages. There was a perceived loss of the natural ability to correctly pronounce and recite the Vedic scriptures. The discussions concerning the need to study Sanskrit phonetics as seen in the introductory chapter of the MB of Patañjali (± 100 B.C.) show that the origin of the analytical tradition of Sanskrit phonetics lies in the urge to preserve the standardized pronunciation of the Vedic texts and to protect them from further deterioration.

4.3.2. The earliest scholars who seem to have paid attention to the form of the Vedic texts, especially their wording and pronunciation, are Śākalya, Śūravīra Māṇḍūkeya, and Hrasva Māṇḍūkeya. The Aitareya-Āraṇyaka (3.2.6) points to the fact that Śākalya followed the tradition of the Māṇḍūkeyas to a large extent:[2]

> अथ हास्मा एतत्कृष्णहारितो वाग्ब्राह्मणमिवोपोदाहरति । प्रजापतिः प्रजाः सृष्ट्वा व्यस्रंसत संवत्सरः । स च्छन्दोभिरात्मानं समदधात् तस्मात्संहिता । तस्यै वा एतस्यै संहितायै णकारो बलं षकारः प्राण आत्मा । स यो हैतौ णकारषकारवनुसंहितमृचो वेद सबलां सप्राणां संहितां वेदायुष्यमिति विद्यात् । स यदि विचिकित्सेत्सणकारं ब्रवाणी३ँ अणकारा३ँ इति सणकारमेव ब्रूयात्सषकारं ब्रवाणी३ँ अषकारा३ँ इति सषकारमेव ब्रूयात्। ते यद् वयमनुसंहितमृचोऽधीमहे यच्च माण्डूकेयीयमध्यायं प्रब्रूमस्तेन नो णकारषकारा उपाप्ताविति ह स्माह ह्रस्वो माण्डूकेयः । अथ यद्वयमनुसंहित-मृचोऽधीमहे यच्च माण्डूकेयीयमध्यायं प्रब्रूमस्तेन नो णकारषकारा उपाप्ता-विति ह स्माह स्थविरः शाकल्यः ।
>
> (Edited by A.B. Keith. Oxford University Press, 1909, pp. 138-9)
>
> Now Kṛṣṇahārīta proclaims this secret doctrine, as it were, regarding speech to him. Prajāpati, the year, after creating creatures, burst. He put himself together by means of the meters, therefore it is the *saṃhitā*. Of that *saṃhitā*, the letter *ṇ* is the strength, the letter *ṣ* the breath, the self. He who knows the *saṃhitā* and the letters *ṇ* and *ṣ*, he knows the *saṃhitā* with its breath and its strength. ... If he is in doubt whether to say it with an *ṇ* or without an *ṇ*, let him say it with an *ṇ*. If he is in doubt whether to say it with an *ṣ* or without an *ṣ*, let him say it with an *ṣ*. Hrasva Māṇḍūkeya says: "If we repeat the verses according to the *Saṃhitā*, and if we recite according to the teaching of the Māṇḍūkeya, then the letters *ṇ* and *ṣ* are obtained for us."

---

2 The Śāṃkhāyana-Āraṇyaka 8.11 (ed. by Bhim Dev, Vishveshvarananda Vaidika Research Institute, Hoshiarpur, 1980) contains an important variant of the Aitareya-Āraṇyaka passage: ते यद्वयमनुसंहितमृचोऽधीमहे यच्च माण्डूकेयीयमध्यायं प्रब्रूमस्तेन नो णकारषकारा उपाप्ताविति ह स्माह ह्रस्वो माण्डूकेयः । अथ यद्वयमनुसंहितमृचोऽधीमहे यच्च स्वाध्यायमधीमहे, तेना नो णकारषकारा उपाप्ताविति ह स्माह स्थविरः शाकल्यः । While the Aitareya-Āraṇyaka passage clearly indicates that Śākalya was a follower of the Māṇḍūkeya school on certain matters, the Śāṃkhāyana-Āraṇyaka makes this relationship a little less clear. The introductory section called Vargadvaya at the beginning of the Ṛgvedaprātiśākhya seems to suggest that the Māṇḍūkeyas were more ancient, and it seems more likely that the relationship as inferred from the Aitareya-Āraṇyaka is historically justified.

> Sthavira Śākalya says: "If we repeat the verses according to the *Saṃhitā,* and if we recite according to the teaching of the Māṇḍūkeya, then the letters *ṇ* and *ṣ* are obtained for us."

4.3.3. These authorities were also perhaps some of the earliest scholarly figures who attempted to construct rules for combining words of the Padapāṭha to produce a continuous scriptural text (*saṃhitā*). The general assumption seems to have been that the continuous Vedic texts needed to be explicitly produced by applying the rules of sandhi to the word-by-word texts provided by scholars like Śākalya (cf. *padaprakr̥tiḥ saṃhitā*, NR 1.17; RPR 2.1). Thus, these early traditions did not offer any details on how to segment the received continuous texts, but they were engaged in figuring out the rules of sandhi which applied to the word-by-word texts to recreate the continuous texts. Thus, the concern of these early phoneticians and exegetes was two-fold, i.e. the proper pronunciation of the Vedic texts and figuring out the rules for performing sandhi operations on the word-by-word texts to produce the continuous texts. The first concern was responsible for developing the analytical study of the articulation of sounds, while the second concern was responsible for the search for features and groupings of these sounds which could be used in formulating the rules of sandhi. In these two concerns, we can see the origins of the phonetic and phonological theories of the ancient Indian phoneticians and grammarians.

4.3.4. The word *śikṣā* refers to training in general, and phonetic or recitational training in particular. It appears in the Taittirīya-Upaniṣad (1.2) which refers specifically to six types of training involved in phonetic education, i.e. *varṇa* 'sounds,' *svara* 'accents,' *mātrā* 'quantity,' *bala* 'force,' *sāma* 'even articulation,' and *santāna* 'continuity in recitation.' In later times, over a hundred texts called Śikṣās were produced by different authorities. Most of the surviving Śikṣā texts are of a relatively late period. The most well known among these Śikṣās is the Pāṇinīyaśikṣā attributed by the tradition to the famous Sanskrit grammarian Pāṇini. Other important Śikṣās include the Vyāsaśikṣā, the Āpiśaliśikṣā, the Yājñavalkyaśikṣā, and the Nāradaśikṣā. A few of these Śikṣā texts, such as the Pāṇinīyaśikṣā and the Āpiśaliśikṣā, are non-"sectarian" in the sense that they do not attach themselves to a particular Vedic school, and deal with the Sanskrit language in a generic way. However, most Śikṣā texts are "sectarian." They are attached to particular Vedic schools, and deal with the recitation of particular Vedic texts. They often provide the most minute details of the recitational practice.

4.3.5. The second category of texts dealing with Sanskrit phonetics, traditionally considered to be more authoritative than the Śikṣās, is represented by the Prātiśākhyas. As the word *prātiśākhya* [< *prati* 'each' + *śākhā* 'branch'] suggests, each branch of the Vedic literature was ideally expected to have a Prātiśākhya text attached to it. Among the surviving texts of this type, we must mention the following important treatises. The Ṛgveda-Prātiśākhya attributed to Śaunaka belongs to the Śaiśirīya branch of the Ṛgveda, which is no longer extant. It refers to the views of Śākalya, whose edition of the Ṛgveda survives, but there is no extant Prātiśākhya attributed to Śākalya. The Taittirīya-Prātiśākhya is attached to the Taittirīya school of the Black Yajurveda. The Vājasaneyi-Prātiśākhya is attached to the White Yajurveda. A text called the Bhāṣika-Sūtra deals with the recitation of the late Vedic prose text of the Śatapatha-Brāhmaṇa belonging to the tradition of the White Yajurveda. There are five texts which fall in the general category of the Prātiśākhyas of the Sāmaveda. Of these five texts, only the Ṛktantra deals with the general discussion of phonetics. There are two texts, i.e. the Atharva-Prātiśākhya and the Śaunakīyā Caturādhyāyikā, associated with the Śaunakīya school of the Atharvaveda. The exact dating of the Śikṣās and the Prātiśākhyas has been a topic of long-standing debates. In general, one can say that the existing Śikṣās seem to be "all of them, young, elaborations of the definitions laid down in the Prātiśākhyas," (Thieme 1935: 85-6). The existing Prātiśākhyas themselves seem to have old and new textual layers in them, some pre-dating the grammarian Pāṇini (± 500 B.C.), others reflecting post-Pāṇinian developments.

4.4. Formation of Sanskrit Alphabet

4.4.1. Referred to by the term *akṣara-samāmnāya* 'collective statement of sounds,' an ordered Sanskrit alphabet, with no reference to writing intended, seems to have come into existence by the time the late Vedic literature (about 700 B.C.) was produced. A distinction between vowels and consonants was already made. The consonants were generally divided into three categories, *sparśa* 'contact sounds,' *antaḥsthā* 'in-between sounds,' and *uṣman* 'aspiration sounds.' The first category included stops and nasals, the second category included semi-vowels, and the third category included spirants. A further amplification resulted in the following generally accepted alphabet:

Vowels:	*a ā i ī u ū r̥ r̥̄ l̥ e o ai au*				
Consonants:					
sparśa:	*k*	*kh*	*g*	*gh*	*ṅ*
	c	*ch*	*j*	*jh*	*ñ*
	ṭ	*ṭh*	*ḍ*	*ḍh*	*ṇ*
	t	*th*	*d*	*dh*	*n*
	p	*ph*	*b*	*bh*	*m*
antaḥsthā:	*y*	*r*	*l*	*v*	
ūṣman	*ś*	*ṣ*	*s*	*h*	

Additional sounds:

Anusvāra	*ṃ*
Visarga	*ḥ*
Jihvāmūlīya	*ḫ* (before *k, kh*)
Upadhmānīya	*ẖ* (before *p, ph*)

4.4.2. The above alphabet, or rather the formal listing of sounds, is accepted with minor differences by all the Śikṣās and Prātiśākhyas. The alphabet shows a tacit awareness of several features of sounds, and a certain ordering of those features. The vowels are grouped into several sub-groups. The first group is represented by the vowels *a, ā, i, ī, u,* and *ū*. These are the basic simple vowels. They are ordered back-to-front in terms of their points of articulation, i.e. throat (*kaṇṭha*), palate (*tālu*), and lips (*oṣṭha*). This order is the reverse of the front-to-back order of listing the sounds in western linguistics, e.g. *p, t, k*. To these basic simple vowels are added the vocalic *r̥, r̥̄, l̥,* (and *l̥̄* for some traditions). All these together, beginning with *a*, are called *samāna* 'simple' vowels. They are grouped into pairs of short and long vowels, and each pair is often subsumed under a common generalization called *varṇa*, e.g. the vowels *a* and *ā* belong to the family or type designated by the term *a-varṇa*. After the simple vowels comes the group of four vowels, i.e. *e, o, ai,* and *au*. These four are generally called *sandhyakṣara*s 'compound-vowels.' Out of these four, the first two are often, though not always, described as monophthongs, while the latter two are most often explicitly called *dvi-varṇa* 'consisting of two sounds,' i.e. diphthongs. The principle of back-to-front ordering in terms of the points of articulations is maintained even in the sub-groups *e, o,* and *ai, au*. As we move to the category of sounds called *sparśa* 'contact sounds, ' i.e. stops and nasals, we see several converging principles at work. The five horizontal groups are each called a *varga* 'group,' i.e. *k(a)-varga, c(a)-varga, ṭ(a)-varga, t(a)-varga,* and *p(a)-varga.* The vertical ordering of these groups shows the same back-to-front ordering, with the *k(a)-varga* at the back end of the spectrum of points of articulation and the *p(a)-varga* at the front end of the same spectrum. The palatal, the retroflex, and the dental groups are ordered between the velar and the labial groups. The vertical lines intersecting these five groups show other phonetic features. The first vertical group, i.e. *k, c, ṭ, t,* and *p,* consists of voiceless unaspirated stops. The second vertical group, i.e. *kh, ch, ṭh, th,* and *ph,* consists of voiceless aspirated stops. The third vertical group, i.e. *g, j, ḍ, d,* and *b,* consists of voiced unaspirated stops. The fourth vertical group, i.e. *gh, jh, ḍh, dh,* and *bh,* consists of voiced aspirated stops. The fifth vertical group, i.e. *ṅ, ñ, ṇ, n,* and *m,* consists of nasals.

4.4.3. The order of consonants in each of the five horizontal groups of stops and nasals is significant for other theoretical reasons as well. Deshpande (1976) shows that there were theorists who reduced the total number of primitive sounds to a much smaller number and argued that other Sanskrit sounds were built by combining these primitive sounds. The principal sources of information on these ancient theories are the RPR (13.13; 13.15) and the ancient Śikṣā text quoted by the Caturādhyāyībhāṣya on CA (1.1.12):

प्रयोक्तुरीहागुणसंनिपाते वर्णीभवन्गुणविशेषयोगात् ।
एकः श्रुतीः कर्मणाप्नोति बह्वीः ॥ ऋ.प्रा. १३.१३ ॥

"When the air (coming up from lungs) is associated with a specific desire of the speaker, that air, being transformed into a sound through specific articulatory effort, attains to various auditory forms, because of the acquisition of various properties."

आहुर्घोषं घोषवतामकारमेकेऽनुस्वारमनुनासिकानाम् ॥
सोष्मतां च सोष्मणामूष्मणाहुः सस्थानेन, घोषिणां घोषिणैव ॥
ऋ.प्रा. १३.१५ ॥

"Some call *a* the voice of the voiced [consonants], and the *ṃ* [the voice] of the nasal [consonants]. They also say that the aspiration of the [voiceless] aspirated [stops] is [due to a combination] with a homorganic spirant, and [the aspiration] of the voiced [aspirated stops] is [due to a combination] with the voiced [spirant, i.e. *h*]."

Ancient Śikṣā quoted in CAB on CA (1.1.12):

‘सस्थानैरूष्मभिः पृक्तास्तृतीयाः प्रथमाश्च ये ।
चतुर्थाश्च द्वितीयाश्च संपद्यन्त इति स्थितिः ॥’
अपर आह । चतुर्थो हकारेणेति ।
‘पञ्चैव प्रथमान् स्पर्शानाहुरेके मनीषिणः ।
तेषां गुणोपसञ्चयादान्यभाव्यं प्रवर्तते ॥
जिह्वामूलीयशषसा उपध्मानीयपञ्चमाः ।
एतैर्गुणैः समन्विता द्वितीया इति तान्विदुः ॥
त एव सह घोषेण तृतीया इति तान्विदुः ।
ऊष्मणा च द्वितीयेन चतुर्था इति तान्विदुः ॥
प्रथमाः सह घोषेण यदा स्युरनुनासिकाः ।
तानाहुः पञ्चमान् स्पर्शांस्तथा वर्णगुणाः स्मृताः ॥

“The thirds and the firsts, combined with homorganic spirants, become the fourths and the seconds. Such is the decision. Another phonetician says: The fourth is [derived] through a combination with *h*. Some scholars say that there are only five stops, i.e. the firsts [of the respective series]. They are transformed into other sounds through their acquisition of different properties. [The firsts, i.e. *k, c, ṭ, t,* and *p*], combined respectively with these factors, i.e. *ḫ* (= *jihvāmūlīya*), *ś, ṣ, s,* and *ẖ* (= *upadhmānīya*), are known as the seconds, [i.e. *kh, ch, ṭh, th,* and *ph*]. The same [firsts], when combined with voice (*ghoṣa*), are known as the thirds, [i.e. *g, j, ḍ, d,* and *b*]. [When the thirds are further] combined with a second element, a spirant, they are known as the fourths, [i.e. *gh, jh, ḍh, dh,* and *bh*]. When the firsts, combined with voice, are nasalized, they are known as the fifths, [i.e. *ṅ, ñ, ṇ, n,* and *m*]. Thus, the properties of the sounds are traditionally recounted.”

Thus, for instance, in the series *k, kh, g, gh,* and *ṅ*, the first consonant *k* is deemed to be a primitive consonant. By adding the voiceless velar aspiration, i.e. *ḫ* (*jihvāmūlīya*), to the primitive *k,* one derives the voiceless aspirate stop *kh*. It is important to note that the aspirated stops are called *soṣman* ‘fused with a spirant’ in Sanskrit indicating their compound nature in terms of these early phonetic theories. My best guess is that this theory developed after the period of the Aitareya-Āraṇyaka, which knows the term *ūṣman,* but not *soṣman.* The latter is obviously derived from the former, and hence comes after the former, at least logically, if not also chronologically. Similarly, the sound *g* is derived by adding the primitive voice (*ghoṣa*) *a* to the primitive consonant *k*. Thus, naturally, the category of voiced consonants is called *ghoṣavat* 'with voice,' indicating that the feature of voice is also looked at as an add-on feature. The sound *gh* is derived by adding the voiced aspiration *h* to *k*. The final nasal of the series, i.e. *ṅ*, is derived by adding the primitive voiced nasal *ṃ* (*anusvāra*) to the primitive consonant *k*. Thus, the order of these consonants represents the results of prior theoretical considerations which are explicitly discussed in texts like the RPR and the ancient Śikṣā quoted in the CAB (Deshpande 1976).

4.4.4. After these 'contact' sounds, the alphabet lists the semi-vowels or 'in-between-sounds' (*antasthā* / *antaḥsthā*), i.e. *y, r, l,* and *v*. At the very end are listed the spirants, *ūṣman* 'aspiration sounds,' i.e. *ś, ṣ, s,* and *h*. The semi-vowels, i.e. *y, r, l,* and *v,* as well as the three sibilants, i.e. *ś, ṣ,* and *s,* also exhibit the back-to-front ordering in terms of the points of articulations of the included sounds. It seems that the phoneticians intended the final *h* as a separate addition to the first three sibilants. The first three are voiceless sibilants, while the final *h,* is a voiced aspiration. Most texts also add the sounds *ṃ, ḥ, ẖ,* and *ḫ*. Among these sounds, the sounds, *ḥ* (*visarga*) is a voiceless *h* sound. The sounds *ḫ* (*jihvāmūlīya*) and *ẖ* (*upadhmānīya*) are variants for *ḥ,* before *k, kh,* and *p, ph,* respectively. The nature of the sound represented by *ṃ,* the *anusvāra,* is highly debated in the ancient texts. The general consensus is that it is an oral-nasal generic sound which changes to homorganic nasals in accordance with what follows. An unchanged or unchangeable *ṃ* is found only before the spirants and *r*. This predominant context of spirants for the *anusvāra* led some texts like the RPR to include this sound in its list of spirants (*ūṣman*). Since there was a feeling that an *anusvāra* could be prolonged in length in recitation, the same text says that an *anusvāra* may be considered to be either a vowel or a consonant. Most of these texts discuss several other sounds and their features. Besides the *ṃ* (= *anusvāra*) which is generally described as an oral-nasal sound, most texts also posit another sound called *nāsikya*, which is deemed to be a pure nasal sound. Additionally, most texts talk about fractional vowels, such as the ones which go in the make-up of a vowel normally represented as *r̥,* i.e. *ərə*. The phonetic treatises also go into details of what are clearly transitional sounds. For instance, the texts talk about a nasal *g̊* (= *ŋ*?) intervening between the consonants *g* and *n* in a word like *agni*. Such consonants are called *Yama*s. The texts also go into details of accents (= pitch variation) and nasalization of vowels, as well as three- and four-moraic vowels. According to these texts, one can also get contextual nasal variants for all vowels, and the semi-vowels *y*, *v*, and *l*, i.e. *ỹ*, *ṽ*, and *l̃*.

4.5. Descriptive Techniques & Terminology

4.5.1. The descriptive and the prescriptive goal of the ancient Indian phonetic tradition was to be able to clearly distinguish between different sounds of Sanskrit, so that one will not be mistaken or mispronounced for another. Verse 10 of the versified Pāṇinīyaśikṣā says:

स्वरतः कालतः स्थानात् प्रयत्नानुप्रदानतः ।
इति वर्णविदः प्राहुर्निपुणं तन्निबोधत ॥

Sounds are distinguished from each other on the basis of accents (*svara*), time or duration (*kāla*), point of articulation (*sthāna*), manner (*prayatna*), and type of phonation (*anupradāna*). Here the term *svara* 'accent' refers to the pitch distinctions denoted by the terms *udātta* 'high,' *anudātta* 'low,' and *svarita* 'rising-falling.' The term *kāla* 'duration' refers to units of time it requires to pronounce a given sound. Consonants are generally considered to be of a half-mora (*ardha-mātrā*) length, while vowels can be of one, two, three and four morae in length. The one-mora vowels are called *hrasva* 'short.' The two-mora vowels are called *dīrgha* 'long.' Vowels with three and four morae length are called *pluta* 'prolonged.' The term *sthāna* 'place, point of articulation' refers to points on the articulatory track, i.e. *uras* 'chest,' *kaṇṭha* 'throat,' *jihvāmūla* 'tongue-root,' *tālu* 'hard-palate,' *mūrdhan* 'cerebrum, roof of the oral cavity,' *dantamūla* 'alveolar ridge, root of teeth,' *danta* 'teeth,' and *oṣṭha* 'lips.' The list of points of articulation sometimes also includes *nāsikā* 'nose.' The term *prayatna* 'manner' refers to how the physical organ called *karaṇa* 'articulator' relates to the point of articulation, i.e. *sparśa* 'contact,' *upasaṃhāra* 'approximation,' *vivṛta* 'open,' etc. The term *karaṇa* 'articulator' generally refers to different parts of the tongue, such as the tip, the middle, and the root, as well as the sides or edges and the middle. It also refers to teeth in the case of labio-dental sounds like *v*, and to the lower lip in the case of labial sounds like *b*. For nasalized vowels such as *ã, ĩ, ũ, ẽ,* and *õ*, the nose is often considered to be the articulator, while for the nasal consonants *ṅ, ñ, ṇ, n,* and *m,* the nose is considered to be the point of articulation (Deshpande 1975: 11-12). The texts show a great diversity of opinion on many of these classifications (cf. Allen 1953, Bare 1976). The final category is that of *anupradāna* 'phonation, emission.' Generally, there are two types of emission, i.e. *śvāsa* 'breath' and *nāda* 'resonance,' resulting from two different positions of the glottal chords, *vivṛta* 'open' and *saṃvṛta* 'close' respectively. The emission of the type of breath further results in voiceless sounds, while the emission of the type of resonance further results in vowels and voiced consonants. Some texts like the Taittirīya-Prātiśākhya claim that there is a third type of emission called *hakāra* 'the *h* sound, voiced aspiration' when the glottal chords are in a position in-between open and close, and this type combines voice or resonance with aspiration and is termed breathy voice in modern phonetics. This type of emission is found in the voiced spirant *h,* as well as in voiced aspirate stops such as *gh, jh, ḍh, dh,* and *bh.* The ancient Indian texts use two different terms, *nāda* and *ghoṣa* to refer to voicing. We are often told that the feature of *nāda* is shared by vowels and *ghoṣavat* consonants, lit. consonants possessed of *ghoṣa*, voiced consonants. Modern scholars have debated the question of whether or not this refers to two different types of resonance. Some have suggested that the distinction has no articulatory basis, but that it is phonologically motivated. Others have suggested a possible articulatory basis, namely that the first, i.e. *nāda*, is produced by the closure of glottal chords, and that the secondary amplification, i.e. *ghoṣa*, is produced by a closure in the oral chamber created by the contact between the articulator and the point of articulation (cf. Deshpande 1976, Cardona 1983).

4.5.2. Certain features are considered as plus/minus features in ancient Indian phonetics, while others are considered as more/less features. The terms *ghoṣavat* (voiced) and *aghoṣa* (voiceless) indicate that the feature of *ghoṣa* 'voice' is a plus/minus feature. On the other hand, the feature of aspiration, especially when designated by the term *prāṇa*, appears as a more/less feature. The sounds which are called unaspirated in Western terminology are called *alpaprāṇa* 'with less *prāṇa,*' while the aspirated sounds are called *mahāprāṇa* 'with greater *prāṇa.*' Similarly, the notion of *prayatna* 'effort, manner' is expressed in some texts in binary terms *spṛṣṭa*/*aspṛṣṭa* 'with or without contact between the articulator and the point of articulation,' while in other texts, this notion is expressed in terms of degrees of openness and contact i.e. *vivṛta* 'open,' *īṣadvivṛta* 'slightly open,' *vivṛtatara* 'more open,' and *vivṛtatama* 'most open,' *spṛṣṭa* 'in contact,' and *īṣatspṛṣṭa* 'in slight contact.'

4.6. What is distinctive?

4.6.1. Several scholars have devoted their attention to a possible distinction between phonetics and phonology in the context of the ancient traditions of Sanskrit phonetics and grammar (cf. Deshpande 1975, Bare 1976,

Cardona 1983). Often the term *varṇa* is translated with the term 'phoneme' in modern expositions of Sanskrit phonetics. The Sanskrit grammarians do indeed discuss minimum pairs like *kūpa/sūpa/yūpa*. However, the term *varṇa* does not strictly refer to a phoneme in modern linguistics. For Sanskrit phoneticians, the sounds *n* and *ñ* are distinct *varṇa*s, while they would be only allophones for a modern linguist. On the contrary, the sounds *a* and *ā* would be separate phonemes for a modern linguist, but they belong to the same *varṇa* for Sanskrit phoneticians and grammarians. On the other hand, the Sanskrit phoneticians and grammarians do indeed have a notion that certain features of sounds are relevant in some descriptive contexts, while they are not relevant in other contexts. Kātyāyana in his comments on Pāṇini's grammar often brings up the notion that the features (*guṇa,* quality) of accent (*svara*), nasality (*ānunāsikya*), and duration (*kāla*) are distinctive (*bhedaka*), See: Deshpande (1975: 50ff; 203, note 442; 207, note 466). According to the fully developed phonetico-grammatical doctrines of Sanskrit grammarians, the term *avarṇa* refers to the whole family (e.g. *avarṇa-kula*) of the following eighteen sounds: *a, ā, ā3, á, ā́, ā́3, à, ā̀, ā̀3, ã, ā̃, ā̃3, ã́, ā̃́, ā̃́3, ã̀, ā̃̀, ā̃̀3.*

4.6.2. The distinctions of length, accent, and nasality are not relevant for inclusion in a *varṇa*. On the other hand, the term *akāra* refers to the six tokens of short *a* differing in accent and nasality, but not in length. The grammarian-phoneticians knew that in formulating some rules of sandhi, they could achieve maximum descriptive economy by resorting to the *varṇa* groupings, while for other rules, the *-kāra* grouping seemed more economical, and for still other rules, one needed to make a highly specific reference to a token with a specific length, nasality, accent etc. The grammarian-phoneticians make several important distinctions in their terminology. For instance, two sound tokens are *sarūpa* 'with identical phonetic shape,' if and only if they have all identical phonetic features, including length, nasality, accents, etc. Two vowel-tokens are grouped in the same *x-kāra* group, if they have the same point of articulation, articulator, manner, and quantity. They could differ in nasality and accent, and still be part of the same *x-kāra* group. Two sounds are *savarṇa* 'homogeneous' with each other if they share the same point of articulation and the same manner. These different groupings were used to formulate different rules in Sanskrit grammar, and allowed descriptive optimization. The notion of maximal featural proximity (*āntaratamya*) is one of the principles used in Sanskrit grammar to determine the choice of a substitute from among a choice of alternatives (cf. Bare 1976, Hueckstedt 1995).

4.6.3. The Sanskrit grammarian-phoneticians were also aware of another distinction, i.e. that of the speed of delivery or tempo, i.e. fast, medium, and slow. These modes of recitation are discussed in Kātyāyana's Vārttikas on Pāṇini 1.1.70 and 1.4.109. Nāgeśabhaṭṭa, in his Uddyota (MB, Vol. I, Pt. I, p. 378) quotes the following verse:

अभ्यासार्थे द्रुता वृत्तिः प्रयोगार्थे तु मध्यमा ।
शिष्याणामुपदेशार्थं वृत्तिरिष्टा विलम्बिता ।।

The verse says that different modes of delivery were considered to be appropriate for different contexts. The fast speed is supposed to be used when a person is reciting the mantras for his own study. In the ritual use of the mantras, one is supposed to use the medium speed. A teacher is supposed to use the slow speed to recite the mantras while teaching his students. Using an inappropriate speed at the wrong occasion creates unacceptable situations, and in this sense, the speed or tempo is a distinctive feature at this level. However, these differences of tempo had no euphonic or grammatical value. This has been clearly recognized by Kātyāyana in his Vārttika: *siddhaṃ tv avasthitā varṇā vaktuś cirāciravacanād vṛttayo viśiṣyante,* MB (Kielhorn edn.), Vol.I, p. 181. Further they noticed that a consonant such as *k* seemed to acquire a certain degree of voicing in intervocalic positions, but that it was not to be distinguished from the generic *k* for all practical purposes.

4.6.4. In the work of Bhartṛhari, the grammarian-philosopher of ± 500 A.D., we find a new representation of these different levels of distinctiveness. These different levels of distinctiveness are seen in terms of a production model. There is a notion that there are ontologically eternal true sounds (*sphoṭa, varṇa*) which are temporally manifested by the physical sounds of two kinds, primary physical sounds (*prākṛta-dhvani*) and secondary physical sounds (*vaikṛta-dhvani*). There are several different views found in Bhartṛhari's Vākyapadīya and in his commentary on Patañjali's MB regarding the relationship between the real sounds, the primary physical sounds, and the secondary physical sounds, and these have been ably discussed in detail by S.D. Joshi (1967: 20-34). For our present purpose, suffice it to say that the level of *sphoṭa* 'true sound,' in general, seems to reflect only the features of point of articulation, manner, voicing, aspiration, etc., but not duration or tempo. The *sphoṭa* level is said to be beyond temporality, while the primary manifesting sounds have the feature of duration or length. The secondary manifesting sounds, which are further reverberations of the primary manifesting sounds, reveal the feature of tempo. Thus, in general, we get concentric circles representing different features. As a production model, I do not think Bhartṛhari's ideas will rank very high in the evaluation of modern phoneticians. On the other hand, the diagrammatic perception of the various phonetic features as concentric circles moving out from more distinctive to less distinctive offers an interesting view of these features and deserves to be explored further.

5. Phonetics vs Phonology in Indian Grammatical Tradition

5.1. 'Phonetics' versus 'Phonology' in Modern Linguistics

5.1.1. There are a number of distinctions made explicitly in modern linguistics for which there are no exact parallels in the traditions of Sanskrit Śikṣās, Prātiśākhyas, and Vyākaraṇa. One such distinction is that between the categories of 'phonetic' versus 'phonemic', or to use a more recent term, 'phonological'. Both phonetics and phonology, in their various brands and branches as practiced in modern linguistics, represent a study of the sound system of a given language. Without getting into too many technicalities, we can describe the difference between these two allied fields in the following way. Phonetics aims at studying the articulatory and the acoustic processes involved in the production of the sounds used by a given language. The very basic material which is being studied may be called phonic material, i.e. the sounds of a language as they are produced and perceived. The next level of understanding may be reached in what may be called phonemic. At this level, an analyst may be looking for features which are distinctive in some sense. The notion of 'phoneme' in structural linguistics attempted to come to grips with this question. There may be two instances of the phonic material which may be different in some respect, and yet may be perceived by both the speaker and the listener as being two instances of the same sound. This kind of an approach leads the analyst to distinguish between differences among the sounds which matter, and the differences which do not matter. Now the whole notion of what matters is a complex notion in itself and later we shall explore this complexity in some detail. At this point, suffice it to say that the traditional notion of 'phoneme' dealt with one such level of what matters, and came up with a concept that for a given language, there was a fixed inventory of distinctive sounds. This lead the structural linguists to work on determining such inventories for various languages, and to debate whether a given phone or sound-instance was an independent phoneme, or merely an allophone, a contextual variant of a phoneme. Eventually, the emphasis on inventories of phonemes, and the debate on a semi-metaphysical question of whether such phonemes exist, gave way to a study of what came to be known as distinctive features. The sounds came to be viewed as bundles of features, some of which were viewed as being distinctive in some sense. The emphasis on the discovery of phonemes then shifted to the determination of a set of distinctive features for a given language. The next level of understanding of the sounds of a language is reached in a branch of linguistics which is now generally called phonology. In terms of the current state of the science of linguistics, the branch of phonemics is very much dead, while the branches of phonetics and phonology are very much alive and prospering. What does phonology deal with? Phonology deals with the study of relationships between the sounds and features of these sounds as part of a system. It focuses on the behavior of sounds in relation to each other, and investigates the questions of how the behavior of sounds can be described in the form of predictable rules. Such rules may make use of various groupings of sounds, their features etc., and can be formulated at increasingly abstract levels. Phonetics and phonology may be studied both in synchronic as well as diachronic aspects. In both such approaches, one can raise the question of not only 'how' the sounds behave, but go further and raise the question of 'why' the sounds behave in a particular way. The answer to the question of 'why' may then be given in various different ways. For a given pattern of behavior of sounds, the answer may lie in the current phonetic features of those sounds, or such a behavior of sounds may simply reflect an inherited pattern of behavior, not fully justifiable in terms of the current features of the given sounds. This leads to some interesting and important possibilities. It is relatively easy to see that phonological groupings of sounds may be motivated by the phonetic features of the given sounds. However, one cannot discount the possibility and the probability that the phonological behavior of sounds may in some cases lead sounds with originally divergent phonetic features to move closer to a more homogeneous phonetic character.

5.1.2. The tradition of Sanskrit phonetics represented in the Śikṣās, Prātiśākhyas, and Sanskrit Grammars clearly does not have any interest in the historical study of Sanskrit, and hence one cannot find any explicit discussions in this tradition in this regard. At the same time, one need not assume that this tradition has been left untouched by the history of the language itself. Similarly, even though the tradition has no explicit separate terms for what we call phonetics and phonology in modern linguistics, one need not assume that the ancient grammarians and phoneticians did not have some of the same concerns. We need to look for what such concerns may have been, and the ways in which such concerns have surfaced in the ancient literature. While we must make every effort to make sure that we are not superimposing a modern set of concepts on the statements of the ancient grammarians, we should leave no stone unturned to find out the distinctions that they made, and the ones which they did not make. A good deal of work has been done in this direction by scholars like George Cardona, Paul Kiparsky, myself, my student James Bare, and more recently by Robert Hueckstedt. In what follows, I shall briefly describe the kind of research which has been going on in this field for the past twenty some years. Many of the details, which I shall report, involve long-standing controversies, though here I shall not proceed in a polemical fashion.

5.2. 'Varṇa' versus 'Phoneme'

5.2.1. In modern expositions of Sanskrit grammar and phonetics, especially the ones coming from India, there has been a tendency to use the term 'phoneme' to render the Sanskrit term *varṇa.* Whatever the historical origins of the term *varṇa,* and we shall not deal with that question here, the term has been used with a wide latitude of reference in Sanskrit literature. Perhaps the term *varṇa* is very much like the English term 'letter,' making an oblique reference to the art of writing. The widest possible meaning of the term *varṇa* is 'sound, letter.' In this wide sense, it appears in expressions like *varṇa-samāmnāya,* where it seems to be identical in meaning with the term *akṣara,* cf. *akṣara-samāmnāya.* If the term *varṇa* refers to sounds listed in the traditional Sanskrit alphabet, including the often unlisted sounds (*ayogavāha*s), e.g. *ṃ* and *ḥ*, can this use of the term *varṇa* be identical in meaning with the sense of the term 'phoneme' in structural linguistics? Most of the sounds listed in the Sanskrit alphabet do qualify for the term 'phoneme,' but not all. In order that a sound should qualify for the term 'phoneme,' we must have minimal pairs of words which differ in just one sound. Patañjali's *kūpa / sūpa / yūpa* analysis does look similar to the analysis with minimal pairs in structural linguistics. However, the fact is that for sounds like *ḥ, ṅ, ñ, ḫ,* and *ẖ,* we cannot find minimal pairs in Sanskrit. For example, we have the pair *bhāna / bhāṇa,* where the change of just one sound produces another word with a distinct meaning. Through analysis like this, we can conclude that the Sanskrit alphabet includes some *varṇa*s which are not phonemes, but are allophones in modern terminology. Why were such sounds considered to be *varṇa*s? Here, the distinctive background of the Sanskrit phonetic tradition must be fully appreciated. There seem to be two possible reasons for treating a sound like *ñ* to be a separate *varṇa.* The first reason seems to be that the distinction of allophones versus phonemes is foreign to the Indian tradition. The Indian tradition was also a *prayoga-śāstra* 'a science of performance,' and obviously it did desire that a reciter should pronounce *ñ,* where it was required, and should not mispronounce it as *n,* or *ṇ.* Even if there are no minimal pairs for *ñ,* every Vaidika knows that *ñ* must be distinguished from other sounds in recitation. Secondly, the phoneme-allophone analysis applies when we are taking into account only one language at a time. Several Śikṣās, including the more popular Pāṇinīyaśikṣā (v. 3), say: त्रिषष्टिः चतुःषष्टिर्वा वर्णाः शम्भुमते मताः । संस्कृते प्राकृते चापि ।, "In the opinion of Śiva, there are 63 or 64 sounds in Sanskrit as well as in Prakrit." Besides the initial uncertainty about the exact number of *varṇas,* the verse clearly points out that these are the *varṇas* for both Sanskrit and Prakrit together. In Prakrit we can find minimal pairs involving *ñ,* e.g. *ñāṇa* versus *nāṇa(ka).* Such a pair may make *ñ* a legitimate phoneme for Prakrit. For Indian phoneticians, *ñ* was simply distinct from *n, ṇ,* and *ṅ.* Thus, the notion of phoneme must be distinguished from that of *varṇa.* We must appreciate the similarities as well as the differences.

5.3. 'Varṇa,' 'Varga,' and 'Savarṇa'

5.3.1. Now we can move to a narrower, and a more technical usage of the word *varṇa.* In this narrow usage, the word *-varṇa* is distinguished from *-kāra.* The word *varṇa,* when affixed to a short vowel, e.g. *i-varṇa,* stands for the whole class of *i*-sounds differing in length, accents, and nasality. Patañjali uses the term *a-varṇa-kula* for such a class. Thus, there is *a-varṇa,* but not *ā-varṇa, ai-varṇa, ka-varṇa,* or *ya-varṇa.* Instead of these, we have *ā-kāra, ai-kāra, ka-kāra,* and *ya-kāra.* The term *a-kāra* is also a generalization in that it refers to varieties of short *a,* which may differ in accent and nasality. For the groups of stops, one could not use the term *varṇa,* but one called the group of *k, kh, g, gh,* and *ṅ,* by the term *ka-varga.* In older works like the Śikṣās and the Prātiśākhyas, membership within a *varṇa*-group, or a *varga*-group was generally defined simply by listing the sounds, cf. द्वे द्वे सवर्णे ह्रस्वदीर्घे, TPR (1.3), also: Deshpande (1975: 85ff). This is generally the meaning of the term *savarṇa* in the Śikṣās and the Prātiśākhyas, i.e. these sounds belong to the same *varṇa.* The term *kavarga* was defined by just picking out the first item of the list and saying: this is the *k-* class.

5.4. From Definitions by Listing to Featural Definitions

5.4.1. As we move from the Śikṣās and the Prātiśākhyas to Pāṇini, we see a qualitative difference in the way the groupings of sounds are defined. Here, there are two modes of defining groups. The first way is to make shortforms (*pratyāhāras*) based on the listings in the Śivasūtras. The second way is to access members of a group through the procedure called *savarṇagrahaṇa* 'accessing a class of *savarṇa*s by referring to a single token.' While the Śikṣās and the Prātiśākhyas defined the phonetic features of Sanskrit sounds, it was Pāṇini who showed a superior ability to define groupings of sounds in terms of their phonetic features. This is how his definition of *savarṇa* differs significantly from the definitions found in most of the Prātiśākhyas: P.1.1.9 (तुल्यास्यप्रयत्नं सवर्णम्). The rule says that any two sounds are called *savarṇa*s of each other if and only if they share the same *āsya-prayatna* 'oral effort.' The term *āsyaprayatna* was eventually interpreted as referring to two features: *sthāna* 'place of articulation' and *ābhyantara-prayatna* 'internal effort,' i.e. the manner in which the *karaṇa* or the articulator was related to the place of articulation.' Pāṇini himself did not specify the phonetic categories he had in mind, although the later Pāṇinian commentators have provided those details for us. Here we shall not go into the question of whether the later Pāṇinian tradition has given us historically reliable phonetic classifications for Pāṇini. In any case, this single generalization in Pāṇini covered the two separate notions in the Prātiśākhyas, i.e. *savarṇa* and *savarga.* Once this was accomplished, Pāṇini introduced his general and limited procedure of *savarṇagrahaṇa* through his rules P.1.1.69 (अणुदित् सवर्णस्य चाप्रत्ययः) and P.1.1.70 (तपरस्तत्कालस्य). In terms of the progress of linguistic theory, this indeed marked an advance.

5.5. Problems of the New Phonology in Pāṇini

5.5.1. The new featural definition of *savarṇa* in Pāṇini, and the procedure of *savarṇagrahaṇa,* achieved new theoretical success, and yet in the wake of this success, it brought with it new problems, which the Prātiśākhyas were generally not faced with. I shall mention here two such problems. The phonetic features assumed by Pāṇini were such that the vowels and the spirants (*ś, ṣ, s,* and *h*) had the same *prayatna,* i.e. the degree of closure or openness between the articulator and the place of articulation. This would have made some vowels *savarṇa*s of some consonants, and the procedure of *savarṇagrahaṇa* would have allowed a vowel to stand for its consonantal *savarṇa*. Pāṇini did recognize the possibility of such undesired over-extension of the notion of *savarṇa,* and to prevent it, he formulated his rule P.1.1.10 (नाज्झलौ). In general terms, the rule is supposed to say that vowels cannot be *savarṇa*s with consonants. This shows the limitations of featural groupings for functional purposes. In spite of the common phonetic features, vowels and consonants must be grouped apart from each other. On the other hand, consider the opposite problem with *a* and *ā*. Traditionally, *ā* was described as an open (*vivṛta*) sound, while *a* was described as a close (*saṃvṛta*) sound. Thus, their *prayatna* being different from each other, they would not become *savarṇa*s of each other, and then they cannot be grouped together. To get over this problem, Pāṇini apparently pronounced an open short *a* throughout his grammar, which was restored to a close short *a* by the last rule of his grammar, i.e. P.8.4.68 (अ अ). This made these two sounds technically *savarṇa*s of each other throughout his grammar, and only the very last rule, invisible to the rest of the grammar, restored it to its true pronunciation. There is a moral to this story. Sounds with common phonetic features can have a different functional load, and sounds with different phonetic features may have the same functional load. This same result has been achieved by some texts by using terms like *savarṇavat.* In the later Pāṇinian tradition, the sounds *ṛ* and *ḷ* were legislated to be each other's *savarṇa*s in spite of the difference in their phonetic features (cf. Vārttika 4 on P. 1.1.10: ऋकारऌकारयोः सवर्णविधिः).

5.6. Varṇarūpa versus Varṇākṛti: From Phonetic Features to Metaphysics

5.6.1. If the difference between the Śikṣās and Prātiśākhyas[3] on the one hand and Pāṇini on the other can be caracterized as a move from groupings by listing to groupings by features, especially in the context of the notion of *savarṇa,* the difference between Pāṇini and Kātyāyana may be characterized as a move from featural phonology to metaphysical phonology. To describe this move briefly, we can say that for Pāṇini, the sounds listed in the Śivasūtras stand for themselves to begin with, and they stand for their *savarṇa* class only as a result of the procedure of *savarṇagrahaṇa.* As we have seen before, membership to the class of *savarṇa* is controlled by the featural definition of the class given by P.1.1.9 (तुल्यास्यप्रयत्नं सवर्णम्). Where the procedure of *savarṇagrahaṇa* does not apply, the given sound stands just for itself. The basic notion of a sound standing for 'itself' is expressed by Pāṇini through the

[3] This is a broad generalization about this literature, and has specific exceptions which may be post-Paninian, e.g. the *Vājasaneyi-Prātiśākhya.*

term *rūpa* 'phonetic shape' of a sound, and this notion has been incorporated in expressions like *sarūpa, asarūpa*, and in the fundamental rule P.1.1.68 (स्वं रूपं शब्दस्याशब्दसंज्ञा). Thus, the form of a word is basically viewed by Pāṇini in terms of its phonetic shape. Moving away from this featural phonology of Pāṇini, Kātyāyana, perhaps under the influence of the emerging philosophical schools such as those of Vājapyāyana and Vyāḍi, proposes a new brand of metaphysical phonology. This proposal says that one should assume that the listing of the Śivasūtras is not a listing of tokens, but a listing of sound-genera or *ākr̥ti*s, which would naturally represent a whole class sharing a given *ākr̥ti*, without any special rules. If such is the case, then one does not need a large part of the Pāṇinian procedure of *savarṇagrahaṇa:* Vt. सवर्णेऽण्ग्रहणमपरिभाष्य-माकृतिग्रहणात्, on P.1.1.69. This proposal of Kātyāyana, which I have discussed at length in Deshpande (1975: 17-31), is fraught with difficulties. I shall briefly mention the following:

1) A metaphysical definition of *ākr̥ti* of a sound becomes impressionistic in terms of one's ability to identify its membership.

2) Generally any member covered by an *ākr̥ti* would be able to stand for the whole class. This obliterates the distinction between sounds directly listed in the Śivasūtras, i.e. the *aṆ* sounds, and the sounds not directly listed in the Śivasūtras, i.e. the non-*aṆ* sounds.

3) The procedure of *ākr̥tigrahaṇa* cannot completely replace the Pāṇinian procedure of *savarṇagrahaṇa*. This is so, because the *ākr̥ti* of *i* can cover *ī*, but the *ākr̥ti* of *k* does not cover *kh, g, gh,* and *ṅ*. This is admitted by Kātyāyana, who suggests that even after accepting the procedure of *ākr̥tigrahaṇa,* one would still need the procedure of *savarṇagrahaṇa* to cover these *varga*s of consonants.

Thus, in general the metaphysical phonology proposed by Kātyāyana has been relatively ineffective and in the later Pāṇinian tradition, there are few supporters for it.

5.7. Phonetics versus Behavior: The Case of Sandhyakṣaras

5.7.1. The treatment of the Sanskrit *sandhyakṣara*s in the Indian tradition is illustrative of several other important points. The sounds *e, o, ai,* and *au* are all generally called *sandhyakṣara*s in Sanskrit texts, implying that the tradition views them as composit sounds in some sense. However, very few texts suggest that all these sounds have distinct components. Generally, the older texts treat the sounds *e* and *o* as monophthongs, and ascribe a single point of articulation to these sounds, even while treating them as *sandhyakṣara*s. On the other hand, all texts treat the sounds *ai* and *au* as diphthongs. The older texts explicitly call these sounds *dvivarṇa* 'consisting of two sounds,' and ascribe to them two points of articulation. However, at the same time, these older texts are quick to point out that for all practical purposes these sounds, i.e. *ai* and *au,* are to be treated as if they are single sounds (CA 1.1.40: सन्ध्यक्षराणि संस्पृष्टवर्णान्येकवर्णवद् वृत्तिः). These sounds behave as if they are single sounds. They do not constitute two syllables either for metrical or grammatical purposes, and phonologically behave as long vowels, rather than as sequences of short vowels. This phonological behavior of these two diphthongs as monophthongs has sometimes clouded even the supposedly phonetic description of these sounds. Several texts tell us that the sounds *e* and *o* are *vivr̥tatara,* the sounds *ai* and *au* are *vivr̥tatama,* and the sound *ā* is still more open. If the sounds *ai* and *au* are phonetically *dvivarṇa* sounds, it makes no sense to say that they are even more open than *e* and *o*. To my mind, the above statement reflects a confusion caused by the lack of proper discrimination between the phonetic and the phonological levels, and the superimposition of one level upon the other. We shall later look at some other cases where the phonological behavior may have colored the phonetic classifications in Sanskrit texts.

5.8. Sthāna versus Karaṇa: The Case of *V*

5.8.1. The featural phonology brings with it the responsibility to explicitly define and specify a finite set of phonetic features for the sounds of a language. Any lack of clarity in the description of the phonological system in this regard can lead to problems which were not faced by those who practiced groupings by listing. As an example, consider the case of the sound *v*. Most of the older Śikṣās and Prātiśākhyas list *v* among the *oṣṭhya* 'labial' sounds without any further comment. These texts must be distinguished from those texts which further specify that the *karaṇa* 'articulator' for *v* is the 'tips of teeth' (cf. VPR 1.81). If the teeth or their tips are only a *karaṇa* for *v,* we can still consider *v* to be an *oṣṭhya* sound, since such terms as *oṣṭhya* are seen as always referring to the point of articulation and not the articulator. The texts which come still later, such as the versified Pāṇinīyaśikṣā say that *v* is a *dantyoṣṭhya* sound. Since many of these late texts pay little attention to the notion of *karaṇa,* the subsequent tradition has interpreted this term to mean that the sound *v* has two points of articulation. This sound is *dantya* as well as *oṣṭhya,* and, therefore, it should be included in both categories. What was Pāṇini's own intention? He has remained silent on the details of the phonetic features, and has left it to his successors to worry about the problems caused by his silence. Consider, for instance, the rule P.7.3.73 (लुग्वा दुहदिहलिहगुहा-मात्मनेपदे दन्त्ये). The rule says that after the listed roots, the affix *-ksa-* of the aorist is optionally (or preferably, if one accepts Kiparsky's interpretation of *vā*) deleted before a middle termination beginning in a *dantya* sound. The affixes *-dhvam* and *-ta* are undoubtedly *dantya*-initial affixes. However, the affix *-vahi* raises doubts. Is it a *dantya*-initial affix, or is it not? If the teeth functioned only as *karaṇa* for *v,* then it is not a *dantya* sound, since the term *dantya* should properly refer only to the point of articulation. However, the KV, relying upon the late phonetic texts says that since *v* is a *dantyoṣṭha* sound, it must be included among *dantya* sounds, as well as among *oṣṭhya* sounds (cf. दन्त्योष्ठ्योऽपि वकारो दन्त्य इति गृह्यते, KV on P.7.3.73). This leads to the derivation of forms like *aduhvahi,* as well as *adhukṣāvahi.* Whether this statement is historically accurate is a major question. This question has been debated elsewhere in detail, cf. Cardona 1964, Deshpande 1975a and 1981. Suffice it to say that the choice of going for featural phonology requires a degree of precision which is sometimes lacking in the Sanskrit texts, and this lack of precision may have contributed to a certain degree of confusion. Similar confusion is also noticeable on the exact status of *nāsikā* 'nose.'

5.9. Āntaratamya versus Yathāsaṃkhya: The Case of *iko yaṇ aci*

5.9.1. In the last several years, a major discussion has taken place among scholars such as myself, George Cardona, and recently, Robert Hueckstedt. This question revolves around the use of the principle of *āntaratamya* 'maximal featural proximity' stated in P.1.1.50 (स्थानेऽन्तरतमः) versus the principle of *yathāsaṃkhya* 'one-to-one substitution' stated in P.1.3.10 (यथासंख्यमनुदेशः समानाम्) in deciding appropriate substitutions in some rules of Pāṇini. There are cases of substitution like P.3.4.101 (तस्थस्थमिपां तान्तन्तामः) where it is beyond doubt that the substitution must be made on the basis of *yathāsaṃkhya.* This rule says that *tas, thas, tha,* and *miP* are replaced by *tām, tam, ta* and *am*, respectively. Similarly, there are cases like P.8.4.53 (झलां जश् झशि), where we must apply the principle of maximal featural proximity or *āntaratamya.* This rule says that *jhaL* sounds are replaced with *jaŚ* sounds, before *jhaŚ* sounds. The group referred to by *jhaL* includes the consonants *jh, bh, gh, ḍh, dh, kh, ph, ch, ṭh, th, c, ṭ, t, k, p, ś, ṣ, s* and *h.* On the other hand, the substitutes denoted by the shortform *jaŚ* include *j, b, g, ḍ* and *d.* The unequal number of originals and substitutes makes it an ideal candidate for the application of the principle of maximal featural proximity. However, rules like P.6.1.77 (इको यणचि) raise difficult questions. Here, the originals are denoted by the shortform *iK,* while the substitutes are denoted by *yaṆ.* If these shortforms are expanded just to *i, u, r̥, l̥,* and *y, v, r, l,* respectively, then one can think of the possibility of one-to-one substitution. However, in order to make sure that the rule would also apply to the change of *ī* to *y* , one must expand the list of originals to cover all the homogeneous varieties of *i, u, r̥* and *l̥,* by P.1.1.69 (अणुदित्सवर्णस्य चाप्रत्ययः). If this is done before effecting the substitution, then one gets unequal numbers of originals and substitutes, and one needs to use the principle of maximal featural proximity. On P.1.1.50, Patañjali (MB, Kielhorn edn., Vol.I., p. 10) says that the problems of P.6.1.77 can be resolved even with *yathāsaṃkhya* : संख्यातानुदेशेनाप्येतत्सिद्धम्. However, on P.1.3.10 (यथासंख्यमनुदेशः समानाम्), he says (MB, Kielhorn edn., Vol.I., p. 267) that the problems of P.6.1.77 can be resolved even with *āntaratamya* : स्थानेऽन्तरतमेनाप्येतत्सिद्धम्. Are there four originals and four substitutes, or is the number of original and substitutes different? This depends upon when exactly we apply *savarṇagrahaṇa* to *ik* and *yaṇ.* Recently, Robert Hueckstedt has published a monograph that reviews the long traditional debate relating to the interpretation of P.6.1.77, and I believe the final conclusion regarding Pāṇini's own intention, if there is one, is still elusive. This example demonstrates that in using listings and features, Pāṇinian grammar at times lacks sufficient clarity, and this has lead to such as-yet-unresolved problems.

5.10. Did Phonology influence Phonetics? The Case of *r̥* and *r*.

5.10.1. Earlier I have mentioned the case of *ai* and *au* which are simultaneously described as being *dvivarṇa* 'composed of two constituent sounds,' and yet being *vivr̥tatama,* i.e. even more open that *e* and *o.* In my view, this situation has occurred either because these sounds are phonetically diphthongs, but phonologically behave as single sounds, or because the conception of these sounds as *dvivarṇa* is the inherited doctrine, while, at least dialectally, these sounds have been reduced to monophthongal pronunciation similar to vowels in the English words *at* and *all*. Since the levels of phonetics and phonology were not sufficiently distinguished, the statements in the texts leave room for speculation.

Such discrepancies are also found as regards the sounds *r* and *r̥*. The older texts generally consider *r̥* as a *jihvāmūlīya* 'velar' sound, and *r* as a *dantamūlīya* 'alveolar' sound. The undoubtedly retroflex sounds are *ṣ*, and the *ṭavarga*. However, notice the fact that the same old texts also specify that a dental *n* coming after *r*, *r̥*, or *ṣ* is retroflexed. This would seem to show that a *dantamūlīya* 'alveolar,' a *jihvāmūlīya* 'velar,' and a *mūrdhanya* 'retroflex' have the same phonological function, i.e. they are cerebralizers, though not all cerebrals themselves. Perhaps such a statement was gradually viewed as being inappropriate, and the later texts started calling *r* and *r̥* also *mūrdhanya* 'retroflex' sounds. Most modern scholars still wonder how these sounds can be phonetically retroflex. It is thus possible that in this case the phonological behavior of sounds has led the ancient phoneticians and grammarians to reclassify the phonetic categories of the concerned sounds to remove the seeming inconsistencies.

Such may also be the case of the oral effort for vowels and spirants. Most ancient works, including Pāṇini, seem to hold that vowels and spirants are all *vivr̥ta* 'open.' Precisely for this reason, Pāṇini had to formulate his rule P.1.1.10 (*nājjhalau*) to prevent the impending *sāvarṇya* 'homogeneity' between vowels and spirants. This rule, to say the least, has created enormous problems of interpretation. To get over these, Patañjali, among others, proposed to differentiate the oral effort for vowels from that of the spirants. The vowels were now classified as 'open' (*vivr̥ta*), while the spirants were classified as 'slightly open' (*īṣad-vivr̥ta*). Whether such a distinction is phonetically justified is not clear. However, this distinction certainly made the phonological statements clearer, and seems to have been greeted with joy by the later grammarians, even at the cost of having to sacrifice P.1.1.10 (*nājjhalau*), cf. Nāgeśabhaṭṭa's statement:

> यदि तु सूत्रवृत्त्यादिषु श्रद्धाजाड्यमपहाय प्रयत्नभेदादेवैतद्व्यावर्त्त्य-सावर्ण्यादीनां न सावर्ण्यमित्युच्यते, तदा सन्तु सप्त प्रयत्नाः, मास्तु च नाज्झलाविति सूत्रम् ।,
>
> Br̥hacchabdenduśekhara, vol. I., p. 48.
>
> "If, however, having set aside the inertia caused by one's trust in the Sūtras, commentaries etc., one can say that there is no homogeneity [between sounds like *i* and *ś*], whose homogeneity P.1.1.10 aims to prohibit, on the basis of a difference in

their articulatory effort, then, [by all means], let there be seven [distinct] articulatory efforts, and let there not be the rule P.1.1.10.

5.11. *Nāda* versus *Ghoṣa*: Phonetic and/or Phonological?

5.11.1. Another such debate which has kept modern scholars busy revolves around the terms *nāda* and *ghoṣa*. Most ancient texts clearly define *nāda* as a type of phonation produced when the glottal chords are closed. The vibration produced by the closed glottal chords is called *nāda.* All voiced sounds have it, including vowels and voiced consonants. Now consider the term *ghoṣa.* Hardly any text defines how *ghoṣa* is produced. However, they all use the terms *ghoṣavat, ghoṣin,* and *aghoṣa,* implying at the very least that *ghoṣa* is a certain feature which some sounds have, and others do not. What complicates the debate is the fact that most older texts say that *nāda* is the phonation for vowels and *ghoṣavat* consonants. This possibly suggests that *ghoṣa* is a feature only for some consonants, but not for vowels.

5.11.2. This last statement is the beginning of the whole controversy. Some scholars have followed up the above conclusion and have attempted to identify what *ghoṣa* as a separate voicing feature may have meant, cf. Deshpande (1976). Cardona (1986) has argued for a different view. I cannot do justice to his extensive treatment of this question here, but to state his conclusion in his own words (p. 79-80): "Though *ghoṣavat* ('voiced') and *aghoṣa* ('voiceless') might at first blush seem to be purely phonetic class names, the use of these terms with reference to voiced and voiceless consonants alone is based on a phonological distinction."

5.11.3. I tend to believe that for the ancient phoneticians, *ghoṣa* was also a phonetic term, which may then have had phonological uses as pointed out by Cardona. Whether modern phonetics can identify two types or degrees of voicing need not decide whether the ancient phoneticians viewed *ghoṣa* to be a phonetic feature of sound, cf. RPR 13.15 (आहुर्घोषं घोषवतामकारमेकेऽनुस्वार-मनुनासिकानाम्), RPR 13.18 (अत्रोत्पन्नावपर ऊष्मघोषौ) and the ancient Śikṣā quoted by the CAB on CA (1.1.12). Such texts lead one to believe that the ancient phoneticians and grammarians did indeed view *ghoṣa* as a *varṇaguṇa* which some sounds have and others do not. Such a view is supported by the lists of *prayatna*s or *varṇaguṇa*s in various texts. Uvaṭa on RPR (13.21) lists *ghoṣatā* and *aghoṣatā* as *varṇaguṇa*s 'features of sound.' The grammatical texts in the Pāṇinian tradition also list *ghoṣa* and *aghoṣa* among the *bāhya-prayatna*s, besides *nāda* and *śvāsa,* and suggest that in their opinion these are phonetic features. If one says that *nāda* and *ghoṣa* are distinct phonological features with no distinct phonetic reality, then one could perhaps say that a lack of clarity between the levels of phonetics and phonology may have led the Sanskrit tradition to come up with pseudo-phonetic features in some cases. On the other hand, this offers us an opportunity to investigate a possible distinction in the kind of voicing involved in the articulation of vowels and voiced consonants. I have suggested that *ghoṣa* may possibly refer to the amplification or perhaps friction added to the original voicing caused by the glottal closure in the pronunciation of voiced consonants. Such an added amplification or friction can be attributed to the partial or complete closure of the oral organs in the utterance of voiced consonants. For example, the implosion for unreleased voiced stops like *b* feels like a form of oral vibration distinct from the vibration of the glottal chords, and it may have been interpreted by the ancient phoneticians as the feature of *ghoṣa*, distinct from *nāda* 'vibration of the glottal chords.' Also see: Ralf Stautzebach 1994: 287.

5.12. No explicit 'phonology' versus 'phonetics'

5.12.1. To reiterate my main point, the Sanskrit phonetic and grammatical traditions did not explicitly distinguish between the phonetic and the phonological levels in their description. However, it is clear that they were faced with many dilemmas in trying to correlate the phonetic features of sounds to their phonological behavior. In doing so, sometimes they made explicit distinctions between what we would call the phonetic character of a sound and its phonological behavior. At other times, the phonological behavior of sounds may have led the ancient grammarians into consciously or unconsciously creating pseudo-phonetic distinctions to match the observed differences in phonological behavior. In any case, the above analysis shows the promise as well as the limitations of the science of phonetics and grammar as practiced in ancient India.

6. Pāṇinian Impact on the Tradition of the CA

6.1. Surya Kanta's Proposal concerning two types of Prātiśākhyas

6.1.1. In the introduction to his magnificent edition of the APR (p. 24), Surya Kanta proposed that the evolution of the Prātiśākhya literature shows that in their formative period, there were essentially two types of Prātiśākhyas.

Type A, represented by the APR, contained exhaustive listings (*gaṇas*) of examples showing certain patterns of linguistic behavior, but no generalized rules. This was the first step.

Type B, represented by the CA, containing generalizations, exceptions to generalizations etc., but not exhaustive lists (*gaṇas*). This was the second step.

Surya Kanta (ibid, p. 25) claims that "the evolution of B would throw into abeyance A", and that "B being descriptive would be easily reduced to the abstract sūtra style."

6.2. Surya Kanta's view of the existing Prātiśākhya texts

6.2.1. We shall briefly summarize below, Surya Kanta's more extensive discussion (ibid, pp. 25ff):

a) Existing Prātiśākhyas represent a mixture of the types A and B, and there are no pure representatives of the types A and B.

b) Surya Kanta assumes that the type A is inherently earlier than the type B, i.e. the listings of instances were made prior to the stage of generalizations. However, on the basis of direct quotations of the CA rules in the APR, he admits that the CA is older than the APR.

Thus, an actual text showing generalizations is older than the text which is primarily a set of listings. In actuality, listings are dependent on generalizations, and generalizations are dependent upon listings.

6.3. Vedic grammar and the grammar of contemporary Sanskrit

6.3.1. We may observe that even the Padapāṭhas presuppose a set of grammatical generalizations, on the basis of which the original Saṃhitā was segmented into Padas, and occasionally into their components. The grammatical theory, though not clearly spelled out by the Padakāras must be assumed to have existed, and can be inferred to a certain extent from the Padapāṭhas, cf. V.N. Jha (1987).

The ancient Padapāṭha/Prātiśākhya type grammars worked under two different pressures or had two slightly divergent targets:

i) *narrow target* = to describe just the text of a particular Śākhā of a particular Veda

ii) *wider target* = to describe the generic Sanskrit language: Vedic and post-Vedic Sanskrit taken together.

Even the Padapāṭha manifests features of post-Vedic dialects of Sanskrit like those of Śākalya and others, cf. Cardona (1991), and is not free from the implicit influence of the grammar of contemporary Sanskrit.

The narrow target of describing the texts of a particular Śākhā, in practice could not be separated from considerations of post-Vedic Sanskrit, and the concerns of a generalized grammar of Sanskrit at large. The Vedic texts were maintained orally by Brahmins who used the more contemporary forms of Sanskrit in their academic and ritual activity, and hence the existence of the Vedic texts was fully circumscribed by the use of the contemporary forms of Sanskrit. Secondly, the recitational segmentations and recombinations often created sequences which were not strictly speaking Vedic, and these were more directly subject to the rules of the contemporary usage of Sanskrit. This is the case, for instance, when Śākalya adds the word *iti* after certain forms in the Padapāṭha, or when the words are reversed in their order in the Jaṭāpāṭha, i.e. *a+b+b+a+a+b*. This phenomenon of active recitational switching between Vedic grammar and the grammar of contemporary Sanskrit is discussed in my paper "Grammars and Grammar-Switching in Vedic Recitational Variations," (Deshpande, 1994). Thus, one may not necessarily assume that there ever existed grammatical texts, some precursors of our Prātiśākhyas, which were strictly related to the facts of a particular Śākhā, and were not at all influenced by or concerned with the general grammar of contemporary Sanskrit.

6.4. The Perceived Role of General Grammar in Relation to Prātiśākhyas

6.4.1. Patañjali indeed asserts that the Padakāras should follow the Grammarians, and the Grammarians should not follow the Padakāras (न लक्षणेन पदकारा अनुवर्त्याः, पदकारैर्नाम लक्षणमनुवर्त्यम्, MB, Kielhorn edn., Vol.II., p. 85).

The Prātiśākhya tradition as we know it does seem to accept a view that its specifications are to be understood on the background of a general grammar of Sanskrit. This is seen from the following discussions

6.4.2. Consider CA 1.1.3-4 (एवमिहेति च विभाषाप्राप्तं सामान्ये). The commentary CAB on this rule says:

> एवमिहेति च । अस्यां शाखायां तत्प्रातिज्ञं मन्यन्ते । 'यरोऽनुनासिकेऽनुनासिको वा' (पा.८.४.४५) इति विभाषाप्राप्तं सामान्ये । किं सामान्यम् । व्याकरणम् । वक्ष्यति 'उत्तमा उत्तमेषु' (च.आ. २.१.५) इति ।
>
> "[On] *thus it is in this [branch]*. In this branch, such is considered to be the [specific, non-optional] doctrine. In the generic [grammar of Sanskrit], namely in P.8.4.45, [the procedure of changing a stop to its corresponding nasal, before a nasal] obtains optionally. What is the generic description? This is the tradition of grammar. [The CA] will state [its own specific, i.e. non-optional, procedure] in 2.1.5."

This suggests the relation between a general grammar of Sanskrit and a Prātiśākhya as that between a generic description of a language comprising all its dialectal and temporal manifestations and a specific description of a specific text. The general grammar of Sanskrit had to introduce a number of options, due to its goal of describing the large variety of linguistic phenomena under its coverage, cf. सर्ववेदपारिषदं हीदं शास्त्रं तत्र नैकः पन्थाः शक्य आस्थातुम्, MB on P.2.1.58 and P.6.3.14, "Indeed this science [of grammar] is concerned with all Vedic traditions [taken together], and hence it is not possible to choose a unique [= non-optional] path [of description, which would apply only to a specific Vedic branch]." On the other hand, the Prātiśākhya literature relates to us the specific choices made by a specific textual tradition.

6.4.3. Uvaṭa, in his introductory commentary on the first Paṭala of the Ṛgveda-Prātiśākhya, discusses this relationship at length. He presents two opposing views. Some claimed that the Prātiśākhyas are statements of exceptions to the rules of a general grammar of Sanskrit, while others claimed them to be independent treatises. Finally, Uvaṭa says: अनयोः पक्षयोर्यतरः पक्षः श्रेयांस्ततरो ग्रहीतव्यः, RPR, Vol.II., p. 23, "Of these two views, one may choose the one which is deemed to be beneficial". However, he has paid greater attention to the first alternative, namely that the relationship of a Prātiśākhya to a general grammar of Sanskrit is that of a specific description to a generic description. He says (RPR, Vol.II., pp. 21-23):

शिक्षाच्छन्दोव्याकरणैः सामान्येनोक्तलक्षणम् ।
तदेवमिह शाखायामिति शास्त्रप्रयोजनम् ।

प्रातिशाख्यप्रयोजनमनेन श्लोकेनोच्यते । शिक्षादिभिर्यत्सामान्येनोत्सर्गेणोक्तं लक्षणं, यथा तावच्छिक्षायां - 'स्युर्मूर्धन्या ऋटुरषाः' - सामान्येन सर्वशाखासु रेफो मूर्धन्य इत्युक्तः । ... एवं सर्वा शिक्षा वर्णेषु स्थानकरणानुप्रदानादि सर्वासु शाखासु विदधाति; न तु नियमतः कस्यां शाखायां रेफो मूर्धन्यः कस्यां दन्तमूलीय इति । अत एतद्व्यवस्थापकमारभ्यते । ... तथा व्याकरणे यत्सामान्येन, यथा 'ऋचि तुनुघमक्षुतङ्कुत्रोरुष्याणाम्' (पा. ६.१.१३३) इति । तद् व्यवस्थापयितुमिदमारभ्यते । न सर्वत्रैतानि पदान्यस्यां शाखायां दीर्घाणि भवन्ति । एवं शिक्षाच्छन्दोव्याकरणैर्यत्सर्वासु शाखासु सामान्येन लक्षणमुच्यते तदेवास्यां शाखायामनेन व्यवस्थाप्यते इत्येतत्प्रयोजनमस्याङ्गस्य । तथा चाथर्वणप्रातिशाख्ये इदमेव प्रयोजनमुक्तम् 'एवमिहेति च विभाषाप्राप्तं सामान्येन' । अस्य सूत्रस्यायमर्थः - सामान्येन लक्षणेन यद् विकल्पप्राप्तं तदेवमस्यां शाखायां व्यवस्थितं भवतीति प्रातिशाख्यप्रयोजनमुक्तम् ।

"The purpose of [this] science [of the Prātiśākhya] is [to clarify] that the rules which are generically expressed in the Śikṣās, metrics (*chandas*) and grammars are [effective] in this branch in a restricted manner. This verse elucidates the purpose of a Prātiśākhya. The rules are stated generically in the Śikṣās and other texts. For example, in the Śikṣā statement '*r̥, ṭ*-series, *r* and *ṣ* should be cerebral,' the sound *r* is generically said to be a cerebral sound in all Vedic traditions. Thus, all the Śikṣās generically prescribe the points of articulation, articulators, phonation etc. for sounds with reference to all Vedic branches, but they do not specifically say in which branch the sound *r* is invariably cerebral, and where it is [invariably] alveolar. Therefore, this [science of the Prātiśākhya] is undertaken to settle such [questions]. Similarly, the grammar makes generic statements, for example P.6.1.133. This [Prātiśākhya] is undertaken to settle this question. The words [listed in P.6.1.133, i.e. *tu, nu, gha* etc.] are consistently free from lengthening in this entire textual tradition [of the RV]. Thus, the rules which are generically stated by the Śikṣās, metrics, and grammars, indifferently with respect to all Vedic branches, are specifically settled by this [Prātiśākhya] with respect to this particular Vedic branch. This is the purpose of this ancillary tradition. The same purpose is expressed in the Prātiśākhya of the Atharvaveda [= CA] in rules CA (1.1.3-4). Such is the significance of this rule: Whatever [procedure] obtains optionally through generic descriptions is settled in a restrictive way in this Vedic branch. This way the purpose of the Prātiśākhya is explained."

6.4.4. On VPR (6.24: परोपापावप्रतिपर्यन्वप्यत्यध्याङ्प्रसन्निर्दुरुन्निविस्वभि), which provides a list of Upasargas, Uvaṭa's commentary says:

एते विंशतिरुपसर्गाः प्रकृतिस्वरा भवन्ति ।... प्रकृतिस्वरस्तु व्याकरण-पठितोऽत्र गृह्यते । तथा च तत् सूत्रम् - 'निपाता आद्युदात्ताः,' 'उपसर्गाश्चाभिवर्जम्' इति ।

"These twenty *upasargas* [as listed in VPR 6.24] retain their natural accent. The natural accent as stated in the grammar is taken for granted in this tradition. Thus, there are the [following] grammatical rules: 'The *nipātas* have their first syllable high-pitched. So do the *upasargas*, except *abhi*.'"

Anantabhaṭṭa's commentary on the VPR also repeats the same Sūtras of some Vyākaraṇa. These rules are not found in Pāṇini's grammar, but are found in the Phiṭsūtras (80, 81) ascribed to Śāntanava. In any case, the discussion assumes that the Prātiśākhyas take for granted the prescriptions of the general grammar of Sanskrit.

6.4.5. The commentary Vaidikābharaṇa by Gopālayajvan on TPR uses the word *mūlaśāstra* "original science" for Pāṇini's rules (cf., on TPR 5.14, 5.33, 7.16, 9.10, 10.9, 11.1, 13.4, 14.4) and views the rules of the TPR as statements of exceptions applicable exclusively to the text of the TS. The TPR (19.5: न पूर्वशास्त्रे न पूर्वशास्त्रे) makes a reference to a *pūrvaśāstra*, a prior grammatical system, and again Gopālayajvan says: अस्य शास्त्रस्य मूलभूतं व्याकरणं पूर्वशास्त्रमित्युच्यते, "The tradition of grammar which forms the basis of this science [of the Prātiśākhya] is referred to as a prior [= foundational] science."

6.4.6. The same term *pūrvaśāstra* is used in the CAB on CA (4.4.27) and seems to have the same reference, namely Pāṇinian grammar.

The above evidence indicates that the Prātiśākhya tradition viewed itself as a description of specific linguistic features found in specific texts, and for more generic facts, it took for granted the prescriptions of the general grammar of Sanskrit. For most of the commentatorial tradition, this general grammar of Sanskrit was non other than that of Pāṇini.

6.5. Which general grammar do the Prātiśākhyas and their commentators assume?

6.5.1. The commentators, as discussed earlier, seem to refer to Pāṇini's grammar while discussing the general grammar taken for granted by the Prātiśākhyas. I would like to make some important historical distinctions in using the term 'grammar.' We must make at least the following distinctions:

a) general grammatical principles taken for granted by the Padakāras, but not spelled out clearly by them.

b) general grammatical principles taken for granted by the authors of the Prātiśākhyas.

c) grammatical system as taken for granted by the commentators.

6.5.2. It is important to make a distinction between these various notions of grammar, so that we may hope to have a clear understanding of the changing historical situation. For example, the Padapāṭha provides us a segmentation of the Saṃhitā as a *fait accompli*. In general, it provides a word-for-word segmentation of the Saṃhitā-text. However, in many cases, it separates the members of compounds, and the base from certain affixes. What we possess is not a theory of segmentation, but the segmentation itself, or the lack of it, and hence we can only indirectly infer the grammatical categories which were used by the authors of the Padapāṭha, cf. V.N. Jha 1987. For instance, we do not know in some cases whether the Padakāra viewed the segments separated by an Avagraha as members of a compound, or as a base and an affix. For instance, the rule CA (4.1.49: कृत्वे समासो वा नानापददर्शनात्) and the commentary CAB on it raise such a question concerning the segment *kr̥tvaḥ*. For Pāṇini, we know that the item *kr̥tvasUC* is indeed an affix, cf. P.5.4.17 (संख्यायाः क्रियाभ्यावृत्तिगणने कृत्वसुच्). On the other hand, the facts of the AV Padapāṭha are such that *kr̥tvas* is sometimes separated by an Avagraha, and sometimes it is not, e.g. *aṣṭa-kr̥tvaḥ* (AV 11.2.9) is separated by an Avagraha, but *daśakr̥tvaḥ* (AV 11.2.9) and *saptakr̥tvaḥ* (AV 12.2.29) are not separated by an Avagraha. The author of the CA says that where it is separated by an Avagraha, it is a case of a Samāsa 'compound.' For Pāṇini, it is a case of affixation. All we know about the Padapāṭha is that *kr̥tvas* is sometimes separated by an Avagraha. We do not know whether the author of the Padapāṭha treated this as a case of compounding or affixation, or whether these specific distinctions between compounding and affixation developed later on. Here, we should note another interesting dimension of this problem. While it is clear that by invoking the category of Samāsa, the author of the CA demonstrates his familiarity with a grammatical system, that grammatical system is indeed not that of Pāṇini. Consider for instance, CA 4.1.50 (जातीयादिषु च). Taken in the context of the previous rule, i.e. CA 4.1.49 (कृत्वे समासो वा ...), this rule also relates to the treatment of a segment as a member of a compound, and its consequent segmentation by an Avagraha. There are two points to be taken into account in this case. The expression *jātīyādi* refers to a Gaṇa or a listing. However, there are no examples of *jātīya* attested in the AV. This means that the CA is indeed bringing in a Gaṇa from some generalized grammar of Sanskrit. However, while the CA, and probably the grammatical source from which it takes this generalized Gaṇa, treat this as a case of compounding (*samāsa*), Pāṇini (5.3.69: प्रकारवचने जातीयर्) clearly treats this as a case of affixation. Thus, one can assert that the author of the CA is familiar with a generalized grammar of Sanskrit, but that grammar need not be identical with that of Pāṇini.

6.6. Generalized description of Sanskrit as the occasional target of the Prātiśākhyas

6.6.1. While the term 'Prātiśākhya' does indeed seem to imply that ideally there should be a specific Prātiśākhya text for each distinct Śākhā, and that the specific text should not aim at linguistic phenomena extending beyond its chosen Vedic Śākhā, the authors of the Prātiśākhyas, for reasons not clearly understood by us, often sojourn into such external territories. Gopālayajvan in his commentary Vaidikābharaṇa on TPR (11.9) discusses this question: स्वशाखायामलब्धावकाशो हि विधिः शाखान्तरविषयत्वकल्पनयोपपादयितव्यः (Mysore edn., p. 317), "Indeed a rule, for which one does not find an example in one's own Vedic branch, should be explained as having examples in other Vedic branches." This issue comes up very often in interpreting the rules of the CA. Consider the following instances:

1) CA (4.2.5-6: षट्पुरसोरुकारोऽन्त्यस्य दशदाशयोरादेश्च मूर्धन्यः). CA (4.2.5: षोडशी सन्देहात्) says that the word *ṣoḍaśī* is not split with an Avagraha in the Padapāṭha, due to doubts regarding the exact boundaries of the member elements. In part, this statement is simply an observation that the word *ṣoḍaśī* is not split with an Avagraha. On the other hand, the remainder of the statement, i.e. *sandehāt,* is a criticism of the author of the Padapāṭha, who apparently could not overcome this alleged *sandeha.* The rules CA (4.2.5-6) in fact

represent a clear effort on the part of the author of the CA to overcome this element of *sandeha,* and in a way mark a grammatical advance over the Padapāṭha. However, of what practical consequence are these rules? The new derivation does not lead to a new segmentation with an Avagraha, but only to a better understanding of the etymology of these words. Such an advance, though indeed praiseworthy, is of little utility in either converting the Padapāṭha into Saṃhitā, or in explaining why a certain segmentation is the way it is. Strictly speaking, this is an advance in the territory of general grammar of Sanskrit, which has its scope extending far beyond that of a Prātiśākhya.

2) CA (1.3.2: कृपे रेफस्य लकारः). This rule, like Pāṇini's rule P.8.2.18 (कृपो रो लः), derivationally links the forms of *kl̥p/kalp* with those of *kr̥p*. What is the practical utility of such a rule for a Prātiśākhya? While it marks an advance in the understanding of the derivation of the forms of *kl̥p,* the sound-change taught by this rule remains unutilized in the crucial area of the Pada<>Saṃhitā relationship. This change does not figure in the process of *samāpatti* or restoration of the supposedly original sounds of an item in Pada and Krama variation. The forms of *kl̥p* are not restored to *kr̥p*. Thus, this remains an advance in the area of grammatical derivation, which is strictly speaking outside the scope of a Prātiśākhya.

3) CA (1.3.25: शान्मान्दानाम्). This rule teaches that the long *ā* of the listed roots becomes nasalized before the affix *-san.* Out of these three roots, only the forms of *mān,* e.g. *mīmāṃsamānāḥ* (AV 9.1.3) is attested in the ŚAV. Why should this text concern itself with other roots? Should we assume with Surya Kanta, that the forms of these other roots may have occurred in a supposedly more genuine Śaunakīya recension? I, rather, tend to agree with Whitney. He shows the similarity of this CA rule with P.3.1.6 (मान्बधदान्शान्भ्यो दीर्घश्चाभ्यासस्य) and suggests that, in the present rule, the CA is simply carried away by the urge to account for facts of the general grammar of Sanskrit.

6.7. Connection of the CA with the traditions of Sanskrit Grammar.

6.7.1. The following examples show how intricately the CA is connected with some traditions of Sanskrit grammar. Some of these features, but not all, look like those of the Pāṇinian grammar, and it is possible that both the texts are drawing upon certain common sources. The CA does not share Pāṇini's ultra-algebraic style, but it shares a number of common terms, and other features. These are a few illustrations:

1) CA (1.3.10: उकारस्येतावपृक्तस्य): *apr̥kta*, cf. P.6.1.67 (वेरपृक्तस्य).
2) CA (1.3.12: ईकारोकारौ च सप्तम्यर्थे): *saptamyartha*, cf. P.1.1.19 (ईदूतौ च सप्तम्यर्थे).
3) CA (1.3.13: द्विवचनान्तौ): *dvivacana*, cf. P.1.1.11 (ईदूदेद् द्विवचनं प्रगृह्यम्).
4) CA (1.3.16: अमी बहुवचनम्): *bahuvacana*, cf. P.7.3.103 (बहुवचने झल्येत्).
5) CA (1.3.19: आमन्त्रितं चेतावनार्षे): *āmantrita* and *anārṣa*, cf. P.6.1.197 (आमन्त्रितस्य च) and P.1.1.16 (सम्बुद्धौ शाकल्यस्येतावनार्षे).
6) CA (1.3.26: वस्वन्तस्य पञ्चपद्याम्): *vasU*, cf. P.8.3.1 (मतुवसो रु ...).
7) CA (1.4.1: वर्णादन्त्यात्पूर्व उपधा): *upadhā*, cf. P.1.1.65 (अलोऽन्त्यात्पूर्व उपधा).
8) CA (2.3.3: समासे सकारः ...): *samāsa*, cf. P.6.1.223 (समासस्य).
9) CA (2.4.3: तद्धिते तकारादौ): *taddhita*, cf. P.4.1.76 (तद्धिताः).
10) CA (2.4.10: उपसर्गाद्धातोः): *upasarga*, *dhātu*, cf. P.6.1.91 (उपसर्गादृति धातौ).
11) CA (2.4.11: अभ्यासाच्च): *abhyāsa*, P.7.3.55 (अभ्यासाच्च).
12) CA (2.4.17: सुञः): *suÑ*, cf. P.6.3.134 (इकः सुञि).
13) CA (3.1.4: उञ इदमूष्वादिषु): *uÑ*, cf. P.1.1.17 (उञः).
14) CA (3.2.10: प्रगृह्याश्च प्रकृत्या): *pragr̥hya, prakr̥tyā*, cf. P.6.1.125 (प्लुतप्रगृह्या अचि नित्यम्) and P.6.1.115 (प्रकृत्यान्तःपादमव्यपरे).
15) CA (3.2.18: पूर्वपरयोरेकः): cf. P.6.1.84 (एकः पूर्वपरयोः).
16) CA (3.2.19: समानाक्षरस्य सवर्णे दीर्घः): *savarṇa, dīrgha,* cf. P.6.1.101 (अकः सवर्णे दीर्घः).
17) CA (3.4.4: विभक्त्यागमप्रातिपदिकान्तस्य): *vibhakti, prātipadika,* cf. P.8.4.11 (प्रातिपदिकान्तनुम्विभक्तिषु च).
18) CA (4.1.42: तातिलि): *tātiL,* cf. P.4.4.142 (सर्वदेवात्तातिल्).
19) CA (4.2.1: न तकारसकाराभ्यां मत्वर्थे): *matvarthe*, cf. P.4.4.128 (मत्वर्थे मासतन्वोः).
20) CA (4.2.2: यत्तदेतेभ्यो वतौ): *vatU*, cf. P.5.2.39 (यत्तदेतेभ्यः परिमाणे वतुप्).

6.7.2. To show that the CA has similarities with the Pāṇinian grammar, but is not exclusively identical to it, consider the following non-Pāṇinian grammatical features:

1) Lack of Pāṇini's algebraic formulations:

CA (1.3.2: कृपे रेफस्य लकारः) versus P.8.2.18 (कृपो रो लः)
CA (1.3.12: ईकारोकारौ च सप्तम्यर्थे) versus P.1.1.19 (ईदूतौ च सप्तम्यर्थे)
CA (1.4.1: वर्णादन्त्यात्पूर्व उपधा) vs. P.1.1.65 (अलोऽन्त्यात्पूर्व उपधा)

2) Non-Pāṇinian terminology:

CA (1.2.15: परस्य स्वरस्य व्यञ्जनानि). Contrast *svara* and *vyañjana* with Pāṇini's algebraic shortforms *aC* and *haL,* respectively.
CA (1.3.26: वस्वन्तस्य पञ्चपद्याम्). Contrast *pañcapadī* with Pāṇini's *sarvanāmasthāna* as defined by P.1.1.43 (सुड-नपुंसकस्य).
CA (2.1.2: पदान्तानामनुत्तमानां तृतीया घोषवत्स्वरेषु). Contrast *tr̥tīya* and *ghoṣavat* with Pāṇini's algebraic shortforms *jaŚ* and *jhaŚ* in P.8.4.53 (झलां जश् झशि).
CA (2.4.7: नामिकरेफात् प्रत्ययसकारस्य). Contrast *nāmi-ka-rephāt* with Pāṇini's *iṆ-koḥ* in P.8.3.57 (इण्कोः).
CA (3.2.26: भूतकरणस्य च). Contrast *bhūtakaraṇasya* with *āṭaḥ* in P.6.1.90 (आटश्च).

3) Non-Pāṇinian procedures: (For details, see Notes on the respective CA rules)

CA (2.1.3: पदान्ते चाघोषाः) vs. P.8.4.56 (वावसाने).
CA (2.1.31: मकारस्य स्पर्शे परसस्थानः) vs. P.8.4.58 (अनुस्वारस्य ययि परसवर्णः).
CA (3.4.25-26: व्यवाये शसलैः, चटतवर्गैश्च) vs. P.8.4.2 (अट्कुप्वाङ्नुम्व्यवायेऽपि).

The conclusion based on the above evidence is that the CA was familiar with grammatical traditions which were in part like Pāṇini's grammar, but in part different from it. It does not look like a text which is a direct reworking of Pāṇini's grammar.

6.8. The early tradition reflected in the metrical authority quoted in the CAB.

6.8.1. The CAB looks like a fairly old commentary, perhaps as old as the KV. The commentary occasionally quotes statements which look like Vārttikas of some sort, and these mark an advance of the tradition, beyond the stage set by the CA itself. The commentary also quotes profusely from a metrical authority, some verses of which are identical with those of the Varṇapaṭala, a Pariśiṣṭa of the Atharvaveda. However, this commentary quotes a large number of verses which are not attested in the currently available text of the Varṇapaṭala. It is likely that the Varṇapaṭala is itself a short selection from a larger older authority. This older authority is probably older than the text of the Māṇḍūkīśikṣā. This Śikṣā was not known to the CAB. Whether the metrical authority quoted to elucidate the contents of the CA is older than the CA itself is a difficult question. CA (1.2.10: पूर्वरूपस्य मात्रार्धं समानकरणं परम्) is identical with the first two quarters of a verse quoted in the CAB on this rule:

पूर्वरूपस्य मात्रार्धं समानकरणं परम् ।
प्रत्ययेन भवेत् कार्यमेतत् संयुक्तमिष्यते ।।

There is indeed a possibility that the metrical authority is older than the text of the CA, though one cannot be completely certain in this matter. In any case, the metrical authority is older than the CAB.

6.8.2. The metrical authority exhibits greater familiarity with the Pāṇinian tradition, as compared to the rules of the Caturādhyāyikā. This can be seen from the following instances:

a) Metrical Authority: एदैतोः, on CA (1.1.19). Here, in the expressions *eT* and *aiT*, the marker *T* is clearly identical with the marker *T* defined in P.1.1.70 (तपरस्तत्कालस्य).

b) Metrical Authority: समानास्यप्रयत्ना ये ते सवर्णा इति स्मृताः, on CA (1.1.27). This is the only known early authority which coincides with P.1.1.9 (तुल्यास्यप्रयत्नं सवर्णम्) in its use of the term *āsyaprayatna*. The CA does not use this term.

c) Metrical Authority: टाशब्दः, on CA (4.1.33) to refer to the instrumental singular affix. Pāṇini (4.1.2: स्वौजसमौट्छष्टा...) also uses the expression *ṭā* for the same affix. The metrical authority seems to take this term for granted.

d) Metrical Authority: अङ्गस्य, on CA (4.1.38). The CA does not use the term *aṅga,* but P.1.3.13 (यस्मात् प्रत्ययविधिस्तदादि प्रत्ययेऽङ्गम्) defines this term. The metrical authority seems to take this term for granted.

e) Metrical Authority: कृत्, on CA (4.1.48-49). The term *kṛt* is not used by the CA. Pāṇini defines it as P.3.1.93 (कृदतिङ्). The metrical authority seems to take this term for granted.

f) Metrical Authority: मतुप् and मयट्, on CA (4.1.49). CA (4.2.1: न तकारसकाराभ्यां मत्वर्थे) knows the first affix as *matu,* and CA (4.1.46: मयेऽसकारात्) knows the second affix as *maya.* Pāṇini refers to these affixes as *matuP* (P.5.2.94: तदस्यास्त्यस्मिन्निति मतुप्) and *mayaṬ* (P.5.4.21: तत्प्रकृतवचने मयट्).

g) Metrical Authority: किकिनौ, on CA (4.1.57). These two affixes are taught by Pāṇini (3.2.171: आदृगमहनजनः किकिनौ लिट् च).

h) Metrical Authority: बहुलं छन्दसि, on CA (4.1.57). This is a reference to a rule in Pāṇini, which occurs a number of times in his grammar, e.g. P.3.2.88.

i) Metrical Authority: अभ्यासस्य च दीर्घत्वं दीर्घोऽकितेति दृश्यते । ... यद्यभ्यासस्य दीर्घत्वं तुजादीनां च यङ्लुकोः । सवर्णे च परोक्षायां ..., on CA (4.3.12). Compare: P.7.4.83 (दीर्घोऽकितः), P.6.1.7 (तुजादीनां दीर्घोऽभ्यासस्य), and P.6.4.78 (अभ्यासस्यासवर्णे).

This evidence amply demonstrates that the versified authority quoted by the CAB was fully familiar with Pāṇini's grammar, and that it quotes it profusely. At the same time, one must make it clear that it is almost totally free from the impact of the Pāṇinīyaśikṣā and the phonetic doctrines of the later Pāṇinian tradition. It is in many ways closer to the tradition represented in the RPR.

6.8.3. To illustrate its relatively more archaic phonetic doctrines, I shall draw attention to the following details. Unlike the metrical Pāṇinīyaśikṣā (verse 18: एऐ तु कण्ठतालव्यावोऔ कण्ठोष्ठजौ स्मृतौ), this cited metrical authority regards only *ai* and *au* as having an initial *kaṇṭhya* element (कण्ठ्यः ... ऐदौतोराद्ययोर्मात्रयोः स्मृतः, on CA 1.1.19), while the sounds *e* and *o* are considered to be *tālavya* and *oṣṭhya,* respectively (cf. ताल्वेयशचवर्गाणामिवर्णस्य च, on CA 1.1.21; उपध्मानीय ओकारो ... तथा (ओष्ठ्याः) मताः, on CA 1.1.25). It holds the sounds *ṛ, ḷ, ka-varga,* and the *jihvāmūlīya* to be *jihvāmūlīya* sounds (cf. जिह्वामूलमृवर्णस्य कवर्गस्य च भाष्यते । यश्चैव जिह्वामूलीय ऌवर्णश्चेति च स्मृतः, on CA 1.1.20). The only retroflex sounds are *ṣ* and the *ṭavarga* (cf. मूर्धा स्थानं षकारस्य टवर्गस्य तथा मतम्, on CA 1.1.22). The sound *r* is treated as a *dantamūlīya,* though the metrical authority is aware of other views on its alternative classifications (cf. रेफस्य दन्तमूलानि ... अपर आह ... हनुमूले तु रेफस्य दन्तमूलेषु वा पुनः । प्रत्यग्वा दन्तमूलेभ्यो मूर्धन्य इति चापरे, on CA 1.1.28). Thus, on the whole, this ancient metrical authority holds fairly archaic phonetic classifications, while exhibiting a wide ranging awareness of Pāṇinian terminology.

6.9. The tradition as reflected in the CAB

6.9.1. The CAB exhibits greater familiarity with the Pāṇinian rules. It quotes some of them directly. Also, while quoting the ancient metrical authority discussed above, it offers phonetic classifications which are more in line with the later Pāṇinian system as represented by the metrical Pāṇinīyaśikṣā.

6.9.2. Direct and Indirect Quotations of Pāṇini's rules

a) CAB on CA 1.1.2.

'लीढ'मित्यत्र हो ढत्वम् (cf. 'हो ढः,' पा. ८.२.३१)। परचतुर्थत्वम् (cf. 'झषस्तथोर्धोऽधः,' पा. ८.२.४०)। ष्टुना ष्टुत्वम् (cf. 'ष्टुना ष्टुः,' पा. ८.४.४१)। ढो ढे लोपो (cf. 'ढो ढे लोपः,' पा. ८.३.१३) दीर्घत्वमिति (cf. 'ढ्रलोपे पूर्वस्य दीर्घोऽणः,' पा. ६.३.१११) वैयाकरणेन वक्तव्यम् ।

b) CAB on CA 1.1.3

एवम् इह इति च । अस्यां शाखायां तत् प्रातिज्ञं मन्यन्ते । 'यरोऽनुनासिकेऽनुनासिको वा' (पा. ८.४.४५) इति विभाषाप्राप्तं सामान्ये । किं सामान्यम् । व्याकरणम् । वक्ष्यति 'उत्तमा उत्तमेषु' (च.आ. २.१.५) इति ।

6.9.3. Non-Atharvan examples which are shared with Pāṇinian commentaries:

a) CAB on CA 1.2.9

अतोऽन्ये व्यञ्जनसंधयः संयुक्ता भवन्ति । अन्ये अभिनिधानात् पदान्तात् स्पर्शाः । अन्तस्थोष्मसु पदादिषु च संयुज्यन्ते । 'गोधुग्याति' । 'विराड् याति' । 'दृषद्याति'। 'त्रिष्टुब्याति' । 'गोधुग्वयति' । 'विराड्वयति' । 'त्रिष्टुब्वयति' । 'गोधुग्रथे' । 'विराड्रथे' । 'षड्रथे' । 'गोधुक्शेते' । 'विराट्शेते'। 'दृषत्शेते' । 'त्रिष्टुप्शेते' । 'गोधुक्षण्डे' । 'विराट्षण्डे' । 'दृषत्षण्डे' । 'त्रिष्टुप्षण्डे' । 'गोधुक्साये' । 'विराट्साये'। 'दृषत्साये' । 'त्रिष्टुप्साये' ।

All the examples cited by the CAB are artificial examples produced by combinations and permutations of a few words. Examples with *śete, sāye,* and *ṣaṇḍe* are found in the KV on P.8.3.28, 29, 30, and 36.

b) CAB on CA 1.4.1:

वर्णादन्त्यात्पूर्वो वर्णः उपधासंज्ञो भवति । 'नाम्युपधस्य रेफः' (च.आ. २.२.३)। 'अग्निरत्र' (not in AV)। 'वायुरत्र' (not in AV)।

The examples *agniratra* and *vāyuratra* provided by the CAB are found in the KV on P.8.2.66 (ससजुषो रुः).

c) CAB on CA 2.1.14:

चटवर्गयोः परतः तकारस्य पर(स)स्थानो भवति । ... 'अग्निचिट्टीकते' (not in AV)। 'सोमसुड्डीयते' (not in AV)।

The example *agniciṭṭīkate* is actually found in the KV on P.8.4.41.

d) CAB on CA 2.1.26:

नकारस्य चटतवर्गेषु अघोषेषु अनूष्मपरेषु विसर्जनीयो भवति । 'भवांश्चिनोति' (not in AV)। 'भवांश्छादयति' (not in AV)। 'भवांष्टीकते' (not in AV)। 'भवांस्तरति' (not in AV)। 'भवांस्तत्र' (not in AV)। अघोषेष्वित्येव । 'बृहन् दक्षिणया' (अ.वे. ६.५३.१)। 'नैनान्नमसा परः' (अ.वे. ७.७.१)। अनूष्मपरेष्वित्येव । 'भवान्त्सरु' (not in AV)। 'महान्त्सरु' (not in AV)।

Most of the examples, not attested in the AV, are found in the KV on P.8.3.7 (नश्छव्यप्रशान्). It is absolutely unconscionable that the commentary does not offer a single example from the text of the Atharvan to illustrate this phenomenon, which is by no means rare in the Atharvan text. By citing the examples which he does, the commentator shows how deeply influenced he is by the of Pāṇinian tradition.

e) CAB on CA 2.4.3:
तद्धिते परतः तकारादौ नाम्युपधस्य सकारस्य षकारो भवति । 'सर्पिष्टरम्' (not in AV)। 'यजुष्टरम्' (not in AV)। 'वपुष्टरम्' (not in AV, ऋ.वे. १०.३२.३)। 'वपुष्टमाम्' ('वपुष्टंमे,' अ.वे. ५.५.६)। तद्धित इति किमर्थम् । 'अग्निस्तक्मानम्' (अ.वे. ५. २२.१)। तकारादाविति किमर्थम् । 'सर्पिस्सात्' (not in AV)। 'यजुस्सात्' (not in AV)। 'वपुस्सात्' (not in AV)।

Most of the unattested examples quoted in the CAB are found in the KV on P.8.3.99 (ह्रस्वात् तादौ तद्धिते).

f) CAB on CA 3.2.19:
समानाक्षरस्य सवर्णे परतः दीर्घो भवति । 'दण्डाग्रम्'। 'दधीन्द्रः' । 'मधूष्णम्' । 'होतॄश्यः' । 'पितॄश्यः' ।

The KV on P.6.1.101 (अकः सवर्णे दीर्घः) cites the examples *daṇḍāgram, dadhīndraḥ, madhūdake,* and *hotṝśyaḥ.* The Osmania edition of the KV notes a manuscript variant *madhūṣṭram* for *madhūdake.* This variant is probably a corruption of *madhūṣṇam.*

6.9.4. Influence of the Late Pāṇinian Phonetic Classifications:

a) The CAB includes *e, ai, o,* and *au,* among the *kaṇṭhya* sounds, implying that the initial elements of all the four are *kaṇṭhya* sounds (cf. CAB on CA 1.1.19). This notion is more in line with the metrical Pāṇinīyaśikṣā (verse 1: एऐ तु कण्ठतालव्यावोऔ कण्ठोष्ठजौ स्मृतौ), and it directly contradicts the doctrines of the cited metrical authority (कण्ठ्यः ... ऐदौतोराद्ययोर्मात्रयोः स्मृतः, on CA 1.1.19, ताल्वेयशचवर्गाणामिवर्णस्य च, on CA 1.1.21; उपध्मानीय ओकारो ... तथा ओष्ठ्याः मताः, on CA 1.1.25).

b) On CA 1.1.22, it includes *r* among the *mūrdhanya* sounds, again contradicting both the cited metrical authority, as well as the direct prescription of the CA 1.1.28 (रेफस्य दन्तमूलानि). This notion is closer to the metrical Pāṇinīyaśikṣā (verse 17: स्युर्मूर्धन्या ऋटुरषाः). The CAB (on CA 1.1.28) says that the 'roots of teeth' (*dantamūlāni*) are the *karaṇa* 'articulator' for *r*. This is believed not to contradict the claim that *r* is a *mūrdhanya* sound. However, it makes little sense to say that the 'cerebrum, top of the oral cavity' is the point of articulation for *r*, and that the 'roots of teeth' are the articulator for it.

c) While the cited metrical authority (in CAB on CA 1.1.25) considers *v* to be an *oṣṭhya* sound, the CAB (on CA 1.1.25) takes it out of the list of *oṣṭhya* sounds, possibly implying that *v* is a *dantyoṣṭhya* 'labio-dental' sound. This is again closer to the doctrines of the metrical Pāṇinīyaśikṣā (verse 18: दन्त्योष्ठ्यो वः स्मृतो बुधैः).

6.10. The Pāṇinian Drift seen in Bhārgava-Bhāskara's Vṛtti

6.10.1. While the CAB is probably closer in date to the KV, the commentary of Bhārgava-Bhāskara and the Pañcasandhi by Kṛṣṇadāsa represent the very late phase of this tradition. These late works indicate that the tradition of the CA has now come under the full Pāṇinian influence as typified by works like Bhaṭṭojī Dīkṣita's SK. This late tradition does not show any awareness of the existence of the older commentary CAB, or of the metrical authority quoted by the CAB. Bhārgava-Bhāskara cites not only Pāṇini's rules, but also the versified Pāṇinīyaśikṣā, and he twists the meaning of the CA rules to fit the interpretations of Pāṇini's rules found in the late texts like the SK. Below we shall briefly review the evidence from Bhārgava-Bhāskara's commentary:

a) On CA 1.1.10: पाणिनीये तु 'वावसाने' (पा. ८.४.५६) इति विकल्पः ।

b) On CA 1.1.16: अत एवोक्तम् 'उच्चैरुदात्तम्' इति वक्ष्यमाणेषु कण्ठादिस्थानेषूच्चार्यमाणो ह्रस्वदीर्घप्लुतस्वरः उच्चैरूर्ध्वभागे उत्पन्नः उदात्तसंज्ञः ऊर्ध्वमात्तः उदात्तः । 'नीचैरनुदात्तम्' । तथाविधस्थानेष्वधोभागेषूच्चार्यमाणः स्वरः अनुदात्तसंज्ञः उदात्तविरुद्धः अनुदात्तः । 'आक्षिप्तं स्वरितम्' । आ उभयार्थकः उभयधर्मावभिव्याप्य क्षिप्तमुच्चारितमक्षरं स्वरितं स्यात् । Compare SK on P.1.2.29, 1.2.30, and 1.2.31.

c) On CA 1.1.17: पाणिनीयेऽपि - 'तस्यादित उदात्तमर्धह्रस्वम्' (पा. १.२.३२) इति ।

d) On CA 1.1.18:
चतुराध्यायीभाष्य- मुखे विशेषा भवन्ति करणस्य । कचटतपाः ।
भा.भा.वृत्ति - मुखे वदनान्तराकाशप्रान्तदेशे । करणस्य स्पृष्टादिसंज्ञक-प्रयत्नस्य विशेषाः । वर्णोच्चारणस्थानभेदाः कथ्यन्ते ।

Contrast the two commentaries. Bhārgava-Bhāskara seems to have confused the notion of *prayatna* as it appears in the Pāṇinian school with that of *karaṇa* in this text. The first term refers to the manner in which the articulator (*karaṇa*) relates to the point of articulation (*sthāna*). On the other hand, the second term refers to the articulator.

e) On CA 1.1.22: मुखबिले ऊर्ध्वायाः हनोर्मध्यदेशः वर्णोच्चारे मूर्धेति संज्ञा । तत्र भवा मूर्धन्याः ऋकारटवर्गौ । ऋटठडढण एषां षण्णां प्रतिवेष्टितं जिह्वाग्रं किञ्चिद्वक्रीकृत्य मूर्धस्थानं स्पृष्ट्वा निमुच्यते ।

Here Bhārgava-Bhāskara includes the sound *ṛ* among the *mūrdhanya* sounds. This is not done either by the metrical authority or by the CAB. While he excludes the sound *r* from the list of *mūrdhanya*s here, later he includes *r* as well among *mūrdhanya*s or near-*mūrdhanya*s.

f) On CA 1.1.28: रेफो मूर्धन्यः । दन्तमूलशब्दः सामीप्यं द्योतयति बहु-वचननिर्देशात्। दन्तमूलस्थानं मूर्धस्थानं च तयोर्मध्ये रेफोच्चारणस्थानं ज्ञेयं तकारटकारोच्चारणस्थानयोर्मध्यस्थानमित्यर्थः ।

g) On CA 1.1.25: वकारस्य तु ऊर्ध्वदन्ताग्राधरस्पर्शेनोच्चारो भवति । पाणिनीये वकारस्य दन्तोष्ठ्यताया आम्नातत्वात् ।

h) On CA 1.1.28: सन्ध्यक्षराणि तु स्थानद्वयोच्चारितानि ज्ञेयानि । तथा च पाणिनीये - 'ए ऐ तु कण्ठतालव्या ओ औ कण्ठोष्ठजौ स्मृतौ' ॥ (पाणिनीयशिक्षा, श्लोक १८) इति शिक्षायां पठितम् ।

i) On CA 1.1.29: कादयो मावसानाः पञ्चविंशतिः स्पर्शाः । तेषां करणमाभ्यन्तरप्रयत्नः स्पृष्टसंज्ञको ज्ञेयः । The term *ābhyantara-prayatna* here and in the following instances is reminiscent of the late Pāṇinian tradition.

j) On CA 1.1.30: अन्तःस्थानां करणमाभ्यन्तरप्रयत्नः ईषत्स्पृष्टो ज्ञेयः ।

k) On CA 1.1.31: एषामूष्मणामाभ्यन्तरप्रयत्नः विवृतसंज्ञः ।

l) On CA 1.1.32: स्वराणां च विवृतसंज्ञः प्रयत्नो ज्ञेयः ।

It is clearly seen from the above evidence that Bhārgava-Bhāskara's commentary has offered a fully late-Pāṇinian interpretation of the CA rules. He has no knowledge of the older commentary CAB or of the metrical authority quoted by the CAB. His authorities include the late Māṇḍūkīśikṣā, but more importantly, the versified Pāṇinīyaśikṣā. Thus the independence of the CA tradition is lost in this process. Since Bhārgava-Bhāskara's commentary is available to us only in an incomplete form, it is difficult to assess what he did with the rest of the CA rules.

6.11. Full Pāṇinianization of the CA rules in Kr̥ṣṇadāsa's Kautsavyākaraṇe Pañcasandhiḥ

6.11.1. Kr̥ṣṇadāsa's Kautsavyākaraṇe Pañcasandhiḥ represents the latest and the most severe case of Pāṇinianization of a Prātiśākhya tradition. The text probably belongs to the period after the SK of Bhaṭṭojī Dīkṣita became popular. It reorganizes the rules of the CA using the model of the SK,[4] and seems to add a whole host of new Sūtras, not found in the CA. Almost at every step, Kr̥ṣṇadāsa compares the CA formulations with those of Pāṇini, and effectively provides a fully Pāṇinian interpretation of the CA rules. In contrast with the CAB as well as Bhārgava-Bhāskara's commentary, Kr̥ṣṇadāsa hardly quotes Atharvan examples. Most of his examples are identical with those found in texts like the SK, and in effect he is trying to build a grammar of the classical language using the rules of the CA, and in this process he stretches the CA rules maximally in the direction of the late Pāṇinian tradition. The following examples are offered to illustrate this phenomenon of maximal Pāṇinianization in Kr̥ṣṇadāsa's work. In my notes on Kr̥ṣṇadāsa's work, I have discussed the parallelisms with the late Pāṇinian works such as the SK more fully. Here, a few instances are noted:

---

[4] In this respect, Kr̥ṣṇadāsa's work resembles the commentary Prātiśākhyajyotsnā on the VPR. For details on this work and its reorganization of the VPR rules along the lines of Bhaṭṭojī Dīkṣita's SK, see: Sunanda R. Abhyankar (1984).

a) Before PS 6: ऋटुरषा मूर्धन्याः ।

b) On *PS* 10: दन्त्यौष्ठ्यो वकारः ।

c) On PS 12: प्रयत्नो द्विधा । आभ्यन्तरो बाह्यश्च । तत्राभ्यन्तरश्चतुर्धा । स्पृष्टेषत्स्पृष्टविवृतसंवृतभेदात् । 'कादयो मावसानाः स्पर्शाः' इति पाणिनीयाः ।

d) On PS 27: विवृतमनूद्य संवृतोऽनेन विधीयते ह्रस्वस्यावर्णस्य प्रयोगे संवृतं प्रक्रियादशायां तु विवृतमेव ।

e) On PS 32: अत्र सूत्रे प्रक्रियाद्वयं दृश्यते 'सरूपाणामेकशेष' ... (पा. १.२.६४) इत्येका वृत्तिः । 'नाज्झलौ' (पा. १.१.१०) इति पाणिनीये आकारप्रश्लेष इवार्थबलात् । 'हलन्त्यम्' (पा. १.३.३) इतिवत् ।

f) ८७. **स्थानार्था षष्ठी** (not found in CA)। षष्ठीनिर्दिष्टं कार्यं तस्यैव स्थाने बोध्यम् । ८८. **पञ्चम्युत्तरस्य** (not found in CA)। ८९. **सप्तमी पूर्वस्य** (not found in CA)। ९०. **आद्यन्तानि टवर्गकवर्गव्यञ्जनानि** (not found in CA)। ९१. **असिद्धं बहिरङ्गमन्तरङ्गे** (not found in CA)। विनाशोन्मुखं कार्यं न कुर्यात् । ९२. **इतो लोपः** (not found in CA)। इत्संज्ञकस्येत्यर्थः । ९३. **विधायकस्य न** (not found in CA)। ९४. **वर्णग्रहे सवर्णमात्रम्** (not found in CA)। ...इति परिभाषाप्रकरणम् ।। This whole section is a new creation in imitation of Pāṇinian rules.

g) On PS 126: समानसंज्ञिकस्य स्वरस्य स्थाने सवर्णे स्वरे परे सति द्वयोरपि स्थाने दीर्घरूप एकादेशः । ... कृष्ण अवलम्ब इत्यत्रोभयोर्ह्रस्वयोरकारयोः दीर्घे आकारादेशे कृष्णावलम्ब इति सिद्धम् । वेदाध्ययनं दैवाधीनमित्यपि च ।

h) On PS 132: अकारस्य स्थाने उवर्णे परे द्वयोरेक ओकारादेशः स्यात् । कृष्ण उपास्यः कृष्णोपास्यः, गङ्गोदकम्, राम ऊनः रामोनः, जाया ऊतिः जायोतिः, इला आ ऊर्ध्वम् इलोर्ध्वम् ।

i) On PS 133: अकारस्य स्थाने ऋवर्णे परे द्वयोरपि स्थाने एकः अर् भवति । अरमिति नपुंसकत्वमार्षम्। कृष्ण ऋद्धिः कृष्णर्द्धिः । जल ऋतुः जलर्तुः । ब्रह्मर्षयः । तव ऌकारः तवल्कारः । सावर्ण्यात्समानः प्रयोगः ।

6.12. The changing nature of the CA tradition

On the basis of the above evidence tracing the historical changes which occurred in the CA tradition, we can draw the following conclusions.

The CA itself was perhaps familiar with Pāṇinian, or perhaps Pāṇini-like, terminology, and occasionally it does venture into explanations of formations which do not occur in the AV, but on the whole it is an authentic description of a particular phase of the Śaunakīya AV. Generally, the text is concerned with the AV, and represents a distinct tradition.

The Metrical Authority, an ancient Śikṣā relating to the AV tradition, predates the later Māṇḍūkīśikṣā. It shows substantial familiarity with Pāṇini's system, and yet it shows a true independent view of Sanskrit phonetics, not colored by what one finds in the versified Pāṇinīyaśikṣā. We can safely assume that this ancient Śikṣā predates the versified Pāṇinīyaśikṣā.

The CAB shows even greater familiarity with the Pāṇinian tradition, perhaps with the KV. Its phonetic description is beginning to show signs of the influence of the late Pāṇinian tradition, though it does not directly quote the versified Pāṇinīyaśikṣā. However, it is clear that its deviations from the quoted Metrical Authority are in the direction of the versified Pāṇinīyaśikṣā. At the same time, it is genuinely related to the Atharvavedic tradition, and it has a very close connection with the APR edited by Surya Kanta.

The commentary of Bhārgava-Bhāskara shows a deep influence of the Pāṇinian tradition. It looks like it has no knowledge of either the CAB or the Metrical Authority quoted by it. On the other hand, it quotes Pāṇini, the Māṇḍūkīśikṣā, and the versified Pāṇinīyaśikṣā. Its interpretations are colored by this late phase of the Pāṇinian tradition. However, at the same time it must be admitted that it is closely linked with the Atharvavedic tradition, and it cites a large number of examples from the text of the Atharvaveda.

The last text, i.e. Kr̥ṣṇadāsa's Kautsavyākaraṇe Pañcasandhiḥ, is a truly different text. It is an SK-style reorganization of the CA rules, clearly dominated by the SK. It is only peripherally part of the Atharvavedic tradition. The examples cited by this commentary are hardly different from those of the SK, and rarely does it cite anything from the AV. It is an effort to write a grammar of the classical language using the rules of the CA, supplemented by a set of new rules based on the Pāṇinian system. Kr̥ṣṇadāsa's work is also largely influenced by Anubhūtisvarūpācārya's Sārasvata-Vyākaraṇa.

The above survey indicates how the tradition of the CA gradually lost its individuality and came under the direct influence of the dominant grammatical paradigm, i.e. the Pāṇinian tradition. This influence perhaps kept the tradition of the CA alive, but in the process of keeping it alive, the CA tradition was gradually drained of its grammatical and phonetic distinctiveness, and, in this sense, the Pāṇinian influence must be viewed as a negative force, and not a positive help in the interpretation of the Prātiśākhya tradition.

7. The AV Prātiśākhyas and the ŚAV Text-Transmission

7.1. General Issues of Saṃhitā Formation and Transmission

7.1.1. In his MB, Patañjali says that the Atharvaveda has nine different recensions (cf. नवधाथर्वणो वेदः, MB, Vol.I, p. 9). However, the Saṃhitā of the Atharvaveda is available to us at present only in two major recensions, i.e. the Śaunakīya and the Paippalāda. The two recensions differ in their overall organization of the material, and the readings for individual verses differ in hundreds of places. The readings found in any one recension are authentic only in so far as they represent that particular recension of the Atharvaveda, and there is no intrinsic claim for any reading to represent the Ur-Atharvaveda, if indeed there was such a thing. With the Vedic Saṃhitās, scholars have proposed two distinct phases of oral transmission. Oldenberg (1890, 1962: 28), referring to the Saṃhitā of the RV, says: "The study of Śaunaka's work [= RPR] affords us the proof that *from that time on* the Vedic hymns, protected by the united care of grammatical and religious respect for letters, have suffered no further appreciable corruptions." However, worth noting are his comments on the pre-redaction textual transmission: "In some cases, isolated details of the additions of prior epochs were caught and clung to with felicitous acumen; in others, no hesitation was had in wiping out of existence entire domains of old and genuine phenomena to suit half-correct theories, so that the most patient ingenuity of modern science will only be able to restore in part what has been lost" (1890, 1962: 27). He further reminds us that "the collection was re-corrected on repeated occasions. It is conceivable enough that thus the original structure, yes, even the existence itself of special hymns was often injured, effaced, or destroyed" (1890, 1962: 26). The first phase represented the pre-redaction period of the oral transmission, uncontrolled and unguided by any systematic efforts at standardization, while the post-redaction phase was characterized by a great deal of systematic standardization of the text in its organization as well as its pronunciation. This second phase began with the work of scholars like Śākalya for the RV, and Śaunaka for the Śaunakīya AV.

Patañjali refers to Śākalya's well-prepared Saṃhitā (cf. शाकल्येन सुकृतां संहितामनुनिशम्य देवः प्रावर्षत्, MB on P.1.4.84, Vol.I, p. 347) of the RV. Śaunaka probably did the same thing for the AV Saṃhitā and prepared its Padapāṭha. As it has been documented more fully for Śākalya, the Padapāṭha reflects his understanding of the words of the Saṃhitā. It also reflects certain features of his own dialect of Sanskrit (Cardona 1991). Finally, the Saṃhitā was to be rebuilt by changing the Padapāṭha by applying the rules of Sandhi, and hence in certain respects, the Saṃhitā, thus arrived at, reflected more modern features, as compared to the original compositions of the Vedic seers which are now lost to us. Thus, a given Saṃhitā represents not precisely the original compositions of the Vedic seers, but compositions as they were received, understood, interpreted, and organized by a particular Saṃhitākāra. As this is true of Śākalya's recension of the RV, so it must be true of Śaunaka's recension of the AV.

7.1.2. With all this, one may develop an impression that such recensions or Saṃhitās, once they were so well put together by the respective Saṃhitākāras, must have been essentially immutable, not susceptible to any further change. As we shall see, such an expectation is wide-spread, but in fact unfounded. For instance, we know that Pāṇini knew Śākalya's RV Saṃhitā, as he directly quotes Śākalya's opinions in several places (cf. लोपः शाकल्यस्य, P. 8.3.19; सम्बुद्धौ शाकल्यस्येतावनार्षे, P.1.1.16). However, can we be certain that he knew Śākalya's recension exactly as we know it today? Did he know the RV with *ḷ* for intervocalic *ḍ*, or did his version not have this feature? In my opinion, the latter alternative is more likely. If the RV recension of Śākalya which has come down to us shows somewhat different features than what were known to Pāṇini, is it possible for us to say that only one of these versions is a true Śākalya recension, and that what survives is not a Śākalya recension in a real sense? Or should we rather abandon the view of the supposed immutability of these recensions, and accept a view that the recensions once formulated by scholars like Śākalya and Śaunaka did undergo a slow process of marginal change. Some of this change was imperceptible phonetic change for a long time, but eventually such changes accumulated over a period of time. In spite of such changes, it was still possible for the successive generations of redactors to believe that they were still maintaining the ancient recension formulated by Śākalya or Śaunaka. If we accept such a view of the transmission of Vedic Saṃhitās, we may have a different understanding of how these Saṃhitās were transmitted. Here we shall investigate some of these questions in relation to the text-transmission of the

Śaunakīya AV Saṃhitā and the exegetical tradition represented by the AV Prātiśākhyas.

7.2. The CA and the text of the ŚAV

7.2.1. Though the 1856 Roth-Whitney edition of the Śaunakīya Saṃhitā of the AV came out before Whitney's 1862 edition of the Caturādhyāyikā, Roth and Whitney were already in possession of the then known single Berlin manuscript of the Śaunakīyā Caturādhyāyikā with the commentary CAB. Although this lone manuscript was terribly corrupt, Whitney was able to extract a working text of the CA before he and Roth finalized the text of their edition of the AV. Since they were editing the Śaunakīya AV, they could see the value of the rules of the CA in the process of establishing the text of the Saṃhitā. However, their AV manuscripts did not always agree with the prescriptions of the CA. Whitney dutifully notes this divergence in his notes on the CA. In such cases, Roth and Whitney were faced with the question of whether to follow the authority of the manuscripts, or to abandon the manuscripts and follow the rules of the Śaunakīyā Caturādhyāyikā in settling the reading to be selected. There were several assumptions to be made in deciding this question. The text to be finally printed as that of the Śaunakīya AV must ideally represent the text as settled by Śaunaka. Secondly, the text which called itself Śaunakīyā Caturādhyāyikā must also be assumed to reflect the opinions of Śaunaka as regards the Saṃhitā and the Padapāṭha of this school. Therefore, on the face of it, it seemed that one could follow the CA in settling the text of the Śaunakīya Saṃhitā. In practice, the Roth-Whitney edition of the ŚAV Saṃhitā follows the CA and rejects the manuscripts in some places, and follows the manuscripts and rejects the CA in other places, and Surya Kanta has rightly criticized Whitney and Roth for this haphazard behavior: "What RW (= Roth-Whitney) have done in such cases is this, that, either they have ignored the CA authority, adopting the unanimous reading of the Vulgate mss., or they have flouted the Vulgate mss., and followed the former" (*APR*, Intro., p. 32).

7.3. Surya Kanta's assumption of the 'lost original Śaunakīya AV'

7.3.1. In 1923, Vishva Bandhu (= Vidyārthī) published a text by the title the Atharvaprātiśākhya, and in 1939, Surya Kanta published his magnificent expanded and annotated edition of the same Atharvaprātiśākhya. All the manuscripts used for this text directly called it Atharvaprātiśākhya. Until then, the title Atharvaprātiśākhya was used with reference to the Śaunakīyā Caturādhyāyikā edited by Whitney. Whitney himself knew that the CA did not call itself a Prātiśākhya, and yet he argued (1862: iii): "The treatise was first brought to light, and its character deter-mined, by Roth. It was recognized by him as being what is indicated by our title, a Prātiśākhya to a text of the Atharvaveda. That it has any inherent right to be called *the* Prātiśākhya to *the* Atharvaveda is not, of course, claimed for it; but, considering the extreme improbability that any other like phonetic treatise, belonging to any other schools of that Veda, will ever be brought to light, the title of Atharvaveda Prātiśākhya finds a sufficient justification in its convenience, and in its analogy with the names given to the other kindred treatises by their respective editors."

The above paragraph from Whitney needs to be read carefully, and one should note that he nowhere asserted that the CA is *the Prātiśākhya of the Atharva-Veda,* an accusation hurled at him unjustly by Surya Kanta (*Atharva-Prātiśākhya, Introduction,* p. 31): "Whitney turns an APr into the APr." Whitney never made such a claim. Whitney's modest claim that the CA was 'a Prātiśākhya' of the AV was clearly not out of line, and now stands supported by a reference in Uvaṭa's commentary on the first Paṭala of the Ṛgveda-Prātiśākhya: (M.D. Shastri's edition, Vol. II, p. 23): तथा चाथर्वणप्रातिशाख्ये इदमेव प्रयोजनमुक्तम् - 'एवमिहेति च विभाषाप्राप्तं सामान्येन' - अस्य सूत्रस्यायमर्थः - सामान्येन लक्षणेन यद् विकल्पप्राप्तं तदेवमस्यां शाखायां व्यवस्थितं भवतीति प्रातिशाख्यप्रयोजनमुक्तम् ।, "Thus, the same purpose is mentioned in the Ātharvaṇa-Prātiśākhya rule *evam iheti ca vibhāṣāprāptaṃ sāmānyena* (= CA 1.1.3-4, Whitney 1.2). The meaning of this rule is as follows: Whatever obtains optionally in a generic grammar of Sanskrit is settled in a particular way in this branch. Thus, the purpose of the Prātiśākhya is explained." Clearly, Uvaṭa refers to CA as an Ātharvaṇa-Prātiśākhya.

7.3.2. Anyway, now we are fortunately in possession of two texts which belong to the category of Prātiśākhyas for the Śaunakīya Atharvaveda, or are we mistaken? If we are to believe Surya Kanta, we are indeed mistaken. To put his claim in his own words: "The Atharva-Prātiśākhya belongs to the AV., and the CA belongs to the Śaunakīya School of this Saṃhitā, and not to the AV. in general" (*APR*, Intro., p. 32). He argues that the APR clearly does not belong to the Paippalāda tradition, nor does it call itself Śaunakīya at any place, and therefore it belongs to a non-Paippalāda and a non-Śaunakīya recension of the AV. This, he calls, *'the AV,'* in contrast with the Śaunakīya recension, which he assumes must be the subject of the Śaunakīyā Caturādhyāyikā. He offers the following arguments to support his case. For each argument, I have provided only a few sample examples, though Surya Kanta has offered a large number of such examples.

7.3.3. Argument a:

7.3.3.1. In a number of places, the Vulgate of the AV, the text represented by the manuscripts, agrees more closely with the description in the APR, than with the description in the CA: "The APR cites 3,236 AV. passages, and the number of citations is probably larger than that contained in any other Prātiśākhya. Out of this large number, there are hardly ten passages, where the Vulgate mss. do not follow the sanction, explicit or implicit, of the APR, while there occur hundreds of passages in the CA., where not a single Vulgate ms. follows the sanction of this treatise, besides those typical cases, where CA specifically prescribes a certain saṃdhi for a chosen passage, but that saṃdhi is not carried out in that passage even by a single Vulgate ms.; and this is significant" (*APR*, Intro., p. 32).

7.3.3.2. For example, consider CA (1.4.3, Whitney 1.94: सोष्मणि पूर्वस्यानूष्मा) and its examples. This rule says that if we have a sequence such as *nicakh-kh-nuḥ,* the first *kh* changes to *k,* and we get the form *nicak-kh-nuḥ.* Thus, we should get *id-dh-ma,* and not *idh-dh-ma; rurud-dh-re,* and not *rurudh-dh-re.* In practice, the manuscripts of the Vulgate do not show forms like *nicak-kh-nuḥ.* We only get *nicakh-nuḥ.* Thus, the CA rule is not obeyed by the manuscripts of the Vulgate. Therefore, the Vulgate is not truly Śaunakīya.

7.3.3.3. Another such example is CA (2.1.6, Whitney 2.6: द्वितीयाः शषसेषु). This rule requires that in a combination like *godhuk-śete,* the final *k* of the first word be replaced by *kh.* This doctrine is explicitly ascribed to Śaunaka by VPR (4.119: असस्थाने मुदि द्वितीयं शौनकस्य). However, the manuscripts of the Vulgate of the AV do not follow this rule, and hence, according to Surya Kanta, the Vulgate is not Śaunakīya.

7.3.3.4. Referring to CA (2.1.9, Whitney 2.9: ङणनेभ्यः कटतैः शषसेषु), Surya Kanta again points out that the Vulgate manuscripts do not show forms like *pratyaṅ-k-śete,* and concludes: "(1) that CA records sandhis for the Śaunaka AV; (2) that these are not observed by the Vulgate mss.; (3) that the Vulgate does not represent the Śaunaka śākhā, but some other" (*APR*, Intro., p. 40).

7.3.4. Argument b:

7.3.4.1. In a number of places, the CA seems to be explaining usages which are not found in the Vulgate text of the AV, and Surya Kanta proposes that such usages must have existed in a genuinely Śaunakīya recension.

7.3.4.2. For example, consider CA rules (1.3.24, Whitney 1.86: हनिगम्योः सनि) and (1.3.25, Whitney 1.87: शान्मान्दानाम्). The first rule refers to desiderative forms of the roots *han* and *gam*. While the desiderative of *han* is attested in the AV, the desiderative of *gam* is not. Similarly, of the three roots cited in CA (1.1.26, Whitney 1.26), only the desiderative forms for *mān* are attested in the Vulgate of the AV, but the desideratives of *śān* and *dān* are not so attested. Surya Kanta argues that the desiderative forms of *gam, śān* and *dān* must have occurred in the original Śaunakīya recension, and their absence in the Vulgate of the AV proves that the Vulgate is not Śaunakīya.

7.3.5. Argument c:

7.3.5.1. The commentary CAB often quotes instances to illustrate the CA rules which are not found in the Vulgate text of the AV. Surya Kanta proposes that such instances must have existed in the genuinely Śaunakīya recension.

7.3.5.2. For example, the CAB on CA (1.1.16, Whitney 1.14-16) quotes an instance which appears in the manuscripts as *prāmū ca roha.* This is not found in the Vulgate of the AV. Surya Kanta cites this as an example which occurred in the so-called genuine Śaunakīya AV, which is now lost. Whitney, I believe correctly, amends the manuscript reading to *prajāṃ ca roha,* AV (13.1.34).

7.3.5.2. To cite another example, the CAB on CA (1.1.28, Whitney 1.28) cites an instance *punā raktaṃ vāsaḥ,* which is not attested in the Vulgate of the AV. Surya Kanta asserts that this example comes from the now lost genuine Śaunakīya recension of the AV.

7.3.6. Argument d:

7.3.6.1. In some places, the APR explicitly goes against the rules of the CA, and in such cases, the manuscripts of the AV generally seem to be closer to the APR, than the CA. Therefore, the AV as found in the currently available manuscripts does not represent the genuine Śaunakīya recension.

7.3.6.2. For example, on CA (2.3.6, Whitney 2.65: कुरुकरंकरत्कृणोतुकृतिकृधिष्वकर्णयोः), the CAB says: कृणोतु इत्यत्र त्रिधात्विति वक्तव्यम् । 'दीर्घमायुष्कृणोतु' (अ.वे. ६.७८.३)। 'अग्निष्कृणोतु भेषजम्' (अ.वे. ६.१०६.३) । 'मणिष्कृणोतु देवजाः' (अ.वे. १०.६.३१). Thus, the CAB says that the change of a *visarga* to *ṣ* before *kr̥ṇotu* occurs [only] in the three listed examples. Referring to the same three instances, the APR (148) says: कृणोत्वित्यत्र त्रिधातु सत्वं न, "There is no change of *visarga* to *s* (and then to *ṣ*) in these three examples." This would suggest that in the view of the APR, one was expected to maintain a visarga in these cases. Surya Kanta points out that the Vulgate manuscripts follow the APR, and not the CA. Then he concludes that the Vulgate is not a Śaunakīya text.

7.3.6.3. Based upon an extensive examination of the CA, CAB, and the APR, in relation to the existing manuscripts of the AV, Surya Kanta arrives at the following conclusions:

1) The APR belongs to the Vulgate.
2) CA goes with the Śaunaka School
3) the two are not one.

Besides these conclusions, Surya Kanta has given a detailed comparison of the readings for the AV as known to the APR and the readings as known to Sāyaṇa. Sāyaṇa shows hundreds of different readings, "more than 300 readings in the first four Kāṇḍas alone" (*APR*, Intro., p. 56). Sāyaṇa claims to represent the Śaunakīya version of the AV, and yet these different readings exist in the text known to him. Surya Kanta suggests that one should check the mss. of Sāyaṇa's commentary to see if they conform to the sanctions of the CA, and then decide whether he really commented on the Śaunakīya recension. In any case, he would like to assert that whatever Śākhā is represented by Sāyaṇa is not the same as the one represented by the APR.

7.4. Surya Kanta's Conclusions:

7.4.1. Based on the above discussion, we can list below the conclusions drawn by Surya Kanta as I understand them.

> ***Conclusion 1:*** The recensions or Saṃhitās, once they were prepared by scholars like Śaunaka, were for all practical purposes immutable.

Conclusion 2: The Śaunakīyā Caturādhyāyikā totally reflects the opinions of Śaunaka, and hence the picture of the Saṃhitā gathered from the CA must be viewed as a faithful representation of the original Saṃhitā prepared by Śaunaka.

Conclusion 3: The CA was designed to deal exclusively with the linguistic facts of the original Śaunakīya Saṃhitā, and nothing more. Therefore, all usages targeted by the rules of the CA must have existed in the original Śaunaka AV, which is not found in the Vulgate mss.

Conclusion 4: The CA and the APR represented different Śākhās of the AV, and are unrelated to each other.

Conclusion 5: The CAB is a completely faithful explanation of the CA rules, and does not represent any change. The CAB, like the CA, is a true Śaunakīya text, and that all the examples cited by the CAB must have occurred in the genuine Śaunakīya AV.

Conclusion 6: Even though Sāyaṇa claims to be commenting on the Śaunakīya AV, his text actually represents a non-Śaunakīya recension.

Some of these conclusions have been explicitly articulated by Surya Kanta, while others can be inferred from his arguments.

7.5. Critique of Surya Kanta's claims and assumptions.[5]

7.5.1. Critique of Surya Kanta's Conclusion 1:

7.5.1.1. In my opinion, this conclusion is unacceptable. It can be demonstrated that while Pāṇini knew the RV Saṃhitā of Śākalya, the form in which he knew it was not totally identical with the form of the RV Saṃhitā as we know it. The Paippalāda as found in Kashmir and in Orissa shows in-

---

[5] In my annotations on the rules of the CA in this critical edition, I have discussed these issues at a number of places. See Notes on the following CA rules: 1.1.10, 1.2.4, 1.2.9, 1.3.15, 1.3.16, 1.3.24, 1.3.25, 2.1.2, 2.1.9, 2.1.12, 2.1.14, 2.1.19, 2.2.1, 2.2.8, 2.2.11, 2.2.12, 2.2.13, 2.3.4, 2.3.6, 2.3.8, 2.3.14, 2.3.15, 2.3.16, 2.3.17, 2.4.6, 3.1.5, 3.1.20, 3.2.10, 3.2.24, 3.2.31, 3.4.5, 3.4.6, 3.4.24, 4.2.16, 4.2.21, and 4.3.13.

credible variation of detail, and there is every reason to believe that these Saṃhitās underwent change in the process of transmission. S.P. Pandit gives a vivid account of his encounters with a reciter of the AV, Keśava Bhaṭ: "he was more shocked that the several mss. of that Veda ... exhibited numerous varieties of reading, and still more horrified when he found that the text he knew by heart and which was as it had been improved by Gaṇeś Bhaṭ Dādā was the worse for improvements." (*AV*, VVRI edition, Vol. I, p. xvii). Pandit amply demonstrates how the Vaidikas practised what they called *Śuddhī-karaṇa* 'purification, restoration', and often knew the inherited traditional reading, besides the improved reading. For the Vaidikas, the results of such a *Śuddhīkaraṇa* did not reflect a change from the original, but, on the contrary, a way of restoring the original. Thus, while in historical terms, a great deal of change occurred in the transmission of a Śākhā, this change was not admitted by the Vaidikas, who continuously tried to restore what they thought was the original. Thus, we cannot maintain any notion of immutability of a Śākhā-text.

7.5.2. Critique of Surya Kanta's Conclusion 2:

7.5.2.1. While the CA does call itself Śaunakīyā, it would not be appropriate to assume that it provides a picture of the Saṃhitā as it was originally prepared by Śaunaka himself. The CA claim to the title Śaunakīyā should only be understood to mean that it respects Śaunaka as the founder of its tradition, and that it belongs to that school. When it comes to details, the CA openly admits that it deviates from the opinions of Śaunaka, and hence represents the Śaunakīya tradition as it had changed over a period of time.

7.5.2.2. For instance, consider CA (1.1.10, Whitney 1.8: प्रथमान्तानि तृतीयान्तानीति शौनकस्य प्रतिज्ञानं न वृत्तिः) and the CAB on this rule: प्रथमान्तानि पदानि तृतीयान्तानीति शौनकस्य आचार्यस्य प्रतिज्ञानं भवति । न तु वृत्तिः । प्रथमान् तृतीयान् विद्यात् । न तु पठेत् क्वचित् । वृत्तेरननुदर्शनात्. Śaunaka's doctrine held that the voiceless unaspirated stops, occurring at the end of words, should be changed to voiced unaspirated stops. However, the CA and the CAB both point out that such a doctrine is not to be applied in actual recitation. Interestingly, Bhārgava-Bhāskara's commentary on this rule refers to Śākaṭāyana's opinion in the RPR (1.15-16: तस्मादन्यमवसाने तृतीयं गार्ग्यः स्पर्शं प्रथमं शाकटायनः), and states: अत्र वेदे तु प्रथमपद्यो गृह्यते शाकटायनानुसरणात्, "Because [we] follow Śākaṭāyana, in [the recitation of] this Veda, [we] accept the first members of the stop-series as word-final [consonants in prepausal situations]." The lesson to be learned from this comment is that a tradition claiming itself to be in the line of Śaunaka felt no hesitation in occasionally deviating from the opinion of

Śaunaka, and following the opinions of another scholar like Śākaṭāyana. Thus, the claim that the CA represents the unsullied views of Śaunaka can not be entertained.

7.5.3. Critique of Surya Kanta's Conclusion 3:

7.5.3.1. In most cases, it is true that the rules of the CA deal exclusively with the linguistic facts of the AV. However, this is not true in absolute terms. Whitney has pointed out numerous cases, where the CA is venturing into an explanation of the facts of Sanskrit beyond what is attested in the AV. This probably occurred because the author of the CA had before him general treatments of Sanskrit at large, and in many cases he drew upon such generalized sources.

7.5.3.2. For example: CA (1.3.25, Whitney 1.87: शान्मान्दानाम्). While the rule relates to the desiderative forms of three roots, only the forms of *mān* are attested in ŚAV. However, these three roots are also grouped together in P.3.1.6 (मान्बधदान्शान्भ्यो दीर्घश्चाभ्यासस्य), and it is very likely that the CA rule was based on a concern for the general grammar of Sanskrit.

7.5.3.3. Consider CA (3.4.24, Whitney 3.92: क्षुभ्नादीनाम्). This rule refers to a Gaṇa, the *Kṣubhnādigaṇa,* and says that in these forms the *n* does not change to *ṇ*. However, no forms of *kṣubh* where this would be applicable are available in the ŚAV. But notice that Pāṇini 8.4.39 (क्षुभ्नादिषु च) prescribes the same thing and refers to the same Gaṇa. Thus, it is safer to assume that occasionally the CA was drawing upon generalized grammars of Sanskrit, and hence occasionally its rules extend beyond the linguistic facts of the AV.

7.5.4. Critique of Surya Kanta's Conclusion 4:

7.5.4.1. This argument is unacceptable for numerous reasons. As Surya Kanta himself notes, several Gaṇas referred to in the CA by the first instance are fully listed in the APR with the same first instance. Similarly, in 95 percent of the cases, the examples quoted in the CAB are simply the first few instances of long lists found in the APR. This could not have occurred unless these two texts were somehow genetically linked.

7.5.4.2. Surya Kanta himself notes that the mss. of the APR are mostly found in the same bundles which also contain the text of the CA, as well as many clearly Śaunakīya texts. The colophons in these ms. bundles indicate that these mss. were copied, preserved and studied by Śaunakīya families (e.g. the Pañcolī family of Gujarat), and the texts of the Vulgate also largely come from these same families. Thus, the Śaunakīyas preserved and studied both of these texts and they also preserved the Vulgate text of the AV, and saw no contradiction.

7.5.4.3. The few cases, where the APR explicitly rejects the formulation of the CA, and where the mss. of the Vulgate follow the APR should be accounted for by resorting to linguistic change within a given tradition over a period of time. Such for instance is the case of CA (2.3.6, Whitney 2.65: कुरुकरंकरत्कृणोतुकृतिकृधिष्वकर्णयोः). As discussed earlier, the CAB says that the change of *visarga* to *s* (and then to *ṣ*) before *kṛṇotu* occurs only in three instances. However, the APR (148) says that one does not change the *visarga* to *s* (and then to *ṣ*) in these three cases. It is possible to account for these statements as reflecting a possible historical development.

7.5.4.4. Whitney, on this rule, says: "In all these (= three) passages, however, the manuscripts read, without dissent, *visarjanīya* before the *k*. ... Other instances in which *kṛṇotu* has an unaltered *visarjanīya* before it are tolerably numerous." Thus, instead of simply talking about two different recensions represented by these two texts, one could make a better case for a possible historical change within the same tradition:

1) CA - Unconditional change of *visarjanīya* to *s* before *kṛṇotu*.
2) CAB - This change occurs only in three instances.
3) APR - The above change does not occur in any instances.

7.5.4.5. Such a general direction of possible change in the oral text is further supported by the following observations of W.S. Allen (1953: 51): "In later, though still ancient, times there appears to have been a tendency for *-ḥ* to extend its usage to contexts other than *in pausa*. The earliest of these extensions was to the position before the initial fricatives *ś-, ṣ-, s-*, where it replaced the homorganic final *-ś, -ṣ, -s* (*indraś śūraḥ* > *indraḥ śūraḥ*, &c). This practice was then extended to the position before the velar and labial voiceless stops: in connexion with this innovation we find mentioned the names of Āgniveśya, Vālmīki, Śākalya, and the Mādhyandina school, whilst the ancient grammarian Śākaṭāyana is quoted as holding to the more conservative practice." Allen also refers to A.H. Fry's view that "the spread of *-ḥ* was due to the writers of Classical Sanskrit operating with a phonemic orthography." The last comment is especially significant, since we are dealing with relatively late manuscripts for editing our texts.

7.5.5. Critique of Surya Kanta's Conclusion 5:

7.5.5.1. There is no reason to believe that the CAB is a totally faithful interpretation of the CA and that it does not add anything to the CA reflecting either historical change in the transmitted text of the Śaunakīya AV, or new influences from other grammatical traditions such as that of Pāṇini.

7.5.5.2. The discussion in the previous section shows a possibility of a gap between the views held by the CA and the CAB. Here is another example. On CA (2.3.3, Whitney 2.62: समासे सकारः कपयोरनन्तःसद्यःश्रेयश्छन्दसाम्), the CAB first discusses all the instances directly referred to by the CA rule, and finally adds: परः परः । पर इति चाम्रेडितसमासे न सकारो भवति । 'त्वत् परः परः' (अ.वे. १२.३.३९). This added instance is not covered by the list of exceptions in the CA rule itself. However, it is covered by the APR (201). Thus, it is possible that this exception was not intended by the author of the CA, but developed later on and was accounted for by both the CAB and the APR.

7.5.5.3. In very many cases, the CAB offers lists of examples which are not found in the AV, but are taken most probably from the Pāṇinian commentaries like the KV. I have already discussed a number of such examples above in section 6.9.3. Considering the profusion of such non-AV Pāṇinian examples in the CAB, one cannot agree with Surya Kanta that every example cited by the CAB, not found in the Vulgate of the AV, must have occurred in the so-called genuine Śaunakīya recension of the AV. I must also point out that Whitney had already cited all these Pāṇinian examples from the CAB in his edition of the CA. However, Surya Kanta remains totally silent about all these examples. If the CAB can cite all these examples, there is no reason to assume that every example cited by the CAB must be a genuine AV example. Even an example like पुना रक्तं वासः in the CAB on CA (1.1.28, Whitney 1.28) which is not traced in the AV, and is ascribed by Surya Kanta to his genuine Śaunakīya recension, is found in the KV on P.1.3.14 (रो रि), and could have been taken from such a Pāṇinian commentary.

7.5.6. Critique of Surya Kanta's Conclusion 6:

7.5.6.1. At the very beginning of his Bhāṣya on the first Kāṇḍa of the AV, Sāyaṇa says:

> शाखायाः शौनकीयायाः पूर्वोक्तेष्वेव कर्मसु ।
> विनियोगाभिधानेन संहितार्थः प्रकाश्यते ।।

> "The meaning of the Saṃhitā of the Śaunakīya branch shall be explained by pointing out its application in the ritual actions mentioned earlier."

This makes it clear that in his own opinion, Sāyaṇa was commenting on the Śaunakīya recension and none other. We should be willing to accept a strong possibility that, like the separate textual transmission of the Paippalāda recension in different regions of India, the Śaunakīya recension also underwent slightly divergent developments in different parts, cf. Mishra, R.C. 1984. These different sub-schools were not always in touch with each other, and probably underwent independent *Śuddhīkaraṇa* 'purification / restoration' (and *a-Śuddhīkaraṇa* for that matter) in different regions. As it has been shown by Vishva Bandhu and Pandit, such regional traits are manifest in the manuscripts of the AV.

> "Looking to the nature of the several MSS., I group them as follows: A, B, C, D, E, R, Sm, Cs, P, P2, J, and Cp, come from Gujarat, though not from the same original source. They are untainted by any attempts to revise the tradition of the text and probably represented the original form of the true tradition of the text. Bp, Bh, K, Km, V, and Dc, are on the other hand representatives of the Atharvaveda as it was revised in the Deccan; where it was introduced about 160 years ago, under the influence of the school of the R̥gvedins and was further subjected to changes in relation to the text of Sāyaṇācārya by Gaṇeś Bhaṭ Dādā after his visit to Śriṅgeri, and his discovery there of Sāyaṇa's commentary" (*AV*, VVRI edition, Vol. I, Intro., p. xxvi).

7.5.6.2. It is also clear that the late commentators of the CA, Bhārgava-Bhāskara and Kr̥ṣṇadāsa, were unaware of the existence of CAB, and were working not on CA, but on what they called Kautsa-Vyākaraṇa. Generally speaking, the CA manuscripts are located in the regions of Gujarat and Rajasthan. The manuscripts which call their text Kautsa-Vyākaraṇa are generally located in Ujjain and Deccan. Not a single manuscript of the CA has been found in the southern parts of India. As Pandit's introduction shows, the Deccan tradition of the AV became aware of Sāyaṇa's commentary at a very late time, when a Maharashtrian AV reciter visited Śriṅgerī and then became aware of its existence. It is also not unlikely that the southern tradition of the

Śaunakīya AV was not aware of the existence of the CA and its commentaries. Sāyaṇa's commentary, which refers to Pāṇini and later grammarians in that tradition hundreds of times, does not refer either to CA or to APR even once. Thus, one can make a probable assumption that the text-tradition of the Śaunakīya AV received by him was not in contact with either the CA or the APR. However, for that reason, one need not discard his claim that he too was working with 'a' Śaunakīya tradition.

7.6. Surya Kanta's 'star example' Re-examined.

7.6.1. Surya Kanta (*APR*, Intro., p. 42) points to a passage in the APR which proves conclusively to him that the currently preserved text of the AV is not that of the true Śaunakīya Saṃhitā. This is a dual reference in APR (140c) and (3g) to the passage *tannastapaḥ* (AV 12.3.12). The question is whether this should be understood as a combination of *taṃ naḥ* or *tat naḥ*. APR (140c: तन्निष्कुरु तन्निदध्मस्तन्नो भूमे तन्नस्तपस्तन्निर्दहत तन्नो गोपायतास्माकमिति षण्मकारान्तानि नकाराबाधे) refers to this passage and says that *tannas* should be analyzed as *tam naḥ*. Referring to the same passage, APR (3g) says: शाखान्तरेऽपि । तन्नस्तपः । अकारान्तं पुंसि वचनम् । नपुंसकं तकारान्तं शौनके ।. Surya Kanta (*APR*, Intro., p. 42) translates this passage as: "Also in another śākhā of the AV; *tan nas tapaḥ* (12.3.12); *tat*, masc., nom. sing. ends in *a* (= *saḥ*); the same in neut. ends in *t*; (this is so found) in the school of *Śaunaka*." For Surya Kanta, "The wording is explicit. *Śaunakas* read in the Pada *tat naḥ*, against *tam naḥ* of the APrŚ. APr. 140c and 3g taken together give: - 1. *tam naḥ*; APrŚ.; so SPP. with all his authorities. 2. *tat naḥ*, Śaunakas; so Whitney with all his mss."

7.6.2. What does this passage mean? One must concede that it refers to an observed difference in the recitation of the Padapāṭha, and that the reading *tat naḥ* is ascribed by the author of the APR to a tradition described as Śaunaka. However, this does not and should not be taken to mean that the reading *tat naḥ* belongs to the so-called pure genuine Śaunakīya Saṃhitā which is now lost. It in fact does not refer to the view of Śaunaka, or directly to the Padapāṭha as constituted by Śaunaka, but to the tradition as constituted by the Śaunakīyā Caturādhyāyikā. This is clear from CA (1.1.10, Whitney 1.8: प्रथमान्तानि तृतीयान्तानीति शौनकस्य प्रतिज्ञानं न वृत्तिः) and the commentaries CAB and Bhārgava-Bhāskara-Vṛtti. It was Śaunaka's doctrine that the words ending in the first members of the stop-series should be recited as ending in the third members, e.g. *tad / naḥ*. However, the rule and the commentaries inform us that such was no longer the practice, and that in the recitation as it was known to the author of the CA, the words were to be recited as ending in the first members of the stop-series, e.g. *tat / naḥ*. Bhārgava-Bhāskara, in his commentary on CA 1.1.10, clearly ascribes the practice of the followers of the CA to the doctrine of Śākaṭāyana: अत्र वेदे तु प्रथमपद्यो गृह्यते शाकटायनानुसरणात्. Thus, it is clear that the word *śaunaka* as used in APR (3g) refers not to some Ur-Śaunakīya recension, now lost, as assumed by Surya Kanta, but to the followers of the CA, who had openly diverged from the genuine doctrine of Śaunaka. Additionally, as Surya Kanta notes himself, these two views, e.g. *tam naḥ* versus *tat naḥ*, continued to manifest in the manuscripts of the Vulgate of the AV, and it is not the case that the manuscripts of the Vulgate took no notice of the view ascribed to *śaunaka* by the APR. What this suggests is a picture of a diversified recitational tradition of the Śaunakīya Saṃhitā. While it is perfectly appropriate to say that the reading *taṃ naḥ* was not followed by the adherents of the CA, the texts as we have them do not distinguish these readings as some being Śaunakīya and others as non-Śaunakīya.

7.7. Need for a new approach to the study of the transmission of the Veda

7.7.1. To conclude, I would like to say that in order to have a realistic notion of what happened to the Vedic Saṃhitās as they were transmitted over centuries in different regions of India, one needs to give up certain stereotypes regarding the nature of the transmission of the Vedic texts. One need not belittle the enormous efforts made by the Vaidikas to transmit these texts without change. However, our critical assessment must not be swayed by such respect. The Vaidikas who transmitted the Śaunakīya Saṃhitā never thought that they were changing anything, and yet change did indeed take place. When they did change something, either this change was unconscious change, or they thought that they were purifying the text and were restoring the pristine original. The CA, the CAB, the APR, the various manuscripts, and Sāyaṇa's commentary must all be looked at for traces of what transpired during this long and diversified process of transmission. All these sources are changing manifestations of the Śaunakīya textual tradition and there is no need to deny the title 'Śaunakīya' to any one of them. Moving away from the unreachable goal of reaching the Ur-form of the Śaunakīya text, or any other Vedic text for that matter, we should look at the changing vicissitudes of a Vedic tradition more carefully. Here, we are more likely to find a realistic historical picture of what real Vaidikas, copyists, reciters, and interpreters did to a text, which had no independent existence from what these custodians did to it. This is all the more significant in the case of the transmission of the Atharvaveda. For reasons which we cannot discuss here in great detail, the population of Vaidikas who pursued the Atharvavedic traditions is minuscule at present, in comparison with the followers of the Ṛgveda and Yajurveda, and there is reason to believe that it was so even in the past. This may have to do with the historically traceable lower status given to the Atharvaveda by the other traditions reflected in its early exclusion from the Trayī, and probably also due to the Ābhicārika rites practiced by the Atharvavedic priests. This is analogous to the social relations of the Brahmaṇa families who perform the funerary rites, and the refusal of even the Atharvavedic reciters to recite the funerary hymns of the Atharvaveda as noted by Pandit. It is indeed the case that the Atharvaveda that we possess today comes to us from extremely limited sources. Most manuscripts found in the Gujarat area seem in fact to point to one single prominent Atharvavedic family, the Pañcolis. From the manuscript colophons alone one can reconstruct several generations of Pañcolis involved in the transmission of the Atharvaveda. With very small numbers of reciters, and often the reciters of the other Vedas taking over the recitation of the Atharvaveda to cater to the demand for the Ābhicārika rites (as reported to me by the late Pt. Nārāyaṇa Śāstrī Raṭāṭe of Banaras), the transmission has indeed suffered through the ages, and hence the Atharvaveda material we possess is in a relatively less authentic state in comparison with other Vedic traditions. In any case, we possess enough material to trace the development of the Atharvaveda transmission in various regions of Western and Southern India. Any detailed discussion of such efforts lies clearly outside the scope of this Introduction. However, the interpretation and the transmission of the CA and the transmission of the Śaunakīya Atharvaveda have been closely related to each other, and this edition hopes to further a clearer understanding of these relations.

॥ शौनकीया चतुराध्यायिका ॥

॥ प्रथमोऽध्यायः ॥
॥ प्रथमः पादः ॥

चतुराध्यायीभाष्य - ॐ नमः सरस्वत्यै नमः । ॐ नमो ब्रह्मवेदाय ।

भार्गवभास्करवृत्ति - श्रीगणेशाय नमः । अथाथर्ववेदाङ्ग-कौत्सव्याकरणस्य चतुराध्यायात्मकस्य वृत्तिप्रारम्भे ग्रन्थप्रयो-जनाद्युपोद्धातं समाम्नायाग्रे सूत्रविवरणं कर्तुमिच्छुः प्रथमा-ध्यायस्य प्रथमपादसूत्राणि भार्गवो भास्करो विवृणोति । ग्रन्थमध्ये मङ्गलं करोति अस्खलितवृत्तिपरिपूर्त्यर्थम् -

श्वेताङ्गं शुक्लवस्त्रं करिवरवदनं भालचन्द्रं सुरेशं
मुक्ताहारैर्निवीतं दशशतवदनाभोगसंलग्नमध्यम् ॥
ऋद्ध्या सिद्ध्या च देव्या मणिगणजटितोद्दण्डयुक्चामराभ्यां
नित्यं संवीज्यमानं सुखदमु(?) भजतां सर्वदानं नमामि ॥१॥

हरिः ॥ ॐ ३ ॥

१.१.१. अथाङ्गिरसः ।

Absent in Whitney. Found in E, F, G, H, I, N, and O. G: 1.1.1.

Translation: Thus [begin the phonetic doctrines in relation to the Veda] of the Aṅgiras.

चतुराध्यायीभाष्य - H and N list this rule without any comment.

भार्गवभास्करवृत्ति - श्रीमद्भगवतोऽङ्गरसात्समुत्पन्ना अङ्गिरस ऋषयः । तथा च गोपथब्राह्मणम् - 'ताया अमू रेतः समुद्रम्' (गोपथब्राह्मणम्, पूर्वभाग, १.७) इति खण्डोक्त-तात्पर्यम् । ब्रह्मतो जलसमुद्रवरुणा जाता मृत्युश्च । 'तद्ब्रह्म पुनरभ्यतपत्तस्य श्रान्तस्य सन्तप्तस्य सर्वेभ्योऽङ्गेभ्यो रसोऽक्षरत् सोऽङ्गर ...' [missing text]

Note: The incomplete quotation in the Bhārgava-Bhāskara-Vṛtti is from the Gopatha-Brāhmaṇa (Pūrvabhāga, 1.7, p.6): तं वरुणं मृत्युमभ्यश्रामयदभ्यतपत्सम-तपत् । तस्य श्रान्तस्य तप्तस्य सन्तप्तस्य सर्वेभ्योऽङ्गेभ्यो रसोऽक्षरत् । सोऽङ्गरसोऽभवत् । तं वा एतमङ्गरसं सन्तमङ्गिरा इत्याचक्षते परोक्षेण । परोक्षप्रिया इव हि देवा भवन्ति प्रत्यक्षद्विषः ।

१.१.२. चतुर्णां पदजातानां नामाख्यातोपसर्गनिपातानां सन्ध्यपद्यौ गुणौ प्रातिज्ञम् ।

Whitney (1.1). Found in B, D, E, F, Hb, I, J, K, L, Nab, O, and P.

Translation: Here are defined the [phonetic/phonological] characteristics of nouns, verbs, prepositions, and particles, the four types of words, as they occur in combination [with the following words, as in the Saṃhitāpāṭha] and before pause [or in isolation, as in the Padapāṭha].

Note: The word *prātijñam* refers to the notion of *pratijñāna* (cf. CA 1.1.10), and this refers to a doctrine or a view explicitly held or stated by a teacher, in contrast with *vṛtti* "recitational practice." In most cases, the *pratijñā* and the *vṛtti* are expected to agree with each other. However, this is not always the case. There is a general expectation that the Prātiśākhyas take the existence of the Padapāṭha for granted and then teach the rules for converting the Padapāṭha into Saṃhitāpāṭha. Such an expectation is created by the statement पदप्रकृतिः संहिता (NR 1.17; RPR 2.1: संहिता पदप्रकृतिः). This statement is interpreted in two opposite ways. The first interpretation is that the Saṃhitāpāṭha is the basis for the Padapāṭha. This is historically valid, since the Padapāṭha is an analysis of the words of the Saṃhitāpāṭha. However, the more commonly accepted interpretation is that the Saṃhitāpāṭha has the Padapāṭha for its basis, i.e. the Saṃhitāpāṭha is derived by applying the rules of Sandhi to the Padapāṭha. With this interpretation in mind, one expects the Prātiśākhyas to provide rules for converting the Padapāṭha into the Saṃhitāpāṭha, and not the other way around. However, as Whitney (1862: 10) notes: "Our own work gives in its fourth chapter the rules for the construction of the *pada*-text itself, as does also the Vājasaneyi Prātiśākhya." This is more in line with the neutral statement of the present rule. It lays equal emphasis on the *sandhya* characteristics, as well as the *padya* characteristics. This is clear in its use of the dual forms: सन्ध्यपद्यौ गुणौ (प्रातिज्ञम्). In general, the Prātiśākhyas are not concerned with the full derivation of grammatical forms, as are the grammars of Sanskrit. This contrast is brought out by the commentary Caturādhyāyībhāṣya. Also see Whitney's comments on TPR (3.1, pp. 82ff): "In the other treatises (Rik Pr vii.-ix., Vāj. Pr. iii. 95-128, Ath. Pr. iii.1-25), the rules tell us in what situations a vowel originally short is lengthened: This is more in accordance with the general method of the Prātiśākhyas, which take for granted, upon the whole, the existence of their Śākhās in the analyzed condition of the *pada*-text, and proceed to construct the *saṃhitā* from it. Here, on the contrary, we are told what vowels, long in the ordinary text, are to be shortened when thrown out of combination with their surroundings. Such dissolution of the continuity of the text takes place, first, in *pada*, whenever a pause - either the *avagraha* separating the two members of a compound, in its repetition after *iti*, or the longer pause that divides between two words - comes to stand between the vowel in question and the consonant which was its next neighbour in *saṃhitā*." I thank Prof. Cardona for drawing my attention to this section of the TPR.

चतुराध्यायीभाष्य - सन्ध्यश्च गुणः पद्यश्च तत् प्रातिज्ञं मन्यन्ते । सन्ध्यो नाम एवमन्तानि पदानि एवमादिषु एवं भवती(न्ती?)ति । पद्यो नाम(H, N: मा) प्रथमान्तानि लिङ्गानि तृतीयान्तानीति शौनकस्य प्रतिज्ञानं न वृत्तिः । सन्ध्यपद्याविति किमर्थम् । 'लीढ'मित्यत्र हो ढत्वम् (cf. 'हो ढः,' पा. ८.२.३१)। पर(H, N: °द, Whitney: °र)चतुर्थत्वम् (cf. 'झषस्तथोर्धोऽधः,' पा. ८.२.४०)। ष्टुना ष्टुत्वम् (cf. 'ष्टुना ष्टुः,' पा. ८.४.४१)। ढो ढे लोपो (cf. 'ढो ढे लोपः,' पा. ८.३.१३) दीर्घत्वमिति (cf. 'ढ्रलोपे पूर्वस्य दीर्घोऽणः,' पा. ६.३.१११) वैयाकरणेन वक्तव्यम् ।

Note: Whitney (1862: 11) expresses some doubt as to whether the commentator here refers to Pāṇini or to some other authority. The expressions used are so obviously Pāṇinian, that we need not entertain any such doubt. The CAB is fully conversant with Pāṇini, and by the term *vyākaraṇa*, it refers to Pāṇini alone. Compare the CAB on the next rule. This need not mean that the CA itself necessarily presupposes Pāṇini. However, the commentatorial tradition is firmly rooted in the awareness of Pāṇini's grammar as the grammar par excellence.

१.१.३. एवमिहेति च ।

Whitney (1.2), Ha, I, Na: एवमिहेति च विभाषाप्राप्तं सामान्ये. B, D, E, F, J, K, L, M, O and P: एवमिहेति च । विभाषाप्राप्तं सामान्ये ।

> **Translation:** [This treatise] also [defines that the phonetic/ phonological features of the words] in this [tradition] are such and such.

Note: Whitney combines this rule with the following one in a single rule, following the CAB. However, having done that, he still feels that the rule is "somewhat obscure and of difficult construction" (Whitney 1862, p. 11). He then refers to Max Müller's rendering of this rule (M. Müller, *RPR*, p. xii): "what by the grammatical text books is left free, that is here thus and thus, so says the Prātiśākhya." Whitney criticizes this interpretation by saying that "it leaves the *ca* unexplained, and supposes the *iti* to be in another place, making the rule to read rather *evam iha vibhāṣāprāptaṃ sāmānya iti; ...* It seems necessary, in order to account for *ca*, to bring down *prātijñam* as general predicate from the preceding rule; and the *iti* must be understood as pointing out that the Prātiśākhya says *evam iha*, 'so and so is proper here,' respecting any matter which the rules of grammar leave doubtful" (Whitney, 1862, p. 11). Whitney is correct in bringing down the word *prātijñam* from the previous rule to give a better account of *ca* in this rule. However, such an interpretation fits better if the portion ending in *ca* is a separate rule, as the majority of mss. now indicate. Additionally, the rule is not obscure, and its interpretation is further assisted by the fact of it being quoted by Uvaṭa in his introduction to the RPR (M.D. Shastri edn., Part II, p. 23) in a discussion of the exact relation between the Prātiśākhya tradition and the tradition of grammar. However, Whitney does make a problematic statement: "it (= CA) does not at all imply or base itself upon the general science of grammar and its text book, but is an independent and a complete treatise as regards its own subject." While it is an independent treatise, it clearly assumes the prior existence of general grammars of Sanskrit, and seems to imply that it is related to the general science of grammar as a statement of particular features of a Veda branch would relate to a generic description of Sanskrit at large.

चतुराध्यायीभाष्य - एवम् इह इति च । अस्यां शाखायां तत् प्रातिज्ञं (H, N: न्यं, Whitney: ज्ञं) मन्यन्ते । 'यरोऽनुनासिकेऽनुनासिको वा' (पा. ८.४.४५) इति विभाषाप्राप्तं सामान्ये । किं सामान्यम् । व्याकरणम् । वक्ष्यति 'उत्तमा उत्तमेषु' (च.आ. २.१.५) इति । 'ऋधंङ्गन्त्रो योनिम्' (अ.वे. ५.१.१)। 'य उदानण्न्यायंनम्' (अ.वे. ६.७७.२)। 'अंर्णवान्मंहतस्परि' (अ.वे. १.१०.४)। 'मदुघान्मधुंमत्तरः' (अ.वे. १.३४.४.)। 'मध्यांन्नीचैः(:,' अ.वे. ४.१.३)। 'य स्तायन् मन्यंते' (अ.वे. ४.१६.१.)। 'त्रिष्टुम्नयति' (not in AV, fabricated example cited in KV on P.8.4.45) ।

१.१.४. विभाषाप्राप्तं सामान्ये ।

A combines this with पदांतः पद्यः.

Translation: [These phonetic/phonological features of the words] obtain optionally in a generic [grammar of Sanskrit].

Note: This rule contrasts the function of a generic grammar of Sanskrit with that of a Prātiśākhya. A Prātiśākhya ideally aims at strictly describing the linguistic features of words as they occur in a particular Vedic Saṃhitā text, and , therefore, it is expected to be highly specific. A general grammar of Sanskrit, on the other hand, is expected to cover all the different textual traditions and dialects of colloquial Sanskrit, and hence it ends up making optional statements. This precisely accords with Patañjali's explanation as to why Pāṇini was forced to use different option-terms. (सर्ववेदपारिषदं हीदं शास्त्रं तत्र नैकः पन्थाः शक्य आस्थातुम्, MB on P.2.1.58 and P.6.3.14). Also see Uvaṭa's introductory comments on the first Paṭala of the RPR (M.D. Shastri edn., Vol.II, p. 23):

शिक्षाच्छन्दोव्याकरणैः सामान्येनोक्तलक्षणम् ।
तदेवमिह शाखायामिति शास्त्रप्रयोजनम् ।

प्रातिशाख्यप्रयोजनमनेन श्लोकेनोच्यते । शिक्षादिभिर्यत्सामान्येनोत्सर्गेणोक्तं लक्षणं, यथा तावच्छिक्षायां - 'स्युर्मूर्धन्या ऋटुरषाः' - सामान्येन सर्वशाखासु रेफो मूर्धन्य इत्युक्तः । ... एवं सर्वा शिक्षा वर्णेषु स्थानकरणानुप्रदानादि सर्वासु शाखासु विदधाति; न तु नियमतः कस्यां शाखायां रेफो मूर्धन्यः कस्यां दन्तमूलीय इति । अत एतद्व्यवस्थापकमारभ्यते । ... तथा व्याकरणे यत्सामान्येन, यथा 'ऋचि तुनुघमक्षुतङ्कुत्रोरुष्याणाम्' (पा. ६.१.१३३) इति । तद्व्यवस्थापयितुमिदमारभ्यते । न सर्वत्रैतानि पदान्यस्यां शाखायां दीर्घाणि भवन्ति । एवं शिक्षाच्छन्दोव्याकरणैर्यत्सर्वासु शाखासु सामान्येन लक्षणमुच्यते तदेवास्यां शाखायामनेन व्यवस्थाप्यते इत्येतत् प्रयोजनमस्याङ्गस्य । तथा चाथर्वणप्रातिशाख्ये इदमेव प्रयोजनमुक्तम् - 'एवमिहेति च विभाषाप्राप्तं सामान्येन' । अस्य सूत्रस्यायमर्थः - सामान्येन लक्षणेन यद् विकल्पप्राप्तं तदेवमस्यां शाखायां व्यवस्थितं भवतीति प्रातिशाख्यप्रयोजनमुक्तम् ।

चतुराध्यायीभाष्य **-** See the commentary on the previous rule.

१.१.५. पदान्तः पद्यः ।

Whitney (1.3), Hab, I, Nab, O: पदान्त्यः पद्यः. A, B, D, E, F, J, K, L, M, P: °दांतः°.

Translation: A sound occurring at the end of a word [i.e. a *pada* in the Padapāṭha] is termed *padya*.

Note: As Whitney (1862: 12) points out, the term *padya* is "not found at all in either of the Yajur-Veda Prātiśākhyas, or in Pāṇini, and in the Rik Prātiśākhya it means 'member of a compound word.'" By its etymology, the word would simply mean 'belonging to a *pada*,' and hence the need for a precise definition.

चतुराध्यायीभाष्य **-** पदान्त्यो वर्णः पद्यो भवति । 'गोधुक्' (अ.वे. ७.७३.६)। 'विराट्' (अ.वे. ८.९.८)। 'दृषत्' (अ.वे. २.३१.१)। 'त्रिष्टुप्' (अ.वे. ८.९.२०)।

१.१.६. अन्लृकारः स्वरः पद्यः ।

Whitney (1.4): अन्लृकारः°. A, B, D, E, F, Hab, I, J, L, M, Nab, O, P: °नृ°.

Translation: [Any] vowel, other than *ḷ*, may occur at the end of a word.

Note: All the manuscripts share the mistaken reading अनृकारः. However, I agree with Whitney's reading. As the CAB clearly shows, the only excluded vowel is *ḷ*. Whitney (1862: 12) provides information on how several other Prātiśākhyas also exclude *ḷ* from the sounds which may occur at the end of words, i.e. *pada*s in the Padapāṭha.

चतुराध्यायीभाष्य - अन्लृकारः स्वरः पद्यो भवति । 'ब्रह्म' (H: ह्मा, Whitney: ह्म, अ.वे. १.१०.४)। 'शालां' (अ.वे. ९.३.१७)। 'नीला' (not found in AV)। 'दधि' ('दधिंवान्,' अ.वे. १८.४.१७)। 'कुमारी' (अ.वे. १०.८.२७)। 'मधु' (अ.वे. १.३४.२)। 'वायू' ('इन्द्रवायू', अ.वे. ३.२०.६)। 'कर्तृ' (Whitney: no such case in AV, ... take instead *pitṛbhiḥ*, e.g. vi.63.3; *pitṛlokam*, xviii.4.64)। 'चंक्षते' (अ.वे. ९.१०.२६)। 'अस्यै' (H, N: स्ये, Whitney: स्यै. अ.वे. २.३६.१)। 'वायो' (अ.वे. २.२०.१)। 'तौ' (अ.वे. ३.२४.७)।

Note: While the ms. H reads *brahmā*, the ms. N reads *brahma*, and this is the reading chosen by Whitney. It seems to be the correct reading in view of the fact that the commentary is clearly offering examples of short and long vowels in a fixed sequence. This would make the reading *brahmā* unsuitable. The word *nīlam* is found in AV (14.2.48), and *nīlena* is found in AV (15.1.8). However, the VVRI concordance does not record any occurrence of *nīlā* in the Vedic Saṃhitās. Whitney (1862: 12) appropriately notes that *ṛ* appears only at the end of the first member of a compound, or before a case affix, but not exactly at the end of inflected words. This reminder is important in view of the fact that the word *pada*, though not defined in this text, applies not only to inflected nominal and verbal items, it also covers nominal bases as they appear in compounds and before certain case terminations. The Padapāṭha typically separates members of compounds, and nominal bases before *bh-* initial case terminations and *-su*. The sound *ṛ* does appear in such environments, and, therefore, it is legitimately a *padya* sound.

१.१.७. लकारविसर्जनीयौ च ।

Whitney (1.5).

Translation: [The sounds] *l* and *ḥ* may also [occur at the end of words].

Note: As Whitney (1862: 13) points out, the RPR (xii.1) and the VPR (i.86) omit *l* from the list of *pada*-final sounds. The other two AV words ending in *l* are *śal* and *phal* "in xx. 135.2, 3, a part of the text of which our treatise takes no account" (Whitney, 1862: 13).

चतुराध्यायीभाष्य - लकारविसर्जनीयौ च पद्यौ भवतः । 'बाल्' (अ.वे. १.३.१)। 'वृ॒क्षः' (अ.वे. ४.७.५)।

१.१.८. स्पर्शाः प्रथमोत्तमाः ।

Whitney (1.6).

Translation: The first and the last [members in each series of] stops [may also occur at the end of words].

चतुराध्यायीभाष्य - स्पर्शाः प्रथमाश्च उत्तमाश्च वर्गाणां पद्या भवन्ति । कचटतपाः । ङञणनमाः ।

Note: In listing the possible *pada*-final stops, the commentary includes *c* and *ñ*. This inclusion must be canceled by the very next rule, which says that members of the *c*-series cannot occur *pada*-finally. Whitney (1862: 13) gives a detailed account of which stops are more or less frequent in the *pada*-final position. Also compare: VPR (i. 85), and RPR (xii. 1).

१.१.९. न चवर्गः ।

Whitney (1.7). B, D, P: °चवर्ग्रः.

Translation: [But] not the [members of the] *c*-series.

Note: Since only the firsts and the lasts of the stop-series qualify to occur at the end of words according to CA 1.1.8, one needs to exclude only *c* and *ñ*, and not the whole *c*-series. Perhaps the expression *cavargaḥ* is felt to be more economical as compared to the expression *cakārañakārau.* The notion of economy often applies at the level of expression, rather than reference.

चतुराध्यायीभाष्य - न चवर्गः पद्यो भवति । चछजझञ ।

भा.भा.वृत्ति - [ms G resumes with folio 4a] नां मध्ये अष्टावेव पद्याः । 'हिरुक्' (अ.वे. ४.३.१)। 'प्रत्यङ्' (अ.वे. ३.२०.२)। 'तुराषाट्' (अ.वे. २.५.३)। 'शीर्ष-ण्वतीम्' (अ.वे.पै.सं. १६.३५.२)। 'वीरुत्' (अ.वे. १.३४. १)। 'पितॄन्' (अ.वे. ५.३०.१)। 'अनुष्टुप्' (अ.वे. ८.९. २०)। 'सहस्रम्' (अ.वे. १.१०.२)।

Note: The incomplete initial word of the Bhārgava-Bhāskara-Vṛtti is most likely *sparśānām.* Thus, the commentary makes it explicit, that among the stops, only eight stops may occur at the end of the *padas*. Concerning the word-final *ṅ*, Whitney (1862: 13) points out that it "appears only as final of masculine nominatives singular of derivatives of the root *añc*." Note that Bhārgava-Bhāskara's example is *pratyaṅ.* The example *śīrṣaṇ-vatīm* offered by Bhārgava-Bhāskara is important, because, as Whitney (1862: 13) notes: "*ṇ*, [occurs] only in a few instances, at the end of the first member of a compound, where, by a specific rule (iv. 99 = CA 4.3.28), it is left in the *pada* in its *saṃhitā* form." Whitney himself came up with the example ब्रह्मण्वतीम् (ŚAV vi.108.2). It is difficult to see why Bhārgava-Bhāskara could not find an example in the ŚAV. The form शीर्षण्वतीं, not शीर्षण्वतीम्, is attested in ŚAV (10.1.2).

१.१.१०. प्रथमान्तानि तृतीयान्तानीति शौनकस्य प्रतिज्ञानं न वृत्तिः ।

Whitney (1.8). J, K, L: प्रथमांतानि तृतीयांतानीति । शौनकस्य प्रतिज्ञानं न वृत्तिः । A, L: तृतीयातानीति. B, D: प्रतिज्ञानं त्र. Ha, Na: वृर्तिः. G: 1.1.10. I: 1.10.

Translation: It is a precept of Śaunaka that the words (= *padas*) ending in the first [members of the stop-series, i.e. voiceless unaspirated stops, should rather] end in the third [members, i.e. voiced unaspirated stops]. [Such, however, is] not the [recitational] practice.

चतुराध्यायीभाष्य - प्रथमान्तानि पदानि तृतीयान्तानीति शौनकस्याचार्यस्य प्रतिज्ञानं भवति । न तु वृत्तिः । 'गो-धुक्' (अ.वे. ७.७३.६)। 'विराट्' (अ.वे. ८.९.८)। 'दृ-षत्' (अ.वे. २.३१.१)। 'त्रिष्टुप्' (अ.वे. ८.९.२०)।

'मावसानानिकान्स्पर्शान्प (W: आ?) द्यानननुनासिकान्। प्रथमान् (H, N: मां, Whitney: मान्) तृतीयान् (H, N: यां, Whitney: यान्, Whitney: प्रथमान्तं तृतीयान्तं?) विद्यात् न तु पठेत् क्वचित् ॥' (Source. ?)

वृत्तेरननुदर्शनात् ।

Note: The verse quoted in the commentary comes to us in a mutilated form. A related verse or a version of the same verse appears to have strayed into the text of this commentary on the next rule. This intrusion appears only in the manuscript H. The intruding passage reads: का(H: जा)दीन् मावसितान् स्पर्शान् पद्यानननुनासिकान् । तृतीयान् शौनकमतात् ... The last statement of the commentary, i.e. वृत्तेरननुदर्शनात् looks like a quarter of a missing Anuṣṭubh verse.

भा.भा.वृत्ति - यानि वर्गप्रथमान्तानि पदानि तानि तृतीयान्तान्यपि पद्यानि भवन्तीति । शौनकस्य प्रतिज्ञानं मतभेदाङ्गीकारः । न तु वृत्तिः । तृतीयान्तः पदान्त इति वर्तनं न करोति । वृत्तिस्तु प्रथमान्तस्यैवाङ्गीकारे तथैव । ऋक्प्रातिशाख्ये शौनकः - 'तस्मादन्यमवसाने तृतीयं गार्ग्यः स्पर्शं

प्रथमं शाकटायनः' (ऋ.प्रा. १.१५-१६) इति । पाणिनीये तु 'वावसाने' (पा. ८.४.५६) इति विकल्पः । अत्र वेदे तु प्रथमपद्यो गृह्यते शाकटायनानुसरणात् ।

Note: Bhārgava-Bhāskara adds some important information, namely that while the CA mentions the opinion of Śaunaka, it does not follow its practice, and that the practice of the AV tradition follows the view of Śākaṭāyana. In view of the fact that we are dealing with the so-called Śaunakīya AV, it is curious to find that the surviving tradition follows the view, not of Śaunaka, but that of Śākaṭāyana. While the CA mentions Śākaṭāyana's views in other contexts, e.g. CA 2.1.24 (लेशवृत्तिरधिस्पर्शं शाकटायनस्य), it does not do so in this case. The view, which the commentator attributes to Śākaṭāyana, is simply assumed to be the default view. The citation of the RPR in Bhārgava-Bhāskara's commentary shows that Śaunaka's view was also shared by Gārgya.

This rule provides a fitting answer to Surya Kanta's excessive claims about the Śaunakīya-ness of this text. It is indeed called Śaunakīyā Caturādhyāyīkā and no doubt belongs to the tradition of Śaunaka. At the same time, one must keep in mind that this tradition was not immutable, and in the course of time, it came to adopt in practice the doctrines of other sages like Śākaṭāyana, which were historically at variance with the views of Śaunaka. Also see CA 4.1.52, and the CAB on that rule.

१.१.११. अधिस्पर्शं च ।

Whitney (1.9). Hb: अधिस्पर्शं चतुर्थाः सोष्माणः. G: 1.1.11.

Translation: [It is] also [the precept of Śaunaka] that [the *pada*-final thirds, i.e. voiced unaspirated stops] have a weak articulatory contact.

चतुराध्यायीभाष्य - अधिस्पर्शं च प्रतिज्ञानं भवति । न तु वृत्तिः । किमधिस्पर्शं नाम । वक्ष्यति । यकारवकारयोः 'लेशवृत्तिरधिस्पर्शं शाकटायनस्य' (च.आ. २.१.२४)। 'क आंसञ्जन्याः के वराः' (अ.वे. ११.८.१)। 'उष्णेनं वाय उदकेनेहिं' (अ.वे. ६.६८.१)। 'अस्या इच्छन्नग्रुवै पतिंम्'

(अ.वे. ६.६०.१)। 'स उं एव मंहायमः' (अ.वे. १३.४.५)। 'ता इमा आपंः' (अ.वे. १५.१५.७)।

Note: Whitney (1862: 15), following Weber's suggestion, correctly removes the following passage from H: जादीन् मावसितान्स्पर्शान्पिद्यानननुनासिकान् । तृतीयान् शौनकमतात्. This intervenes between अधिस्पर्शं च प्रतिज्ञा ... नं भवति. While H has this spurious passage, N does not have it. Also see the note on the previous rule.

भा.भा.वृत्ति - वर्गाणां ये प्रथमास्तृतीयाश्च ते वर्णा अधिस्पर्शसंज्ञका ज्ञेयाः ।

Note: This rule is indeed somewhat unclear. Part of the reason for this lack of clarity is that the expression *adhisparśam* is extremely rare in the Sanskrit phonetic literature. It has been used adverbially in CA 2.1.24 (लेशावृत्तिरधिस्पर्शं शाकटायनस्य), and etymologically it can simply mean "as regards contact." There are several possible interpretations.

a) This interpretation is supported by the CAB. According to this interpretation, the rule simply means: "*Adhisparśa* is also a precept of Śaunaka, though such is not the recitational practice." Then, for the meaning of the term अधिस्पर्शम्, we are referred to CA 2.1.24 (लेशवृत्तिरधिस्पर्शं शाकटायनस्य). According to this rule, in the opinion of Śākaṭāyana, the euphonic *y* and *v* were pronounced slightly (= लेशवृत्तिः) as regards contact (अधिस्पर्शम्), i.e. as weak glides. The same view is then ascribed to Śaunaka in the present rule. Such an interpretation seems less likely, because it would be unnatural that the text would refer a certain view to Śaunaka in one place and to Śākaṭāyana in another place.

b) What seems more likely is that the expression अधिस्पर्शम् is used as an abbreviation for the longer phrase लेशवृत्तिरधिस्पर्शम् found in CA 2.1.24. The phrase then refers to "partial or incomplete articulation." With this generic meaning, one may assume that rule CA 1.1.11 (अधिस्पर्शम् च) is more closely connected to the doctrine as taught in CA 1.1.10. It could then be interpreted to mean: According to the precept of Śaunaka, the *pada*s ending in the first members of the stop-series should rather end in the third members of the stop-series, and that these third members, i.e. voiced unaspirated stops, are articulated incompletely or partially, i.e. without their contact being released. This is my preferred interpretation.

Bhārgava-Bhāskara's commentary proposes that both the firsts and thirds of the stop-series were called अधिस्पर्श according to Śaunaka. Presumably they were all pronounced with a weak articulation according to Śaunaka, though such was not the recitational practice supported by the CA. This inclusion of both the categories has no textual support, though in terms of the general history of Indo-Aryan, all final stops are weak, see: R.L. Turner (1960: 11-19).

According to Allen (1953: 70), this rule, taken along with the previous one, "is perhaps to be interpreted as indicating a realization as voiceless stops, but with the lax articulation characteristic of the voiced stops." It is not clear to me whether the term अधिस्पर्शम् indicates 'lax articulation characteristic of the voiced stops.' I think that this term is more like an equivalent of लघुप्रयत्नतर "having a lighter articulatory effort" or लेशवृत्तिः "a reduced articulation." It is most probably the non-release of the closure making it a weak articulation, rather than a lax articulation. There is a clearer reason for not accepting Allen's interpretation. The rule is not trying to make a generic distinction between voiceless and voiced stops, but a distinction between final voiced stops versus non-final voiced stops. Since all voiced stops have the feature of laxness, one cannot use this feature to distinguish between final and non-final voiced stops. On the other hand, it is clear that while one cannot have unreleased non-final voiced stops, it is possible to have unreleased final voiced stops. Allen also does not recognize the fact that the rules refer to actual recitational or articulatory differences, and not mere theoretical differences. He (1953: 70) renders them as: "Words ending (sc. according to orthodox doctrine) in voiceless stops, end according to Śaunaka in voiced stops, but they are not so treated (sc. phonologically); they have lax contact." As we have noted above, this is not a phonological distinction, but a distinction in recitational practice, and the term *vr̥tti* refers to articulation in recitation.

Whitney (1862: 15) did think of another possibility: "Or is *adhisparśa* to be interpreted as the name of a slighted or imperfect utterance, and did Śaunaka teach such an utterance as belonging to a final mute, which wavered, as it were, between sonant and surd? This appears somewhat more plausible, but not sufficiently so to be accepted as at all satisfactory: there is no question of a difference of contact of the organs (*sparśa*) in such a case." I do not believe that the CA refers to such a wavering pronunciation. It rather refers to two different practices consistently followed by different schools of reciters. However, I agree with Whitney that the term अधिस्पर्शम् is used to refer to incomplete articulation. Whitney (1862: 16) also refers to Weber's conjecture that the passage means that "when the *padyas* enter into *sandhi*, they are to be converted into *tṛtīyas* before nasals (e.g. *tad me*, not *tan me*): but this is only *pratijñānam*, not *vṛtti*." Whitney rejects this interpretation. However, the last part of Weber's interpretation, "but this is only *pratijñānam*, not *vṛtti*," is supported by the commentary CAB. That means that, like the precept of Śaunaka taught in the previous rule, this rule also teaches a precept of Śaunaka, which is not carried out in the recitational practice. If this is true, then it cannot refer to the weakening of euphonic *y* and *v*, since that is part of the recitational practice (cf. CA 2.1.24: लेशवृत्तिरधिस्पर्शं शाकटायनस्य).

I take the rule to refer to the weakening or non-release of the final voiced unaspirated stops. Śaunaka evidently supported the weak pronunciation of the final voiced unaspirated stops, while the recitational practice maintained the voiceless unaspirated stops at the end of words. The weakening of final stops in general can draw support from what happens in the Prakrit languages, see R.L. Turner (1960: 11-19). All final stops are lost in Prakrit, except the nasals are retained in some form or another for a much longer time. It is likely that the recitational practice, perceiving the danger of losing the weak consonants, went in the other direction and strengthened them. Devoicing may have been seen as a move in the direction of preservation. The medial voiceless stops were voiced in most Prakrits, and then were lost in some, as in Mahārāṣṭrī. However, the voiced medial stops were devoiced in the northwestern Paiśācī where they were preserved and protected from loss. For Hinüber (1981: 127) this Paiśācī feature is purely orthographical "without any bearing on Paiśācī phonetics." I am yet to be convinced by this argument.

१.१.१२. द्वितीयचतुर्थाः सोष्माणः ।

Whitney (1.10). A, B, D, I (orig), J, L, M (corr), O: सोष्मणः.

Translation: The seconds and the fourths [in the five stop-series] are termed *soṣman* "aspirated [stops, lit. combined with a spirant]."

Note: The term *soṣman* literally means "with *ūṣman*." Most of the later commentators on phonetic treatises interpret the term to mean "with aspiration," and take the term *ūṣman* to refer to aspiration, cf. अन्वर्थसंज्ञेयम् । ऊष्मा वायुस्तेन सह वर्तन्त इति सोष्माणः, Uvaṭa on RPR 1.13. On the other hand, a more historically apt interpretation is suggested by the ancient Śikṣā text quoted in the CAB. According to this view, the aspirated stops are born through a combination of the unaspirated stop with a voiced or voiceless spirant. Thus, at an earlier period, the term *soṣman* probably meant "combined with a spirant," rather than "combined with aspiration." Compare RPR (13.16-17): सोष्मतां च सोष्मणामूष्मणाहुः सस्थानेन ।। (एके) घोषिणां घोषिणैव ।। The simple fact is that these are different views. However, I believe that the view of *soṣman* as "combined with a spirant" must be the earlier view, since the term *ūṣman* as it is attested in its oldest occurrence in the Aitareya-Āraṇyaka (2.2.4, 3.2.1) and the Chāndogya-Upaniṣad (2.22.2) already seems to refer not to aspiration as such, but to spirants. Thus, historically, it is more likely that the term *soṣman* first meant "combined with a spirant," and then, in certain schools, came to mean "with aspiration." The interpretation "with aspiration" fails to account for the difference between the groups denoted by the terms *ūṣman* and *soṣman*, and points more closely in the direction of the later term *mahāprāṇa*, which does not distinguish between these two sub-groups.

चतुराध्यायीभाष्य - द्वितीयाश्चतुर्थाश्च वर्गाणां सोष्माणो भवन्ति । खछठथफाः । घझढधभाः ।

'सस्थानैरूष्मभिः पृक्तास्तृतीया[ः] प्रथमाश्च ये ।
चतुर्थाश्च द्वितीयाश्च संपद्यन्त इति स्थिति[ः] ।।'

अपर आह । चतुर्थो हकारेणेति ।

'पञ्चैव प्रथमान् स्पर्शानाहुरेके मनीषिणः ।
तेषां गुणोपसञ्चयादान्यभाव्यं प्रवर्तते ।।
जिह्वामूलीयशषसा उपध्मानीयपञ्चमाः ।
एतैर्गुणैः समन्विता द्वितीया इति तान्विदुः ।।
त एव सह घोषेण तृतीया इति तान्विदुः ।
ऊष्मणा च द्वितीयेन चतुर्था इति तान्विदुः ।।
प्रथमाः सह घोषेण यदा स्युरनुनासिकाः ।
तानाहुः पञ्चमान् स्पर्शांस्तथा वर्णगुणाः स्मृताः ।।
न तु द्विव्यञ्जनसन्धि-
रसंयोगो भव(H, N: वे)त्युत (Whitney: भवेत्पुनः)।
संयोगश्च प्रसज्येत क्रमो वाच्यः पुनर्भवेत् ।।
द्वित्वप्राप्तिश्चतुर्थेषु हकारो ह्यत्र कारणम् ।
द्वितीयेषु तु तन्नास्ति सस्थाने तन्निवारणात् ।।

पिप्पल्यादिषु यद् द्वित्वं स्वराच्छब्दविधिः कृतः ।
ज्ञापकश्च (H, N: कंश्च) द्वितीयानां
द्वि(H, N: हि, Whitney: द्वि)त्वप्राप्तेरिति स्थितिः ॥
गुणमात्रा तु(H, N: नु) तत्रैषामपूर्णं व्यञ्जनं
क्वचित्।
अपूर्णे व्यञ्जने क्रमः संयोगश्च कुतो भवेत् ॥
पृथक्सत्त्वानि पश्यामस्तुल्यलिङ्गानि कानिचित् ।
न तेषां लिङ्गसामान्यादेकत्वं प्रतिजायते ॥
सत्त्वपृथक्त्वाद् वै(W: द्वै)लिङ्गं यदेतेषु निबोध तत् ।
तथैव पञ्चवर्गेण गुणमात्रेण तुल्यता ॥' (Source?)

Note: The *pippalyādi gaṇa* and the doubling of consonants in the words listed in this *gaṇa* are dealt with in CA (3.2.5: पिप्पल्यादिषु पूर्वात्). For further information on this gaṇa, see the Note on CA (3.2.5).

भा.भा.वृत्ति - वर्गाणां ये द्वितीयाश्चतुर्थाश्च ते सोष्मसंज्ञका ज्ञेयाः । हकार ऊष्मा । तेन सहिताः सोष्माणः । औरस्य-हकारेण युक्ताः प्रथमाः द्वितीया भवन्ति । तृतीया औरस्य-हकारयुक्ताश्चतुर्था भवन्ति । इमे अधिस्पर्शाः प्रथमे कचट-तप, तृतीयाः गजडदब ।१०। एते सोष्माणः । द्वितीयाः खछठथफ, चतुर्थाः घझढधभ ।१०। एषु सोष्मसु परेषु पूर्वस्य स्वरस्य संयोगनिमित्तं गुरुत्वं नैव स्यात् । औरस्य-हकारस्य लघुप्रयत्नतरत्वात् ।

Note: Bhārgava-Bhāskara offers a more simplistic view. All aspirated stops are produced by a combination of a non-aspirated stop with pulmonary *h* (= *aurasya-hakāra*). Bhārgava-Bhāskara further adds an important clarification. Even though the proposed explanation regards aspirated stops as combinations of unaspirated stops with *h*, the commentator hastens to add that the combination is not regarded as a consonant-cluster, because the *h* sound which is added is a sound with a weaker effort (*laghu-prayatna-tara*). Thus, a short vowel preceding such an aspirated stop does not become a heavy (*guru*) syllable. A better explanation, of course, is that the aspiration, or the *h-* sound, is not an added sound, but is part of the basic phonation (*anupradāna*), cf. Taittirīya-Prātiśākhya (2.6: मध्ये हकारः). However, Bhārgava-Bhāskara does not worry about explaining the difference between voiced and voiceless aspirated stops. The interpretation found in the CAB offers an explanation of this difference.

१.१.१३. उत्तमा अनुनासिकाः ।

Whitney (1.11). G: 1.1.13.

Translation: The final [members of the five stop series] are termed nasal.

चतुराध्यायीभाष्य - उत्तमाः स्पर्शवर्गाणामनुनासिका भवन्ति । ङञणनमाः ।

भा.भा.वृत्ति - पञ्चानां वर्गाणां मध्ये ये उत्तमाः अन्त्याः पञ्चमा वर्णास्तेऽनुनासिकसंज्ञका ज्ञेयाः । ङञणनम ।

Note: Compare the usage of the terms *prathama* and *uttama* in Pāṇini, outside of the context of phonetic lists, referring to the third and the first person forms in the verbal paradigms, cf. Pāṇini 1.4.101 (तिङस्त्रीणि त्रीणि प्रथममध्यमोत्तमाः). The term *prathama* refers to the group which appears first in the list, while the term *uttama* refers to the group which appears at the end of the list. Thus, Bhārgava-Bhāskara's paraphrase of the term *uttama* by *antya* offers the clearest interpretation. One should also note that while the term *anunāsika* is used here to refer to the final members of the stop-series, i.e. *ṅ*, *ñ*, *ṇ*, *n*, and *m*, it is used elsewhere more generically to include the nasal vowels, cf. CA 1.3.6 and CA 1.3.8. Generally, the term *anunāsika* refers to those sounds which involve both the oral and nasal passages in their articulation, cf. CA 1.1.27 (अनुनासिकानां मुखनासिकम्) and P.1.1.9 (मुखनासिकावचनोऽनुनासिकः), and this often leaves sounds like the *anusvāra* and *nāsikya* uncovered by this term.

१.१.१४. श्वासोऽघोषेष्वनुप्रदानः ।

Whitney (1.12). G: 1.1.14.

Translation: In the case of voiceless [consonants], the [type of] phonation [or emission] is *śvāsa* '[voiceless, non-resonant] breath.'

Note: The term *anupradāna* raises a number of conceptual and historical problems. While Whitney generally renders this term by 'emitted material,' he also mentions the view of the RPR (xiii. 2) that *śvāsa* and *nāda* are *prakṛti* 'material cause,' or the original phonic material out of which the different sounds are fashioned. Whitney offers another translation of the term *anupradāna* as 'a giving along forth, a continuous emission.'

In my view, in the period which predated the formation of the available phonetic treatises, the *anupradāna* view originally contrasted with the *prakṛti* view, and these two terms referring to the same phenomenon, in all likelihood, originally represented two somewhat different perspectives on the phonic material covered by the terms *śvāsa* and *nāda.* Instead of the meaning 'along with,' the term more directly stands for 'that which is subsequently contributed.' Such a notion does not make sense in terms of our modern notions of the process of articulation. However, in ancient India, there did exist a school of phonetics which argued that *anupradāna* is like the resounding vibrations of the sound of a bell. The clearest exposition of this view is found in the Āpiśaliśikṣā: "However, others say: When *nāda* 'resonant air-stream' is subsequently contributed to the sound produced by the contact of the point of articulation and the articulator, then through the mixture of *nāda* and that sound, *ghoṣa* 'voice' is produced. When *śvāsa* 'non-resonant air-stream' is subsequently contributed [to the sound produced by the contact of the point of articulation and the articulator], then through the mixture of *śvāsa* and that sound, the *aghoṣa* 'voiceless sound' is produced," अन्ये तु ब्रुवते । तत्र यदा स्थानकरणाभिघातजे ध्वनौ नादोऽनुप्रदीयते, तदा नादध्वनिसंसर्गाद्घोषो जायते, यदा तु श्वासोऽनुप्रदीयते, तदा श्वासध्वनिसंसर्गादघोषो जायते, Āpiśaliśikṣā, cited by K.C. Chatterji (1964: 240). This view cited by the Āpiśaliśikṣā as the view of some other scholars (अपरे तु ब्रुवते) goes hand in hand with the etymological meaning of the term *anupradāna*, and may have had a different significance as compared to the *prakṛti* view represented by the RPR, TPR etc.

Supporting evidence for such an interpretation of the original meaning of the term *anupradāna* may be extracted from some ancient practices of silent or rather airless recitation (*upāṃśu*). In the Brāḥmaṇa literature, a priest is often advised to perform the recitation of a certain Mantra in an *upāṃśu* fashion. For example, the Aitareya-Brāhmaṇa (1.27, Anandashrama edn., Pt. I, p. 115) says: तस्मादुपांशु वाचा चरितव्यम्, 'one should, therefore, act with one's speech in an *upāṃśu* fashion.' Sāyaṇa explains this as: यथा परैर्ध्वनिर्न श्रूयते तथा 'in such a way that others will not hear the sound.' This does not mean that one should recite the Mantra simply in one's mind. In the specific *upāṃśu* mode, one does all the movements of the articulatory organs, except that there is no sound coming out, i.e. there is no phonation. Böhtlingk and Roth in their PW on this term cite passages which clearly distinguish between an *upāṃśu* recitation from a *mānasa* 'mental' recitation. A more technical explanation of the term *upāṃśu* is found in the definition: करणवदशब्दममनःप्रयोगमुपांशु (TPR 23.6): "*Upāṃśu* is without sound, without application of mind, but with articulating action." The commentary Tribhāṣyaratna paraphrases the word *karaṇavat* by *prayatnavat*, and says that this is given specifically to distinguish this form of recitation from silence: करणवदिति तूष्णींभावनिवृत्त्यर्थम्. This conception is very important, because it divides the articulatory process into two parts, phonation and the movements of the articulatory organs. Since the *upāṃśu* mode of recitation clearly assumes the presence of the movements of the articulatory organs without the presence of phonation, one can extrapolate that the addition of phonation leads to a recitation which then becomes audible. Most likely, it is this type of recitational practice which led to the perception of phonation as a secondary or an add-on feature. This closely corresponds to one of the two descriptions of *anupradāna* given by the Āpiśaliśikṣā, as something that is added on to the sound produced by the contact of an articulator and a point of articulation

Such an older meaning for the term *anupradāna* is made likely by the use of the verb *anu+pra+dā* in the Vedic literature. For instance, the TS (2.2.1.4-5) reads: पूषा वा इन्द्रियस्य वीर्यस्यानुप्रदाता पूषणमेव स्वेन भागधेयेनोप धावति स एवास्मा इन्द्रियं वीर्यमनु प्र यच्छति, "Pūṣan is the giver of power and strength, verily he (= sacrificer) has recourse to Pūṣan with his own share; verily he (= Pūṣan) gives to him power and strength." The previous passage speaks: "Verily Indra and Agni he has recourse to with their own share; verily they two place power and strength in him; with power and strength he approaches the battle and conquers in it (TS 2.2.1.3)." Thus, the verb *anu-pra-dā* is used in the sense of contributing something to someone who does not already have it. Also see MS (2.1.1). The word *rasānupradāna* also occurs twice in Yāska's Nirukta (7.10, 10.34). In the first occurrence (NR 7.10), Sarup translates it by 'release' of waters [by Indra by means of slaying of the demon Vṛtra], and in the second occurrence, as 'gift of juice.'

This also goes along with my suggestion (cf. Introduction, 3.2.2) that in the formative stages of Sanskrit phonetics, the distinction between the points of articulation of sounds was probably understood earlier than the distinction between voiced/voiceless consonants, and aspirated/unaspirated consonants. This is what may have allowed some early traditions to view, for example, *k* as the representative consonant, which subsequently came to be differentiated between *k*, *kh*, *g*, *gh* etc. through various combinations of primitive sounds. A similar view is found in the Śikṣā verses cited on CA (1.1.12). Also see RPR (13.5-6), and Deshpande (1976). Thus, the notion of voicing, aspiration, and nasality as added features to a basic non-nasal voiceless unaspirated consonant is a fairly old conception, and it occurs independently of the concerns of the definition of homogeneity (*sāvarṇya*) in these texts. Also compare the term *anunāsika* to *anupradāna*; both share the prefix *anu*, and probably both hint at the 'add-on' character of these features as conceived by some of these old traditions.

However, it looks as if the term *anupradāna* soon lost its original etymological meaning and was shared by most of the schools, including the ones which espoused the *prakṛti* view. This is also clear from the Āpiśaliśikṣā itself, where the other school does not subscribe to the 'subsequent' character of *nāda* and *ghoṣa*, and yet calls them *anupradāna*. In these traditions, the term *anupradāna* has been understood differently. George Cardona (personal communication) suggests that in traditions such as the TPR (2.4-10: संवृते कण्ठे नादः क्रियते । विवृते श्वासः । मध्ये हकारः । ता वर्णप्रकृतयः । नादोऽनुप्रदानः स्वरघोषवत्सु। हकारो हचतुर्थेषु । अघोषेषु श्वासः) the word "*anupradāna* could be derived with *lyuṭ* denoting either an instrument or an object: that by which the sounds are produced or that which is emitted in producing the sounds." This is in accordance with the interpretation of the term *anupradāna* as given by the commentary Tribhāṣyaratna on TPR (2.8): अनुप्रदीयतेऽनेन वर्ण इत्यनुप्रदानं मूलकारणम् । अनुप्रदीयते उपादीयते जन्यत इत्यर्थः ।

However, one may note that the most likely earlier etymological meaning of the term *anupradāna* as an 'added or subsequently contributed factor' is eventually picked up by the later texts when they use the term *bāhyaprayatna* 'external effort' to refer to these types of phonation. While most scholars have translated the term *anupradāna* by 'phonic material,' Allen (1953: 23) renders it by 'secondary feature,' thus capturing the etymological significance of the term. Following the lead of Patañjali and the Āpiśaliśikṣā, he lists *anupradāna* under 'extra-buccal processes' (*bāhyaprayatna*). While this accurately represents the view of Patañjali and the *Āpiśaliśikṣā*, we must keep in mind that such a global division of internal versus external efforts is not common to the Prātiśākhyas. And yet, as has been hinted above, the term *anupradāna* in its etymological meaning may have implied the secondary or external nature of this feature.

A somewhat different explanation is suggested by Cardona (personal communication): "Given that the *Taittirīya-* and *Ṛkprātiśākhyas* very deliberately and carefully distinguish between descriptions of speech production and statement of phonological entities, I think it wise to accept that *anupradāna* was used as equivalent to *prakṛti* with reference to *śvāsa*, *nāda* and their combination (*hakāra* in TPR terms). The other view, which takes *anupradāna* as referring to features added to basic sounds is obviously based on the primacy of *ābhyantaraprayatna* with respect to *savarṇa* sets. ... The RPR/TPR descriptions do indeed describe the articulatory process. The alternative way, wherein one has a basic sound defined by *sthāna* and *prayatna* to which *anupradānas* are added, is patently a blend of phonetics and phonological considerations." For a detailed argument in this direction, see: Cardona (1986).

We may also point out that some texts use the term *anupradāna* as an adjective for the terms *śvāsa* and *nāda*, and hence in these texts the word appears in the masculine gender. However, other texts, such as the Āpiśaliśikṣā (8.11, Yudhishthir Mīmāṃsaka edition: तौ श्वासनादावनुप्रदानमित्याचक्षते), use the term in the neuter gender, indicating that it is used as a substantive. In any case, there is no doubt about the reference of the term.

चतुराध्यायीभाष्य - श्वासः अघोषेषु वर्णेषु अनुप्रदानो भवति । कचटतपाः । खछठथफाः । शषसाः ।

'शषसाश्च यमौ द्वौ च द्वितीयाः प्रथमाश्च ये ।
अघोषा, व्यञ्जनं शेषं घोषवद् दृश्यते बुधैः ।।'
(= वर्णपटलम्, १७)

Note: The commentary on this rule is found only in the manuscript N, and hence was not available to Whitney who worked with only the manuscript H.

भा.भा.वृत्ति - अघोषसंज्ञकेषु वर्णेषु श्वासः अनुप्रदानः बाह्यः प्रयत्नो ज्ञेयः । वर्गाणां प्रथमद्वितीयाः कखचछटठतथपफ ।१०। तेषां यमाः ।१०। विसर्गः । जिह्वामूलीयः । उपध्मानीयः । शषस ।६। एते षड्विंशतिः अघोषाः श्वासानुप्रदाना ज्ञेयाः ।

Note: The categorization of the various types of *anupradāna* as types of *bāhyaprayatna* is not relevant to the Prātiśākhya tradition, but is a reflection of the influence of the Pāṇinian school. The commentator brings in categories from the Pāṇinian school to explain the usage of the Prātiśākhya. To some extent, this is indicative of the fact that the Prātiśākhya traditions, in the course of time, became secondary traditions, and had to be explained in terms of the main-stream paradigm of Pāṇinian grammar. The distinction between *bāhya-prayatna* and *ābhyantaraprayatna* is relevant to the definition of homogeneity within the Pāṇinian school, but has little relevance to the Prātiśākhya tradition, Cf. Deshpande (1975: 11).

There is also an important assertion made in the verse cited by the Caturādhyāyībhāṣya and in Bhārgava-Bhāskara's commentary that the *yama*s or the nasalized twins or transitional nasal allophones of voiceless sounds like *k* and *kh* are also voiceless. Interestingly, the CAB itself does not list these voiceless *yama*s. On the other hand, the CAB on the next rule explicitly lists the voiced *yama*s: *g̊* and *g̊h*. One does not quite know whether the notion of voiceless *yama*s was felt to be somewhat uncomfortable. While other Prāti-śākhyas do list *yama*s for *k*, *kh* etc., there is no explicit indication that these are voiceless. While Whitney (1862: 18) does refer to the sonant nasalized twins for *g* and *gh*, he does not mention the fact that the nasalized twins for *k*, *kh* etc. are listed by the verse cited in the CA as voiceless consonants. In fact, for some reason, Whitney does not refer to the verse cited in that commentary at all, even though it does occur in the ms. of the CAB which was available to him.

१.१.१५. नादो घोषवत्स्वरेषु ।

Whitney (1.13). B (orig), D, F, Hab, O(corr): °वत्सरेषु. G, I, O(orig): °वत्परेषु. A, B: °षो is corrected to घो. G: 1.1.15.

Translation: In the case of voiced [consonants] and vowels, the [type of] phonation [or emission] is *nāda* 'resonance.'

Note: For a critique of Max Müller's and Whitney's refusal to accept the voiced *h*, and the combination of voice and aspiration in sounds like *gh*, *jh*, *ḍh*, *dh*, and *bh*, and the subsequent rebuttal of this early misunderstanding, see: Allen (1953: 35ff). The notion of 'breathy voice' is now commonplace in modern phonetics, see: Peter Ladefoged (1971: 12-13; 1973).

चतुराध्यायीभाष्य - नादः घोषवत्सु च वर्णेषु स्वरेषु चानुप्रदानो भवति । गजडदबाः । घझढधभाः । ङञणनमाः । यरलवाः । हः । गंघं । अआआ३ इईई३ उऊऊ३ ऋॠॠ३ ऌॡॡ३ एए[३] ऐऐ३ ओओ[३] औ(H, N: ओ३) [औ३ not listed in H, N]।

'व्यञ्जनं घोषवत्संज्ञमन्तस्था हः परौ यमौ ।
त्रयस्त्रयश्च वर्गान्त्या अघोषः शेष उच्यते ॥'
(= वर्णपटलम्, १६)

Note: The commentary interestingly lists the long vocalic *ḹ* which does not occur in Sanskrit and is not accepted by most traditions. It is equally unclear whether it is the commentator or the copyist who is responsible for this inclusion.

भा.भा.वृत्ति - (**नादोऽघोषवत्परेषु**) अघोषेषु यथा श्वासः तद्वदघोषेभ्यः परेषु घोषेषु नादोऽनुप्रदानो ज्ञेयः । घोषाः । वर्गाणां तृतीयचतुर्थपञ्चमाः । गघङजझञडढणदधनबभमयरलवह ।२०। तृतीयचतुर्थानां यमाः ।१०। एवं त्रिंशत् घोषाः नादानुप्रदाना ज्ञेयाः । स्वराणां प्रयत्नानाह -

Note: The statement of this rule as well as similar rules in other Prātiśākhyas raise the legitimate question of whether the terms *nāda* and *ghoṣa* are co-extensive with each other. Literally interpreted, the rule would seem to suggest that, while vowels and the *ghoṣavat* consonants share the feature of *nāda*, the separate mention of *ghoṣavat* consonants, apart from vowels, seems to suggest at least a possibility that vowels may not have the feature of *ghoṣa*. The question boils down to this. Is there a phonetic distinction intended between the notions of *nāda* and *ghoṣa*, or is this distinction in some sense phonological and not phonetic? This has led to a lively debate among scholars, cf. Deshpande, (1976); Cardona, (1983, 1986), and Stautzebach (1994: 287).

The commentary of Bhārgava-Bhāskara has been clearly misled by a wrong reading for the rule, i.e. नादोऽघोषवत्परेषु. Such a reading presumes the existence of the term *aghoṣavat*. While the term *ghoṣavat* is a common term, its opposite is always *aghoṣa*, and not *aghoṣavat*. It also comes up with an interpretation which excludes vowels from having the feature of *nāda*. Such a view is not at all acceptable, and it simply shows a deteriorating state of phonetic scholarship reflected in this late commentary. Such a view originates in a certain misunderstanding due to the fact that the emission-features are relegated to the category of *bāhyaprayatna* 'external effort,' and the external effort features are useful in the Pāṇinian phonology only in the context of selecting a substitute with maximal featural proximity (*āntaratamya*). Since, in practical terms, such a consideration of substitutes, in terms of external efforts, applies only to the substitutes for consonants, one develops a misperception that vowels do not have the emission features. This misguided view has been articulated by several late texts, cf. the following statement from Pandit Jagadīśācārya Citrācārya (1969: 13): तत्रोदात्तानुदात्तस्वरितास्त्रयः स्वराणामेव सर्वेषाम् । शेषा अष्टौ विवारादयो व्यञ्जनानामेव.

१.१.१६. समानयमेऽक्षरमुच्चैरुदात्तं नीचैरनुदात्तमाक्षिप्तं स्वरितम् ।

Whitney (1.14-16). All the manuscripts treat this as a single Sūtra. A, B, D, L: समानमक्षरमुच्चै°. G: 1.1.16.

Translation: In one and the same register, a syllable with high [tone, pitch] is termed *udātta*, one with a low (lit. non-high) [tone, pitch] is termed *anudātta*, and one with a falling (lit. cast down, thrust down from high to low) [tone, pitch] is termed *svarita*.

चतुराध्यायीभाष्य - समानयमे(H, N: म)ऽक्षरमुच्चैर्यत्तदुदात्तं भवति । नीचैर्यत्तदनुदात्तं भवति । आक्षिप्तं यत्तत्स्वरितं भवति । 'प्र॒जां॑ (H: प्रा मू, Whitney: प्रजां) च॒ रोह॒' (अ.वे. १३.१.३४)। 'अ॒मा॒वा॒स्यां॑' (अ.वे. ७.७९.२)। 'क॒न्यां॑' (अ.वे. १.१४.२)। [only N:] 'धा॒न्यं॑म्' (अ.वे. ३.२४.२)। 'आ॒चा॒र्यं॑ः' (अ.वे. ११.५.३)। 'रा॒ज॒न्यं॑ः' (अ.वे. ५.१७.९)। 'न्यं॑क्' (अ.वे. ६.९१.२)। 'क्वं॑' (अ.वे. ९.९.४)। 'स्वं॑ः' (अ.वे. २.५.२)।

Note: Whitney, I think, properly amends the mss. reading प्रामू च रोह to प्रजां च रोह which is attested in the known text of the AV. Surya Kanta

(APR, Introduction, p. 40), on the other hand, believes that the ms. reading is probably the genuine Śaunakīya reading, and that it is not found in the currently known Vulgate of the *AV*, because it is not the genuinely Śaunakīya recension.

Allen (1953: 89) particularly commends the CA for making an important specification in this rule: "the *AP*, in describing the *udātta* as high and the *anudātta* as low, made the important specification, 'within the same register' (= *samānayame*); the pitches, that is to say, are relative and not absolute - a point which is specifically made by Patañjali: The terms 'high' and 'low' have no absolute signification." For a detailed discussion of the term *ākṣipta*, see: Allen (1953: 87-88). It is not simply the falling tone, but it carries the meaning of thrusting down.

भा.भा.वृत्ति - समानाश्च यमाश्च समानयमं तस्मिन् समानयमे यदक्षरं तदुदात्तादिसंज्ञं स्यात् । समानाः अआइईउऊऋॠऌ । यमाः । सन्ध्यक्षराणि एऐओऔ । इति स्वराः । स्वरसंज्ञकमक्षरं तु उच्चैरुदात्तम् । ह्रस्वाः पञ्च दीर्घा अष्टौ प्लुता नव । ऌकारस्य दीर्घत्वाभावात् । सन्ध्यक्षराणां ह्रस्वत्वाभावाच्च । सर्वे द्वाविंशतिः । भूर्भुव[:] स्वरिति लोकत्रयनिर्देशार्थं यथा शिरः क्रियते तद्वदत्रापि । भूमिनिर्देशार्थमधः शिरः क्रियते । तद्वदनुदात्तोच्चारः । 'देवस्य' (अ.वे. २.३६.२)। अत्र देकारोऽनुदात्तः । भुवर्दर्शनाय किञ्चिदूर्ध्वं शिरः क्रियते तद्वदुच्चारो यस्य स उदात्तः । 'देवस्य' । अत्र वकार उदात्तः । स्वर्दर्शनायात्यूर्ध्वं शिरः क्रियते तद्वदुच्चारो यस्य सः स्वरितः । 'देवस्य' । अत्र स्यकारः स्वरितः । अत एवोक्तम् 'उच्चैरुदात्तम्' [।] वक्ष्यमाणेषु कण्ठादिस्थानेषूच्चार्यमाणो ह्रस्वदीर्घप्लुतस्वरः उच्चैरूर्ध्वभागे उत्पन्नः उदात्तसंज्ञः ऊर्ध्वमात्तः उदात्तः । 'नीचैरनुदात्तम्' । तथाविधस्थानेष्वधोभागेषूच्चार्यमाणः स्वरः अनुदात्तसंज्ञः उदात्तविरुद्धः अनुदात्तः । 'आक्षिप्तं स्वरितम्' । आ उभयार्थकः उभयधर्मावभिव्याप्य क्षिप्तमुच्चारितमक्षरं स्वरितं स्यात् । पूर्वार्धे

उदात्तमुत्तरार्धेऽनुदात्तमित्यर्थः । उदात्ताः । 'प्र' (अ.वे. ४.३३.३)। 'सम्' (अ.वे. १.१५.१)। 'उद्' (अ.वे. २.९.२)। 'वि' (अ.वे. १.१.३)। 'नि' (अ.वे. १.१.२)। अनुदात्ताः । 'न॒ः' (अ.वे. १.२.२)। 'व॒ः' (अ.वे. १.५.२)। 'ते॒' (अ.वे. १.३.१)। 'मे॒' (अ.वे. १.१.१)। 'वा॒म्' (अ.वे. २.२९.४)। 'नौ॒' (अ.वे. ५.११.१०)। 'त्वा॒' (अ.वे. १.१०.३)। 'मा॒' (अ.वे. १.३३.४)। 'च॒' (अ.वे. १.२.४)। 'वा॒' (अ.वे. १.४.२)। 'ह॒' (अ.वे. २.२७.३)। 'ई॒म्' (अ.वे. ४.३०.४)। 'उ॒' (अ.वे. १.६.४)। 'स्म॒' (अ.वे. १.८.२)। स्वरिताः । 'क्व॑' (अ.वे. ९.१४.४)। 'स्व॑ः' (अ.वे. २.५.२)। 'न्यं॑क्' (अ.वे. ६.९१.२)। स्वरितभेदास्तल्लक्षणानि च तृतीयाध्याये वक्ष्यन्ते । भेदनामान्याह मण्डूकः स्वशिक्षायाम् (Śikṣā-saṃgraha, Māṇḍūkīśikṣā, verse 72) -

'अभिनिहितः प्राश्लि[G: क्श्लि]ष्टो जात्यः क्षैप्रश्च पादवृत्तश्च ॥

तैरोव्यञ्जनः षष्ठस्तिरोविरामश्च सप्तम इति ॥'

भाव्यश्चेत्यष्टमः । अभिनिहितः । 'सो॑ऽध्व॒रान्' (अ.वे. १९.५९.३)। 'ये॒॑स्याम्' (अ.वे. ३.२६.१)। प्राश्लि[G: क्श्लि]-ष्टः । 'अभीद्धे॑' (?, 'अ॒भीन्द्धे॑,' अ.वे. ११.३.१८; 'अ॒भी॑-द्धः,' अ.वे. ७.७३.७, VVRI edn.: ७.७७.७;)। 'अ॒भी॑मे' (अ.वे. ६.१२६.३)। जात्यः । 'क्व॑' (अ.वे. ९.१४.४)। 'क॒न्ये॑व' (अ.वे. ६.२२.३)। 'ध॒न्व॒न्या॒ः॒३॑ शमु॑' (अ.वे. १.६.४) । क्षैप्रः । 'स्व॑ः' (अ.वे. २.५.२)। 'व्यो॑म' (अ.वे. ११.१.३०)। 'त॒न्वे॒॒३॑' (अ.वे. १.३.१)। 'न्य॒१॑ग्वात॑ः' (अ.वे. ६.९१.२)। पादवृत्तः । 'क ई॑ं वेद' (अ.वे. २०.५३.१; २०.५७.११)। 'य ई॑ं च॒कार॑' (अ.वे. ९.१०.१०, VVRI edn.: ९.१५.१०)। तैरोव्यञ्जनः । 'इन्द्र॑ः' (अ.वे. १.७.३)। 'अ॒ग्निना॑' (अ.वे. ३.१२.९)। तिरोविरामः । 'प्र॒जाऽप॑तिः'

(अ.वे. २.३४.४)। 'पुरःऽहिंतम्' (अ.वे. ११.१०.१८, VVRI edn.: ११.१२.१८)। भाव्यस्वरितः परिहारे । 'तनून-पांदिति तनूऽ(G: ३)नपांत्' (क्रमपरिहार, अ.वे. ५.२७.१)। मण्डूक आह (*Śikṣāsaṃgraha*, *Māṇḍūkīśikṣā*, verse 80):

'द्वयोरुदात्तयोर्मध्ये नीचो यः स्यादवग्रहः ।।

तथा भाव्यो भवेत्कम्पस्तनूनपान्निदर्शनम् ।।' इति ।।

एवं 'शचीऽ(G: ३)पतिंः' (part of क्रमपरिहार, अ.वे. ३.१०.१२)।

Note: Following the Pāṇinian school, Bhārgava-Bhāskara says that there is no long *ḹ* in the usage of Sanskrit. Interestingly, Bhārgava-Bhāskara refers to different head movements of the reciter to indicate different accents. The *anudātta* is indicated by the lowering of the head. The *udātta* is indicated by the slight raising of the head. The *svarita* is indicated by raising the head even higher to look upwards to the heaven (*svar*). Especially interesting is his folk-etymological linking of the word *svarita* with *svar* 'heaven,' and the upward movement of the head of the reciter. This also corresponds to the orthographic vertical mark to indicate a *svarita*. While the western scholars have focused upon the 'falling' character of *svarita*, the Indian tradition may have looked at the initial high tone as the distinguishing mark of a *svarita*. Several texts say that the initial portion of a *svarita* is not just a high tone (*udātta*), but that it is a super-high tone (*udāttatara*), cf. RPR (3.45) and Vaidikābharaṇa on TPR (1.41). In Vedic recitation, when an *udātta* is followed by a *svarita*, the tone rises from high to super-high, before falling. For gestures accompanying the different pitches used by different tradition, see: Allen (1953: 91).

The reading of the second verse from the Māṇḍūkīśikṣā quoted in the commentary of Bhārgava-Bhāskara is slightly different from the one seen in the Śikṣāsaṃgraha edition (p. 470):

द्वयोरुदात्तयोर्मध्ये नीचोऽस्ति यदवग्रहः ।
ताथाभाव्यो भवेत्कम्पस्तनूनपान्निदर्शनम् ।।

१.१.१७. स्वरितस्यादितो मात्रार्धमुदात्तम् ।

Whitney (1.17). G: 1.1.17.

Translation: The initial half-mora of a *svarita* is high-pitched (*udātta*), [and, by implication, the rest is low-pitched (*anudātta*)].

चतुराध्यायीभाष्य - स्वरितस्यादितः मात्रार्धमुदात्तं भवति। 'अमावास्या' (अ.वे. ७.७९.२)। 'कन्या' (अ.वे. १.१४.२)। 'धान्यम्' (अ.वे. ३.२४.२)। 'आचार्यः' (अ.वे. ११.५.३)। 'राजन्यः' (अ.वे. ५.१७.९)। 'न्यक्' (अ.वे. ६.९१.२)। 'क्व' (अ.वे. ९.९.४)। (only N:) 'स्वः' (अ.वे. २.५.२)।

Note: The first five examples quoted by the CAB occur in the same order as the first five examples cited under APR (54, p. 43). The next three examples cited by the CAB occur in the same order under APR (53, p. 43). It should also be noted that these are the examples of the *jātya* type of *svarita*. All the same examples appear in the CAB under CA (3.3.8) which defines the *jātya* variety.

भा.भा.वृत्ति - मात्रायाः मात्रयोः मात्राणां च अर्धं मात्रार्धम् । ह्रस्वस्वरितस्य मात्राया अर्धमादितोऽर्धमात्रा उदात्ता । दीर्घस्वरितस्यादौ मात्रयोरर्धमेका मात्रा तावदुदात्तम् । प्लुतस्वरितस्यादौ मात्राणामर्धं सार्धैकमात्रा तावत्कालमुदात्तता । उर्वरितमुत्तरार्धमनुदात्तमर्थतः सिद्धम् । पाणिनीयेऽपि 'तस्यादित उदात्तमर्धह्रस्वम्' (पा. १.२.३२) इति । अथ वर्णोच्चारस्थानान्युपदिशति -

Note: Bhārgava-Bhāskara interprets the rule to mean that the first half, not just a half-mora, is high-pitched. The statement of Pāṇini 1.2.32 (तस्यादित उदात्तमर्धह्रस्वम्) is clearer in saying that a half-short-vowel quantity at the beginning of a *svarita* is *udātta*. It is also certain that the CA rule is identical in meaning with Pāṇini 1.2.32. Therefore, Bhārgava-Bhāskara's interpretation of this rule does not seem to be correct. For him, irrespective of the number of *mātrā*s in a *svarita* vowel, fully the first half portion is *udātta*. If such were the intention, the CA rule might as well be framed with the expression *ardham* alone, and not *mātrārdham.* However, we may note that Bhārgava-Bhāskara's interpretation is in agreement with late Pāṇinian commentaries which disregard the word *hrasva* in *ardhahrasvam*, cf. SK on P.1.2.32 (p. 5): ह्रस्वग्रहणमतन्त्रम् । स्वरितस्यादितोऽर्धमुदात्तं बोध्यम् । उत्तरार्धं तु परिशेषादनुदात्तम् ।

१.१.१८. मुखे विशेषाः करणस्य ।

Whitney (1.18). G:1.1.18.

Translation: In the oral tract (lit. mouth), there are the [following] distinctions of the articulator [*karaṇa* 'the instrument, the moving organ,' in contrast with the relatively static *sthāna*s 'points of articulation'].

Note: The rendering of *mukha* by 'oral tract' needs some comment. It is not always clear whether or not to include *nāsikā* 'nose' as part of *mukha*. While CA (1.1.26: नासिक्यानां नासिका) lists *nāsikā* as an articulator for the pure nasal *nāsikya* sounds under the general heading of our present rule, CA (1.1.27: अनुनासिकानां मुखनासिकम्) mentions oral and nasal tracts separately and says that both of these are used for the articulation of nasalized sounds (*anunāsika*).

चतुराध्यायीभाष्य - मुखे विशेषा भवन्ति करणस्य । कचटतपाः ।

भा.भा.वृत्ति - मुखे वदनान्तराकाशप्रान्तदेशे । करणस्य स्पृष्टादिसंज्ञकप्रयत्नस्य विशेषाः । वर्णोच्चारणस्थानभेदाः कथ्यन्ते ।

Note: Bhārgava-Bhāskara seems to have confused the notion of *prayatna* as it appears in the Pāṇinian school with that of *karaṇa* in this text. The first term refers to the manner in which the articulator (*karaṇa*) relates to the point of articulation (*sthāna*). On the other hand, the second term refers to the articulator. Historically speaking, the term *prayatna* originally did not even have this meaning. Its meaning, most probably, was simply "effort." This is the meaning seen even in Pāṇini's rules like P.8.3.18 (व्योर्लघुप्रयत्नतरः शाकटायनस्य). Here, the term *laghu-prayatna-tara* does not refer to the manner in which the articulator relates to the point of articulation, but to the general articulatory effort. In this case, it refers to a weak articulatory effort. Most probably, the term *prayatna* had the same generic meaning in P.1.1.9 (तुल्यास्यप्रयत्नं सवर्णम्), but that it was explained by the commentators by using more refined categories which were developed in later times. It seems that words like *spṛṣṭa* 'touching, in contact' were originally used as adjectives of the word *karaṇa* 'articulator' to distinguish the different positions of the articulator. This is seen in the CA and in the RPR (13.8ff: तद्विशेषः करणं स्पृष्टमस्थितं ...) These differences of the position of the *karaṇa* later came to be denoted by the term *prayatna*. The VPR (1.43: समानस्थानकरणास्यप्रयत्नः सवर्णः) is probably the earliest text which came to clearly distinguish between the terms *karaṇa* 'articulator' and *āsyaprayatna* 'effort,' see: Deshpande (1975: 9-11, 94-97). The CA clearly first describes the articulators for different sounds, and then it describes the positions of those articulators. However, it does not use the term *prayatna* to refer to these different positions of the articulators (*karaṇa*).

१.१.१९. कण्ठ्यानामधरकण्ठ्यः ।

Whitney (1.19), G: °कण्ठः. A, B, L, M: °मधरं कंण्ठ्यः. G: 1.1.19. Except G, all mss. support the reading कण्ठ्यः. While the reading *adhara-kaṇṭhyaḥ* is clearly justified on the basis of the manuscript evidence, one wonders if *adharakaṇṭhaḥ* was the original reading. The oldest commentary CAB knows the reading *adharakaṇṭhaḥ*. It is possible that *-kaṇṭhyaḥ* was an ancient error which was copied blindly by most manuscript traditions.

Translation: For the glottal sounds, the lower part of the glottal area [is the articulator].

Note: Allen (1953: 59) prefers to render *kaṇṭhya* with 'glottal.' However, it is not clear what is exactly meant by the distinction of lower glottal area versus upper glottal area. Whitney renders *kaṇṭha* with throat. However, the same word *kaṇṭha* is used to describe the production of resonance and voiceless breath, depending upon whether *kaṇṭha* is open or closed. Such a description better fits the glottis, rather than throat in a broad sense. Now what could *adharakaṇṭh(y)a* refer to, in contrast with the rest of the *kaṇṭha* ? If we take *kaṇṭha* to refer just to the glottis, then it is difficult to make the distinction of lower versus upper glottis. However, it is possible that the word *kaṇṭha* referred to the entire throat area inclusive of the glottis. The upper part of this *kaṇṭha* was involved in the production of velar sounds, while the lower part, i.e. the glottis, was involved in the production of the vowel *a* etc. Since, the only moving part of this *kaṇṭha* in the sense of the whole throat area was the glottis, the text could refer to it to be the articulator for the vowel *a* etc. These difficulties of accurate classification probably explain why some texts opted to describe the *k*-series as a *kaṇṭhya* series, while others chose to describe it as a velar series with a distinct point of articulation, i.e. the root of the tongue. In a view that *a* and *k* were both *kaṇṭhya* sounds, one could not truly say that they had the same *karaṇa*. Such a reasoning may have led the ancient phoneticians to differentiate these two by positing different points of articulations for them.

In any case, the description of the process of articulation of these glottal sounds as given in the CAB is very dubious: "the upper *kaṇṭha* is the place of articulation and it is approached by the lower *kaṇṭha*." This reference to lower *kaṇṭha* as the articulator, in spite of its understandable parallelism with the notion of the lower lip as the articulator for labials in CA (1.1.25), hardly makes sense. Perhaps, such absurdities may have led other texts to declare that glottal sounds do not have a distinct *karaṇa* of their own. For them, the point of articulation and the articulator are the same, cf. शेषाः स्वस्थानकरणाः, Āpiśali-śikṣā (2.9, p. 3, Yudhishthira Mimamsaka edition).

Allen (1953: 59) has an enlightening discussion on the classification of *a*, *h*, and *-ḥ* as *kaṇṭhya* 'glottal' sounds: "To class the open vowels as 'glottal' appears at first sight an indefensible procedure. It becomes less so when we perceive the conceptual framework underlying these statements. It will be remembered that the *TP* referred to a 'neutral' position of the articulatory organs, in which the tongue is extended and depressed, and the lips are in the position for *a*. The classification of *a* as glottal begins to make sense if we assume that it was viewed as a 'neutral' vowel in the sense of involving no special intra-buccal articulatory effort." Where the difference of opinion arises is the question of *karaṇa* for these 'glottal' sounds. The CA is perhaps making a unique effort to find a *karaṇa* for these sounds, for which, according to other traditions, there is no distinct *karaṇa* (Allen 1953: 49, 59).

चतुराध्यायीभाष्य - कण्ठस्थानानां वर्णानामधरकण्ठः करणं भवति । किं पुनः स्थानं किं करणम् । उत्तरकण्ठः स्थानमधरकण्ठेन करणेनोपक्रम्यते । यदुपक्रम्यते तत्स्थानम् । येनोपक्रम्यते तत्करणम् । अआआ३ह[विसर्जनीयः] (H, N: वृक्षः)। एऐओऔ ।

'अधः [only N: स्थानानि वर्णानां कण्ठ्योऽवर्ण-
हकारयोः ।
विसर्जनीयस्यैदौतोराद्ययोर्मात्रयोः स्मृतः ॥
शेषस्ताल्वो]ष्ठयोर्वाच्यः स यथासङ्ख्यमिष्यते ।
द्विस्थानत्वं तयोश्चापि वर्गान्त्यानां च शिष्यते ॥'
(= वर्णपटलम्, १८-१९)

Note: The reading for these verses in the printed version of the Varṇapaṭala is slightly different:

अतः स्थानानि वर्णानां कण्ठोऽवर्णहकारयोः ।
विसर्जनीय ऐ औ च स्वाद्ययोर्मात्रयोः स्मृतः ॥१८॥
शेषस्ताल्वोष्ठये(यो?)र्बोध्यः स यथासंख्यमिष्यते ।
द्विस्थानं यमयोश्चापि वर्गान्त्यानां च शिष्यते ॥१९॥ p. 204.

Allen (1953: 17) points out the similarity of the definitions of *sthāna* and *karaṇa* given by the CAB to Kenneth Pike's terms 'point of articulation' and 'articulator.' Also compare TPR (2.31-34): स्वराणां यत्रोपसंहारस्तत्स्थानम् । यदुपसंहरति तत्करणम् । अन्येषां तु यत्र स्पर्शनं तत्स्थानम् । येन स्पर्शयति तत्करणम् ।

The CA does not give us a list of which sounds it considers to be *kaṇṭhya*. That task has fallen to the commentators. The CAB and the ancient Śikṣā text it cites agree that the label of *kaṇṭhya* 'glottal' be given to *a*, *ā*, *ā3*, *h*, and *ḥ*. Then comes the difference. While the cited Śikṣā verse says that the initial elements of the diphthongs *ai*, and *au* are also glottal, the CAB goes one step ahead and adds e and o, implying that these sounds are not monophthongs, and that their initial elements are also glottal. In doing so, it agrees with the statements found in Bhārgava-Bhāskara's commentary on CA (1.1. 28).

***भा.भा.वृत्ति* - (कण्ठ्यानामधरकण्ठः)** अकारहकारविसर्गाः कण्ठ्याः । अहअः । एतेषामुच्चारस्थानमधरकण्ठः कण्ठ-बिलस्याधोभागो ज्ञातव्यः ।

Note: While the CAB appropriately maintains the distinction between the point of articulation (*sthāna*) and the articulator (*karaṇa*), Bhārgava-Bhāskara has confused the two notions. The rule, taken in its proper context, says that the lower *kaṇṭha* is the articulator of those sounds which have *kaṇṭha* as their point of articulation. Bhārgava-Bhāskara interprets the rule to mean: "The point of articulation for these sounds is the lower *kaṇṭha*." This is not correct. This confusion is continued in many of the following rules.

On this particular rule, Bhārgava-Bhāskara does seem to maintain a certain distinction of the CA tradition from that represented by the texts such as the Āpiśaliśikṣā (1.2) and the prose Pāṇinīyaśikṣā (1.2) which treat the *k*-series as *kaṇṭhya*, in addition to *a*, *h*, and *ḥ*. The Āpiśaliśikṣā (1.2) and the prose Pāṇinīyaśikṣā (1.2) say: अकुहविसर्जनीयाः कण्ठ्याः, cf. SK on P.1.1.9: अकुहविसर्जनीयानां कण्ठः. These texts express a view different from that of the metrical Pāṇinīyaśikṣā, which ascribes *kaṇṭha* as the point of articulation for *a* and *h*, while it ascribes *jihvāmūla* to the *k*-series, cf. verses 17-18: कण्ठ्यावहौ, ... जिह्वामूले तु कुः प्रोक्तः.

१.१.२०. जिह्वामूलीयानां हनुमूलम् ।

Whitney (1.20). G: 1.1.20. I: 1.20. Most mss. read *jivhā* for *jihvā*.

Translation: For velar sounds (lit. tongue-root sounds), the base (lit. root) of the jaw [is the articulator].

चतुराध्यायीभाष्य - जिह्वामूलस्थानानां वर्णानां हनुमूलं करणं भवति । ऋ१ऋ३ऋ३ ३कखगघङ । पुरुषᳵखनति । ऌॡ।

'जिह्वामूलमृवर्णस्य कवर्गस्य च भाष्यते ।
यश्चैव जिह्वामूलीय ऌवर्णस्येति स स्मृतः ॥'
(= वर्णपटलम्, २०, *ऌवर्णश्चेति च स्मृतः)

Note: Whitney's emendation for the last quarter of the verse: ऌवर्णश्चेति ते स्मृताः । There is no support for this reading. Also for the difficult-to-read segment ऌॡ, Whitney reads क्लृप्त and refers to AV 10.10.23. Neither H, nor N supports Whitney. A comparison of the way ऌ and ॡ are written in the manuscript N in the commentary on CA 1.1.32 leaves no doubt that the sequence here refers to these two sounds. It may also be noted that the transmission of the CAB and that of the Varṇapaṭala may have occurred independently. The reading ऌवर्णस्येति स स्मृतः is not found among the variants in the Varṇapaṭala manuscripts.

भा.भा.वृत्ति - कवर्गः कखपरो विसर्गश्च जिह्वामूलीयाः ।
कखगघङअ×क अ×ख । एतेषामुच्चारणस्थानमधराया हनो-
मूलं ज्ञेयम् । कण्ठबिलाधोभागात्किञ्चिदन्तःस्थितो देशः ।
हनुमूलं तदेव जिह्वामूलम् । जिह्वामूले भवाः । छः प्रत्ययः ।
जिह्वामूलीयाः ।

Note: Again, the commentators differ as to which sounds are to be listed as velar sounds. The CAB and the Śikṣā it cites list the *k*-series of stops, the *r̥* and *l̥* vowels, and the allophone of *ḥ* before *k*, *kh*, i.e. *ḫ* (*jihvāmūlīya*). For a detailed review of the velar classification for *r̥* and *l̥* vowels, see Hans Henrich Hock (1992). Following the late Pāṇinian tradition, Bhārgava-Bhāskara removes the *r̥*- and *l̥*-vowels from the list of velars. For him, the *r̥*-vowels are retroflex, while the *l̥*-vowels are dental. See Bhārgava-Bhāskara's commentary on CA 1.1.22, 24.

The confusion of the notions of *sthāna* and *karaṇa* continues into this rule in Bhārgava-Bhāskara's commentary. This is explainable in part because he identifies the referents of the words *jihvāmūla* and *hanumūla*. If these two words refer to the same thing, then how can the point of articulation be different from the articulator? It needs to be pointed out that these terms do not refer to the same thing.

Another point to consider is that Bhārgava-Bhāskara does not include the sounds *r̥* and *l̥* among the *jihvāmūlīya*s. For him, *r̥* is a *mūrdhanya* sound, while *l̥* is a *dantya* sound. This is more in line with later texts in the Pāṇinian tradition like the Siddhāntakaumudī. The CAB, on the other hand, seems to reflect an older view.

The final comment of Bhārgava-Bhāskara that the word *jihvāmūlīya* is derived by adding the affix *cha* (⇒ *īya*) to the word *jihvāmūla* shows how he takes the Pāṇinian system for granted both for himself, and for his readers.

In the phonetic literature, there is indeed a good deal of confusion in the case of sounds such as these concerning which of the organs is the point of articulation and which is the articulator. While the CA rule literally seems to say that the *hanumūla* is the articulator and that the *jihvāmūla* is the point of articulation, the TPR (ii. 35: हनुमूले जिह्वामूलेन कवर्गं स्पर्शयति) presents a reverse doctrine. While the CAB seems to offer a straight forward interpretation of the CA statement, Bhārgava-Bhāskara seems to have been influenced by other traditions. Thus, the Āpiśaliśikṣā (2.4: जिह्वामूलेन जिह्व्यानाम्) states that the *jihvā*-

mūla is the articulator for *jihvya* sounds. The same doctrine is found in the prose Pāṇinīyaśikṣā (2.3).

१.१.२१. तालव्यानां मध्यजिह्वम् ।

Whitney (1.21). G: 1.1.21. Most mss. read *jivham.*

Translation: For palatal sounds, the middle of the tongue [is the articulator].

Note: Again, the CA itself does not tell us which sounds are included in the category of palatal sounds. For that we have to rely upon the commentators who differ from each other on this point.

चतुराध्यायीभाष्य - तालुस्थानानां वर्णानां मध्यजिह्वं करणं भवति । एऐयशचछजझञ । इईई३ ।

'ताल्वे (Whitney: ल्वै) यशाचवर्गाणामिवर्णस्य च भाष्यते ।' (= वर्णपटलम्, २१)

Note: The verse cited by the CAB seems to hold a slightly different view as compared to that of the commentary. The commentary, if correctly reproduced by the manuscripts, seems to include both *e* and *ai* among the sounds produced at the palate, besides the *i*-vowels and the *c*-series. On the other hand, out of *e* and *ai*, the verse seems to include only the sound *e*. This may be a reflection of the old view that *e* was a pure monophthongal *tālavya* sound, while *ai*, as a true diphthong, was a composite sound with distinct points of articulation for its two parts, *kaṇtha* for the first part and *tālu* for the second part. The emendation suggested by Whitney does not seem to lead to an acceptable text. It is hard to see how *ai* could be included without the inclusion of *e*. On the other hand, it is easy to see how *e* could be included without the inclusion of *ai*. Bolling and Negelein (1910: 302) report that the mss. A and E of the Varṇapaṭala support the reading **tālvai-*, while the rest of the mss. support the reading *tālve-*.

Allen (1953: 52) also makes an important point: "No difficulty is provided by the description of the *c*-series, which at the period described by out treatises appear still to have been true palatal plosives rather than pre-palatal affricates such as are general in modern Indian pronunciation." The modern pronunciation neither uses the middle of the tongue, nor the point of articulation named as *tālu*. This *tālu* as intended by the Sanskrit phoneticians must have been farther back on the oral dome as compared to the point touched during the pronunciation of the retroflex stops. This must be so given the back-to-front ordering of the consonantal *varga*s. However, the modern pronunciation uses a point slightly above the alveolar ridge and pressed against it not the middle of the tongue, but a portion of the tongue much closer to the tip of the tongue. The historical alternations between palatal and velar consonants are also an indication that the palatal point of articulation was much farther back and closer to the velar point, than being closer to the alveolar ridge as it is in the modern pronunciation.

भा.भा.वृत्ति - इकारश्चवर्गो यकारशकारौ । तालुनि भवास्तालव्याः । इचछजझञयश । एतेषामष्टानां मध्यजिह्वम् । जिह्वाया मध्यस्थलं तालुस्पृष्टमुच्चारस्थानं ज्ञेयम् । जिह्वाग्रमेकाङ्गुलं त्यक्त्वा अनन्तरं जिह्वामध्यदेशस्तेन तालव्यानामुच्चार इति स्फुटम् ।

Note: Bhārgava-Bhāskara includes neither *e* nor *ai* among the pure *tālavya* sounds. This is similar to his exclusion of *o* and *au* from the list of the pure *oṣṭhya* sounds later on. The reason is that he treats these four sounds, in line with the late Pāṇinian tradition, to be sounds with double points of articulation, *kaṇṭhatālu* and *kaṇṭhauṣṭha* respectively for *e*, *ai*, and *o*, *au*, cf. Bhārgava-Bhāskara's commentary on CA1.1.28. This brings out a significant difference between the CAB and the commentary by Bhārgava-Bhāskara. The former is most certainly a relatively earlier text and is relatively free from the influence of the Pāṇinian tradition. It seems that, as time went on, the commentaries were influenced more and more by the Pāṇinian school. This is attributable to the fact that while the Pāṇinian school flourished, the Prātiśākhya tradition became more and more dormant, and the late efforts seen in the commentaries like those of Bhārgava-Bhāskara were essentially efforts to interprete these texts in familiar Pāṇinian terms.

१.१.२२. मूर्धन्यानां जिह्वाग्रं प्रतिवेष्टितम् ।

Whitney (1.22). G: 1.1.22. J, K: परि for प्रति. P reads पति for प्रति. Most mss. read *jivhāgram*.

Translation: For cerebral [or retroflex sounds], the rolled back tip of the tongue [is the articulator].

चतुराध्यायीभाष्य - मूर्धन्यस्थानानां वर्णानां जिह्वाग्रं प्रतिवेष्टितं करणं भवति । रषटठडढण ।

'मूर्धा स्थानं षकारस्य टवर्गस्य तथा मतम् ।'
(= वर्णपटलम्, २१. *तथा मतः)

Note: While the cited verse makes no reference to *r* or *ṛ*, the enumeration in the commentary includes *r*, which is described elsewhere in the CA (1. 1.28) as being alveolar and not cerebral. The inclusion of *r* among the *mūrdhanya*s is relatively late. Thus, the cited verse seems to represent an earlier phase in the development of Sanskrit phonetics. Neither the cited verse nor the commentary makes a reference to *ṛ*, because that sound is considered to be a *jihvāmūlīya* by this text. On the other hand, Bhārgava-Bhāskara's commentary below includes *ṛ* among the *mūrdhanya*s. This is again a reflection of his following the late Pāṇinian tradition. Interestingly, he excludes *r* from the list of *mūrdhanya*s.

Allen (1953: 32) discusses the Indian description of retroflexion and comments that "to consider the retroflex articulations on the same terms as the velars, palatals, dentals, or labials is, even from the point of view of the Indian descriptive framework, not entirely justified." He feels (ibid, p. 33) that "the retroflex series ... is articulated as our treatises recognize, 'by rolling back the tip of the tongue' - that is to say, the place of articulation is not automatically determined by the application of the closure-processes to the apical articulator: there is need of a further *prayatna*, 'articulatory effort,' which might with consistency have been included at this point." I feel that the curling back of the tongue has not been treated as a *prayatna*, firstly because the notion of *prayatna* is defined somewhat narrowly as referring to degrees of contact or lack of it, between the articulator and the place of articulation. Furthermore, given the same point of articulation and the articulator, one does not have a choice of whether or not to curl up one's tongue. Thus, curling up one's tongue is not a feature of choice, with other factors being constant. It is just sheer necessity.

भा.भा.वृत्ति - मुखबिले ऊर्ध्वायाः हनोर्मध्यदेशः वर्णोच्चारे मूर्धेति संज्ञा । तत्र भवा मूर्धन्याः ऋकारटवर्गौ । ऋटठड-

ढण एषां षण्णां प्रतिवेष्टितं जिह्वाग्रं किञ्चिद्वक्रीकृत्य मूर्ध-स्थानं स्पृष्ट्वा निमुच्यते । एतत्क्रियायाः प्रतिवेष्टनमर्थः । एवं मूर्धन्यानामुच्चारो भवति ।

१.१.२३. षकारस्य द्रोणिका ।

Whitney (1.23). G: 1.1.23.

Translation: For the sound *ṣ*, the bowl-[shaped tongue is the articulator].

Note: Whitney feels that *ṣ* should not have been singled out for a special treatment among the cerebral sounds, and that this rule may have been "very possibly a later interpolation in the text of our treatise. ... It can hardly be claimed that this rule adds to the distinctness of our apprehension of the character of this sibilant, which is clearly enough exhibited by its relation to the other lingual sound." In any case, the rule is found in all manuscripts, and there is no reason to consider it to be an interpolation, cf. TPR (2.45): करणमध्यं तु विवृतम्. In contrast to Whitney, Allen (1953: 26) admiringly calls this: "a rather more graphic description," and cites a similar description by Grammont. The commentary of Bhārgava-Bhāskara also adds some graphic description of its own. While for the other cerebral sounds, it is the rolled back tip of the tongue which becomes the articulator, the pronunciation of *ṣ* was supposed to be done in such a way that the middle of the tongue had a dip, and the lower sides of the front edges of the tongue touched the sides of the palatal region. The Āpiśaliśikṣā says that all cerebral sounds are produced with "the part next to the tip, or the under-side of the tip," Allen (1953: 53). It is possible that the CA made a distinction between the rest of the cerebral sounds and the *ṣ*. The CA distinction is at least internally well supported, because it says that the middle of the articulator remains open, i.e. without contact. Thus, the tongue turned into a bowl-like shape, the sides of the front of the touched the sides of the curvature of the oral cavity, leaving the middle without contact. In contrast with this, the tip of the tongue had a direct contact in the pronunciation of cerebral stops.

चतुराध्यायीभाष्य - षकारस्य द्रोणिका करणं भवति । 'षडा॑हुः शी॒तान् षडु॑ मा॒सः' (अ.वे. ८.९.१७)।

भा.भा.वृत्ति - षकारो मूर्धन्यः । तस्योच्चारे जिह्वाया द्रोणिकां कृत्वा जिह्वापार्श्वाधोभागौ मूर्ध(G: र्धा)प्रान्तयोः संस्पर्शयेत् । एवंक्रियाकरणे षकारोच्चारो भवति । अत एवोक्तं द्रोणिकेति ।

१.१.२४. दन्त्यानां जिह्वाग्रं प्रस्तीर्णम् ।

Whitney (1.24). G: 1.1.24. Most mss. read *jivhāgram.*

Translation: For dental sounds, the tip of the tongue spread flat [is the articulator].

Note: Whitney translates *prastīrṇa* as 'thrust forward,' and this might imply that the tip of the tongue was pressed against the upper teeth. The commentary of Bhārgava-Bhāskara, on the other hand, lends support to Allen's (1953: 56) rendering of *prastīrṇa* as 'spread, flat.' The commentary describes the tongue as spread out flat like the leaf of a Vaṭa 'banyan' tree.

चतुराध्यायीभाष्य - दन्तस्थानानां वर्णानां जिह्वाग्रं प्रस्तीर्णं करणं भवति । लसतथदधन ।

'दन्ता(H, N: न्त्या) लसतवर्गाणाम् ।' (वर्णपटलम्, २२)

Note: According to the CAB, the only dental sounds are *l*, *s*, and the *t*-series. The sound *l̥* is included among the velars (*jihvāmūlīya*). In the verse cited in the CAB, the reading **dantyā* for *dantā* is found in the mss. A and E of Varṇapaṭala, but *dantā* is supported by the other mss (Bolling and Negelein, 1910: 303).

भा.भा.वृत्ति - दन्तेषु भवाः दन्त्याः । ऌकारलकारसकार-तवर्गाः (G: र्गः)। ऌलसतथदधन । एतेषामुच्चारणे प्रस्तीर्णं प्रसृतवटपत्रवत् जिह्वाग्रं दन्तमूलस्पर्शि भवति । तदा स्फुट उच्चारः स्यात् ।

Note: In contrast with the CAB and the verse cited therein, the late tradition recorded in Bhārgava-Bhāskara's commentary treats *ḷ* to be a *dantya* sound. It is clear that Bhārgava-Bhāskara follows here the late Pāṇinian school. At the same time, Bhārgava-Bhāskara seems to give an explanation of the articulation of dentals which makes them more like *dantamūlīya*. According to him the tip of the tongue touches the root of the teeth (जिह्वाग्रं दन्तमूलस्पर्शि भवति). If the blade of the tongue is truly flat, we would expect a true dental, rather than an alveolar pronunciation. It is not clear whether Bhārgava-Bhāskara intends the normal pronunciation of dentals to be more like the alveolars, or just that a clear enunciation (*sphuṭa-uccāra*) of the dentals was more like alveolars. One possible interpretation of these comments is that even though the CA calls these sounds dentals, they were pronounced like alveolars in Bhārgava-Bhāskara's own tradition. The RPR (1.9) also supports the alveolar pronunciation for the sounds which are normally considered to be dentals. It is of some interest to note that Bhārgava-Bhāskara generally follows the tradition of the Pāṇinīyaśikṣā, and that there is no support for the alveolar pronunciation of dentals in that text. Thus, the source of this deviation remains somewhat obscure.

१.१.२५. ओष्ठ्यानामधरौष्ठ[च]म् ।

Whitney (1.25), G: 1.1.25: °ष्ठम्. All other manuscripts support the reading given above. However, I wonder whether the reading °ष्ठ्यम् is not an ancient error going back to the archetype of all the available manuscripts.

Translation: For the labial sounds, the lower lip [is the articulator].

चतुराध्यायीभाष्य - ओष्ठस्थानानां वर्णानामधरौष्ठं(H, N: ष्ठ्यं) करणं भवति । किं पुनः स्थानं किं करणम् । उत्तरौष्ठं स्थानमधरौष्ठेन करणेनोपक्रम्यते । यदुपक्रम्यते तत् स्थानम् । येनोपक्रम्यते तत् करणम् । ओओ३औऔ३ पफबभम । पुरुष॒पिबति । उऊऊ३ ।

'सन्ध्यक्षरेषु वर्णेषु वर्णान्तमोष्ठ्यमुच्यते ।
उपध्मानीयमुकारो वः पवर्गश्च (Whitney: no च) तथा
मतः ॥' (Source ?)

Note: Notice that the cited verse includes *v* among the labials, while it is not included in the prose listing, perhaps because it is considered to be a labiodental (*dantyoṣṭhya*) sound. Here again, the cited verse represents an earlier tradition of classification, while the commentary represents a later tradition. There are two slightly different possibilities for *v* being classified earlier as an *oṣṭhya* sound. One possibility is that it was a true glide, more like the English *w*. The other possibility is that many texts considered teeth to be the articulator for *v*, but not its point of articulation, and hence in spite of its labio-dentality, it came to be listed as an *oṣṭhya* sound. The second possibility has greater textual justification in other phonetic treatises. For further details, see: Allen (1953: 57).

Another important factor to note is that many Śikṣā texts do not distinguish between the point or articulation and the articulator for labial sounds, while here the CA seems to make a determined effort to come up with an articulator for each sound. Compare also CA (1.1.19: कण्ठ्यानामधरकण्ठ्यः).

Also compare: Varṇapaṭala 22bcd:

... उवर्णस्त्वोष्ठ्य उच्यते ।
उपध्मानीय ओकारो वः पवर्गश्च तथा मताः ।।

भा.भा.वृत्ति - **(ओष्ठ्यानामधरौष्ठम्)** ओष्ठयोर्भवाः ओष्ठ्याः । उकारः उपध्मानीयः पवर्गश्च वकारोऽपि । उ अ᳹प अ᳹फ पफबभमव । एतेषामुच्चारस्तु अधरः मुखप्रान्ताधोभागः । ओष्ठः । मुखप्रान्तोर्ध्वभागः । अधरश्च ओष्ठश्च अधरौष्ठं प्राण्यङ्गत्वादेकवद्भावः (cf. 'द्वन्द्वश्च प्राणितूर्यसेनाङ्गानाम्,' पा. २.४.२)। अधरौष्ठस्पर्शनेन उच्चारः स्यात् । वकारस्य तु ऊर्ध्वदन्ताग्राधरस्पर्शेनोच्चारो भवति । पाणिनीये वकारस्य दन्तोष्ठ्यताया आम्नातत्वात् ।

Note: Here Bhārgava-Bhāskara lists *v* among the *oṣṭhya* sounds. However, he explains that *v* is an exception to other *oṣṭhya* sounds in that its articulator is *ūrdhvadantāgra* "tips of the upper teeth." For his authority, he refers to the *dantauṣṭhya* "labio-dental" classification for *v* in the Pāṇinian tradition. The Pāṇinīya tradition, however, does not clearly distinguish between the *sthāna* and *karaṇa* for *v*. It is curious to note that the text of CA does not have a separate statement, like some other phonetic treatises, concerning the separate *karaṇa* for *v*. This makes us wonder if the original text did conceive of *v* as a *dantauṣṭya* sound. If *v* did not have a separate *karaṇa* of its own, apart from that of the other *oṣṭhya* sounds, and if it was more like the other *oṣṭhya* sounds, then it must have been a bilabial sound, like the English *w*. This may, perhaps, explain why the gap between *v* and *b* seemed much smaller within the Atharvaveda tradition, and a separate treatise listing the words with these two sounds, i.e. the text called Dantyoṣṭhyavidhi, had to be developed within this tradition. Among modern Indian languages, the merger of *v* with *b* is seen more frequently in Bengali and the related eastern languages, and occasionally in the Hindi-speaking area, cf. Hindi *bīs* 'twenty'. The close connection of the Atharvaveda itself with the tradition of Vrātyas and the region of Magadha makes such an articulation of *v* a very old possibility. This may also hint at the eastern origin of the tradition of CA itself, along with that of the Dantyoṣṭhyavidhi, though no manuscripts of the CA have been found in these eastern parts.

१.१.२६. नासिक्यानां नासिका ।

Whitney (1.26). G: 1.1.26.

Translation: For the sounds with the nose as their point of articulation, the nose [is also the articulator].

Note: Most Sanskrit texts do not distinguish between the point of articulation and the articulator for the nasal sounds. However, as seen in CA (1.1.19) and (1.1.25), the CA makes a unique effort to distinguish between the point of articulation and the articulator for each sound, even though, as in the present case, they turn out to be the same. Also, it is not immediately clear what the reference of the term *nāsikya* is, as distinct from that of the term *anunāsika* in the next rule. The commentaries include under the term *nāsikya* sounds which are generally recognized as *anunāsika*, e.g. *ṅ*, *ñ*, *ṇ*, *n*, and *m*. Whitney suggests that the rule should properly apply to "merely the *nāsikya* and the *yamas*." Here, the term *nāsikya* refers to a peculiar nasal sound, which is inserted between an *h* and the following *n*, *ṇ*, or *m*, and is equivalent to a nasalized *h̐* cf. CA (1.4.9: हकारान्नासिक्येन), also see: Allen (1953: 77). However, the tradition conceives it to be a pure nasal sound, rather than as a nasalized *h*. However, what about the *yamas*? If the *yama* corresponding to *k* is a nasalized *k̐*, then how is it possible to say that this sound is a pure nasal sound. For instance, the Nāradīśikṣā (Śikṣāsaṃgraha, p. 428; Allen, 1953: 76) says that the *yama* which comes between a non-nasal stop and a nasal is a nasal sound homorganic with the preceding stop. Thus, it does not make sense to call it a pure nasal.

चतुराध्यायीभाष्य - नासिकास्थानानां वर्णानां नासिका करणं भवति । 'ब्रह्म' (अ.वे. १.१९.४)। 'पयांसि' (अ.वे. १.९.३)। कंखंगंघं । ङञणनमाः ।

'नासिक्ये नासिका स्थानं तथानुस्वार उच्यते ।
यमा वर्गोत्तमाश्चापि यथोक्तं चैव ते मताः ।।'
(= वर्णपटलम्, २३)

Note: The Varṇapaṭala reads *iṣyate* for *ucyate*. Also note that the notation *kaṃ-khaṃ-gaṃ-ghaṃ* in the commentary refers to the so-called *yamas*, or the nasalized 'twins,' i.e. nasalized transitional segments which come after non-nasal stops, before nasals, cf. CA (1.4.8): समानपदेऽनुत्तमात् स्पर्शादुत्तमे यमैर्यथासंख्यम्. Also compare the doctrine of the TPR (21.12): स्पर्शाद-नुत्तमादुत्तमपरादानुपूर्व्यान्नासिक्याः. The TPR actually uses the term *nāsikya* to refer to these sounds, instead of using the term *yama*. This doctrine of *yama* as an additional transitional segment is different from the doctrine found in the RPR (6. verse 8): स्पर्शा यमाननुनासिकाः स्वान् परेषु स्पर्शेष्वनुनासिकेषु, which teaches that non-nasal stops, before nasal stops, are replaced by the corresponding *yama*s. In this procedure, the *yama*s may be said to be nasalized allophones for non-nasal stops, before nasals. I thank George Cardona for bringing this reference to my attention.

भा.भा.वृत्ति - नासिकायां भवा नासिक्याः । ङञणनमअं । वर्गाणां पञ्चमाः अनुस्वारश्च । तेषां मध्ये अनुस्वारस्य नासिकास्थानमुच्चारणे । अन्येषां तु स्वस्ववर्गस्थानं नासिका चेति स्थानद्वयेनोच्चारो भवति । ङस्य जिह्वामूलनासिकम् । ञस्य तालुनासिकम् । णस्य मूर्धनासिकम् । नस्य दन्त-नासिकम् । मस्यौष्ठनासिकमिति ।

Note: Bhārgava-Bhāskara omits the *yama*s from the list of nasal sounds, and this may also be a reflection of his reliance on the late Pāṇinian school, where the *yama*s are not given a proper place. The *yama*s are included neither in the Śivasūtras, nor referred to in the rules of Pāṇini's Aṣṭādhyāyī. Thus, one can conclude that using the Pāṇinian tradition for the elucidation of a Prātiśākhya text is on the whole a regressive development, and this is what we see in the commentary of Bhārgava-Bhāskara. The confusion of the notion of *nāsikya* and *anunāsika* continues in Bhārgava-Bhāskara's commentary.

१.१.२७. अनुनासिकानां मुखनासिकम् ।

Whitney (1.27). G: 1.1.27. P reads मुखनासिका.

Translation: For the nasalized sounds, the oral [organ, as well as,] the nose [are the articulators].

Note: Like several previous rules, e.g. CA (1.1.19, 25-26), this rule makes a vain effort to distinguish between the articulator and the point of articulation for nasalized sounds, and ends up identifying the same organs as both the point of articulation and the articulator. Here, there is also an additional problem, which neither the CA nor the commentators address clearly. What is the distinction between the *nāsikya* sounds and the *anunāsika* sounds? The commentators are clearly confused over this issue.

चतुराध्यायीभाष्य - अनुनासिकस्थानानां वर्णानां मुखनासिकं करणं भवति । 'द्वे चं मे विंशतिश्चं' (अ.वे. ५.१५.२)। 'तिस्रश्चं मे त्रिंशच्चं' (अ.वे. ५.१५.३)। 'चतंस्रश्च मे चत्वारिंशच्चं' (अ.वे. ५.१५.४)। 'पुमांन् पुंसः' (अ.वे. ३.६.१)। 'तत्रं पुंसवंनम्' (अ.वे. ६.११.१)।

'मुखनासिकेन ये वर्णा उच्यन्ते तेऽनुनासिकाः ।
समानास्यप्रयत्ना ये ते सवर्णा इति स्मृताः ॥'
(= वर्णपटलम्, १२)

Note: Interestingly, the only sound included by the CAB under the category of *anunāsika* is the *anusvāra*. It leaves out the nasal vowels and consonants which are generally referred to by this term in the Sanskrit phonetic texts.

Strangely, the CAB uses the word *anunāsikasthāna* as if the word *anunāsika* referred to a point of articulation. There is no such *sthāna*-expression in

Sanskrit, and the Caturādhyāyībhāṣya is simply giving a paraphrase of the expression *anunāsika*, which is comparable to its paraphrases of expressions in earlier rules, cf. *oṣṭhya* = *oṣṭhasthāna*, *dantya* = *dantasthāna*, *nāsikya* = *nāsikāsthāna*.

In this case, majority of the mss. for the Varṇapaṭala (= ABCETU) give the reading *mukhanāsikena*. This is rejected by Bolling and Negelein in favor of the minority reading *mukhanāsike ye varṇā*. With the concurrence of reading from the mss. of the CAB, the reading *mukhanāsikena* gains in probability.

Whether *nāsikā* is a *sthāna* or *karaṇa* for the *anunāsika* sounds is not quite clear from the statement of the rule, and the commentary does not help either. The expression *mukhanāsika* seems to refer to a joint mode of articulation, without making a further distinction between *sthāna* and *karaṇa*. At the same time, it is to be acknowledged that the term is a popular one. It is seen in the cited Śikṣā text, and is also used by Pāṇini in his rule P. 1.1.8 (मुखनासिकावचनोऽनुनासिकः). For a number of sounds, the Apiśaliśikṣā (2.9: शेषाः स्वस्थानकरणाः) openly declares that the *sthāna* and the *karaṇa* is the same organ. Among these are the *kaṇṭhya*, *oṣṭhya*, *nāsikya*, and *anunāsika* sounds.

The Pāṇinian commentators do make a distinction in the status of *nāsikā* in relation to different sounds. For details, see: Deshpande (1975: 11), Bare (1980: 138). The verse cited in the commentary is also important in that it is the only other ancient text, besides Pāṇini 1.1.9 (तुल्यास्यप्रयत्नं सवर्णम्) and the VPR 1.43 (समानस्थानकरणास्यप्रयत्नः सवर्णः), to use the term *āsyaprayatna* in relation to a definition of the term *savarṇa*, see: Deshpande (1975: 92). Verses 13-15 of the Varṇapaṭala are related to *savarṇa* and *savarṇagrahaṇa*:

ह्रस्वो वर्णपरस्तस्य सवर्णस्य च वाचकः ।
ह्रस्वोत्तरस्तु दीर्घोऽपि तस्मात्तस्यैव वाचकः ।।
वर्गान्तरस्तु वर्गादिर्वर्गस्य ग्राहको मतः ।
वर्गाणां च यथासंख्यं प्रथमादित्वमिष्यते ।।
अकारेणोच्यतेऽतस्तु कारो यस्मात्परो भवेत् ।
तस्य तद्ग्रहणम् बोध्यं ककारोऽत्र निदर्शनम् ।।

भा.भा.वृत्ति - अनुनासिकानां स्वराणां तु मुखशब्देन मुखान्तर्गतकण्ठादिस्थानानि ज्ञेयानि तानि नासिकया सहितानि स्थानानि ज्ञेयानि तद्यथा - अकारस्य कण्ठनासिकम् । इकारस्य तालुनासिकम् । उकारस्य ओष्ठनासिकम् । ऋकारस्य

मूर्धनासिकम् । ऌवर्णस्य दन्तनासिकम् । एऐ अनयोः कण्ठ-तालुनासिकम् । ओऔ अनयोः कण्ठोष्ठनासिकम् । यकारस्य तालुनासिकम् । वकारस्य दन्तोष्ठनासिकम् । लकारस्य दन्तनासिकमिति । 'महाँ असि' (अ.वे. १.२०.४) । 'आ बंभूवाँ३' (अ.वे. १०.२.२८)। 'पणीँरभि' (अ.वे. ५.११.७)। 'दस्यूँरुत' (अ.वे. ४.३२.६)। 'पुरुष्टुतँ एकः' (अ.वे. २०.६१.६)। 'ॐ इति' (पद, अ.वे. १३.४.५)। 'नॄँः प्रणेता' ('प्रणेत्रम्,' ऋग्वेदखिलानि, प्रैषाध्यायः, १.३)। ऋग्वेदे । 'सँय्यंतम्' (अ.वे. १०.४.८)। 'सँव्वत्सरः' (अ.वे. ३.१०.८)। 'जिगीवाँल्लक्षम्' (अ.वे. २०.३४.४)।

Note: Bhārgava-Bhāskara says that nasal *e* and *ai* have *kaṇṭhatālu-nāsikam* as their points of articulation, implying that the non-nasal ones have *kaṇṭhatālu* as their points of articulation. The inclusion of *e*, and similarly the inclusion of *o*, among sounds with double points of articulation is a relatively late phenomenon seen mostly in texts which follow the Pāṇinīyaśikṣā. Bhārgava-Bhāskara on the next rule actually quotes the versified Pāṇinīyaśikṣā to this effect. It is not clear why Bhārgava-Bhāskara does not list the nasal stops under the category of *anunāsika*. His description of these sounds given in the commentary under the previous rule exactly matches the description of *anunāsika* sounds given here.

१.१.२८. रेफस्य दन्तमूलानि ।

Whitney (1.28). G: 1.1.28.

Translation: For *r*, the roots of the teeth (i.e. alveolar ridge) [is the articulator].

Note: This rule indicates that the text of the CA itself is confused over the notions of the point of articulation (*sthāna*) and the articulator (*karaṇa*). Generally, the articulator is the moving organ and the point of articulation is the relatively stationary part in the oral track. Here, one would naturally expect a portion of the tongue, such as the tip of the tongue, to be the articulator, while the alveolar ridge or the roots of the teeth would be the point of articulation. The Śikṣā verse cited by the CAB correctly describes *dantamūla* as a point of articulation (*sthāna*). On the other hand, the CAB itself is philologically accurate in interpreting the CA rule to mean that *dantamūla* is an articulator (*karaṇa*).

चतुराध्यायीभाष्य - रेफस्य दन्तमूलानि करणं भवति । 'शरदः पुरूची रायः' (अ.वे. २.१३.३)। 'पुना रक्तं वासः' (not in known Vedic texts, quoted in the KV on P.1.3.14: *ro ri*)। 'पुना रूपाणि' (अ.वे. १.२४.४)। 'जघ्नू रक्षांसि' (अ.वे. ४.३७.१)। 'अग्नी रक्षांसि' (अ.वे. ८.३.२६)। 'अग्नी रक्षः' (अ.वे. १२.३.४३)।

'रेफस्य दन्तमूलानि प्रत्यग्वा तेभ्य इष्यते ।
इति स्थानानि वर्णानां कीर्तितानि यथाक्रमम् ॥

अपर आह -

हनुमूले तु (Whitney: -लेषु) रेफस्य दन्तमूलेषु वा पुनः ।
प्रत्यग्वा दन्तमूलेभ्यो मूर्धन्य इति चापरे ॥'
(= वर्णपटलम्, २४-२५)

Note: Even the words अपर आह are found in the Varṇapaṭala. This may be an indication that the Varṇapaṭala is itself a conflation of earlier texts. The Varṇapaṭala reads हनुमूले तु रेफः स्यात् for हनुमूले तु रेफस्य.

The example पुना रक्तं वासः cited by the CAB is not found in the Vulgate of the AV, nor in any other Saṃhitā, Brāhmaṇa, Āraṇyaka, or Upaniṣad. Surya Kanta (APR, Introduction, p. 40) suggests that this may have occurred in the genuine Śaunakīya recension of the AV, and that the Vulgate is not the genuine Śaunakīya recension. However, his example is cited in the KV on P. 1.3.14 (रो रि).

भा.भा.वृत्ति - रेफो मूर्धन्यः । दन्तमूलशब्दः सामीप्यं द्योतयति बहुवचननिर्देशात् । दन्तमूलस्थानं मूर्धस्थानं च तयोर्मध्ये रेफोच्चारणस्थानं ज्ञेयं तकारटकारोच्चारणस्थानयोर्मध्यस्थानमित्यर्थः । सन्ध्यक्षराणि तु स्थानद्वयोच्चारितानि

ज्ञेयानि । तथा च पाणिनीये - 'एऐ तु कण्ठतालव्या ओऔ कण्ठोष्ठजौ स्मृतौ' ।। (पाणिनीयशिक्षा, १८) इति शिक्षायां पठितम् । अथ प्रयत्नानाह -

Note: The rule to says that *dantamūla* is the *karaṇa* for *r*. On the other hand, Bhārgava-Bhāskara disregards the context of *karaṇa* for this rule, and treats *dantamūla* not only as a *sthāna*, but as an indication of the vicinity of the real *sthāna* for this sound, namely *mūrdhan*. Treating *r* as a *mūrdhanya*, when the rule clearly says that it is *dantamūlīya*, shows how the characterizations in the Pāṇinīyaśikṣā override the explicit statements of the CA. The Śikṣā cited in the CAB reports that there are different views regarding the point of articulation for *r* and that *mūrdhanya* and *dantamūlīya* are some of the alternative classifications for it. It does not try to interpret the term *dantamūlīya* as a near synonym for *mūrdhanya*, and to this extent, it shows that it is not as much influenced by the Pāṇinian school.

Allen (1953: 54) says that while the Pāṇinīyaśikṣā describes *r* as being a retroflex sound, "the Prātiśākhyas generally require an alveolar articulation (which agrees with the present pronunciation of Sanskrit and the general practice of the modern Indo-Aryan languages)." There are two points to be noted here. The first point, as brought out by Allen (1953: 53), is that *r* (as well as *r̥*) functions phonologically as a member of the retroflex class, in spite of the probable dialectal variation in its phonetic value. I have suggested (Deshpande, 1979: 284) that it is this phonological retroflexion of *r* and *r̥* which was eventually confused with phonetic retroflexion in later times, perhaps under the pressure of facilitating grammatical procedures like substitutions being decided in terms of maximal featural similarity between an original item and its substitute (cf. P.1.1.50: स्थानेऽन्तरतमः). The second point to note is that the notion of *karaṇa* receives only scant attention in the later Pāṇinian tradition, as compared to the notion of *sthāna*. This is also because the maximum featural similarity (*āntaratamya*) between substitutes and their originals is decided in terms of the *sthāna*, but not the *karaṇa*. With a diminishing understanding of factors like *karaṇa*, the later Pāṇinian tradition in fact becomes much less interested in the true phonetic descriptions of the Sanskrit sounds, except as required to facilitate the procedures of *savarṇagrahaṇa* and *āntaratamya*.

The verse 'एऐ तु कण्ठ्यतालव्यौ ...' is also found in the Śaunakaśikṣā (p. 15).

१.१.२९. स्पृष्टं स्पर्शानां करणम् ।

Whitney (1.29). G: 1.1.29.

Translation: In the case of stops (lit. 'contact sounds'), the articulator is in contact [with the point of articulation].

चतुराध्यायीभाष्य - स्पृष्टं स्पर्शानां करणं भवति । कचटतपाः ।

'स्वरमध्ये डढौ यत्र पीडनं तत्र वर्जयेत् ।
मृदुप्रयत्नावुच्चार्याविडां (अ.वे. ५.१२.८) मीढं (अ.वे. ४.२९.४) निदर्शनम् ॥' (Source?)

Note: The Śikṣā verse cited by the CAB says that, in intervocalic contexts, the sounds *ḍ* and *ḍh* are not to be pronounced as normal *sparśa* sounds with full contact of the articulator and the point of articulation, but should be pronounced without pressing the articulator against the point of articulation, and that they should be pronounced with a light articulatory effort. This description makes these sounds into flaps, similar to the intervocalic *ḷ* and *ḷh* of the Ṛgveda. This doctrine is not known to the CA itself, and may have developed later on, perhaps under the influence of the RV tradition. It is also not recorded by the commentary of Bhārgava-Bhāskara, and it is not known to the late text, the Māṇḍūkīśikṣā. It is not clear if the presence of such a description of *ḍ* and *ḍh* points to a distinct source for the ancient Śikṣā cited by the CAB.

भा.भा.वृत्ति - कादयो मावसानाः पञ्चविंशतिः स्पर्शाः । तेषां करणमाभ्यन्तरप्रयत्नः स्पृष्टसंज्ञको ज्ञेयः । पदान्तं स्पृशन्ति ते स्पर्शाः । अत एव तेषां स्पृष्टं करणम् ।

Note: The commentary of Bhārgava-Bhāskara uses the term *prayatna* to refer to different modes of contact between the articulator and the point of articulation. This is the meaning of this term in the Pāṇinian school. On the other hand, the term probably meant articulatory effort in a generic sense, and this is the sense seen in the term *mṛduprayatna* used in the verse cited in the CAB. A similar meaning for the term *prayatna* must be seen in the term *laghu-*

prayatnatara used by Pāṇini (8.3.18: व्योर्लघुप्रयत्नतरः शाकटायनस्य). It seems likely that the term *prayatna* had the same generic meaning of articulatory effort in the term *āsyaprayatna* used by both Pāṇini (1.1.9: तुल्यास्यप्रयत्नं सवर्णम्) and the Śikṣā text quoted the CAB on CA 1.1.27.

१.१.३०. ईषत्स्पृष्टमन्तस्थानाम् ।

Whitney (1.30). G: 1.1.30. I: 30. G alone reads: °मन्तःस्थानाम्, and Whitney has the same reading.

> **Translation:** In the case of semi-vowels, [the articulator] is in slight contact [with the point of articulation].
>
> ***चतुराध्यायीभाष्य*** - ईषत्स्पृष्टमन्तस्थानां करणं भवति ।
>
> ***भा.भा.वृत्ति*** - **(ईषत्स्पृष्टमन्तस्थानाम्)** पदस्यान्तस्तिष्ठन्ति न तु पदान्ते अतोऽन्तस्थाः यरलवाः । अन्तस्थशब्दः स्त्रीपुंसलिङ्गः । तेषां वा तासां वा अन्तःस्थानां करणमाभ्यन्तरप्रयत्नः ईषत्स्पृष्टो ज्ञेयः । पदान्तविरामे नैव दृश्यन्ते । क्षैप्रविसर्गसन्धौ ईषन्मनाक् पदान्तं स्पृशन्ति । अत उक्तमीषत्स्पृष्टमिति ।

Note: It is not clear whether the original term was *anta-sthā* or *antaḥ-sthā*. The problem becomes more complicated because an underlying *antaḥ+sthā* can as well result in the surface form *antasthā* in certain dialects of Sanskrit. As the Aitareya-Āraṇyaka (3.2.1) informs us, the earlier categories recognized by its author's tradition were only three, i.e. vowels (*svara*), stops (*sparśa*), and spirants (*ūṣman*). This text informs us that the scholar Hrasva Māṇḍūkeya proposed the addition of *antaḥsthā*, and that this new addition was not acceptable to its author. One possible explanation of the term *anta-sthā* might refer to this fact of this category being the last addition. The reading *antaḥ-sthā* has been discussed at length by Allen (1953: 29): "The Sanskrit term for the category of semivowels is *anta(ḥ)sthā*, lit. 'standing between'. It is tempting, and has tempted modern commentators, to interpret this term as referring to the postulated 'intermediate' degree of contact discussed above, or, like our term 'semi-vowel', to their phonological alternation. The ending *-sthā*, 'standing', however, is more readily applicable to the place which these letters occupy in the alphabet, viz. between the stops and the fricatives; and it is doubtful whether the ancient sources provide evidence for any other interpretation." Of course, Allen does not consider the reading *anta-sthā*, which is uniformly used by all the manuscripts of the CA. It is, however, clear that the commentary of Bhārgava-Bhāskara explains this word as if it were *antaḥ-sthā*.

Allen (1953: 27-28) further discusses the question of whether a separate *prayatna* for semi-vowels, apart from that of the vowels is justified. Apparently, it seems at first glance like a failure of the Indian phoneticians that they do not see the distinction between vowels and semi-vowels as being phonological, than phonetic. However, Allen appropriately refers to palatographic studies of Indian languages which justify the claim of the Indian phoneticians that the semi-vowels involve a slight degree of contact between the articulator and the point of articulation, as compared to that of the vowels. Also, one should remember that the Indian phoneticians were aware of the various degrees of contact involved in the pronunciation of sounds like *y* and *v*, depending upon whether they occurred word-initially or medially. Thus, the use of expressions like *ati-saṃspr̥ṣṭa-prayatna*, *laghu-prayatna-tara*, and *mr̥du-prayatna* should be sufficient to indicate the fineness of their observations. Many of these are justified by the palatographic evidence, as well as by what happens to these sounds in Prākrit languages. One should also keep in mind that the distinction between 'phonological' versus 'phonetic' is a particularly Western distinction, and while there are echoes of this distinction in the concerns of the Indian grammarians and phoneticians, one should not expect to see it overtly implemented in their works.

The Māṇḍūkīśikṣā does not know the categories of *īṣatspr̥ṣṭa* and *īṣad-vivr̥ta*. It says that the *karaṇa* for stops is *spr̥ṣṭa*, while for the semi-vowels, it is the opposite, i.e. *aspr̥ṣṭa*, see: स्पर्शानां करणं स्पृष्टमन्तःस्थानामतोऽन्यथा (verse 70, Śikṣāsaṃgraha, p. 469).

Bhārgava-Bhāskara's explanation of the *īṣatspr̥ṣṭa* as 'touching (= occurring in) the word-final position lightly (i.e. only as a result of certain external sandhi operations),' is indeed far from what is intended by the text of the CA.

१.१.३१. ऊष्मणां विवृतं च ।

Whitney (1.31). N, L, O: उ for ऊ. A, B, L: °ष्माणां विवृतमं. G: 1.1.31. O: °विवृत्तं च.

Translation: For the spirants, [the articulator remains] also [slightly?] open [or open, besides being in slight contact?].

चतुराध्यायीभाष्य - उष्मणां विवृतं च करणं भवति । ईषत्स्पृष्टं च । शषसहाः ।

भा.भा.वृत्ति - **(ऊष्मणां विवृतम्)** शषसहा ऊ(G: उ)-ष्माणः । पदान्ते स्वरूपेण न दृश्यन्ते । क्वचित्कवर्गटवर्ग-तवर्गतां विसर्गत्वं च संप्राप्य विकृता भवन्ति । 'ऊष रुजा-याम्' (पाणिनीयधातुपाठ, ६८३)। ऊष्माणो विकृता रुग्णा इत्यर्थः । 'विड्भ्यः' (अ.वे. ३.३.३)। 'षट्' (अ.वे. ४.११.१)। 'माड्भ्यः' (अ.वे. ३.१०.१०)। 'गोधुक्' (अ.वे. ७.७३.६)। 'दिग्भ्यः' (अ.वे. ४.४०.८)। 'तुराषाट्' (अ.वे. २.५.३)। एषामूष्मणामाभ्यन्तरप्रयत्नः विवृतसंज्ञः । मुखस्य विवरणाद्विवृतमिति संज्ञा ।

Note: The interpretation of this rule given in the CAB concludes that the articulator of the *ūṣman*s is both *vivṛta* and *īṣatspṛṣṭa*. Following this commentary, Whitney says: "the organ is both in partial contact and open - a rather awkward way of saying, apparently, that its position is neither very close nor very open." Whitney does not reject such an interpretation, and, with the word *ca* in the rule, this is indeed one of the ways to render this rule. Allen (1953: 26) notes that the notion that the spirants do involve some contact and some openness is justifiable on the basis of texts like TPR (ii.45), as well as on the basis of modern palatographic studies of Indian language. TPR (ii.45) suggests that the spirants are produced at the same points of articulation as the homorganic stops, but that in the case of the spirants, the middle of the articulator remains in an open position (करणमध्यं तु विवृतम्).

On the other hand, if we remove the *ca* from this rule following some of the mss. which do not have it, and if we follow Bhārgava-Bhāskara's reading of the rule and its interpretation, we can take this rule to mean that the articulator remains in an open position in the pronunciation of spirants, and, then, by the next rule, so also for vowels. Such a reading is also justified in view of a likely citation of this rule in the MB (on P.1.1.10).

Then there is the possibility that only the word *īṣat*, and not *īṣatspṛṣṭa*, continues into this rule from the previous rule by the force of *ca*. This would give us *īṣadvivṛta* as the mode of articulation for spirants, which accords well with some of the late texts in the Pāṇinian tradition, cf. Laghusiddhāntakaumudī, on P.1.1.9 (ईषद्विवृतमूष्मणां, विवृतं स्वराणाम्). Such an interpretation is suggested by a likely quotation of this rule in the MB (on P.1.1.10), and Patañjali's interpretation of it. Patañjali says: विवृतमूष्मणामीषदित्येव अनुवर्तते. If one accepts this interpretation, then one would have to say that, after this rule, *īṣat* is discontinued, and only the word *vivr̥ta* continues into the next rule describing vowels. This is what Patañjali has proposed. Such an interpretation is also supported by the interpretive maxim: चानुकृष्टं नोत्तरत्र, cf. Paribhāṣendu-śekhara, Paribhāṣā 78.

While the versified Pāṇinīyaśikṣā (verse 21) says that vowels and spirants share the same open (*vivr̥ta*) articulatory effort (स्वराणामूष्मणां चैव विवृतं करणं स्मृतम्), the prose version of the Pāṇinīyaśikṣā (3.6-8) reflects the unresolved situation as described above: ईषद्विवृतकरणा ऊष्माणः, विवृतकरणा वा, विवृत-करणाः स्वराः. One may note with interest the fact that the Māṇḍūkīśikṣā, which is clearly later than the CA, does not seem to know the distinction between *vivr̥ta* and *īṣadvivr̥ta*. It ascribes *vivr̥ta* to both vowels and spirants (विवृतं च स्वरोष्मणाम्, verse 70, p. 469).

As Whitney himself notes, the TPR (ii.44, 45) and RPR (xiii.3, r.11) holds that both spirants and vowels do not involve contact (*aspr̥ṣṭa*). Such also must be Pāṇini's own view, i.e. that the vowels and spirants had the same mode of approximation of the articulator. Only with such an assumption can one explain the formulation of P.1.1.10 (नाज्झलौ). It prohibits homogeneity (*sāvarṇya*) between vowels and consonants. However, the only possibility for vowels and consonants sharing the same point of articulation and oral effort is for vowels and spirants.

१.१.३२. स्वराणां च ।

Whitney (1.32). G: 1.1.32. No such Sūtra in A, B, L, O.

Translation: Also for vowels, [the articulator remains open].

Note: See the Note on the previous rule for a detailed discussion of textual problems.

चतुराध्यायीभाष्य - स्वराणां विवृतं करणं भवति । अआ-आ३ इईई३ उऊऊ३ ऋॠॠ३ ऌॡॡ३ ए[ए३] ऐऐ३ ओ[ओ३] औऔ३ ।

भा.भा.वृत्ति - अत्र स्वराः समानसंज्ञाः सन्ध्यक्षराणि च । अइउऋऌएऐओऔ । एषां नवानां स्वराणां च विवृतसंज्ञः प्रयत्नो ज्ञेयः ।

Note: Note that both the commentaries list the short *a* among vowels while stating that the effort of the vowels is *vivṛta*. This, of course, has to be negated in view of CA (1.1.36) which says that the effort for *a* is *saṃvṛta*.

१.१.३३. एकेऽस्पृष्टम् ।

Whitney (1.33). G: 1.1.33. A, B, and L: no such Sūtra. G and K show the Avagraha.

> **Translation:** Some hold that, [for vowels, the articulator is] not in contact [with the point of articulation, in contrast with saying that the articulator is in an open position].

चतुराध्यायीभाष्य - एकेऽस्पृष्टं स्वराणां करणं ब्रुवते । अपरे विवृतम् । एतान्येवोदाहरणानि ।

Note: Whitney on this rule does not read the Avagraha either in the rule or in the commentary and this has misled him into reading the text as एके स्पृष्टम् and translating it as: "Some consider it as forming a contact." He believed that the rule and the commentator are citing an opinion that "in the utterance of the vowels the organs are in contact; others that they remain open." This interpretation led him to comment: "The former opinion is too obviously and grossly incorrect, one would think, to be worth quoting." Allen (1953: 28) seems to take the reading given in Whitney's edition seriously, and tries to find other evidence from phonetic treatises which say that even vowels involve some contact: "It is presumably to isolated statements such as these (= TPR ii.24, Vyāsaśikṣā 284) that the AP (= CA) is referring when it gives as the opinion of some sources that contact is involved in the vowels, an opinion which Whitney impatiently dismisses as '... too obviously and grossly incorrect, one would think, to be worth quoting.'"

In fact, the entire discussion by Whitney and Allen is now outdated, and one must read the rule as *eke+aspṛṣṭam*, and this is supported by several manuscripts with a clear *avagraha*. This is also clear from both the commentaries. The alternatives are the *aspṛṣta* 'non-contact' view, versus the *vivṛta* 'openness' view, and this makes perfect sense. For details on this division of opinion, see: Deshpande (1976a). The main advantage in choosing the *vivṛta* classification over the *aspṛṣṭa* classification is that, while it is difficult to think of gradations of *aspṛṣṭa* 'non-contact,' it is perfectly possible to think of gradations of *vivṛta* 'open.' Such gradations are seen in the use of the terms *īṣadvivṛta* 'slightly open,' *vivṛtatara* 'more open,' and *vivṛtatama* 'most open.' While the notion of *īṣadvivṛta* may have been merely alluded to in CA (1.1.31), the next rule, i.e. CA (1.1.34), actually uses the term *vivṛtatama*. It thus makes sense to conclude that the *vivṛta* classification was the preferred way for the CA, but it wishes to record the *aspṛṣṭa* alternative upheld by other traditions.

भा.भा.वृत्ति - मुख्याः आचार्याः स्वरमात्रस्य अस्पृष्टं करणमाहुः । न स्पृशति परस्परमोष्ठद्वयम् । मुखमुद्रणं न भवतीत्यर्थः । मुखस्य विवरणे स एवार्थः । एवं च विवृतस्यैवापरपर्यायः अस्पृष्टमिति । स्वराणां पृथक्त्वज्ञानाय असन्देहार्थं करणस्य नामान्तरमुक्तम् । यद्वा अस्पृष्टम् । ईषत्स्पृष्टशब्दात्स्पृष्टशब्दाभावं कृत्वा चकाराद्विवृतमनुवर्त्य ईषद्विवृतमिति स्वराणां प्रयत्नो ज्ञेयः । अयमर्थ एव समीचीनः बहुग्रन्थेष्वपि ईषद्विवृतदर्शनात् । विरामे प्रयत्नविशेषमाह ।

Note: While Bhārgava-Bhāskara is correct in saying that the term *īṣadvivṛta* occurs in a number of texts on Sanskrit grammar and phonetics, he is alone in suggesting that this term refers to the effort for vowels. Such an interpretation cannot be correct. It is also clear that Bhārgava-Bhāskara does not understand the meaning of the term *aspṛṣṭa*. It does not refer to the lips not touching each other or the mouth not closing during the pronunciation of vowels. It rather refers to the fact that the articulator does not touch the point of articulation in the pronunciation of vowels, but only approximates it. The TPR (ii.31-34: स्वराणां यत्रोपसंहारस्तत्स्थानम्; यदुपसंहरति तत्करणम्; अन्येषां तु यत्र स्पर्शनं तत्स्थानम्; येन स्पर्शयति तत्करणम्) uses the term *upasaṃhāra* "approximation/approaching" for this phenomenon, in contrast with the notion of contact (*sparśa*). The RPR (13.11: स्वरानुस्वारोष्मणामस्पृष्टं स्थितम्) uses the term *aspṛṣṭa*, while the Pāṇinian tradition generally uses the term *vivṛta*.

१.१.३४. एकारौकारयोर्विवृततमम् ।

Whitney (1.34), E, F (orig), H, I (orig), J (corr), M, N: एका°. D, J (orig): °र्विवृतमं. F (corr), G, I (corr), K: ऐकारौकारयो°. F (corr), G, I (corr): एकारौकारयोर्विवृततरमैकारौकारयोर्विवृततमम् । G: 1.1.34. A, B, and L: no such Sūtra. O: विवृत्ततमं.

Translation: For *e* and *o*, [the articulator remains in] the most open [position].

चतुराध्यायीभाष्य **-** एकारौकारयोर्विवृततमं करणं भवति। 'एकें तरन्ति' (अ.वे. ६.१२२.२)। 'ओकों अस्य' (अ.वे. ५.२२.५)।

भा.भा.वृत्ति **- (एकारौकारयोर्विवृततरमैकारौकारयोर्विवृत-तमम्)** एकारश्च ओकारश्च अनयोः विरामे प्रयत्नः विवृत-तरो ज्ञेयः । ऐकारश्च औकारश्चानयोस्तु करणं विवृततमं ज्ञेयम् । सूत्रेषु स्पृष्टादीनां क्लीबता तु करणशब्दस्य विशेषण-त्वात् बोध्या ।

Note: The text of this rule and the next rule raises some important questions. The fact that the older commentary, the CAB, supports a version of this rule which deals only with *e* and *o*, and not with *ai* and *au*, makes one support the reading as given here as the older and the original reading. In comparison with other vowels, the vowels *e* and *o* are said to be most open (*vivṛtatama*), and the next rule says that the effort for *ā* is even more open than that. The vowels *ai* and *au* are excluded from this discussion, not necessarily because they are less open, but because they are held to be *dvivarṇa* sounds, i.e. combinations of two vowels each, and hence they are not separately discussed. This must be the original situation.

Later on, as indicated by the later commentaries, these statements were modified to reflect further gradations. Thus, the version of these rules found in the late commentary of Bhārgava-Bhāskara says: *e* and *o* are more open, *ai* and *au* are most open, and *ā* is even more open than that. This version is supported by the Āpiśaliśikṣā, and the prose versions of the Pāṇinīyaśikṣā. The fact that the CAB does not yet show the impact of these other Pāṇinian sources perhaps indicates its relatively early age. The later commentaries are explicit Pāṇinian interpretations of the CA.

One should note that Patañjali himself does not use the notion of *vivṛtatama*, though several Pāṇinian commentators ascribe it to him, cf. Bare (1980: 87), Deshpande (1975: 35). Patañjali differentiates *e* and *o* from *ai* and *au* in a different way. For him, the components of *e* and *o* are thoroughly fused (*praśliṣṭa*) with each other. On the other hand, *ai* and *au* are true composite sounds (*samāhāravarṇau*), cf. एवमप्यवर्णस्य एङोश्च सवर्णसंज्ञा प्राप्नोति । प्रश्लिष्टावर्णावेतौ । अवर्णस्य तर्ह्यैचोश्च सवर्णसंज्ञा प्राप्नोति । विवृततरावर्णावेतौ ।, MB (MLBD edn.), Vol. I, Sec. I, p. 62; and that the components of *ai* and *au*, i.e. *a*, *i*, and *u*, are *vivṛtatara* 'more open', cf. यदत्रावर्णं विवृततरं तदन्यस्मादवर्णाद्ये अपीवर्णोवर्णे विवृततरे ते अन्याभ्यामिवर्णोवर्णाभ्याम्, MB (ibid.), p. 84. Also: इमावैचौ समाहारवर्णौ मात्रावर्णस्य मात्रेवर्णोवर्णयोः, MB (ibid), p. 78.

This discussion offers an important insight into what probably happened to the Sanskrit phonetic traditions in later times. If indeed the sounds *ai* and *au* are true diphthongs, or composed of two *varṇa*s (*dvivarṇa*) as the ancient Indian tradition calls them, then it makes no sense to ascribe *vivṛtatama* effort to these sounds, as their effort can only be the effort of the individual components. The description *vivṛtatama* seems to suggest a more unitary character to these sounds, which is not justifiable in terms of the ancient *dvivarṇa* characterization, but makes sense if the pronunciation of these sounds was something like what it is in modern standard Hindi. In modern standard Hindi, a Sanskrit word like *maithilī* is pronounced with the first vowel being almost equivalent to that in the English word 'at.' This may have been the phonetic basis for saying that *ai* and *au* are *vivṛtatama* sounds. Such early monophthongization of *ai* and *au*, at least in certain dialects, may be suggested by the fact that Sanskrit *ai* and *au* are reduced to *e* and *o* in Prakrits, cf. Sanskrit *maitreya* > Pāli *metteya*.

The other reason to distinguish between the efforts of *e* and *ai*, and *o* and *au*, is that the later tradition considers these sounds to be *kaṇṭhatālavya* and *kaṇṭhauṣṭhya* respectively. Without the differentiation between their efforts, these sounds would become *savarṇa*s with each other, and that would cause a great deal of confusion. Thus, it is possible that such a phonological reasoning may have led the later grammarians to distinguish between the efforts of these sounds.

The importance of the original reading of this rule lies in that the older phonetic texts consider *e* and *o* to be essentially monophthongal like *i* and *u*. In that case, how would one distinguish *i* from *e*, and *u* from *o*? Such a necessity seems to have led to the differentiation in the degree of openness found in this rule and the next. The fact that the CA talks only about *e* and *o* should be taken as an indication of the monophthongal pronunciation for these vowels, and their inclusion in the category of *sandhyakṣara* essentially shows how the levels of phonetic and phonological considerations were blurred into each other. The possibility of such further differentiation in the degree of openness (*vivṛta*) makes this alternative more popular in later phonetic texts as compared to the undifferentiated category of non-contact (*aspṛṣṭa*), which in all likelihood is the earlier categorization.

The lack of finer distinctions between the effort of vowels and sibilants forced Pāṇini to construct an explicit rule prohibiting the impending homogeneity of vowels and consonants, i.e. P.1.1.10 (नाज्झलौ). If Pāṇini did not differentiate between the degree of openness between vowels and sibilants, it seems most unlikely that he differentiated between the degree of openness between the various vowels. Problems created by such a lack of finer differentiation must have led later grammarians and phoneticians to come up with finer distinctions. Thus, the emergence of these finer distinctions in the degree of openness are in all probability related to the emergence of careful thought regarding problems in the application of homogeneity and sound-substitution being decided in terms of featural proximity between the substitute and the original. This shows the possibility that phonological considerations may have led to further developments of phonetic classifications. Later commentators in the Pāṇinian tradition itself have often advocated the position that it is a better thing to accept a finer sub-classification of openness, and not worry about keeping P.1.1.10 (नाज्झलौ), cf. Deshpande (1975: 35, 170-171, notes 121-122).

१.१.३५. ततोऽप्याकारस्य ।

Whitney (1.35). G: 1.1.35.

Translation: [The articulator] for *ā* [remains in an] even more [open position].

चतुराध्यायीभाष्य - ततोऽप्याकारस्य विवृततमं करणं भवति । 'आशांनाम्' (अ.वे. १.३१.१)। 'शालांयाः' (अ.वे. ९.३.१)।

भा.भा.वृत्ति - पूर्वं स्वराणां सामान्यादाकारस्य ईषद्विवृतः प्रयत्न उक्त एव । विरामे प्रयत्नमाह । ततोऽपि पूर्वोक्तप्रयत्ना-दपि अधिकं करणमाकारस्य विरामे स्यात् । अधि(ति?)-विवृतमित्यर्थः ।

Note: It is interesting to note that the text of the CA moves from *vivr̥ta* to *vivr̥tatama* to 'even more open than that.' One would expect perhaps the use of *vivr̥tatara* to describe the position for *e* and *o*, and *vivr̥tatama* to describe the position for *ā*. This felt gap in the terminology is made up by the later version of the previous rule found in Bhārgava-Bhāskara's commentary: *e* and *o* are *vivr̥tatara* 'more open,' *ai* and *au* are *vivr̥tatama* 'most open,' and *ā* is even more open than that. As for Pāṇini, it seems that he probably did not distinguish the degrees of openness, beyond assuming that the short *a* was a *saṃvr̥ta* 'close' sound, in contrast with other vowels which were all open.

१.१.३६. संवृतोऽकारः ।

Whitney (1.36). G: 1.1.36. G and K show the Avagraha.

Translation: The sound *a* is a [relatively] close[r vowel, in comparison with *ā* which is an open vowel].

Note: Note the different syntax of this rule. In the previous rules, words like *vivr̥ta* are neuter words, because they are used to modify the word *karaṇam*, which continues throughout this section. However, here the word *saṃvr̥ta* is used as a qualification of *akāraḥ*, and is, therefore, a masculine word. One can also raise another interesting question. When we say that *ā* is a most open sound, and that *a* is a closer sound, this openness or closeness, as a feature of the *karaṇa* refers not to the openness or closeness of the glottal aperture, but to the gap between the articulator and the point of articulation. For the vowels *a* and *ā*, however, the point of articulation given is *kaṇṭha*, and the articulator mentioned is the lower part of *kaṇṭha*. What sort of openness are we talking about that distinguishes between *a* and *ā*? It cannot be the relative openness of the glottal aperture. It must be the wider opening of the oral cavity, i.e. wider opening of the mouth. This point has not been discussed clearly by any Sanskrit text.

चतुराध्यायीभाष्य - संवृतकरणः अकारो भवति । 'अश्वः' (अ.वे. २.३०.५)। 'अजः' (अ.वे. ४.१४.१)। 'अग्निः' (अ.वे. १.७.४)।

भा.भा.वृत्ति - पूर्वं विवृतप्रयत्नः अकारस्योक्तः । स तु अविरामे ज्ञेयः । अवसाने तु अकारस्य संवृतप्रयत्नो ज्ञातव्यः। तथैवाह भगवान् पाणिनिः 'अ अ' (पा. ८.४.६८) इति । अ अकारः अवसाने अ इति भवति । संवृतो भवतीत्यर्थः । ननु अकारस्य द्विविधः प्रयत्न उक्तः स तु कथमनुभूयेत । श्रोतव्यम् । अविरामे अकारः प्रयुज्यते तदा मुखं विवृतमुद्धाटितं स्यात् । विरामे तु अधः स्थितस्यौष्ठस्य द्रोणिकां कृत्वाऽधोदन्तपङ्क्तिमन्तर्धायोच्चारयेत् । स संवृतसंज्ञः । 'अग्निम्' (अ.वे. १.६.२)। 'च' (अ.वे. १.५.३) ।

Note: The Pāṇinian tradition holds that the short *a* is a *saṃvṛta* sound, while the long *ā* is a *vivṛta* sound. The CA classification is somewhat similar. However, since the CA does not present a featural definition of the notion of *savarṇa*, there is no dilemma within this text about how to have *a* and *ā* become *savarṇa*s of each other, in spite of their featural difference. Pāṇini was indeed faced with such a dilemma, which he sought to resolve by artificially treating (or pronouncing?) *a* as a *vivṛta* sound within the grammatical derivational process, and reinstating the object language *saṃvṛta a* as the last step of all derivations, cf. P.8.4.68 (*a a*). The Śikṣā text quoted by the CAB (on CA 1.1.27), i.e. समानास्यप्रयत्ना ये ते सवर्णा इति स्मृताः, defines the notion of *savarṇa* in a way similar to that of Pāṇini 1.1.9 (तुल्यास्यप्रयत्नं सवर्णम्). However, we have no information on how such a text would resolve the problem of homogeneity between *a* and *ā*. One should also note the interesting explanation given by Bhārgava-Bhāskara. He says that the vowel *a* is pronounced as an open (*vivṛta*) sound in non-final positions, but that it is pronounced as a close (*saṃvṛta*) sound when it occurs in the word-final position. While he describes openness as wider opening of the mouth (मुखं विवृतमुद्धाटितम्), the only such explantion known to me, his explanation of *saṃvṛta* is even more graphic: "having turned the lower lip into the shape of a cup (i.e. having rounded lower lip?), one should cover the lower teeth." Such a description of a close *a* takes it closer to the pronunciation of the Bengali *a* (= *ŏ*). It is very doubtful if the explanation of *saṃvr̥ta* given by Bhārgava-Bhāskara is historically accurate as an interpretation of the CA or of Pāṇini. However, it does seem to have been based on some actual regional trait of pronunciation. This pronunciation of *a* must be clearly differentiated from a truly neutral position of all organs advocated for *a* by texts like TPR (1.113), cf. Allen (1953: 59).

१.१.३७. संस्पृष्टरेफमृवर्णम् ।

Whitney (1.37). G: 1.1.37.

Translation: [The members of] the *r̥* class, [i.e. *r̥*, *r̥̄*, and *r̥̄3*, are] fused with [consonantal] *r*.

Note: The above rule does not clearly define the nature of the fusion of the constituent elements. According to the general description in Sanskrit texts, in the constitution of a *r̥* vowel, a consonantal *r* is flanked by two fractional vowels, i.e. *ərə*. The actual phonetic quality of the vocalic fractions was probably determined by the consonants in the vicinity, though most Sanskrit texts tend to look at these vocalic fractions as partial *a* vowels. Some Sanskrit texts give more precise proportions of the vocalic and consonantal components for *r̥* vowels. Thus, for instance, the Sarvasammataśikṣā (19) says that a short *r̥* has four equal parts: There are two quarter-mora particles of the consonantal *r* in the middle flanked by quarter-mora vowels, i.e. *ərrə*, cf. Allen (1953: 62). The Śikṣā verse cited by the Caturādhyāyībhāṣya seems to offer a close parallel: a half mora quantity of the consonantal *r*, flanked by quarter-mora vowels. Also see the Notes and the commentary on CA 1.4.10-11.

चतुराध्यायीभाष्य - संस्पृष्टरेफमृवर्णं भवति । 'इदं पितृभ्यः प्र भंरामि बर्हिः' (अ.वे. १८.४.५१)। 'पुत्रैर्भ्रातृंभिरदिंतिः' (अ.वे. ६.४.१)। ऋवर्णस्य मध्ये युगपद्व्चनो रः ।

'ऋवर्णे स्वरमात्रायाः (Whitney's emendation: त्रा या)
तस्या मध्येऽर्धमात्रया ।
रेफो भवति संसृष्टो यथाङ्गुल्या नखं तथा ।।
सूत्रे मणिरिवेत्येके तृणे क्रिमिरिवेति च ।
अनेन मात्रस्याद्यायाः (?)
प्रश्लेषे ऊ(तू?) उभयोरपि (Source?) ।।'

Note: Referring to the description given by the Śikṣā verses quoted by the CAB, Allen (1953: 62) says that it is more picturesque than illuminating. The representation of the components of *r̥* in the Sanskrit phonetic texts is further supported by the Avestan parallels such as *pərəθu* and *kərəp* for Sanskrit *pr̥thu* and *kl̥p-*, cf. Wackernagel-Debrunner (1896-1954, Vol.I., p. 32).

भा.भा.वृत्ति - ऋवर्णस्य वैचित्र्यं वर्णयति । सन्धौ स्पृष्टः । मध्ये प्रविष्टः संसृष्टः । संसृष्टः रेफो यस्मिन् सः संसृष्ट-रेफः । एतादृशं वर्णं जानीयात् । अयं भावः । ऋवर्णस्य आदौ अन्ते च स्वरविभागः । मध्ये रेफस्तिष्ठतीति जानी-यात् । 'अर्चन्त्यृग्भिः' (अ.वे. १२.१.३८)। 'प्रशिष्यृतस्य' (अ.वे. ५.१२.११) । 'शंसत्यृभुम्' (?, 'अर्चन्त्यृभुम्,' अ.वे. १.२.३)। 'यद्यृणम्' इत्यत्र ऋवर्णस्यादौ स्वरविभाग-त्वात् पूर्वपदान्तेऽन्तस्थापत्तिः । 'स्वस्ति मात्रे उत पित्रे' (अ.वे. १.३१.४)। 'धात्रे विधात्रे' (अ.वे. ३.१०.१०) इत्यत्र शब्दस्यान्ते स्वरविभागत्वादन्तस्थरेफापत्तिः । एवं चोदाहरणद्वयेनोभयत्र स्वरविभागोऽनुभूयते । 'निर्ऋतिर्' इत्यत्र आदौ विसर्गस्य रेफः ततः स्वरविभागः । ततो रेफः पुनः स्वरविभागः इति । ये तु पूर्वं रेफः पश्चात्स्वरविभाग इति मन्यन्ते तदसत् । तादृङ्ज्ञानने निर्ऋतिशब्दे 'रो रि' (पा. ८.३.१४) इति लोपे पूर्वस्य दीर्घता स्यात् । 'नी-ऋती'ति अनिष्टरूपापत्तेरिदमुपेक्ष्यम् । मध्ये रेफोऽस्तीत्येव-मेवोचितम् ।

Note: The example *śaṃsaty r̥bhum* is not found in any Vedic text. The same is the case of the example *yady r̥ṇam*. Bhārgava-Bhāskara presents some interesting arguments why the *r* element in the vocalic *r̥* must be situated between two vocalic fractions. He quotes an alternative view held by others that the *r* is situated in the beginning, followed by a vocalic fraction. Bhārgava-Bhāskara rejects such a view. It is interesting to note that such a view reflects the latter-day pronunciation of this vowel either as *ri* or *ru*. Such pronunciations, if they were to be taken seriously, would lead to a lot of undesirable phonological consequences. Thus, while the actual pronunciation of *ṛ* did indeed change, its phonological behavior remained like that of a vowel. While the sandhi rules remained an inherited and fixed feature of Sanskrit, the actual pronunciation of Sanskrit sounds was heavily influenced by the local factors.

१.१.३८. दीर्घप्लुतयोः पूर्वा मात्रा ।

Whitney (1.38). G: 1.1.38. O, P: पूर्वमात्रा.

Translation: For long and extra-long [*ṛ* vowels, i.e. *ṝ* and *ṝ3*], the first mora [is fused with the consonantal *r*].

Note: This rule seems to say that in lengthening the *ṛ* vowels, it is the post-*r* vocalic fraction that is lengthened, and not the pre-*r* vocalic fraction. It also makes clear that the lengthening applies only to the vowel portion, and not to the consonantal portion.

चतुराध्यायीभाष्य - दीर्घप्लुतयोस्तु पूर्वा मात्रा संस्पृष्टरेफमृवर्णं भवति । 'कर्तॄन् आचक्ष्व' (?, 'कर्तॄन्नक्षस्व', अ.वे. १०.१.१४)। 'पितॄँरुपेमम्' (अ.वे. १८.४.४०)।

Note: Referring to the text of the commentary संस्पृष्टरेफमृवर्णं भवति as it stands, Whitney says: this "is a palpable blunder for *saṃspṛṣṭarephā bhavati*."

भा.भा.वृत्ति - ह्रस्वऋवर्णस्यैकमात्रिकत्वात् स्वरभागस्य पादमात्रा । ततोऽर्धमात्रा रेफस्य ततः पादमात्रा रेफस्येति ज्ञेयम् । दीर्घप्लुतयोर्ऋवर्णयोस्तु मात्राविभाग उच्यते । दीर्घऋवर्णे द्विमात्रिके पूर्वा मात्रा स्वरस्य । ततोऽर्धमात्रा रेफस्य । ततोऽर्धमात्रा स्वरभागस्येत्यर्थः । प्लुतऋवर्णे पूर्वा मात्रा स्वरस्य । तत एका मात्रा रेफस्य । तत एका मात्रा स्वरस्येति ज्ञेयम् ।

Note: While the CAB on this rule is mostly uninformative, Bhārgava-Bhāskara seems to offer a very strange interpretation. Whitney appropriately interprets the rule to mean that only the first mora for *ṝ* and *ṝ3* is so combined with consonantal *r*. It is the subsequent vocalic element which undergoes lengthening. Whitney states in clear terms: "the *r*-element which it contains is not prolonged." Bhārgava-Bhāskara, disregarding the wording of the rule, says that the middle third portion is the consonantal *r*, i.e. the *r* also undergoes the process of lengthening. For long *r̥̄*, his interpretation is especially strange. According to him. the first entire *mātrā* of long *r̥̄* is purely vocalic, followed by a half-*mātrā* of consonantal *r*, followed by a half-*mātrā* of a vocalic element. This directly contradicts the statement of the rule: पूर्वा मात्रा संस्पृष्टरेफा भवति.

१.१.३९. सलकारम्लृवर्णम् ।

Whitney (1.39). C, Ha, N, E, F, I, O: °ऌ°. A, B, D, J, K, M, P: °मृवर्णं. G: 1.1.39.

Translation: [The members of] the *l̥*-class, [i.e. *l̥*, *l̥̄*, and *l̥̄3* , are fused] with [consonantal] *l*.

Note: This rule, in close parallel with the previous rules, presents the constitution of *l̥* as being equivalent to *ələ*, or to *əllə* if we accept each constituent to be of a quarter-mora quantity. It is interesting to note that the CA uses the term *l̥varṇa*, suggesting that there are more varieties than just the short *l̥*. However, it does not have a specific rule for long (*l̥̄*) and prolonged (*l̥̄3*) vowels, corresponding to CA (1.1.38). The CAB does not cite any example of these long and prolonged varieties, though the Śikṣā verse cited in the commentary does refer to long *l̥̄*.

चतुराध्यायीभाष्य - सलकारम् ऌवर्णं भवति । 'अचीक्लृपत्' (अ.वे. ६.११.३)। 'पञ्चदशेनं क्लृप्ताः' (अ.वे. ८.९.१५)। 'सिनीवाल्यंचीक्लृपत्' (अ.वे. ६.११.३)।

'ऋवर्णवद् ऌवर्णो लः प्रश्लिष्टश्च यदा तयोः ।
ऌॡ इति तदिच्छन्ति प्रयोगं तद्विदो जनाः ।।'
(Source ?)

Note: Whitney corrects the first quarter of the verse to: ऋवर्णे च ॠवर्णे लः. The cited verse is not a quotation from the Varṇapaṭalam, but from some other source. The Varṇapaṭalam (verse 33d: ऌवर्णे नास्ति दीर्घता) explicitly rejects the existence of long $\bar{l}$. On the other hand, the cited verse seems to accept it.

भा.भा.वृत्ति - पूर्वसूत्रद्वयेन ऋवर्णस्य यादृगुक्तं तद्वत्सलकारम्लृवर्णं जानीयात् । स्वरभागयोर्मध्ये लकारं जानीयात् । 'कृपो रो लः' (पा. ८.२.१८) इति पाणिनीये । अत्रापि अग्रे कृपधातोर्ऋवर्णस्थरेफस्य लत्वविधानात् चाक्लृपदित्यादौ एव लृकारस्य दर्शनात् । लृवर्णस्य दीर्घता तु मन्त्रशास्त्रे मातृकागणनेऽस्ति नान्यत्र । प्लुतस्तु क्वचिद्भवति । 'लृकारः प्लुत एव च' (?) इति शौनकाचार्योक्तत्वात् । क्लृप्तक्लृप्तिप्रभृतिशब्देषु 'गुरोरनृत ...' (पा. ८.२.८६) इति प्लुतसम्भवः । 'अनृत' इति पर्युदासः ऋलृवर्णसावर्ण्यादिह नेष्यते । अन्यथा प्लुतत्वासम्भवात् ।

Note: Bhārgava-Bhāskara offers some informative comments on vocalic ḷ. He says that the long $\bar{l}$ is not found in Sanskrit, except in the alphabets found in the Mantraśāstra. For details, see: Ramajñā Pāṇḍeya, *Vyākaraṇadarśanapīṭhikā*, p. 51, Sarasvatī Bhavana Adhyayanamālā 11, Sampūrṇānanda Saṃskṛta Viśvavidyālaya, Banaras. There are actually several texts which accept the long $\bar{l}$, though they cannot cite its occurrence in any attested word, cf. Manomohan Ghosh (1938: 51). On the other hand, it is possible to find an extra-long (*pluta*) $\bar{l}3$ by applying the normal rules of Pāṇini. The *pluta* $\bar{l}3$ is not attested among the Vedic examples of *pluta* vowels, though it is possible, according to the rules of the Pāṇinian system, to have a form with a *pluta* $\bar{l}3$. There is a long debate concerning the inclusion of ḷ in Pāṇini's Śivasūtra: *ṛ-ḷ-K*, and the MB (on the Śivasūtra: *ṛ-ḷ-K*) argues that one must include ḷ in the Śivasūtra *ṛ-ḷ-K*, in order to get a prolonged $\bar{l}3$ in vocative forms like *kḷ3ptaśikha*. Bhārgava-Bhāskara alludes to this discussion.

The quotation लृकारः प्लुत एव च is not found in any known works ascribed to Śaunaka. It is, however, quoted by Ramadev Tripathi (1977: 75) as belonging to verse 5 of the Pāṇinīyaśikṣā. It appears in verse 2 of the Pāṇinīyaśikṣā reconstructed by Manomohan Ghosh (1938: 1). It also occurs in the Agnipurāṇa version of the Pāṇinīyaśikṣā as verse 3; verse 5 of the Pāṇinīyaśikṣā presented by the commentary Pañjikā and Śikṣāprakāśa, the Yajus Recension, and the Ṛk Recension. Manomohan Ghosh (1938: 50, 53) wrongly translates this as: "and the pluta *ḷ̥* is duḥspṛṣṭa." The original verse is simply a continued listing the sounds included in the alphabet and includes the *duḥspṛṣṭa* sound as well as the prolonged *ḷ̥3* as belonging to the total listing. The term *duḥspṛṣṭa* refers to the retroflex *ḷ* (= ळ) found in the Ṛgveda, and is not a description of the prolonged *ḷ̥3* as understood by Ghosh.

१.१.४०. संध्यक्षराणि संस्पृष्टवर्णान्येकवर्णवद्वृत्तिः ।

Whitney (1.40). Hb, Nb: °वृत्ति. G: 1.1.40. I: 40. O: °न्येवर्ण°. P: °संसृष्ट°.

Translation: The composite-sounds [= *e*, *o*, *ai*, and *au*] have, [within each], fused [component] sounds, and [yet] they behave as single sounds.

Note: Whitney and Allen (1953: 63) render the phrase एकवर्णवद् वृत्तिः by 'they are treated as single letters.' In my opinion, a better translation is offered by 'they behave...' The rule thus draws a distinction between the perceived phonetic nature and the phonological behavior. For instance, metrically these vowels form single syllables.

It is clear from the plural form *sandhyakṣarāṇi*, that the text refers by this term to all four sounds, i.e. *e*, *o*, *ai*, and *au*, and not just to *ai* and *au*. As seen earlier, the ancient Śikṣā text cited in the CAB on CA (1.1.21, 25), seems to say that the sounds *e* and *o* have a single point of articulation, in contrast with *ai* and *au*, and that their monophthongal character seems to be supported by CA (1.1.34: एकारौकारयोर्विवृततमम्), the present rule clearly brings them under the term *sandhyakṣara*. The term *sandhyakṣara* is generally translated as 'diphthong,' and this raises the question of why the sounds *e* and *o* should come under this term.

To begin with, we must disabuse ourselves of the notion that the term *sandhyakṣara* refers to a diphthong. It refers literally to a composite-sound, and the composite character is more in terms of their perceived origin, rather than in terms of their current articulation. Thus, phonetically the sounds *e* and *o* were monophthongs for the CA, and yet in terms of their origin they were seen as being born out of a combination. Allen (1953: 64) says: "It will be noted that even where the monophthongal value of **e/o** is phonetically established, the feeling for its phonological equivalence to **a+i/u** still prevails."

However, the combination of elements in *e* and *o*, as compared to the combination in *ai* and *au*, was perceived to be of a different nature by most

Sanskrit texts. The first pair represents a true fusion where the components can no longer be separately perceived, while the second pair has perceptible components. For the first type of combination, Patañjali uses the term *praśliṣta*, while for the second type of combination, he uses the term *samāhāra*, cf. MB (Kielhorn edn), Vol.I., p. 62: एवमप्यवर्णस्य एङोश्च सवर्णसंज्ञा प्राप्नोति । प्रश्लिष्टावर्णावेतौ । Also: इमावैचौ समाहारवर्णौ मात्रावर्णस्य मात्रेवर्णोवर्णयोः, MB (ibid), p. 78.

चतुराध्यायीभाष्य - संध्यक्षराणि संस्पृष्टवर्णानि भवन्ति । एकवर्णवद् वृत्तिर्भवति । ए(?)एए३ ऐ(?)ऐऐ३ ओ(?) ओओ३ औ(?)औऔ३ ।

Note: It is not clear why the commentary offers three varieties of each diphthong. This is probably just an error under the influence of the triple listings for other vowels.

भा.भा.वृत्ति - ए ऐ ओ औ सन्ध्यक्षराणि संस्पृष्टवर्णानि वर्णद्वयजानि । एतेषामेकवर्णवद्वृत्तिः स्वभावो वर्तते । 'गृहे' (अ.वे. १.१४.२)। 'उपैतु' (अ.वे. ७.६६.१)। 'अथो' (अ.वे. १.१४.२)। 'मित्रावरुणौ' (अ.वे. १.२०. २)। किं च पदान्तसन्धौ सन्ध्यक्षराणि पदकाले पुनः प्रस्फुटन्ति । तत्रापि अवर्णान्तपदेन उञा योगे ओकारे जाते पदकालेऽपि नित्यसंहितत्वात् एकवद्वृत्तिरेव । 'अथो इति' (अ.वे. १.१४.२) । 'उतो इति' (अ.वे. ४.१६.३)। 'सो इति' (अ.वे. १८.१.२०)। 'उपो इति' (अ.वे. १३.४.४४, VVRI edn.: १३.७.१६) ।

१.१.४१. नैकारौकारयोः स्थानविधौ ।

Whitney (1.41). G: 1.1.41. E, F, O(orig): °यो स्था°.

Translation: [The behavior of the sounds] *ai* and *au* [as single sounds] does not hold in the context of the prescription of their points of articulation (*sthāna*).

Note: The listing of the four sounds in the commentaries is problematic. The rule clearly uses a dual form, and, after dissolving the sandhi in *naikāraukārayoḥ*, it can be sensibly either *ekāra+okārayoḥ*, or *aikāra+aukārayoḥ*. Out of these two possibilities, Whitney opted for the second one, while Bhārgava-Bhāskara, and the CAB too, would like to have it both ways to include all the four *sandhyakṣara*s.

The interpretation I have given above is supported by Whitney. On this rule, Whitney says: "What the meaning and value of the rule is is not altogether clear: I can see no other application of it than to forbid the inclusion of *ai* among the palatals only, and of *au* among the labials only, since they are both throat-sounds as well. By implication, then, *e* and *o* would admit of being ranked as merely palatal and labial." This is in part because Whitney takes the word *sthānavidhi* to refer to 'prescription of the point of articulation.' The CAB as well as the ancient Śikṣā verse cited therein are unclear on this rule. Whitney derives the following meaning from the verse cited in the CAB: "perhaps the meaning is that, while the beginning and end of *āi*, for instance, are clearly *a* and *i*, a mora in the middle of the sound is of a mixed character." The verse seems to refer to a half-mora element which is of mixed character. I think this is a plausible interpretation.

On the other hand, Bhārgava-Bhāskara's commentary seems to support an interpretation like: "[The behavior] of the sounds *e*/*ai* and *o*/*au* [as single sounds, however], does not [hold] in the context of substitution [*sthānavidhi* , i.e. substitution of the constituents of these sounds by protracted varieties]." Bhārgava-Bhāskara draws our attention to the other possible meaning of the term *sthānavidhi*, i.e. substitution, cf. P.1.1.49 (षष्ठी स्थानेयोगा). With this other meaning of the word *sthānavidhi*, i.e. substitution, there is a different possible context for this rule. In the context of substitution, the sounds *ai* and *au* do not behave as single sounds, i.e. their different components receive different substitutes.

The best example to illustrate this different behavior of the components is offered in the Pāṇinian process of deriving the prolonged versions for *e*, *o*, *ai*, and *au*. Compare Pāṇini's rules P. 8.2.105 (प्लुतावैच इदुतौ) and 8.2.106 (एचोऽप्रगृह्यस्यादूराद्धूते पूर्वस्यार्धस्यादुत्तरस्येदुतौ). The first rule says that when *ai* and *au* are prolonged, it is the *i* and the *u* elements of these composite sounds that get prolonged. Thus, a prolonged *ai* is equivalent to *a+ī3*, and a prolonged *au* is equivalent to *a+ū3*. The next rule says that, for a non-*pragṛhya e*, *o*, *ai*, or *au*, except in a call from afar, the sound *e* and *ai* are prolonged to *ā3+i*, and *o* and *au* to *ā3+u*. Pāṇini's rules clearly refer to the components in the context of substitution.

In the examples *khaṇvakhā3i* and *khaimakhā3i* offered by Bhārgava-Bhāskara, we assume that an original *e* has been changed to *ā3i*, cf. Bhārgava-Bhāskara lists *khaṇvakhe* and *khaimakhe* as the non-*pluta* forms under CA (1.2.22). On the other hand, Whitney guesses on CA (1.4.5 = W 1.96) that the original non-*pluta* forms are 'probably' *khaṇvakhāi* and *khaimakhāi*. If Whitney is correct, we have the change of *ai* to *ā3i*. However, I agree with the Roth-Böhtlingk lexicon in considering these forms to be vocatives of the female frog-names *khaṇvakhā* and *khaimakhā*, and hence the non-*pluta* vocative forms are *khaṇvakhe* and *khaimakhe*, rather than *khaṇvakhai* and *khaimakai*. This is also supported by Sāyaṇa on ŚAV (4.15.15). Bhārgava-Bhāskara also offers an example of an original *o* changing to *ā3u* in the form *vāyā3u* (< *vāyo*). This example is not attested in the ŚAV.

Of these two possible interpretations, the first one is the more likely interpretation, because the rule occurs in the context of describing the articulation of sounds, rather than in the context of substitution. The second argument which goes against the interpretation of Bhārgava-Bhāskara is that the so-called substitution for different parts of a diphthong in the context of *pluta* is never taught as a rule in the CA. It is simply taken for granted, because the *pluta* forms appear both in the Saṃhitāpāṭha and the Padapāṭha. Therefore, Bhārgava-Bhāskara was forced to bring in Pāṇini's substitution rules, which clearly refer to components of the diphthongs.

चतुराध्यायीभाष्य - ऐकारौकारयोः स्थानविधाने एकवर्णवद् वृत्तिर्न भवति । एऐ३ ओऔ३ ।

'ऐकारौकारयोश्चापि पूर्वा मात्रा परा च या ।
अर्धमात्रा तयोर्मध्ये संस्पृ(सृ?)ष्ट इति न (नः?)
स्मृतः ॥' (Source?) ।

Note: The manuscript N has न in the last quarter of the verse, but the syntax of the verse still remains corrupt.

भा.भा.वृत्ति - प्लुतसमये स्थानविधौ कर्तव्ये एकारस्य ओकारस्य च एकवर्णवद्वृत्तिर्न तिष्ठति । किं तर्हि । अकारः प्लुतः स्यात् । ततः परं क्रमात् ह्रस्वः इकारः उकारश्च प्रयुज्यते । 'खण्वखा३इ खैमखा३इ मध्ये' (अ.वे. ४.१५.१५)।

'एहि वाया३उ संतिष्ठ' (not in AV)। 'इदं कल्पितं यज्ञपता३उ' । तैत्तिरीये (तै.सं. ६.६.२)। 'यज्ञपतौ' इत्यौकारस्यापि । 'प्लुतावैच इदुतौ' (पा. ८.२.१०६) इति पाणिनीये चतुर्णां सन्ध्यक्षराणामुक्तम् । अत्र सूत्रे न एकारः न ऐकारः नैकारौकारयोः । अत्र ओकारः औकारः इति पद[च]च्छेदेन चतुर्णां ग्रहणं ज्ञेयम् ।

Note: For the accentuation of the example from AV (4.15.15), see Note on CA (1.4.5). The VVRI Vedic concordance lists RV (9.96.12) as the only Saṃhitā occurrence for *saṃ tiṣṭha*, but the source for एहि वाया३उ सन्तिष्ठ is as yet unknown. There is no occurrence of *saṃ tiṣṭha* in the Brāhmaṇas and Āraṇyakas.

इति प्रथमाध्यायस्य प्रथमः पादः ।

H, N: चतुराध्यायिकायां प्रथमाध्यायस्य प्रथमः पादः । ४१ । एकचत्वारिंशत् । E, F: प्रथमस्य प्रथमः पादः । A, B, D, M, P: प्रथमः पादः । J: इति प्रथमाध्यायस्य प्रथमः पादः । I: ४१ इत्यथर्ववेदे कौत्सव्याकरणे प्रथमाध्यायस्य प्रथमः पादः । G: इत्यथर्ववेदांगकौत्सव्याकरणे प्रथमाध्यायस्य प्रथमपादस्य भार्गवभास्करीयवृत्तिः परिपूर्णा । O: ।।१।।४१।। इत्यथर्ववेदे कौत्सव्याकरणे चतुराध्यायिकस्य प्रथमः पादः ।।

चतुराध्यायीभाष्य - चतुराध्यायिकायां प्रथमस्याध्यायस्य प्रथमः पादः । सूत्र ४१ । एकचत्वारिंशत् ।

भा.भा.वृत्ति - इत्यथर्ववेदाङ्गकौत्सव्याकरणे प्रथमाध्यायस्य प्रथमपादस्य भार्गवभास्करीयवृत्तिः परिपूर्णा ।

॥ प्रथमोऽध्यायः ॥
॥ द्वितीयः पादः ॥

भा.भा.वृत्ति - अथ प्रथमाध्यायस्य द्वितीयपादस्थसूत्राणां वृत्तिरारभ्यते । तत्रादौ सन्ध्यप्रकरणे संज्ञा क्रियते वर्णानां ज्ञानाय । ॐ३म् ।

१.२.१. विसर्जनीयोऽभिनिष्टानः ।

Whitney (1.42), A, G, I, Hac, P: °ष्टानः । B, C, D, E, F, Hb, J, K, M, N, O: °ष्ठानः. G: 1.2.1.

Translation: The *ḥ* (= *visarjanīya*) is an *abhiniṣṭāna* ['off-glide'] sound.

Note: The term *abhiniṣṭāna* is difficult to interpret, because it does not occur elsewhere in the grammatical literature, and because, in its few occurrences in the Gr̥hya-Sūtras etc. it is simply used as a term referring to *visarga;*, for passages in the Gr̥hya-Sūtras, see: Āśvalāyana-Gr̥hya-Sūtra (1.15.4-5), Pāraskara-Gr̥hya-Sūtra (1.17.1-6), and Gobhila-Gr̥hya-Sūtra (2.8.14). For further references, see L. Renou (1942: 376). But the significance of the term itself is hardly accounted for. It looks like an older term for *visarga* or *visarjanīya*, which was discontinued in later Sanskrit.

Secondly, the mss. are divided over the readings *abhiniṣṭāna* and *abhiniṣṭhāna*. Pāṇini (8.3.86: अभिनिसस्तनः शब्दसंज्ञायाम्) derives the formation *abhiniṣṭāna* from *abhi+nis+*√*stan* as a *śabdasaṃjñā* 'technical term referring to a linguistic unit.' However, the other reading is not without some justification. Whitney remarks on this rule: "Pāṇini's rule must be taken as conclusive respecting the derivation and form favored in his time, or by his school; but the analogy of the words *abhinidhāna*, *abhinihita*, *abhinihata*, *abhinipāta* cannot but suggest *abhiniṣṭhāna* as the true form, coming from the root *sthā* with the prefixes *abhi* and *ni*." In my own opinion, the form *abhiniṣṭāna* is the original form, the *lectio difficilior*, and hence probably the original reading.

What does the word *abhiniṣṭāna* mean? Whitney on this rule says: "The Böhtlingk-Roth lexicon gives it ... the meaning 'an expiring or vanishing sound (*ein verklingender Laut*),' but this is merely a conjecture, and by no means so well supported by the etymology of the word (which would suggest rather 'a sounding forth, a resonance') as to be placed beyond the reach of question." Recently, S.M. Katre (1987: 1039) seems to have followed the Böhtlingk-Roth interpretation in translating the term as 'a phoneme that dies away.' Such an interpretation makes no sense in view of the non-technical example offered in the KV on P.8.3.86: अभिनिस्तनति मृदङ्गः. Here it must refer to the reverberations of the sound of the drum. Therefore, I agree with Whitney's interpretation. Perhaps, the best modern technical paraphrase would be 'off-glide.' The meaning of the term *abhiniṣṭāna* is probably close to that of *visarga* or *visarjanīya*, i.e. 'to be released, emitted.'

चतुराध्यायीभाष्य - विसर्जनीयो वर्णः अभिनिष्टा(N: ष्ठा)-नो भवति । 'अ॒ग्निः' (अ.वे. १.७.४)। 'वृ॒क्षः' (अ.वे. ४.७.५)।

भा.भा.वृत्ति - (**विसर्जनीयोऽभिनिष्टानः**) पृथक्पदे परे प्रत्ययोत्तरपदयोश्च विसर्जनीयः जिह्वामूलीयोपध्मानीयतां प्राप्तः अर्धविसर्गसदृशः विसर्गश्च यत्र साक्षात् दृश्यते सोऽभिनिष्टा-नसंज्ञो ज्ञेयः । परेण व्यञ्जनेन सह । पृथक्पदे । 'कᳵ कं॑फो॒डौ' (Whitney's AV: कं॑फौ॒डौ, अ.वे. १०.२.४)। 'याᳵ क्लु॒न्दाः' (अ.वे. २.२.५)। 'शं नं॑ᳵ खनि॒त्रिमा॒ः' (अ.वे. १.६.४)। 'नी॒चैᳵ खं॑न॒न्ति' (अ.वे. २.३.३)। 'ज॒ङ्गि॒डः(ᳵ?) प्रणः॒' (अ.वे. २.४.६)। 'स नं॑ᳶ पि॒ता' (अ.वे. २.१.३)। 'परिं॑ णᳶ पातु' (अ.वे. २.४.२)। 'कᳶ पृश्निं॑म्' (अ.वे. ७.१०४.१)। 'ब॒हु॒लाᳶ फट् कं॑रिक्रति' (अ.वे. ४.१८.३)। 'याᳶ फ॒लिनी॒ः' (?)। आरण्यके (which one?)। 'व॒नस्पतं॑य॒ः शान्ति॒ः' (अ.वे. १९.९.१४)। 'दैवीः॑ षड्डुर्वीः' (अ.वे. ५.३.६)। 'आ॒न॒शा॒नाः सं॑मा॒ने' (अ.वे. २.१.५)। 'नम॒ः क्षेत्रं॑स्य॒ पतं॑ये' (अ.वे. २.८.५)। 'शं न॒ः क्षेत्रं॑स्य॒' (अ.वे. १९.१०.१०)। 'धे॒न॒वः स्यन्दं॑माना॒ः' (अ.वे. २.५.६)। अन्तःपादम् ।

'अरुःस्त्राणम्' (अ.वे. २.३.३)। प्रत्यये परे । 'यशःसु' (?)। 'यशᳲकल्पम्' (?)। 'वेधᳲपाशः' (?)। 'अभिनिस-स्तनः शब्दसंज्ञायाम्' (पा. ८.३.८६) इति पाणिनीये व्यु-त्पादितः ।

Note: Bhārgava-Bhāskara gives a somewhat different interpretation of the term *abhiniṣṭāna.* According to him, it does not refer just to a normal *visarga* (i.e. *ḥ*), but to *visarga* as it changes to *ẖ* (= *jihvāmūlīya*) before *k*, *kh*, or to *ḫ* (= *upadhmānīya*) before *p*, *ph.* Such changes may be due to external or internal sandhi. We have no way of evaluating Bhārgava-Bhāskara's interpretation, except to say that it does not agree with the general usage of the term *abhiniṣṭāna* in the Gṛhya-Sūtras, where it seems to be a plain and simple equivalent of the generic *visarga.* The CAB also seems to interpret this term as a generic equivalent of *visarga*, and the examples it cites are of word-final *visarga* before pause. Therefore, the chances of Bhārgava-Bhāskara being correct are slim.

The example याः फलिनीः is found in RV (10.97.15), TS (4.2.6.4), and VS (12.89). It is also found in the Mantra-Brāhmaṇa (1.5.1), edited by Satyavrat Sāmaśramī, Calcutta, 1947. It is not traced to any known Āraṇyaka. However, Bhārgava-Bhāskara cites it as an Āraṇyaka example. The example यशस्कल्पम् is found in the KV (on P.8.3.38: सोऽपदादौ). For the textual variation concerning the example कः कफोडौ from AV (10.2.4) and its interpretation, see Whitney (*AV Transl.* Vol.II., p. 568).

१.२.२. व्यञ्जनविधारणमभिनिधानः ।

Whitney (1.43), C, E, H, I, N, P: single Sūtra: व्यञ्जनविधारणमभिनिधानः पीडितः सन्नतरो हीनश्वासनादः । A, B, D: two Sūtras: व्यंजनविधारणमभिनिधानः पीडितः । संन(त in D)तरो हीनश्वासनादः । F, G, J, K, M: the first of the two Sūtras ends with °धानः । G numbers the two Sūtras: 1.2.2, 1.2.3.

Translation: Holding a consonant back [i.e. not releasing it, or checking it] is termed *abhinidhāna.*

Note: Following Whitney, Varma (1929: 137) and Allen (1953: 71-72) take CA (1.2.2-3) as representing a single rule. The manuscripts are split half and half on this issue. Among the commentaries, the CAB takes the entire stretch (CA 1.2.2-3) as being a single rule, a definition or description of *abhi-*

nidhāna. Bhārgava-Bhāskara's commentary, on the other hand takes these two to be separate rules. The first rule is a definition of *abhinidhāna*, while the second one a definition of the term *sannatara*. I have given these as two rules, because mss. from different groups seem to treat these as two rules. The manuscript G numbers these two rules separately, and with this numbering, the CA 1.2.10 appears as 1.2.10 in both I and G. On the other hand, I do not agree with Bhārgava-Bhāskara's notion that rule 1.2.3 defines a separate term, i.e. *sannatara*. I think rule 1.2.3 is simply a supplement to 1.2.2, and, hence is a further description of *abhinidhāna*.

Whitney uses the terms implosion and explosion to refer to the two phases involved in the pronunciation of consonants. The first step, especially clear in the case of stops, is indicated by the formation of contact between the articulator and the point of articulation. The sound becomes more audible with the release of that contact, referred to by Whitney by the term explosion. When a stop is followed by another stop, or by a pause, then the utterance of the first stop basically ends with the first phase, and there does not follow a clear release of the contact, making the consonant weakly audible. Whitney generally treats this as a description of indistinct pronunciation. He saw many difficulties in this description, and explained those difficulties "by supposing that the Hindus had not made a complete physical analysis of the phonomenon, and hence that their descriptions of it partake of vagueness and inconsistency; and also, that they have brought together under the name *abhinidhāna* things not entirely accordant, although analogous, in character."

Since Whitney was unhappy with the first explanation of the notion of incomplete utterance, he came up with a second hypothesis (p. 36): "An alternative view to which I have myself been somewhat attracted is that by the *abhinidhāna* is meant the instant of silence which intervenes between the closure of the organs for the first mute, and their opening for the second: that the Hindu theory regards, in the word *āpta*, for example, the utterance of the *p* as complete by the closure of the lips upon the preceding *ā*, and that of the *t* as complete by the unclosure of the tongue before the following *a*, while the brief interval of suspended utterance separating the two acts is *abhinidhāna*." A few modern scholars have taken this to represent Whitney's final view, cf. Vijay Shankar Pandeya (1987: 183). It is, however, not clear whether Whitney's statements concerning the 'Indian notions of the complete utterance of a stop' are correct.

On the other hand, Whitney finally arrives at the following understanding (p. 36): "Fatal objections, however, to this explanation are: the treatment of the phenomenon as something affecting the former consonant, not interposed after it; the difficulty of assuming any such interval of silence in the case of a concurrence with sonant and nasal mutes; and the non-applicability of the theory to the case of a final consonant. The term *vyañjanavidhāraṇa* must therefore be understood as used simply in antithesis to the *saṃyuktam* of rule 49 (= CA 1.2.9: अतोऽन्यत् संयुक्तम्): whereas, in other cases of concurrence of consonants, there is actual combination, with partial assimilation of the latter to the former (rule 50 = CA 1.2.10), here each is held apart from the other as distinct." Whitney realizes that this explanation may not be applicable to the word-final consonants, but states that "it is allowable to regard as contemplated in a general description or designation of a phonetic phenomenon its principal case only."

Allen (1953: 70ff.) comes up with a more positive understanding of this phenomenon. More than an interval of silence, the term *abhinidhāna* refers to an unreleased consonant, either before another consonant making the conjunction weak and excludable from the notion of *saṃyukta* 'conjunct consonants,' or occurring at the word-final position, making the consonant midway between a voiced or a voiceless consonant, as debated in CA (1.1.10: प्रथमान्तानि तृतीयान्तानीति शौनकस्य प्रतिज्ञानं न वृत्तिः). Allen (1953: 71) describes *abhinidhāna* as: "the non-release of a consonant, more particularly a stop, when followed by a stop, and parallels the French term 'implosion.'" The notion of 'implosion' makes eminent sense in the case of a stop followed by a stop, particularly when we see deaspiration of the first stop, aspiration being a feature of the release or 'explosion.' However, the term *abhinidhāna* seems to refer to overall weakening of the initial consonant of a consonant-cluster, and of the final consonant before pause. This overall weakening makes such consonants subject to changes of all kinds, especially subject to progressive assimilation in sandhis and loss of final consonants in Prakrits. Allen (1953: 70ff) correctly links this non-release of the consonant with both the contexts, i.e. a not-too-tight consonantal contact as well as the word-final position.

It must be noted that the notion of *abhinidhāna*, its nature, and scope, were a highly disputed topic among the various traditions, and the phenomenon probably also varied dialectally, cf. Varma (1929: 133-147). For another recent discussion of this term, also see: Ralf Stautzebach (1994: 312-313).

चतुराध्यायीभाष्य - व्यञ्जनविधारणमभिनिधानो भवति । पीडितश्च श्वासनादाभ्याम् । अपर आह । व्यञ्जनविधारणम-भिनिपातो(ऽ?)मात्रो जपनो भवति पीडितश्च श्वास-

नादाभ्याम् । अपर आह । व्यञ्जनविधारणमभिनिपा-
तो(ऽ?)मात्रो जपने गुरुता भवति ।

अन्तःपदे पदान्ते वा पीडितः सन्न एव तु ।
अवकृष्टतर(ः?)स्थानादवसन्नतरश्च सः ।
हीनश्च श्वासनादाभ्यां यो यत्रार्थे(H: र्थो)ऽभिधीयते ।
(source?)

***भा.भा.वृत्ति* -** यो विसर्गः व्यञ्जनरूपं धारयति तस्य परेण व्यञ्जनेन सह योगे द्वयोरभिनिधानसंज्ञा । संयोगसंज्ञाया अवान्तरभेदः । विसर्गस्य रेफशषसा भवन्ति । रेफः । बहिः। ‘बहिर्बालिति’ (अ.वे. १.३.६)। ‘स्व१र्ण’ (अ.वे. २.५.२, not *ṇ*, but *n* in Whitney's AV)। ‘स्वर्षाम्’ (अ.वे. २०.३५.३)। ‘स्वर्पतीन्’ (स्वर्पतिम्, अ.वे. २०.५४.२)। ‘चतुर्भ्यः’ (अ.वे. १.१२.४)। ‘धूर्षु’ । ऋग्वेदे (ऋ.वे. १.१००.१६)। ‘आभिरप्सरासु’ (अ.वे. २.२.३)। ‘आहुर्यतः’ (अ.वे. २.२.३)। ‘दुरिता’ (अ.वे. २.६.५)। शत्वम् । ‘शणश्च मा जङ्गिडश्च’ (अ.वे. २.४.५)। ‘यश्चकार’ (अ.वे. २.९.५)। ‘मधोश्चकानः’ (अ.वे. २.५.१)। ‘प्रदिशश्चतस्रः’ (अ.वे. २.६.१)। ‘मन्युतश्शपात्’ (अ.वे. २.७.२)। षत्वम् । ‘द्यौष्ट्वा’ (अ.वे. २.२८.४)। ‘अग्निष्टे’ (अ.वे. ७.४३.२)। ‘वायुष्टान्’ (अ.वे. २.३४.४)। ‘अग्निष्टत्’ (अ.वे. ७.४३.३)। सत्वम् । ‘क्रुन्दास्तमिषीचयः’ (अ.वे. २.२.५)। ‘इन्द्रस्तुराषाट्’ (अ.वे. २.५.३)। ‘अञ्जस्समुद्रम्’ (अ.वे. २.५.६)। उपचारोऽप्यत्रैव । ‘अधस्पदम्’ (अ.वे. २.७.२)। ‘निष्करत्’ (अ.वे. २.९.५)।

Note: Bhārgava-Bhāskara takes *abhinidhāna* as a continued description of the *visarga* and its contextual substitutes. For him, when a *visarga*, or its contextual substitute, combines with the following consonant, both the consonants together are called *abhinidhāna*. This interpretation cannot be correct.

१.२.३. पीडितः सन्नतरो हीनश्वासनादः ।

Whitney (1.43) combines with the previous Sūtra.

Translation: [The sound termed *abhinidhāna* in the previous rule is] squeezed, weaker, and has reduced breath or voice.

Note: As explained in the Note on the earlier rule, I have treated this as a separate rule, and yet I think it is a continuation of the previous description. The term *vyañjanavidhāraṇam*, in the previous rule, referring to "holding apart or back" of a consonant, seems like a description of the consequences of a certain phonetic process, and that process is described more fully in the present rule. The three terms contained in this rule describe different dimensions of this articulatory process. The term *pīḍita*, lit. 'pressed,' seems to refer to the non-release of the contact between the articulator and the point of articulation. The term *hīnaśvāsanāda* refers to weak emission involved, whether the consonant be voiced or voiceless.

The term *sannatara* presents some further difficulties. It is translated by Whitney (p. 34) as 'quite weakened,' and Varma (1929: 137) and Allen (1953: 72) generally follow Whitney. The term *avasannatara* appears in the Śikṣā verse cited in the Caturādhyāyībhāṣya on the previous rule. Elsewhere, i.e. P.1.2.40 (उदात्तस्वरितपरस्य सन्नतरः), the term *sannatara* is used to describe the lowest pitch level, lower than the normal low-pitch (*anudātta*). This is for a low-pitch syllable which precedes an *udātta* 'high-pitch' or a *svarita* 'rising-falling' syllable. Thus, *sanna* in this context refers to low-pitch, and *sannatara* refers to a pitch lower than the normal low-pitch. It is not clear if there is any shared value in the use of the same term in these two different contexts. Perhaps, the term implies in a generic manner the low level of effort involved in both the lowest-pitch vowels, and the unreleased stops, and in this sense may be comparable to the term *laghu-prayatna-tara*.

चतुराध्यायीभाष्य - See the commentary on the previous rule.

भा.भा.वृत्ति - द्वयोर्वर्णयो[:] स्वरव्यञ्जनयोः स्वरयोर्वा मध्ये पीडितः । हीनश्वासनादः सन् नश्यति विकृतो वा भवति स

सन्नतरसंज्ञो ज्ञेयः । अः । अ॒क । अ॒प । श । ष । स । एते श्वासप्रयत्नकाः । य । र । एतौ नादप्रयत्नकौ । एतद्रूपैर्हीनो विसर्गः इत्यर्थः । अर्थात् उत्वं प्राप्तो वा । लुप्तः कृतदीर्घो वा । लुप्तो वा । सन्नतरः । अदृष्ट इत्यर्थः । उत्वे ओत्वं प्राप्तः । 'अ॒न्यो रसे॑भ्यः' (अ.वे. २.४.५)। 'म॒यो॒भुव॒ः' (अ.वे. १.५.१)। 'च॒तु॒र्भ्यो॒ अङ्गे॑भ्य॒ः' (अ.वे. १.१२.४)। 'शं नो॑ दे॒वीः' (अ.वे. १.६.१)। 'न॑म॒स्यो॑ वि॒क्षु' (अ.वे. २.२.१)। लुप्तः कृतदीर्घः । 'प्रा॒ता रात्री॑' (अ.वे. ६.१२८.२)। 'सार॑थी रे॒ष्मा' (अ.वे. १५.२.१)। 'ज॒घ्नू॒ रक्षां॑सि' (अ.वे. ४.३७.१)। लुप्तः । 'स ए॒व' (अ.वे. २.९.५)। 'ए॒ष पू॒र्तम्' (अ.वे. ९.६.३१, VVRI edn.: ९.८.१)। 'ए॒ष स्य ते॑' (अ.वे. २०.६७.६)। 'स इत्' (अ.वे. १४.१.२९)। 'प्र॑थम॒ज ऋ॒तस्य॒' (अ.वे. ८.९.१६)। 'वा॒श्रा इ॑व' (अ.वे. २.५.६)। 'या॒तु॒धाना॑ अ॒त्रिण॒ः' (अ.वे. १.७.३)। 'ग॒न्ध॒र्व आ॑सीत्' (अ.वे. २.२.३)। 'विश्वा॑ आदित्य' (अ.वे. १३.२.२८)। 'क ईं वेद' (अ. वे. २०.५३.१)। 'एकं॑ ए॒व' (अ.वे. २.१.३)। 'दे॒वा अ॒मृतं॑म्' (अ.वे. २.१.५)। 'सु॒तास॑ इन्द्र' (अ.वे. २.५.४)। 'उ॒प॒जीका॒ उत्' (अ.वे. २.३.४)। 'नम॒ इत्' (अ.वे. २.२.४)। 'आ॒प ओष॑धयः' (अ.वे. २.३.६)। 'ब्रा॒ह्म॒णा इ॒मे' (अ.वे. २.६.३)। 'नमं॑ ईषायु॒गेभ्यः॑' (अ.वे. २.८.४)। 'ब्र॒ह्माणं॑ उ॒त' (अ.वे. २.९.४)। व्यञ्जने परे । 'या वि॒श्वाव॑सुम्' (अ.वे. २.२.४)। 'अ॒क्षका॑मा मनो॒मुह॑ः' (अ.वे. २.२.५)। 'इ॒मा या दे॒वीः' (अ.वे. २.१०.४)।

Note: Bhārgava-Bhāskara takes this rule to be a definition of the term *sannatara* which he claims applies to a *visarga* which changes in certain sandhis in such a way that it survives neither as a sibilant, nor as a *y* or an *r*. It is doubtful if the rule has any such meaning. The term *hīna-śvāsa-nāda* is taken by Bhārgava-Bhāskara to mean a sound which has neither *śvāsa* nor *nāda*. This is clearly unacceptable.

१.२.४. स्पर्शस्य स्पर्शेऽभिनिधानः ।

Whitney (1.44). G: 1.2.4. O: °भिधानः.

Translation: Before a stop [lit. 'contact consonant,' including the nasals *ṅ*, *ñ*, *ṇ*, *n*, and *m*], there is *abhinidhāna* [i.e. lack of release] of a stop.

Note: The CA unconditionally refers to all stops, including nasals, in this rule. This includes conjuncts of homorganic as well as non-homorganic stops, and it also includes combinations of nasals and non-nasals. One of the interpretations proposed for *abhinidhāna* by Whitney was a moment of silence between the consonants. However, as Whitney himself recognized, such a moment of silence does not seem possible between, for example, a voiced unaspirated stop and a homorganic nasal, because the transition between such sounds is far smoother. Therefore, the best conception of *abhinidhāna* is represented by 'unreleased' articulation.

चतुराध्यायीभाष्य - स्पर्शस्य स्पर्शे परतः अभिनिधानो भवति । 'बृहद्भिः' (अ.वे.पै.सं. १०.९.७)। 'समिद्भिः' (ऋ.वे. ३.१.२)। 'मरुद्भिः' (अ.वे. २.२९.४)।

Note: As Whitney notes, out of the three examples cited by the CAB, only the last example is found in the (Ś)AV. The form *samidbhiḥ* is not found in AV, and the references listed for this word in Vishva Bandhu's *A Grammatical Word-Index to Atharvaveda* (p. 622) are actually references for the word *samidhaḥ*, wrongly ascribed to *samidbhiḥ*. One may also note that Surya Kanta has not made the expected suggestion that the first two forms cited by the CAB, which are not found in the Vulgate of the AV, probably occurred in the real Śaunakīya recension of the AV which is now lost and that the Vulgate does not represent the true Śaunakīya recension.

भा.भा.वृत्ति - कादयो मावसानाः पञ्चविंशतिः स्पर्शाः । स्पर्शयोर्योगः अभिनिधानसंज्ञः । 'मुमुग्धि' (अ.वे. ६.११२.१)।

Note: According to Bhārgava-Bhāskara, the whole cluster of stops gets the designation *abhinidhāna*. This does not seem to be correct. The phrase स्पर्शस्य ... अभिनिधानः is comparable to substitution or alteration, in the classical Pāṇinian fashion, where the genitive case represents the *sthānin* 'item undergoing substitution, item being replaced,' and the item in the nominative represents the *ādeśa* 'substitute,' cf. P.1.1.49 (षष्ठी स्थानेयोगा).

१.२.५. पदान्तावग्रहयोश्च ।

Whitney (1.45). G: 1.2.5.

Translation: Also at the end of a word [before pause in the Padapāṭha] and [at the end of the first member of a compound, or at the end of a nominal base] in separation [of the members of a compound or of the base from the case-ending in the Padapāṭha, a stop is reduced to *abhinidhāna*].

Note: Heffner (1952: 119): "The contact and hold phases are usually easy to observe, the release may be obscured, notably for instance, when the stop is the final element of the breath group. In the phrase, *and then he went to sleep*, the final [p] of *sleep* is often not released by the labial "explosion," but by the lowering of the velum for the resumption of normal breathing, the lips having simply remained closed. Such a release is usually not audible."

चतुराध्यायीभाष्य - पदान्ते अवग्रहे च स्पर्शस्य स्पर्शे परतः अभिनिधानो भवति । 'तान् । वः । यः । देवानांम्' (पद, अ.वे. ११.१.५)। 'अप्ऽसु' (पद, अ.वे. १.६.२)। 'सालाऽवृकान्ऽइंव' (पद, अ.वे. २.२७.५)। 'खल्वांन्ऽइव' (पद, अ.वे. २.३१.१)।

Note: Whitney correctly points out that the phrase स्पर्शस्य स्पर्शे परतः "has no business here: that case is included in the preceding rule, and the present precept applies to the pronunciation of a final as a final, without any reference to what may follow." In all the cases cited by the commentator, the word-final stop is followed by a pause, rather than by another stop.

भा.भा.वृत्ति - पदान्तग्रहणात् पूर्वसूत्रमपा(प?)दान्तार्थं ज्ञेयम् । पदान्तस्पर्शस्य पदादिस्पर्शे परे उभयोः स्पर्शयोर्योगः अभिनिधानसंज्ञः । किं च । अवगृह्यपदे स्पर्शयोः सन्धौ सैव संज्ञा । पदान्तग्रहणेनावग्रहस्यान्तःपातित्वात् । अवग्रहशब्देन निषिद्धावग्रहपदानि संज्ञादिषूक्तानि । तत्र पदान्तसन्धौ भवत्वेतदर्थं पृथग्ग्रहणम् । पदान्तसन्धि । अवगृह्यपदम् । 'दम्ऽपंती' (पद, अ.वे. १२.३.१४)। 'सम्ऽगमंनम्' (पद, अ.वे. १८.१.४९)। 'घर्मसत्ऽभिः' (पद, अ.वे. १८.३.४७)। निषिद्धावग्रहम् । 'हिरण्मयम्' (अ.वे.पै.सं. ७.५.८)। 'मरुतः' (अ.वे. २.२९.५)। 'अधरात्तात्' (ऋ.वे. १०.३६.१४, not in AV, but found in the late text Gaṇeśa-Atharvaśīrṣa)। 'इत्थम्' (अ.वे. ३.१३.७)। स्पर्शयोः किम् । 'उत्ऽश्वञ्चमाना' (पद, अ.वे. १८.३.५१)। 'उत् । श्वञ्चस्व' (पद, अ.वे. १८.३.५०)।

Note: Bhārgava-Bhāskara also brings the words *sparśasya sparśe pare* into this rule and says that this rule applies to a stop which occurs at the end of a word and is followed by the initial stop the next word. With this interpretation, he says that the previous rule applies to stops in non-final position.

For Bhārgava-Bhāskara to be correct, one must assume that one is dealing with external sandhi applications, and not with what happens to the word-final stop in the Padapāṭha before pause. In that case, the rule would be dealing with two entirely unrelated situations, one a situation of a word-final stop followed by a word-initial stop, and the second a situation where the word-final stop is followed by an avagraha, a mini-pause to mark the separation of the members of a compound in the Padapāṭha. This seems to be a very unlikely combination. The best way is to take this rule to apply to the word-final stops before pause in the Padapāṭha.

Another feature of Bhārgava-Bhāskara's interpretation is that he views the term *abhinidhāna* as applying to both the stops involved in a conjunct. This does not seem to be correct.

It is interesting to note that all the instances of the word *hiraṇmaya-* listed in Vishva Bandhu's *Grammatical Word-Index to the Atharvaveda* (p. 678) are from the Paippalāda Atharvaveda. However, it should be noted that the word *hiraṇmaya* as a variant for *hiraṇyaya* does occur in the mss. of the ŚAV. See the variants given for *hiraṇyayīm* in AV (10.2.33) in the VVRI edition.

१.२.६. लकारस्योष्मसु ।

Whitney (1.46). G: 1.2.6.

Translation: The consonant *l* [is reduced to *abhinidhāna*] before spirants.

Note: Whitney notes that "only spirants before which *l* is found actually to occur in the Atharvaveda are *ś* and *h*." Whitney has discussed the details of how this notion is highly eclectic and that other treatises propose different treatments for *l* under similar circumstances. His own response to this prescription, however, is: "I must confess myself unable to explain why either *l* before a spirant, or the nasals before *h*, as taught in the next rule, should suffer or be regarded as suffering the obscuring process of *abhinidhāna*." As far as the case of the *abhinidhāna* taught by the present rule is concerned, Varma (1929: 147) says: "This probably refers to a sporadic phenomenon in some of the dialects, for in the majority of cases we should expect Svarabhakti after *l* or *r* before fricatives. The fact that this sporadic phenomenon actually existed in some dialects is corroborated by Prākrit *vassa-*, side by side with, in the majority of cases, *varisa-*, *valiśa-*."

चतुराध्यायीभाष्य - लकारस्य ऊष्मसु परतः । अभिनिधानो भवति । 'श॒तब॑ल्शा॒ वि रो॑ह' (अ.वे. ६.३०.२)। 'स ग॑मिष्यति॒ बल्हिकान्' (अ.वे. ५.२२.९)। 'वि॒हल्हो॒ नाम॑' (अ.वे. ६.१६.२)।

Note: Referring to the expression *balhikān* cited as an example of this rule, Whitney (*AV Transl.* Vol.I., p. 260) says: "The Prāt. rule i.46 (= CA

1.2.6) applies, if we may trust the comment, to the name in d (in AV 5.22.5) and proves it to be *bálhika*, and not *báhlika*; the mss. vary between the two, the majority giving *-lh-;* but the testimony of no ms. is of any authority on this particular point; Ppp. appears to have *-hl-*." The APR (175: गल्हे विल्हौ हकारान्तः संयोगः) supports the CA rule. Witzel informs (in personal communication) that the Orissa mss regularly have *-lih-, -liś-* etc. The last two examples cited by the CAB are also found, though in reverse order, in APR (175). Contrast *balśā* of the CAB and the *valśā* of Bhārgava-Bhāskara.

भा.भा.वृत्ति - शषसहा ऊष्माणः । एषु परेषु लकारस्य योगे द्वयोर्व्यञ्जनयोः योगस्य अभिनिधानसंज्ञा । 'शतवंल्शा' (अ.वे. ६.३०.२)। 'सहस्रंवल्शा' तैत्तिरे (तै.सं. १.१.२.१)। 'बल्हिंकेषु' (अ.वे. ५.२२.५)। 'मल्हाम्' तैत्तिरे (तै.सं. १.८.१९.१) । ऊष्मसु इति किम् । 'सङ्कल्पकुंल्मलाम्' (अ.वे. ३.२५.२)। अत्र लद्वयस्य स्पर्शसंयोगः । 'तिल्पिञ्जम्' (अ.वे. १२.२.५४)। 'शुल्कम्' (अ.वे. ५.१९.३)। 'अलाण्डून्' (अ.वे. २.३१.२)। 'गल्दा' ऋग्वेदे ('गल्दंया,' ऋ.वे. ८.१.२०)। 'गुल्फौ' (अ.वे. १०.२.१)। 'उल्बंः' (अ.वे. ४.२.८)। 'प्रगल्भः' तैत्तिरीये (तै.सं. २.५.५.३)। 'शल्यः' (अ.वे. २.३०.३)। 'तंङ्गल्वा[३]त्' (अ.वे. ८.६.२१)।

Note: Half of Bhārgava-Bhāskara's commentary is occupied in giving examples of the combinations of *l* with non-spirants, where he says the *abhinidhāna* does not occur. The examples show his familiarity with the Ṛgveda, and the Taittirīya school of the Kṛṣṇa Yajurveda. It is, however, not clear why the example *alāṇḍūn* is offered. Here, we have an instance of *l* followed by a vowel.

१.२.७. ङणनानां हकारे ।

Whitney (1.47). G: 1.2.7.

Translation: The sounds *ṅ*, *ṇ*, and *n* [are reduced to *abhinidhāna*] before *h*.

Note: Whitney on the previous rule expresses his inability to explain why the change prescribed by the present rule should occur, and for some reason, Varma's (1929) extensive discussion of *abhinidhāna* does not cover the cases which come under the present rule. The only real examples from the AV are those of *ṅ* and *n* being followed by *h*. This occurs only for word-final *ṅ* and *n* before word-initial *h*, in the Saṃhitāpāṭha. In the Padapāṭha, the word-final *ṅ* and *n* would be followed by a pause, and hence would be reduced to *abhinidhāna* by CA (1.2.5). These sequences do not occur word-internally. The example with *sugaṇ* offered in the commentaries is an artificial example. It is, then, not entirely clear why *ṇ* was included in this rule. Fabricated examples with *gaṇ* or *sugaṇ* are found in the CAB on CA (2.1.9) and (3.2.2), and also in the Śikṣā verse cited in the CAB on CA (3.2.2). The late commentators in the Paṇinian tradition also resort to *sugaṇ*, cf. Siddhāntakaumudī on P.8.3.32 (ङमो ह्रस्वादचि ङमुण्नित्यम्). One may note that the KV on the same rule comes up with an example with an artificial *vaṇ*.

चतुराध्यायीभाष्य - ङणनानां हकारे परतः अभिनिधानो भवति । 'प्रत्यङ् हि' (अ.वे. ४.१९.७)। 'गण् हि' (not in AV)। 'क्रिमीन् हन्तु' (अ.वे. २.३२.१)। 'अमून् हेतिः' (अ.वे. ६.२९.१)।

भा.भा.वृत्ति - ङणनानां हकारे परे द्वयोर्योगे अभिनिधान-संज्ञा । 'प्रत्यङ् ह' (not in AV)। 'सुगण् हरः' (not in AV)। 'हिन्वन् हरयः' (अ.वे. २०.३१.२)।

१.२.८. आस्थापितं च ।

Whitney (1.48). G: 1.2.8.

Translation: [The *abhinidhāna* is] also called *āsthāpita* ['arrested'].

Note: The CAB seems to say that *āsthāpita* is simply another name for the *abhinidhāna*. Whitney has followed the CAB in interpreting *āsthāpita* as just another name for the *abhinidhāna*. He says that this alternative title "does not notably help our comprehension of it (= *abhinidhāna*): the word admits of being translated, in accordance with the explanation of *abhinidhāna* offered above, 'made to stand up to, or against;' but it may also be rendered 'stopped,' that is, 'silenced,' and so may favor another theory of the phenomenon." Allen (1953: 72) follows Whitney, except that he translates the term *āsthāpita* as 'arrested,' and takes it to be just another name for *abhinidhāna*.

RPR (4.1) uses the term *āsthāpita* to refer to consonant+consonant sandhi. It is therefore likely that the terms *āsthāpita* and *abhinidhāna* would have a largely overlapping area of application.

चतुराध्यायीभाष्य - आस्थापितसंज्ञश्च भवति । अभिनिधानश्च । एतान्येवोदाहरणानि ।

भा.भा.वृत्ति - आ मध्ये स्थाप्यते स्म तत् आस्थापितम् । आगम इत्यर्थः । स आगमः पूर्वोत्तरव्यञ्जनेन सह अभिनिधानसंज्ञः स्यात् । 'बट्त्सूर्य' (अ.वे. २०.४८.४) । 'तान्त्संवितः' (W: तां सवितः, अ. वे. ७.१५.१) । 'प्रत्यङ्ङुदेषि' (अ.वे. १३.२.२०) । 'आवत्स्यंन्नंमन्यत' (अ.वे. १५.६.७)। 'सर्वाञ्च्छलुनान्' (W: सर्वां, अ.वे. २.३१.२)। 'इच्छन्ति' (अ.वे. २०.१८.३)।

Note: Quite a different interpretation for the rule is proposed by Bhārgava-Bhāskara in his commentary. He takes the term *āsthāpita* as being equivalent to *āgama* 'augment, appended item,' in the Pāṇinian tradition. According to his explanation, the consonantal augments inserted between either two consonants, or between a consonant and a vowel, are referred to by the term *āsthāpita*. According to him, such a consonantal augment, along with the preceding and the following consonant is given the name *abhinidhāna*.

For instance, in an example like *tān+savitaḥ*, by following CA (2.1.9: ङणनानां कटतैः शषसेषु), a euphonic *t* is inserted between the final *n* and the initial *s*, giving us *tān-t-savitaḥ*. According to the interpretation suggested by Bhārgava-Bhāskara, this euphonic *t* would be reduced to an *abhinidhāna*, i.e. 'an unreleased stop.' The dialectal instability of such augments is indicated by the fact that these are made optional in Pāṇini (8.3.28-31). The *abhinidhāna* character of such a sound would indeed manifest in such instability. However, we do not have any way to confirm independently that the term *āsthāpita* was used to refer to such 'augments.'

The examples प्रत्यङ्ङुदेषि and आवर्त्स्यन्नंमन्यत need to be distinguished from other examples. Here, the augments *ṅ* and *n* are immediately preceded by *ṅ* and *n*, but are followed by vowels.

It may also be noted that the manuscripts of the AV do not exhibit these readings with the added augments.

१.२.९. अतोऽन्यत्संयुक्तम् ।

Whitney (1.49). G: 1.2.9. A, B, D: °त्य° for °न्य°.

Translation: [A consonant, involved in a consonant+consonant combination], other than these [i.e. listed under the category of *abhinidhāna*], is called *saṃyukta* 'conjunct.'

Note: It should be noted that the scope of the notion of *saṃyoga* is different from that of the term *saṃyukta*, though both of these terms are etymologically related. The term *saṃyoga* as used in CA (1.2.11: ह्रस्वं लघ्वसंयोगे) and CA (1.4.7: व्यञ्जनान्यव्यवेतानि स्वरैः संयोगः) encompasses all consonant+consonant combinations, including those covered under *abhinidhāna*. On the other hand, the term *saṃyukta* excludes the cases of *abhinidhāna*. It would seem that the distinction between *abhinidhāna* and *saṃyukta* was phonetically relevant, but not grammatically. Probably for this reason, Pāṇini used only the broad notion of *saṃyoga*, cf. P.1.1.7 (हलोऽनन्तराः संयोगः), and dispensed with the distinction between *abhinidhāna* and *saṃyukta*.

चतुराध्यायीभाष्य - अतोऽन्ये व्यञ्जनसंधयः संयुक्ता भवन्ति । अन्ये अभिनिधानात् पदान्तात् स्पर्शाः (Whitney's emendation: पदान्तस्पर्शाः)। अन्तस्थोष्मसु पदा(भि?)दिषु च संयुज्यन्ते । 'गोधुग्याति' । 'विराड्याति' । 'दृषद्याति' । 'त्रिष्टुब्याति' । 'गोधुग्वयति' । 'विराड्वयति' । 'त्रिष्टुब्वयति' । 'गोधुग्रथे' । 'विराड्रथे' । 'षड्रथे' । 'गोधुक्शेते'। 'विराज(ट्?)शेते(?)'। 'दृषत(?)शेते' । 'त्रिष्टुप्शेते' । 'गोधुक्षण्डे' । 'विराड्(ट्?)षण्डे' । 'दृषत्षण्डे' । 'त्रिष्टुप्षण्डे' । 'गोधुक्साये' । 'विराड्(ट्?)साये'। 'दृषत्साये' । 'त्रिष्टुप्साये' ।

Note: Both the manuscripts write त्रि as तृ or नृ. All the examples cited by the CAB are artificial examples produced by combinations and permutations of a few words. It is again interesting to note that Surya Kanta does not claim these as belonging to the so-called lost recension of the genuine Śaunakīya AV. Surya Kanta's overall argument is weakened by the obvious existence of such a large number of non-AV examples in this commentary. Examples with *śete*, *sāye*, and *ṣaṇḍe* are found in the KV on P.8.3.28, 29, 30, and 36. These examples are not textual quotations, but possible usages.

The wording of the CAB, i.e. अन्ये अभिनिधानात् पदान्तात्, creates an impression that the term *saṃyoga* applies to cases of contact between a final and an initial, but, as Whitney correctly notes, such is not the case.

भा.भा.वृत्ति - अभिनिष्टानाभिनिधानसन्नतरसंज्ञाभ्योऽन्यत् व्यञ्जनयोर्योगः अनुस्वारव्यञ्जनयोगश्च संयुक्तसंज्ञो ज्ञेयः । कः सः । स्पर्शान्तस्थसंयोगः । लकारस्य स्पर्शान्तस्थसंयोगः । ङणनानां हसंयोगवर्जम् । 'सत्यम्' (अ.वे. २.१५.५)। 'संवत्सरः' (अ.वे. ३.१०.८)। 'अराय्यः' (अ.वे. १.२८.४)। 'वायव्यान्' (अ.वे. १९.६.१४)। 'आचार्यः' (११.५.३)। 'शल्यम्' (अ.वे. ७.१०७.१, VVRI edn.: ७.११२.१)। 'आश्यम्' (?)। 'हविष्यम्' (अ.वे.पै.सं. १.८९.३, no occurrence in ŚAV)। 'सस्यम्' (अ.वे. ७.११.१, VVRI edn.: ७.१२.१)। 'गृह्यं[ाः]' (अ.वे. ५.२०.४)। 'व(वा?)-य्वोः' (not in AV)। 'सर्वः' (अ.वे. १.७.४)। 'तंङ्गल्वा-[३]त्' (अ.वे.८.६.२१)। 'अश्वः' (अ.वे. २.३०.५)। 'दु[ष्]-ष्वप्न्य[म्]' (अ.वे. ६.४६.३)। 'स्वः' (अ.वे. १.१९.३)। 'अह्वे' (अ.वे. ४.२७.१)। 'सुव्रतम्' ('सुव्रतानाम्,' अ.वे. ७.६.२) । 'श्रथय' ('श्रथयां,' अ.वे. १.११.३)। 'ह्ना-(ह्रा?)दुनी' (अ.वे.पै.सं. १२.७.८, not found in ŚAV)। 'सहस्रम्' (अ.वे. १.१०.२)। 'अर्कः' (अ.वे. ४.१५.५)।

Note: Bhārgava-Bhāskara adds another important consideration, namely that the term *saṃyukta* not only excludes the cases of *abhinidhāna*, but that it also excludes the cases of *abhiniṣṭāna* as defined in CA (1.2.1: विसर्जनीयोऽभिनिष्टानः). Additionally, he includes the combination of an *anusvāra* with a consonant under the term *saṃyukta*. Such a separate listing of the *anusvāra* is prompted by the unclear position of the *anusvāra* in relation to the distinction between vowels and consonants. The RPR (1.22: अनुस्वारो व्यञ्जनं च) also lists *anusvāra* separately, because of the ambiguous position of the *anusvāra*, cf. RPR (1.5: अनुस्वारो व्यञ्जनं वा स्वरो वा).

१.२.१०. पूर्वरूपस्य मात्रार्धं समानकरणं परम् ।

Whitney (1.50). G: 1.2.10. I: 10.

Translation: The final half-mora of the previous [consonant, in a case of consonant+consonant combination) has the same *karaṇa* [= articulator or mode of articulation?] as the following [consonant].

Note: Whitney first says that the word *karaṇa* in the rule should not be restricted to the notion of 'organ,' or articulator, but should be broadly interpreted in the sense of 'mode of production.' He then points out the main difficulty in interpreting this rule: "Of the accuracy of the physical observations which could discover any actual assimilation of the first element of these (e.g. *ts*, *st*) and other similar combinations, in its final portion, to the latter, I find it hard to say much in praise: I am unable to discover that any part of the *t* in *vatsau* becomes an *s*, or any part of *s* in *vaste* a *t*, any more than the *s* and *t*. One way of interpreting this rule is to say that in combinations like *ts*, the transition between *t* and *s* is marked by something like *th* which shares the features of both *t* and *s*. The rule in general may mark the propensity toward progressive assimilation."

Also compare Heffner (1952: 120): "The precise nature of the movements made to effect the contact of a stop consonant are determined (a) by the position or positions at which the stop is produced, and (b) by the position or positions from which the articulating organs have to move to get there. Any sound produced during these movements is inevitably a constantly changing sound: the contact phase or the onset of stop consonants is therefore sometimes called the on-glide of the consonant. Usually the audible sound produced by this onset is a modification of the preceding speech sound, whether vowel or consonant." The CA may be hinting at a modification of this type.

चतुराध्यायीभाष्य - पूर्वरूपस्य मात्रार्धं समानकरणं परं परेण भवति । 'वत्सौ(H, N: त्सो) विराजः' (अ.वे. ८.९.१)। 'स्तोमा आसन्' (अ.वे. १४.१.८)। 'अयं वंस्ते' (अ.वे. १३.१.१६)। अपर आह -

पूर्वरूपस्य मात्रार्धं समानकरणं परम् ।
प्रत्ययेन भवेत्कार्यमेतत्संयुक्तमिष्यते ।

Note: Whitney draws our attention to the fact that this rule is itself a half Śloka and as such seems to have been quoted from another metrical source, and that the commentary quotes it as the first half of a verse. This raises a possibility that the metrical authority is older than the CA. It seems less likely that a text would take a line from the CA and would turn it into a full Śloka by adding a second half.

भा.भा.वृत्ति - अभिनिष्टानादिसंज्ञकेषु संयोगेषु पूर्वरूपस्य व्यञ्जनस्य विसर्गानुस्वारादेश्च परं व्यञ्जनं समानकरणं स्यात् । पूर्वाङ्गतां प्राप्नुयादित्यर्थः । तेन तदुच्चारे मात्रार्धं कालः स्यान्नाधिकः । व्यञ्जनस्यापि मात्रार्धः कालस्तथैवाभिनिष्टानप्रभृतीनामित्यर्थः । 'कꣳ कंफोडौ' (Whitney's AV: कंफौडौ, अ.वे. १०.२.४)। 'चतुर्भ्यः' (अ.वे. १.१२.४)। 'दिवस्पृष्ठम्' (अ.वे. ४.१४.२)। 'शतवंल्शाः' (अ.वे. ६.३०.२)। 'दुःष्वप्न्यम्' (अ.वे. ६.४६.३)। 'सपत्नीम्' (अ.वे. ३.१८.१)। 'आर्त्नियोः' ('आत्न्योः,' अ.वे.पै.सं. १४.२.१३, not in ŚAV, 'आर्त्नियोः,' तै.सं. ४.५.१.३)।

१.२.११. ह्रस्वं लघ्वसंयोगे ।

Whitney (1.51). G: 1.2.11.

Translation: A short [syllable, i.e. a syllable with a short vowel], when not followed by a consonant cluster, is [metrically called] light.

Note: Whitney correctly takes the rule as referring to a syllable: "The distinction of syllables, as regards their metrical value, is properly into light (*laghu*) and heavy (*guru*); long (*dīrgha*) and short (*hrasva*) are terms to be used of vowels only. The neuter gender of the terms in the rule is to be explained by their agreement with *akṣaram*, 'syllable,' understood." While the CAB does not explicitly refer to the agreement with the term *akṣaram*, this is clearly seen in Bhārgava-Bhāskara's commentary.

चतुराध्यायीभाष्य - ह्रस्वं लघुसंज्ञं भवति । असंयोगे । 'दधिँ' (अ.वे. २०.१२७.९)। 'मधुँ' (अ.वे. १.३४.२)।

भा.भा.वृत्ति - ह्रस्वमक्षरं लघुसंज्ञकं स्यान्न तु संयोगे । संयोगोऽत्राभिनिष्टानादीनामुपलक्षणम् । 'च' (अ.वे. १.२.४)। 'वि' (अ.वे. १.१.४)। 'नु' (अ.वे. २.५.५)। 'कृ-तम्' (अ.वे. ३.९.२)। 'च[ा]क्लृपे' (अ.वे. ७.८७.१, VV-RI edn.: ७.९२.१)। संयोगे परे तु गुरुत्वं स्यात् । 'अप्सु' (अ.वे. १.४.४)। 'पत्नीँ' (अ.वे. २.१२.१)। 'व्यन्तुँ' (अ.वे. ७.४९.२, VVRI edn.: ७.५१.२)। 'कᳲ कंफोडौ' (Whitney's AV: कंफौडौ, अ.वे. १०.२.४)। 'तिस्रः' (अ.वे. ३.२४.६)। 'जिग्ये' (not attested in any known Vedic text)। 'विश्वंम्' (अ.वे. १.१०.२)। 'निन्दा' (निन्दाः, अ.वे. ११.८.२२, VVRI edn.: ११.१०.२२)। 'उत्सः' (अ.वे. ६.१०६.१)। 'रुद्रः' (अ.वे. १.१९.३)। 'शुक्लंम्' (अ.वे.पै.सं. १६.१२७.१-५, not in ŚAV)। 'शुष्कंम्' (not in AV, अ.वे. पै.सं. १७.१४.४, ऋ.वे. २.१३.६)। 'बुध्नम्' (अ.वे.पै.सं. ८.१४.८)। 'वृक्षः' (अ.वे. ४.७.५)। 'कृष्णम्' (अ.वे. ६.२२.१)। 'गृत्संम्' (ऋ.वे. ३.१९.१)। 'पृक्तम्' (not attested in any known Vedic text)। 'नृत्यम्' (शां.ब्रा. २९.५, not attested in any Saṃhitā)। 'क्लृप्तिः' (माध्यं.शु.य.सं. १८.११; काण्व.शु.य.सं. १९.३.२; तै.सं. ४.७.२.२.; मै.सं.

२.११.३)। 'क्रुम्तम्' (अ.वे.पै.सं. ५.१६.५)। 'अंशः' (अ.वे. ६.४.२)। 'इन्द्रः' (अ.वे. १.७.३)। 'मुञ्च' (अ.वे. १.१२. ३)। 'कृन्तति' (कृन्तती, अ.वे. १.२७.२)। 'हृदः' (अ.वे. ३.२५.६)। 'कलशः' (अ.वे. ९.१.६)। 'यः पतिः' (अ.वे. ९.४.१७)। 'नॄँ× पात्रम्' (शौनकशिक्षा, श्लोक २७, पृ. २२, ed. by K.N.M. Divakara Dvijendra, Tripunithura, 1962)।

Note: For नॄँ× पात्रम् and similar other examples, see: RPR (4.78): नॄँ× पतिभ्यो नॄँ× प्रणेत्रं नॄँ× पात्रं स्वतवाँ× पायुः । सन्धिर्विक्रान्त एवैषः ।

१.२.१२. गुर्वन्यत् ।

Whitney (1.52). G: 1.2.12.

Translation: [Any] other syllable [is called] heavy.

Note: Under the category of heavy syllable, we include (a) syllables with long vowels, and (b) syllables with short vowels followed by consonant clusters. Bhārgava-Bhāskara also adds syllables which end in consonants and *visarga*. He adds one more category, i.e. syllables with specially accented vowels, i.e. syllables with *svarita* vowels. This last category is not substantiated by any other text, and probably rests on a faulty citation from Piṅgala's Chandaḥsūtra. Bhārgava-Bhāskara's citation reads तथा स्वरव्यञ्जनान्तम्, and this forces him to come up with this last category. The original reading from Piṅgala is: प्लुतस्वरं व्यञ्जनान्तम्. Here Piṅgala specifically adds the tri-moraic *pluta* vowels. This would be automatically taken care of by our CA rule.

What is the purpose of defining the terms *laghu* and *guru*? These notions are not purposefully used ever again in the CA, the way they are used either by Pāṇini, or by the metrical texts. The commentary of Kṛṣṇadāsa on this rule clearly says: अत्र शास्त्रे लघुगुरुप्रयोजनाभावः, 'there is no purpose for the terms light and heavy in this system.'

चतुराध्यायीभाष्य - गुरु भवति अन्यत् । ह्रस्वं च संयोगे । दीर्घप्लुतौ च । 'तक्षति' (अ.वे. ९.१०.२१)। 'रक्षति'

(अ.वे. ८.९.१३)। 'शालाः' (अ.वे. ८.६.१०)। 'भूया३ इदा३म्' (अ.वे. ९.६.१८)।

भा.भा.वृत्ति - लघुसंज्ञायाः अन्यदक्षरं गुरुसंज्ञम् । तथा च छन्दःशास्त्रे चोक्तं पिङ्गलनागाचार्येण (छन्दःसूत्र, १.४) -

दीर्घं संयोगपरं तथा स्वरव्यञ्जनान्तमूष्मान्तम् ।
सानुस्वारं च गुरु क्वचिदवसानेऽपि लघ्वन्त्यम् ॥

इति । दीर्घं गुरु स्यात् । 'अश्विना' (अ.वे. ३.३.४)। 'पृथिवी' (अ.वे. २.१५.१)। 'बाहू' (अ.वे. ४.२.५)। 'पितृणाम्' (अ.वे. २.१२.४)। 'तन्वे' (अ.वे. १.३.१)। 'है' (अ.वे. ६.५०.२)। 'ओ' (अ.वे. १८.१.१)। 'देवौ' (अ.वे. ३.२९.६)। प्लुतं गुरु स्यात् । 'आ बभूवाँ३' (अ.वे. १०.२.२८)। संयोगपरम् । 'सत्यम्' (अ.वे. २.१५.५)। 'विष्णुः' (अ.वे. ३.२७.५)। 'चित्रम्' (अ.वे. १३.२.३४)। 'पुत्रः' (अ.वे. १.२५.३)। 'गृह्णाति' (अ.वे. ६.७६.४)। 'क्लृप्तिः' (not in AV, कठ.सं. २८.८, माध्यं.शु.य.सं. १८.११, काण्व.शु.य.सं. १९.३.२, तै.सं. ४.७.२.२, मै.सं. २.११.३, काठक.सं. १८.८)। स्वरः । स्वरितः । 'स्व१रा-भरत्' (अ.वे. १३.२.३९) । व्यञ्जनान्तम् । अस्वरे परे । 'बट्' (अ.वे. १३.२.२९)। 'अस्मिन्' (अ.वे. १.९.१)। 'अग्निम्' (अ.वे. १.६.२)। 'बाहुम्' (अ.वे. १८.१.११)। 'त्रिष्टुप्' (अ.वे. ८.९.२०)। 'सकृत्' (अ.वे. २०.११६.२)। ऊष्मान्तम् । ऊष्मा विसर्गः । 'अपः' (अ.वे. १.४.३)। 'अग्निः' (अ.वे. १.७.४)। 'ऋतुः' (अ.वे. ७.४९.२, VVRI edn.: ७.५१.२)। सानुस्वारं व्यञ्जने परे । 'इन्द्रं वै' (तां.म.ब्रा. १२.६.८)। 'अग्निं च' (अ.वे. १.६.२)। 'शत्रुं च' (?)। 'अवंतु' (अ.वे. १८.३.१५)। पदान्तस्य विरामे तु नानुस्वारः किन्तु मकार एव । 'अग्निम्ऽइव' (अ.वे.

७.४५.१, VVRI edn.: ७.४७.१)। 'देवम्' (अ.वे. ४.२५.७)। यस्य छन्दसः पादान्ते गुरुरेव विहितः तत्र लघ्वक्षरमागतं चेत् तद् गुरुरेवेति विज्ञेयम् । छन्दःशास्त्रे आर्याप्रभृतिषु द्रष्टव्यम् । 'न वदति सद्वै करोत्येव' (source?)। अत्र[ा]न्ते वकारो लघुरपि गुरुः स्यादिति ज्ञेयम् । 'विप्राद् द्विषड्गुणयुतादरविन्दनाभः' (source?) इत्यत्र पादान्ते भकारो गुरुरेव 'वसन्ततिलका त्भौ जौ गौ' (छन्दःसूत्र ७.८) इति गुरुस्थाने प्रयुक्तत्वात् लघोरपि गुरुत्वम् ।

१.२.१३. अनुनासिकं च ।

Whitney (1.53). G: 1.2.13.

Translation: [A syllable with] a nasalized [vowel is] also [heavy].

Note: From a metrical point of view of the late MIA period, there is a distinction between nasalizing a vowel and adding an *anusvāra*. For instance, referring to Jaina Prakrits, A.M. Ghatage (1941: 11) says: "The Anunāsika does not change the quantity of a syllable, but Anusvāra makes it long." It is not quite clear what the situation was in Sanskrit, because the nasalized vowels are not attested in metrical texts where the nasalization would make metrical difference. Pāṇini distinguishes an *anunāsika* from an *anusvāra*, cf. P.8.3.4 (अनुनासिकात् परोऽनुस्वारः). It is clear that nasalization has nothing to do with the light/contrast. What is not clear is whether an *anusvāra* made a vowel long.

However, the CA does not make any such clear distinction between an *anusvāra* and an *anunāsika* vowel, and while it does use the term *anunāsika*, it does not use the term *anusvāra*. Varma (1929: 148) argues that in spite of the fact that the CA does not use the term *anusvāra*, it has the same notion of *anusvāra* as other phonetic texts. For a detailed discussion of the complicated issues, see: Varma (1929: 148ff); Allen (1953: 40ff). In any case, the CA considers a nasalized short vowel to form a heavy syllable. In terms of its metrical value, the notion of *anunāsika* in the CA is functionally identical with that of *anusvāra* elsewhere. For instance, verse (1.4) from Piṅgala's Chandaḥsūtra quoted in Bhārgava-Bhāskara's commentary on the previous rule makes a *sānusvāra* 'a vowel with the [following] *anusvāra*' into a heavy syllable.

चतुराध्यायीभाष्य - अनुनासिकं च गुरु भवति । 'द्वे चं मे विंशतिश्चं मे' (अ.वे. ५.१५.२)। 'तिस्रश्चं मे त्रिंशच्चं मे' (अ.वे. ५.१५.३)। 'चतंस्रश्च मे चत्वारिंशच्चं मे' (अ.वे. ५.१५.४)। 'पुमांन् पुंसः' (अ.वे. ३.६.१)। 'तत्रं पुंसवंनम्' (अ.वे. ६.११.१)।

भा.भा.वृत्ति - ह्रस्वं यदनुनासिकतां प्राप्तं तदपि गुरु स्यात् । 'पुरुष्टुतँ एकः' (अ.वे. २०.६१.६) ।

१.२.१४. पदान्ते च ।

Whitney (1.54). G: 1.2.14. I: पादान्ते च ।

Translation: Also at the end of a word [before pause, as in the Padapāṭha, a syllable is considered to be heavy].

Note: The Sanskrit tradition is more familiar with short syllables at the end of metrical lines being treated heavy for metrical purposes. This accounts for the variant reading पादान्ते च in ms. I. Also see Bhārgava-Bhāskara's commentary on CA (1.2.12).

The examples cited by the CAB make Whitney think that the rule is restricted to such final syllables as end with a consonant, and in corroboration, he refers to TPR (xxii. 14. 15). However, Bhārgava-Bhāskara's commentary includes word-final short vowels, as well as final syllables with short vowels, ending in a consonant. This would indicate that in the recitation of the ŚAV Padapāṭha as known to Bhārgava-Bhāskara, the word-final short vowels were recited as long vowels. This possibility is missed by Whitney and Allen (1953: 85). Since such a recitational practice was commonplace for short vowels occurring at the end of metrical feet, it seems likely to have been extended to all final vowels before pause.

चतुराध्यायीभाष्य - पदान्ते च गुरु भवति । 'गोधुक्' (अ.वे. ७.७३.६)। 'विराट्' (अ.वे. ८.९.८)। 'दृषत्' (अ.वे. २.३१.१)। 'त्रिष्टुप्' (अ.वे. ८.९.२०)।

भा.भा.वृत्ति - विरामे ह्रस्वम् । ह्रस्वोपधं च गुरु स्यात् । 'स्म' (अ.वे. १.८.२)। 'हि' (अ.वे. १.५.१)। 'तु' (अ.वे. ४.१८.६)। 'तत्' (अ.वे. १.१६.२)। 'इत्' (अ.वे. १.२.४)। 'त्रिष्टुप्' (अ.वे. ८.९.२०)। 'कृत्' (अ.वे. २.२७.६)। 'इन्द्रः' (अ.वे. १.७.३)। 'अग्निः' (अ.वे. १.७.४)। 'क्रतुः' (अ.वे. ८.९.२२)।

१.२.१५. परस्य स्वरस्य व्यञ्जनानि ।

Whitney (1.55). G: 1.2.15.

Translation: [In the syllabic segmentation], consonants belong to the following vowel.

Note: As Whitney notes, most Prātiśākhyas agree with each other on this doctrine. Thus, the word *dadhi* would be segmented into *da-dhi*, and *madhu* would be segmented into *ma-dhu*. Varma (1929: 55ff) has gone into a detailed examination of the rules of syllabication in the Prātiśākhyas. Also see: Allen (1953: 81ff). This is of course a general rule. Bhārgava-Bhāskara's commentary offers many examples of word-initial consonant-clusters which go with the following vowel.

Allen (1953: 82) considers the CA treatment of syllabic division as representing the generic rules. He also shows that other Prātiśākhyas hold differing views on this matter: "the *RP* allows either the division of a medial consonant-group or its attachment in toto to the following vowel, and the *TP* attaches to the following vowel a group consisting of consonant+semivowel or stop+fricative." Allen refers to Chatterji's opinion that the Nāgarī graphic system may be based on such a syllabic structure. My own conjecture is that the syllabic division allowed by these two texts may have been a result of confusing the notion of written syllable with a spoken syllable, as is certainly evidenced by the syllabic division of the famous Gāyatrī mantra found in one of the Atharva-Pariśiṣṭas, i.e. Anulomakalpa (p.146, Atharvaveda-Pariśiṣṭa, edited by Ram Kumar Rai, Chowkhamba Orientalia, Banaras, 1976): त--त्स--वि--तु--र्व--रे--णि--यं--भ--र्गो--दे--व--स्य etc.

चतुराध्यायीभाष्य - परस्य स्वरस्य व्यञ्जनानि भवन्ति। 'दधि' (अ.वे. २०.१२७.९)। 'मधु' (अ.वे. १.३४.२) ।

भा.भा.वृत्ति - स्वराः केवले सव्यञ्जनाश्चाक्षरसंज्ञाः सन्ति । अतो व्यञ्जनानि कस्याक्षरस्याङ्गानि भवन्तीत्युच्यते । व्यञ्जनानि परस्य स्वरस्याङ्गं भवन्तीत्यर्थः । 'स्वस्मै' (not attested in known Vedic texts)। 'कात्स्न्र्ये' (not attested in known Vedic texts)। 'विश्चपत्न्या' (?, 'विश्वपत्न्या,' अ.वे.पै.सं. १.४१.३, 'विश्पत्न्यै,' अ.वे. ७.४६.२)। 'स्फ्ये' ('स्फ्यौ,' अ.वे. ११.३.९)। 'च' (अ.वे. १.२.४)। 'प्र' (अ.वे. ४.३३.३)। 'नि' (अ.वे. १५.११.२)। 'श्रीः' (अ.वे. ११.७.३, VVRI edn.: ११.९.३)। 'नु' (अ.वे. २.५.५)। 'द्रु' (only in combinations like 'द्रुपदात्,' अ.वे. ६.११५.२)। 'द्यु' (only in forms like द्युवम्, अ.वे. ७.५०.९, VVRI edn.: ७.५२.९)।

१.२.१६. संयोगादि पूर्वस्य ।

Whitney (1.56). G: 1.2.16. G: °दिः°.

Translation: [A consonant occurring] at the beginning of a consonantal cluster belongs to the previous [syllable].

चतुराध्यायीभाष्य - संयोगादि पूर्वस्य स्वरस्य भवति । 'अत्र सति' (आत्रसति?)। 'आद्रवति' (the only AV form, 'आद्रवत्,' अ.वे.पै.सं. २.३१.२)। 'प्रद्रवति' (no attested AV forms for प्र+द्रु)। अपर आह - हसयमं पूर्वस्येति (सयमं पूर्वस्येति?)।

Note: Compare a similar passage in the commentary on CA (3.2.3) and the Note thereupon for a possible reconstruction as: अपर आह - सयमं पूर्वस्येति.

Also compare the wording of VPR (1.102: संयोगादिः पूर्वस्य).

While Whitney may be right in criticizing the CAB for offering fabricated examples like *atra sati*, it is not clear to me what to make of Whitney's following comment: "he (= commentator) does not note for us the fact that, in the combinations which he presents, the former consonant is to be doubled, by iii. 28, and then inform us to which of the two products of duplication the precept of the rule applies." The rule seems to be a generic enough rule, giving a basic principle, and it does not matter at this stage what the length of the consonant-cluster is.

The passage of the commentary अपर आह हसयमं पूर्वस्येति probably restores to अपर आह - सयमं पूर्वस्येति. This comment would then mean that an initial consonant of a cluster, along with *yama*, belongs to the previous syllable.

भा.भा.वृत्ति - पदान्तसन्धिकरणे पूर्वपदान्तव्यञ्जनमेकं वा द्वे व्यञ्जने वा अनुस्वारो वा विसर्गो वा अक्षरवर्णने व्यञ्जने परे संयोगे परे वा पूर्वस्याङ्गं भवति । संयोगस्यादि । संयोगे परे आदिरिति द्विविधसमासकरणात् । संयोगस्यादिः । 'तच्चक्षुंः' (ऋ.वे. ७.६६.१६)। 'रिषᳶ पांतु' (अ.वे. ८.३.१)। 'कᳵ कंफोडौ' (Whitney's AV: 'कंफौडौ,' अ.वे. १०.२.४)। 'शतं ते' (अ.वे. ३.११.४)। संयोगपरे आदिः । 'ऊर्ग्भिः' (not attested in Vedic known texts)। 'हायनान्द्वे' (अ.वे. ८.२.२१)। 'अदब्धान्स्पृणुहि' ? (Whitney: 'आरंब्धान्त्स्पृणुहि,' अ.वे. ८.३.७)। पदान्तसन्धीति किम् । 'अक्षैः' (अ.वे. ७.५०.१, VVRI edn.: ७.५२.१)। 'विश्वंम्' (अ.वे. १.१०.२)। 'अन्तंः' (अ.वे. ९.१०.१४, VVRI edn.: ९.१५.१४)। 'इन्द्रंः' (अ.वे. १.७.३)। 'आर्त्नीं' (अ.वे. १.१.३)। 'विश्पत्नैः' ? ('विश्पत्न्यैं,' अ.वे. ७.४६.२)। अत्र भत्वम् । अयस्मयादित्वात् । तेन शकारस्थितिः । व्यञ्जनत्रयसंयोगे किञ्चिद्विशेषो ग्रन्थान्तरात् । अक्षरनिर्देशो

विवक्षुणा यथेच्छमुच्चार्यते । द्विसंयोगः त्रिसंयोगो वा । इन्द्र-शब्दे द्रशब्दः । स्फ्य इत्यत्र फ्यकार इत्यादि ज्ञेयम् । एवं व्यञ्जनचतुष्कादौ च । 'कार्त्स्न्यम्' (not attested in known Vedic texts, late epic form)। 'आवर्त्स्यन्' (अ.वे. १५.६.७)।

१.२.१७. पद्यं च ।

Whitney (1.57). G: 1.2.17.

Translation: A word-final consonant [before pause] also [belongs to the previous syllable].

Note: The term *padya* has been defined in CA (1.1.5: पदान्तः पद्यः) as referring to the sound occurring at the end of a *pada*. Also see the Note on CA (1.1.7) for further clarification of the meaning of *pada*. Though the term generally refers to an inflected item, it occasionally refers to members of compounds and to pre-affixal nominal bases. The CAB examples only illustrate the standard word-final consonants.

चतुराध्यायीभाष्य - पद्यं च पूर्वस्वरस्य भवति । 'गोधुक्' (अ.वे. ७.७३.६)। 'विराट्' (अ.वे. ८.९.८)। 'दृषत्' (अ.वे. २.३१.१)। 'त्रिष्टुप्' (अ.वे. ८.९.२०)।

भा.भा.वृत्ति - अवसाने पदान्ते यद् व्यञ्जनं । चात् व्यञ्जने परेऽनुस्वाराभिनिष्टानौ पूर्वस्यैवाङ्गं स्यात् । 'तत्' (अ.वे. १.१६.२)। 'षट्' (अ.वे. ४.११.१)। 'तम्' (अ.वे. १.१६.४)। 'सः' (अ.वे. १.८.१)। 'ऊर्क्' (not in AV)। 'सुहार्द्(र्त्?)' (अ.वे. २.७.५)। 'सुहाः' (अ.वे. २.७.५)।

Note: The manuscript variation *suhārt* / *suhāḥ* for AV (2.7.5) is noted in the VVRI edition, as well as in the VVRI concordance, Sec. I, Pt. V, p. 3440.

Bhārgava-Bhāskara also points out that by the force of *ca* 'and,' the rule also refers to *anusvāra* and *visarga* as they occur before consonants (व्यञ्जने परे). This would assume that the rule applies to the Saṃhitāpāṭha, where the final sound of the previous word is immediately followed, without a gap, by the initial of the next word. It is doubtful whether the rule is meant to apply to word-final consonants in other than pre-pausal situations. In all probability, the rule applies only to the Padapāṭha.

१.२.१८. रेफहकारक्रमजं च ।

Whitney (1.58). G: 1.2.18.

Translation: [A consonant] resulting from doubling (*krama*) [on account of the preceding] *r* and *h* [also belongs to the previous syllable along with the preceding *r* and *h*].

चतुराध्यायीभाष्य - रेफहकारक्रमजं च पूर्वस्य स्वरस्य भवति । 'अर्कः' (अ.वे. ४.१५.५)। 'अर्थः' (माध्यं.शु.य.सं. १८.५; काण्व.शु.य.सं. १९.५.३; तै.सं. ४.७.५.२; मै.सं. २.११.५; not in AV, Whitney's emendation: 'अर्चं,' अ.वे. २०.५१.१)। 'गर्त्ते' (ऋ.वे. ५.६२.५; not in AV, Whitney's emendation: 'वर्तः,' as in 'अभीवर्तः,' अ.वे. १.२९.३)। 'भग्नः' (?, षड्विंशब्राह्मण १.४.१६; not in any Saṃhitā, Whitney's emendation: 'भर्गः,' अ.वे. १९.३७.१)। 'प्राह्णः' (not in Vedic Saṃhitās)। 'पूर्वाह्णः' (not in AV, 'पूर्वाह्णे,' ऋ.वे. १०.३४.११)। 'अपराह्णः' (अ.वे. ९.६.४६)। 'अपब्रह्मलयति' (not in known Vedic texts, Whitney's emendation: 'अप ह्मलयति,' not in known Vedic texts)। 'विह्मलयति' (not in known Vedic texts)। 'अपह्नुते' (not in known Vedic texts)। 'विह्नुते' (not in known Vedic texts)। 'ब्रह्म' (अ.वे. १.१९.४)।

Note: Whitney justifiably complains about the lack of specificity in the explanation given by the CAB, and the lax orthography of the examples as found in the mss. does not offer any help either.

However, what the rule means is clear. CA (3.2.8: रेफहकारौ परं ताभ्याम्), like P.8.4.46 (अचो रहाभ्यां द्वे), prescribes doubling of the consonant following *r* and *h*. Thus, for instance, in the example *arkaḥ*, by applying CA (3.2.8), we get the sequence *arkkaḥ*. The present rule then says that the first of the doubled consonant, along with the preceding *r* or *h*, becomes part of the previous syllable, i.e. the syllabic division is *ark-kaḥ*, rather than *ar-kkaḥ*. The writing of the mss. does not show these doubled consonants in the examples.

Whitney includes the example विह्नुते on the basis of other passages in his manuscript, though this example is not found in the commentary on this rule in the manuscript H which was the only manuscript accessible to Whitney. Interestingly, the manuscript N supports Whitney's inclusion of this example. Also see the commentary on CA (3.2.8) and the Note thereupon. The only Saṃhitā form attested for *vi*+√*hnu* is a manuscript variant *vihnutasya* for *vi-hvṛtasya* in PAV (20.13.8). Also compare the text of the commentary on CA 3.2.8. The readings of the examples there support Whitney's emendations in most cases.

भा.भा.वृत्ति - क्रमः व्यञ्जनस्य द्वित्वं तृतीयाध्याये द्वितीय-पादे वक्ष्यते । रेफहकाराभ्यां स्वरात्पराभ्यां परस्य व्यञ्जनस्य द्विर्भावो यत्र भवति तत्र क्रमजं व्यञ्जनं रेफहकारेण सह पूर्वाङ्गं स्यात् । 'अर्क्कः' (अ.वे. ४.१५.५)। 'गृह्ण्णाति' (अ.वे. ६.७६.४)।

Note: We are happily surprised that Bhārgava-Bhāskara's commentary answers all the objections Whitney had against the CAB. It gives a crisp interpretation, and the ms. G shows the doubled consonants in writing. Besides other elements in the interpretation, Bhārgava-Bhāskara appropriately points out that this doubling of the consonant after *r* or *h* occurs only if this group comes after a vowel (स्वरात् पराभ्याम्). This condition on CA (3.2.8: रेफ-हकारौ परं ताभ्याम्) is provided by the continuing expression *svarāt* from CA (3. 2.3). Unfortunately, the CAB on CA (3.2.3) does not make this clear. With this condition, CA (3.2.8) becomes a close equivalent of P.8.4.46 (अचो रहाभ्यां द्वे).

१.२.१९. एकमात्रो ह्रस्वः ।

Whitney (1.59). G: 1.2.19. Most mss. read *rhasvaḥ*.

Translation: [A vowel] with one mora [duration] is called "short."

चतुराध्यायीभाष्य - एकमात्रो ह्रस्वो भवति । 'दधिं' (अ.वे. २०.१२७.९)। 'मधुं' (अ.वे. १.३४.२) ।

भा.भा.वृत्ति - यस्याक्षरस्योच्चारणे एकमात्राकालो जायते तदक्षरं ह्रस्वसंज्ञं ज्ञेयम् । 'च' (अ.वे. १.२.४)। 'प्र' (अ.वे. ४.३३.३)। 'स्म' (अ.वे. १.८.२)। 'क्वं' (अ.वे. ९.९.४, VVRI edn.: ९.१४.४)। 'नि' (अ.वे. १५.११.२)। 'वि' (अ.वे. १.१.४)। 'स्फ्य' (only attested AV form: 'स्फ्यौ,' अ.वे. ११.३.९)। 'स्व' ('स्वः,' अ.वे. १.१९.३)।

Note: Referring to the Indian attempts to fix the duration of vowels etc. in minute units of 1/8 of a mora etc., Allen (1953: 84) says: "this unphonological approach undergoes a further degeneration in statements such as the following (from the *Pāṇinīya-Śikṣā* verse 49): '1 *mātrā* is equivalent to the cry of the blue jay, 2 *mātrās* to that of the crow, 3 *mātrās* to that of the peacock, and 1/2 *mātrā* to that of the mongoose.'" I certainly agree with Allen that such descriptions are unphonological. However, I do not believe that it represents any degeneration. Part of the problem lies in using the dichotomy of phonetic versus phonological in reference to Indian texts, which know of no such overt theoretical distinction. I have discussed some of these issues in the Introduction. Secondly, once we realize that a *mātrā* is a unit of time, there ought to be at least an approximate indication of how long a unit of time a *mātrā* is and such a need is fulfilled by the statements like the one quoted from the Pāṇinīya-Śikṣā. Another reason I am not willing to accept the notion of degeneration is that it assumes that the earlier texts were free from this practice. However, even the great Pāṇini seems to refer to a rooster-call in his rule defining the duration of short, long and extra-long vowels, cf. P.1.2.27 (ऊकालोऽज्झस्वदीर्घप्लुतः). Whitney also refers to RPR (xiii. 20) which "attempts to fix the length of the short, long, and protracted vowels, by comparing them with the cries of certain birds." Many texts in Indian music also define the various musical notes by referring to bird-calls. In a pre-modern age, these were the only available means of approximately indicating the length, pitch etc.

The one point which goes against trying to fix the absolute duration of short, long etc. is that the Sanskrit grammarians do admit that there are different modes of delivery (*vṛtti*) such as fast (*druta*), medium (*madhya*), and slow (*vilambita*), and that fixing absolute durations would militate against the notion of different speeds of delivery. Whitney, I believe, is correct in saying: "It is the fundamental measure, which cannot itself be defined by anything else."

१.२.२०. व्यञ्जनानि च ।

Whitney (1.60). G: 1.2.20.

Translation: The consonants too [are of one-mora duration each].

Note: Almost all other texts consider consonants to be of half-mora length. The commentary of Bhārgava-Bhāskara struggles in vain to reconcile the CA view with thc general view. It does bring up the topic of the possible metrical value of setting a specific duration for consonants, but does not tackle it successfully. For a clear analysis of this subject, see: Allen (1953: 86).

चतुराध्यायीभाष्य - व्यञ्जनानि च एकमात्राणि भवन्ति । 'दधि' (अ.वे. २०.१२७.९)। 'मधु' (अ.वे. १.३४.२) ।

भा.भा.वृत्ति - व्यञ्जनान्यप्येकमात्राकालजानीति वेदितव्यम् । तानि कानि । उच्यते । स्वरात्पराणि पदान्ते स्थितानि संयोगपराणि (।) संयोगादीनि वा पद्यानि वा एकमात्राणि स्युः । अन्यत्र बहुसंयोगेऽपि यत्र यत्र पराङ्गत्वं तस्यार्धमात्रैव ज्ञेया । 'तत्' (अ.वे. १.१६.२)। 'तम्' (अ.वे. १.१६.४)। 'स्वः' (अ.वे. २.५.२)। 'न्यक्' (अ.वे. ६.९१.२)। एतादृशानामेकमात्रिकत्वादक्षरस्य गुरुत्वे मात्राद्वयं स्यात् । 'तच्चक्षुः' (ऋ.वे. ७.६६.१६)। 'अद्भ्यः' (अ.वे. ३.३.३)।

१.२.२१. द्विमात्रो दीर्घः ।

Whitney (1.61). G: 1.2.21.

Translation: [A vowel] with two-mora [duration] is a long [vowel].

चतुराध्यायीभाष्य - द्विमात्रो दीर्घो भवति । 'शाला' (अ.वे. ९.३.१७)।

भा.भा.वृत्ति - यस्याक्षरस्योच्चारणे द्विमात्रकः कालो जायते स स्वरः दीर्घसंज्ञः । 'आ' (अ.वे. १.१४.३)। 'पृथिवी' (अ.वे. २.१५.१)। 'बाहू' (अ.वे. ४.२.५)। 'मातॄः' (अ.वे. ९.९.१०, VVRI edn.: ९.१४.१०)। 'पितॄन्' (अ.वे. ५.३०.१)। 'सर्वै' (अ.वे. १.७.५)। 'वन्दध्यै' (अ.वे. २०. ३५.५)। 'उपो' (अ.वे. १३.७.१६) । 'देवौ' (अ.वे. ३. २९.६)।

१.२.२२. त्रिमात्रः प्लुतः ।

Whitney (1.62). G: 1.2.22. I: 21.

Translation: [A vowel] with three-mora [duration] is a prolonged (*pluta*) [vowel].

Note: By convention, number 3 is written after a long vowel to indicate a *pluta* vowel. Also note that Patañjali occasionally refers to *pluta* vowels with four *mātrā*s, cf. MB on P.1.1.51, (Kielhorn edn.), Vol. I, p. 120. On P.8.2.106, Patañjali clearly says that a *pluta* of four mora duration is desirable: इष्यत एव चतुर्मात्रः प्लुतः. As Allen (1953: 84) notes: "The *pluta* or protracted vowel ... is of rare occurrence and is bound to a very limited series of contexts; it represents the over-lengthening of the final vowel of a word or phrase and is used 'in cases of questioning, especially of a balancing between two alternatives, and also of calling to a distance or urgently. For most phonological purposes, however, the *pluta* vowel may be ignored." We need to keep in mind that there are occasions for non-final vowels undergoing protraction, cf. P.8.2.86 (गुरोरनृतोऽनन्त्यस्याप्येकैकस्य प्राचाम्). Also see CA (4.4.21: प्लुतश्चाप्लुतवत्), CA (1.4.6: अवशा आ बभूवाँ३ इतीतावेकारोऽप्लुतः) and P.6.1.129 (अप्लुतवदुपस्थिते) for non-*pluta*-like behavior of *pluta* vowels in certain contexts. All *pluta* vowels found in the text of the ŚAV are listed under CA (1.4.14).

चतुराध्यायीभाष्य - त्रिमात्र(:) प्लुतो भवति । 'भूंया३ इ॒दा३म्' (अ.वे. ९.६.१८)।

भा.भा.वृत्ति - यस्य स्वरस्य ह्रस्वस्य दीर्घस्य वा प्लुतता विधीयते तदुच्चारणे मात्रात्रयं कालः स्यात् । त्रिमात्रः स्वरः प्लुत इत्यर्थः । आ । बभूव । 'आ बभूवाँ' (अ.वे. १०.२. २८)। ऋग्वेदे । विन्दति । 'वि॒न्द॒ती॒ँ३' (ऋ.वे. १०. १४६.१)। खण्वखे । खैमखे । 'खण्व॒खा३इ॒ खैम॒खा३इ॒ मध्येँ' (अ.वे. ४.१५.१५)। प्लुत उदात्तः । एतद्वेदस्थानि प्लुतान्यग्रे सङ्ग्रहीष्यन्तेऽध्याये ।

इति प्रथमाध्यायस्य द्वितीयः पादः ।

H, N: प्रथमस्य द्वितीयपादः । ६२ । C, E, F: प्रथमस्य द्वितीयः पादः । A, B, D, J, M, P: द्वितीयः पादः । I: इति प्रथमाध्यायस्य द्वितीयः पादः । G: इत्यथर्ववेदांग-कौत्सव्याकरणस्य भार्गवभास्करीयवृत्तौ प्रथमाध्यायस्य द्वितीयपादव्याख्या संपूर्णा। O: इति प्रथमाध्यायस्य द्वितीयः पादः ।। २ ।। सूत्राणि ।। २१ ।।

चतुराध्यायीभाष्य - प्रथमस्य द्वितीयः पादः ।६२।

भा.भा.वृत्ति - अथाथर्ववेदाङ्गकौत्सव्याकरणस्य भार्गवभा-स्करीयवृत्तौ प्रथमाध्यायस्य द्वितीयपादव्याख्या संपूर्णा । २ ।

॥ प्रथमोऽध्यायः ॥
॥ तृतीयः पादः ॥

भा.भा.वृत्ति - अथाथर्ववेदाङ्गकौत्सव्याकरणस्य भार्गव-भास्करीयवृत्तौ प्रथमाध्यायस्य तृतीयपादस्थसूत्रव्याख्यारभ्यते । तत्रादावादेशबोधनमुच्यते । ॐ३म् ।

१.३.१. षट्पुरसोरुकारोऽन्त्यस्य [।] दशदाशयोरादेश्च मूर्धन्यः ।

Whitney (1.63), G, O, P: combine this rule with the following. G: 1.3.1. B, C (corr), D, Hc, J, M (corr): षो for सो. E, G, I, Na (corr) read °पुरसो°, but others read °पुरुसो°. Na (orig), Ha: षुट्पुसो°. O: °षट्परसोदुका°. A, B, C, D, M: °रादेश्च°, others: °रादेशाश्च°

Translation: The final [consonants] of *ṣaṣ* and *puras* are replaced with *u* before the words *daśa* and *dāśa*, respectively, and the initial [*d*] of these two words is replaced with a cerebral [*ḍ*].

Note: Whitney points out that the words *ṣoḍaśa* and *puroḍāśa* are not analyzed in the Padapāṭha, and are not restored to their theoretical original form in their repetition. This point is also made by Bhārgava-Bhāskara: अनयोर्नित्य-मेवंविधं रूपम् । न त्ववग्रहो, न समापत्तिः. In a way, Whitney is right in saying: "and our treatise, accordingly, according to its own programme, has nothing to do with them: and the same is true of the words referred to in the three following rules." The original reason why these words are not analyzed in the Padapāṭha may be identical with *sandehāt* 'excessive fusion / confusion of the constituents' given in CA (4.2.5: षोडशी सन्देहात्). See the Note on CA (4.2.5). The rules here mark progress of the analytical tradition beyond the state of *sandeha* manifest in the Padapāṭha. This is a move in the direction of general grammar.

चतुराध्यायीभाष्य - (**षट्पुरसोरुकारोऽन्त्यस्य दशदाशयो-रादेश्च मूर्धन्यः**) षट् पुरस्(H: पुरुष, N: पुरुस) इत्ये(H, N: त्य)तयोः उकारो भवति । अन्त्यस्य वर्णस्य । दशदाशयोः

परतः उत्तरपदादेश्च मूर्धन्यो भवति । 'षोडशः' ('षोडशम्', अ.वे. ३.२९.१)। 'पुरोडाशौ' (अ.वे. ९.६.१२)।

भा.भा.वृत्ति - (**षट्पुरसोरुकारोऽन्त्यस्य दशदाशयोरादेश्च मूर्धन्यः**) षट्शब्दस्य दशशब्दे परे पुरःशब्दस्य दाशशब्दे परे पूर्वपदान्तस्य षस्य सस्य च उत्वमुत्तरपदादेर्दस्य डत्वं भवति। षष् । पुरस् । 'षोडश' ('षोडशम्,' अ.वे. ३.२९.१)। 'पुरोडाशः' ('पुरोडाशाः,' अ.वे. ८.८.२२)। अनयोर्नित्यमेवंविधं रूपम् । न त्ववग्रहो न सगापत्तिः ।

१.३.२. कृपे रेफस्य लकारः ।

Whitney (1.64). G: 1.3.2.

Translation: The *r* of [the root] √*kṛp* is replaced by *l*.

Note: The rule is expected to apply to both, the *r* which is inside the vowel *ṛ* (*ərə*), as well as *r* occurring independently. Thus, effectively the rule changes *kṛp* to *kḷp*, and *karp* to *kalp*. The commentary CAB on this rule is missing in the manuscript H, and hence was not available to Whitney. It is, however, found in the ms. N. The Caturādhyāyībhāṣya offers examples of *kṛp* changing to *kḷp*, but not of *karp* changing to *kalp*. Such examples from the text of the ŚAV are offered by Bhārgava-Bhāskara. This rule also marks an advance beyond the Padapāṭha, which does not change *l* > *r*. There is also no Samāpatti of *l* to *r*. Thus, one may make a conjecture that the awareness of such a linkage of *kṛp* to *kḷp* may have arisen in the post-Padapāṭha period. Compare P.8.2.18 (कृपो रो लः). Also note that Pāṇini refers to the root as *kṛp*, while the CA refers to the root with the form *kṛpi*, with *kṛpeḥ* as a genitive.

Whitney also makes an interesting comment: "None of the other Prātiśākhyas offers anything equivalent. If our treatise has set itself to note the words in which a *l* appears in the place of a more original *r*, it should not pass over the words in which the root *car* becomes *cal*, as *avicācala*, *puṃścalī*, etc., *glaha* and *glahana*, which are hardly to be separated from the root *grah*, *udumbala* (viii.6.17), etc." One can perhaps derive a different inference from the rule as it stands, as well as from a number of rules that follow. While in this case, the change of *kṛp* to *kḷp* is taught by the rule, suggesting that an etymological linkage was acceptable to Indian grammarians, other cases mentioned by Whitney may not have been so acceptable to them. For example, Pāṇini's Dhātupāṭha separately lists *car*, *cal*, *grah*, and *glah*. On the other hand, as CA (1.3.4: लकारस्य रेफः ...) indicates, the author of the CA asks us to change *l* to *r* in a number of words, where modern linguists may perhaps think of the reverse direction of historical change. In any case, the rule does not indicate any 'historical' change. It does indicate, however, that for some not very explicit reasons, the *r* was felt to be derivationally more basic in some words, while in other words the sound *l* was felt to be more basic. For a similar discussion, see: Patañjali on P.8.2.18 (कृपो रो लः).

चतुराध्यायीभाष्य - कृपे रेफस्य लकारो भवति । 'अचीं-क्लृपत्' (अ.वे. ६.११.३)। 'पञ्चदशेनं क्लृप्ताः' (अ.वे. ८.९.१५)। 'सिनीवाल्यंचीक्लृपत्' (अ.वे. ६.११.३)।

भा.भा.वृत्ति - कृपेः कृपधातोः ऋवर्णस्थरेफस्य लत्वं स्यात् । ततो गुणोऽपि यत्र भवितव्यः । 'चक्लृपे' ('चाक्लृपे,' अ.वे. ७.९२.१)। 'क्लृप्तम्' (अ.वे.पै.सं. ५.१६.५)। 'क्लृप्तिः' (not in AV, कठ.सं. २८.८, माध्यं.शु.य.सं. १८.११, काण्व. शु.य.सं. १९.३.२, तै.सं. ४.७.२.२, मै.सं. २.११.३, काठक.सं. १८.८)। 'सङ्क्लृप्यकुंल्मलाम्' (अ.वे. ३.२५.२)। 'कल्पनम्' (not in AV, 'कल्पना', काठक.सं. ३५.५, कठ. सं. ४८.६)। 'कल्पयित्वा' (अ.वे. १३.१.५२)। 'अकंल्पत' (अ.वे. १३.१.४६)। 'कल्पंमानः' (अ.वे. ३.८.१)। इत्या-दिसर्वव्याकरणेष्वयमेवैकः ऌकारः प्रयोगार्हः नान्यः ।

१.३.३. न कृपादीनाम् ।

Whitney (1.65). G: 1.3.3.

Translation: [However, the change of *r* to *l* in the forms of the root *kṛp*] does not occur in words like *kṛpā*.

Note: As Whitney points out: "This is the first instance in our treatise of a rule stated in this form, the words or phrases to which the precept contained in the rule refers being conceived to form a series, or *gaṇa*, of which the first only is given in the rule, and the others comprehended in an *et cetera*. The form of statement is characteristic of the Atharva Prātiśākhya (= CA) and of Pāṇini." It is possible that the CA itself intended 'et cetera,' and may not have had a fixed list in mind. No fixed list is known to the APR, or the commentators. Patañjali, under P.8.2.18 (कृपो रो लः), also makes a similar statement: कृपणादीनां प्रतिषेधो वक्तव्यः । कृपणः, कृपाणः, कृपीटम्. Referring to *kṛpaṇaḥ* and *kārpaṇyam*, Whitney says: "If these two words, which come from altogether another root, actually belong to the *gaṇa*, it should contain also *kṛpamāṇasya* (v.19.13) and *akṛpran* (xviii.3.23)."

चतुराध्यायीभाष्य - न कृपादीनां रेफस्य लकारो भवति । 'कृपा पांवक' (अ.वे. १८.४.५९)। 'कृपात्स्वंः' (अ.वे. ७.१४.२)। 'कृपणः' ('कृपणाः,' अ.वे. ११.८.२८)। 'कार्पण्यम्' (not in known Vedic texts, a late epic form)।

Note: While the manuscript H contains the reading कृपस्विः, Whitney's conjecture कृपात्स्वः is supported by the manuscript N. Whitney's edition of the AV and his *Index Verborum* also read कृपात्स्वंः. However, he thinks that the reading कृपात्स्वंः "doubtless is a corrupt one, and should be *kṛpā svaḥ*, as is read by both the Sāma and Yajur-Vedas, in their corresponding verses." The VVRI edition (Vol. 2, p. 897-8) records कृपात्स्वंः, but notes that several sources, including Sāyaṇa's commentary, do offer the reading कृपा स्वंः.

भा.भा.वृत्ति - कृपधातोरुत्पन्नानां कृपादिशब्दानां पूर्वसूत्रोक्तं लत्वं नैव । 'कृपा' (अ.वे. १८.४.५९)। 'कृपणम्' (अ.वे. पै.सं. १९.४१.५)। 'कृपाणः' (not in known Vedic texts, a classical form)। 'कार्पण्यम्' (not in known Vedic texts, an epic form)। 'कर्पट' (not in known Vedic texts, a classical form)।

Note: By citing examples like *kṛpāṇa*, *kārpaṇya*, and *karpaṭa*, which do not appear in Vedic texts, the commentaries are using the Prātiśākhya rules to account for words of the later classical language.

१.३.४. लकारस्य रेफः पादमङ्गुरिमित्येवमादीनाम् ।

Whitney (1.66), Hac: °लि° for °रि°. A, B, P(corr): Daṇḍa after रेफः. G: 1.3.4.

Translation: In *pādam aṅgurim* etc., the sound *l* is replaced by *r*.

Note: In his translation, Whitney says 'In *pādam aṅgulim* etc.' This is because, following his lone ms. H, he reads the rule itself as '... *pādam aṅgulim* ...' This is not supported by other manuscripts. However, Whitney did guess correctly: "It is not in accordance with the usage of our treatise elsewhere to give, in citing a word or phrase in a rule, another form than that which it actually has it in the text: we should have expected here पादमङ्गुरिमि°." Whitney's expectation is supported by the mss. Again it is not clear here if the text of the CA intended a fixed set of instances. The commentary of Bhārgava-Bhāskara probably correctly says that the expression *ādi* in the rule is to refer to this type of examples: आदिशब्दः प्रकारार्थः.

चतुराध्यायीभाष्य - लकारस्य रेफो भवति । पादमङ्गुरिमित्येवमादीनाम् । 'शश्रे पादमङ्गुरिम्' (अ.वे. ४.१८.६; ५.३१.११)। 'सह मूरानन दह' (अ.वे. ५.२९.११)। 'याहि मयूररोमभिः' (अ.वे. ७.११७.१)। 'अश्वस्य वारः प(H, N: पु)रुषस्य वारः' (अ.वे. १०.४.२)। आदिग्रहणं किमर्थम् । 'अङ्गुलिभ्यो नखेभ्यः' (अ.वे. २.३३.६)। 'बालास्ते प्रोक्षणीः सन्तु' (अ.वे. १०.९.३)।

भा.भा.वृत्ति - आदिशब्दः प्रकारार्थः । अङ्गुल्यादिशब्दानां रेफस्य लकारो व्यवस्थितविभाषया ज्ञेयः । तथा च लस्य रेफोऽपि । 'व्याख्यानतो विशेषप्रतिपत्तिर्न हि सन्देहादलक्षणम्' (Mahābhāṣya, on the Śivasūtra 'लण्,' Kielhorn-edn.,

Vol.I., p. 35) इति परिभाषया सूत्राद्बाह्योऽप्यर्थोऽङ्गीक्रियते । पादमङ्गुलिम् । पादमिति किम् । 'अङ्गुरिंम्' (अ.वे. ४.१८. ६)। अलम् इत्यस्य अरम् । 'अरंङ्कृतः' (अ.वे. २.१२. ७)। 'अरङ्गमासं[ः]' (अ.वे. १३.२.३३)। लघोः रघुः । 'रघुष्य(G: ष्प)दः' (अ.वे. ३.७.१)। मूलस्य 'मूरंम्' (अ.वे. १.२८.३)। 'वारः' (अ.वे. १०.४.२)। 'बालः' ('बालाः', अ.वे. ९.७.८, VVRI edn.: ९.१२.८)। 'वारंवन्तम्' (ऋ.वे. १.२७.१) ऋग्वेदे । 'बाल' ('बालाः,' अ.वे. ९.७.८, VVRI edn.: ९.१२.८)। 'अश्रील' ('अश्रीरम्,' अ.वे. ४. २१.६)। 'अश्लीलः' ('अश्लीला,' अ.वे. १४.१.२७)। 'संमिश्र' (not in Vedic texts)। 'संमिश्ल' ('संमिंश्लः,' अ.वे. २०.३८.५)। 'विसर्पकः' (not in AV)। 'विसल्पक' ('विसल्पंकः,' अ.वे. ६.१२७.३, Whitney's AV: 'विसल्यं-कः')। पुरु । 'पुलुकामः' (ऋ.वे. १.१७९.५)। 'पुल्वघ[ः]' (अ.वे. २०.१२६.२२)। उरू(रु?) । 'उलुलयः' (अ.वे. ३.१९.६)। 'सलिल' ('सलिलम्,' अ.वे. ८.९.२)। 'सरि-रस्य' तैत्तिरीये (तै.सं. ४.२.१०.१)। 'आश्लेषा' ('आश्ले-षाः,' अ.वे. १९.७.२)। 'आश्रेषा' (not in AV, a variant for *āśleṣā* in मै.सं. २.१३.२०)। 'श्री' ('श्रीः,' अ.वे. ११.७.३, VVRI ed., ११.९.३)। 'श्लीपदम्' (not in Vedic texts; *śrīpada* attested in Gāyatrī-Brāhmaṇa 119.11, Kāṭhaka-Brāhmaṇa-Saṅkalana, ed. by Surya Kanta, Lahore, 1943; *śīpatha* in Baudhāyana-Śrauta-Sūtra 2.5.18)। 'बभ्रु' ('बभ्रुः,' अ.वे. ५.२३.४)। 'बभ्लुशाय' तैत्तिरीये (तै.सं. ४.५.२.१)। 'कसर्णीरः' (not in AV, तै.सं. १.५.४. १)। 'कसर्णील' ('कसर्णीलंम्,' अ.वे. १०.४.५)। 'रोम' ('रोमाणि,' अ.वे. पै.सं. १६.१३९.१८; 'रोमशम्,' अ.वे. २०.१२६.१६)। 'लोमं' (अ.वे. ४.१२.५)। 'रराटम्' (not in AV, माध्यं.शु.

य.सं. ५.२, काण्व.शु.य.सं. ५.५.९, तै.सं. १.२. १३.३, मै.सं. १.२.९, काठक.सं. २.१०, कठ.सं. २.४)। 'ललाटम्' (अ.वे. ९.७.१, VVRI edn., ९.१२.१)। इत्यादि ।

Note: Referring to the testimony of the Vedic reciters used by S.P. Pandit, Lanman says: "The student should bear in mind the especial weight of the oral testimony in cases where errors of the eye, as distinguished from errors of the ear, are probable. Thus the testimony of the reciters, at ix.8(13).20, establishes the reading *visalpa-*, as against *visalya-* of the Berlin text. Save in AV., the word is otherwise unknown, and, the ms.-distinction between *lya* and *lpa* in such a case is worthless, the instance is a typical one to show the value of the reciters' reading: see W's note to vi.127.1," Editor's introduction, Whitney's *AV translation*, Vol. I, pp. lxvi-lxvii. It may thus be said that, to some extent, Bhārgava-Bhāskara's reading *visalpaka* is closer to the reading offered by the Vedic reciters. Also, it may be noted that while one does observe the variation *visalpaka / visarpaka*, the same cannot be said for the word *visalyaka*, which marks a greater deviation. As Whitney (*AV Transl.* Vol.II., p. 967) informs: "For *visalpakas* (in *AV* 19.44.3), the comm. gives *visarpakas*, explaining it as *vividhaṃ saraṇaśīlo vraṇaviśeṣaḥ;* Ppp. has *viśalyakas*."

In his commentary, Bhārgava-Bhāskara has given a very interesting collection of examples where the sounds *r* and *l* occur as variants. Some of these examples are also offered by Patañjali on P.8.2.18: वालमूललघ्वलमङ्गुलीनां वा लो रमापद्यत इति वक्तव्यम् । अश्वबालः अश्ववारः । मूलदेवः मूरदेवः । वरुणस्य लघुस्यदः वरुणस्य रघुस्यदः । अलं भक्ताय अरं भक्ताय । सुबाहुः स्वङ्गुलिः सुबाहुः स्वङ्गुरिः। संज्ञाछन्दसोर्वा कपिलकादीनामिति वक्तव्यम् । कपिरकः कपिलकः । तिल्विरीकः तिल्विलीकः। रोमाणि लोमानि । पांसुरं पांसुलम् । कर्म कल्म । शुक्रः शुक्लः ।

१.३.५. नकारमकारयोर्लोपे पूर्वस्यानुनासिकः ।

Whitney (1.67). G: 1.3.5.

Translation: In the case of a deletion of *n* and *m*, the previous [vowel] is nasalized.

चतुराध्यायीभाष्य - नकारमकारयोर्लोपे पूर्वस्य वर्णस्य अनुनासिको भवति । 'विँशतिः' (अ.वे. ५.१५.२)। 'पयाँसि' (अ.वे. १.९.३)।

भा.भा.वृत्ति - पदान्तयोर्नकारमकारयोर्लोपे पूर्वस्वरस्यानुनासिकः स्वरे परे । वनशब्दे च । महान् । 'बण्महाँ असि' (अ.वे. १३.२.२९)। पणीन् । 'पणीँरभि' (अ.वे. ५.११.७)। दस्यून् । 'दस्यूँरुप' (not in AV, 'दस्यूंरुत,' अ.वे. ४.३२.६)। पितॄन् । 'पितॄँरुप' (अ.वे. १८.२.४)। वृक्षान् । 'वृक्षाँ वनानि' (अ.वे. ६.४५.१)। मकारग्रहणमुत्तरार्थम् ।

Note: Referring to the CAB, Whitney says: "The commentator offers here only the words *viṃśatiḥ* (e.g. v.15.2) and *payāṃsi* (e.g. i.9.3) - which are very ill chosen, since, though each offers an example of a nasalized vowel, neither exhibits an elision of an original nasal mute, according to any rules contained in this treatise." One must however point out that in the example *payāṃsi*, at least according to the Pāṇinian derivation, one would have a deletion of an *n*. Compare the examples offered by the commentators under P.8.3.24 (नश्चापदान्तस्य झलि). One crucial difference is that the Pāṇinian commentators assume that a form like *yaśāṃsi* is derived from the string *yaśāns+i*, where the *n* is replaced by the *anusvāra* by P.8.3.24. Instead of the notion of an *anusvāra*, the CAB speaks of an *anunāsika* as a replacement for the vowel preceding the deleted *n*. It is, however, not clear if such examples were intended by the author of the CA, and whether he intended a similar derivation for forms like *payāṃsi*.

The deficiency pointed out by Whitney is made up by some of the examples offered by Bhārgava-Bhāskara. However, some of his examples, would properly come under the next rule. Additionally, Bhārgava-Bhāskara says that the inclusion of *m* serves no purpose in this rule, except that *n* and *m* together continue into the following rules. For the last example quoted by Bhārgava-Bhāskara, see CA 2.1.28.

१.३.६. यरोष्मापत्तौ च ।

Whitney (1.68). G: 1.3.6. E, F, G, I, J (corr), O: परो° for यरो°.

Translation: Also when [*n* and *m*] are changed [in sandhi] to *y*, *r*, or a spirant.

चतुराध्यायीभाष्य - यकाररेफोष्मापत्तौ च पूर्वस्य वर्णस्यानुनासिको भवति । 'रथाँ इव' (अ.वे. ५.१३.६)। 'सालावृकाँ इव' (अ.वे. २.२७.५)। 'खल्वाँ इव' (अ.वे. २.३१.१)। 'ऋतूँर्ऋतुभिः' (अ.वे.पै.सं. १६.१५१.७)। 'ऋतूँरुत्सृजते वशी' (अ.वे. ६.३६.२)। 'मो षु पणीँरभि' (अ.वे. ५.११.७) (H adds: 'मो इति')। 'दस्यूँरुत बोधि' (अ.वे. ४.३२.६)। ऊष्मणो ग्रहणात्सिद्धे पुनर्ग्रहणेन किम् । नित्यत्वं न स्यात् । 'ऋतूँरुत्सृजते वशी' (अ.वे. ६.३६.२)।

Note: The example ऋतूँर्ऋतुभिः cited by the CAB is not found in the Vulgate of the AV, and Surya Kanta (APR, Introduction, p. 40) suggests that this may have occurred in the genuine Śaunakīya recension of the AV, and that the Vulgate is not the genuine Śaunakīya recension. The last three examples cited by the CAB are found under APR (197).

The last comment made by the CAB is not immediately clear. What does the term *punar-grahaṇa* refer to? Whitney says: "As the *n* must always be converted into the spirant *visarjanīya* before it becomes *y*, it seems superfluous to make separate mention of the latter in the rule. The commentator apparently feels this objection, and ventures for once a defense, as follows: *ūṣmaṇo grahaṇāt siddhe punargrahaṇena kim : nityatvaṃ na syāt : ṛtū̃r utsṛjate vaśī;* 'when the matter is made certain by the use of the term *ūṣman*, why any farther mention? It is because this does not apply to all cases, as is shown by the instance *ṛtū̃r utsṛjate vaśī.*' I do not see the point of this defense: it does, indeed explain the mention of *r* in the rule, but it has nothing to do with that of *y*."

CA 2.1.29 (ऋतूँरुत्सृजते वशीत्येवमादीनाम्) requires the obligatory change of an *n* into an *r* in the listed examples. Thus, in this case, *r* is not covered by the term *ūṣman*, and hence its separate mention is necessary. How about *y*? Whitney says, an *n* must first change to a *visarjanīya* before it becomes *y*. If such is the case, then why is it mentioned again? I think the explanation given by the commentator applies more aptly to the case of *y*, though his example only illustrates the case of *r*. In an example like *rathān iva*, the final *n* first changes to a *visarjanīya* by CA (2.1.27: आकारोपधस्योपबद्धादीनां स्वरे). Then the *visarjanīya* is changed to *y* by CA (2.2.2: स्वरे यकारः). Finally, by CA (2.1.21: स्वराद्यवयोः पदान्तयोः), this *y* is deleted. The commentator assumes the following dilemma. One could apply CA (1.3.6) at the stage *rathāḥ iva* and change this to *rathā̃ḥ iva*, with the assumption that the vowel *ā* is followed by *ḥ*, an *ūṣman*. However, if one chose not to do so, and change *ḥ* first to *y*, then, in the stage *rathāy iva*, one may not be able to nasalize *ā* without a distinct mention of *y*. In part, this brings up the question of whether a substitute can be treated as being a functional equivalent of the original (*sthānivadbhāva*). The fact that the rule separately mentions *y* may be taken as an indication that the CA implicitly had a doctrine of *sthānivadbhāva* (cf. P.1.1.56 स्थानिवदादेशोऽनल्विधौ), where the restriction *analvidhau* 'not in operations dependent on the specific sound' would have prevented the substitute *y* from being attributed the phonological properties of the *ḥ* it replaced.

The reading found in Bhārgava-Bhāskara's commentary, however, is परोष्मापत्तौ च, and it has been interpreted in a substantially different manner by this commentary. The significant thing to note is that this reading is not unique to Bhārgava-Bhāskara, but is supported by a number of other manuscripts, i.e. E, F, G, I, J (corr), O. This includes the entire Kautsa-Vyākaraṇa tradition. In spite of the manuscript support, I do not believe that this is the original reading.

***भा.भा.वृत्ति* - (परोष्मापत्तौ च)** नकारमकारयोः परतः ऊष्मण आपत्तौ नकारमकारयोर्लोपे पूर्वस्यानुनासिकः । सम् सुट् । 'सँस्कृंतः' (अ.वे. २०.५३.३)। 'सँशिंतम्' (अ.वे. ३.१९.१)। अपदान्ते । 'हँसः' (अ.वे.पै.सं. १६.२३.१)। 'अँशांः' (अ.वे. ६.४.२)। 'दृँहं' (अ.वे. ६.१३६.२)। 'तपूँषि' (अ.वे. २.१२.६)। 'सिँहः' (अ.वे. ५.२०.१)।

Note: Vishva Bandhu's *Grammatical Word-Index to Atharvaveda*, p. 671, lists ŚAV (11.6.21) for an instance of *haṃsaḥ*. The verse does not contain *haṃsaḥ*, but *aṃhasaḥ*, and its inclusion is a simple error which should be corrected.

१.३.७. अनुनासिकस्य च पूर्वेणैकादेशे ।

Whitney (1.69). G: 1.3.7. P: °णैकादशे.

Translation: Also, when a nasalized [vowel] combined with a preceding [non-nasal] vowel is replaced by a single substitute, [that single substitute becomes nasalized].

Note: The existence of a rule such as this may be an indication that a doctrine similar to Pāṇini's rule P. 1.1.50 (स्थानेऽन्तरतमः) is not fully developed in the CA tradition. Pāṇini's procedure requires that a substitute should be maximally similar in phonetic features to the original it replaced. Such a generic convention obviates the need for further specialized rules like CA (1.3.7). Bhārgava-Bhāskara's commentary correctly says that the author of the CA feared that, without such a special rule, the combined result of a nasal and a non-nasal vowel would be a non-nasal [lit. *śuddha* 'pure'] vowel. The example illustrates how Pāṇini was working with a more refined and comprehensive phonological apparatus as compared with that of the CA.

चतुराध्यायीभाष्य - अनुनासिकस्य पूर्वेण सह एकादेशे कृते अनुनासिको भवति । 'उभावुंपाँशु प्रंथमा पिंबाव' (अ.वे. ४.३२.७)। 'सोमंस्याँशो (N: शवो)' (अ.वे. ७.८१.३)। 'ये व्रीहयो यवा निरुप्यन्तेँऽशवंः' (अ.वे. ९.६.१४)।

Note: Regarding the last example quoted by the commentary, Whitney (*AV Transl.* Vol.II., p. 540) points out: "The Anukr. requires *-yante aṃś-* to be read, although the passage is quoted under Prāt. 1.69 (= CA 1.3.8) as an example of the elision of initial *a* with the transfer of its nasalization to the eliding *e*." The mss. in this case follow the CA prescription, and it is difficult to see why there is not a single ms. which follows the Anukramaṇī.

भा.भा.वृत्ति - एकादेशे अनुनासिकस्य शुद्धः स्वरः स्यादित्याशङ्क्य पुनरनुनासिकादेशो विधीयते । 'उपऽअँशुः' (not in AV)। 'उपाँशुः' (not in AV, 'उपाँशु,' अ.वे. ४.३२.७)। 'पुष्टोँऽशः' (not in AV)। 'साराँशः' (not in AV)।

१.३.८. पुरुष आ बभूवाँ३ इत्यवसाने ।

Whitney (1.70), C, Hb, N, O: do not have ३. E, F: use ऽ for ३. G: 1.3.8.

Translation: In the passage *puruṣa ā babhūvā̃3* (AV 10.2. 28), [the final vowel of the word *babhūva* is replaced by a protracted nasalized vowel] before the pause.

Note: The expression *avasāne* is used to restrict this change only to the pre-pausal environment. Therefore, this change does not take place when *babhūva* is combined with *iti* in the Parihāra which is part of the Krama recitation. It is not immediately clear whether the rule says anything about what happens in the Saṃhitā, or applies only negatively in the Krama recitation. Whitney seems to prefer almost a negative interpretation: "The *pada* text reads simply *puruṣaḥ : ā : babhūvā̃3* : and there would be no call for such a rule as that given here, but for the requirements of the *krama* text, in which *babhūva* as the last word in a verse, must suffer *parihāra* (iv.117 = CA 4.4.18), or repetition with *iti* interposed, and in which it might be made a question whether the nasality of the vowel should or should not be preserved before *iti*. This rule teaches us that the nasal quality is lost before the *iti*." I believe Whitney's interpretation is too indirect. The straight forward interpretation is that the final vowel of the expression पुरु॑ष॒ आ ब॑भूव becomes [prolonged, and] nasalized, before a pause. The fact that it remains non-nasal before *iti* is an indirect consequence. By mentioning the whole sequence पुरु॑ष॒ आ ब॑भूवाँ३, the CA indicates that this change occurs only in this sequence, and not in every case of *babhūva*.

Whitney's dilemma arises because of the fact that the Padapāṭha already has *babhūvā̃3*, and hence such a rule is not needed either for the Pada text or the Saṃhitā. However, the CA may not always be proceeding from the Pada form to Saṃhitā form, but occasionally it seems to proceed from the normal form, e.g. *babhūva* to both the Pada and Saṃhitā forms.

चतुराध्यायीभाष्य - पुरुष आ बभूवाँ इत्यवसानेऽनुनासिको भवति । 'पुरु॑ष॒ आ ब॑भूवाँ[३]' (अ.वे. १०.२.२८)। अवसान इति किमर्थम् । 'बभूवेति बभूवाँ[३]'।

भा.भा.वृत्ति - बभूवशब्दः लिट्प्रथमैकवचनान्तः अवसानेऽर्धर्चविरामे टेः प्लुतत्वेन प्लुत[ः] । 'अणोऽप्रगृह्यस्य' (पा. ८.४.५७) इति पाणिनीयेनानुनासिक उक्तः । स तु 'पुरु॑ष॒ आ ब॑भूवाँ३' (अ.वे. १०.२.२८)। पदद्वयपूर्व[ः] बभूव-

शब्दः। अवसाने एव प्लुतानुनासिकः । 'पुरुष आ बंभूवाँ३' (अ.वे. १०.२.२८)। नान्यत्र । 'बभूवाँ३' इति शब्दः प्रकारार्थः । तेन वेदान्तरे । 'न त्वा भीरिंव विन्दतीइँ' । ऋग्वेदे (ऋ.वे. १०.१४६.१)।

Note: Bhārgava-Bhāskara assumes that the word *babhūvā̃3* is cited to refer to the a class of similar examples, and thus the rule also accounts for similar examples in RV. Or perhaps he means: *itiśabdaḥ prakārārthaḥ.* In any case, he wishes to extend the scope of this rule beyond its intention. This indicates that the late commentators on the Prātiśākhyas were under the generalizing influence of systems like that of Pāṇini. The rule is originally intended to apply only to the word *babhūva* as it occurs in the specified context, and not to any other instance, let alone to other examples in texts like the RV.

१.३.९. ऋवर्णस्य रेफात्परं यत् ।

Whitney (1.71). G: 1.3.9.

Translation: [In becoming nasalized], for *ṛ* vowels [= *ərə*], the [vocalic] part following *r* [becomes nasal, i.e. *ərə̃*].

चतुराध्यायीभाष्य - ऋवर्णस्य अनुनासिकस्य रेफात्परं यत् तदनुनासिकं भवति । 'भूमिदृँहमच्युतं पारयिष्णु' (अ.वे. ५.२८.१४)। 'दृँहं प्रत्नान्' (अ.वे. ६.१३६.२)। 'जनांन् दृँहन्तम्' (अ.वे. १२.२.९)।

भा.भा.वृत्ति - ऋवर्णस्य मध्ये यो रेफः तस्मात्परस्य स्वरभागस्यानुनासिकः स्यात् । नृन् ..... 'नृँ× प्रणेता' ('नृँ× प्रणेत्रम्,' ऋग्वेदखिलानि, VSM edn. of the RV, Vol. 4, प्रैषाध्याय, पृ. ९८३, ऋक्प्रातिशाख्य ४.७८)।

Note: Commenting upon this rule, Whitney says: "Here we learn that, when such a vowel is nasalized, the nasal quality does not affect the *r*, but only the part of a vowel which follows it. Anyone may perceive, however, upon trying the experiment, that there is no physical difficulty in the way of nasalizing the *r* itself." Whitney clearly disregards the fact that the entire tradition of Sanskrit grammar and phonetics is united in declaring that there is no nasal counterpart for *r*, as indeed there are for *y*, *v*, and *l*. Thus, there was no question of nasalizing the *r* element. However, it was a legitimate question whether the first vocalic element which precedes the *r* also becomes nasal. The question becomes all the more necessary, since, in passages like ऋतूँरुत्सृंजते (AV 6.36.2), the consonant *r* is preceded by a nasal vowel.

An explanation of why the latter vocalic fraction becomes lengthened or is nasalized, and not the previous one, may be found in the fact that the vowel *r̥* was pronounced in most of the historical period as either *ri* or *ru*, and in these pronunciations, the preceeding vocalic fraction almost went unrepresented, and the following vocalic fraction was given a more distinct form. From the present rule, one can infer that the pronunciation of *r̥* known to the CA was closer to *ri* or *ru*, and hence the only vowel which could be lengthened or nasalized was the vowel following the consonantal *r*. This is also known indirectly from earlier evidence; i.e., *dreśya*, see: Wackernagel, I. 31.

१.३.१०. उकारस्येतावपृक्तस्य ।

Whitney (1.72). G combines this with the next rule and numbers it 1.3.10.

Translation: The *u* as a monophonic [morpheme] is nasalized before the word *iti* [in the Padapāṭha].

Note: The term *apr̥kta* literally means 'uncombined.' However, P.1.2.41 (अपृक्त एकाल्प्रत्ययः) defines it as referring to an affix that consists of a single sound. In the usage of the CA (1.3.10, 1.3.17, and 4.4.14), it refers to particles which consist of a single vowel. Cf. TPR (1.54) and VPR (1.151).

चतुराध्यायीभाष्य - उकारस्य इतौ परतः अपृक्तस्य अनुनासिको भवति । ऊँ इति ।

भा.भा.वृत्ति - **(उकारस्येतावपृक्तस्य दीर्घः प्रगृह्यश्च)** अपृक्तस्य उकारस्य प्रगृह्यसंज्ञा दीर्घता च । अनुनासिकानुवर्तनादनुनासिकत्वं च अवैदिके इतौ परे । 'शमु' (अ.वे.

१.६.४)। 'शम् । ॐ इत्यूँ' । तथा च ऋक्प्रातिशाख्ये शौनकः । 'रक्तोऽपृक्तो द्राघितः शाकलेन' (ऋग्वेदप्रातिशाख्य १.७५) इति । तैत्तिरीयादौ तु पदकाले उ इत्येव प्रयुञ्जन्ति । रञ्जनं दीर्घतां च न कुर्वन्ति ।

Note: Whitney says: "In the *pada-* text of the Atharvan, as in those of the other Vedas, the particle *u* is always written *ū̃ iti.*" Bhārgava-Bhāskara on the other hand informs us that this practice is not followed by some schools like the Taittirīyas. This is supported by the printed text of the Padapāṭha of the TS (e.g. 1.1.4, VSM edn, Vol.I., Pt.I., p 71).

१.३.११. दीर्घः प्रगृह्यश्च ।

Whitney (1.73). E, F: omit the Visarga. G combines this with the preceding. I: 16.

Translation: [The monophonic particle *u*, before the word *iti* in the Padapāṭha] is also lengthened and is treated as a *pragṛhya* [i.e. is not combined in sandhi with the following *iti*].

Note: Whitney starts out by saying, "Any satisfactory reason why the particle *u* should be treated in this peculiar manner by the framers of the *pada-*text is not readily apparent," but comes up with the most likely explanation: "It seems as if the protraction must have been made in order to give the word more substance as an independent *pada* in the disjoined text, it being the only instance of a single short vowel possessing such a value; and as if the nasalization and addition of *iti* were intended to mark it more distinctly as an exceptional case, requiring a different treatment in the *saṃhitā*-text. Pāṇini (i.1.17, 18) allows it to be read either *u* or *ūn̐*." Also see the MB on P.1.1.17 for problems involved in interpreting Pāṇini's rules. As Bhārgava-Bhāskara notes on the previous rule, the Padapāṭha of the Taittirīya-Saṃhitā does not show lengthening, nasalization, or the addition of the word *iti* to *u*.

चतुराध्यायीभाष्य - दीर्घश्च भवति प्रगृह्यश्च । 'ॐ इति' ।

भा.भा.वृत्ति - See the previous rule.

१.३.१२. ईकारोकारौ च सप्तम्यर्थे ।

Whitney (1.74). C, Hb, N: omit च. Hb, Nb: इ for ई. G̣: 1.3.11.

Translation: [Word-final] *ī* and *ū*, when the formation has a locative sense, are also treated as *pragṛhya* [i.e. are not combined in *sandhi* with the following vowel, e.g. *i* of *iti* added after a *pragṛhya* word in the Padapāṭha].

Note: The significance of this rule, and the rules which follow, lies in that they offer us some insight into the fact that the Padapāṭha occasionally gives indications of a syntactic-semantic understanding of the words of the Saṃhitā. Generally speaking, the Prātiśākhyas do not concern themselves with matters of syntax, except when such syntactic/semantic matters are explicitly reflected in the Padapāṭha. Another curious fact may also be noted. The CA rule, as well as Pāṇini (1.1.19: ईदूतौ च सप्तम्यर्थे), treat forms like *āṣṭrī* and *urvī* as being in the sense of a locative (*saptamy-arthe*), rather than being irregular Vedic locative forms. It is clear that these forms are viewed by the Padapāṭha as being exceptional forms. Perhaps, after noticing the absence or deletion of the normal locative affix, there was a certain hesitation to categorize them clearly as locatives (*saptamī*), though it was clear that the forms had a locative meaning. Also see: MB on P.1.1.19.

As Whitney notes, in all these instances, these forms are given as *pragṛhya*s in the Padapāṭha, followed by *iti*. However, that by itself does not tell us whether the author of the Padapāṭha intended these forms to be duals, or forms in the locative sense. In any case, the commentators seem to be in further disarray. On RV (9.12.3), both Venkaṭamādhava and Sāyaṇa paraphrase the form *gaurī* with *gauryām*, and Sāyaṇa says: गौर्यामधि । अधीति सप्तम्यर्थानुवादः. The AV examples, on the other hand, have been treated rather in an inconsistent way by [Pseudo]Sāyaṇa. The form *āṣṭrī* (AV 6.27.3) is simply paraphrased with the locative *āṣṭryāṃ*. The form *tanū* (AV 4.25.5) is actually treated as a locative form, with the locative affix deleted: तन्वाम् । 'सुपां सुलुक्' (पा.७.१.३९) इति सप्तम्या लुक् । 'ईदूतौ च सप्तम्यर्थे' (पा.१.१.१९) इति प्रगृह्यसंज्ञा. On the other hand, the form *urvī* (AV 18.1.32) is taken as an accusative dual and is paraphrased with *urvyau*. Even though this does not understand the word in the locative sense, it at least accounts for why the word is treated as a *pragṛhya* in the Padapāṭha. Finally, the form *mahī* (AV 18.1.39) is taken either as an irregular accusative singular (महतीमित्यर्थः । अमः स्थाने सुः), or it is construed with *vātāḥ* in the same verse (अथ वा महीत्युत्तरत्र वाता इत्यनेन सम्बध्यते). In either case, the explanations do not account for why the word should be treated as a *pragṛhya* by the Padapāṭha.

चतुराध्यायीभाष्य - ईकारोकारौ च सप्तम्यर्थे प्रगृह्यौ भवतः । 'आष्ट्री पदं कृणुते अग्निधाने' (अ.वे. ६.२७.३)। (पद ⇒) 'आष्ट्री इति' । 'अतो जातासो धारयन्त उर्वी' (अ.वे. १८.१.३२)। (पद ⇒) 'उर्वी इति' । 'मही नो वाताः' (अ.वे. १८.१.३९)। (पद ⇒) 'मही इति'। 'तनू दक्षमा सुवताम्' (अ.वे. ४.२५.५)। (पद ⇒) 'तनू इति'। सप्तम्यर्थ इति किमर्थम् । 'धीती वा ये' (अ.वे. ७.१.१)। 'तस्यामू सर्वा' (अ.वे. १३.४.२८)।

Note: The CAB cites all the same examples as found under APR (63), though in this case the examples occur in a slightly different order. One should also note that the CA rule is identical in wording with APR (63). This means that at least for these two texts, the forms concerned are all in the sense of the locative case. Also note the reading आष्ट्र्यां पदम् ... found in RV (10.165.3) which proves the equivalence of *āṣṭrī* and *āṣṭryām.*

भा.भा.वृत्ति - प्रगृह्यश्चेत्यनुवर्तते सूत्रदशकपर्यन्तम् । सप्तम्यर्थे पर्यवसन्नं यत् ईकारान्तमूकारान्तं च पदं प्रगृह्यसंज्ञं स्यात् । प्रगृह्यसंज्ञायाः प्रयोजनं स्वरे परे विवृत्तसन्धिः । अत एव पदकाले प्रगृह्यपदस्य इतिकरणं भवति । (पदपाठ ⇒) 'तनू इति । दक्षम् । आ । सुवताम् । सुऽशेवम् ।' (संहिता ⇒) 'तनू दक्षमा सुवतां सुशेवम्' (अ.वे. ४.२५.५)। प्रातिशाख्ये ऋग्वेदे । 'सोमो गौरी अधि श्रितः' (ऋ.वे. ९.१२.३)।

Note: The example from the RV is cited by Uvaṭa in his commentary on RPR (2.52: स्वरेषु चार्ष्याम्). It would seem that Bhārgava-Bhāskara is here referring to Uvaṭa's commentary on the RPR.

१.३.१३. द्विवचनान्तौ ।

Whitney (1.75). G: 1.3.12.

Translation: [The vowels *ī* and *ū*] occurring as finals of dual forms [are also called *pragṛhya*].

Note: The words which are designated as *pragṛhya* by this rule are followed by *iti* in the Padapāṭha, and are not combined in sandhi with the following vowels either in the Saṃhitā or in the Padapāṭha. While for all the AV examples for the previous rule, the absence of sandhi can be illustrated only for Padapāṭha citations, that is not the case for the examples of the present rule. Here, in a number of cases listed by the CAB, the lack of sandhi is manifest in the Saṃhitā as well.

Another curious feature may also be noted. By using dual forms *īkāro-kārau* in the previous rule, and *dvivacanāntau* in the present rule, the CA, at least on the face of it, seems to be designating these sounds, rather than the words ending in these sounds, by the term *pragṛhya*. Interestingly, in this case, Pāṇini seems to be somewhat inconsistent. P.1.1.19 (ईदूतौ च सप्तम्यर्थे) resembles CA (1.3.12: ईकारोकारौ च सप्तम्यर्थे). On the other hand, P.1.1.11 (ईदूदेद् द्विवचनं प्रगृह्यम्) contrasts with CA (1.3.13: द्विवचनान्तौ). In this case, Pāṇini seems to treat the whole words as *pragṛhyas*, while the CA seems to be explicitly referring to the final vowels alone.

चतुराध्यायीभाष्य - द्विवचनान्तौ च ईकारोकारौ प्रगृह्यौ भवतः । 'केन॒ पार्ष्णी॒ आभृ॑ते॒' (अ.वे. १०.२.१)। (पद ⇒) 'पार्ष्णी॒ इति॑' । 'इ॒न्द्र॒वा॒यू उ॒भौ' (अ.वे. ३.२०.६)। (पद ⇒) 'इ॒न्द्र॒वा॒यू इति॑' । 'उ॒भावि॑न्द्रा॒ग्नी आभ॑रताम्' (अ.वे. ५.७.६)। (पद ⇒) 'इ॒न्द्रा॒ग्नी इति॑' ।

भा.भा.वृत्ति - द्विवचनस्यान्ते यावीकारोकारौ प्रगृह्यसंज्ञौ स्तः । विवृत्तसन्धिः 'द्यावा॑पृथि॒वी इति॑' (पद, अ.वे. २.१.४)। 'बा॒हू इति॑' (पद, अ.वे. ४.२.५)। 'इ॒न्द्रा॒ग्नी इति॑' (पद, अ.वे. १.३५.४)। 'इ॒न्द्र॒वा॒यू इति॑' (पद, अ.वे. ३.२०.६)। 'अह॑नी॒ इति॑' (पद, अ.वे. १३.२.३)। 'अ॒ग्नी

इति' (पद, अ.वे. ११.५.११, VVRI edn., ११.७.११)। 'रोदंसी इति' (पद, १.३२.३)। 'द्यावांपृथिवी इति' (पद, अ.वे. २.१.४)

१.३.१४. एकारश्च ।

Whitney (1.76). A, B, D: °स्य for °श्च. G: 1.3.13.

Translation: [The sound] *e* [occurring as the final of a dual form] is also [called *pragṛhya*].

Note: In contrast with CA (1.3.13-14), Pāṇini combines all three types of duals ending in *ī*, *ū*, and *e*, under a single rule: P.1.1.11 (ईदूदेद् द्विवचनं प्रगृह्यम्). For further contrast, see Note on the previous rule.

चतुराध्यायीभाष्य - एकारश्च द्विवचनान्तः प्रगृह्यो भवति । 'अत्रा दधेते' (अ.वे. ५.१.३)। (पद ⇒) 'दधेते इति' । 'रोधंचक्रे वावृधेतें' (अ.वे. ५.१.५)। (पद ⇒) 'वावृधेते इति' । 'सं पिंतरावृत्विंये' (अ.वे. १४.२.३७)। (पद ⇒) 'ऋत्विंये इति' ।

भा.भा.वृत्ति - द्विवचनान्ते यस्त्वेकारः स प्रगृह्यः स्यात् । अविशेषात् सुबन्तं तिङन्तं च द्विवचनं गृह्यते । 'शीर्षऽकपाले इति शीर्षऽकपाले' (पद, अ.वे. १५.१८.४)। 'नासिंके इति' (पद, अ.वे. १५.१८.४)। 'द्वे इति' (पद, अ.वे. १३.२.२८)। 'रूपे इति' (पद, अ.वे. १३.२.२८)। 'नानांरूपे इति' (पद, अ.वे. १३.२.३)। 'अहोरात्रे इति' (पद, अ.वे. १०.७.६)। 'वसांने इति' (पद, अ.वे. १३.३.११)। 'इमे इति' (पद, अ.वे. ३.३१.४)। 'श्रिते इति' (पद, अ.वे. १३.१.३७)। 'ईजाते इति' (पद, अ.वे. १३.१.४७)। मंत्रे । 'ये [इति । ...?] ते इति' (?, पद, अ.वे. ४.२६.१)।

Note: The last example quoted by Bhārgava-Bhāskara is somewhat unclear. AV (4.16.6) has the passage beginning with *ye te*. However, the words *ye* and *te* in this instance are not dual forms. They are nominative plurals agreeing with *pāśāḥ*. The commentator must have intended dual forms, as they occur in AV (4.26.1). However, here they do not occur consecutively. Also, these forms are nowhere followed by *iti* in the *mantra* (= *saṃhitā*), but only in the Padapāṭha for AV (4.26.1). Thus, it is not clear why Bhārgava-Bhāskara would cite this example prefixed with the word *mantre*.

१.३.१५. अस्मे युष्मे त्वे मे इति चोदात्तः ।

Whitney (1.77), P: °त्ताः. D, J, M, P(corr): Daṇḍa after अस्मे, युष्मे, त्वे, and मे. G: 1.3.14.

Translation: Also [the] high-pitch [sound *e* occurring at the end of the forms] *asmé*, *yuṣmé*, *tvé*, and *mé*.

Note: Whitney points out: "The specification 'when accented' is, of course, meant only for the two latter of the words named, as the others would never occur otherwise than accented. Of the four, *yuṣmé* and *mé* never occur in the Atharvan text." Compare the wording of the verse cited in the CAB with the wording of APR (59, p. 53): एकारो विभक्त्यादेशश्छन्दसीति. Also note that the examples listed under APR (59) cover only *tve* and *asme*. Since those are the only forms occurring in the ŚAV, one can clearly relate the APR with the Śaunakīya tradition. On the other hand, Surya Kanta (*Atharva-Prāti-śākhya, Introduction*, p. 39) says that the forms *yuṣmé* and *mé* do not occur in the Vulgate of the AV, but suggests that they may have occurred in a genuine Śaunakīya recension of the AV.

There is a great deal of confusion of readings in the mss. of the AV, and Whitney points out: "*tvé* is found once, in a Rik passage (AV. v.2.3 = RV. x.120.3), and also, according to the manuscripts, in viii.9.9, twice repeated, and each time written in the *pada*-text *tvé iti*, as a *pragṛhya:* but the accent and the addition of *iti* are hardly to be regarded otherwise than as a blunder of the tradition, since the word is evidently the enclitic or accentless *tva* of the Vedic language: no forms of this enclitic pronoun are found elsewhere in the Atharvan. The fourth, *asmé*, is also hardly an Atharvan word. It is found in three Rik passages, viz. iv.21.1 (RV. vi.28.1), xviii.1.3 (RV. x.10.3), 42 (RV. x.17.8) : in another passage (iv.31.3), where the Rik (x.84.3) reads *asmé*, all the Atharvan manuscripts have *asmai*, which has been altered to *asmé* in the edition, in obedience to the requirement of the sense, and the authority of the

Rik reading. Another precisely similar case is xix.40.4 (RV. i.46.6). The only passage where the Atharvan gives *asmé* independently is v.1.3, where all the manuscripts except P. and M. (copies of the same original, by the same scribe) agree in reading it (pada *asmé iti*) : here also, however, the edition reads *asmai*."

In contrast with Whitney's views, it should be born in mind that the APR (59) deals with *tvé* and *asmé* examples, and therefore the inclusion of *asmé* forms under *pragr̥hya*s was clearly acceptable to both the CA and the APR. The APR lists AV (8.9.9) as a case of accented *tvé*. In AV (4.21.1), (18.1.3), (18.1.42), and (5.1.3), the APR reads *asmé*, and its non-inclusion of AV (4.31.3) suggests that it had the reading *asmai*. In all these listed cases, the Padapāṭha clearly treats these forms as *pragr̥hya*s, and adds *iti* after them. Thus, it is most likely that Whitney's choice of readings in these cases is not only against the mss. of the AV, but also against the authority of the Padapāṭha, and the APR, which was indeed not known to him.

The KV on P.1.1.13 (शे) claims that the only Vedic example of one of these *pragr̥hya*s listed in this rule being followed by a vowel in the Saṃhitāpāṭha is RV (4.49.4): अ॒स्मे इ॑न्द्राबृहस्पती.

चतुराध्यायीभाष्य - अस्मे युष्मे त्वे मे इति उदात्तः प्रगृह्यो भवति । 'अ॒स्मे इति॑' (पद, अ.वे. ४.२१.१)। 'यु॒ष्मे इति॑' (पद, अ.वे.पै.सं. ९.४.९)। 'त्वे इति॑' (पद, अ.वे. ५.२.३)। 'मे इति॑' (पद, वा.सं. ४.२२)।

'निगमे युष्मदस्मद्भ्यां विभक्तेरेत्वमिष्यते ।'

(source?)

युष्माकम् अस्माकम् त्वम् अहम् इति प्राप्ते अस्मे युष्मे त्वे मे इति च विभक्त्यादेशः क्रियते ।

भा.भा.वृत्ति - सर्वाविभक्तिकशेप्रत्ययान्तानि चत्वारि पदानि प्रगृह्याणि स्युः । उदात्तग्रहणमस्मदादेशस्य अनुदात्तस्य 'मे॒' एतच्छब्दस्य व्यावृत्त्यर्थम् । किञ्च सर्वनामसंज्ञस्य अनुदात्तस्य 'त्वे॒' एतत्पदस्य प्रथमाबहुवचनान्तव्यावृत्त्यर्थः एकारः उदात्तः प्रगृह्यश्चेत्यर्थः । 'अ॒स्मे इति॑' (पद, अ.वे. ४.२१.१)।

'युष्मे इति' (पद, अ.वे.पै.सं. ९.४.९)। 'त्वे इति' (पद, अ.वे. ५.२.३)।

१.३.१६. अमी बहुवचनम् ।

Whitney (1.78). G: 1.3.15.

Translation: [The word] *amī*, when it is a plural form, [is also *pragṛhya*].

चतुराध्यायीभाष्य- अमी बहुवचनं प्रगृह्यं भवति । 'अमी ये युधम्' (अ.वे. ६.१०३.३)। (पद ⇒) 'अमी इति' । 'अमी ये विव्रताः' (अ.वे. ३.८.५)। (पद ⇒) 'अमी इति' । 'अमी अशश्रे' (not attested in Vedic Saṃhitās)। 'अमी इति' (पद, अ.वे. ३.८.५)। बहुवचनमिति किमर्थम् । 'शम्यत्र' (not in Vedic texts)।

Note: The example *amī aśaśre* (not *āśaśre* as cited by Surya Kanta) cited by the CAB is not found in the Vulgate of the AV, and Surya Kanta (*APR*, *Introduction*, p. 40) suggests that this may have occurred in the genuine Śaunakīya recension of the AV, and that the Vulgate is not the genuine Śaunakīya recension. M.A. Mehendale, Bhandarkar Oriental Research Institute, Pune, suggests in a personal exchange that if the form *aśaśre* is read as *āśaśre*, this could possibly be an irregular past perfect 3rd plural form of *ā-√śā* (*śiśāti*), similar to the form *duhre*. In any case, no such form is attested in any known Vedic text. The form *śaśre* by itself is attested several times in the AV as a perfect form in the singular (e.g. AV 4.8.6; 5.31.11). This form is derived by Sāyaṇa from the root *śṛ*, *śṛṇāti*.

The counter-example *śamyatra* cited by the CAB suggests that the commentator took the expression *amī* in the rule as not referring to the form *amī*, but as referring any expression ending in the sequence *amī*. Such an interpretation is strengthened by the addition of the condition *bahuvacanam* in the rule. Whitney says that the counter-example *śamy atra* is plainly a fabrication of the commentator. The same counter-example is also given in the KV on P.1.1.12 (अदसो मात्), though for a different reason.

Referring to the addition of the condition *bahuvacanam*, Whitney says: "nor can I find that the text contains anything which should render that addition necessary. The Vāj. Pr. says (i.98) '*amī*, when a word by itself;' the other treatises (R. Pr. i.19, r. 19, r. 73, lxxiv; Taitt. Pr. iv. 12) see no reason for appending any such limitations." A possible reason for the inclusion of such a condition may be that the dividing line between phonology and morphology could not be clearly conveyed, and hence the author of the CA suspected that a mere enunciation of the sequence *amī* could possibly overextend to those cases where the sequence *amī* occurred, but not as an independent word. To avert such a presumed over-extension, the condition *bahuvacanam* was added.

भा.भा.वृत्ति - अदःशब्दस्य अमू इत्यस्य द्विवचनान्तत्वेन प्रगृह्यता सिद्धा । ईदन्तत्वेऽपि बहुवचनान्तत्वादप्राप्तविधिरारभ्यते । 'अमी इति' (पद, अ.वे. १३.२.१३)। अमी इति सूत्रारम्भादेव सिद्धे बहुवचनमिति किमर्थम् । श्रोतव्यम् । अमधातोः ('अम गतौ,' पा. धातुपाठ, ४६५; 'अम रोगे,' पा. धातुपाठ, १७२०) 'सर्वधातुभ्य इन्' ('इन्,' उणादिसूत्र १.४६ दशपादी, ४.१२६ पञ्चपादी)। 'कृदिकारादक्तिनः' (गणसूत्र, बह्वादिगण, पाणिनीयगणपाठ. Also: काशिका on P.4.1.45) इति ङ्यन्तोऽमीशब्द उत्पद्यते । 'हल्ङ्याब्भ्यः ...' (पा. ६.१.६८) इति सोर्लोपः । एवंभूतस्य प्रगृह्यसंज्ञा मा भूदित्येतदर्थं बहुवचनग्रहणम् ।

Note: Bhārgava-Bhāskara makes a desperate attempt to prove the necessity of the qualification *bahuvacanam* in the rule by showing that there can be another expression *amī* derived from the root *am*, which is a feminine nominative singular of a stem in long *ī*. The qualification *bahuvacanam* is intended to prevent the application of this rule to such an instance. No such expression is attested in Sanskrit usage, and it is purely a theoretical creation of the commentator. The CAB provides a better counter-example in this respect, i.e. *śamī+atra*. This counter-example is also found in the KV on P.1.1.12.

१.३.१७. निपातोऽपृक्तोऽनाकारः ।

Whitney (1.79). G: 1.3.16.

Translation: A monophonic particle, except *ā*, is also *pragr̥hya.*

Note: P.1.1.41 (अपृक्त एकाल्प्रत्ययः) defines the term *apr̥kta* as applying to a monophonic affixal element. Since a *nipāta* 'particle' is not an affixal element, the term *apr̥kta* could not be used for a monophonic particle in Pāṇini's system. Thus, he was forced to formulate his rule differently, cf. P.1.1.14 (निपात एकाजनाङ्). However, the CA use of the term *apr̥kta* is not constrained by such a limitation, and hence it could be used to qualify a particle. While practically, all the elements qualified by the term *apr̥kta* in the CA are particles consisting of a single vowel, it is not clear whether one should translate the term as 'consisting of an uncombined vowel,' as done by Whitney.

Whitney clearly perceives that the particle *o* illustrated by the examples cited in the CAB is 'composed of *ā* and *u*.' This is made explicit by Bhārgava-Bhāskara. However, it would seem to me that the author of the Padapāṭha and the author of the CA probably did not treat it that way, but perceived it as a single particle, which needed a separate treatment.

Whitney, however, does have a point: "The form of this rule is not a little strange : why *o* should thus be made an exception from the next rule, and why, when there is no other particle, except *ā*, composed of a single vowel, it should be treated as if one of a class, it is very difficult to see : we cannot help suspecting here the influence of the general grammar : compare Pāṇ. i.1.14, the virtual correspondence of which with our rule is as close as possible." It seems clear that Pāṇini had a larger class of monophonic particles in his mind. Bhārgava-Bhāskara cites such Pāṇinian examples, which are, of course, not attested in the text of the AV.

चतुराध्यायीभाष्य - निपातः अपृक्तः अनाकारः प्रगृह्यो भवति । 'ओ चित् सखायम्' (अ.वे. १८.१.१)। (पद ⇒) 'ओ इति' । 'श्रातं हविरो षु' (अ.वे. ७.७२.२)। (पद ⇒) 'ओ इति' । अनाकार इति किमर्थम् । 'पुनरेहि वाचस्पते' (अ.वे. १.१.२)।

भा.भा.वृत्ति - अपृक्त एक एव स्वरः निपातसंज्ञश्चेत्प्रगृह्यः स्यात् । न त्वाङ् । 'इ इन्द्रः' । 'उ उमेशः' । 'ए अनन्त'। 'आ एवमस्ति किम्' । अनाङ् किम् । 'आऽअंक्ता' ।

'आत्तां' (अ.वे. १०.१.२५)। 'आ । इहि' । 'एहि' (अ.वे. १.१.२)। आङः उञा योगे एकवद् वृत्तौ 'ओ इति' (पद, अ.वे. १८.१.१)। अयं प्रगृह्य एव उञा योगात् । अपृक्तः किम् । 'ईम्' (अ.वे. ४.३०.४)। 'स्म' (अ.वे. १.८.२)। 'च' (अ.वे. १.२.४)। 'मा' (अ.वे. १.१.४)। 'वि' (अ.वे. १.१.४)। 'तु' (अ.वे. ४.१८.६)। 'हे' (not in AV)। 'है' (अ.वे. ६.५०.२)। 'नेत्' (ऋ.वे. ७.८६.६)। 'इत्' (अ. वे. १.२.४)। इत्यादि ।

Note: Compare the terminology used by the CAB and the commentary of Bhārgava-Bhāskara. While the first uses the sūtra term *anākāraḥ*, the latter replaces it with *anāṅ*, a usage from Pāṇini (1.1.14: निपात एकाजनाङ्). It also replaces the term *ukāra* of CA 1.3.11-12 with the Pāṇinian term *uñ*, cf. P.1.1.17-18 (उञः, ऊँ). This shows how Bhārgava-Bhāskara is fully utilizing, and taking for granted, the terminology of the Pāṇinian grammar. By offering examples, which are not specifically Atharvan, and which are commonplace in Pāṇinian commentaries, he is in effect offering a Pāṇinian interpretation of this Prātiśākhya. The examples इ इन्द्रः and उ उमेशः are found in the Siddhānta-Kaumudī on P.1.1.14 (निपात एकाजनाङ्). We also find there the instances आ एवं नु मन्यसे and आ एवं किल तत्.

१.३.१८. ओकारान्तश्च ।

Whitney (1.80). G: 1.3.17.

Translation: Also [a polyphonic particle] ending in *o* [is *pragṛhya*].

Note: Whitney raises an important concern regarding the notion of a particle ending in *o* as understood in this rule: "This is a strangely inaccurate description: it was bad enough to have the *upasarga* or preposition *ā* treated as a *nipāta* by the last rule, when combined with *u* : but here we have nouns, verbs, prepositions, and particles all confounded together under the same name. ... In the form of the rule is perhaps to be seen again the influence of the general grammar : compare Pāṇ. i.1.14." What Whitney fails to point out is that in all these cases, the final *o* is arrived at by a combination of a word with the following particle *u*, and yet this combination is treated by the Padapāṭha as an indivisible combination, making the combined form a *nipātānta*, if not strictly a *nipāta*, cf. Bhārgava-Bhāskara's commentary.

One also needs to comment on Whitney's statement: "it was bad enough to have the *upasarga* or preposition *ā* treated as a *nipāta* by the last rule." This statement assumes that *nipāta* and *upasarga* refer to exclusive classes. Such an impression could have been created perhaps by the statement in the Nirukta (1.12) which lists *nāma*, *ākhyāta*, *upasarga*, and *nipāta* as four classes of words. However, this is clearly not the only treatment of these two categories. Pāṇini (1.4.56, 58, 59) considers *upasarga* and *nipāta* as overlapping categories, with the latter subsuming the former, cf. गत्युपसर्गकर्मप्रवचनीयसंज्ञाभिः सह निपातसंज्ञा समाविशति, KV on P.1.4.56 (प्राग्रीश्वरान्निपाताः). Also see: प्राग्वचनं क्रियते निपातसंज्ञाया अनिवृत्तिर्यथा स्यात् । अक्रियमाणे हि प्राग्वचनेऽनवकाशा गत्युपसर्गकर्मप्रवचनीयसंज्ञा निपातसंज्ञां बाधेरन् । ता मा बाधिषतेति प्राग्वचनं क्रियते । अथ क्रियमाणेऽपि प्राग्वचने यावतानवकाशा एताः संज्ञाः कस्मादेव न बाधन्ते । क्रियमाणे हि प्राग्वचने सत्यां निपातसंज्ञायामेता अवयवसंज्ञा आरभ्यन्ते तत्र वचनात्समावेशो भवति ।, MB on P.1.4.56.

चतुराध्यायीभाष्य - ओकारान्तश्च निपातः प्रगृह्यो भवति । 'दोषो गाय' (अ.वे. ६.१.१)। (पद ⇒) 'दोषो इति' । 'अङ्गो न्वर्यमन्' (अ. वे. ६.६०.२)। (पद ⇒) 'अङ्गो इति' । 'अत्तो हवींषि' (अ.वे. १८.३.४४)। (पद ⇒) 'अत्तो इति' । 'दत्तो अस्मभ्यंम्' (अ.वे. १८.३.१४)। (पद ⇒) 'दत्तो इति' ।

भा.भा.वृत्ति - अवर्णान्तं पदम् उञा निपातेन योगे ओकारान्तं नित्यसंहितं पदमुत्पद्यते । सः शब्दः ओकारान्तः निपातान्त इत्यर्थः [।] प्रगृह्यसंज्ञः स्यात् । 'नो इति' (पद, अ.वे. १.३२.१। 'चो इति' (पद, ऋ.वे. ५.२९.१३)। 'सो इति' (पद, अ.वे.पै.सं. १७.२३.४)। 'प्रो इति' (पद, अ.वे. २०.९५.२)। 'क्वों इति' (पद, ऋ.वे. १.३८.३)। 'अथो इति' (पद, अ.वे. १.१४.२)। 'उतो इति' (पद, अ.वे. ४.१६.३)। 'तत्रो इति' (पद, ऋ.वे. ८.५६.४)।

'अर्यमो इति' (not found in known Vedic texts)। आख्यातं पदमपि । 'अत्तो इति' (पद, अ.वे. १८.३.४४)। 'विद्मो इति' (पद, अ.वे. १.२.१)।

Note: Bhārgava-Bhāskara quotes many more examples as compared to the CAB. However, Whitney provides a comprehensive listing: "The particles, it is true, greatly preponderate in number and in frequency : thus we have *atho* (about 130 times in the whole Atharvan text), *mo* (15 times), *no* (12 times), *uto* (7 times), and *iho*, *yado*, *aṅgo*, *evo*, *doṣo* (once each); but of prepositions we have *o* and *upo* (twice each), and *pro* (once); of verbs, *vidmo*, *datto*, *atto* (once each); and of nouns (pronouns), *teno* (twice), *yo* and *so* (once each)." Bhārgava-Bhāskara lists additional non-AV forms.

१.३.१९. आमन्त्रितं चेतावनार्षे ।

Whitney (1.81). G: 1.3.18. Ha, Na: °र्थे for °र्षे.

Translation: A vocative form, [ending in *o*], is also [*pragṛhya*], before an *iti* which is not a part of the Saṃhitā text [lit. which does not come from the ancient seers who 'saw' the Vedic saṃhitās].

Note: The present CA rule corresponds to P.1.1.16 (सम्बुद्धौ शाकल्यस्येतावनार्षे), where this doctrine is ascribed to Śākalya. The rule raises some interesting questions and Whitney has brought out some of these: "The vocatives in *o*, from themes in *u*, are not in a single instance treated as *pragṛhyas* in the *saṃhitā* of the Atharvan, but are always euphonically combined with the following vowel. In the *pada*-text, however, they are invariably written as if they were *pragṛhyas*, with the usual *iti* annexed. The object of this rule, then, is to teach that they are exempt from euphonic combination only in the *pada*-text, while in other situations they are to be treated according to the general euphonic rules." This sounds good enough. The CAB, raising the question इताविति किमर्थम्, says that before words other than *iti*, the vocative forms in *o* are not *pragṛhya*s. On the other hand, Bhārgava-Bhāskara raises the question *anārṣe iti kim*. This is answered by pointing out that before an *iti* of the saṃhitā-text, the vocative in *o* is not treated as a *pragṛhya*. Of course the example he offers is not from the Atharvan text, but it is a Vedic example nonetheless.

Whitney questions: "This whole state of things is something very peculiar. Why, when the *o* of *vāyo* is really no more exempt from change than the *e* of *agne*, should it be regarded by all the *pada*-texts as a *pragṛhya*, causing so much trouble to the different treatises to explain its treatment?" This may possibly suggest dialect differences among the Padakāras, see Cardona (1991).

चतुराध्यायीभाष्य - आमन्त्रितं च ओ(H, N: ओँ)कारान्तमितौ परतः अनार्षे प्रगृह्यं भवति । 'त्वय्युदिते प्रेरते चित्रभानो' (अ.वे. ४.२५.३)। (पद ⇒) 'चित्रभानो इति' । 'युवं वायो सविता' (अ.वे. ४.२५.३)। (पद ⇒) 'वायो इति' । 'मन्यो वज्रिन्' (अ.वे. ४.३२.६)। (पद ⇒) 'मन्यो इति' । इताविति किमर्थम् । 'वाय ऊतये' (अ.वे. ४.२५.६)। 'मन्य ईडिता' (अ.वे. ४.३१.४)। 'बभ्र आ मे शृणुत' (अ.वे. ५.१३.५)।

Note: The CAB, under the query इताविति किमर्थम्, cites the first 3 examples out of a list of six found in the APR (143).

भा.भा.वृत्ति - ऋषिर्वेदः । सर्वज्ञानहेतुत्वात् । तत्रत्यः आर्षः अनार्षस्तु यो वेदोक्तादन्यः । अनार्षे इतिशब्दे परे ओकारान्तमामन्त्रितं प्रगृह्यं स्यात् । 'वायो इति' (पद, अ.वे. ४.२५.३)। 'विष्णो इति' (पद, अ.वे. ७.२६.३)। 'सूनो इति' (पद, अ.वे. १८.१.२४)। 'यो इति' (G: य हो) (पद, अ.वे. ११.४.९)। इतौ किम् । 'वाय उदकेन' (अ.वे. ६.६८.१)। 'वायवा याहि' (ऋ.वे. ५.५१.५)। 'वायविन्द्रश्च' (ऋ.वे. १.२.५)। 'मन्य ईडिता(G: तः)' (अ.वे. ४.३१.४)। (पद ⇒) 'मन्यो इति' । 'वषट् ते विष्णवास आ' (ऋ.वे. ५.९९.७)। अनार्षे किम् । 'ब्रह्मबन्धवित्यब्रवीत्' ('एता गा ब्रह्मबन्ध इत्यब्रवीत्,' काण्व.शु. य.सं. १०.६)।

Note: The example ब्रह्मबन्धवित्यब्रवीत् is cited in the KV on P.1.1.16 (सम्बुद्धौ शाकल्यस्येतावनार्षे). Note that while Pāṇini ascribes this view to Śākalya, it is cited here without any such comment, and is the only available procedure.

१.३.२०. आर्त्नी इवादिष्विवादितिपरः ।

Whitney (1.82): °दितिः परः. G: 1.3.19. I: 20.

Translation: In [passages such as] *ārtnī iva* (AV 1.1.3), [in the *pada*-text], the word *iti* follows [the word *iva*, rather than the strictly *pragṛhya* word *ārtnī* etc.].

Note: The peculiarity of this formation needs to be clearly understood. The Vedic exegetical tradition almost unanimously agrees that the word *iva* is compounded with the preceding word. Given this notion, how should one deal with forms like *ārtnī* before *iva*? Here, Bhārgava-Bhāskara states clearly that there is no *sandhi* between such *pragṛhya* words as *ārtnī* with the following *iva*, i.e. there is a *pragṛhya* inside a compound expression. However, the *pada*-text marks the *pragṛhya* character by adding an *iti* after the compound expression ending in *iva*.

Whitney points out that the *pada*-text of the AV actually reads *ārtnī ivety ārtnī 'iva*, but the commentary CAB records only the first portion *ārtnī iveti*, and leaves out the repetition of the compound.

चतुराध्यायीभाष्य - आर्त्नी इवादिषु इवात् इतिपरो भवति । 'आर्त्नी इवेति' (पद, अ.वे. १.१.३)। 'घर्मदुघे इवेति' (पद, अ.वे. ४.२२.४)। 'नृपती इवेति' (पद, अ.वे. ८.४.६)। 'यमे इवेति' (पद, अ.वे. १८.३.३८)।

Note: All the examples cited by the CAB occur under APR (58, examples 45-47, p. 52). Surya Kanta informs us that the example AV (8.4.6) occurs only in the mss. Vn. However, the fact that it also appears in the CAB makes it almost certain that it is part of the genuine APR text, because of the close correspondence between the examples cited in the CAB and the APR.

भा.भा.वृत्ति - आर्त्नी इवादिषूदाहरणेषु अन्तःपदं प्रगृह्यतास्ति । तत्र इवशब्दस्य परत्वादेव इतिशब्दपरत्वं ज्ञेयम् ।

अयं भावः । इतिशब्दः स्वरादिः विवृत्तसन्धिनिदर्शनाय पद-काले प्रयुज्यते [।] यत्र इवशब्देन विवृत्तसन्धिः स्फुटः तत्र इतिकारस्य प्रयोजनं नास्ति [।] अतः अवग्रहानन्तरमिति-कारो न प्रयुज्यते [।] तैत्तिरीया(G: र्यी)दौ तु इवशब्दः पद-काले विगृह्यते तत्र प्रगृह्यस्य इतिकरणमुचितमेव ।

Note: Bhārgava-Bhāskara draws our attention to the fact that the *pada*-text of the TS does not follow this pattern, i.e. it adds the word *iti* directly after the *pragṛhya* word, and not after the word *iva*. This is illustrated, for instance, by the cxample वाससी इव (TS 1.5.10). Here, the dual word *vāsasī* is a *pragṛhya* and is followed by the word *iva* in the Saṃhitā. However, the Pada-text goes: वासंसी इति । इव. In view of the example from the TS, and its distinctive practice mentioned by Bhārgava-Bhāskara, we need to modify Whitney's belief that the doctrine enunciated by the present rule was "adopted by all the *pada*-texts."

१.३.२१. अनुनासिकोऽन्तःपदे ह्रस्वः ।

Whitney (1.83). G: 1.3.20. Most mss. read *rhasvaḥ*.

Translation: A nasal [vowel] occurring in the interior of a word [i.e. in the non-final position] is [as a general rule] short.

Note: Whitney thinks that the doctrine taught by this rule and its exceptions does not enter into the proper province of a Prātiśākhya. However, he commends Uvaṭa on the RPR who "is at much pains to explain its introduction into the Prātiśākhya, into whose proper province such a matter does not enter." Whitney then explains the "little inconsistencies and redundancies of this kind, which are exhibited by all the treatises; they aid in the general purpose of a Prātiśākhya, which is to preserve the traditional text of the school from corruption." Whitney's discussion has a built-in circularity, though I do not disagree with his final conclusion.

It must be pointed out again that this treatise does not distinguish between *anusvāra* and *anunāsika*. Therefore, the point of the rule is not to say that such a vowel as discussed here is a nasal vowel, instead of being a pure vowel followed by an *anusvāra*. The point of the discussion is that it is a short vowel. However, note that according to this text, cf. CA (1.2.13: अनुनासिकं च),

every nasal vowel is metrically treated as a heavy (*guru*) vowel / syllable. This removes the possible metrical difference between a short nasal vowel, and a short pure vowel followed by an *anusvāra*.

> ***चतुराध्यायीभाष्य*** - अनुनासिकः अन्तःपदे ह्रस्वो भवति । 'द्वे चं मे विँशतिश्च' (अ.वे. ५.१५.२)। 'तिस्रश्चं मे त्रिँशच्चं' (अ.वे. ५.१५.३)। 'चतंस्रश्च मे चत्वारिँशच्चं' (अ.वे. ५.१५.४)। 'पुमांन् पुँसः' (अ.वे. ३.६.१)।

> ***भा.भा.वृत्ति*** - अन्तःपदे पदस्य मध्ये योऽनुनासिकः स ह्रस्व एवेति ज्ञातव्यः । 'अँशः' (अ.वे. ६.४.२)। 'अँशुः' (अ.वे. ५.२९.१२)। 'हँसः' (not in ŚAV, अ.वे.पै.सं. १६.२३.१)। 'संपिँषन्ति' (अ.वे. १४.१.३)। 'वँशः' ('वँश,' अ.वे. ३.१२.६)। 'शिँशपा' (शिँशपाः, अ.वे. २०.१२९.७)। 'शिँशुमारः' (अ.वे.पै.सं. २०.५८.६; 'शिँशुमाराः,' अ.वे. ११.२.२५)। 'सिँहः' (अ.वे. ५.२०.१)।

१.३.२२. दीर्घो नपुंसकबहुवचने ।

Whitney (1.84). G: 1.3.21.

Translation: [The nasal vowel occurring] in neuter plural forms is long.

Note: This is an exception to the previous rule, which stipulated that nasal vowels, in general, are short. Again it should be kept in mind that the CA does not differentiate between a nasal vowel and a pure vowel followed by an *anusvāra*.

> ***चतुराध्यायीभाष्य*** - दीर्घः अनुनासिको भवति नपुंसकबहुवचने । 'परूँषि यस्यं संभाराः' (अ.वे. ९.६.१)। 'यजूँषि होत्रां ब्रू(H, N: क्र)मः' (अ.वे. ११.६.१४)। 'अत्तो हवीँषि' (अ.वे. १८.३.४४)।

भा.भा.वृत्ति - नपुंसकलिङ्गस्य प्रथमाद्वितीययोर्बहुवचने योऽनुनासिकः स दीर्घो ज्ञेयः । 'यशाँसि' (not in *AV*) । 'ज्योतीँषि' (अ.वे. ९.५.८) । 'वपूँषि' (अ.वे. ५.१.२) ।

१.३.२३. पांसुमांसादीनाम् ।

Whitney (1.85). E (orig), F, G: पाँशुमाँसा°. G and F (corr) add उ at the beginning of the rule. G: 1.3.22. O: पांशु°.

Translation: [Also, the nasal vowels] of the words *pāṃsu* (= *pā̃su*), *māṃsa* (= *mā̃sa*) etc. [are long].

Note: The mss. do not consistently distinguish between a nasal vowel from an *anusvāra*, nor does the CA make any clear distinction. Thus, as before, the main point of this rule is that these nasal vowels are long, and not to contrast between a nasal vowel versus a pure vowel followed by an *anusvāra*.

चतुराध्यायीभाष्य - पाँसुमाँस इत्येवमादीनां दीर्घः अनुनासिको भवति । 'पाँसू(H, N: सु)नक्षेभ्यः' (अ.वे. ७.१०९.२) । 'माँसं माँसेन' (अ.वे. ४.१२.४) । 'शाँशपेन(H: °यत)' (अ.वे. ६.१२९.१) । 'शिला भूमिरश्मा पाँसुः' (अ.वे. १२.१.२६) ।

Note: Concerning the reading *śāṃśayena* for AV (6.129.1), Whitney's note on this rule hesitantly asks us to correct the form to *śāṃśapena* : "should be *śāṃśapena?* the manuscripts blunder somewhat over the word, but W.E. and H. read distinctly *śāṃśapena*." This hesitation is gone in his note to the translation of this verse (*AV Transl.* Vol.I., p.378): "The mss. blunder over the word *śāṃśapéna*. SPP. reports only *śāṃśaphéna* as variant (read by two of his); ours have that, and also *śāṃsayéna* and *sāṃśayéna;* our text reads wrongly *śāṃśayéna* ⌊correct to *śāṃśapéna*⌋." The VVRI edition finally chooses *śāṃśapéna*, and I have followed that reading. However, the mss. of the CAB probably intended *-yena*. This is also the reading of the APR (p. 150).

भा.भा.वृत्ति - (उपाँशुमाँसादीनाम्) उपाँश्वादीनामेकादेशतां प्राप्तानामनुनासिकानां माँसादिशब्दानां च योऽनुनासिकस्तस्य च दीर्घतास्तीति ज्ञातव्यम् । 'उपऽअँशु' । 'उपाँशु' (अ.वे. ४.३२.७)। 'अमृताँशुः' (not in AV)। 'माँसम्' (अ.वे. ४. १२.४)। 'काँस्य' (not in AV)। 'पाँसून्' (अ.वे. ७.१०९. २) । 'पाँसुरे' (अ.वे. ७.२६.४)।

Note: The two commentaries show that they seriously commented on two different readings. It would seem that an original reading *pā̃su* was first corrupted to *pā̃śu*, and then a few manuscripts further changed it to *upā̃śu*. These two readings are restricted to those manuscripts which call the CA either Caturādhyāyī-Vyākaraṇa, or Kautsa-Vyākaraṇa, and thus share a common branching.

१.३.२४. हनिगम्योः सनि ।

Whitney (1.86). C, Hb, J, Nab, P: °सनिः. Ha: °सतिः. G: 1.3.23.

Translation: [The nasal vowel is long also] in the desiderative forms of the roots *han* and *gam* [lit. the nasal vowel of the roots *han* and *gam*, when followed by the desiderative affix *san*, is long].

Note: One needs to assume that when there is a reduplication of the root, the first occurrence is treated as the reduplication, while the second occurrence is treated as the original root.

As Whitney notes, there is no desiderative form of *gam* found in the present text of the AV, unless we decide to amend यदा स्याम जिघाँसति (AV 12.4.29-30) to जिगांसति on the basis of the present rule. No manuscript of the AV supports this emendation. However, note that Bhārgava-Bhāskara seems to cite the form *jigā̃sati*, besides *jighā̃sati*. In all probability, this is simply to illustrate the two roots given in the rule, and need not truly suggest that the text of the AV as known to Bhārgava-Bhāskara had the form *jigā̃sati*.

Secondly, it is interesting to note the use of *san* in this text where the *n* is identical with the metalinguistic marker *n* in Pāṇini's desiderative affix *san*. The CA simply takes this marker for granted, and does not define its function as Pāṇini does, cf. P.6.4.16 (अज्झनगमां सनि). This may possibly indicate a post-Pāṇinian layer in the CA, but one cannot be certain.

Surya Kanta (*APR*, *Introduction*, p. 39) suggests that the currently available Vulgate of the AV is not a genuinely Śaunakīya version, and that a genuinely Śaunakīya AV may have contained the desiderative of *gam*.

चतुराध्यायीभाष्य - हनि गमि इत्येतयोः सनि परतः दीर्घः अनुनासिको भवति । 'जिघाँसति' (अ.वे. ४.१८.३)। 'यदा स्थाम् जिघाँ (Whitney's emendation: गां)सति' (अ.वे. १२. ४.२९-३०)।

भा.भा.वृत्ति - हनिगमिधात्वोः सन्प्रत्यये परे योऽनुनासिकः स दीर्घः स्यात् । 'जिघाँस-' ('जिघाँसति,' अ.वे. ४.१८. ३)। 'जिगाँ(G: गां)स-' (?'यदा स्थाम् जिघाँ[Whitney's emendation: गां]सति,' अ.वे. १२.४.२९-३०)।

१.३.२५. शान्मान्दानाम् ।

Whitney (1.87). G: 1.3.24.

Translation: [Also, the nasal vowel in the desiderative forms of the roots] *śān*, *mān*, and *dān* [is long].

Note: Of the three listed roots, only the forms of *mān* occur in the available text of the ŚAV. Surya Kanta (*APR*, *Introduction*, p. 39) suggests that desiderative forms of *śān* and *dān* may have actually occurred in a genuinely Śaunakīya recension of the AV, which the currently available Vulgate is not. Whitney points out that P.3.1.6 (मान्बधदान्शान्भ्यो दीर्घश्चाभ्यासस्य) also groups these three roots together, besides the root *badh*, and suggests that a similar occasional urge to indulge in the provisions for a general grammar of Sanskrit may account for several rules in the CA. Whitney's suggestion does have some merit, and that one need not posit, like Surya Kanta, the existence of a so-called true Śaunakīya recension of the AV which supposedly contained all these untraceable forms.

चतुराध्यायीभाष्य - शान् मान् दानाम् इत्येतेषां सनि परत(:) दीर्घः अनुनासिको भवति । 'शीशाँसति' (not in AV)। 'मीमाँसमानाः' (अ.वे. ९.१.३)। 'दीदाँसति' (not in AV)।

भा.भा.वृत्ति - शान् । मान् । दान् । एषां धातूनां सनि अनुनासिको दीर्घ एव ज्ञेयः । 'शीशाँस-' (not in AV)। 'मीमाँ(G: मां)समानस्य' (अ.वे. ९.६.२४, VVRI edn.: ९.७.७)। 'दीदाँस-' (not in AV)।

१.३.२६. वस्वन्तस्य पञ्चपद्याम् ।

Whitney (1.88). A, B (orig): वस्यंत°. Hb, Nb: वस्वतस्यं°. G: 1.3.25.

Translation: [Also, the nasal vowel appearing] in the first five case forms [i.e. nominative sg., du., and pl., and accusative sg. and du.] of [a nominal stem] ending in [the perfect participial affix] *vasU* [is long].

Note: The inclusion of the nominative singular form in this rule is somewhat intriguing, because such a form ends in *n*, e.g. *pareyivān*, and has neither a nasal vowel, nor a pure vowel followed by an *anusvāra*. Perhaps, the author of the rule has in his view examples like *śuśruvā̃* (< *śuśruvān*) found in RV (10.71.5d).

चतुराध्यायीभाष्य - वस्वन्तस्य पञ्चपद्यां दीर्घः अनुनासिको भवति । 'परेयिवाँसः' ('परेयिवाँसम्,' अ.वे. १८.१.४९)। 'प्रविशिवाँसः' ('प्रविशिवाँसम्,' अ.वे. ४.२३.१)। 'उत्त-स्थिवाँसः' (अ.वे. ६.९३.१)। 'पपिवाँसः' (अ.वे. ७.९७.३)।

भा.भा.वृत्ति - क्वसुप्रत्ययान्तस्य पञ्चपद्यां दीर्घोऽनुनासिको ज्ञेयः । प्रथमाया वचनत्रयं द्वितीयाया द्वयं पञ्चपदी । 'जागृ-

वान्' (not in AV)। 'जागृवाँसौ' (not in AV)। 'जक्षिवाँसः' (अ.वे. ७.९७.३)। 'पपिवाँसः' (अ.वे. ७.९७.३)। 'परेयिवाँसम्' (अ.वे. १८.१.४९)। 'उत्तस्थिवाँसः' (अ.वे. ६.९३.१)। 'सासह्वाँसम्' (अ.वे. २०.४६.१)। क्वचिन्न । 'दाश्वांसम्' (अ.वे. ७.४०.२)।

Note: The last comment of Bhārgava-Bhāskara is somewhat intriguing. What does he mean in saying that this long nasal vowel does not occur in some instances? His example दाश्वांसम् might make sense perhaps if we assume that he makes a distinction between forms which have a nasal vowel versus those which have a pure vowel followed by an *anusvāra*. Such a distinction is not assumed by the rules of the CA, and the mss. of the AV do not show any such distinction. If Bhārgava-Bhāskara's comment is taken seriously, it may suggest changes which occurred in certain oral traditions.

The CA rule itself uses the expression *vasu* for the affix *vas*. The final *u* must be a marker sound, as the same marker is found in Pāṇini. Pāṇini adds one more marker, making the affix *vas* appear as *KvasU*, cf. P.3.2.107 (क्वसुश्च). Bhārgava-Bhāskara uses the expression *KvasU*, even though the CA uses only *vasU*, thus indicating an advanced degree of Pāṇinianization of this tradition.

१.३.२७. ईयसश्च ।

Whitney (1.89). A, Hb, Nbc, O: इ for ई. A, B, D: °शश्च for °सश्च. G: 1.3.27, comes after विदेश्च.

Translation: [Also, the nasal vowel appearing in the first five case forms i.e. nominative sg., du., and pl., and accusative sg. and du.] of [a nominal stem] ending in [the comparative affix] *īyas* [is long].

चतुराध्यायीभाष्य - ईयसश्च पञ्चपद्यां दीर्घः अनुनासिको भवति । 'श्रेयान्' (अ.वे.पै.सं. १७.३४.६)। 'श्रेयाँसौ' (not in AV)। 'श्रेयाँसः' (not in AV)।

Note: Whitney says the only form of the stem श्रेयस्, relevant in the present context, occurring in the ŚAV is श्रेयांसम् (15.10.2). This form also occurs in AV (2.11.1-5).

भा.भा.वृत्ति - ईयसुन्प्रत्ययान्तस्य च पञ्चपद्यामनुनासिको दीर्घः बोद्धव्यः । 'भूयाँसः' (अ.वे. ७.६०.७, VVRI edn.: ७.६२.७)। 'तीक्ष्णीयाँसः' (अ.वे. ३.१९.४)। 'सहीयाँसम्' (अ.वे. १७.१.१-५)।

Note: Again notice that the CA and the CAB refer to the affix as *īyas*, but Bhārgava-Bhāskara uses the Pāṇinian term *īyasUN*. This is an indication of an advanced stage of Pāṇinianization of this tradition.

१.३.२८. विदेश्च ।

Whitney (1.90). G: 1.3.26. O: विदेश्चः. G, I: comes before ईयसश्च. I: ईयसश्च२ विदेश्च१.

Translation: Also, [the nasal vowel appearing in the first five case forms i.e. nominative sg., du., and pl., and accusative sg. and du.] of the root *vid* [ending in the perfect participial affix *vasU* is long].

Note: As Whitney notes, Pāṇini treats the formation *vid+vas* as an exceptional case of a present participle, cf. P.7.1.36 (विदेः शतुर्वसुः), where the perfect participle affix *vas* is used for a present participle. Whitney raises two appropriate objections: "There are two damaging objections to be made to this rule : in the first place, it ought to be brought in, if at all, after rule 88 (= CA 1.3.26), in order that *vasvantasya* as well as *pañcapadyām* may be implied in it by inference from its predecessor; and in the second place, there is no need of any such precept at all, since there is no good reason why *vidvān*, the word to which it alone applies, should not be considered a *vasvanta*, and therefore regarded as disposed of by rule 88." Whitney's concern about rule ordering was apparently felt by a few copyists as well, and therefore we have two manuscripts, G and I, which invert the order of CA 1.3.27-28, and place this rule immediately after CA 1.3.26 (= W 1.88). Unfortunately, the manuscript evidence is overwhelmingly against this inversion. No manuscript omits this rule either. Just looking at the textual evidence, one must say that the author of the

CA could not lump the forms of *vidvas* together with the perfect participle forms like those of *pareyivas*, and in this separation he had reasons similar to Pāṇini's.

चतुराध्यायीभाष्य - विदेश्च पञ्चपद्यां दीर्घः अनुनासिको भवति । 'विद्वान्' (अ.वे. २.१.२)। 'विद्वाँसौ' (not in AV)। 'विद्वाँसः' (अ.वे. ६.११५.१)। 'विद्वाँसम्' (अ.वे. १५.२.१)। 'विद्वाँसौ' (not in AV)। 'विद्वान् स व्रात्यः' ('विद्वाँसं व्रात्यम्,' अ.वे. १५.२.१)।

भा.भा.वृत्ति - 'विदेः शतुर्वसुः' (पा. ७.१.३६) इति वस्वन्तस्य । चात् मत्वर्थे वसुः । तदन्तस्य च पञ्चपद्यां दीर्घोऽनुनासिकः । 'विद्वान्' (अ.वे. २.१.२)। 'विद्वाँसौ' (not in AV)। 'विद्वाँसः' (अ.वे. ६.११५.१)। 'विद्वाँसम्' (अ.वे. १५.२.१)। 'भक्तिवाँसः' (अ.वे. ६.७९.३)।

Note: Bhārgava-Bhāskara tries to extend this rule beyond the forms of *vid*, by overinterpreting *ca* to mean that the rule applies to other cases of *vas*, such as the affix *vas* as a possessive affix. This is done in order to account for the form भक्तिवाँसः (AV 6.79.3). It is not clear if this form could be taken care of by CA (1.3.26). But, then, the forms of *vidvas* can as well be taken care of by that rule.

१.३.२९. पुंसश्च ।

Whitney (1.91). E, F, G: पुँ°. G: 1.3.28. I: 29.

Translation: Also, [the nasal vowel appearing in the first five case forms i.e. nominative sg., du., and pl., and accusative sg. and du.] of the word *puṃs* [= *pūs* is long].

चतुराध्यायीभाष्य - पुंसश्च पञ्चपद्यां दीर्घः अनुनासिको भवति । 'पुमान्' (अ.वे. १.८.१)। 'पुमाँसौ' (not in AV)। 'पुमाँसः' (अ.वे.पै.सं. ५.२१.४)। 'पुमाँसम्' (अ.वे. ३.

२३.३)। 'पुमाँसौ' (not in AV)। पञ्चपद्यामिति किमर्थम्। 'पुँसि वै रेतो भवति' (अ.वे ६.११.२)।

भा.भा.वृत्ति - पञ्चपद्यां पुंशब्दस्यानुनासिकः चात् तद्धिते परेऽपि दीर्घश्च ह्रस्वश्च। 'पुमान्' (अ.वे. १.८.१)। 'पुमाँसौ' (not in Vedic texts)। 'पुमाँसः' (अ.वे.पै.सं. ५.२१.४)। 'पुमाँसम्' (अ.वे. ३.२३.३)। तद्धिते। 'पौँस्यम्' ('पौँस्यं,' अ.वे. २०.७३.६)। 'पौँस्नः' (not in Vedic texts)। 'पुँस्त्वम्' (not in Vedic texts)। 'पुँस्ता' (not in Vedic texts)। पञ्चपद्यां किम्। 'पुँसः' (अ.वे. ३.६.१)। 'पुँसि' (अ.वे. ६.११.२)। 'पुँसु' (अ.वे. १२.१.२५)। स्पर्शे। 'पुँभिः' (not in Vedic texts)।

Note: Both the commentaries raise the question: why have the condition *pañcapadyām*? The simple answer is that the rule should not apply beyond the five forms referred to by *pañcapadī*, i.e. the first five forms of the nominal paradigm. Again, we must keep in mind that the intended contrast between the forms *pumā̃sam* and *pū̃si* is only as regards the length of the nasal vowel, and not that one form is with a nasal vowel, while the other should be with a pure vowel followed by an *anusvāra*. Such a distinction is not made by this text, and it is only our orthography which forces us to be over-specific.

Also, Bhārgava-Bhāskara over-interprets this rule to extend it to cases of *taddhita* formations like *paũsnya*. This word is attested in AV (20.73.6) and was possibly not in the AV as known to the author of the CA. Whitney has made a justifiable argument that the CA is familiar with only the first 18 books of the ŚAV, and that the last two books are a later addition.

इति प्रथमाध्यायस्य तृतीयः पादः ।

H, N: प्रथमस्य तृतीयपादः । C, E, F: प्रथमस्य तृतीयः पादः । A, B, D, J, M, P: ।३। तृतीयः पादः । G: इत्यथर्ववेदांगकौत्सव्याकरणस्य भार्गवभास्करीयवृत्तौ प्रथमाध्यायस्य तृतीयपादसूत्रव्याख्यानं संपूर्णं । H, N: add number 91 to indicate the cumulative number of rules in the first three Pādas of the first Adhyāya. O: ।।३।। सूत्राणि ।।२९।। प्रथमस्य तृतीयः पादः ।।

चतुराध्यायीभाष्य- प्रथमस्य तृतीयः पादः । ९१।

भा.भा.वृत्ति - इत्यथर्ववेदाङ्गकौत्सव्याकरणस्य भार्गवभास्करीयवृत्तौ प्रथमाध्यायस्य तृतीयपादसूत्रव्याख्यानं संपूर्णम् ।

॥ प्रथमोऽध्यायः ॥
॥ चतुर्थः पादः ॥

भा.भा.वृत्ति - अथाथर्ववेदाङ्गकौत्सव्याकरणस्य भार्गव-भास्करीयवृत्तौ प्रथमाध्यायस्य चतुर्थपादस्थसूत्रगणव्याख्यानमारभ्यते । ॐ३म् ।

१.४.१. वर्णादन्त्यात्पूर्व उपधा ।

Whitney (1.92). G: 1.4.1.

Translation: The sound which precedes the final sound [i.e. the penultimate sound] is termed *upadhā*.

Note: Whitney points out that this definition of *upadhā* is 'precisely the same' as the definition in the VPR (i.35), but further says: "In the Rik Pr. the word has a more general use, as 'preceding letter or word' (*upa-dhā*, 'a setting against or next to'): it is probably on account of this less restricted signification current in some schools that the two treatises first spoken of deem it necessary to limit the term by a specific definition." Also see Renou (1942: 395-6). P.1.1.65 (अलोऽन्त्यात् पूर्व उपधा) is also identical with the present CA rule. One may speculate that Pāṇini's wording is based on something similar to the wording of the CA, in that the masculine form *pūrvaḥ* in Pāṇini's rule seems to have the assumed masculine qualificand *varṇa* (= *aL*).

चतुराध्यायीभाष्य - वर्णादन्त्यात्पूर्वो वर्णः उपधासंज्ञो भवति । 'नाम्युपधस्य रेफः' (च.आ. २.२.३)। 'अग्निरत्र' (not in AV)। 'वायुरत्र' (not in AV)। 'आकारोपधस्य लोपः' (च.आ. २.२.१६)। 'अश्वा भवथ' (अ.वे. १.४.४)।

भा.भा.वृत्ति - अन्त्याद्वर्णात्पूर्वो वर्ण उपधासंज्ञो बोध्यः [।] अकारोपधान्मकारोपधान्मतोर्मस्य वत्वमित्यादिविधिषु उपधासंज्ञायाः प्रयोजनं ज्ञेयम् । सरः, 'सरस्वती' (अ.वे. ५.२३.

१)[।] लक्ष्मी[:], 'लक्ष्मीवान्' (not in known Vedic literature)। [भगम्], 'भगंवन्तः' (अ.वे. ३.१६.४)।

Note: The difference between these two commentaries is noteworthy. In order to show the purpose of the technical term *upadhā* defined here, the CAB cites two rules from the CA which make use of this term. On the other hand, Bhārgava-Bhāskara alludes to P.8.2.9 (मादुपधायाश्च मतोर्वोऽयवादिभ्यः) which uses this same term. However, this rule teaches where the possessive affix *-matUP* changes to *-vatUP*. There is no such rule in the CA. To say that the Prātiśākhya defines the term *upadhā* so that it may used in rules similar to P.8.2.9 is absurd. However, this only goes to show how the Pāṇinian tradition has been internalized by this commentator, so that he almost fails to recognize that the CA is not part of this tradition.

The examples अग्निरत्र and वायुरत्र provided by the CAB are found in the KV on P.8.2.66 (ससजुषो रुः).

१.४.२. स्वरोऽक्षरम् ।

Whitney (1.93). G: 1.4.2.

Translation: A vowel is called a syllable.

Note: Whitney comments: "The precise scope of this rule it is not easy to determine; it seems to be rather a general and theoretic doctrine than a precept which enters in any active and practical manner into the system of rules of our treatise. ... We may perhaps regard our rule as a virtual precept that the accentuation, which in later rules (iii.55 = CA 3.3.1 etc.) is taught especially to the vowels, extends its sway over the whole syllable : or, on the other hand, that the accents, which in rules 14-16 (= CA 1.1.16) above were declared to belong to syllables, affect especially the vowels. With the subject of accent the commentator seems, at any rate, to bring it into special connection." Additionally, one may perhaps connect this rule with the metrical notion of syllable, where the number of syllables is basically identical with the number of vowels. The term *akṣara* in the sense of a metrical syllable is historically attested all the way from the oldest stratum of the Vedic literature. Also cf. VPR (1.99).

चतुराध्यायीभाष्य - स्वरः अक्षरसंज्ञं भवति । 'किमक्षरस्य स्वर्यमाणस्य स्वर्यते । अर्धं ह्रस्वस्य पादो दीर्घस्येत्येके ।

सर्वमिति शाङ्खमित्रिः (H: त्रः)। अक्षरस्यैषा विधा न (H: धानं, N: विधानं, Whitney: विधान) विद्यते यद् द्विस्वरीभावः (H, N: यद् यद् विरस्वराभावः, Whitney: विश्वरीभावः)' (च.आ. ३.३.३१-३४)। स्वरमक्षरमित्याहुः स्वरादन्यद् व्यञ्जनं सर्वं पृथक् वर्णसामान्यं द्व्यक्तांव्यंज्यते बुधैः (?)।

Note: The CAB here quotes CA 3.3.31-34 to illustrate the use of the term *akṣara* just as it has quoted two CA rules on the previous sūtra to illustrate the term *upadhā*. These rules were not admitted by Whitney as being part of the text of the CA. All the manuscripts contain these rules, and now it is clear that even the CAB, the oldest commentary on this text, admits them as sūtras belonging to the CA. At the same time, it is a puzzle as to why the CAB does not directly comment on these rules.

Whitney, who treated the cited passages as belonging to the commentary, rather than to the text of the CA, yet offered a translation, 'though not without some misgivings,': "what part of a circumflexed syllable is circumflexed? Some say, half a short one, quarter of a long one : Śāṅkhamitri says, the whole : here is found no rule for a syllable [*hrasva* and *dīrgha* are said of vowels only, see note to r. 51 above]; since, in each case, the vowel alone is contemplated [??] : now the vowel is declared to be the syllable." Whitney notes that his manuscript has the reading शाङ्खमित्रः in this place, though elsewhere (CA 2.1.6 and 3.3.30) the reading is शाङ्खमित्रिः, and hence in his translation, he selects the latter. This choice is now supported by the second manuscript, N.

Given the confirmed reading अक्षरस्यैषा, the next unclear portion can be confidently reconstructed as विधा न विद्यते, यद् द्विस्वरीभावः, and can be translated as: "It is not the norm of a syllable to have two accents [within one and the same syllable]." This seems be the continuation of Śāṅkhamitri's doctrine that the whole, and not part of a syllable, is circumflexed.

Also for some reason, Whitney says about the commentary: "Omitting his usual explanatory paraphrase (a small loss : it would doubtless have been *svaro 'kṣaram bhavati*), he proceeds at once to give an exposition, of which a part occurs again at the close of the third section of the third chapter." This is inaccurate. Both the manuscripts of the commentary CAB contain the initial phrase: स्वरः अक्षरसंज्ञं भवति. This paraphrase is also found in the lone manuscript H, which was available to Whitney, but for some reason, he missed it while reading or copying it.

भा.भा.वृत्ति - अश्नुते वाग्जालं व्याप्नोति अक्षरं मध्योदात्तम्। 'क्षरः सर्वाणि भूतानि कूटस्थोऽक्षर उच्यते' (भगवद्गीता १५.१६) इत्यादिषु नञ्समासोत्पन्नः आद्युदात्तः अक्षरः । आकाशादौ मध्योदात्तमक्षरम् । स्वरः ह्रस्वो वा दीर्घो वा प्लुतो वा अक्षरसंज्ञो ज्ञेयः । अ आ इ ई उ ऊ ऋ ॠ ऌ ए ऐ ओ औ एतान्यक्षराणि । व्यञ्जनानि परस्य स्वरस्याङ्गानि इत्युक्तं पूर्वमेव (cf. 'परस्य स्वरस्य व्यञ्जनानि,' च.आ. १.२.१५)। च, स्म, स्फ्य, सा, ग्ना, नि, त्रि, धी, स्त्री, तु, क्षु, भू, भ्रू, नृ, ते, द्वे, वै, त्वै, नो, प्रो, तौ, स्वौ एतान्यप्यक्षराणि । पद्याः पूर्वाङ्गमित्युक्तत्वात् (cf. 'पद्यं च,' च.आ. १.२.१७) तत् षट् ... (break in the Ms)

Note: By referring to the derivation of the word *akṣara* from the verb *aśnute*, the commentator probably alludes to Patañjali's MB: अक्षरं न क्षरं विद्यात् अश्नोतेर्वा सरोऽक्षरम्। अश्नोतेर्वा पुनरयमौणादिकः सरन्प्रत्ययः । अश्नुते इत्यक्षरम्, (cf. MB, Kielhorn edn., Vol. I., p. 36). This verse has been partially cited also by the CAB.

१.४.३. सोष्मणि पूर्वस्यानूष्मा ।

Whitney (1.94), C (orig), P: नु for नू. A, B, D, E, F, Ha, J, M, Na, O, P: Daṇḍa after सोष्मणि, and join the rest with the next rule. J, M: °पूर्वस्यानूष्मण. Ha, Na: Daṇḍa after पूर्वस्यानूष्मा. J, D: सोष्मणिं°. I: single rule: सोष्मणि पूर्वस्यानूष्मांतर्येण वृत्तिः.

Translation: Before an aspirated stop, the preceding [aspirated stop] is replaced by a non-aspirate [stop].

Note: As Whitney correctly points out: "The proper application of this rule, within the sphere of the Prātiśākhya, is only to cases of the doubling of the first or second consonants of a group, by the *varṇakrama*, as taught in rules iii.26 (= CA 3.2.1) etc., yet its form of statement is general, and there can be no doubt that it should apply to all cases arising in the course of derivation and inflection, and that forms such as *mṛḍhḍhi*, containing a double lingual sonant aspirate, are strictly excluded by it." Whitney then points out that such double aspirates occur in all manuscripts of Vedic texts, and he gives a list of occurrences in the text of the AV. He corrected all of these in accordance with the precept taught in the present rule.

चतुराध्यायीभाष्य - सोष्मणि परतः पूर्वस्यानूष्मा, सोष्म(H, N: ष्मा)णः अनूष्मा भवति । 'इ[द्?]ध्मम्' (अ.वे. १०.६.३५; H: इंधं; Whitney: इद्ध्मम् as in 'समिंद्धम्,' अ.वे. ७.७४.४)। 'दुग्धम्' (अ.वे. १०.६.३१)। 'नन्वा रुरुध्रे(द्ध्रे?)' (अ.वे. ४.३१.३)। 'यो दध्रे(द्ध्रे?)' (अ.वे. १८.३.६३)। 'वलगं (H: वल्गं) वा निचख्नुः(क्ख्नुः?)' (अ.वे. १०.१.१८)।

प्रथमाश्च द्वितीयानां संयोगे प्रत्यनन्तरा(?, Whitney's emendation: रम्) ।
तृतीयाश्च चतुर्थानामेतत्सर्वत्र लक्षणम् ।। (Source?)

Note: The manuscripts of the AV generally do not show the forms *iddhmam*, *ruruddhre*, *daddhre*, *nicakkhnuḥ*. We find only the forms *idhmam rurudhre*, *dadhre*, and *nicakhnuḥ*. Thus, it would seem that while the doctrines laid down in the CA refer to oral traditions, the orthography of the manuscripts of the AV reflects a choice of not carrying out these doublings. Even the manuscripts of the commentaries on the CA do not show the doubling in the very examples cited to illustrate this phenomenon. As far as manuscripts of the commentary are concerned, they do not properly indicate the sequence of a non-aspirate followed by the aspirate. In most cases, the preceding non-aspirate is not shown in writing. For example, the mss. offer the example *idhmam.* Written in this fashion, it does not illustrate the operation of the present rule. What is assumed is that the *dh* in *idhmam* undergoes doubling giving us the stage *idhdhmam*, which is then reduced to *iddhmam* by the present rule. Thus, the intended citation must be *iddhmam.* The remaining citation forms as intended must be *ruruddhre*, *daddhre*, and *nicakkhnuḥ*. Only in the case of *dugdham*, one need not posit *dugddham*. This, is because the form *dugdham* can be properly thought of as having been derived from *dugh+dha*, cf. P.8.2.32 (दादेर्धातोर्घः), where the sound *gh* is reduced to *g* by the present rule. For a discussion on the reading *rurudhre*, see Whitney (*AV Transl.* Vol.I., p. 202).

The verse cited in the commentary is translated by Whitney as: "First mutes are substituted for seconds, when directly preceding the latter in a group; and thirds in like manner for fourths : this is a rule of universal application."

१.४.४. आन्तर्येण वृत्तिः ।

Whitney (1.95). See notes on the previous rule.

Translation: The substitution is [effected] in accordance with [maximal featural] proximity [between the substitute and the replaced items].

चतुराध्यायीभाष्य - आन्तर्येण वृत्तिर्भवति । 'मकारस्य स्पर्शे परसस्थानः' (च.आ. २.१.३१)। 'तत(ङ्?)कुर्वन्ति' । 'तञ्चित्रयन्ति' । 'तण्टीकयन्ति' । 'तन्तारयन्ति' । 'तम्पाचयन्ति' । 'विसर्जनीयस्य परसस्थानोऽघोषे' (च.आ. २.२.१)। 'वृक्ष[श्]छिनत्ति' । 'वृक्ष[श्]छादयति' । 'स्वरे नामिनोऽन्तस्थाः' (च.आ. ३.२.१६)। 'दध्यत्र' । 'मध्वत्र' । 'मात्रर्थम्' । 'पित्रर्थम्' ।

Note: After pointing out the fact that the commentator cites three CA rules where this term is used, Whitney further observes: "There are other rules to which the present precept applies; so, in explaining the one next preceding, it may be looked upon as determining the non-aspirate into which the duplication of an aspirate is converted to be surd or sonant according as the aspirate is surd or sonant (a matter which, in the other treatises, is expressly prescribed in the rules themselves, and not left for inference) : and possibly its bearing upon that rule is the reason why it is introduced here, rather than elsewhere in the treatise. Similar prescriptions are found in the Rik Pr. (i.14, r.56, lvii) and the Vāj. Pr. (i.142)." This procedure is also very close to P.1.1.50 (स्थानेऽन्तरतमः).

The commentary supports the view that the replacement of vowels by semi-vowels occurs, not on the basis of the principle of one-to-one replacement or *yathāsaṃkhya* 'one-to-one substitution for identically numbered substitutes and originals,' but on the basis of maximal featural proximity or *āntaratamya*. For recent discussions on this issue relating to the interpretation of Pāṇini's rule इको यणचि (P.6.1.77), see: Deshpande (1981), Cardona (1980-81), and Hueckstedt (1995). The examples cited here are all made-up examples and are not citations from the Atharvan text. The examples दध्यत्र and मध्वत्र occur in the KV on P.6.1.77. The example वृक्षश्छादयति is found in the KV on P.8.4.40 (स्तोः श्चुना श्चुः).

१.४.५. खण्वखा३इ खैमखा३इ इत्याकारादिकारोऽनुदात्तः ।

Whitney (1.96), F, I: इ after खैमखा ३. O: °इत्यका कौ. व्या. रादिकारो-नुदात्तः.

Translation: In the forms *kháṇvakhā́3i* and *kháimakhā́3i* (both from AV 4.15.15), [in the *pluta* (protracted) vowel, i.e. *ā́3i*], the *i* following the *ā́*[*3*] is unaccented.

Note: There is a good deal of confusion regarding the accentuation of these forms in the manuscripts and the editions of the ŚAV. As Whitney (1862: 62, footnote) points out: "E. I. and H. read the first word *khaṇvakhā́3i*, with a single accent only, and the printed text [i.e. the text of the Whitney-Roth edition of the AV : खण्वखा३इ खैमखा३इ मध्ये तदुरि] has, wrongly, as it seems to me - followed their authority instead of that of the other manuscripts : and also, by some inexplicable oversight, signs of accent have become attached to the *pluti* figures, as if the preceding *ā*-s were circumflex, and the following *i*-s acute. The line ought to read as follows: खण्वखा३इ खैमखा३इ मध्ये तदुरि." The VVRI edition follows Whitney's corrected reading, while noting other deviant accentuations in the footnote. This reading shows that these two words contain two accented syllables each. The initial syllables of these words have the derivational or lexical *udātta* accent, while the *pluta ā́3* gets the prosodic *udātta* accent which does not override the former. Other examples with dual *udātta* syllables are found in the Vedic literature: *yajñápatā́3u*, TS 6.6.2.3; *súślokā́3ṃ súmaṅgalā́3ṃ*, TS 1.8.16.2; *úpahūtā́3m*, TS 2.6.7.3; *ágnā́3 íti*, TS 6.5.8.4; *juhávānī́3*, TS 6.5.9.1; *páśavā́3*, MS 1.8.2; *utsṛ́jyā́3m*, TS 7.5.7.1; *bahávā́3 íti*, ŚB 10.5.2.16; *kúmārā́3*, ŚB 14.9.1.1. Cf. Wackernagel and Debrunner (1896-1954), I: 298-99; Delbrück (1888: 552-553); and Strunk (1983: 70, 99).

Some of the Padapāṭha manuscripts, as noted in the VVRI edition, offer the following readings: खण्वखा३इं । खैमखा३इं । Such pada readings probably represent the hyper-corrected accentuation, on the basis of the assumed general rule that a word should have no more than one *udātta* syllable. Even the Whitney-Roth edition of the AV seems to have been based on this impression, and overlooked the exceptional nature of the *pluta* accent, which does not seem to override the lexical or derivational accent of the word. As noted above, Whitney did correct his error later. His *Index Verborum to the*

AV offers the corrected readings with dual *udāttas*. The corrected readings are followed by Wackernagel and Debrunner (1896-1954), Vol.I., p. 298.

For additional discussion of these examples, see Note on CA (1.1.41).

चतुराध्यायीभाष्य - खण्वखा३इ खैमखा३इ इति आकारात्पर इकारः अनुदात्तो भवति । 'खण्वखा३इ खैमखा३इ' इति (अ.वे. ४.१५.१५)।

१.४.६. अवशा[३] आ बभूवाँ३ इतीतावेकारोऽप्लुतः ।

Whitney (1.97). A, B, C, I, J, P: ३ after वाँ. E, F, H, M, N, O: omit ३. A, B, D, E, F, H, K, N, P: °वां°. A, B, E, F, H, J, M, N, O(orig): °इति ताबे°.

Translation: In the [instances] *ávaśā3* (AV 12.4.42) and *ā́ babhūvā̃3* (AV 10.2.28), when followed by *iti*, the *e* [resulting through the combination of *ā́3+i*] is not protracted.

Note: As Whitney accurately notes, these two examples are somewhat different from each other in the circumstances of this euphonic combination. In the first case, the word *ávaśā3* is followed by *íti* in the text of the Saṃhitā itself which reads *ávaśéti*. But, the Padapāṭha offers the two *padas* as: *ávaśā3 / íti /*, with the first word ending in the *pluta* vowel.

Regarding this first example, Whitney comments: "All the *saṃhitā* manuscripts, however, observe the precept of our treatise in making the combination of *avaśā3* with the succeeding word, and accordingly its protraction, which is assured by this rule and by i.105 (= CA 1.4.14), and which is exhibited by the *pada*-text, entirely disappears in *saṃhitā* - a strange imperfection of the latter text, and one which, if it did not exhibit itself in all the manuscripts, we should be very loth to introduce, upon the sole authority of this rule of the Prātiśākhya." Whitney (*AV Transl.* Vol.II., p. 699) says: "The more proper reading in b (in AV 12.4.42) would seem to be *ávaśā3íti*, but all the *saṃhitā*-mss. read *ávaśé' ti*, as in our text, although the *pada* gives the sign of protraction (*3*) also after *avaśā*, as it should be. But the Prāt. (i.97 = CA 1.4.6) requires *-śé' ti* simply: see the rules i.97 (= CA 1.4.6) and 105 (= CA 1.4.14), and notes to them."

Whitney's doubts whether this rule should apply to the Saṃhitāpāṭha are strengthened by P.6.1.129 (अप्लुतवदुपस्थिते). The rule teaches something similar to the present CA rule, except that the word *upasthita* is interpreted by Patañjali on this rule as अनार्षः इतिकरणः, "the word *iti* which does not stem from a *Ṛṣi* (= Saṃhitāpāṭha)," i.e. the word *iti* which appears in the Pada, Krama, etc. This would suggest that the rule did not apply to the Saṃhitāpāṭha. However, as Whitney points out, all the manuscripts of the AV exhibit the saṃhitā form *ávaśéti*, and hence we must accept that reading. Interestingly, even the Paippalāda (17.20.2, Raghuvir edn.) reading agrees with the Śaunakīya reading in this case. Thus, the assumption that the word *avaśā3* ends in a *pluta* vowel is not directly based on the Saṃhitāpāṭha, but on the understanding of the text as exhibited by the author of the AV Padapāṭha, an understanding which is in close agreement with the precepts of Pāṇini, cf. P.8.2.97 (विचार्यमाणानाम्). Also see Strunk (1983: 67, 81-82, 97).

In the second case, the word *babhūvā̃3* ending in the *pluta* vowel already appears in the Saṃhitā, and it is not followed by *íti*, either in the Saṃhitā or in the Padapāṭha. Such a combination arises only in the Kramapāṭha : बभूवेतिं बभूवाँ३.

चतुराध्यायीभाष्य - अवशा आ बभूवाँ इति इतौ परतः ए(H, N: इ)कारः प्लुतो न भवति । 'अवशेतिं' (संहिता, अ.वे. १२.४.४२)। 'बभूवेतिं' (क्रमपाठ, अ.वे. १०.२.२८)।

भा.भा.वृत्ति - (वि)रामे प्लुतोऽनुनासिकः । तस्य चर्चायां सन्धौ अप्लुतवद्भावं विधाय इतिशब्देन सन्धौ अप्लुतः अननुनासिकः एकारः स्यात् । 'बभूवेतिं बभूवाँ३' (क्रमपाठ, अ.वे. १०.२.२८)। एवं च 'अवशेतिं' (संहिता, अ.वे. १२.४.४२) 'बभूवेतिं' (क्रमपाठ, अ.वे. १०.२.२८) सन्धीभवतः ।

१.४.७. व्यञ्जनान्यव्यवेतानि स्वरैः संयोगः ।

Whitney (1.98). A, B, C, D, M, P: °व्यपेतानि°. A, B: व्यञ्जनात्परव्यपेतानि°. E, F: व्यञ्जनान्यववे°. K reads °व्यञ्जनान्येवापेतानि°, and Kṛṣṇadāsa's commentary justifies this reading. G: 1.4.7.

Translation: Consonants, not separated by [intervening] vowels, are termed *saṃyoga* 'conjunction.'

Note: As Whitney notes, the term *saṃyoga* 'conjunction' is more comprehensive than the scope of the term *saṃyukta* defined in CA (1.2.9). For the distinction between these conceptions, see Notes on CA (1.2.2) and CA (1.2.9).

चतुराध्यायीभाष्य - व्यञ्जनानि अव्यवेतानि स्वरैः संयोगो भवति ।

'अग्निरिन्द्रश्च तुष्टश्च वृक्षः प्लक्षो निदर्शनम् ।'
(Source?) ।

भा.भा.वृत्ति - द्वयोर्द्वयोर्व्यञ्जनयोः संयोगसंज्ञा । बहूनां व्यञ्जनानामप्येका संज्ञेति मतान्तरम् । '[स]फ्यः' ('स्फ्यौ,' अ.वे. ११.३.९, 'स्फ्यः,' तै.सं. १. ६. ८.२), 'ऊर्क्' (not found in AV, तै.सं. १.१.११.१), 'विश्पत्न्यै' (अ.वे. ७. ४६.२, VVRI edn.: ७.४८.२), 'दुःष्वप्न्यम्' (अ.वे. ६.४६. ३), 'सहस्राह्ण्यम् (H, N: ह्वयं)' (अ.वे. १०.८.१८) शेषः । (Referring to यज्+न ⇒ यज्ञ) नस्य द्वित्वम् असिद्धवच्च, 'स्तोः श्चुना श्चुः' (पा. ८.४.४०) इति नस्य ञत्वे प्राप्ते व्यत्ययेन तवर्गयोगे चवर्गस्य तवर्गः । तेन जकारस्य दकारः । तस्यासिद्धत्वाच्चुत्वेन द्वितीयनकारस्य ञकारः । मध्यम-नकारेण व्यवधानं न तस्यासिद्धत्वात् । एवं च दनञानां संयोगः द्न्ञ । अस्याक्षरस्य लेखने संकेतितं रूपं 'ज्ञ' इति । 'यज्ञस्य' (अ.वे. २.३५.३) । पदादौ तु आचार्येणोपदिष्टः ज्ञाधातुः 'ज्ञप मिच्च' (पाणिनीयधातुपाठ, सिद्धान्तकौमुदी, धातुक्रमाङ्क १६२५), 'प्रसंभ्यां जानुनो ज्ञुः' (पा. ५.४. १२९) इति निर्देशात् पूर्वोक्तरचनायाः सामीचीन्यं ज्ञेयम् । वेदान्तरे चुत्वे प्राप्ते व्यत्ययेन 'चोः कुः' (पा. ८.२.३०) इति जकारस्य गकारः । तस्यासिद्धत्वान्नस्य ञत्वम् । ग्ञ अस्य

लिपिभेदः । जग्येन जग्यम् । मध्ये द्वितीयनकारकल्पने तस्य नकारस्यापि कुत्वेन ङत्वम् । जग्ङ्ञेन गङ्ञानां संयोगः । अत्र मध्ये नकारः इत्युपलक्षणार्थं पूर्वोत्तरवर्णधर्मवान् सम-संज्ञक इत्यर्थः ।

Note: Here, Bhārgava-Bhāskara displays his expertise in the Pāṇinian system by quoting a number of Pāṇinian rules. Of course, building a Pāṇinian argument to account for the divergent pronunciations of *jña* is nothing but an exercise in futility. Also this whole discussion has little relevance to the context of the Prātiśākhya rule.

१.४.८. समानपदेऽनुत्तमात्स्पर्शादुत्तमे यमैर्यथासंख्यम् ।

Whitney (1.99). A, B (corr), Nb: °नुत्तमास्पर्शा°. G: 1.4.8.

Translation: Within the same word, after [a stop], other than the last [member of a stop series, i.e. after a non-nasal stop], its numerically corresponding twin [*yama* = nasalized version of the stop] is [inserted], before a last [member of a stop series, i.e. nasal stop].

Note: Here, the distinctive notion is that of a different principle of selection for the insertion, i.e. the principle of numerical correspondence (*yathāsaṃkhya*). This is the same principle which is enunciated in P.1.3.10 (यथासंख्यमनुदेशः समानाम्). The idea is as follows. For the set of four non-last stops in each series of stops, e.g. *k*, *kh*, *g*, and *gh*, there is a corresponding set of four nasalized twins or *yama*s, e.g. *k̐*, *kh̐*, *g̐*, *gh̐*. The insertion of these *yama*s takes place in accordance with their numerical correspondence, e.g. after *k*, we can insert only *k̐*, and not any other *yama*.

On this rule, Whitney has a long note discussing the notion of *yama*, and the core of Whitney's analysis is as follows: "If, now, we pronounce a *t* before a following *m*, as in *ātma*, the *t*, in the first place, suffers *abhinidhāna*, losing the explosion which is essential to its full utterance : the organs pass, without intervening unclosure, from the dental contact to the labial contact, by which latter the *m* is produced, with expulsion of sound through the nose. ... But if we utter sound through the nose before transferring the organs from the dental to the labial contact, we give origin to a kind of nasal counterpart to the *t*, as a transition sound from it to the *m*. If this is not the *yama* of the Hindu grammarians, I am utterly at a loss to conjecture what the latter sound should be. The theory which recognizes it might be compared with that which, in rule 50 (= CA 1.2.10), above, taught a general assimilation of the former consonant of a group, in its final portion, to the latter; it is still more nearly analogous with the surd which, by ii. 9 (= CA 2.1.9), is inserted between a final nasal and a following sibilant : this arises, like the *yama*, by an exchange of the emission (the *anupradāna*) belonging to the former letter for that belonging to the latter before the transfer of the organs from the one position to the other; and the *t* thus introduced, for example, between a *n* and a *s* has just as good a right to be called the *yama* or counterpart of the former letter, as has the *n* inserted after *t* before *m*."

On the whole, Whitney's account is substantially accurate, except that his valuation of the contribution of the Indian phoneticians was not without hesitation. On the other hand, Max Müller and Regnier, who held the Indian phoneticians in high esteem, wrongly believed the *yama* to be a nasal articulation preceding the stop. For a review, see: Allen (1953: 75-7).

Whitney also mentions the two dominant views on *yama* found in the Sanskrit phonetic texts: "The ancient commentators themselves seem to have been somewhat in doubt as to how many different *yamas* there are, whether twenty, one for each of the non-nasal mutes, or a smaller number. The orthodox doctrine of the Rik Pr. seems to be that of twenty : but its commentator says that there are only four; one for all the first mutes, one for all the seconds, and so on." Rightly calling the second alternative indefensible, Whitney also has an important criticism of the first alternative: "Physically, it would seem necessary that a nasal transition sound between two mutes should be of the nature either of the first or of the second : if the second, and that second a nasal, it would be indistinguishable from it; of the first, it would be identical with the nasal of that series, and so the same for all the mutes of the series."

Another question raised by Whitney relates to the possibility of a *yama* after an aspirated stop: "A much more serious difficulty is, that the theory of the *yama* allows its occurrence between an aspirate mute and a nasal : and we should suppose that the unclosure and brief emission of unintonated breath constituting the aspiration would form an impassable barrier between the two letters, the nasal utterance being unable to precede it, and the position of contact of the former letter to follow it, so that no nasal counterpart to the former letter could be uttered. I see no way of getting over this difficulty, excepting by supposing an inaccuracy in the analysis of the Hindu phonetists." As is now shown by Allen (1953: 176-7), the two processes of breath and nasality may overlap, whether partially or wholly, and that this was the case with Sanskrit.

One should also note that Whitney did not admit the possibility of voiced aspiration, and that modern phonetics clearly admits voiced aspiration or breathy voice.

In spite of some of these valid doubts, Whitney is correct in assuming that the CA seems to have opted for the doctrine of twenty *yamas*. Both the commentaries seem to support such a view.

> ***चतुराध्यायीभाष्य*** - समानपदेऽनुत्तमात् स्पर्शात् उत्तमे पर-(त): स्पर्शे यमैर्व्यवधानं भवति । यथासंख्यम् । 'सप-त्त्ँनं(म्)' (अ.वे. ७.१०९.३, VVRI edn.: ७.११४.३)। 'श्रध्ध्ँनाति' (not found in *AV*)। 'यज्ज्ँञः' (४.११.४)। 'गृह्णा(Whitney em.: भ्णा ⇒ भ्भ्ँणा)ति'।

Note: The form *gr̥hṇāti* is attested in AV (6.76.4), but cannot have a *yama*. The form *gr̥bhṇāti* is not attested in AV. However, we do have the form *gr̥bhṇāmi* in AV (3.8.6), which, with the insertion of the *yama*, would read *gr̥bh+bh̐+ṇāmi*. For *śradhnāti* which is not attested in AV, Whitney says: "the word most nearly resembling it is *śrathnānaḥ* (xiv.1.57), for which it may not impossibly be a false reading of the manuscript." With the insertion of the *yama*, the form *śrathnānaḥ* should read *śrath+th̐+nānaḥ*. Whitney's guess is probably on the mark, as the VVRI edition notes the variant *śradhnānaḥ* in the manuscript K for *śrathnānaḥ* in AV (14.1.57). It is possible that our commentary belongs to the tradition represented by the manuscript K recorded in the VVRI edition. Of course, no manuscripts ever record the *yamas*.

> ***भा.भा.वृत्ति*** - एकस्मिन् पदे अनुत्तमात् स्पर्शात् प्रथम-द्वितीयतृतीयचतुर्थस्पर्शात् उत्तमे पञ्चमे स्पर्शे परे मध्ये यथासंख्यं स्वस्ववर्गोक्तप्रथमादिस्पर्शसमैर्यमैर्भवितव्यम् । यमे पूर्वोत्तरवर्णधर्मौ ज्ञेयौ । प्रथमः यमः 'असिक्क्ँनीः' (अ.वे. ८.७.१), 'रुक्क्ँमाम्(H, N: क्कां)' ('रुक्मा,' अ.वे. ९.५. २५-२६), 'याच्च्ँञैः' ('याच्ञाय,' अ.वे. १२.४.३०), 'अ[ा?]ट्ट्ँणारः' (तै.सं. ५.६.५.३), 'पत्त्ँनी' (अ.वे. २. १२.१), 'आत्त्ँमा' (अ.वे. ५.१.७), 'अप्प्ँन्यः' (not found

in Vedic Saṃhitās), 'पाप्म्ँमा' (अ.वे. ६.२६.५), 'वृ-क्कँणम्' (अ.वे. ८.१२.२)। द्वितीययमः 'चख्ँन्तुः' (not found in Vedic Saṃhitās), 'यछ्छ्ँञ्नु' (not found in Vedic Saṃhitās)... (incomplete manuscript)

Note: The manuscripts do not show the *yama*s in writing. I have indicated the *yama*s with nasalized consonant signs in Devanagari.

१.४.९. हकारान्नासिक्येन ।

Whitney (1.100). D, F, Ha, J, M, Na, P: हकारां°. O: °रांनांसिक्येन. A, B: °नासिकान.

Translation: After *h*, there is [insertion of] a *nāsikya* [= *h̐*?], [before a nasal stop].

Note: CA (1.1.26: नासिक्यानां नासिका) refers to the sound or sounds called *nāsikya* '[pure?] nasal.' See the Note on CA (1.1.26). Whitney expresses his doubts: "What the sound may be which is thus taught to form the step of transition from the aspiration to a following nasal, it is hard to say with confidence. I can only conjecture it to be a brief expulsion of surd breath through the nose, as continuation of the *h*, before the expulsion of the sonant breath which constitutes the nasal." Whitney suggests that, in a word like *brahma* : "the Hindu phonetists doubtless regarded the *h* as belonging with and uttered like the *a;* and noticing at the same time the utterance, scarcely to be avoided, of at least a part of the *h* in the position of the *m*, they took account of it as a separate element, and called it *nāsikya*." One of the misconceptions of Whitney was that he could not accept Sanskrit *h* to be a *voiced aspiration*, because he did not think such a thing was possible. Thus, the *nāsikya*, if it involved aspiration, was not a 'surd' aspiration, but voiced nasal aspiration. Such nasal voiced aspirates are attested for a modern IA language like Marathi, e.g. n^h (as in *tin*^{h}*ī*), $ṇ^h$ (as in *kaṇ*^{h}*aṇe*), and, m^h (as in *tum*^{h}*ī*). Also see Allen (1953: 77).

चतुराध्यायीभाष्य - हकारात् नासिक्येन समानपदे व्यव-धानं भवति । 'प्राह्णः' [⇒ °ह्ँण°] (not in AV)। 'पूर्वा-

ह्णः' [⇒ °ह्ँण°] (not in AV)। 'अपराह्णः' [⇒ °ह्ँण°] (अ.वे. ९.६.४६)। 'अपह्मलयति' [⇒ °ह्ँम°] (not in AV)। 'विह्मलयति' [⇒ °ह्ँम°] (not in AV)। 'विह्नुते' [⇒ °ह्ँनु°] (not in AV)। 'ब्रह्म' [⇒ °ह्ँम°] (अ.वे. १.१९.४)।

Note: The sound called *nāsikya* is represented by the Nagari ligature ँ in the above notations. The manuscripts do not show the *nāsikya* in writing. For details on the cited examples, see the commentary on CA 1.2.18 (रेफहकार-क्रमजं च).

१.४.१०. रेफादूष्मणि स्वरपरे स्वरभक्तिरकारस्यार्धं चतुर्थमित्येके ।

Whitney (1.101).

Translation: After an *r*, and before a spirant followed by a vowel, there is an insertion of a vocalic fraction (*svarabhakti*), which is [equivalent to] half of a short *a*, or quarter according to some [authorities].

Note: Calling it a perfectly intelligible theory, Whitney says: "The theory evidently is, that a *r* cannot be pronounced in immediate combination with any following consonant : there must always be slipped between them a little bit of a transition-vowel, varying in length, according to different authorities, from a half to an eighth of a mora, and longer before a sibilant or *h*, if these be followed in turn by a vowel, than before other consonants; while in quality it coincides with the *a*."

Whitney, however, was not able to discern the reason why the fractional vowel inserted before spirants must be longer than before other consonants, though he does note the practice of the AV manuscripts of writing *r̥* for *r* before spirants. Referring to Wackernagel and Debrunner (1896-1954), Vol.I., § 50, Allen (1953: 73) points out that, in such cases, "the metre also occasionally requires the pronunciation of a vowel which is not noted in our texts (e.g. *darśata* = 4 syllables)." Besides the variation of the length of the inserted vowel fraction, different texts suggest that the vowel is *r̥*, *a*, *i*, *e*, or *u*, cf. Allen (1953: 73).

चतुराध्यायीभाष्य - रेफादूष्मणि स्वरपरे स्वरभक्तिर्भवति । अकारस्य अर्धं चतुर्थमित्येके । अपर आह । ऋकारस्वर-भक्तिः । ऊष्मसु स्वरपरेष्वर्धाकारवर्णो व्यञ्जनं शेष इति ।

'रेफादन्यदृकारे यत्तस्यार्धं पूर्वसस्वरम् ।
वचनेन व्यवेतानां संयोगत्वं विहन्यते ।।
ऋवर्णेऽपि तु रेफस्य चार्धमात्रा प्रतिज्ञया ।
अर्धमात्रा स्वरं विद्यात्सा चैवं क्रियते पुनः ।।
तान्ह्रस्वोभयतः कुर्याद्यथा मात्रा भवेदिति ।
दर्शो वर्षं तथा तर्सः (W's em.:ऋतवः) बर्हिश्चात्र
निदर्शनम् ।।
एतामृतिं विजानीयात्स्वरभक्तिर्यदा भवेत् ।'
(source?)

Note: The words *varsam* and *tarsam* are cited as examples in the MB on P.8.3.59. Referring to the verses cited in the commentary, Whitney says: "Next follow several verses, a part of which are of a character which would render their introduction under rule 37 (= CA 1.1.37), above, more approppriate, while one line, the second, belongs rather under rule 98 (= CA 1.4.7). Placing the responsibility for the inelegance of these verses upon the commentator or the manuscript, Whitney offers the following translation: "Half of what there is in the *r̥*-vowel different from *r* is of the same character with the preceding vowel. Of consonants separated by audible sound, the conjunction is destroyed. In the *r̥*-vowels there is, by express rule, half a mora of *r*, half a mora is to be recognized as vowel, and that, again, is thus managed : put the parts upon both sides of the short vowel, so as to make out a mora : examples are *darśa*, *varṣa*, *tatha r̥tavaḥ*, [and] *barhiḥ* : know this to be the way when a *svarabhakti* is to be produced."

There seems to be an important distinction between the *svarabhakti* of longer duration and the *svarabhakti* of the shorter duration. With the *svarabhakti* of the longer duration, as the verses here seem to say, a consonant cluster is broken apart, by the creation of an additional syllable. On the other hand, as CA 1.4.13, below, shows, the *svarabhakti* of the shorter duration did not lead to the break-up of a cluster.

१.४.११. अन्यस्मिन्व्यञ्जने चतुर्थमष्टमं वा ।

Whitney (1.102). A, B, D: Avagraha after °चतुर्थम.

Translation: [After *r*], before another consonant [= non-spirant], [the inserted fractional vowel is equivalent to] a quarter or an eighth [of a short *a* in duration].

Note: See the Note on the previous rule.

चतुराध्यायीभाष्य - अन्यस्मिन् व्यञ्जने रेफात् अकारस्य चतुर्थं वा अष्टमं वा भवति । 'अर्यमा' (अ.वे. १.११.१)। 'पर्व' (अ.वे. १.१२.२)। 'धर्मणा' (अ.वे. ६.१३२.१)।

१.४.१२. तदेव स्फोटनः ।

Whitney (1.103). P separates this rule from the previous rule by adding a daṇḍa as a correction.

Translation: That [i.e. insertion of the shorter fractional vowel of $^1/_8$ or $^1/_4$ mora duration] is itself [called] *sphoṭana.*

Note: There seems to be a difference of opinion between Whitney and others on what this rule means. Whitney does not seem to identify the *sphoṭana* with the shorter *svarabhakti*, but only admits that a *sphoṭana* is of the same duration: "(Trans:) Of the latter value is *sphoṭana*. (Comment:) That is to say, if I do not misapprehend the meaning of the rule, *sphoṭana*, like the shorter *svarabhakti*, has a quarter or an eighth the quantity of a short *a* : or it may be that the emphatic *eva* would restrict the reference to the latter value, the eighth, alone."

Allen (1953: 74) seems to understand that the *svarabhakti* of the length of $^1/_8$ *a* to be the element referred to as *sphoṭana*. Allen further clarifies: "From a later passage (= CA 2.1.38: *vargaviparyaye sphoṭanaḥ pūrveṇa ced virāmaḥ*) we learn that this occurs in groups where a stop is followed by another of a more back series, especially a velar (e.g. in *vaṣaṭ-kr̥tam*, *tad gāyatre*). ... This would appear to indicate a type of *svarabhakti*, whether voiced or voiceless, the infinitesimal duration of which is suggested by the specification of a value $^1/_8$ *a*, in fact a minimal audible release. The mechanism of the feature referred to is perhaps the release of the front closure during the formation but before the completion of the back closure, resulting in the momentary outflow of an air-stream attenuated by the back constriction."

In my view, *sphoṭana* is just another name for the shorter *svarabhakti* of the duration of a quarter of or an eighth of an *a*, and is not different from such a *svarabhakti*.

> **चतुराध्यायीभाष्य** - तदेव स्फोटनो व्यञ्जको भवति । 'वषट्कारेण' (अ.वे. ५.२६.१२)। 'अव(N: व्य)त्कम्' (अ.वे. २.३.१)। 'एजत्काः' (अ.वे. ५.२३.७)। 'त्रिष्टुब्गायत्री' (अ.वे. १८.२.६)।

Note: On the citation from AV (2.3.1), Whitney (*AV Transl.* Vol.I., p. 40) says: "*Avatká* (p. *avat°kám :* quoted in the comment to Prāt. i.103 = CA 1.4.12; ii.38 = CA 2.1.38; iv.25 = CA 4.1.25) is obscure, but is here translated as from the present participle of root *av* (like *ejatká*, v.23.7 ⌊cf. *abhimādyatká*, ŚB., *vikṣiṇatká*, VS.⌋)."

१.४.१३. पूर्वस्वरं संयोगाविघातश्च ।

Whitney (1.104), C, Hb, I (orig), Nb, O: °विघातश्च. A, B, D, F, I (corr), J, K, M, P: °भिघातश्च. E, F: Visarga after पूर्व. J, M: पूर्वसः स्वरं°. A, B, D: पूर्वसः स्वरसंयो°. Ha, Na: °विविघातश्च. P: °पूर्वसस्वरं°.

> **Translation:** [With the shorter *svarabhakti* called *sphoṭana*, it carries] the accent of the previous syllable [lit. vowel], and there is no dismemberment of the consonant cluster.

Note: Whitney takes this rule to mean that all the phonetic insertions taught in this section "are to be reckoned as belonging to the preceding vowel, and sharing in its accent; and whereas it might seem that the insertion of the vowel-fragment, and of its kindred *sphoṭana*, dissolved the conjunction of the consonants between which they were inserted ... the contrary is expressly declared to be true." He further states: "The Rik Pr. alone, besides our treatise, thinks it necessary to say (vi. 10, r. 35, ccccxi) that the *svarabhakti* does not dissolve the conjunction : in the Vāj. Pr. it is left to be pointed out by the commentator."

In my opinion, the present rule is restricted to the shorter *svarabhakti* alias *sphoṭana*, and does not extend to the cases of longer *svarabhakti*, where as pointed out by Allen (1953: 73): "the metre also occasionally requires the pronunciation of a vowel which is not noted in our texts (e.g. *darśata* = 4 syllables)." Support for such a restricted interpretation is derived clearly from the CAB, which refers only to the shorter *svarabhakti* (cf. यत्तद्रेफादकारस्य चतुर्थं वा भवत्यष्टमं वा), and all the examples it cites are identical with the examples for the shorter *svarabhakti* offered under CA (1.4.11).

चतुराध्यायीभाष्य - पूर्वपूर्वस्वरं च तद्भवति संयोगस्य चाविघातः । यत्तद्रेफादकारस्य चतुर्थं वा भवत्यष्टमं वा । 'अ॒र्य॒मा' (अ.वे. १.११.१)। 'पर्व॑' (अ.वे. १.१२.२)। 'धर्म॑णा' (अ.वे. ६.१३२.१)।

१.४.१४. खण्व॒खा३इ॒ खैम॒खा३इ॒ मध्ये॑ तदुरि (अ.वे. ४.१५.१५)। इ॒दं भू॑या३ इ॒दा३मिति॑ (अ.वे. ९.६.१८)। ऊ॒र्ध्वो नु सृ॑ष्टा३स्ति॒र्यङ् नु सृ॑ष्टा३ः सर्वा॒ दिश॒ः पुरु॑ष॒ आ बभू॒वाँ३ (अ.वे. १०.२.२८)। परा॑ञ्चमोद॒नं प्राशी३ः प्र॒त्यञ्चा३मिति॑ (अ.वे. ११.३.२६)। त्वमो॑द॒नं प्राशी३स्त्वामो॑द॒ना३इति॑ (अ.वे. ११.३.२७)। व॒शेया३मव॒शेति॑ (अ.वे. १२.४.४२)। यत्तदासी॑३दिदं नु ता३दि॒ति॑ (अ.वे. १२.५.५०)। इति प्लुतानि । इत उत्तरमधिकम् । किमर्थः परिपाठः । एतावत्स्वार्थोऽपि । बहुविधास्त्रिविधाः प्लुतयो भवन्ति । स्वरपरा अभिनिष्टानपरा व्यञ्जनपरास्तासां याः समानाक्षरपरास्ता इतावप्लुतवद्भवन्ति । इतावप्लुतवद्भवन्ति ।

Whitney (1.105): ends with °दिति प्लुतानि, the rest being cited as part of the commentary. C: omits the entire passage. E, F: omit beginning with इत उत्तरमधिकम्. B, D: तदुरी इदं. A, D: omit Repha in °त्यूर्ध्वो°. H, N: omit नु after तिर्यङ्. A, B, D, H, K, N: °बभूवां. B, D: omit पुरुष after सर्वा दिशः. H, N: °प्राशीःस्त्वा°. F, H, N: place ३ after °मवशेति°. A, B, D: °मुता३दिति° for °नुता३दिति°. H, N: किमर्थः परिपाठः before इत उत्तरमधिकम्. E, F: omit किमर्थः

परिपाठः. H, N: place Daṇḍa after एतावत्स्वार्थोऽपि. A, B, D, J, K, M: °एतावत्प्लुतवद्भवन्ति°. The repetition of the passage इतावप्लुतवद्भवन्ति indicates that this is the end of the Adhyāya. O places इत उत्तरमधिकम् at the very end of the passage, while P omits it. O places a daṇḍa after स्वरपरा.

> **Translation:** There are the following cases of protracted vowels [in the ŚAV]: AV (4.15.15), (9.6.18), (10.2.28), (11.3. 26), (11.3.27), (12.4.42), and (12.5.50). Why is this listing made? Any instances beyond this [listing] are in excess [i.e. do not belong to the ŚAV]. The following is also the intrinsic purpose [of the listing], [namely, to point out that] protractions are of various types, specifically, three types: followed by vowels, followed by *abhiniṣṭāna* [= *visarjanīya*, *ḥ*], and followed by consonants. Among them, those which are followed by simple vowels are treated as if non-protracted before *iti*, [e.g. *ávaśéti*, AV (12.4.42), Pada: *ávaśā3 / íti /*].

Note: Concerning the variant readings and interpretations for the first passage, see Whitney (*AV Transl.* Vol.I., p. 175). On the passage from AV (11.3.27), Whitney (*AV Transl.* Vol.II., p. 627) has some important remarks: "The *pluta-* or protracted syllables in this and the next verse are quoted in Prāt. i.105 (= CA 1.4.14), but nothing is said as to their accentuation, from which it seems most plausible to infer that the protraction made no difference in the accent; and though in the Brāhmaṇas a protracted syllable is always accented, that is not the invariable rule in the Vedic texts." Lanman (ibid.) also notes the great variety of mss. readings for the passage concerned. Also see Whitney's comments on AV 9.6.18 and 10.2.28, and Strunk (1983: 68).

The passage after *iti plutāni* is treated by Whitney as part of the commentary, and translated as follows: "for what reason is this enumeration made? because any other instance than these is in excess : within these limits the protracted vowel is pointed out by its own meaning (?). Protractions are various; namely, of three kinds: those which affect a syllable ending in a vowel, in *visarjanīya*, and in a consonant, respectively; among these, those which affect syllables ending in simple vowels assume their unprotracted form before *iti*." I have given my own translation above, and I believe it is an improvement over Whitney's.

Whitney, on this rule, discusses in some detail, problems of accentuation of the cited examples. However, in most cases, the accents cannot be decided on the basis of either the CA rules or manuscripts. The only case, where the CA rule is relevant for the accent of a pluta syllable is AV (4.15.15). For a discussion of the accents of this example, see the Note on CA (1.4.5). Also see Strunk (1983: 90).

For the accents of examples from AV (10.2.28) and AV (11.3.26, 27), I have followed the readings of the VVRI edition, rather than those of Roth-Whitney edition. See CA (4.1.28) and the Note on it for further discussion on these examples. Also see Strunk (1983) for an extensive discussion.

चतुराध्यायीभाष्य - The manuscripts H and N contain this entire passage. However, there is no Bhāṣya on it.

इति प्रथमाध्यायस्य चतुर्थः पादः । प्रथमोऽध्यायः समाप्तः ॥

H, N: चतुराध्यायिकायां च प्रथमोध्यायः समाप्तः ॥१३॥. C: चतुराध्यायिकायां च प्रथमोऽध्यायः समाप्तः ॥१०३॥. E, F: प्रथमस्य चतुर्थः पादः । आथर्वणे चतुराध्यायिकायां प्रथमोध्यायः ॥. A, B, D, M: चतुर्थः पादः । प्रथमोऽध्यायः समाप्तः ॥. I: इति प्रथमाध्याये चतुर्थः पादः ॥ इत्यथर्ववेदे कौत्सव्याकरणे चतुराध्यायिकायां प्रथमोऽध्यायः समाप्तः ॥१॥ सूत्राणि ११०. O: सूत्राणि ॥१९॥ इत्यथर्ववेदे कौत्सव्याकरणे चतुराध्यायिकायां प्रथमस्य चतुर्थः पादः ॥४॥ प्रथमोध्यायः समाप्तः ॥ P: चतुर्थः पादः ॥ प्रथमोध्यायः ॥

Note: Notice the difference in the number of rules mentioned for this Pāda and the cumulative numbers given for the first Adhyāya in the colophons of different manuscripts. Not only do the manuscripts H and N list only 13 Sūtras for this Pāda, the last Sūtra, i.e. 1.4.14 is most probably not considered to be a Sūtra by the CAB. On the other hand, the manuscript O says that there are 19 rules in this Pāda. The manuscript C omits this entire last rule and offers the cumulative number of Sūtras for this Adhyāya to be 103. On the other hand, the manuscript I lists the cumulative number of rule for this Adhyāya to be 110. It not only includes the last passage as part of the Sutra text, it probably counted its separate parts as seven different Sūtras. It would seem that this passage is indeed not part of the CAB itself, as it was once thought by Whitney. This must be the case because this passage does not comment on some earlier rule. However, its inclusion in the manuscripts of the CAB indicates that the copyists of this commentary knew that this passage had been admitted as part of the Sūtra text, though the CAB does not comment on it.

चतुराध्यायीभाष्य - चतुराध्यायिकायां च प्रथमोऽध्यायः समाप्तः ।।१३।।

॥ द्वितीयोऽध्यायः ॥
॥ प्रथमः पादः ॥

२.१.१. संहितायाम् ।

Whitney (2.1). P adds a daṇḍa after this rule as a correction.

Translation: [The following rules apply] in [the context of] combining [the separated words given in the Padapāṭha to form a continuous text, i.e. the Saṃhitāpāṭha].

Note: In general, the Prātiśākhya literature took for granted the existence of the Padapāṭha, and assumed that the Saṃhitāpāṭha was derived by explicitly combining the separated words given in the Padapāṭha, following the rules of sandhi. This rule is a general heading (*adhikāra*) with its scope extending over the second and the third chapters of the CA. However, as Whitney warns: "We shall see, however, that our treatise does not everywhere strictly limit itself to what concerns the conversion of *pada*-text into *saṃhitā*."

चतुराध्यायीभाष्य - संहितायामित्येतदधिकृतं वेदितव्यम् । इत उत्तरं यदनुक्रमिष्यामः ।

२.१.२. पदान्तानामनुत्तमानां तृतीया घोषवत्स्वरेषु ।

Whitney (2.2). A, B, D: °तृतीयो°. J, M (corr): Daṇḍa after °नुत्तमानां.

Translation: Word-final stops, except the last [members of the stop-series], are replaced with the [corresponding] thirds [of the series, i.e. voiced aspirate stops], before voiced consonants and vowels.

Note: Whitney observes: "Considering that, by i. 6 (= CA 1.1.8), only the first and last of each series of mutes can occur as finals, this rule might have said *prathamānām*, 'first mutes,' instead of *anuttamānām*, 'mutes not nasal;' both this and the following rules, however, seem constructed in view of the disputed character of the final non-nasal mute, and of the doctrine of Śaunaka himself that it is a *media*, and not a *tenuis*." One should note that the

Padapāṭha lists the separated words as ending in the first stops, i.e. voiceless unaspirated stops, e.g. *yat / yatra*, AV (2.1.1); *tasmāt / vāḥ*, AV (3.13.3). However, the present rule is formulated in a generic way. One may see here not only the need to accommodate the doctrine of Śaunaka, as noticed by Whitney, but also the influence of the generic grammars of Sanskrit of the type represented by Pāṇini, cf. P.8.4.53 (झलां जश् झशि), which subjects all non-nasal stops, as well as spirants, to substitution by an appropriate voiced unaspirated stop. However, Pāṇini's rule applies to internal, as well as external, sandhis, and interestingly does not specify this change explicitly before vowels. In a procedure somewhat reminiscent of Śaunaka's view noted above, cf. CA (1.1.10), Pāṇini, as a generic procedure, changes all word-final non-nasal stops, and spirants, to the appropriate voiced unaspirated stops, cf. P.8.2.39 (झलां जशोऽन्ते). It is, however, appropriate to note that Pāṇini is not dealing with word-finals before pause, as is the case with Śaunaka's doctrine.

We must mention another dilemma raised by this rule. Since the rule refers to *ghoṣavat* 'possessed of *ghoṣa*, voiced' and *svara* 'vowel' as separate classes, a question is raised whether the term *ghoṣavat* did not include vowels (*svara*) because vowels do not have the feature of *ghoṣa*, or whether, for some reason, the term *ghoṣavat* was used only for consonants to distinguish voiced consonants from voiceless consonants. If the first alternative is valid, then one could argue for two modes of voicing, one represented by *ghoṣa*, which belonged only to voiced consonants, and *nāda*, which belonged to both the voiced consonants and vowels. On the other hand, some have argued that there is no phonetic distinction between *nāda* and *ghoṣa*, and that the term *ghoṣavat* is used to refer to voiced consonants, with no intention of denying the feature of *ghoṣa* to vowels. For the details of this debate, see: Deshpande (1976, 1976a), Cardona (1983, 1986). Also see: Introduction, section **5.11.**

चतुराध्यायीभाष्य - पदान्तानामनुत्तमानां तृतीया भवन्ति घोषवत्सु वर्णेषु स्वरेषु च परतः । 'यद्यत्र विश्वम्' (अ.वे. २.१.१)। 'यद्यामं चक्रुः' (अ.वे. ६.११६.१)। 'तस्माद्वार्नाम' (अ.वे. ३.१३.३)। 'वेविंषद्विषः' (अ.वे. ५.१७.५)। 'यद्राजानः' (अ.वे. ३.२९.१)। 'सुहस्तो गोधुगुत' (अ.वे. ७.७३.७)। 'सा विराड्टृषयः' (अ.वे. ८.९.८)। 'तदभू(H: मू, N: म्व)तम्' (not in AV)। 'त्रिष्टु(H, N: तृषु)बत्र' (not in AV)।

Note: The example तदभूतम् cited by the CAB is not found in the Vulgate of the AV, and Surya Kanta (*APR*, *Introduction*, p. 40) suggests that this may have occurred in the genuine Śaunakīya recension of the AV, and that the Vulgate is not the genuine Śaunakīya recension. It is clear that, in making such claims, Surya Kanta did not consult the original manuscripts, H and N. Otherwise, his so-called genuinely Śaunakīya examples may have been तदम्वतम् (N) or तदमूतम् (H). Surya Kanta makes no allowance for either the inaccuracies of the copyists, or for the possibility that the commentator may occasionally quote a passage which is not Atharvan. Interestingly, Whitney also reports another example, i.e. त्रिष्टुबत्र cited by the commentator which does not occur in the AV. However, Surya Kanta does not use that example for raising the same claims. The example त्रिष्टुबत्र is found in the KV on P.8.2.39 (झलां जशोऽन्ते).

२.१.३. पदान्ते चाघोषाः ।

Whitney (2.3). D, I (corr): °वाघोषाः.

Translation: Further, at the end of a word, [before a pause, as in the Padapāṭha, or at the end of a metrical foot in the Saṃhitāpāṭha, the non-nasal stops] are replaced with [the corresponding] voiceless [unaspirated stops].

Note: Whitney comments: "This, in view of i. 6 (= CA 1.1.8), is a superfluous precept, and its introduction is only to be accounted for by the considerations adverted to under the last rule." I do not believe that the rule is superfluous at all. CA (1.1.8) is more of the nature of a listing of what could occur in the word-final position. On the other hand, this rule is an operational rule achieving that result. Since the inputs to this rule are represented by the word *anuttamānām* in the previous rule, it represents a theoretically wider procedure replacing all possible word-final non-nasal stops with the corresponding voiceless unaspirated stops. The rule is followed by the Saṃhitā and the Padapāṭha manuscripts for the ŚAV.

Pāṇini 8.4.56 (वावसाने) says that the change of word-final non-nasal stops to voiceless stops is optional, or preferable (if we follow Kiparsky's view, cf. Kiparsky 1979, on the meaning of *vā* in Pāṇini). The Kiparskyan interpretation of Pāṇini brings him closer to the view of the CA. However, the traditional commentators view this rule as being simply optional, and this may have influenced the reading in the two CA manuscripts, D, I (corr): °वाघोषाः.

चतुराध्यायीभाष्य - पदान्ते चाघोषा भवन्ति पदान्तानामनुत्तमानाम् । 'गोधुक्' (अ.वे. ७.७३.६)। 'विराट्' (अ.वे. ८.९.८)। 'दृषत्' (अ.वे. २.३१.१)। 'त्रिष्टुप्' (अ.वे. ८.९.२०)।

२.१.४. अघोषेषु च ।

Whitney (2.4). B, D: °अंघोषे°.

Translation: Also, before voiceless [consonants, the word-final non-nasal stops become voiceless].

Note: As with the previous rule, Whitney says: "Also an unnecessary specification; since final surds do not require to become surds before succeeding initial surds, but simply remain unchanged." The rule takes a more generic view of the word-final consonants as inputs for this rule, possibly assuming that there are words which, in derivational or recitational terms, may be assumed to end in voiced stops. Such a recitational tradition was attributed to Śaunaka, cf. CA (1.1.10: प्रथमान्तानि तृतीयान्तानीति शौनकस्य प्रतिज्ञानं न वृत्तिः). The rule may be understood as saying that, even if one assumes that the Padapāṭha could have words ending in non-nasal voiced stops, these must be changed to their voiceless counterparts in sandhi combinations imminent in the Saṃhitāpāṭha. Compare P.8.4.55 (खरि च). Note that Pāṇini's rule does not distinguish between external versus internal sandhi. The present CA rule, though it applies to the transformation of the Padapāṭha into Saṃhitāpāṭha, may apply to those internal sandhis, where the Padapāṭha splits the base from the affix, or members of a compound. For example, the word *apsu* (AV 1.4.4) is split in the Padapāṭha as *ap+su*. One wonders if the Padapāṭha reading could have been *ab+su*, in accordance with Śaunaka's precept, cf. CA (1.1.10). Assuming, such a possibility, the present rule would change the *b* to *p* in the Saṃhitāpāṭha. The same sort of dilemma may be perceived in a form like *uttarasmin* (AV 1.9.1), which is split up in the Padapāṭha as *ut+tarasmin*. A Padapāṭha which strictly followed the precept of Śaunaka could have had the reading *ud+tarasmin*.

चतुराध्यायीभाष्य - अघोषेषु च अघोषा भवन्ति पदान्तानामनुत्तमानाम् । 'वाक्चेंन्द्रियं चं' (अ.वे. १२.५.७)।

'विराट् प्रजापंतिः' (अ. वे. ९.१०.२४)। 'त्रिष्टुप्पंञ्चदशेन' (अ.वे. ८.९.२०)।

२.१.५. उत्तमा उत्तमेषु ।

Whitney (2.5). B, D: Daṇḍa after उत्तमा.

Translation: [The non-nasal word-final stops] are replaced with [the corresponding] nasal [stops, lit. last members of the stop-series], before nasal [stops, lit. last members of the stop-series].

Note: Whitney makes an important observation: "The Prātiśākhyas are unanimous in this requirement. ... Pāṇini, as has already been noticed (under i.2 = CA 1.1.3), [cf. P.8.4.45: यरोऽनुनासिकेऽनुनासिको वा], allows either the unaspirated sonant or the nasal before a nasal, while the manuscript usage is almost, if not quite, invariably in favor of the nasal." Whitney's view of Pāṇini may now be revised in view of the interpretation proposed by Kiparsky (1979) that *vā* in Pāṇini refers to a preferred option. This would suggest that Pāṇini's preferred option is more in agreement with the Prātiśākhyas and the practice of the manuscripts.

चतुराध्यायीभाष्य - उत्तमा भवन्ति उत्तमेषु परतः पदान्तानामनुत्तमानाम् । 'ऋधंङ्मन्त्रो योनिम्' (अ.वे. ५.१.१)। 'य उदानण्म्यायंनम्' (अ.वे. ६.७७.२)। 'अंर्णवान्मंहतस्परिं' (अ.वे. १.१०.४)। 'मदुघान्मधुंमत्तरः' (अ.वे. १.३४.४.)। 'मध्यांन्नीचैः,' (अ.वे. ४.१.३)। 'य स्तायन्मन्यंते' (अ.वे. ४.१६.१.)। 'त्रिष्टुम्नयति' (not in AV, cited in KV on P.8.4.45)।

Note: As Surya Kanta (*APR*, *Introduction*, p. 62) points out, the APR (136: उत्तमा उत्तमेष्विति) directly refers to our present rule. Referring to AV (1.34.4), Whitney (*AV Transl.* Vol.I., p. 35) says: "The majority of our mss. (nor Bp.I.E.D.) read here *madhúghāt* in b, as do also the Prāt. mss. in both the places (ii.5c = CA 2.1.5; iv.16 = CA 4.1.38) where the verse is quoted; but at vi.102.3 all read *-du-* ; SSP. reads *-du-* (as does our text), and makes no report of discordance among his authorities. The comm. (= Sāyaṇa) has *-du-*, and derives the word from *madhudugha*." Contrary to Whitney's report, both the manuscripts of the CAB have the reading *madughāt* on both the rules referred to by him, and not *madhughāt*.

For a discussion of different readings for AV (4.16.1), i.e. *yas tāyat* or *ya(s) stāyat*, see Whitney (*AV Transl.* Vol.I., p. 176, also p. 464).

२.१.६. द्वितीयाः शषसेषु ।

Whitney (2.6).

Translation: Before *ś*, *ṣ*, and *s*, [the word-final non-nasal stops] become second [members of the series, i.e. voiceless aspirated stops].

चतुराध्यायीभाष्य - द्वितीया भवन्ति शषसेषु परतः पदान्तानामनुत्तमानाम् । 'गोधुख(H, N: क)शेते' (not in AV) । 'विराठ्(H, N: ड्)शेते' (not in AV) । 'दृषथ्शेते' (not in AV) । 'त्रिष्टुफ(H, N: ͨ)शेते' (not in AV) । 'गोधुख(H, N: क)षण्डे' (not in AV) । 'विराठ्(H, N: ड्)षण्डे' (not in AV) । 'दृषथ(N: त)षण्डे' (not in AV) । 'त्रिष्टुफ(H, N: ͨ)-षण्डे' (not in AV) । 'गोधुख्साये' (not in AV) । 'विराठ्(H, N: ड्)साये' (not in AV) । 'दृषथ(H, N: त)साये' (not in AV) । 'त्रिष्टुफ(H, N: ͨ)साये' (not in AV) । अपदान्तानामपि शषसेषु द्वितीया भवन्ति इति शाङ्ख(H, N: ख्य)मित्रिशाकटायनवात्स्याः । 'तस्यां अग्निर्वथ्सः' (H, N: त्सः) (अ.वे. ४.३९.२) ।

Note: Except for the last example offered by the commentary, all the examples are fabricated examples. The same examples are found in the CAB on CA (1.2.9). Also see the Note on CA (1.2.9).

Surya Kanta (*APR*, *Introduction*, p. 28-29, 40) points out that the VPR (4.119: असस्थाने मुदि द्वितीयं शौनकस्य) is a patent reference to CA (2.1.6). However, rejecting Weber's claim that the CA is later than the VPR, Surya Kanta says that "the kernel of the VPr. is older than is yet supposed to be.

Such references (to CA) can only show the various recasts each work of this class has undergone." While it is probably the case that the kind of phonetic changes taught in this rule were genuinely part of Śaunaka's doctrine, such a doctrine is followed neither by the manuscripts of the AV, nor by the manuscripts of the CAB. Whitney, on this rule, points out the disagreements between the different Prātiśākhyas, but finally says: "The manuscripts of the Atharvan read always the simple surd before the sibilant, and in the printed text we have of course followed their authority rather than that of the Prātiśākhya." This particular doctrine is not followed by Pāṇini, but is ascribed by a Vārttika on P.8.4.48 to a teacher named Pauṣkarasādi (चयो द्वितीयाः शरि पौष्करसादेः). Even while intending to exemplify this rule, the manuscripts of the commentary do not show the change in writing.

२.१.७. तेभ्यः पूर्वचतुर्थो हकारस्य ।

Whitney (2.7).

Translation: After them [i.e. word-final non-nasal stops, the following] *h* is replaced by the fourth [member of the stop-series, i.e. the voiced aspirated stop], corresponding to the preceding [word-final stop].

Note: As Whitney notes, the Prātiśākhyas generally follow this rule, but that Pāṇini (8.4.62: झयो होऽन्यतरस्याम्) allows this change optionally. The mss. of both the AV, as well as those of the CAB, almost universally follow the rule. All the examples cited by the commentator are examples of a word-final *t*, as given in the AV Padapāṭha, combined with the following *h*. In all the cases, the Pāṇinians are likely to treat the first member as ending in *d*, rather than in *t*, cf. P.8.2.39. However, the CA tradition converts all prepausal non-nasal stops to voiceless unaspirated stops. Pāṇinian commentators offer examples of other word-final non-nasal stops combined with the word-initial *h*. Macdonell (1916, 1971: 39), offers Vedic examples like *sadhryàg ghitā́* from *sadhryàk + hitā́*, and *ávāḍ ḍhavyā́ni* from *ávāṭ + havyā́ni*. While the CA rule is a generic rule, the examples offered in the commentary do not exhibit the variety required to justify this generality. It is possible that the rule shows the occasional shift of the CA in the direction of the general grammar of Sanskrit.

चतुराध्यायीभाष्य - तेभ्यः पदान्तेभ्यः अनुत्तमेभ्यः पूर्वचतुर्थो भवति हकारस्य । 'उद्धर्षन्तां मघवन्' (अ.वे. ३.

१९.६)। 'उद्धर्॑षय॒ सत्व॑ना॒म्' (अ.वे. ५.२०.८)। 'उ॒द्ध॒र्षि-(H, N: °र्ष°)णं॒ मुनिं॑(H, N: °नी°)केशम्' (अ.वे. ८.६.१७)। 'कद्धं॑ नू॒(H, N: °र्द्धमू°)नम्' (अ.वे. १८.१.४)। 'पृ॒थि॒व्याम॑स्तु॒ यद्धं॑रः' (अ.वे. १८.२.३६)। 'तेज॑स्व॒द्धरं॑ः' (अ.वे. १८.३.७१)।

Note: Surya Kanta (*APR*, *Introduction*, p. 60) states that the APR (163) and the CAB on the present rule cite identical examples. However, note that, in this case, the APR cites only the first three examples out of the total of six cited by the CAB. One should also point out that this is not a case of a *gaṇa* or a complete listing, and the examples are only illustrative in both the texts. Also see APR (p. 110).

२.१.८. टकारात्सकारे तकारेण ।

Whitney (2.8). P adds a daṇḍa after this rule as a correction, while O crosses out a daṇḍa as a correction.

Translation: After a [final] *ṭ*, a [dental] *t* [is inserted], before an [initial] *s*.

Note: The insertion of *t* between *ṭ* and *s* facilitates the transition from *ṭ* to *s*. It suggests that after an unreleased *ṭ*, there is first a shift of the organs to the position of a dental stop, before moving on to the dental spirant. The closure begins at the retroflex position and then shifts, without release to the dental position.

चतुराध्यायीभाष्य - टकारात्सकारे परतः तकारेण व्यवधानं भवति । 'वि॒राट्त्स्व॒(H, N: ड्स्व)राज॑म्' (अ.वे. ८.९.९)। 'पृ॒त॒ना॒षाट्त्सु॒(H, N: ड्सु)वीरः॑' (अ.वे. ११.१.२)। 'त्रि॒श॒ताः षट्त्स(H, N: ड्स)ह॒स्राः' (अ.वे. ११.५.२)।

Note: The examples offered by the commentators illustrate the juncture of one word with the next, the juncture of a base with an affix, and the juncture of the first member of a compound with the second. In all these cases, the Padapāṭha splits the components.

Referring to the first example cited above, Whitney and Lanman (*AV Transl.* Vo.II., p. 508) make some important observations: "No ms. ⌊of ours⌋ inserts *t* between *-rā́ṭ* and *sva-* in b ⌊but four of SSP's do so⌋, as required by Prāt. ii.8 (under which this is one of the passages quoted)." Given this condition of the mss., one needs to seriously investigate, whether certain mss. or groups of mss. follow the rules of the CA more consistently, and whether this reflects a somewhat separate transmission.

The manuscripts of the CAB, while offering examples for this rule show neither the Padapāṭha form, nor the Saṃhitāpāṭha form, but read a final *ḍ* followed by an initial *ś*, without showing the insertion of *t*.

२.१.९. ङणनेभ्यः कटतैः शषसेषु ।

Whitney (2.9). E, F (orig): ङणनेमः°. I: 10. O adds a daṇḍa after ङणनेभ्यः.

Translation: After [final] *ṅ*, *ṇ*, and *n*, [respectively] the [sounds] *k*, *ṭ*, and *t* [are inserted], before *ś*, *ṣ*, and *s*.

Note: Whitney says: "The form of this rule is a little ambiguous, since we might be left by it to query whether, for instance, after *ṅ*, was to be inserted *k* before *ś*, *ṭ* before *ṣ*, and *t* before *s*, or only *k* before all the three sibilants - in other words, whether the transition-sound should adapt itself to the character of the following or of the preceding letter. The commentator either does not notice, or does not deign to relieve, this difficulty; he offers no explanation of the rule, and, in the instances which he cites, the manuscript persistently omits to write the transition-sound."

While the manuscripts are unclear because of the lack of writing the transition-sound, the commentary does clear one doubt. The one-to-one matching (*yathāsaṅkhya*) does not work across the board. The commentary does clearly indicate that a final *ṅ* may be followed by *ś*, *ṣ*, and *s*. The same holds true for final *ṇ* and *n*. As far as the CA rule is concerned, Whitney also correctly assumes: "For phonetic reasons, however, it cannot be doubted that the latter is determined by the preceding letter, and that after *ṅ* is to be uttered a *k*, after *ṇ* a *ṭ*, and after *n* a *t*, before all the sibilants." However, it is not clear whether such an assumption was widely shared by all the different grammatical traditions. For instance, Pāṇini treats *ṅ* and *ṇ* differently from *n*. P.8.3.28 (ङ्णोः कुक्टुक् शरि) says that, after *ṅ* and *ṇ*, optionally, the augments *kUK* and *ṭUK* are respectively inserted, before *ś*, *ṣ*, and *ś*. Then P.8.3.30 (नश्च) says that, after *n*, the augment *dhUṬ* (*dh*>*t*) is optionally inserted before *s*. Finally,

P.8.3.31 (शि तुक्) says that, after *n*, the augment *tUK* is inserted before *ś*. None of these rules cover the case of a word final *n* being followed by an initial *ṣ*. On the other hand, the CAB clearly offers an attested case of a word-final *n* followed by an initial *ṣ*, e.g. *śītān+ṣaṭ* (AV 8.9.17).

The manuscripts of the AV are irregular at best in showing these transitional sounds, and the manuscripts of the CAB do not show them at all.

The logic of this phenomenon is elucidated by Whitney as follows: "The insertion of these *tenues* after the nasals is a purely physical phenomenon, and one which is very natural, and liable to occur in any one's pronunciation. There is to be made, in each case, a double transition in utterance: from the sonant nasal to the surd oral emission, and the former is made an instant earlier than then latter, if the nasal resonance is stopped just before, instead of exactly at the same time with, the transfer of the organs to the position of the sibilant, a *tenues* of the same position with the nasal becomes audible. It is, as already remarked under i. 99 (= CA 1.4.8), the counterpart of the nasal *yama*, asserted by the Hindu phonetists to be heard between a mute and following nasal. It is also closely analogous with the conversion of *nś* into *ñch*, as will be pointed out below (under rule 17 = CA 2.1.17)."

The artificial examples cited under this rule by the CAB are comparable in general to examples found in the KV on P.8.3.28-30.

चतुराध्यायीभाष्य - ङणनेभ्यः कटतैर्व्यवधानं भवति शषसेषु परतः । 'प्रत्यङ्क्शो(H, N: ङ्शो)ते' (not in AV)। 'प्रत्यङ्क्षण्डे' (H, N: °ङ्क्षेते) (not in AV)। 'प्रत्यङ्क्सा(H, N: °ङ्सा)ये' (not in AV)। 'गण्ट्शो(H, N: °ण्शो)ते' (not in AV)। 'गण्ट्ष(H, N: °ण्ष)ण्डे' (not in AV)। 'गण्ट्सा(H, N: °ण्सा)ये' (not in AV)। 'षडाहुः शीतान्त्ष(H, N: °न्ष)डुंमासः' (अ.वे. ८.९.१७)। 'तान्त्स(H, N: °न्स)त्यौजाः' (अ.वे. ४.३६.१)।

Note: Surya Kanta (*APR*, *Introduction*, p. 40) points out that this rule is not followed by the Vulgate mss. for the AV. From this, and such other facts, he concludes "(1) that *CA* records saṃdhis for the *Śaunaka AV*; (2) that these are not observed by the Vulgate mss.; (3) that the Vulgate does not represent the *Śaunaka* śākhā, but some other." Surya Kanta, fully convinced of his own conclusions, does not notice the fact that the sandhis prescribed by the CA are not applied by the manuscripts of the CAB to the very examples which are supposed to illustrate those sandhis. Whitney himself has noted this fact many times, and the present edition also makes that amply clear. Thus, if the manuscripts of the very CA and its commentary fail to apply the sandhis taught by this very text, so could, and probably did, the manuscripts of the very Śaunakīya AV itself. This happened most probably because the Śaunakīya tradition itself underwent significant change, as evidenced by the APR. Surya Kanta forgets to notice the significance of the fact that a significant number of manuscripts of the CA also contain the text of the APR, and the manuscript tradition has consistently treated both of these texts as belonging to the Śaunakīya tradition. See the manuscripts B, M, P, VR, and V (*APR*, *Introduction*, p. 1-3). All these manuscripts have also been used for the present edition of the CA. The manuscripts, as the final colophons show, were copied and meant to be studied by the Brahmins who did not distinguish between the śākhās of these two texts, and who were all followers of the Śaunakīya AV. For instance, the final colophon for the *Jyotiṣagrantha* included in the mss. B used by Surya Kanta (ibid, p. 1) says: एवं शौनकशाखायां ब्रह्मवेदस्याङ्गं ज्योतिषग्रंथं ब्रह्मकाश्यपानुवादं समाप्तम्. The same manuscript contains the texts of CA and APR, and the whole mss. was meant for the study of a Brahmin named Bṛhaspatiji in the Pañcoli family from Anahilapurapattana. Descendants of this Pañcoli family are followers of the Śaunakīya AV till this very day, and the last few surviving reciters of the Śaunakīya AV come from this family.

Concerning this rule, Whitney (*AV Transl.* Vol.I., Intro., p. cxxiv) says: "Pr. ii.9 ordains that between *ṅ*, *ṇ*, *n* and *ś*, *ṣ*, *s* respectively, *k*, *ṭ*, *t* be in all cases introduced; the first two thirds of the rule never have an opportunity to make themselves good, as the text offers no instance of a conjunction of *ṅ* with *ś* or of *ṇ* with *ṣ*; that f final *n* with initial *s*, however, is very frequent, and the *t* has always been introduced by us. The usage of the mss. is slightly varying ['exceedingly irregular,' says W. in his note to the present rule of CA]: there is not a case perhaps where some one of them does not make the insertion, and perhaps hardly one in which they all do so without variation." On AV 6.51.1, Whitney (*AV Transl.* Vol.II., p. 319) remarks: "The Atharvan reading, according to the Prāt. phonetic rule ii.9 (= CA 2.1.9), ought to be *pratyáṅk* before a following *ś;* but (as explained in the note to that rule) the mss. read simple *ṅ*, and both printed texts adopt it."

२.१.१०. नकारस्य शकारे ञकारः ।

Whitney (2.10). A, B: नकारः for ञकारः. O: यकारः for ञकारः. P: शकार for शकारे.

Translation: Before *ś*, *n* is replaced with *ñ*.

Note: This rule needs to be understood in conjunction with CA (2.1.17: तवर्गीयाच्छकारः शकारस्य), which changes *ś* to *ch*, after a dental stop. The examples as cited by the commentator show the change of *-n+ś-* to *-ñ+ch-*. These two rules raise interesting questions as regards the order of their application. However, such theoretical questions are not discussed by the commentary. The dilemmas, however, are transparent. If we apply CA (2.1.10) first, and change the *n* to *ñ*, then we cannot apply CA (2.1.17), because that rule changes *ś* to *ch* after a dental stop, and *ñ* is not a dental stop. On the other hand, if we first apply CA (2.1.17), and change *ś* to *ch* after *n*, then we can no longer apply CA (2.1.10) which changes *n* to *ñ* before *ś*, and there is no longer a *ś* after *n*. Also see Note under CA (2.1.17).

चतुराध्यायीभाष्य - नकारस्य शकारे परतः ञकारो भवति । 'अस्माञ्छंत्रूयतीमभि' (अ.वे. ३.१.३)। 'दिवि षञ्छुक्रः' (अ.वे. १८.४.५९)।

२.१.११. चवर्गीये घोषवति ।

Whitney (2.11). A, B: °र्ग्गी°.

Translation: [The final *n* changes to *ñ*, also] before a voiced [stop] belonging to the *c*-series.

Note: As Whitney points out: "That is to say, before *j;* since *jh*, as already noticed, never occurs, and *ñ* is never found as initial." The exclusion of voiceless stops *c* and *ch* is important, because the final *n* behaves differently before these sound, cf. *devān+ca* > *devā̃śca* / *devāṃśca*. The manuscripts of the AV do not consistently show this change, and, instead of the expected *ñ*, sometimes we find an *anusvāra*, or a dental *n*. For example, on AV (1.33.2), Whitney (*AV Transl.* Vol.I., p. 33) notes that only about half of the mss. carry out the prescribed sandhi. The Whitney-Roth edition generally has an *anusvāra*. S.P. Pandit's edition and the VVRI edition read *-an j-* without applying this sandhi rule.

चतुराध्यायीभाष्य - चवर्गीये परतः घोषवति नकारस्य ञ-कारो भवति । 'अवपश्यञ्जनां(H: जाता)नाम्' (अ.वे. १. ३३.२)। 'तृणहाञ्जनम्' (अ.वे. ५.८.७)। 'प्रैष्यञ्जनमिव' (अ.वे. ५.२२.१४)। 'विवाहाञ्ज्ञातीन्' (अ.वे. १२.५. ४४)।

Note: The CAB here lists the first four instances out of a total list of 10 instances found in the APR (138). The examples occur exactly in the same order. Surya Kanta (*APR*, *Introduction*, p. 58) mistakenly cites CA (2.2, from Whitney's edition), instead of the present rule.

२.१.१२. टवर्गीये णकारः ।

Whitney (2.12).

Translation: [The final *n* is changed to] *ṇ* before a [voiced stop] belonging to the *ṭ*-series.

Note: As Whitney points out, no lingual stop is found at the beginning of "any word in the Atharvan, any more than in the other Vedas, and this rule is as unnecessary as is the inclusion of *ṇ* along with the other nasals in rule 9 of this chapter (= CA 2.1.9), and as is more than one rule or part of a rule in that which is to follow: such specifications are made merely for the sake of a theoretical completeness."

चतुराध्यायीभाष्य - टवर्गीये परतः घोषवति नकारस्य ण-कारो भवति । 'भवाण्डी(H, N: र्णी)यते' (not in AV)। 'महाण्डी(H, N: र्णी)यते' (not in AV)।

Note: The readings भवाण्डीयते and महाण्डीयते are based on Whitney's conjectures which are clearly preferable to the reading in the manuscripts, which as they stand cannot even illustrate this rule. These are clearly artificial examples, not attested in the known text of the AV. However, with respect to these examples, Surya Kanta does not raise his claim that these instances may have occurred in the genuine text of the Śaunakīya recension.

The corruptions भवार्णीयते and महार्णीयते in both the mss. for the original भवाण्डीयते and महाण्डीयते are comparable to the corruption of खड्वैडका to खड्वैरगा on CA 3.2.27. These corruptions, which seem to change *ḍ* to *r*, seem to be indications of the probable Rajasthani origin of the manuscripts, cf. Ernest Bender (1992: 90-91)

२.१.१३. तकारस्य शकारलकारयोः परसस्थानः ।

Whitney (2.13). A, B, D: °परमःस्थानः. Ha, J, M, N, P: °परसःस्थानः.

Translation: Before *ś* and *l*, *t* is changed to a sound sharing the same point of articulation as the following sound.

Note: Whitney points out that the sandhi of *t* with *ś* is not complete without rule CA (2.1.17), which changes *ś* to *ch* after a dental stop.

The term *parasasthāna* refers to a sound which has the same point of articulation as the following sound. In comparison with other treatises, we know that a final *t* is changed to *c* before *ś*, and to *l* before *l*. The first change is more obvious than the second, because *t* and *l* share the same *sthāna* 'point of articulation,' i.e. both are dental (*dantya*), and hence it is not clear why this rule should change a *t* to *l* before *l*. Since, *t* and *l* are already *sasthāna* of each other, the formulation of the rule is basically faulty. Pāṇini's formulation averts such a difficulty by using the term *parasavarṇa* instead of the term *parasasthāna*, cf. P.8.4.60 (तोर्लि) with *parasavarṇaḥ* continuing from P.8.4.58. The term *sasthāna* simply refers to the sharing of a common point of articulation, while the term *savarṇa*, as defined by P.1.1.9 (तुल्यास्यप्रयत्नं सवर्णम्), refers to those sounds which share the same point of articulation (*sthāna*) as well as the internal effort (*prayatna*). While *t* and *l* are *sasthāna* 'having a common point of articulation,' they are not *savarṇa* 'having a common point of articulation and internal effort.' Pāṇini asks us to replace a dental stop, before *l*, with a sound which is *parasavarṇa*. The only sounds which share the same point of articulation and internal effort with *l*, are *l* itself and its nasal variety, i.e. *l̃*. Thus, a final *t* is changed to *l*, and a final *n* is changed to *l̃*. Neither the CAB, nor Whitney, show any awareness of these theoretical difficulties. This also raises a significant question about how much of this text is pre-Pāṇinian.

चतुराध्यायीभाष्य - तकारस्य शकारलकारयोः परसस्थानो भवति । 'उच्छिंष्टे नामं' (अ.वे. ११.७.१)। 'घृतादुल्लुंप्तम्' (अ.वे. ५.२८.१४)।

Note: The manuscripts of the AV, as well as those of the CA, most often do not fully observe this sandhi as it relates to the juncture of *t* and *ś*, and write *ch* for *cch*.

२.१.१४. चटवर्गयोश्च ।

Whitney (2.14). A, B: चटर्गीयोश्च.

Translation: Before the consonants of the *c*-series and *ṭ*-series, [a final *t* is changed to a consonant which shares the same point of articulation as the following consonant].

Note: This rule also shows that the CA makes certain assumptions which are not brought out by the CAB. One such assumption is that out of the possible substitutes, one selects a replacement which is closest to the original in terms of phonetic features. This principle is stated by Pāṇini in P.1.1.50 (स्थानेऽन्तरतमः), and CA (1.4.4: आन्तर्येण वृत्तिः). For example, when a final *t* is followed by *c*, we are told that *t* changes to a consonant which is *parasasthāna* 'shares the same point of articulation as the following sound.' The sounds *i*, *e*, *c*-series, and *ś*, all share the same point of articulation. They are all *tālavya* 'palatal.' The principle given in CA (1.4.4) tells us that we replace *t* with *c*, and not with some other sound.

चतुराध्यायीभाष्य - चटवर्गयोः परतः तकारस्य पर(स)-स्थानो भवति । 'उच्चं तिष्ठ' (अ.वे. २.६.२)। 'यज्जामयं:' (अ.वे. १४.२.६१)। 'अग्निचिट्टीकते' (not in AV)। 'सोमसुड्डीयते' (not in AV)।

Note: The fact that there are no examples attested in the Vulgate of the AV for illustrating a *t* followed by a retroflex stop is taken by Surya Kanta (*APR*, *Introduction*, p. 39) as a possible indication that the Vulgate is not a genuinely Śaunakīya recension, and that a genuinely Śaunakīya recension may have contained such examples. On the other hand, I believe that Whitney is probably correct in suggesting that a rule like this is perhaps an indication of this text straying occasionally into the requirements of a general grammar for Sanskrit, and he points to similar examples in the commentaries on P.8.4.40-41 (स्तोः श्चुना श्चुः, ष्टुना ष्टुः). The example अग्निचिट्टीकते is actually found in the KV on P.8.4.41.

२.१.१५. ताभ्यां समानपदे तवर्गीयस्य पूर्वसस्थानः ।

Whitney (2.15). A, B, D, J, M, P: °चवर्गीयस्य पूर्वसःस्थानः. O combines a portion of this rule with CA 2.1.17, and omits CA 2.1.16: ताभ्यां समानपदे तवर्गीयाछकारःश्छकारस्य.

Translation: Within the same word, after these [= stops of the *c*-series, i.e. palatal stops, and the *ṭ*-series, i.e. retroflex stops], a member of the *t*-series [i.e. a dental stop] is replaced with a sound which shares the same point of articulation as the previous [palatal or retroflex stop].

चतुराध्यायीभाष्य - ताभ्यां चटवर्गाभ्यां समानपदे तवर्गीयस्य पूर्वसस्थानो भवति । 'मूढा अमित्राः' (अ.वे. ६.६७.२)। 'तेषां वो अग्निमूढानाम्' (अ.वे. ६.६७.२)। चवर्गीयान्नकारस्य च । 'यज्ञेनं यज्ञम्' (अ.वे. ७.५.१)। 'सोमाय राज्ञे' (अ.वे. २.१३.२)। 'सोमस्य राज्ञः' (अ.वे. ६.६८.१)।

Note: Whitney points out that all the cases of this rule illustrated by the commentary fall in the category of internal sandhi which results only if one is interested in the derivation of the word *mūḍha*, and not its relationships with the preceding or the succeeding word, which is the proper area for a Prātiśākhya. The CAB on CA (1.1.2) says:

सन्ध्यपद्याविति किमर्थम् । 'लीढ'मित्यत्र हो ढत्वम् (cf. 'हो ढः,' पा. ८.२.३१)। पर(H, N: °द, Whitney: °र)चतुर्थत्वम् (cf. 'झषस्तथोर्धोऽधः,' पा. ८.२.४०)। ष्टुना ष्टुत्वम् (cf. 'ष्टुना ष्टुः,' पा. ८.४.४१)। ढो ढे लोपो (cf. 'ढो ढे लोपः,' पा. ८.३.१३)दीर्घत्वमिति (cf. 'ढ्रलोपे पूर्वस्य दीर्घोऽणः,' पा. ६.३.१११) वैयाकरणेन वक्तव्यम् ।

The word *mūḍha* is derived in the same way, where the root *muh* is followed by the past participle affix *-ta*. The CAB, and perhaps the CA, seem to assume a derivational process analogous to the Pāṇinian process cited in the commentary passage above. The *h* of the root *muh* is replaced with *ḍh* before the affix *-ta*. Then the present CA rule changes *t* of *-ta*, coming after *ḍh*, to *ḍh*, giving us the stage *muḍh+ḍha*. The present CA rule does not go beyond this stage. According to Pāṇinian derivation, however, *ḍh* is deleted before *ḍh* by P.8.3.13 (ढो ढे लोपः), and the preceding vowel is lengthened by P.6.3.111 (ढ्रलोपे पूर्वस्य दीर्घोऽणः). Whitney is, however, correct is saying that such a derivational process does not truly concern a Prātiśākhya, a point also made by the CAB on CA (1.1.2).

Whitney also suggests: "The only practical application of the precept is one which is not recognized, or at least not illustrated, by the commentator; namely, to those cases in which an initial *s* followed by a *t* or *th* is, by later rules (ii. 90 = CA 2.4.10 etc.), converted to *ṣ* : the following dental then becomes by this rule a lingual." While the change indicated by Whitney does indeed take place in forms like *anuṣṭhita*, it cannot take place by the present CA rule, because the present CA rule strictly applies to a dental stop which follows a palatal or a retroflex stop, and not something that follows any palatal or retroflex sound. The change indicated by Whitney does, however, take place by the following CA rule, i.e. CA (2.1.16).

In any case, this rule, along with several successive rules, illustrates the relatively less common process of regressive assimilation. Generally, Sanskrit shows progressive assimilation.

२.१.१६. षकारान्नानापदेऽपि ।

Whitney (2.16). F, I: °रांतांनाना°. O omits this rule.

Translation: After an *ṣ*, even in a different word [i.e. even across a word-boundary], [a dental stop is replaced with a sound which has the same point of articulation as the preceding *ṣ*].

चतुराध्यायीभाष्य - षकारान्तान्नानापदे अपिशब्दात्समान-पदेऽपि तवर्गीयस्य पूर्वसस्थानो भवति । 'षष्टिः' (अ.वे. ५.१५.६)। 'षण्णवतिः' (not in AV, 'षण्णवत्यै,' तै.सं. ७.२.१५.१, काठकसं. ४२.५)।

Note: Whitney says that the example *ṣaṣṭiḥ* properly 'belongs under the preceding rule.' This is not quite true. The preceding rule, as pointed out earlier, applies only to dental stops which follow palatal or retroflex stops, and not which follow palatal or retroflex sounds across the board. In any case, an example like *ṣaṣṭiḥ* constitutes an example of internal sandhi, which concerns the process of word-derivation, which strictly speaking is not the concern of a Prātiśākhya. However, as Whitney indicates on the preceding rule, one can think of a 'word-internal' application for this rule, where the initial *s* of a root is changed to *ṣ* because of the preceding vowel across the word-boundary. The dental stop following such an *ṣ* then changes to a retroflex stop, e.g. *anu+ sthita* > *anu+ṣthita* > *anu+ṣṭhita.* Numerous examples of this kind can be found in the text of the Atharvan.

The example *ṣaṇṇavatiḥ* is offered in the KV on P. 8.4.42 (न पदान्ताट्टोर-नाम्), to illustrate the Vārttika: अनाम्नवतिनगरीणामिति वाच्यम्. Since the example *ṣaṇṇavatiḥ* is not attested in the AV, what would be a proper AV example? In this case, Whitney rightly points out: "The precept was evidently only intended for such combinations as *bahiṣ ṭe* (i.3.1), in which, by the rules contained in the fourth section of this chapter, an original final *s* becomes lingualized, and the following *t* is assimilated to it."

२.१.१७. तवर्गीयाच्छकारः शकारस्य ।

Whitney (2.17). A, B (corr), D, J: तवर्गीयाः°.

Translation: After a member of the *t*-series [i.e. a dental stop], *ś* is replaced with *ch*.

Note: This rule works in conjunction with rules 2.1.10 and 2.1.13 above. See Notes on those rules for problems regarding the mutual relations between these rules as formulated. Whitney also points out: "This rule, taken in connection with rules 10 (= CA 2.1.10) and 13 (= CA 2.1.13), above, determines the form to be assumed by the combinations *t+ś* and *n+ś*. Exception may fairly be taken, however, to the method in which the change is taught. By the other rules referred to, *t* and *n* are to become *c* and *ñ* before *ś*: and if those rules are first applied, there will be no dental mutes for *ś* to follow; while, if the present rule be first applied, the others are rendered wholly or in part superfluous, by the non-occurrence of *ś* after *t* and *n*. In the case of *t* there comes in the still farther difficulty that rule 6 of this chapter (= CA 2.1.6) has converted it into *th*, so that a part of rule 13 is thereby also rendered incapable to application. These are incongruencies such as the authors of the Prātiśākhyas are very seldom guilty of. What is the intention of our treatise is, indeed, sufficiently clear." The kind of problems pointed out by Whitney in the application of CA rules have been handled with far greater sophistication in the Pāṇinian system with devices like a) *sthānivadbhāva* 'treating a substitute as if it had some of the same properties as the original,' b) rule ordering and well-defined procedures for conflict-resolution and priority, and c) treating a rule or it result as if it is not in effect for some other rules (*asiddha*).

चतुराध्यायीभाष्य - तवर्गीयादुत्तरस्य शकारस्य छकारो भवति । 'देवाञ्छ्लोकः' (अ.वे. १८.१.३३)। 'अस्मांञ्छंत्रूयतीमभि' (अ.वे. ३.१.३)। 'दिवि षञ्छुक्रः' (अ.वे. १८.४.५९)।

Note: Whitney points out: "The commentator cites examples only of the combination of *n* and *ś*. ... As an example illustrative of the other part of the rule, we may take *ārāc charavyāḥ* (i.19.1)."

Whitney further points out that the manuscripts "with hardly an exception, write simply *ch*, instead of *cch*." While this observation is beyond doubt, Whitney draws some debatable conclusions: "This orthography (i.e. *ch*, rather than *cch*) is also, to my apprehension, a truer representation of the actual phonetic result of combining *t* with *ś*. That these sounds fuse together into a *ch* is very strong evidence that the utterance of the Sanskrit surd palatals did not differ materially from that of our *ch* (in *church* etc.); and I conceive that the constant duplication of the *ch* and *jh* (wherever the latter occurs) between two vowels is to be looked upon simply as an indication of the heaviness of those consonants, and of their effect to make the preceding vowel long by position." I think Whitney seems to overlook the fact that the representation *cch* is not a mere orthographic representation, but that the processes of syllabication would require that the initial *c* be part of the previous syllable, with the next syllable beginning with *ch*. Such a syllabic division was obligatory in Sanskrit, especially, if the previous syllable had a short vowel. In NIA languages like Hindi and Marathi, however, we can have a *ch* preceded by a short vowel forming a light syllable in words like *bichānā* > *bi-chā-nā*. In Sanskrit, there is no reason to believe that *ch* was always a heavy consonant. After long vowels and sentence-initially, one has no reason to assume that *ch* must be a heavy consonant.

Assuming the compound nature of *ch*, Whitney says: "The conversion of *nś* into *ñch*, on the supposition of the compound nature of the palatal, as made up of a mute and a sibilant element, would be almost precisely analogous with that of *ns* into *nts*, as taught in rule 9, above, and would be readily and simply explainable as a phonetic process." While there is indeed some commonality between these two cases, one must note that the Sanskrit tradition treated *ch* as a single sound, while *ts* was always treated as a consonant cluster. In the cluster *ts*, after the initial closure for *t*, one has the continuant *s*. On the other hand, *ch* is unlike *n+c+ś*, in that *ch* has aspiration as part of it release, but does not have the continuant feature of *ś*. Such a distinction allows *ts* to be split in a syllabic division as *-t+s-*. Such a division is not available for *ch*.

२.१.१८. लोप उदः स्थास्तम्भोः सकारस्य ।

Whitney (2.18). Ha, Na: उदस्थाः°. J, M, Hb, Nb, P: उदस्थास्तंभोः°. E, F: लोपोदँस्थाः°. A, B: लोपे उदस्थाः स्तंभोः°. O: लोपोदँस्थास्तंभोसकारस्य.

चतुराध्यायीभाष्य - लोपो भवति उद उत्तरयोः स्थास्तम्भोः सकारस्य । 'मा घोषा उत्थुः' (अ.वे. ७.५२.२)। 'ततस्त्वोत्थापयामसि' (अ.वे. १०.१.२९)। 'उत्थापय सीदंतः' (अ.वे. १२.३.३०)। 'सत्येनोत्तंभिता' (अ.वे. १४.१.१)।

Note: Referring to the form *utthuḥ* in AV (7.52.2), Whitney (*AV Transl*. Vol.I., p. 422) remarks: "SSP. strangely reads, with the comm. and the majority of his authorities, and with part of ours (P.?O.R.), *ut sthur* in c, against both general grammar and the Prātiśākhya (ii.18; its commentary quotes this passage as an illustration of the rule)." In all the cases of *ut+sthā* cited by the commentary, the Padapāṭha clearly retains the *s* of *sthā*. However, as Whitney points out: "Wherever, however, the preposition receives the accent, and enters into a more intimate combination with the root, as in the participle *útthita*, the *pada*-text (by iv. 62 = CA 4.2.16) does not separate the compound, or restore the original *s*, but reads the same form which appears in *saṃhitā*. Of this kind is also the only example of the root *stambh* combined with the preposition *ud* which our text presents, viz. *satyeno 'ttabhitā* (xiv.1.1), where the *pada* reads *úttabhitā*, and not *út-stabhitā*." Also compare this rule with P.8.4.61 (उदः स्थास्तम्भोः पूर्वस्य). The CA rule is closer to Pāṇini as compared to other Prātiśākhyas, as Whitney points out: "The Vāj. Pr. (iv. 95) notices the loss of *s* from the root *stambh*, but, as Weber remarks with surprise, omits all mention of *sthā*. The Taitt. Pr. (v. 14) includes these cases in a more general rule, that *s* is dropped when preceded by *ud* and followed by a consonant."

२.१.१९. रेफस्य रेफे ।

Whitney (2.19).

Translation: *R* [is deleted] before *r*.

Note: As Whitney notes: "The *r* which is thus dropped must itself, of course, be the product of euphonic processes taught elsewhere (ii. 42, 43 = CA 2.2.3-4). The protraction of a preceding short vowel when an *r* is thus dropped is prescribed in a later rule (iii. 20 = CA 3.1.20)." However, the CA rules must be clearly contrasted with Pāṇinian rules P.8.3.13 (ढो ढे लोपः) and P.6.3.111 (ढ्रलोपे पूर्वस्य दीर्घोऽणः), which prescribe additionally a deletion of a *ḍh* before *ḍh*, and the lengthening of the preceding vowel. The CAB on CA (1.1.2) knows these Pāṇinian rules, and the same commentary on CA (2.1.15), if not CA (2.1.15) itself, seems to presuppose such rules. See Notes on CA (1.1.2) and CA (2.1.15).

चतुराध्यायीभाष्य - रेफस्य रेफे परतः लोपो भवति । 'शरदः पुरूची(ः) रायः' (अ.वे. २.१३.३)। 'पुना रक्तं वासः' (not in known Vedic texts, quoted in the KV on P.1.3.14)। 'पुनां रूपाणि' (अ.वे. १.२४.४)। 'जघ्नू रक्षांसि' (अ.वे. ४.३७.१)। 'अग्नी रक्षांसि' (अ.वे. ८.३.२६)। 'अग्नी रक्षः' (अ.वे. १२.३.४३)।

Note: The example पुना रक्तं वासः cited by the CAB is not found in the Vulgate of the AV and is actually not found in the known Vedic literature. Surya Kanta (*APR*, *Introduction*, p. 40) suggests that this may have occurred in the genuine Śaunakīya recension of the AV, and that the Vulgate is not the genuine Śaunakīya recension. However, the fact that it occurs in the KV may perhaps mean that it could have been taken by our commentary from a grammatical source like the KV.

२.१.२०. स्पर्शादुत्तमादनुत्तमस्यानुत्तमे ।

Whitney (2.20).

Translation: After a last member [of a stop-series, i.e. a nasal stop], and before a non-last [member of a stop-series, i.e.

non-nasal stop], a non-last [member of a stop-series, i.e. a non-nasal stop, is deleted].

Note: This rule is interesting in that it does not seem to apply to the transformation of the words given in the Padapāṭha to their Saṃhitā versions, or vice versa, and hence it does not fit a strict definition of the purpose of a Prātiśākhya. To make sense of the inclusion of such rules, one may perhaps propose that the CA is trying to clearly distinguish its recitational practice from the norms of generic Sanskrit, and from other traditions, cf. Whitney: "Neither of the other known Prātiśākhyas teaches the same omission, or even notices it as prescribed by any authority." Concerning the practice taught by this rule, Whitney (*AV Transl.* Vol. I., Intro., p. cxxv) says: "Abbreviation of the consonant-groups: as in *paṅkti* and the like. -- By ii.20 (= CA 2.1.20) a non-nasal mute coming in the course of word-formation between a nasal and a non-nasal is dropped: so *paṅti; chintam* and *rundhi* in stead of [*paṅkti*], *chinttam* and *runddhi;* etc. The manuscripts observe this rule quite consistently, although not without exceptions; and it has been uniformly followed in the edition. At xii.1.40, *anuprayuṅktām* is an accidental exception; and here, for once, the mss. happen to agree in retaining the *k*. ⌊Cf. the Hibernicisms *stren'th*, *len'th*, etc.⌋" Note that the comments enclosed between the L-brackets '⌊' and '⌋' are added by Lanman. On the other hand, the VVRI edition does not follow this rule, and maintains the *k*/*g* in its readings.

This rule also needs to be contrasted with CA (2.1.9: ङणनानां कटतैः शषसेषु), which prescribes: "After [final] *ṅ*, *ṇ*, and *n*, [respectively] the [sounds] *k*, *ṭ*, and *t* [are inserted], before *ś*, *ṣ*, and *s*." While CA (2.1.9) has parallels elsewhere, the present rule does not.

चतुराध्यायीभाष्य - स्पर्शात् उत्तमात् अनुत्तमस्य स्पर्शस्य अनुत्तमे परतः स्पर्शे लोपो भवति । 'पङ्ति (H, N: ङ्क्ति) - रत्र' (not in *AV*)। 'पाङ्तं (H, N: ङ्क्तं) छन्दः' (अ.वे. १२.३.१०)। 'सपत्नांन्मे भङ्धि (H, N: भवति)' (अ.वे. १०.३.१३)। अनुत्तम इति किमर्थम् । 'तस्यां वायुर्वत्त्सः (H, N: त्सः)' (अ.वे. ४.३९.४)। 'उत्त्सों (H, N: त्सो) वा तत्त्र (H, N: त्र)' (अ.वे. ६.१०६.१)। 'अप्प्स (H, N: प्स) रसः

सधमादं मदन्ति' (अ.वे. १४.२.३४)। 'नुदामं एनमपं रुद्ध्मः(H: ध्सः, N: धाः)' (अ.वे. १२.३.४३)।

Note: The deletion taught by this rule is not practiced by the mss. of the CAB. The consonant groups as assumed in the counter-examples are not seen either in the manuscripts of the AV, nor in those of the CAB. Also the counter-examples are not chosen with proper care in that several of them contain multiple violations of the conditions at a time, rather than illustrating strictly the single condition referred to by the query अनुत्तम इति किमर्थम्. In the text of the commentary above, I have given the examples with the consonant clusters as expressly intended by the commentary, and noted the manuscript readings which do not actually illustrate the intended clusters.

२.१.२१. स्वराद्यवयोः पदान्तयोः ।

Whitney (2.21). I: 20.

Translation: After a vowel, word-final *y* and *v* [are deleted].

Note: As Whitney points out: "This rule applies, on the one hand, to the *y* and *v* of the syllables *ay*, *av*, *āy*, *āv* (the latter, however, being excepted by the following rule), into which, by iii. 40 (= CA 3.2.17), *e*, *o*, *ai*, and *au* are converted before a vowel; and, on the other hand, to the *y* into which, by ii. 41 (= CA 2.2.2), *visarjanīya* theoretically passes before an initial vowel." I object to the word 'theoretically' used by Whitney. While it is true that the CA seems to demand unconditional deletion of a *y* derived from a *visarjanīya*, and, therefore, this *y* becomes a seemingly theoretical entity, other schools were not so categorical about this deletion, and hence this *y* could appear in the final result, cf. KV on P.8.3.19 (लोपः शाकल्यस्य) says: शाकल्यग्रहणं विभाषार्थम् । तेन यदापि लघुप्रयत्नतरो न भवत्यादेशस्तदापि व्योः पक्षे श्रवणं भवति. Also contrast the fact that such a deletion takes place, according to Pāṇini, before *aŚ*, i.e. vowels and voiced consonants. The CA rule is a statement of unconditional deletion. In any case, this procedure was widely disputed, and Whitney records the wide spectrum of views in the traditional phonetic literature concerning these disputes.

चतुराध्यायीभाष्य - स्वरादुत्तरयोः यकारवकारयोः पदान्तयोर्लोपो भवति । 'क आंसञ्जन्याः के वराः' (अ.वे. ११.८.

१)। 'उष्णेनं वाय उदकेनेहिं' (अ.वे. ६.६८.१)। 'अस्या इच्छन्नग्रुवै पतिंम्' (अ.वे. ६.६०.१)। 'स उं एव मंहायमः' (अ.वे. १३.४.५)। 'ता इमा आपंः' (अ.वे. १५.१५.७)।

Note: While the CAB quotes *asyā icchan* to show that there is no recombination, Whitney (*AV Transl.* Vol.I., p. 327) points out that "the meter shows that the irregular combination *asye 'cchan* requires to be made, and the Anukr. apparently winks at it."

२.१.२२. नाकाराद्वकारस्य ।

Whitney (2.22). A, B, D, P: नकारा°.

Translation: [However], [a word-final] *v* occurring after *ā* is not [deleted].

चतुराध्यायीभाष्य - नाकारात् उत्तरस्य वकारस्य लोपो भवति । 'द्वाविमौ वातौं वातः' (अ.वे. ४.१३.२)। 'इन्द्र-वायू उभाविह' (अ.वे. ३.२०.६)। 'उभाविन्द्राग्नी आ भंर-ताम्' (अ.वे. ५.७.६)।

Note: Whitney says: "This rule is uniformly observed in the Sanhitā of the Atharvan, excepting in a couple of cases in book xix, which book the Prātiśākhya does not recognize as forming part of the Atharvan text: these are *pādā ucyete* (xix.6.5), and *citrā imā vṛṣabhau* (xix.13.1)." One cannot discount the possibility that the 19th book represents a somewhat different linguistic tradition and constitutes a relatively late addition to the rest of the books. However, note that the Padapāṭha does not render *citrā* of the Saṃhitā with *citrau* as Whitney seems to assume, but leaves it as *citrā.* If such be the case, then it would not come under the scope for the present rule.

२.१.२३. गविष्टौ गवेषण इति च ।

Whitney (2.23). O: गविष्ठौ°.

Translation: Also, [there is no deletion of the word-final *v* in the forms] *gaviṣṭau* [< *go+iṣṭau*] and *gaveṣaṇaḥ* [< *go+eṣaṇaḥ*].

Note: In the two cases listed in the rule, the Padapāṭha breaks down the compounds as indicated in the brackets.

चतुराध्यायीभाष्य - गविष्टौ गवेषण इति च न वकारस्य लोपो भवति । 'इषुंमन्तं गविंष्टौ' (अ.वे. ४.२४.५)। 'गवेषंणः सहंमानः' (अ. वे. ५.२०.११)।

Note: Whitney says: "Other like cases, as *gavāśir* and *gaviṣ*, occur in the twentieth book of the text, but with that book the Prātiśākhya has nothing to do."

APR (155), which seems to be referring to our CA rule, also teaches that in *gaviṣṭau* and *gaveṣaṇaḥ* the *v* is not elided. Surya Kanta makes a case that making such a rule which can apply to the Saṃhitā text was originally not the function of the APR, which was originally supposed to describe only the peculiarities of the Pada text, and that such rules were added later to it. On the other hand, he argues that the CA was from the very beginning a treatise dealing with the conversion of the Padas into Saṃhitā, and that a rule such as the present one is more genuinely suited to it. See: *APR*, *Introduction*, pp. 25-26.

२.१.२४. लेशवृत्तिरधिस्पर्शं शाकटायनस्य ।

Whitney (2.24). A, B, D: °स्पृर्शं°. O: °स्पर्शा°.

Translation: According to Śākaṭāyana, there is a weak articulation [of the word-final *y* and *v* discussed in the earlier rules], as regards the feature of contact [between the articulator and the point of articulation].

Note: As Whitney's survey of the various texts shows, the doctrine ascribed to Śākaṭāyana here is offered as an option by most texts, and is occasionally ascribed to other scholars like Vātsapra. P.8.3.18 (व्योर्लघुप्रयत्नतरः शाकटायनस्य) ascribes the same view to Śākaṭāyana, but uses a slightly different term: *laghuprayatnataraḥ* "relatively weaker articultory effort." Pāṇini 8.3.19 (लोपः शाकल्यस्य) ascribes the deletion of final *y* and *v* to Śākalya. By default, it would seem that these sounds were neither deleted nor weakened, but were pronounced with the normal force in Pāṇini's own school. This gives us a wide range of pronunciation for final *y* and *v* across the various dialects of Sanskrit. What is noteworthy, however, is that the view of deletion, which is ascribed by Pāṇini expressly to Śākalya, is the default view in CA. While it does care, for some reason, to record the view of Śākaṭāyana, it does not care to record the view of normal pronunciation of *y* and *v*. It should be noted that there is a close relationship of the CA tradition to the views expressed by Śākaṭāyana, cf. Bhārgava-Bhāskara's commentary on CA (1.1.11-12) and the Notes on these rules.

चतुराध्यायीभाष्य - लेशवृत्तिर्भवति अधिस्पर्शं शाकटायनस्य आचार्यस्य । 'क आंसञ्जन्याः के वराः' (अ.वे. ११.८.१)। 'उष्णेनं वाय उदकेनेहिं' (अ.वे. ६.६८.१)। 'अस्या इच्छन्नग्रुवै पतिंम्' (अ.वे. ६.६०.१)। 'स उं एव मंहायमः' (अ.वे. १३.४.५)। 'ता इमा आपंः' (अ.वे. १५.१५.७)।

२.१.२५. पुमो मकारस्य स्पर्शेऽघोषेऽनूष्मपरे विसर्जनीयोऽपुंश्चादिषु ।

Whitney (2.25). E, F: पूँ for पुं. J, M: °यो अपुं°. O: °पूंश्चा°.

Translation: Before a voiceless stop not followed by a spirant, the *m* of *pum* is changed to a *visarjanīya* [i.e. *ḥ*], except in *puṃśca* etc.

Note: Whitney's frustration with the rule and the commentary is manifest in his comments: "This is a rule very hard to get along with. In the first place, it is altogether unnecessary and uncalled for, since of all the words to which it is intended to apply, but a single one, *puṃścalī*, is found in the Atharvan text, and that one is written by the *pada*-text precisely as in *saṃhitā*, and so requires no explanation from the Prātiśākhya."

Besides the fact that the rule seems to step into the un-Prātiśākhyan territory of general grammatical derivation, the condition *apuṃścādiṣu* creates a number of problems. The first problem is that the form *puṃśca* already seems to show the operation of the rule. If so, then what is being excluded by saying *apuṃścādiṣu*? The CAB offers *puṃścora* as a counter-example. However, as Whitney agonizes: "But *puṃścora*, 'he-thief,' is as regular an instance of the application of the rule as *puṃskāmā* or *puṃścalī;* nor does it seem possible to find in *apuṃścādiṣu* itself any form which constitutes an exception to the previous specifications. I can only conjecture that the reading is corrupt, and was corrupt before the commentator set himself at work upon it, and that his explanation was as unintelligible to himself as it is to us. The specification may have been intended for such words as *puṃkhyāna*, which constitutes an actual exception to the rule, and it is cited as such in Böhtlingk's note to Pāṇini viii.3.6, as from the Siddhānta-Kaumudī."

It is now quite clear that *apuṃścādiṣu* is an ancient corruption. It is shared by all the manuscripts, and, as Whitney correctly assumes, it must have been there already when the author of the CAB attempted to explain the word. Whitney's comment quoted above, led me to look for a possible emendation. Having looked at the shapes of the letters *kh* and *c* in Gupta and pre-Gupta scripts, it seems very likely that these two letters were confused, and a possible *apuṃkhādiṣu* was misread as *apuṃścādiṣu.* The expression *apuṃkhādiṣu* would not only exclude *puṃkhyāna* cited by Whitney, but also the relatively earlier expression *puṃkha*, which is traditionally etymologized as *pum+kha* [< *pumāṃsaṃ khanati*, *pum+khan+Ḍa*, etymology offered in Śabdakalpadruma, Vol. 3, p. 163].

Another possible reading is *apuṃkṣādiṣu*, which would exclude cases like *puṃkṣīraḥ* and *puṃkṣuraḥ.* However, these examples are already taken care of by the exclusion *anūṣmapare*, and one would not need a separate exclusion to be stated. Therefore, the reading *apuṃkhādiṣu* seems to be a better emendation. Another word which fits in the same category as *puṃkha* is *puṃkheṭa*, which is analyzed by Roth-Böhtlingk (*PW*, Vol. 4, p. 752) as *puṃs+khe 'ṭa*, and explained as: "ein männlicher Planet, (ref:) Ind. St. 2,258, N." Indeed the word *puṃkha* is at least as old as the epics, cf. Böhtlingk, *PW*, Vol. 4, p. 752, and, even though it is unattested in Vedic literature, it could have been on the mind of the author of the CA as an exception to the rule. It is also attested in Varāhopaniṣad (2.82, *Yogopaniṣadaḥ*, p. 482). However, this is a late Upaniṣad, and the verse containing this word is in the meter Vasantatilakā, a late classical meter.

Whitney rightly suspects that the reading *apuṃścādiṣu* was corrupted from some now-unknown original before this commentary was written. On the other hand, his comment that this whole rule is probably an interpolation, because the word *visarjanīya* is repeated again in the following rule, is not justified, since Whitney's reading of CA 2.1.26: नकारस्य चटतवर्गेष्वघोषेष्वनूष्मपरेषु विसर्जनीयः is not supported by a single manuscript. By mistake, Whitney has taken the elaboration in the commentary to be the text of the rule.

चतुराध्यायीभाष्य - पुमो मकारस्य स्पर्शे अघोषे अनूष्मपरे विसर्जनीयो भवति अपुंश्चादिषु । 'पुंस्कामा' (not in Vedic texts)। 'पुंस्पुत्रा' (not in Vedic texts)। 'पुंश्चली' (अ.वे. १५.२.१)। स्पर्श इति किमर्थम् । 'पुंयानम्' (not in Vedic texts)। अघोष इति किमर्थम् । 'पुंदानम्' (not in Vedic texts)। अनूष्मपरे इति किमर्थम् । 'पुंक्षुरः' (not in Vedic texts)। 'पुंक्षारः' (not in Vedic texts)। अपुंश्चादिष्विति किमर्थम् । 'पुंश्चोरः' (not in Vedic texts)।

Note: Except for one, all the examples cited by the commentator are unattested in the AV. Many of these examples are found in the KV on P.8.3.6 (पुमः खय्यम्परे). The example *puṃkṣārah* may be a corruption of *puṃkṣīra* which occurs in the KV on P.8.3.6. For *puṃyānam* and *puṃścoraḥ*, the Petersburg Lexicon finds the only known attestations in the CAB on the present rule.

२.१.२६. नकारस्य चटतवर्गेषु ।

Whitney (2.26): नकारस्य चटतवर्गेष्वघोषेष्वनूष्मपरेषु विसर्जनीयः. A, B, C, D, E, F, J, M, Na, O: °चटवर्गेषु°. P: °चटवर्ग्रेषु°.

Translation: Before voiceless [stops] of the *c*-series, *ṭ*-series, and *t*-series [i.e. palatal, retroflex, or dental stops], [not followed by a spirant], the [final] *n* [is changed to a *visarjanīya*, i.e. *ḥ*].

Note: As Whitney points out, this rule is uniformly applied by the manuscripts of the ŚAV. Whitney's further contribution lies in pointing out that the doctrine proposed by this rule amounts to an insertion of a sibilant, and the *n* is subsequently replaced by the nasalization of the preceding vowel. Whitney offers a historical explanation: "It is sufficiently evident that this insertion of a sibilant after a final *n* before a surd mute is no proper phonetical process: the combination of the nasal and following non-nasal is perfectly natural and easy without the aid of a transition sound, nor can any physical explanation be given of the thrusting in between them of a sibilant, which only encumbers the conjunction. ... The historical rather than phonetical origin of the *r* which is appended (see rule 29 = CA 2.1.29, below) to a few accusatives plural in the Vedic language before a vowel has been long since pointed out by Bopp; and a kindred explanation of the conversion of *ān* into *ām̐* before a vowel (see rule 27 = CA 2.1.27, below) was added by him in his Comparative Grammar. He has refrained from tracing the insertion of a sibilant before *c* and *t* to the same cause, doubtless, because of the numerous instances in which the insertion is made after a word which is not entitled by origin to a final *s*. But nothing is more natural than that an insertion originally organic, but of which the true character was forgotten, and which had come to seem merely euphonic, should considerably extend its sphere of occurrence, and should be by degrees, and more and more, applied to cases to which it did not historically belong. Now a very large majority of the words ending in *n* are accusatives plural and nominatives singular, to both of which cases comparative grammar clearly shows that a final *s* belongs as case-ending; and I can entertain no doubt that the whole phenomenon of the insertion of the sibilant arose from its preservation in these forms, and from the inorganic extension of the same mode of combination, by analogy, to the much smaller classes of vocative, locative, and verbal forms." I have quoted Whitney's explanation in full, because it is an explanation which has been subsequently accepted without any challenge. In his footnote (1862: 86-87), Whitney offers statistical information pertaining to the occurrence of this type of sandhi.

चतुराध्यायीभाष्य - नकारस्य चटतवर्गेषु अघोषेषु अनूष्मपरेषु विसर्जनीयो भवति । 'भवांश्चिनोति' (not in Vedic texts) । 'भवांश्छादयति' (not in Vedic texts) । 'भवांष्टीकते' (not in Vedic texts) । 'भवांस्तरति' (not in Vedic texts) । 'भवांस्तत्र' (not in Vedic texts) । अघोषेष्वित्येव । 'बृहन् दक्षिंणया' (H, N: णायाः) (अ.वे. ६.५३.१) । 'नैनान्नमंसा परः' (अ.वे. ७.७.१) । अनूष्मपरेष्वित्येव । 'भवान्त्सरु' (not in Vedic texts) । 'महान्त्सरु' (not in Vedic texts) ।

Note: Most of the examples, not attested in the AV, are found in the KV on P.8.3.7 (नश्छव्यप्रशान्). Again we must note that Surya Kanta does not suggest that these examples are from the so-called now lost genuine Śaunakīya recension. It is absolutely unconscionable that the commentator does not offer a single example from the text of the Atharvan to illustrate this phenomenon, which is by no means rare in the Atharvan text. By citing the examples which he does, he shows how deeply influenced he is by the tradition of Pāṇinian grammar.

२.१.२७. आकारोपधस्योपबद्धादीनां स्वरे ।

Whitney (2.27). E (orig), F (orig): आकारोपबद्धा°. P: °स्यौप°.

Translation: In words like *upabaddha* [i.e. *upabaddhān*], [the final *n*], preceded by *ā*, [is changed to a *visarjanīya*, i.e. *ḥ*], before a vowel.

Note: While the previous rule survives in the classical language, the present rule is applicable only to Vedic language. Here, the *visarjanīya* is eventually replaced with *y* by CA (2.2.2), and by CA (2.1.21), this *y* is deleted. The other change taking place is the compensatory nasalization of the preceding vowel by CA (1.3.6). Thus, the sequence *upabaddhān+iha* is changed in the Saṃhitāpāṭha to *upabaddhā̃ iha.* In the classical usage, this would remain *upabaddhāniha.* It is not immediately obvious why the sandhi of *devān+ca* resulting in *devāṃśca* should retain the historical dimension down to the classical usage, while the combination *upabaddhān+iti* should lose that historical dimension.

As Whitney points out, "All the cases in which this loss of a final *n* occurs are accusatives plural or nominatives singular, which originally possessed a final *s* after the *n*, and the loss of the *n* before the sibilant, with accompanying nasalization of the preceding vowel, and then the disappearance of the sibilant itself, as in other cases after *ā* and before a vowel, are unquestionably the cause of the sandhi as it finally presents itself." The interesting thing is that there is no synchronic generalization of this rule to all cases with final *-ān* followed by a vowel, but the phenomenon is limited to a set of defined cases. For example, *yātumān+ayam* in AV (1.7.4) does not change to *yātumā̃ ayam.* Whitney himself notes: "The loss of the *n* with nasalization of the vowel is evidently an old-style *sandhi*, going out of use, and no longer appearing except sporadically. It is interesting, as regards this *sandhi* and that taught in the preceding rule - which have both ... the same historical origin - to note the relations of the Rik and the Atharvan usage to one another and to the practice of the classical Sanskrit. The insertion of the *s*, which has become a necessary proceeding under the modern euphonic rules, is almost universal in the Atharvan, and comparatively rare in the Rik: the conversion of the *n* into *anusvāra*, of which the general Sanskrit grammar knows nothing, is only infrequently observed in the Atharvan, while it is made in the Rik with but few exceptions."

चतुराध्यायीभाष्य - आकारोपधस्य नकारस्य विसर्जनीयो भवति । उपबद्धादीनां स्वरे । ‘उप॑बद्धाँ इ॒हा व॑ह’ (अ.वे. १.७.७)। ‘शा॒स इ॒त्था म॒हाँ अ॑सि’ (अ.वे. १.२०.४)। ‘यो अ॒स्माँ अ॑भि॒दास॑ति’ (अ. वे. १.१९.३)। ‘सर्वा॒न् म॒च्छपथाँ॒ अधि॑’ (अ.वे. २.७.१)।

Note: There is a slight error when Whitney says that the commentator cites five instances. The commentary cites only four instances. However, Whitney collects a complete list of such cases in the text of AV. The *gaṇa* referred to in this CA rule is fully spelled out by the APR (196), and out of a total of 76 instances listed by the APR, the CAB cites the first four in the same order. This, in spite of Surya Kanta's view to the contrary, indicates a very close connection between the CAB and the APR.

One should also note that Whitney's listing does not completely match the listing of the *gaṇa* as found in the APR, and the differences between these listings need to be further explored. All the instances listed under APR (196) are covered by Whitney's listing, but Whitney's listing contains substantially more instances. Below, I am listing those cases which are listed as showing a case of this rule, which are listed by Whitney, but are not found in the listing under APR (196): 1.19.3; 4.19.5; 4.19.7; 5.23.8; 6.15.1-2; 6.54.3; 6.69.2; 7.57.1; 7.65.1; 9.1.19; 10.3.14; 10.3.15; 11.9.22; 11.9.24; 13.2.5; 13.2.18; 13.2.21; 13.2.29; 14.1.45; 14.1.55; 14.2.10; 18.2.13; 18.2.18. Whitney also lists the following instances from the 19th and the 20th Kāṇḍa of the AV, which are completely left out of consideration by the APR (196): 19.6.8; 19.13.8; 19.26.3; 19.32.7; 19.36.4; 19.50.4; 19.59.2; 20.127.7; 20.128.4; 20.128.5; 20.128.8; 20.136.15. One needs to study all these instances individually. However, at first glance, it seems plausible that the scope of the application of this rule went on increasing even after the *gaṇa* was fully listed by the APR. Such an increasing scope for this application is indeed puzzling, especially since it is not represented in the classical language. One possible reason for it may be sought in the generally accepted Ṛgvedic influence on the AV tradition. As Whitney points out, this rule is applied in the "Rik with but few exceptions," the Ṛgvedic influence may have led the AV tradition in the direction opposite to that of the classical language.

२.१.२८. वृक्षाँ वनानीति वकारे ।

Whitney (2.28). A, B, D, P: °क्षां°. E, F: °क्षाँऽ°. Hb, Nb: वृक्षान्°. O: °क्षँ वनानाति°.

Translation: In the sequence *vṛkṣān vanāni*, [the final *n* changes to a *visarjanīya*] before *v*.

Note: The rule specifically mentions the phrase *vṛkṣān vanāni* to restrict this change to this instance. However, as Whitney points out: "The counter-examples [e.g. *vṛkṣān vātaḥ* and *vṛkṣān vayāḥ* cited by the CAB], however, are fabricated: no such passages occur in the Atharvan. Nor is the citation of *vanāni* in the rule necessary, although excusable enough: a *v* follows *vṛkṣān* in no other passage of the text, except in xii.1.51, where it is separated from it by an *avasāna*, and so exercises upon it no euphonic influence." In the example above, the *n* is changed to a *visarjanīya*, which is subsequently deleted, and the preceding vowel is nasalized. This is also a type of sandhi which is not attested in the classical language.

चतुराध्यायीभाष्य - वृक्षाँ वनानीति वकारे नकारस्य विसर्जनीयो भवति । 'वृक्षाँ वनानि सं चर' (अ.वे. ६.४५.१)। सोपपदस्य ग्रहणमे(H, N: मै)तावत्त्वार्थम् । इह मा भूत्। 'वृक्षान् वातो वृक्षान् वयाः' (not in AV)।

२.१.२९. नाम्युपधस्य रेफ ऋतूँरुत्सृजते वशीत्येवमादीनाम् ।

Whitney (2.29): °मादीनास्. D, J, K, M, Nb, O, P: Daṇḍa after रेफः. E, F: place ऽ after रेफ.

Translation: [The final *n*], preceded by a *nāmin* [i.e. any vowel other than *a* or *ā*], is changed to *r*, in the passages *ṛtūn utsṛjate vaśī* etc.

Note: Whitney criticizes the formulation: "The Prātiśākhya is to be reprehended here for not treating the cases to which this rule applies in the same manner as those coming under the preceding rules, by prescribing the conversion of *n* into *visarjanīya*, and leaving it for rule 42 (= CA 2.2.2), below, to change the latter into *r*."

चतुराध्यायीभाष्य - नाम्युपधस्य नकारस्य रेफो भवति । ऋतूंरुत्सृजते वशीत्येवमादीनाम् । 'ऋतूँरुत्सृंजते वशी' (अ.वे. ६.३६.२)। 'मो षु पणींरभि' (अ.वे. ५.११.७)। 'दस्यूँरुत बोधि' (अ.वे. ४.३२.६)।

Note: The *gaṇa* referred to in this CA rule has been fully listed by the APR (197), and out of a total of eight instances listed therein, the CAB quotes the first three in the same order. Whitney points out that there are nine cases of this rule in the text of the Atharvan. The APR lists *ṛtū̃r anyaḥ* (AV 14.1.23), which is excluded in Whitney's listing. In this case, the Whitney-Roth text actually agrees with the APR. Whitney additionally lists 6.61.2 and 7.81.1, which are excluded by the APR listing. It is likely that the scope of this sandhi slightly increased after the listing of the APR was made.

२.१.३०. न समैरयन्तादीनाम् ।

Whitney (2.30). A, B, D: °तामित्येवमादीनाम्.

Translation: [The change of *n* taught in the preceding rules to *visarjanīya* or *r*] does not take place in cases such as *sam airayan tām*.

चतुराध्यायीभाष्य - न समैरयन्तादीनां नकारस्य यत्प्राप्तं तद्भवति । 'समैरयन्तां व्यूर्णुवन्तु' (अ.वे. १.११.२)। 'कुलपा राजन् ताम् उं ते' (अ.वे. १.१४.३)। 'अस्मिन् तिंष्ठतु याः' (अ.वे. १.१५.२)।

Note: Whitney, referring to these three examples, says: "The three happen to be typical examples of the three principal classes of cases - verbal forms, vocatives, and locatives - in which we should not expect to see the sibilant inserted, since the forms did not originally end in a sibilant." Expansion of the insertion of a sibilant in these cases can then be dated to a post-AV period. On rule CA (2.1.26 = Whitney 2.26), Whitney offers a 'complete list of exceptions' in a footnote. The APR (198) follows a different strategy. Instead of formulating a *gaṇa* of exceptions, it lists cases where the final *n* is preceded by a short vowel and followed by *t*, where the *n* changes to a *visarjanīya*.

After providing a listing of such cases, the APR says: इत्यतोऽन्यत्र ह्रस्वोपधस्य तवर्गे प्रकृत्या. This makes it difficult to directly compare Whitney's data with those offered by the APR.

Regarding the expression समैरयन्तादीनाम्, Whitney (*AV Transl*, Vol. I., p. 11) points out the ambiguity involved in the form of the citation: "The word (*tam* or *tāṃ*) and its predecessor are quoted in the Prāt. (ii.30 = CA 2.1.30), ... but the form of the quotation (*samairayantādīnām*) prevents our seeing whether its authors read *tā́m* or *tám;* the comm. gives *tām.*"

२.१.३१. मकारस्य स्पर्शे परसस्थानः ।

Whitney (2.31). H, J, M, Na, P: °सःस्थानः. A, B: मकारस्पर्शे°.

Translation: [A final] *m*, before a stop, is changed to a consonant which has the same point of articulation as the following [stop].

Note: In conjunction with CA (1.4.4: आन्तर्येण वृत्तिः), this rule changes the final *m* to a nasal consonant of the same point of articulation as the following stop. The CAB on CA (1.4.4) cites our present rule as an example where the principle of maximal featural proximity enunciated in CA (1.4.4) must apply. Thus, the present rule changes the word-final *m* to *ṅ*, *ñ*, *ṇ*, *n*, or *m*, depending upon which stop follows *m*. We should note that Pāṇini allows the change of *m* to an *anusvāra* and its maintenance before any consonant as an option to its change to a nasal homorganic with the following stop. Pāṇini also allows the change of *m* to nasal *ỹ*, *ṽ*, or *l̃*, before *y*, *v*, and *l*. CA (2.1.35) makes allowance for only *l̃*.

चतुराध्यायीभाष्य - मकारस्य परसस्थानो (H, N: परःस्थानो) भवति स्पर्शे परतः । 'सङ्कांशयामि वहतुम्' (अ.वे. १४.२.१२)। 'उदागांञ्जीवः' (अ.वे. १४.२.४४)। 'तण्डयमानम्' (not in Vedic texts)। 'सन्नस्तेभिः' (अ.वे. २.३५.२)। 'सन्तैः पशुभिः' (अ.वे. ४.३६.५)। 'सन्नष्टेन' (अ.वे. ७.९.४)। 'सन्त्वयैंधिषीमहि' (अ.वे. १४.२.१७)। 'मा त्वां वृक्षः सम्बांधिष्ट' (अ.वे. १८.२.२५)। शान्तस्तान्नान्तः (H,

N: न्नोदात्तः)पदे तवर्गे प्रकृत्या । 'दुर्णाम्नीः सर्वाः' (अ.वे. ४.१७.५)।

Note: Whitney reads the ms. H: शान्तस्तान्नेदान्तःपदे तवर्गे प्रकृत्या. He is unable to read the first half, which he suspects to be an additional citation, and translates the second half as: "in the interior of a word, *m* remains unchanged before a dental." The manuscripts do not exactly support Whitney's reading, though the passage still remains largely corrupt. I suggest the following emendation: शान्तस्तान्नान्तःपदे तवर्गे प्रकृत्या. I take the last portion of this passage exactly in the same way as done by Whitney, i.e. अन्तःपदे तवर्गे प्रकृत्या. The first two expressions, i.e. *śāntaḥ* and *tānna*, may be taken to illustrate the rule 2.1.31. The expression *śāntaḥ*, AV (3.21.9), illustrates the change of *m* to *n*, with the etymology from √*śam-ta*, and the expression *tānna*, AV (5.18.7), stands for *tām-na.*

Is the expression *sannaṣṭena* (AV, 7.9.4) a misinterpretation for *saṃnas-tena* ? On *sannastebhiḥ* in AV (2.35.2), Whitney (*AV Transl.* Vol.I., p. 80) says: "All the *saṃhitā*-mss. make the absurd combination *naṣṭébhiḥ* in d, seeming to have in mind the participle *naṣṭá;* SSP. retains *naṣṭébhis* in his text, while ours emends to *nas tebhiḥ*, as given in the comment to Prāt. ii.31 (= CA 2.1.31)."

२.१.३२. अन्तस्थोष्मसु लोपः ।

Whitney (2.32). E, F, Nb: No Visarga after लोप.

Translation: Before semi-vowels and spirants, [the word-final *m* is] deleted.

Note: After deleting the *m* before semi-vowels and spirants, the previous vowel is nasalized by CA (1.3.5: नकारमकारयोर्लोपे पूर्वस्यानुनासिकः). The CA procedure differs from Pāṇini in that Pāṇini allows the change of *m* to nasal *ỹ*, *ṽ*, *or l̃*, before *y*, *v*, and *l*. The CA (2.1.35) makes allowance for only *l̃*. Before any consonant, Pāṇini also allows the maintenance of an *anusvāra*. The *anusvāra* is left out of consideration by the CA in favor of the nasalized vowel. Whitney on this rule surveys the variegated practice of the Prātiśākhyas.

चतुराध्यायीभाष्य - अन्तस्थोष्मसु परतः मकारस्य लोपो भवति । 'वृक्षँ यद्गावः' (अ.वे. १.२.३)। 'पितरँ वरुंणम्'

(अ.वे. १.३.३)। ‘सँ॒रा॒धय॑न्त॒ः सधु॑रा॒ः’ (अ.वे. ३.३०.५)। ‘परा॒द्य दे॒वा वृ॑जि॒नँ शृ॑णन्तु’ (अ.वे. ८.३.१४)। ‘न्यो॒ष(H, N: ए)तँ ह॒तम्’ (अ.वे. ८.४.१)। ‘सँ सुभू॑त्या’ (अ.वे. ३.१४.१)। ‘भवसि सँ समृ॑द्ध्या’ (अ.वे. १२.३.२१)।

Note: Whitney is undoubtedly right in saying that this deletion of *m* carries with it the nasalization of the preceding vowel. However, both the manuscripts simply show the *anusvāra* where one would expect a nasal vowel.

२.१.३३. ऊष्मस्वेवान्तःपदे ।

Whitney (2.33). A, B, D, O: उ° for ऊ°.

Translation: Within the same word, [the *m* is deleted] only before spirants.

Note: After the deletion of *m*, the preceding vowel is nasalized by CA (1.3.5: नकारमकारयोर्लोपे पूर्वस्यानुनासिकः).

चतुराध्यायीभाष्य - ऊष्मस्वेव अन्तःपदे मकारस्य लोपो भवति । ‘द्वे च॑ मे विँश॒तिश्च॑’ (अ.वे. ५.१५.२)। ‘ति॒स्रश्च॑ मे त्रिँ॒शच्च॑’ (अ.वे. ५.१५.३)। ‘चत॑स्रश्च मे चत्वा॒रिँशच्च॑’ (अ.वे. ५.१५.४)। ‘पुमा॑न् पुँ॒सः’ (अ.वे. ३.६.१)। ‘तत्र॑ पुँ॒सु(H, N: स)व॑नम्’ (अ.वे. ६.११.१)। ऊष्मस्वेवेति किमर्थम् । ‘पति॒र्यः प्र॑तिका॒म्य॑ः’ (अ.वे. २.३६.८)।

Note: In all the above examples, the manuscripts simply show *anusvāras* where the rule stipulates deletion of *m* and the subsequent nasalization of the preceding vowels. The commentary cites only one counter-example: *pratikāmyaḥ* (AV 2.36.8). Whitney points out: "Instances of *m* before *r* in like position would not be hard to give - e.g. *tāmradhūmrāḥ* (x.2.11) - but it is found before *l* only in root syllables, as in *malimlucam* (viii.6.2), and before *v* only in the case which forms the subject of rule 37 (= CA 2.1.37), below." Whitney also appropriately points out that "this rule and the next concern matters with which the Prātiśākhya properly has no concern," because they deal with internal sandhis which are not altered during the transformations between the Padapāṭha and the Saṃhitāpāṭha.

२.१.३४. नकारस्य च ।

Whitney (2.34).

Translation: Also, *n* [is deleted before sibilants within a given word].

Note: This rule, like the previous rule, also deals with what may be strictly called an internal sandhi, which one would encounter only in the derivation of a given word, rather than in transformations between the Padapāṭha and the Saṃhitāpāṭha. In that sense, as Whitney points out, these rules exceed the strictly defined scope of a Prātiśākhya.

Interestingly, these rules provide us some insight into the grammatical derivations of words as understood by the CA. For instance, this rule assumes that a form like *parū̃ṣi* is derived from *parūnṣi*, while the previous rule assumes that a form like *vĩśati* is derived from *vimśati*. For instance, in the derivation of the form *parū̃ṣi*, Pāṇini starts with *parus+i*. Then, P.7.1.72 (नपुंसकस्य झलचः) prescribes the augment *nUM*, which goes after the *u* of *parus*, leading to *paruns+i*. The CA seems to assume a somewhat similar process.

चतुराध्यायीभाष्य - नकारस्य ऊष्मस्वेव अन्तःपदे लोपो भवति । 'परूँषि यस्यं सम्भाराः' (अ.वे. ९.६.१)। 'यजूँषि होत्रां ब्रूमः' (अ.वे. ११.६.१४)। 'अत्तो(N: त्रा) हवीँषि' (अ.वे. १८.३.४४)। ऊष्मस्वेवेत्येव । 'तौदी नामांसि कन्यां' (अ.वे. १०.४.२४)।

Note: Again the manuscripts show merely the *anusvāra*, where one would expect to find a nasalized vowel.

२.१.३५. उभयोर्लकारे लकारोऽनुनासिकः ।

Whitney (2.35). A, B, D, J: °भकारो° for °लकारो°.

Translation: Both [i.e. *m* and *n*] are changed to a nasal *l̃* before an *l*.

Note: Unlike Pāṇini, the CA does not make provision for *ỹ* and *ṽ* for *m* before *y* and *v*.

चतुराध्यायीभाष्य - उभयोः नकारमकारयोः लकारे परतः लकारः अनुनासिको भवति । 'तल्ँलोकम्' (अ.वे. ३.२८.५)। 'अविल्ँल्लोकेन' (अ.वे. ३.२९.३)। 'प्रति(H, N: ती)-माल्ँलोकाः' (अ.वे. १८.४.५)। 'दुर्गन्धील्ँल्लोहितास्यान्' (अ.वे. ८.६.१२)। 'सर्वाल्ँल्लोकान्' (अ.वे. ४.३८.५)।

Note: Referring to the citation from AV (18.4.5), Whitney (*AV Transl*. Vol.II., p. 873) says: "The reading and sense at the beginning of **c** are very doubtful; the *pada*-mss. all give *prati-mā́m*, as if it were accustive of *pratimā́;* most of the *saṃhitā*-mss. have *pratīmā́m* (our Bs. has *pratímā́m* ⌊!⌋, and P.M. *pratimā́m;* T. has *pratīmám*), and it is quoted in the comment to the Prāt. (ii.35 = CA 2.1.35 : so the ms.) as the same ⌊that is, I presume, in the form *pratīmām*⌋. SPP. emends to *prátī' mā́m*, since, with his usual disregard of the accent, the comm. so reads, explaining *imām* as referring to *pṛthivīm;* our edition has *pratimā́m*, with the majority of our earlier mss. The translation implies *práti mā́m*, simply on account of superior intelligibility; doubtless the true AV. reading is *pratīmā́m*." We should note that the reading found in both the mss. of the CAB actually agrees with Whitney's final conclusion.

२.१.३६. न समो राजतौ ।

Whitney (2.36).

Translation: [The *m*] of *sam* is not [deleted] before [the *r* of the root] *rāj*.

चतुराध्यायीभाष्य - न सम् इत्यस्य मकारस्य राजतौ परतः यत्प्राप्तं तद्भवति । 'सम्राडेको वि राजति' (अ.वे. ६.३६.३)। 'सम्राज्ञ्येधि श्वशुरेषु सम्राज्ञ्युत देवृषु । ननान्दुः(H, N: न्दूषु) सम्राज्ञ्येधि सम्राज्ञ्युत श्वश्र्वाः' (अ.वे. १४.१.४४)।

Note: A possible counter-example to this rule may be the form *saṃ-[sā?]rādhayantaḥ* in AV (3.30.5).

Both the manuscripts of the commentary show the *anusvāra* in addition to retaining the *m*. As the rule goes, there is no place for an *anusvāra* in these examples.

२.१.३७. सन्ध्ये च वकारे ।

Whitney (2.37). A, B (corr), K, P: संध्ये वकारे. B (orig), D, M: °चकारे. J: °चाकारे.

> **Translation:** Also before *v* resulting from a sandhi, [the *m* is not deleted].

> ***चतुराध्यायीभाष्य*** - न सम् इत्यस्य मकारस्य यत्प्राप्तं तद्भवति संध्ये वकारे परतः । 'सम्वास्नाहं आस्यम्' (अ.वे. ६.५६.३)।

Note: Here, the sequence *sam v āsnā* is derived by the change of *u* to *v* before the following *ā*. The Mss H adds *ūṃ iti* at the end.

२.१.३८. वर्गविपर्यये स्फोटनः पूर्वेण चेद्विरामः ।

Whitney (2.38). A, B, D, K, P(corr): place Daṇḍa after स्फोटनः, and treat the rest as a separate Sūtra. Ha, Na: °स्फोष्टनः.

> **Translation:** [In a stop+stop combination], in the reverse order of the stop-series [i.e. reverse of the normal order: *k*-series, *c*-series, *ṭ*-series, *t*-series, and the *p*-series], there is an insertion of a *sphoṭana* [i.e. a vocalic particle of one-eighth mora length, between the stops], if the first [stop of the combination] occurs at the end [of a *pada*].

Note: The term *sphoṭana* has been discussed at length in the Note to CA (1.4.12: तदेव स्फोटनः). Referring to *sphoṭana*, Allen (1953: 74) says: "This would appear to indicate a type of *svarabhakti*, whether voiced or voiceless, the infinitesimal duration of which is suggested by the specification of a value 1/8 *a*, in fact a minimal audible release. The mechanism of the feature referred to is perhaps the release of the front closure during the formation but before the completion of the back closure, resulting in the momentary outflow of an air-stream attenuated by the back constriction."

I agree with Whitney that the term *viparyaya* refers to not just 'difference of the series,' but to their reverse order, i.e. where a stop is followed by another stop belonging to a series pronounced farther back on the oral track. All the instances offered by the commentary fit this pattern: *ṭ+k*, *t+k*, *b+k*, and *d+g*. Whitney says: "That the Hindu theory allows *sphoṭana* in the combination of the phrase only in the case two mutes meet in the inverse order of the *vargas* to which they belong has something of arbitrariness in it, yet is not without foundation; for it may be noted, I think, that it is perceptibly harder to change from a contact farther forward in the mouth to one farther back, than to make a like transfer in the contrary direction, without allowing any intervening escape of breath or sound: and the order of the *vargas* follows the advance in the mouth of the place of formation." Allen's explanation given above is not very different from Whitney's.

चतुराध्यायीभाष्य - वर्गाणां विपर्यये स्फोटनः संध्यो भवति पूर्वेण चेद्विरामो भवति । 'वषट्कारेण' (अ.वे. ५.२६.१२)। 'अवत्कम्' (अ.वे. २.३.१)। 'एजत्काः' (अ.वे. ५.२३.७)। 'त्रिष्टुब्गांयत्री' (अ.वे. १८.२.६)। 'यद्गांयत्रे' (अ.वे. ९.१०.१)। पूर्वेणेति किमर्थम् । 'क्रमान् को अंस्याः' (अ.वे. ८.९.१०)। विराम इति किमर्थम् । 'वेणोरद्गां इव' (अ.वे. १.२७.३)।

'वर्गाणां विपरीतानां सन्निपाते निबोधत ।
व्यवायी स्फोटनाख्यस्तु यद्गांयत्रे निदर्शनम् ॥'
(source?)

Note: Referring to the citation of AV (1.27.3), Whitney (*AV Transl.* Vol.I., p. 28) says that Sāyaṇa's reading is *udgās* for *adgās* as given by the CAB, and that neither word is quotable from elsewhere.

For Whitney's comment on *avatkám*, see the Note on CA (1.4.12).

Whitney criticizes the interpretation of the term *pūrveṇa* assumed by the CAB. For the commentary, the term *pūrva* 'previous,' seems to mean non-final, i.e. non-nasal. The term *pūrva* simply refers to the earlier member in a consonant-cluster. The commentary seems to exclude the combinations of nasals with non-nasals from the occurrence of *sphoṭana*. Whitney suggests that these must be included, and offers the following examples: *keśān+*

khādantaḥ (AV 5.19.3), *vidvān+gandharvaḥ* (AV 2.1.2), and *devān+ghṛtavatā* (AV 3.10.11). Whitney supports his interpretation by pointing out that "the Vāj. Pr. makes no such exception of the nasals."

२.१.३९. न टवर्गस्य चवर्गे कालविप्रकर्षस्त्वत्र भवति तमाहुः कर्षण इति ।

Whitney (2.39). A, B, D, M: न टवर्ग्रस्य चवर्ग्रे ... भवति । तमाहुः कर्षण इति ॥. P also divides the rule in the same way. Ha, Na: °र्षस्तत्र. I: 39.

Translation: There is [no insertion of a *sphoṭana*] when a stop of the *ṭ*-series is followed by a stop of the *c*-series. However, here there is a prolongation of time [needed to pronounce the cluster], and that [prolongation] is called *karṣaṇa* [i.e. 'dragging'].

Note: The term *karṣaṇa* is not met with in the phonetic literature elsewhere. Whitney remarks: "It is easy to see the physical ground of this exception to the rule prescribing *sphoṭana.* The same close relationship with respect to place of utterance which causes the final palatal to pass often into a lingual instead of reverting to the guttural out of which it originally grew, causes the lingual, in coming before the palatal, to virtually double it only. The transfer of position of the organs is too slight and easy to necessitate the emission of an intervening sound." Also see Allen (1953: 74-75). Perhaps, the CA needs an interpretation different from the one offered by Whitney. The extension of duration (*kālaviprakarṣa*) in this case is explainable by referring to the fact that the retroflex stops require the curling of one's tongue and touching the top of the oral cavity with the underside of the tip of the tongue. On the other hand, the pronunciation of the palatal stops requires touching the *tālu* by the middle of the tongue. Making a switch from the one to the other obviously involves a major rearrangement of the articulatory organs. The reason that there is no *sphoṭana* is that there is no discontinuity of the contact of the tongue-tip moving from the retroflex to palatal position, and hence no intermediate release of breath.

चतुराध्यायीभाष्य - न टवर्गस्य चवर्गे स्फोटनः संध्यो भवति । कालविप्रकर्षस्त्वत्र भवति तमाहुः कर्षण इति ।

'षट् चेमाः' (अ.वे. ४.२०.२)। 'षट् च मे षष्टिश्च' (अ.वे. ५.१५.६)। 'षड् जाता' (अ.वे. ८.९.१६)।

इति द्वितीयाध्यायस्य प्रथमः पादः ।

C, E, F, H, N: द्वितीयस्य प्रथमः पादः. A, B, D, M, P: प्रथमः पादः. I, J: इति द्वितीयाध्यायस्य प्रथमः पादः. O: च. द्वितीयस्य प्रथमः पादः ॥ सूत्राणि ॥ ३९ ॥

चतुराध्यायीभाष्य **-** द्वितीयस्य प्रथमः पादः ॥

॥ द्वितीयोऽध्यायः ॥
॥ द्वितीयः पादः ॥

२.२.१. विसर्जनीयस्य परसस्थानोऽघोषे ।

Whitney (2.40). A, B, D, Ha, J, M, Na, P: °सःस्थानो°. O: °नोपोषे.

Translation: The *visarjanīya* [= *ḥ*], before a voiceless [consonant], is changed to a [maximally similar consonant] which has the same point of articulation as the following [voiceless consonant].

Note: This rule clearly works in conjunction with CA (1.4.4: आन्तर्येण वृत्तिः) in ensuring that of all possible sounds which share the same point of articulation as the following voiceless consonant, only the consonant which is maximally similar with a *visarjanīya* will be substituted. The CAB on CA (1.4.4) cites the present rule as an illustration for the use of the general principle of finding a substitute which is maximally similar to the original. For instance, in a case like *yaḥ+ca*, the possible substitutes include all the sounds which share the same point of articulation as *c*, i.e. *i*-vowels, *e*, *c*-series, and *ś*. Of all these possible substitutes, CA (1.4.4) will permit only *ś* to replace *ḥ* in the above example, because *ś* is maximally similar to *ḥ*, i.e. it is voiceless and a spirant. Thus, the above rule predicts that the *ḥ* becomes a *jihvāmūlīya*, i.e. *ẖ*, before *k*, and *kh;* it becomes *ś* before *c*, *ch*, and *ś*; it becomes *ṣ* before *ṭ*, *ṭh*, and *ṣ*; it becomes *s* before *t*, *th*, and *s*; and it becomes *upadhmānīya*, i.e. *ẖ*, before *p*, and *ph*.

Whitney notes that "The theory of the Prātiśākhya, however, is not at all the practice of the manuscripts, and the latter, rather than the former, has been followed by us in the printed text." Other editions of the AV also follow the same practice. Whitney points out that none of the AV manuscripts distinguish the *jihvāmūlīya* and the *upadhmānīya* from the *visarjanīya*, and approvingly he says: "as we cannot but think, with much reason: since the division of this indistinct and indefinite sound into three different kinds of indefiniteness savors strongly of an over-refinement of analysis." On the one hand, Whitney's discussion is suggestive of the distinction of phonemic versus allophonic sounds as it developed later in linguistics. On the other hand, it is also indicative of the emphasis he put on the written versus oral comprehension of the text of the AV, and the fact that the texts like CA were not aimed at describing the practice of writing, but at the accurate pronunciation of the Vedic texts. The best Vedic recitation even today distinguishes between these three sounds, though they are not represented in the manuscripts. For a critique of Whitney's views, see: Allen (1953: 50).

While Whitney concentrated primarily on the written evidence, Allen (1953: 51) offers a historical understanding which bridges the early descriptions of pronunciation and the later practice of writing: "In later, though still ancient, times there appears to have been a tendency for *-ḥ* to extend its usage to contexts other than in pausa. The earliest of these extensions was to the position before the initial fricatives *ś-*, *ṣ-*, *s-*, where it replaced the homorganic final *-ś*, *-ṣ*, *-s* (*indraś śūraḥ* > *indraḥ śuraḥ*, etc.). This practice was then extended to the position before the velar and labial voiceless stops: in connexion with this innovation we find mentioned the names of Āgniveśya, Vālmīki, Śākalya, and the Mādhyandina school, whilst the ancient grammarian Śākaṭāyana is quoted as holding to the more conservative practice. These changes have been generally accepted so far as the writing of Sanskrit is concerned, and A.H. Fry in his article 'A Phonemic Interpretation of Visarga' has suggested that the spread of *-ḥ* was due to the writers of Classical Sanskrit 'operating with a phonemic orthography'. Though the term 'orthography' once again begs the vexed question of writing, it is possible that this extension had a phonological rather than a phonetic basis." A history of the actual recitational practice is difficult to reconstruct, though occasionally one does come across reciters who exhibit clear differences between the pronunciation of these sounds. Therefore, conclusions based solely on manuscript material are not an appropriate reflection of the recitational practice. Whitney provides a detailed survey of the views of different Prātiśākhyas in his comments.

चतुराध्यायीभाष्य - विसर्जनीयस्य परसस्थानो भवति अघोषे । कवर्गे । 'अन्तःकोषमिंव' (अ.वे. १.१४.४)। चवर्गे । 'यश्चं द्विषन्' (अ.वे. १.१९.४)। टवर्गे । 'वृक्ष-ष्टीकते' (not in Vedic texts)। तवर्गे । 'मयंस्तोकेभ्यंः' (अ.वे. १.१३.२)। 'अविंस्तोकानि' (अ.वे. ५.१९.२)। 'बल्हिंकान् वा परस्तराम्' (अ.वे. ५.२२.७)। 'युजंस्तुजे जनांः' (अ.वे. ६.३३.१)। 'यथा पसंस्तायादरम्' (अ.वे. ६.७२.२)। 'प्रावंन्तु नस्तुजये' (अ.वे. ७.४९.१)। 'त्रय-

स्त्रिंशेन जगंती' (अ.वे. ८.९.२०)। 'मखस्तंविष्यतें' (अ.वे. १८.१.२३)। पवर्गे । 'ततः परि प्रजांतेन' (अ.वे. ६.८९.-१)। सकारे । 'वातंभ्रजास्स्तनयंन्' (अ.वे. १.१२.१)। 'अरुस्स्राणं(H: णा, N: णो)म्' (अ.वे. २.३.३)। 'विव्रंता-स्स्थ(H, N: स्थ)नं' (अ.वे. ३.८.५)। 'अतिं दुर्गास्स्रो(H, N: स्रो)त्याः' (अ.वे. १०.१.१६)।

Note: Whitney rightly says: "before *k* and *kh* it (= *visarjanīya*) becomes *jihvāmūlīya*, and, before *p* and *ph*, *upadhmānīya* -- these last two spirants being, as already noticed, clearly implied in this rule, although nowhere referred to by name as belonging to the scheme of spoken sounds recognized by the treatise." The mss. do not orthographically distinguish these two sounds from the *visarjanīya*. Referring to this rule, Surya Kanta (*APR*, *Introduction*, p. 39) says: "The prescription is unmistakable, and must have been carried out by the *Śaunakīyas*. This is not followed by the Vulgate mss., which, instead, drop the visarjanīya altogether before a sibilant followed by a surd or sonant mute, a usage sanctioned by the APr. 80. Compare Vyāsaśikṣā 156 for this against TPr. 9.1., which is ignored by the TS. mss.; thus indicating a hopeless mixture of śākhā variations." Here Surya Kanta is again looking for homogeneous and authentic śākhā manuscripts. However, the kind of change which is advocated by the CA perhaps became so outdated by the time the AV was committed to writing, that even the Śaunakīyas may have disregarded the explicit prescription of their own tradition under the pressure of the more current practice of writing Sanskrit. For such a possible historical development, see: Allen (1953: 51). This possibility cannot be easily discounted. By Surya Kanta's own admission, the APR represents a somewhat later formulation as compared to CA, and it may have impacted the writing of the AV even in the Śaunakīya tradition.

The example वृक्षष्टीकते, which is not attested in a Vedic text, is found in the KV on P.8.2.41 (ष्टुना ष्टुः). It is interesting to note that Surya Kanta does not suggest that this instance belonged to the so-called genuine Śaunakīya recension of the AV which is now supposedly lost.

For a discussion of related textual problems, see Lanman (*AV Transl.* Vol.II., p. 976): "The rationale of the corruption is not hard to see: the hiatus between **c** and **d** being once covered by the fusion of the final of *jambhaya* with the *ā́* of *ā́ stenam*, nothing was easier than to see a form *jambhayās* in the first part of the combination, and then to substitute *téna* for the vastly less common *stenám* or for the meaningless *tenám* (which might be read out of the combination: see Prāt. ii. 40, note); the exigency of the meter occasioned by the blunder with *jambhayās* then made the insertion of *tám* easy. With the Berlin solution of the corruption, the meter is in perfect order." For AV (19.47.8), Whitney-Roth read जम्भया स्तेनं (from assumed *jambhaya ā stenam*), while the VVRI edition reads जम्भयास्तेन तं, with the Padapāṭha: जम्भयाः । तेन । तम्.

२.२.२. स्वरे यकारः ।

Whitney (2.41). C: °शकारः.

Translation: Before a vowel, [a *visarjanīya*, i.e. *ḥ*] is changed to *y*.

Note: Whitney says: "It is very hard to say whether the conversion into *y* is a matter of grammatical theory only, or whether it gives account of an actual process of phonetic transition." For a fuller discussion of this issue, see the Note on CA (2.1.21). For a survey of other Prātiśākhyas, see Whitney on this rule.

The examples as cited in the commentary do not show this change to *y*, but jump to the next stage and delete it, cf. CA (2.1.21).

चतुराध्यायीभाष्य - स्वरे परतः विसर्जनीयस्य यकारो भवति । 'यस्यां उ॒पस्थं उ॒र्व[१॒]न्तरिक्षम्' (अ.वे. ७.६.४)। 'म॒ध्यन्दिंन॒ उद्गांयति' (अ.वे. ९.६.४६)। 'अ॒भि॒पश्यंत ए॒व' (अ.वे. १०.८.२४)। 'सर्वं आपः' (अ.वे. १६.४.६)।

Note: The H reading is *sa āpaḥ* and the N reading is *sarva āpaḥ*. Referring to the former, which was the only reading accessible to Whitney, he says: "perhaps the reading is corrupt, and *va āpaḥ* (iii.13.7) or *na āpaḥ* (xii.1.30) is the passage intended." Now the manuscript N has provided the proper reading *sarva āpaḥ* which is attested in AV (16.4.6).

२.२.३. नाम्युपधस्य रेफः ।

Whitney (2.42).

Translation: [The *visarjanīya*, i.e. *ḥ*], preceded by a *nāmin* [i.e. a vowel other than *a* and *ā*], is changed to *r*, [before a vowel].

चतुराध्यायीभाष्य - नाम्युपधस्य विसर्जनीयस्य स्वरे परतः रेफो भवति । 'अग्निरासींनः' (अ.वे. ९.७.१९)। 'वायुरमित्रांणाम्' (अ.वे. ११.१०.१६)। '°स्याहं मन्योरव ज्यामिंव' (अ.वे. ५.१३.६)। 'तैरमित्रांः' (अ.वे. ५.२१.८)।

२.२.४. घोषवति च ।

Whitney (2.43). A, B, D: °ती°.

Translation: Also, before a voiced [consonant, the *visarjanīya*, preceded by a vowel other than *a* and *ā*, is changed to *r*].

Note: This rule, in conjunction with the preceding rule, raises some questions about the meaning of the term *ghoṣavat*, and why the vowels are not covered by this term. These same questions are also raised by the usage of this term in other rules. For a discussion, see the Note on CA (1.1.5), and Introduction, section **5.11.**

चतुराध्यायीभाष्य - घोषवति परतः नाम्युपधस्य विसर्जनीयस्य स्वरे परतः रेफो भवति । 'तस्यां अग्निर्वत्सः' (अ.वे. ४.३९.२)। 'तस्यां वायुर्वत्सः' (अ.वे. ४.३९.४)। 'अग्नेर्भागः स्थ' (अ.वे. १०.५.७)। 'अरातीयोर्भ्रातृंव्यस्य' (अ.वे. १०.६.१)। 'तैर्मेदिनो अङ्गिंरसः' (अ.वे. १०.६.२०)।

Note: On the preceding rule, and its commentary, Whitney says: "There is here another *lacuna* in the manuscript: immediately upon the citation *tair amitrāḥ* follow *tasyā agnir vatsaḥ* and the other illustrations of the conversion of *visarjanīya* preceded by an alterant vowel into *r* before a sonant consonant, and then follow the words *ghoṣavati ca*, before the rule *āvaḥ* etc. It is evident that the copyist has leaped over the rule *ghoṣavati ca*, together with its own paraphrase, the final repetition of the preceding rule, and perhaps some of the illustrative citations belonging to one or both of them. There is no reason whatever to suppose that anything more than this is omitted, or that any rule is lost altogether." Fortunately, this lacuna is fully made up by the second manuscript, N, now available to me.

२.२.५. आवः करकश्च वि वरबिभरसर्वनाम्नः ।

Whitney (2.44). A, D, Hab, O, P: °विभर°. A, B, D: °म्नाः. Nb, Hb: आवष्क°. P adds a daṇḍa at the end of this rule as a correction.

Translation: [Also, the *visarjanīya*, i.e. *ḥ*, of] *āvaḥ*, *kaḥ*, *akaḥ*, *ca vi vaḥ*, and *abibhaḥ* [is changed to *r*, before a vowel or a voiced consonant], when [these] are not pronominal [expressions].

Note: As Whitney points out, "In this and the following rules, as far as the 49th (= CA 2.2.10) inclusive, are treated the words whose final *visarjanīya* represents an original *r*, and not *s*, and in which, accordingly, the *r* is liable to reappear before a sonant initial, even though *a* or *ā* precede." One should note that the CA itself does not have a notion of an 'original *r*.' The starting point of the rule for the CA is not some abstract derivational or lexical sequence, but the expression as found in the Padapāṭha, i.e. a word as it would appear before pause. The recitational tradition converted the so-called 'original' *r* to a *visarjanīya* before pause, and then this *visarjanīya* became the starting point for our rule. For instance, the CA does not have a rule parallel to P.8.3.15 (खरवसानयोर्विसर्जनीयः) which says: "Before a voiceless consonant (= *khaR*) or a pause (*avasāna*), an *r* is replaced with a *visarjanīya*." The CA rule takes off from where P.8.3.15 leaves a derivation.

Whitney also points out that there is some built-in 'superfluity.' The commentary says that some instances are cited along with a few associated words to avoid generalization and to limit the listing to these specific cases. Whitney says that the final condition added to the rule, i.e. exclusion of pronominal usages achieves the same purpose, and, therefore, there is 'superfluity.'

In all the examples cited by the commentary, except AV (6.81.3), the *visarjanīya* is not followed by either a vowel or a voiced consonant in the Saṃhitāpāṭha. Thus, where would one see the change of *visarjanīya* to *r*? The commentary offers examples of repetition (*parihāra*) of the word concerned with an interposed *iti*. This creates an occasion for the change of *visarjanīya* to *r* before *iti*. Concerning this cited repetition, Whitney makes a very significant observation: "It will be observed that the commentator repeats each word to which the rule applies with *iti* interposed, except in the last case, where the *r* appears in *saṃhitā*. This is in accordance with the usage of the *pada*-text of the Rigveda, but not with that of the Atharvan, which in no single instance performs *parihāra* of a word ending in a *riphita visarjanīya;* and we must accordingly regard the repetitions as taken from the *krama*-text, which would give such a form to the words in question, as standing at the end of a line." He also points to the deviant behavior of the 20th Kāṇḍa: "Excepting in the twentieth book, whose *pada*-text is shown by this and other peculiarities to be merely a putting together of extracts from that of the Rik." The fact that the CA does not note the deviant behavior of the 20th Kāṇḍa probably indicates that the 20th Kāṇḍa was added to the AV after the formation of the CA. The examples cited by the commentary are mostly found among the examples on APR (141).

The CA rule lists instances which show this phenomenon neither in the Saṃhitāpāṭha, nor in the Padapāṭha, but only in the Kramapāṭha. [However, we have *prātar iti* in the Padapāṭha for RV 4.35.7a]. This is nowhere clearly stated in the rule or in the commentary, but is an inference of Whitney. Unfortunately, I have not been able to confirm this practice with modern-day reciters of the AV, none of whom could recite the Krama. I have now found a few manuscripts of the Kramapāṭha and Jaṭāpāṭha for the ŚAV, but unfortunately not for the sections containing these instances.

चतुराध्यायीभाष्य - आवः । कः । अकः । च वि वः । हस्तमबिभः । इति असर्वनाम्नो विसर्जनीयस्य रेफो भवति । आवः । 'सुरुचों वेन आंवः' । (क्रम ⇒) 'आवरित्यावः' (अ.वे. ४.१.१)। आवः कः । 'सरस्वति(H, N: ती) तमिह धातवे कः' । (क्रम ⇒) 'करिति कः' (अ.वे. ७.१०.१)। करकः । 'अशं निर्ऋत्या अकः' । (क्रम ⇒) 'अकरित्यकः' (अ.वे. २.२५.१)। अकश्च वि वः । 'सतश्च योनिमसतश्च वि वः' । (क्रम ⇒) 'वरिति वः' (अ.वे. ४.१.१)। सोपपदग्रहणमेतावत्त्वार्थम् । च वि वरबिभः । 'यं परिहस्तमबिंभरदितिः पुत्रकाम्या' (अ.वे. ६.८१.३)। असर्वनाम्न इति किमर्थम् । 'हिरण्यवर्णा अतृपं यदा वः' । (क्रम

⇒) 'व इति वः' (अ.वे. ३.१३.६)। 'यत्रेदं वेशयामि वः' (अ.वे. ३.१३.७)।

२.२.६. द्वार्वारिति ।

Whitney (2.45).

Translation: [Also, the *visarjanīya* of the forms] *dvāḥ* and *vāḥ* [is changed to *r*, before a vowel or a voiced consonant].

Note: Since these expressions are not followed by a vowel or a voiced consonant either in the Saṃhitāpāṭha or the Padapāṭha, Whitney makes a reasonable assumption that the citations द्वारिति द्वाः and वारिति वाः refer to the practice of the Kramapāṭha. This is comparable with the situation of the examples of the previous rule. Thus, as with the previous rule, we must assume that the listing here was meant to cover the practice of the Kramapāṭha.

चतुराध्यायीभाष्य - द्वार्वारिति विसर्जनीयस्य रेफो भवति । 'प्रथमा द्वाः' । (क्रम ⇒) 'द्वारिति द्वाः' (अ.वे. ९.३.२२)। 'तस्माद्वार्नाम' (अ.वे. ३.१३.३)। 'दिव्यं घृतं वाः'। (क्रम ⇒) 'वारिति वाः' (अ.वे. १८.१.३२)।

२.२.७. अजहातेरहाः ।

Whitney (2.46). D, Ha, K, M (corr), P: °ह्यतेरहाः. J, M (orig): °ह्येतेरहाः.

Translation: [The *visarjanīya*, i.e. *ḥ*, of the form] *ahāḥ* [is also changed to *r* before a vowel or a voiced consonant], except if it is from the root √*hā*.

चतुराध्यायीभाष्य - अहारिति विसर्जनीयस्य रेफो भवति । 'इन्द्रस्तान्पर्यहार्दाम्ना' (अ.वे. ६.१०३.२, ३)। 'इह राष्ट्रमाहाः' (अ.वे. १३.१.४)।[should add: (क्रम ⇒) 'अहारित्यहाः' ।] 'अग्निष्टदाहाः' ('अग्निष्टदाहार्निर्ऋतेः,'

अ.वे. ७.५३.३)। 'अहारित्यहाः' [? no place for *parihāra* for *ahāḥ* in AV 7.53.3)। अजहातेरिति किमर्थम् । 'अहा अरातिम्' (अ.वे. २.१०.७)।

Note: Whitney suggests an alternative formulation for this rule: "An equivalent and, one would think, preferable form for this rule would have been *harater ahāḥ*, '*ahāḥ* when coming from the root *har* (*hṛ*)." Whitney's suggestion has the merit of brevity. The commentary of [pseudo-]Sāyaṇa, on AV (6. 103.2-3, and 7.53.3) paraphrases the form *āhāḥ* with root *hṛ*, and AV (13.1.5) refers back to the form *āhāḥ* in (13.1.4) with *ā ahārṣīt*. Thus, all the three examples are from the root *hṛ* (*harati*).

With the examples cited for this rule, it is clear that the rule applies to a few cases in the Saṃhitāpāṭha such as AV (6.103.2, 3) and (7.53.3); and that there is a counter-example from the Saṃhitāpāṭha, i.e. AV (2.10.7). The instance in AV (13.1.4) must be assumed as a case of Kramapāṭha.

Referring to the passage 'इह राष्ट्रमाहाः' (अ.वे. १३.१.४)। 'अग्निष्टदाहाः' (अ.वे. ७.५३.३)। (क्रम ⇒) 'अहारित्यहाः' in the CAB, Whitney makes an important observation: "*iha rāṣtram ā 'hāḥ* (xiii.1.4: the commentator, or the copyist, omits to add *ahār ity ahāḥ*), and *agniṣ ṭad ā 'hāḥ* (vii.53.3: here is added *ahār ity ahāḥ*, but it is out of place, the word not standing in pausa; perhaps the *parihāra* has slipped away from its proper place after the preceding citation to this: but then the word following *ahāḥ* should also have been quoted in the last passage, and it should read *agniṣ ṭad ā 'hār nirṛteḥ*)." The kind of ill-arrangement of the text of the commentary referred to by Whitney must have taken place at a relatively early period, since it is shared by both the available manuscripts, H and N.

Referring to AV (2.10.7), Whitney says: "The comment to Prāt. ii.46 (= CA 2.2.7) quotes *ahās* in this verse as not *ahār*, i.e. as from *hā*, not *hṛ*" (*AV Transl.* Vol.I., p. 52). The commentary of [pseudo-]Sāyaṇa also paraphrases *ahāḥ* in this passage with *ahāsīḥ atyākṣīḥ*.

२.२.८. एकामन्त्रिते रौद्विवचनान्तस्य ।

Whitney (2.47), C, Hbc, N: °रौ°. Other mss. read °रो°. A, B, D: °तै°. A, B: °द्विवचनस्य.

Translation: [Also, the *visarjanīya*, i.e. *ḥ*], belonging to a vocative singular of [a noun] which has a dual form ending in -*rau*, [is changed to *r*, before a vowel or a voiced consonant].

Note: Concerning the formulation of this rule, Whitney makes an important observation: "Here, as in more than one other instance, our treatise shows a greater readiness than the others to avail itself of the help of grammatical categories in constructing its rules: all the other Prātiśākhyas laboriously rehearse in detail, one by one, the words which are here disposed of as a class, in one brief rule." The procedure is also to be contrasted with Pāṇini. For Pāṇini, it is not the case that one takes the forms of words as they would appear before pause, and then combine them by removing the pause. Certain forms may lexically or derivationally end in *r*. Such *r*-final forms may then be followed either by pause or by other words beginning with vowels or consonants. P.8.3.15 (खरवसानयोर्विसर्जनीयः) says that a final *r* is changed to a *visarjanīya* before voiceless consonants, or before pause. Thus, by exclusion, it is left unchanged before vowels and voiced consonants. Thus, Pāṇini neither needs, nor has, a rule which changes the word-final (pre-pausal) *visarjanīya* to *r* in some cases, after removal of that pause. The construction of the Saṃhitāpāṭha from the Padapāṭha essentially amounts to the removal of pause between the separated items.

चतुराध्यायीभाष्य - रौद्विवचनान्तं यस्यामन्त्रितस्य तस्य रौद्विवचनान्तस्य यदेकवचनं तस्मिन् एकामन्त्रिते रौद्विवचनान्तस्य विसर्जनीयस्य रेफो भवति । 'धातर्देहि' (not in AV) । 'सवितर्देहि' (not in AV) । 'पुनर्देहि' (अ.वे. १८.३.७०) । 'भूमें मातर्नि धेहि' (अ.वे. १२.१.६३) । 'त्वचंमेतां विंशस्तः' । (क्रम ⇒) 'विशस्तरिति विशस्तः' (अ.वे. ९.५.४) । एकामन्त्रितमिति किमर्थम् । 'दैवा (H, N: व्या) होतांर ऊर्ध्वम्' (अ.वे. ५.२७.९) । रौद्विवचनान्तस्येति किमर्थम् । 'तविषस्यं प्रचेतः' । (क्रम ⇒) 'प्रचेत इति प्रचेतः' (अ.वे. ४.३२.५) । प्रचेतसौ द्विवचनान्तम् ।

Note: The example(s) धातर्देहि and सवितर्देहि are not found in the Vulgate of the ŚAV. Whitney rightly points out that पुनर्देहि belongs properly under the next rule. Whitney first makes a suggestion: "but possibly the three phrases form a single passage together, and are a genuine citation from some other text." Surya Kanta (*APR*, *Introduction*, p. 40), carrying Whitney's suggestion forward, construes these three to be part of a single passage suggests that this may have occurred in the genuine Śaunakīya recension of the AV, and that the Vulgate is not the genuine Śaunakīya recension. In any case, there is no trace of these in any known Vedic text. One finds several instances of धाता दधातु in AV, e.g. AV (7.17.1-3), and it is possible that the commentator created the example धातर्देहि from such associations. An actual instance धातरीशांनः is found in AV (7.18.1).

२.२.९. अन्तःपुनःप्रातःसनुतःस्वरव्ययानाम् ।

Whitney (2.48). O: अंतः । पुनः । प्रातः । सनुतः । स्वरव्ययानां ॥

Translation: [Also, the *visarjanīya*, i.e. *ḥ*] of the indeclinables *antaḥ*, *punaḥ*, *prātaḥ*, *sanutaḥ*, and *svaḥ* [is changed to *r*, before vowels and voiced consonants].

Note: Whitney observes: "The other treatises exclude the noun *ánta* by defining the accent of *antáḥ*, and the Rik Pr. treats *sváḥ* in the same way -- a method which renders necessary considerable additional limitation and explanation." For the Pāṇinian procedure, see the Note on CA (2.2.8).

चतुराध्यायीभाष्य - अन्तःपुनःप्रातःसनुतःस्वरित्येतेषाम् अव्ययानां विसर्जनीयस्य रेफो भवति । अन्तः । 'अन्तर्दावे जुंहुत' (अ.वे. ६.३२.१)। अन्तः । पुनः । 'पुनर्मैत्विंन्द्रियम्' (अ.वे. ७.६७.१)। पुनः । प्रातः । 'प्रातर्भगं पूषणंम्' (अ.वे. ३.१६.१)। प्रातः । सनुतः । 'सनुतर्युंयोतु' (अ.वे. ७.९२.१)। सनुतः । स्वः । 'स्व[१']र्णोऽपं त्वा' (अ.वे. २.५.२)। अव्ययानामिति किमर्थम् । 'यो नः स्वो यो अरंणः सजातः' (अ.वे. १.१९.३)। 'समंग्रः समंन्तः । समग्र इति सम्ऽअग्रः । समंन्तो भूयासम् । समन्त इति सम्ऽअन्तः' (क्रम, संहिता ⇒ 'समंग्रः समंन्तो भूयासम्,' अ.वे. ७.८१.४)।

Note: Whitney's text for AV (2.5.2) does not show the change of *n* to *ṇ*. However, he says (*AV Transl.* Vol.I., 44): "In the third interpolation, SV. combines *svàr ná* and AŚS. ŚŚS. *svàr ṇá;* and the mss. vary between the two; our edition reads the former with the majority of our mss.; SSP. has the latter, with the majority of his."

२.२.१०. स्वर्षाश्च ।

Whitney (2.49). Ha, Na: स्वर्षा च. I: 10. P(orig): धर्षाश्च. P(corr): स्वर्षाश्च.

> **Translation:** Also, [the *visarjanīya*, i.e. *ḥ*, of the word *svaḥ*, in the combination] *svarṣāḥ* (< *svaḥ+sāḥ*).

> ***चतुराध्यायीभाष्य*** - स्वर्षा इति विसर्जनीयस्य रेफो भवति। 'शूषमंग्रि॒यः स्व॒र्षाः' (अ.वे. ५.२.८)। पदग्रहणमघोषार्थम् । संहितायामित्येव । (क्रम ⇒) 'स्व॒ःसा इतिं स्व॒ःऽसाः' ।

Note: The commentary points out that the full expression *svarṣāḥ* is mentioned to indicate that the change of *ḥ* of *svaḥ* to *r* takes place here in spite of the fact that the following consonant is a voiceless spirant. The previous rules make this change only before vowels and voiced consonants. Then, the commentary says that this change takes place only in the Saṃhitāpāṭha. Whitney notes that this implies that the above change does not take place in the Padapāṭha. Since the Padapāṭha actually separates the components *svaḥ* and *sāḥ* from each other, the item *svaḥ* is in fact followed by a pause, rather than by *sāḥ*. Therefore, Whitney comments: "This last is rather a gratuitous piece of information." Actually, the commentary is quoting not the Padapāṭha, but the *parihāra* or repetition of a final word interposed with *iti* as it appears in the Kramapāṭha. In the Kramapāṭha, the second time the word appears, its components are separated from each other, but not when it appears the first time. However, even in the first occurrence, changes like *s*>*ṣ* are restored, cf. CA (4.3.6: क्रमे परेण विगृह्यात्) and the commentary CAB on this rule. Thus, in the *parihāra* for *svarṣāḥ*, we do not get *svarṣāḥ* in either repetition. The first time the word is given, *svaḥ* is not separated from *sāḥ*, and yet *ḥ* is not changed to *r*, nor is *s* changed to *ṣ*. Thus, the comment of the CAB seems to have a proper place, and need not be discarded following Whitney. This instance of Krama is now attested from AV 20.11.4 in the BORI ms. 133/1879-80, folio 6.

Another point one should note is that the term *saṃhitā* in the commentary is used in the sense of Saṃhitāpāṭha, rather than its normal later meaning of sandhi or absence of separation. In the *parihāra*, the word is first given as *svaḥsāḥ*. Here, by classical standards, we have an occasion for sandhi, since there is no separation of components. However, this is not the same thing as the Saṃhitāpāṭha.

२.२.११. अहर्नपुंसकम् ।

Whitney (2.50). Ha, Na: no Repha.

Translation: [Also, the *visarjanīya*, i.e. *ḥ*, of] the word *ahaḥ*, if neuter, [is changed to *r*, before vowels and voiced consonants].

चतुराध्यायीभाष्य - अहरिति विसर्जनीयस्य रेफो भवति नपुंसकं चेद्भवति । 'यदहंरहरभिगच्छांमि' (अ.वे. १६.७.११)। 'अहर्मात्यंपीपरः' (अ.वे. १७.१.२५)। नपुंसकमिति किमर्थम् । 'सप्ता(H: प, Whitney: म)हो वर्तते' । 'द्वादशाहोऽपि' ('द्वादशाहेन' अ.वे. ९.६.४३)।

Note: The example समहो वर्तते (as read by Whitney) cited by the CAB is not found in the Vulgate of the AV, and Surya Kanta (*APR*, *Introduction*, p. 40) suggests that this may have occurred in the genuine Śaunakīya recension of the AV, and that the Vulgate is not the genuine Śaunakīya recension. The mss. H reads सपहो, which Whitney reported as समहो without even noting the actual mss. reading. Now the mss. N provides a much more acceptable reading सप्ताहो. Surya Kanta did not consult the original mss. readings while making his claims. Whitney may have been misled by the word समह which occurs in AV (5.4.10, and 5.24.1). However, this is not a masculine word and has nothing to do with *ahar*.

२.२.१२. न विभक्तिरूपरात्रिरथन्तरेषु ।

Whitney (2.51).

Translation: However, [the *visarjanīya*, i.e. *ḥ*, of *ahaḥ*] does not [change to *r*], before a case-ending, or before the words *rūpa*, *rātri*, and *rathantara*.

चतुराध्यायीभाष्य - न तु खलु विभक्तिरूपरात्रिरथन्तर इत्येतेषु परतः अहरिति विसर्जनीयस्य रेफो भवति । विभक्ति । 'अहोभ्याम्' । 'अहोभिः' (अ.वे. १८.१.५५)। विभक्ति । रूप । 'यदहोरूपाणि दृश्यन्ते' (not in AV, 'अहोरूपाणाम्,' जै.ब्रा. २.२१०; २१३)। रूप । रात्रि । 'अहोरात्राभ्यां नक्षत्रेभ्यः' (अ.वे. ६.१२८.३)। 'अहोरात्रे इदं ब्रूमः' (अ.वे. ११.६.५)। रात्रि । रथन्तर । 'यदाहोरथन्तरं साम गीयते' (not in knownVedic texts)।

Note: Surya Kanta (*APR*, *Introduction*, p. 39-40) says that the combination of *áhas* with *rūpá* and *rathaṃtará* does not occur in the Vulgate of the AV, and suggests that a genuinely Śaunakīya version of the AV probably contained such examples. I believe, Whitney was correct in his suggestion: "It is a very suspicious circumstance that a vārttika to a rule of Pāṇini's (viii.2.68, *ahno ruvidhau rūparātrirathantareṣūpasaṃkhyānaṃ kartavyam*) mentions the same three exceptions which our rule gives: and it is very probable that our treatise in this case, as in several others, has constructed its rule so as to include all the cases noted as occurring in general usage; and hence, that the two phrases quoted are not necessarily to be regarded as having constituted a part of the Atharvan text for which the Prātiśākhya was composed." This is a far more realistic explanation. Whitney did not suggest that these were merely "slips of memory on the part of the CA-writer," as alleged by Surya Kanta (*APR*, *Introduction*, p. 39). The reading as cited by Surya Kanta (p. 40), i.e. °*sāma gāyati*, is not supported either by Whitney, or by mss. H and N.

२.२.१३. ऊधोऽम्नोभुवसाम् ।

Whitney (2.52). P: ऊध्सोम्नो°. P adds a daṇḍa after this rule as a correction.

Translation: [The *visarjanīya*, i.e. *ḥ*,] of [the words] *ūdhaḥ*, *amnaḥ*, and *bhuvaḥ* [is not changed to *r*].

Notes: Whitney observes: "This rule is utterly idle in our treatise, since no precept has been given which should in any way require or authorize the conversion into *r* of the final of these words. The original form of *ūdhas*, however, is *ūdhar*, as is clearly shown by the comparison of the kindred languages, ..., and by its treatment in the Rig-Veda; and the Rik. Pr. ... Neither of the other treatises takes notice of it or of either of the words here associated with it. All three, however, are noted by Pāṇini (viii.2.70, 71), as words which may or may not, in Vedic use, change their final into *r*." The *svarādi-gaṇa* mentioned in P.1.1.37 (स्वरादिनिपातमव्ययम्), as given in Böhtlingk (1887: 144), includes *bhuvar*, *amnas*, and *amnar*.

While Whitney is absolutely correct in saying that there is no rule in the CA to authorize the change of *ḥ* of these words into *r*, the very existence of the present rule, combined with the information given by Pāṇini, would make it understandable that this matter did weigh on the mind of the author of the CA. It seems that this rule may have been intended to distinguish the ŚAV recitational tradition from the traditions of the other Vedas. In the larger context of other traditions, the author of the CA assumes a possibility of the *visarjanīya* in these words being changed to *r*, perhaps unwittingly, and the present rule simply wards off such a possibility. Clearly, the inherited texts of the AV, i.e. the Saṃhitāpāṭha and the Padapāṭha do not show a case of the *visarjanīya* of any of these words changing to *r*. Perhaps, the author of the CA was really concerned with such a change happening in cases of *parihāra* in the Kramapāṭha, such as would be occasioned for the word *ūdhas* in AV (8.10.12), where the word occurs at the end of the line: गायत्र्यंभिधान्यभ्रमूधंः. With the present rule, the author of the CA perhaps wanted to ensure the *parihāra* as ऊध इत्यूधः, rather than as ऊधरित्यूधः. If the tradition of the AV was coming under an increasing influence of the RV tradition, then such a fear may be understandable.

चतुराध्यायीभाष्य - ऊधस्, अम्नस्, भुवस् इति न विसर्जनीयस्य रेफो भवति । 'यो अंस्या ऊधो न वेदं' (अ.वे. १२.४.१८)। 'ये अम्नो जातान्मारयंन्ति' (अ.वे. ८.६.१९)। 'भुवो विश्वेंषु सवंनेषु यज्ञियंः' (ऋ.वे. १०.५०.४)। 'भुवों विवस्वांनन्वा तंतान' (अ.वे. १८.२.३२)।

Note: Surya Kanta says that the example भुवो विश्वेंषु भुवंनेषु यज्ञियंः as a passage cited by the CAB is not found in the Vulgate of the AV, and he (*APR*, *Introduction*, p. 40) suggests that this may have occurred in the genuine Śaunakīya recension of the AV, and that the Vulgate is not the genuine Śaunakīya recension. Here again it is obvious that he has confused Whitney's statements. Whitney says that the example भुवो विश्वेंषु भुवंनेषु यज्ञियंः is found in the commentaries on Pāṇini (8.2.70, 71), and that the CAB gives भुवो विश्वेषु सवनेषु यज्ञियः, which is not found in the AV. Now the new critical edition of the KV (Osmania University edn., Vol. 2, p. 927), based on mss. evidence gives exactly the same example as given by our commentary, and it refers it to RV 10.50.4, which is the same reference given for भुवो विश्वेषु भुवनेषु यज्ञियः by Surya Kanta. The text of RV 10.50.4 unambiguously reads *savaneṣu* and not *bhuvaneṣu* as cited by Surya Kanta.

२.२.१४. अकारोपधस्योकारोऽकारे ।

Whitney (2.53). J, M, O: आकारो°.

Translation: [A *visarjanīya*, i.e. *ḥ*], preceded by *a*, is changed to *u*, before *a*.

Note: This rule works in conjunction with other rules. After the *visarjanīya* is changed to *u*, this *u* is combined with the preceding *a* to yield an *o* by CA (3.2.22: उवर्णे ओकारः), and then the following *a* is combined with the preceding *o* to yield an *o* by CA (3.2.30: एकारौकारान्तात् पूर्वः पदादेरकारस्य).

चतुराध्यायीभाष्य - अकारोपधस्य विसर्जनीयस्य उ(H, N: ओ, W: उ)कारो भवति अकारे परतः । 'परोऽपेंह्यसमृद्धे' (अ.वे. ५.७.७)। 'परोऽपेंहि मनस्पाप' (अ.वे. ६.४५.१)।

Note: The CAB, or perhaps the copyists, render the rule incorrectly by stating that the *visarjanīya* changes to *o*. That would have led to the wording of the original rule to be *akāropadhasya+okāraḥ+akāre* > *akāropadhasyaukāro 'kāre*. This is not supported by any manuscript. Without noting the deviant explanation of the CAB, Whitney correctly translates: "*visarjanīya* becomes *u*." In fact, he cites the commentary as: *akāropadhasya visarjanīyasyo 'kāro bhavati*. However, this is a reading corrected by Whitney. The original reading of both the manuscripts is given above in the text. The commentary of Kṛṣṇadāsa on this rule (= *PS* 267) also correctly interprets this rule: अकारोपधस्य विसर्गस्य उकारो भवति अकारे परे ।.

About the text of the rule as given by the manuscript H, Whitney comments: "This rule is much mutilated by the copyist, both in its first statement (*akāro 'kāre*) and in its final repetition (*akāropadhasyokāre*), so that its true form is only restorable from the commentator's paraphrase. ... Evidently the triple recurrence of the syllables *kāro*, *kāro*, *kāre* bothered the copyist's weak head, and he stumbled from the one to the other of them in an utterly helpless manner." It is to Whitney's credit that, in spite of the mutilated text in the manuscript H, he correctly guessed the proper wording of this rule, which is now fully confirmed by the second manuscript, N. Evidently, the copyist for the second manuscript did not have what Whitney called a "weak head," and he was not bothered by the triple recurrence of the syllables *kāro*, *kāro*, and *kāre*. On the whole, the manuscript N presents a better state of the text of the commentary and the rules. It is also chronologically slightly earlier than the manuscript H.

२.२.१५. घोषवति च ।

Whitney (2.54).

Translation: [The *visarjanīya*, i.e. *ḥ*, preceded by *a*, is changed to *u*], also before a voiced [consonant].

Note: This rule works in conjunction with CA (3.2.22: उवर्ण ओकारः), which combines *a* and *u* into an *o*.

चतुराध्यायीभाष्य - घोषवति च परतः अकारोपधस्य विसर्जनीयस्य उकारो भवति । 'तथां सप्तऋषयों विदुः' (अ.वे. ४.११.९)। 'तद्वै ब्रंह्मविदों विदुः' (अ.वे. १०.८.४३)। 'तस्यां नरो वपत् बीजंमस्याम्' (अ.वे. १४.२.१४)।

२.२.१६. आकारोपधस्य लोपः ।

Whitney (2.55). A, B, D, M, P: अकारो°. Hb, Nb: °लोपलोपः.

Translation: [A *visarjanīya*, i.e. *ḥ*,] preceded by *ā*, is deleted [before a voiced consonant].

Note: As Whitney notes, "the case of *āḥ* before a vowel was included in ii. 41 (= CA 2.2.2: *svare yakāraḥ*)."

चतुराध्यायीभाष्य - आकारोपधस्य विसर्जनीयस्य घोषवति परतः लोपो भवति । 'अनमीवा विंवक्षवः' (अ.वे. २.३०.

३)। 'धीरा देवेषु' (अ.वे. ३.१७.१)। 'एकंशतं ता जनता या भूमिः' (अ.वे. ५.१८.१२)।

२.२.१७. शेपहर्षणीं वन्दनेव वृक्षम् ।

Whitney (2.56). J, M: °वंदहनेव°.

Translation: [The *visarjanīya*, i.e. *ḥ*, is also deleted in the expressions] *śepaharṣaṇīm* [< *śepaḥ+harṣaṇīm*] and *vandane 'va* [< *vandanaḥ+iva*].

Note: By normal rules of sandhi, the first combination would have given us *śepoharṣaṇīm* and *vandana[#]iva*.

Referring to the first of these two cases, Whitney says: "The former is a striking case of arbitrariness in etymologizing on the part of the authors of the *pada*-text, for there is neither necessity nor plausibility in treating the compound as if made up of *śepas* and *harṣaṇa:* the former member is evidently *śepa*, which in the Atharvan is much the more common of the two forms of this word." On another occasion, Whitney (*AV Transl.* Vol.I., p.149) further adds: "The *pada*-reading of the last word is *śepaḥ-harṣaṇīm*, and Prāt ii.56 (= CA 2.2.17) prescribes the loss of the *visarga* of *śepaḥ* in *saṃhitā;* the comment to Prāt. iv.75(74?) (= CA 4.3.2) gives the reading thus: *śepoharṣaṇīm iti śepaḥ-harṣaṇīm;* and one of our *pada*-mss. presents it in the same form, adding *kramakāle* 'this is the *krama*-reading'; and the comm. has *śepoha-*; but Ppp., *śepaharṣiṇī*. As *śépa* is as genuine and old a form as *śépas*, there seems to be no good reason for the peculiar treatment of the compound."

Whitney is clearly misguided in view of the fact that his own *Index Verborum* cites (p. 294) no other occurrence for *śepa-* than the expression *śepaharṣaṇīm*. On the other hand, it lists nine occurrences of *śepas*. This is also confirmed by *A Grammatical Word-Index to Atharvaveda*, VVRI, 1963. Thus, there is good justification for the treatment given to *śepaharṣaṇīm* by the present rule.

Referring to the second case, he says: "As for the other case, of elision of the *visarjanīya* before *iva* and contraction of the two vowels into a diphthong, it is equally surprising to find this one singled out to be so written, from among the many in the text which are to be so read."

Whitney's more general comments are as follows: "For the contraction of a final syllable, ending either in an original *s* or *m*, with the following particle of comparison *iva*, so that the two together form but two syllables, is the rule rather than the exception in the Atharva-Veda. Out of 59 instances in the text, in which a final *aḥ* occurs before *iva*, there are only 13 in which the metre shows the *sandhi* to be regular: in 46 cases we are to read *e 'va*; *am iva* is contracted in the same manner 25 times out of 40; *āḥ iva*, only 4 times out of 19; *im iva*, 3 times out of 5; *iḥ iva*, 7 times out of 10; *uḥ iva*, 6 times, or in every instance the text contains; *um iva*, only once out of 3 times: and there are single sporadic cases of a similar elision after the terminations *eḥ*, *āu*, *ān*, *ad*, *ud*, which would pass without notice, as mere irregularities of metre, were it not for their analogy with the others I have mentioned, but which, considering these latter, are worth adverting to, as illustrations of the same general tendency."

A primary fact Whitney fails to mention is that the rules in the CA are not given to account for those cases where modern scholars restore the irregular meter to its regularity by assuming that the 'original' text read differently from what has been transmitted to us. The CA rules are not restorative in this sense, but descriptive of the Saṃhitāpāṭha and the Padapāṭha as they were received at that time.

चतुराध्यायीभाष्य - शेपहर्षणीं वन्दनेव वृक्षमिति विसर्जनीयस्य लोपो भवति । 'ओषंधिं (H, N: धीं) शेपहर्षंणीम्' (पद ⇒ शेपःऽहर्षंणीम्, अ.वे. ४.४.१)। 'वन्दंनेव वृक्षम्' (पद ⇒ वन्दंनःऽइव, अ.वे. ७.११५.२)। संहितायामित्येव। (क्रम ⇒) 'शेपोहर्षणीमिति शेपः हर्षणीम्' । 'वन्दन इवेति वन्दनः इव' ।

Note: The VVRI edition of the AV cites the Padapāṭha for AV (7.120.2 = W: 7.115.2) as वन्दंनाऽइव, and offers the variant वन्दंनःऽइव in the footnotes. One should also note that the commentary of [Pseudo]-Sāyaṇa adopts the first of these readings (cf. वन्दना लताविशेषः), and shows no awareness of the reading as assumed by the CA. In this connection, it may also be noted that, as far as my reading of [Pseudo]-Sāyaṇa's commentary goes, he shows no knowledge of the CA. This may also be explained by the fact that no manuscript of the CA has been found to the south of Maharashtra, and that it is likely that {Pseudo]-Sāyaṇa may have had no access to this text.

Whitney points to a case which he believes the Prātiśākhya should have taken care of. This is the expression *yakṣmodhām* in AV (9.8.9). Whitney

(*AV Transl.* Vol.II., p. 550) says: "The *pada*-text reads in c *yakṣmaḥ-dhā́m*. The Prāt. takes no notice of the irregular form of the first member of the compound, as it does, superfluously (ii. 56 = CA 2.2.17), of the contrary treatment of *śepas* in *śepa-harṣaṇīm*." Also see the Note on CA (3.2.12) for more possible examples which could have been listed under this rule.

२.२.१८. एष स व्यञ्जने ।

Whitney (2.57). O: °व्यजने.

Translation: [The *visarjanīya*, i.e. *ḥ*,] of the words *eṣaḥ* and *saḥ* [is deleted] before a consonant.

चतुराध्यायीभाष्य - एषः सः इति व्यञ्जने परतः विसर्जनीयस्य लोपो भवति । 'एष प्रियः' (अ.वे. २.३६.४)। 'स सेनां मोहयतु' (अ.वे. ३.१.१)।

Note: This rule is identical with the first *pāda* of APR (99).

२.२.१९. न सस्पदीष्ट ।

Whitney (2.58). A, B, D: °ष्टः. J, M: °सस्यदीर्घः. O: नसस्यदीष्ट. P(orig): °दीर्घः.

Translation: [The *visarjanīya*, i.e. *ḥ*, in the expression] *sas padīṣṭa* [< *saḥ+padīṣṭa*] is not [deleted].

चतुराध्यायीभाष्य - न सस्पदीष्टेति विसर्जनीयस्य लोपो भवति । 'अधरः सस्पदीष्ट' (अ.वे. ७.३१.१)।

२.२.२०. दीर्घायुत्वायादिषु च ।

Whitney (2.59), F, Ha, Na, O: omit च. A, B, D: दीर्घायुत्वादिषु च. I: 20. P: °युत्वयोदि°.

Translation: Also, in *dīrghāyutvāya* etc., [the *visarjanīya*, i.e. *ḥ*, is dropped].

Note: The syntax of this rule seems strange, especially coming after the previous rule. Normally, one would have expected the force of *na* in the previous rule to continue into this rule. However, the examples as given do indeed show the deletion of a theoretically possible *visarjanīya*, e.g. *dīrghāyutva* < *dīrghāyuḥ+tva*. Whitney notes an important point that "in all these cases, it will be noticed, the *lopa* of the *visarjanīya* is made in the *pada*-text, as well as in *saṃhitā*, as is directed in a later rule (iv. 100 = CA 4.3.29: *dīrghāyutvāyādīnāṃ ca*)."

चतुराध्यायीभाष्य - दीर्घायुत्वायादिषु विसर्जनीयस्य लोपो भवति । 'दीर्घायुत्वाय' (अ.वे. १.२२.२)। 'अथो सहस्र-चक्षो त्वम्' (अ.वे. ४.२०.५)। 'बर्हिषदः' (अ.वे. १८.१.४५, ५१)।

Note: Whitney correctly assumes that in the first two examples, there is an actual substitution of the stems *āyu* and *cakṣu*, for the stems *āyus* and *cakṣus*. However, he has some hesitation in assuming a similar substitution of the stem *barhi* for *barhis* in the last example.

The *gaṇa* referred to in this rule of the CA has been fully listed in the APR (200). The CAB cites the first three instances of this *gaṇa*, which contains a total of 10 instances.

इति द्वितीयाध्यायस्य द्वितीयः पादः ।

H, N: ।।५९।। द्वितीयस्य द्वितीयपादः. C, E, F: द्वितीयस्य द्वितीयः पादः. A, B, D, J, M, P: द्वितीयः पादः. I: इति द्वितीयाध्याये द्वितीयः पादः. O: च. द्वितीयस्य द्वितीयः पादः ।। सू.।।२०।।

चतुराध्यायीभाष्य - ।।५९।। द्वितीयस्य द्वितीयः पादः ।।

॥ द्वितीयोऽध्यायः ॥
॥ तृतीयः पादः ॥

२.३.१. दुर उकारो दाशे परस्य मूर्धन्यः ।

Whitney (2.60). Ha, Na: °मूर्द्धन्यः.

Translation: [The *visarjanīya*, i.e. *ḥ*,] of *duḥ* [< *dur*] is changed to *u*, before *dāśa*, and [the *d*] following [*ḥ*] is changed to a retroflex [*ḍ*].

Note: It is assumed that after *duḥ+dāśa* is changed to *duu+ḍāśa*, the two *u* vowels coalesce into a long *ū*, yielding the formation *dūḍāśa*.

चतुराध्यायीभाष्य - दुर इति विसर्जनीयस्य उकारो भवति दाशे परतः परस्य च मूर्धन्यो भवति । 'येना॑ दू॒डाशे॒ अस्य॑सि' (अ.वे. १.१३.१)। संहितायामित्येव । (क्रम ⇒) 'दु॒र्दाश॒ इति॑ दुः॒ऽदाशे॑' । अपर आह - 'धानाशदाशदभध्ये(H, N: ये)षु लुप्यते उपधायाश्च दीर्घः तवर्गीयस्य टवर्गीय' इति । 'दूडाशः' ('दूडाशे,' अ.वे. १.१३.१)। (missing: 'दूणाशः,' ऋ.वे.खिल. ४.४.१)। 'दूडभः' (not in AV, 'दूळभा॑सः,' ऋ.वे. ७.६०.६)। 'दूढ्यः' (not in AV)। 'अप॑(H, N: व) दू॒ढ्यो॑ जहि' (ऋ.वे. १.९४.९)।

Note: The commentary brings up an important issue by saying this change occurs only in the Saṃhitāpāṭha. We must interpret संहितायामित्येव as referring specifically to the Saṃhitāpāṭha, and not referring to the generic sandhi or the lack of a pause in between the recited items. Thus, the Padapāṭha reading *duḥ* / *dāśe* does not occasion this rule, because the components are separated by a short pause. However, in the *parihāra* of the Kramapāṭha, the word is first repeated with its components combined. Then it is followed by *iti*, followed by the repetition of the word broken into its components. In the first repetition, one would expect the normal sandhi rules to apply. Thus, we have *duḥ+dāśa* changing to *durdāśa.* However, since this is not the Saṃhitāpāṭha, the present rule does not apply. The same important distinction between sandhi versus Saṃhitāpāṭha is found in several other cases, e.g. CA (2.2.17).

It should be noted that the CA appropriately limits itself to the formation *dūḍāśa* which is attested in the AV. However, the more generalized formulation appearing in the commentary extends the same procedure to other formations occurring elsewhere. Also note that while the generalized formulation includes *dūṇāśa,* Whitney points out that "the Atharvan has *duḥ-naśa* (v.11.6), but treats it according to the regular methods of combination, making *durṇaśa* in *saṃhitā.*" Thus, the generalized formulation, introduced with *apara āha,* seems to take care of *dūṇāśa,* which is not an Atharvan expression, and fails to take care of *durṇaśa* which is an Atharvan expression. Thus, the Vārttika-like passage cited by the commentary offers a glimpse into an unknown [non-Atharvan?] grammatical text. Compare the Vārttika (दुरो दाशनाशदभध्येषु) on P.6.3.109, which is expanded by Patañjali to: दुरो दाशनाशदभध्येषूत्वं वक्तव्यमुत्तरपदादेश्च ष्टुत्वम्.

२.३.२. शुनि तकारः ।

Whitney (2.61).

Translation: Before *śun,* [the *visarjanīya,* i.e. *ḥ,* of *duḥ*] is changed to *t.*

Note: This rule helps the transition of the Padapāṭha reading *duḥ / śunā* to the Saṃhitāpāṭha reading *ducchunā.* The initial *duḥ+śunā* is changed to *dut+śunā* by this rule. Then, with the application of CA (2.1.13: तकारस्य शकारलकारयोः परसस्थानः) and CA (2.1.17: तवर्गीयाच्छकारः शकारस्य), we finally get *ducchunā.*

Since the forms *ducchunām* and *ducchunā* are not analyzed into their components in the Padapāṭha, Whitney believes that this rule is "properly superfluous, and we have a right to wonder that it was introduced into our treatise." The same sentiment is echoed by Surya Kanta (*APR,* p. 142). In my opinion, this rule, like several others, indicates that the author of the CA occasionally goes into grammatical analysis beyond the limits of the Padapāṭha, rather than this rule being a later addition to the text. All the manuscripts have the rule and the oldest commentary comments on it, and hence, if the rule is a 'later' addition, it must have taken place very early.

There is good reason why the Padapāṭha does not break this word down into its components. Its etymology is elusive. Sāyaṇa on RV (1.116.21) paraphrases the word with *duṣṭasukha* = *duḥkhasya kartā*, and says that the word *suna* refers to happiness. However, this word is not independently attested. Skandasvāmin paraphrases the word with *durbhikṣa*. Surya Kanta (1981: 343) derives it as *dut+śuna*, but then also seems to link it with the root *du* 'burn.' He quotes a paraphrase as *duṣṭacitta* for this word occurring in TS (iv.6.6.7). The denominative verb *ducchunāyase* in RV (7.55.3) is paraphrased by Sāyaṇa with *bādhase*, while *ducchunāyate* in VS (xix. 33) is paraphrased with *daridraṃ karoti*. Thus, this word would qualify for not being split into its components in the Padapāṭha, because of the confusion concerning its components, cf. *sandeha* in CA (4.2.5: षोडशी सन्देहात्). On the other hand, the present CA rule represents an humble effort to suggest an etymology for the word.

चतुराध्यायीभाष्य - शुनि परतः दुरिति विसर्जनीयस्य तकारो भवति । 'दुच्छुनां ग्रामम्' (अ.वे. ५.१७.४)। 'तद्राष्ट्रं हन्ति दुच्छुना' (अ.वे. ५.१९.८)।

२.३.३. समासे सकारः कपयोरनन्तःसद्यःश्रेयश्छन्दसाम् ।

Whitney (2.62). A, B: °सद्यश्रेयः छंदसां. D, M, O, P: °सद्यः श्रेयः छन्दसां. O: °श्रेयःश्छन्दसां.

Translation: In a compound, [a *visarjanīya*, i.e. *ḥ*, occurring at the end of the first member,] is changed to *s*, before *k* and *p*, except for the words *antaḥ*, *sadyaḥ*, *śreyaḥ*, and *chandaḥ*.

चतुराध्यायीभाष्य - समासे विसर्जनीयस्य सकारो भवति कपयोः परतः अन्यत्र अन्तः सद्यः श्रेयः छन्दस् इत्येतेषाम् । 'अधस्पदम्' (अ.वे. २.७.२)। 'पीबस्फाकम्' (अ.वे. ४.७.३)। 'नमस्कारेण' (अ.वे. ४.३९.९)। 'यो विश्वतंस्पाणिरुत विश्वतंस्पृथः' (अ.वे. १३.२.२६)। अनन्तःसद्यःश्रेयश्छन्दसामिति किमर्थम् । 'अन्तःकोशमिंव' (अ.वे. १.१४.४)। 'अन्तःपात्रे रेरिंहतीम्' (अ.वे. ११.९.१५)। 'संद्यःक्रीः'

(अ.वे. ११.७.१०)। 'श्रेयःकेतः' (अ.वे. ५.२०.१०)। 'छन्दःपक्षे' (अ.वे. ८.९.१२)। परःपरः । पर इति चाम्रेडितसमासे न सकारो भवति । 'त्वत्परःपरः' (अ.वे. १२.३.३९)।

Note: The last counter-example, i.e. AV (12.3.39), cited by the commentary is not directly accounted for by the CA rule. Its very presence in the commentary suggests that either the commentator is adding something that the author of the Sūtras unintentionally left out, or that there was a change in the oral tradition, and that the commentator was faced with an instance which did not occur in the text as known to the author of the Sūtras. This instance is indeed listed in the APR (201) as an exception, and it is clear that the CAB has recorded this exception from the APR. Whitney suggests another possibility that sequences of repeated words like *paraḥ+paraḥ* were perhaps not treated as compounds by the author of the Sūtras and hence he did not feel the need to make provision for this instance. On the other hand, it is clear that the commentator considers this an instance of compounding, and hence feels that he must explicitly exclude this instance from the operation of the rule. In any case, there is change in the tradition, either linguistic, theoretical, or both. Since this last instance has been explicitly accounted for by the APR (201, p. 120), it is clear that the CAB and the APR are following the same tradition, which is slightly different from the one reflected in the CA. Also see the Note on CA (4.1.62).

This rule is cited in a slightly abbreviated form in APR (201, See: *APR, Introduction*, p. 20). However, identical examples are found under APR (201) and in the CAB on the present rule.

As far as the prescription for *sadyaḥkrīḥ* is concerned, we should note that the later uniform usage of the derivative *sādyaskra* indicates that the prohibition on the change of Visarga to *s* in this form was not generally followed. Sāyaṇa's reading is *sadyaskrīḥ.*

On *pībasphākam*, Whitney says: "I would remark that its treatment by the *pada*-text, and its citation under this rule, seem to depend upon a false etymology, in as much as its final member is plainly not *phāka*, but *sphāka*, a word allied with *sphāna* and *sphāti*, repeatedly met with elsewhere." On the same word in AV (4.7.3), Whitney (*AV Transl.* Vol.I., p. 155) says: "In b, all our mss. (as also the comment on Prāt. ii.62 = CA 2.3.3) read *pībasphākám* (p. *pībaḥ-phākám*, which the comment just quoted ratifies), as our edition reads; SPP., on the other hand, prints *pībaspākám* (comm. *pīvaspākam*, explained as 'fat-cooking') and declares this to be the unanimous reading of his authorities: this discordance of testimony is quite unexplainable. The translation implies emendation of the *pada*-reading to *pībaḥ-sphākám*." Lanman further adds (ibid.): "In a supplementary note, Roth reports: Ppp. has *pivassākam;* R. has, p.m., *pibaspā-*, corrected to *pībasphā-*; T. has *pīvaspā-*."

On *chandaḥpakṣe* in AV (8.9.12), Whitney (*AV Transl.* Vol.II., p. 509) says: "The Pet. Lexx. give the first word in the form *chándaspakṣa*, although Prāt. ii. 62 expressly requires *-aḥpa-*, and all the mss. read it except Bp., which has *-aṣpa-*."

२.३.४. निर्दुराविर्हविरसमासेऽपि ।

Whitney (2.63). P does not have a daṇḍa between this rule and the next.

Translation: [The *visarjanīya*, i.e. *ḥ*, of] *niḥ*, *duḥ*, *āviḥ*, and *haviḥ* [becomes *s* before *k* and *p*], even where there is no compounding.

चतुराध्यायीभाष्य - निः दुः आविः हविः इत्येतेषाम् असमासेऽपि विसर्जनीयस्य सकारो भवति । निः । 'कुष्ठ॒(H, N: ष्ट)स्तत्सर्व॒ँ निष्कंरत्' (अ.वे. ५.४.१०)। निः । दुः । 'दु॒ष्कृ॒तम्' (अ.वे. ४.२५.४)। 'दुष्पीतम्' (not in AV)। 'दुराविः (H: वः, N: वाः)' । 'आ॒विष्कृंणुष्व रू॒पाणिं' (अ.वे. ४.२०.५)। 'आविष्कृणुते रूपाणि' (variant for AV 12.4. 29c)। आविः । हविः । 'ह॒विष्कृ॒ण्वन्तंः परिवत्स॒रीणंम्' (अ.वे. ३.१०.५)। ततोऽपवदति । 'ह॒विः पुंरो॒डाशंम्' (अ.वे. १८.४.२)।

Note: Whitney says: "The particle *duḥ* never appears in the Atharvan text except as compounded with other words, but it would seem from this rule that the compounds which it forms are not entitled to the name *samāsa*." However, with respect to any cited form, a conclusion whether it is or it is not a case of compound (*samāsa*) cannot be automatically be drawn, because the condition stated in the rule, 'even when there is no compounding,' allows for examples of compounds, as well as non-compounds. In general, words like *niḥ* are not viewed as being compounded with finite verbs, but are viewed as being compounded with verbal nouns. A somewhat similar distinction seems to hold in Pāṇini's system, cf. P.8.4.14 (उपसर्गादसमासेऽपि णोपदेशस्य) and P.7.1.37 (समासेऽनञ्पूर्वे क्त्वो ल्यप्).

All the AV mss. used by Whitney retain the *visarjanīya* in निः क्रव्यादम् (AV 12.2.16, 42) and निः पृथिव्याः (AV 16.7.6), and so does Whitney's edition. Surya Kanta (*APR*, *Introduction*, p. 38) suggests that here we have the non-Śaunakīya readings preserved in the mss. Concerning the passage आविष्कृणुते रूपाणि which is not attested in the AV, Surya Kanta (ibid, p. 40) makes a suggestion that it may have occurred in the genuine Śaunakīya recension, and that the currently available AV text is not genuinely Śaunakīya. Somehow, he does not raise the same claim about the example *duṣpītam* cited by the commentary which is also not attested in the AV. The example *duṣpītam* is cited by the KV on Pāṇini (8.3.41: इदुदुपधस्य चाप्रत्ययस्य), and it is likely that our commentator cited it from such a source. To illustrate the condition असमासेऽपि, the commentator seems to have found examples of mostly finite verbs with the associated words like *nir*. However, when it came to *dur*, it would seem that he was hard-pressed to find examples of such finite verbs. Thus, he was forced to come up with examples of non-finite forms, out of which one is attested in the AV, and the other the commentator found in commentaries on Pāṇini. One need not posit for this a so-called lost genuine Śaunakīya text of the AV.

The exception introduced by the commentary with the words ततोऽपवदति is important. This exception is not directly accounted for by the CA rule, nor has it been accounted for in the APR. This makes one suspect that the text of the AV as known to the author of the commentary was perhaps slightly different as compared to the text as known to the authors of the CA and the APR. Whitney's edition of the AV follows the statement in the commentary, but it is not clear whether the manuscripts of the AV follow this prescription. The VVRI edition also seems to follow the prescription as given in the commentary.

Whitney (*AV Transl.* Vol.II., p. 698) suggests another possibility for आविष्कृणुते रूपाणि. For AV (12.4.29c), some mss. read आविष्कृणुते रूपाणि, while others read आविष्कृणुष्व रूपाणि. Whitney says: "The translation implies in **b** the reading *kr̥ṇute* instead of *kr̥ṇuṣva*, although the former is found only in O.p.m.D.T. ⌊Three of SSP's *pada*-mss. have *kr̥ṇute*.⌋ The comm. to Prāt. ii.63 quotes *āviṣ kr̥ṇute rūpāṇi*, which is not found in the text unless here." Thus there is no reason to say that this passage is not at all found in the AV. The simplest assumption would be that the CAB knew this reading for AV

12.4.29c. The only other known Vedic text which uses आविष्कृणुते is Jaiminīya-Brāhmaṇa (3.96), but here it does not co-occur with *rūpāṇi*.

२.३.५. त्रिः ।

Whitney (2.64).

Translation: [The *visarjanīya*, i.e. *ḥ*, of] *triḥ* [is changed to *s*, before *k* and *p*].

चतुराध्यायीभाष्य - त्रिरिति विसर्जनीयस्य सकारो भवति। 'अपालामिंन्द्र त्रिष्पूत्वा' (अ.वे. १४.१.४१)। 'त्रिष्क्र-(ष्कृ?)त्वा' (not in Vedic texts)। 'त्रिष्प्रकारेण' (not in Vedic texts)।

२.३.६. कुरुकरंकरत्कृणोतुकृतिकृधिष्वकर्णयोः ।

Whitney (2.65). D, J: °कुरुकरंकरकृ°. O adds daṇḍa after करत्. P: °षि-ष्वकर्णयोः.

Translation: [A *visarjanīya*, i.e. *ḥ*,] except that of *karṇayoḥ*, [is changed to *s*], before the words *kuru*, *karam*, *karat*, *kr̥ṇotu*, *kr̥ti*, and *kr̥dhi*.

चतुराध्यायीभाष्य - कुरु करं करत् कृणोतु कृति कृधि इत्येतेषु परतोऽकर्णयोः विसर्जनीयस्य सकारो भवति । कुरु । 'पितृभ्यंश्च नमंस्कुरु' (अ.वे. १४.२.२०)। कुरु । करम् । 'सुबद्धाममुतंस्करम्' (अ.वे. १४.१.१८)। करम् । करत् । 'स नमस्करत्' (Whitney: 'सम्मंनसस्करंत्,' अ.वे. ७.९४.१)। करत् । कृणोतु । कृणोत्वित्यत्र त्रिधात्विति वक्तव्यम् । 'दीर्घमायुंष्कृणोतु' (अ.वे. ६.७८.३)। 'अग्नि-ष्कृंणोतु भेषजम्' (अ.वे. ६.१०६.३)। 'मणिष्कृंणोतु देव-जाः' (अ.वे. १०.६.३१)। कृणोतु । कृति । 'तस्य त्वमंसि निष्कृंतिः' (अ.वे. ५.५.४)। कृति । कृधि । 'अनमित्रं पुर-

स्कृधि' (अ.वे. ६.४०.३)। 'सेमं निष्कृधि पूरुषम्' (अ.वे. ५.५.४)। अकर्णयोरिति किमर्थम् । 'मिथुनं कर्णयोः कृधि' (अ.वे. ६.१४१.२)।

Note: Whitney says: "The cases to which this rule is meant to apply are of very different frequency of occurrence, and the rule itself is of very different degrees of accuracy as concerns the forms mentioned. ... Not much can be said in praise of the way in which this rule is constructed." While Whitney's frustration is understandable, one must also deal with the fact that he is comparing the text of the AV as we know it today with the rules of the CA which were formulated more than two thousands years ago, and we must make allowance for change in the transmitted text, before assigning blame to the author of the CA. This rule is especially a good example for illustrating the possibility of such changes occurring in the transmitted text.

Surya Kanta (*APR*, *Introduction*, p. 41) brings up a very interesting difference between the CA and the APR. The CAB says that the change of *visarjanīya* to *ṣ* before *kr̥ṇotu* occurs only in three cases listed there. On the other hand, the APR (148) refers to the same three passages and says: कृणोत्वित्यत्र त्रिधातु सत्वं न. Surya Kanta points out that the Vulgate mss. follow the APR, and not the CA prescription, and retain the *visarjanīya* in these cases. This, to Surya Kanta, implies that the Vulgate is not a Śaunakīya text. While not denying the facts pointed out by Surya Kanta, one can think in terms of possible change within the same tradition over a period of time. Such a change could have occurred even between the period of CA and that of the CAB. It is indeed conceivable that the CA did not think of the kind of limitations suggested by the CAB, but that the CAB is making a reference to a changed situation. If such a possibility is granted, one can then think of further change reflected in the APR. Does the APR project a reverse situation, i.e. that there could be an *s* for the *visarjanīya* before *kr̥ṇotu* in all other instances, except these three? Or does it say that in the three cases, where the CAB prescribed the change, no such change occurs, and in these cases, we get a *visarjanīya*, as we get it elsewhere before *kr̥ṇotu*. One would have to accept the second alternative, in view of the testimony of the manuscripts. Whitney says: "In all these (= three) passages, however, the manuscripts read, without dissent, *visarjanīya* before the *k*. ... Other instances in which *kr̥ṇotu* has an unaltered *visarjanīya* before it are tolerably numerous. ... They are vi.40.1, 2; 53.3; 73.3; 83.1; 104.3; vii.32.1; 33.1; 51.1; 91.1; viii.8.4; ix.2.7; 4.2; xi.1.6; xii.1.1, 43." In all these cases, the VVRI edition records a *visarjanīya* before *kr̥ṇotu*, and there are no manuscript varients recorded. Thus, instead of simply talking about two different recensions represented by these two texts, one could make a better case for a possible historical change within the same tradition:

1) CA - Unconditional change of *visarjanīya* to *s* before *kr̥ṇotu*.
2) CAB - This change occurs only in three instances.
3) APR - The above change does not occur in any instances.

Surya Kanta's conceptions are based on several assumptions. The first is that the oral (or even written) textual traditions, once codified by some scholar-sage, were essentially immutable. The second assumption is that the CAB actually forms part of the text of the original CA, and hence the examples and everything else seen in the CAB was somehow identical with the expectations of the original CA. In my opinion, both of these assumptions are seriously questionable. The general direction of possible change in the language is further supported by the following observations of W.S. Allen (1053: 51): "In later, though still ancient, times there appears to have been a tendency for *-ḥ* to extend its usage to contexts other than *in pausa*. The earliest of these extensions was to the position before the initial fricatives *ś-*, *ṣ-*, *s-*, where it replaced the homorganic final *-ś*, *-ṣ*, *-s* (*indraś śūraḥ* > *indraḥ śūraḥ*, &c.). This practice was then extended to the position before the velar and labial voiceless stops: in connexion with this innovation we find mentioned the names of Āgniveśya, Vālmīki, Śākalya, and the Mādhyandina school, whilst the ancient grammarian Śākaṭāyana is quoted as holding to the more conservative practice." Allen also refers to A.H. Fry's view that "the spread of *-ḥ* was due to the writers of Classical Sanskrit operating with a phonemic orthography."

On the inclusion of *kr̥ti* in this rule, Whitney remarks: "The next word, *kr̥ti*, is one which, for a double reason, has no right to a place in the rule: in the first place, it occurs nowhere except in compounds; and secondly, it converts into a sibilant only the preceding *visarjanīya* of *niḥ* and *haviḥ*, and so would be sufficiently provided for by rule 63 (= CA 2.3.4), even if not adjudged to fall under rule 62 (= CA 2.3.3)."

On मणिष्कृणोतु in AV (10.6.31), Whitney and Lanman (*AV Transl*. Vol. II., p. 588) point out: "According to Prāt. ii.65 (= CA 2.3.6), we ought to read *maṇíṣ kr̥-* ; ⌊this is the reading of three of SPP's mss., but of none of W's so far as noted: both texts give *maṇíḥ*⌋."

२.३.७. ततस्परौ ब्रह्मपरे ।

Whitney (2.66). O: °म्ह°.

Translation: [The *visarjanīya*, i.e. *ḥ*, of] *tataḥ* [is changed to *s*], before the word *pari* followed by the word *brahma*.

चतुराध्यायीभाष्य - तत इति विसर्जनीयस्य परौ परतः सकारो भवति । ब्रह्मपरे । 'ततस्परि ब्रह्मणा' (अ.वे. १.१०.१)। ब्रह्मण इति किमर्थम् । 'ततः परि प्रजातेन' (अ.वे. ६.८९.१)।

Note: Whitney points out: "A similar case, in which the suffix *taḥ* becomes *tas* before *pari*, is सिन्धुतस्परि (iv.10.4 and vii.45.1); the Prātiśākhya takes no notice of it, if it be not intended to be included in the *gaṇa* with which the section concludes (ii. 80 = CA 2.3.21)." This *gaṇa*, as we now know, is fully listed under APR (203, p. 121-2), and contains 12 instances. Yet, interestingly enough, it does not contain the instance cited above by Whitney, i.e. सिन्धुतस्परि.

However, that instance could be taken care of by the next rule, i.e. CA (2.3.8). The example is listed neither among the positive cases for changing the *visarjanīya* to *s*, nor among exceptions to APR (202, p. 120-1). My understanding of the APR lists under this rule (i.e. APR 202) is that the list of positive examples is merely illustrative, while the list of exceptions is a complete list. Since सिन्धुतस्परि does not appear in the list of exceptions, it could have been most likely a case of the positive change of *visarjanīya* to *s*. The fact that there are no manuscript varients listed for this instance by any of the editions of the AV also probably points in the same direction.

२.३.८. पञ्चम्याश्चाङ्गेभ्यः पर्यादिवर्जम् ।

Whitney (2.67).

Translation: Also, [the *visarjanīya*, i.e. *ḥ*,] of an ablative form [is changed to an *s*, before *pari*], except in *aṅgebhyaḥ pari* etc.

Note: Whitney points out: "The Rik Pr. (iv. 15) and Vāj. Pr. (iii. 30) give the additional specification that the *pari* must be at the end of a *pāda*, or before a pause, and the addition of that restriction to our own rule would have made it accurate, and obviated the necessity of the *gaṇa*." Whitney records, in a footnote, the instances and the counter-instances for this rule. Since the APR (202, pp. 120-1) also contains similar lists of instances and counter-instances, it is well worth comparing Whitney's listing with the APR listing. Whitney's list of positive instances matches with the one given under APR (202), except that Whitney also adds AV (xix.39.1, 5), and, he, for some reason, does not think of adding सिन्धुतस्परि (AV iv.10.4 and vii.45.1) to this list. The lists of exceptions, have important mismatches: Whitney's list of exceptions includes 10.7.25, 13.1.26, besides several instances from the 19th Kāṇḍa, which are not included in the APR list. On the other hand, the APR list of exceptions includes 3.6.1, 6.89.1, 1.27.1, 4.33.6, and 9.5.6. These cases are not included in Whitney's list of exceptions. Thus, there are major discrepancies, suggesting the possibility of changes in the textual transmission of the ŚAV after the completion of the APR.

चतुराध्यायीभाष्य - पञ्चम्याश्च विसर्जनीयस्य परौ परतः सकारो भवति । अङ्गेभ्यः पर्यादिवर्जम् । 'कुष्ठों(H, N: ष्टो) हिमवंतस्परिं' (अ.वे. १९.३९.१)। 'जातं हिमवंतस्परिं' (अ.वे. ४.९.९; ५.४.२)। 'विद्युतो ज्योतिंषस्परिं' (अ.वे. ४.१०.१)। अङ्गेभ्यः पर्यादिवर्जमिति किमर्थम् । 'प्राणमङ्गेभ्यः पर्याचरंन्तम्' (अ.वे. २.३४.५)।

Note: In a footnote on p. 109, Whitney details instances and counter-instances for this rule. Surya Kanta wishes to use the examples cited by the commentary and the CA rule itself to argue that the CA and the APR belong to two different recensions of the AV. He points out (*APR*, *Introduction*, pp. 40-1) that the APR (202) prescribes the same operation as the present rule in CA, but in the APR the *gaṇa* list of exceptions begins with पुमांन्पुंसः परिंजातः (अ.वे. ३.६.१), the second exception listed being प्राणमङ्गेभ्यः पर्याचरंन्तम् (अ.वे. २.३४.५). Why should the list of exceptions in the CA begin with the second example in the APR list? Surya Kanta argues: "Either CA has omitted *púmān puṃsáḥ*, or APR has added it afterwards. In any case the result is unmistakable. While the APR negatives *satva* in the passage, CA seems to imply it, thus showing that the two schools are different." Surya Kanta also forgets to point out that the first positive example of such a change offered by the commentary, i.e. कुष्ठों हिमवंतस्परिं is absent from the list of examples provided by the APR (202). This example is from the 19th Kāṇḍa of the AV, and both the CA and the APR rarely cite from anything beyond the first 18 Kāṇḍas. It is possible that this is a later addition to the text of the commentary. One more possibility omitted by Surya Kanta from consideration is that the pronunciation may have changed in the period between the CA and the APR, making it necessary for the latter to list or omit a passage. Such a change could have occurred within the same school.

See the Note on the previous rule for a discussion of the example *sindhutas pari* (AV, iv.10.4 and vii.45.1).

२.३.९. दिवस्पृथिव्यां सचतिवर्जम् ।

Whitney (2.68).

Translation: [The *visarjanīya*, i.e. *ḥ*, of] *divaḥ* [is changed to *s*] before the word *pr̥thivī*, except [when it is followed by a form of] the verb *sac*.

चतुराध्यायीभाष्य - दिव इति विसर्जनीयस्य पृथिव्यां परतः सकारो भवति । 'दि॒वस्पृ॑थि॒व्या अ॒न्तरि॑क्षात्समु॒द्रात्' (अ.वे. ९.१.१)। 'दि॒वस्पृ॑थि॒वीम॒भि ये सृ॒जन्ति॑' (अ.वे. ४.२७.४)। सचतिवर्जमिति किमर्थम् । 'आ य॑न्ति दि॒वः पृ॑थि॒वीं स॑चन्ते' (अ.वे. १२.३.२६)।

Note: Whitney comments: "The text affords three others, viz. vi.100.3; 125.2; xix.3.1. The only counter instance is that mentioned in the rule."

२.३.१०. पृष्ठे च ।

Whitney (2.69). O, P: पृष्टे च.

Translation: [The *visarjanīya*, i.e. *ḥ*, of the word *divaḥ* is changed to *s*] also before the word *pr̥ṣṭha*.

चतुराध्यायीभाष्य - पृष्ठे च परतः दिव इति विसर्जनीयस्य सकारो भवति । 'दि॒वस्पृ॒ष्ठे धाव॑मानं सु॒प॒र्णम्' (अ.वे. १३.२.३७)। दिव इत्येव । 'भूम्याः॑ पृ॒ष्ठे व॑द' (अ.वे. ५.२०.६)।

Note: The exception cited by the CAB, i.e. भूम्याः पृष्ठे वद, is listed in APR (147e). Whitney lists several more instances of this change: iv.14.2, xi.5.10, xii.2.12, xiii.4.1, and xviii.1.61. He further points out: "The original sibilant of *divas* also maintains itself before *p* in two other cases, viz. *divas putrau* (viii.7.20) and *divas payaḥ* (xix.44.5). With the latter our treatise has nothing to do: the former it lets fall, apparently, into the *barathrum* of the *gaṇa* which closes the subject and the section (rule 80 = CA 2.3.21)." The *rāyaspoṣādigaṇa* referred to in CA (2.3.21) is listed at length under APR (203, pp. 121-2), and yet it does not contain the instance दिवस्पुत्रौ. Either we must assume that the listing under APR (203) was only illustrative, or we need to accept the possibility of textual change after the period of APR.

२.३.११. यः पतौ गवामस्याः परवर्जम् ।

Whitney (2.70).

Translation: [The *visarjanīya*, i.e. *ḥ*, of] *yaḥ* [is changed to *s*] before *pati*, except when [the word *yaḥ* is preceded by] *gavām* or *asyāḥ*.

चतुराध्यायीभाष्य - य इति विसर्जनीयस्य पतौ परतः सकारो भवति । गवामस्याः परवर्जम् । 'दिव्यो गन्धर्वो भुवनस्य यस्पतिः' (अ.वे. २.२.१)। 'मृडाद्गन्धर्वो भुवनस्य यस्पतिः' (अ.वे. २.२.२)। 'धाता विधाता भुवनस्य यस्पतिः' (अ.वे. ५.३.९)। गवामस्याः परवर्जमिति किमर्थम् । 'गवां यः पतिः' (अ.वे. ९.४.१७)। 'दीर्घायुरस्या यः पतिः' (अ.वे. १४.२.२)।

Note: The first two instances cited in APR (147e) are identical with the two exceptions referred to by the words *gavām* and *asyāḥ* in our rule, and fully by the CAB. Whitney cites two more cases of भुवनस्य यस्पतिः, i.e. AV (13.3.7) and AV (19.20.2). Then he makes an interesting remark: "One cannot but think that a better form for the closing restriction of the rule would have been "whenever *bhuvanasya* precedes." One should also note that the word *para* is used in this rule in a way different from its use in other rules, cf. CA (2.3.7: ततस्परौ ब्रह्मपरे). In the present rule, in view of the known examples, the word is interpreted as "when *yaḥ* is preceded by *gavām* or *asyāḥ*," or "when *yaḥ* follows *gavām* or *asyāḥ*." In CA (2.3.7), *brahmapare* is interpreted in an opposite way: "when the word *pari* is followed by the word *brahma*."

२.३.१२. षष्ठ्याश्चाशच्याः ।

Whitney (2.71).

Translation: [The *visarjanīya*, i.e. *ḥ*,] of a genitive form, except *śacyāḥ*, is also [changed to *s*, before the word *pati*].

Note: As Whitney points out, "the cases coming under this rule are almost innumerable, and it would be a waste of labor to specify them in full. ... The only exception is that which the rule mentions." The manuscripts of the AV do seem to follow the prohibition regarding the formation शच्याः पतिः. No ms. records the form शच्यास्पतिः.

चतुराध्यायीभाष्य - षष्ठ्या इति विसर्जनीयस्य पतौ परतः सकारो भवति अशच्याः । 'वाचस्पतिः' (अ.वे. १.१.१)। 'उषस्पतिः' (अ.वे. १६.६.६)। 'ब्रह्मणस्पतिः' (अ.वे. ६.४.१)। 'जगतस्पतिः' (अ.वे. ७.१७.१)। अशच्या इति किमर्थम् । 'अरात्याः शच्याः पतिः' (अ.वे. १३.४.४७)।

२.३.१३. इडायास्पदे ।

Whitney (2.72). P: इडायाःस्पदे.

Translation: [The *visarjanīya*, i.e. *ḥ*,] of the word *iḍāyāḥ* [is changed to *s*] before the word *pada*.

चतुराध्यायीभाष्य - इडाया इति विसर्जनीयस्य पदे परतः सकारो भवति । 'इडायास्पदम्' (अ.वे. ३.१०.६)। इडा-यास्पदे । इडाया इति किमर्थम् । 'हस्तिन्याः पदेन' (अ.वे. ६.७०.२)।

Note: The counter example हस्तिन्याः पदेन cited by the CAB is also listed under APR (147e). Referring to इडस्पदे in AV (6.63.4), Whitney (*AV Transl.* Vol.I., p. 329) remarks that "the prescription in that rule (= CA 2.3.13) of *s* as the final of only *iḍāyās* before *pada* seems a strong indication that this verse (= AV 6.63.4) was not a part of the AV text as recognized by the Prāt." On the present rule, Whitney says: "That the rule is not so framed as to include also the closely analogous case *iḍas pade* (vi.63.4), the only other one in the text where an original final sibilant is preserved before *pada*, gives reason to suspect that the verse containing it was not in the commentator's Atharvan: a suspicion which is supported by the peculiar mode of occurrence of the verse, at the end of hymn with the subject of which it has nothing to do. It looks as if it had been thrust in at the end of vi.63, because in the Rik text (x. 191) it preceded the verses of which vi.64 is composed."

There are some curious facts which must be mentioned. The text of the commentary repeats इडायास्पदे after citing the actual AV example इडायास्पदम्, before proceeding to ask the question इडाया इति किमर्थम्. This is highly unusual, and one wonders whether this was a misreading for an intended original इडस्पदे. Such a suspicion is strengthened by the fact that the APR (203, p. 121) actually lists the case इडस्पदे. However, it is of course possible that the example was not part of the AV known to the CA and the CAB, and was incorporated in it by the time of APR.

२.३.१४. पितुष्पितरि ।

Whitney (2.73), A, B, D, H, J, K, M, N, and P read पितुः पितरि. Other mss. read: पितुष्पितरि.

> **Translation:** [The *visarjanīya*, i.e. *ḥ*,] of the word *pituḥ* [is changed to *s*] before the forms of *pitṛ*.
>
> ***चतुराध्यायीभाष्य*** - पितुरिति विसर्जनीयस्य पितरि परतः सकारो भवति । 'यस्तानि वेद स पितुष्पितासत्' (अ.वे. २.१.२)। 'यस्ता विंजानात् स पितुष्पितासत्' (अ.वे. ९.९.१५)।

Note: Whitney's manuscript, our H, contained only the first example, and Whitney recorded the second one in his notes: "a similar phrase is found once more in the text (at ix.9.15)". This second example is now found in the manuscript N.

Whitney further says: "On the other hand, we have three cases in the eighteenth book (xviii.2.49; 3.46, 59) in which *pituḥ* stands before *pitaraḥ*, and, by the unanimous authority of the manuscripts, maintains its *visarjanīya*. We must suppose either that the Prātiśākhya and its commentator overlooked these passages, or that they did not stand in the text contemplated by them, or that they stood there with the reading *pituṣ pitaraḥ*." In all these cases, the VVRI edition also offers a reading with the *visarjanīya*, and does not cite any manuscript varients in favor of its change to *ṣ*.

Surya Kanta (*APR*, *Introduction*, p. 38) argues that such violations by the Vulgate text of the AV of the rules of the CA should be interpreted to mean that the Vulgate is not the Śaunakīya recension of the AV, and that the CA must be referring to a genuinely Śaunakīya recension which we do not possess today.

It is curious to note that while the CAB does not explicitly note any exceptions, the APR (147, p. 101) lists ये नः पितुः पितरो ये पितामहाः, AV (xviii.2.49; 3.46, 59) as an exception to the change of *ḥ* to *s*. Since neither the CA nor the CAB show any awareness of this exception, and since the APR explicitly lists it as an exception, the most likely conclusion is that the text of the AV as known to the CA and the CAB did not have this exception, but that the exception had developed prior to the listings made by the APR.

Referring to the mss. variants regarding this phrase in AV (9.9.15), Whitney (*AV Transl.* Vol.II., 554) says: "Some of our mss. (P.s.m.O.K.T.) read *pitúḥ p-* in d; we had the phrase once before, at ii.1.2, and the combination falls under Prāt. ii.73 (= CA 2.3.14)."

२.३.१५. द्यौश्च ।

Whitney (2.74).

Translation: [The *visarjanīya*, i.e. *ḥ*,] of the word *dyauḥ* [is] also [changed to *s*, before a form of *pitṛ*].

चतुराध्यायीभाष्य - द्यौरिति विसर्जनीयस्य पितरि परतः सकारो भवति । 'द्यौष्पितर्यावय' (अ.वे. ६.४.३)। 'द्यौष्पितः' (अ.वे. ६.४.३)। 'न्यङ् अधराङ्' (H, N: 'न्यध-राङ्,') (अ.वे. ५.२२.२)।

Note: Referring to the Vulgate mss. for AV (6.4.3), Whitney says: "All mss., but one, retain visarjanīya." All manuscripts, except I and H, give *dyauṣ* in AV 3.9.1 and so does Whitney's edition. However, later Whitney

(*AV Transl.* Vol.I., p. 98) says "SSP. reads in b *dyāúḥ p-*, which is doubtless preferable to our *dyāúṣ p-*; it is read by the majority of his mss. and by part of ours (H.I.K); Ppp. also has it." At AV (3.23.6, and 8.7.2), almost all mss. retain the *visarjanīya*, and so does Whitney's edition. On the reading in this verse, Whitney (*AV Transl.* Vol.I., p. 128) reports: "The first half verse is found again later, as viii.7.2.c,d; in both places, part of the mss. read *dyāúṣ p-* (here only our O., with half of SPP's); and that appears to be required by Prāt. ii-74 (= CA 2.3.15), although the looser relation of the two words favors in a case like this the reading *dyāúḥ*, which both editions present." Surya Kanta (*APR*, *Introduction*, p.38) refers to this situation and argues that the Vulgate of the AV is not Śaunakīya, but that there is a mixture of the Śaunakīya readings at times in the existing mss. The example AV (6.4.3) is cited as example 21 under APR (28b, p. 27) with *ṣ*, rather than with the *visarjanīya*. The tendencies in the manuscripts of the AV, in this case, seem to show a further shift away from *ṣ*. Such a change is clearly more in the direction of the tendencies reflected in the classical language. See: Allen (1953: 51).

The example न्यङ् अंधराङ् has no place here. The examples द्यौष्पितः (AV 6.4.3) and न्यङ् अंधराङ् (AV 5.22.2) are cited consecutively under APR (53, p. 43), and it is possible that the copyist for the CAB, who may also have copied the APR, confused the citations. This is the best explanation for why these two otherwise unrelated examples might have been juxtaposed in the manuscripts of the CAB. The confusion must have been fairly old to have been found in both the manuscripts H and N.

२.३.१६. आयुष्प्रथमे ।

Whitney (2.75), D, H, J, M, N, and P: आयुः प्रथमे. Other mss: आयुष्प्रथमे.

Translation: [The *visarjanīya*, i.e. *ḥ*,] of the word *āyuḥ* [is changed to *s*], before *prathama*.

चतुराध्यायीभाष्य - आयुरिति विसर्जनीयस्य प्रथमे परतः सकारो भवति । 'आयुंष्प्रथमं प्रजां पोषंम्' (अ.वे. ४.३९.२)।

Note: On this rule, Whitney says that all the AV mss. without dissent read *visarjanīya* whereas the CA rule expects *ṣ* in the example cited by the commentator. In this case, in his edition of the AV, Whitney disregards the unanimous authority of the mss. and follows the CA. Surya Kanta (*APR*, *Introduction*, p. 38) refers to this situation and says that Whitney's decision is arbitrary. However, note that the APR does not record these cases as exceptions to the change of *visarjanīya* to *s*, and the best guess is that the APR knew these cases with the change.

In Surya Kanta's opinion, the AV mss. in this case represent a non-Śaunakīya recension. On the cited example, Whitney (*AV Transl.* Vol.I., p. 216) says: "Our edition combines *ā́yuṣ pr-*, because required by Prāt. ii.75 (= CA 2.3.16); but the mss., except one of SPP's have *ā́yuḥ pr-*, which SPP. retains." Here too, the manuscripts of the AV seem to indicate a progression toward the maintenance of the *visarjanīya*, cf. Allen (1953: 51). In this case, the shift away from the change of *visarjanīya* > *s* > *ṣ*, may have begun after the completion of the APR.

२.३.१७. प्रे मुषिजीवपरे ।

Whitney (2.76).

Translation: [The *visarjanīya*, i.e. *ḥ*, of the word *āyuḥ* is changed to *s*] before *pra*, when it is followed by a form of the verb *muṣ* or *jīv*.

चतुराध्यायीभाष्य - प्रे परतः मुषिजीवपरे आयुरिति विसर्जनीयस्य सकारो भवति । 'मा न आयुष्प्र मोषीः' (अ.वे. ८.२.१७)। 'दीर्घमायुष्प्र जीवसे' (अ.वे. १८.२.३)। मुषिजीवपर इति किमर्थम् । 'जीवानामायुः प्र तिर' (अ.वे. १२.२.४५)।

Note: Whitney points out that all the mss. for AV (8.2.17 and 18.2.3) read *āyuḥ*, and he accepts this reading in his edition. Surya Kanta (*APR*, *Introduction*, p.38) points out how arbitrary Whitney's decisions generally are, and that the manuscripts represent a non-Śaunakīya recension. The Śaunakīya readings as defined by the CA are not always available in the existing AV manuscripts. Regarding AV (18.2.3), Whitney (*AV Transl.* Vol.II., p. 832) himself says: "The Prāt. (ii. 76 = CA 2.3.17) distinctly requires *ā́yuṣ prá* to be read in **d**, but of our mss. only O.s.m. (in margin) gives it; nearly half of SPP's *saṃhitā*-mss., however, have it, and it ought to be received as the true AV. text, though both editions read *ā́yuḥ*." A case such as this suggests that one needs to carefully investigate the groupings of the manuscripts to detect slightly divergent traditions of the transmission of the AV, and see if they are consistent in following or not following the rules of the CA. On the whole, it still seems that there is a general movement away from the change of *visarjanīya* > *s*, a direction discussed by Allen (1953: 51).

Since the APR (147, p. 101) explicitly lists AV (12.2.45) as an exception to the change of *visarjanīya* to *s*, as listed here by the CAB, one may assume that the APR knew other instances as involving this change, and the wholesale movement in the direction away from this change and toward the maintenance of the *visarjanīya* can be dated after the APR.

२.३.१८. परिधिष्पतातौ ।

Whitney (2.77), Ha, J, K, Na: परिधिः पतातौ. Other mss: परिधिष्पतातौ.

Translation: [The *visarjanīya*, i.e. *ḥ*,] of *paridhiḥ* [is changed to *s*] before *patāti*.

Note: Whitney notes: "The manuscripts are unanimous in supporting the reading prescribed by the Prātiśākhya." However, note that the VVRI edition notes the Paippalāda variant as परिधिः पताति. The example cited by the commentary is not listed among exceptions to the change of *visarjanīya* to *s* by the APR, and one may assume that the APR knew this case as involving this change. Why the manuscript tradition should maintain this change, when in other cases it moves in the direction of keeping the *visarjanīya* needs to be explored.

चतुराध्यायीभाष्य - परिधिरिति विसर्जनीयस्य पतातौ परतः सकारो भवति । 'यथा॒ सो अ॒स्य प॑रि॒धिष्पता॑ति' (अ.वे. ५.२९.२,३)।

२.३.१९. निवतस्पृणातौ ।

Whitney (2.78).

Translation: [The *visarjanīya*, i.e. *ḥ*,] of *nivataḥ* [is changed to *s*] before *pr̥ṇāti*.

Note: Whitney notes that the reading with *s* is supported by all of his manuscripts. The VVRI edition also shows no manuscript variants in this respect. The example listed by the CAB is not included among the exceptions to the change of *visarjanīya* to *s* listed by the APR, and hence one may assume that the APR knew this example with the change to *s*. Again, it needs to be investigated why this case has been resistant to the general direction of moving toward maintaining the *visarjanīya*.

चतुराध्यायीभाष्य - निवत इति विसर्जनीयस्य पृणातौ परतः सकारो भवति । 'या(H, N: यो) विश्वा॑ नि॒वत॑स्पृ॒णाति॑' (अ.वे. ६.२२.३)।

२.३.२०. मनस्पापे ।

Whitney (2.79). C, Hb, J, K, O: °स्यापे. P adds a daṇḍa after this rule as a correction.

Translation: [The *visarjanīya*, i.e. *ḥ*,] of *manaḥ* [is changed to *s*] before *pāpa*.

Note: Whitney has an important comment: "The *pada*-text regards *manaspāpa* as a compound, writing it *manaḥ-pāpa*. Its separate mention by the Prātiśākhya would seem to indicate that the latter regards the two words as independent; since, as a compound, it would fall under rule 62, and would need no special notice. The accentuation does not help to settle the question, and the sense is nearly as good one way as the other."

One may point out that the commentary of [pseudo-]Sāyaṇa on AV (6.45.1) treats the expressions *pāpa* and *manaḥ* as separate vocatives, rather than as parts of a compound, though the manuscripts of the Padapāṭha, without exception, treat this expression as a compound.

चतुराध्यायीभाष्य - मन इति विसर्जनीयस्य पापे परतः सकारो भवति । 'प॒रोऽपे॑हि मनस्पाप' (अ.वे. ६.४५.१)।

२.३.२१. रायस्पोषादिषु च ।

Whitney (2.80). I: 21.

Translation: Also, [the *visarjanīya*, i.e. *ḥ*, occurring at the end of the first item is changed to *s* before the second item] in [sequences] such as *rāyaspoṣam*.

चतुराध्यायीभाष्य - राय इति विसर्जनीयस्य पोषादिषु च परतः सकारो भवति । 'रायस्पोषंम्' (अ.वे. १.९.४)। 'परुंष्परुः' (अ.वे. १.१२.३)। 'मा पिंशाचं तिरस्कंरः' (अ.वे. ४.२०.७)।

Note: The wording of the commentary creates an impression that the Gaṇa is simply *poṣādi*. However, it is clear from the cited examples that the entire expression *rāyaspoṣādi* refers to the Gaṇa. The CAB here cites the first three instances out of a total list of 12 examples found in the APR (203). The examples occur in the same order. Whitney also notes a large number of cases, which he thought were not covered by the earlier rules. Whitney's listing has several common instances, but several differences. The instances दिवस्पुत्रौ (AV 8.7.20), दिवस्पयंः (AV 19.44.5), and द्विषतस्पांदयामि (AV 11.1.12, 22) are listed by Whitney, but are not included in the APR (p.121) listing. On the other hand, the APR list includes असितास्परिं (AV 6.137.2), अधंरः सस्पंदीष्ट (AV 7.31.1), जास्पत्यम् (AV 7.73.10), and स्वादुष्किलायम् (AV 18.1.48), which are not listed by Whitney under this rule.

However, comparing such lists is a very difficult task, as Whitney notes: "Unfortunately, it is impossible to tell what is the teaching of the Prātiśākhya with regard to any such cases; we do not even know how accurately it or its commentators had noticed and noted the instances which their text contained. There is no apparent reason why the single cases noted in rules 66, 72, 77, 78, 79 should not have been left to go into the *gaṇa*, if a *gaṇa* was to be established, and neither the accuracy nor the method of the treatise, in dealing with this class of phenomena, is worthy of unqualified condemnation." Even with the addition of the APR to our understanding of the AV tradition, things have not changed completely.

इति द्वितीयाध्यायस्य तृतीयः पादः ।

H, N: ।।८०।। द्वितीयस्य तृतीयपादः. C, E, F: द्वितीयस्य तृतीयः पादः. A, B, D, J, M, P: तृतीयः पादः. I: इति द्वितीयाध्यायस्य तृतीयः पादः. O: च.।। द्वितीयस्य तृतीयः पादः ।। ३ ।। सू.।। २१ ।।.

चतुराध्यायीभाष्य - ।।८०।। द्वितीयस्य तृतीयपादः ।।

॥ द्वितीयोऽध्यायः ॥
॥ चतुर्थः पादः ॥

२.४.१. अत्र नाम्युपधस्य षकारः ।

Whitney (2.81).

Translation: Here [i.e. in the context of the section beginning with CA (2.3.3: *samāse sakāraḥ kapayor* ...) teaching the change of a *visarjanīya*, i.e. *ḥ*, to *s*], *s* is changed to *ṣ*, if preceded by a *nāmin* [i.e. any vowel other than *a* and *ā*].

Note: The change of *s* to *ṣ* taught by this rule is already apparent in the examples of a number of previous rules, e.g. CA (2.3.4-6; 14-8; 21). Its scope also extends to rules which follow, e.g. CA (2.4.3-6). The commentary CAB continues the words नाम्युपधस्य सकारस्य षकारः into these following rules. As Whitney points out, this rule applies "whether the *s* to which the rules relate is original, or comes from *visarjanīya*." In the Prātiśākhyas, this phenomenon is generally referred to by the term *nati* "bending [= retroflexion]," and the vowels which condition this change are called *nāmin* "bender [= retroflexing vowel]." Whitney translates the term *nāmin* as "alterant vowel."

चतुराध्यायीभाष्य - यदेतत् - 'समासे सकारः कपयो-रनन्त...' (च.आ. २.३.३) इत्यनुक्रान्तः । अत्र नाम्युपधस्य सकारस्य षकारो भवति । एतान्येवोदाहरणानि । नाम्युपध-स्येत्येवं द्रष्टव्यम् । इत उत्तरं यदनुक्रमिष्यामः ।

२.४.२. सहेः साड्भूतस्य ।

Whitney (2.82). C, E, F, I, O: °ड्रूपस्य. B, D, J, N: °द्भूतस्य.

Translation: [The *s*] of the root *sah*, when transformed to *sāṭ*, [is changed to *ṣ*].

Note: From the examples given by the commentary, we understand that the condition *nāmyupadhasya* is not relevant for this rule, and that the change of *s* to *ṣ* takes place, even when the form *sāṭ* is not preceded by a *nāmin* vowel, a vowel other than *a* and *ā*.

If *sāḍbhūtasya* in the CA rule is intended to prevent the application of this rule to the form *prasahanam*, and if *prasahanam* is not attested in Vedic literature, then it is clear that like Pāṇini 8.3.56 (*saheḥ sāḍaḥ saḥ*), the CA too, consciously or unconsciously, could not dispense with the contemporary language while framing its rules.

Whitney points out, "That *sāḍbhūta* means 'when it becomes *sāṭ*,' and not 'when it becomes *sāh*,' appears from the instances *amitrasāha* and *sātrāsāha* (see under iii.23 = CA 3.1.23), in which, although the vowel of the root is lengthened, the sibilant remains unaltered."

Whitney also objects to the rule itself, and its location in the text: "There is no real necessity for any such rule as this, since all the words to which the commentary regards it as relating have precisely the same form in *pada* as in *saṃhitā*." A positive way of putting the same thing may be to say that this rule, like many others, shows progress of linguistic analysis beyond the stage represented in the Padapāṭha. The rule is a close parallel to Pāṇini 8.3.56

As for its location, Whitney says: "But there is a graver objection to the rule than its dispensability: it is quite out of place where it stands. In the first place, it treats of an initial *s*, while the treatise otherwise puts off such cases until after all those of a final *s* are disposed of; and, much worse, it interrupts the *anuvṛtti* of *nāmyupadhasya*, which must necessarily take place from rule 81 (= CA 2.4.1) to those that follow; since, in the majority of the cases which it concerns, the sibilant is preceded by long *ā*. Either there is here an unusual degree of awkwardness and inconsistency of method on the part of the author of the treatise, or the rule is an interpolation." Since the rule is found in all the manuscripts, and since the CAB comments on it, the chance of this rule being an interpolation is drastically reduced. The question of the location of the rule, however, cannot be easily solved.

The problem has been resolved in Pāṇini's grammar in an interesting way: P.8.3.55 (अपदान्तस्य मूर्धन्यः) states the general conditions: "[in the following rules], the words 'of the non-word-final' and 'cerebral' [should be continued]." Then comes the rule P.8.3.56 (सहेः साडः सः): "The *s* of the root *sah*, transformed into *sāṭ*, [is changed to a cerebral *ṣ*]." Then comes the rule P.8.3.57 (इण्कोः): "after the sounds [included in the shortforms] *iṆ* and *kU*." The term *iṆ* refers to the sounds *i*, *u*, *ṛ*, *ḷ*, *e*, *o*, *ai*, *au*, *h*, *y*, *v*, *r*, and *l*. Among other things, this list includes all the *nāmin* vowels referred to in CA (2.4.1). The term *kU* refers to the consonants *k*, *kh*, *g*, *gh*, and *ṅ*. Thus, Pāṇini's system has taken care to place the condition *iṇkoḥ* after P.8.3.56, and avoid the problem of this condition becoming vacuous in this rule. I now doubt the traditional view that the CA follows Pāṇini. A large portion of the CA probably predates Pāṇini, or follows pre-Pāṇinian traditions, and Pāṇini's formulations seem to improve upon the inadequacies of this or a similar older tradition.

चतुराध्यायीभाष्य - सहेः साड्भूतस्य सकारस्य षकारो भवति । 'तुराषाट्' (अ.वे. २.५.३)। 'प्राषाट्' (अ.वे.पै.सं. २०.३५.२)। 'शत्रूषाप्नीषाट्' (अ.वे. ५.२०.११)। 'अभीषाडस्मि विश्वाषाट्' (अ. वे. १२.१.५४)। साड्भूतस्येति किमर्थम् । 'प्रसहनम्' (not in Vedic texts)।

Note: The examples listed by the CAB are found in APR (p. 146).

२.४.३. तद्धिते तकारादौ ।

Whitney (2.83).

Translation: Before a *t*-initial *taddhita* affix, [the *s*, preceded by a vowel other than *a* and *ā*, is changed to *ṣ*].

Note: As Whitney notes, none of the other Prātiśākhyas give "a grammatical definition of the phenomenon, like that of our treatise." *Taddhita* affixes are affixes added to nominal stems to derive secondary nominal stems. This rule, unlike the previous rule, has a proper application within the normal scope of a Prātiśākhya. For instance, वपुंष्टमे in AV (5.5.6) is represented as *vapuḥ-tame* in the Padapāṭha. Based on such examples, we know that the author of the AV Padapāṭha did separate certain affixes from their bases, affixes which were explicitly called *taddhita* by Pāṇini and the CA. Compare Pāṇini's rule P.8.3.101 (ह्रस्वात्तादौ तद्धिते), which has an additional condition *hrasvāt* "after a short vowel," to prevent from this change applying after long vowels. The CA version can dispense with such a condition, because it is primarily concerned with examples as they appear in the ŚAV, and not with Sanskrit at large.

चतुराध्यायीभाष्य - तद्धिते परतः तकारादौ नाम्युपधस्य सकारस्य षकारो भवति । 'सर्पिष्टरम्' (not in Vedic texts)।

'यजुष्टरम्' (not in Vedic texts)। 'वपुष्टरम्' (not in AV, ऋ.वे. १०.३२.३)। 'वपुष्टमाम्' ('वपुष्टमे,' अ.वे. ५.५.६)। तद्धित इति किमर्थम् । 'अग्निस्तक्मानम्' (अ.वे. ५.२२.१)। तकारादाविति किमर्थम् । 'सर्पिस्सात्' (not in Vedic texts)। 'यजुस्सात्' (not in Vedic texts)। 'वपुस्सात्' (not in Vedic texts)।

Note: Most of the unattested examples quoted in the CAB are found in the KV on P.8.3.101 (ह्रस्वात्तादौ तद्धिते).

२.४.४. युष्मदादेशे तैस्त्वमादिवर्जम् ।

Whitney (2.84).

Translation: [The *s*, preceded by a vowel other than *a* and *ā*, is changed to an *ṣ*], before [*t*-initial] allomorphs [lit. 'substitutes'] of *yuṣmat*, except in passages such as *tais tvam*.

Note: The relevant allomorphs of *yuṣmat* in this context are *tvam*, *tvā*, and *te*, as well as *tubhyam* and *tava* not included by Whitney. In a footnote, Whitney lists all cases of this phenomenon he found in the text of the ŚAV. However, he does not list the *gaṇa*, which forms the exceptions: "This *gaṇa* I have not thought it worth while to take the trouble to fill up, deeming it of more interest to give the complete list of the cases in which the change of the sibilant did, rather than of those in which it did not, take place. The former are, I believe, the more numerous of the two classes." Methodologically, of course, Whitney's procedure is exactly opposite of the one chosen by the CA.

Also note that the *gaṇa* referred to in the above CA rule is fully listed in the APR (204). The APR lists a total of 18 instances in this *gaṇa*, and the CAB cites the first three instances exactly in the same order. The examples listed in this *gaṇa* also include instances of *tubhyam* and *tava*, indicating that our present rule did indeed cover these forms as well.

There are other significant differences between the listings of Whitney and the listing given by the APR. Whitney lists अथो यो मन्युष्टे (AV 7.74.3) as a positive case of change, while the list of exceptions to this change in the APR (p. 122) includes this example, indicating that the APR knew this instance without cerebralization.

चतुराध्यायीभाष्य - युष्मदादेशे (H, N: युष्मदस्मदादेशे) तकारादौ नाम्युपधस्य सकारस्य षकारो भवति तैस्त्वमादिवर्जम् । 'बहिष्टे अस्तु' (अ.वे. १.३.१)। 'ऋतुभिष्ट्वा वयम्' (अ.वे. १.३५.४)। 'द्यौष्ट्वा पिता' (अ.वे. २.२८.४)। 'ताभिष्ट्वमस्मान्' (अ.वे. ९.२.२५)। 'तैष्टे रोहितः' (अ.वे. १३.१.३५)। तैस्त्वमादिवर्जमिति किमर्थम् । 'तैस्त्वं पुत्र(म्)' (अ.वे. ३.२३.४)। 'वध्रि(H: ध्रि, N: कध्रे)स्त्वम्' (अ.वे. ४.६.८)। 'पवस्तैस्त्वा' (अ.वे. ४.७.६)।

Note: The manuscripts of the commentary both contain the reading युष्मदस्मदादेशे, where the reference to *asmad* is clearly an error of some copyist. Also compare P.8.3.103 (युष्मत्तत्ततक्षुःष्वन्तःपादम्). The condition अन्तःपादम् "within a metrical foot" in Pāṇini eliminates certain instances, which the APR (p. 122) had to explicitly list as exceptions, e.g. अदब्धेभिः परि पाह्यक्तुभिः । तवेद्विष्णो, AV (17.1.9). It is, however, not clear how the Pāṇinian system would take care of many of the other examples listed in the APR as exceptions, except through some global rules like बहुलं छन्दसि.

२.४.५. तत्तानग्रादिषु ।

Whitney (2.85) adds च. E, F, I, O, P(corr): °नग्रा°.

Translation: [The *s*, preceded by a vowel other than *a* and *ā*, is changed to *ṣ*] also before *tat*, *tān agre* etc.

Note: Whitney says that the relevant forms of *tat* covered by this rule "are *tam*, *tat*, and *tān*." If *tān* is thus included by the generic reference to *tat*, then what is the point of listing '*tān agre* etc'? Normally, such phrasal citations are meant to limit a given generalization to the instances with the whole phrases. If we thus take this reference to तानग्रे as limiting this change to those instances of *tān* which are followed by *agre*, then some cases in the AV pose a dilemma, e.g. अग्निष्टानस्मात्, AV (18.2.28). This case is listed by Whitney as a case where the rule applies. The CA, perhaps, knew this case without cerebralization, and that the present text represents an analogical extension of cerebralization. However, since the rule refers to a Gaṇa, which is not fully illustrated by the CAB, we cannot be certain.

चतुराध्यायीभाष्य - तत्तानग्रादिषु च परतः नाम्युपधस्य सकारस्य षकारो भवति । 'अग्निष्टद्धोतां' (अ.वे. ६.७१.१)। 'अग्निष्टानग्रैं' (अ.वे. २.३४.३)। 'वायुष्टानग्रैं' (अ.वे. २.३४.४)। 'दुष्टरो' (Whitney: नो) ('दुष्टनो,' अ.वे. ४.७.३; 'दुष्टरंम्,' अ.वे. ६.४.१)। 'निष्टं भंज' (अ.वे. ४.२२.२)। 'निष्टक्वंरी(म्)' (अ.वे. ५.२२.६)।

Note: The CAB additionally offers a few examples which do not strictly come under the purview of the present rule. The manuscripts actually read *duṣṭaro*, while Whitney reports *duṣṭano*, and then comments: "The word *duṣṭara* (vi.4.1) would seem to come properly under it, but its treatment by the *pada*-texts (it is written *dustara*, not *duḥ-tara*) indicates, I should think, that the Hindus regarded it as an irregular compound of *duḥ* and *stara*, from the root *star* (*stṛ*); hence it would fall under the next rule, or else under rule 98 (= CA 2.4.18)." The manuscript reading *duṣṭaro* looks like a conflation of *duṣṭano* and *duṣṭaram*. The most likely intended form must be दुष्टनो (AV 4.7.3), which is split by the Padapāṭha as दुस्तनो इति दुःऽतनो.

२.४.६. स्तृतस्वस्वपिषु ।

Whitney (2.86). I have accepted Whitney's reading against all the mss, because each manuscript contains numerous errors. H, Nb: स्तृतः स्व°. A, B, D, E, F, O: स्तृतस्य स्वपिषु. Na: स्तृतिः स्व°. I: स्तृतस्त्यस्वपिषु. C: स्त्रितः स्वस्वपिषु. J, M: स्त्रितस्त्वस्वपिषु. P: स्त्रितस्यस्वपिषु.

Translation: Before *stṛta*, *sva*, and forms of the root *svap*, [the *s*, preceded by a vowel other than *a* or *ā*, is changed to *ṣ*].

Note: The manuscripts of the CA, and also of the AV, do not reflect the predicted double sibilant in these forms, but the forms are read with a single cerebral *ṣ*. The printed editions follow the manuscripts in this respect.

However, in the examples, as intended by the rule and the commentary, one must assume that, after a final *s* has been changed to *ṣ*, by this rule, before one of these forms, the initial *s* of these forms further undergoes cerebralization. Whitney here notices a gap in the coverage of sandhi rules in the CA. He points out that the rule as literally interpreted would yield the 'barbarous and impossible forms' like *aniṣstṛtaḥ*, *niṣsvā*, and *duṣsvapnyam*, and that there is no express prescription to change the *s* of the roots to *ṣ* due to its conjunction with an *ṣ*. Pāṇini 8.4.41 (*ṣṭunā ṣṭuḥ*) expressly takes care of such a situation. However, as Whitney correctly states: "... we are compelled to look upon *aniṣṣṭr̥taḥ*, *niṣṣvā*, and *duṣṣvapnyam* as the forms which the Prātiśākhya intends to sanction." Also, Whitney (*AV Transl.* Vol.I., p. 370) remarks: "The proper readings in (AV 6.121.1) c are (see note to Prāt. ii.86 = CA 2.4.6) *duṣṣvápnyam* and *níṣṣva*, which the mss. almost without exception abbreviate to *duṣvap-* and *níṣva*, just as they abbreviate *dattvā* to *datvā*, or, in 2 a, *rájjvām* to *rájvām*. SPP. here gives in his *saṃhitā*-text *ní ṣva*, with all his authorities; our text has *níḥ ṣva*, with only one of ours (O.): doubtless the true metrical form is *níṣ ṣuvā 'smát*."

In AV (7.82.3) etc., the CA rule enjoins double *ṣṣ*, which is not seen in any mss. Surya Kanta (*APR*, *Introduction*, p. 39) says that the mss. drop the *ṣ* according to the APR 80. Surya Kanta argues that the mss. thus represent a non-Śaunakīya tradition. However, it may be that even the Śaunakīyas disregarded their own precepts, when it came to writing down the text of their tradition, under the pressure of the contemporary practice of writing Sanskrit, where the writing of such double *ṣṣ* is hardly ever practiced. Thus, one needs to make a distinction between the original Śaunakīya precepts, and what later happened to the transmitted text under the pressure of the latter-day practice of Sanskrit orthography, and perhaps, pronunciation.

चतुराध्यायीभाष्य - स्तृतस्वस्वपिषु परतः नाम्युपधस्य सकारस्य षकारो भवति । 'अग्निष्ट्रृतः' (?, Whitney: 'अनिंष्टृतः,' अ.वे. ७.८२.३)। 'दुष्ष्वप्न्यम्' (अ.वे. ६.४६.३)। 'दुरितं निष्ष्वास्मत्' (अ.वे. ६.१२१.१; ७.८३.४)।

Note: Referring to *aniḥ-str̥taḥ* in AV (7.82.3), Whitney (*AV Transl.* Vol.I., p. 449) remarks: "All the *pada*-mss. read at the end *ániḥ-str̥taḥ*, and this is required by Prāt. ii.86 (= CA 2.4.6); but SPP. alters to *áni-str̥taḥ* -- which, to be sure, better suits the sense. The RV. *pada*-text also has (viii.33.9) *ániḥ-str̥taḥ;* TS. (and by inference MS., as the editor reports nothing), *ániṣṭr̥taḥ*, unchanged."

२.४.७. नामिकरेफात्प्रत्ययसकारस्य ।

Whitney (2.87). A, B, D, P: split the rule after °प्रत्ययः. H, J, M, N, O: °प्रत्ययः सकारस्य. P(orig): हकारस्य for सकारस्य.

Translation: The [initial] *s* of a suffix [is changed to *ṣ*] after a vowel other than *a* and *ā*, *k*, or *r*.

Note: There is a shift beginning with this rule to the change of an initial *s*. The conditioning sounds belong to a different morpheme, and hence we should note that the change takes place across a morpheme-boundary. Elements across such morpheme-boundaries are occasionally split by the Padapāṭha, but not always so. In all the three examples cited here, the Padapāṭha does not split the constituents.

The comparable rules in Pāṇini are P.8.3.57 (इण्कोः) and P.8.3.59 (आदेशप्रत्यययोः). While the present CA rule refers to *k*, rather than *ka-varga*, cf. Pāṇini's *kU* in P.8.3.57, the CAB renders it as *kavarga*, possibly under the influence of the Pāṇinian rules. Or perhaps, as Whitney suggests: "He explains *ka* in the rule by *kavargāt*, 'after a guttural,' probably in view of the requirements of some authorities (see under ii. 6 = CA 2.1.6) that the *k* should become *kh* before the sibilant."

चतुराध्यायीभाष्य - नामिनश्च कवर्गाच्च रेफाच्चोत्तरस्य प्रत्ययसकारस्य षकारो भवति । 'फालांज्जातः करिष्यति' (अ.वे. १०.६.२)। 'इयंक्षमाणा भृगुंभिः' (अ.वे. ४.१४.५)। 'हविषाहांर्षमेनम्' (अ.वे. ३.११.३)।

Note: Rules such as this one indicate that a transition from the original purposes of the Prātiśākhya and Śikṣā literature to those of a general grammar of Sanskrit has already begun. This rule deals with a kind of juncture which is not separated even in the Padapāṭha, and hence one would not be expected to make this sandhi in the process of combining the Padas to derive the Saṃhitāpāṭha. This juncture is purely internal.

२.४.८. स्त्रैषूयम् ।

Whitney (2.88).

Translation: [The change of *s* to *ṣ* also takes place in the form] *straiṣūyam* [< *strai+sūyam*].

Note: Whitney comments: "Why, among the words mentioned in iv.83 (= CA 4.3.11), it should be singled out to be made thus the subject of a special rule, is not at all clear. The position of the rule, too, thrust in between the two closely related rules 87 (= CA 2.4.7) and 89 (= CA 2.4.9), and disturbing their connection, is in a high degree awkward, and calculated to inspire suspicion of an interpolation." Since all the manuscripts contain this rule in this very position, this rule must have been a very ancient interpolation, if indeed it is an interpolation.

In any case, the instance accounted for in this rule is of an exceptional character. It is not covered by प्रत्ययसकारस्य in CA (2.4.7), because the *s* of *sūya* does not belong to an affix. Similarly, it is not covered by rules like CA (2.4.10), because *sūyam* is not preceded by an *upasarga*. This form would probably be derived by P.8.3.106 (पूर्वपदात्), which is a nebulous rule saying that, according to some teachers, in Vedic texts, an *s*, preceded by an appropriate conditioning sound belonging to the preceding word, is cerebralized.

चतुराध्यायीभाष्य - स्त्रैषूयमिति सकारस्य षकारो भवति । 'स्त्रैषूयमन्यत्र' (अ.वे. ६.११.३)।

२.४.९. नलोपेऽपि ।

Whitney (2.89).

Translation: Even when the [intervening] *n* has been deleted, [the initial *s* of an affix, preceded by an appropriate conditioning sound, cf. CA (2.4.7), is changed to cerebral *ṣ*].

Note: As Whitney notes, the rule "is intended to apply to such cases as *yajū̃ṣi*, *havī̃ṣi*, where, by ii. 34 (= CA 2.1.34), there has been a loss of *n* before the ending *si*, accompanied, by i.67 (= CA 1.3.5), with nasalization of the preceding vowel, when the ending itself is converted into *ṣi* after the alterant vowel, although the latter is nasal." It is to be contrasted to Pāṇini 8.3.58 (नुम्विसर्जनीयशर्व्यवायेऽपि). P.8.3.58, in part, says that the *s* of the following affix changes to *ṣ*, if preceded by an appropriate conditioning sound, in spite of the intervention of sounds like *nUM* (> *anusvāra*). Since the *anusvāra* is considered to be a consonantal nasal sound, Pāṇini thinks of its intervention in examples like *yajūṃṣi*. For the CA, which does not have the conception of an *anusvāra*, the *n* is deleted, and the preceding vowel is nasalized. Therefore, it speaks of "even after the deletion of the intervening *n*." Another point brought up this rule is the conception of the deletion as held by the CA. One may possibly infer that, according to the CA, a deletion may be considered to be like a positive zero, whose intervention may block the operation of a rule like CA (2.4.7).

चतुराध्यायीभाष्य - नकारस्यापि लोपे नामिनश्चोत्तरस्य सकारस्य षकारो भवति । 'परूंषि यस्यं सम्भाराः' (अ.वे. ९.६.१)। 'यजूंषि होत्रां ब्रूमः' (अ.वे. ११.६.१४)। 'अत्तो हवींषि' (अ.वे. १८.३.४४)।

Note: On this rule, Whitney says: "This rule attaches itself immediately and closely to rule 87 (= CA 2.4.7), from which it has been blunderingly separated by the intrusion of rule 88 (= CA 2.4.8)." On the basis of the contents of the rule, one feels like agreeing with Whitney. Note that the parallel rules in Pāṇini, i.e. P.8.3.57 (इण्कोः), P.8.3.58 (नुम्विसर्जनीयशर्व्यवायेऽपि), and P.8.3.59 (आदेशप्रत्यययोः), are consecutive rules. However, rule CA (2.4.8) must have been a very early intrusion, since it is uniformly supported by all the manuscripts as well as by the oldest commentary, i.e. the CAB.

२.४.१०. उपसर्गाद्धातोः ।

Whitney (2.90). A, B, D: °र्ग्रा°. I: 10.

Translation: After [an appropriate conditioning sound, cf. CA (2.4.7), at the end of a] preverb (= *upasarga*), [the initial *s*] of a verb root [is changed to *ṣ*].

Note: We should note that, in this case, the Padapāṭha clearly analyses the forms *pariṣasvajānāḥ* and *viṣitam* into *pari-sasvajānāḥ* and *vi-sitam*. The first occurrence of the reduplication of the root in *sa+svaj* is treated here as representing the root. Here, the counter-examples are fabricated examples, but, as noted by Whitney, "The proper exceptions to the rule are detailed below, in rules 102-107 (= CA 2.4.22-27)."

चतुराध्यायीभाष्य - उपसर्गस्थान्निमित्तात् धातुसकारस्य षकारो भवति । 'वृक्षं यद्गावंः परिषस्वजाना अंनुस्फुरम्' (अ.वे. १.२.३)। 'विषितं ते वस्तिबिलम्' (अ.वे. १.३.

८)। उपसर्गादिति किमर्थम् । 'दधि सिञ्चति' । 'मधु सिञ्चति' ।

Note: The counter examples दधि सिञ्चति and मधु सिञ्चति are found in the KV on P. 8.3.65 (उपसर्गात्सुनोतिसुवतिस्यतिस्तौतिस्तोभतिस्थासेनयसेधसिचसञ्जस्वञ्जाम्).

२.४.११. अभ्यासाच्च ।

Whitney (2.91). No such rule in A and B.

Translation: [The initial *s* of a verb-root is changed to *ṣ*] after [an appropriate conditioning sound, cf. CA (2.4.7), in] the reduplication.

Note: For all the examples cited by the commentator, the Padapāṭha offers the dental *s* unchanged, e.g. *suṣūdata : susūdata*, *siṣyade : sisyade*. It is not, however, clear how one would avoid double retroflexion in a case like अभि सिष्यदे, AV (5.5.9). Why would rule CA (2.4.10) not apply to this example to change the *s* of the reduplication to *ṣ*, as it does in the form परिषस्वजानाः? The answer may lie in the way the Padapāṭha treats these forms. The form परिषस्वजानाः in AV (1.2.3) is represented as *pari-sasvajānāḥ* in the Padapāṭha, indicating this as a case of compounding. On the other hand, अभि सिष्यदे in AV (5.5.9) is represented as *abhi* / *sisyade* in the Padapāṭha, indicating that these are treated as two separate padas, and hence *abhi* is not an *upasarga*. In this context, *abhi* is a preposition (*karmapravacanīya*) connected with the accusative *vṛkṣān*.

चतुराध्यायीभाष्य - अभ्यासाच्चोत्तरस्य धातुसकारस्य षकारो भवति । 'सुषूदत' (अ.वे. १.२६.४)। 'अभि सिष्यदे' (अ.वे. ५.५.९)। 'आ सुष्वदे' (only in N, not found in Vedic texts)। 'आ सुष्वयन्ती' (अ.वे. ५.१२.६; ५.२७.८)। 'तत्सिंषासति' (अ.वे. १३.२.१४)। 'सुषुवे' (अ.वे. १४.१.४३)।

२.४.१२. स्थासहिसिचीनामकारव्यवायेऽपि ।

Whitney (2.92). E, F, I, O: °व्यवधायेपि. No such rule in A and B. E (corr), F (corr), Ha: °नामकारस्य व्य°. O: स्थासहितसिची°.

Translation: [The *s* of the roots] *sthā*, *sah*, and *sic*, [is changed to *ṣ* after an appropriate conditioning sound, cf. CA (2.4.7), in the *upasarga*], even when there is an intervening [past-tense marker] *a*.

Note: There is an interesting theoretical issue concerning the application of this rule which has not been brought out either by the CAB or by Whitney. For example, in the example *abhyaṣṭhām*, the components are *abhi+a+sthām*. On the face of it, the rule assumes that the change of *s* to *ṣ* takes place before the *i* of *abhi* is changed to *y*. CA (2.4.7: नामिकरेफात्प्रत्ययसकारस्य) does not include the sound *y* among the conditioning sounds for this change, while the category of *nāmin* includes the sound *i*. On the other hand, the conditioning sounds for this change, as listed in P.8.3.57 (इण्कोः), include *y*, besides *i*, in the abbreviation *iṆ*, cf. Padamañjarī on P.8.3.63 (प्राक् सितादड्व्यवायेऽपि) says: अभ्यषुणोदिति । ... प्रागेव यणादेशात्षत्वम्, कृते वा यणि यकारमेवाश्रित्य षत्वम्. Thus, Pāṇini can afford to make the change of *s* to *ṣ*, either before or after changing *abhi* to *abhy*. On the other hand, the CA seems to expect us to make change of *s* to *ṣ*, before changing *abhi* to *abhy*.

चतुराध्यायीभाष्य - स्थासहिसिचीत्येतेषाम् अकारव्यवायेऽपि उपसर्गस्थान्निमित्तात् सकारस्य षकारो भवति । 'अभ्यंष्ठां विश्वाः' (अ.वे. १०.५.३६; १६.९.१)। 'तेनं देवा व्यंषहन्त' (अ.वे. ३.१०.१२)। 'येनाक्षा अभ्यषिंच्यन्त' (अ.वे. १४.१.३६)।

Note: The manuscript H presents the first sentence simply as: स्थासहिसिचीनामकारस्य षकारो भवति । Whitney rightly felt that this was mutilated and incomplete, and he restored the sentence as: स्थासहिसिचीनामुपसर्गस्थान्निमित्तादकारव्यवायेऽपि धातुसकारस्य षकारो भवति। While this is not exactly identical with the text as now found in the second manuscript, N, it is very close to it, and we must admire Whitney's acumen in restoring the missing text.

For the examples cited by the commentary, the Padapāṭha and the printed editions offer different treatment. The example *abhyaṣṭhām* in AV

(10.5.36) is represented in the Padapāṭha as two words: *abhi / asthām*. The VVRI edition reads *vyasahanta* in AV (3.10.12), while it notes the manuscript variant *vyaṣahanta*. The Padapāṭha splits it as: *vi / asahanta*. The form *abhyaṣicyanta* in AV (14.1.36) is represented in the Padapāṭha as: *abhi-asicyanta*. All the three forms are given with cerebrals in the Whitney-Roth edition.

२.४.१३. अभ्यासव्यवायेऽपि स्थः ।

Whitney (2.93).

Translation: Even with the intervention of a reduplication, [the *s*] of *sthā* [is changed to *ṣ*, after an appropriate conditioning sound, cf. CA (2.4.7), in the preverb (*upasarga*)].

Note: In the examples cited by the commentary, the Padapāṭha restores the 'original' dental sibilant, e.g. *vi taṣṭhire : vi / tasthire*.

चतुराध्यायीभाष्य - अभ्यासव्यवायेऽपि उपसर्गस्थान्निमित्तात् स्थः सकारस्य षकारो भवति । 'सप्त सिन्धंवो वि तष्ठिरे' (अ.वे. ४.६.२)। 'ब्रह्मं पुरुरूपं वि तंष्ठे (H: ष्ठिरे)' (अ.वे. ९.१०.१९)।

Note: Whitney's text for AV (9.10.19) does not show the application of this rule, but reads: *vi tasthe*. Whitney says that this was given erroneously and that there is manuscript evidence to support the reading *vi taṣṭhe*. This reading is also supported by the VVRI edition, AV (9.15.19 = W: 9.10.19).

Whitney further points out: "We have in two other passages (ix.9.2, xiv.2.9) *adhi tasthuḥ* (not *taṣṭhuḥ*); this apparently constitutes an exception to the rule which has escaped the notice both of the treatise and of the commentator : possibly, however, the *adhi* is not in these passages regarded as standing in the relation of *upasarga* to the root *sthā*, since it does, in fact, belong rather, in a prepositional relation, to preceding ablative cases, than to the verbal form as its prefix : and this is the more clearly indicated by its retaining its independent accent before the accented verb." The VVRI edition agrees with Whitney's reading, and cites no manuscript variants. It is just not clear what ablative cases Whitney is referring to in the cited examples. The preposition (कर्मप्रवचनीय) *adhi* in both instances seems to echo the locatives in the context: यत्रेमा

विश्वा भुवनाधिं तस्थुः, AV (9.9.2); ये गंन्धर्वा अंप्सरसंश्च देवीरेषु वांनस्पत्येषु येऽधिं तस्थुः, AV (14.2.9).

२.४.१४. परमेभ्योऽनापाके ।

Whitney (2.94). P: °नापाने.

Translation: [The initial *s* of *sthā* is changed to *ṣ*] after *parama* etc., but not after *āpāke*.

Note: The CAB does not explicitly continue the word *sthaḥ* from the previous rule, though all the examples it cites are examples of the root *sthā*, and it makes eminent sense to continue the word into this rule. It may be noted that all the examples of the *paramādi gaṇa* listed under APR (205, pp. 122-3) involve the element *stha*. There are two instances included here which actually involve the superlative affix *-iṣṭha*, but seem to have been evidently wrongly etymologized as involving *stha*, i.e. *śreṣṭha* and *prathiṣṭha*. These two words are not analyzed by the Padapāṭha. However, in all the examples cited by the CAB, the Padapāṭha analyses the components, and reduces the *ṣ* to *s*, e.g. *parameṣṭhī : parame-sthī*.

चतुराध्यायीभाष्य - परमादिभ्यः पूर्वपदेभ्यः अनापाके उत्तरपदस्थस्य सकारस्य षकारो भवति । 'परमेष्ठी' (अ.वे. ४.११.७)। 'भुवनेष्ठाः' (अ.वे. २.१.४)। 'मध्यमेष्ठाः' (अ.वे. २.६. ४)। 'अङ्गेष्ठाः' (अ.वे. ६.१४.१)। अनापाक इति किमर्थम् । 'आपाकेस्थाः प्रंहासिनंः' (अ.वे. ८.६.१४)।

Note: The *gaṇa* referred to in this CA rule is fully listed in the APR (205). It contains a total of 9 instances, of which the CAB lists the first three instances in the same order. One should also note an interesting fact that the CA rule contains the exception: अनापाके, which allows the exclusion of the example आपाकेस्थाः प्रंहासिनंः. The APR (200), on the other hand, does not contain any such explicit statement of exception, but perhaps excludes the above example simply by not listing it. However, one must say that rule APR (200: अनुपसर्गात्षकारः) would apply in this case, and one should have had a list of exceptions. One may possibly make a guess that the original CA notion of such *gaṇa*s was more like the notion of *ākṛtigaṇa*s in the Pāṇinian system, and therefore, one needed exceptions like अनापाके included. Once full listings of *gaṇa*s were made, the need for stating such exceptions diminished. One needs exceptions stated, only when one does not have full lists of instances, and has only generic rules. The examples *bhuvaneṣṭhāḥ*, *madhyameṣṭhāḥ*, and *aṅgeṣṭhāḥ* occur in the same order as examples 114-116 under APR (79).

The VVRI edition, which is basically a reprint of the SSP edition, reads AV (8.6.14): आपाकेष्ठाः प्रंहासिनंः, while it lists the reading approved by the CA, आपाकेस्थाः प्रंहासिनंः, as a manuscript variant. Most likely this is a case of the spread of retroflexion to examples where it did not occur in an earlier period. Whitney's reading matches what is approved by the CA, but one cannot be certain whether he was influenced by the CA in the choice of his reading. Criticizing SSP., Whitney (*AV Transl.* Vol.II., p. 496) says: "In (AV 8.6.14)c, he (= SSP.) adopts *āpākeṣṭhā́s*, with a small minority of his mss., and directly against Prāt. ii.94 (= 2.4.14), which prescribes *-sthā́s*."

२.४.१५. अपसव्याभ्यां च ।

Whitney (2.95).

Translation: Also after *apa* and *savya*, [the *s* of *sthā* is changed to *ṣ*].

Note: As Whitney notes, in these cases "the change takes place irregularly after *a*, instead of after an alterant vowel." The Padapāṭha does not analyze the components of *apāṣṭhāt*, AV (4.6.5), and does not reduce the cerebral sibilant to dental, but it does analyze *savyaṣṭhāḥ*, AV (8.8.23) into *savya-sthāḥ*. Pāṇini 8.3.97 (अम्बाम्बगोभूमिसव्यापद्वित्रिकुशेकुशङ्क्वङ्गुमञ्जिपुञ्जिपरमेबर्हिर्दिव्यग्निभ्यः स्थः) lumps *apa* and *savya* along with *parame*, and several others. This rule allows the formations *ambaṣṭha* and *āmbaṣṭha* which also lack phonological motivation for this change. Pāṇini also has a special rule to account for an equally exceptional *praṣṭha*, cf. P.8.3.92 (प्रष्ठोऽग्रगामिनि).

चतुराध्यायीभाष्य - अप सव्य इत्येताभ्यां चोत्तरस्थसकारस्य षकारो भवति । 'अपाष्ठाच्छृङ्गात्' (अ.वे. ४.६.५)। 'इन्द्रः सव्यष्ठाश्चन्द्रमाः' (अ.वे. ८.८.२३)।

Note: On *apāṣṭhāt* in AV (4.6.5), Whitney (*AV Transl.* Vol.I., p. 154) says: "Prāt. ii.95 (= CA 2.4.15) regards *apāṣṭha* as from *apa-sthā*, doubtless correctly".

२.४.१६. अग्नेः स्तोमसोमयोः ।

Whitney (2.96). A, B, D, E, Ha, J, M, Na, P: अग्नेस्तो°. F, O: अग्ने-स्तोमयोः.

Translation: [The *s*] of *stoma* and *soma* [is changed to *ṣ*] after *agni*.

Note: These cases are covered by a closely similar rule in Pāṇini: P.8.3.82 (अग्नेः स्तुत्स्तोमसोमाः). However, while the form *agniṣṭomena*, AV (9.6.40), is reduced in the Padapāṭha to *agni-stomena*, the form *agnīṣomau*, AV (8.9.14) is not so analyzed.

Whitney also points out *agniṣvāttaḥ*, AV (18.3.44: *Pada: agni-svāttaḥ*), which he says should have been included in this rule: "We can hardly suppose that it was intentionally omitted here, to be included in the *gaṇa* of rule 98 [= CA 2.4.18], below: either it must have been overlooked by the maker of the treatise, or the verse which contains it was not in his Atharvaveda : that it was, however, contained in the text recognized by the commentator, is shown by the fact that he several times (under i.80 = CA 1.3.18; i.84 = CA 1.3.22; and ii.34 = CA 2.1.34) cites the phrase *atto havīṃṣi*, which forms part of its second line."

Whitney's inference may not be so cogent, especially because the parallel rule in Pāṇini, i.e. P.8.3.82, also excludes the consideration of this form. Secondly, the APR (206, pp. 123-4) precisely does what Whitney considers to be most unlikely, namely it lists this example among a *gaṇa*, which begins with *tri*, the *gaṇa* which is referred to in CA (2.4.18). One may assume that the CA also intended this example to be included in this *gaṇa*.

चतुराध्यायीभाष्य - अग्नेरुत्तरयोः स्तोमसोमयोः सकारस्य षकारो भवति । 'यावंदग्निष्टोमेन' (अ.वे. ९.६.४०)। 'अग्नीषोमांवदधुः' (अ.वे. ८.९.१४)। अग्नेरिति किमर्थम् । 'अभि सोमों अवीवृधत्' (अ.वे. १.२९.३)।

२.४.१७. सुञः ।

Whitney (2.97). A, B: सुपः.

Translation: [The *s*] of the particle *su* [is also changed to *ṣ* after an appropriate conditioning sound in the preceding word].

Note: Pāṇini 8.3.107 (सुञः) is identical with CA (2.4.17). Pāṇini's rule 8.3.107 comes immediately after P.8.3.106 (पूर्वपदात्), which says that a change like the one taught by the present rule takes place after the conditioning sound in a preceding word, i.e. पूर्वपदात्. This is also made explicit in APR (206: पूर्वपदात् षकारः), which precedes APR (207a) which deals with the examples covered by the present rule. All the examples offered by the CAB are found listed in the same order under APR (207a, p. 124).

चतुराध्यायीभाष्य - सुञः सकारस्य षकारो भवति । 'इदमू षु' (अ.वे. १.२४.४)। 'तदू षु' (अ.वे. ५.१.५)। 'पर्यू षु' (अ.वे. ५.६.४)। 'महीमू षु' (अ.वे. ७.६.२)। 'अन्य ऊ षु' (अ.वे. १८.१.१६)। 'स्तुष ऊ षु' (अ.वे. १८.१.३७)। 'त्यमू षु' (अ.वे. ७.८५.१)।

Note: Whitney misses the example पर्यू षु which is found in both the manuscripts. On *anya ū ṣu* (AV 18.1.16), Whitney (*AV Transl.* Vol.II., p. 819) remarks: "RV. x.10.14 has for **a** the much better version *anyám ū ṣú tvám*. ... Our D., and a single ms. of SPP's (with the comm.), also have *anyam* ⌊at the beginning⌋, and SPP. accordingly admits *anyám* into his text, in spite of the absence of *tvám*. But the comment on the Prāt. three times (under ii.97 = CA 2.4.17; iii.4 = CA 3.1.4; vi.98 = CA 4.3.27) reads *anya ū ṣu*, and it cannot well be questioned that this is the true text of our AV."

२.४.१८. त्र्यादिभ्यः ।

Whitney (2.98). A, Hac, Nc: त्रा°. P: आदिभ्यः corrected to त्र्यादिभ्यः.

Translation: [The initial *s* of a word] preceded by words such as *tri* [is changed to *ṣ*].

Note: The examples cited by the commentary to illustrate this rule are analyzed by the Padapāṭha into their components and are presented with their original form without the cerebral sibilant, e.g. *triṣaptāḥ : tri-saptāḥ*.

चतुराध्यायीभाष्य - त्र्यादिभ्यः पूर्वपदेभ्यः उत्तरपदस्थस्य सकारस्य षकारो भवति । 'ये त्रिंषप्ताः' (अ.वे. १.१.१)।

'गोषेधाम्' (अ.वे. १.१८.४)। 'रघुष्यदोऽधि' (अ.वे. ३.७. १)।

Note: Referring to the expression *tryādi*, Whitney says: "Here is another of those convenient *gaṇas*, set as a catch-all for whatever cases may not have been otherwise provided for, and rendering it impossible for us to ascertain the precise degree of accuracy with which the authors of the treatise examined and excerpted their text." Now, the *gaṇa* referred to in this CA rule is fully listed in APR (206). It contains a total of 16 instances, out of which the CAB quotes the first three instances exactly in the same order. Also see the Note under CA 2.4.16.

Whitney further says: "He (= commentator) also, in his paraphrase, limits the application of the rule to cases of this character, in which an alterant vowel at the end of the first member of a compound comes before an initial *s* of the following member." The commentator simply says त्र्यादिभ्यः पूर्वपदेभ्यः, and makes no explicit reference to the *nāmin* vowels at the end of these words. It is, true, however, that all the cited examples fit Whitney's description. But the examples listed in this *gaṇa* under APR (206, pp. 123-4) are not examples of compounds. They contain a number of phrasal sequences, e.g. नि ष हींयताम्, AV (8.4.10).

Whitney offers a number of cases which might potentially become members of this class. Whitney's listing overlaps with the listing of this *gaṇa*, as found under APR (206, pp. 123-4). As noted above, the *gaṇa* under APR (206) contains several phrasal sequences, while Whitney's listing includes only compound expressions. The APR *gaṇa* contains the following compound expressions, not covered by Whitney's listing: *gaviṣṭhiram* (4.29.5), *viṣāsahiḥ* (1.29.6), *abhimātiṣāhaḥ* (4.32.4), and *agniṣvāttāḥ* (18.3.44). It additionally contains the phrasal sequences *ni ṣa hīyatām* (8.4.10) and *hi ṣmā* (18.1.33). On the other hand, Whitney lists the following compounds, which are not listed under APR (206): *suṣṭuti* (6.1.3), *suṣūman* (7.46.2), *anuṣṭup* (8.9.14), *triṣṭup* (8.9.14), *traiṣṭubha* (9.10.1), and *diviṣṭambhaḥ* (19.32.7).

२.४.१९. ऋकारान्तात्सदेः ।

Whitney (2.99).

Translation: After a word ending in short *ṛ*, [the initial *s*] of the root *sad* [is changed to *ṣ*].

चतुराध्यायीभाष्य - ऋकारान्तादुत्तरस्य सदिसकारस्य षकारो भवति । 'होतृषदंनम्' (अ.वे. ७.९९.१)। 'पितृषदंनाः पितृषदंने त्वा' (अ.वे. १८.४.६७)।

Note: Whitney adds: "To these may be added *pitṛṣad* (xiv.2.33 : p. *pitṛ-sad*); and in *nārṣada* (4.19.2 : p. *nārsada*) is also implied *nṛṣad*."

२.४.२०. बर्हिपथ्यप्सुदिविपृथिवीति च ।

Whitney (2.100). F: °प्सुदिवीति च. I: °पृथिवीभ्यश्च. J, M, P(corr): °पथाप्सु°. I: 20.

Translation: [The *s* of the root *sad* is changed to *ṣ*] also after *barhi*, *pathi*, *apsu*, *divi*, and *pṛthivi*.

Note: Whitney comments: "We have reason to be surprised that the root *sad* is treated in this manner, being made the subject of these two separate rules. If the compounds into which it enters as final member are to be excepted from the general *gaṇa* of rule 98 (= CA 2.4.18), we should expect to find it directed that the *s* of *sad* should always be lingualized after an alterant vowel, as is actually the case. Not only is there, by the method adopted, a loss of that brevity which treatises of the *sūtra* class are wont to aim at almost as their chief object, but there is also a loss of completeness : the only remaining compound of *sad* of this class, *suṣad* (e.g. ii.36.4), is left out, to be provided for in the general *gaṇa*. Or is it possible that *su* is regarded as falling under rule 90 (= CA 2.4.10), as if a proper *upasarga* or preposition? If so, the forms into which it enters would be sufficiently provided for; since, excepting in the cases noted in the later rule (102 = CA 2.4.22 etc.), it always lingualizes the initial *s* of a root, while it has no effect upon that of a preposition or adverb, as in *susaha* (vi.64.3 : p. *su-saha*) and the numerous compounds in which it is followed by *sam*, as *susaṃrabdha*." There is no exactly parallel rule or rules in Pāṇini which deals specifically with the formations involving the root *sad*.

We may note that no forms of *sad* are noted in the *gaṇa* under APR (206), which is probably the same *gaṇa* as referred to by the term *tryādi* in CA (2.4.18). Whitney's discussion regarding the status of *su* needs an extensive consideration. For a parallel discussion, see the KV on P.8.3.88 (सुविनिर्दुर्भ्यः) and P.8.3.98 (सुषामादिषु च).

चतुराध्यायीभाष्य - बर्हि पथि अप्सु दिवि पृथिवीत्येतेभ्य-श्चोत्तरस्य सदिसकारस्य षकारो भवति । बर्हि । 'बर्हिषदः पितरः' (अ.वे. १८.१.५१)। बर्हि । पथि । 'पथिषदी नृचक्षसा' (अ.वे. १८.२.१२)। पथ्यप्सु । 'अप्सुषदोऽप्यग्नीन्' (अ.वे. १२.२.४)। अप्सु । दिवि । 'ये देवा दिविषदः' (अ.वे. १०.९.१२)। दिवि । पृथिवि । 'पृथिविषद्भ्यः' (अ.वे. १८.४.७८)।

२.४.२१. हिदिविभ्यामस्तेः ।

Whitney (2.101).

Translation: After *hi* and *divi*, [the initial *s*] of the verb *as* [is changed to *ṣ*].

Note: It is understood from the context that the rule applies only to those forms of the verb *as*, where the initial *a* is deleted, and the forms become *s*-initial.

चतुराध्यायीभाष्य - हि दिवि इत्येताभ्यामुत्तरस्य अस्ति-सकारस्य षकारो भवति । 'आपो हि ष्ठा' (अ.वे. १.५.१)। 'ये देवा दिवि ष्ठ' (अ.वे. १.३०.३)। ततोऽपवदति । 'विमुचो हि सन्ति' (अ.वे. ६.११२.३)।

Note: What is the source of this exception referred to in the passage ततोऽपवदति । विमुचो हि सन्ति in the CAB*?* APR*?* This could be a case of the author of the CA inadvertently forgetting to mention an exception, or a case of textual change. In this case, the manuscripts of the AV do follow this exception, and Whitney as well as the VVRI edition read विमुचो हि सन्ति. One, however, cannot be certain that this was the reading known to the CA.

Referring to the preceding section, Whitney makes the following general comments: "But there are still left in the Atharvan text a few instances of the same conversion, which can hardly be regarded as included in any of the preceding rules, since they are analogous with none of the other cases there treated of: unless something has been lost from this final section of the chapter

- of which there are no indications - the treatise-makers and their commentator must lie under the imputation of having been careless enough to overlook them. The passages referred to are as follows: आदुं ष्टेनम् (iv.3.4), तमुं ष्टुहि (vi.1.2), नि ष हींयताम् (viii.4.10), and चिद्धि ष्मां (xviii.1.33). There would be little plausibility in a claim that the verses containing these passages were not included in the Atharvaveda accepted by the school to which the treatise belonged, or that the readings of the school were different."

Now we find that the last two of the examples are mentioned in the *tryādi gaṇa*, which is referred to in CA (2.4.18), and is extensively listed under APR (206, pp. 123-4). Besides this, Whitney's assumption that the CAB was expected to give complete lists of all examples and counter-examples found in the text of the ŚAV is baseless. Even in the APR, it appears that lists of positive examples are not complete catalogues, while the lists of exceptions are so. In contrast, the CAB is almost always illustrative, rather than exhaustive.

२.४.२२. न सृपिसृजिस्पृशिस्फूर्जिस्वरतिस्मरतीनाम् ।

Whitney (2.102). Ha, Na: °स्पृषि°. J, M: °स्यूर्जि°. E (corr): °मृशि° for °स्पृशि°. F (corr): omits सृजि.

Translation: Not, [however, the *s*] of the roots *sṛp*, *sṛj*, *spṛś*, *sphūrj*, *svṛ*, and *smṛ*.

Note: Whitney makes the following comment: "This is evidently a rule of kindred sphere with rule 106 (= CA 2.4.26), below, and the two might well enough have been combined into one, which should teach that a root containing a *r*, either semivowel or vowel, was not liable to the changes prescribed in this section." However, from the behavior of the treatise, one may infer that the CA does not intend to cover the consonantal and the vocalic *r* under a common generalization. This suspicion is further strengthened by the separate mention of *ṛ* and *r* in one and the same rule, e.g. CA (3.4.1: ऋवर्णरेफषकारेभ्यः समानपदे नो णः). Pāṇini 8.3.110 (न रपरसृपिसृजिस्पृशिसवनादीनाम्) also separately refers to roots containing consonantal and vocalic *r*.

Whitney further says: "As so stated, it would require the notice of but a single exception, *vi ṣphurat* (vi.56.1 and x.4.8). As the rules now stand, they are slightly inexact, for in neither of them are included *anusphuram* (i.2.3), *atisara* (v.8.2 etc.), and *pratisara* (e.g. ii.11.2), although other forms of the root *sar* are contemplated in rule 106 (= CA 2.4.26)."

Again, we now find that the instances of *atisara* (v.8.2 etc.), and *pratisara* (e.g. ii.11.2) are listed in the *gosanyādi gaṇa* referred to in the next rule,

CA (2.4.23), and fully listed under APR (147f, p. 101). As for *anusphuram* (1.2.3) mentioned by Whitney as an exception to cerebralization, the VVRI edition notes several manuscripts which have the reading *anuṣphuram.* Further, the absence of *anusphuram* in the *gosanyādi gaṇa* listed exhaustively under APR (147f, p. 101) may be taken as an indication that the APR also knew the form as *anuṣphuram*, rather than as *anusphuram.* On the other hand, P.8.3.76 (स्फुरतिस्फुलत्योर्निर्निविभ्यः) says that after *nir*, *ni*, and *vi*, the *s* of *sphurati* and *sphulati* is optionally (or 'preferably' *a la* Kiparsky) changed to *ṣ*. The tradition understands this rule in such a way, that without this rule, there would be no cerebral *ṣ* in any forms of these roots: एतयोरपि पूर्ववदप्राप्त एव मूर्धन्यो विधीयते, Nyāsa on KV on P.8.3.76. This would predict the form *anusphuram.* One could conceivably argue that a more original AV form *anuṣphuram* was reduced to *anusphuram* under the pressure of the Pāṇinian tradition.

चतुराध्यायीभाष्य - न तु खलु सृपिसृजिस्पृशिस्फूर्जिस्वरतिस्मरतीनाम् इत्येतेषां सकारस्य षकारो भवति । सृपि । 'विसृपो विरप्शिन्' (not in AV, वा.सं. १.२८)। सृपि । सृजि । 'अतिसृष्टो अपां वृषभः' (अ.वे. १६.१.१)। सृजि । स्पृशि । 'विस्पृशः' (?, Whitney: perhaps a corrupted reading for 'उपरिस्पृशः,' अ.वे. ५.३.१०)। स्पृशि । स्फूर्जि । 'वाश्यमानाभि स्फूर्जति' (अ.वे. १२.५.२०)। स्फूर्जि । स्वरति । 'विदथाभिस्वरन्ति' (अ.वे. ९.९.२२)। 'निर्ऋथो यश्च निस्वरः' (अ.वे. १२.२.१४)। स्वरति । स्मरति । 'प्रति स्मरेथां तुजयद्भिः' (अ.वे. ८.४.७)।

Note: The instances cited by the commentary, not traced to the AV, are found in the KV on P.8.3.108 (न रपरसृपिसृजिस्पृशिसवनादीनाम्). The APR (147g: रपरसृपिसृजिस्पृशिस्पृहिस्फूर्जिस्वरतिस्मरतीनां च) looks like a combination of the CA rule and the Pāṇinian rule. All the examples cited by the CAB are found in the same order in APR (147g). We must also note that the APR readings of the examples support Whitney's conjecture that *vispṛśaḥ* of the mss. is a corruption for *uparispṛśaḥ.*

२.४.२३. गोसन्यादीनां च ।

Whitney (2.103). B, D: °संन्या°. P: गोसन्यासादीनां च.

Translation: Nor [the *s*] of *gosani* etc.

चतुराध्यायीभाष्य - गोसन्यादीनां च सकारस्य षकारो न भवति । 'गोसनिंम्' (अ.वे. ३.२०.१०)। 'वि सींमतः' (अ.वे. ४.१.१)। 'अभि सिंष्यदे' (अ.वे. ५.५.९)। 'अनु सूतुं सविंतवे' (अ.वे. ६.१७.१-४)।

Note: The example *gosanim* is included in the *savanādigaṇa* mentioned in P.8.3.108 (न रपरसृपिसृजिस्पृशिसवनादीनाम्). It is found in the list of this Gaṇa as given in the KV. However, the whole *gosanyādigaṇa* is listed in APR (147f, p. 101-102) where the examples cited by the CAB appear in the same order. Also see the Note on the previous rule. However, one cannot be certain that the membership of such *gaṇa*s as mentioned in the CA was necessarily identical with the *gaṇa*s as listed in the APR. For example, the *gosanyādigaṇa* as listed under APR (147f, p. 101) also includes the examples *adhi skanda* (5.25.8) and *abhi skandam* (5.14.11), while the CA provides the next rule to take care of these examples, as if they were not included in the *gosayādigaṇa*.

२.४.२४. अध्यभिभ्यां स्कन्देः ।

Whitney (2.104). O: अध्यबिभ्यां°.

Translation: [The *s*] of the root *skand*, after *adhi* and *abhi*, [is not changed to *ṣ*].

चतुराध्यायीभाष्य - अधि अभि इत्येताभ्यामुत्तरस्य स्कन्दि-सकारस्य षकारो न भवति । 'अधिं स्कन्द वीड(Whitney: र)यंस्व' (अ.वे. ५.२५.८)। 'अभि स्कन्दं मृगीवं' (अ.वे. ५.१४.११)। अध्यभिभ्यामिति किमर्थम् । 'एकंशतं विष्कंन्धानि' (अ.वे. ३.९.६)।

Note: The VVRI edition accepts the reading *vīrayasva* for AV (5.25.8), but notes the manuscript variant *vīḍayasva*. The examples cited by the CAB appear in the same order as examples 40-41 on APR (147f). However, see the Note on CA (2.4.23).

Whitney notes, "As counter-instance, the commentator brings forward *ekaśataṃ viṣkandhāni* (iii.9.6), which is a blunder - unless, indeed, the commentator's grammatical system derives *skandha*, 'shoulder,' from the root *skand*. An actual example of the kind he seeks to give is *pariṣkanda* (xv.2.1 etc.)."

Whitney's suspicion that, for the commentator, the word *skandha* in *viṣkandha* may have been derived from the root *skand* finds support in [pseudo-]Sāyaṇa' commentary on the word *viṣkandham* in AV (1.16.3): विष्कन्धमिति । स्कन्दिर्गतिशोषणयोः । भावे घञ् । प्रादिसमासे 'वेः स्कन्देरनिष्ठायाम्' (पा. ८.३.७३) इति षत्वम् । व्यत्ययेन धकारः.

We should note that on *pariṣkanda*, the VVRI edition notes that a substantial number of manuscripts have the reading *pariskanda*. Apparently, the northwestern form was cerebralized, while the central and the eastern form was non-cerebralized, according to Pāṇini, cf. P.8.3.74 (परेश्च) and P.8.3.75 (परिस्कन्दः प्राच्यभरतेषु).

२.४.२५. परेः स्तृणातेः ।

Whitney (2.105). All mss read परेस्तृणातेः. However, I agree with Whitney's addition of the Visarga.

Translation: [The *s*] of the root *stṛ*, after *pari*, [is not changed to *ṣ*].

चतुराध्यायीभाष्य - परेरुत्तरस्य स्तृणातिसकारस्य न षकारो भवति । 'परिं स्तृणीहि परिं धेहि वेदिंम्' (अ.वे. ७.९९.१)। 'परिस्तरंणमिद्धविः' (अ.वे. ९.६.२)। परेरिति किमर्थम् । 'विष्टारी जातः' (अ.वे. ४.३४.१)।

Note: On the counter-example offered by the commentator, Whitney remarks: "As counter-example, he can find only *viṣṭārījātaḥ* (iv.34.1). *Viṣṭārin* doubtless comes from the root *star*; yet, as the *pada*-text does not analyze it, but writes it in its *saṃhitā* form, it might have been neglected, and the root *star* added to those rehearsed in rule 102 (= CA 2.4.22), with which it evidently belongs."

२.४.२६. रेफपरस्य च ।

Whitney (2.106). Hb: रेफस्य च. I: रेफस्य परस्य च.

Translation: [The *s*] followed by *r* [is not changed to *ṣ*].

Note: Rules CA (2.4.22) and the present rule together provide a large class of exceptions to the roots whose initial *s* changes to *ṣ* after an appropriate conditioning sound. The common factor shared by these roots is that they contain, after their initial *s*, either a vocalic or a consonantal *r*. A similar grouping of roots resistant to cerebralization is found in Pāṇini 8.3.110 (न रपरसृपिसृजिस्पृशिस्पृहिसवनादीनाम्). Also see the Note on CA (2.4.22).

चतुराध्यायीभाष्य - रेफपरस्य च सकारस्य न षकारो भवति । 'सिस्रतां नारीं' (अ.वे. १.११.१)। 'परिस्रुतः कुम्भः' (अ.वे. ३.१२.७)। 'प्र भानवः सिस्रते' (अ.वे. १३.२.४६)।

२.४.२७. अभि स्याम पृतन्यतः ।

Whitney (2.107). A, B, D, O: °तंन्यतः. I: ष्याम for स्याम. I: 26.

Translation: [There is no cerebralization of *s* in] *abhi syāma pṛtanyataḥ.*

चतुराध्यायीभाष्य - अभि स्याम पृतन्यत इति सकारस्य षकारो न भवति । 'वयमभि स्याम पृतन्यतः' (अ.वे. ७.९३.१)। सोपपदग्रहणमेतावत्त्वार्थम् । इह मा भूत् । 'विश्वाः पृतना अभि ष्यांम' (अ.वे. १३.१.२२)।

Note: For the citation from AV (7.93.1), all the mss., except W, used by Whitney read *ṣyāma* and this reading, violating the present rule in the CA, is chosen by Whitney in his edition. Later Whitney changed his mind. He (*AV Transl.* Vol.I., p. 456) remarks: "Most of the *saṃhitā*-mss. give *ṣyāma* (our W.O., and two fifths of SPP's authorities, *sy-*), and both printed texts read it; but the Prāt. (ii.107 = CA 2.4.27) expressly requires *syāma*, and that accordingly should be the accepted text." Surya Kanta (*APR*, *Introduction*, p. 38-39) points out that Lindenau again reversed the reading to fit it with the CA prescription, but that the mss. reading probably represents the non-Śaunakīya recension of the AV. On AV (13.1.22), Whitney (*AV Transl.* Vol.II., p. 714) points out that "M.p.m. ⌊and SPP's C.⌋ read at end *syāma;* the passage is quoted as an instance of *-ṣy-* in the comm. to Prāt. ii. 107 (= CA 2.4.27)."

With respect to the variation in AV (7.93.1), it is more likely that the situation as seen in the majority of the manuscripts represents an analogical spread of retroflexion in later times. It is non-Śaunakīya only in the sense that it does not represent the situation as codified by the CA. However, one must not preclude the possibility of change within the Śaunakīya oral tradition, as is done by Surya Kanta. The VVRI edition offers the reading अभि ष्यांम पृतन्यतः for AV (7.98.1 = W: 7.93.1), but notes the reading अभि स्यांम पृतन्यतः as a manuscript variant. It would probably be reasonable to assume that there was further spread of retroflexion after the period of the CA, and such a spread accounts for the retroflexion seen in such instances.

Secondly, this rule again brings into sharp focus the possibility that the *gaṇas* such as the *gosanyādigaṇa* referred to in CA (2.4.23) and APR (147f, p. 101-2) may have had different composition in the two traditions. While the instance *abhi syāma pṛtanyataḥ* appears in the list of the *gosanyādigaṇa* in the APR, its separate treatment by the CA may indicate that the *gosanyādigaṇa* as conceived by the CA was a smaller collection of exceptions. For another similar case, see the Note on CA (2.4.23).

इति द्वितीयाध्यायस्य चतुर्थः पादः ।
द्वितीयोऽध्यायः समाप्तः ।

H, N: ।।१०६।। इति द्वितीयोऽध्यायः समाप्तः. E, F: द्वितीयस्य चतुर्थः पादः । आथर्वणे चतुराध्यायिकायां द्वितीयोऽध्यायः. C, J: इति द्वितीयोध्यायः. A, B, D: ।।४।। इति द्वितीयोऽध्यायः समाप्तः. M: ।।४।। चतुर्थः पादः ।। द्वितीयोऽध्यायः. I: इति द्वितीया-ध्यायस्य चतुर्थः पादः ।।४।। इत्यथर्ववेदे कौत्सव्याकरणे चतुरध्यायिकायां द्वितीयोऽध्यायः ।।२।। सूत्र १०७ ।। ऐक्यं २१७. O: इत्यथर्ववेदे कौत्सव्याकरणे चतुराध्यायिकायां द्वितीयस्य चतुर्थपादः ।। द्वितीयोऽध्यायः समाप्तः ।। सूत्राणि ।। ३७ ।। (The number 37 given in the ms. O is obviously an error for 27). P: ।।४।। द्वितीयोऽध्यायः समाप्तः ।।

चतुराध्यायीभाष्य - ।।१०६।। इति द्वितीयोऽध्यायः समाप्तः।।

॥ तृतीयोऽध्यायः ॥
॥ प्रथमः पादः ॥

३.१.१. सहावाडन्ते दीर्घः ।

Whitney (3.1).

Translation: Before [a form of] the root *sah*, ending in *āṭ*, [the preceding vowel] becomes long.

Note: As Whitney notes, the qualification *āḍ-anta* 'ending in *āṭ*' in this rule achieves the same goal as achieved by the qualification *sāḍbhūtasya* in CA (2.4.2). Whitney says: "It would not do to say 'before *sah* when it becomes *sāh*,' because of the words *amitrasāha* and *abhimātiṣāha*, in which, though the vowel of the root is lengthened, the preceding final remains unchanged."

Whitney also notes: "This rule also belongs in the category of the supererogatory, since in none of the words to which it relates does the *pada*-text afford a different reading from that of the *saṃhitā*." A more positive way of interpreting this rule may be to say that it marks a stage of grammatical analysis beyond the stage reached by the Padapāṭha, and hence, even though it does not relate to the conversion of the *pada*s into *saṃhitā*, it shows us the progression of the grammatical science, cf. P.8.3.56 (सहेः साडः सः).

चतुराध्यायीभाष्य - सहौ परतः आडन्ते दीर्घो भवति । 'प्राषाट्' (not in AV)। 'तुराषाट्' (अ.वे. २.५.३)। 'पृतनाषाट्' (अ.वे. ५.१४.८)। 'शत्रूषाप्नीषाट्' (अ.वे. ५.२०.११)। 'अभीषाडस्मि विश्वाषाट्' (१२.१.५४)। आडन्त इति किमर्थम् । 'प्रसहनम्' (not in Vedic texts)।

Note: While *prāṣāṭ* is not attested in the ŚAV as we know it, it is listed in the APR (p. 146), along with the other examples cited by the CAB.

३.१.२. अष्ट पदयोगपक्षपर्णदंष्ट्रचक्रेषु ।

Whitney (3.2).

Translation: [The final *a* of] *aṣṭa* [is lengthened] before *pada, yoga, pakṣa, parṇa, daṃṣṭra*, and *cakra*.

चतुराध्यायीभाष्य - अष्टेत्यस्य दीर्घो भवति पदयोगपक्षपर्णदंष्ट्रचक्र इत्येतेषु परतः । 'अष्टापंदी चतुरक्षी' (अ.वे. ५.१९.७)। 'अष्टापंक्षाम्' (अ.वे. ९.३.२१)। 'अष्टायोगैः' (अ.वे. ६.९१.१)। 'अष्टापर्णः' । 'अष्टादंष्ट्रम्' । 'अष्टाचंक्रा नवंद्वारा' (अ.वे. १०.२.३१)। 'अष्टाचंक्रं वर्तते' (अ.वे. ११.४.२२)।

Note: Whitney remarks that "the rule, moreover, is an unnecessary one, since the *pada*-text everywhere offers the same reading with the *saṃhitā*, as is expressly directed by a later rule." Surya Kanta (*APR, Introduction,* p. 39) suggests that combinations of *aṣṭá* with *parṇá* and *dáṃṣṭra,* which are not attested in the Vulgate of the AV, may have existed in a genuinely Śaunakīya recension of the AV. I tend to think that these are indications of the CA occasionally straying into provisions for a general grammar of Sanskrit. However, in this case, it should be noted that these examples are not found in the KV on P.6.3.125 (अष्टनः संज्ञायाम्). The word *aṣṭādaṃṣṭraḥ* is found in Āśvalāyana-Śrauta-Sūtra (12.99.9) and Āpastamba-Śrauta-Sūtra (24.8.6), but not in the earlier Vedic texts. The fact that the rule of the CA includes *daṃṣṭra,* though it is evidently a late usage, shows that the author of the CA was already leaning toward a general grammar of Sanskrit.

३.१.३. व्यधावप्रत्यये ।

Whitney (3.3). B, J: °वत्प्र°. E, F, I, O, P(orig): व्यवधावप्रत्यये. M: विधाव°.

Translation: Before the root *vyadh*, when it does not end in any affix, [the preceding vowel is lengthened].

Note: In the examples of this rule, the Padapāṭha is identical with the Saṃhitāpāṭha reading, and hence we need to look at this rule as an advance of grammatical analysis beyond the stage represented by the Padapāṭha.

The rule asserts that in a formation like *śvā-vit* < *śvā-vidh* < *śvā-vyadh*, the root *vyadh* is *apratyaya* 'does not end in an affix.' However, it is clear that here it is a verbal noun. The CA deals with a root-noun as a root without an affix. This needs to be contrasted with Pāṇini's procedure which adds an affix such as *KvIP*, where ultimately each component of this affix is deleted, leaving behind a Ø-affix. Pāṇini's rule which provides lengthening in such cases explicitly refers to the Ø-affix *KvI,* i.e. P.6.3.116 (नहिवृतिवृषिव्यधिरुचिसहितनिषु क्वौ). Patañjali, however, uses the term *apratyaya* to refer to such zero-affixes like *KvIP*, see: MB and Pradīpa on P.1.1.6 with reference to *pipaṭhīḥ*.

On the expression *marmāvidham,* AV (11.10.26), [pseudo]-Sāyaṇa's commentary offers a Pāṇinian derivation by adding the affix *KvIP* to the root *vyadh*.

> ***चतुराध्यायीभाष्य*** - व्यधौ परतः [अ]प्रत्यया[न]ते दीर्घो भवति । 'श्वावित्' (अ.वे. ५.१३.९)। 'हृदयाविधम्' (अ.वे. ८.६.१८)। 'मर्माविधम्' (only in N, अ.वे. ११.१०.२६)। अप्रत्यय इति किमर्थम् । 'प्रविध्यन्तो नाम' (अ.वे. ३.२६.४)।

Note: The three examples cited by the CAB are listed under APR (p. 146) in the same order.

३.१.४. उञ इदमूष्वादिषु ।

Whitney (3.4). Hb, Nb: उभयादि°. After this rule, A, B, D, J, M add: ऊंइसु इतिष्विवादितिपरः. C, E, F, H, I, and N: no such rule.

> **Translation:** In [the sequences] *idam ū ṣu* etc., the particle *u* (= *uñ*) [is lengthened].

> ***चतुराध्यायीभाष्य*** - उञ इदमूष्वादिषु दीर्घो भवति । 'इदमू षु' (अ.वे. १.२४.४)। 'तदू षु' (अ.वे. ५.१.५)। 'पर्यू षु' (अ.वे. ५.६.४)। 'महीमू षु' (अ.वे. ७.६.२)।

'अ॒न्य ऊ॒ षु' (अ.वे. १८.१.१६)। 'स्तु॒ष ऊ॒ षु' (अ.वे. १८.१.३७)। 'त्यमू॒ षु' (अ.वे. ७.८५.१)।

Note: Evidently, Whitney is listing some missing instances: "the other cased afforded by the text are *pary ū ṣu* (vi.6.4), and *para ū te* (xviii.3.7)." Of these two, the first one is actually found in the text of the CAB, and Whitney just missed it. It is found in both the manuscripts, one of which, i.e. H, was available to Whitney.

About the second example, i.e. *para ū te* (xviii.3.7), Whitney comments: "Were it not for this last case, the rule of our treatise might have been constructed like that of the Vāj. Pr., which says (iii.109) that *u* before *su* is lengthened." The *gaṇa* referred to in this CA rule is fully spelled out in APR (207a) and the examples listed there occur exactly in the same order as in the CAB. The example which is added by Whitney and which is not given by our commentary here is the last example in the APR list. It is not clear why the CAB did not list this example. It could be an example of omission, or it may represent a change in usage. Compare this rule with Pāṇini 6.3.134 (इकः सुञि), which has slightly wider coverage, but represents a generalization of the type demanded by Whitney in his comments cited above.

३.१.५. ओषधेरपञ्चपद्याम् ।

Whitney (3.5).

Translation: [The final *i*] of the word *oṣadhi* [is lengthened] before [case endings] other than the first five [i.e. nominative sg., du., pl., and accusative sg., and du.].

Note: Whitney translates the condition *apañcapadyām* as 'except in the strong cases,' and then assumes that this condition leaves everything else open, including a situation where *oṣadhi* occurs as the first member of a compound, and is followed by the second member. With such a wider interpretation, he comments: "Since the rule does not restrict itself to forms of declension, it is guilty of an oversight in taking no account of the compound *oṣadhija* (x.4.23 : p. *oṣadhi-ja*) as a farther exception. In the only other compounds which the text affords - viz. *oṣadhīsaṃśita* (x.5.32 : p. *oṣadhi-saṃśita*), and *oṣadhīmant* (xix.17.6; 18.6) - the rule of the Prātiśākhya is observed."

The closely similar rule in Pāṇini's grammar, i.e. P.6.3.132 (ओषधेश्च विभक्तावप्रथमायाम्), clearly seems to restrict this lengthening before a case ending, other than the nominative, and it seems likely that the CA rule also applies before case endings alone, and not to the situations of compounds. If so, how would one deal with the examples of compounds brought up by Whitney? The APR may provide some assistance in this direction. The example *oṣadhī-saṃśita* is included in a *gaṇa* of compound expressions showing similar lengthening of the final vowel of the first member, cf. APR (208, pp. 125-6). Though, it is true that there is no specific CA rule which would take care of this lengthening. On the other hand, the text of the Padapāṭha, as given by the VVRI edition reads: *oṣadhī-saṃśitaḥ*. This is different from the *pada*-reading cited by Whitney. But, if this reading is somehow valid, then this may not have been viewed as a case of lengthening at all, since the long vowel was already there in the Padapāṭha. The instance *oṣadhīmant* is clearly taken care of by CA (3.1.17: बहुलं मतौ).

चतुराध्यायीभाष्य - ओषधेः अपञ्चपद्यां दीर्घो भवति । 'ओषधीभिः' (अ.वे. २.१०.२)। 'ओषधी(H, N: धि)भ्याम्' (not in AV)। 'ओषधीभ्यः' (अ.वे. ६.२०.२)। 'ओषधीनाम्' (अ.वे. ३.५.१)। 'ओषधीषु' (अ.वे. १.३०.३)। अपञ्चपद्यामिति किमर्थम् । 'इयं ह मह्यं त्वामोषधिः' (अ.वे. ७.३८.५)।

Note: The manuscript H mostly writes ॐ for ओ.

३.१.६. जीवन्तीमोषधीम् ।

Whitney (3.6). O: जीवंतीमोषधीमहं.

Translation: [The *i* of the word *oṣadhi* is also lengthened in the word *oṣadhīm* only in the phrase] *jīvantīm oṣadhīm*.

Note: Pāṇini 6.3.132 (ओषधेश्च विभक्तावप्रथमायाम्) prescribes lengthening of *oṣadhi* before all non-nominative case-endings, and hence जीवन्तीमोषधीम् would be a normal formation in that system, while इमां खनाम्योषधिम् would be an exceptional case. The situation is reverse with the CA formations.

चतुराध्यायीभाष्य - जीवन्तीमोषधीमिति च दीर्घो भवति । 'जीवन्तीमोषंधीमहम्' (अ.वे. ८.२.६; ७.६)। सोपपदग्रहणमेतावत्त्वार्थम् । इह मा भूत् । 'इमां खंनाम्योषंधिम्' (अ.वे. ३.१८.१)। 'ओषंधिं शेपहर्षंणीम्' (अ.वे. ४.४.१)।

Note: [Pseudo-]Sāyaṇa reads *oṣadhīm* in AV (3.18.1), but *oṣadhim* in AV (4.4.1). Could this be taken as an indication that [Pseudo-]Sāyaṇa was not familiar with the rules of the CA, which he fails to quote even once in his entire commentary?

३.१.७. साढः ।

Whitney (3.7).

Translation: [The vowel *a* in the root *sah* in the form] *sāḍha* [is lengthened].

Note: Whitney comments: "The rule is one of the most utterly superfluous presented by our treatise, which, of course, has nothing to do with the mode of formation of such words. Moreover, if it was inclined to do a work of supererogation as regards them, it should not have omitted to notice also *rūḍhvā, rūḍha, mūḍha, gūḍha*, and other like forms which the text contains. Probably the reason why this particular one was noticed, and not the others, is that the regular form, according to the rules of the general grammar, is *soḍha*." Whitney's last comment is the correct reason. Pāṇini too provides special treatment only for this form, and not the other ones, which are derived by the normal rules of his grammar. The normal rule, i.e. P.6.3.112 (सहिवहोरोदवर्णस्य), changes the *a* of the root *sah* to *o* to derive the form *soḍha*. However, the next rule, i.e. P.6.3.113 (साढ्यै साढ्वा साढेति निगमे), admits as *nipātana*s exceptional forms like *sāḍha* for the Vedic language (*nigame*). For some reason, *sāḍheti* in P.6.3.113, is analyzed by the *Kāśikāvṛtti* as साढा इति, rather than as साढ इति, and the commentary takes *sāḍhā* to be a nominative form of *sāḍhṛ-* : साढेति तृचि रूपमेतत्. However, it does not cite any example for it. The SK on this rule offers the example *sāḷhā* (= *sāḍhā*). But, interestingly, the commentary Subodhinī says that the rule should also be applicable to the past participle *sāḍha* : सूत्रे इतिशब्दः प्रकारार्थः । तेन निष्ठायामपि निपातनं बोध्यम् । 'अषाळ्हो अग्ने वृषभः ।' In general, the Pāṇinian commentators show little familiarity with the AV tradition.

चतुराध्यायीभाष्य - साढश्च दीर्घो भवति । 'वाचा साढः परंस्तराम्' (अ.वे. ५.३०.९)।

३.१.८. बहुलं रात्रेः ।

Whitney (3.8).

Translation: [The final *i*] of *rātri* is diversely [lengthened].

Note: Whitney takes the author of the CA to the woodshed: "This is rather a discreditable confession on the part of our treatise, whose business it is to settle authoritatively the reading of its school in all cases admitting of any doubt, that it does not feel equal to dealing with the irregularities of the word in question. Nothing like it has hitherto met us, but we shall find several instances in that which follows." It is understandable that a similar appeal to diversity and irregularity of Vedic usage is found in Pāṇini 4.1.31 (रात्रेश्चाजसौ). However, Pāṇini's appeal is more acceptable, since he aimed at describing the diversity of Sanskrit at large. On the other hand, we do indeed expect a more exact accounting from a Prātiśākhya text. The use of *bahulam* in this and other rules again indicates occasional leanings of the author of the CA in the direction of a general grammar of Sanskrit. This is also apparent from Whitney's comment: "It is also a very unnecessary acknowledgment; for, in the first place, there was no such rule as this absolutely called for, since the *pada*-text everywhere reads all the forms of *rātri* like the *saṃhitā*."

To look a little deeper into the wording of the rule, one may point out that the genitive *rātreḥ* suggests that, for the author of the CA, as for Pāṇini - cf. P.4.1.31 -, the basic stem form was *rātri,* and not *rātrī*, and the CA rule may be taken literally to indicate the deemed deviant character of this word, a stem in short *i*, occasionally providing forms in the text of the AV unpredictably (*bahulam*) as if it were a stem in long *ī*. However, I agree with Whitney's criticism that we should expect from a Prātiśākhya a more exact account. For some reason, the APR also does not take account of the diverse behavior of *rātri*.

चतुराध्यायीभाष्य - बहुलं रात्रेः दीर्घो भवति । 'रात्रीं(H, N: त्रि)भिः' (अ.वे. १८.१.१०)। 'रात्रींभ्याम्' । 'रात्रीं-भ्यः'। 'रात्रींणाम्' (अ.वे. ४.५.४)। 'रात्रीषु' । बहुल-

ग्रहणात् न च भवति । 'व्रात्य एकां रात्रिंम्' (अ.वे. १५. १३.१)।

Note: Whitney's text for AV (18.1.10) reads *rātrībhiḥ*. The manuscripts H and N both read *rātribhiḥ*. However, considering the later comment in the commentary, i.e. बहुलग्रहणात् न च भवति, I suspect that the reading intended by the commentator must have been *rātrībhiḥ*. This reading is also supported by the VVRI edition.

३.१.९. विश्वस्य नरवसुमित्रेषु ।

Whitney (3.9).

Translation: [The final *a*] of *viśva* is [diversely lengthened] before *nara, vasu,* and *mitra*.

Note: Whitney points out that the examples brought together here are heterogeneous. The word *viśvānara* is not broken up in the Padapāṭha into its components. On the other hand, *viśvāvasu* of the Saṃhitā is represented as *viśva-vasu* in the Padapāṭha. The word *viśvāmitra* is unchanged in the Padapāṭha, while the word *viśvamitrāḥ* in AV (18.3.63, 4.54) is analyzed in the Padapāṭha as *viśva-mitrāḥ*. Whitney also argues that it is difficult to justify the continuity of the word *bahulam* into this rule from the previous rule. However, his arguments against the continuity of *bahulam* are not strong. Compare Pāṇini 6.3.128 (विश्वस्य वसुराटोः), 6.3.129 (नरे संज्ञायाम्), and 6.3.130 (मित्रे चर्षौ). Pāṇini makes a semantic distinction between *viśvānara* vs *viśvanara,* and *viśvāmitra* vs *viśvamitra*. The lengthened forms are names, while non-lengthened forms are descriptions. For example, on *viśvamitrāḥ* in AV (18.3.63), the commentary of [pseudo-]Sāyaṇa renders it as सर्वजनमित्रभूताः, and not as members of Viśvāmitra's clan. Also see Whitney's note on this verse (*AV Translation,* Vol.II., p. 866).

चतुराध्यायीभाष्य - विश्व इत्येतस्य बहुलं दीर्घो भवति नरवसुमित्र इत्येतेषु परतः । 'विश्वानंरे अक्रमत(H, N: त्)' (अ.वे. ४.११.७)। 'या विश्वावंसुम्' (अ.वे. २.२.४)। 'विश्वामिंत्र जमंदग्ने' (अ.वे. १८.३.१६)। न च भवति । 'तमंर्चत विश्वमिंत्राः' (अ.वे. १८.३.६३; १८.४.५४)।

३.१.१०. शुनः पदे ।

Whitney (3.10).

Translation: [The *a*] of *śvan* [is diversely lengthened] before *pada.*

चतुराध्यायीभाष्य - शुन इत्यस्य पदे परतः बहुलं दीर्घो भवति । 'अथो॒ सर्वं॒ श्वापंदम्' (अ.वे. ११.९.१०)। 'श्वापंदो॒ मक्षिंकाः' (अ.वे. ११.१०.८)। 'उ॒त वा॒ श्वापंदः' (अ.वे. १८.३.५५)। न च भवति । 'व्या॒घ्रः श्वपंदामिव' (अ.वे. ८.५.११; १९.३९.४)।

Note: Whitney raises an objection to the continuation of the word *bahulam* into the last two rules, and states that it certainly does not continue into the next rule. However, how do we then account for the exceptional behavior of the examples introduced by the commentator with the phrase: न च भवति? We should also note that the exception is followed by all the editions of the AV and is supported by the manuscripts. Whitney (*AV Transl.* Vol.II., p. 492) says, "Prāt. iii.10 (= CA 3.1.10) notes the double form *śvápad* and *śvā́pad.*"

However, one must agree with Whitney that the rules do not have any clear indications about the continuation and cessation of *bahulam.* It certainly does not continue into the next rule. However, looking at the examples available in the AV text, the commentary is justified in continuing this word in these two rules.

३.१.११. उपसर्गस्य नामिनो दस्ति ।

Whitney (3.11). A, B, D, J, M, P: omit स्य. A, B, D: °र्ग्र°. I: 11.

Translation: [The final] *nāmin* [i.e. any vowel other than *a* and *ā*] of a pre-verb [is lengthened] before *t* of the root *dā.*

Note: Whitney notes that the two attested examples cited by the commentator appear in an identical form in the Padapāṭha and the Saṃhitāpāṭha.

चतुराध्यायीभाष्य - उपसर्गस्य नाम्यन्तस्य ददातौ परतः तकारादौ दीर्घो भवति । 'नीत्ता(H, N: ता)' (not in Vedic texts)। 'वीत्ता' (not in Vedic texts)। 'परीत्तिः' (not in Vedic texts)। 'अप्रंतीत्तम्' (अ.वे. ६.११७.१)। 'परीत्तः' (अ.वे. ६.९२.२)। नामिन इति किमर्थम् । 'प्रत्तम्' (not in AV, तै.सं. २.२.८.४, मै.सं. १.६.९)। 'अवत्तम्' (not in AV, तै.सं. ६.३.१०.४, मै.सं. ३.१०.१)।

Note: The commentator quotes a number of forms not attested in the AV. The forms *apratīttam, parīttaḥ, prattam, avattam* are listed under APR (217, p. 145). Also see the examples cited in the KV under Pāṇini 6.3.124 (दस्ति), which include *nīttam, vīttam, parīttam, prattam,* and *avattam.*

३.१.१२. वर्तादिषु ।

Whitney (3.12). E, F, H, N, O, P: °र्ता°. A, B, C, D, Hb: वा°.

Translation: Before *varta* etc., [the final vowel of the preceding item is lengthened].

चतुराध्यायीभाष्य - वर्तादिषु परतः दीर्घो भवति । 'अभीवर्तेन' (अ.वे. १.२९.१)। 'विश्वंमन्यामंभीवारे' (अ.वे. १.३२.४)।

Note: Whitney, reading only from the manuscript H, believed that the paraphrase of this rule had some missing words, which, if restored, would read: उपसर्गस्य नाम्यन्तस्य वर्तादिषु परतः दीर्घो भवति. However, the second manuscript, N, does not support this wording. The *gaṇa* referred to in this rule is fully listed in APR (207b). It contains a listing of 21 instances. The CAB quotes the first two instances from this list. It may have also contained the cases listed under APR (208).

APR (207b, p. 124): उपसर्गस्योत्तरपदे दीर्घः, and the 21 cases listed under this rule take care of the cases of the *nāmin* vowel of an *upasarga* being lengthened before *varta* etc. However, Whitney lists a whole host of expressions where the preceding is not an *upasarga,* nor does it necessarily end in a *nāmin* vowel, and yet one finds lengthening. Many of these cases are found listed under the next rule of the APR, i.e. APR (208, p. 125-6). One may assume that, contrary to Whitney's expectation, the present CA rule had a general application, not restricted to *upasargas* ending in a *nāmin* vowel, and that it may have intended to encompass the examples covered by the two consecutive rules of the APR, i.e. APR (207b, and 208).

I would just like to note in passing, that the lists of examples offered by Whitney do not completely match the ones found under APR (207b, and 208), and the discrepancies need to be individually investigated. They may possibly indicate changes in the transmitted text of the AV.

३.१.१३. अकारस्याभ्यासस्य बहुलम् ।

Whitney (3.13).

Translation: The *a* of a reduplication is diversely [lengthened].

Note: The word *bahulam* in the rule seems to be there to take care of examples like *sasahe* cited by the commentator. It may be noted that the APR (209, p. 126) reads अभ्यासस्य दीर्घश्छन्दसि. It is a somewhat strange formulation in that one would expect a text like the APR to be concerned with the language of *chandas* alone, and, therefore, one sees no purpose in the use of *chandasi,* except to indicate that the forms where this kind of lengthening does not take place are more like the non-*chandas* language. The *gaṇa* listed under this rule cites examples of lengthening alone. The APR rule is also not restricted to the vowel *a* of the reduplication. The rule contains no such restriction, and the *gaṇa* contains the example *jīhīḍa*, the only case of non-*a* vowel. This example is taken care of by the next rule of the CA.

Whitney draws our attention to the forms *rūrupaḥ* (iv.7.5), *rīriṣaḥ* (v.3.8), and *śūśucaḥ* (xviii.2.4), and says: "The Prātiśākhya may intend to include these forms in the *gaṇa* of rule 21 (= CA 3.1.21), below, but they would much more properly have been provided for in the present rule." Indeed, the *nārakādigaṇa* referred to in CA (3.1.21), and as fully elaborated under APR (212, p. 129) contains the first two examples cited by Whitney. However, it is not clear why these examples were not covered by APR (209).

चतुराध्यायीभाष्य - अकारस्याभ्यासस्य बहुलं दीर्घो भवति। 'दाधृषुः' (अ.वे. १.२७.३)। 'अभिवावृधे' (अ.वे.

१.२९.१)। 'वावृधेते' (अ.वे. ५.१.५)। 'जीतस्य वावृतुः' (अ.वे. ५.१९.१३)। न च भवति । 'अनेन [विश्वा] ससहे' (अ.वे. १.१६.३)। 'न संसहे शत्रून्' (अ.वे. २.५.३)।

Note: Whitney (*AV Transl.* Vol.I., p. 17) points out that "the short *a* in the reduplication of *sasahe* in c, though against the meter and in part against usage, is read by all the mss., and in the comment to Prāt. iii.13 (= CA 3.1.13)." On AV (2.5.3), Whitney has further describes how certain texts, as well as manuscripts of the AV, rectify the metrical deficiency by reading the form as *sasāhé* (*AV Transl.* Vol.I., p.44). Whitney (ibid., p. 28) notes that Sāyaṇa's commentary on AV (1.27.3) reads *dādr̥śuḥ.*

The first four examples, excluding the counter-examples, are cited under APR (209).

३.१.१४. जीहीडाहम् ।

Whitney (3.14).

Translation: [Also, in the form *jīhīḍa* in the phrase] *jīhīḍāham,* [the vowel of the reduplication is lengthened].

चतुराध्यायीभाष्य - जीहीडाहमिति च दीर्घो भवति । 'अक्रतुर्जीहीडाहम्' (अ.वे. ४.३२.५)। न च भवति । 'यद्वा पितापराद्धो जिहीडे' (अ.वे. ६.११६.२)।

Note: Whitney rightly objects to the continuation of *bahulam* into this rule as is clearly implied by the commentator. The counter-example given by the commentary does not contain the word *jīhīḍāham,* but merely the word *jihīḍe.* The form *jīhīḍa* is listed as a case of lengthening of the reduplication under APR (209, p. 127). The APR rule says that this lengthening of the reduplication occurs *chandasi.* However, it does not make any effort to show how such lengthening is avoided in the form *jihīḍe,* except by not listing it in the *gaṇa.* In this case, the CA rule foregoes the generalization, and cites the specific case where the lengthening takes place.

On the reading *jīhīḍāham* in AV (4.32.5), Whitney (*AV Transl.* Vol.I., p. 204) points out that the RV reading is *jihīḍāham,* "although the AV. *saṃhitā* reading is unquestionably *jīhīḍ-*; the *saṃhitā* mss. have this almost without exception (all ours save O.), the *pada*-mss. put after the word their sign which shows a difference between *pada* and *saṃhitā* reading, and *jīh-* is twice distinctly prescribed by the Prāt. (iii.14 = CA 3.1.14; iv.87 = CA 4.3.15)."

३.१.१५. साह्याम ।

Whitney (3.15). C, Hc, Nc: स°.

Translation: [Also, in the form] *sāhyāma* [the vowel of the root *sah* is lengthened].

Note: Quite clearly, this is not a case of the lengthening of a reduplication, and hence needed to be dealt with separately. The APR (212, p. 129) lists this form in the *nārakādigaṇa* referred to also in CA (3.1.21). Obviously, the membership of these *gaṇas* as conceived by these texts was different. Under the present rule, Whitney cites a number of "causative forms from verbal roots which show in the first or radical syllable a short *a* in *pada* and a long *ā* in *saṃhitā*, and which are not specially noted in this section, being left, apparently, to fall into the *gaṇa* of rule 21 (= CA 3.1.21), below. ... They are *yāvaya* etc. (e.g. i.20.3), from *yu; cyāvayati* etc. (e.g. x.1.13), from *cyu; vānayantu* (vi.9.3), from *van; yāmaya* (vi.137.3), from *yam;* and *glāpayanta* (ix.9. 10), from *glā*." Most of these forms, except the forms of *yam,* are listed in the *nārakādigaṇa* of the APR (212, pp. 129-130), which is also referred to by CA (3.1.21).

चतुराध्यायीभाष्य - साह्यामेति च दीर्घो भवति । 'साह्याम दासमार्यम्' (अ.वे. ४.३२.१)।

३.१.१६. विद्मादीनां शरादिषु ।

Whitney (3.16). C: विघ्नादीनां°.

Translation: [The final vowels] of *vidma* etc. [are lengthened] before *śara* etc.

चतुराध्यायीभाष्य - विद्मादीनां शरादिषु परतः बहुलं दीर्घो भवति । 'विद्मा शरस्य पितरम्' (अ.वे. १.२.१)। 'एवा

रोगं चास्नावम्' (अ.वे. १.२.४)। 'एवा मे प्राण मा बिभेः'
(अ.वे. २.१५.१)।

Note: The APR does not have a single *gaṇa* which encompasses all of these examples. The examples of the lengthening of *eva* are listed under APR (216c, p. 134). But this list does not include verbs like *vidmā*. Verbs with similar lengthening are listed under APR (215c, 215d, p. 132), but these lists do not include the form *vidmā*.

Whitney has given the full statistics of both of these Gaṇas as they are found in the text of the AV. Unlike the Gaṇapāṭha in the Pāṇinian school, we have no complete listings of Gaṇas mentioned in the CA. Also, it is clear that there is no reason to continue the word *bahulam* into this rule. Had the word *bahulam* continued into this rule, there would be no need to mention it expressly in the following rule: बहुलं मतौ.

३.१.१७. बहुलं मतौ ।

Whitney (3.17). Hb, Nb: बहुमतविच्छायां.

Translation: Before the [affix] *mat*, [the preceding vowel is] diversely [lengthened].

Note: Whitney notes that *mat* in this rule also covers *vat*. It is the same affix for Pāṇini with the change of *m* to *v*, cf. P.8.2.9. The examples in the commentary here cover only the latter. The same coverage is found in APR (210, pp. 127-8). The only example of *mat* is *tviṣīmat*. Its instances are included in the APR list, and the same example is cited by Whitney.

The APR (210) offers a long list of instances, out of which the CAB quotes the first three instances. Here, a major difference emerges between the treatment of the same topic by these two texts. Since the CA frames its rules in a generic way, it uses the term *bahulam*, and then the commentator is forced to offer instances where the lengthening does not take place. On the other hand, the APR expects to provide full listings where the particular change takes place, and hence it often does not feel the need to cite the exceptions.

चतुराध्यायीभाष्य - मतौ परतः बहुलं दीर्घो भवति ।
'शालेऽश्वावती' (अ.वे. ३.१२.२)। 'अश्वावतीर्गोमतीः'
(अ.वे. ३.१६.७)। 'अश्वावतीं प्र तर' (अ.वे. १८.२.३१)।

न च भवति । 'वीरवंतीः सदंम्' (अ.वे. ३.१६.७)। 'घृत-वंती पयंस्वत्युच्छ्रंयस्व' (अ.वे. ३.१२.२)।

३.१.१८. इच्छायां च यकारादौ ।

Whitney (3.18), A, B, C, D, E, F, H, J, M, N, O, P: °छायां°. I: °च्छायां°.

Translation: Also, in a desire-expressing form, before a *y*-initial [suffix], [the final vowel of the base is diversely lengthened].

चतुराध्यायीभाष्य - इच्छायां च यकारादौ बहुलं दीर्घो भवति । 'अध्वरीयताम्' (अ.वे. १.४.१)। 'वृषायमांणः' (अ.वे. २.५.७)। 'शंत्रूयतीमभि' (अ.वे. ३.१.३)। न च भवति । 'अरातियात्' (अ. वे. ४.३६.१)। 'जनियन्तिं' (अ.वे. १४.२.७२)। 'पुत्रियन्तिं' (अ.वे. १४.२.७२)। 'मृगयुः' (अ.वे. १०.१.२६) प्रभृतीनि च ।

Note: By referring to the corresponding RV (vii.96.4a, b) forms *janī-yántaḥ* and *putrīyántaḥ,* Whitney (*AV Transl.* Vol.II., p. 767) remarks: "That our denominatives [in AV] have a right to their short *i* is further vouched for by their quotation as examples for it under Prāt. iii.18 (= CA 3.1.18)." The examples cited by the CAB are found in the same order on APR (154: यकारादौ बहुलं दीर्घः), including the exceptions. Even the word प्रभृतीनि च is found in the APR (p. 108). Also see the examples on APR (211, pp. 128-129). This close correspondence shows that the CAB and the APR belong to the same basic tradition.

३.१.१९. तृतीयान्तस्य ।

Whitney (3.19).

Translation: The final [vowel] of an instrumental form [is diversely lengthened].

Note: Whitney notes: "In the form of this rule there is nothing which continues the implication of *bahulam*, but such an implication is, of course, unavoidably necessary, and is made by the commentator." Whitney has provided statistics for *tenā* and *yenā*, cf. Whitney (1862: p. 132). Additionally, he points to forms *sahasyenā, bhadreṇā, amṛtenā, kāvyenā,* and *martyenā* each of which occurs only once. I have not located any treatment of these lengthened forms in the APR.

चतुराध्यायीभाष्य - तृतीयान्तस्य बहुलं दीर्घो भवति । 'येनां सहस्रं वहसि येनांग्ने सर्ववेदसम्' (अ.वे. ९.५.१७)। न च भवति । 'केन श्रोत्रियमाप्नोति' (अ.वे. १०.२.२०)।

३.१.२०. रलोपे ।

Whitney (3.20). E, F, I, O: रलोपे पूर्वस्य.

Translation: When [a final] *r* is deleted [before an initial *r*, the preceding vowel is lengthened].

Note: See the Note on CA (2.1.19), which prescribes the deletion of an *r* before an *r*.

चतुराध्यायीभाष्य - रलोपे दीर्घो भवति । 'पुना रक्तं वासः' (not in Vedic texts)। 'पुनां रूपाणि' (अ.वे. १.२४.४)। 'जघ्नू रक्षांसि' (अ.वे. ४.३७.१)। 'अग्नी रक्षांसि' (अ.वे. ८.३.२६)। 'अग्नी रक्षः' (अ.वे. १२.३.४३)। किमर्थमिदं नोदाह्रियते । 'पुरूची रायः' (अ.वे. २.१३.३)। यद्यपि रलोपो दीर्घ एवैषः ।

Note: The example *punā raktaṃ vāsaḥ* cited by the CAB is not found in the Vulgate of the AV, and Surya Kanta (*APR, Introduction,* p. 40) suggests that this may have occurred in the genuine Śaunakīya recension of the AV, and that the Vulgate is not the genuine Śaunakīya recension. This example is cited in the KV on P.8.3.14 (*ro ri*).

Whitney's reading of the last few sentences of the commentary was: *kim artham idam nodārddhate : purūcī rāyaḥ : yady api ralopo dīrgha evaivaḥ.*

With both the manuscripts in my possession, I have now been able to give a better reading.

३.१.२१. नारकादीनां प्रथमस्य ।

Whitney (3.21).

Translation: For words like *nāraka* [or words listed in the *nārakādi-gaṇa*?] the first [vowel is lengthened].

चतुराध्यायीभाष्य - नारकादीनां प्रथमस्य दीर्घो भवति । 'नारंकम्' (अ.वे. १२.४.३६)। 'सादंनम्' (अ.वे. २.१२. ७)। 'आसंत इन्द्र' (अ.वे. ८.४.८)।

Note: The *gaṇa* referred to in this rule is fully listed in the APR (212: प्रथमस्य दीर्घः). It contains a total of 28 instances, out of which the CAB quotes the first three instances in exactly the same order. However, for many words listed in the *nārakādigaṇa* in the APR, the CA has separate rules, and hence the membership of this list as intended by the CA and the APR could not have been identical, cf. Notes on CA (3.1.13, and 3.1.15).

Surya Kanta (*APR,* p. 75) points out: "Whitney cites *sūyamān* (AV 4. 27.1) on *nārakādīnām prathamasya* III.21, which is not found in the printed AV. text and is contradicted by our treatise." Surya Kanta is referring to the reading as *suyamān.* Whitney, however, does note the variation of the mss. readings, cf. *AV Transl.* Vol.I., p. 196, and is not as absolute in his opinion as implied by Surya Kanta.

३.१.२२. दीदायादीनां द्वितीयस्य ।

Whitney (3.22). B, M, N: दीर्घदाया°. J: No such rule.

Translation: For words like *dīdāyat*, the second [vowel is lengthened].

चतुराध्यायीभाष्य - दीदायत् आदीनां द्वितीयस्य दीर्घो भवति । 'दीदायत्' (अ.वे. ३.८.३)। 'उषासों वीरवंतीः' (अ.वे. ३.१६.७)। 'उषासानक्तां' (अ.वे. ५.१२.६)।

Note: The *gaṇa* referred to in this rule is fully listed in APR (213: द्वितीयस्य दीर्घः). It contains a total of seven instances, and the CAB quotes the first three instances in exactly the same order. Whitney says: "The only other word of like character which I have noted in the Atharvan is *śrathāya* (vii.83.3: p. *śrathaya*)." The *gaṇa* as listed in the APR contains *śrathāya*.

३.१.२३. सात्रासाहादीनामुत्तरपदाद्यस्य ।

Whitney (3.23). O: °दीनांमुत्त°.

Translation: For [compound expressions like] *sātrāsāha*, the first vowel of the second member [is lengthened].

चतुराध्यायीभाष्य - सात्रासाहादीनाम् उत्तरपदाद्यस्य दीर्घो भवति । 'सात्रासाहस्य' (अ.वे. ५.१३.६)। 'अमित्रसाहः' (अ.वे. १.२०.४)। 'विषासहिः' (अ.वे. १.२९.६)।

Note: The *gaṇa* referred to in this rule is fully listed in APR (214). Out of a total of seven instances listed, the CAB quotes the first three in exactly the same order. Whitney adds *abhimātiṣāhaḥ* (AV 4.32.4), *nyāyanam* (AV 6.77.2), and *ukthaśāsaḥ* (AV 18.3.21). On the last one, he says: "which the *pada*-texts of the Rik and White Yajus write *uktha-śasaḥ, ...* is read in our *pada* (xviii.3.21) *uktha-śāsaḥ.*" Of these three examples, the first and the last are listed in the *sātrāsāhādigaṇa* under APR (214, p. 131). Also, the Padapāṭha for *ukthaśāsaḥ* is given as *uktha-śasaḥ* in the VVRI edition, and by Surya Kanta (*APR*, p. 131). The VVRI edition notes *uktha-śāsaḥ* as a variant *pada*-reading. However, the inclusion of this instance in the *sātrāsāhādigaṇa* in the APR makes the *pada*-reading *uktha-śāsaḥ* less likely. The APR list also includes *yama-sādana* (AV 12.5.64), which is not cited by Whitney.

३.१.२४. ऋत वृधवरीवानेषु ।

Whitney (3.24). Hb, Nb: °वध°.

Translation: [The final *a* of] *ṛta* [is lengthened], before *vṛdha, varī,* and *vāna.*

चतुराध्यायीभाष्य - ऋतेत्यस्य दीर्घो भवति वृधवरीवाने-त्येतेषु परतः । वृध । 'ऋतावृधः (H, N: °म्)' (अ.वे. ११. ६.१९)। वृध । वरी । 'ऋतावरी यज्ञिये' (अ.वे. ६.६२. १)। वरी । वान । 'ऋतावानं वैश्वानरम् (N: रः)' (अ.वे. ६.३६.१)।

Note: All the examples cited in the commentary here are found as examples 16-18 under APR (208). However, the order of the examples is: *-vṛdha, -vāna*, and *-varī*.

३.१.२५. अध त्यंधीःपरवर्जम् ।

Whitney (3.25). P: °परि°.

Translation: [The final *a* of] *adha* [is lengthened], except when followed by *tyam* or *dhīḥ*.

चतुराध्यायीभाष्य - अधेत्यस्य दीर्घो भवति त्यंधीःपर-वर्जम् । 'अधा यथा नः' (अ.वे. १८.३.२१)। 'अधा पितॄँ-रुपं द्रव' (अ.वे. १८.२.२३)। त्यंधीःपरवर्जमिति किमर्थम्। 'अध त्यं द्रप्सम्' (अ.वे. १८.१.२१)। 'अध धीरजायत' (अ.वे. १८.१.२१)।

'अधेति व्यञ्जने (H,N: न, Whit., APR 216b: °ने) दीर्घो
वर्जयित्वा त्यधी (APR 216b: त्यं धीः) परम् ।
स्वरादा (H, N: °दारा, W: रादा) वथ (N: वथ, Whitney: वपि, Surya Kanta: वध) सर्वत्र
व्यञ्जने ह्रस्व (Surya Kanta: °नेऽह्रस्व) एव तु ॥'
(= APR 216b)

Note: The phenomenon covered by the present CA rule is covered by APR (216b, p. 133), and the verse cited in the CAB is identical with APR (216b), except that in b it reads: त्यं धीः परं. Except the first example of the CAB, all the other examples are found under APR (216b).

Whitney, who could read the cited verse only imperfectly from his manuscript, renders it as: "*adha* is long before a consonant, excepting the cases in which it is followed by *tyam* and *dhīḥ;* but before a consonant preceded by a vowel (?) it is everywhere only short." The same verse in APR (216b, Notes, p. 63) is rendered by Surya Kanta as: "The final of *adha* is lengthened before a consonant, except *tyam* and *dhīḥ*. It is invariably *adha* (with a short *a*) before the initial vowel of the following word; but before a consonant it is long." The way this meaning is extracted from the verse is by slightly emending verse. Surya Kanta says: "Emend MS, *atha* into *adha* and put an avagraha mark between *-ne* and *hra-* (= *ne 'hra*)."

Whitney points to "yet another case in the text in which the final vowel is left short, and which has been overlooked both by treatise and commentator: it is *adha syāma* (xviii.3.17)." Surya Kanta (*APR*, Notes, p. 63) says that even though the manuscripts report this reading without variants, it "may be, accordingly, corrected into *adhā*." The VVRI edition reads *adha syāma*, but notes that the manuscripts P and P[2] for the Padapāṭha give the reading *adhā syāma*. The absence of this example in the listing of examples as well as counter-examples provided under APR (216b, pp. 133-4) needs a careful answer. One way to sort this out is to assume that the APR list of positive examples is illustrative and not exhaustive. Then, since the present case is not covered by the exceptions, we assume that the APR knew this instance as *adhā syāma*. A similar argument must be made for the example *adhā yathā naḥ* (AV 18.3.21), which is offered by the CAB, but is not found in the list given under APR (216b).

इति तृतीयाध्यायस्य प्रथमः पादः ।

H, N: तृतीयस्य प्रथमपादः. E, F: तृतीयस्य प्रथमः पादः. A, B, D, M, P: प्रथमः पादः. I: इति तृतीयाध्यायस्य प्रथमः पादः. O: तृतीयस्य प्रथमः पादः ॥ सूत्राणि ॥ २५ ॥

चतुराध्यायीभाष्य - तृतीयस्य प्रथमः पादः ॥

॥ तृतीयोऽध्यायः ॥
॥ द्वितीयः पादः ॥

३.२.१. पदान्ते व्यञ्जनं द्विः ।

Whitney (3.26).

Translation: At the end of a word, a consonant is doubled.

चतुराध्यायीभाष्य - पदान्ते व्यञ्जनं द्विर्भवति । 'गोधुक्क्' (अ.वे. ७.७३.६)। 'विराड्ड्' (अ.वे. ८.९.८)। 'दृषत्त्' (अ.वे. २.३१.१)। 'त्रिष्टुप्प्' (अ.वे. ८.९.२०)।

Note: Whitney's remarks on this rule are most virulent: "The subject of the duplicated pronunciation of consonants, or of the *varṇakrama*, ... is one of the most peculiar in the whole phonetical science of the Hindus. It is also the one, to my apprehension, which exhibits most strikingly their characteristic tendency to arbitrary and artificial theorizing; I have not succeeded in discovering the foundation of fact upon which their superstructure of rules is based, or explaining to myself what actual phonetic phenomena, liable to occur in a natural, or even a strained, mode of utterance, they supposed themselves to have noted, and endeavored thus to reduce to systematic form." On the other hand, as Whitney himself notes: "The *varṇakrama*, however, forms a not inconspicuous part of the phonetic system of all the Prātiśākhyas, and is even presented by Pāṇini (viii.4.46-52), although the latter mercifully allows us our option as to whether we will or will not observe its rules." However, one should note that Pāṇini's rules cited by Whitney do not relate to the doubling of consonants in the word-final position.

Referring to this rule, Lanman *(AV Transl.* Vol.II., p. 832) comments: "Considering the exaggerated nicety of the theory of the Hindus respecting consonant groups (cf. Whitney, AV Prāt., p. 584-90), and in particular their doctrine of the *varṇakrama* ('at the end of a word, a consonant is pronounced double,' *padānte vyañjanaṃ dviḥ,* Prāt. iii. 26 = CA 3.2.1), it is strange that the mss. sometimes fail to come up even to the simple requirements of orthography as set by grammar and sense. On the other hand, it can hardly be said that the mss. in the cases of these shortcomings are a less truthful representation of the actual connected utterance of the text than would be for instance the graphical representation of the English *some more* by the words *some ore*." It is of course correctly assumed by Lanman that the reciters and the copyists have no inkling of the meaning of the expressions being recited or copied, and hence such multiple mechanical reproductions are all the more likely.

Neither the manuscripts of the AV, nor those of the CA, show this doubling of the final consonants. This also goes against the general tendency of the language reflected in Pāṇini 8.2.23 (संयोगान्तस्य लोपः). Perhaps this doctrine represents a deliberate effort to counter the weakening of the final consonants as evidenced by Prakrits. This may also be an ancient interpretation of the final unreleased unexploded consonant, cf. RPR (6.39-42). To make the non-release clear, one needs to lengthen the silence. I owe this suggestion to Professor A.M. Ghatage, Bhandarkar Oriental Research Institute, Pune.

As I have pointed out above, Pāṇini does not support the doubling of word-final consonants. However, a Vārttika cited in the KV on P.8.4.47 (अनचि च) reads: अवसाने च यरो द्वे भवत इति वक्तव्यम्: "It should be stipulated that, before a pause, a consonant other than *h* is doubled." The examples cited are: वाक्क्, वाक्, त्वक्क्, त्वक्, षट्ट्, षट्, तत्त्, तत्. These examples look very much like the ones cited by the CAB on the present rule. This Vārttika appears as अवसाने च in the MB on P.8.4.47, and, on this Vārttika, Patañjali rejects the necessity of making such a separate statement, but derives the same doctrine by reinterpreting P.8.4.47: तत्तर्हि वक्तव्यम् । न वक्तव्यम् । नायं प्रसज्यप्रतिषेधः - अचि नेति । किं तर्हि? पर्युदासोऽयम् - यदन्यदच इति. Patañjali says that the condition अनचि च does not mean: "the doubling does not occur, when followed by *ac* = a vowel," but it means: "the doubling occurs, when followed by something other than a vowel." This last phrase "something other than a vowel" is interpreted broadly to include consonants, as well as pause (*avasāna*). Kaiyaṭa disputes the correctness of this reading of the MB: पाठोऽयं लेखकप्रमादान्नष्टः - पर्युदासे ह्यच्सदृशस्य वर्णान्तरस्य निमित्तत्वेनोपादानादवसाने द्विर्वचनस्याप्रसङ्गात् । तस्मात् - नायं पर्युदासो यदन्यदच इति । किं तर्हि? प्रसज्यप्रतिषेधोऽचि न - इत्ययं पाठः । तत्र प्रसज्यप्रतिषेधे विधिरनुमीयते । अच उत्तरस्य यरो नूनं द्विर्वचनं सर्वत्रास्ति यतोऽचि प्रतिषिध्यते. However, he finally concludes: एवं चानैमित्तिकं द्विर्वचनमवसानेऽपि भवति : "Thus, the unconditional doubling of a [final] consonant occurs even before a pause." With all the confusion concerning the exact reading of the MB, this seems to be the intention of Patañjali. I have a strong feeling that Pāṇini does not sanction such a doctrine, but it is sanctioned by Patañjali. The agreement of Patañjali's doctrine with that of the present CA rule may perhaps indicate the eastern origin of the CA. It is possible that the diglossic gap between Sanskrit and Prakrit being much wider in the east than in the west, some 'protective' modes of pronunciation of final consonants developed specifically in the east.

The other question which is left unclear by the present CA rule is whether the doubling of the word-final consonant takes place unconditionally, i.e. irrespective of what follows, or does it take place specifically before pause. The rule does not contain the word अवसाने, comparable to the Vārttika discussed above.

Whitney thinks as follows: "If the first rule of the second chapter (= CA 2.1.1: *saṃhitāyām*) is to be strictly applied, we must conclude that the makers of the Prātiśākhya recognized the duplicated methods of pronunciation as of force only in the *saṃhitāpāṭha*, and not in the utterance of the disjoined text, or the *padapāṭha*. This interpretation is somewhat supported by the fact that both the Rik Pr. (vi.3, r. 14, cccxc) and Pāṇini (viii.4.51) attribute to Śākala or Śākalya, the teacher to whom the invention of the *padapāṭha* is generally ascribed, a denial of all duplicated utterance."

This argument does not seem to be cogent. The next rule of the CA says: "The final *ṅ*, *ṇ*, and *n*, preceded by a short vowel, are doubled before a vowel." Such a rule would not make sense if the previous rule were to prescribe unconditional doubling of a final vowel, irrespective of what followed. The best resolution of the confusion is to conclude that rule CA (3.2.2) applies under the condition of sandhi between two words, while the previous rule applies before an *avasāna* 'pause.' Thus, the rule may apply to words, before pause, in the Padapāṭha, as well as in the Saṃhitāpāṭha. One can agree with Whitney that the present rule "is directly in contravention with the doctrine of the other treatises (R. Pr. vi.2, r. 7, ccclxxxiv; V.Pr. iv. 114; T. Pr. xiv. 15), which unanimously teach that a consonant is not duplicated in pausa." However, that need not deter us from accepting that the CA has a distinctive doctrine of its own. The similarity of the CA view with the view given in the Vārttika (अवसाने च) on P.8.4.47 has been pointed out above.

३.२.२. ङणना ह्रस्वोपधाः स्वरे ।

Whitney (3.27). A, B, D, E, F, Hb, J, M, Nb: °धा स्वरे°. E, F: °ह्रस्वो°. A, B, D: ङणनां°. Most mss. read: न्ह for ह्र.

Translation: The [word-final] *ṅ*, *ṇ*, and *n*, preceded by a short vowel, [are doubled] before an [initial] vowel [of the next word].

Note: For the implication of this rule that the previous rule applies to final consonants before a pause, see the Note on CA 3.2.1.

Whitney says: "Pāṇini and the Taitt. Pr. very properly treat this doubling of a final nasal as something apart from and unconnected with the phenomena of the *varṇakrama*, by teaching it in a different part of their texts from that which deals with the latter subject; and in the Rik Pr., also, the rule rather follows next after, than is introduced among, those which prescribe the other duplications." This rule is distinct from other consonant doublings in being obligatory both in Vedic and the classical language, and Pāṇini explicitly calls this doubling *nityam* 'obligatory,' cf. P.8.3.32 (ङमो ह्रस्वादचि ङमुण्नित्यम्). Procedurely, we may point out that Pāṇini teaches front-end augments to the word-initial vowels, rather than doubling of the word-final consonant. However, this is simply for system-internal reasons, which do not tolerate consonant clusters at the end of a *pada*, cf. P.8.2.23 (संयोगान्तस्य लोपः).

चतुराध्यायीभाष्य - ङणनाः पदान्ता ह्रस्वोपधाः स्वरे परतः द्विर्भवन्ति । 'प्रत्यङ्ङृणोति' (not in AV)। 'प्रत्यङ्ङुदेंषि' (अ.वे. १३.२.२०)। 'उद्यन्नांदित्यः' (अ.वे. २.३२.१)। 'सुगण्णास्ते' (not in AV)। ह्रस्वोपधा इति किमर्थम् । 'अर्वाङ् आकूंत्या चर' (अ.वे. ३.२.३)। स्वर इति किमर्थम् । 'उदंङ्जातः' (अ.वे. ५.४.८)।

'ङणनास्तु पदान्ता ये ह्रस्वपूर्वाः स्वरोदयाः ।
तेषां द्विर्भावमिच्छन्ति प्रत्यङ्ङ् उद्यन्न् सुगण्ण् इति।।'
(source?)

Note: The form *ṛṇoti* is found in Nighaṇṭu (2.14), but it is not attested in any known Vedic text. The example सुगण्णास्ते is an artificial example. No instance of word-final *ṇ* is found in the AV text. The rule thus represents a phonetic generalization applicable to the general grammar of Sanskrit. This tendency is manifest here in the CA rule, in the CAB, as well as in the cited versified authority. The Pāṇinian commentators were also forced to offer the same kind of artificial examples, because in the natural usage of Sanskrit, we do not find word-final *ṇ*. See the KV on P.8.3.32 (ङमो ह्रस्वादचि ङमुण्नित्यम्). It is difficult to see the real need of including the treatment of word-final *ṇ* in this rule.

३.२.३. संयोगादि स्वरात् ।

Whitney (3.28).

Translation: The first consonant of a cluster is doubled after a vowel.

चतुराध्यायीभाष्य - संयोगादि स्वरात्परतः द्विर्भवति । 'अग्निः' (अ.वे. १.७.४)। 'वृक्षः' (अ.वे. ४.७.५)। [There is a lacuna in H, which resumes with CA 3.2.6. N continues:] 'आत्रसति' । 'त्रसति' । 'आद्रवति' 'प्रद्रवति' । अपर आह । स(N: सं)यमं । पूर्वस्योति ।

Note: The doubling prescribed by this rule is not exhibited by the manuscripts of either the AV or the CA. There is a similar passage in the CAB on CA (1.2.16): संयोगादि पूर्वस्य स्वरस्य भवति । अत्र सति (?)। आद्रवति (the only AV form, आद्रवत्, अ.वे.पै.सं. २.३१.२)। प्रद्रवति (no attested AV forms for प्र+द्रु)। अपर आह - हसयमं पूर्वस्येति (?)। Considering the context, the last segment of this passage probably reconstructs to: अपर आह - सयमं पूर्वस्येति । This could be interpreted to mean that a consonant, along with its *yama,* goes with the previous vowel, in the context of syllabication. This could apply to an example like *aggniḥ,* especially if we interpret the sequence *gg* as a sequence of *g* followed by its *yama,* i.e. गँ्. Thus, while the initial consonant of a consonant cluster goes with the previous vowel, a consonant followed by its *yama* may go with the previous vowel, along with that *yama.* The rest of the passage probably reconstructs to: आत्त्रसति । त्रसति । आदद्रवति । प्रदद्रवति. Here, three out of the four examples would show doubling of the initial consonant of a cluster after a vowel, while the example *trasati* shows the absence of such doubling, since the consonant cluster does not follow a vowel.

The verb *ā-√tras* is not attested in Vedic literature, but *trasantu* is found in AV (5.21.8).

The lone manuscript H, which Whitney used, has a number of missing rules. Now, with the second manuscript of the commentary, N, and the rest of the manuscripts of the CA, we are able to confidently fill the *lacuna* which distressed Whitney a great deal.

३.२.४. छकारश्च ।

Whitney, H: no such rule. E, F, I, N, O: श्च, while other mss: स्य.

Translation: The consonant *ch* [is doubled after a vowel].

Note: In an example like *puccha* cited by the commentary, one must assume *pucha* to be the original form. With the doubling taught by the present rule, we get *puchcha*, which is finally reduced to *puccha* with the deaspiration of the first *ch* taught by CA (1.4.3: सोष्मणि पूर्वस्यानूष्मा).

Pāṇini achieves this same final outcome by prescribing an end-augment *t* (= *tUK*) to the vowel preceding *ch*. This *t* is then changed to *c* by other rules. While the CA rule has a wide obligatory coverage, Pāṇini's rules note variation regarding this phenomenon, cf. P.6.1.73-76). One should especially note that Pāṇini makes this procedure optional (or preferred *a la* Kiparsky), when a word-final long vowel is followed by word-initial *ch*, cf. P.6.1.76 (पदान्ताद्वा).

Also see the Notes on CA 2.1.17 for a further discussion on *ch*.

चतुराध्यायीभाष्य-छकारश्च स्वरात्परतः द्विर्भवति। 'इच्छति' । 'यच्छति' । 'पुच्छं वातस्य देवस्य' (अ.वे. ९.४.१३)। 'नडमिवा च्छिन्द्धि' (अ.वे. ४.१९.१)। 'आ च्छिंनद्मि स्तुकामिव' (अ.वे. ७.७४.२)।

Note: This rule and the commentary are missing in H, but are found in N, which was not available to Whitney.

३.२.५. पिप्पल्यादिषु पूर्वात् ।

Whitney, H: no such rule. P: पिष्पल्यादिषु°.

Translation: In [words] such as *pippalī*, [the consonant] after the first [vowel is doubled].

चतुराध्यायीभाष्य - पिप्पल्यादिषु पूर्वात् स्वरात् परतः द्विर्भवति । 'पिप्पली' (अ.वे. ६.१०९.१)। 'पिप्पलम्' (अ.वे. ९.१४.२०)। 'पित्तम्' (अ.वे. १.२४.१)। 'चित्तम्' (अ.वे. १.३४.२, probably 'वित्तम्,' अ.वे. १८.४.८९)।

'मिछं' (?)। 'मज्जा' (अ.वे. ४.१२.३)। 'मज्जु:' (?, probably 'रज्जु:,' अ.वे. ४.३.२)।

Note: Whitney's edition did not have either this rule or the commentary. However, in his "Collation of the Second Manuscript of the Atharvaveda Prātiśākhya" (1880, p. 161), Whitney says: "The second rule declares that 'in *pippali* etc. there is duplication after the first vowel of the word.' The cases here contemplated, judging from the word taken as example, are of a wholly different character from the others to which the rules of duplication relate, being such as have a double letter as part of their original and proper orthography. I do not, therefore, think it at all worth to look through the Atharvan text in order to pick out the other words which may have been included in the *gaṇa*." One of the assumptions in the rule seems to be that the double consonant cannot be etymologically derived, but must be a surface level phonological rule. This suggests some interesting ideas about the possible intended etymologies for these words. Such intended etymological connections can be guessed for some words, e.g. *pittam* < √*pā* and *cittam* < √*ci*. The examples *pippalī* and *pippalam* seem to suggest that the author of the CA held the forms *pipalī* and *pipalam* to be more basic, cf. *pīpal* in Hindi. The forms *majjā* and *majju* were probably derived from *maj+ā* and *maj+u* respectively, and the consonants were doubled later on. The form *majjuḥ,* though unattested, may be possibly related to the form *majjūka* cited in the Nirukta (9.5), which is, according to the Roth-Böhtlingk dictionary, related to the word *maṇḍūka.* The most mysterious form is *miccham.* Even if one takes this as an error for *piccham,* this form would be covered by the previous rule, and there is no need to offer it here. A number of mss. of the AV offer the reading *piṣpalī* for *pippalī.* It is not clear whether *pippalī* is a Prakritization of *piṣpalī,* or whether *piṣpalī* is a hyper-correction for *pippalī.* See: Whitney *(AV Transl.* Vol.I., pp. 359-360).

As for *cittam,* one may perhaps also refer to the occurrence of this word in AV (18.4.14). Referring to the mss. variants, Whitney *(AV Transl.* Vol.II., p. 876) points out: "The mss. vary in **a** between *citám* and *cittám;* our text reads the latter; SPP's the former, which is doubtless correct, and which is implied by the translation." It is an undeniable possibility that the CAB knew the reading *cittám,* and yet it felt that the word must be derived by doubling the consonant of an original *citám,* which alone fits the context, as correctly guessed by Whitney. Also see the same problem in AV (18.4.37), cf. AV *Transl.* Vol.II., p. 881.

A perusal of the APR helps clear a good deal of confusion regarding the citations given under this rule. Rules APR (106-111a, pp. 76-77) deal with words containing the geminates *yy* (106), *jj* (107), *ll* (108), *pp* (109), *tt* (110), and *nn* (111a). APR (107) deals with the words *majjā* (AV 4.12.3) and *rajjuḥ* (AV 4.3.2). APR (109) deals with *pippalī* (AV 6.109.1), *pippalaṃ* (AV 9.9.20), and *pippalyaḥ* (AV 6.109.2). APR (110) deals with *pittam* (AV 1.24. 1; 18.3.5) and *vittam* (AV 18.4.89). In all likelihood, the present CA rule refers to the same collection of instances. The main difference between the CA and the APR seems to be that while the CA speaks of doubling, suggesting some prior stage of derivation without such doubling, the APR simply represents an enumeration of instances with specific geminated consonants. It may also be noted that the manuscript Vn for the APR records the reading *cittam*, where other manuscripts read *vittam.*

The *pippalyādi gaṇa* and the doubling of consonants in the words listed in this *gaṇa* is referred to in a verse cited in the CAB on CA (1.1.12).

३.२.६. न विसर्जनीयः ।

Whitney (3.29). H omits न. Whitney suspects the presence of न, and this conjecture is supported by the manuscripts.

Translation: A *visarjanīya,* i.e. *ḥ*, is not doubled.

चतुराध्यायीभाष्य - न विसर्जनीयस्य द्विर्भवति । 'अ॒ग्निः' (अ.वे. १.७.४)। 'वृ॒क्षः' (अ.वे. ४.७.५)।

३.२.७. सस्थाने च ।

Whitney (3.30).

Translation: [A consonant], when followed by another consonant with the same point of articulation, [is not doubled].

चतुराध्यायीभाष्य - सस्थाने न च द्विर्भवति । 'इन्द्रः' (अ.वे. १.९.१)। 'च॒न्द्रः' (अ.वे. २.१५.३)। 'म॒न्द्रः' (अ.वे. १८.१.३०)। 'उष्ट्रः' (not in AV)। 'क्रोष्ट्रः'

('क्रोष्ट्रे,' अ.वे. ११.२.२)। 'भ्राष्ट्रम्' (not in AV)। 'नेष्ट्रम्' (not in AV)। 'राष्ट्रम्' (अ.वे. ३.४.१)।

Note: The examples *indraḥ, candraḥ, uṣṭraḥ, rāṣṭram,* and *bhrāṣṭram* are cited by the KV on P.8.4.50 (त्रिप्रभृतिषु शाकटायनस्य). Śākaṭāyana held that there was no doubling of consonants involved in triple clusters. There seems to be a close relationship between the CAB and the Pāṇinian commentaries.

Other treatises offer similar rules, but there are differences. For details, see: Whitney (1862: 142), and Deshpande (1975: 208).

Whitney further observes: "The instances are wanting in variety, as illustrating our text, since they all present groups of three consonants, while we must suppose our rule to apply no less to groups of two, and to forbid duplication in such words as *antaḥ, asti, aṣṭa,* etc."

३.२.८. रेफहकारौ परं ताभ्याम् ।

Whitney (3.31). A, B: °लोताभ्यां. P(orig): हफहकारौ°.

Translation: *R* and *h*, [at the beginning of a cluster, are not doubled. However, the consonant] following those two [is doubled].

चतुराध्यायीभाष्य - रेफहकारौ संयोगादी न द्विर्भवतः (H, N: ति) । परं तु ताभ्यां द्विर्भवति । 'अर्क्कः' (अ.वे. ४.१५.५)। 'अर्च्चः' ('अर्चं,' अ.वे. २०.५१.१)। 'वर्त्तः' (as in 'अभीवर्तः,' अ.वे. १.२९.३)। 'भर्ग्गः' (अ.वे. १९.३७.१)। 'प्राह्ण्णः' (not in AV) । 'पूर्वाह्ण्णः' (not in AV, RV 10.34.11)। 'अपराह्ण्णः' (अ.वे. ९.६.४६)। 'अपह्म्मलति' (not in AV)। 'विह्म्मलति' (not in AV)। 'अपह्न्नुते' (not in AV)। 'निह्न्नुते' (not in AV)। 'ब्रह्म्म' (अ.वे. १.१९.४)।

Note: Neither manuscript shows the doubling of consonants required by the rule. Also, compare the commentary on CA (1.2.18):

रेफहकारक्रमजं च पूर्वस्य स्वरस्य भवति । 'अर्क:' (अ.वे. ४.१५.५)। 'अर्थ:' (not in AV, Whitney's emendation: 'अर्चं,' अ.वे. २०.५१.१)। 'गर्त्ते' (not in AV, Whitney's emendation: 'वर्त:,'as in 'अभीवर्त:,' अ.वे. १.२९.३)। 'भग्न:' (not in AV, Whitney's emendation: 'भर्गः,' अ.वे. १९.३७.१)। 'प्राह्ण:' (not in AV)। 'पूर्वाह्ण:' (not in AV)। 'अपराह्ण:' (अ.वे. ९.६.४६)। 'अपब्रह्मलयति' (Whitney's emendation: 'अप ह्मलयति' (not in AV)। 'विह्मलयति' (not in AV)। 'अपह्नुते' (not in AV)। 'विह्नुते' (not in AV)। 'ब्रह्म' (अ.वे. १.१९.४)।

The text of the commentary on CA (3.2.8) shows that Whitney's emendations of the text of the commentary on CA (1.2.18) were mostly correct. Neither the manuscripts of the CA, nor those of the AV, show this doubling.

The CAB does not explicitly continue the condition *svarāt* from CA (3.2.3), but that word must continue into this rule. This is clear from Bhārgava-Bhāskara's commentary on CA (1.2.18), and the near equivalence of this rule with P.8.4.46 (अचो रहाभ्यां द्वे), cf. Notes on CA (1.2.18).

We say that this rule is a near equivalent of P.8.4.46, rather than identical with it, because the two rules predict slightly different results in a few cases. Consider for instance a form like *arhati*. Here, in the cluster *rh,* the CA rule would require doubling of *h,* since it applies to all consonants coming after *r* or *h*. This would give us the form *arhhati*. Pāṇini's rule 8.4.46, on the other hand, prescribes the doubling of *yaR* consonants. The abbreviation *yaR* refers to all consonants, except *h,* and, therefore, P.8.4.46, will not lead to the doubling of *h* in *arhati*. The doubling of *h* was not universally accepted by Sanskrit phoneticians, cf. Varma (1929: 114-115).

३.२.९. शषसा: स्वरे ।

Whitney (3.32).

Translation: The consonants *ś, ṣ,* and *s*, [are not doubled], before a vowel.

चतुराध्यायीभाष्य - शषसा: स्वरे परे न द्विर्भवन्ति । 'कर्षति' ('कर्षेत्,' अ.वे. १५.१३.१२)। 'वर्षति' (अ.वे. पै.सं. १५.२१.५, 'वर्षन्ति', अ.वे. ९.१.९)। 'आदर्श:' (?, 'आ दंर्शति,' अ.वे. ५.२.७)। 'अक्षतर्श:' (not in Vedic Saṃhitās)। 'ततर्ष(H, N: र्शं)' (not in Vedic

Saṃhitās)। 'पुरोडाशम्' (अ.वे. १८.४.२)। स्वर इति किमर्थम् । 'बाष्ष्पो(H: वाष्यो, N: बाष्पो, Whitney: वर्ष्यो)-दकेन यजेत' (not in Vedic Saṃhitās)।

Note: Surya Kanta says that the example वार्ष्योदकेन यजेत cited by the CAB is not found in the Vulgate of the AV, and he *(APR, Introduction,* p. 40) suggests that this may have occurred in the genuine Śaunakīya recension of the AV, and that the Vulgate is not the genuine Śaunakīya recension. Here, Whitney cites the example from the commentary as वर्ष्ष्योदकेन and not as वार्ष्योदकेन, as reported by Surya Kanta. Secondly, Whitney does not report the actual reading in the mss. H: वष्योदकेन. Thirdly, the second manuscript of the commentary offers the reading: बाष्पोदकेन. None of the mss. provide the doubling of *ṣ* as required by the rule. Surya Kanta is claiming the possible Śaunakīya status for a ghost reading. However, the word वर्ष्याः is found in AV 19.2.1 referring to rain-water, and this makes the original reading वर्ष्योदकेन a likely reading.

On this rule, Whitney points out that "the manuscripts of the AV., so far as known to me, do not, save in very infrequent and entirely sporadic cases, follow any of the rules of the *varṇakrama* proper, excepting the one which directs duplication after a *r* ; and even in this case, their practice is as irregular as that of the manuscripts of the later literature."

This rule is similar to P.8.4.49 (शरोऽचि). Compare the examples cited by the KV on this rule: कर्षति, वर्षति, आकर्षः, अक्षदर्शः । अचीति किम् । दश्र्य्यते ।. The first several examples of the CAB seem to have been taken over from the KV, and the copyists have probably garbled them up.

३.२.१०. प्रगृह्याश्च प्रकृत्या ।

Whitney (3.33). I, O: °ह्यश्च°. A, B, D: प्रगृह्यश्चेमाकृत्य. I: 10. O: °प्रकृत्याः.

Translation: The *pragṛhya* [vowels, as defined in CA (1.3. 11-19)] remain unaltered.

Note: Regarding an anomalous case, Whitney observes: "The text offers a single case in which a final *pragṛhya* vowel is combined with a following initial: it is *nṛpatī 'va* (viii.4.6). The same passage is found in the Rig-Veda (vii.104.6), exhibiting the same anomalous *sandhi*. ... That no reference is made to the passage in our treatise is possibly to be taken as an indication that the true Atharvan reading is *nṛpatī iva*, as is actually given by E. and I." The VVRI edition reads *nṛpatī iva*, and the Padapāṭha clearly supports this reading as a *pragṛhya*: *nṛpatī iveti nṛpatī 'iva*. The VVRI edition also notes that a large number of manuscripts read *nṛpatīva*. The complicating factor with *iva* is that the tradition treats *nṛpatī iva* as a compound form. This instance is listed as *nṛpatīva* under APR (105, p. 76), though a late manuscript Vn records the reading *nṛpatī iva*. A few deviant instances such as *maṇīva* < *maṇī+iva* were known to Pāṇinian commentators, and an apocryphal Vārttika : मणीवादीनां प्रतिषेधो वक्तव्यः came up to deal with such exceptional cases. For a discussion of this statement, see: Kaiyaṭa's Pradīpa on the MB on P.1.1.11. In any case, I tend to agree with Whitney's guess that the original Atharvan reading was most probably *nṛpatī iva,* but, I suspect that under the influence of the RV tradition, it was unconsciously altered by the reciters to *nṛpatīva.*

चतुराध्यायीभाष्य - प्रगृह्याश्च प्रकृत्या भवन्ति । 'केन पार्ष्णी आ भृंते' । (पद ⇒) 'पार्ष्णी इति' (अ.वे. १०.२.१)। 'इन्द्रवायू उभौ' । (पद ⇒) 'इन्द्रवायू इति' (अ.वे. ३.२०.६)। 'उभाविन्द्राग्नी आ भंरताम्' । (पद ⇒) 'इन्द्राग्नी इति' (अ.वे. ५.७.६)।

३.२.११. एना एहा आदयश्च ।

Whitney (3.34). D, Hb, J: एता for एना. I: 11.

Translation: In passages like *enā ehāḥ,* [there is no sandhi of adjacent vowels].

चतुराध्यायीभाष्य - एना एहा आदयश्च प्रकृत्या भवन्ति । 'एना एहाः परिं' (अ.वे. १२.३.३३)। 'यथा मन्नापंगा असंः' (अ.वे. १.३४.५; २.३०.१; ६.८.१-३)। 'पृथिवी उत द्यौः' (अ.वे. १८.१.५)।

Note: The CAB cites all the same examples in the same order as are found under APR (103). Whitney, however, points out additional cases which are not covered by the citations in the commentary, e.g. Whitney *(AV Transl.*

Vol.I., 459) refers to *sádanā akarma* in AV (7.97.4) as a case of hiatus, and says: "the irregular hiatus must be regarded as falling under Prāt. iii.34 (= CA 3.2.11), although the passage is not quoted by the commentary to that rule."

The example *sadanā akarma* (AV 7.97.4) raises further complicated questions. It is cited under APR (100, p. 71) as an example of an *ekādeśa* combination, where there may be doubt as to the original long vowels. All the examples cited under this rule show that a vowel combination has taken place, except the example *sadanā akarma*. My guess is that this example too must have been read as *sadanākarma* (< *sadanā* + *akarma*) by the person who included it in the APR list of *ekādeśa*s, though it is clear that the meter requires it to be read as *sadanā akarma*. In any case, it is clear that it does not come under the present rule, or under APR (103).

३.२.१२. यवलोपे ।

Whitney (3.35).

Translation: When the [final] *y* and *v* are dropped [by CA (2.1.21), the preceding vowel does not combine with the following vowel].

चतुराध्यायीभाष्य - यकारवकारलोपे च प्रकृत्या भवति । 'क आंसञ्जन्याः के वराः' (अ.वे. ११.८.१)। 'उष्णेनं वाय उदकेनेहिं' (अ.वे. ६.६८.१)। 'अस्या इच्छन्नग्रुवै पतिंम्' (अ.वे. ६.६०.१)। 'स उं एव मंहायमः' (अ.वे. १३.४.५)। 'ता इमा आपंः' (अ.वे. १५.१५.७)।

Note: The examples cited here by the CAB are identical with the ones cited under CA (2.1.21).

Whitney, in his comments on the present rule, point to several anomalous cases. For example, AV (9.4.19) reads ब्राह्मणेभ्य ऋषभं दत्त्वा, while the meter requires the sandhi: ब्राह्मणेभ्यर्षभं दत्त्वा. On the other hand, on AV (10.1.15), Whitney *(AV Transl.* Vol.II., p. 564) says: "All the *saṃhitā*-mss. ⌊or rather, most of them: see also note to Prāt. iii.35 (= CA 3.2.12)⌋ combine *kṛtyé'ti* ⌊and thus indeed the meter requires us to pronounce⌋; but our edition restores the more correct reading ⌊*kṛtya íti*⌋, since the Prāt. does not countenance the irregularity; we should expect to find it with *vandane'va* (in ii.56 = CA 2.2.17)." The VVRI editions sticks to the manuscripts and keeps the reading *kṛtyeti*. However, we must note that the exceptional behavior of *kṛtyeti* is noticed neither by the CA, nor by the APR, and it makes one wonder whether the reading as known to these texts was the expected regular form *kṛtya iti* < *kṛtye iti*.

३.२.१३. केवल उकारः स्वरपूर्वः ।

Whitney (3.36). Hb, Nb: °उका स्वर°. O: °स्वरः पूर्वः.

Translation: An *u*, when a word by itself, preceded by a vowel, [is not combined with the following vowel].

Note: For example, in स उ एव, AV (13.4.5), the combination of *saḥ+u* results in *sa u*, by the previous rule. The present rule makes the *u* in such combinations immune from combinations with the following vowels.

चतुराध्यायीभाष्य - केवल उकारः स्वरपूर्वः प्रकृत्या भवति । 'स उं एव मंहायमः' (अ.वे. १३.४.५)। 'स उ अश्मांनमस्यति' (अ.वे. १३.४.४१)। .

३.२.१४. नमौ सन्ध्यौ ।

Whitney (3.37). J.K: न समौ सन्ध्यौ. Kṛṣṇadāsa's commentary in K attempts to justify this reading.

Translation: The sounds *n* and *m*, resulting from euphonic combinations, [remain unchanged].

चतुराध्यायीभाष्य - नकारमकारौ च सन्ध्यौ प्रकृत्या भवतः (H, N: ति)। 'नदीन्तरति (H, N: नंदी°)' । 'त्रिष्टुम्न-(H, N: न्न)यति' ।

Note: The second example is found in the KV on P.8.4.45 (यरोऽनुनासिकेऽनुनासिको वा).

Besides pointing out that the examples offered by the commentator are fabricated examples, Whitney informs: "The former is intended to show that a *n* which is the result of the assimilation of a final *m*, by ii. 31 (= CA 2.1.31), before an initial *t*, is not liable to a farther insertion of a sibilant before that *t*, by

ii. 26 (= CA 2.1.26); the latter, that a *m* which grows out of the assimilation of a final labial to a following initial dental, by ii. 5 (= CA 2.1.5), is not then, by ii. 31 (= CA 2.1.31), convertible into *n* by a second assimilation."

Whitney also makes an important observation: "This rule ... is replaced, or rendered unnecessary, in the other treatises, by the general precepts there referred to." For example, in the Pāṇinian system P.8.4.45 (यरोऽनुनासिकेऽनुनासिको वा) converts a final labial stop to *m* before a nasal. A final *m* is converted to an *anusvāra* by P.8.3.23 (मोऽनुस्वारः), and then the *anusvāra* is converted to a homorganic nasal before a non-spirant consonant by P.8.4.58 (अनुस्वारस्य ययि परसवर्णः). Now, the rule P.8.2.1 (पूर्वत्रासिद्धम्) institutes a convention by which, in the following sections of the Aṣṭādhyāyī, a given rule does not recognize the outputs of the following rules, but recognizes the outputs of the preceding rules. Thus, in the example *triṣṭumnayati* < *triṣṭup+nayati*, P.8.3.23 (मोऽनुस्वारः) does not recognize the change of *p* > *m* brought about by P.8.4.45 (यरोऽनुनासिकेऽनुनासिको वा), and hence it does not convert this *m* into an *anusvāra*. In the absence of an *anusvāra*, P.8.4.58 (अनुस्वारस्य ययि परसवर्णः) does not operate with respect to our example. This is how the form **triṣṭunnayati* is prevented in the Pāṇinian system.

३.२.१५. आकारः केवलः प्रथमं पूर्वेण ।

Whitney (3.38). A, B: °प्रथमः°. P adds a daṇḍa after केवलः.

Translation: The sound *ā*, [forming a separate word] by itself, is first [combined] with the preceding vowel, [and then with the following vowel].

Note: Different systems of grammar followed different strategies. For example, Pāṇini assumes that the combination of *ā* with the following form takes place first, e.g. *dhiyā+ā+ihi* > *dhiyā+ehi*. However, after this has been done, the combination of *dhiyā+ehi* must exceptionally provide *dhiyehi*, rather than the normal expected result *dhiyaihi*. To achieve this exceptional result, he composed a special rule: P.6.1.95 (ओमाङोश्च). The KV notes that this is an exception to the normal *vṛddhi* rule, P.6.1.88 (वृद्धिरेचि): वृद्धिरेचीत्यस्यापवादः. The present CA rule, like RPR 2.7: आनुपूर्व्येण सन्धीन्, achieves the same result with a different procedure. First we combine *dhiyā+ā* > *dhiyā*, and then we combine *dhiyā+ihi* to derive the expected *dhiyehi*. This is achieved by stipulating the order of combinations. One may infer from this that the normal order of these combinations, without the present exception-rule, might have been the other way around. Whitney seems to draw a reverse conclusion: "The latter is the true method of making the two successive *sandhis*, as we are taught by this rule, and by corresponding rules in the other treatises; which, however, express themselves in a more general manner, declaring that all *sandhis* must be made in the order of their occurrence." The reason why the linear order of sandhis may not have been looked at as the necessary order is that a relationship between a preverb and a verb is viewed as a more 'interior' relationship, in comparison with the relationship of the preverb with a non-verb item. In most of the examples cited by the commentator, the *ā* is followed by a verb form.

चतुराध्यायीभाष्य - आकारः केवलः प्रथमं पूर्वेण स्वरेण सन्धीयते । 'धियेहि' (पद ⇒ 'धिया । आ । इहि,' अ.वे. २.५.४)। 'जुषस्वेन्द्र' (पद ⇒ 'जुषस्व । आ । इन्द्र,' अ.वे. २.५.४)। 'स्तनयित्नुनेहि' (पद ⇒ 'स्तनयित्नुना । आ । इहि', अ.वे. ४.१५.११)। 'कुष्ठेहि' (पद ⇒ 'कुष्ठ । आ। इहि,' अ.वे. ५.४.१)। 'उदकेनेहि' (पद ⇒ 'उदकेन । आ । इहि,' अ.वे. ६.६८.१)। 'अव पश्यतेत' (पद ⇒ 'अव । पश्यत । आ । इत,' अ.वे. १८.४.३७)।

Note: All the examples cited by the CAB are cited in the same order under APR (8), which also cites the present CA rule. One may also note that the APR sorts its examples into two categories, those where the *ā* is followed by *i*, and those where the *ā* is followed by *e*. The first is dealt with by APR (8), while the second is dealt with by APR (9). In the cases listed under APR (9), the order of sandhis does not seem to really make any difference, e.g. *ihaitu* < *iha+ā+etu,* AV (1.15.2).

On *dhiyéhi* (AV 2.5.4), Whitney *(AV Transl.* Vol.I., p. 44) says: "The first half-verse is vs. 5 in AŚS., where it reads: ... *dhiyā hiyānaḥ*. Of the two versions of the last pāda, that of AŚS. is doubtless the original, though ours (the *pada* has *dhiyā́ ā́ ihi ā́ naḥ*) is ingenious enough to give a fair sense; the reading *dhiyéhi* is authenticated by the Prāt. comment, which quotes it more than once (to iii.38 = CA 3.2.15; iv. 113-115 = CA 4.4.14-16)."

Whitney *(AV Transl.* Vol.II., p. 564) points to another example which is subject to this rule, though the *pada*-text does not clearly indicate it in this fashion: "The *pada*-mss. have in b *upa-eyimá,* and the combination to *upeyimá* falls under the rule Prāt. iii.38, although the *ā* contained in *eyimá* (= *ā-īyimá*) does not appear as *ā* in the *pada*-text." Since, in this case, the finite verb is accented, the unaccented upasargas are compounded with the verb by CA (4.1. 23: उपसर्गं आख्यातेनोदात्तेन समस्यते), and with two *upasarga*s involved in this compound, only the first juncture is separated with an *avagraha* in the *pada*-text.

३.२.१६. स्वरे नामिनोऽन्तस्थाः ।

Whitney (3.39): °न्तःस्थाः. No manuscript supports Whitney. A, B: °मिनांतस्थाः.

Translation: Before a vowel, the *nāmin*s, i.e. vowels other than *a* and *ā*, are changed to [appropriate] semi-vowels.

Note: The rule as stated is indeed too broad, and its domain is brought down to its proper size by the subsequent exception rules which follow. Finally, its actual scope is limited to the vowels *i, u, r̥,* (and theoretically *l̥*) changing respectively to *y, v, r,* (and *l*), before dissimilar vowels. The choice of appropriate substitutes is governed by CA (1.4.4: आन्तर्येण वृत्तिः). The CAB on CA (1.4.4) specifically refers to the present rule as a case for the application of CA (1.4.4) which says that the choice of a substitute is determined in terms of maximal featural proximity to the original sound. Also: Hueckstedt (1995).

चतुराध्यायीभाष्य - स्वरे परतः नामिनः अन्तस्था भवन्ति। 'दध्यत्र' । 'मध्वत्र' । 'मात्रर्थम्' । 'पित्र(H, N: तृ)र्थम्' ।

Note: As Whitney rightly observes, these examples are fabricated examples and are identical with those found in the commentaries on Pāṇini's rule 6.1.77 (इको यणचि). This fact may perhaps allow us to set the upper limit for the date of this commentary, if we can date the first appearance of these examples in Pāṇinian commentaries. At the very least, it is quite clear that the commentator is substantially under the influence of the Pāṇinian tradition, though, unlike the other two commentaries, he does not directly cite Pāṇini's rule. Interestingly, Surya Kanta selectively omits these examples from his claim that such unattested examples belong to the so-called genuine Śaunakīya recension.

३.२.१७. सन्ध्यक्षराणामयवायावः ।

Whitney (3.40). M, Na: °यवः.

Translation: The diphthongs [i.e. *e, o, ai,* and *au,* before vowels, are respectively, replaced by] *ay, av, āy,* and *āv.*

चतुराध्यायीभाष्य - सन्ध्यक्षराणां स्वरे परतः अयवायावो भवन्ति । 'अग्न आसाम्' (?)। 'वाय आसाम्' (?)। 'अग्न ऊतये' (?)। 'वाय ऊतयें' (अ.वे. ४.२५.६)। 'अस्मा उद्धर' (?)। 'असावांदित्यः' (अ.वे. १५.१०.७)। 'च(H, N: श्व)यनम्' । 'चा(H, N: वा)यकः' । 'लवनम्' । 'लाव-(H, N: य)कः' । 'पव(H:, N: च)नम्' । 'पाव(H, N: च)-कः' ।

Note: The first several examples, which are examples of external sandhis, do not show the *y* or *v* of *ay, av, āy,* and *āv,* but show the stage of their deletion by CA (2.1.21-22), and the remaining vowels are immune from combination with the following vowels by CA (3.2.12).

The examples *cayanam, lavanam, cāyakaḥ, lāvakaḥ* and *pāvakaḥ* are stock examples in the Pāṇinian tradition right from Patañjali's MB. Also see the KV on P.6.1.78 (एचोऽयवायावः). Again, as Whitney notes, the commentator prefers to give stock examples from the Pāṇinian tradition, rather than real examples from the text of the AV. However, Whitney correctly notes that these last "are examples of applications of the rule which the Prātiśākhya does not contemplate." These last examples illustrate the present rule in the situation of internal sandhi.

३.२.१८. पूर्वपरयोरेकः ।

Whitney (3.41).

Translation: The preceding and the following [vowels are combined into] a single [substitute, in the following operations].

Note: Whitney comments: "The technical language of the Prātiśākhyas has no recognized method of indicating the fusion of two sounds into one, and the form of the following rules is ambiguous, since rule 44 (= CA 3.2.21), for instance, literally means, according to the phraseology of the treatise, that *a* before *i* becomes *e*, and not *a* with *i*. Hence the necessity of this special rule of interpretation." One may add that Pāṇini is not different from the Prātiśākhyas in this respect, cf. P.6.1.84 (एकः पूर्वपरयोः) and the following rules. Also curious is the inversion of the word-order in the statement of the rule, as compared to Pāṇini 6.1.84.

चतुराध्यायीभाष्य - पूर्वपरयोरेको भवति । एतदधिकृतं वेदितव्यम् । इत उत्तरं यदनुक्रमिष्यामः ।

३.२.१९. समानाक्षरस्य सवर्णे दीर्घः ।

Whitney (3.42). Hc, Nc: सामान्याक्षरस्य°.

Translation: A simple vowel, followed by a member of the same *varṇa* group, becomes long.

Note: The wording of this rule is very similar to Pāṇini's rule 6.1.101 (अकः सवर्णे दीर्घः). However, the main difference lies in the fact that while Pāṇini 1.1.9 (तुल्यास्यप्रयत्नं सवर्णम्) explicitly defines the term *savarṇa* as referring to a sound sharing the same point of articulation and the manner as the sound in question, the CA does not define the term *savarṇa*. In the CA, this term occurs only once. The CAB on CA (1.1.27) quotes an ancient Śikṣā verse which defines the term *savarṇa* as: समानास्यप्रयत्ना ये ते सवर्णा इति स्मृताः, which closely parallels P.1.1.9. However, a closer study of the CA shows that the CA seems to be using the term in a more basic meaning, i.e. member of the same *varṇa*, e.g. *i* and *ī* are members of the same *varṇa*, and are hence represented by the term *ivarṇa*. For an extensive study of the different notions of *savarṇa*, see: Deshpande (1975: 91-93).

चतुराध्यायीभाष्य - समाना(H, N: सामान्या°)क्षरस्य सवर्णे परतः दीर्घो भवति । 'दण्डाग्रम्' । 'दधीन्द्रः' । 'मधूष्णम्' । 'होतॄश्यः' । 'पितॄश्यः' ।

Note: Notice that Surya Kanta has conveniently made no claim for the cited examples as belonging to his so-called genuine Śaunakīya recension. The KV on P.6.1.101 (अकः सवर्णे दीर्घः) cites the examples *daṇḍāgram, dadhīndraḥ, madhūdake,* and *hotṝśyaḥ*. The Osmania edition of the KV notes a manuscript variant *madhūṣtram* for *madhūdake*. This variant is probably a corruption of *madhūṣṇam*. Also noteworthy is the absence of an example of *-ḷ+ḷ-*.

This is natural for the CA since one does not have any words ending in *ḷ*, and this fact has been explicitly stated in CA (1.1.6: अन्ऌकारः स्वरः पद्यः).

३.२.२०. सीमन्ते ह्रस्वः ।

Whitney (3.43). Hb, Nb: सीमंतऱ्हस्वः. Most mss. read ऱ्ह for ह्र.

Translation: In *sīmanta* [< *sīma+anta*, the combination resulting from *a+a*] is a short [*a*].

चतुराध्यायीभाष्य - सीमन्ते ह्रस्वो भवति । 'जिनतो वज्र त्वं सीमन्तम्' (अ.वे. ६.१३४.३)। सीमन्ते केशवेष्टेति वक्तव्यम् । यो हि सीम्नो अन्तः सीमान्तः सः ।

Note: Whitney argues that the theme here is *sīmant* and not *sīmanta.* He however acknowledges that the rule seems to presuppose a derivation as *sīmanta* coming from *sīma+anta.* Whitney notes that the Padapāṭha does not analyze this word into its components. The APR (p. 137) lists *sīmanta* in the *samudrādi gaṇa*, a list of words which are not analyzed because of unclear components and unclear combinations.

However, as in other cases, the CA rule marks an effort to move the grammatical analysis of words beyond the stage of the Padapāṭha. The CA and the CAB are indeed not alone in deriving *sīmanta* from *sīma(n)+anta.* On P.6.1.94 (एङि पररूपम्), Kātyāyana offers a Vārttika: शकन्ध्वादिषु च. This list begins with the word *śakandhu* < *śaka+andhu*, where the combination of *a+a* results in *a*, rather than *ā.* One of the additional examples on this Vārttika offered by Patañjali is *sīmanta*, which he explicitly analyzes as *sīma+antaḥ.* Then Patañjali says: केशेष्विति वक्तव्यम् । यो हि सीम्नोऽन्तः, सीमान्तः स भवति. The passage in the CAB reminds one of the MB passage. I wonder whether the reading केशवेष्टेति is a garbled form for the original केशेष्विति .

३.२.२१. अवर्णस्येवर्ण एकारः ।

Whitney (3.44). J, M (corr), P: °स्येववर्ण°.

Translation: A member of the *a-varṇa* [i.e. *a, ā* etc.] followed by a member of the *i-varṇa* [i.e. *i, ī* etc.] is replaced with *e*.

चतुराध्यायीभाष्य - अवर्णस्य इवर्णे परतः एकारो भवति। 'खट्वेन्द्रः' । 'मालेन्द्रः' ।

Note: The manuscript H reads: *ravadgomālendrah,* and by comparing this with examples under Pāṇini (vi.1.87), Whitney restored this to *khaṭvendraḥ, mālendraḥ.* These examples are also found in the KV on P.6.1.84 (एकः पूर्वपरयोः), and in the MB on P.6.1.87 (आद्गुणः). This restoration is now clearly supported by the second manuscript, N.

३.२.२२. उवर्ण ओकारः ।

Whitney (3.45). A, B, D, Hb: °उकारः for °ओकारः.

Translation: [A member of the *a-varṇa,* i.e. *a, ā* etc.] followed by a member of the *u-varṇa* [i.e. *u, ū* etc.] is replaced with *o.*

चतुराध्यायीभाष्य - अवर्णस्य उवर्णे परतः ओ(H: ॐ)-कारो भवति । 'खट्वोदकम्' । 'मालोदकम्' ।

Note: The example *khaṭvodakam* is found in the KV on P.6.1.87 (*ād guṇaḥ*). Both of these examples are found in the MB on P.6.1.87.

Commenting on an anomalous form, Whitney says: "There is a single instance in the text, in which this rule is not observed, and *a+ū* ar not combined into *o,* but into *au :* it is the word *prauḍhaḥ* (xv.15.4 : p. *pra-ūḍhaḥ*). B., indeed, reads *proḍho*, but doubtless only by an error of the copyist. We must suppose, either that the authors and commentator overlooked this word, or that its *pada* as well as *saṃhitā* reading in their text would be *prauḍhaḥ*, or that the passage containing it was not in their Atharva-Veda - of which suppositions, I should regard the first as the most plausible, and the last as the least likely." The VVRI edition finds one more manuscript, O, which shares the reading *proḍho*, but the edition chooses the majority reading *prauḍhaḥ.*

Pāṇini is probably familiar with the form *proḍha*, as it appears in the *gaṇa* mentioned in P.2.1.17 (तिष्ठद्गुप्रभृतीनि च). [Of course one cannot be totally certain if all the words in such lists go back to Pāṇini.] The formation *prauḍhaḥ* is not provided for by Pāṇini, but is provided for by Kātyāyana's Vārttika : प्रादूहोढोढ्येषैष्येषु on P.6.1.89 (एत्येधत्यूठ्सु). It is also interesting to find that Kaiyaṭa on this Vārttika still attempts to derive the expression प्रोढा

प्र+आ+ऊढा प्रोढाशब्दे आ+ऊढा ओढा, प्र+ओढा इति स्थिते 'ओमाङोश्च' इति पररूपं भवति, MB, (MLBD edn, Vol. II., p. 745). It is thus possible that the oldest reading was indeed *proḍha*, which was gradually supplanted by *prauḍha*, and under the pressure of the post-Kātyāyana Pāṇinian tradition, the Atharvan reciters almost completely replaced an older *proḍha* with a later form *prauḍha*. Such a speculation is further supported by the fact that the APR also makes no effort to account for an anomalous *prauḍha*.

३.२.२३. अरमृवर्णे ।

Whitney (3.46).

Translation: [A member of the *a-varṇa*, i.e. *a*, *ā* etc.] followed by a member of the *r̥-varṇa* [i.e. *r̥*, *r̥̄* etc.] is replaced with *ar*.

चतुराध्यायीभाष्य - अरम् भवति अवर्णस्य ऋवर्णे परतः । 'तस्यंर्षभस्याङ्गांनि' (अ.वे. ९.४.११)। 'अवंर्तिः' (अ.वे. ४.३४.३)। 'यज्ञर्तः' (अ.वे. ८.१०.४)। 'काम(H, N: मा)र्तः' (not in AV)। 'नैनानवंर्तिः' (अ.वे. ४.३४.३)।

Note: Whitney's AV text for 9.4.11 reads: तस्यं ऋषभस्याङ्गांनि । Whitney *(AV Transl.* Vol.II., p. 530) points out: "All our mss. (save O.) read, like the edition, *tásya r̥ṣa-* in c, although the passage is quoted as example under the Prāt. rule (iii.46 = CA 3.2.23) that *a* and *ā*+*r̥* make *ar*." The same reading is maintained by SPP and VVRI editions. One wonders whether this is a case of the influence of the Pāṇinian grammar on the text-tradition of the AV, cf. P.6.1.128 (*r̥ty akaḥ*). It is also clear from the context that the instance must be *kāmartaḥ* < *kāma+r̥taḥ,* and not *kāmārtaḥ* < *kāma+ārtaḥ* as cited by the manuscripts. There is some disagreement concerning the interpretation of the word *ávartiḥ* in AV (4.34.3). Whitney *(AV Transl.* Vol.I., p. 206) says: "The *pada*-text writes *ávartiḥ* without division, yet the comment to Prāt. iii.46 (= CA 3.2.23) quotes the word as exemplifying the combination of final *a* and initial *r̥*; the comm. understands and explains it as *a-vartti!*"

On this rule, Whitney has extensive comments on the practice of the manuscripts of the AV, and the phonetic implications of that practice: "They follow a method of their own, in which is to be recognized the influence of a doctrine agreeing with or resembling that of our Prātiśākhya respecting the *svarabhakti*, or figment of vowel sound, assumed to be thrust in between *r* and a following consonant (see i.101, 102 = CA 1.4.10-11). Where the phonetical theory requires the insertion of the longer *svarabhakti*, or where a sibilant follows, there the manuscripts usually and regularly give the vowel *ṛ* instead of *r*, reading *iva ṛṣabhaḥ* (iii.6.4), *svasa ṛṣīṇām* (vi.133.4), etc.; before any other consonant, or where our treatise and the Rik. Pr. interpose the shorter *svarabhakti* after the *r*, and the other Prātiśākhyas require no insertion at all, there our manuscripts regularly make the combination according to the rule now under discussion, writing *ṛtasya rtena* (vi.114.1), *iva rbhuḥ* (x.1.8), *sa rcām* (x.8.10), etc. These rules are not, however, altogether without exceptions."

३.२.२४. उपर्षन्त्यादिषु च ।

Whitney (3.47). Ha, Na: omit च. J, M: उपरिषन्त्या°. P: उपरिषांत्या°.

Translation: [The final *a* of an *upasarga* combines with the initial *ṛ* of the verb to yield *ar*] also in forms like *uparṣanti*.

Note: This rule is an exception to the next rule, i.e. CA (3.2.25) which predicts the result *ār* in a combination of a final *a* of an *upasarga* and the initial *ṛ* of a verb.

चतुराध्यायीभाष्य - उपर्षन्त्यादिषु च अरं भवति अवर्णस्य ऋवर्णे परतः । 'या हृदंयमुपर्षन्ति' (अ.वे. ९.८.१४)। 'याः पार्श्वे उंपर्षन्ति' (अ.वे. ९.८.१५)। 'यास्तिरश्चीरुप-र्षन्ति' (अ.वे. ९.८.१६)।

Note: Surya Kanta *(APR, Introduction,* p. 43) points out that the APR (13), examples 34-36, indicate a reading *upariṣánti,* rather than *uparṣánti* as expected by CA (3.2.24). He concludes from this that the Vulgate, which follows the APR, is not a Śaunakīya text, and that a genuine Śaunakīya text had the reading as expected by the CA. As I have shown above, the mss. J and M read *upariṣantyādiṣu,* and would lead one to believe that the same tradition which copied and maintained knowledge of the CA was perhaps conversant with the different reading, and that reading shows up even though it contradicts the very rule of the CA. Such a situation would indicate a change within a tradition, rather that the existence of two entirely separate and unrelated traditions. The variation in the mss. of the AV noted by both Whitney and Surya Kanta may also indicate the same situation, i.e. that some manuscripts represent a more conservative reading, while others represent a latter-day changed pronunciation. Both Whitney (on CA 3.2.24 = W: 3.47) and the VVRI editions note the existence of the manuscript variation of the readings: *uparṣanti, upa r̥ṣanti,* and *upariṣanti.*

३.२.२५. उपसर्गस्य धात्वादावारम् ।

Whitney (3.48). A, B, D, J, P: उपसर्गधात्वादाचारं.

Translation: [The final *a* or *ā*] of an *upasarga* is replaced with *ār*, before verb-initial [*r̥* or *r̥̄*].

Note: Strictly speaking, the rule refers to *avarṇa* at the end of an *upasarga* and *r̥varṇa* at the beginning of the verb-form. The word *avarṇasya* continues from CA (3.2.21) and *r̥varṇe* from CA (3.2.23). Thus, in theory, the rule refers to classes of *a*-vowels and *r̥*-vowels, irrespective of the length of the instances. However, the CAB speaks of *r̥kārādau,* restricting the rule to verb-initial short *r̥.* This is done probably for two reasons. In practice, we do not have verb-initial *r̥̄.* Secondly, Pāṇini's rule 6.1.91 (उपसर्गादृति धातौ) which deals with the same phenomenon also refers to short *r̥.*

चतुराध्यायीभाष्य - उपसर्गस्य अवर्णान्तस्य ऋकारादौ परतः धातौ आरं भवति । 'उपार्षति' । 'प्रार्षति' । 'उपार्च्छति' । 'प्रार्च्छति' । 'उपार्ध्नोति' । 'प्रार्ध्नोति' ।

Note: The examples *upārcchati, prārcchati,* and *upārdhnoti* are found in the KV on P.6.1.91 (उपसर्गादृति धातौ).

None of the instances cited by the commentator are attested in the AV. Whitney says: "The only case arising under the rule in the Atharva-Veda is *ārcchatu*, at ii.12.5. Our treatise might, then, like the Vāj. Pr. (iv. 57), have restricted the operation of the rule to the preposition *ā*. The Taitt. Pr. (x.9) states the principle in the same general form in which it is given here." This is clearly an instance of the CA moving closer to the format of a generic grammar of Sanskrit.

३.२.२६. भूतकरणस्य च ।

Whitney (3.49).

Translation: Also, the [*a*] of the past-tense marker, [before the verb-initial *ṛ*, is replaced with *ār*].

Note: Whitney remarks: "This rule, of course, in a treatise whose subject is the *sandhyapadyau guṇau* of words (i.1 = CA 1.1.2), is out of place and superfluous." The rule, like many others of this kind, represents an interest on the part of Prātiśākhya authors to occasionally move in the direction of a generic grammar of Sanskrit, cf. P.6.1.90 (आटश्च).

चतुराध्यायीभाष्य - भूतकरणस्य च अवर्णान्तस्य ऋकारादौ परतः धातोश्चारं भवति । 'स आर्ध्नोत्' (अ.वे. ४.३९.१)। भूतकरणस्येति किमर्थम् । 'कतमा सर्चाम्' (अ.वे. १०.८.१०)।

Note: Whitney's AV text for 10.8.10 reads: कतमा स ऋचाम् । The example *ārdhnot* is found in the KV on P.6.1.90 (आटश्च).

३.२.२७. एकारैकारयोरैकारः ।

Whitney (3.50). Ha, Na: एकारैकारयोरैकः. O: एकारैकारयोरिकारः.

Translation: [Word-final *a* and *ā*], combined with [word-initial] *e* and *ai*, are replaced with *ai*.

चतुराध्यायीभाष्य - एकारैकारयोः ऐकारो भवति । 'खट्वैरगाः' (Whitney: °का) । 'मालैरगाः' (Whitney: °काः)। 'खट्वैति (H: भि) कायनः (H, N: °मानस) :' (Whitney: खट्वैतिकायनः)। मालैतिकाय (H, N add: मा) नः ।

Note: The examples *khaṭvaiḍakā* and *khaṭvaitikāyanaḥ* are found in the KV on P.6.1.88 (वृद्धिरेचि). The fact that the text of the commentary has *khaṭvairagā* instead of *khaṭvaiḍakā,* may mean that either the author of the CAB, or some early copyist, was from a western regions like Rajasthan. For the interchange of *ḍ* and *r,* and *k* and *g*, in Rajasthani dialects of medieval times, see: Ernest Bender (1992: 90-91). Such a possibility is strengthened by the fact that most of the manuscripts of the CA are found in Rajasthan and Gujarat. Also see the Note on CA 2.1.12 for another similar case.

३.२.२८. ओकारौकारयोरौकारः ।

Whitney (3.51). A, D: ओकारो°. O: ओकारौकायोरौकारः.

Translation: [Word-final *a* and *ā*], combined with [word-initial] *o* and *au*, are replaced with *au*.

चतुराध्यायीभाष्य - ओकारौकारयोः औकारो भवति । ब्रंह्मौदनं पंचति (अ.वे. ११.१.१)। तस्यौंदनस्य (अ.वे. ११.३.१)। ब्रह्मौपगवः (not in AV)।

Note: The examples *brahmaudanaḥ* and *brahmaupagavaḥ* are cited in the KV on P.6.1.88 (वृद्धिरेचि).

३.२.२९. शकल्येष्यादिषु पररूपम् ।

Whitney (3.52). A, B: वाकल्ये°. M, N: °शादिषु°. K: शाकल्येष्वादिषु°.

Translation: In sequences such as *śakalyeṣi*, [the final vowel of the preceding word combined with the initial of the following] is replaced with the following [initial] sound.

चतुराध्यायीभाष्य - शकल्येष्यादिषु पररूपं भवति । 'शकल्येषि यदिं वा ते जनित्रंम्' (पद ⇒ 'शकल्यऽएषि,' अ.वे. १.२५.२)। 'अनमीवा उपेतंन' (पद ⇒ 'उपऽएतंन,' अ.वे. ३.१४.३)। 'अर्वाची गौरुपेंषतु' (पद ⇒ 'उपं । एषतु,' अ.वे. ६.६७.३)। 'उपेषंन्तमुदुम्बलंम्' (पद ⇒ 'उपऽएषंन्तम्,' अ.वे. ८.६.१७)।

Note: Whitney remarks: "Of these cases (cited by the CAB), the first would equally admit of being regarded as a case of regular *sandhi*, and analyzed as *śakali-eṣi* : the second is analogous with the combinations to which rule 38 of this chapter (= CA 3.2.15) relates, the preposition *ā* being in *saṃhitā* combined with *upa*, and then the resulting *upā* with *itana*. Of this kind, the text presents one additional instance, in *upeyima* (x.1.10: p. *upa-eyima;* it is made up of *upa-ā-īyima*) : it is the only passage falling under the rule which the commentator does not give."

Whitney's comments given above may be tempered down in view of the fact that the CAB cites all the same examples which are listed under APR (62) and the CA rule is identical in wording with APR (62). This shows that the traditional understandings of these form were quite different from what Whitney proposed for them.

Whitney (*AV Transl.* Vol.I., p. 25) points out: "The *pada*-reading *śakalya-eṣi* in b is assured by Prāt. iii.52, but the meaning is extremely obscure. Ppp. has the better reading *śākalyeṣu* 'among the shavings'; *janitram* rather requires a locative. The comm. guesses it as loc. of *śakalyeṣ*, from *śakalya* explained as a 'heap of shavings,' and root *iṣ* 'seek,' and so an epithet of fire; BR. conjecture 'following the shaving, i.e. glimmering.'"

३.२.३०. एकारौकारान्तात्पूर्वः पदादेरकारस्य ।

Whitney (3.53). E, F, Hb, I, Nb, O: °पूर्वपदादे°.

Translation: After final *e* and *o*, the word-initial *a* [becomes one] with the preceding [vowel].

चतुराध्यायीभाष्य - एकारौकारान्तात्पूर्वो भवति । पदादेः अकारस्य । 'तेऽवदन्' (अ.वे. ५.१७.१)। 'तेऽब्रु(H: क्र)वन्' (तै.सं. २.५.१.३)। 'सोऽब्रवीत्' (अ.वे. १५.३.२)। 'योऽस्य दक्षिणः कर्णः' (अ.वे. १५.१८.३)। 'सोऽरज्यत' (अ.वे. १५.८.१)।

Note: The reading *te 'kravan* of H led Whitney to suggest an emendation to *te 'kṛṇvan*, which "also is not to be found in the Atharvan." The manuscript N offers a better reading: *te 'bruvan.*

The example *te 'vadan* is cited in the KV on P.6.1.115 (प्रकृत्यान्तःपादमव्यपरे). However, this instance is also traceable to RV (10.109.1), and hence we cannot be sure if the KV is citing this passage from the AV. This rule is in part comparable to APR (99). We should note that all the examples in the CAB are found in the same order as examples 68-71 on APR (100).

While admitting that this is an "exceedingly common *sandhi*," Whitney observes: "The physical explanation of this combination is exceedingly difficult." Perhaps, one may suggest that as one moves from *e* or *o* to the consonant after the word initial *a*, one inevitably goes from a more open sound to a point of a relative oral constriction. If *a* is itself a close (*saṃvr̥ta*) sound, then it is just like a point in the normal transition from an open sound to a constriction. For other detailed explanations, see: Allen (1962: pp. 39ff) and Cardona (1987).

३.२.३१. क्वचित्प्रकृत्या ।

Whitney (3.54). I: 31. O: °प्रकृत्याः.

Translation: Sometimes, [the word-initial *a*] remains unchanged.

चतुराध्यायीभाष्य - क्वचित्प्रकृत्या भवति । 'ये अग्रयः' (अ.वे. ३.२१.१)। 'सहस्रार्घ(H, N: र्च)मिडो(H, N: डे) अत्र' (अ.वे. १८.१.४३)।

Note: One may note that these exceptions are not specifically taken care of by the APR, except that the APR (100) refers to a nebulous rule: बहुलं छन्दसि. The present CA rule is comparable to P.6.1.115 (प्रकृत्यान्तःपादमव्यपरे) and the following rules.

Surya Kanta *(APR, Introduction,* p. 40) suggests that the example सहस्रर्चमिडे अत्र which is not attested in the Vulgate of the AV, possibly belongs to the now lost genuine Śaunakīya recension of the AV. Whitney cites the example as सहास्रर्चम्, while both the manuscripts offer the reading सहस्रार्चम्.

The reading सहस्रार्चमिडे अत्र is obviously a corruption for सहस्रार्घमिडो अत्र (AV 18.1.43). This shows the fallacy of Surya Kanta's hypothesis.

इति तृतीयाध्यायस्य द्वितीयः पादः ।

H, N: तृतीयस्य द्वितीयपादः. E, F: तृतीयस्य द्वितीयः पादः. A, B, D, J, M: ।।२।। छ ।। इति द्वितीयः पादः. I: इति तृतीयाध्यायस्य द्वितीयः पादः. O: च. तृतीयस्य द्वितीयः पादः ।। सूत्र ।।३१।। P: ।।२ द्वितीयः पादः ।।

चतुराध्यायीभाष्य - तृतीयस्य द्वितीयपादः ।।

॥ तृतीयोऽध्यायः ॥
॥ तृतीयः पादः ॥

३.३.१. षडेव स्वरितजातानि लाक्षणाः प्रतिजानते ।
पूर्वं पूर्वं दृढतरं म्रदीयो यद्यदुत्तरम् ॥

Translations: The authorities [lit. makers of definitions] recognize only six types of circumflex (*svarita*) accent. Of these, [in the order in which they are explained], each preceding one is harder [than the succeeding one, and] the succeeding one is softer [than the preceding one].

Note: Whitney (p. 154) cites the five verses beginning with this verse as belonging to the commentary in the mss H. However, these verses are found in all the mss. which provide only the text of the CA. Since the CAB does not comment on these verses, it is possible that at one time they belonged to that commentary itself, but were incorporated later into the text of the CA. Whitney (1880: 162) says: "The passage introductory to the third section of this chapter and which, in the edition, I treated as a part of the commentary, is found in B., as if belonging to the text. That it belongs to the text, however, as an original and proper part of it, is by no means to be believed; it is, rather (along with the two similar passages to be noted later), the interpolation of some reworker. This is evidenced both by its own character and by the fact that the comment takes no notice of it; it did not belong to the treatise which the commentator took in hand to explain." There is also a strong possibility, as suggested by Whitney, that these passages may be interpolations of a later period. However, since these verses are found in all manuscripts, including those that call themselves Kautsa-Vyākaraṇa, this incorporation must have taken place at a reasonably early time. Therefore, I have decided to treat these verses as part of the text of the CA as it can be reconstructed on the basis of our manuscripts. A, B, D: षडेच. E, F, I, O: लक्षणानि प्रति°. Surya Kanta (APR, Intro., p. 61) makes a far looser claim for incorporation of all sorts of portions of the commentary into what he styles the *older* CA: "A deeper analysis of CCA (= CAB) should suggest that the portion now styled as *comment*, is, in reality, nothing but relics of the *older* CA., that the metrical portions betokened by Whitney as citations from some *ancient authority* are mutilated parts of the *older* CA., and that longer metrical portions thrown into *Additional Notes* by the editor are definitely so. They are so, all the more, because in all the mss. of the CA., they are read as part of the Sūtra-text; they must, accordingly, be reinstated to their proper position." Not all the verses cited in the CAB are treated by the other manuscripts as belonging to the Sūtra-text, and one must make a careful distinction between these two classes of verses. The fact that certain verses are treated by most manuscripts as being part of the Sūtra-text does not by itself prove that they must be part of the original CA. They could very well be ancient interpolations into the Sūtra-text from the commentary. It is also true that the later text-tradition did treat them as being part of the Sūtra-text.

As Whitney points out: "Precisely what is meant by 'sharp' (*tīkṣṇa*) and 'hard' (*dṛḍha*) on the one hand, and 'soft' (*mṛdu*) on the other, is not very clear: but that the proper circumflex, which arises upon the combination into a single syllable of an original acute and an original grave element, is more strongly marked and distinct in its quality of double pitch than that circumflex which is only enclitic, need not be doubted."

Some light is shed on this question by the possibility that different kinds of svaritas represent different levels of musical pitch. S. Varma (1929: 156), referring to Pāriśikṣā, informs us that the types *jātya*, *abhinihita*, and *kṣaipra* are pronounced with *niṣāda*, or the 7th note on the Indian musical scale. The types *tairovyañjana* and *pādavṛtta* are pronounced with *dhaivata*, or the 6th note. The types *praśliṣṭa* and *pratihata* are pronounced with *pañcama*, or the 5th note. On the whole, one may conclude that higher musical pitch is referred to by the terms 'sharp' or 'hard,' and the lower musical pitch is referred to by the term 'soft.' This distinction is still common in the Indian classical music till today, where the term *tīvra* 'sharp' refers to higher pitch, and the term *komala* 'delicate, soft' refers to lower pitch. The order of the types of *svarita* given by the present CA verse does not completely match the one given by the Pāriśikṣā, but one does notice some shared features, and this indeed seems to be the intended difference between the various types of *svarita*. Unfortunately, the reciters of the ŚAV I met in India were not able to demonstrate these differences in their recitation, and it would seem that these distinctions have been lost in the recitation of the AV.

३.३.२. अभिनिहितः प्राश्लिष्टो जात्यः क्षैप्रश्च तावुभौ ।
तैरोव्यञ्जनपादवृत्तावेतत्स्वरितमण्डलम् ॥

Whitney (p. 154). A, B: °प्रास्त्विष्टो°. E, F, I, J, M: °प्राक्श्लिष्टो°. Whitney: °ता उभौ. A, B, D: °जात्यक्षैप्रश्च पादवृत्तश्च°. J, M, P: °जात्यः क्षैप्रश्च पादवृत्तश्च°. H, N: °पादवृत्तामेत°. O: °प्राश्लिष्टजात्यः°.

Translation: *Abhinihita*, *Prāśliṣṭa*, and both *Jātya* and *Kṣipra*, as well as *Tairovyañjana* and *Pādavṛtta*, - this is the group of svarita [varieties].

Note: The order of the different types of *svarita*s given in this verse, and assumed in all the first four verses of this section is directly correlated to the order in which these types are defined in the rules that follow, i.e. *abhinihita* (3.3.6), *praśliṣṭa* (3.3.7), *jātya* (3.3.8), *kṣaipra* (3.3.9-12), *tairovyañjana* (3.3.13), and *pādavṛtta* (3.3.14). This matching shows that the verses are integrally related to the rules that follow. The verses present the notions of relative hardness and softness of these types, but do not define their exact nature, while the later rules define the exact circumstances of each type, without going into the question of their relative hardness. However, both the sections assume the same order of presentation of these types, and hence are clearly complementary to each other.

३.३.३. सर्वतीक्ष्णोऽभिनिहितस्ततः प्राश्लिष्ट उच्यते ।
ततो मृदुतरौ स्वारौ जात्यः क्षैप्रश्च तावुभौ ॥

Whitney (p. 154). A, B, E, F, I, J, M: °प्राक्श्लिष्ट°. I: °प्राश्लिष्ट°. H, N: °प्रायश्चि°. M: स्वरौ for Svara=. O: °भिनिहितःस्ततः°.

Translation: The *abhinihita* is the sharpest of all. [Softer] than that is said to be the *prāśliṣṭa*. Softer than that is the next pair of accents, i.e. *jātya* and *kṣipra*.

Note: The verse is found in the Māṇḍūkīśikṣā (verse 82), Śikṣāsaṃgraha, p. 470.

३.३.४. ततो मृदुतरः स्वारस्तैरोव्यञ्जन उच्यते ।
पादवृत्तो मृदुतर इति स्वारबलाबलम् ॥

Whitney (p. 154). A, B, D, J, M, P: °मृदुतरस्वार°. H, N: °स्वारः तै°. E, F, N: °पादवृत्तौ°. B, D: °मृदुत्तर°. O: °स्वारःस्तैरो°. P adds इति as a correction.

Translation: Softer than those is said to be the accent called *tairovyañjana*. The *pādavṛtta* is softer [than that]. Such are the relative strengths and weaknesses of the *svarita* varieties.

Note: This verse is also found in the Māṇḍūkīśikṣā (verse 83), Śikṣā-saṃgraha, p. 470.

३.३.५. अपर आह - तैरोव्यञ्जनपादवृत्तौ तुल्यवृत्ती इति । उदात्तः पूर्वः । परोऽनुदात्तः । स्वरितः सन्धिः ।

Whitney (p. 154). E, F, I, O: अपरः प्राह. O: °तुल्यवृत्तीत्युदात्तः°. D, E, F, J, M, O: °पूर्वपरो° for °पूर्वः । परो°. O, P: °स्वरितसंधिः.

Translation: Another [phonetician] says: "*Tairovyañjana* and *Pādavṛtta* are of similar utterance." [In a *svarita*], the first [portion] is high-pitched (*udātta*). The following [portion] is low-pitched (*anudātta*). A *svarita* is a combination of these two.

Note: The tag phrase *apara āha* clearly indicates that this was in all probability originally not part of the text of the CA, but that of a commentary. However, the entire passage is found in all the CA-text-only manuscripts. One may also note the curious fact that the text of the Varṇapaṭala, a Pariśiṣṭa of the AV, contains verses introduced with the phrase अपर आह, and the verses along with the tag phrase are cited in the CAB. See the commentary and the Note on CA (1.1.28: रेफस्य दन्तमूलानि).

Whitney had assigned the entire preceding portion to the commentary. However, regarding उदात्तः पूर्वः, परोऽनुदात्तः, स्वरितः सन्धिः he said: "I am not altogether confident that this is not the first rule of the section, since, as we shall see, the two rules which follow are defective in form, and need some such predecessor. Considering, however, the faulty construction of the whole section, the limited applicability of the words in question as an *adhikāra* or heading for that which follows, their inconsistency with rule 66 (= CA 3.3.17) below, and the absence of the paraphrase and repetition which ought to follow them, if they are a rule, I have not ventured to regard them as a part of the treatise; they are more probably an addition of the commentator, intended to supply the deficiency of the next two rules." As I pointed out in my Note on CA (3.3.1), Whitney was not willing to accept this initial portion as part of the text of the CA even after the discovery of a second manuscript of the CA which contained this portion. Now it is clear that each and every manuscript of the CA contains this initial portion, and we have to accept it as part of the text of the CA. However, it could have been a very early addition, which remained somewhat unassimilated even up to the composition of the CAB.

३.३.६. एकारौकारौ पदान्तौ परतोऽकारं सोऽभिनिहितः ।

Whitney (3.55). Ha, Na: एकारौ पदांतौ°. A, B: ऐकारौ°. E, F, I, O: °परतोऽकारः°.

> **Translation:** [Where] the final *e* or *o* [are merged with] the following *a* [resulting into *e* and *o* respectively], that [*svarita*] is [called] *abhinihita.*

Note: The commentary adds significant information which is not explicit in the rule itself. The commentator specifies that it is a combination of the final high-pitched *e* or *o* with the following low-pitched *a*. This general information is derived from the immediately preceding rule, CA (3.3.5). This rule is an exception to CA (3.3.17: एकादेश उदात्तेनोदात्तः), which prescribes that a combination of a high-pitched vowel with a non-high-pitched vowel, resulting in a single substitute for both (*ekādeśa*), is high-pitched. Whitney criticizes the CA : "the treatise nowhere informs us under what circumstances a circumflex accent arises in connection with the meeting of a final *e* or *o* and an initial *a*, or even that it arises at all." Indeed the treatise, CA (3.2.30: एकारौकारान्तात् पूर्वः पदादेरकारस्य), teaches the single substitute in such cases. The present section, headed by CA (3.3.5) tells us that, under certain circumstances, such combinations become *svarita*s, and the present rule tells us that this specific combination of a high-pitched *e* or *o* with the following low-pitched *a* becomes a specific type of *svarita*, i.e. *abhinihita*.

Whitney believes that the CA should have combined all this with the fact that such a svarita combination is an exception to CA (3.3.17), and the fact that the author of the CA has not done so leads Whitney to say: "We can hardly avoid supposing that the constructors of this part of the treatise have not been skillful enough, or careful enough, to combine the two subjects of the section in such a manner as to give completeness to both." There is indeed an internal logic to the presentation of the CA rules, including the initial verses of this section, which Whitney misses. For details, see the Note on CA (3.3.2).

चतुराध्यायीभाष्य - एकारौकारौ पदान्तौ उदात्तौ परतः अकारम् पदादि अनुदात्तं स अभिनिहितः स्वरो भवति ।

'तेँऽवदन्' (अ.वे. ५.१७.१)। 'तेऽब्रु(H: क्र)वन्' (तै.सं. २.५.१.३)। 'सोँऽब्रवीत्' (अ.वे. १५.३.२)। 'योँऽस्य दक्षिँणः कर्णः' (अ.वे. १५.१८.३)। 'सोँऽरज्यत' (अ.वे. १५.८.१)।

Note: The example *te 'bruvan*, TS (2.5.1.3) is cited as an example of *abhinihata* in the commentary Vaidikābharaṇa on TPR (20.10). We should note that all the examples in the CAB, including the unattested *te 'bruvan*, are found in the same order as examples 68-71 on APR (100). The same examples are cited in the CAB on CA 3.2.30.

Whitney notes that in *parataḥ akāram* 'with a following' the commentator treats the word *akāram* as a neuter nominative. A nominative with *parataḥ,* in the sense of 'with *x* following' or '*x* is on the other side,' is not uncommon in Sanskrit, cf. *yaḥ* and *parataḥ* in यो बुद्धेः परतस्तु सः, Bhagavadgītā (3.42d). What is uncommon is the neuter gender of the word *akāra.* The MB also uses the word *varṇa* in both masculine and neuter genders.

३.३.७. इकारयोः प्राश्लिष्टः ।

Whitney (3.56). D, E, F, H, I (corr), J, M (corr), N, P: °प्राक्श्लिष्टः.

Translation: [The *svarita* arising out of a combination] of two short *i* vowels is [called] *prāśliṣṭa.*

Note: While a combination of any two *i* vowels, long or short, results in a long *ī* vowel, not all such resulting long *ī* vowels are evidently eligible for the title of *prāśliṣṭa.* The second constraint, as explained by the commentary, and evidently implied in this case by the continuing force of CA (3.3.5), is that of these two short *i* vowels being combined, the first one is originally high-pitched, and the second one is originally low-pitched. Thus, this rule also becomes an exception to CA (3.3.17) which says that a combination of a high-pitched vowel with a non-high-pitched vowel, resulting in a single substitute, becomes high-pitched.

Whitney finds that if the first high-pitched vowel is a long *ī* and the following low-pitched vowel is a short *i*, "it is very natural that, as the more powerful element, it should assimilate the weaker grave vowel, and make the whole compound accute." But the reverse situation is more problematic. "The cases in which a long unaccented *ī*, on the other hand, is preceded by a short accented *í*, are exceedingly rare. ... We should, however, expect that in such a compound, especially the circumflex would not fail to appear; for if, in the fusion of *í* and *i*, the grave accent of the second element is represented in the accentuation of the resulting vowel, by so much the more, should this be the case in the fusion of *í* + *i*, where the second element is the stronger. The teachings of the accentual theory are so obvious and explicit upon this point that it is hardly possible to avoid the conclusion that the Hindu grammarians, in establishing their system, overlooked or disregarded the combination *í*+*ī*, on account of its rarity, and that the accent of the cases later noted was made to conform to the rule, instead of the rule being amended to fit the cases."

Perhaps, Whitney has been a bit too impatient. First, there is no globally accepted accentual theory, which predicts results for each Vedic school, and, as Whitney himself notes, the different schools disagree on the scope and nature of *prāśliṣṭa svarita.* Given the fact that the *prāśliṣṭa* ranks the second highest in hardness or sharpness of musical pitch, it seems natural that what the early AV reciters were looking for in a *prāśliṣṭa* is the musical height of the high portion of the *prāśliṣṭa*, rather than the prominence of the low-pitched part, as Whitney seems to imply above.

There are major differences on the scope of *prāśliṣṭa* among the various phonetic and grammatical authorities, and Whitney has eminently surveyed these different views in his comments on the present rule.

चतुराध्यायीभाष्य - इकारयो(:) उदात्तानुदात्तयोः प्राश्लिष्टः स्वरो भवति । 'अ॒भी॑हि मन्यो॑' (अ.वे. ४.३२.३)। 'भि॒न्धी॒[इ॒॑]दम्' (अ.वे. ७.१८.१)। 'दि॒शी॒[इ॒॑]तः' (अ.वे. ११.२.१२)। इकारयोरिति किमर्थम् । 'मा व॒निं॑ मा वाचं॑ नो॒ वीर्त्सी॑ः' (अ.वे. ५.७.६)। परो दीर्घः । इह अस्मात्प्राश्लिष्टो न भवति । 'अती॑व॒ यः' (अ.वे. २.१२.६)। (क्रम ⇒) 'अ॒तीवेत्यति॑ इव' । तैरोव्यञ्जन इत्येषः ।

'इकारयोः(H: इकारः, Whitney: ई°) प्राश्लिष्टो
यदा स्यादुदात्तः पूर्वः परोऽनुदात्तः ।
स प्राश्लिष्टः स्वर्यत एव नित्यं
सन्धिजं स्वरितं नान्यदाहुः ॥' (source?)

'दि॒वी॑व चक्षुः॑' (अ.वे. ७.२६.७)। 'दि॒वी॑व॒ ज्योतिः॑' (अ.वे. ६.९२.३)। (क्रम ⇒) 'दि॒वी॑वेति॑ दि॒वि इं॑व' ।

Note: Whitney (1862: 159) translates the end portion of the commentary beginning with *atīva* : "in the passage *átī 've yáḥ* (ii.12.6) - where the krama-text would read *átī 'vé' ty áti-iva* - the circumflex of the *ī* is *tairovyañjana* (see rule 62 = CA 3.3.13). When an *ī* is the result of *praśleṣa*, the former element being acute and latter grave, the result of *praśleṣa* is always made circumflex. No other circumflex accent is declared to arise from the sandhi. Instances are *divì 'va cákṣuḥ* (vii.26.7), *divì 'va jyótiḥ* (vi.92.3), where the krama-text reads *divì 'vé 'ti diví-iva*." He is not sure of his interpretation, and thinks that "its significance is evidently of the smallest."

The first point to make, which apparently escaped Whitney's attention, is that there is a verse cited here. Secondly, the manuscript N offers the reading *ikārayoḥ* which fits the meter better and is probably the original reading. Third, the cited verse offers a context for CA (3.3.5) to be brought down to bear on the interpretation of the present rule of the CA, indicating that CA (3.3.5) is in all likelihood a genuine part of the CA. Finally, the verse adds support to the (3.3.7) itself, in reinforcing the view that, in the AV tradition of recitation, the *prāśliṣṭa svarita* was limited to the combination resulting from *í+i*. Finally, it says that it is always pronounced as a *svarita*, indicating that it is no longer a prosodically variable syllable, but always remains *svarita*. The last quarter of the verse still remains enigmatic to me.

३.३.८. अनुदात्तपूर्वात्संयोगाद्यवान्तात्स्वरितं परमपूर्वं वा जात्यः ।

Whitney (3.57). A, B, D: °ता स्वरि°. J: अनुदात्तात्पूर्वसंयोगा°. O reads सरितं for स्वरितं. P: °संयोगाद्यवात्तात्स्व°.

> **Translation:** A *svarita*, which follows a consonant cluster ending in *y* or *v*, - a consonant cluster which is either preceded by an unaccented vowel, or is not preceded by any vowel - is [called] *jātya*.

Note: The term *jātya* indicates that this particular variety of *svarita* is an integral part of a word, it is born with it. It is lexical, rather than born out of discourse or prosody. Whitney notes: "no syllable in Sanskrit has an independent circumflex accent except as it results from the conversion of an original accented *í* or *ú* (short or long) into its corresponding semivowel *y* or *v*." The important thing to note, however, is that it arises "in connection with the combination of syllables into words, rather than of words into a sentence." Thus, the *jātya svarita* arises as part of derivation of a word, or as a result of internal sandhi, rather than as a result of an external sandhi (= *kṣaipra svarita*).

Whitney complains: "The definition or description of the *jātya* circumflex given by our treatise is after all imperfect, since it fails properly to distinguish the *jātya* from the *kṣaipra*. Such *kṣaipra* accents as are instanced by *abhy àrcata* (vii.82.1), *nv èténa* (v.6.5), and the like, answer in every particular to the defined character of the *jātya*. The word *pade*, 'in an independent or uncombined word,' or something equivalent, needs to be added to the rule."

Whitney's problem lies in confusing his understanding of the historical evolution of Sanskrit and its derivational morphology with the assumptions made by the authors of the Prātiśākhya. The CA rules 3.3.8 and 3.3.9, defining the *jātya* and *kṣaipra* varieties make a very important and subtle distinction. CA (3.3.8) speaks of *jātya* as a *svarita* coming after a consonant cluster ending in *y* or *v*, and makes no reference to *y* and *v* being results of sandhi, or being substitutes for some 'original' *í* or *ú*, like Whitney. Ideally, the Pratiśākhya is not interested in internal word-derivation, and, therefore, the morph+morph sandhi, or internal sandhi, is of no value to it, unless it somehow participates in *pada* <> *samhitā* transformations. Therefore, the results of the so-called internal sandhi are not treated by the Prātiśākhya as results of any transformation, but as given facts. In contrast with CA (3.3.8), the wording of CA (3.3.9), defining the *kṣaipra svarita*, clearly makes a reference to sandhi-transformation - *antaḥsthāpatti* - of *í* and *ú* into *y* and *v* before unaccented vowels. By such a transformative process, the Prātiśākhya refers only to external sandhi. In a word like *kvà*, the modern linguist may see a derivational process from *kú+a*. However, the Prātiśākhya does not call this process *antaḥsthāpatti* - transformation of vowels into semivowels. It takes the form *kvà* for granted, and this is what makes this type of *svarita* a *jātya svarita* 'born with the word.' Thus, Whitney's criticisms of the formulation of these rules shows a certain lack of comprehension of the assumptions made by the CA, which can be easily recovered from the wording of the rules. Thus, the CA can clearly separate the *jātya* variety from the *kṣaipra* variety. While the CAB does not make these assumptions explicit, it offers the correct examples for the *jātya* and the *kṣaipra* varieties.

चतुराध्यायीभाष्य - अनुदात्तपूर्वात् संयोगात् यवान्तात् स्वरितं परम् अपूर्वम् वा जात्यस्वरो भवति । 'अ॒मा॒वा॒स्यां॑' (अ.वे. ७.७९.२)। 'क॒न्यां॑' (अ.वे. १.१४.२)। 'धा॒न्यं॑म्' (अ.वे. ३.२४.२)। 'आ॒चा॒र्यः॑' (अ.वे. ११.५.३)। 'रा॒ज॒-

न्यः' (अ.वे. ५.१७.९)। 'न्यंक्' (अ.वे. ६.९१.२)। 'क्व' (अ.वे. ९.९.४)। 'स्वः' (अ.वे. २.५.२)।

Note: The CAB on CA (1.1.17) offers exactly the same examples. Also see the Note on CA (1.1.17). It may be noted that somehow the *jātya svarita* is the most basic *svarita* of all the types.

३.३.९. अन्तस्थापत्तावुदात्तस्यानुदात्ते क्षैप्रः ।

Whitney (3.58). No mss reads अन्तः°, though Whitney has this reading. A, B: °नुदात्ते क्षैप्रः.

Translation: When, [in external sandhi], a high-pitched vowel is transformed into a semi-vowel, before a low-pitched vowel, the resulting *svarita* is [called] *kṣaipra*.

Note: For a clear distinction between the *jātya* and *kṣaipra* varieties, and the assumptions made by the CA rules, see the Note on CA (3.3.9).

चतुराध्यायीभाष्य - अन्तस्थापत्तौ उदात्तस्यानुदात्ते परतः क्षैप्रः स्वरो भवति । 'अभ्यंर्चत' (अ.वे. ७.८२.१)। 'वीत्तंङ्गः' (अ.वे. ६.१२५.१)। 'मात्रर्थम्' (not in AV)। 'पित्रर्थम्' (not in AV)।

Note: The KV on P.6.1.77 (इको यणचि) cites the example *kartrartham*.

३.३.१०. अन्तःपदेऽपि पञ्चपद्याम् ।

Whitney (3.59). B, D: °पादे°.

Translation: Even within the same word, in the first five case-forms [i.e. nominative sg., du., and pl., and accusative sg., and du., when a high-pitched vowel is transformed into a semi-vowel, before a low-pitched vowel, the resulting *svarita* is called *kṣaipra*].

Note: Whitney comments: "Not one of the other treatises offers anything corresponding; they would all, apparently, class as jātya the circumflex accents here treated of, not distinguishing them from the others which occur within the limits of a word, or in the uncombined text. The rules, however, are not without some interest, as showing that the authors of our text appreciated the entire analogy which the circumflex accents with which they deal have with the ordinary *kṣaipra*. Thus *nadyàs* is equivalent to *nadī́.as*, as *nadyàsti* would be to *nadī́ asti*, while *nadyā̃i*, *nadyā́s* represent *nadī-ā̃i*, *nadī-ā́s*; the terminations of the strong cases showing no trace of that tendency which is exhibited by the other case-endings to draw away upon themselves the accent of the final vowel of the theme: compare *tudántam, tudántau, tudántas*, with *tudatā́, tudatós, tudatás*."

चतुराध्यायीभाष्य - अन्तःपदेऽपि पञ्चपद्यामन्तस्थापत्तौ उदात्तस्यानुदात्ते परतः क्षैप्रः स्वरो भवति । 'नद्यो३ं नामं स्थ' (अ.वे. ३.१३.१)। 'पिप्पल्य१ः सम्' (अ.वे. ६.१०९.२)। 'रुदत्य१ः पुरुषे हते' (अ.वे. ११.९.१४)। पञ्चपद्यामिति किमर्थम् । 'तयां सहस्रपर्ण्या हृदंयम्' (अ.वे. ६.१३९.१)।

'अन्तोदात्ता नदी न्यायाद्धस्वनामि च यत्तथा ।
अपञ्चपद्यां वचनमुदात्तः क्षैप्र उच्यते ।।' (source?)

Note: The text of the verse given above is based largely on the manuscript N. The reading in H is even more corrupt: अन्तोदात्ता नदी न्याया ह्रस्वनामि चत्तथा.

APR (57, p. 48), as given by Surya Kanta reads: चत्वारि क्षैप्रश्च पञ्चपद्यामन्तोदात्तादीनि यात्. For the last portion, Surya Kanta cites the mss. variants अन्तोदात्तादीनि न्यायात्, अन्तोदातादीनि न्यायात्, and अन्तोदात्तानि दीयात्. If Surya Kanta has reconstructed the correct reading for this APR rule, then, assuming that a similar confusion may have taken place with our verse quoted in the CAB, the verse could be partially restored as:

अन्तोदात्तादीनि यात् ह्रस्वनामि च यत् तथा ।
अपञ्चपद्यां वचनमुदात्तः क्षैप्र उच्यते ।।

Surya Kanta (APR, Notes, p. 24) offers the following interpretations for some of the words which appear in APR (57): "*antodāttādīni = antodāttaḥ (ī́+am) ādir yeṣāṃ tāni. yāt* = through *y* letter *(ī́+a = yà)*, *vilīḍhī́+am= vilīḍhí-am=yà.*" With all this partial restoration, the verse still remains metrically irregular.

I propose an alternative interpretation of the verse, as it now reads in the text given above:

'अन्तोदात्ता नदी न्यायाद्ध्रस्वनामि च यत्तथा ।
अपञ्चपद्यां वचनमुदात्तः क्षैप्र उच्यते ।।'

"[For] feminine stems ending in *ī́* and *ū́*, in accordance with the rule [= *nyāyāt*], and [for the feminine stems ending in] short *nāmin* [i.e. *í* and *ú*] which also [occasionally] behave like [the feminine stems in *ī́* and *ū́*], in weak cases [= *apañcapadyām*], the high-pitched vowel is pronounced. [In strong cases = *pañcapadyām*, by contrast], a *kṣaipra svarita* is pronounced."

I suspect that the word *nadī* in the verse is used in its Pāṇinian technical meaning, i.e. a feminine stem ending either in *ī* or *ū*, cf. P.1.4.3 (यू स्त्र्याख्यौ नदी). Here, the verse seems to refer to *antodāttā nadī,* "feminine stems ending in *ī́* and *ū́*." I admit that this interpretation also requires a good deal of "constructive imagination," and I would welcome a better proposal.

३.३.११. उकारस्य सर्वत्र ।

Whitney (3.60): ऊकार°. P: उकारश्च°.

Translation: [When a final] *ú* [and *ū́* are transformed into *v* before a low-pitched vowel], in all cases [i.e. strong as well as weak cases, the low-pitched vowel is pronounced as a *kṣaipra svarita*].

Note: The major confusion regarding this rule is whether it should read *ukārasya* as all the manuscripts have it, or as *ūkārasya* as Whitney emends it, or something still different. Whitney says: "The manuscript reads in this rule *ukārasya*, 'if the final is *u*,' but the facts seem to require the amendment to *ū*, and the method of writing of our copyist is too careless to make his authority of much weight against it." Part of APR (57, p. 48) also reads *ukārasya sarvatra* and is clearly a related rule. Surya Kanta (*APR*, Notes, p. 24) says "better *ūkārasya*" and refers to the present CA rule, without realizing that Whitney gave the reading *ūkārasya*, while his manuscript actually read *ukārasya*.

The dilemma arises because if the rule is *ukārasya*, it will cover only the examples in short *u*, while *ūkārasya*, as suggested by Whitney and Surya Kanta, will cover only the examples in long *ū*. Among the examples cited by the CAB, the stems *tanū*, *camū*, and *vadhū* end in long *ū*. On the other hand, the CAB cites a number of exceptions, and among these exceptions, two stems, i.e. *pr̥dāku* and *urvāru*, end in short *u*, while *śvaśrū* ends in long *ū*. Somehow,

Whitney does not notice that two of these exceptions have stems ending in short *u*, as he clearly acknowledges in his Index Verborum. If the rule is read *ūkārasya*, then the exceptions with stems in short *u* do not make any sense. On the other hand, if the rule is read *ukārasya*, as justified by the manuscripts, the positive examples with stems in long *ū* do not make any sense. Perhaps, what one needs is the reading *uvarṇasya*, which no manuscript supports.

चतुराध्यायीभाष्य - उकारस्य सर्वत्र अन्तस्थापत्तौ उदात्तस्य अनुदात्ते परतः क्षैप्रस्वरो भवति । 'तन्वां' (अ.वे. १.३३.४)। 'तन्वे[३]' (अ.वे. १.३.१)। 'उत्तानयोंश्चम्वो-[३]ः' (अ.वे. ९.१०.१२)। 'वध्वंश्च वस्त्रंम्' (अ.वे. 'पृदाक्वाः' (अ.वे. १०.४.५)। 'श्वश्र्वै' (H, N: श्वशुरः, Whitney: 'श्वश्र्वै') (अ.वे. १४.२.२६)। 'श्वश्र्वाः' (अ.वे. १४.१.४४)।

Note: Surya Kanta (APR, Introduction, p. 60-61) points out that the APR (57b) shares with the CAB even the corrupt reading *śvaśuraḥ* for the required *śvaśrvai*. This is explainable by referring to the fact that a large number of the mss. of the APR and the CA are found in the same bundles, are copied by and meant for the same person. However, in this case, the two texts do not cite all identical examples. Under ततोऽपवदति, the CAB cites the first four examples out of the five listed by the APR. In this case, even the phrase ततोऽपवदति is shared with the APR (57b). It should also be pointed out that while the examples cited as exceptions to the rule are mostly identical in both the texts, the positive examples are not so identical. What this perhaps indicates is that one should not assume that the CAB directly copied its examples from the APR. Most probably, there existed a list of *gaṇa*s, like the Gaṇapāṭha of the Pāṇinian tradition, which was used by both. However, where the examples were only illustrative, and not part of a closed *gaṇa*, the two texts cited independent illustrations. There is no indication in the CA rule of there being exceptions to this rule. However, the CAB and the APR both share the same list of exceptions. Thus, it is conceivable that the original rules did not envision any such exceptions, and that the commentary reflects a changed state of the Atharvan text.

After listing the exceptions cited by the CAB, Whitney adds: "to which is to be added *vadhvā̆i* (xiv.2.9, 73)." The *gaṇa* as listed in the APR already contains this instance. Then Whitney observes: "All these exceptional forms, it will be remarked, have a heavy ending, while those which exhibit the circumflex accent the ending is light in every instance but one (*tanvā̀m*)."

Whitney's additional exceptions: "The words *bāhvós* (e.g. vii.56.6) and *ūrvós* (xix.60.2) are instances - and, if my search has been thorough, the only ones which the text presents - of like forms from themes in *u*, which are not to be regarded as contemplated by the rule."

३.३.१२. ओण्योश्च ।

Whitney (3.61). O: ॐण्योश्च.

Translation: Also in the form *oṇyòḥ,* [the final syllable from -*ṇí*+*oḥ* is a *kṣaipra svarita*].

चतुराध्यायीभाष्य - ओण्योश्च क्षैप्रः स्वरो भवति । 'ओण्योंः कविक्रंतुम्' (अ.वे. ७.१४.१)।

Note: The example *oṇyòḥ* cited by the CAB is listed under APR (55, p. 55). However, there is no indication in APR whether this represents a *kṣaipra.*

३.३.१३. व्यञ्जनव्यवेतस्तैरोव्यञ्जनः ।

Whitney (3.62). E, F, I: °व्यपेत°. A, B: °व्यवेते°. O: °व्यपेतःस्तैरो°.

Translation: [The *svarita*] which is separated [from the preceding high-pitched vowel] by consonants is called *tairo-vyañjana.*

Note: Whitney observes: "There is here a notable change of subject and of implication. We have passed without any warning, from considering the necessary or independent circumflex to treating of that which is enclitic only, arising, according to following rules (rules 67-70 = CA 3.3.18-21), in an unaccented syllable, which is preceded by an acute, and not again immediately followed by an acute or circumflex." Whitney discusses other subdivisions of this type as prescribed by other texts, e.g. *tairovirāma*, in which the preceding high-pitched vowel belongs to the first member of a compound-word, separated in the Padapāṭha by an avagraha, or a brief pause, for example *prajā́-vat*, where the unaccented a of vat is prosodically changed to a *svarita*.

चतुराध्यायीभाष्य - व्यञ्जनव्यवेतस्तैरोव्यञ्जनः स्वरो भवति । 'इदं देवाः' (अ.वे. २.१२.२)। 'इदमिन्द्र' (अ.वे. २.१२.३)।

३.३.१४. विवृत्तौ पादवृत्तः ।

Whitney (3.63). B, D: विवृतौ°.

Translation: Where there is a hiatus [between the preceding high-pitched vowel and the following low-pitched vowel, the resulting *svarita* for the low-pitched vowel is called] *pādavr̥tta*.

Note: Whitney notes that the RPR calls this type *vaivr̥tta*, 'arising in connection with a hiatus,' and further observes: "The term *pādavr̥tta* is evidently a mutilated substitute for *pādavivr̥tta* or *pādavaivr̥tta*, 'arising in connection with a hiatus between two words.'" Whitney's footnote further clarifies: "The definition of the Taitt. Pr. (xx.6) brings out this derivation more distinctly than our own; we read there *pada-vivr̥ttyām pādavr̥ttaḥ*." The important point clarified by the TPR definition is that this type of *svarita* has to do with a hiatus between two padas 'words,' rather than between two *pādas* 'metrical feet.'

चतुराध्यायीभाष्य - विवृत्तौ पादवृत्तः स्वरो भवति । 'याः कृत्या आङ्गिरसीर्याः कृत्या आसुरीर्याः कृत्याः स्वयंकृता या उं चान्येभिराभृताः' (अ.वे. ८.५.९)।

Note: The manuscript N has a lacuna. After the word *svayaṃkr̥tā,* the manuscript resumes with the end portion of the commentary on CA 3.3.24.

३.३.१५. अवग्रहे सविधः ।

Whitney (3.64).

Translation: With the separation [of members of compound-words by a brief pause, the accents of the separated parts remain] of the same pattern [as before the separation].

Note: The recitational tradition, in the context of the Padapāṭha, thus distinguishes between a longer pause between the words which produces prosodically discontinuous segments and the brief pause (*avagraha*) between members of compound-words which does not produce prosodically discontinuous segments. Of the several possible interpretations of this rule, Whitney prefers this wider interpretation: "Notwithstanding an *avagraha*, the accent of a following syllable remains just what it would be were there no such pause; a hiatus conditioning a *pādavṛtta*, and the intervention of consonants a *tairovyañjana*." Whitney points out that such a wider interpretation "is supported by the authority of the Rik. Pr., which lays down the general principle (iii.15, r.23, ccx) that where syllables are separated by *avagraha*, there accentuation is the same as if they were connected with one another according to the rules of sandhi."

The CAB, on the other hand, seems to prefer a narrower interpretation, applying only to those cases of *avagraha*, where a hiatus is created by splitting the vowels apart due to an *avagraha*, which had been merged by sandhi in the Saṃhitāpāṭha. Such a narrow interpretation is indicated by the kind of examples cited by the commentary.

चतुराध्यायीभाष्य - अवग्रहे सविधः स्वस्वरो भवति । 'उक्षऽअंन्नाय, वशाऽअन्नांय' (पद, अ.वे. ३.२१.६)। 'यज्ञऽऋतंः' (पद, अ.वे. ८.१०.४)। 'शतऽओंदना' (अ.वे. १०.९.१)। 'शतऽआंयुषा' (अ.वे. ३.११.३, ४)। 'दीर्घऽआंयुषा' (not in AV)। 'दीर्घऽआंयुषः' (not in AV)।

Note: Whitney notes that the nominative *dīrghá-āyuḥ* is found at AV (xiv.2.2, 63).

३.३.१६. अभिनिहितप्राश्लिष्टजात्यक्षैप्राणामुदात्तस्वरितोदयानामणुमात्रा निघातो विकम्पितं तत्कवयो वदन्ति ।

Whitney (3.65). E, F, I (corr), M (corr): °प्राक्श्लिष्ट°. A, D, J: अभिनिहितः । ... स्वरितोदयामणु°. O, P: अभिनिहितः. O: °प्राश्लिष्टजात्यः°.

Translation: Of [the four types of *svarita,* i.e.] *abhinihita, prāśliṣṭa, jātya*, and *kṣaipra*, followed by a high-pitched or circumflex, a quarter-mora quantity is made to fall [below the normal level of low-pitch accent], and that [phenomenon] is called *vikampita* 'oscillation' by the wise.

Note: Whitney has a very long discussion on this rule, and to do full justice to it would need a dissertation by itself. To respond to his main thrust, Whitney seems to look at the entire discussion of the accents in the Prātiśākhyas as a matter of grammatical theory, rather than as facts of a recitational tradition. Referring to Hindu grammar, Whitney says: "Whether the Hindu grammar is much the gainer by this intense elaboration of the accentual theory may fairly be questioned: whether, indeed, it has not lost more than it has gained by the exaggeration, and even the distortion, in more than one particular, of the natural inflections of the voice. To me, I must acknowledge, it seems clear that those ancient grammarians might better have contented themselves with pointing out in each word the principal accent and its character, leaving the proclitic and enclitic accents, the claimed involuntary accompaniments of the other, to take care of themselves; or, if they could not leave them unnoticed, at least stating them in a brief and general way, as matters of nice phonetic theory, without placing them on a level with the independent accents, and drawing our a complete scheme of rules for their occurrence." In his comments, Whitney seems to foreshadow the distinction between *phonetic* versus *phonemic*, which developed in later times, and seems to feel that the function of the authors of the Prātiśākhyas was, or should have been, closely similar to that of the modern grammarians of Sanskrit. Here, he completely misses the main point of the Prātiśākhyas. They are, first and foremost, description of recitational practice, rather than that of some abstract theory. Consider the distinction between *pratijñā* 'doctrine' and *vr̥tti* 'recitational practice' drawn by CA in 1.1.1. The second point missed by Whitney is that the accent as understood by the Prātiśākhyas, and as observed in the recitational practice, is already fully musical, and hence, in theory as well as in practice, afforded a far wider latitude of up and down pitch movement, as compared to accent in natural speech. The statements at the beginning of this *pāda* of the CA, indicate that the various types of *svarita* rank differently in terms of the sharpness of the musical note reached in their utterance. Thus, the notion of phonological redundancy of all this phonetic or recitational detail is a peculiarly western theoretical problem, and shows a lack of comprehension of the function of the Prātiśākhyas.

Within the description of the CA it makes eminent sense why a feeling of vibration or *kampa* would be created only for some varieties of *svarita* than for others. The rising portion of the different varieties of *svarita* rises to different musical heights, and the first four varieties, i.e. *abhinihita, prāśliṣṭa, jātya,* and *kṣaipra* rise higher than *tairovyañjana* and *pādavṛtta.* Then, before a high-pitched *udātta* or a *svarita,* with its initial rising element, the falling segment of these four varieties of *svarita* falls below the normal level of *anudātta.* From this lower than the low position, the pitch then rises again to the high of the following *udātta*, or to the higher than high of the following *svarita.* This naturally creates a feeling of vibrating or swinging up and down the musical scale.

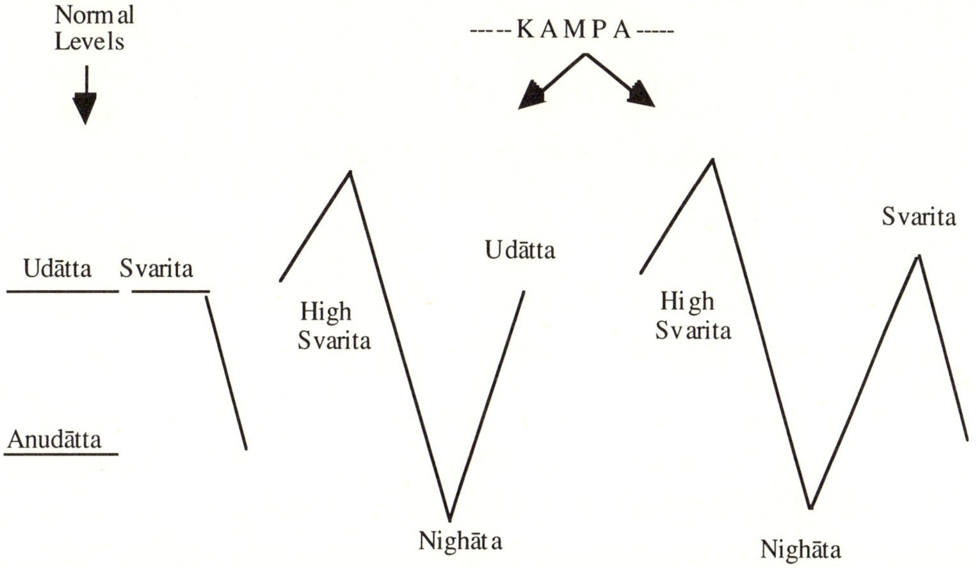

Different manuscripts have different methods of marking accents, cf. Witzel (1974) for a comprehensive discussion. The printed editions have generally opted for the method used in the Ṛgveda. For the notation of *kampa*, Whitney points out: "A *svarita* immediately preceding an *udātta* cannot receive simply the usual *svarita* sign, lest the following syllable be deemed a *pracaya* instead of *udātta.* The method followed in such a case by the Rik is to append to the circumflexed vowel a figure 1 or 3 - 1 if the vowel be short, 3 if it be long - and to attach to this figure the signs of both *svarita* and of *anudātta.*" In the text of the commentary below, I have placed these figures in square brackets, since they do not appear in the manuscripts of the commentary, but are provided from the printed text of the AV. Whitney has additionally given a plausible explanation for the origin of this notation, cf. Whitney (1862: 169).

चतुराध्यायीभाष्य - अभिनिहितप्राश्लिष्टजात्यक्षैप्र इत्येषामुदात्तस्वरितोदयानाम् अणुमात्रा निघातो(H: ता) भवति । विकम्पितं तत् कवयो वदन्ति । अभिनिहितः । 'यो[३]भि-

यांतः' (अ.वे. ११.२.१३)। 'ये[३]स्याम्' (अ.वे. ३.२६.१)। 'सोऽर्थम्' ('सो[३]भ्वम्,' correction suggested by Whitney, अ.वे. १३.४.२५)। अभिनिहितः । प्राश्लिष्टः । 'भिन्धी[३]दम्' (अ.वे. ७.१८.१)। 'दिशी[३]तः' (अ.वे. ११.२.१२)। प्राश्लिष्टः । जात्यः । 'अमावास्या[३]' (अ.वे. ७.७९.२)। 'स्व[१]ः' (अ.वे. २.५.२)। जात्यः । क्षैप्रः । 'नद्यो[३] नाम(H: मी) स्थ' (अ.वे. ३.१३.१)। 'पिप्पल्य[१]ः सम्' (अ.वे. ६.१०९.२)। 'रुदत्य[१]ः पुरुषे हते' (अ.वे. ११.९.१४)।

३.३.१७. एकादेश उदात्तेनोदात्तः ।

Whitney (3.66). Identical with P.8.2.5.

Translation: [As a general principle], the single replacement for a high-pitched vowel [combined with a non-high-pitched vowel] is high-pitched.

Note: This is a general rule, and has a few exceptions, i.e. CA (3.3.6-7): The vowels *é* and *ó*, when they absorb the following *a*, become *è* and *ò*, and *í*+*i* become *ī̀*.

चतुराध्यायीभाष्य - एकादेशः उदात्तेन सह उदात्तो भवति । 'धियेहि' (पद ⇒ 'धिया । आ । इहि,' अ.वे. २.५.४)। 'जुषस्वेन्द्र' (पद ⇒ 'जुषस्व । आ । इन्द्र,' अ.वे. २.५.४)। 'स्तनयित्नुनेहि' (पद ⇒ 'स्तनयित्नुना । आ । इहि,' अ.वे. ४.१५.११)। 'कुष्ठेहि' (पद ⇒ 'कुष्ठ । आ । इहि,' अ.वे. ५.४.१)। 'उदकेनेहि' (पद ⇒ 'उद-केन । आ । इहि', अ.वे. ६.६८.१)। 'अव पश्यतेत' (पद ⇒ 'अव । पश्यत । आ । इत,' अ.वे. १८.४.३७)।

Note: All the examples cited here by the CAB are cited in the same order under APR (8).

३.३.१८. उदात्तादनुदात्तं स्वर्यते ।

Whitney (3.67). J: स्वरितादनुदात्तं°.

Translation: A low-pitched vowel, following a high-pitched [syllable], becomes circumflexed.

Note: The *svarita* or the circumflex accent defined here is the enclitic *svarita*. As Whitney points out, "it is, as we have seen above (rules 62, 63 = CA 3.3.13-4), subdivided into the two kinds called *tairovyañjana* and *pāda-vr̥tta*, according as one or more consonants, or only a hiatus, intervene between the acute vowel and its successor."

It is to be noted here that the first element of a *svarita* was, for many of its varieties, higher than the normal height of an *udātta*, while the *anudātta* preceding an *udātta* remained *anudātta* according to CA (3.3.21), or became lower than the normal low according to Pāṇini, cf. P.1.2.40 (उदात्तस्वरितपरस्य सन्नतरः). The printed editions of the AV follow the Pāṇinian or the R̥gvedic method of marking the *sannatara*. Thus, the two most noticeable peaks of musical notes during the recitation were the higher than the high of the *svarita* and the lower than the low of the *sannatara*. Otherwise, for the recitational purposes, the intermediate high and low levels represented by the normal *udātta* and the normal *anudātta* actually collapsed into a single level, as indicated by CA (3.3.22) which says that the *anudātta* syllable after a *svarita* has the same pitch as that of the *udātta*. Thus, the historical values of *udātta* and *anudātta* collapsed into an unmarked pitch level. The initial high of the *svarita* moved up from this level, and the lower-than-low of *sannatara* moved down from this level. Thus, from a purely recitational point of view, the historical *udātta* could not be distinguished from the *anudātta*. This clearly indicates the nature of the recitational tradition.

Burrow (1955: 114) remarks: "According to the usual system, that adopted in the R̥gveda for instance, the principle is to mark the syllable preceding the udātta, the sannatara, with a subscript line, and the dependent svarita following the udātta by a vertical stroke above. The udātta itself is left unmarked. ... The modern recitation of the R̥gveda follows the notational system to the extent of pronouncing the sannatara lowest and the svarita highest musically of syllables and ignoring the udātta altogether. This is a secondary development although it may be old, and at variance with the teachings of Pāṇini which are in complete agreement with the findings of comparative philology." It is clear that Pāṇini, who specifically defines the occasion for *sannatara*, knew that it was pronounced lower than the normal *anudātta*. Similarly, the CA, as discussed above, knew that many varieties of *svarita* rose above the normal level of *udātta*, and their falling levels went below the normal level of *anudātta*. Similarly, the CA clearly says that the *anudātta*s, which follow an *udātta* or a *svarita* have the same *śruti* 'auditory quality' as the *udātta*. This is a clear proof of the unmarked *udātta* and unmarked *anudātta* having fallen together to a common unmarked middle pitch level. While, I agree with Burrow that this is a secondary development, it is indeed very old. To the extent it is true to the recitational practice, one need not follow Burrow (ibid, p. 113) in calling the notational system as "unnecessarily complicated." Strictly speaking, according to the CA description, the first part of the dependent *svarita* is not higher than *udātta*, and the *anudātta* before an *udātta* or a *svarita* remains an *anudātta*, and does not become *sannatara*, the marking system adopted by many manuscripts, and by all the printed editions, shows the *svarita* with a vertical line, and the *anudātta* before an *udātta* or a *svarita* with a subscript line. These markings hint at the Ṛgveda-like recitation of the AV. The AV reciters I have heard do not distinguish the AV recitation from the RV recitation in these respects. Thus, there may indeed be a strong RV influence on the AV recitational tradition, driving it somewhat farther away from the description of the accents as given in the CA.

चतुराध्यायीभाष्य - उदात्तादनुदात्तं स्वर्यते । 'इदं देवाः' (अ.वे. २.१२.२)। 'इदमिन्द्र' (अ.वे. २.१२.३)।

३.३.१९. व्यासेऽपि समानपदे ।

Whitney (3.68). A, B: व्यप्यपि°.

Translation: Even with the separation [of words from each other by pauses in the Padapāṭha], within the same word, [an *anudātta* syllable following an *udātta* syllable is circumflexed].

Note: As Whitney notes: "By their *adhikāra* (ii.1 = CA 2.1.1), all rules in the second and third chapters should apply only to the *saṃhitā,* or combined text; hence it must here be specifically taught that in *pada*, as well as in *saṃhitā,* the syllable following an acute is enclitically circumflex, if the latter be in the same word with the former, and so not separated from it by a pause or *avasāna*." The pauses between the separated words of the Padapāṭha create discontinuous segments, and yet, as the present rule indicates, within each word unit, the same prosodic rules apply. This contrasts with the next rule, where an *avagraha*, or a brief pause separating members of compound-words, does not create prosodically discontinuous segments as far as accentuation is concerned. In Whitney's words: "Although, in the *pada*-text, the pause which separates each independent word from the one following it breaks the continuity of accentual influence, so that a final acute of the one does not render circumflex the initial grave of the other, yet the lesser pause of the *avagraha*, which holds apart the two members of a compound word, causes no such interruption; on the contrary, an acute at the end of the former member calls forth the circumflexed utterance in the first syllable of the latter member." In my view, it is not anything in the phonetic nature of the pauses that causes this behavioral difference. As we are told by CA (3.3.35), all these different pauses are of one mora duration, and hence, as durations of silence, they are identical with each other. It must be theoretical assumptions made by the authors of the Padapāṭha that cause this difference. In one case, one is separating words from each other, in the other, only components of compound-words. The authors of the Padapāṭha have assumed that the first kind of separation creates independent units, while the second kind creates dependent units.

चतुराध्यायीभाष्य - व्यासेऽपि समानपदे उदात्तात्परमनुदात्तं स्वर्यते । 'अ॒युत॑म्' (अ.वे. ८.२.२१)। 'अ॒मृत॑म्' (अ.वे. १.४.४)। 'अ॒न्तरि॑क्षम्' (अ.वे. २.१२.१)।

३.३.२०. अवग्रहे च ।

Whitney (3.69).

Translation: Also, when there is a separation [with *avagraha*, a brief pause, of the members of compound-words, an *anudātta* syllable following an *udātta* syllable is circumflexed].

Note: See the Note on the previous rule for a distinction between separation of words by *avasāna*s and separation of members of compounds by *avagraha*s.

चतुराध्यायीभाष्य - अवग्रहे च उदात्तात्परमनुदात्तं स्वर्यते। 'सुऽसं॑शितः' (पद, अ.वे. ६.१०५.२)। 'सुऽयं॑तः' (पद, अ.वे. ६.१११.१)। 'सुऽशृं॑तम्' (पद, अ.वे. ७.७२.३)।

'सुऽदृंढम्' (पद, अ.वे. १०.२.३)। 'सुऽभृंतम्' (पद, अ.वे. ६.३९.१)। 'सुऽहुंतम्' (अ.वे. ६.७१.१)।

Note: All these examples occur exactly in the same order as examples 13-18 under APR (31b, p. 34). This shows that both the texts are drawing upon identical lists of examples.

३.३.२१. नोदात्तस्वरितपरम् ।

Whitney (3.70). Ha: °स्वरिततरं°. O: नोदात्तः°.

Translation: However, [a low-pitched (*anudātta*) syllable], followed by a high-pitched (*udātta*) or a circumflex (*svarita*) syllable, is not [circumflexed].

Note: As Whitney explains: "A syllable originally grave remains grave before a following *udātta* or *svarita*, even though preceded by an *udātta*, and hence, by the last rules, regularly entitled to the enclitic circumflex." Whitney's theoretical conclusion is as follows: "The proclitic accent thus appears, in the estimation of the Hindu phonetists, to be more powerful than the enclitic, and the law which requires the voice to plant itself upon a low pitch in order to rise to the tone of acute or independent circumflex to be more inviolable than that which prescribes a falling tone in the next syllable after an acute."

While according to the rule of the CA, such a syllable remains merely *anudātta*, according to the RV notation used by many manuscripts and by the printed editions, such a syllable is marked with a horizontal subscript. In Pāṇinian terms, such a syllable becomes *sannatara*, with pitch lower than the low of the *anudātta*. The post-CA tradition of the AV reciters seems to have moved more in the direction of the RV in this respect.

चतुराध्यायीभाष्य - न उदात्तपरं च स्वरितपरं च अनुदात्तं स्वर्यते । 'शं न आपंः' (अ.वे. १.६.४)। 'यो अस्य विश्वजंन्मनः' (अ.वे. ११.४.२३)। 'अस्य सुतस्य स्व१ः' (अ.वे. २.५.२)।

३.३.२२. स्वरितादनुदात्तमुदात्तश्रुतिः ।

Whitney (3.71): °नुदात्त उदात्त°.

Translation: A low-pitched [syllable], after a circumflex, assumes the high-pitch [of the *udātta*].

Note: Whitney says: "All the other treatises (R. Pr. iii. 11, r. 18, ccv; V. Pr. iv. 138, 139; T. Pr. xxi. 10) lay down the same principle, stating also distinctly what must be regarded as implied in our precept, that not only the single grave syllable which immediately follows the circumflex receives the acute utterance, but those also which may succeed it, until, by rule 74 (= CA 3.3.25), the proximity of an acute or circumflex causes the voice to sink to the proper *anudātta* tone." The significance of this rule cannot be overstated. This shows that the accentual system of the Vedic texts as they were being recited was already on its way to major collapsing of levels, and this collapse is further indicated by the traditional RV notation, also used for many AV manuscripts and all the AV editions, supports this collapsing of *udātta* and the syllables described in the present rule. Most other Prātiśākhyas refer to this syllable by the term *pracaya*, which is sometimes used as a name for a distinct accent. Pāṇini 1.2.39 (स्वरितात् संहितायामनुदात्तानाम्) provides that all low-pitched vowels after a circumflex are pronounced with *ekaśruti* 'monotone.'

चतुराध्यायीभाष्य - स्वरितात् परम् अनुदात्त[म्] उदात्तश्रुतिर्भवति । 'देवीर्द्वारो बृहतीर्विश्वमिन्वः' (अ.वे. ५.१२.५)। 'माध्वी धर्तारा विदथस्य सत्पती' (अ.वे. ७.७३.४)।

३.३.२३. व्यासेऽपि समानपदे ।

Whitney (3.72).

Translation: Even when separation [of words from each other occurs in the Padapāṭha], within the same word, [an *anudātta* syllable after a *svarita* syllable is pronounced like an *udātta*].

चतुराध्यायीभाष्य - व्यासेऽपि समानपदे स्वरितात्परम् अनुदात्तम् उदात्तश्रुतिर्भवति । 'उरुझऽीगूलांयाः' (पद, अ.वे. ५.१३.८)। 'ककाटिंकाम्' (पद, अ.वे. १०.२.८)।

Note: The commentary cites these examples without specifically telling us that these are to be understood as Padapāṭha citations, which is what they must be in order to illustrate this rule. The rule is comparable to CA (3.3.19).

३.३.२४. अवग्रहे च ।

Whitney (3.73).

Translation: Also, when there is a separation [e.g. of the members of a compound-word with an *avagraha* 'brief pause,' an *anudātta* 'low-pitched' syllable after a *svarita* 'circumflex' syllable is pronounced like an *udātta* 'high-pitched' syllable].

Note: Whitney comments: "That is to say, again, the *avagraha*, or pause of division, does not interfere with the influence of the circumflex, any more than (by rule 69 = CA 3.3.20) with that of an acute, upon the following unaccented syllables." See the Notes on CA 3.3.19-20.

चतुराध्यायीभाष्य - अवग्रहे च स्वरितात्परम् अनुदात्तमुदात्तश्रुतिर्भवति । 'श्वंन्ऽवतीः' (पद, अ.वे. ११.९.१५)। 'स्वंःऽवती' (पद, अ.वे. १८.१.२०)। 'अश्मंन्ऽवती' (पद, अ.वे. १२.२.२६)।

Note: The manuscript N resumes with the word *aśmanvatī.*

३.३.२५. स्वरितोदात्तेऽनन्तरमनुदात्तम् ।

Whitney (3.74). A, B: °नंत्तर°. F, O: °नंतरमुदात्तं.

Translation: Before a circumflex or a high-pitched syllable, the immediately preceding [low-pitched] syllable remains low-pitched.

Note: In the system of accents as laid out by the CA, this is the only kind of syllable which remains truly *anudātta* after all the prosodic changes are made. The *anudātta* after an *udātta* turns into a *svarita*. The *anudātta* after a *svarita* turns into an *udāttaśruti* 'syllable sounding like an *udātta*.' Thus, the only *anudātta* which is left unaltered in this system is the one prescribed by this rule.

However, we should note that the Pāṇinian system, cf. P.1.2.40 (उदात्तस्वरितपरस्य सन्नतरः), treats exactly the same syllable as a *sannatara* syllable, i.e. syllable with a note lower than the normal level of *anudātta*. The RV notation used to mark the accents for the AV in printed editions and many manuscripts seems to treat this syllable more like a *sannatara*, if indeed this is the implication of the horizontal line below the syllable.

For further discussion, see the Notes on CA (3.3.18, 21, 22).

चतुराध्यायीभाष्य - स्वरिते च परतः उदात्ते च अनन्तरमनुदात्तं भवति । 'अजस्तद् दंदृशे क्व' (अ.वे. १०.८.४१)। 'इदं देंवाः शृणुत ये' (अ.वे. २.१२.२)। 'इदमिंन्द्र शृणुहि सोमप यत्' (अ.वे. २.१२.३)।

३.३.२६. अस्वराणि व्यञ्जनानि ।

Whitney (p. 174) quotes this as part of the commentary. H, I, N connect this with the following rule.

Translation: Consonants have no accents.

Note: The Sūtras beginning with CA 3.3.26 are simply listed in the manuscripts H and N, and may have either been part of the commentary itself, or may be an early interpolation. Here they are treated as Sūtras because they are found in all the Sūtra-only manuscripts.

३.३.२७. स्वरवन्तीत्यान्यतरेयः ।

Whitney (p. 174) quotes this as part of the commentary. E, F, P: °तरेयाः. H, I, N: connect this rule with the previous one.

Translation: Ānyatareya says that [consonants] do have accents.

Note: For a discussion of accent-bearing consonants, see: Allen (1953: 83).

३.३.२८. किं सन्धेः स्वरितम् ।

Whitney (p. 174) quotes this as part of the commentary. Whitney, H, N: add भवति at the end. O, P: किं संधेस्वरितं.

Translation: Which part of a combination is circumflexed?

३.३.२९. पूर्वरूपमित्यान्यतरेयः ।

Whitney (p. 174) quotes this as part of the commentary. O: °त्यांन्यतरेयः. P: °त्यान्यतरेयाः.

Translation: Ānyatareya says that it is the former constituent.

३.३.३०. उत्तररूपं शाङ्खमित्रिः ।

Whitney (p. 174) quotes this as part of the commentary. A, B: °मत्रिः. P: °शाख°.

Translation: Śāṅkhamitri says that it is the latter constituent.

३.३.३१. किमक्षरस्य स्वर्यमाणस्य स्वर्यते ।

Whitney (p. 174) quotes this as part of the commentary. A, B, D, J, M, P: किमक्षरस्य स्वर्यते. The CAB on CA (1.4.2: स्वरोऽक्षरम्) cites the rules CA (3.3.31-34) as Sūtras to illustrate the use of the term *akṣara*. Thus, it would seem that this commentary treats these as part of the text of the CA. However, the absence of any comments on these Sūtras is perhaps an indication of their lack of full incorporation into the text of the CA. Such a situation is perhaps to be explained by an assumption that these were relatively recent interpolations into the text of the CA, and that the author of the CAB had ambivalent feelings about these rules. For further details, see the Note on CA (1.4.2).

Translation: Of a syllable being circumflexed, which part is it that is circumflexed?

Note: Whitney (1862: 174) cannot locate any context for this whole discussion: "In the absence of any illustrations, I am at a loss to see to what kind of combinations this question and its answers are to be understood as applying." It would seem that it was commonplace to think of a *svarita* as being composed of two portions. It is also my guess that the verb *svaryate* is probably used in the sense of 'markedly raised,' and that it was this raising the initial part of the *svarita* that was the most noticeable part of a *svarita* for the Indian phoneticians and Veda reciters. For further discussion, see the Note on the Bhārgava-Bhāskara-Vṛtti on CA (1.1.16).

३.३.३२. अर्धं ह्रस्वस्य पादो दीर्घस्येत्येके ।

Whitney (p. 174) quotes this as part of the commentary. B, D: अर्द्धं स्वरस्य पादो°. H, N: पदौ for पादो. Most mss. read ऱ्ह for ह्र.

Translation: Some say that [the first] half of a short vowel, and the [first] quarter of a long vowel [is circumflexed].

Note: The doctrine here generally agrees the one stated in CA (1.1.17) that the first half-mora of a *svarita* is high-pitched. This naturally gives the first quarter of the long *svarita* vowel as being high-pitched. However, this general view leads to the recitation of each *svarita* vowel as having two distinct accents for their initial and final portions. While this is the standard view shared by most authorities, a minority opposition is voiced in the next rule by Śāṅkhamitri.

३.३.३३. सर्वमिति शाङ्खमित्रिः ।

Whitney (p. 174) quotes this as part of the commentary.

Translation: Śāṅkhamitri says that the entire [syllable is circumflexed].

Note: This rule and the next represent Śāṅkhamitri's argument against having a *svarita* vowel with two parts, and he apparently proposed that the entire syllable be pronounced with a raised pitch with no falling portion. Śāṅkhamitri is a lone voice in Sanskrit phonetics, as no one else is known to have expressed the same view.

३.३.३४. अक्षरस्यैषा विधा न विद्यते यद् द्विस्वरीभावः ।

Whitney (p. 174) quotes this as part of the commentary. A, B, D: °विधाने°. E, F, O: °विधानं°. Whitney: °यद् यद् विश्वरीभाव°. H, J, M, N, P: °यद् यद्विस्वरी°. A, B (corr), C, E, F, I, M (corr), O: °यद्विस्वरीभावः. B, D: °यद्यत् द्विस्वरीभावः.

> **Translation:** [Continuation of Śāṅkhamitri's view?]: [This should be so, since] it is not the pattern of a [single] syllable to have two accents [within itself].

Note: With the reading यद् यद् विश्वरीभावः, Whitney could only say: "A renewed consideration affords me no new light upon this passage." I believe that now there is enough manuscript support for the reading I have offered, and that it is clearly a continuation of Śāṅkhamitri's argument why the whole of a syllable must be circumflexed, and not just its initial segment.

३.३.३५. ऋगर्धर्चपदान्तावग्रहविवृत्तिषु मात्राकालः कालः ।

Whitney (p. 174) quotes this as part of the commentary. Whitney, H: °पदांतनाव°. C, N: °पदांतराव°. A, B: °पदांनाव°.

> **Translation:** [The pause] at the end of a half-verse, at the end of a word [in the Padapāṭha, before the next word], the *ava-graha*, [e.g., the pause between the separated members of a compound-word in the Padapāṭha], and for the hiatus [in the Saṃhitāpāṭha] is of one mora duration.

Note: This is a very important rule. It is important to note that the various pauses are phonetically identical, i.e. they are all stretches of silence for the duration of one mora. However, they have different theoretical and recitational consequences. See the Note on CA (3.3.19).

इति तृतीयाध्यायस्य तृतीयः पादः ।

H, N: तृतीयस्य तृतीयपादः. C, E, F: तृतीयस्य तृतीयः पादः. A, B, D, J, M, P: तृतीयः पादः. I: इति तृतीयाध्यायस्य तृतीयः पादः. O: इत्य. तृतीयस्य तृतीयः पादः ॥ ४० ॥.

चतुराध्यायीभाष्य - तृतीयस्य तृतीयः पादः ॥

॥ तृतीयोऽध्यायः ॥
॥ चतुर्थः पादः ॥

३.४.१. ऋवर्णरेफषकारेभ्यः समानपदे नो णः ।

Whitney (3.75).

Translation: Within the same word, after *r̥*-vowels, *r*, and *ṣ*, *n* is replaced with *ṇ*.

Note: The significant point to note is that this rule makes it quite clear that the author of the CA does not attempt to cover consonantal *r* and vocalic *r̥* under a common generalization. This is also clear elsewhere, cf. Note on CA (2.4.22). In this respect, contrast Pāṇini 8.4.1 (रषाभ्यां नो णः समानपदे). In this case, Pāṇini's rule seems to make a generic reference to *r* and *r̥* by just mentioning *r*. Elsewhere, Pāṇini's practice is more like that of the CA, cf. Note on CA (2.4.22). For a further discussion of this issue, see Deshpande (1975: 159-60, notes 50-56).

In the formulation of the rules of the CA and Pāṇini, there is another major difference. The CA rule assumes that the conditioning sound and the *n* that undergoes cerebralization need not be contiguous. All the examples offered by the CAB are of this non-contiguous type. Later rules like CA (3.4.25: व्यवाये शसलैः) and CA (3.4.26: चटतवर्गैश्च) specify that the intervention of certain sounds blocks the change of *n* to *ṇ*. In contrast with this, Pāṇini 8.4.1 (रषाभ्यां नो णः समानपदे) assumes that the conditioning sound and the *n* undergoing the change are contiguous. With this assumption, Pānini then specifies that this change can take place even with the intervention of certain sounds, cf. P.8.4.2 (अट्कुप्वाङ्नुम्व्यवायेऽपि). Thus, the theoretical assumptions made by these two texts are reverse of each other.

चतुराध्यायीभाष्य - ऋवर्णाच्च रेफाच्च षकाराच्चोत्तरस्य समानपदे नकारस्य णकारो भवति । 'परिं स्तृणीहि परिं धेहि वेदिंम्' (अ.वे. ७.९९.१)। 'परिस्तरंणमिद्धविः' (अ.वे. ९.६.२)। 'कोषणम्' (not in AV)। 'तोषणम्' (not in

AV)। समानपदे इति किमर्थम् । 'स्वर्नयति' । 'प्रातर्नयति'।

Note: For parallels to the examples not attested in the AV, see the KV on P.8.4.1 (रषाभ्यां नो णः समानपदे): कुष्णाति, पुष्णाति, ... समानपदे इति किम् । अग्निर्नयति । वायुर्नयति.

३.४.२. पूर्वपदाद् द्रुघणादीनाम् ।

Whitney (3.76). P: °दादुघणादीनां.

Translation: In *drughaṇa* etc., [the change of *n* to *ṇ* takes place] after [the conditioning sound in] the preceding word [i.e. preceding member of the compound-expression].

Note: The CA seems to assume a *drughaṇādigaṇa*. However, there is no record of this *gaṇa* in the APR. Whitney, in his note on this rule, lists a large number of examples of this type from the text of the Atharvaveda. P.8.4.3 (पूर्वपदात् संज्ञायामगः) teaches a similar doctrine, though it has a few additional conditions. One of the conclusions to be derived from the very existence of such rules is that the process of compounding was not viewed as completely obliterating the individuality of the member words, and that the boundary between the members of a compound was often a barrier to processes like retroflexion. The fact that retroflexion did take place across such boundaries in certain compound-words, but not in others, is one of the indications of the sporadic weakening of this boundary.

चतुराध्यायीभाष्य - पूर्वपदस्थान्निमित्तात् द्रुघणादीनां नकारस्य णकारो भवति । 'द्रुघणः' ('द्रुऽघनः,' पद, अ.वे. ७.२८.१)। 'सूता ग्रामण्यः' (H: °ण्या) ('ग्रामऽन्यः,' पद, अ.वे. ३.५.७)। 'रक्षोहणं वाजिनम्' ('रक्षःऽहनम्,' पद, अ.वे. ८.३.१)। 'बृहस्पतिप्रणुत्तानाम्' ('बृहस्पतिऽप्रनुत्तानाम्,' पद, अ.वे. ८.८.१९)। 'पृषदाज्यप्रणुत्तानाम्' ('पृषदाज्यऽप्रनुत्तानाम्,' पद, अ.वे. ११.१०.१९)। 'दुर्णिहितैषिणीम्' ('दुर्निहितऽएषिणीम्,' पद, अ.वे. ११.९.१५)।

Note: On the last example given by the CAB, Whitney remarks: "The latter case, we should think, is one of somewhat ambiguous quality, since in the form of the word, as given by the *pada*-text, there is nothing to show that *dur* stands in the relation of *pūrvapada*, or former member of a compound, to *nihita*, they being unseparated by *avagraha*." This is not a good objection, since, as is well known, the Padapāṭha generally shows only one separation for a compound with more than two members. This is not a denial of other embedded compounds, but a practice based on the theoretical assumption that, at a time, we combine only two units, and the Padapāṭha only shows the final stage of such combinations.

Whitney further says: "The same objection lies against the two preceding instances; but also the much more serious one that they are examples properly belonging under rule 79 (= CA 3.4.5), below, the converted *n* being that of a root after a preposition." This is also not a good objection, since the true force of CA (3.4.5: उपसर्गाद्धातोर्नानापदेऽपि) is conveyed by the phrase: नानापदेऽपि "even [when the conditioning sound appears in the preceding] separate word." Compare the condition असमासेऽपि in Pāṇini 8.4.14 (उपसर्गादसमासेऽपि णोपदेशस्य). The present rule does relate to the preceding word, but only in the sense of the preceding member of a compound-expression. The KV on P.8.4.14 says: असमासेऽपीति किम् । पूर्वपदाधिकारात्समास एव स्यादिति तदधिकारनिवृत्तिद्योतनार्थम् ।. The term *nānāpada* in CA (3.4.5) refers to a sequence of uncompounded words.

Beginning with the paraphrase of this rule, the manuscript N has missing folios, except the very last folio of the manuscript. Therefore, the text of the commentary from here on is based solely on the manuscript H.

३.४.३. अकारान्तादह्नः ।

Whitney (3.77). Most mss. read न्ह for ह्न.

Translation: [The *n*] of *ahan* [is changed to *ṇ*] after [the appropriate conditioning sound in the preceding member of the compound] ending in *a*.

Note: As Whitney notes, "Pāṇini's rule, viii.4.7 (*ahno 'dantāt*), is precisely coincident with this, and the illustrative citations of its scholiasts are in good part those which our commentator gives us, and which are all strange to the Atharvan." One may, however, point out the intriguing contrast in the word order. A similar contrast is seen in CA (3.2.18: पूर्वपरयोरेकः) and P.6.1.84 (एकः पूर्वपरयोः). It is not immediately clear whether such changes in the word-order reflect some consistent principles, or whether they are purely accidental.

चतुराध्यायीभाष्य - अकारान्तात् पूर्वपदस्थान्निमित्तात् अह्नो नकारस्य णकारो भवति । 'प्राह्णः' । 'पूर्वाह्णः' । अकारान्तादिति किमर्थम् । 'निरह्नः' (H: ह्नेः) । 'पर्यह्नः' । 'दुरह्नः'।

Note: All these examples are absent from the AV. Whitney points out: "Our text has only the two examples *aparāhṇaḥ* (ix.6.46: p. *apara-ahnaḥ*) and *sahasrāhṇyam* (e.g. 10.8.18: p. *sahasra-ahnyam*), and furnishes no counter-examples at all, so that the rule evidently finds its justification in the observed phenomena of the general language, and not in those of the Atharva-Veda." For parallels to the unattested examples, see the KV on P.8.4.7 (अह्नोऽदन्तात्).

३.४.४. विभक्त्यागमप्रातिपदिकान्तस्य ।

Whitney (3.78). A, B, D: °गमः प्राति°. Hb: °गमाप्राति°.

Translation: [After the conditioning sound in the preceding member of the compound-word, the change of *n* to *ṇ* also applies to the *n*] of a case-ending, of the augment, and, [to the *n*] occurring at the end of a nominal stem.

Note: This rule is a close parallel to Pāṇini 8.4.11 (प्रातिपदिकान्तनुम्विभक्तिषु च). The rule also clearly assumes the existence of a general derivational grammar of Sanskrit, and its morphological categories. The term *prātipadika*, as defined by Pāṇini 1.2.45 (अर्थवदधातुरप्रत्ययः प्रातिपदिकम्), refers to the underived nominal stems, and, as defined by P.1.2.46 (कृत्तद्धितसमासाश्च), it covers derived nominal stems, such as verbal nouns (*kṛdanta*), secondary nouns derived from primary nouns through affixation (*taddhita*), and compounds (*samāsa*). The CA seems to assume the same meaning for this undefined term. The term *āgama* is used here as it is used by the Pāṇinian commentators to refer to adjunct items which are added to other items to become integral parts of those items. Here, the term is used to refer to *n* in forms like *durgāṇi*, where the original affix is simply *i*. However, by P.7.1.72 (नपुंसकस्य झलचः), the nominal stem *durga* gets the augment *nUM*, before the affix *i*, which, by the force of the marker *M*, attaches to the nominal stem after its final vowel, cf. P.1.1.47 (मिदचोऽन्त्यात् परः). The sequence *durgan+i* ultimately yields *durgāṇi*. Here, both the CA and Pāṇini seem to assume that this augment *n* will not be covered by the reference to the nominal stem or the case-ending, and must be specifically mentioned.

Whitney translates the term *vibhakti* as 'case-ending,' and L. Renou (1942: 495) follows Whitney in interpreting this term in the present rule as: "désigne spécialement les désinences casuelles." However, the term theoretically covers both the case-endings as well as finite verb-endings, according to the definition given by Pāṇini, cf. P.1.4.104 (विभक्तिश्च). However, the CAB gives only an example of *n* as part of a case-ending, and does not offer an example of *n* as part of a finite verb ending. If the rule is intended to derive word-internal cerebralization in a form like अति तराणि (AV 4.35.1-6), then we need to interpret the term *vibhakti* in a larger sense to include the verbal endings. Here, the affix *-āni* of the first person singular active imperative may need to be included in the wider notion of *vibhakti*. Sanskrit grammatical texts sometimes use this term in the narrower meaning of 'case-ending,' as for example APR (59: एकारो विभक्त्यादेशश्छन्दसि). L. Renou (ibid. p. 495) also notes the wider usage of this term in the ancient grammatical literature. If the condition पूर्वपदस्थान्निमित्तात् is assumed to continue into this rule, as suggested below, then we do not need this rule to account for forms like *tarāṇi*, and we may be correct in choosing the narrower interpretation for the word *vibhakti* as case-endings.

There is another significant question concerning the interpretation of this rule. The commentary CAB does not expressly continue the phrase पूर्वपदस्थान्निमित्तात् into this rule. On the other hand, the KV on P.8.4.11 (प्रातिपदिकान्तनुम्विभक्तिषु च) continues this expression into this rule. This makes one wonder whether the interpretation as offered by the commentary needs to be amended. Such a condition is needed to explain the form *paryāyiṇaḥ* in AV (6.76.4), which is split in the Padapāṭha as: *pari-āyinaḥ*. Also, in the example *durgāṇi* in AV (7.63.1), the Padapāṭha breaks it down to *duḥ-gāni*. Though the word *svargeṇa* is not attested in the AV, the word *svarga* is analyzed by the Padapāṭha as *svaḥ-ga*, (e.g. AV 9.5.16). In all these examples, the conditioning sound, i.e. *r*, belongs to the previous member of the compound expression. Only the example *varāheṇa* is not split by the Padapāṭha, and hence does not present the same situation. However, the commentator may have an etymology for the word *varāha* in mind where the *r* belongs to the first member of a compound expression. Indeed, such an etymology is proposed by Yāska in his NR. Yāska (NR, V.4) cites a Brāhmaṇa passage: वरमाहारमहार्षीदिति हि ब्राह्मणम्, and derives the word from *vara+āhāra*, cf. Siddheshwar Varma (1953: 36, 171). The KV seems to assume that, if the conditioning sound is in the same word, one does not need a separate rule, but can manage with the basic rules

P.8.4.1 (रषाभ्यां नो णः समानपदे) and P.8.4.2 (अट्कुप्वाङ्नुम्व्यवायेऽपि). However, if the conditioning sound is in the previous member of the compound-word, then P.8.4.11 is needed. All the examples offered by the KV are compound-words. I suspect that the CA has a similar interpretation intended for this rule, something that is not clearly stated by the CAB, but assumed by the examples offered in it.

चतुराध्यायीभाष्य - विभक्तिनकारस्य आगमनकारस्य प्रातिपदिकान्तस्य नकारस्य णकारो भवति । 'स्वर्गेण लोकेन' (not in known Vedic texts)। 'वराहेणं पृथिवी सं-विदाना' (अ.वे. १२.१.४८)। 'अतिं दुर्गाणि विश्वा' (अ.वे. ७.६३.१)। 'नैनं घ्नन्ति पर्यायिणः' (अ.वे. ६.७६.४)।

Note: The example *svargeṇa lokena* cited by the CAB is not found in the Vulgate of the AV, and Surya Kanta (*APR, Introduction,* p. 40) suggests that this may have occurred in the genuine Śaunakīya recension of the AV, and that the Vulgate is not the genuine Śaunakīya recension. The expression *svargāṇām* is found in the Kāṭhaka-Saṃhitā (33.6).

३.४.५. उपसर्गाद्धातोर्नानापदेऽपि ।

Whitney (3.79). B, C, D: °र्ग्रा°. O: °पदेष्वपि.

Translation: After [a conditioning sound in] a pre-verb (*upasarga*), even if [the conditioning sound happens to be] in a separate word [i.e. uncompounded pre-verb, the *n*] of a verb root [is replaced with a *ṇ*].

Note: The phrase नानापदेऽपि in this rule has the same force as the phrase असमासेऽपि in P.8.4.14 (उपसर्गादसमासेऽपि णोपदेशस्य). For a further discussion of this condition, see the Note on CA (3.4.2). The other important difference between Pāṇini and the CA rule is that the CA rule is phrased as a general rule for all verbs with *n*. Pāṇini takes a different path. He first makes a distinction between verbs with *n* which is not likely to change and verbs with *n* which is likely to change. The second class of verbs are listed in the Dhātupāṭha already with a retroflex *ṇ*, and these verbs are called *ṇopadeśa*, verbs taught with retroflex *ṇ*. Then Pāṇini unconditionally converts this retroflex *ṇ* to dental *n*, for all normal contexts, cf. P.6.1.65 (णो नः). Then, P.8.4.14

reconverts this *n* to *ṇ*, after a conditioning sound in a pre-verb. Perhaps, since the CA was concerned only with the roots as they occurred in the text of the AV, it did not feel the need to make such large classes, cf. Whitney on this rule: "The initial *n* of a root it almost always cerebralized by the preceding preposition in the Atharvan."

Whitney further says: "the only exceptions are the combinations of *nabh* with *pra* (vii.18.1, 2), and of *nart* with *pari* (e.g. iv.38.3) and *pra* (e.g. viii.6.11)." The first of these exceptions, i.e. *pra+nabh* is taken care by CA (3.4.18: नभेः) which was not available to Whitney. The exception of *pari+nṛt* is taken care of by the inclusion of the root *nṛt* in the *kṣubhnādi gaṇa* mentioned in CA (3.4.24: क्षुभ्नादीनाम्), and the CAB on that rule cites examples of *pra+nṛt* without retroflexion of *n*.

चतुराध्यायीभाष्य - उपसर्गस्थान्निमित्तात् धातुनकारस्य णकारो भवति नानापदेऽपि । 'अपः प्र णंयति' (अ.वे. ९.६.४)। 'या एव यज्ञ आपः प्र णीयन्ते' (अ.वे. ९.६.५)। 'जीवामृतेभ्यः परिणीयमांनाम्' (अ.वे. १८.३.३)।

Note: Surya Kanta says that this rule should give us a retroflexion even in *pra nabhasva* (AV 7.18.1, 2), *pari nṛtyati* (AV 4.38.3), and *parinṛtyantaḥ* (AV 8.6.11). However, as Surya Kanta (*APR, Introduction,* p. 39) points out, all mss. retain *n* in all these passages. Surya Kanta concludes: "It is obvious that the CA. is prescribing saṃdhis, which must have been current in the *Śaunaka* school; these are not observed by the Vulgate mss.; hence *Vulgate is not Śaunakīya*." The cases of *pra+nabh* and *pari+nṛt* are now meaningfully taken care of, without the assumptions made by Surya Kanta, cf. See the Note above.

३.४.६. प्रपराभ्यामेनः ।

Whitney (3.80). A, B: omit प्र. O has no daṇḍa between this and the next rule.

Translation: [The *n*] of *ena* [is cerebralized] after [the preceding uncompounded words] *pra* and *parā*.

Note: The word *enaḥ* clearly refers to forms of *idam* or *etad* where these two pronominal stems are substituted with *ena*, cf. P.2.4.34 (द्वितीया-

टौस्वेनः). However, while the word *enaḥ* in Pāṇini's rule is a nominative from the base *ena*, in the present CA rule, the context requires us to read *enaḥ* as a genitive form, evidently from the base *en*. The CAB clearly takes it as a genitive: उत्तरस्य एनो नकारस्य.

> ***चतुराध्यायीभाष्य*** - प्र परा इत्येताभ्यामुत्तरस्य एनो नकारस्य णकारो भवति । 'प्रैणांञ्छृणीहि' (अ.वे. १०.३.२)। 'प्रैणान्वृक्षस्य' (अ.वे. ३.६.८)। 'परैणान्देवः' (अ.वे. ८.३.१६)। प्रपराभ्यामिति किमर्थम् । 'पर्येना(H: णा)-न्प्राणः' (अ.वे. ९.२.५)।

Note: While the mss. H reads the counter-example as *paryeṇān,* Whitney corrects it to *paryenān,* without mentioning the actual reading in the mss. It is quite clear that, as the intended counter-example to the rule, it must read *paryenān*. However, it is to be noted that the passage as cited under APR (28, p. 26, example 13) reads *paryeṇān.* Whitney's edition of the AV reads *paryenān,* perhaps under the influence of our CA rule. Whitney's mss. mostly supported his reading, though there was one deviant ms. Whitney (*AV Transl.* Vol.II., p. 522) says: "O. reads *páry eṇān* in d; but the passage is quoted under Prāt. iii. 80 (= CA 3.4.6) as one in which the lingualization of *n* does not take place." This case seems to have escaped Surya Kanta's attention. However, it would seem that the Vulgate of the AV in this case did follow the CA rule, except the ms. O. It is also interesting to note that the commentary on the CA clearly intended to give the form *paryenān,* and yet the copyist, under the influence of the general grammatical tradition, offered the form *paryeṇān.* Thus, the apparent misreading in the manuscript H may be an indication of the influence of the general rules of Sanskrit grammar on the copyists, even when the tradition of the AV mss. in this case retained the non-retroflexed form.

Referring to the missing rules which were not known to Whitney in 1862, he adds: "Perhaps the treatise next took note of another case which the text affords of the lingualization of the nasal of *ena*, viz. *ā jabhārāi 'ṇām* (v.31.10). Possibly there followed also a mention of the passage *asṛjan nir eṇasaḥ* (ii.10.8); but this is very questionable, as the reading itself is doubtful." In both of these examples, the VVRI edition shows that the cerebralized reading is supported by the majority of manuscripts.

३.४.७. नसश्च ।

Missing in Whitney and H. No CAB on CA 3.4.7-12. This is a case of missing text, though most likely these rules originally did have the commentary. This is clear from the fact that the manuscript jumps from प्रपराभ्यामेन: to पुनर्णयामसि, though there is no commentary on the latter rule. Whitney (1862: 178) tries to guess what these missing rules may have looked like: प्रपरिभ्यां न: and आशीरुरुष्यगृहेषुशिक्षेभ्यश्च. However, the missing rules, as now known from the other manuscripts are somewhat different from Whitney's guesses.

Translation: Also, [the *n*] of *nas* [= *naḥ*, is cerebralized after the conditioning sound in the preceding pre-verb (*upasarga*)].

Note: In the absence of a commentary on this rule, one can only speculate about what the rule means. As Whitney (1880: 163) has astutely noted, this rule along with the two next rules "have the aspect of representing the three items of a rule of Pāṇini, *naś ca dhātusthoruṣubhyaḥ* (viii.4.27)." We may perhaps also bring in the next rule of Pāṇini, P.8.4.28 (उपसर्गाद्बहुलम्).

Whitney (1880: 163) assumes that the expression *praparābhyām* continues into this rule, and then he remarks: "The first rule, *nasaś ca*, must mean 'the *n* of *naḥ* also is changed to *ṇ* after *pra* and *parā*.' So far as *pra* is concerned, this is well enough; the cases of *pra ṇaḥ* are twelve in the Atharvan. ... But the text offers no example of *naḥ* after *parā;* while, on the other hand, there are eight cases ... in which *naḥ* follows *pari* and is changed to *ṇaḥ*, all the manuscripts agreeing. The form of rule 80 (= CA 3.4.6), then, as here implied, needs absolutely to have been *praparibhyām*, instead of *praparābhyām.* How to get over the difficulty I do not see. We cannot amend rule 80 (= CA 3.4.6) to *praparibhyām*, because there is in the Atharvan a single case of *eṇ* after *parā*, and a single phrase (repeated) in which it remains *en* after *pari;* both are quoted by the commentator under rule 80 (= CA 3.4.6)."

The other most plausible way is the follow the lead given by Pāṇini as mentioned above. If we take into account P.8.4.28 (उपसर्गाद्बहुलम्), which says that *naḥ* is diversely cerebralized after a conditioning sound in the preceding *upasarga*, a similar interpretation is suggested for the present CA rule. To get at that, we may continue the generic condition *upasargāt* from CA (3.4.5), instead of the limited condition *praparābhyām.* This, effectively allows us a wider interpretation for the rule to take care of the difficulties mentioned by Whitney.

One may also passingly mention that the cerebralization of *naḥ* after *pari* is ascribed by the VPR (3.87: परि ण इति शाकटायन:) specifically to

Śākaṭāyana. This means that it was not a universal phenomenon, and the incidence of *pari ṇaḥ* in the AV text could possibly be due to the AV reciters following the lead of Śākaṭāyana, as they expressly aknowledge elsewhere, cf. Bhārgava-Bhāskara's commentary on CA (1.1.10).

३.४.८. धातुस्थादयकारात् ।

Missing in Whitney and H. F: °स्थाद्यकारात्. I: °स्थात्षकारात्. P has no daṇḍa between this and the next rule. All other manuscripts read: धातुस्थादयकारात्.

> **Translation:** [The *n* of *nas* is cerebralized] after [the appropriate conditioning sound] in the verb root which is not combined with *y*.

Note: We do not have the commentary on this rule, and the rule seems to present major difficulties of interpretation. After discovering this rule in a second manuscript of the CA, Whitney (1880: 164) says: "There remains the rule *dhātusthād ayakārāt*, which can hardly signify anything else than 'after an altering letter contained in a root, unless combined with *y*,' and must be understood as applying only to *naḥ*. But the only case of altered *n* in the text falling under the rule as thus understood is *śikṣā ṇo asmin* (xviii.3.67) : all the manuscripts read *ṇo*. But the specification *ayakārāt*, if I interpret it correctly, can only be intended to exclude *uruṣya* (vi.4.3); and there all the *saṃhitā* MSS. save E. give *uruṣyā ṇaḥ*, which has accordingly been received into the edited text." Here one may point out that the VVRI edition, while it follows Whitney in giving the reading *uruṣyā ṇo*, mentions two more manuscripts, B and K, as giving the reading *uruṣyā naḥ*. Since, we have at least three manuscripts providing the reading *uruṣyā naḥ*, one needs to seriously consider the possibility that the author of the CA knew the reading *uruṣyā naḥ*, and tried to exclude it from cerebralization with the condition *ayakārāt*.

Whitney further says: "And, on the other hand, we have *mīmr̥ṣo naḥ* at iii.15.4, and *rīriṣo naḥ* at xi.2.29, in which *ṇ* is not read by a single manuscript." Even the VVRI edition does not have any manuscripts reading *ṇ* in these cases, and, one wonders how the present rule would exclude these, unless one makes an assumption that the author of the CA knew these examples with *ṇaḥ*. I am not certain we have enough evidence at this point to be able to draw any firm conclusions.

One may also mention a remote possibility concerning these two instances. P.8.4.28 (उपसर्गाद्नोत्परः), as read by the MB, offers a view that *naḥ* preceded by a conditioning sound in an *upasarga*, which is not followed by an *o*, changes to *ṇa*. The instance offered by the MB is *pra+u+naḥ* > *pro naḥ*, without cerebralization. One wonders whether the fact that the forms *mīmr̥ṣo* and *rīriṣo* end in *o* in the Samhitāpāṭha may have, at some point in the oral transmission, led to a similar exclusion of cerebralization of *naḥ*. Again, this is simply a speculation, and needs further research. The rule P.8.4.28 is read as (उपसर्गाद्बहुलम्) by the KV, and hence the text of the rule itself is to some extent uncertain.

Whitney (1880: 165) discusses further possible complications with the interpretation of the term *dhātusthāt*, but these cannot be resolved in the present state of the manuscript variants.

One may also note that the manuscript I offers a significant variant for the rule: धातुस्थात् षकारात्. If this has any validity, it may then eliminate those examples pointed out by Whitney (1880: 165), where the root contains an *r* as a possible conditioning sound for the change of *naḥ* to *ṇaḥ*. The only examples for *dhātusthāt* offered in the KV under P.8.4.27 are examples involving *ṣ*. However, the manuscript I is the only manuscript with this reading.

३.४.९. उरु ।

Missing in Whitney and H.

Translation: [The *n* of *naḥ* is cerebralized after the word] *uru*.

Note: Most manuscripts offer the reading *urū*. However, a comparison of this rule with the wording of P.8.4.27 (नश्च धातुस्थोरुषुभ्यः) leads me to choose the short *u* reading *uru*. Whitney (1880: 164) points to a possible dilemma with this rule: "The rule *uru* affords fewer difficulties of interpretation. But the only passage in which *naḥ*, or any other word beginning with *n*, follows *uru*, is *uru naḥ kr̥ṇota* (v.3.6), where P.M., to be sure, have *ṇaḥ*, but E.I.H. read *naḥ*, which was received into the edited text, because the passage is found also in the Rig-Veda, and is expressly exempted by the Rik. Prāt. (v. 27) from the operation of the rule requiring in general *ṇaḥ* after *uru* (v. 26). If this rule of our own treatise is to be respected, the correct Atharvan reading is *uru ṇaḥ*." While the VVRI edition gives *uru naḥ* for its choice of reading, it mentions several additional manuscripts which have *uru ṇaḥ* for this passage, i.e. A, D, K^m, R, S^m. It is thus most likely, as Whitney suggests, that the original Atharvan reading known to the author of the CA was *uru ṇaḥ*. It was changed to *uru naḥ* by some reciters, perhaps under the pressure of the RV tradition.

Whitney further adds: "Possibly *urūṇasau* (xviii.2.13), which I had regarded as included in the *gaṇa* of rule 76 (= CA 3.4.2), is to be brought under the present precept." The *drughaṇādi gaṇa* mentioned in CA (3.4.2) is not listed in the APR and hence its membership cannot be verified.

३.४.१०. ब्रह्मण्वत्यादीनाम् ।

Missing in Whitney and H. I: 10. O reads म्ह for ह्म. P has no daṇḍa between this and the next rule.

> **Translation:** [The *n*] in the forms *brahmaṇvatī* etc. [is changed to *ṇ*].

Note: Whitney (1880: 163), who found this rule in the second manuscript which became available to him after the publication of his edition in 1862, remarks: "Of the remaining rules, one, *brahmaṇvatyādīnām*, is clear enough in its bearing; it applies to the cases (referred to also in iv.99 = CA 4.3.28, and there rehearsed in the note) in which, against iii.89 = CA 3.4.21, a *n* becomes *ṇ* (in *pada* as well as *saṃhitā* text) even when final." Some idea of what kind of examples are included in this class can be gained from the CAB on CA (4.3.28):

> ***चतुराध्यायीभाष्य*** - ब्रह्मण्वत्यादीनां च न समापत्तिर्भवति । 'ब्रह्मंण्ऽवतीम्' (पद, अ.वे. ६.१०८.२, संहिता ⇒ 'ब्रह्मंण्वतीम्')। 'पश्यंत् । अक्षण्ऽवान्' (पद, अ.वे. ९.९.१५, संहिता ⇒ 'पश्यंदक्षण्वान्')। 'शीर्षण्ऽवती' (पद, अ.वे. १०.१.२, संहिता ⇒ 'शीर्षण्वती')। 'वृषण्यन्तींऽइव । कन्यला' (पद, अ.वे. ५.५.३, संहिता ⇒ 'वृषण्यन्तींव कन्यला')।

३.४.११. निपातस्य स्वः ।

Missing in Whitney and H. C, E, F, I: निपातस्य°. I (corr): निपातस्वः. O: निपातस्य रवः. Remaining mss. read: निपातश्च स्वः .

> **Translation:** After [lit. 'of'] the particle *su* [or rather, when it appears as *ṣu*, the *n* of *naḥ* changes to *ṇ*].

Note: The syntax of this rule is quite confusing. Whitney (1880: 163-4) says: "It appears capable of meaning only 'of the particle *su*,' while it ought to mean 'after *ṣu*, when particle,' and so to read *nipātāt ṣvaḥ*." An original *nipātāc ca* could have been conceivably altered through scribal error to *nipātaś ca* or *nipātasya* as we find in the manuscripts. In any case, Whitney's guess that the rule has to do with the particle *su*, or when it appears as *ṣu*, derives added support from P.8.4.27 (नश्च धातुस्थोरुषुभ्यः). The rule deals with three conditions, *dhātustha*, *uru*, and *ṣu*. Of these three conditions, the first and the second are taken care of by CA (3.4.8-9), and the remaining *ṣu* is taken care of by the present rule. As Whitney (1880: 163) notes, the reference to *ṣu* as a *nipāta* is necessary to avoid cerebralization of *naḥ* in a case like *gr̥heṣu naḥ*. The rule thus takes care of the commonly found sequence *ṣu ṇaḥ*. The parallel rule of Pāṇini clearly applies only to *naḥ* after *ṣu*, and not to any other *n*-initial word after *ṣu*. Whitney (1880: 164), however, argues that the intervention of ब्रह्मण्वत्यादीनाम् between CA (3.4.8-9) and the present rule "seems to dissociate it from *naḥ*, and mark it as applying to any word whatever with initial *n*." However we interpret the rule, there are some major problems in relating the rule to the phenomena found in the text of the AV. As Whitney notes: "There is then the further and not unimportant objection that no example of *ṇ* for *n* after *ṣu* is to be found in the text (of the AV). The altered *ṣu* is not once followed by *naḥ*; the only initial *n* that comes in contact with it is at xviii.1.37, where we have *stuṣa ū ṣu nr̥tamāya*, not a single manuscript reading *ṇr̥tamāya*. Unless, therefore, all the manuscripts are wrong here, and we have to alter to *ṇr̥tamāya*, I cannot see what purpose this rule answers." One can only say that in this case, the author of the CA is simply attempting to imitate some generic grammar of Sanskrit, such as represented by P.8.4.27. The cases of *naḥ* changing to *ṇaḥ* after *ṣu* are common in the RV, and are cited by the commentators under P.8.4.27.

This rule seems to have been mistakenly applied to the sequence *gr̥heṣu naḥ* by some transmitters. Whitney (1880: 164) says: "the phrase ... occurs twice in the Atharvan, most of the manuscripts reading each time *ṇaḥ*. I think that, in view of the absence of authority for this reading in the Prātiśākhya, the adoption of *naḥ* in the edited text is to be approved." Also see Whitney's note on this rule (W: iii.80).

३.४.१२. पुनर्णयामसि ।

Whitney (3.81). While the manuscript H resumes with part of this rule, the commentary on the rule is still missing.

Translation: [The *n* of] *nayāmasi* [after] *punar* [is changed to *ṇ*].

Note: The rule takes care of the sequence पुनर्णयामसि in AV (5.14.7). Beginning with CA (3.4.6), the manuscript H jumped to this rule, skipping the intermediate text: प्रपराभ्यामेर्णयामसि, and, on the basis of his knowledge of the AV, Whitney reconstructed the rule as पुनर्णयामसि. On this reconstruction, Whitney (1862: 178) remarked: "Whether I have given the form of the rule correctly is not quite certain, a portion of it being lost altogether." Now, all the newly found manuscripts of the CA support Whitney's reconstructed text.

३.४.१३. नवतेश्च ।

Whitney (3.82).

Translation: [The *n*] of the root *nu* [is cerebralized after *punar*].

Note: All the examples cited by the commentator contain the word *nava* 'new,' rather than any verb-forms from the root *nu*. Whitney observes: "The authors of our treatise, then, must have derived *nava,* 'new,' from the verbal root *nu*, 'to praise,' instead of from the pronominal word *nu*, 'now.'" Yāska's Nirukta (III.19) derives *nava* from *ā+nayati.* Siddheshvar Varma (1953: 120) says: "But Indo-Eur. *neuos*, 'new,' Gr. *néos* 'new.'" Kṣīrasvāmin's commentary on Amarakośa (3.77) derives *nava* from *nu*, and this is further supported by his commentary Kṣīrataraṅgiṇī on Pāṇini's Dhātupāṭha, which derives the words *nava* and *praṇava* from the root *nu* (= *ṇu* of the *Dhātupāṭha)* by applying the Uṇādisūtra : नुदंशोर्गुणश्च (rule 6.54, Daśapādī-Uṇādisūtra), Kṣīrataraṅgiṇī (p. 173). Thus, it is clear that a derivation for the word *nava* from the root *nu* is well established in the Indic tradition. While the word *nava* can be technically derived by the general rule P.3.3.57 (ऋदोरप्) by adding the affix *aP* to the root *nu*, there is no specific rule relating to the derivation of *nava* in Pāṇini.

चतुराध्यायीभाष्य - नवतेश्च नकारस्य णकारो भवति । 'चन्द्रमाश्च पुनर्णवः' (अ.वे. १०.७.३३)। 'या रोहन्ति पुनर्णवाः' (अ.वे. ८.७.८)। 'पुनरागाः पुनर्णवः' (अ.वे. ८.१.२०)।

Note: On AV (8.1.20), Whitney (*AV Transl.* Vol.II., p. 475) notes that the citation here is similar with RV (10.161.5), except that the RV has the vocative *punarnava* without a retroflex *ṇ,* a reading which it shares with AVP (16.2.9), as well as with Sāyaṇa's commentary on AV (8.1.20). The lack of retroflexion in the RV reading may indicate that it is the earlier reading, relatively less affected by the increasingly greater pressure for retroflexion. For the question of retroflexion in the RV, see: Deshpande (1979).

३.४.१४. पूर्याणः ।

Whitney (3.83). E, F, I, O: दूर्याणः.

Translation: [After the word] *pūr*, [the *n* of the word] *yāna* [is cerebralized].

Note: The compound-expression *pūryāṇa* (AV 18.1.54) is split into *pūḥ-yāna* by the Padapāṭha. Whitney observes: "There is small reason to be seen for singling out this word in order to make it the subject of a special rule, and the same is true of those treated in the two following rules: they might all have been as well left to fall into the *gaṇa* of rule 76." Since this *gaṇa* is not fully listed in the APR, we have no exact way of ascertaining its membership as intended by the CA or by its commentators.

The commentary of [Pseudo-]Sāyaṇa on AV derives the word *pūryāṇa* from *pums+yāna*, and then says that the word is grammatical because of its inclusion in the *pr̥ṣodarādi gaṇa* referred to in P.6.3.109 (पृषोदरादीनि यथोपदिष्टम्). However, the tradition considers this list to be an open-ended list (*ākr̥tigaṇa*), and this is simply a way of saying that this is an irregular formation. It is unlikely that the word is actually derived from *puṃs+yāna.* Whitney, I think quite correctly, renders this word as "(the roads) that go to the stronghold." In his note on AV (18.1.54), (*AV Translation*, Volume II, p. 828), Whitney says: "The commentary absurdly explains the word as = *pumāṃso yena ... yānti!* for the *pur*, compare x.2.28 ff.; xix.17 and 19." The phrase *puram praimi* appears in each verse of AV (19.17), and the phrase *puram pra ṇayāmi* occurs in each verse of AV (19.19). Whitney, (*AV Translation,* Volume II, p. 828), further points out, "The Anukr. takes no notice of the metrical irregularity in the verse." To this comment, Lanman adds: "It is due to the displacement of *pūrviébhis* by *pūryāṇais :* the secondary character of the latter (occurring elsewhere only at 18.4.63 below) is palpable in more ways than one."

Commenting on *pūryāṇaiḥ* in AV (18.4.63), Whitney points out that MS (i.10.3) reads *pūrvyebhiḥ* for our *pūryāṇaiḥ*, while the ĀŚS (ii.7.9), "with K. and Kap. S., as pointed out by Schröder" (*AV Translation* , Vol. II, p. 889), reads *pūrviṇebhiḥ*. One may suggest the possibility that the reading *pūrviṇebhiḥ* indicates a possible transition between *pūrvyebhiḥ* and *pūryāṇaiḥ*.

चतुराध्यायीभाष्य - पू(H: भू)रित्यस्मात् यानो नकारस्य णकारो भवति । 'प॒थिभिः॑ पू॒र्याणैः॑' (अ.वे. १८.१.५४)।

Note: What case is *yāno* in *yāno nakārasya* in the commentary, a genitive for *yān*? The rule itself simply seems to cite the word *pūryāṇa* in the nominative. However, probably under the influence of the clear genitive in *durṇāmnaḥ*, the commentator interprets *-yāṇaḥ* as a genitive. For a similar question, see the note on CA (3.4.6: प्रपराभ्यामेनः).

३.४.१५. दुर्णाम्नः ।

Whitney (3.84). P has no daṇḍa between this and the next rule.

Translation: [After] *dur*, [the initial *n* of] the word *nāman* [is cerebralized].

Note: The Padapāṭha splits the expression into *duḥ-nāman*.

चतुराध्यायीभाष्य - दुरित्येतस्मादुत्तरस्य नाम्नो नकारस्य णकारो भवति । 'दु॒र्णाम्नीः॒ सर्वाः॑' (अ.वे. ४.१७.५)। 'दु॒र्णामा॒ तत्र॒ मा गृ॑धत्' (अ.वे. ८.६.१)। 'दु॒र्णामा॒ च सु॒नामा॑ च' (अ.वे. ८.६.४)।

३.४.१६. अवग्रहादृकारात् ।

Whitney (3.85). Hb: °हादकारात्. B, D: °हात् दृकारात्.

Translation: After a *ṛ* [at the end of a] separable [member of compound, the *n* of the following member is cerebralized].

चतुराध्यायीभाष्य - अवग्रहात् ऋकारात् नकारस्य णकारो भवति । 'दे॑व॒यानाः॑ पितृ॒याणाः॑' (पद ⇒ 'पि॒तृ॒ऽयानाः॑,' अ.वे. ६.११७.३)। 'पि॒तृ॒याणैः॒ सं व॒ आ रो॑हयामि' (पद

⇒ 'पितृऽयानैः,' अ.वे. १८.४.१)। 'नृमणा नाम' (पद ⇒ 'नृऽमना,' अ.वे. १६.३.५)।

Note: The KV on P.8.4.26 (छन्दस्यृदवग्रहात्) cites passages with the same expressions, i.e. *pitṛyāṇa* and *nṛmaṇā*. The KV interprets this rule to suggest that this change takes place only if the first part containing the sound *ṛ* is liable to be separated with an *avagraha* in the Padapāṭha. The rule does not mean that this change occurs in the Padapāṭha, even when the members are actually separated with an *avagraha*. The Padapāṭha for these examples separates their components with an *avagraha*, and then does not show retroflexion, e.g. *pitṛyāṇa* < *pitṛ-yāna*, *nṛmaṇā* < *nṛ-manā*. Thus the Padamañjarī on the KV on P.8.4.26 says: अवग्रहणभूतो य ऋकारस्तदन्तादिति । संहिताधिकाराच्च संहिताकाल एतेषां णत्वं, पदकाले चावग्रहः क्रियते, तेनावग्रहयोग्यत्वादृकारोऽवग्रह इत्युक्तः, न तु तद्दशापन्नः । तथा चावग्रहं दर्शयता णत्वं न प्रयुक्तम्. The commentary Nyāsa clarifies the dilemma even better: अपरे तु मन्यन्ते - यथानृत्यन्नपि नर्तनयोग्यत्वान्नर्तक इत्युच्यते, तथानवगृह्यमाणोऽपि ऋकारोऽवग्रहयोग्यत्वादवग्रह इत्युक्तः । अत एतदुक्तं भवति - अवग्रहयोग्यादृकाराण्णत्वं भवति, एवं सत्यवग्रहग्रहणे संहिताधिकारात् संहितायामेव णत्वं भवति, नावग्रहादिति.

Whitney mentions *nṛpāṇa* (AV xix.58.4) as an additional example. However, neither Whitney, nor the commentator on CA, nor Pāṇini offers a counter-example, i.e. an example where *n* does not change to *ṇ*, because the previous member, though ending in *ṛ*, is not separable with an *avagraha*.

The wording of Pāṇini's rule indicates that not only was he familiar with the Padapāṭhas, but that at least some of his rules were indented for building up the Saṃhitā text starting from the Padapāṭha.

३.४.१७. न मिनन्ति ।

Whitney (3.86): °मिनाति. E, F, I: प्रमिनंति. I (corr): °मिनातेः. O offers both readings as separate rules: प्रमिनंति ।। नमिनंति ।।.

Translation: However, [the *n* of] the verb *mī* [is not changed to *ṇ* after a conditioning sound in the preceding pre-verb].

चतुराध्यायीभाष्य - न मिनन्तीत्यस्य नकारस्य णकारो भवति । 'प्र मिंनीज्जनिंत्रीम्' (अ.वे. ६.११०.३)। 'प्र

मिंनन्ति व्रतानिं' (अ.वे. १८.१.५)। 'प्र मिंनाति सङ्गिरः' (अ.वे. १८.४.६०)।

Note: Whitney points to an additional example *pramināma vratāni* (xix.59.2). He further observes: "The rule itself is to be understood, it may be presumed, as giving exceptions to rule 79 (= CA 3.4.5: उपसर्गाद्धातोर्नानापदेऽपि) above: yet the latter would seem to apply only to conversions of the nasal of a root itself, and not of the appended conjugational syllable." Whitney's concern seems to be fully justified, especially when we find Pāṇini making a separate rule to take care of the forms *prahiṇoti* and *pramīṇāti*, cf. P.8.4.15 (हिनुमीना). This rule may be taken as an indication that under normal circumstances, the *n* of the infixes *nu, nā* etc. is not cerebralized. On the other hand, the CA rule as an exception would imply that such infixes would be cerebralized by the normal rules, unless their cerebralization is specifically prevented. This may perhaps suggest that by the term *dhātu* in CA (3.4.5), the author of the CA may have intended the verbal base before the final endings. This is further supported by the fact that CA (4.3.24: हिनोतेः), as well as APR (147c: हिनोतेः, p. 100), already take for granted the fact of cerebralization in forms like *pratiprahiṇmaḥ*, (AV 10.1.5) and simply point out that the cerebral in these forms is not restored to dental in the Padapāṭha. Neither of these treatises have a separate rule like P.8.4.15 (हिनुमीना) prescribing cerebralization of the infix. Also comparable is the prohibitory rule CA (3.4.20: परेर्हिनोतेः), which presumes that without such a rule, the cerebralization will take place in *pari hinoti*.

All the examples cited in the CAB are found as examples 62-64 on APR (147h).

३.४.१८. नभेः ।

No such rule in Whitney. A, B: नेभेः. P has no daṇḍa between this and the next rule.

Translation: Also, [the *n*] of the root *nabh* [is not cerebralized after a conditioning sound in the preceding pre-verb].

चतुराध्यायीभाष्य - नभेश्च नकारस्य णकारो (न?) भवति । ...

Note: It is difficult to understand why Whitney did not include this rule in spite of the fact that at least an incomplete commentary on this rule exists in the manuscript H. After consulting a second manuscript of the CA, however, Whitney (1880: 165) acknowledged his "want of acuteness," and cited the examples *pra nabhasva* and *pra nabhatām* (vii.18.1, 2). Also see the Note on CA 3.4.5 concerning some misconceptions of Surya Kanta which are now corrected by the discovery of this rule.

APR (147h, p. 102) lists *pra nabhasva* (AV 7.18.1) and *pra nabhatām* (AV 7.18.2) as exceptions to cerebralization, and it is obvious that these are the same cases intended by the present CA rule.

३.४.१९. भानोश्च ।

Whitney (3.87). P: भानोःश्च.

Translation: Also, [the *n*] of *bhānu* [is not changed to *ṇ* after a conditioning sound in the preceding word].

चतुराध्यायीभाष्य - .... 'चित्रभानो' (अ.वे. ४.२५.३)। 'प्र भानवः सिस्रते' (अ.वे. १३.२.४६)।

Note: The CAB offers two examples to illustrate this phenomenon. The first example seems to be a genuine example for this rule, because the cerebralization of *n* would otherwise take place by CA (3.4.2). One may, however, wonder why this could not be taken care of by simply excluding this instance from the *drughaṇādi* list referred to in that rule. The only conclusion one can draw is that the CA list was not a complete list, but simply an open-ended list hinted by the token *drughaṇa*. This is what occasions the present rule.

On the other hand, the example *pra bhānavaḥ sisrate* (AV 13.2.46), as Whitney himself noted, "cannot be forced under any rule that has been laid down." This is because, the pre-verb *pra* is not semantically related to *bhānavaḥ*, but to the verb *sisrate*. Therefore, there is no possibility of *pra* cerebralizing the *n* of *bhānavaḥ*.

One may note a curious fact, corroborating the criticism above, that the APR (147h, p. 102) lists only the example *citrabhāno* in its list of exceptions to cerebralization, and makes no mention of *pra bhānavaḥ sisrate*.

३.४.२०. परेर्हिनोतेः ।

Whitney (3.88).

Translation: [The *n*] of *hinoti* [is not cerebralized] after [the prefix] *pari*.

चतुराध्यायीभाष्य - परेरुत्तरस्य हिनोतेर्नकारस्य णकारो [न] भवति । 'परिहिनोमिं मेधयां' (अ.वे. ८.४.६)। परेरिति किमर्थम् । 'प्र हिंणोमि दूरम्' (अ.वे. १२.२.८)।

Note: The form *pari hinomi* (AV 8.4.6) is listed among the exceptions to cerebralization under APR (147h, p.102). Whitney reminds us: "A strict application of rule 79 = CA (3.4.5: उपसर्गाद्धातोर्नानापदेऽपि), then, to the nasal only of a root itself, would render this rule also unnecessary." But, then how would one get the cerebral *ṇ* in the attested counter-examples, where Whitney indeed admits the presence of cerebral *ṇ*? For theoretical issues relating to the assumptions behind this and other similar rules, see the Note on CA (3.4.17: न मिनन्ति). The counter-example *pra hiṇomi* (AV 12.2.8) is also listed under APR (147c, p. 100) among examples where in the Padapāṭha, the cerebralization does not revert to the dental original. Other forms listed are *pratiprahiṇmaḥ* (AV 10.1.5) and *pra hiṇuta* (AV 18.4.40).

३.४.२१. पदान्तस्पर्शयुक्तस्यं ।

Whitney (3.89). E, F, O: °दांतात्स्प°. P: °स्पर्शउक्तस्य.

Translation: Neither a word-final [*n*], nor [an *n*] combined with a stop [is cerebralized].

चतुराध्यायीभाष्य - पदान्तस्पर्शयुक्तस्य च नकारस्य णकारो [न] भवति । 'पूषन् तवं व्रते' (अ.वे. ७.९.३)। 'संक्रन्दंनः' (अ.वे. ५.२०.९)। 'पाशों ग्रन्थिः' (अ.वे. ९.३.२)।

Note: Whitney points out: "To the first part of this rule would need to be made the exceptions noted at iv. 99 (= CA 4.3.28: ब्रह्मण्वत्यादीनाम्), but that, by the operation of that precept, they are made to read in *pada* as in *saṃhitā*, and so are withdrawn from the ken of the Prātiśākhya." There is a positive precept now in CA (3.4.10: ब्रह्मण्वत्यादीनाम्), which was not available to Whitney when he prepared his edition which prescribes the change of word-final *n* in certain exceptional cases. However, we should note that in all those cases, the *n* occurs at the end of the first member of a compound word, and not at the absolute end of the word as in the case of *pūṣan* in AV (7.9.3) cited by the commentary.

The first condition stated in this rule of the CA is taken care of by Pāṇini with a specific rule, P.8.4.37 (पदान्तस्य), with identical import. As far as the second condition is concerned, Pāṇini's grammar handles the absence of cerebralization in a very different way. In an example like *granthi*, P.8.3.24 (नश्चापदान्तस्य झलि) converts the non-final *n* to an *anusvāra* before non-nasal stops and spirants. This form *graṃthi* is then changed back to *granthi* by P.8.4.58 (अनुस्वारस्य ययि परसवर्णः) which says that an *anusvāra* is replaced by a consonant homorganic with the following non-spirant consonant. By the convention set by P.8.2.1 (पूर्वत्रासिद्धम्), the cerebralization rule, P.8.4.1 (रषाभ्यां नो णः समानपदे), considers only the results of the preceding rules as having taken effect, and does not consider the results of the succeeding rules as having taken effect. Thus, for P.8.4.1, the form *granthi* has not been brought into existence. It still sees the form *graṃthi*, to which cerebralization of *n* cannot apply, because there is no *n* in that form. This complicated logic, system-internal as it is, is explained by Bhaṭṭojī Dīkṣita with reference to the form *kurvanti* in his SK on P.8.4.58 (SK, p. 29): कुर्वन्तीत्यत्र णत्वे प्राप्ते तस्यासिद्धत्वादनुस्वारे परसवर्णे च कृते तस्यासिद्धत्वान्न णत्वम्.

३.४.२२. नशेः षान्तस्य ।

Whitney (3.90). P: नशेषांतस्य, and no daṇḍa between this and the next rule.

Translation: [The *n*] of the root *naś*, when it ends in *ṣ*, [is not changed to *ṇ* after a conditioning sound in the pre-verb].

चतुराध्यायीभाष्य - नशेः षान्तस्य च नकारस्य न णकारो भवति । 'प्रनष्टः' (not in Vedic Saṃhitās) । 'परिनष्टः' (not in Vedic Saṃhitās) । 'निर्नष्टः' (not in Vedic Saṃhitās) । 'दुर्नष्टः' (not in Vedic Saṃhitās) । षान्तस्येति किमर्थम् । 'दुर्णशं चिद्र्वाक्' (अ.वे. ५.११.६) ।

Note: With respect to this rule, Whitney says: "it belongs rather to the general grammar than to a Prātiśākhya of the Atharvan, since our text does not furnish a single case to which it should apply." However, the counter-example is indeed attested in the text of the AV, i.e. *durṇaśaṃ cid arvāk* (AV 5.11.6), and it is possible that the existence of the counter-example occasioned the presence of the rule, which, as Whitney rightly says, comes from a general grammar of Sanskrit. We should noted that the APR (147h, p.102), which provides a list of exception to cerebralization makes no mention of these examples, perhaps for a simple reason that they do not occur in the text of the AV.

This rule is identical with P.8.4.36. For parallel examples, see the KV on P.8.4.36. An example to the contrary is found in the TS 2.4.4.1 (*nirṇāśaya*).

३.४.२३. स्वरलोपे हन्तेः ।

Whitney (3.91).

Translation: [The *n*] of the root *han*, when its vowel is deleted, [is not cerebralized].

चतुराध्यायीभाष्य - स्वरलोपे कृते हनिनकारस्य न णकारो भवति । 'वृत्रघ्न स्तोमाः' (अ.वे. ४.२४.१)। 'इन्द्रेण वृत्रघ्ना मेदी' (अ.वे. ३.६.२)। स्वरलोप इति किमर्थम् । 'रक्षोहणं वाजिनम्' (अ.वे. ८.३.१)।

Note: Whitney observes: "Unless *sparśayukta*, in rule 89 (= CA 3.4.21), meant only 'combined with a following mute,' which is very unlikely, the present precept is superfluous, as merely specifying a case already sufficiently provided for elsewhere."

On the other hand, Whitney points out that "Pāṇini (viii.4.22: *hanter atpūrvasya*) looks at this matter from the opposite point of view, and teaches that the *n* of *han* is lingualized whenever it is preceded by *a*."

As I pointed out in my note on CA (3.4.21), Pāṇini's grammar does not have a rule similar to the condition स्पर्शयुक्तस्य in CA (3.4.21), but that it takes care of the same phenomenon in a different way. However, the method used in Pāṇini's grammar to avoid the cerebralization of *n* in a form like *kurvanti* cannot apply to the example *vṛtraghna*. Here, the *n* of the root cannot be first converted to an *anusvāra*, and then back to *n*, invisible to the cerebralization rule P.8.4.1 (रषाभ्यां नो णः समानपदे). Therefore, Pāṇini's formulation of

P.8.4.22 (हन्तेरत्पूर्वस्य) remains significant in restricting cerebralization of *n* in the root *han* only to those instances where the *n* is preceded by an *a*. Such indeed is not the case with the present CA rule. Therefore, Whitney's criticism of it still remains valid.

३.४.२४. क्षुभ्नादीनाम् ।

Whitney (3.92). O: क्षुभ्णादीनां. P adds a daṇḍa after this rule as a correction.

Translation: [The *n*] of the forms of *kṣubh* etc. [is not cerebralized].

चतुराध्यायीभाष्य - क्षुभ्नादीनां च नकारस्य न णकारो भवति । 'क्षुभ्नाति' । 'परि नृत्यंन्त्योरिव' (अ.वे. १०.७.४३)। 'मधुंना प्रपींनाः' (अ.वे. १२.३.४१)। 'परिं नृत्यन्ति केशिनीः' (अ.वे. १२.५.४८)।

Note: The fact that there is no attested example of the root *kṣubh* in the Vulgate of the AV is taken as an indication by Surya Kanta (*APR, Introduction,* p. 39) that the Vulgate is not genuinely Śaunakīya, and that such examples may have occurred in a genuinely Śaunakīya recension. I tend to agree with Whitney that the similarity of this rule with Pāṇini (viii.4.39: क्षुभ्नादिषु च) suggests that the CA is relying here upon a source which dealt primarily with the general grammar of Sanskrit. Also see my Note on CA (3.4.5).

३.४.२५. व्यवाये शसलैः ।

Whitney (3.93). O: °शाषलैः.

Translation: [The cerebralization of *n* due to the preceding *r*, *ṛ*, and *ṣ* does not take place] when there is an intervention by [the sounds] *ś*, *s*, and *l*.

चतुराध्यायीभाष्य - व्यवाये शकारसकारलकारैः नकारस्य न णकारो भवति । 'कः पृश्निं धेनुम्' (अ.वे. ७.१०४.१)।

'गर्भे अन्तरदृश्यमानः' (अ.वे. १०.८.१३)। 'सविता प्रसवानाम्' (अ.वे. ५.२४.१)।

Note: In comparison with this rule, and the following rule, of the CA, Pāṇini's grammar takes a wholly different strategy. For a discussion, see my Note on CA (3.4.1).

३.४.२६. चटतवर्गैश्च ।

Whitney (3.94). A, B, D, J, M, P: चटवर्गैश्च.

Translation: Also, [there is no cerebralization of *n* if the preceding conditioning sound is separated by stops belonging to] the *c*-series, *ṭ*-series, and *t*-series.

Note: For a further discussion of the formulation of this rule, and its contrast with Pāṇini's grammar, see my Note on CA (3.4.1). Also see the Note below.

चतुराध्यायीभाष्य - चटतवर्गैश्च व्यवाये नकारस्य न णकारो भवति । 'उपेहोपपर्चनास्मिन् गोष्ठ उप पृञ्च नः' (अ.वे. ९.४.२३)। 'रेषयैनान्' (अ.वे. ११.१.२०)। 'यथासों मित्रवर्धनः' (अ.वे. ४.८.६)। 'तं वर्तनिः' (अ.वे. ७.२१.१)।

Note: Referring to the example *reṣayainān,* Whitney correctly observes: "this, however, is no example under the rule." Later, he (*AV Transl.* Vol.II., p. 616) observed that even though the commentary ms. reads *reṣayainān,* the fact that it is "quoted as an example of a palatal or lingual or dental mute interposed between *r* and *n,* which would imply *recaya.* ⌊That is, it implies the mute (*c*) rather than the sibilant (*ś*), the intervention of which was treated in the preceding rule, iii. 93 (= CA 3.4.26).⌋"

It should be noted that while several mss. offer the variant *reśaya,* none offers the reading *recaya.* The rules 3.4.25-6 provide a statement which is different from that of P.8.4.2 (अट्कुप्वाङ्नुम्व्यवायेऽपि). Pāṇini's rule lists those sounds whose intervention does not prevent the change of *n* to *ṇ.* On the other hand, the CA lists those sounds whose intervention prevents this change. This shows a certain difference in the orientation of these two texts. Also, the initial rule in Pāṇini, i.e. P.8.4.1 (रषाभ्यां नो णः समानपदे) assumes that the procedure applies only to *n* immediately preceded by *r* and *ṣ*. Then the next rule, P.8.4.2, allows this procedure to situations with intervention of certain sounds. On the other hand, the initial rule in CA seems to assume that *n* changes to *ṇ* as long as it is somehow preceded by *r* and *ṇ*. Then the text stipulates that this change does not take place if certain sounds intervene.

Whitney offers an excellent explanation of why the intervention of these sounds prevents cerebralization of the following *n*: "The physical explanation of the effect of the sounds mentioned in these two rules to prevent the lingualization of the nasal is obvious: they are all of them such as cause the tongue to change its position. When this organ is once bent back in the mouth to the position in which the lingual sibilant, semivowel, and vowels are uttered, it tends to remain there, and produce the next following nasal at that point, instead of at the point of dental utterance; and it does so, unless thrown out of adjustment, as it were, by the occurrence of a letter which calls it into action in another quarter."

३.४.२७. पदेनावर्जितेन ।

C, E, F, I, Hcb, O: °तेन. Whitney (3.95) and the rest of the manuscripts: °ते च.

> **Translation:** With [the intervention] of a [whole] word [between *n* and the conditioning sound, there is no cerebralization], unless [the intervening word is] *ā*.

> ***चतुराध्यायीभाष्य-*** पदेन आकारवर्जितेन व्यवाये नकारस्य न णकारो भवति । 'परीमे गामनेषत' (अ.वे. ६.२८.२)। आकारवर्जितेति किमर्थम् । 'पर्याणद्धम्' (अ.वे. १४.२.१२)।

Note: Whitney points out that "Pāṇini, however, takes due note of it (viii.4.38: *padavyavāye 'pi*), but omits to except the preposition *ā*, so that (unless he makes the exception by some other rule which I have not observed) he would read *paryānaddha*."

We should note that the VVRI edition provides the reading *paryāṇad-dham*, but notes that a large number of manuscripts have the reading *paryānad-dham* without the cerebralization of *n*.

३.४.२८. तुविष्टमः ।

Whitney (3.96). I: 29. O: तुविष्टभः.

Translation: The form *tuviṣṭama* [from *tuvi+tamaḥ* is correct].

चतुराध्यायीभाष्य - तुविष्टम इति सकारागमो भवति । 'इन्द्रः पतिंस्तुविष्टंमः' (अ.वे. ६.३३.३)। संहितायामित्येव। (क्रम ⇒) 'तुवितंम इतिं तुविऽतंमः' । अनधिकारे सूत्रनिर्देशः । सूत्रार्थस्तद्यो(H: र्द्यो)गश्च चर्चापरिहारयोर्वचनं मा भूदिति ।

Note: The comment अनधिकारे सूत्रनिर्देशः । सूत्रार्थस्तद्योगश्च चर्चापरिहार-योर्वचनं मा भूदिति indicates that the commentator has indeed thought about the organization of the rules in the CA. Whitney renders the first part of this comment as: "in the absence of an explanatory heading." A better rendering would be, "the rule is enunciated in an inappropriate section." The reason for the deviation is then given in the following comment. Whitney, however, makes a significant observation: "The same word is found more than once in the Rig-Veda, but is written by the *pada*-text *tuviḥ-tama,* so that there is nothing irregular in the *saṃhitā* form, and it requires and receives no notice from the Rik Prātiśākhya. It is a legitimate matter for surprise to find the rule thrust in this place, in connection with a subject to which it stands in no relation whatever: we should expect to meet it in the second chapter, along with rules 25 and 26 of that chapter, or after rule 30, or elsewhere. Its intrusion here, and the indefiniteness of its form, cannot but suggest the suspicion of its being an interpolation, made for the purpose of supplying an observed deficiency in the treatise." However, it must be a very early interpolation, since it is found in all the manuscripts, and also since the commentary CAB comments upon this rule, even though it is evidently unhappy with its location.

इति तृतीयाध्यायस्य चतुर्थः पादः । तृतीयोऽध्यायः समाप्तः ।

H: ।।१०५।। इति तृतीयोध्यायः. O: इति तृतीयोध्यायः. E, F: तृतीयस्य चतुर्थः पादः ।। आथर्वणे चतुराध्यायिकायां तृतीयोध्यायः. A, B, D, P: तृतीयोध्यायः समाप्तः. I: इति तृतीयाध्यायस्य चतुर्थः पादः ।।४।। इत्यथर्ववेदे कौत्सव्याकरणे चतुराध्यायिकायां तृतीयोऽध्यायः समाप्तः ।। सू १२५. O: इत्यथर्ववेदे कौत्सव्याकरणे चतुराध्यायिकायां तृतीयस्य चतुर्थः पादः ।। तृतीयोऽध्यायः समाप्तः ।। सूत्राणि ।।२९।।.

चतुराध्यायीभाष्य - ।।१०५।। इति तृतीयोऽध्यायः ।।

Note: Note the different numbers of the rules in this Adhyāya given in the colophons for H and I. This suggests that there is a difference of opinion regarding 20 statements, which are regarded as part of the Sūtra-text by some manuscripts, while they are not considered to be part of the Sūtra-text by others. Especially, the manuscript of the CAB, H, shows the smaller number. Thus, it is clear that while this mss. contains all these extra-passages, without any commentary upon them, they are not counted as being part of the Sūtra-text. Whether they were part of the commentary, and therefore were not commented upon again, or whether they were included under the influence of the other text-tradition seen in the rest of the manuscripts is not clear.

॥ चतुर्थोऽध्यायः ॥
॥ प्रथमः पादः ॥

४.१.१. समासावग्रहविग्रहान्पदे
यथोवाच छन्दसि शाकटायनः ।
तथा प्रवक्ष्यामि चतुष्टयं पदं
नामाख्यातोपसर्गनिपातानाम् ॥

Whitney (p. 261) quotes this as part of the commentary. C: no such verse. A, B, D, J, K: °विग्रहां°. P(orig): °समासावग्रहां पदे° corrected to °समासावग्रहविग्रहां पदे°. Whitney: °तथा वक्ष्यामि°. A, B, D: °पसर्ग्रं°. The verses which are given hear as CA 4.1.1-23 either formed part of the commentary, or were a very early interpolation into the text. In any case, they are found in all Sūtra-only manuscripts and were accepted as being part of the text of the CA. The only manuscript which does not contain these verses (CA 4.1.1-23) is C. Whether it represents an older tradition of the Sūtra-text, going to a time before these verses were incorporated, or whether it simply left them out, is difficult to say. It does not provide a count of the rules either for this Pāda or the Adhyāya, and, therefore, we do not know what to make of this omission. To confuse the matter further, the mss. C does include other passages in the 3rd Pāda of the 3rd Adhyāya which are left out by Whitney as belonging to the commentary. Thus, most probably, this represents an eclectic decision on the part of someone to leave out these verses.

Translation: As Śākaṭāyana has explained for the Veda, the compounding, the disjoining of the compounded expressions, and the separation of words in the Padapāṭha, so will I explain the fourfold word - noun, verb, pre-verb, and particle.

Note: As for the structure of this passage, Whitney (1862: 184, fn) says: "With the slight alteration of *yatho' vāca* to *yathā" ha*, we should have here three equal successive *pādas* of a metrical verse: but the impossibility of forcing the last compound into any such metrical form, as a fourth *pāda*, renders it very doubtful whether this is anything more than a curious coincidence, and whether the words are not meant for simpler prose." With all the mss. variants at hand, it is still not possible to restore the correct metrical form of this passage, if indeed it had any originally.

४.१.२. आख्यातं यत्क्रियावाचि नाम सत्त्वाख्यमुच्यते ।
निपाताश्चादयोऽसत्त्व उपसर्गास्तु प्रादयः ॥

Whitney (p. 261) quotes this as part of the commentary. C: no such verse.

> **Translation:** The word which expresses action is the verb. The word which names an object is said to be a noun. Words like *ca*, when they do not refer to an object, are particles. However, words like *pra* are pre-verbs.

Note: The verse represents a mixture of the doctrines which are found in diverse texts like Pāṇini's grammar, Yāska's NR, and other Prātiśākhyas. The definitions of verb and noun given here are more in line with those given by the NR (p. 23): भावप्रधानमाख्यातम्, सत्त्वप्रधानानि नामानि. Also see RPR (12.17-19): तन्नाम येनाभिदधाति सत्त्वम्, तदाख्यातं येन भावं सधातु. Patañjali's MB (MLBD edn., Vol.II., p. 625) uses *kriyā* instead of *bhāva* : क्रियाप्रधानमाख्यातं भवति । द्रव्यप्रधानं नाम. Pāṇini, on the other hand, offers non-semantic formal definitions for the categories of noun and verb, cf. P.1.2.45 (अर्थवदधातुरप्रत्ययः प्रातिपदिकम्), P.1.2.46 (कृत्तद्धितसमासाश्च), P.1.3.1 (भूवादयो धातवः). For a detailed discussion of the differences between these definitions, see: Deshpande (1992: 10-15). The definition of *nipāta* reminds us of P.1.4.57 (चादयोऽसत्त्वे), and the definition of *upasarga* by referring to a list beginning with *pra* reminds us of P.1.4.58 (प्रादयः) and P.1.4.59 (उपसर्गाः क्रियायोगे). However, we must keep in mind that the categories of *nipāta* and *upasarga* are not exclusive categories for Pāṇini, and both of these are ultimately subsumed for him in the category of *prātipadika* 'nominal stem.' For details, see the Note on CA (1.3.18). The fourfold division, on the whole, represents a non-Pāṇinian tradition, though it is referred to and utilized by the post-Pāṇinian grammarians commenting on Pāṇini, cf. Deshpande (1992: 13ff).

४.१.३. नाम नाम्नानुदात्तेन समस्तं प्रकृतिस्वरम् ।
न युष्मदस्मद्वचनानि न चामन्त्रितमिष्यते ॥

Whitney (p. 261): °नाम्नानुदात्तेन° quoted as part of the commentary. A, B: Daṇḍa after °मुदात्ते. C: no such verse. Most mss. read: नाम्नामुदात्तेन. However, I agree with Whitney's emendation to °नाम्नानुदात्तेन°, though Whitney does not call it an emendation. His ms. actually reads नाम्नामुदात्तेन.

> **Translation:** A noun, brought together with an unaccented noun, retains its natural accent. However, not desired [in this context] are (enclitic) forms of *yuṣmad* or *asmad*, or a vocative.

Note: Whitney (1862: 263) interprets the first half of the verse to mean: "a noun which has its natural accent is compounded with another which is unaccented." As examples of the first part of this verse, Whitney says: "thus we must combine *tri : saptā́ḥ* (i.1.1), *śatá : vr̥ṣṇyam* (i.3.1), into *tri-ṣaptā́ḥ*, *śatá-vr̥ṣṇyam*."

I have a slightly different understanding of the term *samastam.* In my opinion, the term does not refer to compounding as it is understood in a limited sense in the Pāṇinian grammar, but it probably is equivalent to the wider post-Pāṇinian conception of *vr̥tti* as found in Kātyāyana, Patañjali, and the later grammarians like Bhartr̥hari. It becomes inclusive of the traditional notion of compounding (*samāsa*), but additionally includes processes like the addition of the *taddhita* and *kr̥t* affixes, and the formation of secondary verbs. In some of these cases, the Padapāṭha does not completely isolate the items, but separates their members with an *avagraha.* For a discussion of this conception of *vr̥tti*, in the context of Padapāṭha, see K.V. Abhyankar (1974: 5ff).

Thus, we can point to *áṅge aṅge* (AV 1.12.2) as a positive example of this rule. Here, the Padapāṭha treats these two as members of a compound-expression and separates them only with an *avagraha*: *áṅge-aṅge.* On the other hand, consider the following counter-examples. In *vásoṣpate* (AV 1.1.2), the unaccented *pate* is a vocative, and the Padapāṭha does not treat this as a compound word: *vásoḥ* / *pate* /. Similarly, the unaccented enclitic forms of *asmad* and *yuṣmad,* such as *te* and *naḥ*, are not treated by the Padapāṭha as forming a compound-expression with the preceding accented noun: *ténā te* (AV 1.3.3) : Pada - *téna* / *te; tā́ naḥ* (AV 1.4.2) : Pada - *tā́ḥ* / *naḥ.*

४.१.४. नामानुदात्तं प्रकृतिस्वरो गतिरनुच्चो वा नाम चेत्स्यादुदात्तम् ।

Whitney (p. 261) quotes this as part of the commentary. A, B: °वेश्या° for °चेत्स्या°. C: no such rule.

Translation: An unaccented noun and a naturally accented particle [= *gati*, are treated in the Padapāṭha as a compound-expression]. Or, if the noun is accented, then with an unaccented particle, [it is treated as a compound-expression in the Padapāṭha].

Note: The term *gati* is repeatedly used by these rules without strictly defining it. It is defined by P.1.4.60-79 as applying to a whole host of prepositions and particles, and particle-like items, compare the expression *upasarga-vr̥tti* 'items which behave like an *upasarga*' in CA (4.1.22).

We may offer the following examples to illustrate the teachings of this rule. In *úpahūtaḥ* (AV 1.1.4), the accented particle *úpa* is compounded with the unaccented *hūtaḥ,* cf. Padapāṭha : *úpa-hūtaḥ*. On this expression, the commentary of [Pseudo-]Sāyaṇa says: 'गतिरनन्तर' (पा.६.२.४९) इति गतेः प्रकृतिस्वरत्वम् । 'उपसर्गाश्चाभिवर्जम्' (फिट्सूत्र ४.१३) इत्युपशब्द आद्युदात्तः. In *niṣécanam* (AV 1.3.1), the unaccented *ni* is compounded with the accented word *sécanam*, cf. Padapāṭha : *ni-sécanam.* In this example, by P.6.2.139 (गतिकारकोपपदात् कृत्), the word *sécana* is allowed to retain its derivational accent, and the particle *ní* loses its original accent and becomes unaccented. While Pāṇini's grammar, as part of its derivational process, teaches us how an item which is 'originally' (*prakr̥tisvara* = lexical accent) accented can lose its accent in the process of being combined with other words in compounding etc., the Prātiśākhya simply looks at the result that the particle *ni* in the example cited above is unaccented. While the Prātiśākhya does not clearly specify the circumstances under which a particle may lose its accent, it does have the conception of its original or lexical accent.

४.१.५. क्रियायोगे गतिः पूर्वः समासो यावन्तोऽनुच्चाः समर्थास्तान्समस्येत् ।

Whitney (p. 261) quotes this as part of the commentary. Whitney, H: °समर्थांस्तान्°. Whitney, H, J: °समस्यते. E, F, I: Daṇḍa after क्रियायोगे. A, B: °समासोर्या°, °स्तात्समस्येत्. C: no such rule. O: °गतिपूर्वः°.

Translation: A preceding [unaccented] particle (*gati*) is compounded with a verb. As many semantically related unaccented particles there may be, they should all be compounded [with the following verb].

Note: The verse here deals with the compounding of the pre-verbs with finite verbs. Thus, a proper example may be *pariyánti* (AV 1.1.1), where an unaccented *pari* is compounded with an accented verb: Padapāṭha : *pari-yánti*, with an *avagraha* indicating that this is a compound-expression. On this expression, the commentary of [Pseudo]-Sāyaṇa says: उदात्तवता तिङा गतेः समासवचनमिति परिशब्दस्य तिङन्तेन समासः । 'तिङि चोदात्तवति' (पा.८.१.७१) इति गतेरनुदात्तत्वम्. An accented pre-verb is not compounded with the following unaccented verb.

The second part of the verse lays down a rule which, as far as I understand, is repeated in part in CA (4.1.6) and CA (4.1.24: अनेकोऽनुदात्तेनापि). The CAB on CA (4.1.24) offers a number of examples, where several unaccented pre-verbs, followed by an accented pre-verb, are all compounded with the following verb form:

> ***चतुराध्यायीभाष्य*** - अनेक उपसर्गः अनुदात्तेनापि आख्यातेन सह समस्यते। 'उत्ऽअवंस्यति' (पद, अ.वे. ९.६.५४, VVRI edn.: ९.११.६)। 'सम्ऽ-आचिंनुष्व । अनुऽसम्प्रयांहि' (पद, अ.वे. ११.१.३६)। 'उपऽसम्परांन(H: ण)यात्' (पद, अ.वे. १८.४.५०)। उपसर्गवृत्तिभिश्च । 'अच्छऽआवंदामसि' (पद, अ.वे. ७.३८.३, VVRI edn.: ७.३९.३)। 'अभिऽहिङ्कृंणोत' (पद, अ.वे. १२.३.३७)।

The present rule, as well as CA (4.1.24), seem to also allow a host of unaccented pre-verbs to be compounded with an accented verb. However, all the instances in the CAB on CA (4.1.24) are of unaccented verb preceded by an accented pre-verb, preceded by one or more unaccented pre-verbs. We need to find instances in the AV of an accented verb compounded with a plurality of unaccented pre-verbs. A.A. Macdonell (1916: 469) offers an instance of this type: *pariprayāthá* (RV 4.51.5), RV-Padapāṭha : *pari-prayāthá.* It seems that such an instance is difficult to find in the AV, in view of the APR rule (12c, p. 11), which says that when an accented verb is preceded by two *upasargas*, the first of them is isolated as a separate word. All the instances offered under this rule have the first *upasarga*, treated here as a *karmapravacanīya* and is accented, e.g. *abhí vipáśyāmi* (AV 12.1.33).

४.१.६. यत्रानेकोऽनुदात्तोऽस्ति परश्च प्रकृतिस्वरः ।
आख्यातं नाम वा यत्स्यात्सर्वमेव समस्यते ॥

Whitney (p. 261) quotes this as part of the commentary. A, B, D, M: °प्रकृतिः स्वरः°. E, F, I, O: यत्रानेकोप्यनुच्चोस्ति°. C: no such verse.

Translation: Where there is more than one unaccented [particle/preverb = *gati*], and where the following [word? particle/preverb = *gati* ?] retains its original accent [i.e. remains *udātta*], the following verb or noun is compounded with all these.

Note: Examples of unaccented verbs, compounded with the preceding accented *upasarga*, preceded further by one or more unaccented *upasargas*, are found in the CAB on CA 4.1.24: अनुऽसम्प्रयांहि' (पद, अ.वे. ११.१.३६)। 'उपऽसम्परांनयात्' (पद, अ.वे. १८.४.५०)।

As I have indicated by the question-mark in my translation, the phrase *paraś ca prakr̥tisvaraḥ* could perhaps mean 'where the following word retains its original accent,' and this may be taken to refer to the following verb or noun maintaining its original accent. In my Note on the previous rule, I have mentioned that the APR rule (12c, p. 11) seems to be against the possibility of an accented verb being compounded with more than one unaccented pre-verb. However, we do find examples of a plurality of unaccented pre-verbs compounded with a verbal noun, if we include a gerund among verbal nouns: *abhyudétya* (AV 15.11.2), Padapāṭha : *abhi-udétya*. This is a combination of *abhi+ud+ā* with the gerund form *ítya*, which retains its accent in the compound-expression.

४.१.७. सोपसर्गं तु यन्नीचैः पूर्वं वा यदि वा परम् ।
उदात्तेन समस्यन्ते तथैव सुप्रतिष्ठितम् ॥

Whitney (p. 261) quotes this as part of the commentary. H, J, M, P: °यदि वा परः°. D, E, F, I, O, P: °यथैतत्सुप्रतिष्ठितं. I: °समस्येते°. C: no such verse. D omits उदात्तेन समस्यन्ते.

Translation: An unaccented word, accompanied by a preverb, is compounded with an [another?] accented [preverb], [irrespective of?] whether [the accented preverb] is the first one or the second one. Thus is the example *súpratiṣṭhitam.*

Note: This is verse 5 in Whitney's (1862: 263) text, and he says: "Verse five has for its subject such compounds as are instanced by *súpratiṣṭhitam* (xii.1.63 : p. *sú-pratiṣṭhitam.*" Here, *prati+ṣṭhitam* is unaccented and is compounded further with the accented preverb *sú*. As an instance illustrating the second *upasarga* being the accented one, we can cite *upā́kr̥tam* (AV

2.34.2), Padapāṭha : *upa-ā́kr̥tam*. Here, the basic word, *kr̥tam* is unaccented. However, of the two *upasargas*, it is the second one which is the accented *upasarga*, in contrast with the example *súpratiṣṭhitam*.

४.१.८. उदात्तस्तु निपातो यः सोऽनुदात्तः क्वचिद्भवेत् ।
समस्यन्ते तथाविधमितिहासो निदर्शनम् ॥

Whitney (p. 261) quotes this as part of the commentary. H, I: °विधिः मिति°. D, O: °समस्यते°. E, F, O: °यथाविधमिति°. Others: °तथाविधिमिति°. C: no such verse. O: °सानुदात्तः°.

Translation: A particle which is [normally] accented can occasionally become unaccented, and as such is compounded. An instance of that kind is *itihāsáḥ*.

Note: The word *itihāsáḥ* (AV 15.6.4) is analyzed by the Padapāṭha as *itiha-āsáḥ*. The lexical accent of *iti* is *íti*, and the *ha* is lexically unaccented. However, the item *íti* loses its accent in the process of compounding.

४.१.९. नघारिषां सुसहेत्येवमादीन्युदाहरेत् ।
सहेत्यनेनानुदात्तं परं नाम समस्यते ॥

Whitney (p. 261) quotes this as part of the commentary. Whitney: °सुसहे°. B, D: °सहसहे°. C: no such verse. O: °सहेत्येनानुदात्तं°. P: नघरिषां°. All other mss. read ससहे°, and Whitney reads °सुसहे°, though his manuscript actually reads ससहे°. In any case, in spite of the fact that no manuscript directly supports it, I believe that Whitney's emendation offers the correct original reading, and I have adopted it in the text of the verse. Also see the Note below.

Translation: [Additionally, for the preceding rule], one should offer examples such as *naghāriṣā́m* and *súsaha*. [The next rule:] An unaccented noun is compounded with the preceding *sahá*. [Examples in the next verse *ab*.]

Note: The form *naghāriṣām* occurs in AV (7.7.6). Whitney (AV *Transl.* Vol.II., 499) remarks: "The mss. again are much at variance as to the reading of *naghāriṣā́m*, Bp.I.M.p.m.E.p.m.O. read ⌊Bp. with *-ghă-*⌋ *naghār̥ṣā́m*. ⌊Ppp. reads *naghāriṣām* (as does Berlin ed.).⌋"

The reading found in most mss., i.e. *sasahe*° makes no sense in this context, and probably represents the confusion of *susaha* and *sasahe*, enhanced by the presence in the AV of the form *sasahe* (AV 1.16.3; 2.5.3). However, this is a verb form with reduplication, and does not illustrate anything in the present context.

The examples *naghāriṣā́m* (AV 8.2.6, 7.6) and *sú́saha* (AV 6.64.3) are intended to illustrate the rule given in the previous verse. Normally, *ná* is an accented particle, but it loses its accent in the first example. Similarly, *sahá* is normally accented on the last syllable. However, it loses its accent in the compound-expression *sú́saha*.

४.१.१० अनुदात्तेन चोदात्तं सभावो यत्र चोच्यते । सहसूक्तवाकः सान्तर्देशाः शतक्रतो [सकृतौ?] निदर्शनम् ॥

Whitney (p. 261) quotes this as part of the commentary. E, F, I, O: °चोदात्तमभावो°. C: no such verse. O: °सातदेशाः°. Other mss. read स्वभावो. The reading सभावो is my emendation. See the Note below.

> **Translation:** [Continuing the previous topic of compounding of *sahá*]: And, where the change [of *sahá*] to *sa* is taught, an accented word is compounded with the unaccented [*sa*]. The illustrations are *sahásūktavākaḥ*, *sā́ntardeśāḥ*, and *śatakrato*.

Note: I have translated the first part of the verse, assuming the emendation *sabhāvo* referring to the change of *sahá* to *sa*. In my opinion, the manuscript readings *codāttaṃ svabhāvo* and *codāttam abhāvo* are corruptions for *codāttaṃ sabhāvo*, because the copyists could not understand the word *sabhāvo*, and replaced it with the more familiar words, which actually make no sense in the context.

The examples *sahásūktavākaḥ* (AV 7.97.6) and *sā́ntardeśāḥ* (AV 9.5.37) illustrate the two types of combinations. In the first combination, the accented word *sahá* is combined with the unaccented *sūktavākaḥ*. In the second combination, the unaccented *sa* is combined with the accented *ántardeśāḥ*, cf. Padapāṭha : *sa-ántardeśāḥ*. As for the example *śatakrato* (AV 14.1.41), Whitney (1862: 263) comments: "*śatakrato* is also added, but apparently only by a blunder; or rather, the reading is probably false and corrupt, as the metre helps to show." All the manuscripts have this reading, and yet the reading makes no sense in this context. I would like to suggest that *śatakrato* is an ancient error of a copyist for *sakṛ́tau* (AV 11.1.10) which is analyzed by the

Padapāṭha as *sa-kṛ́tau*, a compound of an accented word with the unaccented *sa* for *sahá*. This copyist's error must be truly ancient to get into all the available manuscripts. This may indicate that ultimately all our existing manuscripts go back to a common source which had this error.

४.१.११. अनुदात्तो गतिर्मध्ये पूर्वपरौ प्रकृतिस्वरौ । पूर्वेण विग्रहस्तत्र पुरुषेऽधि समाहिते ॥

Whitney (p. 262) quotes this as part of the commentary. A, B, D, P: अनुदात्तानुगति°. Other mss. read: अनुदात्तोऽनुगतिर्मध्ये. Whitney's emendation: अनुदात्तो गतिर्मध्ये°, °समाहितः. C, E, F, I, O: in a different location. J: no such verse. I have adopted Whitney's emendation over the manuscripts. The reading अनुदात्तोऽनुगतिः probably developed due to the scribal confusion with उदात्तोनुगतिः in the next verse. The prevalence of this confusion in most manuscripts also hints at its presence in the archetype from which probably all our surviving manuscripts are derived. For a similar phenomenon, see my Note on the preceding verse.

> **Translation:** Where there is an unaccented pre-verb [= *gati*] in between the preceding and the following [pre-verbs], both of which have their natural accent [*udātta*], the first of these is isolated [in the Padapāṭha as a separate word], for example: *púruṣé 'dhi samā́hite* (AV 10.7.15).

Note: In the example cited by the verse, there are three pre-verbs [*gati, upasarga*], such that the first and the third are *udātta,* while the second one is unaccented, i.e. *ádhi+sam+ā́.* The verse says that in such a sequence, the first preverb is isolated in the Padapāṭha as an independent word, namely that it is not treated as part of a compound. This is confirmed by the Padapāṭha. Here, one may say that *ádhi* is syntactically related to *púruṣe*, rather than with *samā́hite*, and, hence, to use the Pāṇinian terminology, it is a true preposition (*karmapravacanīya*), rather than a preverb (*upasarga*). Both categories are subsumed under the wider category of *gati* in the Pāṇinian grammar, as is apparently the case with these verses. The phrase *púruṣé 'dhi samā́hitāḥ* appears in the same verse. The grammatical theory as expressed in the verse pays attention only to the sequence of accented or unaccented items, but does not seem to pay much attention to the syntactic component.

४.१.१२. उदात्तोऽनुगतिर्यत्रानुदात्तं परं पदम् ।
पूर्वेण विग्रहस्तत्र संसुभूत्या निदर्शनम् ॥

Whitney (p. 262) quotes this as part of the commentary. B, D, M: उदात्तौ नु गतिर्यत्रा°. E, F, J: अनुदात्तोनुगतिर्यत्रा°. C: no such verse. O, P: उदात्तो-नुगति°. Others: उदात्तानुगति. The meter requires a hiatus: यत्र अनुदात्तं.

Translation: Where an accented [pre-verb, particle, *gati*] is followed by a pre-verb, and where the following word is unaccented, in such a case, the first [pre-verb, particle, *gati*] is isolated [in the Padapāṭha as a separate word], for example: *sáṃ súbhūtyā* (AV 3.14.1).

Note: Whitney (1862: 263) describes this verse as: "where two accented prepositions precede an unaccented noun, the former of them is to be made independent." The Padapāṭha for the example reads: *sám / sú-bhūtyā /*. The verse does not clearly say that both the pre-verbs must be accented. However, given that the noun is said to be unaccented, this makes the compounded pre-verb an accented item.

We should note that, the logic of this verse is not entirely clear. The actual practice of the AV Padapāṭha, which is also corroborated by 54 examples listed under APR (10, pp. 9-11), seems to provide a somewhat generalized rule. When an accented or unaccented verbal noun (*kr̥danta*) is preceded by two *upasarga*s, with the first one being an accented *upasarga / karmapravacanīya*, it is isolated as a separate word in the Padapāṭha. For instance, *ápa durmatím* (AV 14.2.6). Here, *dur* is unaccented, *matím* is accented, and yet the Padapāṭha isolates *ápa* as an independent word. There is a large number of examples of this kind.

४.१.१३. यत्रोभे प्रकृतिस्वरे पूर्वं यच्च परं च यत् ।
वर्जयित्वाद्युदात्तानि सर्वमेव विगृह्यते ॥

Whitney (p. 262) quotes this as part of the commentary. E, F, O: यत्रो-भेदप्रकृतिस्वरे°. Whitney: °पूर्वे°. F, M: °त्वाद्युत्तादानि°. E, F, I, O: °सर्वमेव विगृह्यते. Others: सर्वमेव समस्यते. C: no such verse.

Translation: Where both the first and the second [*upasarga*s] are naturally accented (*udātta*), in such cases, after isolating the initial accented items [as independent words in the Padapāṭha], all the items are separated.

Note: On this verse, Whitney (1862: 263) remarks: "Verse 11 has no example, and, although easily enough translated, its meaning is to me obscure."

To begin to make sense of this verse, we need to properly interpret the term *ādyudātta*.

On the one hand, the term *ādyudātta* understood as 'an item with its initial syllable with the *udātta* accent,' distinguishes between accented and unaccented preverbs, and then distinguishes between those which are accented on the first syllable, and the ones which are accented on the last syllable. Such a distinction is possible only with polysyllabic *upasarga*s. CA (4.1.19-21) below tell us that all the twenty *upasarga*s are naturally accented. Out of the eleven polysyllabic *upasarga*s, *abhí* is the only one which is accented on the final syllable. All the others are accented on the first syllable. If the verse above, as translated here, is to be meaningful, it refers to a difference of behavior between *abhí* and the rest of the *upasargas*. I have not been able to detect any clear behavioral difference.

Therefore, I have chosen to interpret the term *ādyudāttāni* in the verse to refer to 'initial accented items.' If this meaning is accepted, then we can find examples to illustrate this verse. As far as I can see, all the 57 examples listed under APR (13c, pp. 12-14) would fall into this category. Here, typically, an unaccented verb is preceded by two accented *upasarga*s, and the Padapāṭha isolates all of these as separate words. For example: *úpa prā́gāt* (AV 1.28.1), Padapāṭha : *úpa / prá / agāt /*.

I should note here that over half the mss. read सर्वमेव समस्यते instead of सर्वमेव विगृह्यते. I have chosen the latter reading, and I admit, along with Whitney, that I cannot make any sense of the former.

४.१.१४. नाख्यातानि समस्यन्ते न चाख्यातं च नाम च । नाम नाम्नोपसर्गैस्तु संबद्धार्थं समस्यते ॥

Whitney (p. 261) quotes this as part of the commentary. E, F, I, O: नामाख्यातानि समस्यंते°. A, B, D, P: °पसर्ग्रै°. C: no such verse. P: नाख्यानि समस्यंते°. O: °नाम्नोपसर्गेस्तु°. H: संवधार्थं. Others: संबंधार्थं.

Translation: Verbs are not compounded [with each other], nor is a verb and a noun compound [with each other]. However, a semantically related noun is compounded with a noun or with a pre-verb (*upasarga*).

Note: The reading *sambandhārtham*, as supported by most manuscripts, and by Whitney (1862: 262), would literally mean: 'for the sake of relationship.' However, taking a hint from the reading संवधार्थं in H, I have chosen to amend the text to संबद्धार्थं. The word *sambaddhārtha* as an equivalent to *samartha* is found in the MB on P.2.1.1 (Kielhorn edn., Vol.I., p. 365): सम्बद्धार्थः समर्थः. Also relevant in the context is the fact that the APR (3, p. 3) is identical with P.2.1.1 (समर्थः पदविधिः), and that the APR often brings up the notion that no compounding takes places between items which are *asamartha,* cf. APR (13b, p. 12). I suspect that the present verse is making a similar statement. The statement सम्बद्धार्थं समस्यते of this verse is comparable to APR (13b, p. 12):

उपसर्गपूर्वमाख्यातं यत्रोभाभ्यां समस्यते ।
सामर्थ्यमुभयोस्तत्रासामर्थ्येषु विग्रहः ॥.

४.१.१५. न युष्मदस्मदादेशा अनुदात्ताः पदात्परे । नामोपसर्गगतिभिः समस्यन्ते कदाचन ॥

Whitney (p. 262) quotes this as part of the commentary. A, B: °अनुदात्तान्पदा°. I, M, P: °अनुदात्ताः पदा°. Others: °अनुदात्तात्पदा°. C: no such verse. P: °नाम्नोपसर्गगतिभिः ... कदाचनः°.

Translation: The unaccented forms of *yuṣmad* and *asmad* which occur after [other words, i.e. are enclitic,] are never compounded with nouns, preverbs and prepositional items.

Note: Examples for this verse are found in the first half of the next verse.

४.१.१६. मामनुप्रतेप्रवामित्येवमादीन्युदाहरेत् । एतदश्चानुदात्तानि इदमश्च तथैव च ॥

Whitney (p. 262) quotes this as part of the commentary. Whitney: °मित्येवमा°, °एतदश्चोनुदात्तानि°. A, B, D: °दींन्यु°. E, F, I, O: मामनुप्रते पुत्रमित्येव°. Others: मामनुप्रतेप्रवामी°. E, F, I, O: एतदश्चानुदात्तानीदमश्च°. A, B, D, J, M: °पदमस्य तथैव च. Others: एतदस्यानुदात्तानि इदमस्य. C: no such verse.

Translation: [To illustrate the rule in the previous verse], one should offer examples such as: *mā́m ánu prá te* (AV 3.18.6) and *prá vām* (AV 7.73.5). [The second half of this verse goes with the next verse, and is translated below].

Note: The Padapāṭha isolates *prá* from *te* and *vām* in these examples to indicate that they are separate words, and not members of compounds.

४.१.१७. नामोपसर्गगतिभिः समस्यन्ते कदाचन ।
बृहन्नेषां य एनां वनिमायन्ति पर्येनान्
पर्यस्येति निदर्शनम् ॥

Whitney (p. 262) quotes this as part of the commentary. C: no such rule. P: एनं for एनां.

Translation: [Beginning with the second half of the previous verse]: The unaccented forms of *etad*, as well as those of *idam*, are never compounded with nouns, pre-verbs, and prepositional items. The examples are: *bṛhánn eṣām* (AV 4.16.1), *yá enāṃ vaním āyánti* (AV 12.4.11), *páry enān* (AV 9.2.5), and *páry asya* (AV 15.12.7).

Note: It is clear that this must be a prohibitory rule. However, the text of the verses does not contain an explicit *na*. We need to continue the force of *na* in the previous rule into this rule, perhaps indicated by *ca* "also." The Padapāṭha clearly separates the forms *eṣām, enām, enān,* and *asya* from the neighboring words to indicate that there is no compounding.

४.१.१८. अनुदात्तो गतिः सर्वैः समस्तः स्वरितादिभिः ।
संस्राव्येण दुरर्मण्य आचार्येति निदर्शनम् ॥

Whitney (p. 262) quotes this as part of the commentary. E, F, I, O: reads CA 4.1.11 in this place, and read this verse in another location. E, F, H, I, M: अनुदात्तोनुगतिः सर्वैः समस्तस्वरितादिभिः°. E, F, I: °सँस्राव्येण निर्दुरर्मण्य°. E, F, H, I, O: °आचार्येति°. Others: आचार्य इति. C: no such verse. O: °संस्राव्येण निदुर्मण्य°. P: °संस्राव्ये दुर्मण्य°.

Translation: An unaccented prepositional item is compounded with all kinds of words which have circumflex and other accents, for example: *saṃsrāvyèṇa* (AV 1.15.1), *durar-maṇyàḥ* (AV 16.2.1), and *ācāryàḥ* (AV 11.5.3).

Note: Given the fact that the reading *svaritādibhiḥ* is supported by all mss., it can either mean '*svarita* etc.' or 'those which begin with a *svarita* syllable.' Since the second meaning does not seem to be even remotely applicable, we must accept the first meaning. Whitney (1862: 263) takes this to mean 'however accented,' and then says that the verse "illustrates only their composition with a circumflexed word." All the three illustrations demonstrate the same type, i.e. compounding of an unaccented prepositional item with the following word with a *svarita* accent. How about the compounding of an unaccented prepositional item with words with *udātta* or *anudātta* accents? If our understanding of the verse is correct, this should be possible.

We can find a large number of instances where an unaccented prepositional item is compounded with the following word with an *udātta* syllable, e.g. *sumatím* (AV 4.25.6). However, it is not easy to find an unaccented prepositional item compounded with an unaccented (*sarvānudātta*) word. The only cases I can locate in the text of the AV are those where a previous compound becomes completely unaccented through further embedding, e.g. *ṛtáprajātā* (AV 1.11.1), where the segment *prajātā* becomes completely unaccented because of its further compounding with *ṛtá*. Otherwise, the word would be accented as *prájātā* (AV 1.34.1).

The AV mss. read *durarmaṇya* (AV 15.2.1). However, Whitney (AV *Transl.* Vol.II., p. 795) remarks: "The translation implies the change of *durar-maṇyàs* to *duradmanyàs,* as proposed by the Pet. Lexx. (add TB. iii.3.9[9] as a reference for *duradmanī́*). The reading of the mss. is, however, assured by its quotation in the Prāt., and three times in the Kāuś."

४.१.१९. प्रपराणिसमादुर्णिरवाधिपरिवीति च ।
अत्यपिसूदपाभीत्युपानुप्रति विंशतिः ॥

Whitney (p. 262) quotes this as part of the commentary. A, B, H: °सामा°. E, F, I: °समानिर्दु°. O: °समासाभिर्दुरवाधि°. Whitney, H: °परिवीनि°. A, B, D, J, M: °अव्यपि सूदयाभी°. A, B, D: °सूदयाभीत्पुनायानु°. C: no such verse. O: °सूदपाभीत्युपानु°. P: °भीत्युपादानुप्रति°.

Translation: *Prá, párā, ní, sám, ā́, dúr, nír, áva, ádhi, pári, ví, áti, ápi, sú, úd, ápa, abhí, úpa, ánu,* and *práti* are the twenty [*upasarga*s].

Note: For the second half of the verse, the meter requires us to read: अत्यपिसूदपाभीति उपानुप्रति विंशतिः.

४.१.२०. एकाक्षरा उदात्ता आद्युदात्तास्तथापरे । अभीत्यन्त उपसर्गाः क्रियायोगे गतिस्तथा ॥

Whitney (p. 262) quotes this as part of the commentary. I: एकाक्षरा उदात्तास्त आद्यु°. K: अभीत्यन्ता. Other mss. and Whitney: °अभीत्यन्त उप°. A, B, D: °सर्गा क्रिया°. C: no such verse. O: एकाक्षरमुदात्ता°.

> **Translation:** Of these, the monosyllabic ones have the high-pitch accent. Others have their first syllable with the high-pitch accent, [except for] *abhí* [which has its] final [syllable with the high-pitch accent]. In conjunction with verbs, these items are called *upasarga,* as well as *gati.*

Note: The lone reading in I, i.e. एकाक्षरा उदात्तास्त आद्यु° looks like an effort to regularize a line which is otherwise metrically deficient, and this indicates that the metrically deficient reading, supported by most manuscripts, is the earlier reading.

The expression *abhītyanta(ḥ)* must be interpreted to mean *abhītyantodāttaḥ.* The final part of the verse उपसर्गाः क्रियायोगे गतिस्तथा calls to mind P.1.4.59 (उपसर्गाः क्रियायोगे) and P.1.4.60 (गतिश्च).

४.१.२१. आद्युदात्ता दशैतेषामुच्चा एकाक्षरा नव । विंशतेरुपसर्गाणामन्तोदात्तस्त्वभीत्ययम् ॥

Whitney (p. 262) quotes this as part of the commentary. A, B, D, M: °सर्ग्रा°. C: no such verse. O: °दशैतेषाउच्चा°.

> **Translation:** Of these twenty *upasarga*s, ten [polysyllabic ones] have their initial syllable high-pitched, nine monosyllabic ones are high-pitched, and *abhí* has its final syllable high-pitched.

Note: This verse is quoted in the Prātiśākhyapradīpaśikṣā (Śikṣāsaṃgraha, p. 267). It is prefaced with *tathā coktam,* and the first and the second lines are reversed. In the same form, this verse occurs in the RPR (12.22-24). Uvaṭa's comment on this verse runs as: प्र, आ, निः, दुः, वि, सम्, नि, सु, उत्,

इत्येतेषामुपसर्गाणां नवसंख्या एकाक्षराः उच्चाः उदात्ताः इत्यर्थः । एतेषामुपसर्गाणां दशाद्युदात्ता वेदितव्याः । परा, अनु, उप, अप, परि, प्रति, अति, अधि, अव, अपि इत्येते । एतेषामेवोपसर्गाणां मध्ये अभि इत्ययमन्तोदात्तो वेदितव्यः ।

४.१.२२. अच्छारमस्तंहस्तलांगूलंतिरःपुरःपुनर्णवश्येतीवातीफलीहिंस्रुग्वषड्डुलुलाककजास्वाहास्वधाश्रत्स्वरललेत्युपसर्गवृत्तीनि यथाम्नातस्वराणि ।

Whitney (p, 262) quotes this as part of the commentary. All mss: °हस्तोलांगूलं°. Whitney: °हस्तलांगूलं°, °पुनर्णमः°, °क्षितीवाती°, °वषट्प्रादुरुलाककजा°, °यथास्तातस्वराणि°. All mss: °पुनर्णवः°. B, D: °अच्छादमस्तं°. E, F, I, O: °श्येतीवाती°. H: °क्षितीवाती°. Others: °सिनीवाली°. E, F: °वषुड्डुला°. E, F, H, I: °श्रत्स्वरल°. O: °श्रत्स्वररला इत्यु°. Other: °सृक्स्वर°. A, B, D: °पसर्ग्र° for °पसर्ग°. E, F, I, O: °यथाम्नातः स्वराणि°. Others: यथाम्नातस्वरितानि. C: no such rule. P: °तिरः पुनः पुनर्णवः ... सिनीवाती ... वषड्डुला ... स्तरललेत्यपसर्ग्र°. H: °वषड्गुदुरुला°. This is probably the most corrupt passage in this entire text.

Translation: The following items, [though not listed as *upasargas*], behave like *upasargas*, and their accents are as recited: *áccha, áram, ástam, hásta, lāṅgūlam, tiráḥ, puráḥ, púnaḥ, nava, śyetī́, vātī́, phalī, híṃ, srúk, váṣaṭ, ululā , kakajā́, svā́hā, svadhā́, śrat, svàr, alalā.*

Note: Whitney (1862) took great pains to make sense of this passage, for which he had only one manuscript. We shall begin by noting his comments (1862: 263-4): "Finally, the last verse (or prose passage) attempts to give a list of those words which are treated as if they were prepositions, although properly belonging to what it includes and what it omits. A part of the forms which it contains are in frequent use, and familiarly known as bearing marked analogies with the prepositions proper. Such are *achā, tiraḥ, puraḥ, punaḥ, hiṅ, prāduḥ,* and *śrat*. Others, as *aram* and *astam*, are more remotely connected with the same class. *Vaṣaṭ, svāhā*, and *vātī* are in the Atharvan compounded only with *kāra* and *kr̥ta*, and hardly in such a manner as should require their inclusion in the list. *Svadhā* and *sruk* form no other compounds than *svadhākāra* and *srukkāra* (ix.6.22); *phalī* forms *phalīkaraṇa* (xi.3.6); *kakajā* forms *kakajākr̥ta* (xi.10.25). *Namas* enters into *namaskāra, namaskr̥ta*, and *namaskr̥tya* (vii.102.1), which last affords actually good ground for special treatment, as does *hastagr̥hya* (e.g. v.14.4), on account of which *hasta* is ranked with the others. For *lāṅgūla, kṣitī,* and *ulā*, I can find nothing at all in the Atharvan :

there is room in the case of the two last, and especially of the third, to suspect corrupted readings. What may be hidden in *svaralalā*, I have not been able to discover, nor how the last word in the extract, which apparently has to do with the accent of the words treated of, is to be amended into intelligibility."

With the new set of manuscripts at our disposal, and with further thought on the listed items, I think it is now possible to advance beyond Whitney's difficulties. We shall look at the listed items individually:

1. *Áccha*. For example: *ácchā vada* (AV 3.20.2). Compare P.1.4.69 (अच्छ गत्यर्थवदेषु), which treats *áccha* as a *gati*.

2. *Áram (= álam)*. For example: *áraṅkṛtam* (AV 12.1.22). Compare P.1.4.64 (भूषणेऽलम्), which treats *álam* as a *gati*.

3. *Ástam*. For example: *astameṣyaté* (AV 17.1.23). Compare P.1.4.68 (अस्तं च), which treats *ástam* as a *gati*.

4. *Hásta*. For example: *hastagṛ́hya* (AV 5.14.4). Compare P.1.4.77 (नित्यं हस्ते पाणावुपयमने), which treats *haste* as a *gati*. The mss. reading *hasto* is probably a corruption of *haste*, as it is found in P.1.4.77.

5. *Lāṅgūlam*. The word *lāṅgūla* is attested in the Paippalāda AV (9.8.1) in the expression *lāṅgūla-gṛhya*, which is directly comparable with *hasta-gṛ́hya* (AV 5.14.4). Such an occurrence accounts for its being listed as an *upasarga-vṛtti* item. In my view, this is the best explanation. However, I would like to mention two further possibilities.

A possible reading is *uluṅgulam*. All manuscripts have the reading *hastolāṅgūlaṃ*, which Whitney amended to *hastalāṅgūlam*. This did not account for the *o* in *hasto*. My guess is that *hastoluṅgulaṃ* could be analyzed as *hasta+uluṅgulaṃ*. Here, the word *uluṅgulam* is in all probability a portion of the name of the Apsaras mentioned in Paippalāda AV (15.19.1-12: इदमुलुङ्-गुलुकाभ्योऽप्सराभ्योऽकरं नमः). With the final agentive affix *-uka*, the formation *uluṅgulukā* looks like a derivation from a denominative verb *uluṅgulati*, from the sound-imitation *uluṅgula-*. Such sound-imitations, especially in combination with verbs like *kṛ* are called *gati*, cf. *ulalā* and *alalā* below. The word *uluṅgulukā* has been provided with a somewhat unclear folk-etymology in Paippalāda AV (15.18.6: उलमालस्य यो गुलस्तदगश्छन्त्यासुरैः).

I would also like to mention one more possibility. A reading such as *hastolūgaluṃ* may contain three words: *hasta, ulū,* and *galuṃ*. Here, the word *ulū* could be the first member of the word *ulū́khala* (AV 9.6.15) which is left unanalyzed by the Padapāṭha. The next item *galuṃ* may be the first portion of the expression *galuntáḥ* (AV 6.83.3). This expression is not split by the Padapāṭha. However, Sāyaṇa explains this expression as: गडून् तस्यति इति

गडुन्तः । तसु उपक्षये । अस्मात् औणादिकः क्विप्. Thus, if the word is traditionally derived from *galu+tas*, the *ṃ* could be explained on the analogy of forms like *aruntuda*, cf. P.6.3.67 (अरुर्द्विषदजन्तस्य मुम्). It is possible that Śākaṭāyana listed the form *galuṃ* as an *upasargavṛtti* item.

6. *Tiráḥ*. For example: *tiráskaraḥ* (AV 4.20.7). Compare P.1.4.71 (तिरोऽन्तर्द्धौ), which treats *tiráḥ* as a *gati*.

7. *Puráḥ*. For example: *puraḥsaraú* (AV 15.2.1-4). Compare P.1.4.67 (पुरोऽव्ययम्), which treats *puráḥ* as a *gati*.

8. *Púnar*. For example: *punardā́ya* (AV 5.17.11). On P.1.4.60 (गतिश्च), Kātyāyana's *Vārttika* (पुनश्चनसौ छन्दसि) adds *púnar* as a *gati*.

9. *Náva*. There is a strong possibility that *náva,* in the sense of 'newly, recently,' may have been treated as a *gati* in an instance like *navagát* (AV 3.10.4), which is split by the *Padapāṭha* as *nava-gát*. Also see: Wackernagel, *Altindische Grammatik,* Vol. II., Pt. I., *Nachträge zu Band II1,* von Albert Debrunner, p. 21: "*nava-* im Sinn von **návam* 'neulich' (vgl. gr. *νεο~γενης* usw. zu *νεον*) z.B. v. *nava-sū́-* 'eine Kuh, die kürzlich gekalbt hat' Schwyzer Mél. Boisacq 2, 236." All the manuscripts read *punarṇavaḥ.* It is easy to see how the combination in the list of *punar+nava* may have been identified by the copyists with the AV word *punarṇavaḥ* (AV 8.1.20).

Against his manuscript, and now against all manuscripts, Whitney amended the text to read *punarṇamaḥ. Námas* is attested in AV. For example: *namaskārḗṇa* (AV 4.39.9). The word *namaḥ* is included in the *sākṣātprabhṛtīni* list of items treat as *gati* in combination with the root *kṛ*, cf. P.1.4.74 (साक्षात्प्रभृतीनि च), and the KV on this rule. However, given the above explanation in favor of *náva*, we need not go for Whitney's emendation.

10. *Śyetī́*. This reading is supported by mss. E, F, I, and O, and probably is the source of the reading *kṣitī* in H. The item *syetī* as a *cvi*-form appears in combination with the verb *kṛ* in the Taittirīya-Saṃhitā (5.5.8: *śyaiténa śyetī́ akuruta ... śyaiténa śyetī́ kurute*). This form, along with *mithunī,* is mentioned in TPR (x.18: न श्येती मिथुनी). While the AV does not have the usage of *śyetī́+kṛ*, the word *śyaita* is attested in AV (15.2.4). The similarity of the formations *śyetī́+kṛ* with *vātī+kṛ* below is inescapable.

I would like to mention *sani* as another possibility, though not a very strong one. In the form *saniṣyadā́ḥ* (AV 19.2.1), the portion *sani* is actually part of reduplication of the root in the intensive form. However, several manuscripts of the Padapāṭha place an *avagraha* between *sani* and *syadā́ḥ,* suggesting that somebody at sometime may have looked at *sani* as a first member of a compound-expression, cf. Whitney, *Index Verborum to AV*, p. 304, and the VVRI edition, Part IV, Fasc. I., p. 1790. Whitney (*AV Translation,* Vol. II.,

p. 899) says: "Our *saniṣyadā́s* in **c** is an emendation, and called for ⌊see *Skt. Gram.* § 1148. 4. k., near the end⌋; all the mss., and SPP., accent *saniṣyádās*. ... The *pada*-mss. make the absurd division *sani°syádāḥ*." While Whitney's view may be historically correct, there is no reason to reject out of hand the strong possibility that some traditions analyzed the word differently. This is especially so in view of the different accentuation for the word found in the manuscripts. The combination *sani-vātī* in the list was easily misunderstood and changed to *sinīvālī* by some copyists.

11. *Vātī́*. For example: *vātī́kr̥tasya* (AV 6.109.3). Such forms are included under P.1.4.61 (ऊर्यादिच्विडाचश्च).

12. *Phalī*. For example: *phalīkáraṇāḥ* (AV 11.3.6). The item *phalīkr̥tya* is listed by the KV under P.1.4.61 (ऊर्यादिच्विडाचश्च).

13. *Híṃ*. For example: *hiṅkārā́ḥ* (AV 11.7.5). Compare the items *hum, ghum* etc. which are listed among *nipātas* under P.1.4.57 (चादयोऽसत्त्वे), cf. the KV on P.1.4.57. As imitations of sounds, these are covered as *gatis* under P.1.4.62 (अनुकरणं चानितिपरम्).

14. *Srúk*. For example: *srukkārḗṇa* (AV 9.6.22). This expression appears in the same verse which has the more familiar expression *vaṣaṭkārḗṇa*, and the items listed next in our list is *váṣaṭ*.

15. *Váṣaṭ*. For example: *vaṣaṭkārḗṇa* (AV 9.6.22). The item *váṣaṭ* is listed as a *gati* in the *ūryādigaṇa* in P.1.4.61 (ऊर्यादिच्विडाचश्च), cf. the KV on P.1.4.61.

16. *Ululā* . This is my suggested emendation. The mss. readings vary: *uḍulā, gudurulā, ulā*. The form *ululā* is made likely by the fact that AV (3.19.6) has the expression *ghóṣā ululáyaḥ*. Sāyaṇa's commentary has the reading *ullulayáḥ*, which he explains as अनुकरणशब्दोऽयम् । उल्लुलु इत्येवमात्मका घोषाः. If *ululu* or *ullulu* is a sound-imitation, then to combine it with a verb like *kr̥* in the sense of making that sound, P.1.4.62 (अनुकरणं चानितिपरम्), the sound-imitation is given the designation *gati*. Also P.5.4.57 (अव्यक्तानुकरणाद् द्व्यजवरार्धादनितौ डाच्) prescribes the affix *ḍāc* to be added to a sound-imitation like *ululu* to turn it into *ululā* before it is compounded with a verb like *karoti*. In fact, the expressions *ululākuru* and *ululākr̥taḥ* are attested in Paippalāda AV (5.34.2, and 2.55.5). Thus, we can confidently have the form *ululā* eligible for inclusion in the present list. Compare the other included sound-imitation *alalā*.

17. *Kakajā́*. For instance: *kakajā́kr̥tā* (AV 11.10.25). This belongs to the same type of *gatis* listed under P.1.4.61 (ऊर्यादिच्विडाचश्च).

18. *Svā́hā*. For example: *svāhākārám* (AV 15.14.8). The item *svā́hā* is listed as a *gati* under P.1.4.61 (ऊर्यादिच्विडाचश्च).

19. *Svadhā́*. For example: *svadhākārā́m* (AV 15.14.7). The item *svadhā́* is listed as a *gati* under P.1.4.61 (ऊर्यादिच्विडाचश्च).

20. *Śrát*. For example: *śraddhéyam* (AV 4.30.4). The item *śrát* is listed as a *gati* under P.1.4.61 (ऊर्यादिच्विडाचश्च).

21. *Svàr*. For example: *svargáḥ* (AV 9.5.16) analyzed by the Padapāṭha as *svaḥ-gáḥ*. P.1.1.37 (स्वरादिनिपातमव्ययम्) includes *svar* among indeclinables.

22. *Alalā*. There is no example for *alalā* in AV. However, *alalā* is found compounded in the following usage: *alalābhávantīḥ* (RV 4.18.6) 'making the sound *alalā*,' cf. Sāyaṇa: अललेत्येवंरूपं शब्दं कुर्वत्यः.. Such compounding be covered by P.1.4.62 (अनुकरणं चानितिपरम्), giving the status of *gati* to the sound-imitation *alalā*. This solves the puzzle of *svaralalā* which Whitney was unable to solve. It also shows that this list is not restricted to items from the AV, but includes items from other textual traditions.

Whitney further comments: "There are two words which we especially miss in this list of *upasargavr̥ttīni*, and can hardly believe to have been originally absent from it: they are *antaḥ* and *āviḥ* : I cannot, however, find by emendation any place for them in the text as it stands." It is difficult to say why these words are not included in the list. These are examples of *gati*s in the Pāṇinian tradition. The word *antaḥ* as a *gati* is covered by P.1.4.65 (अन्तरपरिग्रहे), and *āvis* as a *gati* is covered under P.1.4.61 (ऊर्यादिच्विडाचश्च).

Perhaps another enumeration ascribed to Śākaṭāyana did include the particle *antar*. Referring to Śākaṭāyana's view, the Br̥haddevatā (2.95) says:

अच्छश्रदन्तरित्येतानाचार्यः शाकटायनः ।
उपसर्गान्क्रियायोगान्मेने ते तु त्रयोऽधिकाः ।।

Finally, I believe that this entire initial portion probably represents a very ancient incorporation into the text of the original CA. However, since all manuscripts of the CA, except C, contain them, I believe that the text of the CA, as it can be reconstructed on the basis of the manuscripts, must incorporate these passages. Clearly, the archetype of all our manuscripts must have had this portion. However, it is most likely that they were incorporated into the text of the CA after the CAB. While the CAB itself probably did not know these verses as part of the text of the CA, and therefore did not comment on them, the copyists of the manuscripts of the CAB definitely knew them, and they did incorporate these uncommented verses in their manuscripts. Also see the note on the colophon for this Pāda for a serious disagreement on the number of rules in this Pāda.

A possible hint is provided by Bhārgava-Bhāskara for the importance of the views of Śākaṭāyana to the later followers of Śaunakīya AV, that, while professing themselves to be followers of Śaunaka, they often disregarded Śaunaka's precepts in preference to those of Śākaṭāyana, cf. Bhārgava-Bhāskara's commentary on CA (1.1.10): अत्र वेदे तु प्रथमपद्यो गृह्यते शाकटायनानुसरणात्. The presence of such a large extract supposedly from a work of Śākaṭāyana, or a work from his tradition, may be an indication of such influence on the CA tradition. Also see CA 4.1.52, and the CAB on that rule.

४.१.२३. उपसर्ग आख्यातेनोदात्तेन समस्यते ।

Whitney (4.1). A, B, C: °र्ग°. D: उपसर्ग आख्यातेनोदात्ते । न समस्यते. O: °आख्यातेन चोदात्तेन°.

Translation: A pre-verb (*upasarga*) is compounded with an accented verb.

Note: In the situation envisioned by this rule, the pre-verb (*upasarga*) is unaccented and the verb is accented. Whitney says: "This is the well-known usage of all the Vedic *pada*-texts, at least so far as they have been brought to general knowledge. With a true appreciation of the slightness of the bond which connects a verb with its prefix, the constructors of the disjoined text have ordinarily treated the two as independent words: unless, indeed, by laws of accentuation of the sentence, the usually enclitic verb retains its accent and becomes proclitic; and then the two are written together as a compound."

चतुराध्यायीभाष्य - उपसर्ग आख्यातेनोदात्तेन सह समस्यते। 'परियन्ति' (अ.वे. १.१.१, पद ⇒ 'परिऽयन्ति')। 'समभंरः' (अ.वे. १.९.३, पद ⇒ 'सम्ऽअभंरः')। 'संस्रवंन्ति' (अ.वे. १.१५.३, पद ⇒ 'सम्ऽस्रवंन्ति)। उपसर्गवृत्तिभिश्च । 'यम् । अराते । पुरःऽधत्से' (पद, अ.वे. ५.७.२)। 'यम् । अमी इतिं । पुरःऽदधिरे' (पद, अ.वे. ५.८.५)। उदात्तेनेति किमर्थम् । 'यातुऽधानांन् । वि । लापय' (पद, अ.वे. १.७.२)।

Note: This rule is comparable to part of APR (12a). However, the examples listed under APR (12a) are not identical with the examples cited here by the CAB. Since the positive examples of the rules do not form a closed *gaṇa,* one can guess that there was no standard list of such examples.

The distinction between *samāsa* and non-*samāsa* manifests itself in the Padapāṭha, where an *upasarga* combined as a *samāsa* with the verb form is separated in the Padapāṭha by an *Avagraha.* On the other hand, an *upasarga* which is not combined as a *samāsa* with the verb is separated from that verb in the Padapāṭha as a separate word.

The commentary makes an interesting observation. It refers to two classes of items, the *upasargas* and the *upasargavṛttis* 'words which behave like *upasargas*, but are not *upasargas*.' Items like *puras* have been categorized as *upasargavṛtti* in CA (4.1.22). As discussed in the note on that rule, it is not clear whether the author of the CAB was familiar with the verses at the beginning of this Pāda. It is also likely that it was the CAB that cited the entire passage in the beginning, and then, for some reason, it was incorporated into the text of the CA.

४.१.२४. अनेकोऽनुदात्तेनापि ।

Whitney (4.2).

Translation: When there is more than one pre-verb [preceding the verb], they are [all] compounded even with an unaccented verb.

Note: It may be noted that CA (4.1.5-6) formulate this rule in a somewhat different way, and it seems most likely that they were not part of the 'original' CA, but were extracted from a different grammatical tradition and added to the text of the CA at some point.

As Whitney points out: "If more prepositions than one are compounded with an unaccented verb, only one of them, the one next the verb, is accented, the others becoming proclitic. In such a case, the constructors of the *pada*-text have very properly combined all with the verb, instead of simply putting the prepositions together, since it is not the relation of the former to the latter preposition that costs the former its accent, but rather their common relation to the verb : we have not a compound preposition, but a duplicate verbal compound. A later rule (rule 7 = CA 4.1.29, below) teaches us that in such a combination the first of the prepositions is separated by *avagraha* from the rest."

The rule seems to leave open the possibility, not discussed by Whitney, that a multiplicity of pre-verbs may be compounded with an accented verb as well. However, all the examples offered here are examples of unaccented verbs. See the Notes on CA (4.1.5-6).

चतुराध्यायीभाष्य - अनेक उपसर्गः अनुदात्तेनापि आख्यातेन सह समस्यते । 'उत्ऽअवंस्यति' (पद, अ.वे. ९.६.५४, VVRI edn.: ९.११.६)। 'सम्ऽआचिंनुष्व । अनुऽसम्प्रयांहि' (पद, अ.वे. ११.१.३६)। 'उपऽसम्परांन(H: ण)यात्' (पद, अ.वे. १८.४.५०)। उपसर्गवृत्तिभिश्च । 'अच्छऽआवंदामसि' (पद, अ.वे. ७.३८.३, VVRI edn.: ७.३९.३)। 'अभिऽहिङ्कृंणोत' (पद, अ.वे. १२.३.३७)।

Note: On the citation from AV (18.4.50), Whitney (AV *Transl.* Vol.II. p. 884) points out: "Three of out *pada*-mss. (Bp.Kp.D., but D. not accented) make the anomalous division *upa°sám : parānayāt;* the other (Op.) has *upa°sampárānayāt,* which is the regular and proper form: see Prāt. iv. 2 (= CA 4.1.24) and note, and iv.7 (= CA 4.1.29)."

४.१.२५. अनर्थककर्मप्रवचनीयान्ययुक्तैर्विग्रहोऽभिवितन्वादिषु ।

Whitney (4.3): अनर्थकर्म°. O: °युक्तैर्गृहोभिवि°.

Translation: [However], meaningless prepositional items, prepositional items syntactically linked with nouns (*karma-pravacanīya*), and those which are related in some other way, are separated [from the verb in the Padapāṭha as independent uncompounded words], as in examples such as: *abhí / ví / tanu* (AV 1.1.3).

चतुराध्यायीभाष्य - अनर्थकैश्च कर्मप्रवचनीयैश्च अन्ययुक्तैश्च विग्रहो भवति अभिवितन्वादिषु । 'इह । एव । अभि। वि । तनु' (पद, अ. वे. १.१.३)। 'सम् । सम् । स्रवन्तु' (पद, अ.वे. १.१५.१)। 'सु । प्र । साधय' (पद, अ.वे. १.२४.४)। 'उपं । प्र । अगात्' (पद, अ. वे. १.२८.१)।

Note: The CAB lists here the first four instances out of a total list of fifty-seven instances found in the APR (13). The instances are cited exactly in the same order. The CA rule is itself identical with, and perhaps is a quotation in, APR (13c). The notion that certain prepositional items are *anarthaka* in certain contexts is also seen in P.1.4.93 (अधिपरी अनर्थकौ). The KV on this rule says that the items *adhi* and *pari* are given the designation *karmapravacanīya*, when not bearing any meaning, in order to prevent the designations *gati* and *upasarga* : गत्युपसर्गसंज्ञाबाधनार्था कर्मप्रवचनीयसंज्ञा विधीयते. Our rule here, and the commentary on it, seem to differentiate between the categories *anarthaka* and *karmapravacanīya*. Neither the CAB nor the APR explain as to which examples are offered to illustrate which type. However, a related discussion of some of these issues is found under APR (3, p. 4):

> 'पूषा त्वेतश्च्यावयतु प्र विद्वान्' (१८.२.५४)। अत्र च *प्र विद्वान्* विगृह्यते । समासोऽन्यत्र । किं कारणम्? प्रेत्यस्य च्यवतिना सामर्थ्यम् । पूषा त्वेतः प्रच्यावयतु विद्वान् इति ।
>
> 'कर्मन्कर्मन्नाभंगम्' - कर्मन्ऽकर्मन् । आऽभंगम् (४.२३.३)। *आभंगम्* इति समस्यते । विग्रहोऽन्यत्र । किं प्रयोजनम् । कर्मणि कर्मण्याभगम् ।
>
> 'अधिंश्रितेऽग्निहोत्रे' - अधिंऽश्रिते । अग्निऽहोत्रे (१५.१२.१)। अधिशब्दस्य श्रितशब्देन सह समासः । विग्रहोऽन्यत्र । कस्मात् ? कर्मप्रवचनीयत्वात् ।

Whitney (1862: 186) says: "The term *anyayukta* probably means 'belonging to another verb,' but such cases are quite rare in the text : an instance of the kind intended is perhaps *níḥ stuvānásya pātaya* (i.8.3), where the preposition *niḥ* belongs to the verb *pātaya*, and not the intervening participle, to which it would otherwise be attached, with loss of its own accent. Pāṇini's *karmapravacanīya* is comprehensive enough to include all the cases to which our rules apply."

A similar example of *anyayukta* is offered by the APR passage cited above, e.g. AV (18.2.54), where *pra* is not compounded with *vidvān*, since *pra* is semantically related to *cyāvayatu*, rather than to *vidvān*. To this extent, Whitney's understanding seems to be correct.

However, Whitney is not correct in suggesting that cases like these would be subsumed under Pāṇini's notion of *karmapravacanīya*. As I have pointed out above, Pāṇini's notion of *karmapravacanīya*, subsumes the instances of *anarthaka*, cf. P.1.4.93. However, there is no reason to believe that instances of *anyayukta* would be covered under his notion of *karmapravcanīya*. The compounding of *anyayukta* items would be prevented by the general convention set by P.2.1.1 (समर्थः पदविधिः), which lays down the rule that processes like compounding take place only for the items which are semantically and syntactically related to each other. Interestingly, the APR (3), which is identical with P.2.1.1, has the same import, and the APR specifically prohibits compounding because of the lack of *sāmarthya* 'semantic/syntactic relationship,' cf. APR (13b, p. 12):

उपसर्गपूर्वमाख्यातं यत्रोभाभ्यां समस्यते ।
सामर्थ्यमुभयोस्तत्रासामर्थ्येषु विग्रहः ॥

Commenting on the present rule, Whitney exerts to bring together a large collection of instances for "this and the two following rules, since they evidently form a single class, and are only formally distinct from one another." Now that we have access to Surya Kanta's APR, we can be certain that these two *gaṇa*s were treated as distinct *gaṇa*s, and they are listed separately in that text. The examples offered by the CAB appear to be the first few citations of the long lists found in the APR. Further, the APR brings out some crucial differences which are not overtly mentioned by the CA, or the CAB.

४.१.२६. पूर्वेणाभिविपश्याम्यादिषु ।

Whitney (4.4). O: °पश्यांम्या°.

Translation: In *abhi vipaśyāmi* etc., the first [prepositional item is separated as an independent word].

Note: Whitney says that, in these instances, "a preposition retaining its accent and independence before another preposition which is itself made proclitic and combined with a following accented verb."

चतुराध्यायीभाष्य - पूर्वेण उपसर्गेण विग्रहो भवति अभि विपश्याम्यादिषु । 'यावंत् । ते । अभि । विऽपश्यांमि' (पद, अ.वे. १२.१.३३)। 'मनंसा । अभि । सम्ऽविदुः' (पद, अ.वे. ३.२१.५)। 'यावंत् । सा । अभि । विऽजङ्गंहे' (पद, अ.वे. ५.१९.४)। 'यः । विश्वां । अभि । विऽपश्यंति' (पद, अ.वे. ६.३४.४)।

Note: The CAB lists here the first four instances out of a total of seven listed in the APR (12c). The passages occur exactly in the same order as found in the APR. The APR rule (12c) says: "When an accented verb is preceded by two prepositions, separated (from the second preposition+verb) are such items as are used without significance, or as *karmapravacanīyas*, or connected with something else." While the CA rule simply makes a reference to a list, the APR (12c) provides a more detailed description, and a reasoning. It still leaves a logical possibility open that an accented verb could be compounded with two pre-verbs, which are not *anarthaka, karmapravacanīya*, or *anyayukta*. However, I have not found any such instances.

४.१.२७. योनावध्यैरयन्तादिषु च ।

Whitney (4.5).

Translation: [The preverb is separated from the verb as an independent word in the Padapāṭha] in examples such as *yónāv ádhy aírayanta* (AV 2.1.5).

Note: Whitney says: "This rule applies to such cases ... as show an accented and independent preposition immediately before an accented verb."

चतुराध्यायीभाष्य - योनावध्यैरयन्तादिषु च उपसर्गेण विग्रहो भवति । 'समाने । योनौं । अधिं । ऐरंयन्त' (पद, अ.वे. २.१.५)। 'अधिं । तस्थुः' (पद, अ.वे. ९.९.२, VVRI edn.: ९.१४.२)। 'ये । असंतः । परिं । जज्ञिरे' (पद, अ.वे. १०.७.२५)। 'समुद्रात् । अधिं । जज्ञिषे' (पद, अ.वे. ४.१०.२)। 'परिं । भूमं । जायंसे' (पद, अ.वे. १३.२.३)।

Note: As Surya Kanta *(APR, Introduction,* p. 56) points out the *gaṇa* referred to in this CA rule occurs fully in APR (12b), and the CAB lists all the examples exactly in the same order.

Referring to the last example cited by the CAB, Whitney says: "The citation of the last passage seems to imply that the commentator regarded *bhūma* as a verbal form, from the root *bhū*; but he can hardly, except in the forgetfulness of a moment, have been guilty of so gross a blunder." Also see:

Surya Kanta *(APR,* Notes, p. 6). While one must agree with Whitney and Surya Kanta that *bhūma* is not a verb, it is now clear that the CAB was not alone in including this example in this list, but the APR (p. 11) also includes it in the same list, and the shared example shows a close connection between these two texts, to the point of having shared conceptual errors.

४.१.२८. आशीर्बभूवेति प्लुतस्वरस्य सिद्धत्वात् ।

Whitney (4.6): °प्लुतस्वरस्य सिद्धत्वात्°. C, E, F, I, O, P(corr): °प्लुतः स्वरस्यासिद्धत्वात्. H, M: °प्लुतः स्वरस्य सिद्धत्वात्. Others: °प्लुतस्वरस्य सिद्धत्वात्.

> **Translation:** [There is separation of the pre-verb from the verbs] *āśī3ḥ* (AV 11.3.26) and *babhūvā́3*, because the prolonged [i.e. *pluta,* vowel of the verbs] is [already] effected (*siddha*).

> ***चतुराध्यायीभाष्य*** - आशीर्बभूवेति प्लुतः स्वरस्य सिद्धत्वात् उपसर्गेण विग्रहो भवति । 'परांञ्चम् । ओदनम् । प्र। आशी[३]ः' (पद, ११.३.२६)। 'आ । बभूवाँ३' (पद, अ.वे. १०.२.२८)।

Note: On this rule, Whitney says: "That is to say, if I do not misapprehend the meaning of the rule, owing to the recognition of the final syllable of each word as a protracted one. To what end the precept is given, unless the words referred to (x.2.28 and xi.3.26, 27) have an irregular accent on the protracted syllable, I do not see. If accented, they would have a right, by the first rule of this chapter (= CA 4.1.23), to combination with the preceding preposition; but, the present rule virtually says, they are seen to lose this right upon a recognition of the fact that the accented vowel is protracted, and that its accent is therefore of an anomalous character. It has been already noticed (under i. 105 = CA 1.4.14) that a part of our manuscripts accent *babhūvā́3* in the latter of the two passages referred to : not one gives an accent to *āśī3ḥ*, in either case of its occurrence."

The VVRI edition goes with the majority of the manuscripts and gives the accent of *babhūvā́3* as *antodātta*, while it notes the unaccented reading given by the Whitney-Roth edition in the footnote. Also in *prá āśī3ḥ* (AV 11.3.26, 27), the VVRI edition gives the accented reading. In view of the fact that P.8. 2.97 (विचार्यमाणानाम्) which sanctions the *pluta* vowel also ensures the *udātta* accent for the *pluta* vowel, this reading seems appropriate. In contrast with this, the non-*pluta* reading for *prá āśīḥ* in AV (11.3.28) is unaccented, and, as the Padapāṭha shows, the accented preverb *prá* is compounded with the unaccented *āśīḥ* in AV (11.3.28). On the other hand, in AV (11.3.26, 27), the accented preverb *prá* is not compounded with the accented pluta form *āśī́3ḥ*.

It is in the process of becoming pluta that the vowel also becomes accented. Pāṇini's rules for pluta and its accent are in the section beginning with P.8.2.82 (वाक्यस्य टेः प्लुत उदात्तः), and the convention set by P.8.2.1 (पूर्वत्रासिद्धम्) says that, for rules preceding P.8.2.1, the results of rules coming afterwards are treated as if not effected (*asiddha*), and that even among the rules which follow P.8.2.1, any given rule does not recognize the following rules and their results. The words *siddha* and *asiddha* are crucial in this context, and perhaps the CA is alluding to some such distinction. The CA seems to be saying that, in the context of compounding with the pre-verb, the accent of the pluta vowel is to be treated as a fully valid result. In both the examples cited under this rule, the pre-verbs are accented, as well as the verbs, and hence there is no compounding. The Padapāṭha generally does not have a compound-expression with two *udātta* syllables in it. This is probably what goes against the compounding in the present case, and this is also probably why the rule uses प्लुतस्वरस्य सिद्धत्वात् as a reason.

४.१.२९. पूर्वेणावग्रहः ।

Whitney (4.7). B, D, J, M: पूर्वेणाविग्रहः. I: 48. The numbering in I indicates that the earlier verses were considered to be part of the text of the CA. Perhaps, the verses were broken down into multiple rules in some text-traditions.

> **Translation:** [In the Padapāṭha], there is separation with an *avagraha* [i.e. pause marking the separation of a member of a compound-expression, as contrasted with *virāma* or a pause marking the separation of independent words,] of the first [of the many preverbs from the rest, which are left joined to the verb].

चतुराध्यायीभाष्य - पूर्वेण उपसर्गेण अवग्रहो भवति । 'उप॒ऽअवैति' (पद, अ.वे. ९.६.५३, VVRI edn.: ९.११.५) । 'उत्ऽअवंस्यति' (पद, अ.वे. ९.६.५४, VVRI edn.: ९.

११.६)। 'समुऽआचिंनुष्व । अनुऽसंप्रयाहि' (पद, अ.वे. ११.
१.३६)। 'उपऽसंपरांनयात्' (पद, अ.वे. १८.४.५०)।

Note: Whitney observes: "The *avagraha*, or pause of separation between the two parts of a compound word, is defined by two of the Prātiśākhyas (as has been already remarked, in the note following iii. 74 = CA 3.3.25) as having the length of a mora. From here to the end of section II (rule 72 = CA 4.2.26), the treatise is occupied with rules for its employment or omission. And, in the first place, with however many prepositions a verbal form may be compounded, it is always the first of them that is separated from the rest of the compound by *avagraha*." Rule CA (3.3.35: ऋगर्धर्चपदान्तावग्रहविवृत्तिषु मात्राकालः कालः), also says that the *avagraha* is of one mora duration, but so is the pause between words (*padānta*). See Notes on CA (3.3.19) and CA (3.3.35). Another general principle is that irrespective of the number of members a compound-expression may have, there is only one *avagraha*.

४.१.३०. यातुमावत् ।

Whitney (4.8). I: 49. P combines this with the following rule.

Translation: In the expression *yātumāvat,* [the former member, i.e. *yātu*, is separated from the rest of the members with an *avagraha*].

Note: Whitney says: "It comes in rather awkwardly here, as only prepositions have been contemplated, thus far in the chapter, as former constituents of compounds." However, it is clear that, as an exceptional item, it had to be taken care of somewhere. The assumption seems to be that the word has three members, i.e. *yātu-mā-vat*. However, in the Padapāṭha, only the first item is separated with an *avagraha*.

The CAB also cites another view that *-māvat* is a single affix having the same meaning as *-mat*.

The word *yātumāvat* appears several times in the RV (1.36.20; 7.1.5; 7.104.23; and 8.49.20), where the Padapāṭha follows the same division as prescribed by our rule. However, perhaps through oversight, Surya Kanta (1981: 546) cites this expression divided as *yātumā́+vat*.

चतुराध्यायीभाष्य - यातुमावदिति च पूर्वेणावग्रहो भवति। 'यातुऽमावंत्' (पद, अ.वे. ८.४.२३)। मत्वर्थे वायं मावच्छब्दो मतु(H: नु)पो मकारस्य वकारः । आकारागम(H: ०त्य): (?)।

४.१.३१. समासे च ।

Whitney (4.9). I: 50.

Translation: Separation [of the members] by *avagraha* [takes place in the Padapāṭha] also for a compound.

Note: Whitney says: "The *ca* in the rule evidently continues the implication simply of *avagraha* from rule 7 (= CA 4.1.29), and the connection of the text casts upon *yātumāvat* the suspicion of being an interpolation." While one feels like agreeing with Whitney, one must note that all manuscripts contain the rule *yātumāvat*, and, therefore, if this is an interpolation, it must be a very ancient interpolation, certainly predating the composition of the CAB.

चतुराध्यायीभाष्य - समासे च अवग्रहो भवति । 'उपंऽहूतः' (पद, अ.वे. १.१.४)। 'भूरिंऽधायसम्' (पद, अ.वे. १.२.१)। 'भूरिंऽवर्पसम्' (पद, अ.वे. १.२.१)। 'भूरिंऽधनाः' (पद, अ.वे. ७.६०.४, VVRI edn.: ७.६२.४)।

४.१.३२. उपजाते परेण ।

Whitney (4.10). P adds a daṇḍa after this rule as a correction.

Translation: When [a pre-existing compound is expanded with a] newly added [member], the latter [i.e. newly added member, is separated with an *avagraha*, and not the members of the old compound].

चतुराध्यायीभाष्य - उपजाते परेण पर्वणा अवग्रहो भवति। 'प्रजाऽपंतिः' (पद, अ.वे. २.३४.४)। प्रजानां पतिः । 'प्रजा-पंतिऽसृष्टः' (पद, अ.वे. १०.६.१९)।

Note: As Whitney explains: "The word *prajā* is itself divisible as a compound - thus, *pra-jā* (e.g. vii.35.3); upon farther adding *pati*, the former division is given up in favor of that between the old compound and its added member, and we have *prajā-pati* (e.g. ii.34.4); and a similar addition and removal of the pause of separation gives us *prajāpati-sr̥ṣṭaḥ* : while we might have, did the words occur, the yet farther change *prajāpatisr̥ṣṭaḥ-iva,* or *prajāpatisr̥ṣṭi-bhiḥ*, and *prajāpatisr̥ṣṭibhiḥ-iva*. In no compound is the separation by *avagraha* made at more than one point, and it is always the member last appended which is entitled to separation."

This rule presents a very important observation as regards the division of compounds. It implicitly recognizes that certain compounds are already in use and are fully entrenched in the language, and then other members are added to them. Thus, one should not assume that a compound with three members, e.g. ABC, could be split in all sorts of possible ways. One must take into account which members are entrenched in the usage. Otherwise, one could possibly argue that *pra* has been added to a prior compound *jāpati*. This is unacceptable, because no expression like *jāpati* is in use. On the other hand, the expression *prajā* is in use. Thus, the practice of separating compounds by *avagraha* provides us significant insight into how the ancient grammarians looked at the relation of the linguistic usage and the grammatical theory. Compare P.2.1.4 (सह सुपा), which, with the continuation of *sup* from P.2.1.2, lays down the general principle that, at a time, only one noun is compounded with another noun. Thus, generally, a multi-member compound must be successively built through incorporation of prior compounds. This general discussion is also taken up by the Vārttikas (25 ff.) on P.2.1.1, MB (Kielhorn edn., Vol.I., pp. 372-3. For a detailed discussion, see: S.J. Joshi (1968: 168-208). It may be noted that the grammarians did not bother themselves with the question of *avagraha*, and that dimension was left for the Prātiśākhyas.

४.१.३३. सुप्राव्या च ।

Whitney (4.11). A, B, D, H, M: सुप्राच्या च.

Translation: Also in the expression *suprāvyā* (AV 4.30.6), [the last member is separated with an *avagraha*].

Note: As Whitney says: "In the word specified the last member is separated from the rest of the compound, and not the first, as would be more in accordance with the general analogies of the system of separation." Normally, with a verbal noun with two preverbs, the first preverb is separated with an *avagraha*, cf. CA 4.1.7 and the Note on this rule.

चतुराध्यायीभाष्य - सुप्राव्येति च परेण पर्वणा अवग्रहो भवति । 'सुप्रऽअव्यां । यजंमानाय' (पद, अ.वे. ४.३०.६)।

'अवतेः [सु]प्रपूर्वस्य टाशब्दः स्वरितः परः ।
सुप्रावीति तृतीयायाः क्षैप्रः छन्दसि स्वर्यते ॥'
(source?)

Note: For the expression *ṭāśabdaḥ* in the verse, Whitney proposes the emendation *yaśabdaḥ*. However, the expression *ṭā* here refers to the instrumental singular affix in the Pāṇinian tradition, cf. Pāṇini 4.1.2. Thus, this tradition looks at the word *suprāvyā* as a feminine instrumental singular from the base *suprāvī*. Whitney mistakenly interprets the verse as suggesting a derivation with the desiderative suffix *yā*, but then says: "Such an explanation, of course, would be futile, being sufficiently disproved by the accent alone." As is clear, the verse does not propose such an interpretation in the first place.

Sāyaṇa offers the reading *suprāvye,* perhaps under the influence of RV (10.125.2). The same reading is recorded by some AV manuscripts as noted in the VVRI edition. This perhaps shows the increasing influence from the RV tradition upon that of the AV in the post-CA period. For further discussion of the RV and the AV readings, see Whitney (*AV Transl.* Vol.I., p. 201). Also note that the RV Padapāṭha separates members of this word in the same way as taught by this rule, and it may be that the exceptional character of this division is influenced by the RV tradition.

The word *suprāvī* appears several times in the RV (1.34.4, 1.60.1, 1.83.1, 2.13.9, and 4.26.5), and in each case the word is split as *supra-avī* in the Padapāṭha. The word *duṣprāvī* also appears in RV (4.25.6) and it is split in an analogous way in the Padapāṭha. The word *prāvī* also appears in the RV (4.9.2), where the Padapāṭha splits its as *pra-avī.*

The exceptional division of the word in the Padapāṭha may imply that, somehow, the words *su* and *dus* were not deemed by the author of the Padapāṭha as modifying the whole compound *prāvī*, but just the portion *pra* in it. This is analogous to the use of the adverb 'very' in English in a phrase like *a very good person.* Here, *very* goes with *good*, rather than with *person.* However, the presence of the compound *prāvī,* and the absence of just *supra* or *duṣpra* made it seem like, the normal *avagraha* may have been like *su-prāvī* or *duḥ-prāvī.* Since this was not the case, a separate rule to note the exception had to be given.

४.१.३४. अनिङ्गेन पूर्वेण ।

Whitney (4.12). I: °निंग्ये°. O: °निंग्येण°. P adds a daṇḍa after this rule as a correction.

> **Translation:** When [the new compounding is with an indivisible item], the old [member is separated with an *avagraha*].
>
> ***चतुराध्यायीभाष्य*** - अनिङ्गेनोपजाते । अनिङ्गेन विशेष-लक्षणेन अविकृषितेन द्वयोः संशये जाते पूर्वेण अवग्रहो भवति । 'सुऽक्षेत्रिया । सुऽगातुया' (पद, अ.वे. ४.३३.२)। 'सहऽसूंक्तवाकः' (पद, अ.वे. ७.९७.६, VVRI edn.: ७.१०२.६)। 'सऽअंन्तर्देशाः' (पद, अ.वे. ९.५.३७)। 'सुऽप्रजाः' (पद, अ.वे. ४.११.३)।
>
> 'द्वे यत्रावग्रहस्थाने पूर्वेणेति परेण वा ।
> पूर्वेणावग्रहस्त(H: सू)त्र ...
> सुक्षेत्रिया सान्तर्देशाः सुप्रजाश्च निदर्शनम् ॥'
> (source?)

Note: Here, the assumption seems to be that the original compounding in the form *sukṣetriyā* is with *su+kṣetri,* to which the new member *yā* is added. However, this new member *yā* being inseparable, the separation with an *avagraha* is carried out with the old member *su.* This is the same logic with the example *sugātuyā.* CA (4.1.52) and the CAB on it specify that the separation with *yā* occurs only in five forms, and nowhere else. See the CAB on CA (4.1.52):

वसुअवस्वप्नसुम्न(H: म्न)साध्वित्येतैः सह याशब्दे परतः अवग्रहो भवति ।
'वसुऽया' (पद, अ.वे. ४.३३.२)। 'अवऽया' (पद, अ.वे. २.३५.१)।
'स्वप्नऽया' (पद, अ.वे. ५.७.८)। 'सुम्न(H: म्न)ऽया' (पद, अ.वे. ७.५५.१)।
'साधुऽया' (पद, अ.वे. १०.४.२१)।

'पञ्चैवावग्रहानाह याशब्दे शाकटायनः ।
अन्तोदात्तः पदत्वं च विभक्त्यर्थे भवेत्तु या ॥' (source?)

Thus, while we agree with Whitney that *yā* is not a universally *aniṅgya* affix, he fails to take due notice of the fact that it is divisible only in the five forms cited above, and nowhere else. This is what makes the two cited cases *su-kṣetriyā* and *su-gātuyā* proper examples.

However, the situation with the three additional examples offered by the CAB is different. Why are the compounds *sā́ntardeśāḥ, sahásūktavākaḥ,* and *suprajā́ḥ* offered as examples of this rule? The CAB seems to assume that the original compound is *sāntar,* which is then connected to an indivisible *deśa.* Similarly, it seems to assume that *sahasūkta* is an original compound, which is subsequently compounded with an indivisible *vākaḥ.* Finally, it assumes that *supra* is the original compound, which is subsequently compounded with an indivisible *ja.* Such assumptions are difficult to comprehend. We must agree with Whitney: "I do not see how this statement can be accepted as a correct one; for, of the compounds consisting of more than two members, the last is even more often separated from the first two than the first from the last two."

My own guess is that the original CA rule applies appropriately to *su-kṣetriyā́* and *su-gātuyā́.* However, the CAB has mixed up several unrelated rules and their examples. The first two examples are not there in the text of the cited verses, and the verses seem to refer to a slightly different doctrine: "Where there are two possible places for separation, an earlier one and a later one, the separation takes place with the earlier one. This is illustrated by *su-kṣetriyā́, sá-antardeśāḥ,* and *su-prajā́ḥ.*" This doctrine has nothing to do with the present rule, and thus the confusion. Here, the words *pūrva* and *para* are used in spacial sense, rather than in temporal order in which the compound develops.

The disparate nature of these examples is also indicated by the fact that the APR accounts for them in diverse ways. APR (122, p. 83) reads: सु इत्येतेनोपसर्गेण. There is separation of the *upasarga su* with an *avagraha.* As examples are offered *su-kṣetriyā́* and *su-gātuyā́* from AV (4.33.2). One suspects that *su-prajā́ḥ* (AV 4.11.3) would be accounted for by the same rule. The example *sá-antardeśāḥ* (AV 9.5.37) is accounted for under APR (128-129, p. 90) which says that *sá-*, the reduced form of *sahá,* is separated with an *avagraha.* Also see CA (4.1.10) for a different explanation for *sahá-sūktavākaḥ* and *sá-*

antardeśāḥ. The only reason the CAB was able to bring all these examples together is that in all these the separation with an *avagraha* takes place with the first item. This surface similarity, in addition to the word *pūrveṇa* in the CA rule and in the cited verse, seems to have led the CAB to bring all these examples together. They could all come together under the rule as phrased in the cited verse, but not under the rule as phrased in CA (4.1.34).

४.१.३५. तद्धिते धा ।

Whitney (4.13). P adds a daṇḍa after this as a correction.

Translation: *Dhá*, when it is a *taddhita*-suffix, [is separated with an *avagraha* in thc Padapāṭha].

चतुराध्यायीभाष्य - तद्धिते परतः धाप्रत्यये अवग्रहो भवति । 'चतुःऽधा । रेतः' (पद, अ.वे. १०.१०.२९)। 'अष्टऽधा । युक्तः' (पद, अ.वे. १३.३.१९)। 'नवऽधा । हिताः' (पद, अ.वे. १३.४.१०)। 'द्वादशऽधा' (पद, अ.वे. ६.११३.३)। व्यत्यय[:] स्वश्रद्दीर्घेभ्यो धाप्रत्यये न अवग्रहो भवति ।

Note: Referring to an exception, Whitney says: "On the other hand, the text offers a single exception to the rule, *viśvádhā* (vi.85.3), which neither the Prātiśākhya nor its commentary notices : it is accented on the penult, while all the other compounds with *dhā* accent the suffix itself." Here, it may be noted that, for the *viśvádhā yatīḥ* of the AV text, Sāyaṇa reads *viśvadhāyanīḥ,* and Paippalāda AV (19.6.3) reads *viśvadhāyasaḥ,* suggesting that we have here a suspect reading which may not have been known as *viśvádhā* to the author of the CA or the CAB.

Also, referring to the added rule in the commentary, Whitney says: "*vyatyayasvaśraddīrghebhyo dhāpratyaye na avagraho bhavati;* 'the suffix *dhā* does not suffer separation after ... (?), *sva, śrat,* and a long vowel.' The words *svadhā* and *śraddhā*, into which the root *dhā* enters as last member, are here referred to, and perhaps *godhā* (iv.3.6); but to what the first item in the enumeration refers, I have not succeeded in discovering." The first word, by adding a visarga after it, is nothing but the word *vyatyayaḥ*, which also appears in Patañjali's MB (on P.1.4.9, Kielhorn edn., Vol.I., p. 315, etc.) in the sense of transposition or deviation. Thus, the cited rule seems to be saying that, in deviation from the normal CA rule, the item *dhā* is not separated after *sva, śrat,* and a long vowel. The words *śraddhā* and *svadhā* are not analyzed by the Padapāṭha. However, this really cannot be an exception to the normal CA rule, since the present CA rule applies only if *dhā* is a *taddhita* affix. Clearly *svadhā* and *śraddhā* are not *taddhita* formations, but derived from the root *dhā*. For *dhā* coming after a long vowel, Whitney suggests "perhaps *godhā* (iv.3.6)." A genuine *taddhita* formation with a long vowel before *dhā* is the word *tredhā́* (AV 1.12.1) which is not divided by the Padapāṭha with an *avagraha*, cf. CA (4.2.20).

४.१.३६. त्राकारान्ते ।

Whitney (4.14).

Translation: Also the affix *trā,* when it ends in *ā,* [is separated with an *avagraha*].

Note: The qualification *ākārānte* is to distinguish *trā* from the affix *tra*. While the former is separated with an *avagraha* in the Padapāṭha, the latter is not. Whitney makes an important observation: "Doubtless it is the character of the forms to which *tra* is attached, as being pronominal roots, that prevents its separation from them, rather than anything in the suffix itself. The ablative suffix *tas* is not separated, even when it follows a word having an independent *status* in the language, as in *abhitas*."

चतुराध्यायीभाष्य - त्राप्रत्यये आकारान्ते अवग्रहो भवति । 'दे॒व॒ऽत्रा । च॒ । कृ॒णु॒हि॒' (पद, अ.वे. ५.१२.२)। 'पु॒रु॒ऽत्रा । ते॒ । व॒(H: म)न्व॒ता॒म्' (पद, अ.वे. ६.१२६.१)। आकारान्त इति किमर्थम् । 'यत्र॑ दे॒वा अ॒मृत॑म्' (अ.वे. २.१.५)। 'तत्रा॒मृत॑स्य॒ चक्ष॑णम्' (अ.वे. ५.४.३)।

४.१.३७. थानेकाक्षरेण ।

Whitney (4.15). O: थ्याने°. P adds a daṇḍa after this rule as a correction.

Translation: The affix *thā* [is separated with an *avagraha* in the Padapāṭha] when [added after a word] of more than one syllable.

चतुराध्यायीभाष्य - थाप्रत्यये अनेकाक्षरेण पदेन अवग्रहो भवति । 'ऋतुऽथा । वि । चक्षते' (पद, अ.वे. ९.१०.२६, VVRI edn.: ९.१५.२६)। 'नामऽथा । स[ः] । मन्येत' (पद, अ.वे. ११.८.७, VVRI edn.: ११.१०.७)। अनेकाक्षरेणेति किमर्थम् । 'अध । यथा । नः' (पद, अ.वे. १८.३.२१)। 'तथा । तत् । अग्ने' (पद, अ.वे. ५.२९.२)।

Note: Whitney observes: "Here, again, it is evidently not the length of the words to which the suffix is appended, as monosyllables or polysyllables, that determines its separability, but the character of the former as pronominal roots and of the latter as nominal themes." A crucial example to test Whitney's assessment might be a word like *sarvathā*. However, it does not appear in the ŚAV. It appears in Paippalāda AV (9.10.5), but the Padapāṭha for PAV is not available to us, if it ever existed. Also, there is no known Prātiśākhya for it.

४.१.३८. तरतमयोः ।

Whitney (4.16). P adds a daṇḍa after this rule as a correction.

Translation: Also [the comparative and the superlative affixes] *-tara* and *-tama* [are separated with an *avagraha*].

चतुराध्यायीभाष्य - तरतमयोश्च परतः अवग्रहो भवति । 'मधोः । अस्मि । मधुऽतरः । मदुघात् । मधुमत्ऽतरः' (पद, अ.वे. १.३४.४)। 'उत्ऽतमः । असि । ओषधीनाम्' (पद, अ.वे. ६.१५.१)। 'अहम् । अस्मि । यशःऽतमः' (पद, अ.वे. ६.३९.३)। 'नृणाम् । च । भगवत्ऽतमः' (पद, अ.वे. २.९.२)। तरतमयोरिति किमर्थम् । 'अश्वतरस्य' (पद, अ.वे. ४.४.८)। 'अश्वतर्यः' (अ.वे. ८.८.२२)। इह कस्मात् (न?) अवग्रहो भवति । 'कतरः' ।

'कतमः' । 'यतरः' । 'यतमः' । नैतौ स्तः तरतमावन्या-
वेतावकारादी प्रत्ययौ ।

'अङ्गस्यात्रादिमात्रं तु (H: उ) शिष्यते लुप्यते परम् ।
स्वरादी प्रत्ययावेतौ पदत्वं नात्र शिष्यते ॥'
(source?)

गोतमः प्रतिषेधो वक्तव्यः । 'यौ । गो(H: गौ)तंमम् । अवंथः' (पद, अ.वे. ४.२९.६)।

'संज्ञायां रूढिशब्दो धा(?)
तमोऽ(H: मा)त्रानतिशायने ।
असमानः स(H: सोम)मुद्रादि-
स्तस्मान्नेत्यतिगोतमः (?)॥' (source?)

Note: Referring to the counter-examples *aśvatarásya* (AV 4.4.8) and *aśvataryàḥ* (AV 8.8.22), Whitney comments: "The citation of these words in this manner, as if they were excluded by the very form of the rule itself from falling under its operation, suggests as the true reading and interpretation of the rule *taratamapoḥ*, '*tara* and *tama* when unaccented,' giving to the indicatory letter *p* the same force which it has as appended to the same suffixes by Pāṇini (e.g. v.3.55, 57). My copy of the manuscript, indeed, gives m everywhere *taratamayoḥ;* but, considering the small difference between *y* and *p* when hastily formed, I cannot be confident that the Hindu scribe did not mean to write the latter." Now that we have a large number of manuscripts, Whitney's expectation is not supported.

My guess is that the commentator, in asking the question तरतमयोरिति किमर्थम्, means to suggest that by juxtaposing the affixes *tara* and *tama* in this fashion, the rule naturally makes it clear that these words refer to comparative and superlative affixes, and not to just any homophonic affixes. Such an inference excludes *aśvatarásya* etc., since the affix *-tara* in this example does not have the meaning of the comparative affix.

Then, the commentator takes up the question as to why there is no separation in the forms *katará* and *katamá*, *yatará* and *yatamá*. This is answered by saying that these are not the affixes *-tara* and *-tama*, but a different set of affixes, i.e. *-atara* and *-atama*. The verse cited after this says that when an affix like *-atara* is added, only the initial consonant of the base remains, the rest is deleted, i.e. *yat+atara* > *y+atara* > *yatara*.

Commenting on this discussion, Whitney remarks: "This distinction of the suffixes as applied to pronominal roots from those applied to other themes is evidently artificial and false. The difference is that the roots themselves are not, like derivative themes, detachable from the suffixes appended to them - as we have seen to be the case under the two preceding rules." Whitney does not note that the commentator is following a standard method, also found in Pāṇinian grammar, where these special suffixes are given with a special marker *Ḍ*, i.e. *ḌataraC* and *ḌatamaC*, and by the force of this marker *Ḍ,* the final portion of the base beginning with its final vowel (= *ṬI*) is deleted, cf. P.5.3.92 (किंयत्तदो निर्द्धारणे द्वयोरेकस्य डतरच्) and P.5.3.93 (वा बहूनां जातिपरिप्रश्ने डतमच्), P.6.4.143 (टेः). Thus, Pāṇini's procedure is exactly the same as that given by the CAB. Whitney also misses a major distinction. While the comparative and superlative affixes are unaccented affixes, marked with *P* by Pāṇini, i.e. *-taraP* and *-tamaP*, the affixes in forms like *katará* and *katamá* are accented affixes, marked with the marker *C* by Pāṇini, i.e. *ḌataraC* and *ḌatamaC*. Thus, Whitney is not accurate in saying that the distinction of the suffixes as applied to pronominal roots from those applied to other themes is evidently artificial and false. It is a real difference recognized by both Pāṇini and the CAB.

The last verse cited by the commentator refers to words in the *samudrādigaṇa* referred to in CA (4.2.8) and fully listed in APR (217c, examples 59ff). Words in the *samudrādigaṇa* are not separated by an *avagraha* in the Padapāṭha. The APR (p. 155) lists *gótamaḥ, kataráḥ, katamáḥ, yatarā́, yatamáḥ, aśvatarásya,* and *aśvataryàḥ* in the *samudādi gaṇa,* and the verse cited by the CAB seems to make a reference to it. However, a substantial portion of the verse remains unintelligible, unless d is read as: *tasmān neṅgati gotamaḥ.*

As the VVRI edition of the AV shows, a number of manuscripts support the reading *gautamam* for AV (4.29.6). The manuscript H may have derived this reading from this tradition. However, looking at the context of the discussion, the reading intended by the CAB must be *gotamam.* The verse in the commentary points out that the affix *-tama* in the word *gótama* is not in the superlative sense (*anatiśāyane*), and therefore it is not analyzed in the Padapāṭha.

For a discussion of the example AV (1.34.4), see the note on CA (2.1.5).

४.१.३९. मतौ ।

Whitney (4.17). P adds a daṇḍa after this rule as a correction.

Translation: Before the affix *matU*, [the base is separated in the Padapāṭha with an *avagraha*].

Note: The affix *mat* is referred to here as *matU*, and this marker *U* is reminiscent of the way Pāṇini mentions this affix: *matUP*, cf. P.5.2.94 (तदस्यास्त्यस्मिन्निति मतुप्).

चतुराध्यायीभाष्य - मतौ च परतः अवग्रहो भवति । 'मधुंऽमत्' (पद, अ.वे. १.३४.३)। 'गोऽमंत्' (पद, अ.वे. १८.३.६१)।

४.१.४०. वकारादौ च ।

Whitney (4.18). O: ककारादौ°.

Translation: Also before a *v*-initial [*taddhita* affix, the base is separated with an *avagraha* in the Padapāṭha].

चतुराध्यायीभाष्य - वकारादौ च परतः अवग्रहो भवति । 'अत्रिऽवत् । वः । क्रिमयः । हन्मि । कण्वऽवत् । जमदग्निऽवत्' (पद, अ. वे. २.३२.३)। 'ऋतऽवांनम्' (पद, अ.वे. ६.३६.१)। 'सत्यऽवांनम्' (पद, अ.वे. ४.२९.१, २)। 'अश्वंऽवान्' (पद, अ.वे. ६.६८.३)। 'अञ्जिऽवम्' (पद, अ.वे. ८.६.९)। 'केशऽव[ा]ः' (पद, अ.वे. ८.६.२३)। 'राण्ऽवतः' (?)। 'मार्तऽवत्सम्' (H: वस) (पद, अ.वे. ८.६.२६)। 'आऽवयम्' (पद, अ.वे. ८.६.२६)। 'वाधूंऽयम्' (पद, अ.वे. १४.१.२९)। विनः (H: ज्ञो) प्रतिषेधो वक्तव्यः । 'द्रुवयः । (H: हवयोः) विऽबंद्धः' (पद, अ.वे. ५.२०.२)। 'उभयाविनंम्' (पद, अ.वे. ५.२५.९)। 'आमयावी' । 'मेखलावी' । 'मेधावी' ।

Note: Referring to the examples *mā́rta-vatsam, ā-vayám,* and *vā́dhū-yam,* Whitney says: "He must have been nodding when he added the last three words, of which the third has no suffix beginning with *v,* and the two others are not formed by suffixes, but by composition." Also see Whitney (AV *Transl.* Vol.II., p. 498). As for *mā́rtavatsam*, it is clear that there is no *taddhita* affix beginning with *v*, though clearly the word is a secondary *taddhita* formation from an original *mr̥tavatsa*. Contrast with *ā-vayám* (AV 8.6.26), the indivisible example *ā́vayaḥ* (AV 6.16.2). Both of these are specifically mentioned in the APR (217g, p. 158) precisely in the same context. Thus, the examples of the CAB are appropriate as far as their divisibility is concerned, though their grammatical characterizations are not always accurate.

Whitney (AV *Transl.* Vol.I., p. 255) notes that "the *pada*-text does not divide *druváyaḥ*, but the case is quoted in the comment to Prāt. iv.18 (= CA 4.1.40) as an exceptional one, *vaya* being regarded as a suffix added to *dru*." However, we should note that the expression *druváyaḥ* is not listed by the APR in its *samudrādi-gaṇa,* a list of indivisible words, and hence there is room to speculate whether it was divisible for the APR.

Referring to two more examples in the commentary, Whitney says: "It is curious that both *ā-vayam* and *mārta-vatsam* are quoted in the commentary to Prāt. iv.18 (= CA 4.1.40), as if their second member were a *taddhita* beginning with *v*." To recognize that the APR and the CAB are genetically linked, we should note that the unattested examples *āmayāvī, mekhalāvī, medhāvī* quoted by the CAB are also found in APR (p. 156) which lists words whose members are inseparable. The CAB tries to cover these examples with an exception rule, while the APR tries to cover these examples by incorporating them in the *samudrādigaṇa*, a list of indivisible words.

४.१.४१. शसि वीप्सायाम् ।

Whitney (4.19). I: 60. P adds a daṇḍa after this rule as a correction.

Translation: Also before the affix *śas*, in the distributive meaning, [the base is separated with an *avagraha* in the Padapāṭha].

चतुराध्यायीभाष्य - शसि परतः वीप्सायाम् अवग्रहो भवति । 'परुऽशः । कल्पय । एनम्' (पद, अ.वे. ९.५.४)। 'धामऽशः । स्थात्रे । रेजन्ते । विऽकृ॑तानि । रूपऽशः' (पद, अ.वे. ९.९.१६)। वीप्सायामिति किमर्थम् । 'अङ्कुशः'

(पद, अ.वे. ६.८२.३)। 'की̱नाशा॑ः' (पद, अ.वे. ३.१७.
५)।

Note: Whitney remarks with respect to the counter-examples in the CAB : "cases which it was very unnecessary to cite, since their suffix, if they have one, is *śa*, not *śas*." However, one may point out that the Prātiśākhya may be looking at a more basic surface level, where the expressions end in *śaḥ*. The citation *kīnā́śāḥ* is probably suggestive of the singular form *kīnāśaḥ* which ends in *śaḥ*.

It may be noted that the APR (p. 139) mentions *aṅkuśáḥ* in its *samudrādigaṇa*, a list of indivisible words, but not *kīnā́śāḥ*. The APR (p. 137) lists *śúnāsīrā*, from the same verse (AV 3.17.5) in which the word *kīnā́śāḥ* appears, among indivisible items. This leaves open a possibility that the APR knew *kīnā́śāḥ* as a divisible word.

४.१.४२. तातिलि ।

Whitney (4.20). E, F, I, O: तातये. A, B, C, D: तालिलि. P adds a daṇḍa after this rule as a correction.

Translation: Also before the affix *tātiL*, [the base is separated with an *avagraha* in the Padapāṭha].

Note: Pāṇini's rule 4.4.142 (सर्वदेवात्तातिल्) prescribes the affix *tātiL*, and interestingly, the CA seems to cite this affix along with its marker *L*, which indicates that the syllable preceding the suffix is *udātta*, cf. P.6.1.193 (लिति). Whitney also notes that "the related suffix *tā* is never separated from the theme to which it is appended."

The verses cited in the CAB under CA (4.1.49) also list *tātiL*. The word *ariṣṭátāti* is derived by P.4.4.143 (शिवशमरिष्टस्य करे).

चतुराध्यायीभाष्य - तातिलि परतः अवग्रहो भवति । 'म̱ह्यै । अ̱रि̱ष्टऽतांतये' (पद, अ.वे. ३.५.५)। 'ह̱विष्मं-न्तम् । मा̱ । व̱र्द्ध̱य̱ । ज्ये̱ष्ठऽतांतये' (पद, अ.वे. ६.३९.
१)।

४.१.४३. उभयाद् द्युभि ।

Whitney (4.21). E, F, I, O: °भयाद्युसि. J: °याद्युभिः. P: °याद्युभि.

Translation: [The affix] *dyuBH* [is separated with an *avagraha* in the Padapāṭha] after *ubhaya*.

चतुराध्यायीभाष्य - उभयाद् द्युभि परत अवग्रहो भवति । 'उभयऽद्युः । अभिऽएति' (पद, अ.वे. १.२५.४)। 'उभयऽद्युः । उप । हरन्ति' (पद, अ.वे. ८.१०.२१, VVRI edn.: ८.१३.८)। उभयादिति किमर्थम् । 'यः । अन्येद्युः' (पद, अ.वे. १.२५.४)।

'अन्यस्य (H: स्या) द्युभि त्वेत्वं
स्यादन्यो वा द्यु (H: द्य) भिरिष्यते (?)।
लोप एद्युभि चान्त्यस्य
सिद्धो वायं पुनर्द्युभि (?)।।' (ref?)

(See the note below for an emended version.)

Note: Whitney wonders whether the original reading might have been *dyusi,* instead of *dyubhi,* because the indicatory letter *bh* is not known even in Pāṇini, and that it would be better to assume the stem-form to be *dyus.* This conjecture is supported by the manuscripts E, F, and I. However, the rest of the manuscripts, and especially the commentary, clearly seem to have the reading *dyubhi,* and I have retained that reading. The same word appears in the verses cited under CA (4.1.49). Noting that even Pāṇini does not use *bh* as an indicatory letter, Whitney says: "one is tempted to conjecture that the authors of our system may have regarded *dyus* in these compounds as a contraction for the instrumental plural *dyubhis*."

Regarding the verse cited in the CAB, Whitney says: "This evidently has to do with the formation of *anyedyus*, accounting for the *e* which precedes the suffix : but I can offer no entirely satisfactory restoration of the text." My emended text reads as follows:

'अन्यस्य द्युभि त्वेत्वमन्ये वा द्युभिरिष्यते ।
लोप एद्युभि चान्त्यस्य सिद्धो वायं पुनर्द्युभि।।'

The verse seems to discuss a number of possible ways of dealing with the derivation of *anyedyuḥ.* The first quarter of the verse seems to say that before the affix *dyu,* the final vowel of *anya* changes to *e* (= *etvam*). The second quarter seems to say that one could prescribe the affix *dyu* after the form *anye*. The third alternative is to say that the affix is *edyu*, and that the final vowel of *anya* is deleted. I cannot however make any clear sense of the last quarter of the verse. We may note that P.5.3.22 offers *anyedyuḥ* as a *nipātana*, an unanalyzed word. On the other hand, Kātyāyana in his Vārttika on this rule (6: पूर्वान्यान्यतरेतरापराधरोभयोत्तरेभ्यः एद्युसुच्) suggests the affix *edyusUC* after words like *anya*. Adding this affix, also implies the deletion of the final vowel of *anya*, cf. P.6.4.148 (यस्येति च). Kātyāyana's Vārttika (7: द्युश्चोभयात्) derives *ubhayadyuḥ* by adding the affix *dyus* after the word *ubhaya*.

४.१.४४. मात्रे च ।

Whitney (4.22). A, B, D, M, P: omit च. P adds a daṇḍa after this as a correction.

Translation: Also before the affix *mātra*, [the base is separated with an *avagraha* in the Padapāṭha].

चतुराध्यायीभाष्य - मात्रे च परतः अवग्रहो भवति । 'अतिऽमात्रम् । अवर्धन्त' (पद, अ.वे. ५.१९.१)। 'ये । आत्मानंम् । अतिऽमात्रम्' (पद, अ.वे. ८.६.१३)।

Note: Whitney observes: "This is most palpably a rule which has its ground in the observed phenomena of the general language, and not in those of the Atharva-Veda; for although, in the later language, *mātra* came to be used in such a mode and sense as to give some ground for its treatment as a suffix, it is in the Atharvan nothing but a noun." We should note that P.5.2.37 (प्रमाणे द्वयसज्दघ्नञ्मात्रचः) prescribes the affix *mātraC*, where the marker *C* ensures that the final syllable of the formation is *udātta.* Thus, the practice of the Prātiśākhya is paralleled by that of Pāṇini. It should also be noted that *mātra* is cited as an affix in the verses quoted in the CAB under CA (4.1.49).

४.१.४५. विश्वाद्दानीमि ।

Whitney (4.23), C, E, F: °श्वाद्दानीमि. Others: °श्वादानीमि. O: विश्वहानीभि.

Translation: After *viśva*, before the [affix] *dānīm*, [there is a separation with an *avagraha* in the Padapāṭha].

चतुराध्यायीभाष्य - विश्वात्(H: न्) दानी(H: री)मि परतः अवग्रहो भवति । 'विश्वऽदानींम्' (पद, अ.वे. ७.७३.११, VVRI edn.: ७.७७. ११)। विश्वादिति किमर्थम् । 'तदानींम्' (पद, अ.वे. १०.८.३९)।

Note: Whitney points out: "Here, again, is an instance of a suffix remaining attached in *pada* to a pronominal root, while it is separated from a nominal theme (compare under rules 14-16 = CA 4.1.36-8)." The affix *-dānīm* is listed in the verses in the commentary CAB on CA (4.1.49).

४.१.४६. मयेऽसकारात् ।

Whitney (4.24). P adds a daṇḍa after this as a correction.

Translation: Before [the affix] *maya*, after [the base] not ending in *s*, [there is a separation with an *avagraha* in the Padapāṭha].

चतुराध्यायीभाष्य - मये परतः असकारात् अवग्रहो भवति। 'शकऽमयंम् । धूमम्' (पद, अ.वे. ९.१०.२५, VVRI edn.: ९.१५.२५)। असकारादिति किमर्थम् । 'अनंः। मनस्मयंम्' (पद, अ.वे. १४.१.१२)।

Note: Whitney notes that *manasmayam* is the singular example of non-separation. For some reason, the APR does not include this word among its *samudrādigaṇa*, list of indivisible words, and this raises a possibility that certain traditions may have considered this word as a separable word. This is especially significant since the APR cites other parts of this verse, without noting this peculiarity. Finally, we should note that the affix *maya* is listed in the verses cited by the CAB on CA (4.1.49).

४.१.४७. के व्यञ्जनात् ।

Whitney (4.25).

Translation: Before [the affix] *ka*, after [a base ending in] a consonant, [there is separation with an *avagraha* in the Padapāṭha].

चतुराध्यायीभाष्य - के परतः व्यञ्जनात् अवग्रहो भवति । 'अवत्ऽकम्' (पद, अ.वे. २.३.१)। 'एजत्ऽकाः' (अ.वे. ५.२३.७)। व्यञ्जनादिति किमर्थम् । 'तुण्डिकः' (पद, अ.वे. ८.६.५)। 'शिपविलुकाः' (पद, अ.वे. ५.२३.७)।

Note: For Whitney's comments on *avatkám,* see Note on CA (1.4. 12). The two counter-examples given by the CAB are the first two examples in a list in the APR (p. 161) under a rule which deals with the same issue from the opposite point of view: स्वरात् कशब्दे नेङ्गयेत्, "after a word ending in a vowel, before the affix *ka*, there should be no separation."

४.१.४८. त्वे चान्तोदात्ते ।

Whitney (4.26).

Translation: In a word accented on the final syllable, before the affix *tvá*, [the base is separated with an *avagraha* in the Padapāṭha].

चतुराध्यायीभाष्य - त्वे च परतः अन्तोदात्ते अवग्रहो भवति । 'महिऽत्वा । कस्मै' (पद, अ.वे. ४.२.४)। 'अमृतऽत्वम् । आनशुः' (पद, अ.वे. ९.१०.१, VVRI edn.: ९.१५.१)। 'शुचयः । शुचिऽत्वम्' (पद, अ.वे. १२.३. २८)। अन्तोदात्त इति किमर्थम् । 'अदितिः । जनित्वम्' (पद, अ.वे. ७.६.१)।

'जनित्वमदितेः परं नेङ्ग्यते कृज्जनपरतः (?)।
इत्वो वा स्याज्जनस्तेन पदत्वं नात्र शिष्यते (?)।।'
(source?)

इह कस्मात् समासो न भवति । 'एकऽज । त्वम्' (पद, अ.वे. ४.३१.३)। 'महि । त्वम्' (पद, अ.वे. १२.१.५५)।

‘एकज त्वं महि त्वं च तदुभयं [न?] समस्यते ।
आमन्त्रितं तयोः पूर्वं युष्मद[स्?]त्वं परं पदम् ॥’
(source?)

इह कस्मादवग्रहो न भवति । ‘अग्रे(ग्ने?)पित्व’ (?, ‘पि॒त्वो अं॑ग्ने,’ पद ⇒ ‘पि॒त्वः । अ॒ग्ने॒,’ अ.वे. ८.४.१०)।

‘तद्धितेऽवग्रहः शिष्टः पदत्वं नात्र शिष्यते ।
पिबतेस्तन्निबोधत इत्वं छान्दसमिष्यते ॥’
(source?)

Note: Whitney understands the first verse cited by the commentator as saying: “*janitva* following *aditi* is not to be treated as separable, as being formed from the root *jan* by the suffix *itva*, which is not taught to be an ending capable of constituting an independent word.” Cardona (personal communication) suggests that the reading *kṛjjanaparataḥ* is to be restored most likely to *kṛjjanaparaḥ* or *kṛjjaniparaḥ*. Such an emendation allows an overall better interpretation for the verse: (my translation): “[In the word] *janitva* [after the word *aditi* in AV 7.6.1], the *kṛt* [affix *tva*] after *jani* is not separated. Or [perhaps, in the word *janitva*], there is the affix *-itva* after [the root] *jan*. Therefore, [*jan*] is not treated as a [separable] *pada*.” The second alternative is similar to the one taught by the Uṇādisūtra (4.104) which teaches the affix *itvaN* after the root *jan,* where the marker *N* ensures that the first syllable of the word becomes *udātta*. This is the explanation offered by Sāyaṇa on AV 7.6.1.

With reference to the example *mahi tvam,* Surya Kanta *(APR, Introduction,* p. 40) appropriately points out Whitney's error. Somehow, he was unable to trace this example in AV, perhaps because he, for some unexplained reason, treated these two words as one word in his edition of the AV (12.1.55). This was quite clearly an error, and one must read: दे॒वै॒रुक्ता व्यसं॑र्पो महि॒ त्वम्. Here the word *mahi* is a feminine vocative, uncompounded with *tvam*. In fact, the same matter is explained in the verse cited by the commentary. One should also note that the VVRI edition makes the same mistake as Whitney, and it reads *mahitvam* as a single word in the Saṃhitā, and *mahi-tvam* with an *avagraha* in the Padapāṭha. Assuming that the Padapāṭha as given by the VVRI edition reflects the manuscripts, this error must have been an old error, and we need not fault Whitney. The context, however, supports the interpretation of *mahi* as a vocative followed by the separate word *tvam*.

Whitney interprets the third verse cited in the commentary as saying that the word *pitva* is derived from the root *pā* with the Vedic suffix *itva*. I doubt if this is what the verse means. The verse teaches the derivation from the root *pā* , and then says that the *ā* of the root changes to *i* and that this change is irregular, i.e. Vedic. The word *itvam* in the verse does not refer to an affix -*itva,* but to the change of *ā* to *i*. As evidenced by Sāyaṇa's commentary on AV (8.4.10), the word *pitvaḥ* is a genitive singular of the stem *pitu-* and is paraphrased by Sāyaṇa with the word *annasya.* The discussion is occasioned by the fact that, on the face of it, the word has the element *tva,* and it is *udātta,* and hence it should be subject to this rule. The verse points out that there is no *taddhita* affix in this form, and hence it is not subject to the present rule.

४.१.४९. कृत्वे समासो वा नानापददर्शनात् ।

Whitney (4.27). B, J, M, P: °दर्शितात्. A, B: तत्वे समासो°. Ha: क्तसमासो वा°. P adds a daṇḍa after this as a correction.

Translation: The affix *kṛtva* is optionally compounded, since one diversely sees it separated or not as an independent word.

चतुराध्यायीभाष्य - कृत्वे अवग्रहो भवति । कुतः नानापददर्शनात् । 'चतुः । नमः । अष्टऽकृत्वः । भवाय । दश । कृत्वः' (पद, अ.वे. ११.२.९)। 'त्रिः । सप्त । कृत्वः' (पद, अ.वे. १२.२.२९)। नन्वेवं कथम् । व्यवस्थितेन विकल्पेन वाशब्देन प्रतिपादितत्वात् । तथा हि ।

'करोतेर्दशसप्तभ्यां त्वशब्दः कृद्विधीयते ।
संख्याया अनुदात्ताया अष्टशब्दात्समस्यते ।।
उदात्तात् दश सप्तेति एवं पूर्वेण विग्रहः ।
धाप(H: य)र्यन्तास्तद्धिता ये तेष्वेवावग्रहो भवेत् ।।
अतोऽन्येन पद(H: दे)त्वेऽपि युवत्यादिषु तद्धितम् ।
धा-त्रा(H: त्वा)-था(H: प्या)-तातिलि-शसि-
दानीम्-तरतमौ(H: मो)-मतुप् ।
व-मात्र-द्युभि(H: ति)-के-त्वापि
मयट्-कृत्वेष्ववग्रहः ।।' (source?)

Note: On some occasions, *kr̥tvas* is separated as an independent word in the Padapāṭha, for example *dáśa / kŕ̥tvaḥ* (AV 11.2.9) and *saptá / kŕ̥tvaḥ* (AV 12.2.29). On the other hand, it is compounded with a number word in some instances, i.e. *aṣṭa-kŕ̥tvaḥ* (AV 11.2.9). The CA rule simply says that this happens optionally because of the diverse behavior in the Padapāṭha.

The CAB looks at the same situation and says that this is a case of *vyavasthitavibhāṣā* "settled option," namely that in certain known cases the compounding takes place, and in certain other known cases it does not, and it is not that in each case the compounding is optional.

This is further supported by the fine analysis presented in the first cited verse. It says that the item *kŕ̥tvaḥ*, which is an accented item, is compounded with unaccented number words like *aṣṭa*. However, it is not compounded with accented number words *saptá* and *dáśa.* This goes far beyond the rule of the CA in providing a rational reason for the diverse behavior of this item. Also note the use of the word *samāsa* for a juncture of a *taddhita* affix in the CA rule. On the other hand, perhaps to get over this oddity, the cited verse does not treat *kr̥tvas* as a *taddhita* affix, but as a verbal noun, derived from the root *kr̥* with the *kr̥t* affix *-tva*. This makes it seem more like a normal compound in Pāṇinian terms. This perhaps shows that the cited verses are more sensitive to the categories of the Pāṇinian grammar. Also note that the forms in which the affixes are cited in the verses are closer to their Pāṇinian forms, cf. *matup* and *mayaṭ*, P.5.2.94 (तदस्यास्त्यस्मिन्निति मतुप्) and P.5.4.21 (तत्प्रकृतवचने मयट्). The CA rules (4.1.39) and (4.1.46) refer to *matu* and *maya*, rather than to *matup* and *mayaṭ.*

The recognition that the last verse quoted in the commentary provides an enumeration of all the suffixes thus far treated of as separable allows us to reconstruct the text of that verse in a much more satisfactory way, in spite of the sorry state of the manuscript. As a parallel to युवत्यादिषु तद्धितम् in the cited verses, we find युवत्यादिषु तद्धिते in APR (217a). The wording धापर्यन्ताः in our verses here may have a parallel in धोपनतेः in APR (217a).

४.१.५०. जातीयादिषु च ।

Whitney (4.28). C, M: this rule comes before CA 4.1.49. O omits च.

Translation: Also, [there is separation of the base with an *avagraha* in the Padapāṭha] before [the affixes] such as *-jātīya.*

चतुराध्यायीभाष्य - जातीयादिषु च परतः अवग्रहो भवति । 'पटुऽजातीयः' । 'मृदुऽजातीयः' । 'पण्डितऽजातीयः' । 'शोभनऽजातीयः' । 'भागऽधेयम्' (पद, अ.वे. ६.१११.१)। 'रूपऽधेयम्' (रूपऽधेयानि, पद, अ.वे. २.२६.१)। 'नामऽधेयम्' (पद, अ.वे. ७.१०९.६, VVRI edn.: ७.११४.६)।

Note: Surya Kanta (*APR, Intro.*, p. 39) points to the fact that the examples of *jātīya* are not found in the Vulgate of the AV, and argues that, therefore, the Vulgate is not a genuine Śaunakīya recension, suggesting that examples of *jātīya* must have occurred in a genuinely Śaunakīya text. However, as Whitney notes, the examples of *jātīya* cited by the commentator are identical with examples appearing in commentaries on Pāṇini (5.3.69: प्रकारवचने जातीयर्). This would suggest that even the commentator did not find any examples in the AV text known to him, and got his examples from his exposure to the Pāṇinian tradition. It is thus very likely that the Gaṇa *jātīyādi* itself was not a purely Atharvan Gaṇa, but was taken by the author of the CA from some general grammar of Sanskrit. Whitney says: "What other frequently occurring final members of compounds it may have pleased the authors of our treatise to regard as suffixes, and to include in this *gaṇa*, I do not know. I have noted no actual suffixes as needing to be comprehended in it."

It must be noted, however, that this general grammar used as a source of information by the author of CA was not identical with Pāṇini's grammar in every respect. Thus, Pāṇini himself treats *jātīya* as an affix, and not as a separate word forming a compound with another word. The CA, on the other hand, thinks of some affixes being compounded with their bases. Also, there is no *jātīyādigaṇa* in Pāṇini's grammar.

४.१.५१. यादाविच्छायां स्वरात् कर्मनामतन्मानिप्रेप्सुषु ।

Whitney (4.29). A, B, D: °कर्मेनाम°. A, B: °नामे°. I numbers यादाविछायां as 70, and स्वरात् as 71. E, F, O: °स्वस्वरात्°. P places a daṇḍa after कर्मनाम.

Translation: [There is separation with an *avagraha* in the Padapāṭha] after [a base ending in] a vowel, before a *y*-initial desire-expressing [affix], in verbal nouns, derivatives in the sense of "thinks of oneself like *x*," and agent nouns in the sense of "desirous of doing *x*."

चतुराध्यायीभाष्य - यादौ इच्छायां स्वरात् अवग्रहो भवति कर्मनामतन्मानिप्रेप्सुषु । 'अध्वरिऽयताम्' (पद, 'अध्वरीयताम्,' संहिता, अ.वे. १.४.१)। 'अघऽयुः' (पद, 'अघायुः,' संहिता, अ.वे. ४.३.२)। 'वृषऽयमाणः' (पद, 'वृषायमाणः,' संहिता, अ.वे. २.५.७)। 'शत्रुऽयतीम् । अभि' (पद, 'शत्रूयतीमभि,' संहिता, अ.वे. ३.१.३)। यादाविति किमर्थम् । 'तत् । सिसासति' (पद, 'तत्सिंषासति,' संहिता, अ.वे. १३.२.१४)। स्वरादिति किमर्थम् । 'येनं । श्रवस्यवः' (पद, 'येनं श्रवस्यवः,' संहिता, अ.वे. ३.९.४)।

Note: Whitney remarks: "Not one of the technical terms used in this rule is known to me to occur elsewhere than in the grammatical language of our treatise. ... *Karmanāma*, then, I have without much hesitation rendered by 'participle;' and *tanmānin* seems to me to mean 'implying the making or doing of that which the theme indicates,' and so to be applicable to such words as *śatrūyanti, aghāyanti,* where the signification is not simply desiderative : but of this I do not feel altogether confident, and I have at one time sought in the word a designation of the middle participles having the termination *māna; prepsu* I think must belong to such derivative adjectives as *devayu, śravasyu*."

The term *karmanāma* is found in the Nirukta (2.13) in the sense of action-noun, e.g. व्रतमिति कर्मनाम, as contrasted with *sattvanāma* 'noun referring to an object,' Nirukta (1.1). The word *karmanāma* probably has an extended sense of a noun derived from a verb, as evidenced by the fact that it is used to refer to such words as *apaḥ, apnaḥ, daṃsaḥ* etc., cf. Nirukta (3.1): कर्मनामान्युत्तराणि षड्विंशतिः. Its further derivative कार्मनामिकः (संस्कारः) is also found in the Nirukta (1.13) where it refers to a proper derivation of a noun from a verb. Durga's commentary on this passage says: कर्मकृतं नाम कर्मनाम । पाचकलावकादि । तस्मिन् भवः कार्मनामिकः संस्कारः. Here, in the CA rule, Whitney may be correct in assuming that the word is used in a more restricted sense of participle.

The expression *tan-mānin* is not found elsewhere in grammar, but its meaning is similar to the meaning of आत्ममाने in Pāṇini (3.2.83: आत्ममाने खश्च). Examples of this rule, such as दर्शनीयमानिन्, mean दर्शनीयमात्मानं मन्यते, namely, 'though someone is actually not good-looking, he thinks himself to be good-looking.' This type of meaning is ascribed to the forms *vṛṣāyámāṇaḥ* and *śatrūyátīm,* i.e. acting like x.

The word *prepsu* simply means 'desirous,' and is exemplified by *aghāyúḥ* and *śravasyavaḥ.*

For a related rule and examples, see: CA (3.1.18: इच्छायां च यकारादौ), and APR (154: यकारादौ बहुलं दीर्घः). The examples in the CAB on the present rule are identical with the examples on APR (154).

४.१.५२. वस्ववस्वप्नसुम्नसाधुभिर्या ।

Whitney (4.30). A, B, D, P: °सुन्म°. J, M: वस्ववच°.

Translation: [There is separation with an *avagraha* in the Padapāṭha of the affix] *yā* combined with *vasu, ava, svapna, sumna*, and *sādhu.*

Note: The verse cited in the CAB reports Śākaṭāyana's view that separation with an *avagraha* occurs only in five words involving *yā*. The enumeration, both in the CA rule and in the cited verse, is important because *yā* is not separated with an *avagraha* in other instances, e.g. *su-kṣetriyā́* and *su-gātuyā́* in AV (4.33.2). These two words are offered as instances in the CAB on CA (4.1.34). There are other words ending in *-yā́* which are not divisible and are listed in the APR (p. 154-3) as members of the *samudrādi-gaṇa*, a list of indivisible words, e.g. *mithuyā́* (AV 4.29.7), *amuyā́* (AV 5.22.1), *bhadráyā* (AV 3.30.3), *urviyā́* (AV 5.12.5). Here, *bhadráyā* has been included with other forms, and yet its different accentuation shows that it is a different kind of word. It is not clear why the division takes place in some words, and not in others.

चतुराध्यायीभाष्य - वसुअवस्वप्नसुम्न(H: म्र)साध्वित्येतैः सह याशब्दे परतः अवग्रहो भवति । 'वसुऽया' (पद, अ.वे. ४.३३.२)। 'अवऽया' (पद, अ.वे. २.३५.१)। 'स्वप्नऽया' (पद, अ.वे. ५.७.८)। 'सुम्न(H: म्र)ऽया' (पद, अ.वे. ७.५५.१)। 'साधुऽया' (पद, अ.वे. १०.४.२१)।

'पञ्चैवावग्रहानाह याशब्दे शाकटायनः ।
अन्तोदात्तः पदत्वं च विभक्त्यर्थे भवेत्तु या ॥'
(source?)

Note: On the example *ava-yā,* Whitney rightly says: "The second of them is classed with the rest only by a blunder, since it is evidently *avayās,* the irregular nominative singular of *ava-yāj,* and ought to be written by the pada-text *ava-yāḥ,* instead of *ava-yā.*" While Whitney is philologically correct, the form as sanctioned by the CA indicates that the form was understood differently by the Indian tradition. The VVRI edition reads अवऽयाः, but notes the manuscript variant अवऽया. Sāyaṇa reads अवयाः and refers to P.8.2.67 for the *nipātana* of the form अवयाः. The example *sumna-yā* is cited under APR (7, example 31). The VVRI edition reads सुऽगातुया for AV (4.33.2), but notes the manuscript variant सुगातुऽया, and also refers to the Padapāṭha of the RV for this alternative division. This may also be a possible influence from the RV tradition on some AV reciters.

Referring to *sumnayā́* in AV 7.55.1, Whitney (*AV Transl.* Vol.I., p. 425) remarks: "The construction seems so decidedly to call for a locative in **c** that *sumnayā́* (p. *sumna-yā́,* by Prāt. iv. 30 = CA 4.1.52) is rendered as if it were for *-yāú,* from *-yú;* the comm. glosses it with *sumne sukhe.*"

Looking at the verse cited in the commentary, it seems that this rule represents a practice which was instituted by Śākaṭāyana. The rule makes no reference to Śākaṭāyana, but the commentary makes this clear. This is somewhat similar to CA 1.1.10, cf. Bhārgava-Bhāskara's commentary on CA 1.1.10.

४.१.५३. भिर्भ्याम्भ्यःसु ।

Whitney (4.31). A, B, D, J, P: भिभ्यांभ्यः°.

Translation: Before the affixes *bhiḥ, bhyām,* and *bhyaḥ,* [the base is separated with an *avagraha* in the Padapāṭha]..

चतुराध्यायीभाष्य - भिर्भ्याम्भ्यःसु परतः अवग्रहो भवति । 'पञ्चऽभिः । अङ्गुलिऽभिः' (पद, अ.वे. ४.१४.७)। 'उरुऽभ्याम् । ते । अष्ठीवद्ऽभ्याम् । पार्ष्णिऽभ्याम् । प्रऽपदाभ्याम्'

(पद, अ.वे. २.३३.५)। 'अस्थिऽभ्यः । ते । मज्जऽभ्यः । स्नावंऽभ्यः । धमनिंऽभ्यः' (पद, अ.वे. २.३३.६)।

Note: For a related rule, see APR (218: दीर्घाद्भिर्भ्यांभ्यःसु) which combines into one rule CA (4.1.53) and CA (4.1.55). However, the APR rule prohibits the separation after a base ending in a long vowel, before these affixes.

४.१.५४. सौ च ।

Whitney (4.32). P has no daṇḍa after this rule.

Translation: Also, before the [locative plural affix] *su*, [the base is separated with an *avagraha* in the Padapāṭha].

चतुराध्यायीभाष्य - सौ च परतः अवग्रहो भवति । 'अंहंऽसु' (पद, अ.वे. ६.३५.२)। 'अप्ऽसु' (पद, अ.वे. १.४.४)। 'वयम् । राजंऽसु' (पद, अ.वे. ७.५०.७, VVRI edn.: ७.५२.७)।

Note: On the expression *áṃhasu* (AV 6.35.2), Whitney (*AV Transl.* Vol.I., p. 307) remarks: "The translation [= 'in our distresses'] given implies that *áṅhasu* (which is read by all the mss. without exception, and is quoted so in the commentary to Prāt. iv.32 [= CA 4.1.54]) is the same with the usual *áṅhaḥsu;* no stem *áṅhan* is found anywhere else. The commentary foolishly explains it by *abhigantavyeṣu,* adj. to *ukthеṣu*."

For an identically worded rule, see APR (218b: सौ च). However, like APR (218: दीर्घाद्भिर्भ्यांभ्यःसु), APR (218b) says that after a base ending in a long vowel, there is no separation with an *avagraha* before *su*.

४.१.५५. न दीर्घात् ।

Whitney (4.33). P adds a daṇḍa after this as a correction.

Translation: There is no [separation with an *avagraha* in the Padapāṭha of *bhis, bhyām, bhyas,* and *su*] after [a base ending in] a long vowel.

Note: See the Notes on the preceding two rules for comparison with the APR. Whitney points out: "No case ending is separable after a long final vowel, whether this be an original long final of the theme, or the result of a prolongation according to the rules of declension." This prohibition is there, perhaps, because it is difficult to tell immediately whether the long vowel is an original one or lengthened before the affix. Thus, it fits the notion of *sandeha* 'confusion, lack of clarity' as a reason for not separating parts of a word, cf. CA (4.2.5: षोडशी सन्देहात्).

चतुराध्यायीभाष्य - न दीर्घात् अवग्रहो भवति भिस्भ्यांभ्यःसु परतः सौ च । 'याभिः । सत्यम् । भवति' (पद, अ.वे. ९.२.२५)। 'ताभिः । त्वम् । अस्मान्' (पद, अ.वे. ९.२.२५)। 'अक्षीभ्याम् । ते । नासिकाभ्याम् । कर्णाभ्याम्' (पद, अ.वे. २.३३.१)। 'गोभ्यः । अश्वेभ्यः' (पद, अ.वे. ३.२८.३)। 'आसु । इतरासु' (पद, अ.वे. ३.१०.४)।

४.१.५६. विनामे च ।

Whitney (4.34). A, B: व for च.

Translation: [No separation of *su* takes place] also when there is the change of *s* [of *su*] to *ṣ*.

चतुराध्यायीभाष्य - विनामे च परतः न अवग्रहो भवति । 'प्रति । तिष्ठ । दिक्षु' (पद, अ.वे. ४.१४.९)। 'नमस्यः । विक्षु (H: विष्णु) । ईड्यः' (पद, अ.वे. २.२.१)। 'मानुषीषु । दिक्षु' (पद, अ.वे. ५.११.८)। 'मरुतः । विक्षु' (पद, अ.वे. ८.४.१८)। 'यम् । च । विक्षु' (पद, अ.वे. ९.५.१९)। 'परि । पश्य । विक्षु' (पद, अ.वे. ८.३.१०)। 'सुऽवृजनासु। दिक्षु' (पद, अ.वे. १८.१.४६)।

४.१.५७. वसौ ह्रस्वात् ।

Whitney (4.35). Most mss. read ऱ्ह for ह्र. P adds a daṇḍa after this rule as a correction.

Translation: After [the base ending in] a short [vowel], before [the affix] *vasU,* [the base is separated with an *avagraha* in the Padapāṭha].

चतुराध्यायीभाष्य - वसौ परतः ह्रस्वात् अवग्रहो भवति । 'चकृऽवान्' (पद, अ.वे. २.३५.३)। 'पपिऽवान्' (पद, अ.वे. १४.१.३)। ह्रस्वात् किम् । 'विद्वान्' (अ.वे. २.१.२)।

'अपदेऽवग्रहः शिष्ट इकारेण पदादिना ।
धात्वन्ताच्च वसौ ह्रस्वाच्चकृवान् पपिवानिति ॥
उपसर्गसमासेऽपि वसावेवावगृह्यते ।
किकिनावविशेषेण भूते ताभ्यां विधीयते ॥
वसु[:] स्वार्थे तयो[:] ल[H: लु]ब्धं बहुलं छन्दसीति च ।
वा तयोः कृतोः समासश्चो[Whitney: साच्चा]पजायेत
वस्तुतः ॥
अवकारे पदत्वं न पूर्वेणैवावगृह्यते ।
अह्रस्वेऽपि पदत्वं स्यात् प्राप्तस्तत्राप्यवग्रहः ॥
अह्रस्वे छान्दसत्वात्तु रुत्वमाहुर्मनीषिणः ।' (source?)

Note: About the verses cited in the commentary, Whitney remarks: "The meaning of some of these lines is very clear, and they are seen to cover the ground of our present rule and of the two following : others are obscure, and need emendation before they can be intelligently rendered." However, now we can indeed make better sense of these verses. They provide further insights into how some of these derivations were viewed by this tradition.

The form *cakr̥-vā́n* did not pose a major problem because the base *cakr̥* is viewed as naturally ending in a short vowel. However, the form *papi-vā́n* did apparently pose a problem. In this form, this tradition did not believe that the root ended in *i.* The element *papi-* was viewed as being made up of *pap* [from √*pā*] followed by an affix *i*. This affix *i* is identified in the verses with the affixes *Ki* or *KiN* prescribed by P.3.2.171 (आदृगमहनजनः किकिनौ लिट् च), which yields forms like *papi, dadi, jagmi.* The cited verse says that the affix *vasU* is added to *pap-i,* to express no additional meaning, but that of the base (*svārthe*), to yield *pap-i-vas*, cf. P.3.2.107 (क्वसुश्च). The KV on this rule offers the examples *jakṣivān* and *papivān.* By the convention बहुलं छन्दसि (= e.g. P.3.2.88), which says that grammatical rules apply diversely in Vedic texts, the two *kṛt* affixes *i* and *vasU* are compounded into *ivasU,* cf. वा तयोः कृतोः समासश्चोपजायेत तत्वतः. Thus, the vowel *i* in *pap+ivas* occurs at the beginning of the *pada,* i.e. *ivas*, rather than at the end of the preceding base, and yet in this exceptional case, an *avagraha* has been prescribed after *i* of *ivas,* cf. अपदेऽवग्रहः शिष्टः इकारेण पदादिना.

We should note that the standard Pāṇinian tradition derives the forms *jakṣivān* and *papivān* differently from the process outlined here in these verses, cf. Nyāsa on KV on P.3.2.107: जक्षिवानिति । 'लिट्यन्यतरस्याम्' (पा.२.४.४०) इत्यदेर्घस्लादेशः, 'वस्वेकाजाद्धसाम्' (पा.७.२.६७) इतीट्, 'घसिभसोर्हलि च' (पा.६.४.१००) इत्युपधालोपः, ... पपिवानिति । पा पाने । पूर्ववदिट् । 'आतो लोप इटि च' (पा.६.४.६४) इत्याकारलोपः. The important point to note is that the Pāṇinian tradition does not view these formations as containing *Ki* or *KiN* followed by *vasU*, but as formations with the affix *KvasU,* with an initial augment *iṬ*.

The line उपसर्गसमासेऽपि वसावेवावगृह्यते teaches the same rule as CA (4.1.58).

The line अवकारे पदत्वं न पूर्वेणैवावगृह्यते teaches the same rule as CA (4.1.59).

The final verse seems to relate to those forms where *vas* is preceded by a long vowel (*ahrasva*), such as *jigīvā́n* (AV 4.22.6), which is not split in the Padapāṭha. The last line seems to refer to the fact that the Padapāṭha form *jigīvā́n* appears as *jigīvā̐* in the Saṃhitāpāṭha through the irregular Vedic (छान्दसत्वात्) change of the final *n* to *rU* (रुत्वम्) [*rU* > *y* > *Ø*], with the concomitant nasalization of the preceding vowel, cf. P.8.3.7 (नश्छव्यप्रशान्), P.8.3.8 (उभयथर्क्षु), and P.8.3.2 (अत्रानुनासिकः पूर्वस्य तु वा).

Note that CA (4.1.57) uses the expression *vasu-,* where the final *u* is a marker sound, similar to Pāṇinian usage. Such markers are, however, nowhere defined in the CA. The verses cited by the commentary show a thorough familiarity with the Pāṇinian system. They use the Pāṇinian expressions *Ki-Kinau* and *rU*.

४.१.५८. तेनैवोपसृष्टेऽपि ।

Whitney (4.36). E, F, Ha, O: °स्पृष्टे°.

Translation: Even when [the verb is compounded] with a preverb (*upasarga*), the separation [with an *avagraha* in the Padapāṭha takes place] with that [affix *vasU*] alone.

चतुराध्यायीभाष्य - तेनैव अवग्रहो भवति । उपसृष्टेऽपि वसौ । 'परेयिऽवांसम्' (पद, अ.वे. १८.१.४९)। 'प्रविशिऽ-वांसम्' (पद, अ.वे. ४.२३.१)। 'जक्षिऽवांसः, पपिऽवांसः' (पद, अ.वे. ७.९७.३, VVRI edn.: ७.१०२.३)। 'उत्तस्थिऽ-वांसः' (पद, अ.वे. ६.९३.१)।

Note: As Whitney notes, the examples *jakṣi-vāṃsaḥ* and *papi-vāṃsaḥ* are wrongly included here in the CAB perhaps by the mistake of the copyist. The rule applies to verbs with preverbs. A verse cited in the CAB on CA (4.1.57) teaches the same rule: उपसर्गसमासेऽपि वसावेवावगृह्यते.

४.१.५९. उपसर्गेणावकारे ।

Whitney (4.37). A, B, C: °र्ग्रे°. O: उपसर्गेणवकारे.

Translation: Also, when [the affix *vasU* appears as] non-*v*-initial [i.e. *us*, the separation with an *avagraha* in the Padapāṭha] applies to the preverb (*upasarga*).

चतुराध्यायीभाष्य - उपसर्गेण अवग्रहो भवति अवकारादपि वसौ । 'आऽजग्मुषः । अनुऽमते' (पद, अ.वे. २.२६.२)। 'वशा । प्रऽददुषे । दुहे' (पद, अ.वे. १२.४.३५)।

'यदा प्रसारणं तस्य पदत्वं नेष्यते तदा ।
पूर्वेणावग्रहः सिद्धो यतः तज्जीयते पदम् ॥'
(source?)

Note: Whitney says: "That is to say, when the suffix is contracted into *uṣ*, in the weak forms of declension, it is no longer separable, and the *avagraha* remains where it was before, between the preposition and the verb." This rule is also stated in the verse cited in the CAB on CA (4.1.57): अवकारे पदत्वं न पूर्वेणैवावगृह्यते. The verse cited in the CAB on the present rule is rendered by Whitney as: "when the suffix suffers contraction, its capability of standing as an independent *pada* is not taught : the former constituent then maintains the *avagraha*, as having a superior right to it (?)." The word *prasāraṇa* in the verse is identical with *samprasāraṇa* of Pāṇini 1.1.45 (इग्यणः सम्प्रसारणम्), and is better translated as 'expansion [e.g. of *v* into *u*],' rather than as 'contraction.'

It should also be noted that there is no *avagraha* in forms like *ábibhyuṣīḥ* (AV 3.14.3) and *babhūvúṣī* (AV 9.10.21), because in these forms too the original affix *vas* changes to *us*. The form *babhūvúṣī* is especially interesting, because, here seemingly there is an affixal element *vúṣī*, beginning with *v*. We do not know exactly how the Prātiśākhya tradition conceptualized the derivation of such a form. However, Pāṇini prescribes an end-augment *vUK* to the root, cf. P.6.4.88 (भुवो वुग्लुङ्लिटोः), giving us the division *babhūv+úṣī*, leaving the affix as a non-*v*-initial form of the original *vasU*.

४.१.६०. समन्तः पूरणे ।

Whitney (4.38). I: 80.

Translation: The word *samanta*, [only] in the sense of 'full,' [is split with an *avagraha* in the Padapāṭha].

चतुराध्यायीभाष्य - समन्त इति पूरणार्थेऽवग्रहो भवति । 'पुष्करिणीः । सम्ऽअन्ताः' (पद, अ.वे. ४.३४.५)। 'सम्ऽअग्रः । सम्ऽअन्तः । भूयासम्' (पद, अ.वे. ७.८१.४)। पूरण इति किमर्थम् । 'यथा । वृक्षम् । लिबुजा । समन्तम्' (पद, अ.वे. ६.८.१)। समन्तं सर्वतोऽर्थेऽन्तोदात्तं नावगृह्यते। आद्युदात्तमवगृह्यते । पूरणार्थे - 'पुष्करिणीः । सम्ऽअन्ताः' (पद, अ.वे. ४.३४.५)।

Note: Whitney faults the commentator for making pseudo-semantic distinctions between the two uses of the word *samanta*. He translates the word *pūraṇa* as 'completion' and *sarvataḥ* as 'wholly.' Thus translated, the meanings are indeed not sufficiently distinct. However, *pūraṇa* rather refers to being full, endowed with everything. On the other hand, the expression *sarvataḥ* refers to 'on all sides.' This is the distinction intended by the commentator, and it is a valid distinction. Sāyaṇa, on AV (6.8.1), paraphrases the word *samantam* with *sarvataḥ,* while, on AV (7.81.4), he paraphrases the same word with *sampūrṇa*.

The passage समन्तः सर्वतोऽर्थेऽन्तोदात्तं नावगृह्यते, आद्युदात्तमवगृह्यते पूरणार्थे is comparable to APR (p. 157).

४.१.६१. अनतौ विसंभ्यां प्राणाख्या चेत् ।

Whitney (4.39). B, C, J, M, P: Daṇḍa after विसंभ्यां. A, D, E, F, H, O, P: अनंतौ. I: अनितौ.

Translation: After the [preverbs] *vi* and *sam*, before the [forms of the verb-root] *an*, [there is separation with an *avagraha* in the Padapāṭha], if [the resulting word is] a name of [one of] the breaths.

चतुराध्यायीभाष्य - अन(H: नं)तौ वि सम् इत्येताभ्याम् अवग्रहो भवति । प्राणाख्या चेद् गम्यमाना(H: ने) । 'विऽआनः(H: नं) । आयुः' (पद, अ.वे. १८.२.४६)। 'समऽआनम् । अस्मिन् । कः' (पद, अ.वे. १०.२.१३)। विसंभ्यामिति किमर्थम् । 'प्राणोऽपानः' (?, 'प्राणो अपानः,' पद ⇒ 'प्राणः । अपानः', अ.वे. १८.२.४६)। प्राणाख्या चेदिति किमर्थम् । 'समानम् । अस्तु । वः । मनः' (पद, अ.वे. ६.६४.३)।

Note: Whitney remarks: "We should have expected this rule to be stated the other way; namely, that the root *an* was not separated from *pra* and *apa* (in the compounds *prāṇa* and *apāna*, which are always thus written in *pada*, without division). This would, one the one hand, be theoretically preferable, since the general rules for division would lead us to expect the *pada* readings *pra-āna*, *apa-āna*, *vi-āna*, and *sam-āna*, and we therefore ought to have the first two denied, rather than the last two ratified, by a special rule : and, on the hand, it would be practically more accurate, since *udāna*, which occurs in the combination *vyāna-udānau*, is doubtless a separable compound, and is in fact so regarded by the commentator, under rule 42 (= CA 4.1.64) below. Why *prāṇa* and *apāna* should not also be divided, it is far from easy to see."

Note that the AV form is *prāṇati* corresponding to the RV and the Classical form *prāṇiti*. This justifies the wording of this rule, e.g. *anatau*. The reading *anitau* found in the manuscript I is either under the influence of the Ṛgvedic tradition or an unconscious classicalization. Also see: CA (4.2.11: प्राणति प्राणन्ति). The discussion in the commentary that the word *vyānaḥ* is separated in the *pada*-text with an *avagraha,* but the words *prāṇa* and *apāna* are not so separated matches with what we find in the mss. of the Padapāṭha. However, it is not immediately clear why such should be the case. One possibility is that the divisions of these two words were easily perceived in a natural pronunciation of *vyāna* as *vi(y)āna* and of *samāna* as *sam āna*. On the other hand, no such natural separation was possible in the pronunciation of the words *prāṇa* and *apāna*. This seems to have been the explanation offered by thc APR (p.135: प्राणोऽपानति वेदितः प्रापाभ्यां दीर्घसंशयात्). If one is to venture an explanation beyond this statement, one could say that such a state of affairs reflects a very early phase in the development of ideas about *sandhi,* and the Padakāras have shied away from those cases of possible segmentation which might have involved what the CA calls *sandeha,* cf. CA (4.2.5: षोडशी सन्देहात्). The word *sandeha* obviously have both the meanings, fusion and confusion!

Some examples of the CAB are found in APR (p. 157). Also compare the formulation of APR (217f, p. 157):

समानमस्मिन्को देव (अ.वे. १०.२.१३) इत्येतदेवावगृह्यते ।
अतोऽन्यानि समानानि नेङ्गयेत्सर्वदा कविः ॥

४.१.६२. काम्याम्रेडितयोः ।

Whitney (4.40). A, B, D: °म्यांम्रे°. J, M, P: कम्यांम्रे°.

Translation: [There is separation with an *avagraha* in the Padapāṭha] before the [affix] *kāmya* and [before] a repeated word.

चतुराध्यायीभाष्य - काम्ये च परतः आम्रेडिते च अवग्रहो भवति । 'अश्रद्धाः । धनऽकाम्या' (पद, अ.वे. १२.२.५१)। 'अनृतम् । वित्तऽकाम्या' (पद, अ.वे. १२.३.५२)। 'भूयःऽभूयः । श्वःऽश्वः' (पद, अ.वे. १०.६.५)।

Note: It is clear that the author of the Padapāṭha separates *kāmyā* with an Avagraha. While Pāṇini treats this as a case of affixation (e.g. *kāmyaC*), cf.

P.3.1.9 (काम्यच्च), the CA treats this as a case of an affix being compounded with its base. Whitney remarks: "This is a strange rule. In the first place, the Atharva-Veda furnishes no ground whatever for the treatment of *kāmya* as a suffix, even though it be regarded as such in certain combinations in the general grammatical system (see Pāṇ. iii.1.9 etc.). We find it only in such compounds as the commentator instances, which would fall under rule 9 of this chapter (= CA 4.1.31) without occasioning any difficulty or hesitation. In the second place, I can discover no possible reason for combining together in one rule things so utterly unconnected and incongruous as the occurrence of this suffix and that of words repeated in an emphatic or a distinctive sense. The dual termination, however, is our warrant that we have not here, as in the case of rules 12 and 13 of the first chapter (= CA 1.1.14-15), two rules written and explained together by the commentator."

It may be observed that CA (4.1.31: समासे च) seems to refer to combinations which are traditionally considered to be *samāsa* 'compounds' by the systems of general grammar. However, the CA considers many cases of affixation as cases of compounding, since the members are so separated with an *avagraha* in the Padapāṭha. One may assume that traditions of general grammar, such as reflected in Pāṇini's grammar, had already classified *kāmya* as an affix, and the CA was simply responding to such a classification by including it here as a case of affixal compound.

As for the *āmreḍita* 'repeated word,' the CAB on CA (2.3.2) uses the term *āmreḍita-samāsa* to refer to *paraḥparaḥ* in AV (12.3.39). The CA inclusion of *āmreḍita* here indicates a concern that this is not considered to be a compound (*samāsa*) by the traditional general grammars of Sanskrit, and hence needs to be included explicitly. K.V. Abhyankar in his own recent work on the Padapāṭha formulates a rule: द्विर्वचनवृत्तौ समासवदवग्रहः, (Abhyankar, 1974, p. 19). Note here the expression *samāsavat,* which suggests a similar hesitation about using the term *samāsa* to refer to such a phenomenon. Abhyankar brings it under a wider category of *vṛtti*, which may be translated as 'composition,' to distinguish it from a narrower notion of compound. See my note on CA (2.3.2). Also see George Cardona (1996)

४.१.६३. इवे च ।

Whitney (4.41).

Translation: Also, before *iva*, [the preceding word is separated with an *avagraha* in the Padapāṭha].

चतुराध्यायीभाष्य - इवे च परतः अवग्रहो भवति । 'सालावृकान्ऽइंव' (पद, अ.वे. २.२७.५)।

Note: It is clear that the CA suspected that the combination of *iva* with the preceding word may not be included in the traditional notion of compound, and hence needed to be mentioned separately. Pāṇini had clearly not intended this to be a compound. However, under the pressure of the Prātiśākhya tradition, Kātyāyana suggests that compounding with *iva* be accepted by the grammarians, cf. Vārttika: इवेन विभक्त्यलोपः पूर्वपदप्रकृतिस्वरत्वं च, on P.2.1.4 (सह सुपा). Patañjali on this Vārttika explicitly uses the term *samāsa:* इवेन सह समासो विभक्त्यलोपः पूर्वपदप्रकृतिस्वरत्वं च वक्तव्यम्, MB, (Kielhorn edn., Vol. I., p. 378). Here, the word *vaktavyam* is significant in that it indicates that this is a new prescription, not available from Pāṇini's rules.

४.१.६४. मिथोऽवगृह्ययोर्मध्यमेन ।

Whitney (4.42). B, D: °ध्येमेन. C, J, M, P: °मध्येन. O: °थोवावगृ°. P: no daṇḍa after this rule.

> **Translation:** The separation [with an *avagraha* in the Padapāṭha is effected at the juncture] in between two separable [compound-expressions, when they are further joined to form a new compound].

Note: For example, *āñjana* is separable as *ā-añjana* and *abhyañjana* is separable as *abhi-añjana*. When these two are further compounded, their new joint is separated in the Padapāṭha with an *avagraha.* This shows a great awareness of the derivational history of a larger compound, and shows that compounding is not simply a flatland concatenation of disparate items, but a step-by-step process.

Whitney criticizes the formulation of this rule: "The Vāj. Pr. finds no need of such a rule as this, nor does it seem imperatively called for, all possible cases being already disposed of by rules 10 and 12 above (CA 4.1.32, 34). Still less is to be seen the necessity of adding to it the two which next follow, and which it obviously includes."

While CA (4.1.32, 34) deal with a new accretion to a previously compounded unit, the present rule deals with a second level combination of two independent compound-expressions, and hence has a somewhat different subject matter. Secondly, the formulation of the next two rules indicates that not all combinations were easily categorized as *samāsa*s, and hence had to be listed separately. Not all *avagṛhya*s were readily categorized as compounds. It indicates a historically important dimension of the term *samāsa*, namely that it had originally a narrower meaning, and that its scope was slowly widened in some traditions. The CA shows the transitional phase where there is still some hesitation about the exact scope of the term, and hence the need for specific rules. On the other hand, the verses cited in the CAB on CA (4.1.66) seem to take the expanded meaning of term *samāsa* for granted and hence lump all the examples together under a single category of *pṛthak-iṅgya-samāsa*. This is not done either by the CA or by the CAB. Thus, the cited verses seem to mark a further movement of the grammatical generalization.

चतुराध्यायीभाष्य - मिथोऽवगृह्ययोः पदयोः एकपदीभावे मध्यमेन पर्वणा अवग्रहो भवति । 'यत् । आञ्जनऽ-अभ्यञ्जनम्' (पद, अ.वे. ९.६.११)। 'प्रजाऽअमृतत्वम् । उत । दीर्घम् । आयुः' (पद, अ.वे. ११.१.३४)। 'व्यानऽ-उदानौ । वाक्' (पद, अ.वे. ११.८.४, VVRI edn.: ११.१०.४)।

४.१.६५. समासयोश्च ।

Whitney (4.43).

Translation: [There is separation with an *avagraha* in the Padapāṭha at the joint] between two compound-expressions.

Note: See the note on the rule above.

चतुराध्यायीभाष्य - समासयोश्च । 'अघशंसऽदुःशंसाभ्याम् । करेण' (पद, अ.वे. १२.२.२)।

४.१.६६. द्विरुक्ते चावगृह्ये ।

Whitney (4.44), D, Hac, J, M: °चावगृह्ये. Other mss read °वावगृह्ये. P adds a daṇḍa after this rule as a correction.

Translation: Also, [there is separation with an *avagraha* in the Padapāṭha at the juncture between] the repeated occurrences of a separable word.

Note: See the note on CA (4.1.64).

चतुराध्यायीभाष्य - द्विरुक्ते च अवगृह्ये मिथोऽवगृह्ययोः पदयोः एकपदभावे मध्यमेन पर्वणावग्रहो भवति । 'कुर्व-तीम्ऽकुर्वतीम् । एव' (पद, अ.वे. ९.५.३२)। 'संयतीम्ऽ-संयतीम् । एव' (पद, अ.वे. ९.५.३३)। 'पिन्वतीम्ऽ-पिन्वतीम् । एव' (पद, अ.वे. ९.५.३४)। 'उद्यतीम्ऽ-उद्यतीम् । एव' (पद, अ.वे. ९.५.३५)। 'अभिभवन्तीम्ऽ-अभिभवन्तीम् । एव' (पद, अ.वे. ९.५.३६)।

'पृथगिङ्ग्य (H: ण्य, Whitney: ङ्ग्य) समासे च
मध्ये कुर्यादवग्रहम् ।
संयतीं (H: ती) संयतीं (H: ती) चैव
व्यानोदानौ निदर्शनम् ।।' (source?)

४.१.६७. वसुधातरः सहस्रसातमेति वसुसहस्राभ्याम् ।

Whitney (4.45). P adds daṇḍas after वसुधातरः and सहस्रसातमेति.

Translation: In the expressions *vasudhātara* and *sahasra-sātama*, [separation with an *avagraha* in the Padapāṭha is made] after *vasu* and *sahasra* respectively.

चतुराध्यायीभाष्य - वसुधातरः सहस्रसातमेति वसुसहस्रा-भ्याम् अवग्रहो भवति । 'वसुऽधातरः । च' (पद, अ.वे. ५.२७.६)। 'सहस्रऽसातमा । भव' (पद, अ.वे. ३.२८.४)। वसुधातर इति षष्ठ्यन्तेन समासः । समासे अवग्रहो भवति। वसूनि वा दधाति । 'वसुऽधातरः' । समासे अवग्रहो भवति।

'साधा(H: सनि, Whitney: साधा) भ्यां च कृदन्ताभ्यां
विहितौ तद्धितौ परौ ।
ताभ्यां षष्ठीसमासश्च
पूर्वेणावग्रहः स्मृतः ।।' (source?)

Note: Whitney says: "It is not without reason that the Prātiśākhya takes note of these cases; for, since the suffixes *tara* and *tama* are separable (by iv. 16 = CA 4.1.38), and are plainly the last added members, the words they form should read, in *pada*, *vasudhā-tara* and *sahasrasā-tama*."

Whitney understands the commentary as offering the first alternative that the word *vasudhā́taraḥ* as "the plural of *vasu-dhātar*." If indeed such were the case, there would be nothing exceptional about the separation of this compound as *vasu-dhātaraḥ*. Whitney responds to this interpretation: "It would be, in fact, in its Atharvan connection, much more easily interpretable in this manner, but that the accent speaks strongly for the other mode of derivation." It is, however, not certain from the wording of the commentary that it is proposing a derivation from *vasudhātr̥-*. The commentary simply says that it is a genitive compound. However, the cited verse relates this notion of a genitive compound with the explanation: *dhā+taraḥ*, then *vasūnaṃ dhā+taraḥ*.

The commentary gives as the second alternative, the derivation *vasudhā+tara*. The first part *vasudhā* is explained as *vasūni vā dadhāti*, an agentive root-noun.

Whitney was not able to interpret the verse properly, since he misunderstood it as saying "after *sā* and *dhā* (?), as *kr̥t* -endings." The verse says that the words *sā* and *dhā* are *kr̥dantas*, i.e. these words end in *kr̥t*-affixes, and not that they are themselves *kr̥t* endings. Then the *taddhita* affixes *-tara* and *-tama* are added after these *kr̥danta* formations, yielding *dhātaraḥ* and *sātamaḥ*. The words *vasu* and *sahasra* are then compounded with these in genitive Tatpuruṣas. The tradition thus looks at the words *dhā* and *sā* as agentive root-nouns, with zero-affixes such as *VIC* or *VIṬ*, which turn a root into an agentive noun.

For the Pāṇinian derivation of *sā* in *sahasrasā́tamā*, see: षणु दाने । 'जनसनखनक्रमगमो विट्' (पा.३.२.६७) । 'विड्वनोरनुनासिकस्यात्' (पा.६.४.४) इति आत्वम् । ततः आतिशायनिकस्तमप् ।, Sāyaṇa on AV (3.28.4).

For example, the word *viśvapā* is explained as: विश्वं पाति रक्षतीति विग्रहे 'पा रक्षणे' इत्यस्मात् 'आतोनुपसर्गे ...' (पा.३.२.३) इति कं बाधित्वा 'आतो मनिन्क्वनिब्वनिपश्च' (पा.३.२.७४) इति चकाराद्विजिति व्याख्यातारः । इह छन्दसि 'आतो मनिन् ...'

इति विच्, लोके तु 'अन्येभ्योपि दृश्यते' (पा.३.२.१७४) इत्यनेनेति विवेकः, Tattva-bodhinī on SK on P.6.3.110, p. 56. The traditional explanation for *vasudhā* would be similar.

For AV (3.28.4), Whitney records a different accent for the word सहस्रं-सातमा. This variant is noted by the VVRI edition, but I have followed the reading as recorded by the VVRI edition. Whitney (*AV Transl.* Vol.I., p. 135) says: "All the manuscripts agree in giving the false accent *sahásrasātamā* in b; it should be *sahasra-sā́tamā* --- or to rectify the meter, simply *-sā́*." The VVRI edition, without specifying the reason, seems to have followed Whitney's suggested change in giving the reading *sahasrasā́tamā,* though it notes the original manuscript reading (= *mūlakośa*) *sahásra-sātamā* as a variant.

४.१.६८. सुभिषक्तमस्तमे ।

Whitney (4.46). E, F, I, O: °क्तमे.

Translation: [In the expression] *subhiṣaktama*, [there is separation with an *avagraha* in the Padapāṭha] before [the affix] *-tama.*

चतुराध्यायीभाष्य - सुभिषक्तम इति तमे परतः अवग्रहो भवति । 'सुभिंषक्ऽतमाः' (पद, अ.वे. ६.२४.२)। शोभनः भिषक् । सुभिषक् ।

'भिषजा हि सुशब्दोऽयं पुंलिङ्गेन समस्यते ।
उपजातस्तमस्तस्मात्पूर्वेणावग्रहः स्मृतः ।।'
(source?)

Note: Whitney translates the cited verse as: "here *su* is compounded with the masculine *bhiṣaj*, and *tama* is farther appended : separation by *avagraha* is made of the latter."

Whitney criticizes the formulation of this rule: "I can see no reason at all for any such rule as this : the case specified is simply one in which the separation by *avagraha* takes place normally, according to the general rules, and a score more of precisely similar cases might easily be quoted from the Atharvan text: instances are *bhágavat-tama* (ii.9.2) and *bhágavat-tara* (iv.13.6), *sphātimat-tama* (iii.24.6), *mr̥támanaḥ-tara* (vi.18.2), and *vr̥trahán-tama* (vii.110.1)."

Whitney's criticism is not justified in view of the fact that the expression *bhiṣák-tarāḥ,* without the initial *su,* is attested in AV (19.2.3), leading one to think of the possibility of first having the expression *bhiṣak-tama* and then compounding it with *su*. In such a case, the juncture of *su* with *bhiṣaktama* being the most recent juncture, the *avagraha* would fall between *su* and *bhiṣaktama*.

Such an understanding of this compound is further strengthened by the fact that the expression *bhiṣáktamam* without *su* also appears in *bhiṣáktamaṃ tvā bhiṣájāṃ śr̥ṇomi* (RV 2.33.4), which is comparable to *bhiṣájāṃ súbhiṣaktamāḥ* (AV 6.24.2). In contrast with this, the expression *subhiṣaj* by itself is not attested in the Vedic Saṃhitās.

The CA rule is most likely based on such an understanding of the compound, and then stating the exceptional behavior of the *avagraha*. On the other hand, the cited verse normalizes the *avagraha* by suggesting that *su* is compounded with *bhiṣak,* and that *tama* is added to *subhiṣak*. On such an understanding of the derivation, the *avagraha* becomes normal, and does not require a special rule.

इति चतुर्थाध्याये प्रथमः पादः ।

H: ।।४७।। चतुर्थस्य प्रथमः पादः ।। चतुरध्यायीभाष्ये चतुर्थस्य प्रथमः पादः समाप्तः. E, F: चतुर्थस्य प्रथमः पादः. A, B, C, D, J, M, P: प्रथमः पादः. I: ।।९८।। इति चतुर्थाध्याये प्रथमः पादः. O: इत्य. चतुर्थस्य प्रथमः पादः ।। सूत्राणि ।। ९९ ।।. Notice the difference between the number of rules for this Pāda given by H (47), I (98), and O (99). This is an indication of two textual traditions, one with the initial verses, and the one without. However, the majority of the manuscripts supports inclusion of these verses in the text of the CA. One may conjecture that the inclusion of the verses was explicitly done first by the manuscripts of the Kautsavyākaraṇa, as evidenced by the number of rules recorded in I and O. However, the verses are physically present in all the manuscripts, even though not counted in the number of rules, cf. H (47). Thus, they must have been present in the archetype reconstructible on the basis of the existing manuscripts. However, given the abnormal length of this Pāda, it seems unlikely that the initial portion was part of the 'original' CA.

चतुराध्यायीभाष्य - ।।४७।। चतुर्थस्य प्रथमः पादः ।। चतुराध्यायीभाष्ये चतुर्थस्य प्रथमः पादः समाप्तः ।।

॥ चतुर्थोऽध्यायः ॥
॥ द्वितीयः पादः ॥

४.२.१. न तकारसकाराभ्यां मत्वर्थे ।

Whitney (4.47). B, D: °मन्वर्थे. J, M, P(orig): नकारसकाराभ्यां°. P adds a daṇḍa after this rule as a correction.

Translation: After [words ending in] *t* and *s*, there is no [separation with an *avagraha* in the Padapāṭha] before [an affix] in the sense of [the affix] *matU* [i.e. a possessive affix].

चतुराध्यायीभाष्य - न तकारसकाराभ्यां मत्वर्थे अवग्रहो भवति । 'दत्वती' (H adds: म्) (पद, अ.वे. ४.३.२)। 'गरुत्मान्' (पद, अ.वे. ४.६.३)। 'मरुत्वान्' (पद, H: त्) (अ.वे. ६.१०४.३)। 'ऊर्जस्वान्' (ऊर्जस्वन्तः, पद, अ.वे. ७.६०.२)। 'पयस्वान्' (पद, अ.वे. ७.७३.५)। 'ऊर्जस्वती' (पद, अ.वे. ३.१२.२)। 'पयस्वती' (पद, अ.वे. ३.१०.१)।

Note: While the commentary does not provide counter-examples, Whitney provides them: *āsan-vat* (AV vi.12.2), *asthan-vantam* (AV ix.9.4), and *brahmaṇ-vatīm* (AV vi.108.2). These expressions are split with an *avagraha* in the Padapāṭha. Whitney points out: "The only consonants other than *t* and *s* which are found to occur before the suffix *vant* are *n* and *ṇ*, which allow separation. ... The rule is an exception under rule 17 (= CA 4.1.39) above." It is also an exception to CA (4.1.40).

The expression *matvartha* implies that *matU* was looked as a prototypical possessive affix. Indeed, the possessive affix *vat* is derived by Pāṇini by changing the *m* of *matUP*, cf. P.8.2.9 (मादुपधायाश्च मतोर्वोऽयवादिभ्यः).

४.२.२. यत्तदेतेभ्यो वतौ ।

Whitney (4.48). Ha: °मतौ. Hc, J, M, P: °वंतौ. P adds a daṇḍa after this rule as a correction.

Translation: After *yat, tat,* and *etat,* [there is no separation with an *avagraha* in the Padapāṭha], before *vatU.*

Note: While prohibiting the separation of *vat*, the rule informs us that forms like *yāvat* are derived by adding the affix *vat* to *yat* etc., cf. P.5.2.39 (यत्तदेतेभ्यः परिमाणे वतुप्). This rule is an exception to CA (4.1.40). Pāṇini 6.3.91 (आ सर्वनाम्नः) prescribes the replacement of the final sound of a pronoun with *ā* before the affixes *dṛk, dṛś,* and *vatU,* e.g. *yad+vat* > *ya+ā+vat* > *yāvat.* However, there were other grammarians who prescribed the affix *ḌāvatU,* which led to the deletion of the final portion of the pronoun beginning with the final vowel, *yad+ḌāvatU* > *y+ḌāvatU* > *y+āvat* > *yāvat,* cf. Vārttika : डावतावर्थवैशेष्यात् ..., on P.5.2.39. Referring to this Vārttika, the Tattvabodhinī points out: इह शास्त्रे वतुपं विधाय तस्मिन् परे आत्वं विहितम् । पूर्वाचार्यास्तु डावतुं विदधिरे, on SK on P.5.2.39, p. 298. The CA procedure is more like that of Pāṇini.

चतुराध्यायीभाष्य - यत् तत् एतत् इत्येतेभ्यः वतौ तत्र च न अवग्रहो भवति । यत् । 'यावंत् । ते । अभि । विऽपश्यांमि' (पद, अ.वे. १२.१.३३)। य(H: ाव)त् । त(H: ाव)त् । 'तावंत् । सम्ऽऐतुं । इन्द्रियम्' (पद, अ.वे. ३.२२.५)। एतत् । 'एतावंत् । अस्य । प्राचीनंम्' (पद, अ.वे. ४.११.८)। यत्तदेतेभ्य इति किमर्थम् । 'सूनृताऽवत्' (पद, अ.वे. ५.२०.६)। 'अपाष्ठऽवंत्' (H: अपाऽष्टवत्) (पद, अ.वे. १४.१.२९)।

Note: The reason for prohibition here seems to be *sandeha* 'doubt' as to the exact shape of the base, after which the separation is to take effect, cf. CA 4.2.5 (षोडशी सन्देहात्) below.

Referring to the counter-examples cited by the CAB, Whitney remarks that these are "hardly called for." I assume Whitney means that the rule is so obvious, there is no need for counter-examples, and not that there is anything wrong with these counter-examples. The *avagraha* in the counter-examples is effected by CA 4.1.40 (वकारादौ च). The present rule is an exception to that rule.

४.२.३. देवताद्वन्द्वे च ।

Whitney (4.49).

Translation: Also, [no separation of members with an *avagraha* takes place] in a copulative compound of divinity-names.

चतुराध्यायीभाष्य - देवतानां द्वन्द्वो देवताद्वन्द्वः । तत्र चावग्रहो न भवति । 'इन्द्राग्नी' (पद, अ.वे. १.३५.४)। 'इन्द्रवायू' (पद, अ.वे. ३.२०.६)। 'भवारुद्रौ' (पद, अ.वे. ११.२.१४)। 'भवाशर्वौ' (पद, अ.वे. ४.२८.१)। 'वातापर्जन्या' (पद, अ.वे. १०.४.१६)। 'अग्नीषोमा' (पद, अ.वे. १.८.२)। 'मित्रावरुणा' (पद, अ.वे. ३.४.४)। 'इन्द्रावरुणा' (पद, अ.वे. ७.५८.१)। 'इन्द्रासोमा' (पद, अ.वे. ८.४.१)।

'देवतानामिह द्वन्द्वे
दीर्घत्वं य(Whitney adds: दि?) दृश्यते ।
अनिङ्ग्यं तत् (H: अनित्यत्, W: अनिङ्ग्यं तत्) पदं
वाच्यम्
अग्नीषोमौ (अ.वे. १.८.२) नि(H: ति)दर्श[नम्] ॥
देवासुराणां द्वन्द्वेऽ-
प्यवगृह्यं कथं पदम् ।
शाकल्यस्येङ्गिते नित्यं
यथा 'सत्या(H: संख्या, W: सत्या)नृते'
(अ.वे. १.३३.२) तथा ॥
ब्रह्मप्रजापतिः (अ.वे. १९.९.१२) त्वह(त्विह?)
नावगृह्यं कदाचन ।

आनङः प्रतिषेधश्च
वायोश्चोभयतः परम् ।।
इन्द्रवाय्वादिषु (अ.वे. ३.२०.६) कथं
दीर्घो यत्र न(H: त, W: न) दृश्यते ।
द्वन्द्वमात्रे नि(H: न)षेधस्त्वम्(?)
अहोरात्रे निदर्शनम् ।।' (source?)

Note: Referring to the cited verses, Whitney says: "A number of verses follow in the commentary, in the usual corrupt condition of the text : *devatānām iha dvandve dīrghatvaṃ yati dṛśyate : aniṅgyaṃ tat padaṃ vācyam agnīṣomau nidarśanam :* thus much is clear, and is a virtual repetition of our rule, but with a restriction to cases in which a long vowel appears at the end of the first member of the compound, which requires a specification farther on of the single exception *indravāyū;* what follows is more obscure, and I have not been able, with what time I have given to it, to restore the text to an intelligible form." I think we can now make better sense of most, if not all, of these verses.

The second verse says that, if, as stated in the first verse, a *devatādvandva* that has a long vowel is not divisible, then how come the compound *devāsurā́ḥ* (AV 6.141.3) is divisible in the Padapāṭha as *deva-asurā́ḥ*? Here, the long vowel is due to the merger of the two words, and not due to lengthening of the final vowel of *deva*. This is similar to the compound *satyānṛté* (AV 1.33.2), which is divisible in the Padapāṭha as *satya-anṛté*.

On the face of it, the line discussing the expression *bráhma prajā́patiḥ* (AV 19.9.12) is unclear. It seems to say that this is never separated. However, the available Padapāṭha reads: *bráhma / prajā́-patiḥ.* However, note that Kātyāyana in his Vārttika : ब्रह्मप्रजापत्यादीनां च on P.6.3.25 (आनङ् ऋतो द्वन्द्वे) says that in the *dvandva* compound *brahmaprajāpatī,* one does not have *ānAṄ* for the final vowel of the first member. Thus expression आनङः प्रतिषेधः च in our verses is not difficult to comprehend. The present verse seems to say that in a compound like *brahmaprajāpatī*, there is no separation. The *dvandva* compound *brahmaprajāpatī́* is not attested in AV. It is, however, attested in the Taittirīya-Āraṇyaka (4.1.1).

The line वायोश्चोभयतः परम् is comparable to Kātyāyana's Vt. देवताद्वन्द्वे उभयत्र वायोः प्रतिषेधः on P.6.3.26 (देवताद्वन्द्वे च), which says that neither is the word *vāyu* as a first member of a *devatādvandva* lengthened, nor is another word, before *vāyu* is lengthened, e.g. *vāyvagnī, agnivāyū.* The AV example of this phenomenon is *indravāyū́* (AV 3.20.6) which is not divided in the Padapāṭha, even though there is no lengthening.

The last verse is somewhat unclear. It seems to be saying that this prohibition of *avagraha* should apply to all *dvandva*s, and an example of this would be *ahorātre* (AV 6.128.3). See CA (4.2.6) below.

In view of the fact that CA (4.2.4) below specifically relates to those *dvandva*s where the first member has its final vowel lengthened, the proper examples for the present rule can only be compounds like *indravāyū́* (AV 3.20.6), where we do not have lengthening of the final vowel of the first member.

४.२.४. यस्य चोत्तरपदे दीर्घो व्यञ्जनादौ ।

Whitney (4.50).

Translation: [There is no separation of members of a *dvandva* compound with an *avagraha* in the Padapāṭha] where [the final vowel of the first member is] lengthened, before the consonant-initial second member.

चतुराध्यायीभाष्य - यस्य द्वन्द्वस्य उत्तरपदे दीर्घो व्यञ्जनादौ तत्र चानवग्रहो भवति । 'इ॒ष्टा॒पू॒र्तम्' (पद, अ.वे. २.१२.४)। 'पि॒तापु॒त्रौ' (पद, अ.वे. ६.११२.२)। 'ह॒सा॒मु॒दौ' (पद, अ.वे. १४.२.४३)। 'द्यावांपृथि॒वी' (पद, अ.वे. २.१.४)। 'द्यावांभूमी' (पद, अ.वे. १८.१.३१)। 'उ॒षासा॒नक्तां' (पद, अ.वे. ५.१२.६)। व्यञ्जनादावि(H: मि)ति किमर्थम्। 'स॒त्या॒नृ॒ते इतिं स॒त्य॒ऽअ॒नृ॒ते' (पद, अ.वे. १.३३.२)।

> 'इडा(W: रा?)मीवापुरोभ्यश्च प्रकृत्या दीर्घ एव सः ।
> ह्रस्वस्य यत्र दीर्घत्वं स द्वन्द्वो नावगृह्यते ॥'
> (source?)

Note: Examples cited by the CAB on this rule are found listed under APR (217, pp. 136-7) in the same order.

This rule and the commentary on this rule answer some of the questions raised in the verses cited in the commentary on the previous rule. The condition *vyañjanādau* excludes the compound *satyānṛté* from being indivisible. Here, the second member, i.e. *anṛta* begins in a vowel, and the lengthening in *satyā-* comes about through euphonic combination *-a+a-,* rather than as lengthening of the final vowel of the first member, before the second member. The verses cited in the commentary on the previous rule also bring up the example *devāsurā́ḥ* (AV 6.141.3).

As far as the verse cited in the commentary on this rule, Whitney has justifiable criticisms. He renders the verse as: "After *irā, amīvā,* and *puraḥ* [*avagraha* comes in], for in those cases the vowel is long by nature; but where a short vowel is lengthened, there no division by *avagraha* takes place." Then, he remarks: "This is a very blundering statement, so far as concerns the instances given in the first *pāda: puraḥ*, of course, could form no copulative compound; *amīva* forms none such in the Atharvan, and it also, though a feminine with a long final vowel, as a separate word, always shortens its final in composition (*amīva-cātana*, e.g. i.28.1; *amīva-han*, e.g. RV. i.18.2); *irā*, too, is found only in the compound *irā-kṣīrā* (x.10.6), which is not copulative."

Of the three words cited by the verse, for *amīvā*, there is a plausible example from the Paippalāda AV (1.10.1): *amīvāyātucātanam.* A variant for this is cited as *amīvāyās tu cātanam.* However, if we accept the reading *amīvā+yātu+cātanam*, then the first portion, i.e. *amīvā+yātu* could be a kind of *dvandva* referred to by the verse. This reading is rejected by Vishvabandhu, in favor of *amīvāyās tu cātanam,* cf. *VVRI Vedic Word Concordance, Saṃhitā* Section, Pt.I., p.385, footnote **e**. However, considering the reference to *yātu* in the same hymn, PAV (1.10.3), there is some reason to support the reading *amīvā+yātu+cātanam.*

For *iḍā* in the verse, one could possibly point to the compound *iḍā+prāśitrá* (ŚB, 2.6.1.33).

४.२.५. षोडशी संदेहात् ।

Whitney (4.51).

Translation: [Members of the word] *ṣoḍaśin* [are not separated with an *avagraha* in the Padapāṭha], due to [con-]fusion.

चतुराध्यायीभाष्य - षोडशी सन्देहात् । न अवग्रहो भवति। 'इ॒ष्टा॒पू॒र्तस्यं । षो॒ड॒शम्' (पद, अ.वे. ३.२९.१)। 'षो॒ड॒शी । स॒प्त॒ऽरा॒त्रः' (पद, अ.वे. ११.७.११, VVRI edn.: ११.९.११)।

Note: Whitney has some important comments on this rule. We agree with his opinion "that the rule reads *ṣoḍaśī* in stead of *ṣoḍaśa* is surprising, since both words (each in but a single passage) occur in the text." On the statement of the rule that the word *ṣoḍaśī* is not split because of *sandeha,* which Whitney translates as 'interfusion,' he comments: "Or, it may be, 'on account of doubt'- that is to say, of doubt as to the form to which the constituents should be restored, their mode of combination being an entirely anomalous one. It is to be observed, however, that our treatise has itself (at i.63 = CA 1.3.1) given special directions as to how *ṣaṭ* and the following *daśa* are combined together, so that to the student of the Prātiśākhya the *pada*-reading *ṣaṭ-daśa* ought to occasion no difficulty." Whitney has pointed his finger at a very important dilemma. In stead of saying that there is behavioral contradiction, however, one may understand the situation somewhat differently. It is difficult to say that the rules given in this or any other Prātiśākhya were actually the ones followed by the creators of the Padapāṭhas. The Prātiśākhyas, on the other hand, seem to take the existence of the Padapāṭha for granted, and then try to account for it. This being the case, the author of the Prātiśākhya was obligated to observe that the word *ṣoḍaśī* was not divided in the Padapāṭha, and the expression *sandehāt* refers to his own rationalization as to why the Padapāṭha did not divide this word. On the other hand, the rule CA 1.3.1 is almost a rule of word-derivation, showing the leanings of the author of the Prātiśākhya in the direction of general grammatical theory. Whitney himself has given ample proof of such leanings on the part of this text, which go well beyond the narrow scope of a Prātiśākhya.

The notion of *sandeha* as a cause for non-separation is also found in APR (217a, p. 134): सन्देहाद्वर्णलोपाच्च व्यत्ययान्नावगृह्यते. The examples of this rule are also found in APR (p.137). Also cf. VPR (5.34: पाङ्त्रानुद्द्रोऽभ्राय संशयात्) and (5.38: उत्तम्भनादीन्यादिसंशयात्).

४.२.६. अहोरात्रे ।

Whitney (4.52). P adds a daṇḍa after this rule as a correction.

Translation: [There is no separation of members with an *avagraha* in the Padapāṭha in the word] *ahorātra*.

चतुराध्यायीभाष्य - अहोरात्रे इति च न अवग्रहो भवति । 'अहोरात्राभ्यांम् । नक्षंत्रेभ्यः' (पद, अ.वे. ६.१२८.३)। 'अहोरात्रे [इतिं]। इदम् । ब्रूमः' (पद, अ.वे. ११.६.५)।

Note: Whitney says: "There is nothing in the character of either *ahorātre* or *ṣoḍaśa,* so far as I can discover, which should withdraw them from the action of rule 50 (= CA 4.2.4), and render their separate mention necessary." I feel that Whitney is overlooking here the reason *sandehāt* given by the author of the Prātiśākhya in CA 4.2.5, which most likely continues into this rule. As I see, these are irregular changes. The change of *ṣaṭ* + *daśa* to *ṣoḍaśa* is irregular by all counts. Similarly, the behavior of the first member in the compound *ahorātre* is equally irregular, and hence the confusion. The stem form is *ahan,* which changes to *ahar,* and, especially in this compound, behaves like *ahas.* Thus, these cases are indeed more complicated than the cases listed under CA 4.2.4, where we have nothing more than simple lengthening of the final vowel of the first member of the compound.

We should note another curious fact. While the APR (217, p. 137) lists *ahorātré* among its examples of indivisible words, it does not list *ahorātrā́bhyāṃ.* On the other hand, it lists both *ṣoḍaśam* and *ṣoḍaśī.* This makes one wonder whether the expression *ahorātrā́bhyām* was intended as an indivisible word. However, no editions record any variants.

४.२.७. अञ्चतिजरत्पर्वसु ।

Whitney (4.53), C, Hcb: °पर्वसु. Others: पूर्वसु. A, B: अवति°. P: °एतत्पूर्वसु.

Translation: [There is no separation in the Padapāṭha with an *avagraha*] for the root *añc*, as well as for older junctures [i.e. junctures of older constituents of a compound-expression].

चतुराध्यायीभाष्य - अञ्चतौ च जरत्पर्वसु च न अवग्रहो भवति । 'प्राचीः' (पद, अ.वे. ५.२८.११)। 'प्रतीचीं' (पद, अ.वे. ३.२७.३)। 'उदींचीः' (पद, अ.वे. १२.१.३१)। 'शंतांतिऽभिः । [अथो इतिं] । अरिष्टतांतिऽभिः' (पद, अ.वे. ४.१३.५)।

'यत्रोभे प्रतिवि[षि?]ध्येते
उपजातं जरच्च(H: जरं च) यत् ।
जरतावग्रहः कार्य
ऋक्सामाभ्यां निदर्शनम् ।।' (source?)

Note: Consider Whitney's criticism of the commentary: "The commentator ends with a verse which seems to say precisely the opposite of the rule of his text. ... 'when both members are severally separable, both the newly added and the ancient, separation by *avagraha* is to be made of the ancient one: an instance is *r̥k-sāmābhyām.*' But this is mere non-sense, as it stands, the word cited being a case where the last-appended element is inseparable, as following a long vowel (see rule 33 = CA 4.1.55, above), and where, therefore, the division be suffered to remain between the two original constituents of the compound. If the theme of the declension had been *r̥k-sāman,* instead of *r̥ksāma,* we should have an instrumental dual *r̥ksāma-bhyām,* which would be a true illustration of the rule. One may conjecture that the last line originally read *jare nāvagrahaḥ kārya r̥ksāmabhyāṃ nidarśanam,* and that it was amended to its present form by some copyist who knew that the Atharvan read, not *r̥ksāma-bhyām,* but *r̥k-sāmābhyām,* but who was careless enough to overlook the discordance which he thus introduced between the text and its comment."

I do agree with Whitney that there is discord between the rule and the verse as it stands. However, Whitney's emendation of the verse and his attributing to the copyist so much of the initiative do not seem appropriate. Perhaps, we do not fully understand the meaning of the expression *pratividhye te* or *pratividhyete* in the cited verse. In my view, it is most likely that this is a mistake for an original *pratiṣidhyete.* Assuming this to be the reading, the verse would mean: "Where the separation is prohibited for both the old and the new members, the separation should be carried out with the old member, for example in *r̥k-sāmābhyām.*" Here, the *avagraha* is prohibited before *-bhyām,* because it is preceded by a long vowel, and it is prohibited between *r̥k* and *sāmābhyām,* because it is an old joint. In such a case, the verse says that the *avagraha* should be done between the old-members. Such an understanding removes the dilemma posed by this verse for Whitney.

The first three examples quoted on this rule by the CAB to illustrate the formations with the root *añc* are found listed under APR (217, p. 136).

४.२.८. समुद्रादिषु च ।

Whitney (4.54). C: omits च.

Translation: [No separation of members with an *avagraha* in the Padapāṭha occurs] in the words such as *samudra*.

चतुराध्यायीभाष्य - समुद्रादिषु च ...(missing commentary) ।

Note: The missing commentary is clearly due to the carelessness of the copyist. However, Whitney unjustly criticizes the commentator: "This, however, gives us reason to believe that the commentator had performed his work in his usual brief and unsatisfactory style, and had done very little toward filling up the *gaṇa*." I do not see how the copyist's carelessness can give reason to believe such a thing.

Invaluable help is offered by the fact that the *samudrādigaṇa* is fully listed in the APR (217c, examples 59ff.). This is a list of words whose seeming parts should not be separated in the Padapāṭha. Given the close relationship between the CAB and the APR, there is every reason to believe that the commentator would have cited the first few words from the APR list. For a possible reference to the *samudrādigaṇa* in the CAB, see CA (4.1.38).

We must, however, keep in mind that the membership of the *samudrādigaṇa* as intended by the CA must have been somewhat smaller as compared to the list found in the APR, because a large number of cases of indivisible expressions listed by the APR in the *samudrādigaṇa* are taken care of by the CA with specific rules, cf. CA (4.2.1-7).

Since Whitney had no access to the APR edited by Surya Kanta, he made a determined effort on his own to fill out this *gaṇa*. However, now we have a historically more authentic collection in the APR and we need not dwell upon Whitney's collection, except as a reflection of what one finds in the manuscripts of the AV.

४.२.९. वृद्धेनैकाक्षरेण स्वरान्तेन ।

Whitney (4.55). Hb: वृद्धौ°. D: वृत्तेनै°. O: वृद्धै°. P adds a daṇḍa as a correction after वृद्धेनैकाक्षरेण.

Translation: A monosyllabic word, ending in a *vṛddhi* vowel [i.e. *ā, ai,* and *au*, is not separated with an *avagraha* in the Padapāṭha].

चतुराध्यायीभाष्य - वृद्धेन एकाक्षरेण स्वरान्तेन अवग्रहो [न?] भवति । 'सापत्नः' (पद, अ.वे. २.७.२)। 'सौमनसः' (पद, अ.वे. ३.३०.७)। 'सौमनस(H: स्य)म्' (पद, अ.वे. १३.१.१९)। 'सौधन्वनाः' (पद, अ.वे. ६.४७.३)। 'त्रैष्टुं-भम्' (पद, अ.वे. ९.१०.१)। 'सौभंगम्' (पद, अ.वे. २.३६.१)। 'सौभांग्यम्' (पद, अ.वे. १४.१.४२)। वृद्धेनेति किमर्थम् । 'सुऽपर्णः' (पद, अ.वे. १.२४.१)। एकाक्षरे-णेति किमर्थम् । 'ऐराऽवतः' (पद, अ.वे. ८.१०.२९, VVRI edn.: ८.१४.१५)। 'मार्तांऽवत्सम्' (पद, अ.वे. ८.६.२६)। 'वाधूंऽयम्' (पद, अ.वे. १४.१.२९)। स्वरान्तेनेति किमर्थम् । 'नैःऽबाध्येंन (H: नौबाऽध्येन) । हविषां' (पद, अ.वे. ६.७५.१)। 'दौःऽस्वंप्न्यम् । दौःऽजींवित्यम्' (पद, अ.वे. ४.१७.५)।

'अवगृह्यात्पदाद्यं तु (W: पदाद् यं तु)
तद्धितो वृद्धिमान्भवेत् ।
एकात् वृद्धिस्वरान्तेषु (H: सु) न चैवावग्रहो भवेत् ।।
ऐरावतो मा(H: म)र्तवत्सं वाधूयं च निदर्शनात् ।'
(source?)

Note: The CA uses the term *vṛddha* without defining it. Pāṇini defines this term as P.1.1.73 (वृद्धिर्यस्याचामादिस्तद्वृद्धम्). Something similar is intended by the CA. Referring to the example *airā-vatáḥ* (AV 8.10.29), Whitney (*AV Transl.* Vol.II., p. 515) says: "*Āirā-vatáḥ* is quoted under Prāt. iv.55 (= CA 4.2.9) as an example of a word divided in the *pada*-text, not withstanding its secondary formation with initial *vṛddhi*."

All the positive examples of the CAB are found under APR (219, pp. 165-6). We should note that the APR (219) attributes this view to Śākalya:

समस्तमेकाक्षरं वृद्ध्या यद्भवेद्विकृतम् पदम् ।।
स्वरान्तं नावगृह्णीयाच्छाकल्यस्य तथा मतम् ।।

४.२.१०. अवर्णान्तेनैकाक्षरेण प्रतिषिद्धेनाप्रयावादिवर्जम् ।

Whitney (4.56). B, D, J, M, P: Daṇḍa after °क्षरेण. A: only प्रतिषिद्धेना-प्रयावादिवर्जम्.

Translation: [There is no separation with an *avagraha* in the Padapāṭha] for a monosyllabic item ending in *a*, which is also negatived [with an initial *a* or *an*], except in expressions like *aprayāvan*.

चतुराध्यायीभाष्य - अवर्णान्तेन एकाक्षरेण प्रतिषिद्धेन नावग्रहो भवति । 'असं(H: सं)बन्धुः' (पद, अ.वे. ६.१५.२)। 'असंपत्नः' (पद, अ.वे. १.१९.४)। 'अप्रजाः अप्रजाताः' (not in known Vedic texts)। अवर्णान्तेनेति किमर्थम् । 'अग्ने । अक्रव्यऽअत्' (पद, अ.वे. १२.२.३)। प्रतिषिद्धेनेति किमर्थम् । 'यः । सऽप(H: य)त्नः' (पद, अ.वे. १.१९.४)। प्रयावादिवर्जमिति किमर्थम् । 'अप्रंऽयावन्' (पद, अ.वे. ३.५.१)। 'अप्रंऽमादम्' (पद, अ.वे. १२.१.७)। 'अप्रंऽहितौ' (पद, अ.वे. ६.२९.२)। 'अप्रंऽचङ्कशाः' (पद, अ.वे. ८.६.१६)।

'एकाक्षरसवर्णान्तं यद् भवेत् पदमुत्तरम् ।
तत्पदं नाव(H: प)गृह्णीयादप्रयावादिवर्जितम् ।।'
(source?)

Note: Whitney criticizes the formulation of this rule as follows: "The form of statement which our treatise has adopted for its rule respecting the separability of negative compounds is not particularly well chosen." However, compare the CA rule to APR (220, p.166):

एकाक्षरमवर्णान्तं यद्भवेन्नञ उत्तरम् ।
तत्पदं नावगृह्णीयादप्रयावादिवर्जितम् ।।

The verse cited by the CAB is clearly a mutilated version of APR (220). The APR (220) itself, in Surya Kanta's edition reads **b:** यद्भवेन्नय उत्तरम्, which I have emended to यद्भवेन्नञ उत्तरम्. We should also note that all the positive examples of this rule offered by the CAB including the unattested *aprajātāḥ* are the first few examples of a long list of examples offered by the APR. The APR (p. 167) also illustrates the condition *aprayāvādivarjitam* with the examples *ápra-yāvam* (AV 3.5.1) and *ápra-yucchan* (AV 2.6.3). Whitney also draws our attention to the form *ápra-yucchan.*

Regarding the indivisible example *ásabandhuḥ* (AV 6.15.2), Whitney points out that this word in its occurrence in AV (6.54.3) is divided by his Padapāṭha manuscript as *ása-bandhuḥ*. Whitney says that this is "probably a copyist's error." The VVRI edition does not even note such a manuscript variant.

Concerning the form *aprayāvan* in AV (3.5.1), Whitney (*AV Transl.* Vol. I., p. 91) says: "*Áprayāvan* in d, which is read by all the mss. (hence by both editions) and the comm. (= Sāyaṇa), is unquestionably to be emended to -*yāvam;* the word is quoted in the Prāt. text (iv.56 = CA 4.2.10), but not in a way o determine its form (*aprayāvādi-*). ... The commentary raises no objection to *áprayāvan,* and explains it as either *māṃ vihāyā 'napagantā san* (with irregular exchange of case-forms), or else *aprayātar,* i.e. *sarvadā dhāryamāṇa.*" The manuscript H for the CAB clearly reads *aprayāvan,* and, in his CA edition, Whitney also reads *aprayāvan.* For Lanman's vigorous defense of Whitney's emendation to the form *áprayāvam,* see: *AV Transl.* Vol.II., p. 991. Whitney's emendation to *aprayāvam* is now supported by the APR (p. 167).

४.२.११. प्राणति प्राणन्ति ।

Whitney (4.57). A, B, D: first word प्रणति. A, B: second word प्राणति.

Translation: [There is no separation of components with an *avagraha* in the Padapāṭha] in [the forms] *prāṇati* and *prāṇanti*.

चतुराध्यायीभाष्य - प्राणति प्राणन्तीति न अवग्रहो भवति। 'यः । प्राणति' (पद, अ.वे. ४.३०.४)। 'यत् । च । प्राणति' (पद, अ.वे. ११.४.१०, VVRI edn.: ११.६.१०)। 'येनं । प्राणन्ति' (पद, अ.वे. १.३२.१)। 'यस्मात् । प्राणन्ति' (पद, अ.वे. १३.३.३)।

Note: Whitney observes: "But the rule is an exceedingly insufficient exposition of the treatment by the *pada*-text of the forms of the root *an* with the prefix *pra*. Division is, in fact, omitted only when the verb, and not the preposition, has the accent; but then not in the two forms specified only, but also in the participles - as *prāṇát* (e.g. x.8.2), *prāṇaté* (xi.4.8), *prāṇatás* (iv.2.2), *prāṇatā́m* (iii.31.9), and *prāṇatī́nām* (viii.9.9) -- and in the causative as *prāṇáyati* (xiii.3.3). On the other hand, if the prefix takes the accent, it is disjoined from the verb, according to the general usage in such cases, and we read *prá : ana* (iii.31.9), and *prá : anati* (x.8.19, xi.4.14). If the root is compounded with *apa*, also, the same usage is followed, and we have *apānaté* (xi.4.8) and *ápa : anati* (xi.4.14)." The APR (pp. 135-6) takes care of Whitney's concerns by providing a much fuller list of finite verb forms and participial forms where the division does not take place, and is, on the whole, a more adequate accounting of the facts of the Atharvan. One way to soften Whitney's criticism is to say that the CA rule applies only to those cases, where *prá* is compounded with the root *an*, and not where it remains apart as an independent word, due to the retaining of its *udātta* accent. In any case, either the rule should have been more specific, or there should have been a more adequate listing, as in the APR (pp. 135-6).

It should be noted that the AV form is *prāṇati,* while the corresponding RV form is *prāṇiti.* That is also the form found in the Taittirīya-Brāhmaṇa (3.12.6.1). This justifies the wording of the rule: अनतौ विसंभ्यां प्राणाख्या चेत्, CA (4.1.61). For a parallel, see under APR (217a, p. 135): प्राणोऽपानति वेदितः प्रापाभ्यां दीर्घसंशयात्. Compare the explanation *saṃśayāt* here with *sandehāt* in CA (4.2.5: षोडशी सन्देहात्).

४.२.१२. संपरिभ्यां सकारादौ करोतौ ।

Whitney (4.58). O: करौति for करोतौ.

Translation: [There is no separation with an *avagraha* in the Padapāṭha], after [the preverbs] *sam* and *pari*, before *s*-initial forms of *kr̥*.

चतुराध्यायीभाष्य - सम् परीत्येताभ्यां सकारादौ करोतौ अवग्रहो न भवति । 'संस्कृत(H: तं)त्रम्' (पद, अ.वे. ४.२१.४)। 'संस्कृतम्' (पद, अ.वे. ११.१.३५)। 'परिष्कृता' (पद, अ.वे. ९.३.१०)।

Note: The VVRI edition notes the manuscript variant संस्कृतऽत्रम्, and notes that this is supported by the Ṛgveda Padapāṭha. This may also be a case of the influence of the Ṛgvedic tradition on the AV tradition. Whitney's *Index Verborum* gives the RV form, which Whitney later admitted was a case of oversight (*AV Transl.* Vol.I., p. 187). The examples quoted by the CAB are found in the same order in APR (p. 145).

४.२.१३. सर्वस्मिन्नेवागमसकारादौ तुविष्टमवर्जम् ।

Whitney (4.59). C, F: °न्नेवासकारादौ°. F: तुविष्टमवर्जं as a separate rule. O: सर्वास्मित्रेवागमसकारादौ°.

> **Translation:** [No separation with an *avagraha* in the Padapāṭha is made] in any case where there is an inserted *s*, except in the form *tuviṣṭama* (AV 6.33.3).

चतुराध्यायीभाष्य - सर्वस्मिन्नेवागमसकारादौ न अवग्रहो भवति । तुविष्टमवर्जम् । 'अतस्करम्' (पद, अ.वे. १२.१.४७)। 'तस्करः' (पद, अ.वे. ४.३.२)। 'वनस्पतिः' (पद, अ.वे. ४.३.१)। 'बृहस्पतिः' (पद, अ.वे. २.१३.२)। तुविष्टमवर्जमिति किमर्थम् । 'इन्द्रः पतिस्तुविष्टमः' (पद ⇒ 'तुविऽतमः,' अ.वे. ६.३३.३)।

Note: Referring to the examples cited by the CAB, Whitney says: "Their citation under such a precept implies the acceptance of some such etymological theories of their derivation and form as given by the Vāj. Pr. (iii.49, 51), which explains *taskara* and *bṛhaspati* as from *tat-kara* and *bṛhat-pati* respectively, with loss of *t* and insertion of *s*, and *vanaspati* as from *vana-pati*, with the insertion of *s;* but it is unnecessary to remark that such explanations are futile : *taskara* is obscure, and the other two are without much doubt compounds of *pati* with the preceding genitive of an obsolete noun, being analogous with *bráhmaṇas páti, vācás páti, śubhás páti,* etc.; and they would doubtless be separated by the *pada*-text into two independent words, like these, but for their frequency of occurrence, and, yet more, the irregularity of the accent of their former members as genitives of a monosyllabic theme."

We may additionally note that Pāṇini derives these forms in an analogous way, cf. P.6.1.157 (पारस्करप्रभृतीनि च संज्ञायाम्), and the *gaṇasūtra :* तद्बृहतोः

करपत्योश्चोरदेवतयोः सुट् तलोपश्च. Instead of castigating the Indian grammarians for not recognizing the 'obsolete' genitives, one may recognize that their procedure of viewing these as *s*-insertions, marks a similar fact, namely that these are not synchronically to be treated as genitives. The Padapāṭha, the Prātiśākhyas, and Pāṇini, all treat the classical language as the norm, and the Vedic language as a deviation from that norm, and hence there is great deal to be learned from their works about the synchronic perception of language.

The Padapāṭha for RV (1.186.6) reads तुविःऽतमः, in contrast with the AV Padapāṭha reading तुविऽतमः, suggesting that that tradition did not view the *s* in the form *tuviṣṭamaḥ* as an *āgama,* but that it was simply a normal transformation of the *visarga.* The CA rule and the AV Padapāṭha imply a different intended derivation for the same word. Also see CA (3.4.28) which deals with the same form.

The examples offered by the CAB on the present rule occur in the same order in the APR (p. 145).

४.२.१४. विश्पतिर्विश्पत्नी ।

Whitney (4.60).

Translation: [There is no separation of the components with an *avagraha* in the Padapāṭha] in [the expressions] *viśpátiḥ* and *viśpátnī.*

चतुराध्यायीभाष्य - विश्पतिर्विश्पत्नी न अवग्रहो भवति । 'स्वप्नं । विश्पतिः' (पद, अ.वे. ४.५.६)। 'या । विश्पत्नी' (पद, अ.वे. ७.४६.३, VVRI edn.: ७.४८.३)।

'विश्पतिर्विश्पत्नी यस्य
पतिर्विश्वस्य विश्पतिः ।
व(H: च)शब्दो(H: ब्दौ) लुप्यते पत्यौ
विशां वा पतिर्विश्पतिः ॥' (source?)

Note: These two examples are listed in APR (p. 145). The verse cited by the commentary offers two different derivations for *viśpáti,* namely *viśvasya patiḥ* or *viśām patiḥ.* Whitney remarks: "The indivisibility of the compound is doubtless owing to the rarity of the consonantal conjunction *śp*, and the embarrassment which would acompany the restoration of the *saṃhitā* form from a *pada*-reading *viṭ-pati*." It may perhaps also be the perceived lack of clarity regarding the derivation of the words, which leads to their indivisibility, cf. VPR (5.39: विशौजा इत्यन्यायसमासात्).

Whitney on CA (4.2.14 = W: 4.60) mistakenly refers to *svaptu viśpatiḥ* as AV (ix.5.6). It should read AV (iv.5.6).

४.२.१५. ददातौ तकारादौ ।

Whitney (4.61), Ha, J, M, O: insert च after ददातौ. Hbc, J, M, P: °नकारादौ.

Translation: [There is no separation with an *avagraha* in the Padapāṭha of the preverb] before a *t*-initial form of the root *dā*.

चतुराध्यायीभाष्य - ददातौ(H: ददौ) च त(H: न)कारादौ न अवग्रहो भवति । 'नीत्ता(H, N: ता)' (not in AV)। 'वीत्ता' (not in AV)। 'परीत्ता' (not in AV)। 'परीत्तिः' (not in AV)। 'अप्रंतीत्तम्' (पद, अ.वे. ६.११७.१)। 'परींत्तः' (पद, अ.वे. ६.९२.२)। 'प्रत्त(H: त्तं)म्' (not in AV)। 'अवत्तम्' (not in AV)।

Note: It is important to note that along with the attested examples *apratīttam* and *parīttaḥ,* the APR (p. 145) also cites the unattested examples *prattam* and *avattam,* and this is one of those few occasions when both the CAB as well as the APR are citing the same unattested examples, indicating a close relationship between these texts.

Whitney observes: "The difficulty of making out an acceptable analysis of them for the *pada*-text is reason enough for their being treated in that text as indivisibles." On the forms *parītta* and *avatta* cited as indivisible in VPR (5.45), Uvaṭa's commentary says: तत्र तावत् परीत्तः अवत्तानां सग्धिः एतानि धात्वेकदेश-लोपान्नावगृह्यन्ते. Uvaṭa cites a verse generalizing the principles for indivisibility:

आदिमध्यान्तलुप्तानि समासान्य[drop न्य?]न्यायभाञ्जि च ।
नावगृह्णन्ति कवयः पदान्यागमवन्ति च ।।

The words *prattam* and *avattam* are also cited in NR (2.1), and Surya Kanta (APR, p. 145) refers us to Skanda's commentary on NR : लौकिकाश्चात्र शब्दाः प्रत्तमवत्तमित्यादय उदाहर्तुं प्रक्रान्ताः. This informs us that Yāska was already possibly aware of these forms being non-Vedic.

४.२.१६. उद हन्तिहरतिस्थास्तम्भिषु ।

Whitney (4.62), I: उदो हंति°. J, M: °स्तंतिषु. O: °स्थाःस्तंभिषु. P: °हंति । हरतिष्टास्तनिषु.

Translation: [The preverb] *ud* [is not separated with an *avagraha* in the Padapāṭha] before [forms of the roots] *han, hṛ, sthā,* and *stambh.*

चतुराध्यायीभाष्य - उदः न अवग्रहो भवति हन्तिहरतिस्थास्तम्भीत्येतेषु परतः । 'उद्धतः' (not in AV)। 'उद्धृंता(H: तां)' (पद, अ.वे. १२.५.३४, VVRI edn.: १२.९.७)। 'उद्ध्रियमांणा(H: णः)' (पद, अ.वे. १२.५.३४)। 'उद्धृंतेषु' (पद, अ.वे. १५.१२.१)। '[उ]त्तंभिता' (पद, अ.वे. १४.१.१)। 'उत्थातुः' (पद, अ.वे. ९.४.१४)। 'उत्थिंतः' (पद, अ.वे. ६.४३.२)।

Note: Whitney notes that the combination of *ud* + *han* is not attested in the known AV. Surya Kanta (*APR, Introduction,* p. 39) takes this as an indication that the Vulgate is not a genuinely Śaunakīya recension. A more likely possibility is that the CA rule incorporates considerations of general grammar. It should be noted that the APR (pp. 145-6) quotes all the same examples as cited by the CAB including the first unattested example *uddhataḥ.* This shows that there is a more genuine linkage between these texts and their transmission.

Whitney makes some important observations: "The *pada*-text, however, appears to treat the combinations as inseparable only where there is actual composition, as in the participles, and as would also be the case if the unaccented preposition preceded the accented verb, for we find *út : hara* in three passages (iv.14.7, ix.6.19, xii.3.36). For *sthā* with *ud,* ... it has already been noticed (under ii.18 = CA 2.1.18) that where the preposition would be, by the general rules of combination, disjoined from the verb, it is actually so disjoined, and that the *pada* accordingly has *út : sthuḥ, út : sthāpaya,* etc., where the *saṃhitā* has *útthuḥ, útthāpaya,* etc." This makes it clear that the Padapāṭha saw no difficulty in separating the members where it thought they were not compounded, and therefore, we need to make a clear distinction between *vigra-*

ha and *avagraha*. The complexities which prevented *avagraha*, did not always prevent the *vigraha*.

However, Whitney correctly observes: "One would have thought it especially desirable that the *pada*-text should separate *ut-hṛta* etc., in order to mark the forms as coming from the root *har*, and not from *dhar*."

४.२.१७. दधातौ च हकारादौ ।

Whitney (4.63). J: °नकारादौ.

Translation: [There is no separation of the preverb with an *avagraha* in the Padapāṭha] before an *h*-initial [form of the root] *dha*.

चतुराध्यायीभाष्य - दधातौ च हकारादौ [न?] अवग्रहो भवति । 'ये । दृग्धाः । ये । च । उद्धिंताः' (पद, अ.वे. १८.२.३४)।

Note: The example *úddhitāḥ* is also listed as an indivisible word in the APR (p. 146).

On *uddhitā* in AV (19.42.2), Whitney (*AV Transl.* Vol.II., p. 964) says: "In **b**, our *pada*-mss. have *út°hitā,* ⌊a word-division⌋ which is contrary to Prāt. iv. 63 (= CA 4.2.17) and to the usage of the AV. hitherto; SPP. reads in his *pada*-text *úddhitā,* and makes no note upon the matter; ⌊he had in fact a note stating that his P.P.[2]J. also read *út°hitā :* but, as appears from his 'Corrections' to vol. iv., p. 446, his note was disordered in printing;⌋ the comm. has instead *uddhṛtā*." The VVRI edition does not split the word in its *pada*-text, but cites *út-hitā* as a manuscript variant.

As an exception to this rule, Whitney mentions the form *uddhí* (viii.8. 22), and says: "our *pada*-text leaves it undivided, although it does not fall under this rule, being composed of *ud* and *dhi*." There is a doubtful listing of *uddhí* in APR (p. 145) as an indivisible word. The VVRI edition does not split this word in its *pada*-text. One wonders if this form was listed in the *samudrādi-gaṇa*, a list of indivisible words, as conceived by the CA, cf. CA (4.2.8).

४.२.१८. जास्पत्यम् ।

Whitney (4.64). P adds a daṇḍa after this rule as a correction.

Translation: [There is no separation with an *avagraha* in the Padapāṭha of the constituents of the expression] *jāspatyam.*

चतुराध्यायीभाष्य - जास्पत्यमिति च न अवग्रहो भवति । जास्पत्यम् । 'सम् । जास्पत्यम्' (पद, अ.वे. ७.७३.१०)। जायापत्यम् । यापत्यम् । याशब्दो लु(H: लुं)प्यते(H: त्ये) पत्यौ । असंतुरूष्माशु(?) द्व्यक्षरो जायाः वा जाभावः।

Note: Concerning the last portion of the commentary, Whitney says: "Although much corrupted, it is evident that this teaches the same etymology with that given by the Vāj.Pr. (at iv.39: *yakārākārayor jāspatye pade*): *jāspatya* for *jāyās-patya*." In the present state of the manuscript, this passage cannot be restored to its correct original. The verse seems to say that the word *jāspatyam* is derived from *jāyā+patyam*, with the deletion of *yā*, and insertion of *s*. The other suggested alternative is to replace the word *jāyā* with *jā*.

While the CA clearly says that there is no Avagraha for the word *jās-patyam*, the VVRI edition for AV (W: 7.73.10 = VVRI 7.77.10) reads the Padapāṭha as जाःऽपत्यम्, and notes no manuscript variant, except that it points out that the Padapāṭha on RV (5.28.3) reads: जाःपत्यम्. Whitney, on this CA rule, also notes: "This rule and one in the next section (iv.83), taken together, show that the true *pada* reading recognized by our treatise is *jāḥpatyam*; our *pada* manuscript, however, gives *jāḥ-patyam*, with *avagraha*." In this instance, it would seem that the manuscripts have deviated from the CA rule, while the CA rule represents a situation similar to that in the Ṛgveda Padapāṭha. Whitney (*AV Transl.* Vol.I., p. 439) remarks: "The Prāt. iv.64 (= CA 4.2.18), 83 (= CA 4.3.11) prescribes *jāḥpatyám* as pada-reading in c, but all the pada-mss. read *jāḥ-patyám*, divided, and SPP. accordingly gives that form in his pada-text. The RV. pada reads *jāḥpatyám* and *jā́ḥpátiḥ*, but, strangely, *jā́ḥ-patim* (the two latter occurring only once each)."

४.२.१९. मनुष्यत् ।

Whitney (4.65). I: °ष्वत्. P adds a daṇḍa after this rule as a correction.

Translation: [There is no separation of components with an *avagraha* in the Padapāṭha in the expression] *manuṣyat.*

चतुराध्यायीभाष्य - मनुष्यदिति च न अवग्रहो भवति । 'इडा । मनुष्यत्' (पद, अ.वे. ५.१२.८)। मनुष्यवत् मनुष्यत् । यशब्दो लुप्यते वकारस्य च यकारः ।

Note: Whitney and Roth had chosen *manuṣvát* in their edition of the AV. On the present CA rule, Whitney admitted: "It is unfortunate that, the Atharvan form of the word being thus fully established [as *manuṣyát*], and its treatment having been prescribed by the Prātiśākhya with so much care, it should have been altered in the edited text to *manuṣvát*, even though the latter is theoretically decidedly the preferable reading, and is presented by the Rig-Veda in the corresponding passage (x.110.8)." Elsewhere, Whitney is even more emphatic on *manuṣyát* : (*AV Transl.* Vol.I., p. 241): "All our mss. have *manuṣyát* in b ⌊and so have all SPP's authorities⌋, and this form is authenticated by Prāt. iv.65 (= CA 4.2.19), the comment explaining how it is derived from *manuṣyavat*. As being, therefore, the indubitable AV. reading, it should not have been altered in our edition to *-ṣvát,* to conform with the four other texts, even though doubtless a corruption of *-ṣvát*. ⌊SPP. also alters it.⌋" With such clear admissions of error on the part of Whitney, it is unclear why the VVRI edition still opts for the reading *manuṣvat*. The reading *manuṣvát* is found in RV (10.110.8), Mādhyandina Śukla-Yajurveda (29.33), and Taittirīya Brāhmaṇa (3.6.3.4). The manuscript I for the CA also has the reading *manuṣvát*.

The APR (p. 148) also has the reading *manuṣyat*.

४.२.२०. त्रेधा ।

Whitney (4.66). P has no daṇḍa after this rule.

Translation: [There is no separation of components with an *avagraha* in the Padapāṭha in the expression] *tredhā*.

चतुराध्यायीभाष्य - 'त्रेधा' (पद, अ.वे. १.१२.१) इति च अवग्रहो (न?) भवति । ... (missing commentary) ।

Note: The word *tredhā́* is an exception to CA (4.1.35: तद्धिते धा). The example *tredhā́* is listed among inseparable words in the APR (p. 149).

Concerning the lacuna in the manuscript, Whitney says: "It is impossible to say, of course, whether a rule or two has not dropped out." With sixteen more manuscripts, we know that no rule has been dropped. Only a small portion of the commentary has been missing.

४.२.२१. संज्ञायाम् ।

Whitney (4.67). A, B: °यं. P adds a daṇḍa after this rule as a correction.

Translation: [There is no separation of components with an *avagraha* in the Padapāṭha] in a name.

चतुराध्यायीभाष्य - (missing commentary)... 'अश्वत्थाः । न्यग्रोधाः' (पद, अ.वे. ४.३७.४)। 'कश्यपः' (पद, अ.वे. ४.३७.१)। 'विश्वामित्रः' (पद, अ.वे. १८.३.१५)। बहुलमिति च वक्तव्यम् । जमदग्न्याद्यर्थम् (H: थर्वं)। 'जमत्ऽअग्ने' (पद, अ.वे. १८.३.१६)। 'भरत्ऽवाजम्' (पद, अ.वे. ४.२९.५)। 'पराऽशरः' (पद, अ.वे. ६.६५.१)। 'वामऽदेव' (पद, अ.वे. १८.३.१६)।

Note: Surya Kanta says that the example *jamadagnyātharvaṇa* cited by the CAB is not found in the Vulgate of the AV, and he (*APR, Introduction,* p. 40) suggests that this may have occurred in the genuine Śaunakīya recension of the AV, and that the Vulgate is not the genuine Śaunakīya recension. In this particular case, the lone manuscript actually reads *jamadagnyātharvaṃ,* which Whitney amends without notice to *jamadagnyātharvaṇa,* which is now claimed by Surya Kanta as possibly belonging to a long-lost genuine Śaunakīya recension of the AV. The manuscript reading can be best emended to *jamadagnyādyarthaṃ*. Then follows a list of names beginning with *Jamadagni.* Thus, this is another case of a ghost word claimed by Surya Kanta as possibly belonging to the so-called genuine Śaunakīya recension.

Another matter to be noted is that the passage बहुलमिति च वक्तव्यम् and the following exceptions may indicate either a lapse on the part of the author of the CA, or a change in the AV traditions. In any case, the AV manuscripts do seem to follow this statement of exceptions, rather than following a general prohibition of Avagraha for the proper names suggested by the CA rule. The examples of divisible names offered by the CAB must have been divisible for the APR as well, as the APR does not list them among its list of indivisible words.

It may be pointed out that at least some of these divisible names also appear as adjectives, e.g. *parāśara* : *índro yātūnā́m abhavat parāśaráḥ* (AV 8.4.21). Here, [Pseudo]-Sāyaṇa paraphrases *parāśaráḥ* as: *parāśātayitā.*

For a parallel to the doctrine taught in this rule, see APR (217a):

रूढिशब्दार्थसंज्ञा ये नेङ्ग्यन्ते ककुभादयः ।
तच्छास्त्रं शब्दमित्यर्थं यथासूत्रे निपातितम् ॥

The first four examples cited by the CAB are found in the same order in the APR (p. 139).

४.२.२२. व्यधौ ।

Whitney (4.68), C, E, H: व्यधौ. I: व्यृद्धौ. O: व्यृधौ. Other mss: व्याधौ. P has no daṇḍa after this rule.

Translation: [There is no separation with an *avagraha* in the Padapāṭha of the first constituent of a compound-expression] before [a form of the root] *vyadh.*

चतुराध्यायीभाष्य - व्यधौ च न अवग्रहो भवति । 'हृदयाविधंम्' (पद, अ.वे. ८.६.१८)। 'मर्माविधम्' (पद, अ.वे. ११.१०.२६, VVRI edn.: ११.१२.२६)।

Note: The VVRI edition, p. 1129, points out that the word *hṛdayāvidham* occurring in the Padapāṭha of RV (1.24.8) does have an Avagraha. However, it does not cite any manuscripts of the AV showing this phenomenon. Thus, in this case, the AV tradition has remained unaffected by the RV tradition. The examples cited by the CAB are found in APR (p. 146). Surya Kanta (APR, p. 146) says that the CAB on our rule also cites the example *śvāvit* (AV 5.13.9) cited by the APR. But, this is not supported by the manuscripts of the CAB. However, all the three examples are cited in the CAB on CA (3.1.3).

Whitney observes: "The rule is too broadly stated, and should have been restricted by him [= commentator], as was the preceding one : it is only when a protracted vowel precedes the root that the compound is left undivided; and we have, for instance, *vi-vyādhin, abhi-vyādhin* (both i.19.1), and *kṛta-vyadhanī* (v.14.9)."

४.२.२३. दृशि सर्वनाम्नैकारान्तेन ।

Whitney (4.69), Hc: दृशौ°. P adds a daṇḍa as a correction after दृशि.

Translation: [There is no separation with an *avagraha* in the Padapāṭha] of a pronominal [form] ending in *a* or *i*, before [a form of the root] *dṛś*.

चतुराध्यायीभाष्य - दृशौ च सर्वनाम्ना अकारान्तेन इकारान्तेन च न अवग्रहो भवति । 'तादृक्(H: त्)' । 'तादृशः' । 'यादृक्' । 'यादृशः' । 'ईदृक्' (पद, अ.वे. ४.२७.६)। 'ईदृशः' ('ईदृशें,' पद, अ.वे. ३.१.२)।

Note: As Whitney notes, the form of this rule is rather strange, where apparently *a* and *ī* were fused into *e,* and then combined with *sarvanāmnā* to yield *sarvanāmnaikārāntena.* Whitney proposes to amend the expression to *sarvanāmnekārāntena* to stand for *sarvanāmnā īkārāntena,* since the only forms attested in the AV is *īdṛk.* However, the reading of the rule as it stands is supported uniformly by all the manuscripts, as well as by the commentary. Also, Whitney disregards *dṛśi* given in Ha and Hb, and opts for *dṛśau* found in the commentary. However, the reading *dṛśi* is uniformly supported by the manuscripts. For a parallel to this rule, see APR (217a). The APR (p. 135) cites the two attested AV examples.

The reason these forms are indivisible is that the pronoun to which a form of *dṛś* is compounded undergoes substantial change. For instance, Pāṇini derives *īdṛśa* from *idam*, by replacing the entire *idam* with *ī*, cf. P.6.3.90 (इदंकिमोरीश्की). Also see P.6.3.91 (आ सर्वनाम्नः), which replaces *d* of *tad* with *ā*, before *dṛś.*

४.२.२४. सहावाडन्ते ।

Whitney (4.70). A, B, D, M, P: सह°.

Translation: [There is no separation with an *avagraha* in the Padapāṭha of the first constituent of a compound] before a form of the root *saḥ* ending in *āṭ*.

चतुराध्यायीभाष्य - सहौ च परतः आडन्ते न अवग्रहो भवति । 'प्राषाट्' (not in AV)। 'तुराषाट्' (पद, अ.वे. २.५.३)। 'पृतनाषाट्' (पद, अ.वे. ५.१४.८)। 'शत्रूषाप्नीषाट्' (पद ⇒ 'शत्रूषाट् । नीषाट्', अ.वे. ५.२०.११)। 'अभीषाडस्मि विश्वाषाट्' (पद ⇒ 'अभीषाट् । अस्मि । विश्वाषाट्,' १२.१.५४)। आडन्त इति किमर्थम् । 'प्रसह-(H, N: °हस°)नम्' (not in AV)।

Note: The examples offered by the CAB on this rule are identical with what we find in the same commentary on CA (2.4.2).

४.२.२५. अव्ययानाम् ।

Whitney (4.71). J, M: अप्ययानां. P: अध्ययानां and adds a daṇḍa after this as a correction.

Translation: [Components] of indeclinables [are not separated with an *avagraha* in the Padapāṭha].

चतुराध्यायीभाष्य - अव्ययानां च न अवग्रहो भवति । 'प्रातः' (पद, अ.वे. ३.१६.१)। 'सनुतः' (पद, अ.वे. ७.९२.१, VVRI edn.: ७.९७.१)। 'सनुतः । युयोतु' (पद, अ.वे. ७.९२.१, VVRI edn.: ७.९७.१)। 'प्रातः' (पद, अ.वे. ३.१६.१)। 'उच्चैः' (पद, अ.वे. ४.१.३)। 'उच्चात्' (पद, 'उच्चा,' अ.वे. १३.२.३६)। 'नीचैः' (पद, अ.वे. ४.१.३)। 'नीचा(H: त्वा, Whitney: नीचात्)' (पद, 'नीचा,' अ.वे. १.२१.२)।

Note: Whitney observes: "The rule does anything but credit to the acuteness of the authors of the Prātiśākhya, for no word in the text which would otherwise be entitled to *avagraha* is left unresolved on account of its being an indeclinable."

४.२.२६. आशा दिशि ।

Whitney (4.72). A, B, D: अशा°. I: 29.

Translation: [There is no separation with an *avagraha* in the Padapāṭha of the constituents of the word] *āśā*, when it is used in the sense of 'region.'

चतुराध्यायीभाष्य - आशेत्यस्य दिग्वाचि (H: दिग्यानि) शब्दे न अवग्रहो भवति । 'आशांभ्यः' (पद, अ.वे. १०.५.२९)। 'आशांनाम्' (पद, अ.वे. १.३१.१)। 'आशांः (H: °शाम्) । अनुं' (पद, अ.वे. ७.९.२, VVRI edn.: ७.१०.२)। दिशीति किमर्थम् । 'अभिऽधावांमि । आऽशाम्' (पद, अ.वे. ६.११९.३)।

Note: All the examples as well as the exceptions of the CAB are listed in APR (p. 158). APR (217h, p. 158) reads:

अभिधावाम्याशामाशिष्येतदेवावगृह्यते ।
अतोन्यान्याद्युदात्तानि दिगर्थे नेङ्गयेदसौ ।।

इति चतुर्थाध्यायस्य द्वितीयः पादः ।

E, F, H: चतुर्थस्य द्वितीयः पादः. C: चतुर्थे द्वितीयः पादः. A, B, D, J, M, P: द्वितीयः पादः. I: इति चतुर्थाध्यायस्य द्वितीयः पादः. O: इत्य. चतुर्थस्य द्वितीयः पादः ।। सूत्राणि ।। २९ ।।.

चतुराध्यायीभाष्य - चतुर्थस्य द्वितीयः पादः ।

॥ चतुर्थोऽध्यायः ॥
॥ तृतीयः पादः ॥

४.३.१. प्रकृतिदर्शनं समापत्तिः ।

Whitney (4.73). O: °पतिः.

Translation: The term 'reinstatement' (*samāpatti*) refers to the display of the original form.

Note: Here the term 'original' (*prakṛti*) refers to a stage in the derivation of a word, before changes like lengthening, or retroflexion of *n* or *s* are effected. The state thus obtained offers us a theoretical starting point for the transformations mentioned above, and while the reinstatement often results in undoing of what Whitney (1862: 219) calls "anomalies of Vedic orthoepy," it does not necessarily result into a usable expression of the classical language. This is because the process of reinstatement results in undoing of not only Vedic anomalies, but also of some of the changes which are common in the classical language. Such a reinstatement of the derivationally original form takes place in the Padapāṭha and Kramapāṭha, in accordance with the rules that follow.

Whitney points out that the term *samāpatti* does not occur in any other grammatical treatise, though the related term *samāpādya* occurs once "in one of the later chapters of the Rik Pr. (xiii.11, 12), in a passage so obscure, without the light which the treatment of the subject in our own Prātiśākhya casts upon it, that its meaning has, very naturally, been misapprehended by the learned editor (= Max Müller)." Now we know that the term does occur precisely in the same meaning as our CA rule in APR (147, p. 99): षत्वणत्वोपाचारदीर्घत्वसमापत्तेरपवादः. The finite verb *samāpādyate* is found in the same meaning in APR (214b), which reinstates the final short vowel in the Padapāṭha for words like *jánimā* (AV 2.28.2). The term *samāpādya* also appears in the Māṇḍūkīśikṣā, see the note on the next rule. Further it is also found in the Upalekhasūtra (8.18), which is identical with RPR (13, verse 11, sūtra 30).

A related term *pratyāpatti* occurs in Kātyāyana's Vārttika on the Śivasūtras, cf. लिङ्गार्था तु प्रत्यापत्तिः, MB (Kielhorn edn., Vol.I., p. 14). While this term has the sense of reinstatement of an original stripped of unwanted alterations, it has nothing to do with the Padapāṭha. However, the term *pratyāpatti* has been used in a sense identical with *samāpatti* by K.V. Abhyankar (1974: 25-27).

चतुराध्यायीभाष्य - प्रकृतिदर्शनं षत्वादीनां समापत्तिर्भवति । अत्रैवोदाहरिष्यामः ।

४.३.२. षत्वणत्वोपाचारदीर्घटुत्वलोपान्पदानां चर्चापरिहारयोः समापत्तिः ।

Whitney (4.74), C, M: °लोपान्पदानां°. Other mss: °लोपात्पदानां°. E, F, Ha, O: °त्वोपचार°. C, E, F, Ha: °पदानां°. P adds this rule in the margin as a correction. P: °लोपान्पदांतानां°.

Translation: In the repetition of a word in the Padapāṭha (= *carcā*) and in the repetition of a word in the Kramapāṭha (= *parihāra*), there is reinstatement of the original form in the cases involving the change of *s* to *ṣ*, of *n* to *ṇ,* of *ḥ* to *s* before *k* and *p*, lengthening of a vowel, change of a dental stop to a cerebral stop, deletion of an element, and the change of a final *ān* to *āḥ*.

चतुराध्यायीभाष्य - षत्वणत्वोपाचारदीर्घटुत्वलोपान्(H: त्)पदानां चर्चापरिहारयोः समापत्तिर्भवति । षत्व । 'निषेचंनम् । निसेचंनमितिं निऽसेचंनम्' (क्रम, अ.वे. १.३.१)। षत्व । णत्व । 'परायंणम् । परायंनमितिं पराऽअयंनम्' (क्रम, अ.वे. १.३४.३)। णत्व । उपाचारः । 'अधस्पदम् । अधःपदमितिं अधःऽपदम्' (क्रम, अ.वे. २.७.२)। उपाचार । दीर्घ(:)। 'अभीवर्तेनं । अभिवर्तेनेत्यंभिऽवर्तेन' (क्रम, अ.वे. १.२९.१)। दीर्घ । टुत्व । 'यो विंष्टभ्नातिं । विस्तभ्नातीतिं विऽस्तभ्नातिं' (क्रम, अ.वे. १३.१.२५)। टुत्व। लोप । 'शेपहर्षंणीम् । शेपोहर्षंणीमितिं शेपःऽहर्षंणीम्' (क्रम, अ.वे. ४.४.१)। लोप । आन्पद (H: आनंपद) । 'सालावृकाँ इंव । सालावृकानिवेतिं सालावृकान्ऽइंव' (क्रम, अ.वे. २.२७.५)।

Note: As Whitney explains: "*Carcā*[1] (see iv. 123 = CA 4.4.24) designates the repetition, with *iti* interposed, made in the *pada*-text of a divisible compound which is also *pragṛhya*, or which ends in a vowel not subject to the ordinary rules of combination: for example, *satyānṛté íti satya-anṛté* (i.33.2); *parihāra* (see iv. 117 = CA 4.4.18) is the like repetition made in the *krama*-text of a *pragṛhya*, a divisible compound, a word requiring restoration to its natural form, and the last word before a pause." The term *upācāra* refers to the change of *ḥ* to *s* before *k* and *p* by CA (2.3.3 etc.). The term *ṭutva* reminds one of the usage in P.8.1.41 (ष्टुना ष्टुः), and refers to the change of *t*-series to *ṭ*-series. The marker *U* added to the initial stop of a stop series becomes a notation for the whole series of five members, cf. P.1.1.69 (अणुदित् सवर्णस्य चाप्रत्ययः). The CA seems to have taken such conventions for granted and saw no need to explicitly define them.

Compare the following verse of the Māṇḍūkīśikṣā (verse 108), Śikṣā-saṃgraha, p. 472:

षत्वणत्वमुपाचारो दीर्घीभावस्तथैव च ।
यस्मिन् पदे निपद्यन्ते तत् समासा(पा?)द्यलक्षणम् ।।

For *ān-pada,* also see: RPR (4.67). For further discussion on *śepa-harṣaṇīm,* see Note on CA (2.2.17). The terminology used in our CA rule is comparable to the wording of APR (147).

Whitney (1862: pp. 220-221) notes some major problems, for which I must quote him at length:

> "A quite embarrassing question now presents itself, in connection with the part of the text contained in this and the following rules; namely, with reference to the constitution of the *pada*-text which they imply. The actual *pada*-text of our manuscripts is very sparing in its use of *carcā*, or repetition with *iti* interposed : it avails itself of that expedient only in the case already referred to as prescribed by iv.123 (= CA 4.4.24) or when a *pragṛhya* is likewise *avagṛhya*. ... Now when we find put forth in our treatise, as its leading and principal direction for the restoration of the natural form in *pada*, a rule like the one here given, which classes *pada* repetitions and *krama* repetitions together, and corresponds, as regards the *pada*, so nearly with the Vāj. Pr., we cannot help suspecting that it contemplates a *pada*-text in

[1] The word *carcāpadāni* is also used with reference to split up words of the rules of Pāṇini by Patañjali in his MB, न केवलानि चर्चापदानि व्याख्यानम् - वृद्धिः आत् ऐजिति ।, Vol. I, p. 11.

which, as in that of the Vāj. Saṃhitā, the repetitions of *krama* and *pada* extend over nearly the same classes of cases. It is actually the fact that, if we allow the *pada*-text to be of the form in which our manuscripts give it, there are but about half a dozen words in the whole Atharvan text to which this rule and the two following, all together, have any application : while on the other hand, the Prātiśākhya is found to give no direction at all for the use of *iti* alone in *pada* after a *pragṛhya*, or for the innumerable restitutions of natural form which are made in words not repeated. I find myself, I must acknowledge, hardly able to avoid the conclusion that this part of our Prātiśākhya was framed to suit a *pada*-text in which all *pragṛhya*s, divisible words, and words requiring restoration to normal form, were alike repeated, or suffered *carcā* : such seems to me to be the only intelligible and consistent interpretation of its rules. That the fourth section of the chapter contains a direction for *carcā* agreeing with the nature of our extant *pada*-text, would find its explanation in the evident character of that section as a foreign addition to the main body of the work; we should have to assume that the school to which the treatise as a whole belonged, in its present form, framed its *pada*-text in the manner there taught, and probably suffered that rule to take the place of one of another character formerly contained in this section, and now omitted from it; while yet they did not so recast the section as to adapt it fully to their new method of construction of the *pada*. This may seem like a violent and improbable supposition; but it appears to me, after making every possible attempt to avoid it, to involve less difficulty that the interpretation of the rules of this section in such a manner as to make them suit the *pada*-text of the manuscripts. ... One other solution of our difficulties, less satisfactory, but also less violent, deserves to be suggested. If we could omit the words *carcāparihārayoḥ* from the rule altogether, leaving the latter to authorize a restoration of normal form in the *pada* generally, we could perhaps make shift to get along with such inconcinnities and omissions as would still remain -- of which the principal would be that the treatise made no provision for the use of *iti* after a *pragṛhya* word, and that it did not direct what form words should have in the numerous repetitions of the *krama*-text."

In response to Whitney's proposals, we must make the following observations. The text of the CA as reconstructed on the basis of all the available manuscripts does not support Whitney's second solution of omitting the words *carcāparihārayoḥ* from the present rule.

Secondly, the rules do not specify where *carcā* occurs in the Padapāṭha, but what to do when it occurs, thus giving us no direct clue to the extent of *carcā* to be carried out in the Padapāṭha. Thus, there is really no reason to claim that the CA assumes a different Padapāṭha in which *carcā* was carried out more massively, as compared to the Padapāṭha available in the manuscripts. Actually, the fact that the existing Padapāṭha for the ŚAV deviates from the Padapāṭha of the RV and VS, would itself be an indication of its independent transmission. As Whitney himself observes elsewhere, the Padapāṭha for the 19th Kāṇḍa considerably deviates from the rest of the earlier Kāṇḍas, and the fact that this deviation is in the direction of the RV Padapāṭha would suggest that the Padapāṭha that we have for the first 18 *Kāṇḍa*s is fairly authentic.

Finally, we should note that in citing examples of repetitions, the commentary nowhere specifies whether it is citing from the Padapāṭha, or from the Kramapāṭha. Whitney (1862: 222) remarks: "The commentator does not state whether he takes his instances from the *pada* or from the *krama* text : according to the construction of our present *pada,* they could only come from *krama*, if the conclusion drawn above as to the original *pada* contemplated by our text is correct, they may illustrate both." Now, it is safer to assume that most of the instances of repetitions are from the Kramapāṭha, where they occur on a vastly larger scale, than to assume that all these examples are equally representative of a now-lost original Padapāṭha.

It seems to me that the CA (4.4.24: प्रगृह्यावगृह्यचर्चायां क्रमवदुत्तरस्मिन्नवग्रहः) provides some clue that the scope of *carcā* and *parihāra* was different. The repetitions were carried out on a much larger scale in the Kramapāṭha as compared to the Padapāṭha, and that is why the rule says *kramavat*, namely that the rules of restoration in repetitions were primarily meant to apply to the Kramapāṭha, and were to be extended by analogy to the smaller corpus of repetitions in the Padapāṭha. Such is my conclusion based on the CA rule, and this agrees with Whitney's observation that "the actual *pada*-text of our manuscripts is very sparing in its use of *carcā*, or repetition with *iti* interposed : it avails itself of that expedient only in the case already referred to as prescribed by iv.123 (= CA 4.4.24), or when a *pragṛhya* is likewise *avagṛhya*." This is supported by the CAB on CA (4.4.24).

यस्मिन्नवगृह्यत्वं [प्रगृह्यत्वं च] एकस्मिन्नेव युगपद्भवति तत्प्रगृह्यावगृह्यम् । तत्र(H: व) चर्चायां क्रमवद्भवति । चर्चा द्वि(H: दि)र्वचनमित्युक्तम् । पदकालेऽपि तच्च क्रमकाले इव भवति । तस्य क्रमकालस्य रूपं परिहरेत्। प्रगृह्याणि चावगृह्याणि च परे क्रमे परिक्रि(ह्नि?)यन्ते । प्रगृह्यावगृह्यं पुनः पदेष्वेव परिक्रि(ह्नि?)यते । तत्र चावग्रहः कथम् । उत्तरस्मिन्नवग्रहः । उत्तरस्मिन्नेव द्वितीयेऽवग्रहः कार्यः । न प्रथमे । 'विरूपे इति विऽरूपे' (अ.वे. १०.७.६, ४२)।

Comparable to the use of the expression *kramavat* in CA (4.4.24) is the use of the expression *padavat* in the Upalekhasūtras (5.1, 5.3, 6.6, 6.7, 7.9 etc.), where the basic rules describe what happens in the Padapāṭha, and the description of what happens in the Kramapāṭha takes place by simply referring to *padavat*.

S.S. Pandit (*AV edition*, Vol.I., p. 5) refers to "a Vaidika of the Atharvaveda from Māhulī; his full name is Keśava Bhaṭ bin Dājī Bhaṭ. He knew the Saṃhitā and Pada texts by heart as also the Krama of the first four Kāṇḍas." Later (*ibid*., p. 8), Pandit refers to another reciter: "This is Venkaṇ Bhatjī otherwise known as Venku Dājī. ... He knew the whole of the Saṃhitā and the Pada text by heart and a considerable portion in the form of Krama and Jaṭā." Unfortunately, Pandit did not make any record of the Krama and the Jaṭāpāṭha recitations, and that information is now mostly lost to us, since none of the present day AV reciters are capable of reciting these versions. Whitney too was merely theorizing about the Kramapāṭha, and had, as far as I can tell, no access to a manuscript of Krama. Now I have found three important manuscripts at the Bhandarkar Oriental Research Institute, which give us at least a glimpse of these advanced recitational versions. There are two manuscripts (BORI, Mss. 128/1879-80 and 83/1880-81) which provide the Jaṭāpāṭha for the 15th and the 17th Kāṇḍas, respectively. There is also a manuscript (BORI: 133/1879-80) of the Kramapāṭha for the 20th Kāṇḍa. I have been currently transcribing these manuscripts and hope to publish these texts along with my analysis in future. While I do not wish to go into details of these texts at this point, I would like to mention a few important differences from the manner of citations in our commentary and the pattern found in the manuscripts of Krama and Jaṭāpāṭha. The examples of *samāpatti* cited in the CAB typically read like: / 'निषेचंनम् । निसेचंनमितिं निऽसेचंनम्' (क्रम, अ.वे. १.३.१). This gives an impression that the reinstatement phrase like *nisecanam iti ni 'secanam* immediately follows after the original Pada: *niṣecanam*. The pattern noticed in the manuscripts of Jaṭā and Kramapāṭha is somewhat different. In the Kramapāṭha, if we have a sequence of three Padas, e.g. *a, b,* and *c*, with the Pada *b* undergoing reinstatement, we get the following sequence: *ab / bc / b iti b*. For example, notice the reinstatement for the word *puruṣṭuta* (AV 20.15.4, BORI ms 133/1879-80, folio 12): वयं पुरुष्टुत । पुरुष्टुत ये । पुरुस्तुतेति पुरु॰स्तुत. A minor feature to note is that the BORI manuscripts for Krama and Jaṭā use a small circle to indicate the *avagraha*. A similar general pattern for reinstatement is noticed in the manuscript for the Jaṭāpāṭha. In a sequence of Padas, such as *a, b,* and *c*, if the Pada *b* requires reinstatement, we get the following recitational sequence: *abbaab / bccbbc / b iti b*. To illustrate this pattern, I can offer the following example from AV (15.2.6, BORI ms 128/1879-80, folio 11): च परिष्कन्दौ परिष्कन्दौ चं च परिष्कन्दौ । परिष्कन्दौ मनो मनः परिष्कन्दौ परिष्कन्दौ मनः । परिस्कन्दाविति परि॰स्कन्दौ. However, the general features of reinstatement as described by the CA and the CAB are confirmed by the newly found manuscripts of Kramapāṭha and Jaṭāpāṭha.

४.३.३. पूर्वपदनिमित्तानाम् ।

Whitney (4.75), E, F, Hac, O: add च. P adds a daṇḍa after this rule as a correction.

> **Translation:** [In the repetitions of the Padapāṭha and Kramapāṭha, there is reinstatement of the originals of also those transformations] which are caused by [conditioning elements residing in] the preceding words [i.e. preceding components of compounds].

> ***चतुराध्यायीभाष्य*** - पूर्वपदनिमित्तानां च षत्वादीनां समापत्तिर्भवति । एतान्येवोदाहरणानि । पूर्वपदनिमित्तानामिति किमर्थम् । 'परिरापिणमिति परिऽरापिणम्' (क्रम, अ.वे. ५.७.२)। 'सुत्रामाणमिति सुऽत्रामाणम्' (क्रम, अ.वे. ७.६.३)।

Note: The commentary does not offer any new positive examples of reinstatement, but refers us to examples on the preceding rule, such as: 'निषेचनम् । निसेचनमिति निऽसेचनम्' (क्रम, अ.वे. १.३.१)। 'परायणम् । परायनमिति पराऽअयनम्' (क्रम, अ.वे. १.३४.३)।. However, it does offer counter examples where the reinstatement does not take place, because the cause for the transformations is within the same word.

Whitney, along with a small number of manuscripts, has the reading पूर्वपदनिमित्तानां च. With this reading in mind, Whitney objects to the treatment given to this rule by the commentator: "He cites no examples, but says 'the illustrations are those already given:' namely, under the preceding rule. According to this exposition, the present rule would seem merely an explanatory appendage to its predecessor. But this is clearly inadmissible: not only ought we to have it, in that case, combined with the other, so as to form part of it, but more especially, it would not contain the particle *ca*, 'and,' which positively stamps it as something added to the latter. We cannot avoid, as it seems to me, understanding rule 74 (= CA 4.3.2) of the abnormal changes of disjoined and independent words, and rule 75 (= CA 4.3.3) of such as are produced by an altering influence in the prior member of a compound." A good deal of the force of Whitney's argument is lost when we realize that a majority of the manuscripts do not have *ca* in the rule, and I have not reconstructed it in my critical text.

४.३.४. इङ्ग्यानाम् ।

Whitney (4.76). A, B, C, D, Hcb, J: इग्यानां. P adds a daṇḍa after this rule as a correction.

> **Translation:** [There is also reinstatement in the repetitions in the Padapāṭha and Kramapāṭha of the original forms for transformations of the words] which are divisible [with an *avagraha* in the repetitions].

चतुराध्यायीभाष्य - इङ्ग्यमानानाम् अवगृह्यमाणानां च षत्वादीनां समापत्तिर्भवति । एतान्येवोदाहरणानि । इङ्ग्यानामिति किमर्थम् । 'परिंष्कृता' (क्रम ⇒ 'परिंऽस्कृता', अ.वे. ९.३.१०)। 'प्राणन्तिं' (क्रम ⇒ 'प्रऽअनन्तिं,' अ.वे. १.३२.१)।

'अनिङ्ग्यत्वात्समापत्तिरेषु नेलपदेषु(?) तु ।
उत्पन्नेऽवग्रहे चात्र समापत्तिस्तथैव च ।।
'सूनृतांवत्' (अ.वे. ५.२०.६) 'अपाष्ठ(H: ष्ट)वंत्' (अ.वे. १४.१.२९) इत्युदाहरेत् ।' (source?)

Note: It should be carefully noted that the reinstatement (*samāpatti*) prescribed here does not occur in the normal Padapāṭha for these words. The normal Padapāṭha readings for the above forms are परिष्कृता, प्राणन्तिं, सूनृताऽवत्, and अपाष्ठऽवंत्, respectively, and show no restoration taught by this rule. We, however, understand that there is *samāpatti* in the Kramapāṭha.

Also, as Whitney notes: "The rule, as these illustrations help to show, is not a mere additional specification to the one preceding, affecting only the cases to which the other applies : in that case it would have been incorporated with it, not made to follow it, as an independent precept; but it concerns all changes occurring in the interior of divisible words, whether in the former or the latter member, and a part of the commentator's examples, rehearsed under rule 75 (= CA 4.3.3) belong to it, and not to the latter."

The APR (147, p. 99) lists the examples *sūnŕ̥tāvat* (AV 13.1.1) and *apāṣṭhávat* (AV 14.1.29) as exceptions to the procedure of *samāpatti*, and Surya Kanta interprets this as saying that we do not get the restored forms *sunŕ̥tā-vat* and *apasthá-vat*.

४.३.५. अन्येनापि पर्वणा ।

Whitney (4.77). A, B, D: अंन्ये°.

Translation: [There is also reinstatement in the in the Padapāṭha and Kramapāṭha of the original forms for transformations of the words], even when a separation [with an *avagraha*] occurs at a different joint [than the one which led to the transformation in the first place].

चतुराध्यायीभाष्य - अन्येनापि पर्वणा इङ्ग्यमानानां च षत्वादीनां समापत्तिर्भवति । 'विसिंतऽस्तु (H: सु)पः' (पद-क्रम, संहिता ⇒ 'विषिंतस्तुपः,' अ.वे. ६.६०.१)। 'अभिऽ-निःपतंन् (H: निष्पतत्) (क्रम, संहिता ⇒ 'अभिनिष्पतंन्'), अपींपतत्' (अ.वे. ७.६४.१, VVRI edn.: ७.६६.१)। 'विस्थिंताःऽइव' (पद-क्रम, संहिता ⇒ 'विष्ठिंता इव,' अ.वे. ७.११५.४)। 'बृहस्पतिंऽप्रनुत्तानाम्' (पद-क्रम, संहि-ता ⇒ 'बृहस्पतिंप्रणुत्तानाम्,' अ.वे. ८.८.१९)। 'पृषदाज्यऽ-प्रंनुत्तानाम्' (पद-क्रम, संहिता ⇒ 'पृषदाज्यप्रंणुत्तानाम्,'

अ.वे. ११.१०.१९, VVRI edn.: ११.१२.१९)। 'दुर्निहितऽ-एषिणीम्' (पद-क्रम, संहिता ⇒ 'दुर्णिहितैषिणीम्', अ.वे. ११.९.१५)।

'प्रकृत्या ष(H: म)त्वणत्वं यदवगृह्ये तथैव तत् ।
उपतिष्ठन्ती (अ.वे. १२.५.२४)
प्रपणादीन्युदाहरेत् ॥' (source?)
('प्रपणः,' अ.वे. ३.१५.४)

Note: Whitney translates this rule as: "In which case restoration is made, even when the word is farther compounded with another member." This translation is further explained: "That is to say : a compound which, being divisible by *avagraha*, is entitled to restoration of the normal form of its constituent parts, retains its right even when, by farther composition, the division of its original members is lost."

The commentary CAB seems to take a more justifiable approach. It continues the word इङ्ग्यानाम् into this rule: अन्येनापि पर्वणा इङ्ग्यमानानाम्. For example, in the word *víṣitasrupaḥ* (AV 6.60.1), the change of *s* to *ṣ* occurs because of compounding *ví+sita*. Once this joint were separated with an *avagraha*, one would expect the dental *s* to be restored. However, in the *carcā* and *parihāra* type of repetitions, the expression *víṣitasrupaḥ* is separated at another juncture, e.g. *vísita-srupaḥ*. Here, the old joint between *ví* and *sita* remains unseparated, and yet, by the present rule, there is restoration of the original *sita*, giving us *vísita-srupaḥ*.

Whitney considers the cited verse to be "more than usually mutilated and obscure," and he refuses to translate it. He reads *matvaṇatvaṃ* and *avagr̥hyet tathaiva*. Of these, *matva* is clearly a mistake for *ṣatva*, and the second expression clearly reads in H as: *avagr̥hye tathaiva*. With these corrections, the verse no longer remains mutilated and obscure. The verse says that the retroflex *ṣ* and *ṇ*, which are part of the original form (*prakr̥tyā*), remain unaltered even after the separation of constituent members of a word with an *avagraha*. For example, in the form *upatíṣṭhantī* (AV 12.5.24), the occurrence of *ṣ* is not caused by joining *upa* to the root, and hence, the separation of *upa* does not lead to the reinstatement of *ṣ* to *s*. Similarly, in the example *prapaṇáḥ* (AV 3.15.4), the retroflex *ṇ* is part of the original root, and is not brought about by the combination of that root with *pra*. Therefore, separation of that preverb does not lead to the reinstatement of *ṇ* to *n*.

In most of the above examples, the Pada as well as Krama show the result of *samāpatti,* even when no repetition (*carcā* or *parihāra*) is involved. Thus, this is a more generic rule, as compared to the previous rules. The only case where the Pada text given in the VVRI edition does not show *samāpatti* is AV (7.66.1 = W: 7.64.1): अभिऽनिष्पतंन्. It is not clear why there is no *samāpatti* in this case, as it is seen in others. Whitney also notes this anomaly and suggests that the writing of *ṣ* in such examples may simply be an attempt at representing the labial spirant, i.e. *upadhmānīya.* He cites other cases where the same thing happens for the *jihvāmūlīya.* Concerning the textual variation, Whitney (*AV Transl.* Vol.I., p. 431) says: "Prāt. iv.77 (= CA 4.3.5) appears to require as *pada*-reading in b *abhi-niḥpátan;* but all the *pada*-mss. give *-niṣp-,* and SPP. also adopts that in his *pada*-text: *abhinipatan* would be a decidedly preferable reading." One should also note the fact that while the CA rule would require *samāpatti* in the form of *abhi-niḥpatan,* the lone manuscript of the commentary reads *-niṣpatat.* Thus, the manuscripts of the commentary CAB seem to come under the influence of the majority of the later mss. of the AV, and this influence often manifests in the citations of forms which violate the very rules which they are supposed to illustrate.

Whitney offers several more examples for this rule: *viskandha-dūṣaṇa* (AV 2.4.1), *atisthā-vant* (AV 3.22.6), *su-pranīti* (AV 5.11.5), *durnāma-cātana* (AV 8.6.3), *anu-visicyate* (AV 8.10.33), *abhimoda-mud* (AV 11.7.26), *jāgrat-suḥsvapnyam* and *svapne-duḥsvapnyam* (AV 16.6.9), *pṛthivisat-bhyaḥ* (AV 18.4.78). Exceptions to this rule are made in rule CA (4.3.25).

४.३.६. क्रमे परेण विगृह्यात् ।

Whitney (4.78). J, M (corr): °विगृह्यते.

Translation: In the Kramapāṭha, [reinstatement of a given word to its original form, away from its transformations] caused by the disjoinable [previous or the following word, is made when that given word is] joined together with another word [and disjoined from the word which caused that transformation].

चतुराध्यायीभाष्य - क्रमे परेण प्रसन्धाने विगृह्यान्निमित्तात् षत्वादीनां समापत्तिर्भवति । 'आपो हि ष्ठा मयोभुवः' (अ.वे. १.५.१, क्रम ⇒ 'आपो हि । हि ष्ठ । स्था

मंयोभुवंः')। 'परिं णो वृङ्धि' (अ.वे. ६.३७.२, क्रम ⇒ 'परिं णः । नो वृङ्धि')। विगृह्यादिति किमर्थम् । 'पृथिव्यां तें । ते निषेचंनम् । निषेचंनं बहिः । निसेचंनमितिं निऽसेचंनम्' (क्रम, अ.वे. १.३.१)। 'आयंने ते । आयंन इत्याऽअयंने । ते परायंणे । परायंणे दूर्वा । परायंन इतिं पराऽअयंने' (क्रम, अ.वे. ६.१०६.१)।

Note: As Whitney explains: "*Vigṛhya* denotes a word which is altogether independent, and therefore disjoined from others in the *pada*-text, a *nānāpada*, in distinction from *avagṛhya*, which means 'divisible into its constituents (*pūrvapada* and *uttarapada*), as a compound.' In the construction of the *krama*-text, then, where each word is in succession taken along with its predecessor and its successor, a word which in *saṃhitā* has an abnormal form, under the influence of the former or of the latter, retains that form when in the same *kramapada* with the alternating word, but is restored to its natural form when making a *kramapada* with any other word."

Thus, when the original sequence *āpo hi ṣṭhā mayobhuvaḥ* is changed into its Krama version, we get the following kramapadas *: āpo hi / hi ṣṭha / sthā mayobhuvaḥ*. Here, in the second kramapada, we get the form *ṣṭha*. Its cerebralization is caused by the *i* that precedes within the same kramapada, but it is stripped of its long *ā*, which is caused in the saṃhitā by its connection with the following word, from which it is disjoined. In the next kramapada, we have the form *sthā*. Here, it has the long vowel caused by its joining the following word, but it is stripped of its cerebrals, because it is disjoined from the preceding word. Thus, this reinstatement of the original form in the Kramapāṭha is a dynamic interactive process, and works feature by feature, depending upon the cause being joined or disjoined.

The BORI manuscript (133/1879-80, folio 49) of the Kramapāṭha provides an example of this kind in AV (20.67.1): सुन्वानो हि । हि ष्मं । स्मा यजंति. Folio 51 offers an example from AV (20.68.11): नि षींदत । सीदतेन्द्रंम्.

Whitney explains the counter-examples: "Here the *ṣ* of *niṣecanam* and *ṇ* of *parāyaṇe* are maintained wherever the words containing them enter into a *kramapada,* and only suffer restoration (by rule 75 = CA 4.3.3 above) to *s* and *n* in the repetition or *parihāra*." Compare the example from AV (20.88.1) found in the BORI manuscript (133/1879-80, folio 64): बृहस्पतिंस्त्रिषधस्थः । त्रिषधस्थो रवेंण । त्रिसधस्थ इतिं त्रिऽसधस्थः.

४.३.७. दीर्घस्य विरामे ।

Whitney (4.79).

Translation: [There is reinstatement] of a long vowel [appearing in the Saṃhitāpāṭha to the original short vowel] before pause [in the Padapāṭha and Kramapāṭha].

चतुराध्यायीभाष्य - दीर्घस्य विरामे समापत्तिर्भवति । ‘आप॑ः । हि । स्थ । म॒य॒ःऽभुव॑ः’ (पद, अ.वे. १.५.१, संहिता ⇒ ‘आपो॒ हि ष्ठा म॑यो॒भुव॑ः,’ क्रम ⇒ ‘हि ष्ठ । स्था म॑यो॒भुव॑ः’)। ‘पर्व॑ । अ॒स्य॒ । ग्रभी॑ता’ (पद, अ.वे. १.१२.२, संहिता ⇒ ‘पर्वा॑स्या॒ ग्रभी॑ता,’ क्रम ⇒ ‘पर्वा॑स्य। अ॒स्या॒ ग्रभी॑ता’)। विराम इति किमर्थम् । ‘आपो॒ हि ष्ठा म॑यो॒भुव॑ः’ । ‘पर्वा॑स्या॒ ग्रभी॑ता’ ।

Note: As Whitney explains: “The rule, however, evidently applies not less to the *krama* than to the *pada* text, and is even intended chiefly for the former : it is our authority for shortening a protracted final when it comes to stand at the end of a *kramapada,* while it is left long when taken together with its successor.” For an example attested in the BORI Krama manuscript, see the note on the preceding rule.

४.३.८. चतूरात्रोऽवग्रह एव ।

Whitney (4.80). A, B, Hb: चतु°.

Translation: In the expression *catūrātráḥ* (AV 11.7.11), [reinstatement of *ū* in *catū* to original short *u*] takes place only when [the component *catū* is] separated with an *avagraha* [from the following component *rātráḥ* in the Padapāṭha and Kramapāṭha].

चतुराध्यायीभाष्य - चतूरात्र इति अवग्रह एव समापत्तिर्भवति । ‘च॒तू॒रा॒त्रः प॑ञ्चरा॒त्रः’ (अ.वे. ११.७.११)। (क्रम ⇒) ‘च॒तू॒(H: तु)रा॒त्र इति॑ चतुःऽरा॒त्रः’ ।

Note: Whitney explains: "From rule 74 (= CA 4.3.2), which prescribes restoration of the normal form of a lengthened vowel in both parts of a repetition, one might draw the conclusion that the word here in question should be written, when repeated, *caturātra iti catuḥ-rātraḥ* : hence this rule, which teaches the reading *catūrātra iti catuḥ-rātraḥ.*" Whitney recognizes that the commentator is citing the Kramapāṭha when he says: *catūrātra iti catuḥ-rātraḥ.* However, we must note the fact that this word is separable with an *avagraha* in the Padapāṭha, and the Padapāṭha reading as given in the VVRI edn. shows the application of this rule: *catuḥ-rātraḥ.* Whitney (*AV Translation*, Vol.II., p. 645) himself notes the *pada* reading *catuḥ-rātraḥ* and says that it is the subject of the present CA rule. Thus, on the basis of all known evidence, this rule is applicable to the Padapāṭha as well, where the components of the word are separated with an *avagraha.*

४.३.९. पदान्तविकृतानाम् ।

Whitney (4.81).

Translation: [There is reinstatement of the original forms] of [transformations such as] the change of word-final [*i* before dissimilar vowels to *y*, when the word comes to stand before a pause in the Padapāṭha and Kramapāṭha].

चतुराध्यायीभाष्य - पदान्तविकृतानां च यत्वादीनां समापत्तिर्भवति । 'परिऽएतिं । रक्षंन्(H: त्)' (पद, अ.वे. ४.३८.५, संहिता ⇒ 'पर्येति रक्षंन्')। 'अभिऽऐमिं । देवाः' (पद, अ.वे. ६.११८.३, संहिता ⇒ 'अभ्यैमिं देवाः')।

Note: Whitney has a puzzling remark on the commentary: "The commentator's paraphrase is *padāntavikṛtānām ca ṣatvādīnām samāpattir bhavati,* which would seem to show that he understands the rule as referring to the same series of abnormal alterations which was detailed in rule 74 (= CA 4.3.2). His illustrations, however, put quite another face upon the matter. ... Here the only changes of form which have undergone restoration are the regular conversions of *i* into *y* (by iii.39 = CA 3.2.16) before the following dissimilar vowel. We are thus guided to a different interpretation of the rule: whereas we have heretofore dealt with irregular or abnormal changes only, learning under what circumstances, in *pada* and in *krama,* they become reversed, and the original form restored, here we are taught that all alterations made at the end of a word, by the ordinary as well as the extraordinary combinations of the phrase, undergo restoration when the word comes to stand, in *pada* or in *krama,* before a pause (*virāme,* rule 79 = CA 4.3.7). It should be remarked that the final repetition of this rule is wanting in the manuscript, and that we cannot therefore be certain that we may not have lost with it other examples and farther exposition, which would have set the meaning of the rule, or the commentator's apprehension of it, in a clearer light."

I now have a complete photocopy of the original Berlin manuscript, H, which was handcopied by (or for?) Whitney. The manuscript clearly reads यत्वादीनां समापत्तिर्भवति, and not षत्वादीनां as claimed by Whitney. Additionally, Whitney's claim that "the final repetition of this rule is wanting in the manuscript" is also not supported by the manuscript which clearly shows this final repetition. Thus, one wanders how accurate the hand-copy made by Whitney was. Perhaps, not unlike the original copyist, Whitney himself (or one who copied the text for him) occasionally miscopied the text. Since, the original manuscript was in Germany, and he had no continuous access to it, he was unable to correct his own errors in copying the manuscript. On the other hand, Whitney is absolutely correct that this rule requires reinstatement of the originals of all word-final changes, rather than the restoration of only the 'abnormal' changes.

४.३.१०. अभ्यासविनतानां च ।

Whitney (4.82). A, B, D: °विततनां°. I: 10.

Transformation: [There is restoration of the original form] of cerebralization caused by [the preceding] reduplicated syllable [in the Padapāṭha and Kramapāṭha].

चतुराध्यायीभाष्य - अभ्यासविनतानां च षत्वादीनां समापत्तिर्भवति । 'सुसूदत' (पद, अ.वे. १.२६.४, संहिता ⇒ 'सुषूदत')। 'अभि । सिस्यदे' (पद, अ.वे. ५.५.९, संहिता ⇒ 'अभि सिष्यदे')। 'आ । सुस्वयंन्ती' (पद, अ.वे. ५.१२.६, संहिता ⇒ 'आ सुष्वयंन्ती')। 'सिसासवः । सिसासथ' (पद, अ.वे. ६.२१.३, संहिता ⇒ 'सिषासवः सिषासथ')। 'सिसासति' (पद, अ.वे. १३.२.१४, संहिता ⇒ 'सिषा-

सति')। 'सुसुवे' (पद, अ.वे. १४.१.४३, संहिता ⇒ 'सुषुवे')।

Note: As Whitney notes: "The Prātiśākhya now goes on to inform us where restoration must be made of alterations which have taken place in the interior of a word, and not under the influence of any cause lying outside of the word itself. The rules in this portion of the work are in great part the reverse of others formerly given, when the subject under treatment was the conversion of *pada* into *saṃhitā*. Thus, the present precept is the correlative of ii.91 (= CA 2.4.11)."

Restorations of this kind are now confirmed for the Kramapāṭha in the BORI manuscript 133/1879-80. Folio 49 provides the following instance from AV (20.67.1): इत्सिंषासति । सिषासति सहस्रां । सिसासतीतिं सिसासति.

We should also note that the so-called 'original' form restored by rules like these in the Padapāṭha is simply a stage in the derivation of the word, prior to the application of the cerebralization rule. It is 'original' in a theoretical sense, namely it is prior in the derivational sequence.

४.३.११. स्त्रैषूयं नार्षदेन दुष्टरं त्रैष्टुभं त्रैहायणाज्जास्पत्यम् ।

Whitney (4.83). A, B: त्रैषूय°. Hc, I, M, O: omit त्रैष्टुभं. A, B: °त्रैहायणा°. P adds daṇḍas after each of the first three words of this rule, and it adds a daṇḍa after the last word as a correction.

Translation: [There is reinstatement, in the Padapāṭha and Kramapāṭha, of the originals of the various transformations in the expressions] *straiṣūyam, nārṣadena, duṣṭaram, traihāyaṇāt,* and *jāspatyam.*

चतुराध्यायीभाष्य - स्त्रैषूयं नार्षदेन दुष्टरं त्रैहायणात् जास्पत्यमिति च समापत्तिर्भवति । 'स्त्रैसूयम्' (पद, अ.वे. ६. ११.३, संहिता ⇒ 'स्त्रैषूयम्')। 'नार्सदेन' (पद, अ.वे. ४. १९.२, संहिता ⇒ 'नार्षदेन')। 'दुस्तरम्' (पद, अ.वे. ६. ४.१, संहिता ⇒ 'दुष्टरम्')। 'त्रैस्तुभम्' (पद, अ.वे. ९. १०.१, VVRI edn.: ९.१५.१, संहिता ⇒ 'त्रैष्टुभम्')। 'त्रैहायनात्' (पद, अ.वे. १०.५.२२; १२.४.१६, संहिता

⇒ 'त्रैहायणात्')। 'जाःपत्यम्' (पद, अ.वे. ७.७३.१०, संहिता ⇒ 'जास्पत्यम्')।

Note: Whitney appropriately notes that the alterations in these words are restored, even though these are not *avagr̥hya* words. However, the Pada manuscripts do show *jāḥ-patyam* as an *avagr̥hya* form. It is not clear whether this is simply the copyist's error in the Pada manuscripts, or a reflection of a different of opinion. However, the CA and the APR (p. 145) agree on treating *jāspatyam* as an indivisible expression. For a discussion on *jāspatyam,* see Note on CA (4.2.18).

On *nārṣdena* (AV 4.19.2), Whitney (*AV Transl.* Vol.I., p. 183) says: "The *pada*-mss. waver between *nārsadéna* and *nārṣ*- (our Bp. emends *ṣ* to *s*; Op. is altered obscurely; D.K. have *s*), but *s* is certainly the true reading, as required by Prāt. iv.83 (= CA 4.3.11); SPP. has wrongly chosen *ṣ* for his *pada*-text." The VVRI edition reads *nārṣadena* in its Padapāṭha, while it notes the variant *nārsadena* in the footnotes.

Referring to *duṣṭara,* Surya Kanta (APR, p. 142) suggests: "The Pada-reading *dustá*- instead of *duḥ-tá*- indicates that the authors of that text regarded it as an irregular compound of *duḥ* and *stára* from the root *star*." Restoration of this word in the Kramapāṭha is now confirmed by the BORI manuscript 133/1879-80. Folio 51 offers an instance from AV (20.67.2): च दुष्टरं॑म् । दुस्तरमिति॑ दुस्तरं॑म्.

४.३.१२. अभ्यासस्य परोक्षायाम् ।

Whitney (4.84). B, D: °परोक्षयां.

Translation: [There is reinstatement, in the Padapāṭha and Kramapāṭha, of the original shape] of the reduplication in a perfect form.

चतुराध्यायीभाष्य - अभ्यासस्य परोक्षायां समापत्तिर्भवति । 'ततृपुः' (पद, अ.वे. ११.७.१३, संहिता ⇒ 'तातृपुः')। 'ववृतुः' (पद, अ.वे. ५.१९.१३, संहिता ⇒ 'वावृतुः')। परोक्षायामिति किमर्थम् । 'लालंपीति' (पद-संहिता, अ.वे. ६.१११.१)। 'रारंजीति' (पद-संहिता, अ.वे. ६.७१.२)।

'अभ्यासस्य च दीर्घत्वं दीर्घोऽकितेति दृश्यते ।
न(H: त) तस्येष्टा समापत्तिर्लालपीति निदर्शनम् ।।
यद्यभ्यासस्य दीर्घत्वं
तु(H: नु)जादीनां च यङ्लु(H: ल)कोः ।
सव(H: र्व)र्णे च परोक्षायां
न समापद्य(H: द्ये)ते क्व(H: क)चित् ।।' (source?)

Note: Concerning the verses quoted in the commentary, Whitney says: "I have not succeeded in amending the text so as to be able to translate the whole passage." Now we can make sense of these verses without any major difficulties.

The segment दीर्घोऽकितेति refers to Pāṇini 7.4.83 (दीर्घोऽकितः) which prescribes lengthening of the reduplication of the root in intensive forms like *lālapīti*. What Whitney read as नुजादीनाम् in the manuscript H, needs to be amended to तुजादीनाम्, and refers to Pāṇini 6.1.7 (तुजादीनां दीर्घोऽभ्यासस्य) which prescribes lengthening of the reduplication of the root in forms like *tūtujānaḥ*. The expression which the manuscript and Whitney read as यङ्लकोः clearly stands for यङ्लुकोः. This expression refers to the affix *yaṄ* prescribed by Pāṇini in forms like *lālapyate,* and its deletion (*luk*) in forms like *lālapīti*. Lengthening of the reduplication of the root in such forms is prescribed by Pāṇini 7.4.83 cited above. The segment सवर्णे च परोक्षायाम् also refers to Pāṇini 6.4.78 (अभ्यासस्यासवर्णे). This rule says that a reduplication of a root which ends in *i* or *u,* followed by a non-homogeneous vowel, has these sounds substituted by *iyaṄ* and *uvaṄ* respectively. Thus, in the example *uvokha,* the reduplication *u* is changed to *uv,* before *okha*. On the other hand, in the form *ūkhatuḥ,* the reduplication *u* is followed by *ukh+ atuḥ*. Since, the *u* is followed by a *savarṇa* "homogeneous" vowel, it is not replaced by *uv,* but is combined with the following *u* to yield a long *ū*. The verse cited by the commentary refers to such forms and says that the long vowels in such forms are not to be restored to short vowels in their Pada form. Thus, the verse is no longer enigmatic.

Also compare the examples listed under CA (3.1.13: अकारस्याभ्यासस्य बहुलम्) and APR (209, pp. 126-7).

Restorations of this kind for the Kramapāṭha are now confirmed by the BORI manuscript 133/1879-80. Folio 57 offers an instance from AV (20.73.6): तविंषीं वावृधे । वावृधे शवंः । ववृध इतिं ववृधे.

४.३.१३. वावृधानप्रभृतीनां च ।

Whitney (4.85).

Translation: [There is reinstatement in the Padapāṭha and Kramapāṭha of the original shapes of reduplications] also in forms such as *vāvr̥dhāna*.

चतुराध्यायीभाष्य - वावृधानप्रभृतीनां च षत्वादीनां समापत्तिर्भवति । 'ववृधानःऽइव' (not in AV)। 'ससहि[:]' (पद, अ.वे. ३.१८.५, संहिता ⇒ 'सासहिः')। 'ववृधानः' (पद, अ.वे. १.८.४, संहिता ⇒ 'वावृधानः')।

Note: The passage *vāvr̥dhāna iva* cited by the CAB is not found in the Vulgate of the AV, and Surya Kanta (*APR, Introduction,* p. 40) suggests that this may have occurred in the genuine Śaunakīya recension of the AV, and that the Vulgate is not the genuine Śaunakīya recension.

About the *gaṇa* referred to in the rule, Whitney says: "The *gaṇa* might be filled up from the material collected and presented in the notes to the first section of the third chapter, but I have no taken the trouble to put it together, as it is uncertain how much and what the authors of the treatise meant the precept to cover." Unfortunately, no such *gaṇa* is collected in the APR either, and hence we are unable to determine its exact membership.

However, note that the APR (209, pp. 126-127) lists the examples *sāsahānaḥ* (AV 3.6.4, *pada* = *sasahānaḥ*) and *sāsahim* (AV 3.21.3, *pada* = *sasahim*). Curiously, the passage in which the form *sāsahānaḥ* occurs is *sāsahānaḥ iva*, and one wonders whether the unattested *vāvr̥dhānaḥ iva* of the CAB is simply an error for an original *sāsahānaḥ iva*.

Restorations of this kind for the Kramapāṭha are now confirmed by the BORI manuscript 133/1879-80. Folio 7 offers an instance from AV (20.11.1): तन्वां वावृधानः । वावृधानो भूरिंदात्रः । ववृधान इतिं ववृधानः. The accent-marking in the repetition is somewhat peculiar, but not uncommon. The restoration of *sāsahiḥ* in the Kramapāṭha is also found on folio 17 in AV (20.19.6): वाजेंषु सासहिः । सासहिर्भव । ससहिरितिं ससहिः.

४.३.१४. कृपिरुपिरिषीणामनह्वानाम् ।

Whitney (4.86). A, B, C, D, J, O: °ऋषीणा°. P: °रुषी°.

Translation: [There is reinstatement in the Padapāṭha and Kramapāṭha of the original short vowel for the long vowel appearing in the reduplications of the roots] *kr̥p, rup,* and *riṣ*, in the augmentless [aorist injunctive, *anahva = anaṭka?*, forms].

चतुराध्यायीभाष्य - कृपिरुपिसंसः (?)। 'न । रुरुपः' (पद, अ.वे. ४.७.३, ५-६, संहिता ⇒ 'रूरुपः')। 'एनंसः । देव। रिरिषः' (पद, अ.वे. ६.५१.३, संहिता ⇒ 'रीरिषः')। 'मा। नः । रिरिषः' (पद, अ.वे. ५.३.८, संहिता ⇒ 'रीरिषः')। अनह्वानामिति किमर्थम् । 'न । अमीमदः । न। अरूरुपः' (पद, अ.वे. ४.६.३)। [H also adds: 'मा । रिरिषः । नः' (पद, अ.वे. ११.२.२९, संहिता ⇒ 'रीरिषः'?)]। 'सिनीवाली । अ[ची]क्लृपत्' (पद, अ.वे. ६.११.३)।

Note: The explanatory paraphrase of the rule is missing from the manuscript of the commentary, and it is not clear what the term *anahva* stands for. Looking at the instances cited in the commentary, Whitney suggests that, "so far as these instances go, *anahva* might be understood as designating an aorist form which has lost its accent; or virtually, an aorist subjunctive." K.V Abhyankar and J.M. Shukla (1977: 19) refer to our CA rule, but mistakenly explain the term *anahva* as "a tech. term used by the authors of the Prātiśākhya works for frequentative formations such as *rīriṣaḥ, cākl̥pat* etc." These forms are not frequentative forms. They are augmentless aorists, or aorist injunctives.

Renou (1942: 364) refers to Weber's suggestion that *anahva* may be a misreading for *anaṭka*, meaning 'dépourvu d'augment.' Pāṇini (6.4.71: लुङ्लङ्लृङ्क्ष्वडुदात्तः) uses the term *aṬ* to refer to the past tense augment in imperfect and aorist forms, and says that this augment is dropped if these forms are used in conjunction with *mā*, or even otherwise in Vedic, cf. P.6.4.74 (न माङ्योगे) and P.6.4.75 (बहुलं छन्दस्यमाङ्योगेऽपि). This is how Pāṇini accounts for what modern scholars refer to as aorist injunctive. Thus, the term *anaṭka* could easily refer to an augmentless aorist, or better, as Whitney recognizes, an aorist subjunctive, an injunctive in modern terminology. The counter-examples of the commentary then make sense, because they are examples of augment-retaining aorists. The vertical Devanagari cluster for *ṭka* (= ट्क)could have been easily misread as *hva* (ह्व).

For the intruding *mā rīriṣaḥ naḥ* AV (11.2.29), the VVRI Pada reading is *ririṣaḥ*. However, it is not clear why this example is cited by the commentary. Whitney rightly criticizes the commentator and says: "this is, however, no counter-example, but precisely analogous with the two already cited for the same word." Once we take this example out, the term *anaṭka* becomes applicable to the remaining counter-examples.

We should, however, note that if *anahva* is a copyist's error for *anaṭka*, it must have been a very ancient error going all the way back to the archetype of all our available manuscripts.

Concerning another matter, Whitney says: "The text (of AV) affords one other word, *śuśucaḥ* (xviii.2.4: s. *śūśucaḥ*), of the same class with those treated in this rule. Its omission must be understood as signifying, either that the verse containing it was not in the Atharvan text of the authors and commentator of our Prātiśākhya, or that their text read, with the Rig-Veda (x.16.1), *śocaḥ,* or, finally, that the word escaped their notice." Whitney (*AV Transl.* Vol.II., p. 833) further informs us: "Our Bp. appears to give in **a** *śuśucaḥ*, as it ⌊apparently⌋ ought to do according to Prāt. iv. 86 (= CA 4.3.14), though the example is not quoted in the comment on that rule; but the other *pada*-mss. ⌊and SPP.⌋ have *śūśucaḥ*."

As far as the examples cited by the commentator are concerned, there is some variation in the manuscripts and editions. For AV (4.7.3), the VVRI edition offers the Padapāṭha reading *rūrupaḥ,* but mentions *rurupaḥ* as a manuscript variant. For AV (6.51.3), it offers the Pada reading *rīriṣaḥ,* without noting any manuscript variants. On AV (4.6.3), Whitney (AV *Transl.* Vol.I., p. 155) says: "The construction of the augmentless aorist-form *rūrupas* with *ná* instead of *mā́* is against all rule and usage; the easiest emendation would be to *nā́rūrupas;* Ppp. gives *na rūrūpaḥ*. SPP. unaccountably reads *rūrupaḥ* in *pada*-text, both here and in 5d, and 6d, against all but one of his *pada*-mss. in this verse, and also against Prāt. iv.86 (= CA 4.3.14), which distinctly requires *rurupaḥ;* and (in all three cases alike) the *pada*-mss. add after the word the sign which they are accustomed to use when a *pada*-reading is to be changed to something else in *saṃhitā*." It is to be noted that the *pada*-reading for AV (4.6.3) given by the CAB in fact completely supports Whitney's suggested emendation.

The examples *rūrupaḥ* and *rīriṣaḥ* are listed under APR (212, p. 129) as examples of lengthening, and seem to belong to the *nārakādigaṇa*, referred to in CA (3.1.21: *nārakādīnām prathamasya*). However, the *nārakādigaṇa* as found in APR (212, pp. 129-130) lists no form of *kṛp* in this category. No example of *kṛp* is offered by the CAB either. Whitney comments: "For the root *kṛp*, either the commentator furnished no instances, or the manuscript has omitted them : the only derivative of that root, so far as I can discover, which the rule can have any concern with, is *cākḷpat* (vi.35.3 : p. *cakḷpat*); since *cakḷpuḥ* and *cakḷpe* would properly fall under rule 84 (= CA 4.3.12)." All the three forms are, however, listed by the APR under APR (209, pp. 126-127), and not as part of the *nārakādigaṇa*. Given the demonstrable dependence of the CAB on the APR, the dislocation of these examples in the APR may have led the CAB to not citing any example here for the root *kṛp/kḷp*.

४.३.१५. जीहीडाहम् ।

Whitney (4.87).

Translation: [There is reinstatement in the Padapāṭha and Kramapāṭha of the original short vowel for the long vowel appearing in the reduplication in the form] *jīhīḍa* [in *jīhīḍāham*, AV 4.32.5].

चतुराध्यायीभाष्य - जीहीडाहमिति च समापत्तिर्भवति । 'अक्रतुः । जिहीड । अहम्' (पद, अ.वे. ४.३२.५, संहिता ⇒ 'जीहीडाहम्')।

Note: The VVRI edition gives जिहीडाहम् for the Saṃhitā, but offers the manuscript variant जीहीडाहम्. Whitney's edition also offers जिहीडाहम् as the Saṃhitā reading. This change in the AV reading may have occurred under the influence of the RV tradition. The RV (10.83.5) reads: जिहीळाहम्. For further discussion, see Note on CA (3.1.14). The APR (209, pp. 126-127) lists this form as a case of lengthening of the reduplication in the Saṃhitāpāṭha.

४.३.१६. साह्याम ।

Whitney (4.88). B, C, D, H, P: सह्याम. P adds a daṇḍa after this rule as a correction.

Translation: [There is reinstatement in the Padapāṭha and Kramapāṭha of the original short vowel of the root in the form] *sāhyāma*.

चतुराध्यायीभाष्य - स(ा?)ह्यामेति च समापत्तिर्भवति । 'सह्यामं । दासंम्' (पद, अ.वे. ४.३२.१, संहिता ⇒ 'साह्यामं')।

'सह्यामेति(H: ज्ञि) च(H: य) सहेः
दीर्घत्वं यद् दृश्यते ।
न तस्येष्टा समापत्तिर्
या(H: यः)शब्दो दीर्घ एव सः ।।
आख्यातेऽन्तःपदे ह्रस्वो
न समापद्यते पुनः ।' (source?)

Note: Whitney cites the text of the quoted verses without any comment. The verse warns against mistakenly reinstating a short vowel for the long *ā* in *yā* of *sahyāma*. It says that such a reinstatement of *yā* to *ya*, yielding the form *sahyama*, is not desirable.

४.३.१७. दीदायत् ।

Whitney (4.89).

Translation: [There is reinstatement in the Padapāṭha and Kramapāṭha of the original short vowels in the second syllable of words like] *dīdāyat*.

चतुराध्यायीभाष्य - दीदायदिति च समापत्तिर्भवति । 'दीदयत्' (पद, अ.वे. ३.८.३, संहिता ⇒ 'दीदायत्')। 'उषसंः । वीरऽवंतीः' (पद, अ.वे. ३.१६.७, संहिता ⇒ 'उषासंः')। 'उषसानक्तां' (पद, अ.वे. ५.१२.६, संहिता ⇒ 'उषासानक्तां')।

Note: Whitney appropriately says that this rule refers to a *Gaṇa*, and that ideally it should have been worded: *dīdāyādīnām*. Compare CA 3.1.22 (दीदायादीनां द्वितीयस्य). However, no manuscript supports the reading *dīdāyādīnām*. The commentary here cites the same examples as are cited under

CA (3.1.22), clearly suggesting that by the present rule, it recognizes the same *gaṇa* as referred to in CA (3.1.22).

CA (3.1.22) teaches the reverse doctrine that the second syllable of words like *dīdāyat,* read as *dīdayat* in the Padapāṭha), should be lengthened in the Saṃhitāpāṭha. The present rule teaches the reinstatement of the short vowel in the Padapāṭha. Also see the Note on CA (3.1.22).

४.३.१८. नारकादीनाम् ।

Whitney (4.90). Hac, I, J, M: तार°. P adds a daṇḍa after this rule as a correction.

Translation: [There is reinstatement in the Padapāṭha and Kramapāṭha of the original short vowels for the first syllables] of words such as *nāraka.*

चतुराध्यायीभाष्य - नारकादीनां च समापत्तिर्भवति । 'नरंकम्' (पद, अ.वे. १२.४.३६, संहिता ⇒ 'नारंकम्')। 'सदंनम्' (पद, अ.वे. २.१२.७, संहिता ⇒ 'सादंनम्')। 'असंतः । इन्द्र' (पद, अ.वे. ८.४.८, संहिता ⇒ 'आसंत इन्द्र')।

Note: Compare CA 3.1.21 (नारकादीनां प्रथमस्य). The *gaṇa* referred to in this rule is listed under APR (212), though it is clear that the intended membership of this *gaṇa* could not be completely identical for the CA and the APR, because for a large number of words included in the *nārakādigaṇa* in the APR (212), the CA has independent rules. For the details, see the Note on CA (3.1.21).

४.३.१९. च्यावयतेः कारितान्तस्य ।

Whitney (4.91). A, F, Hab, J: व्यावयतेः°.

Translation: [There is reinstatement in the Padapāṭha and Kramapāṭha of the original short vowel] of the root *cyu* ending in a causative affix.

चतुराध्यायीभाष्य - च्यावयतेः कारितान्तस्य णिजन्तस्य समापत्तिर्भवति । 'आ । च्यवयन्तु । सख्याय' (पद, अ.वे. ३.३.२, संहिता ⇒ 'च्यावयन्तु')। 'यथा । वातः । च्यवयति' (पद, अ.वे. १०.१.१३, संहिता ⇒ 'च्यावयति')। 'अङ्गात्ऽअङ्गात् । प्र । च्यवय' (पद, अ.वे. १०.४.२५, संहिता ⇒ 'च्यावय')। 'च्यवयन् । च । वृक्षान्' (पद, अ.वे. १२.१.५१, संहिता ⇒ 'च्यावयन्')। 'देवताः । च्यवयन्तु' (पद, अ.वे. १२.३.३५, संहिता ⇒ 'च्यावयन्तु')। 'पूषा । त्वा । इतः । च्यवयतु' (पद, अ.वे. १८.२.५४, संहिता ⇒ 'च्यावयतु')।

Note: Whitney points out that these are all the cases which the text of the Atharvaveda furnishes. All the examples cited by the CAB are found in the same order under APR (212). Restorations of this kind for the Kramapāṭha are now confirmed by the BORI manuscript 133/1879-80. Folio 37 offers an instance from AV (20.37.1): कृष्टीश्च्यावयति । ... च्यवयतीति च्यवयति. Folio 64 offers another instance from AV (20.89.2) आ च्यावय । च्यावय मघदेयाय । च्यवयेति च्यवय. Also note the use of the Pāṇinian term *ṇic* by the CAB.

४.३.२०. यावयतेराख्याते ।

Whitney (4.92).

Translation: [There is reinstatement in the Padapāṭha and Kramapāṭha of the original short vowel] in the finite verb forms of the root *yu*.

चतुराध्यायीभाष्य - यावयतेराख्यातप्रत्यये परतः समापत्तिर्भवति । 'वरीयः । यवय । वधम्' (पद, अ.वे. १.२०.३, संहिता ⇒ 'यावया')। 'अस्मत् । यवयतम्' (पद, अ.वे. १.२०.२, संहिता ⇒ 'यावयतम्')। 'वरुण । यवय' (पद, अ.वे. १.२०.३, संहिता ⇒ 'यावय')।

Note: The examples cited by the CAB are found listed under APR (212). About the condition *ākhyāte* in the rule, Whitney says: "He (= the commentator) does not explain the meaning of the restriction *ākhyāte* added to the rule, nor cite any counter-example. I can discover no other reason for it than the occurrence of the word *yavayāvānaḥ*, at ix.2.13 : this may have been deemed by the authors of the treatise to contain the causative (*kāritānta*) *aya*, and therefore to require the rule to be so framed as to exclude it. But the word is divided by the *pada*-text *yava-yāvānaḥ*, as if composed of *yava* and *yāvan*, from *yā* : and this seems the best account to be given of it." This form is not listed by the APR (212, pp. 129-130) among other forms of *yu* which are the appropriate positive examples for our present rule. However, the APR (147, 7j, p. 106) clearly lists as exception to reinstatement of the original short vowel for the long vowel of the *saṃhitā* (दीर्घत्वसमापत्तेरपवादः) the following examples: *śapatha-yā́vanīm* (AV 4.17.2) and *yava-yā́vānaḥ* (AV 9.2.13). Here, we do not get reinstatement to *yávanīm* and *yávānaḥ*. Thus, Whitney's guess turns out to be absolutely correct.

४.३.२१. वनियमिश्रथिग्लपीनाम् ।

Whitney (4.93): °ग्लापि. A, B, D, J, M, P: no such rule. O: वनी°.

Translation: [There is reinstatement in the Padapāṭha and Kramapāṭha of the original short vowels in the forms] of the roots *van, yam, śrath,* and *glap*.

चतुराध्यायीभाष्य - वनियमिश्रथिग्ल(ा)पि तेषां समापत्तिर्भवति । वनि । 'अमूम् । सम् । वनयन्तु' (पद, अ.वे. ६.९.३, संहिता ⇒ 'वानयन्तु')। वनि यमि । 'वि । मध्यंम् । यमय' (पद, अ.वे. ६.१३७.३, संहिता ⇒ 'यामय')। यमि श्रथि । 'मध्यमम् । श्रथय' (पद, अ.वे. ७.८३.३, VVRI edn.: ७.८८.३ संहिता ⇒ 'श्राथय')। श्रथि ग्लपि । 'ईम् । अवं । ग्लपयन्त' (पद, अ.वे. ९.९.१०, संहिता ⇒ 'ग्लापयन्त')।

Note: All the examples cited by the CAB are found under APR (212) except for the example of *śrath* which is found under APR (213).

Whitney's reading for this rule, based on his lone manuscript H, was: *vani-yami-śrathi-glāpi*. However, he says: "The form of our rule 93 (= CA 4.3.21), it may be remarked, is somewhat unusual: we should expect at the end of it the genitive plural ending: thus, °*glāpīnām*." Whitney's expectation is supported by all the other manuscripts which contain this rule.

४.३.२२. इङ्ग्यवच्च ।

Whitney: no such rule. A, B, C, D, P: इग्य°.

Translation: [There is reinstatement in the Padapāṭha and Kramapāṭha of the original forms for compound-expressions] which contain components separable with an *avagraha* (*iṅgya* = *avagr̥hyamāṇa*).

चतुराध्यायीभाष्य - इङ्ग्यवच्च ।... missing commentary.

Note: Just working with the defective manuscript H, Whitney says: "The manuscript contains no final repetition of this rule (= CA 4.3.21), but offers, after the last citation, the words *iṅgyavac ca*. What to make of these words I do not precisely know: they may be part of a cited verse, of which the rest, along with the repetition of the rule, is lost; or they may possibly belong to an omitted rule: but I can hardly suppose the latter to be the case, not seeing what the meaning of the phrase should be, as a rule or a part of one."

Obviously, Whitney was wrong. This is a rule and this fact is supported by most manuscripts. Unfortunately, the commentary on this rule is missing. Even after finding this rule in the second manuscript, Whitney (1880: 169) says: "The words *iṅgyavac ca* are in fact found in B. as the next rule; but, in the absence of a comment and illustrations to show what is the meaning, I do not venture to attempt the interpretation of a phrase so indefinite."

Besides this rule, the term *iṅgya* appears in CA 4.3.4 (इङ्ग्यानाम्) and the related term *aniṅga,* which should perhaps be read as *aniṅgya,* is found in rule CA 4.1.34 (अनिङ्गेन पूर्वेण). The commentary CAB on CA 4.3.4 renders the term *iṅgya* by *avagr̥hyamāṇa* and the term refers to forms which undergo division, or separation by *avagraha.* CA 4.3.4 says that restoration of pre-change forms is made only in such compounds which are resolved into their constituent elements in the Padapāṭha. One wonders whether CA 4.3.4 applies to restoration in the Padapāṭha, and whether an extension of the same restoration of *iṅgya* words to Kramapāṭha is enjoined by the present rule *iṅgyavac ca.* Perhaps, this rule was necessary, so that a prohibition of *samāpatti* for *aṣṭan* etc. could be taught by the next rule precisely for separable compounds of various kinds in the following rules.

४.३.२३. नाष्टनः ।

Whitney (4.94). O: नार्ष्टनः. P adds a daṇḍa after this rule as a correction.

Translation: [There is] no [reinstatement] of *aṣṭan* [i.e. of *aṣṭā* to *aṣṭa*, in the Padapāṭha and Kramapāṭha].

चतुराध्यायीभाष्य - न अष्टनः समापत्तिर्भवति । ‘अ॒ष्टाप॑दी चतु॒रक्षी’ (अ.वे. ५.१९.७, पद ⇒ ‘अ॒ष्टाऽप॑दी’)। ‘अ॒ष्टाऽयो॑निः’ (अ.वे. ८.९.२१, संहिता ⇒ ‘अ॒ष्टायो॑निः’ ?)। ‘अ॒ष्टाऽप॑क्षाम्’ (पद, अ.वे. ९.३.२१, संहिता ⇒ ‘अ॒ष्टाप॑क्षाम्’)। ‘अष्टाऽपर्णः’ (not in AV)। ‘अ॒ष्टा॒ऽयो॒गैः’ (पद, अ.वे. ६.९१.१, संहिता ⇒ ‘अ॒ष्टा॒यो॒गैः’)। ‘अ॒ष्टाऽप॑दी’ (पद, अ.वे. ५.१९.७, संहिता ⇒ ‘अ॒ष्टाप॑दी’)। ‘अष्टाऽदंष्ट्रः’ (not in AV)। ‘अ॒ष्टाऽच॑क्रा । नव॑ऽद्वारा’ (पद, अ.वे. १०.२.३१, संहिता ⇒ ‘अ॒ष्टाच॑क्रा’)। ‘अ॒ष्टाऽच॑क्रम् । व॒र्त॒ते॒’ (पद, अ.वे. ११.४.२२, संहिता ⇒ ‘अ॒ष्टाच॑क्रम्’)।

Note: Concerning the example *aṣṭā-yoniḥ* cited by the commentator, Whitney says that this is a blunder "for the word is read with a short vowel in both *pada* and *saṃhitā* in our Atharvan manuscripts, nor is *yoni* mentioned (iii.2 = CA 3.1.2) by the Prātiśākhya among words before which the final vowel of the numeral is made long." The same reading is exhibited by the VVRI edition. There are indeed no manuscript variants cited which agree with the reading as given by the CAB. Such instances may perhaps reflect a process of analogical extension of this lengthening in certain recitational traditions which instinctively made this change, without realizing that there was no authority for such a change in the Prātiśākhya.

Whitney comments: "He (= the commentator) also interposes, between the first and third examples, *aṣṭā-yoniḥ*; but this is a blunder, for the word is read with a short vowel in both *pada* and *saṃhitā* (viii.9.21), in our Atharvan manuscripts, nor is *yoni* mentioned (iii.2 = CA 3.1.2) by the Prātiśākhya among words before which the final vowel of the numeral is made long."

It should also be noted that the examples *aṣṭāyoniḥ, aṣṭāparṇaḥ,* and *aṣṭādaṃṣṭraḥ* are not found in the corresponding list of examples in the APR (147b). The rest of the examples are found in the APR (147b) exactly in the same order. It is possible that the additional examples found in the CAB are a later addition to an old list. The APR (147b: *aṣṭanaḥ*) also seems to be directly referring to our present rule.

Also, see the Note on CA (3.1.2).

४.३.२४. हिनोतेः ।

Whitney (4.95).

Translation: [There is no reinstatement in the Padapāṭha and Kramapāṭha of *ṇ* to *n* in the forms] of the root *hi*.

चतुराध्यायीभाष्य - हिनोतेश्च न समापत्तिर्भवति । 'प्रतिऽप्रहिण्मः' (पद, अ.वे. १०.१.५, संहिता ⇒ 'प्रति-प्रहिण्मः')। 'प्र । हिणोमि । दूरम्' (पद, अ.वे. १२.२.४, संहिता ⇒ 'प्र हिंणोमि')। 'प्र । हिणुत (H: ताम्) । पितृन्' (पद, अ.वे. १८.४.४०, संहिता ⇒ 'प्र हिंणुत')।

Note: I agree with Whitney's statement that the *Pada* usage as regards the forms *pra* / *hiṇomi* and *pra* / *hiṇuta* is quite anomalous. He further says: "I can only conjecture that it may have been adopted in order to mark the euphonic alteration as itself of anomalous and exceptional character: there being, so far as I have been able to find, no other cases in which a preposition lingualizes the nasal of a conjugational sign." The exceptional character of such changes is noted by Pāṇini in his rules P.8.4.15 (हिनुमीना) and P.8.4.16 (आनि लोट्). The change is exceptional on two counts. First, it occurs when the cause of this change is in a separate uncompounded word (असमासेऽपि, in P. 8.4.14). Second, the *n* undergoing this change does not belong to the root, but to the affix. Thus, it is possible, as Whitney suggests, that the Padapāṭha marked this exceptional nature by proposing to maintain the retroflexion of *n* even in the Pada version, where theoretically there is no phonological motivation for such a change.

APR (147c) directly refers to our present rule, and the examples cited under APR (147c, p. 100) are identical with those cited by the CAB.

४.३.२५. बोधप्रतीबोधौ केसरप्राबन्धाया अभ्यघायन्ति पनिष्पदातिष्ठिपं दाधार जागार मीमायेति ।

Whitney (4.96). E, F, O, P: °प्राबंधायां°. A, B, D: °अभ्यच्चायंति°. O: daṇḍa after °प्राबंधायां°. O, P: °तिष्टिपं°. P(orig) adds a daṇḍa after °बोधप्रतीबोधौ°, and adds daṇḍas after °केसरप्राबंधायां° and at the end of the rule as corrections.

Translation: [There is no reinstatement in the Padapāṭha and Kramapāṭha of the original forms of the following words]: *bodhapratībodhau, kesaraprābandhāyāḥ, abhyaghāyanti, panispadā, atiṣṭhipam, dādhāra, jāgāra,* and *mīmāya.*

चतुराध्यायीभाष्य - बोधप्रतीबोधौ केसरप्राबन्धाया अभ्यघायन्ति पनिष्पदातिष्ठिपम् दाधार जागार मीमायेति न समापत्तिर्भवति । 'बोधऽप्रतीबोधौ' (पद, अ.वे. ५.३०.१०, संहिता ⇒ 'बोधप्रतीबोधौ')। 'केसरऽप्राबन्धायाः' (पद, अ.वे. ५.१८.११, संहिता ⇒ 'केसरप्राबन्धायाः')। 'अभिऽअघायन्ति' (पद, अ.वे. ५.६.९, संहिता ⇒ 'अभ्यघायन्ति')। 'पनिष्पदा' (पद, अ.वे. ५.३०.१६, संहिता ⇒ 'पनिष्पदा')। 'अतिष्ठिपम्' (पद, अ.वे. ७.९५.२, VVRI edn.: ७.१००.२, संहिता ⇒ 'अतिष्ठिपम्')। 'दाधार' (पद, अ.वे. ४.२.७, संहिता ⇒ 'दाधार')। 'जागार' (पद, अ.वे. ५.१९.१०, संहिता ⇒ 'जागार')। 'मीमाय' (पद, अ.वे. ५.११.३, संहिता ⇒ 'मीमाय')।

Note: Without this rule, we may have had the undesired forms with reinstatements of 'original' features such as: *pratibodhau, kesaraprābandhāyāḥ, aghayanti, paniḥpadā, atisthipam, dadhāra, jagāra,* and *mimāya.* These unreinstated forms are 'original' only in the sense that they represent prior states in a grammatical derivation. A rule like this shows that, even when the Padapāṭha is identical with the Saṃhitāpāṭha, the ancient Indian grammarians knew the notion of a sequential grammatical derivation of a word passing through various stages of morphophonemic changes. It is also the case in some of these forms, that the 'original' form implied is closer to the form as found in the classical language. However, this is not always the case.

The APR (147d) seems to be quoting the whole of our present rule and the CAB quotes all the same examples which are cited in the APR in the same order. For the last instance, however, note that AV (9.10.21, VVRI edn. 9.15.21: *gaur in mimāya ...*) offers *mimāya* in both the Saṃhitā and Padapāṭha. As this verse is a variant of the RV (1.164.41: *gaurīr mimāya ...*), it is likely that an earlier *mīmāya* was altered to *mimāya* under the influence of the Ṛgvedic tradition. Most probably, the reading of AV (9.10.21) known to the author of the CA was *mīmāya*.

Whitney further points out: "Of the class of the first three cases is *sam-niṣadya* (iv.16.2), which equally calls for inclusion in this rule, unless the reading in our *pada* manuscript is a copyist's error, and should be amended to *sam-nisadya*." The APR (147) does not include this case among those where reinstatement of the original is prohibited. The Padapāṭha in the VVRI edition reads *sam-niṣadya,* and no manuscript variants are mentioned..

४.३.२६. प्रपणः पणतेरेव ।

Whitney (4.97). Ha: प्रयणः°.

Translation: [There is no reinstatement in the Padapāṭha and Kramapāṭha of *ṇ* by *n* in the form] *prapaṇa*, only if it is derived from the root *paṇ*.

चतुराध्यायीभाष्य - प्रपण इति पणतेरेव (H: परतैरक) समापत्तिर्न भवति । 'येनं । धनेंन । प्रऽपणं । चरांमि' (पद, अ.वे. ३.१५.५, संहिता ⇒ 'प्रपणम्')। 'शुनम् । नः । अस्तु । प्रऽपणः' (पद, अ.वे. ३.१५.४, संहिता ⇒ 'प्रपणः')।

Note: Referring to the reading of the commentary in H, Whitney says: "In his paraphrase, the commentator says *prapaṇa iti parataíraka samā-pattir na bhavati;* but what *parataíraka* is, I do not know." My own best guess is that *paratairaka* is a corruption by the copyist of the phrase *paṇatereva*. My guess is based on the following reasoning. In a sequence such as *paṇatereva,* the initial part of *ṇ* [perhaps originally written in a way similar to the North Indian Nagari ण] was read as *r*, and the remaining part was read as a Pṛṣṭhamātrā for the next syllable, i.e. *te*. This syllable *te* with an added Pṛṣṭhamātrā was then interpreted as *tai*. Finally, the *reva* was miscopied as *raka*.

Again, referring to the commentary on this rule in the manuscript H, Whitney says: "Its (=of the rule) repetition before the one next following is wanting in the manuscript: possibly, then (as in the case of rule 81 = CA 4.3.19, above), we have lost something in the way of exposition or illustration which would have farther enlightened us." My photocopy of the same manuscript which was hand-copied by Whitney clearly shows the final repetition of this rule, and this is one of those cases where Whitney missed something while hand-copying the text from the Berlin manuscript, H.

४.३.२७. इदमूष्वादिषु त्रिपदत्वात् ।

Whitney (4.98), J: इदमूष्वादिषु पदत्वात्. A, B, D, Hc, J, M, P: °तृपदत्वात्. O: °त्रिपादत्वात्.

Translation: [There is no reinstatement of in the Kramapāṭha of the original words in sequences such as] *idam ū ṣu*, because [in the Kramapāṭha] these three words are combined into a single unit [= *tripada*].

चतुराध्यायीभाष्य - इदमूष्वादिषु त्रिपदत्वान्न समापत्तिर्भवति । 'इदमू षु' (अ.वे. १.२४.४, क्रमपद ⇒ 'इदमू षु')। 'तदू षु' (अ.वे. ५.१.५, क्रमपद ⇒ 'तदू षु')। 'पर्यू षु' (अ.वे. ५.६.४, क्रमपद ⇒ 'पर्यू षु')। 'महीमू षु' (अ.वे. ७.६.२, क्रमपद ⇒ 'महीमू षु')। 'अन्य ऊ षु' (अ.वे. १८.१.१६, क्रमपद ⇒ 'अन्य ऊ षु')। 'स्तुष ऊ षु' (अ.वे. १८.१.३७, क्रमपद ⇒ 'स्तुष ऊ षु')।

Note: Whitney is not correct in saying that "the commentator paraphrases *padatvāt* by *tripadatvāt*." All the manuscript evidence, including the manuscript H, supports the reading of the rule given above as: *idam ūṣvādiṣu tripadatvāt*. Whitney is, however, correct in saying that the rule applies only to the *krama-* text, and that the *pada* reading of the passages referred to does not deviate in any manner from the usual norm: we have *idam : ūn̐ iti : su,* etc. The term *tripada* refers to those *kramapada*s which, by rule 113 = CA (4.4.14), below, are composed of three words, instead of, as usual, two only.

For AV (18.1.16), Whitney's edition agrees with the reading given in the CAB. However, the VVRI edition gives the reading *anyam ū ṣu,* while noting the manuscript variant *anya ū ṣu.* It should be noted that the reading *anyam ū ṣu* is identical with the reading found in RV (10.10.14). Thus, one can surmise that the deviation from the reading given by the CA tradition may have come about through the influence of the Ṛgvedic tradition. All these examples are cited in the same order in APR (207a, p. 124), and the APR reading for AV (18.1.16) agrees with the one found in the CAB. The APR (207a) has one more passage which is not cited by the CAB : *pará ū ta ékam* (AV 18.3.7), and we do not know whether this passage was intended to be included in this *gaṇa* by the CA and the CAB. Also see the Note on CA (3.1.4).

४.३.२८. ब्रह्मण्वत्यादीनाम् ।

Whitney (4.99). O: म्ह for ह्म.

Translation: [There is no reinstatement in the Padapāṭha and Kramapāṭha of the original *n* for *ṇ* in forms] such as *bráhmaṇvatī.*

चतुराध्यायीभाष्य - ब्रह्मण्वत्यादीनां च न समापत्तिर्भवति । 'ब्रह्मंण्ऽवतीम्' (पद, अ.वे. ६.१०८.२, संहिता ⇒ 'ब्रह्मंण्वतीम्')। 'पश्यंत् । अक्षण्ऽवान्' (पद, अ.वे. ९.९.१५, संहिता ⇒ 'पश्यंदक्षण्वान्')। 'शीर्षण्ऽवती' (पद, अ.वे. १०.१.२, संहिता ⇒ 'शीर्षण्वती')। 'वृषण्यन्तींऽइव । कन्यला' (पद, अ.वे. ५.५.३, संहिता ⇒ 'वृषण्यन्तींव कन्यला')।

Note: Whitney says: "The irregularity which renders necessary the rule is the retention of the lingual *ṇ* as final, against the principle of rule iii.89 (= CA 3.4.21), above. The last case cited, however, does not belong with the rest, since the denominative ending, by rule 29, above, is separable only after a vowel, and we read *vṛṣaṇyantyāḥ* (vi.9.1) and *vṛṣaṇyataḥ* (vi.70.1-3), without *avagraha :* hence there is no ground for restoration."

Whitney's reasoning about *vr̥ṣaṇyantīva* is correct only as far as the Padapāṭha goes. However, in the process of *parihāra* in the Kramapāṭha, there can be reinstatement of the original sounds, even when there is no *avagraha*, and this has led the commentator to include this example here. Compare the examples on CA (4.3.2). The *parihāra* 'repetition with an *iti* interposed' becomes applicable to the example *vr̥ṣaṇyantīva,* since the tradition considers this as a divisible compound of *vr̥ṣaṇyantī+iva,* and such divisible compounds are subject to *parihāra* in the Kramapāṭha. This is not the case with the other two examples pointed out by Whitney.

४.३.२९. दीर्घायुत्वायादीनां च ।

Whitney (4.100), Ha, I: omit °या°. I: 30.

Translation: [There is no reinstatement in the Padapāṭha and Kramapāṭha of the original forms in expressions] such as *dīrghāyutva.*

चतुराध्यायीभाष्य - दीर्घायुत्वायादीनां च न समापत्तिर्भवति । 'दीर्घायुऽत्वायं' (पद, अ.वे. १.२२.२, संहिता ⇒ 'दीर्घायुत्वायं')। 'सहस्रचक्षो इतिं सहस्रऽचक्षो । त्वम्' (पद, अ.वे. ४.२०.५, संहिता ⇒ 'सहस्रचक्षो त्वम्')। 'बर्हिऽसदंः' (पद, अ.वे. १८.१.४५, ५१, संहिता ⇒ 'बर्हिषदंः')।

Note: The same examples are offered in the commentary on CA (2.2.20). The *gaṇa* referred to in this rule is also referred to in CA (2.2.20) and it has been fully listed in the APR (200). The CAB cites the first three instances of this *gaṇa,* which contains a total of 10 instances. Also see the Note on CA (2.2.20).

इति चतुर्थाध्यायस्य तृतीयः पादः ।

H: ।।१०२।। चतुर्थस्य तृतीयः पादः. E, F: चतुर्थस्य तृतीयः पादः. I: इति चतुर्थाध्यायस्य तृतीयः पादः. A, B, C, D, J, M, P: तृतीयः पादः. O: इत्य. चतुर्थस्य तृतीयः पादः ।। सूत्राणि ।। ३० ।।.

चतुराध्यायीभाष्य - ॥१०२॥ चतुर्थस्य तृतीयः पादः ॥

Note: Referring to the cumulative count of the rules mentioned in the colophon of the manuscript H, Whitney says: "unless rule 53 is to be divided into two, or unless the copyist's count is inaccurate, we have lost, somewhere in the course of the second and third sections, one of the rules of the text." As Whitney was to realize after the discovery of a second manuscript: "The restoration of *iṅgyavac ca* (after rule 93), and the reckoning of the introduction to the chapter as a rule, would make out the number 102, given in A (= H) as that of the rules in the first three sections," Whitney (1880: 169). One must, however, keep in mind that other manuscripts show inclusion of the initial verses of the fourth Adhyāya as part of the text of the CA, and hence their counts are significantly different.

॥ चतुर्थोऽध्यायः ॥
॥ चतुर्थः पादः ॥

४.४.१. वेदाध्ययनं धर्मः ।

Whitney (4.101).

Translation: Study of the Veda is a merit-producing act.

चतुराध्यायीभाष्य - वेदाद्ध(H: ध)र्मः कर्मशेषभूतात् वेदाद्धर्ममाहुर्याज्ञिकाः । वेदेन कर्माणि क्रियन्ते । कर्मणो धर्मः । अनेन प्रकारेण वेदाद्ध(H: ध)र्ममाहुर्याज्ञिकाः । 'स्वर्गकामो अघायताम्' (source?) इत्यनेन मन्त्रेण शतौदनाख्यं(H: °नास्तख्यं) कर्म कृत्वा स्वर्गं साधयेदिति याज्ञिकाम्नानम् । 'यज्ञततिर्न पृथग्वेदेभ्यः' (च.आ. ४.४.४)। यज्ञस्य ततिर्यज्ञततिस्ततिर्विस्तारः । सा न पृथग्वेदेभ्यो भवति । न विना वेदैर्यज्ञस्तायते । यज्ञाद्धर्मो वेदाद्यज्ञः । एवं वेदाध्ययनाद्धर्मः । 'वेदाध्ययनं धर्म' (च.आ. ४.४.१) इत्यादिसूत्रम् ।

Note: The manuscript H here does something unusual. At the beginning of this Pāda, it firsts lists all the sūtras by themselves, and then it takes up each sūtra to comment. Since we do not possess the second manuscript for this portion, it is not clear why this change of pattern came about in the text.

४.४.२. प्रेत्य ज्योतिष्कं कामयमानस्य ।

Whitney (4.102). A, B, D, Ha: प्रेत्यये°. P: °योनिष्कं°.

Translation: [Study of the Veda is a merit-producing act] for [a person] desiring to become a luminescent heavenly body after having gone forth [from this world after death to the world beyond].

चतुराध्यायीभाष्य - प्र इत्य प्रकर्षेण गत्वेत्यर्थः । कुतः प्रकर्षेण गत्वा । अस्माल्लोकान्त(H: त्त, Cardona suggests: °ल्लोकाल्लोकान्त)रं गमनं प्रकर्षगमनाल्लोकान्तरं गत्वा प्रेत्य ज्योतिष्ट्वं कामयमानस्य । ज्योतिर्भावो ज्योतिष्ट्वम् । उक्तं हि 'ये वा इह यज्ञैरार्ध्नुवंस्तेषामेतानि ज्योतींषि यान्यमूनि नक्षत्राणीति' (source?)। ज्योतिर्दीप्तिभावमित्य[न]र्थान्तरम् । कथं तन्मे(H: ताम) स्यादित्येवमर्थं कामयमानस्य । 'वेदाध्ययनं धर्मः' (च.आ. ४.४.१)। वेदस्याध्ययनं धर्मः । तेन हि धर्मोऽभिव्यज्यते । धर्मो ज्योतिर्भावो भवति । किमध्ययनमात्रो धर्मः । नेत्युच्यते । किं तर्हि ।

४.४.३. याज्ञिकैर्यथा समाम्नातम् ।

Whitney (4.103). O: याज्ञिकौर्यथा°.

Translation: This is so, [in accordance with the textual authority] as it has been traditionally recited by the ritualists.

चतुराध्यायीभाष्य - यज्ञमधीते यज्ञं विदुर्वा ते याज्ञिकास्ते यथा समामनन्ति वेदाध्ययना(H: नां)त्(H: त) धर्मस्तथा भवति । नाध्ययनमात्रात् । यथा समाम्नातमित्युक्तम् । आम्ना(H: त्म)नं पठनम् । कथं च याज्ञिकाः पठन्ति । 'स्वर्गकामो अघायताम्' (source?) इत्यने(H: न्ये)न स्वर्गं साधयेदिति । ननु कर्म एतत् । न वेदाध्ययनम् । ततः कर्मणो धर्मः न वेदाध्ययनात् । नैतदेवम् ।

४.४.४. यज्ञततिर्न पृथग्वेदेभ्यः ।

Whitney (4.104). F, I, O: °पति° for °तति°.

Translation: There can be no continuity of the sacrificial performances apart from [the understanding and maintenance of] the Vedas.

चतुराध्यायीभाष्य - यज्ञस्य ततिः यज्ञविस्तारः । सा वेदेभ्यः पृथक् न भवति । कारणे कार्योपचाराद(H: व)ने(H: ते)न वेद[ा]ध्ययनादेव धर्म इति निरवद्यं वेदा(H: देवा)-ध्ययनं धर्म इति ।

४.४.५. यज्ञे पुनर्लोकाः प्रतिष्ठिताः ।

Whitney (4.105). J, M: °प्रतिताः.

Translation: [All the three] worlds are in turn firmly established in the sacrifice.

चतुराध्यायीभाष्य - द्यौर्वियदवनिस्त्रयो लोका यज्ञे प्रतिष्ठिताः । कथं निर्वापादिसंस्कृतं हविरङ्गुष्ठपर्वमात्रेण शकयावत्तम्(?) अन्तर्निधनस्वाहाकारे(H: र)ण अग्नौ हुतं ज्योतिर्ध(H: ध)र्म(Whitney: धूम)भावेन परिणतं ज्योतिर्भावेन द्यौलोकं धूमभावेनान्तरिक्षं पुनर्वृष्टिभावेन परिणतं पृथिवीं यात्येवं यज्ञे लोकाः प्रतिष्ठिताः ।

४.४.६. पञ्चजना लोकेषु ।

Whitney (4.106).

Translation: The five communities of men [are firmly established] in the worlds.

Note: The term *pañca janāḥ* most probably refers to the four Varṇas, plus those who are outside the Varṇa classification. The term has been variously interpreted in the Śabdakalpadruma : a) one who is born from five great elements, b) Gandharvas, fathers, gods, Asuras, and Rākṣasas. The CAB simply interprets the word to mean 'men.'

चतुराध्यायीभाष्य - पञ्चजना मनुष्य[ा]स्ते लोकेषु(H: लोकाः) प्रतिष्ठिताः । लोका यज्ञे प्रतिष्ठिताः । यज्ञा वेदे

प्रतिष्ठिताः । वेदाश्च धर्मशेषभूताः । धर्मा दैवतमतिदान्शात्-(?)कर्मणि शेषतां च(H: व) गच्छन्ति ।

४.४.७. पदाध्ययनमन्तादिशब्दस्वरार्थज्ञानार्थम् ।

Whitney (4.107). A, D, M, P: °स्वरार्थं°.

Translation: The study of the Padapāṭha is for the purpose of gaining understanding of the ends and initials of words, their accents and their meaning.

चतुराध्यायीभाष्य - अभिधानाभिधेयसंबन्धे(II: धौ) अन्त-[ज्ञा]नं च पदाध्ययनमन्तरेण न भवति । अन्तज्ञा(H: र्ज्ञा)नं च पदाध्ययनमन्तरेण न सिध्यतीत्यवश्यं मन्त्रार्थज्ञानाय प(H: प्र)दान्यध्येयानि । पदानि वाधीयमानेनावश्यं संशयच्छेदाय प्रातिशाख्यमध्येयम् । इमानि च पुनः पदाध्ययनस्य प्रयोजनानि । 'पदाध्ययनमन्तादिशब्दस्वरार्थज्ञानार्थम्' । अन्तश्च। आदिश्च । शब्दश्च । [स्वरश्च]। अर्थश्च । अन्तादिशब्द-स्वरार्थाः । तेषां तु ज्ञानमर्थः प्रयोजनं यस्य तत्पदा-ध्ययनमन्तादिशब्दस्वरार्थज्ञानार्थम् । तत्कथम् । उ(H: व)-च्यते । शं नो देव्याः (ref: 'शं नों देवीः,' अ.वे. १.६.१) पादैरुदकाचमनं विहितम् । तन्न(H: त्र) 'शं नों देवी-रभिष्टंये' पदाध्ययनमन्तरेण एकारान्तो ज्ञायते । अष्टका-याम् 'ऋतुभ्यंस्त्वा' (VVRI reading: 'ऋतुभ्यंष्वा,' अ.वे. ३.१०.१०) इति (H: ऋतुमभ्यस्त्येति) विग्रहमष्टौ । 'ऋतुभ्यस्त्वा यजे' इति 'आर्तवेभ्यस्त्वा यज(H: त)' इत्य-त्राकारादि न तु ज्ञायते । पदाध्ययनं विना वैदिकाः शब्दा न ज्ञायन्ते । तद्यथा । 'अश्वंऽवतीम्' (पद, अ.वे. १८.२.३१, संहिता ⇒ 'अश्वांवतीम्'), 'स्त्रैसूंयम्' (पद, अ.वे. ६.११.३, संहिता ⇒ 'स्त्रैषूंयम्') इत्येवमादयः संहितायामन्यरूपाः 'अश्वांवतीम्,' 'स्त्रैषूंय'मित्येवंरूपाः शब्दाः । तस्मादध्येयानि

पदानि । ब्रह्मयज्ञा(H adds ना)दि त्रैस्वर्येण विहितम् । तत्रा-पदाध्यायी पदेषु अप्रवीणः । तत्र 'ब्रह्मौदनं पंचती' (अ.वे. ११.१.१)त्येवमादिषूदात्तश्रुत्या एकश्रुत्या तानस्वरेण अधी-यीत । यस्त(H: त्त)त्र स्वरहीनमन्त्रदोषो दृष्टः स मा भूदिति । आथर्वणेषु च कर्मसु यागवर्जितेषु मणिबन्धनादिषु यज्ञ इवेह (H: यज्ञवेहे) त्रैस्वर्ये(H: र्ग्ये)ण मन्त्रप्रयोग-मिच्छति । मन्त्रार्थश्च पदाध्ययनाद्विना न ज्ञायते । वाक्यं हि पदशो विभक्तमनुव्यनक्ति । तच्च पदाध्यायी सन्धिं च पदे छेदं तु शक्नुयाद्विभक्तम्[°क्तुम्?]। 'वि हंर (अ.वे. ५.२०. ९)'। 'अलसालां(H: त्वा)सि' (अ.वे. ६.१६.४)। 'यवान्ने-ददान्(H: त्)' (अ.वे. ६.५०.१)। 'ऊँ इतिं' (पद, अ.वे. १.६.४)। 'स(H: श)म्वास्नाहं आस्यंम्' (अ.वे. ६.५६.३)। 'तद्वंस्य रेतंः' (अ.वे. ९.४.४)। इत्येवमादिषु संहितायां च भवति । य(H, Whitney: र्य)जतीत्यत्र सां(Whitney: सं)-हितिकः स प्रकुर्यात् ।तथा उदात्तस्वरितोदयेन वि[नि?]घातम् (cf. CA 3.3.21: 'नोदात्तस्वरितपरम्') अजानन् - 'ये अस्मा-कं तन्वंम्' (अ.वे. २.३२.५)- अन्यत्रापि निहन्येत । 'स्वा-द्वं१द्मीतिं' (अ.वे. ५.१८.७)। अत्र च स्वरितं कुर्यात् । तथा उदात्तान्तस्य पूर्वपदस्यानुदात्ता(H: °त्तआ°)दावुत्तरपदे तत्तस्यान्तस्थापत्तौ स्वरितम्(cf. CA 3.3.9: 'अन्तस्थापत्तावु-दात्तस्यानुदात्ते क्षैप्रः') 'अक्षंनर्थे जनस्यार्थे(?)'त्यन्यत्रापि त-[त्]कुर्यात् । एवमाद्यन्यत्राप्यपदाध्यायी संहितां(H: ता) विनाशयेत् । तस्मादेभिः कारणैरवश्याध्येयानि [पदानि]। किं च ।

Note: The above passage in the commentary is one of the most difficult to restore. The lone manuscript H is bad enough, but Whitney occasionally faults it for his own copying errors. For example, the commentary cites the forms *traisūyam* (= *pada*) and *traiṣūyam*. (= *saṃhitā*). Whitney's note on

p. 235 says: "Ms., both times, *traisūyam*." The photocopy of the Berlin manuscript which I have in my possession correctly distinguishes between the two instances of the word, and Whitney's comment could have been a result of only his own error in hand-copying the manuscript.

A statement comparable to the present rule is found in APR (3): ऋषिप्रोक्तमन्त्रादिशब्दस्वरज्ञानार्थः पदविभागः.

Referring to the reading *ṛtubhyas tvā* in AV (3.10.10), Whitney (*AV Transl.* Vol. I., p. 102) says: "All the *saṃhitā*-mss. combine in a *-bhyaṣ ṭvā,* and SPP. accepts the reading in his text; ours emends to *-bhyas tvā;* such treatment of final *as* is common in Ppp., and sporadic examples of it are found among the AV. mss., but it is hardly to be tolerated in a text like ours; and the comment to Prāt. iv. 107 (= CA 4.4.7) quotes the passage as *-bhyas tvā*." For a similar passage in AV (19.38.4) and its extensive discussion by Whitney, see: *AV Transl.* Vol.II., p. 957.

४.४.८. संहितादार्ढ्यार्थम् ।

Whitney, H: no such rule. A, B, D: °दाद्यार्थं°. J, M: संहितापदा°. P: °दाढ्यार्थं°.

Translation: [The study of the Padapāṭha is] for the purpose of firmly grasping the text of the Vedic Saṃhitās.

चतुराध्यायीभाष्य - संहितादार्ढ्यार्थं च पदान्यध्येयानि । दृढस्य भावो दार्ढ्यम् । वर्णदृढादित्वात् ष्य(H: ध्य)ञ् (cf. P.5.1.123: 'वर्णदृढादिभ्यः ष्यञ् च')। तत्रापदाध्यायी संहितायां सन्देह उत्पन्ने(H: त्ते) संशयच्छेदं न (H: च्छेदनं) कुर्यात् । यदि पदाध्ययनेन संदेहापनयो(H: °नायो) भवति, तर्हि किं क्रमाध्ययनेन । तत्राह ।

Note: With the lone manuscript H in his possession, Whitney was unable to distinguish the two rules: CA 4.4.8 and CA 4.4.9. He argues that there must be only one rule, and that one rule is identical with CA 4.4.9 (= Whitney iv. 108). This is, however, proven wrong by all the manuscripts in our possession. Clearly, there are two rules. The first refers to the importance of studying the Padapāṭha, while the second refers to the importance of studying the Kramapāṭha. One should study the Padapāṭha in order to strengthen one's control over the Saṃhitā. One should study the Kramapāṭha in order to strengthen one's control over both the Padapāṭha and the Saṃhitā. In (1880: 169), after the discovery of the second manuscript, Whitney admits that there must be two rules. He also presents a "somewhat amended" version of the text of the commentary given above. The manuscript as it stands reads: तत्रापदाध्यायी ... संशयच्छेदनं कुर्यात्. Whitney amends it to: तत्र पदाध्यायी ... संशयच्छेदनं कुर्यात्. A better way to amend it is: तत्रापदाध्यायी ... संशयच्छेदं न कुर्यात्. Whitney also amends the manuscript passage वर्णदृढादित्वात् ध्यञ् directly to Pāṇini 5.1.123: वर्णदृढादिभ्यः ष्यञ् च. There is no justification to do so. The passage should be amended simply to: वर्णदृढादित्वात् ष्यञ्, and should be interpreted as simply alluding to Pāṇini 5.1.123.

४.४.९. क्रमाध्ययनं संहितापददार्ढ्यार्थम् ।

Whitney (4.108). A, B, D, M: °पदाद्यार्थं. P: क्रमानां संहितापददाढ्यार्थं°.

Translation: The study of the Kramapāṭha is for the purpose of firmly grasping the Saṃhitāpāṭha and the Padapāṭha.

चतुराध्यायीभाष्य - संहितात्र(Whitney: च for त्र) स्वसंस्था च भवति । यवामण्ये(?)कपदद्विपदाच्च प्रगृह्यावगृह्य(H: ह्यं)सन्देहापनोदनम् । इदं वा(Whitney: चा)परं कारणं क्रमाध्ययनस्य ।

Note: The reading of the commentary is in part unintelligible.

४.४.१०. स्वरोपजनश्चादृष्टः पदेषु संहितायां च ।

Whitney (4.109). C, E, F, I, O: Daṇḍa after °दृष्टः. I: Sūtra ending in °दृष्टः numbered 10. A, B: °श्चादृष्टपदेषु°. J: Daṇḍa after °पजनश्च. P: °श्चादष्टपदेषु°, and adds a daṇḍa after this as a correction.

Translation: There is emergence of accents [in the Kramapāṭha] which is not seen in the Padapāṭha or in the Saṃhitāpāṭha.

चतुराध्यायीभाष्य - स्वरस्योपजन उत्पत्तिरदृष्टः पदकाले । स स्वरस्योपजनो भवति क्रमकाले । यथा 'स्वाद्वं१द्मीतिं' (H:

प्री, Whitney: च्री, अ.वे. ५.१८.७) अत्र पदेष्वन्तोदात्तोऽ-नुदात्तं स्वरितः संहितायामपि निघातः । क्रमे पुनः स्वरितः । स न(H: च) संहितायां न पदेषु दृष्टः । तस्य क्रमाध्ययन-मन्तरेण विज्ञानं न स्यात्तस्मात्क्रमोऽध्येयः । अधुना तस्य लक्षणम् । कीदृशोऽसौ क्रम इत्याह ।

Note: The intent of this rule seems to be to say that the Kramapāṭha has distinct accents as compared to the Padapāṭha and the Saṃhitāpāṭha. This new accent pattern emerges, because, in the Kramapāṭha, each *pada* is combined with the next *pada*, but this duo stands in isolation from the preceding and the following *pada*s. Thus, the Kramapāṭha creates entirely new prosodic circumstances producing a distinct accent pattern. Whitney seems to interpret this statement somewhat differently: "That is to say -- as we are doubtless to understand it -- in the *pada* we have before us only the accent of the uncompounded elements; in the *saṃhitā*, only that of the combined phrase : how the one grows out of the other is shown by the *krama*, which gives everything in both its separate and combined state."

Referring to the cited example *svādv àdmíti* (AV 5.18.7), Whitney says: "here, in *pada,* we have an oxytone and an unaccented syllable, which form a circumflex, while in the *saṃhitā* the circumflex farther suffers depression (*nighāta,* the *vikampita* of our rule iii.65 = CA 3.3.16, above), and the circumflex itself only appears in *krama* (in *svādv àdmi,* where the cause of depression of the *svarita* is not present)."

४.४.११. द्वे पदे क्रमपदम् ।

Whitney (4.110).

Translation: Two [consecutive] words [combined together] form a *krama*-word.

चतुराध्यायीभाष्य - क्रमाध्ययनेऽपि प्रसिद्धे द्वे पदे संहिते एकं क्रमपदं भवति । तयोः सन्धा(H: न्ध्य)नमुपरिष्टाद्व-क्ष्यति । यथाशास्त्रमिति (ref: CA 4.4.23) ।

४.४.१२. तस्यान्तेन परस्य प्रसन्धानम् ।

Whitney (4.111).

Translation: With the final [or rather the second member of a Krama-word], the combination of the next word is made [to form the next Krama-word].

चतुराध्यायीभाष्य - तस्य क्रमपदस्यान्तेनावसानेन परस्य पदस्य प्रसन्धानं कुर्यात् । तस्याप्यन्तेन परस्य तस्यापि परस्येत्येवं द्वे द्वे पदे प्रसन्धाय क्रमो भवति । अथ किमर्थं द्वे पदे क्रमपदमित्युक्तम् । पुनस्तस्यान्तेन परस्येत्युच्यते । यदि नोच्यते । प्रथमे द्वे पदे क्रमपदं कृत्वा तत्रापि परे तृतीयचतुर्थे तद् द्वितीयं क्रमपदं कुर्यात् । तत्रापि परे ये पञ्चषष्ठे तृतीयमित्येवं क्रमः स्यादित्येवं मा भूदित्येवमुच्यते । तस्यान्तेनेति । तत्कथं नाम क्रमे(H: म) द्वितीये तृतीयं तृतीये चतुर्थमित्येवं प्रसन्धानं स्यादिति । तस्माद्वक्तव्यम् ।

Note: Whitney says: "The term *antena* is explained by *avasānena,* 'close, end:' we might have rather expected the reading *antyena*, 'with the last word of each *krama*-word as already defined.'" While Whitney's expectation is appropriate, it is not supported by a single manuscript of the CA. However, I have translated the rule as if the word *antena* was synonymous with *antyena.* The CA seems to be using the word *anta* in the sense of *antya* in other rules as well, cf. CA (1.1.5: पदान्तः पद्यः), CA (2.1.2: पदान्तानामनुत्तमानाम् तृतीया ...), CA (3.4.21: पदान्तस्पर्शयुक्तस्य), CA (4.3.9: पदान्तविकृतानाम्).

As an illustration of Krama, Whitney cites the last line of the first hymn of the AV (i.1.4 c, d) and constructs its Krama*: saṃ śrutena : śrutena gamemahi : gamemahi mā : mā śrutena : śrutena vi : vi rādhiṣi : rādhiṣīti rādhiṣi*. Now we have at least one manuscript of Kramapāṭha (Kāṇḍa 20, ms. # 133/1879-80) and two manuscripts of Jaṭāpāṭha (Kāṇḍa 15, ms # 128/1879-80; Kāṇḍa 17, ms # 83/1880-81) available at the Bhandarkar Oriental Research Institute. With these manuscripts, we can now confirm at least some of the features of Krama discussed by the CA and the CAB.

४.४.१३. नान्तगतं परेण ।

Whitney (4.112). E, F, I, O: नांतर्गतं°. P: तांतगतं°.

Translation: A word occurring at the end [of a half-verse, i.e. first two metrical feet, or at the end of a verse] is not [combined] with the following [i.e. the initial word of the third metrical foot, or the initial word of the next verse].

चतुराध्यायीभाष्य - अतिप्रसक्तं तस्यान्तेन परस्येति क्वचिन्नेष्यते । तत्प्रतिषेधार्थमिदमुच्यते । नान्तगतमिति । अर्धर्चान्तगतं परेणार्धर्चादिना पदेन न(H: म) सन्धेयम् । द्वे पदे क्रमपदमित्युक्तम् ।

Note: Each verse is divided into two parts, each followed by a pause. The first pause occurs at the end of the second metrical foot, and the second pause occurs at the end of the verse. The present rule says that a Kramapada is not to be formed across a pause at either of these locations. The final word, thus occurring before a pause, undergoes a repetition (*parihāra*) by CA (4.4.18). This pattern is now fully confirmed by the BORI manuscript (133/1879-80) containing the Kramapāṭha for the 20th Kāṇḍa. Consider the first verse of the 20th Kāṇḍa and its Kramapāṭha provided by the manuscript on its first folio:

AV (20.1.1): इन्द्रं त्वा वृषभं वयं सुते सोमें हवामहे ।
स पांहि मध्वो अन्धंसः ।।

Kramapāṭha: इन्द्रं त्वा । त्वा वृषभं । वृषभं वयं । वयं सुते । सुते सोमें ।
सोमें हवामहे । हवामह इतिं हवामहे ।
स पांहि । पाहि मध्वंः । मध्वो अन्धंसः । अन्धंस इत्यन्धंसः ।।

४.४.१४. त्रीणि पदान्यपृक्तमध्यानि ।

Whitney (4.113). P: °दान्यपृ°.

Translation: Three [consecutive] words, with the middle word being a single vowel, [are combined to form a single Krama-word].

चतुराध्यायीभाष्य - क्वचित्त्रीणि त्रीणीष्यन्ते । तदा त्रीणि पदान्यपृक्तमध्यानि । अपृक्तं पदं येषां मध्ये तान्यपृक्तमध्यानि। पृक्तं मिश्रमित्यर्थः । किं च पदस्य मिश्रमुच्यते । स्वरान्तं व्यञ्जनैर्मिश्रीयते । तत्र येषां पदानां(H: पदां) मध्यमं पदम-व्यञ्जनमिश्रशुद्धकेवलस्वरो भवति, तानि तादृक[?]लक्षणानि त्रीणि क्रमपदं भवति । 'धिया । आ । इहि' (पद, अ.वे. २.५.४, क्रम ⇒ 'धियेहि') इति यथा । अत्र प्रयोजनमुच्यते । कस्मादपृक्तमध्यानि त्रीणि एवं भवति ।

Note: The term *apṛkta* also occurs elsewhere in the CA, cf. CA (1.3.10: उकारस्येतावपृक्तस्य) and CA (1.3.17: निपातोऽपृक्तोऽनाकारः). See the Note on CA (1.3.17). The commentary offers the example of the triple Krama-word: *dhiyā́+ā́+ihi* (*AV* 2.5.4). Here, the Krama-sequence, in terms of the previous rules might have been like: *dhiyā́ (= dhiyā́+ā́)/ éhi (= ā́+ihi).* The present rule says that we are supposed to combine all the three words together into a single Krama-word: *dhiyéhi*. For Whitney's comment on *dhiyéhi,* see Note on CA (3.2.15).

Whitney further remarks: "It is doubtless to point out and call attention to this mode of treatment of the *ā* in the *krama*-text, that our Atharvan *pada* manuscripts quite frequently write a figure 3 after the word which follows it : thus, in the instance cited, the manuscript gives *dhiyā : ā : ihi : 3,* at i.1.2, *punaḥ : ā : ihi : 3*, etc."

This pattern of a Tripada in the Kramapāṭha is now confirmed by the BORI manuscript 133/1879-80. For the initial words for AV (20.4.1: अयमु त्वा विचर्षणे), the Kramapāṭha (folio 2) reads: अयमुंत्वा । ऊँ इत्यूँ । त्वा विचर्षणे । Here, the first segment अयमुंत्वा is a Tripada, with the monophonic middle Pada *u*.

४.४.१५. एकादेशस्वरसन्धिदीर्घविनामाः प्रयोजनम् ।

Whitney (4.114). J, M: omit the Visarga. A, B, C: एकादश°. P: एकादेशः°.

Translation: The reasons [for considering three words combined together as a single Krama-word as described above] are the fusion of two vowels into one, combination of vowels, lengthening of a vowel, and the change of *s* to *ṣ* [after vowels other than *a* and *ā*].

चतुराध्यायीभाष्य - एकादेशादीनि चत्वारि प्रयोजनानि अपृक्तमध्यस्य त्रिपदस्य तान्युच्यन्ते । 'धि॒या । आ । इ॒हि॒' (पद, अ.वे. २.५.४)। इत्यत्र समानाक्ष[र]स्येति (च.आ. ३.३.१९) दीर्घत्वे ति[ए?]कत्वे कृते 'धि॒या' इति पदम् । तस्य पदस्याकारो यः स्वर 'इहि' [इ]त्यादाविकारः तयोरेकारे च कृते 'धि॒येहि' इत्येकमेव पदं भवति । तस्मादित्यनेन सन्धानेन भवितव्यम्। अन्यथा क्रमपदमेव न स्यात् । तत्र 'इह्या' इति । 'आ न' इत्यत्रापि (= क्रम ⇒ 'इ॒ह्या । आ नः,' पद ⇒ 'इ॒हि॒ । आ। न॒ः,' अ.वे. २.५.४)। 'स्वरे नामिनोऽन्तस्था' (च.आ. ३.२.१६) इति [इ]कारस्य स्वरसन्धिः क्रियते । 'इ॒दम् । ऊँ॒ इतिं । सु' (पद, अ.वे. १. २४.४) इत्येतदप्येकं पदं मतम् । तस्य(H: स्या) च न सन्धिः । तथा हि । इद(H: ह)मूष्वादिष्वसां(H: सं)हितिकं दीर्घत्वम् । चर्चास्य त्रिपदस्य मध्यभावादिष्यते । इदमूष्वित्येवंभूतस्यैव रूपाख्यतायामवश्यं त्रिपदं वंशक्रमेण भवितव्यम्। अत्रैव अपदत्वम् । तदपि त्रिपदमध्यावयवम् । तस्मादे(H: दि)भिः कारणैः अपृक्तमध्यानि त्रिपदानि क्रमपदं भवति ।

Note: A good deal of the last portion of the above commentary is still unclear, though I have now given on the whole a better text than Whitney. Also, AV (2.5.4) presents a more complicated sequence: *dhiyā́ / ā́ / ihi / ā́ / naḥ*. It is not clear from the commentary whether it proposes to turn this sequence into two *krama*-words: *dhiyéhi (= dhiyā́+ā́+ihi)* and *ihyā́naḥ (= ihi+ā́+naḥ)*. Whitney remarks: "For the second item, he selects the example *ihi : ā : naḥ* (ii.5.4) : here, if we compound *ihy ā* and *ā naḥ*, a vowel-combination (*svarasandhi*) is made of the *i*, by the rule *svare nāmino 'ntasthāḥ* (iii.39 = CA 3.2.16). How this vowel combination furnishes the ground for the *krama*-word *ihy ā naḥ*, he does not point out." Similarly, referring to the example *idam ū ṣu*, Whitney says: "The prologation of the *u* in this and similar cases would indeed seem to furnish a reason for the construction of the *krama*-word out of three members, since the long vowel could not properly appear if the particle were made the final of one such word and the beginning of another; but I am unable to see how the lingualization of the sibilant should have any effect in the same direction, since there would be no difficulty in reading *u ṣu* as a *krama*-word, if the *u* were treated in the ordinary manner." A more detailed account of the reasons for combining three or more words into a single Krama-word is found in the XIth Paṭala of the RPR. For a confirmation of the Tripada Krama of this type from the BORI Krama manuscript, see the note on the previous rule.

४.४.१६. आकारौकारादि पुनः ।

Whitney (4.115). B, D, M, P: °दिषु न°. A, B, C, D, J, M, Ha, P(orig): a single rule combined with CA 4.4.17. P adds a daṇḍa after उकारः of the next rule as a correction, suggesting that the first rule was: आकारौकारादिषुनरुकारः.

> **Translation:** The *ā* and *o* [which are first treated as the middle members included in a triple Krama-word] are again taken as the initial [members of a subsequent Krama-word].

> ***चतुराध्यायीभाष्य*** - आकारौकारादिषु त्रि(H: संस्त्रि)पदे परतः प्र(H: प्रा)त्यारम्भः । स पुनरुच्यते । तद्यथा । 'गोपायतास्माकंम्' (त्रिपदक्रम, अ.वे. १२.३.५५, पद ⇒ 'गोपायत । आ । अस्माकंम्')। 'आस्माकंम्' (क्रम, पद ⇒ 'आ । अस्माकंम्')। तथा । 'धियेहिं' (त्रिपदक्रम, अ.वे. २.५.४, पद ⇒ 'धिया । आ । इहिं')। 'एहिं' (क्रम, पद ⇒ 'आ । इहिं')। 'हविरोषु' (त्रिपदक्रम, अ.वे. ७.७२.२, पद ⇒ 'हविः । ओ [इतिं] । सु')। 'ओ षु' (क्रम, पद ⇒ 'ओ । सु')। 'ओ इत्यो' (=परिहार)।

Note: This behavior is now confirmed by the BORI Krama manuscript (133/1879-80). Folio 4 offers an instance from AV 20.6.2: Saṃhitā: पिबा वृंषस्व, Pada: पिबं । आ । वृषस्व, Krama: पिबा वृंषस्व । आ वृंषस्व.

४.४.१७. उकारः परिहार्य एव ।

Whitney (4.116). B: नकारः परिहार्य एव.

Translation: The [monophonic particle] *u* must indeed be repeated (*parihāra*).

चतुराध्यायीभाष्य - एवम् उकारो(एवकारो?)ऽन्ययोगनिवृत्त्यर्थः । श्रीनारायणः (?)। अयोगनिवृत्त्यर्थष्व[°स्त्व?]परिहार्य एव । परिहारश्चर्चा द्विर्वचनमित्यनर्थान्तरम् । उकारो न पुनरुच्यते। किन्तु परिक्रि[ह्रि?]यते । त(H: य)द्यथा । 'स उ सूर्यः' (अ.वे. १३.४.५)। 'ॐ इत्यूँ इति' । 'स उं एव' (अ.वे. १३.४.५) (अ)त्र 'ॐ इत्यूँ इति'।

Note: The wording of the commentary is not quite clear. However, Whitney says: "This rule is, as the commentator explains it, intended to forbid the combination of *u* (like *ā* and *o*) with the next following word to form a new *krama*-word (*anyayoganivṛttyarthaḥ*)." The commentary seems to be making some distinction between *anyayoganivṛtti* and *ayoganivṛtti* for the particle *u*. In technical Sanskrit, these terms are used to explain the meaning of the particle *eva*, and hence the first line could be emended to: *evakāro 'nyayoganivṛttyarthaḥ*. *Ayoganivṛtti* may mean "obligatory combination, lit. prohibition on lack of combination." For *u* in B.O.R.I. Krama ms., cf. note on CA 4.4.19.

४.४.१८. प्रगृह्यावगृह्यसमापाद्यान्तगतानां द्विर्वचनं परिहार इतिमध्ये ।

Whitney (4.117). A, B, D, O: °वगृह्यास°. I: °द्यानामंतर्ग°. O: °समापद्या°. P adds daṇḍas after द्विर्वचनं and मध्ये as corrections. All mss. °न्तर्गतानां°.

Translation: Repetition with *iti* interposed [i.e. 'x *iti* x'] is applied to *pragṛhya*s, compound-words divisible with an *avagraha*, of those requiring reinstatement of the original form, and those which occur at the end [of a half-verse, or at the end of the verse].

Note: All manuscripts have the reading *antargatānāṃ*, and so does the manuscript of the commentary CAB. Whitney restores it to *antagatānāṃ*, without reporting the original reading. I agree with Whitney's restoration, since it agrees with the practice of *parihāra,* or *parigraha* as it is called in the RPR (iii.23: परिग्रहे त्वनार्षान्तात् ...) and *sthitopasthita* as it is called in the VPR (4.190, 4.196: अवसाने च). The misreading *antargata* for *antagata* is also found in several manuscripts for CA (4.4.13: नान्तगतं परेण).

> ***चतुराध्यायीभाष्य*** - प्रगृह्यं च अवगृह्यं च समापाद्यं च अन्तग(H: र्ग)तं च । प्रगृह्यावगृह्यसमापाद्यान्तग(H: र्ग)तानि चैषां प्रगृह्यादीनां द्विर्वचनं कर्तव्यम् । क्रमकाले द्विर्वक्तव्यानि। तस्य द्विर्वचनस्य परिहार इति संज्ञा । स च इतिमध्यः परिहारः कार्यः । तयोर्द्विर्वचनयोरेकमुक्त्वा तत(H: त्) इति । ततो द्विर्वचनं । मध्ये तु प्रगृह्यादीनि । एकेन इतिना परिहार्याणि ।

Note: Whitney provides a comparative view of *parihāra* in the various traditions: "The forms to be repeated are, according to the doctrine of he Vāj. Pr. (iv.187-193), a divisible word (*avagṛhya*), one in the interior of which appears a prolongation or a lingualization, a *pragṛhya*, a *riphita* of which the *r* does not appear in the *saṃhitā*, and a word preceding a pause *(avasāna)*. The first and the last three of these classes are, indeed, treated in the same manner by all the other authorities (compare R. Pr. x.6-8, r. 7-9, and xi. 13-14, r. 25; Up(alekhasūtra) iv. 4-11); but as regards the words which in *saṃhitā* undergo an abnormal alteration of form, there is a less perfect agreement among them. The Rik. Pr. and Up. specify as requiring repetition in *krama* (but sundry special and anomalous cases), words having their initial vowel prolonged, and those in the interior of which there is a change not brought about by external influences - that is to say, due to euphonic causes within the word itself. Whether the Vāj. Pr. includes among the repeatable words those having a prolonged initial, or whether any cases of this kind occur in the text to which it belongs, I do not know. Our own *krama*-system, it will be noticed, while in one respect more chary of the repetition than the others, in that it repeats no *riphita* words, in another respect is vastly more liberal of its use, applying it in the case of every word which requires restoration from an abnormal to a normal form, according to the rules given in the preceding section of this chapter. There is no limitation made, either by the text or the commentary, of the term *samāpādya*; so far as I can see, every word in the text which undergoes in *saṃhitā* any of the changes detailed in rule 74, above, must suffer *parihāra.*

The Atharvan *krama* is thus made a more complete and elaborate index of the euphonic irregularities occurring in its text than is that of either of the other Vedas."

Note that Whitney's conception of the Kramapāṭha for the AV is purely inferential, and is not based on either perusal of the manuscripts of the Krama-pāṭha or its actual recitation. Now the BORI Krama manuscript (133/1879-80) confirms the description given by the CA and the CAB. The *parihāra* is also carried out in the Jaṭāpāṭha as shown by the BORI manuscripts 128/1879-80 and 83/1880-81.

४.४.१९. द्वाभ्यामुकारः ।

Whitney (4.118). I: 20. O: द्वाध्यांमुकारः.

Translation: [The *parihāra* repetition for] *u* [is carried out] by [placing] two [*iti*-s, namely one after each occurrence of *u*].

चतुराध्यायीभाष्य - द्वाभ्यामितिकरणाभ्यामुकारः परिहार्यः । 'ऊँ इत्यूँ इतिं' यथा । किं प्रयोजनम् । सर्वाणि प्रगृह्याण्येकेनेतिनावेष्ट्यन्ते उकारस्तु द्वाभ्यामित्युच्यते ।

Note: Whitney points out that this exceptional treatment of *u* is unique to the AV tradition: "None of the other treatises supports this reading : all would prescribe simply *ūn̐ ity ūn̐*." In this respect, the BORI Krama manuscript (133/1879-80) does not follow the CA prescription and uses *iti* only once. However, the BORI Jaṭāpāṭha manuscript (128/1879-80, folio 36-7) shows the application of the present CA rule: ऊँ इत्यूँ इतिं (AV 15.10.6-7). Since the Krama manuscript is available only for the 20th Kāṇḍa, the difference between the treatment of *u*, may be historically significant. The Krama of the 20th Kāṇḍa may have been influenced more by the RV tradition. The Jaṭā manuscript, however, shows that the CA rule was indeed followed.

४.४.२०. अनुनासिकदीर्घत्वं प्रयोजनम् ।

Whitney (4.119). B, D: अनुनासिकादी°.

Translation: [The use of *iti* after each of the repeated occurrences of *u* is] for the purpose of [maintaining] nasalization and lengthening [of *u*].

चतुराध्यायीभाष्य - तस्य उकारस्य इतिपरस्य त्वनुनासिकत्वं विहितम् 'उकारस्येतावपृक्तस्य' (च.आ. १.३.१०) इति । तद्यदा द्वितीय इतिर्ना(H: ना)द्रियेत तदेतिपरमनु(H: °रमंनासि°)नासिकं व्याहन्येत । तथा दीर्घत्वम् । तेनावश्यमनुनासिकदीर्घत्वव्याख्यानाय(H: °नेय) उकारो द्वाभ्यां नित्यं परिहर्तव्यः ।

Note: As the commentary points out, CA (1.3.10: उकारस्येतावपृक्तस्य) prescribes that the particle *u* is nasalized before *iti*. CA (1.3.11: दीर्घः प्रगृह्यश्च) further says that *u* is lengthened before *iti* and that it becomes a *pragṛhya*, namely that it is not combined in sandhi with the following *iti*. The commentator says that, unless each occurrence of *u* in the repetition were followed with *iti*, it would not be possible to keep it long and nasalized, i.e. as *ū̃*.

४.४.२१. प्लुतश्चाप्लुतवत् ।

Whitney (4.120). P adds a daṇḍa after this as a correction.

Translation: A prolated vowel, [in *parihāra* repetition], is treated like a non-prolated one.

चतुराध्यायीभाष्य - प्लुतश्चाप्लुतवच्च परिहर्तव्यः अप्लुतेन तुल्यतां प्रावहितव्यः । परिहारकाले 'पुरुंषः । आ । बभूवाँ३' (अ.वे. १०.२.२८) अत्र 'आ' इत्या(H: त्य)कारः प्लुतः । सः अप्लुतवता परिहर्तव्यः । 'आ बभूवाँ३' इति बभूवेति वक्तव्यम् ।

Note: A *pluta* vowel, like a *pragṛhya*, is not combined with the following vowel in sandhi, cf. P.6.1.125 (प्लुतप्रगृह्या अचि नित्यम्). Though there is no specific rule in the CA teaching this feature of a *pluta* vowel, this seems to have been taken for granted by the present rule.

Whitney remarks: "The reading of the manuscript is unfortunately corrupt at the end, where the required *Krama* is to be given." The commentary further confuses the issue by interpreting the word *aplutavat* as a non-adverbial, by paraphrasing it as: सः अप्लुतवता परिहर्तव्यः. Whitney translates this phrase as: "it (= protracted *a*) must be repeated along with [or, in the form of] an unprotracted *a*." In the original rule, the expression *aplutavat* is adverbial in the same manner as it is in P.6.1.129 (अप्लुतवदुपस्थिते). Pāṇini's rule makes it somewhat more transparent that by the term *aplutavat* we are given permission to combine a *pluta* vowel with the following vowel of *iti*, something which was otherwise not permitted by P.6.1.125. Thus, the CA rule says that when in the *parihāra* repetition, the word *babhūvā̃3* is followed by *iti*, the final *ā̃3* is treated as if it were not *pluta*, i.e. it is allowed to combine with the following *i* of *iti*.

४.४.२२. अनुनासिकः पूर्वश्च शुद्धः ।

Whitney (4.121). M: अनुनासिकश्च°. P adds a daṇḍa after this as a correction.

Translation: [The vowel, which is seen] previously [i.e. in the Saṃhitā and Pada] as a nasal [vowel], is [restored to] a pure [i.e. non-nasal, vowel before the *iti* of a *parihāra* repetition].

चतुराध्यायीभाष्य - यः पूर्वमनुनासिको दृष्टः स परिहारकाले शुद्ध[:?] कृत्वा परिहर्तव्यः । एतदेवोदाहरणम् । अत्रैव 'पुरुष आ बभूवाँ३ इत्यवसाने' (च.आ. १.३.९) इति अवसाने आ इतिपूर्वमनुनासिको दृष्टः शुद्धः परिहर्तव्यः । 'बभूवेतिं बभूवाँ३' । 'यथाशास्त्रं प्रसन्धानम्' (च.आ. ४.४.२३) उक्तम् । 'तस्यान्तेन परस्य प्रसन्धानम्' (च.आ. ४.४.१२) इति । तत्र सन्धानविधानं नोक्तम् । उच्यते ।

Note: Thus, in a *parihāra* repetition, when *babhūvā̃3* is combined with *iti*, the previous rule gives us the permission to treat *ā̃3* as if it were not a prolated vowel and hence to combine it with *iti*. However, even if it were to be treated as a non-prolated vowel, it would still remain a nasal *ā̃*, and combined with the following *i*, it would yield a nasal *ẽ* in *babhūvẽti*. The present rule says that the nasal vowel should be first restored to a non-nasal vowel and then combined with the following vowel. Thus we get the desired form *babhūveti*. The full *krama* repetition reads as: *babhūveti babhūvā̃3*. CA (1.3.8) ensures that the form *babhūva* in the phrase *puruṣa ā babhūva* appears as *babhūvā̃3* before a pause.

Whitney's discussion on this rule is entirely misguided. He seems to think that the present rule would teach the *krama* reading *babhūveti babhūva*, while CA (1.3.8) would have us read *babhūveti babhūvā̃3*. He, therefore, says: "It may be, however, that we ought to confess a discordance between the teachings of our treatise here and in the first chapter." Whitney is misled to this conclusion because he gives CA (4.4.21) an interpretation which is too wide. It is not that a *pluta* vowel is treated as a non-*pluta* anywhere in the *parihāra* repetition, but that it is treated as a non-*pluta* before *iti* of the repetition. The present CA rule applies to the same context, and therefore there is no contradiction in our treatise.

४.४.२३. यथाशास्त्रं प्रसन्धानम् ।

Whitney (4.122). C, E, F, O: यथाशास्त्रप्र°.

Translation: The combination [of two successive words into a Krama-word] is made in accordance with the [general] rules [of sandhi].

Note: The rules which are used to combine Padas to form Saṃhitā are the same rules which are used to combine Padas to form a Krama-word. Compare the use of the expression *yathāśāstram* in APR (170, p.111).

चतुराध्यायीभाष्य - यद्यच्छास्त्रं यथाशास्त्रं यद्यत्पदशास्त्रे पदानां सन्धानलक्षणमुक्तमिहापि तदेकस्य क्रमपदस्य भवति। क्रमपदत्वादन्यशब्दशङ्कयोच्यते । तदेव मा स्यादिति ।

४.४.२४. प्रगृह्यावगृह्यचर्चायां क्रमवदुत्तरस्मिन्नवग्रहः ।

Whitney (4.123). A, B, J: °ह्याचर्चा°. P: °ह्याचगृह्य°.

Translation: In the *carcā* repetition of *pragṛhya* words whose members are separable with an *avagraha* (in the Padapāṭha), [the *carcā* repetition is to be made] in a manner like the *krama*-[-*parihāra*] repetition, [with separation of the divisible members] with an *avagraha* in the second occurrence [of the repetition].

चतुराध्यायीभाष्य - यस्मिन्नवगृह्यत्वं [प्रगृह्यत्वं च] एकस्मिन्नेव युगपद्भवति तत्प्रगृह्यावगृह्यम् । तत्र(H: व) चर्चायां क्रमवद्भवति । चर्चा द्वि(H: दि)र्वचनमित्युक्तम् । पदकालेऽपि तच्च क्रमकाले इव भवति । तस्य क्रमकालस्य रूपं परिहरेत् । प्रगृह्याणि चावगृह्याणि च परे(दे?) क्रमे परिक्रि[°ह्रि?]यन्ते । प्रगृह्यावगृह्यं पुनः पदेष्वेव परिक्रि[°ह्रि?]यते । तत्र चावग्रहः कथम् । उत्तरस्मिन्नवग्रहः । उत्तरस्मिन्नेव द्वितीयेऽवग्रहः कार्यः । न प्रथमे । 'विरूपे इति विऽरूपे' (अ.वे. १०.७.६, ४२)।

Note: For a detailed examination of Whitney's views, see the Note on CA (4.3.2).

४.४.२५. समापाद्यानामन्ते संहितावद्वचनम् ।

Whitney (4.124). I: °पद्या°.

Translation: Words which require reinstatement of the original form, if they occur at the end [of half-verse or verse], should be [first] recited [without such reinstatement] as in the *saṃhitā* [and then should be subjected to the *parihāra* repetition].

चतुराध्यायीभाष्य - यानि समापाद्यानामन्तग(H: र्ग)तान्यर्धर्चे(H: ते) यानि भवन्ति । तेषां संहितावद्वचनं कर्तव्यम् । यथा संहिताकाले भवन्ति तथा तानि । 'सा वृक्षाँ(H: त्ताँ)अभि सिंष्यदे' (अ.वे. ५.५.९, पद ⇒ 'सिस्यदे')। सिष्यद इत्येवं पुनर्वक्तव्यम् । ततः परिहारः । 'सिस्यद इतिं सिस्यदे' । तथा 'प्रणींतये' (अ.वे. ६.२३.२, पद ⇒ 'प्रऽनींतये') इत्यादयः सर्वे उदाहार्याः समानपदस्थाः ।

Note: The words *siṣyade* and *praṇītaye* occur at the end of half-verse. In their *krama-parihāra* repetition, we are asked to first recite the words as they are given in the *saṃhitā*, before reciting the *parihāra*. Thus we get the sequences: *siṣyade / sisyada íti sisyade,* and *práṇītaye / prá́nītaya íti prá-nītaye.* Whitney says that "this special point is left untouched in all the other *krama* treatises." It is perhaps peculiar to the AV tradition.

The BORI manuscript (133/1879-80) of Krama for the 20th Kāṇḍa shows a slightly different state of affairs. In all the cases of *samāpādyas*, not just the ones that occur at the end of half-verses, one finds that the word as read in the Krama portion is always in its shape as seen in the Saṃhitā, and only in its *parihāra* does it show the restoration. For example, the words हर्य पुरुष्टुत occur at the end of the second Pāda of AV (20.6.2). Their Krama in the manuscript (folio 3) reads: हर्य पुरुष्टुत । पुरुस्तुतेतिं पुरु०स्तुत. However, the same treatment is seen in this Krama manuscript for *samāpādya* words which do not occur at the end of a half-verse. Compare the Krama (folio 3) for the words प्र णों धितावांनं यज्ञं in AV (20.6.3) which do not occur at the end of a half verse: प्र णों । नो धितावांनं । धितावांनं यज्ञं । धितवांनमितिं धित०वांनं. This behavior is different from the prescription of the CA and the CAB. The BORI manuscripts (128/1879-80; 83/1880-81) of the Jaṭāpāṭha show the same behavior as seen in the Krama manuscript. It is not immediately clear how to account for this difference.

४.४.२६. तस्य पुनरास्थापितं नाम ।

Whitney (4.125). C: °रास्थितं नाम.

Translation: This [Saṃhitā-like recitation of a word which needs reinstatement of its original form] is given the designation *āsthāpita.*

चतुराध्यायीभाष्य - तस्य संहितावद्वचनस्य आस्थापितमित्येवं संज्ञा भवति । यत्र निमित्तनैमित्तिके एकत्र भवतः । यथा 'सिष्यदे' । अत्र हि अभ्यासकृतं षत्वमनुभवति । अभ्यास(H: स्य)षत्वयोरेकप[द]त्वात् । इह न भवति । 'स्त्रियामनुं षिच्यते' (अ.वे. ६.११.२)। 'तत् । स्त्रियाम् । अनुं । सिच्यते' (=पद)। इति न संहितावद्भवति । कुतोऽस्मान्निमित्तनैमित्तिकानां भिन्नपदार्थत्व[पदस्थत्व?]मुच्यते । अन्वित्युपसर्गः ।

'उपसर्गात्सि(H: नि)चेः षत्वं स च नानापदे श्रुतः ।
तेनात्र मेदं(H: मिदि) भूदित्येतदर्थमिदमुच्यते ।।'

(source?)

Note: The phenomenon of *āsthāpita* takes place only when the transformation which is restored to its original is caused by word-internal causes, and not by causes in the preceding word. Thus, it applies to the form *siṣyade*, because the cerebralization here is caused by the vowel *i* in the same word. On the other hand, in the expression *anu ṣicyate*, the cerebralization is caused by the preceding *u* of *anu* which is treated as a separate word by the Padapāṭha. Whitney points out: "It might still seem doubtful, after all this lengthy exposition, whether such a word as *sicyate* was regarded by the commentator as not to be separately spoken at all, or as to be separately spoken, only not in *saṃhitā* form, as follows: *striyām anu : anu ṣicyate : sicyate : sicyata iti sicyate;* but the latter interpretation seems to me the more probable." The pattern *anu ṣicyate : sicyate : sicyata iti sicyate* reconstructed above by Whitney is not met with in the BORI Krama manuscript. However, we do find different treatment of word-internal and word-external changes. Contrast the following examples. After the Krama सुषावं हर्यश्व (AV 20.117.1, folio 78), we get the *parihāra* in the form: सुसावेतिं सुसावं. In this instance, the retroflexion is caused by word-internal conditions. However, we do not get any such *parihāra* in the example of AV (20.113.2, folio 79): प्रथमो नि । नि षींदसि । सीदसि सोमंकामं. This is not followed by सीदसीति सीदसि. Since the Padapāṭha treats *ni* as a separate Pada, the same treatment is continued in the Kramapāṭha. Once the context of *ni* is removed in the Kramapāṭha in a sequence such as सीदसि सोमंकामं, the retroflexion naturally goes away, and there is no need to deliberately go for another explicit restoration.

The passage निमित्तनैमित्तिकानां भिन्नपदार्थत्वम् in the CAB almost certainly must be emended to निमित्तनैमित्तिकानां भिन्नपदस्थत्वम्, cf. the CAB on CA 4.4.27.

४.४.२७. स एकपदः परिहार्यश्च परिहार्यश्च ।

Whitney (4.126). I: 28.

Translation: The word [thus defined as an *āsthāpita* in the preceding rule] is a single-word [unit in the Kramapāṭha] and it is to be repeated [with an *iti* interposed in *parihāra*].

चतुराध्यायीभाष्य - परिहर्तव्यश्च स (Whitney:) आस्थापितसंज्ञैकपदः (H: आस्थितसंज्ञपदृशः)। योऽसौ संहि[ता]व[द्] द्विर्वचनेन निर्दिश्यते । निमित्तनैमित्तिकयो[:] भिन्नपदस्थ (H: स्य) त्वात् । स परिहार्यश्च भवति । संहितावद्विडाचि (?) बहुलमिति

'[शास्त्रे पुराणे कविभिर्दृष्टमेतत्
वर्णलिङ्गस्वरविभक्तिवाक्यव्यत्य]यश्छन्दसीति'।
(= APR 222, p. 168)
'वर्ण (H: र्णा) लोपागमह्रस्वदीर्घप्लुतआत्मने-
[भा]षापरस्मै (H adds: वि) भाषा अपियन्ति' ॥
(= APR 223, p. 168)
'न तर्क (H: की) बुद्ध्या न च शास्त्रदृष्ट्या
यथाम्नात (H: न) मन्यथा नैव कुर्यात् ।
आम्नातं परिषत्त (H: न्न) स्य शास्त्रं
दृष्टो विधिर्व्यत्ययः पूर्वशास्त्रे' ॥
(= APR, p. 169)
'आम्नातव्यमनाम्नातं
प्रपाठेऽस्मिन् क्वचित्पदम् ।
छन्दसोऽपरिमेयत्वात्
परिषत्तस्य लक्षणं परिषत्तस्य लक्षणमिति॥'
(= APR, p. 169)

Note: The final portion of the Caturādhyāyāyībhāṣya has a close parallel in the final portion of the APR, and this also establishes a close connection between these two texts:

शास्त्रे पुराणे कविभिर्दृष्टमेतत्
वर्णलिङ्गस्वरविभक्तिवाक्यव्यत्ययश्छन्दसीति ।
वर्णलोपागमह्रस्वदीर्घप्लुतात्मने-
भाषा परस्मैभाषा अपियन्ति ॥

न तर्कबुद्ध्या न च शास्त्रदृष्ट्या
यथाम्नातमन्यथा नैव कुर्यात् ।
आम्नातं परिषत्तस्य शास्त्रं
दृष्टो विधिर्व्यत्ययः पूर्वशास्त्रे ॥
आम्नातव्यमनाम्नातं
प्रपाठेऽस्मिन् क्वचित् पदम् ।
छन्दसोऽपरिमेयत्वात्
परिषत्तस्य लक्षणं परिषत्तस्य लक्षणमिति ॥

इति चतुर्थाध्यायस्य चतुर्थः पादः । चतुर्थोऽध्यायः समाप्तः । समाप्ता चतुराध्यायिका ॥

H: इति शौनकीयं चतुराध्यायिके चतुर्थः पादः । चतुरध्यायिभाष्य समाप्तः. F: चतुर्थस्य चतुर्थः पादः । आथर्वणे चतुराध्यायिकायां चतुर्थोध्यायः । ग्रंथसंख्या ५८०. G: इति चतुर्थाध्यायस्य चतुर्थः पादः । सूत्राणि १७४ । इति चतुर्थोध्यायः. I: प्र. सू ११० । द्वि. सू. १०७ । तृ. सू. १२५ । च. सू. १७४ । इत्यथर्ववेदे कौत्सव्याकरणे चतुराध्यायिका समाप्ता । सूत्रैक्यं ५१६ । इति कौत्सव्याकरणं समाप्तम्. O: इत्यथर्ववेदे कौत्सव्याकरणे चतुराध्यायिकायां चतुर्थोध्यायस्य चतुर्थः पादः ॥ समाप्तः सूत्राणि ॥२७॥ चतुर्थोध्यायः ॥४॥. The numbers of rules in each Adhyāya given in these colophons are useful only in a general way. Since the manuscripts do not fully agree with each other, we cannot take the numbers too seriously. However, one must keep in mind that different numberings probably refer to different interpretive traditions.

॥ श्रीमदथर्वकौत्सव्याकरणे पञ्चसन्धिः ॥

॥ कृष्णदासप्रणीतः ॥[1]

॥ श्रीगणेशाय नमः ॥

ॐ अथर्वाणमृषिं देवं हयग्रीवशिरोधरम्।
कर्तुमाङ्गिरसव्याख्यां नमस्ये शिरसासकृत् ॥१॥[2]
चत्वारि वाक्परिमितानि पदानि यस्मात्
पर्युद्भवन्ति पुरुसम्मतभाञ्जि नित्यम् ॥
ओङ्कारमादिपुरुषं सगुणं सशब्दम्
मात्राक्षराधिपतिमीश्वरमानतोऽस्मि ॥२॥
शब्दार्णवो दुरवगाहन एव यस्य
निर्मन्थनाय विबुधा अपि यद्विषेदुः ॥
तद्रत्नजातमलभत्स (?) तु कोऽपि नासी-
च्चेल्लभ्यते विहगवाहनमामतेयात् ॥३॥
श्रीकेशवस्य चरणद्वितयाश्रयेण
हंसस्य योगमधिगम्य तु कृष्णदासः ॥
कर्तुं समीहति यथामति पञ्चसन्धि-
माथर्वणाङ्गिरससूत्रमतप्रपाठीम् ॥४॥

---

[1]This edition is based on the lone manuscript (K) of this commentary found at the Vaidika Saṁśodhana Maṇḍaḷa, Pune. I have numbered the Sūtras and placed them in bold-face.

[2]The first two quarters of this verse are comparable with the first two quarters of the first verse of Dantyoṣṭhyavidhi : अथर्वाणमृषिं देवं देवं हयशिरोधरम्.

शास्त्रप्रशंसा

तत्र तावच्छास्त्रप्रशंसा । इदं व्याकरणं शब्दशास्त्रमित्यभिधीयते । शब्द इति निगमेषु वाचो नाम । वाक् सरस्वती । तस्या भगवतो वैराजस्य मुखे निवासार्हत्वात्तत्राग्नेरपि निवाससामानाधिकरण्यात्सरस्वत्यास्तेजस्वित्वमुक्तम् । अत एव शब्दशास्त्रमज्ञानान्ध्यं दूरीकृत्य प्रकाशं कुरुते । तच्छब्दशास्त्रं तपोबलं विना न प्राप्यते । तदुक्तं यास्केन - 'सेयं विद्या श्रुतिमतिबुद्धिस्तस्यास्तपसा पारमीप्सितव्यम् । तदिदमायुरिच्छता न निर्वक्तव्यम्' (निरुक्त १३.१३) इति । मन्त्रेऽपि च । 'क्वस्विदस्याः परमं जंगाम' (ऋग्वेद ८.१००.१०), 'धेनुर्वागस्मानुप सुष्टुतैतु' (ऋग्वेद ८.१००.११) इति सिद्धान्तः । तपः षड्विधम् ।

'अर्चाकोटिगुणं स्तोत्रं स्तोत्रात्कोटिगुणो जपः ।
जपाद् ध्यानं ततो ज्ञानं ज्ञानात्कोटिगुणो लयः ॥'

इति योगशास्त्रे (source?)। अथ च यदा भगवतो महापुरुषस्य नाभिकमलाद् ब्रह्माजायत तमितिकर्त्तव्यताभ्रमेण मूढं ज्ञात्वादभ्रकरुण आदिपुरुषस्तप तपेत्युपदिदेश । ततो ब्रह्मा मननेन सविकल्पकं ध्यानेन निर्विकल्पकं च तप्त्वा उत्पन्नबोधो नाभिनालद्वारान्तः प्रविवेश तत्र ब्रह्माण्डगोलं सृष्टिचक्रं वेदांश्च ददर्श । तत्र निगमानां वेदमूलत्वाद्भगवता निघण्टुषु यानि पदानि चतुर्थपञ्चमाध्यायगतानि तानि दर्शितानि । ततो नामाख्यातजातदार्ढ्याय ब्रह्मणाध्यायत्रयं पठितम् । इति भाति एकार्थानेकशब्दत्वात् । अयमेवोपदेशः श्रीभागवते प्रोक्तोऽस्ति वानेकार्थैकशब्दत्वादध्यायद्वयस्य यास्कोक्तत्वाच्चतुर्थाध्यायस्यातिगहनत्वाच्च । 'तेने ब्रह्म हृदा य आदिकवये मुह्यन्ति यत्सूरयः' (भागवतपुराण १.१.१b) इत्युक्तमस्ति । अत्र युक्तमयुक्तं श्रीगुरुर्जानाति । इति वेदोत्पत्तिमूलम् ।

अथ व्याकरणोत्पत्तिमूलम् । तदुक्तमैतरेयेण । 'प्रजापतिरकामयत । प्रजायेय भूयान्स्यामिति । स तपोऽतप्यत । स तत इमाँल्लोकानसृजत पृथिवीमन्तरिक्षं दिवम् । तेभ्यः क्रमेण त्रीणि ज्योतींष्यजायन्ताग्निर्वायुरादित्य इति । तेभ्योऽभितप्तेभ्यस्त्रयो वेदा अजायन्त । ऋग्वेदोऽग्नेर्यजु-

वेंदो वायोः सामवेद आदित्यात् । तेभ्यस्तप्तेभ्यस्त्रीणि बीजान्यजायन्त । भूर्ऋचो भुवो यजुषः स्वः साम्नः । तेभ्यस्त्रयो वर्णा जज्ञिरेऽकार उकारो मकार इति । तानेकत्राकरोत्'[3]। अत्रैक्यकरणाय व्याकरणमुदभूत् । तेन सन्धिः साधितः । तदोमिति सिद्धम् । अस्य ब्रह्मरूपत्वान् माहात्म्यमैतरेयः[4] । 'ओमिति वै दैवं तथेति मानुषम् । दैवेन चैवैनं तन्मानुषेण च पापात्प्रमुञ्चति'[5]। अतः प्रणवः परं ब्रह्म । तदुपासनार्थं नम इति पदम् । तदुक्तं मन्त्रे 'यो नमसा स्वध्वर' (ऋग्वेद ८.१९.५c) इति । आश्वलायनस्तु 'नमस्कारेण वै खल्वपि न वै देवा नमस्कारमति (K: °न्ति)'। अतिक्रामन्तीत्यर्थः । 'यज्ञो वै नम इति हि ब्राह्मणं भवति[6] इति' । अतः

---

[3]The passage, as it appears in the Aitareya-Brāhmaṇa (25.7, Vol. II., p. 667), reads: प्रजापतिरकामयत प्रजायेय भूयान्स्यामिति स तपोऽतप्यत स तपस्तप्त्वेमाल्ँलोकानसृजत पृथिवीमन्तरिक्षं दिवं ताल्ँलोकानभ्यतपत्तेभ्योऽभितप्तेभ्योऽभितप्तेभ्यस्त्रीणि ज्योतींष्यजायन्ताग्निरेव पृथिव्या अजायत वायुरन्तरिक्षादादित्यो दिवस्तानि ज्योतींष्यभ्यतपत्तेभ्योऽभितप्तेभ्यस्त्रयो वेदा अजायन्त ऋग्वेद एवाग्नेरजायत यजुर्वेदो वायोः सामवेद आदित्यात्तान्वेदान् अभ्यतपत्तेभ्योऽभितप्तेभ्यस्त्रीणि शुक्राण्यजायन्त भूरित्येव ऋग्वेदादजायत भुव इति यजुर्वेदात्स्वरिति सामवेदात् । तानि शुक्राण्यभ्यतपत्तेभ्योऽभितप्तेभ्यस्त्रयो वर्णा अजायन्ताकार उकारो मकार इति तानेकधा समभरत्तदेतदोमिति । Kshitish Chandra Chatterji (1948, 1964: 286) refers to this passage and says that the element *-kāra* appears to occur for the first time with letters of the alphabet in AB (xxv.7). Thus, Kr̥ṣṇadāsa has indeed referred to one of the earliest references to individual sounds and their combination.

[4]Compare: Aitareya-Brāhmaṇa (25.7, Vol.II., p. 668): यदेतत्त्रय्यै विद्यायै शुक्रं तेन ब्रह्मत्वमकरोत् ।

[5]Compare: Aitareya-Brāhmaṇa (33.6, Vol.II., p. 859): ओमिति वै दैवं तथेति मानुषं दैवेन चैवैनं तन्मानुषेण च पापादेनसः प्रमुञ्चति ।

[6]This is a citation from the Āśvalāyanagr̥hyasūtra (1.1.5): य इमं स्वाध्यायमधीयते इति यो नमसा स्वध्वर इति नमस्कारेण वै खल्वपि न वै देवा नमस्कारमति यज्ञो वै नम इति हि ब्राह्मणं भवति । The Āśvalāyanagr̥hyasūtra quotes RV (8.19.5c): 'यो नमसा स्वध्वरः.' Other citations are comparable to 'नमो नम इति यज्ञो वै नमो यज्ञेनैवेनानेतन्नमस्कारेण नमस्यति,' Śatapatha-Brāhmaṇa (7.4.1.20, and 9.1.1.16) and 'न हि नमस्कारमति देवाः' Gopatha-Brāhmaṇa (2.2.1.18). The Śāṃkhāyana Āraṇyaka (1.5) also has a similar passage. For the sources of the Āśvalāyanagr̥hyasūtra, see: V.M. Apte (1940-41), Vol.III, Nos. 2-7, pp. 5-6.

'ॐ नमः सिद्धम्'[7] । यद्वा कञ्चित् सिद्धं नमस्करोत्याचार्यः । 'उपपदविभक्तेः कारकविभक्तिर्बलीयसी'ति (महाभाष्य on P.1.4.96; परिभाषेन्दुशेखर, परिभाषा ९४) चतुर्थ्यर्थे द्वितीया । ॐ नमः सिद्धायेति भावः । तर्हि सिद्धः कः । सिद्धः पदसमाम्नायः । पदसमाम्नायः कः । अत्र यास्कः - 'समाम्नायः समाम्नातः स व्याख्यातव्यस्तमिमं समाम्नायं निघण्टव इत्याचक्षते । निघण्टवः कस्मान्निगमा इमे भवन्ति' (निरुक्त, १.१) । अतो वेदपुरुषाय नमः इत्यर्थः । पदसमाम्नायश्चतुर्धा । नामाख्यातोपसर्गनिपातभेदेन । 'पदप्रकृतिः संहिता'[8] (निरुक्त, १.१७;

---

[7]It almost looks like the initial Sūtra of the work that Kṛṣṇadāsa is commenting upon. However, no manuscripts of the CA or Kautsa-Vyākaraṇa contain this as a Sūtra. This is comparable to Mugdhabodha-Vyākaraṇa (1.1: ॐ नमः शिवाय). We may also note that in the region of Maharashtra, the traditional education of a child began by the words ओनामासीधम्, which is nothing but a vernacularized form of ॐ नमः सिद्धम्. This practice presumably has its origin in the Jain tradition. The Marāṭhī Jain work Ādinātha-Purāṇa (7.95) says that the education of a child began with the mantra ॐ नमः सिद्धेभ्यः, and then the child was introduced to the alphabet (see: Subhashchandra Akkole, 1968, p. 209). The word *siddha* is associated with the alphabet also in the Kātantra Vyākaraṇa (1.1.1: सिद्धो वर्णसमाम्नायः). The salutation ॐ नमः सिद्धेभ्यः also occurs at the beginning of the Kātantrarūpamālāvyākaraṇa (p. 1). It is not clear whether it is part of the original text, or something added by the editor. In any case, the connection with Jain traditions is unmistakable, because the editor views Śarvavarman, the author of the Kātantra-Vyākaraṇa, to be a Jain, and Bhāvasena Traividyadeva, the author of the Kātantrarūpamālā, is indeed a Jain author.

[8]This statement is interpreted in two opposite ways by different traditions. Generally, the later grammarians interpret it to mean that the Saṃhitāpāṭha is the source of the Padapāṭha, in the sense that the words given as separate items in the Padapāṭha are isolated from the Saṃhitā. This view is found in the commentary of Puṇyarāja on Vākyapadīya (2.1-2). The reverse interpretation is generally found in the Prātiśākhya tradition which believes that the Saṃhitāpāṭha is produced by applying the rules of sandhi to the isolated words given in the Padapāṭha, and hence the latter is the source of the former. This is stated clearly by Uvaṭa in his commentary on RPR (2.1): पदानि प्रकृतिभूतानि यस्याः संहितायाः सा पदप्रकृतिः संहितात्र विकारः । तथा हि षत्वणत्वादयो

'संहिता पदप्रकृतिः,' ऋग्वेदप्रातिशाख्य, २.१) इति न्यायेन तत्साधकं व्याकरणम् । तदुक्तमाथर्वणिके - **१. चतुर्णां पदजातानाम् (च.आ. १.१.२)** इति शास्त्रप्रशंसा ॥१॥ अत्र षट् प्रकरणानि । शास्त्र-प्रशंसा ॥१॥ स्थानप्रयत्नविवेकः ॥२॥ संज्ञाप्रकरणम् ॥३॥ परिभाषा-प्रकरणम् ॥४॥ सन्धिसाधनम् ॥५॥ स्वरसाधनम् ॥६॥[9]

शास्त्रप्रशंसा प्रथमा द्वितीयः स्थानप्रयत्नस्य विवेककल्पः ।
संज्ञा तृतीया परिभाषणं च सन्धिः स्वरज्ञानमितीह षट्कम् ॥

स्थानप्रयत्नविवेकः

तत्र तावत् सन्ध्युपयोगाय स्थानप्रयत्नविवेकः । 'तुल्यास्यप्रयत्नं सवर्णम्' (पा. १.१.९) इति पाणिनिः । तुल्यं स्थानं प्रयत्नश्च यस्याक्षरस्य येनाक्षरेण तन्मिथः सवर्णं स्यात्[10] । संहितायां सवर्णधर्मं प्राप्नोति । स्थानविवेको यथा । **२. मुखे विशेषाः करणस्य (च.आ. १.१.१८)।** वर्णोच्चारस्येति भावः । 'साधकतमं करणम्' (पा. १.४.४२) इति

विकाराः संहिताया एव भवन्ति । प्रकृतिभूतत्वाच्च पदानां सिद्धत्वम् । In contrast with the view of Puṇyarāja mentioned above, Cardona (1991: 129) has argued that "Pāṇini fits right in with a long tradition of considering the *padapāṭha* the source text by means of which the *saṃhitāpāṭha* and recitations such as the *kramapāṭha* are accounted for." Kṛṣṇadāsa seems to be within this latter view.

[9]There is a certain ambiguity about the actual extent of the sections referred to here as *sandhisādhana* and *svarasādhana*, since these terms are not used again in the text. For instance, does the word *sandhisādhana* refer to the preliminaries of the sandhi section, or does it refer to all the sandhi sections taken together? Similarly, does the word *svarasādhana* refer to vowel-sandhi section, later referred to as *svarasandhi*, or does it refer to accents? The verse that follows would perhaps support a view that *sandhisādhana* referred to all sandhi sections taken together, and that the word *svarasādhana* was equal to *svarajñāna* in the sense of treatment of accents. However, the text as we have it does not have any systematic treatment of accents.

[10]Compare: ताल्वादिस्थानमाभ्यन्तरप्रयत्नश्चेत्येतद् द्वयं यस्य येन तुल्यं तन्मिथः सवर्णसंज्ञं स्यात् । SK on P.1.1.9, p. 5.

पाणिनिः । स्वरहकारविसर्जनीयानां[11] कण्ठः । ३. **कण्ठ्यानामधरकण्ठ्यः** (च.आ. १.१.१९)। कवर्गस्य जिह्वामूलम् । ४. **जिह्वामूलीयानां हनुमूलम्** (च.आ. १.१.२०)। तत्र नामिस्वराणां प्रत्येकं स्थानद्वयम् । हकारस्यापि पञ्चमैर्वर्णैर्योगादन्तस्थाभिर्वा योगाद्ध्रुदयम्[12] । एऐइचुयशास्तालव्याः । ५. **तालव्यानां मध्यजिह्वम्** (च.आ. १.१.२१)। जिह्वामध्यभागस्पर्शी उच्चारः । ऋटुरषा मूर्धन्याः । ६. **मूर्धन्यानां जिह्वाग्रं परिवेष्टितम्** (च.आ. १.१.२२)। ७. **षकारस्य द्रोणिका** (च.आ. १.१.२३)। ८. **रेफस्य दन्तमूलानि** (च.आ. १.१.२८)। ऌतुलसा दन्त्याः । ९. **दन्त्यानां जिह्वाग्रं प्रस्तीर्णम्** (च.आ. १.१.२४)। ओऔउपूपध्मानीया औष्ठ्याः । १०. **औष्ठ्यानामधरौष्ठ्यम्** (च.आ. १.१.२५)। दन्त्यौष्ठ्यो वकारः[13] । केवलोऽनुस्वारो नासिक्यः[14] । ११. **नासिक्यानां नासिका** (च.आ. १.१.२६)। अन्ये वर्णा ङञणनमास्ते वर्गेषु उत्तमा अनुनासिकाः । १२. **अनुनासिकानां मुखनासिकम्** (च.आ. १.१.२७)। इति स्थानानि । प्रयत्नो द्विधा । आभ्यन्तरो बाह्यश्च । तत्राभ्यन्तरश्चतुर्धा । स्पृष्टेषत्स्पृष्टविवृतसंवृतभेदात्[15] । कादयो

---

[11]The inclusion of all *svaras* among *kaṇṭhya* sounds is inexplicable. Contrast: SK on P.1.1.9 (p. 4): अकुहविसर्जनीयानां कण्ठः । However, after PS 4, below, Kṛṣṇadāsa says: तत्र नामिस्वराणां प्रत्येकं स्थानद्वयम्, namely that the *nāmin* vowels, i.e. vowels other than *a* and *ā* each have two points of articulation. This probably means that he seriously believes that all vowels are minimally *kaṇṭhya*, and some may have an additional point of articulation. No other text on Sanskrit grammar or phonetics entertains such a notion.

[12]This refers to the notion that the sound *h* is an *aurasya* 'pulmonary' when it is combined with nasals and semi-vowels, but it is *kaṇṭhya* 'glottal' when uncombined. This is conveyed by the Pāṇinīyaśikṣā (verse 16): हकारं पञ्चमैर्युक्तमन्तःस्थाभिश्च संयुतम् । औरस्यं तं विजानीयात्कण्ठ्यमाहुरसंयुतम् ॥

[13]This view is imported from the late Pāṇinian commentators

[14]The text of the CA actually makes no reference to *anusvāra*. The general view is that the CA does not have the notion of *anusvāra*, and that it accepts only the nasalized vowels.

[15]Compare: इति स्थानानि । यत्नो द्विधा । आभ्यन्तरो बाह्यश्च । आद्यश्चतुर्धा । स्पृष्टेषत्स्पृष्टविवृतसंवृतभेदात् । SK on P.1.1.9, p. 5.

मावसानाः स्पर्शाः[16] इति पाणिनीयाः । **१३. स्पर्शाः प्रथमोत्तमाः (च.आ. १.१.८)**। प्रथमपञ्चमा इत्यर्थः[17] । **१४. प्रथमान्तानि तृतीयान्तानि (च.आ. १.१.१०)** इति (।) यः प्रथमस्य प्रयत्नः स एव तृतीयस्येति ज्ञेयम्[18] । **१५. न चवर्गः (च.आ. १.१.९)**। वर्गस्य प्रयोजनं सर्वत्र समानमिति न[19] । **१६. विभाषाप्राप्तं सामान्ये (च.आ. १.१.४)**। सामान्ये शास्त्रे यत्प्राप्तं तद्विभाषा नाम विकल्पः । 'सामान्यशास्त्रतो नूनं विशेषो बलवान्भवेत्' [20] इति । **१७. शौनकस्य प्रतिज्ञानं न वृत्तिः (च.आ. १.१.१० अंशः)**। **१८. अधिस्पर्शं च (च.आ. १.१.११)**। स्पर्शेष्वधिकारो यस्य तदपि च । प्रातिशाख्ये यमाः प्रसिद्धास्तेऽपि स्पर्शाः[21] । **१९. द्वितीयचतुर्थाः सोष्माणः (च.आ. १.१.१२)**। वर्गेषु द्वितीयचतुर्था वर्णास्ते स्पर्शा एव परन्तु किञ्चिदधिकश्वासोच्चारसहिता[22] अत एव सोष्माणः । **२०. स्पृष्टं स्पर्शानां करणम् (च.आ.**

---

[16]Compare: कादयो मावसानाः स्पर्शाः । SK on P.8.2.1, p. 6.

[17]Kṛṣṇadāsa offers no real interpretation for this rule, unless somehow his comment is taken to mean that the first and the final members of the series are called *sparśa*s. Even this does not make any sense. The rule is actually meant to say that, among all the *sparśa*s, the first and the final members can occur word-finally (*padya*).

[18]This interpretation is substantially far off from what the original rule is supposed to mean. See the other commentaries and notes on CA (1.1.10). Also note that Kṛṣṇadāsa has split the original rule into two separate rules: PS 14 and 17.

[19]The rule CA (1.1.9) is actually an exception to CA (1.1.8 = PS 13), and means that members of the *c*-series do not occur word-finally. Kṛṣṇadāsa's paraphrase does not bring out this meaning. It seems to say: "It is not the case that the purpose of the/a *varga* is everywhere the same." I am not quite sure what he intends to say.

[20]This appears to be a citation from the Sārasvata-Vyākaraṇa (p. 9). The complete verse is as follows: सामान्यशास्त्रतो नूनं विशेषो बलवान्भवेत् । परेण पूर्वबाधो वा प्रायशो दृश्यतामिह ॥

[21]Compare: यमो नाम पूर्वसदृशो वर्णः प्रातिशाख्ये प्रसिद्धः । SK on P.8.2.1, p. 5.

[22]Compare RPR (13.19): शीघ्रतरं सोष्मसु प्राणमेके. Uvaṭa on this rule: सर्वेषु वर्णेषु स्थानकरणानुप्रदानानि त्रयो गुणाः समानाः । सोष्मसूष्मा गुणोऽधिकः ।

१.१.२९)। स्पर्शानां स्पृष्टः प्रयत्नः । यरलवा अन्तस्थाः । **२१. ईषत्स्पृष्टमन्तस्थानाम् (च.आ. १.१.३०)**। अन्तस्थानामीषत्स्पृष्टः प्रयत्नः । शषसहा ऊष्माणः । अआइईउऊएऐओऔअंअः इति स्वराः[23] । **२२. ऊष्मणां विवृतं च (च.आ. १.१.३१)**। **२३. स्वराणां च (च.आ. १.१.३२)**। 'स्वराणामूष्मणां चैव विवृतं करणं स्मृतम्' (पाणिनीयशिक्षा, २१) इति शिक्षायाम्[24] । **२४. एकेऽस्पृष्टम् (च.आ. १.१.३३)**। एओ विवृततरौ[25] । **२५. ऐकारौकारयोर्विवृततमम् (च.आ. १.१.३४)**। **२६. ततोऽप्याकारस्य (च.आ. १.१.३५)**। एतानि स्फुटार्थानि । **२७. संवृतोऽकारः (च.आ. १.१.३६)**। विवृतमनूद्य संवृतोऽनेन विधीयते[26] ह्रस्वस्यावर्णस्य प्रयोगे संवृतं प्रक्रियादशायां तु विवृतमेव[27] ।

---

[23]One may perhaps justify the exclusion of *r̥, r̥̄,* and *l̥* from this listing, because these vowels contain consonantal constituents, but the inclusion of *aṃ* and *aḥ* among vowels makes no sense. The author is misled by the fact that in most traditional *mātr̥kā* alphabets, *aṃ* and *aḥ* follow the vowels. This is the way the sounds named *anusvāra* (= *ṃ*) and *visarga* (= *ḥ*) are traditionally cited, cf. VPR (8.21: अं इत्यनुस्वारः) and VPR (8.22: अः इति विसर्जनीयः). Perhaps, the author is influenced by the Tāntric view of Sanskrit alphabet, which often included these two sounds among vowels. For a detailed exposition of the Tantrik view, see: Rāmājñā Pandey (1986: 26, 38, 48).

[24]From this citation, it is clear that Kr̥ṣṇadāsa does not interpret PS 22 (= CA 1.1.31) to mean that the effort for the spirants is *īṣad-vivr̥ta.* For further discussion, see the notes on CA (1.1.31).

[25]The original CA rule (1.1.34) was simply एकारौकारयोर्विवृततमम्, but it was expanded in certain sub-schools to एकारौकारयोर्विवृततरम् ऐकारौकारयोर्विवृततमम्। See the notes on CA (1.1.34)..

[26]Compare: विवृतमनूद्य संवृतोऽनेन विधीयते । SK on P.8.4.68, p. 5. Kr̥ṣṇadāsa would have us believe that the CA had open (*vivr̥ta*) short *a* in the derivational process, but the present rule, like P.8.4.68 (अ अ), reinstates the close (*saṃvr̥ta*) *a* in the usable utterance. There is no reason to believe that the CA had any such notion. The rule here is a straight forward description that short *a* is a close sound. Pāṇini needed to make an adjustment of this sort to have the sounds *a* and *ā* become *savarṇa* 'homogeneous' with each other by P.1.1.9 (तुल्यास्यप्रयत्नं सवर्णम्). The original CA does not have any such definition of the term *savarṇa*, and hence does not need such an accommodation.

२८. **संस्पृष्टरेफमृवर्णम्** (च.आ. १.१.३७)। २९. **दीर्घप्लुतयोः पूर्वा मात्रा** (च.आ. १.१.३८)। संस्पृष्टेत्यर्थः । ३०. **सलकारम्लृवर्णम्** (च.आ. १.१.३९)। लृवर्णमपीत्यर्थः । ३१. **सन्ध्यक्षराणि संस्पृष्टवर्णान्येकवर्णवद् वृत्तिः** (च.आ. १.१.४०)। निपातवद् वृत्तिरित्यर्थः[28] । परन्तु ३२. **नैकारौकारयोः स्थानविधौ** (च.आ. १.१.४१) इति आभ्यन्तरम् । अत्र सूत्रे प्रक्रियाद्वयं दृश्यते 'सरूपाणामेकशेष' ... (पा. १.२.६४) इत्येका वृत्तिः[29] । 'नाज्झलौ' (पा. १.१.१०) इति पाणिनीये आकारप्रश्लेष इवार्थबलात्[30] । 'हलन्त्यम्' (पा. १.३.३) इतिवत्[31] । बाह्यप्रयत्नोऽपि चतुर्धैवोपयोगार्थः । श्वासनादघोषाघोषभेदात् ।[32]

For further details, see: Deshpande (1975: 13, 91-93).

[27]Compare: ह्रस्वस्यावर्णस्य प्रयोगे संवृतम् । प्रक्रियादशायां तु विवृतमेव । SK on P.1.1.9, p. 5.

[28]This is a somewhat cryptic remark. It is not clear what Kṛṣṇadāsa finds common between a diphthong and a particle. It is possible that *nipātavat* is a scribal error for *nipātanavat*. A *nipātana* is a word which is approved as a whole, without making any effort to separate its constituents. Thus, a *nipātana* may be viewed as a word which has seeming parts, but is treated as if it is partless. Similarly, a diphthong has parts, and yet it is treated as a single sound (*ekavarṇavat*).

[29]As far as I can make sense of this comment, Kṛṣṇadāsa is proposing that CA (1.1.41) be given two readings a) *na ekāra-okārayoḥ,* and b) *na aikāra-aukārayoḥ*. Both the readings, after sandhi, lead to the same text: *naikāraukārayoḥ*. For further discussion, see notes on CA (1.1.41).

[30]Commenting on P.1.1.10 (नाज्झलौ), Bhaṭṭojī Dīkṣita splits this rule as *na+ā+ac+halau*, instead of what would normally be *na+ac+halau*. The insertion of *ā* in the rule here is termed *ākārapraśleṣa*. See: 'नाज्झला' विति निषेधो यद्यप्याक्षरसमाम्नायिकानामेव तथापि हकारस्याऽऽकारो न सवर्णः, तत्राऽऽकारस्यापि प्रश्लिष्टत्वात् । तेन विश्वपाभिरित्यत्र 'हो ढ' इति ढत्वं न भवति । SK on P.1.1.69, p. 6.

[31]The rule P.1.3.3 (हलन्त्यम्) is traditionally given two interpretations, by repeating it twice. For details, see: Deshpande (1975: 41-42).

[32]While the SK on P.8.2.1 (p. 5) offers an eleven-fold division of the *bāhyaprayatna*s, Kṛṣṇadāsa here focuses upon only four of them. Perhaps, the other kinds of *bāhyaprayatna*s are viewed as being not relevant in the context of the sandhis he discusses. He does not deal with the interaction of accents in sandhis.

'खयां यमाः खयःकःपौ विसर्गः शर एव च ।
एते श्वासानुप्रदाना अघोषाश्च विवृण्वते ॥
कण्ठमन्ये तु घोषाः स्युः संवृता नादभागिनः ।'[33]

इति पाणिनीयाः । कखचछटठतथपफा एषां यमाश्च । जिह्वामूलीयोपध्मानीयविसर्गाः शषसाश्चैते अघोषश्वासानुप्रदानाः । 'अन्ये तु' । गघङजझञडढणदधनबभमाः एषां यमाश्च यरलवहाः एते विंशतिर्वर्णा घोषनादभागिनः । नादलक्षणं तु[34] । **३३. पीडितः सन्नतरो हीनश्वासनादः (च.आ. १.२.३)।** उच्चारणे दृब्ध इत्यर्थः । बाह्यप्रयत्नाश्च यद्यपि सवर्णसंज्ञां न प्राप्नुवन्ति तथापि स्थानकार्यं कुर्वन्ति[35] । इति बाह्यप्रयत्नः । इति श्रीमदथर्वकौत्सव्याकरणे स्थानप्रयत्नविवेकः[36] ॥

संज्ञाप्रकरणम्

आचार्यनाम्नो विभाषा ज्ञेया[37] (।) परिभाषा 'वर्णे वर्णे कारट्'[38] । वर्णजातौ प्रत्येकवर्णे कारट्प्रत्ययः स्यात् । 'अइउऋऌ समानाः'[39] । एषां

---

[33]These verses are not found in the standard versions of Pāṇinīyaśikṣā, but are cited in the SK on P.8.2.1 (p. 5). The commentary Tattvabodhinī on these verses says that the external efforts were listed in verses by someone for easier comprehension: बालबोधनाय बाह्यप्रयत्नाः कैश्चित्सुगमोपायेनोपनिबद्धाः। Tattvabodhinī on SK on P.8.2.1 (p. 5).

[34]What follows is quite clearly not a *nādalakṣaṇa* 'definition of *nāda*.' For better interpretations, see notes on CA (1.2.3).

[35]Compare: बाह्यप्रयत्नाश्च यद्यपि सवर्णसंज्ञायामनुपयुक्तास्तथाप्यान्तरतम्यपरीक्षायामुपयोक्ष्यन्त इति बोध्यम् । SK on P.8.2.1 (p. 6).

[36]Compare: इति स्थानप्रयत्नविवेकः । SK on P.8.2.1 (p. 6).

[37]This is an interesting formulation. Wherever Pāṇini refers to the views of other grammarians by citing their names, he probably intends to refer to dialectal variation in Sanskrit. On the other hand, Kātyāyana and Patañjali interpret such references as being no more than indications of options. For a detailed consideration of this question, see: Deshpande (1978).

[38]Compare Kātyāyana's Vārttika: वर्णात्कारः on P.3.3.108. The marker sound *Ṭ* in the affix *kāraṬ* is intriguing. It is not clear what it was intended for in the system from which this statement is cited.

पञ्चस्वराणां ह्रस्वदीर्घप्लुतभेदेऽपि समाना इति संज्ञा । एतेषां निपाताधिकारात्सन्धिर्न[40] । **३४. निपातोऽपृक्तोऽनाकारः (च.आ. १.३.१७)।** असंश्लिष्टः स्वरः सन्धिं न प्राप्नोतीत्यग्रे प्रकृतिभावगतं सूत्रम् । तत्र आकारो न । 'अपृक्त एकाल्प्रत्ययः' (पा. १.२.४१)। 'निपात एकाजनाङ्' (पा. १.१.१४) इति पाणिनिः । समानत्वं किम् । ह्रस्वदीर्घप्लुतानुनासिकाननुनासिकोदात्तानुदात्तस्वरितभेदेन प्रत्येकमेते पञ्च स्वरा अष्टादशधा तुल्यं धर्मं प्राप्नुवन्ति[41] । अनुनासिकाः स्वराः नपुंसकलिङ्गविभक्तिसाधकाः । **३५. अनुनासिकोऽन्तःपदे ह्रस्वः (च.आ. १.३.२१)। ३६. दीर्घो नपुंसकबहुवचने (च.आ. १.३.२२)।** 'प्रश्ने प्लुते च'[42] इति सूत्रसामर्थ्यात् ज्ञायते । 'प्रतिज्ञानुनासिक्याः पाणिनीयाः'[43] । **३७.**

---

[39]This is probably a citation of Sārasvata-Vyākaraṇa (1.1, p. 1). Pāṇini does not use the term *samāna*, but the Prātiśākhyas use the term *samāna* or *samānākṣara* to refer to simple vowels.

[40]This concern as to why the sounds listed as *samāna*s do not undergo sandhi in the very listing is analogous to the concern expressed by the Pāṇinian grammarians about the sound-listing in the Śivasūtras. Kṛṣṇadāsa's explanation is very similar to the explanation found in the commentary Tattvabodhinī on SK (pp. 1-2): वर्णानामसंदिग्धत्वेन बोधनाय संहिताया अविवक्षणादेतेष्वसंधिः। स्वराणां चादिषु पाठात् 'चादयोऽसत्त्वे' इति निपातसंज्ञायां 'निपात एकाजनाङ्' इति प्रगृह्यत्वे प्रकृतिभावान्न संधिरित्यन्ये । The Sārasvata-Vyākaraṇa (p. 1) also expresses the same conclusion, though it offers a different reason for it: नैतेषु सूत्रेषु संधिरनुसंधेयोऽविवक्षितत्वात् । It looks like Kṛṣṇadāsa cites the rule from the Sārasvata-Vyākaraṇa, but derives the explanation for the absence of sandhi from Pāṇinian commentators.

[41]The term *samāna* is normally interpreted to mean a simple vowel. Here, Kṛṣṇadāsa takes it in the sense of 'equal.' In what sense are the five simple vowels equal? This question is answered by saying that each of them has eighteen types of manifestations due to the distinctions of length (3), nasality (2), and accents (3). This is generally not conceded for *ḷ*, which is traditionally said to have short and prolated varieties, but no long varieties.

[42]There is no such rule in CA. However, compare P.8.2.100 (अनुदात्तं प्रश्नान्ताभिपूजितयोः) and P.8.2.105 (अनन्त्यस्यापि प्रश्नाख्यानयोः). It is not clear where such additional rules in Kṛṣṇadāsa's works are coming from.

[43]See the KV on P.1.3.2 and P.7.1.1. Also the SK on P.1.3.2 (p. 3). The

मात्राकालः कालः (च.आ. ३.३.३५ अंशः)। उच्चारस्येत्यर्थः । ३८. **एकमात्रो ह्रस्वः** (च.आ. १.२.१९)। एका मात्रा यस्योच्चारकाले स स्वरो ह्रस्वसंज्ञः स्यात् । ३९. **व्यञ्जनानि च** (च.आ. १.२.२०)। व्यञ्जनान्यप्येकमात्रोच्चाराणि । चकारात्स्वरहीनान्यर्धमात्राणि ज्ञातव्यानि[44] । 'व्यञ्जनं चार्धमात्रम्'[45] इति केचित् । अत्रैव लघुगुरुलक्षणम् । ४०. **ह्रस्वं लघ्वसंयोगे** (च.आ. १.२.११)। असंयोगे परे पूर्वं यद्ध्रस्वमक्षरं तल्लघुसंज्ञं भवति । ४१. **गुर्वन्यत्** (च.आ. १.२.१२)। 'ह्रस्वं लघु, संयोगे गुरु, दीर्घं च' (पा. १.४.१०-१२) गुर्विति पाणिनिः । अत्र शास्त्रे लघुगुरुप्रयोजनाभावः । परन्तु सूत्रचारितार्थ्याय गृह्यते[46] । गुर्विति ४२. **अनुनासिकं च** (च.आ. १.२.१३)। ४३. **पदान्ते च** (च.आ. १.२.१४)। ४४. **परस्य स्वरस्य व्यञ्जनानि** (च.आ. १.२.१५)। ४५. **संयोगादि पूर्वस्य** (च.आ. १.२.१६)। ४६. **पद्यं च** (च.आ. १.२.१७)। ४७. **रेफहकारक्रमजं च** (च.आ. १.२.१८)।

'दीर्घं संयोगपरं तथा स्वरव्यञ्जनान्तमूष्मान्तम् ।
सानुस्वारं च गुरु क्वचिदवसानेऽपि लघ्वन्त्यम् ।।'[47]

---

commentary Tattvabodhinī on SK explains this as: यद्यपि सूत्रकारकृतोऽनुनासिकपाठ इदानीं परिभ्रष्टः, तथापि वृत्तिकारादिव्यवहारबलेन यथाकार्यं प्राक् स्थित इत्यनुमीयत इति ।

[44]The CA rule says that consonants also have one-mora duration. Kṛṣṇadāsa tries to change the meaning of this rule to match the citation which says that consonants have a half-mora duration.

[45]This seems to be a reference to the commonly cited verse: एकमात्रो भवेद् ह्रस्वो द्विमात्रो दीर्घ उच्यते । त्रिमात्रस्तु प्लुतो ज्ञेयो व्यञ्जनं चार्धमात्रकम् ।। This is not found in any version of the Pāṇinīyaśikṣā. It is cited in the Sārasvata-Vyākaraṇa (p. 2).

[46]This is a significant comment. While the CA defines the terms *laghu* and *guru*, there is no occasion within the system of CA to purposefully use these terms. In contrast, Pāṇini's grammar finds purposeful utilization of this distinction, e.g. P.8.2.86 (गुरोरनृतोऽनन्त्यस्याप्येकैकस्य प्राचाम्) and P.7.2.7 (अतो हलादेर्लघोः). It is not clear why Kṛṣṇadāsa feels compelled to include these rules.

[47]This verse is also cited with the same reading in Bhārgava-Bhāskara's Vṛtti

इति पिङ्गलः (छन्दःसूत्र, १.४)। **४८. द्विमात्रो दीर्घः (च.आ. १.२.२१)। ४९. त्रिमात्रः प्लुतः (च.आ. १.२.२२)।** मात्रोच्चारोदाहरणं तु -

'चाषस्तु वदते मात्रां द्विमात्रं त्वेव वायसः ।
शिखी रौति त्रिमात्रं तु नकुलस्त्वर्धमात्रकम् ॥'

इति शिक्षा (पाणिनीयशिक्षा ४९)। कुक्कुटोऽपि मात्रात्रयमेककालावच्छेदेन[48] पृथक् पृथक् प्रब्रूते । उ१ ऊ२ ऊ३ ॥ अत एव[49] पाणिनिनोक्तम् 'ऊकालोऽज्झ्रस्वदीर्घप्लुतः' (पा. १.२.२७) इति । **५०. समानयमेऽक्षरमुच्चैरुदात्तं नीचैरनुदात्तमाक्षिप्तं स्वरितम् (च.आ. १.१.१६)।** समानः तुल्यश्चासौ यमः[50] ह्रस्वदीर्घप्लुतधर्मश्च तस्मिन् यदुच्चैरुपलभ्यमानमक्षरं तदुदात्तमित्युच्यते । एवमग्रेऽपि । नीचैरुच्चार्यमाणमनुदात्तम् । उभयधर्मौ आक्षिप्तौ यस्मिन् तत्स्वरितम् । **५१. स्वरितस्यादितो मात्रार्धमुदात्तम् (च.आ. १.१.१७)।** 'उच्चैरुदात्तः,' 'नीचैरनुदात्तः,' 'समाहारः स्वरितः' (पा. १.२.२९-३१) इति पाणिनिः । 'तस्यादित उदात्तमर्धह्रस्वम्' (पा. १.२.३२) इति च ।

---

on CA (1.2.12). For a discussion of the different readings of this verse, see the note on CA (1.2.12).

[48]The phrase *ekakālāvacchedena* is somewhat strange in this context. It normally means, 'within the same time-span.' In a rooster-call, we here different lengths of *u* successively, and normally one would not expect the use of the above phrase.

[49]The notion that Pāṇini chose the vowel *u* to demonstrate the different durations of short, long, and prolated vowels, because this is naturally seen in the call of a rooster (*kukkuṭa*), is explicitly stated in the works of Nāgeśabhaṭṭa. The Bṛhacchabdenduśekhara (vol.I., p. 28) says: कुक्कुटरुते उकार एव एकमात्रत्वद्विमात्रत्वादीनां प्रसिद्धेरकारादयो नोक्ताः सूत्रकारेण । The same comment in found in Nāgeśabhaṭṭa's Laghuśabdenduśekhara (p. 82).

[50]Kṛṣṇadāsa takes the term *yama* to be equivalent of vowel-length. The term actually refers to 'range of vowel pitch, register.' For details, see the note on CA (1.1.16).

'उदात्तश्चानुदात्तश्च स्वरितश्च स्वरास्त्रयः ।
आयामविश्रम्भाक्षेपैस्त उच्यन्तेऽक्षराश्रयाः ।।'

इति प्रातिशाख्ये (ऋग्वेदप्रातिशाख्य, ३.१-२; पाणिनीयशिक्षा, श्लोक ११)। ए ऐ ओ औ इत्यत्र ह्रस्वाभावात् प्रत्येकं द्वादशभेदात्तेभ्यः पूर्वोक्त-स्वरेभ्यः किञ्चिदूनत्वात्तत्समानत्वं नेति दिक्[51] । तरतमानि सन्ध्य-क्षराणि[52] । एषां सन्ध्यक्षराणीति संज्ञा । सन्ध्यक्षरत्वं किम् । पूर्वोक्ताः पञ्च स्वराः पदान्ते एव सन्धिं सम्पादयन्ति । एतानि तु यत्र तत्रापि । नायकः, पावकः, भवतीत्यत्र पदमध्येऽपीत्यर्थः[53] । उभये स्वराः । अइउ-ऋऌ ५ एऐओऔ ४ एषां स्वरा इति संज्ञा[54] । स्वरत्वं किम् । **५२. स्वरोऽक्षरम् (च.आ. १.४.२)।** स्वेनैव राजते न तु पराश्रयेणेति स्वरः । यद्वा उदात्तादिभेदैः स्वर्यते इति स्वरः । अक्षरं न क्षीयते अन्या-श्रयमभिलषते इत्यक्षरम् । स्वर एव पूर्णाक्षरम् । अन्यान्यर्धमात्राणि । **५३. अस्वराणि व्यञ्जनानि (च.आ. ३.३.२६)।** स्वरं विना यान्यक्ष-राणि तानि व्यञ्जनानीति संज्ञा । 'स्वरहीनं व्यञ्जनम्' (सारस्वत-व्याकरण, p. 3) इति केचित्[55] । इमानि स्वरं संप्राप्यैव सुखोच्चाराय

---

[51]If the phrase तत्समानत्वं न is used simply to point to the fact that the diphthongs have only twelve varieties each, and therefore they are not equal in regard to the number of varieties with the preceding vowels, this makes sense. However, Kṛṣṇadāsa is simultaneously attempting to explain why these sounds are not included in the category of *samāna* vowels. Elsewhere, he attempts to explain the technical term *samāna* for simple vowels by pointing out that they are *samāna* 'equal' in each having 18 varieties. See his commentary on PS 34: समानत्वं किम् । ह्रस्वदीर्घप्लुतानुनासिकाननुनासिकोदात्तानुदात्त-स्वरितभेदेन प्रत्येकमेते पञ्च स्वरा अष्टादशधा तुल्यं धर्मं प्राप्नुवन्ति ।

[52]This is most likely a reference to the notion that *e* and *o* are *vivṛtatara,* while *ai* and *au* are *vivṛtatama*. See PS rules 25, 59 and 60 below. For a detailed discussion, see the note on CA (1.1.34).

[53]This is an unusual explanation of the term *sandhyakṣara* and is not supported by any other text.

[54]This looks like a direct reflection of the Sārasvata-Vyākaraṇa (1.4, p. 2): ४ **उभये स्वराः** । अकारादयः पञ्च, एकारादयश्चत्वारश्चोभये स्वरा उच्यन्ते ।

[55]See the comment in the Sārasvata-Vyākaraṇa (p. 3): स्वरहीनं व्यञ्जनम् । स्वरे-

भवन्तीति[56] । व्यज्यन्ते स्वरेण स्पष्टीक्रियन्ते इति व्यञ्जनानि । **५४. व्यञ्जनान्येवापेतानि स्वरैः संयोगः (च.आ. १.४.७, पाठान्तरम्)।** स्वरैरपेतान्येव व्यञ्जनानि तेषां संयोग इत्यपि च संज्ञा । 'हलोऽनन्तराः संयोगः' (पा. १.१.७) इति पाणिनिः । संयुज्यते स्वरेणेति[57] । **५५. अ-संवृताः स्वराः नामिनः[58] (not found in CA)।** अकारः संवृतः तं विनाऽन्ये स्वरा नामिन उच्यन्ते । नामित्वं किम् । नामसंबन्धिषु स्वादिषु विभक्तिषु प्रक्रियाः संपाद्यन्ते यैस्ते नामिनः[59] । अं अः इत्यत्र प्रक्रिया-कालेषु अकारस्यापि विवृतत्वमस्त्येव । अकारेण केवलेन विभक्तिरिति क्वापि न सम्भाव्यते । 'अवर्जा नामिनः'[60] (सारस्वतव्याकरण १.५) इति केचित् । अकारान्तपुंलिङ्गसंबोधने तु विभक्तिलोपः न विभक्तिरिति । **५६. सस्थानकरणं सवर्णम्[61] (not found in CA)।** तुल्यं स्थानं करणं च

भ्योऽन्यत् स्वरहीनम् । अन्यथा स्वरेषु स्वरो नास्तीति तेषां स्वराणामपि व्यञ्जनता स्यात् ।

[56]The original CA rules 3.3.26-7 appear in the context of a discussion of whether consonants have accents (*svara*). Kṛṣṇadāsa, perhaps under the influence of the cited Sārasvata-Vyākarana statement, takes the term *svara* to refer to vowels, rather than to accents.

[57]This interpretation of *saṃyoga* as conjunction with a vowel is not supported by any text in Sanskrit grammar or phonetics.

[58]This definition is inaccurate, because it does not exclude *ā* from the scope of the term *nāmin.* The vowel *ā* is not *saṃvṛta*, and yet it must be excluded from the scope of the term *nāmin.*

[59]The term *nāmin* has nothing to do with *nāman*, as alleged by Kṛṣṇadāsa. It is derived from the causative form *namayati* in the sense of 'to bring about change.' See: K.C. Chatterji (1948, 1964).

[60]This rule is interpreted in the Sārasvata-Vyākaraṇa as: अवर्णवर्जाः स्वराः नामिन उच्यन्ते । This properly excludes both *a* and *ā* from the scope of *nāmin*, since both of them are covered by the term *avarṇa.*

[61]The wording of this rule is indeed intriguing, unless the word *karaṇa* is used in the sense of *prayatna* 'effort, manner,' and not in the sense of 'articulator.' The possibility that Kṛṣṇadāsa means *prayatna* by the term *karaṇa* is enhanced by his gloss on PS 20 (= CA 1.1.29) above, where the term *karaṇa* is glossed by *prayatna.* This would make this definition identical with that offered by Pāṇini 1.1.9 (तुल्यास्यप्रयत्नं सवर्णम्). If the term *karaṇa* were to mean 'articulator,' there are very few parallels in the grammatical literature. One

यस्य येन तत् सवर्णसंज्ञं स्यात् । **५७. वर्णैक्यं संहिता** (not found in CA)। वर्णानां यदैक्यमेकीभवनं तत् संहितेति संज्ञा । 'परः सन्निकर्षः संहिता' (पा. १.४.१०९) इति पाणिनिः । स्थानप्रयत्नबलात्स्वरैः सह व्यञ्जनानां सावर्ण्यं प्राप्तम् । **५८. नैकारौकारयोः स्थानविधौ (च.आ. १.१.४१)** इति सूत्रे ह्रस्वदीर्घप्लुतानां स्वराणां परसन्निकर्षणात् अइएऐउओऔ एभिर्व्यञ्जनानां सन्धौ सावर्ण्यं नेति निषेधः ।[62] 'नाज्झलौ' (पा. १.१.१०) इति पाणिनिः । मित्रवदागमः[63] । प्रत्ययश्च[64] । शत्रुवदादेशः[65] । आगमादेशबलात्तु कार्यं सिध्यति । नित्यादपवादो बलीयानिति[66] । सामान्याद्विशेषोऽपि । **५९. विवृततरौ गुणः** (not found in

---

such parallel is found in the Varṇaratnapradīpikāśikṣā, verse 38, Śikṣāsaṃgraha (p. 120):

यद्यद्यस्य भवेत्स्थानं करणं वा विशेषणम् । सवर्णत्वेन संग्राह्य आस्ययत्नस्तु भिद्यते ।।

Also compare the definition given in VPR (1.13): समानस्थानकरणास्यप्रयत्नः सवर्णः which uses the notion of *karaṇa* besides *āsyaprayatna*. For a detailed discussion of issues involved, see: Deshpande (1975: 94ff, 104ff, and 118-119).

[62]This is indeed a very unlikely interpretation. It is difficult to see how one can extract all the listed vowels, i.e. *a, i, e, ai, u, o,* and *au*, including all the short, long, and extra long varieties from the expression *naikāraukārayoḥ*. Also it is difficult to see how the rule can be additionally made to say that vowels are not homogeneous with consonants. Bhārgava-Bhāskara's commentary also offers a different, but an equally unlikely explanation. See the notes on CA (1.1.41).

[63]Identical with Sārasvata-Vyākaraṇa (1.19, p. 4).

[64]The Sārasvata-Vyākaraṇa does not extend the analogy of *mitravat* to *pratyaya*s. This may be Kṛṣṇadāsa's innovation. The behavior shared by the augments and affixes is that they are both add-on elements, and do not replace anything.

[65]Identical with Sārasvata-Vyākaraṇa (1.20, p. 4). Kshitish Chandra Chatterji (1948, 1964: 317) quotes a parallel verse:

स्थाने शत्रुवदादेशा भाले पुण्ड्रवदागमाः ।
दन्तानामिव लोपः स्याच्छत्रवत्प्रत्ययाः परे ।।

[66]Compare Paribhāṣā (Paribhāṣenduśekhara 38: पूर्वपरनित्यान्तरङ्गापवादानामुत्तरोत्तरं बलीयः).

CA)। विवृततरौ एओकारौ गुणसंज्ञौ स्तः[67] । **६०. विवृततमा वृद्धिः** (not found in CA)। आऐऔकारा विवृततमा वृद्धिसंज्ञाः स्युः[68] । **६१. द्रव्यार्थदिशा धातवः** (not found in CA)। द्रव्याणां विषयाणामर्थानुपदिशन्ति ते । 'भूवादयो धातवः' (पा. १.३.१) इति पाणिनिः संज्ञपते । **६२. साधकतमा विभक्तिः** (not found in CA)। विभक्तिरेवार्थान् संपादयति । **६३. पदान्तः पद्यः (च.आ. १.१.५)**। 'सुप्तिङन्तं पदम्' (पा. १.४.१४) इति पाणिनिः । पद्यते संपद्यतेऽर्थोऽनेनेति भावः । 'विभक्त्यन्तं पदम्' (सारस्वतव्याकरण १२१) इति केचित्[69] । कमीमिद्विति[70] निपाता एकस्वराश्च[71] । निपाता धात्वर्थरञ्जका अनेकार्थाश्च[72] । **६४. प्रपरेत्युपसर्गाः**[73] (cf. **च.आ. ४.१.१९**)। धातूनां संयोगेऽर्थान्तरगमकाः । **६५. अभीत्यन्ता उपसर्गाः क्रियायोगे गतिस्तथा**

---

[67]PS rule 59 and the commentary exclude *a* from the list of *guṇa* vowels, cf. P.1.1.2 (अदेङ् गुणः). The featural description *vivṛtatara* can apply to *e* and *o* within the system as understood by Kṛṣṇadāsa, but not to *a*, which is a close (*saṃvṛta*) vowel.

[68]This rule and the commentary presumably try to lump *ai, au,* and *ā* together as *vivṛtatama* vowels. The CA (1.1.34-35) distinguish between the degree of openness for *ai* and *au* on the one hand, and *ā* on the other. The vowel *ā* is treated by the CA as being even more open than *ai* and *au*, which are described as *vivṛtatama*.

[69]Also compare: ते विभक्त्यन्ताः पदम्, न्यायसूत्र, २.२.५१.

[70]Compare Yāska's Nirukta (1.9): अथ ये प्रवृत्तेऽर्थेऽमिताक्षरेषु ग्रन्थेषु वाक्यपूरणा आगच्छन्ति पदपूरणास्ते मिताक्षरेष्वनर्थकाः कमीमिद्विति. The same list is referred to in Bṛhaddevatā (2.91) which explicitly refers to these items as *nipāta*s in (2.89).

[71]While the *nipāta*s cited here have one vowel each (*ekasvarāḥ*), it is not exactly clear why this qualification has been mentioned here. It almost seems like a reflex of the words *nipāta ekāc* of P.1.1.14 (निपात एकाजनाङ्).

[72]The wording of Kṛṣṇadāsa is confusing at best. The Nirukta (1.9) and Bṛhaddevatā (2.90-91) say that the *nipāta*s like *kam, īm, it,* and *u* are meaningless (*anarthakāḥ*), but that "there are also such particles as have various senses (*anekārthāḥ*), e.g. *iva, na, cid,* and *nu* - these are the four having the sense of comparison" (Bṛhaddevatā 2.91).

[73]Compare Sārasvata-Vyākaraṇa (355, p. 75): प्रादिरुपसर्गः, and the list of *Upasarga*s begins with *pra, parā* etc.

(च.आ. ४.१.२०cd)। 'उपसर्गाः क्रियायोगे, गतिश्च' (पा. १.४.५९-६०) इति पाणिनिः । ६६. **विकल्पो विभाषा** (not found in CA)। ६७. **अवसानं विरामोऽन्तश्च** (not found in CA)। वर्णाभावे विरामादि-संज्ञा[74] । ६८. **वर्णादन्त्यात्पूर्व उपधा** (च.आ. १.४.१)। अन्त्याद्वर्ण-मात्रात्पूर्वो यो वर्णः स उपधेति । ६९. **अन्त्यः स्वरः सोत्तरावयवष्टिः**[75] (not found in CA)। ७०. **प्रत्यये व्यञ्जनमित्** (not found in CA)। ७१. **उपरिष्टाद् बिन्दुरनुस्वारः**[76] (not found in CA)। ७२. **पार्श्वबिन्दु-द्वयो विसर्गः** (not found in CA)। ७३. **अ꞉क꞉पौ जिह्वामूलीयो-पध्मानीयौ** (not found in CA)। ७४. **ईऊए द्विवचने प्रगृह्यम्** (not found in CA)। ७५. **वर्णकार्यादर्शनं लोपः** (not found in CA)। ७६. **विसर्जनीयोऽभिनिष्ठा (ष्टा?) नः** (च.आ. १.२.१)। ७७. **व्यञ्जनवि-धारणमभिनिधानः** (च.आ. १.२.२)। पूर्वसूत्राणि स्पष्टार्थानि । व्यञ्जनविधारणं संयोगस्याद्यक्षरमभि[नि]धानसंज्ञं स्यात् । ७८. **स्पर्शस्य स्पर्शे पदान्तावग्रहयोश्च** (च.आ. १.२.४-५)। ७९. **लकारस्योष्मसु** (च.आ. १.२.६)। ८०. **ङणनानां हकारे** (च.आ. १.२.७)। ८१. **आस्थापितं च** (च.आ. १.२.८)। ८२. **अतोऽन्यत्संयुक्तम्** (च.आ. १.२.९)। ८३. **स्पर्शेषु सस्थानः स्ववर्गः** (not found in CA)। वर्ग इति संज्ञा । ८४. **अविभक्ति नाम प्रातिपदिकं च**[77] (not found in

---

[74]Compare: P.1.4.110 (विरामोऽवसानम्), and SK on it: वर्णानामभावोऽवसानसंज्ञः स्यात्।

[75]Compare Sārasvata-Vyākaraṇa (26, p. 5): अन्त्यस्वरादिष्टिः ।

[76]This rule and the next one, interestingly offer a graphic, rather than a phonetic, description of the Anusvāra and the Visarga. Compare Sārasvata-Vyākaraṇa (32, p. 4): वर्णशिरोबिन्दुरनुस्वारः । The Pāṇinian grammarians generally do not offer graphic descriptions of sounds. However, occasionally this does happen. For *jihvāmūlīya* and *upadhmānīya* sounds, the SK on P.8.2.1 (p. 6) says: ꞉क꞉पाविति कपाभ्यां प्रागर्धविसर्गसदृशौ जिह्वामूलीयोपध्मानीयौ। Commenting on this line, the Tattvabodhinī says: सादृश्यमुच्चारणे लेखने च बोध्यम् ।

[77]This looks like an effort to combine Sārasvata-Vyākaraṇa (122: अविभक्ति नाम) with the Pāṇinian term *prātipadika* for the nominal stem, cf. P.1.2.45 (अर्थवदधातुरप्रत्ययः प्रातिपदिकम्). The commentary excludes *nipāta*s and *upasarga*s from the scope of this term. This is not the case with Pāṇinian rules.

CA)। विभक्तिरहितं निपातोपसर्गवर्जितं नामेति संज्ञा प्रातिपदिकमिति च । ८५. **सर्वादीनि सर्वनाम**[78] (not found in CA) इति । ८६. **अनाख्यातं कृदन्तम्**[79] (not found in CA) इति । इति श्रीमदथर्वकौत्सव्याकरणे संज्ञाप्रकरणम् ॥

परिभाषाप्रकरणम्

८७. **स्थानार्था षष्ठी**[80] (not found in CA)। षष्ठीनिर्दिष्टं कार्यं तस्यैव स्थाने बोध्यम् । ८८. **पञ्चम्युत्तरस्य**[81] (not found in CA)। ८९. **सप्तमी पूर्वस्य**[82] (not found in CA)। ९०. **आद्यन्तानि टवर्गकवर्गव्यञ्जनानि**[83] (not found in CA)। ९१. **असिद्धं बहिरङ्गमन्तरङ्गे** (not found in CA)। विनाशोन्मुखं कार्यं न कुर्यात् । ९२. **इतो लोपः** (not found in CA)। इत्संज्ञकस्येत्यर्थः । ९३. **विधायकस्य न**[84] (not

---

It appears that this exclusion is to make this rule compatible with the Prātiśākhya tradition which distinguishes nominal stems from the categories of *nipāta* and *upasarga*, cf. CA (1.1.2: चतुर्णां पदजातानां नामाख्यातोपसर्गनिपातानां सन्ध्यपद्यौ गुणौ प्रातिज्ञम्). For further details, see: Deshpande (1992: 10-15).

[78]This looks like an incomplete expression, since the plural of *sarvādīni* does not match the singular of *sarvanāma*. Compare P.1.1.27 (सर्वादीनि सर्वनामानि). However, the singular usage is more in accordance with Sārasvata-Vyākaraṇa (148: सर्वादेः स्मट्) and सर्वादिः सर्वनामाख्यः in a verse cited in the Sārasvata-Vyākaraṇa (p. 23).

[79]Compare P.3.1.93 (कृदतिङ्).

[80]Compare P.1.1.49 (षष्ठी स्थानेयोगा).

[81]Compare P.1.1.67 (तस्मादित्युत्तरस्य).

[82]Compare P.1.1.66 (तस्मिन्निति निर्दिष्टे पूर्वस्य).

[83]Compare P.1.1.46 (आद्यन्तौ टकितौ). The rule as stated by Kṛṣṇadāsa refers to *ṭa-varga* and *ka-varga*, rather than just the marker consonants *ṭ* and *k*.

[84]The term *apratyayaḥ* in P.1.1.69 (अणुदित्सवर्णस्य चाप्रत्ययः) is interpreted by Bhaṭṭoji Dīkṣita in his SK on this rule as being equal to *avidhīyamānaḥ*. This is interpreted to mean that an item which is prescribed is not capable of representing its homogeneous sounds. Historically, such an interpretation goes back to the MB of Patañjali who derives the maxim भाव्यमानेन सवर्णानां ग्रहणं न. For a detailed discussion of this maxim, see: Deshpande (1975:

found in CA) । ९४. **वर्णग्रहे सवर्णमात्रम्**[85] (not found in CA) । ९५. **कारे सत्यसहवर्णो:**[86] (?, not found in CA) । व्यञ्जनानां परैः संयोगः कार्यः संहितायाम्[87] । इति परिभाषाप्रकरणम् ।।

[सन्धिसाधनम्?][88]

९६. **संयोगे पूर्वं व्यञ्जनं पूर्वमुत्तरमुत्तरम्** (not found in CA) । ९७. **पूर्वं रेफश्चेत्स ऊर्ध्वगः**[89] (not found in CA) ।

[स्वरसन्धिप्रकरणम्]

अथ स्वरसन्धिः । अभ्यागतः पूज्य इत्यत्र अभि आगत इति स्थितौ ९८. **संहितायाम्** (**च.आ. २.१.१**) इत्यधिकृत्य । ९९. **स्वरे**

71ff). This notion manifests in different grammars as a distinct rule, and the rule विधायकस्य न in Kṛṣṇadāsa's work is in all likelihood a statement expressing this notion. Compare Bhoja's Sarasvatīkaṇṭhābharaṇa, rule 1.2.4 (अविधीयमानोऽण् ससवर्णः).

[85]Compare: Sārasvata-Vyākaraṇa (p. 6): वर्णग्रहणे सवर्णग्रहणम् ।

[86]While the reading here is corrupt, the component *asaha* may be compared with the expression *kevala* in Sārasvata-Vyākaraṇa (p. 6): कारग्रहणे केवल-ग्रहणम्. The rule probably means: "A letter appended with the affix *-kāra* does not stand for the associated sounds, i.e. stands just for itself."

[87]This statement probably belongs to the next section, introducing rule PS 96.

[88]I am not sure about this section. The text says earlier that there is a section titled *sandhisādhanam* between the *paribhāṣā* section and the *svarasandhi* or *svarasādhana* section. However, it is strange to find just two rules, without any indication of the beginning or the end of the section.

[89]Compare the graphic description of *repha* found in the Sārasvata-Vyākaraṇa (pp. 7-8):

तुम्बिका तृणकाष्ठं च तैलं जलसमागमे ।
ऊर्ध्वस्थानं समायान्ति रेफाणामीदृशी गतिः ।।
जलतुम्बिकान्यायेन रेफस्योर्ध्वगमनम् -
रेफः स्वरपरं वर्णं दृष्ट्वारोहति तच्छिरः ।
पुरःस्थितं यदा पश्येदधः संक्रमते स्वरम् ।।

नामिनोऽन्तस्थाः (च.आ. ३.२.१६)। पदान्ते इत्यनुवृत्तिः । सन्ध्यक्षरं विना नामिसंज्ञस्य स्वरस्य स्थाने स्वरसंज्ञे वर्णे परेऽन्तस्था भवन्ति । अन्तस्थाश्चतस्रः तासां मध्यात् कस्याः प्राप्तिरत्र । यो यस्य सस्थानः स एव सन्धिविषये प्राप्तुं शक्नोति नान्यः । आगमादेशकाले तु विशेषस्य बलवत्त्वात् । अतः सस्थानत्वबलादिकारस्य स्थाने यकारः । अभ्य् इति स्थिते । **१००. पदान्ते व्यञ्जनं द्विः (च.आ. ३.२.१)** इत्यनुसृत्य । **१०१. संयोगादि स्वरात् (च.आ. ३.२.३)।** स्वरात् संयोगसंज्ञस्य वर्णस्यादिभूतं यद् व्यञ्जनं तद् द्विः स्यात् । इति भकारस्य द्वित्वम् । **१०२. पदान्ते व्यञ्जनं द्विः (च.आ. ३.२.१)।** पदान्ते यद् व्यञ्जनं तद् द्विः स्यात् । अत्र इकारस्थाने यकारः पदान्ते तस्यापि द्वित्वम् । तदा अभ्भ्य्य् इति स्थितम् । यकारस्य स्वरस्य सस्थानत्वमाशङ्क्य[90] । नेत्यनुवृत्त्या **१०३. सस्थाने च (च.आ. ३.२.७)।** स्वराणां सस्थाने व्यञ्जने परे संयोगो द्विर्न भवति । इति द्वित्वनिषेधे प्राप्ते **१०४. न समौ सन्ध्यौ (cf. च.आ. ३.२.१४)।** सन्धिस्थसन्धिस्थानादेशीयवर्णौ समानधर्मौ न स्तः इति स्थानिशङ्कानिरासः । **१०५. तृतीयान्तानि (from च.आ. १.१.१०)** इत्यनुवर्त्त्य । **१०६. अधिस्पर्शं च (च.आ. १.१.११)।** स्पर्शाक्षरात्पूर्वं स्पर्शाक्षरमधिस्पर्शं तदपि तृतीयान्तं स्यात् संयोगे परे अनेन पूर्वभकारस्य बकारः । तदा ब्भ्य्य् इति जाते । पुनर्द्वित्वे प्राप्ते । लोप

---

[90] In the stage *abh-bh-y* + *āgataḥ*, Kr̥ṣṇadāsa argues that one may suspect that *y* is followed by a *sasthāna* 'homorganic' vowel *ā*, and then deny reduplication to *y* by PS 103. This argument is based on several assumptions. The first assumption is that the substitute *y* can be treated as having the same features as the original *i*, cf. *sthānivadbhāva* in Pāṇini, which, however, contains the restriction *analvidhau* in P.1.1.56. Even if *y* is treated as having the same features as *i*, how can it be treated as being *sasthāna* 'homorganic' with *ā*? This cannot happen in any other system, except the one set up by Kr̥ṣṇadāsa. He, on PS 2, argues that all vowels are minimally *kaṇṭhya*, and that vowels other than *a* and *ā* may have a second point of articulation, cf. स्वरहकारविसर्जनीयानां कण्ठः and नामिस्वराणां प्रत्येकं स्थानद्वयम्. This allows the possibility of *i* and *ā* being treated as *sasthāna*. No other system of grammar known to me would support such a position.

इत्यनुवर्त्त्य **१०७. स्पर्शादुत्तमादनुत्तमस्यानुत्तमे (च.आ. २.१.२०)।** स्पृष्टप्रयत्नमात्राद्वर्णात् प्रथमाद् द्विरुक्तिविषयेऽपरस्य व्यञ्जनस्य स्थानेऽपरस्मिन् सजातीये व्यञ्जने प्राप्ते सति लोपः स्यादिति पुनर्द्वित्वप्रतिषेधः[91] । **१०८. लेशवृत्तिरधिस्पर्शं शाकटायनस्य (च.आ. २.१.२४)।** स्पर्शमधिकृत्येत्यधिस्पर्शो यस्मिन्नित्यधिस्पर्शं सजातीयस्य लेशमात्रे वर्तनं यस्येदृशो लोपः स्यादिति शाकटायनस्य मतम्[92] । 'सरूपाणामेकशेष' ... (पा. १.२.६४) इति पाणिनिः[93] । तेन द्वितीयस्य यकारस्य लोपो वा । तत्र ब्भ्य्य् [and ब्भ्य्य्] इति रूपद्वयस्थितौ । **१०९. व्यञ्जनं परतः सन्धयेत्**[94] (not found in CA)। तदा सन्धौ अब्भ्यागतः । अब्भ्य्यागतः । सरूपैकशेषे[95] भकारद्वयस्य सारूप्येऽभ्यागत इति रूपत्रयं सिद्धम् । रूपचतुष्टयं[96] च यकारद्वयेन । अभ्य्यागत इति । सर्वत्र शाकल्यस्य[97] मतेन द्वित्वं न । गौरि एहि इत्यत्र यकारादेशः पूर्ववत् । रेफस्य द्वित्वे प्राप्ते । **११०. रेफहकारौ परं ताभ्याम् (च.आ. ३.२.८)।** ताभ्यां व्यञ्जनस्वराभ्यां रेफहकारौ द्विर्न स्तः इति परम् । पूर्वस्मात् शास्त्रात्परं

---

[91]Contrast the more standard interpretations of CA (2.1.20). The rule applies to a situation where an *uttama* 'list-final' nasal consonant is followed by one of the first four members (= non-list-final) of the stop-series. Under no circumstances can the rule apply to the sequence *b-bh-y-y*.

[92]The rule does not say that the consonant under consideration is deleted according to Śākaṭāyana, but that it has a reduced articulation. P.8.3.18 (व्योर्लघुप्रयत्नतरः शाकटायनस्य) and P.8.3.19 (लोपः शाकल्यस्य) clearly distinguish between these alternatives. The deletion alternative is ascribed to Śākalya.

[93]Kṛṣṇadāsa implies that this rule of Pāṇini also applies to phonology, so that a sequence of two identical consonants could be reduced to a single consonant. The original context of the rule does not have anything to do with phonology.

[94]Compare Cāndravyākaraṇa (36: स्वरहीनं परेण संयोज्यम्) and Kātantravyākaraṇa (1.1.21: व्यञ्जनमस्वरं परं वर्णं नयेत्).

[95]This repeats the view that P.1.2.64 (सरूपाणामेकशेष एकविभक्तौ) teaches that a cluster of two identical consonants can be reduced to a single consonant.

[96]Compare the SK on P.8.2.23, referring to the sandhi of *sudhī+upāsyaḥ* : तदिह धकारयकारयोर्द्वित्वविकल्पाच्चत्वारि रूपाणि । एकधमेकयम् । द्विधं द्वियम् । द्विधमेकयम्। एकधं द्वियम् ।

[97]This refers to P.8.4.51 (सर्वत्र शाकल्यस्य).

शास्त्रं बलवत् । 'विप्रतिषेधे परं कार्यम्' (पा. १.४.२) इति पाणिनिः । अनेन रेफस्य द्वित्वं न । अन्यत्पूर्ववत् । गौर्येहीति सिद्ध(K: द्धिं)म् । मह्यम्बेति मही अम्बा अत्र हकारस्यापि सूत्रबलाद् द्वित्वं न । वधू आननमित्यत्र ऊ(K: उ)कारस्थानेऽन्तस्थानां मध्याद्वकार एव प्राप्तः ऊ(K: उ)कारवकारयोः सस्थानत्वादू(K: दु)कारस्य वकारः । द्वित्वादि पूर्ववत् । वध्वाननं सिद्धम् । मध्वरिरिति । पितॄ(K: तृ)णामाज्यमन्नं वा पितृअन्नम् [पित्]ऋआज्यम् । ऋकारस्य रेफः पित्र् परसंयोजनात् पित्रन्नम् । विकल्पात्[98] पित्राज्यम् । द्विर्न । [पित्]राज्यमिति सिद्धम् । **१११. ऋवर्णरेफषकारेभ्यः समानपदे नो णः (च.आ. ३.४.१)।** एभ्यः एक-पदाश्रये नकारस्य णत्वं स्यात् । ऋअनम् रणम् ऋआवनः रावणः[99] । बृंहणम् सर्पणम् । अर्चनम् दर्शनम् रटनम् इत्यत्र नकारानुवर्तनात् । **११२. व्यवाये शषलैः (च.आ. ३.४.२५)। ११३. चटतवर्गैश्च (च.आ. ३.४.२६)।** एभिर्व्यवधानात् णत्वं नेति । रेफस्य दन्तमूल-त्वात् लकारस्यापि दन्त्यत्वात् । **११४. लकारस्य रेफः पादम् ... (च.आ. १.३.४)।** इति सूत्रबलाद्रेफलकारयोर्ऋॡवर्णयोः [च] साव-र्ण्यम् । तेन ॡअवनम् लवनं[100] लवणं च ॡअवनम् इत्यत्रान्तस्था-मध्याल्लकारादेशः परेण स्वरेण योगाल्लवनमिति सिद्धम् । लम्भनम् रम्भणम् च रलयोः सावर्ण्यात् । शाकलानां मूर्धन्यलकारोच्चारणात् डलयोरप्य-भेदः । दुर्दभ इत्यत्र दुरो रेफात्परस्य दकारस्य मूर्धन्यादेशं डकारं कृत्वा डकारस्य रेफलकाराभ्यां सस्थानत्वं मत्वा 'रो रि' (पा. ८.३.१४) इति-वद्रेफस्य लोपे पूर्वस्योकारस्य दैर्घ्यमालक्ष्य 'परि ते दूळभो रथः' (ऋग्वेद ४.९.८a) इति पठन्ति । **स्वरे** (from **च.आ. ३.२.१६**) इत्यनुवर्त्त्य

98This probably refers to the two possible forms *pittrājyam* and *pitrājyam*.

99The etymologies of the words *raṇa* and *rāvaṇa* are intriguing.

100Generally, the word *lavanaṃ* is derived from the verb *lu* plus the affix *ana*, and not from a combination of *ḷ+avana*. The Pāṇinian commentators look at *lavaṇa* as an irregular formation sanctioned by its inclusion in the *nandyādi-gaṇa*, cf. P.3.1.134 (नन्दिग्रहिपचादिभ्यो ल्युणिन्यचः), and the SK (p. 488) on this rule: नन्द्यादिगणे निपातनाण्णत्वम्.

११५. सन्ध्यक्षराणामयवायावः (च.आ. ३.२.१७)। एओऐऔ एतेषां सन्ध्यक्षराणां स्थाने विवृततरविवृततमक्रमेण अय् अव् आय् आव् एते प्रत्ययाः[101] संभवन्ति प्रत्येतीति प्रत्ययः । वर्णं प्रति यातीत्यर्थः । **११६. प्रत्ययव्यञ्जनमित्** (not found in CA) प्रत्यये यद् व्यञ्जनं तदित्स्यात् । **११७. इतो लोपः** (not found in CA) इति यवयोर्लोपे प्राप्ते **११८. विधायकस्य न** (not found in CA)। कार्यं विधीयतेऽनेनेति विधायकः । तस्य लोपो न । यवयोर्लोपे तु अयावादिविधानमपि न सिद्ध्येत्[102] । वे उ न इति स्थिते । वे इत्यस्य एकारस्य स्थाने अय्प्रत्ययो जातः । तदा व् अय् उ नग् इति परसंयोगात् वयुनं नयनमिति सिद्धम् । गवां सादृश्यमेतीति गवयः कश्चित् पशुः । गो अयः इत्यत्र ओकारस्य स्थाने अव् । परेण योगात् गवय इति सिद्धिः । भो अनं भवनम् । हो अनं हवनम् । रायो धनस्य आप्तिः रै आप्तिः । अत्राय्प्रत्ययः रै इत्यत्र रेफादुत्तरस्य ऐकारस्य तदा र् आय् आप्तिः इति स्थिते परैर्योगे रायाप्तिः सिद्धा । नै अकः नायकः दायकः वायक इति । श्रौ अकः इत्यत्र औकारस्य आव्, तदा श्र् आव् अकः योगः पूर्ववत् । श्रावकः धावकः[103] पावकः । इति सिद्धम् । **११९. गोरगर्धं पूर्णं च स्वहव्ये यत्प्रत्ययेऽक्षेन्द्राध्वनि च अजिनाग्रयोर्विभाषा[104]** (not found in CA)। गोशब्दात् स्वाङ्गजे हव्ये

---

[101]Here the term *pratyaya* is used in the sense of a substitute (*ādeśa*), and not in the sense of an affix. K.C. Chatterji (1948, 1964: 91ff) surveys the various meanings of this term in the grammatical literature, but has not found any usage of the term in the sense of substitute.

[102]The question of why the *y* and *v* at the end of the substitutes *ay, av, āy,* and *āv* are not deleted is of importance even in the Pāṇinian system, cf. SK on P.6.1.78 (एचोऽयवायावः) and P.1.3.9 (तस्य लोपः) इति यवयोर्लोपो न । उच्चारणसामर्थ्यात् । एवं चेत्संज्ञापीह न भवति ।

[103]This assumes a derivation from *dhau+aka*. Such a possibility occurs even in the Pāṇinian system which prescribes the substitute *dhau* for the verb root *sṛ*, cf. P.7.3.78 (पाघ्राध्मास्थाम्नादाण्दृश्यर्तिसर्तिशदसां पिबजिघ्रधमतिष्ठमनयच्छपश्यर्च्छधौशीयसीदाः)

[104]In the Pāṇinian tradition, the forms derived by this rule are derived by a number of different rules, cf. P.6.1.79 (वान्तो यि प्रत्यये), P. 6.1.122 (सर्वत्र

तत्रैव यत्प्रत्ययेऽध्वपरिमाणजे यकारे परे च अगागमः ककारः स्थानप्रदेशार्थ इत् । अकार उच्चारणार्थो वा । अत्र सरूपाणामेकशेषत्वादर्धस्याकारस्य पूर्णस्याकारस्यापि कार्यमतः कार्यद्वयं दृश्यते । यकारे परेऽर्धस्य स्वरे तु पूर्णस्य । **१२०. अकारस्यार्धं चतुर्थमित्येके ... (च.आ. १.४.१०)** इति सूत्रबलात् न दीर्घत्वं पूर्णत्वाभावात् । **१२१. रेफादूष्मणि स्वरपरे स्वरभक्तिरकारस्यार्धं चतुर्थमित्येके (च.आ. १.४.१०)।** रेफात् स्वर-परे स्वरः परो यस्य तस्मिन्नूष्मणि स्वरभक्तिः नाम स्वरभागः संयोगः अकारस्यार्धं चतुर्थांशं वा । **१२२. अन्यस्मिन् व्यञ्जने चतुर्थमष्टमं वा (च.आ. १.४.११)।** इति अकारार्धे गो अ् (K: अ) यम् इति स्थिते ओकारे अव्प्रत्ययः तदा ग् अव् अ्[105] यम् जातं संयोगात् गव्यं सिद्धम् । क्रोशद्वयं गव्यूतिः । पूर्णे स्वरे तु ग् अव् अ अक्षः संयोजनात् सवर्णे दीर्घात् गवाक्ष इति सिद्धम् । गवाजिनम् । गवाग्रमित्यपि । विकल्पे गोजिनम् गोग्रमिति । **१२३. अजिनाग्रयोर्विभाषेति नौधात्वोश्चार्धम्**[106] (not found in CA)। नौ च धातुश्च तयोः परतः यप्रत्यये अर्धाकारागमेन

विभाषा गोः), P.6.1.123 (अवङ् स्फोटायनस्य), P.6.1.124 (इन्द्रे च), and the Vārttikas : गोर्यूतौ छन्दस्युपसङ्ख्यानम् and अध्वपरिमाणे च on P.6.1.79. What distinguishes Kṛṣṇadāsa's statement is that there is some notion of a half and a full *a*. As the following discussion shows, he assumes that in the formation *gavyam*, at the stage *go+ya*, there is a reduced *a* as an end-augment after *go*, i.e. *go*^{a}*+ya*. The reduced *a* allows the change of *go* to *gav*. The reduced *a* is like the *svarabhakti*. This is a distinctive interpretation, and differs significantly from Pāṇini's procedure in P.6.1.79 (वान्तो यि प्रत्यये), which prescribes the change of *go* to *gav* before a *y*-initial affix. It may perhaps indicate occasional tri-syllabic pronunciation of words like *gavyam* and *nāvyam* in the AV tradition. Wackernagel, *Altindische Grammatik*, Vol.I., p. 201ff. discusses the variation of the suffixal elements *-ya* and *-iya*. However, the tradition here may indicate a different, more *a*-like pronunciation of the initial vocalic element, e.g. *gav*^{a}*ya* rather than *gav*^{i}*ya*. While the original CA does not have this view, Kṛṣṇadāsa is certainly citing this from some as yet unknown source.

[105] The manuscript K uses the ligature अ् to indicate the half or reduced *a* (*akārārdha*).

[106] The term *ardham* here again refers to the notion of *akārārdham* which has been explained in the notes above.

नावा तार्यं नाव्यम् । लाव्यमिति ओकारात् लव्यम् । **१२४. पूर्वपरयोरेकः (च.आ. ३.२.१८)।** पूर्वपरयोः स्वरयोः स्थाने एकाधिकाररूपस्य स्वरस्यादेशः स्यात् । **१२५. पूर्वस्यान्ते परस्यादौ**[107] (not found in CA)। इत्यधिकृत्य **१२६. समानाक्षरस्य सवर्णे दीर्घः (च.आ. ३.२.१९)।** समानसंज्ञिकस्य स्वरस्य स्थाने सवर्णे स्वरे परे सति द्वयोरपि स्थाने दीर्घरूप एकादेशः । रेफे ऋकारः ऌकारो दीर्घो न भवति प्लुतो भवति[108] । कृष्ण अवलम्ब इत्यत्रोभयोर्ह्रस्वयोरकारयोः दीर्घे आकारादेशे कृष्णावलम्ब इति सिद्धम् । वेदाध्ययनं दैवाधीनमित्यपि च । ह्रस्वादकाराद्दीर्घे आकारे परे सति संयोगे त्रिमात्रत्वं प्लुतत्वमाशङ्क्य । **१२७. आकारः केवलः प्रथमं पूर्वेण (च.आ. ३.२.१५)।** इति पठति स्म । आकारः प्रथममिति पदादिश्चेत्पूर्वेण ह्रस्वेन(K: ण) अकारेण संयोगं प्राप्य केवलः नामस्वरूपेण दैर्घ्येणैवावतिष्ठते[109] । न त्रिमात्रत्वमेति । एवं दिक्प्रदर्शनेन ह्रस्वात् पूर्वोऽप्याकारः संयोगे ज्ञातव्यः । एवमेव ईऊॠ(K: ॠ)कारा ज्ञातव्याः । **१२८. कार्ये प्लुतः (not found in CA)।** प्लुतकार्यं भिन्नं तत्रैव प्लुतो भवितुमर्हति[110] । प्लुतकार्यमग्रे प्रवक्ष्यामः । **१२९. सीमन्ते ह्रस्वः (च.आ. ३.२.२०)।** सीमन्तादिगणे सावर्ण्यसंयोगे प्राप्तेऽप्यकारो ह्रस्वः । टेर्लोपात् ।

'सीमन्तः केशभागे स्यात्सारङ्गः पशुपक्षिणोः ।
मार्तण्डोऽर्कोऽञ्जलीषान्धुः कुलटादौ टिलोपतः ।।' (source?)

---

[107] Compare P.6.1.85 (अन्तादिवच्च).

[108] This statement is not very clear, but seems to refer to the possible homogeneity of *r* and *ṛ* on the one hand, and *ṛ* and *ḷ* on the other.

[109] This interpretation strays substantially from the intent of CA (3.2.15). PS 126 (= CA 3.2.19) specifically says that the combination of two similar simple vowels results in a long vowel, and there is no reason to suspect that it could become a prolonged (*pluta*) vowel.

[110] Compare the Vārttika cited in the MB on P.1.2.17: प्लुतश्च विषये स्मृतः, and Patañjali's explanation: विषये प्लुत उच्यते यदा च स विषयो भवितव्यमेव तदा प्लुतेन.

"Rot genug, Lachlan. Du solltest besser mitkommen, du könntest dein Geld verlieren, wenn du es nicht tust."

"Oh, *Maister* Alic, Liebling, sagt nicht, dass mein Gesicht rot ist - es ist nicht rot, Maister Alic - es ist nicht *vera* rot", plädierte der arme Kerl.

"Kommst du mit oder nicht?" sagte M'lan, als er die Zügel in seiner Hand aufnahm und die Peitsche ergriff.

In diesem Moment kamen drei oder vier Fahrer aus einem Zelt in der Nachbarschaft, und Lachlan hörte, wie sein Name gerufen wurde.

"Ich gehe zurück für meinen Hut. Es wäre nicht anständig, ohne Hut mit Gentlemen zu fahren;" und er zog seine Hand zurück.

Die Viehzüchter riefen erneut und dieser zweite Schrei zog Lachlan an, wie das Licht die Motte anzog.

"Sein Gesicht wird vor dem Abend rot genug sein", sagte M'lan, als wir wegfuhren.

Nachdem wir ungefähr eine Viertelstunde gefahren waren und uns völlig vom Markt befreit hatten, rief M'lan, der seine Augen mit einer gekrümmten Handfläche vor der Sonne abschirmte, plötzlich aus: "Da sitzt ein roter Hund am Straßenrand, ein Stück weiter. Es sieht aus wie John Kellys."

Als wir aufstanden, wedelte der Hund mit dem Schwanz und winselte, behielt aber seine liegende Position bei.

"Kommt", sagte M'lan. "Der Hund spielt die Rolle eines Wächters, und ich gehe davon aus, dass wir seinen Herrn finden werden."

Wir stiegen dementsprechend aus und stellten bald fest, dass John sich auf dem Heidekraut ausstreckt hatte und heftig schnarchte, seine Krawatte war nicht

[illegible]

[illegible]

[illegible]

अत इति अनेन सह लोपात पत (पत?) अञ्जलिरिति पदान्ताभावात [illegible]

[illegible]

अन्त्यस्य पृषादरत्वाल्लोप मन्यन्ते[111] । ह्रस्वयोरिकारयोर्योगे कवीन्द्रः । पूर्व दीर्घ करीन्द्रः । उकाराभ्यां भानूदयः । भानूध्व(K: द्धु)म् । वधूाच्छ- [illegible] । ऋकारस्तु स्वतोऽधमात्रः । [illegible] (K: ऋ) कारद्वययोगादेको मात्रा [illegible]

[illegible]

[111] This refers to Varttika (शकन्ध्वादिषु च) on P.6.1.94. However, the citation of [illegible] 1, p. 64) on P.6.1.94 for the same examples. The final comment is even more closely comparable to the Praudhamanorama on SK (p. 194): [illegible] It is clear that Bhattoji refers to this view as a rejected view, and this is made clear by Haridiksita in his commentary Laghusabdaratna: अत्रारुचिबीजं तु वचनद्वयव्यापारो व्यर्थः, पृषोदरादि- [illegible] N. D. W[illegible] [illegible] Praudhamanorama and Sabdaratna (Vol. 3, pp. 132-3), identifies the view being rejected as that of Śrikrsnapandita, the author of the commentary Prakāśa on Rāmacandra's Prakriyākaumudī. Śrīkṛṣṇapaṇḍita (Prakāśa on Prakriyākaumudī, Vol.I., p. 112) says: [illegible] ... मनस ईषा । असः पररूप पृषोदरादित्वात्सलोपऽकारस्य वा । ... पतञ्जलिरिति ... [illegible] अन्ये तु पततीति पत इत्यजन्तेन पतशब्देन विग्रहोऽकारस्य पररूपमाहुः । The modern Sanskrit commentary Rasmi on Prakasa by the editor Muralidharamisra explains (p. 112): पतञ्जलिरित्यत्र पृषोदरादित्वादन्त्यलोपे पश्चात्पररूपम् । टेः पररूप [illegible] pandita. The Bhattoji tradition prefers the derivation of the word patañjali [illegible] from [illegible] rather than from [illegible]. The commentary [illegible] on Nagesa's [illegible] (p. [illegible]) points out that Nagesa prefers the former derivation, and casts aside the latter which was offered by a grammarian referred to as Ratnākara: एतेन पतन्नञ्जले- रिति विगृह्णन् रत्नाकरः कटाक्षितो, लडर्थस्य बाधात् । For earlier explanations of the words *manīṣā* and *manīṣita* along the lines of Prakāśa, see Mallinātha's commentary on Kumārasambhava (1.28 and 5.4). I am grateful to Cardona for providing the reference to Mallinātha.

अकारद्वयं सिद्धम् । पूर्वेणापि सिद्ध्येत् । पितृ ऋणं पितृणं मातृ ऋतुः मातृतुः । अयं प्रयोगः वैदिके न दृश्यते सौत्र एवेति[118] । **१३०. अवर्णस्येवर्ण एकारः (च.आ. ३.२.२१)।** अकारस्थाने इवर्णे परे द्वयोरपि स्थाने एकारादेशः स्यात् । उदाहरणमत्रैव स्य इ इति स्थिते द्वयोरेकारः स्ये इति सिद्धम् । येन इदं येनेदम् । च इति चेति । दीर्घे रमेश इति । गवेन्द्र इत्यगागमात्सिद्धम्[119] । **१३१. दीर्घप्लुतव्यवधाने च** (not found in CA)। अवर्णस्य स्थाने दीर्घेण प्लुतेन च व्यवधाने इकारे ई ई३ परे एकारादेशः स्यान्नत्वैकारः । गङ्गा आ इदं गङ्गेदम् । शिव आ इति शिवेति । अवर्णस्यानुवृत्तिः । **१३२. उवर्ण ओकारः (च.आ. ३.२.२२)।** अकारस्य स्थाने उवर्णे परे द्वयोरेक ओकारादेशः स्यात् । कृष्ण उपास्यः कृष्णोपास्यः, गङ्गोदकम्, राम ऊनः रामोनः, जाया ऊतिः जायोतिः, इला आ ऊध्वम् इलोर्ध्वम् । **१३३. अरमृवर्णे (च.आ. ३.२.२३)।** अकारस्य स्थाने ऋवर्णे परे द्वयोरपि स्थाने एकः अर् भवति । अरमिति नपुंसकत्वमार्षम् । कृष्ण ऋद्धिः कृष्णर्द्धिः । जल ऋतुः जलर्तुः । ब्रह्मर्षयः । तव ऌकारः तवल्कारः । सावर्ण्यात्समानः प्रयोगः[120] । **१३४. उपसर्गाद्धात्वादावारम् (च.आ. ३.२.२५, पाठान्तरम्)।** उप-

---

[118]This statement draws an interesting contrast between *vaidika* and *sautra*. It says that examples like *pitṝṇam* and *mātṝtuḥ* are not attested in Vedic texts, but are found only in illustrating rules of grammar. I think the word *sautra* is used here not in the sense of 'occurring in the *sūtra*,' but in the broad sense of 'illustrating the rules of grammar.' One may, however, note that this simultaneously admits that such expressions are not found in the classical language either. One needs to consider the possibility whether the consonant-initial pronunciation of *ṛ* as *ri* or *ru* makes it resistant to this type of sandhi in actual usage.

[119]This also refers to PS 119 above which, among other things, prescribes the augment *aK* to the word *go* before the word *indra*, i.e. *go+a+indra* > *gav+a+indra* > *gava+indra* > *gavendra*.

[120]This statement is deemed necessary because the original CA rules do not provide for the change of *a+ḷ* to *al*. For similar issues in the Pāṇinian system, see Deshpande (1975: 24-25).

सर्गात् उपसर्गस्य अकारात् धातोरादिभूते ऋकारे परे अर् इत्यस्य स्थाने आरं विजानीयादिति पूर्वत्राप्यन्वयः । प्रार्छत् । उपार्छति । अवार्छेत् । उप लृकारः उपाल्कारः । अयं रेफः पूर्वस्वरस्यान्ते तत्र पदान्ते विसर्जनीयत्वमाशङ्क्य सूत्रविधानसामर्थ्यान्नित्युत्तरम्[121] । प्रकृतिभावोऽपि नेति ।

१३५. **ऋणवत्सतरकम्बलवसनदशानामृणे**[122] (not found in CA) ।
ऋणार्णं प्रार्णं दशार्णो देशः । नदी च [।] ऋणशब्दो दुर्गभूमौ जले च[123] ।
१३६. **वा सुपि**[124] (not found in CA) । प्रार्षभीयति प्रार्षभीयति । प्राल्कारीयति । प्राल्कारीयति । उप ऋते उपर्ते उपार्ते । १३७. **तृतीयासमासे च**[125] (not found in CA) । शीतेन ऋतः शीतार्तः इति ।

---

[121] The argument assumes that the replacement *ār* for *-a+r̥-* can be treated as occurring at the end of the previous word or at the beginning of the following word, cf. PS 124-125 above.

[122] The source of this statement can be ultimately traced to the Vārttikas (प्रवत्सतरकम्बलवसनानां चर्णे) and (ऋणदशाभ्यां च) on P. 6.1.89. While the KV keeps these two as separate statements, they are combined by the Prakriyākaumudī on P.6.1.89 into प्रवत्सतरवत्सरकम्बलवसनदशानामृणे and SK on P.6.1.89 into प्रवत्सतरकम्बलवसनदशानामृणे. Kr̥ṣṇadāsa's rule seems to be a modification of the SK statement. It does not include the word *vatsara* which is found in the formulation of the Prakriyākaumudī. Apparently, it was included in the Prakriyākaumudī on the basis of its inclusion by Durga in his commentary on the Kātantravyākaraṇa, cf. Prakāśa on Prakriyākaumudī (Vol.I., p. 109). The word *pra* is not included in Kr̥ṣṇadāsa's formulation as given by the manuscript K. However, the citation of the example *prārṇam* suggests that it was included in his original formulation.

[123] Compare: SK on P.6.1.89 (p. 20): दशार्णो देशः । नदी च दशार्णा । ऋणशब्दो दुर्गभूमौ जले च ।

[124] Compare P.6.1.92 (वा सुप्यापिशलेः). It seems like the reference to Āpiśali was omitted by Kr̥ṣṇadāsa, as it was grammatically deemed to be unnecesary, cf. SK on P.6.1.92: आपिशलिग्रहणं पूजार्थम् । At the beginning of his Samjñāprakaraṇa, Kr̥ṣṇadāsa says: आचार्यनाम्नो विभाषा ज्ञेया. Since P.6.1.92 already contains the word *vā*, the reference to Āpiśali providing another indication of option was clearly deemed to be unnecessary. For an extensive treatment of this general question, see: Deshpande (1978).

[125] Compare Kātyāyana's Vārttika (ऋते च तृतीयासमासे) on P.6.1.89.

परत्वाद्दीर्घेन । उपऋकारीयति उपर्कारीयति । **१३८. एकारैकारयोरैकारः (च.आ. ३.२.२७)।** अवर्णस्थाने एऐकारयोः परतो सतोः पूर्वपरयोः पदान्तपदाद्योः स्वरयोः स्थाने एक ऐकारादेशः स्यात् । अम्ब एषा अम्बैषा ते पूजा अम्बैश्वर्यं तव । गङ्गैश्वर्यं गङ्गैषा राधैति कृष्णैधते । प्रैषः प्रैष्यः । **१३९. न दीर्घोपधे** (not found in CA)। ईषगतिः प्रेष्यः[126] । **१४०. शकल्येष्या (K: ष्वा) दिषु पररूपम् (च.आ. ३.२.२९)।** 'एङि पररूपम्' (पा. ६.१.९४) इति प्रेजते उपोषति । विकल्पात् उपैडकीयति उपेडकीयति[127] । **१४१. अनिश्चये एवे च**[128] (not found in CA)। क्वेवं भोक्ष्यसे । क्व एवम् । अद्य एवम् अद्येवम् । निश्चये तु अद्यैवम् इहैवैधि । नियोगे तु तवैव न किलैवं ननु किलैवमिति । **१४२. स्वादीरेरिणोर्वृद्धिः**[129] (not found in CA)। पदादेर्दीर्घस्यापि । स्वेनेरितुं शीलमस्येति स्वैरी स्वैरिणी च । स्व ईरम् ईकारस्य एत्वे संयोगे पररूपत्वे स्वैरी[130] । **१४३. ओकारौकारयोरौकारः (च.आ. ३.२.२८)।** अवर्णस्थाने ओकारे औकारे च परे द्वयोः स्थाने एक औकारादेशः पदान्तपदाद्योः । गङ्गा ओघः गङ्गौघः, कृष्ण औत्कण्ठ्यम् कृष्णौत्कण्ठ्यम्[131] ।

---

[126]Probably originates in SK on P.6.1.89 (p. 20): इष इच्छायां तुदादिः । इष गतौ दिवादिः । इष आभीक्ष्ण्ये क्र्यादिः । एषां घञि ण्यति च एषः एष्यः इति रूपे । तत्र पररूपे प्राप्तेऽनेन वृद्धिः । प्रैषः प्रैष्यः । यस्तु ईष उञ्छे । यश्च ईष गतिहिंसादर्शनेषु । तयोर्दीर्घोपधत्वात् । ईषः ईष्यः । तत्राद्गुणे । प्रेषः । प्रेष्यः ।

[127]Probably originates in SK on P.6.1.94 (p. 20): **एङि पररूपम् ।** ६.१.९४ । आदुपसर्गादेङादौ धातौ परे पररूपमेकादेशः स्यात् । प्रेजते । उपोषति । इह वा सुपीत्यनुवर्त्य वाक्यभेदेन व्याख्येयम् । तेन एङादौ सुब्धातौ वा । उपेडकीयति । उपैडकीयति ।

[128]Compare the Vārttika (एवे चानियोगे) on P.6.1.94. Kṛṣṇadāsa's commentary seems to derive its examples from the KV and SK on this Vārttika.

[129]Compare the Vārttika (स्वादीरेरिणोः) on P.6.1.89. Kṛṣṇadāsa's commentary follows the SK on P.6.1.89 (p. 19): स्वेनेरितुं शीलमस्येति स्वैरी स्वैरिणी च ।

[130]Kṛṣṇadāsa says that in the combination *sva+īra*, the *ī* of *īra* first changes to *e* and then through the *pararūpa* sandhi in *sva+era*, one gets *svaira*. None of this makes any sense. The rule actually says that in the combination *sva+īra* the single substitute for *a+ī* is a *vṛddhi*, i.e. *ai*, rather than the usual *e*.

[131]These examples are found in the Prakriyākaumudī and SK on P.6.1.88.

तव ओदनं तवौदनम् । **१४५. अक्षादूहिन्यां वृद्धिः**[132] (not found in CA)। अक्षौहिणी सेना । **१४६. प्रादूहोढयोर्वृद्धिः**[133] (not found in CA)। प्र ऊहः वृद्धिः औ संयोगे प्रौहः प्रौढः प्रौढिः । ऊठि प्रष्ठौहः[134] । गुणे पररूपे उपोषति । विकल्पेन प्रोघीयति प्रौघीयति[135] । **१४७. ओत्वोष्ठयोः समासे वा**[136] (not found in CA)। अवर्णस्य ओत्वोष्ठयोः परयोः द्वयोः स्थाने वृद्धिरेकादेशः स्यात् । तव ओष्ठः तवौष्ठः ममौतुः इति । समासे विकल्पात् स्थूलोतुः पररूपम् । स्थूलौतुः वृद्धिः । रक्तोष्ठे पर[रूप]म् । बिम्बौष्ठे वृद्धिरेका[देशः] । **१४८. ओमाङोश्च**[137] (not found in CA)। ओमि आङि च पररूपादे... । अद्योम्[138], रामेहि[139]

---

[132]The source for this rule is the Vārttika (अक्षादूहिन्याम्) on P.6.1.89, which Patañjali expands as: अक्षादूहिन्यां वृद्धिर्वक्तव्या. While the Prakriyākaumudī offers the example simply as *akṣauhiṇī*, Bhaṭṭoji's SK on P.6.1.89 (p. 19) reads: *akṣauhiṇī senā*.

[133]This goes back to the Vārttika (प्रादूहोढोढ्येषैष्येषु) on P.6.1.89. Kṛṣṇadāsa seems to have excised the forms *īṣa* and *īṣya*, because they are separately considered earlier.

[134]This is not covered by PS 146, but relates to the element *ūṭh* mentioned in P.6.1.89 (एत्येधत्यूठ्सु), and the example *praṣṭhauhaḥ* is the standard example in the KV and the SK. In *praṣṭha+ūha*, the element *ūha* is derived from the causative of the root *vah*, by the replacement of the initial *va* with *ū (= ūṬH)* by P.6.4.132 (वाह ऊठ्).

[135]The passage beginning with *guṇe* seems to be based on SK on P.6.1.94 (p. 20): **एङि पररूपम्** । आदुपसर्गादेङादौ धातौ परे पररूपमेकादेशः स्यात् । ... उपोषति । इह वा सुपीत्यनुवर्त्य वाक्यभेदेन व्याख्येयम् । तेन एङादौ सुब्धातौ वा । ... प्रोघीयति । प्रौघीयति ।

[136]This is identical with the Vārttika (ओत्वोष्ठयोः समासे वा) on P.6.1.94. The examples *sthūlautuḥ* and *bimbauṣṭhī* are found in the MB on this Vārttika. The example of a non-compounded sequence *tavauṣṭhaḥ* is found in the commentary Prakāśa on Prakriyākaumudī (Vol.I., p. 111), as well as in the SK on P.1.1.64 (p. 21). All three are found in the Sārasvata-Vyākaraṇa (64, p. 11).

[137]This is identical with P.6.1.95.

[138]The SK and the Prakriyākaumudī on P.6.1.95 offer the example *śivāyoṃ namaḥ*. The example *adyom* seems to have come from the Sārasvata-Vyākaraṇa (54, p. 10).

[139]In this case, the SK and the Prakriyāprakāśa on P.6.1.95, and the Sārasvata-

इकारः । **१४९. एकारौकारान्तात्पूर्वः पदादेरकारस्य (च.आ. ३.२. ३०)।** एकारान्तादोकारान्ताच्च पदादेः अकारस्य पूर्वः नाम पूर्वरूप एकादेशः स्यात् । 'तेऽवर्धन्त' (ऋग्वेद १.८५.७) । 'मन्योऽविंधत्' (अ.वे. ४. ३२.१) । हरेऽव । विष्णोऽवेति[140] । **१५०. प्रकृत्या वा**[141] (not found in CA)। गोऽग्रम् । गोअजिनम् । तेअत्र[142] । इति श्रीमदथर्वकौत्सव्याकरणे स्वरसन्धिः ।

[प्रकृतिभावप्रकरणम्]

अथ प्रकृतिभावः । पदान्ते इत्यधिकारः । **१५१. प्रगृह्याश्च प्रकृत्या (च.आ. ३.२.१०)।** स्वरे इत्यनुवृत्तिः । प्रगृह्याः प्रगृह्यसंज्ञिका ये वर्णास्ते याथातथ्येनैवावतिष्ठन्ति । सन्धिं न यान्ति । चकारात् प्लुता अपि प्रथमं प्रगृह्यसन्धिं ततः प्लुतसन्धिमिति वक्ष्यामः क्रमेण । **१५२. उकारस्येतावपृक्तस्य (च.आ. १.३.१०)।** अपृक्तस्य परेणासंपृक्तस्य एकस्यैव उकारस्य स्थाने इतिपदे परे प्रागनुवृत्तेरनुनास्यम् । **१५३. दीर्घः प्रगृह्यश्च (च.आ. १.३.११)।** दैर्घ्यं प्रगृह्यत्वञ्चेति ज्ञेयम् । ऊँ इति पदम् । ऊँ । क्वचित्प्रकृत्या । तम्वभि । इद्ध्वधि । इद्विन्द्रः इति ।

Vyākaraṇa (54, p. 10) offer the example *śiva+ā+ihi* > *śivehi*. Perhaps, as a devout Vaiṣṇava, Kr̥ṣṇadāsa changed it to *rāmehi*.

[140]The examples *hare 'va* and *viṣṇo 'va* are found in the Prakriyākaumudī and the SK on P.6.1.109 (एङः पदान्तादति).

[141]Compare P.6.1.122 (सर्वत्र विभाषा गोः). The example *go 'gram* is found in the SK on P.6.1.122 (p. 22): लोके वेदे चैङन्तस्य गोरति वा प्रकृतिभावः स्यात् पदान्ते । गोअग्रम् । गोऽग्रम् ।

[142]It is not clear whether Kr̥ṣṇadāsa's rule प्रकृत्या वा was meant to cover the additional example *te atra*. The example *te+atra* changing to *te 'tra* is offered by the Sārasvata-Vyākaraṇa (51, p. 9). The example *te atra* as an example of *prakr̥tibhāva* could possibly come under प्रकृत्या वा to make up the syllables of a metrical line in Vedic, cf. P.6.1.115 (प्रकृत्यान्तःपादमव्यपरे). The other possiblity is that the example *te atra* is misplaced here and actually is supposed to go with PS 151 below as an example of an uncombinable dual form (*pragr̥hya*).

१५४. **ईकारोकारौ च सप्तम्यर्थे (च.आ. १.३.१२)।** ईकारश्च ऊकारश्च प्रगृह्यौ सप्तम्यर्थे स्यातां चेत् । सप्तम्यर्थे किम् । १५५. **अधियोगे सप्तम्यर्थे द्वितीया**[143] (not found in CA)। सोमो गौरीम् अधि श्रितः । विभक्तिलोपे 'गौरी अधिं श्रितः' (ऋग्वेद ९.१२.३) इति । प्रतियोगे[144] 'मामकी तनू' (पैप्पलादसंहिता ६.६.८) आविशेति । मामक्यां तन्वामित्यर्थः । वाप्यामश्व इत्यर्थान्तरे मा भूदिति[145] । १५६. **द्विवचनान्तौ (च.आ. १.३.१३)।** औ इति विभक्तिनिर्दिष्टावीऊकारौ च । उ[दाहरणम्] हरी एतौ । विष्णू इमौ । १५७. **एकारान्तश्च (च.आ. १.३.१४, पाठान्तरम्)।** तथैव द्विवचनविभक्तिनिर्दिष्ट एकारः सन्धिं नैति । पचेते इमौ । उदा° 'ते आचरंन्ती' इति मन्त्रे (ऋग्वेद ६.७५.४)। 'घृतवंती भुवंनानाम्' (ऋग्वेद ६.७०.१) इति च (?)। माले एते । १५८. **अस्मे युष्मे त्वे मे इति चोदात्तः (च.आ. १.३.१५)।** १५९. **अमी बहुवचनम् (च.आ. १.३.१६)।** अमी ईशाः । अमी अश्वाः । अमू आसाते । १६०. **निपातोऽपृक्तोऽनाकारः (च.आ. १.३.१७)।** अ अपेहि । विस्मये इ इन्द्रं पश्य । उ उमेश उ उत्तिष्ठ । आ एवम् आः । आ उष्णम् ओष्णम् । आङ् ङिदन्तो न प्रगृह्यः । १६१. **ओकारान्तश्च (च.आ. १.३.१८)।** नो अह । अहो आश्चर्यम् । अथो एवम् । १६२. **आमन्त्रितं चैतावनार्षे (च.आ. १.३.१९)।** आर्षो

---

[143]This formulation offers perhaps the best explanation why CA (1.3.12) uses the expression *saptamyarthe*, rather than considering forms like *gaurī* below as irregular locatives. There was apparently a tradition of viewing these as being non-locative forms with locative meaning. For additional discussion, see notes on CA (1.3.12). Bhaṭṭoji has a different view of these examples, cf. SK on P.1.1.19 (p. 26): 'सुपां सुलुक्' इति सप्तम्या लुक्.

[144]The expression *pratiyoge* is parallel to *adhiyoge* in PS 155. However, the example cited, i.e. मामकी तनू, is not an example of *prati*, but of *adhi*. The full citations from Paippalāda (6.6.8) reads: अध्यस्यां मामकी तनू. The word *āviśeti* in Kṛṣṇadāsa's commentary makes one wonder if he thought of the citation as मामकी तनू आविश. However, I have not been able to trace such a passage.

[145]Both the examples and the counter-example are found in the KV and the SK on P.1.1.19.

वैदिकः तं विना इतौ इतिपदे परे आमन्त्रितं सम्बोधनम् । चकाराद्विकल्पः । आर्षः प्रगृह्यः अन्यो न । विष्णो इति । विष्ण इति । विष्णविति । 'वायवा याहि' (ऋग्वेद १.२.१) । 'अध्वर्यवा तु' (ऋग्वेद ८.३२.२४) । 'इन्दविन्द्रः' (ऋग्वेद ९.६.२) । 'ब्रह्मबन्धविति' (काण्व शु.य.सं. १०.६)[146] अनार्षः । **१६३. आर्त्नी इवादिष्विवादितिपरः (च.आ. १.३.२०)।** आर्त्नी इवादिषु द्विवचनान्तेषु इवात् इवपदात् इतिशब्दः परः बलीयान् । 'आर्त्नी इव ज्यया' (अ.वे. १.१.३) । 'आर्त्नी इमे' (अ.वे.पै.सं. १५.१०.४) । प्र(म?)णीव[147] । 'रोदसीमे'[148] । 'दम्पतीव' (ऋग्वेद २.३९.२) । 'उपधीवं प्रधीवं' (ऋग्वेद २.३९.४) । एते प्रयोगाः क्वचित्प्रकृत्या क्वचित्सन्धिः । **१६४. अनुनासिकोऽन्तःपदे ह्रस्वः (च.आ. १.३.२१)।** पदाभ्यन्तरे योऽनुनासिकः स्वरः स ह्रस्वो भवति । **१६५. सन्धौ पदान्ते च** (not found in CA)**।** दधि । मधुलिट् । अन्तर्वर्तिनीं विभक्तिमाश्रितः । दधिशेषः । चक्रि अत्र चक्र्यत्र । **१६६. न समासे** (not found in CA)**।** वाप्यश्वः । **१६७. ऋवर्णे वा** (not found in CA)**।** ब्रह्मर्षिः । सप्त ऋषयः । इति प्रगृह्यप्रकृतिः ।

[प्लुतप्रकरणम्]

अथ प्लुतानि । **१६८. वाक्यस्य टेः प्लुत**[149] (not found in CA) इत्यधिकृत्य **१६९. दूराद्धाने[150] गाने रोदने शङ्काप्रश्ने आशीर्वचने**

---

[146] Also cited in the KV on P.1.1.16. Also see the SK on P.1.1.16 (p. 26).

[147] For *maṇīva*, see the KV on P.1.1.16. Also SK on P.1.1.11 (p. 24).

[148] One would assume that this is a combination of *rodasī+ime*. However, I have not located this sequence in the Saṃhitās. AV (18.1.31) has *rodasī me*, which may have been misunderstood as a combination of *rodasī+ime*. It may also be a corruption for *rodasīva*, which is cited as a deviant example in the KV on P.1.1.11 along with *maṇīva* and *dampatīva*.

[149] Compare P.8.2.82 (वाक्यस्य टेः प्लुत उदात्तः).

[150] Compare P.8.2.84 (दूराद्धूते च).

प्रेरणे यज्ञाङ्गे च (not found in CA)। **१७०. ओमभ्यादाने**[151] (not found in CA)। **१७१. ये३ यजामहे**[152] (not found in CA)। **१७२. याज्यान्तःप्रणवश्च**[153] (not found in CA)। **१७३. ब्रू३हिप्रे३ष्यश्रौ३षड्-वौ३षडा३वहानामादेः**[154] (not found in CA)। **१७४. अग्नी३त्प्रेषणे**[155] (not found in CA)। **१७५. विभाषा पृष्टप्रतिवचने हेः**[156] (not found in CA)। **१७६. निगृह्यानुयोगे च**[157] (not found in CA)। **१७७. आम्रेडितं भर्त्सने**[158] (not found in CA)। **१७८. अङ्गयुक्तं तिङा-काङ्क्षम्**[159] (not found in CA)। **१७९. विचार्यमाणानाम्**[160] (not found in CA)। **१८०. पूर्वं तु भाषायाम्**[161] (not found in CA)। **१८१. प्रतिश्रवणे चोदात्तम्**[162] (not found in CA)। **१८२. अनुदात्तं प्रश्नान्ता-भिपूजितयोः**[163] (not found in CA)। **१८३. चिदुपमार्थे**[164] (not found in CA)। **१८४. उपरिस्विदासी३दिति च**[165] (not found in CA)। **१८५. है३हे३रामेति गुरोः स्वरादनृकाराच्चेति**[166] (not found in CA)। **१८६. अशूद्राधिकारे आशिषि**[167] (not found in CA)। **१८७. पूर्वस्वरं**

---

[151]Compare P.8.2.7 (ओमभ्यादाने).

[152]Compare P.8.2.88 (ये यज्ञकर्मणि). SK on this rule offers ये३ यजामहे as an illustration on this rule.

[153]Compare P.8.2.89 (प्रणवष्टेः) and P.8.2.90 (याज्यान्तः).

[154]Compare P.8.2.91 (ब्रूहिप्रेष्यश्रौषड्वौषडावहानामादेः).

[155]Compare P.8.2.92 (अग्नीत्प्रेषणे परस्य च).

[156]Compare P.8.2.93 (विभाषा पृष्टप्रतिवचने हेः).

[157]Compare P.8.2.94 (निगृह्यानुयोगे च).

[158]Compare P.8.2.95 (आम्रेडितं भर्त्सने).

[159]Compare P.8.2.96 (अङ्गयुक्तं तिङाकाङ्क्षम्).

[160]Compare P.8.2.97 (विचार्यमाणानाम्).

[161]Compare P.8.2.98 (पूर्वं तु भाषायाम्).

[162]Compare P.8.2.99 (प्रतिश्रवणे च)

[163]Compare P.8.2.100 (अनुदात्तं प्रश्नान्ताभिपूजितयोः).

[164]Compare P.8.2.101 (चिदिति चोपमार्थे प्रयुज्यमाने).

[165]Compare P.8.2.102 (उपरिस्विदासीदिति च).

[166]Seems to combine P.8.2.85 (हैहेप्रयोगे हैहयोः) and 8.2.86 (गुरोरनृतोऽनन्त्यस्या-प्येकैकस्य प्राचाम्).

[167]Compare P.8.2.83 (प्रत्यभिवादे चाशूद्रे).

संयोगाभिघातश्च (**च.आ. १.४.१३**)। पूर्वमक्षरं स्वरेण युक्तं तस्य स्वरस्य संयोगः सन्धिः तस्याभिघातो नाम पृथक्करणम् । **१८८. तदेव स्फोटनः** (**च.आ. १.४.१२**)। स्फोटनसंज्ञः । खण्वखा३इ खैमखा३इ । अत्र सामगायने स्वराभिघातः । **१८९. खैमखे** (**च.आ. १.४.१४**) मूलम् । **१९०. मध्ये तदुरीदं भूया३ इदा३ मित्यूर्ध्वोऽनु सृष्टा३ स्तिर्यङ् नु सृष्टाः३ सर्वा दिशः पुरुष आ बभूवाँ३ पराञ्चमोदनं प्राशीः३ प्रत्यञ्चा३ मिति त्वमोदनं प्राशी३ स्त्वामोदना३ इति वशेया३ मवशेति यत्तदासी३ दिदं नु ता३ दिति प्लुतानि** (**च.आ. १.४.१४**)। **१९१. प्रश्ने** (not found in CA)। ऋकारवर्जितात् स्वरा-द्दीर्घात्प्रत्येकं प्लुतो वा दे३वदत्त[168] । देवद३त्त । देवदत्ता३ । **१९२. आशिषि** (not found in CA)। आयुष्मानेधि अमुकशर्म[ा]३न् वर्म[ा]३न् गुप्ता३ । **१९३. अभिपूजिते** (not found in CA)। न त्वा भीरिव विन्दती३ । **१९४. क्वचिदप्लुतवत्**[169] (not found in CA)। अनार्षे इतिपदे परे प्लुतोऽप्लुतवद्भवति । सन्धिं करोति । सुवचन[ा]३ इति । सुव-चनेति । चिनुही३ इति च चिनुहीति । चिनुही३ इदम् । चिनुहीदम् । प्रगृह्याश्रये प्रकृतिभावे प्लुतस्य श्रवणं न स्यात् अग्नी[३] इति[170] । **१९५. किमर्थः परिपाठ एतावत् स्वार्थोऽपि बहुविधास्त्रिविधाः प्लुतयो भवन्ति । स्वरपरा अभिनिष्ठानपरा व्यञ्जनपरास्तासां याः समाना-क्षरपरास्ता एतावत्प्लुतवद्भवन्तीति** (**च.आ. १.४.१४, अंशः**)। इति श्रीमदथर्वकौत्सव्याकरणे प्लुतसन्धिः ।

---

[168]This is the misplaced commentary on PS 185 above. How do we get the *vā* in the commentary here? Compare SK on P.8.2.86 (p. 24): इह प्राचामिति योगो विभज्यते । तेन सर्वः प्लुतो विकल्प्यते ।

[169]Compare P.6.1.129 (अप्लुतवदुपस्थिते).

[170]Compare the SK on P.6.1.129 (p. 24): तथा च प्रगृह्याश्रये प्रकृतिभावे प्लुतस्य श्रवणं न स्यात् अग्नी३ इति ।

[व्यञ्जनसन्धिप्रकरणम्]

अथ व्यञ्जनसन्धिः । १९६. **संहितायाम्** (च.आ. २.१.१) इत्यधिकारः । १९७. **पदान्तानामुत्तमानाम्**[171] (च.आ. २.१.२, अंशः, पाठान्तरम्) । १९८. **तृतीया घोषवत्स्वरेषु** (च.आ. २.१.२, अंशः, पाठान्तरम्) । उत्तमानां वर्गप्रथमाक्षराणां पदान्तानां स्थाने घोषवत्स्वक्षरेषु च स्वरेषु च परेषु तृतीयाः स्ववर्गतृतीया भवन्ति । १९९. **स्पर्शाः प्रथमोत्तमाः** (च.आ. १.१.८) । स्पर्शेषु ये प्रथमाः वर्णास्ते उत्तमा इत्यत्र संज्ञा[172] । २००. **प्रथमान्तानि तृतीयान्तानीति** (च.आ. १.१.१०, अंशः) । यानि प्रथमान्तानि वर्गप्रथमाक्षरान्तानि पदानि संयोगे तृतीयान्तानि भवन्ति । यानि च तृतीयवर्णान्तानि पदान्ते प्रथमान्तानि भवन्ति प्रथमतृतीययोः परस्परं साधर्म्यम्[173] । २०१. **शौनकस्य प्रतिज्ञानं न वृत्तिः** (च.आ. १.१.१०, अंशः) । अत्र संज्ञायां शौनकस्य प्रतिज्ञैव प्रमाणमासीत् न वृत्तिः । अक्षरार्थ इति । इतरथा तु पञ्चमवर्णस्यैवोत्तमत्वं दृश्यते । २०२. **उत्तमा उत्तमेषु** (च.आ. २.१.५) इति सूत्रात् । वाग्यज्ञः वाक् अर्थः वागर्थः वागीशः । दृग्रूपम् । लुग्जातिः । धिग्डाकिनी । दिग्वासः । भुग्लक्ष्यम् । मुग्दलम् । युग्बाहुः । अज्भ्यः ।

---

[171]This is a misreading for पदान्तानामनुत्तमानाम्. The misreading must go back to the text as it was received by Kṛṣṇadāsa. It has led him to come up with an uncommon interpretation of the term *uttama* under PS 198 and 199 below.

[172]The rule actually means to say that among the members of the five stop series, the firsts (*prathama*) and the lasts (*uttama*) in each series can occur at the end of words (*padya*). Kṛṣṇadāsa thinks that the rule says that the first members (*prathama*) of the series are also called *uttama*. This is clearly inaccurate. However, he is forced to launch into this unlikely meaning for the word *uttama,* because of the wrong reading he inherited for his rule PS 197 (= CA 2.1.2). The correct CA reading for this rule is पदान्तानामनुत्तमानाम्, while Kṛṣṇadāsa's received reading is पदान्तानामुत्तमानाम्. On rule PS 201 below, Kṛṣṇadāsa acknowledges that such an interpretation of the term *uttama* is quite uncommon: इतरथा तु पञ्चमवर्णस्यैवोत्तमत्वं दृश्यते ।

[173]For a more accurate interpretation of this rule, see the notes on CA (1.1.10).

षडङ्गम् । तदन्नम् । अब्यन्त्रम् । जलयन्त्रमिति[174] । **२०३. पदान्ते चाघोषाः (च.आ. २.१.३)।** च पुनस्ते एव प्रथमतृतीया वर्णाः पदान्ते अघोषाः प्रथमवर्णा भवन्ति । ऊर्ग् ऊर्क्, अज् अच्, लिड् लिट्, शरद् शरत्, त्रिष्टुब् त्रिष्टुप् । **२०४. अघोषेषु च (च.आ. २.१.४)।** च पुनः अघोषेषु वर्णेषु परेषु सत्सु अघोषा एव स्युः । प्रथमा एव स्युः । दिक्कल्पः । दिक्चक्रम् । न्यक्टङ्कारः । वाक्तति: (K: न्तिः)। असृक्पटः । अच्कृतिः । अच्तन्तुः । अच्परितः । लृट्कार्यम् । लट्चिह्नम् । लिट्पदम् । स्तुप्कथम् । स्तुप्चिन्ता । स्तुप्टङ्कितम् । एवं द्वितीयवर्णेषु । तत्कर्म[175] । तत्खननम् । तत्परः[176] । **२०५. उत्तमा उत्तमेषु (च.आ. २.१.५)।** उत्तमेषु पञ्चमवर्णेषु परेषु सत्सु प्रथमास्तृतीयाश्च उत्तमाः पञ्चमा वा[177] भवन्ति । दिक् नालम् दिग्नालम् । दिङ्नभः । युक् मित्रम् । युग्मित्रम् । युङ्मित्रम् । पृतनाषाट् नरः । पृतनाषाड्नरः । पृतनाषाण्नरः । षण्णरः । षण्मासाः । चित् मयम् । चिद्मयम् । चिन्मयम् । स्तुप् निधिः । स्तुब्निधिः । स्तुम्निधिः । त्रिष्टुम्मतम् । यवादिगणे दकारनिपातनात् ककुद्मान्(K: द्मी)[178] । **२०६. द्वितीयाः शषसेषु**

---

[174]The examples offered here show voicing of voiceless stops before voiced consonants and vowels, e.g. *vāk+yajñaḥ > vāgyajñaḥ*. These can be treated as examples of CA (2.1.2 = PS 197-8) above. The expression *jalayantram* is not an example, but looks like an explanation of the meaning of the example *abyantram.*

[175]This example does not fit the description एवं द्वितीयवर्णेषु.

[176]This example also does not fit the description एवं द्वितीयवर्णेषु.

[177]The original CA rule (2.1.5) is not an optional rule. Kṛṣṇadāsa offers the optional interpretation most probably under the influence of the optional rule in Pāṇini, cf. P.8.4.45 (यरोऽनुनासिकेऽनुनासिको वा). See the notes on CA (2.1. 5).

[178]The *yavādigaṇa* is referred to in P.8.2.9 (मादुपधायाश्च मतोर्वोऽयवादिभ्यः). Kṛṣṇadāsa makes an interesting observation that the word *kakud* is listed in this *gaṇa* with a final *d*, and hence this *d* is preserved in the formation *kakudmān* and not changed to *kakunmān*. One may note that the word *kakud* is listed in the *yavādigaṇa* as listed in the SK (p.728). The argument of Kṛṣṇadāsa is based directly on Bhaṭṭoji's SK on P.8.4.45 (pp. 28-29): कथं

(च.आ. २.१.६)। शषसेषु परेषु वर्गप्रथमास्ते द्वितीयाः स्युः । अर्वाक् शफः । अत्र कस्य खत्वम् । अर्वाख्शफः । कषयोगे क्षः कस्य खत्वात् (?)। प्रत्यक् सिद्धिः अत्रापि खत्वम् । **२०७. तेभ्यः पूर्वचतुर्थो हकारस्य (च.आ. २.१.७)।** तेभ्यो वर्गाक्षरेभ्यः[179] उत्तरस्य हकारस्य स्थाने यद्वर्गाक्षरेण संयोगे तद्वर्गस्यादिमाक्षराच्चतुर्थवर्णस्यादेशः स्यात् । गोधुक् हरिः । गोधुग्घरिः । गोधुघ्घरिः[180] । अझ्झीनम् । षड्ढस्तः । मरुद्धानिः । ककुप् हारः । ककुभ्भारः । न्यङ् हासः । न्यङ्घासः । **२०८. टकारात्सकारे तकारेण (च.आ. २.१.८)।** टकारात् परे सकारे स एव सकारः तकारेण सहितो भवति । तकारेण सहयोगे तृतीयेत्यर्थबलात्तकारोत्तरः सकारो ज्ञेयः । 'ङः सि धुट्' (पा. ८.३.२९) इति पाणिनिः । षट् सन्तः । षट्त्सन्तः । पृतनाषाट्(K: ड्)त्सुवीरः । साविट्त्सुवीरेति । **२०९. ङणनेभ्यः कटतैः शषसेषु (च.आ. २.१.९)।** प्रत्येकं वा । ङणनेभ्य उत्तरेषु शषसेषु क्रमेण कटतैः सह प्रत्येकं पृथक् पृथक् वा भवन्ति । ङकारयोगे ककारागम ऊष्मसु । णकारयोगे टकारागमः(K: टकारः) । नकारयोगे तकारागमः । **२१०. ङणनेभ्य ऊष्मसु**

तर्हि 'मदोदग्राः ककुद्मन्त' इति । यवादिगणे दकारनिपातनात्. The exact significance of this comment in the SK is debated by the commentaries on the SK. Nāgeśabhaṭṭa argues that this statement of Bhaṭṭoji is based on the view that the *yavādigaṇa* lists not just the word *kakud*, but the whole expression *kakudmān*, cf. Laghuśabdenduśekhara (p. 356): यवादिगणे ककुद्मानिति प्रकृतिप्रत्ययसमुदायः पठ्यते इति मतेनेदम्. The Prauḍhamanoramā on P.8.4.45 seems to back away from the interpretation offered in the SK and offers another alternative.

179 While the CAB on this rule restricts this rule to non-nasal stops, तेभ्यः पदान्तेभ्यः अनुत्तमेभ्यः, Kṛṣṇadāsa extends it to cover the nasals. Also see the example *nyaṅ+hāsaḥ* > *nyaṅghāsaḥ* below. P.8.4.62 (झयो होऽन्यतरस्याम्) excludes the nasals.

180 Some of these examples as given by the manuscript K seem to be impossible: *godhugh-ghariḥ, ajh-jhīnam, ṣaḍh-ḍhastaḥ*, and *kakubh-bhāraḥ*. The retention of the voiced aspirate stop before a voiced aspirate stop goes against all rules, cf. CA (1.4.3: सोष्मणि पूर्वस्यानूष्मा). For further discussion, see the notes on CA (1.4.3).

प्रथमानां द्वितीया वा[181] (not found in CA)। एभ्य एवोष्मसु शषसहेषु परेषु प्रथमानां कटतानां स्थाने खठथा वा स्युः । 'ङ्णोः कुक्टुक् शरि' (पा.८.३.२८) इति पाणिनिः । 'चयो द्वितीयाः शरि'[182] इति पाणिनीयाः । उ०। प्रत्यङ् शीर्णः प्रत्यङ्क्शीर्णः प्रत्यङ्ख्शीर्णः । प्राङ्ख्शीर्णः । सुगण्षष्ठः । सुगण्ट्शीर्णः । सुगण्ठ्शीर्णः । भवान् शान्तः । भवान्थ्शान्तः । एतैर्वर्णैर्मिश्रैः **२११. शकारस्य छकारः (च.आ. २.१. १७, अंशः)**। ततः **२१२. नकारस्य शकारे ञकारः (च.आ. २.१. १०)**। स्पष्टार्थं तदा भवाञ्छान्त इति सिद्धम् । आङ्क्ख्षष्ठः[183] । सुगण्ट्ठ्षष्ठम् । भवान्त्थ्षष्ठम् । प्रत्यङ्क्ख्सिद्धः । सुगण्ट्ठ्सिद्धः । विद्वान्त्थ्सिद्धः । अर्वाङ्क्ख्हस्तः[184] । अर्वाङ्घस्तः । सुगण्ट्ठ्हस्तः ।

---

[181]The optionality of this statement is derived probably from the fact that this view is historically ascribed to the grammarian Pauṣkarasādi in Kātyāyana's Vārttika cited below.

[182]Cf. चयो द्वितीयाः शरि पौष्करसादेः, Vārttika 3 on P.8.4.48 (नादिन्याक्रोशे पुत्रस्य). This Vārttika is cited in the SK under P.8.3.28 (p. 30).

[183]Many of the forms as cited in the manuscript here are impossible forms, e.g. *ākaṅkkhṣaṣṭhaḥ*. It is perhaps possible that this is a shortform method of referring to a pair of forms such as *ākaṅkṣaṣṭhaḥ* / *ākaṅkhṣaṣṭhaḥ*.

[184]The examples involving the word *hasta* as the second member seem to indicate a certain confusion. The rules given above do not speak of the insertion of *k, ṭ, t* etc. before *h*. CA (2.1.9) explicitly says *śaṣaseṣu*, which is identical in its scope to *śari* in P.8.3.28 (ङ्णोः कुक्टुक् शरि) and in the Vārttika : चयो द्वितीयाः शरि पौष्करसादेः on P.8.4.48. In contrast with this, PS 210 (ङणनेभ्य ऊष्मसु प्रथमानां द्वितीया वा) uses the term *ūṣman* which is inclusive of *h*. Kṛṣṇadāsa makes this clear by rendering the word *ūṣmasu* by *śaṣasaheṣu*. This extension to *h* is not supported by any traditions of grammar or phonetics. Also note that the change of *h* to a voiced aspirate stop is prescribed only before non-nasals. In P.8.4.62 (झयो होऽन्यतरस्याम्), the shortform *jhaY* excludes the nasals. Also CA (2.1.7: तेभ्यः पूर्वचतुर्थो हकारस्य) is interpreted by the CAB in a way that excludes the nasals, i.e. तेभ्यः पदान्तेभ्यः अनुत्तमेभ्यः पूर्वचतुर्थो हकारस्य. On the other hand, Kṛṣṇadāsa on PS 207 (= CA 2.1.7) clearly extends this rule to include the nasals: तेभ्यो वर्गाक्षरेभ्यः (including nasals). He offers the example *nyaṅ+hāsaḥ* > *nyaṅghāsaḥ*. This is also not supported by any other traditions. It looks like an analogical extension.

सुगण्ढ्ढस्तः । बलवान्त्थ्द्धस्तः । **२१३. चवर्गीये घोषवति (च.आ. २.१.११)।** नकारस्य स्थाने चवर्गीये घोषवति परे ञकारः स्यात् । अञ्जनम् । तञ्झयम् । **२१४. टवर्गीये णकारः (च.आ. २.१.१२)।** टवर्गीये घोषवत्यक्षरे परे नकारस्य णकारः स्यात् । खण्डम् । षण्ढः । **२१५. तकारस्य शकारलकारयोः परसस्थानः (च.आ. २.१.१३)।** तकारस्य स्थाने शलयोः परयोः परसस्थानो वर्णो भवति । शे छः । ले लः । त[च]छास्त्रम् । सल्लयः[185] । **२१६. चटवर्गीयाच्च (च.आ. २.१.१४, पाठान्तरम्)।** च परं चटवर्गीये व्यञ्जने परे तकारस्य परसस्थानः । तच्चित्रम् । तच्छत्रम् । तज्जातम् । तज(K: ज्झ)झराः । तट्टङ्कनम् । तड्ठा(K: ठ्ठा)नम् । तड्डामरम् । तड्ढा(K: ड्ढा)कनम् । **२१७. ताभ्यां समानपदे चवर्गीयस्य पूर्वसस्थानः (च.आ. २.१.१५)।** ताभ्यां चटवर्गाभ्यां समानपदे चवर्गीयस्य पूर्वसस्थानः स्यात् । **२१८. षकारान्नानापदेऽपि (च.आ. २.१.१६)।** चवर्गीयस्य पूर्ववदिति । **२१९. तवर्गीयाच्छकारः शकारस्य (च.आ. २.१.१७)।** शरद् शशी । शर[च]छशी । **२२०. लोप उदः स्थास्तम्भोः सकारस्य (च.आ. १.२.१८)।** उदः परयोः स्थास्तम्भोः सकारस्य लोपः स्यात् । उथ्थानम्[186] । उत्थानम् । उत्तम्भनम् । **२२१. पदान्ते व्यञ्जनं द्विः (च.आ. ३.२.१)।** पदान्ते यद् व्यञ्जनं तद् द्विर्भवति ह्रस्वानुनासिकस्वरात्परं[187] चेत् ।

---

[185]Compare the example *tallayaḥ* in SK on P.8.4.60 (तोर्लि), p. 29.

[186]There is no way of deriving such a form either in the CA system, or in the Pāṇinian system. However, a form *ut-th-thānam* is derivable within the Pāṇinian system. P.8.4.61 (उदः स्थास्तम्भोः पूर्वस्य) does not prescribe the deletion of the initial *s* of the roots *sthā* and *stambh*, but the change of *s* to a sound homogeneous with the preceding, i.e. *th*. There is an option of deleting this *th*, but if one chooses not to delete it, then we are told that it must remain a *th*, and cannot be deaspirated, cf. SK on P.8.4.61, (p. 29): अत्राघोषस्य महाप्राणस्य सस्य तादृश एव थकारः । तस्य 'झरो झरि' इति पाक्षिको लोपः । लोपाभावपक्षे तु थकारस्यैव श्रवणं न तु 'खरि च' इति चर्त्वम् । चर्त्वं प्रति थकारस्यासिद्धत्वात् । However, this gives us the form *ut-th-thānam*, and not the form *uth-thānam* as it appears in the manuscript.

[187]The CAB does not have the condition ह्रस्वानुनासिकस्वरात् परं चेत्, and there is

२२२. ङणना ह्रस्वोपधाः स्वरे (च.आ. ३.२.२)। ह्रस्वस्वरः उपधा येषां ते ङणना वर्णाः स्वरे परे द्विर्भवन्ति । प्रत्यङ्ङुदेषि । आगमन्नापः । सुगण्णिह । वृत्रहणौ अत्र पदान्तत्वं न[188] । प्राङास्ते अत्र ह्रस्वोपधत्वं न । **२२३. छकारस्य[189] (च.आ. ३.२.४)।** ह्रस्वोपधाच्छकारस्य द्वित्वम् । ऋच्छति । पप्रच्छ । इच्छा । पुच्छमिति । **२२४. पिप्पल्यादिषु पूर्वात् (च.आ. ३.२.५)।** पिप्पल्यादिषु मतेषु पूर्वात् दीर्घादपीत्यर्थः[190] । आच्छिद्य । म्लेच्छः । लक्ष्मीच्छाया । **२२५. मोऽनुस्वारः[191] (not found in CA)।** पदान्ते मकारव्यञ्जनस्यानुस्वारः स्यात् । रामं । गङ्गां । **२२६. मकारस्य स्पर्शे परसस्थानः (च.आ. २.१.३१)।** पदान्ते मकारस्यानु-

no basis for it either in the CA rules, or in Pāṇini.

[188]Kr̥ṣṇadāsa's commentary on PS 222 does not explicitly use the qualification *padāntāḥ* for *ṅaṇanāḥ* as is used by the CAB on CA (3.2.2). However, it is clear from the counter-example *vr̥trahaṇau* that Kr̥ṣṇadāsa intends such a qualification.

[189]This reading is supported by several manuscripts, while others support the reading छकारश्च.

[190]This interpretation cannot be correct, since it does not apply to the word *pippalī* itself. For further discussion, see the notes on CA (3.2.5). It is clear that Kr̥ṣṇadāsa is looking for a way to get rules parallel to P.6.1.75 (दीर्घात्) and P.6.1.76 (पदान्ताद्वा). However, such a meaning cannot be extracted from PS 224 = CA (3.2.5).

[191]Compare P.8.3.23 (मोऽनुस्वारः). However, there is a difference in the way Kr̥ṣṇadāsa interprets this rule. He takes it as an unconditional rule, while the Pāṇinian commentators say that a word-final *m* changes to an *anusvāra* before a consonant, cf. SK on P.8.3.23 (p. 29): मान्तस्य पदस्यानुस्वारः स्याद्धलि । However, Kr̥ṣṇadāsa may have derived his notion of unconditionality of the word-final *m* from some non-Pāṇinian systems. The Sārasvata-Vyākaraṇa (94: अवसाने वा) prescribes optional *anusvāra* for a prepausal *m*, and it (p. 15) further says: कौमारास्त्ववसानेऽप्यनुस्वारमिच्छन्ति । I do not find a rule like this in the *Bibliotheca Indica* edition of the Kātantra-Vyākaraṇa, though the Kātantrarūpamālāvyākaraṇa of Bhāvasena Traividyadeva has the rule (92, p. 16) विरामे वा. Finally, we should note that the CA does not use the term *anusvāra*, and does not seem to recognize *anusvāra* as a nasal element added after a non-nasal vowel.

स्वाराधिकारस्य स्पर्शे वर्णे परे परवर्णस्य सस्थानः पञ्चम एव भवति । तामूताङ्कालीं । अहञ्च त्वञ्च । कण्ठः । त्वण्डामरः षण्ढः शान्तं तन्तुं तनु (?) । माम्पालय । हुम्फट् । कृष्णम्भोजय । **२२७. स्वरे मकारः**[192] (not found in CA) । स्वरे परेऽनुस्वारस्य मकारः । देवमर्च । कृष्णमिच्छ । गुरुमाश्रय । ऋतमृतम् । **२२८. अन्तःस्थोष्मसु लोपः (च.आ. २.१.३२)** । अन्तःस्थाभिः सहिता ये ऊष्माणस्तेषु परेषु च अन्तःस्थासु परासु चोष्मसु परेषु च पदान्तस्य मकारस्य लोपः स्यात् । सरूपाणामेकशेषादर्थद्वयम् । **२२९. नकारमकारयोर्लोपे पूर्वस्यानुनासिकः (च.आ. १.३.५)** । नकारमकारयोर्द्वयोरपि लोपे पूर्वस्वरस्य स्थानेऽनुनासिकस्वरः स्यात् । किम् ह्यः । मकारलोपे पूर्वस्वरोऽनुनासिकः । **२३०. संयोगादि (च.आ. ३.२.३, अंशः)** इति यकारो द्विः । किँय्ह्यः[193] । किँव्ह्वलयति । किँल्ह्लादयति । किँन्ह्नुते । अन्तस्थासु । सँयन्ता । सँवत्सरः । रामँ (K: मं) रट । कृष्णँ (K: ष्णं) लक्ष्ययेति । उष्णँ (K: ष्णं) शीतं पिब । रिपुँ (K: पुं) षड्वर्गं जहि । शिवँ (K: वं) सन्धत्स्व । दुःखँ (K:

---

[192]There is no such rule either in CA or in Pāṇini. However, compare Sārasvata-vyākaraṇa (101: मः स्वरे).

[193]The forms such as *kĩyhyaḥ* are difficult to justify. Kr̥ṣṇadāsa says that after the deletion of *m* in *kim+hyaḥ*, the vowel preceding the *m* is nasalized, and then the initial consonant of the cluster is doubled yielding *kĩyhyaḥ*. Clearly, the initial consonant of the cluster is *h*, and not *y*. Thus, it seems obvious that Kr̥ṣṇadāsa is misled by the late Indo-Aryan metathesized pronunciation of all old *h*-initial clusters. Thus, Kr̥ṣṇadāsa is implicitly thinking of the forms pronounced as *kĩyyhaḥ, kĩvvhalayati, kĩllhādayati,* and *kĩnnhute*. According to Pāṇini 8.3.26-27 (हे मपरे वा, नपरे नः), the word-final *m* can be retained as *m* before *hm*, and can b e changed to *n* before *hn*. A Vārttika of Kātyāyana on P.8.3.26 reads यवलपरे यवला वा. This is taken to mean that a word-final *m* can be changed to *ỹ*, *ṽ*, and *l̃*, before *hy, hv,* and *hl,* respectively. However, this would provide the forms to be officially viewed as *kiỹhyaḥ, kiṽhvalayati, kil̃hlādayati,* and *kinhute*. Kr̥ṣṇadāsa's error points to the fact as to how the changes occurring in the phonology of Sanskrit under the influence of MIA and NIA languages were beginning to confuse the grammarians. For the causation of these changes, see: Deshpande, (1983).

खं) हन्त्यज । अनुस्वारस्य याजुषा रेफोष्मसु ँ॒ पठन्ते[194] । **२३१. ऊष्मस्वेवान्तःपदे (च.आ. २.१.३३)। २३२. नकारस्य च (च.आ. २.१.३४)।** नकारस्योष्मसु परेषु अन्तःपदे पदाभ्यन्तरे एव लोपो भवति पदान्ते न । चकारान्मकारस्यापि[195] । उ° यशाँ(K: ं)सि । क्रँ(K: क्रं)-स्यते । मँ(K: मं)स्यते । मकारोदाहरणे पुँ(K: पुं)सि इति । **२३३. उभयोर्लकारे लकारोऽनुनासिकः (च.आ. २.१.३५)।** उभयोर्मकारनकारयोः स्थाने लकारे परेऽनुनासिको लकारः स्यात् । उ° कृष्णलँ्लि(K: ष्णंल्लि) खामि । विद्वलँ्ल(K: द्वंल्ल)क्षय । **२३४. न समो राजतौ (च.आ. २.१.३६)।** समः सम् इत्युपसर्गस्य मकारो व्यञ्जनं तस्य राजतौ धातुरूपे परे न लोपो भवति । तदा सम्राट् । सम्राज इति । **२३५. सन्ध्ये च वकारे (च.आ. २.१.३७)।** सन्धिभवो यो वकारस्तस्मिन्परे मकारस्य लोपो न स्यात् । तम्वभि इति । **२३६. वर्गविपर्यये स्फोटनः पूर्वेण चेद्विरामः (च.आ. २.१.३८)।** वर्गविपर्यये सन्धिस्थे वर्णे परे सवर्णः स्फोटनो भवति । सन्ध्यक्षरं स्फोटयेत् । द्विधा कुर्यादिति । चेत्पूर्वेण पदान्तस्तदा । पदानां क्रमपाठे पादान्ते चोप-

---

[194]This is the sound called *nāsikya* or *raṅga* in the various texts. This sound is described as a pure nasal sound, with the complete blockage of the oral track. It involves the same sort of velar closure as involved in *g*, but then without releasing this closure and letting the air pass through the oral track, the air is expelled forcefully through the nasal passage. Neither Pāṇini, nor the CA provide for this sound. However, Kr̥ṣṇadāsa provides for it, probably under the influence of the Sārasvatavyākaraṇa (102, p. 16): ँ॒ **छन्दसि** । अनुस्वारश् छन्दसि ँ॒कारमापद्यते शषसहरेफेषु परतः । चतुस्त्रिँ॒शद्वाजिनः । सामयजूँ॒षि । वयँ॒ सोम । सिँ॒ह्यसि । देवानाँ॒ राजा ।

[195]This is an intriguing comment. In the original CA system, CA (2.1.33) applies to *m*, and CA (2.1.34) applies to *n*. Kr̥ṣṇadāsa seems to assume that both the rules basically apply to *n*, and are extended to *m*, on the basis of the word *ca* in CA 2.1.34. Such an interpretation may have been prompted by the analogy of P.8.4.24 (नश्चापदान्तस्य झलि). The SK on this rule (p. 29) reads: नस्य मस्य चापदान्तस्य झल्यनुस्वारः स्यात् । यशांसि । आक्रंस्यते । Kr̥ṣṇadāsa in fact seems to have borrowed the same examples.

योगोऽस्य[196] । २३७. **पुमो मकारस्य स्पर्शेऽघोषेऽनूष्मपरे विसर्जनीयः (च.आ. २.१.२५, अंशः)**। पुमो मकारस्य स्थाने अघोषेऽनूष्मपरे स्पर्शे परे विसर्जनीयादेशः स्यात् द्वित्वं[197] च । रेफसकारौ विसर्जनीयौ तयोः कस्यादेशः । 'विसर्जनीयस्य सः' (पा. ८.३.३४) इति पाणिनिः । **२३८. समासे सकारः ... (च.आ. २.३.३)** इति सूत्रादत्रापि । पुंस्कोकिलः । पुंश्चकोरः । पुंश्चली । पुंष्टिट्टिभः । पुंस्त्राता । पुंस्पुत्रः । अनूष्मपरे किम् । **२३९. द्वितीयचतुर्थाः सोष्माणः (च.आ. १.१.१२)** इति सूत्रवशात् द्वितीयवर्णवर्जिते इत्यर्थः । तेन पुंक्षीरं पुंख्यानमित्यत्र[198] सकारो न । **२४०. संपर्युपेभ्यः करोतौ च क्वचित्**[199] (not

---

[196]The significance of this comment is not clear. None of the Śikṣās or Prātiśākhyas explain how and why the notion of *sphoṭana* is particularly useful in the Kramapāṭha and at the end of each metrical line (*pādānta*). It is possible that the word *pādānta* here is simply an error for *padānta*.

[197]The reference to *dvitva* or doubling is not immediately explicable. The CA rule (2.1.25) itself has no such context. It seems most probable that Kṛṣṇadāsa is referring to doubling of the kind discussed by Bhaṭṭoji Dīkṣita in the context of the form *saṃskartā*, cf. SK on P. 8.3.34 (p. 31).

[198]The word *puṃkṣīra* is excluded from the scope of PS 237 (= CA 2.1.25) by the condition *anūṣmapare*, since the voiceless stop *k* is followed here by the spirant (*ūṣman*) *ṣ*. The example *puṃkhyānam* is an interesting case. To fit this case in the exclusion *anūṣmapare* in CA (2.1.25), Kṛṣṇadāsa would like to claim that the voiceless aspirate stops also come under the term *ūṣman*, and are therefore excluded. This blurs the distinction between *ūṣman* and *soṣman*, and also fudges the interpretation of *anūṣmapare*. That phrase in its own context refers to 'before a voiceless stop which is not followed by an *ūṣman*.' Thus, it will not apply to the case of *kh* in any case. To exclude the case of *puṃkhyānam*, Bhaṭṭoji Dīkṣita cites an apocryphal Vārttika : *khyāñ-ādeśe na*, cf. SK on P.8.3.6 (p. 32). This Vārttika is not found in the MB or the KV. It probably goes back to the comment ख्याधातौ नेति केचित् in the Prakriyākaumudī on P.8.3.4 (Vol.I., p. 155). Referring to this phrase, Śrīkṛṣṇa remarks in his Prakāśa (ibid, p. 158): केचिदिति । भाष्यकारादन्य इति व्याचक्षते । ... तस्मात्परमताभिप्रायेणैवेदमुक्तं न सिद्धार्थ इत्येवं युक्तमालोचयामः । For further discussion on these examples, see the notes on CA (2.1.25).

[199]Compare P.6.1.137 (सम्परिभ्यां करोतौ भूषणे) and P.6.1.39 (उपात्प्रतियत्नवैकृतवाक्याध्याहारेषु च). By omitting the semantic condition, Kṛṣṇadāsa creates an

found in CA)। सम् । परि । उप । एभ्य उपसर्गेभ्यः करोतौ करोतौ परे आदेशादि पूर्ववत् । सँस्कारः । संस्कृतम् । अभावे संकरश्च[200] । **२४१. नाम्युपधस्य सस्य षकारः** (not found in CA)। परिष्कारः । अभावे परिकरः । उपस्करम् । उपकारः । इति । **२४२. नकारस्य चटतवर्गेषु (च.आ. २.१.२६)। २४३. अघोषेषु** (not found in CA)। नकार-व्यञ्जनस्य स्थानेऽघोषेषु चटतवर्गेषु परेषु सः स्यात् । परस्य स्थान एव । **२४४. नकारस्य च (च.आ. २.१.३४)** इति सूत्रात्[201] । भगवाँश्चरति । विप्राँश्छन्दयते । भवाँष्टीकते । भवाँष्ठीवते । भवाँस्तरति । देवाँस्थगयति । शार्ङ्गिँश्छिन्धि । चक्रिँस्त्रायस्व[202] । **२४५. नान्तःपदे सन्ध्ये तकारे च** (not found in CA)। पदमध्ये सकारो न स्यात् सन्धिस्थे संयुक्ते तकारे च । हन्ति । सन्त्सरुः । सन्त्स्तौतीति[203] । **२४६. उः पाकारे उपध्मा वा**[204] (not found in CA)। **२४७. स्वतवसः पाया-**

---

optional rule. There are good grounds for doing it. For example, note Bhaṭṭoji Dīkṣita's comment in his SK on P.6.1.138 (p. 414): संपूर्वस्य क्वचिद-भूषणेऽपि सुट् । 'संस्कृतं भक्षाः' इति ज्ञापकात् । Another point to note is that the KV reading for P.6.1.137 is सम्परिभ्यां करोतौ भूषणे, and could be a probable source for Kṛṣṇadāsa's reading. The KV also notes: संपूर्वस्य क्वचिदभूषणेऽपि सुडिष्यते संस्कृतमन्नमिति । The word *kvacit* is used by both the KV and the SK.

[200]Kṛṣṇadāsa seems to derive the word *saṃkara* from *sam+karoti*, and accounts for it by saying that there is absence of the insertion of *s* because of the provision of *kvacit*. Other grammarians preferred to derive this word from *sam+kirati* and derived words like *saṃkṛti* on another basis, cf. Cāndravyākaraṇa (on rule 5.1.136, Vol.II., p. 155): संकृतिरिति गर्गादिपाठात् सिद्धम् । सङ्कारः सङ्कर इति किरतेर्घञपौ बहुलाधिकारात् ।

[201]The CAB on CA (2.1.34) interprets it in such a way that it applies only word-internally (अन्तःपदे). If that interpretation is valid, then the rule will not apply to the cases of external sandhi cited by Kṛṣṇadāsa.

[202]The two final examples are probably taken from the SK on P.8.3.7 (p. 32)

[203]The two initial examples are probably taken from the SK on P.8.3.7 (p. 32): **नश्छव्यप्रशान् । ८.३.७ ।** अम्परे छवि नकारान्तस्य पदस्य रुः स्यात् । ...पदस्य किम् । हन्ति । अम्परे किम् । सन्त्सरुः ।

[204]Compare P.8.3.10 (नॄन्पे). The *upadhmānīya* is derived in the Pāṇinian system by the generic rule P.5.3.37 (कुप्वोः ᳲक ᳲपौ च). However, note that

देव[205] (not found in CA)। नकारान्तादृकारात् पाकारे परे उपध्मा वा स्यात् । नॄँ꠶पात्रम् । नॄँ꠶पाहि । स्वतवच्छब्दात् पायौ उपध्मा वा स्यात् । 'स्वतवाँ꠶पायुः' (ऋग्वेद ४.२.६) इति । **२४८. नाम्युपधस्य रेफः (च.आ. २.१.२९ अंशः)**। नाम्युपधस्य पदान्तनकारस्य स्वरे परे रेफः स्यात्[206] । 'ऋतूँरनु' (ऋग्वेद १.१५.५) । हरीँरेति । 'पितृँरुप' (अ.वे. १८.२.४) । 'स त्रीँरेकादशाँ इह' (ऋग्वेद ८.३९.९) । **२४९. ऋतूँरुत्सृजते वशीत्येवमादीनाम् (च.आ. २.१.२९, अंशः)**। **२५०. न समैरयन्तादीनाम् (च.आ. २.१.३०)**। स्पष्टमिदं सूत्रम् । **२५१. आकारोपधस्योपबद्धादीनां स्वरे (च.आ. २.१.२७)**। देवान् एतु इति स्थिते । आकारोपधस्य नकारस्य स्थाने उपबद्धादीनामुपसर्गनिपातधातुसम्बन्धिनां पदानां स्वरे परे विसर्जनीयः स्यात् । देवा एतु । **२५२. विसर्गस्य स्वरे यकारः**[207] (not found in CA)। देवायेतु । **२५३. स्वराद्यवयोः पदान्तयोः (च.आ. २.१.२१)** लोपः । **२५४. यवलोपे (च.आ. ३.२.१२)** प्रकृत्या स्वरस्तिष्ठति । देवा एतु । नकारस्थानीयकारलोपे पूर्वस्यानुनासिकः देवाँ एतु सिद्धम् । 'अग्ने देवाँ इहा वह' (अ.वे. २०.१०१.३)[208]। **२५५. वृक्षाँ वनानीति वकारे (च.आ. २.१.२८)**। इति वकारे नस्याभिनिष्ठानं स्यात् । **२५६. आकारोपध-**

Bhaṭṭoji Dīkṣita juxtaposes these two rules and offers the example *nṝ꠶pāhi*.

[205]Compare P.8.3.11 (स्वतवान्पायौ).

[206]The CAB offers a somewhat different interpretation of rule CA (2.2.3: नाम्युपधस्य रेफः): नाम्युपधस्य विसर्जनीयस्य स्वरे परतः रेफो भवति । This rule is given in Kṛṣṇadāsa's work as PS 268. However, the identical looking rule given here is not CA (2.2.3), but the initial portion of CA (2.1.29) नाम्युपधस्य रेफ ऋतूँत्सृजते वशीत्येवमादीनाम्. As noted under CA (2.1.29), a significant number of manuscripts place a daṇḍa after *rephaḥ* in this rule, suggesting that this is a separate rule. Thus, this may not be a new initiative on the part of Kṛṣṇadāsa.

[207]This is just an expanded version of CA (2.2.2: स्वरे यकारः).

[208]It should be noted that while the CA and the CAB do not betray any familiarity with the 19th and the 20th Kāṇḍa of the ŚAV, Kṛṣṇadāsa's example occurs in the 20th Kāṇḍa. However, it is also found in RV (1.12.3a).

स्याभिनिष्ठानस्य लोपः[209] (not found in CA)। **२५७. घोषवति परे**[210] (not found in CA)। **२५८. सस्थाने लोपेऽनुनासिकः**[211] (not found in CA)। वृक्षाँ विमृश । 'दद्वाँ वा यत्' (ऋग्वेद १०.१३२.३) इति । एषां विसर्गादेशानां विकल्पः सर्वत्र[212] । **२५९. न टवर्गस्य चवर्गे कालविप्रकर्षस्त्वत्र भवति तमाहुः कर्षण इति (च.आ. २.१.३९)**। टवर्गस्य चवर्गे परे कालविप्रकर्षो नाम उच्चारणकाले मात्राधिक्यं न भवति । तं कर्षण इत्याहुः । इति श्रीमदथर्वकौत्सव्याकरणे व्यञ्जनसन्धिः ।

[विसर्गसन्धिप्रकरणम्]

अथ विसर्गसन्धिः । **२६०. विसर्जनीयस्य परसस्थानोऽघोषे (च.आ. २.२.१)**। विसर्जनीयस्योष्मणः श्वासस्य परसस्थानः अघोषे परे सति । कखयोः परयोश्चेत् । शषसहा ऊष्माणः । तेष्वत्र कः । अकुहविसर्जनीयानां कण्ठः । विसर्गो नाम किञ्चित् ईषत् हकारसदृशः श्वासैकदेशः । कण्ठेऽपि जिह्वामूले कवर्गोच्चारात्[213] । जिह्वामूले एवार्धविसर्गरूपः श्वासः प्रयोक्तव्यः[214] आᳵ कᳵ खनतीति[215] । चछयोः परयोः

---

[209]This is just an expansion of CA (2.2.16: आकारोपधस्य लोपः).

[210]This may not be an independent rule, but a part of the explanation of PS 256. Compare घोषवति परतः in the CAB on CA (2.2.16).

[211]This probably refers to PS 229 = CA 1.3.5: नकारमकारयोर्लोपे पूर्वस्यानुनासिकः.

[212]The CA system does not provide such an option. However, Kṛṣṇadāsa is probably referring to the option of having either *vṛkṣān* or *vṛkṣā̃.* before *vimṛśa*. The CA is far more specific. See the notes on CA (2.1.28).

[213]This shows an effort to patch two different points of articulation for *k*, i.e. *kaṇṭha* vs *jihvāmūla*. It looks like Kṛṣṇadāsa feels some concern as to how the *visarga* could change to a *jihvāmūlīya* before a *kaṇṭhya k*.

[214]This refers to the pronunciation of *jihvāmūlīya*. The sounds *upadhmānīya* and *jihvāmūlīya* are referred to as *ardhavisargasadṛśa* in the SK on P.8.2.1 (p. 6): ᳵकᳵपाविति कपाभ्यां प्रागर्धविसर्गसदृशौ जिह्वामूलीयोपध्मानीयौ । Bhaṭṭoji's own commentary Prauḍhamanoramā (p. 50) explains that this halfway similarity between the *visarga* and these two sounds is based both on their pronunciation and writing: सादृश्यमुच्चारणे लेखने च बोध्यम् । The commentary

शकारस्य सस्थानत्वात् कश्चरति । कृष्णश्छत्रं नः । टठयोः षकार ऊष्मण आदेशः धनुषष्टङ्कारः । तथयोः सकारः । कृष्णस्तारकः । पफयोः उपध्मानीयोऽर्धविसर्गः । कृष्णᳵ पातु माम् । बुद्धिᳵ फलम् । शषसेषु विभाषा पाणिनीये[216] । हरिः शेते । हरिश्शेते इति ज्ञेयम्[217] । **२६१. संयुक्ते स्वेन धर्मेण**[218] (not found in CA)। संयुक्ते वर्गे परे विसर्ग ऊष्मधर्मेणैव तिष्ठते । कः त्सरुः । देवः क्षरति । रामः स्थाता । हरिः स्फुरति । अत्र सस्थानत्वं न । कस्कादिषु सकारनिपातनात् कस्कः कौतस्कुतः काँस्कानिति[219] । **२६२. रेफसकारयोर्विसर्गः पदान्ते**[220] (not found in CA)। स्पष्टं सूत्रम् । **२६३. स्वरे यकारः (च.आ. २.२.२)**। विसर्जनीयस्य स्वरे यकारः स्यात् । देवाः आगताः । अत्राभिनिष्टानस्य यकारः । देवायागताः इति । **२६४. यवलोपे (च.आ. ३.२.१२)**। यकारवकारयोर्लोपे स्वरः प्रकृत्या तिष्ठति । देवा आगताः । एवमेव सन्ध्यक्षराणां स्थाने अय् अव् आय् आव् एतेषु प्रत्ययेषु परेषु विधिः उ°[221] ते आगत[ाः?] । अय् तयागत[ाः?] । त आगता वसेति(?)। तस्मै आसनं तस्मायासनम् आय् लो°[222] तस्मा आसनम् । अवावोर्लोपस्तु । उओऔषु । ओष्ठ्यस्वरेषु एव नान्यत्र[223] । उ° 'शतक्रत उत्' (ऋग्वेद

Laghuśabdaratna (ibid.) explains this statement: उच्चारणेति । पादमात्रिकौ इमौ इति भावः । लेखने चेति । अर्धवृत्तद्वयात्मकलिपित्वादिति भावः ।

[215]The example कᳵखनति is found in the SK on P.8.3.36 (p. 33).

[216]This refers to P.8.3.36 (वा शरि).

[217]These examples are probably taken from the SK on P.8.3.36 (p. 33).

[218]Compare P.8.3.35 (शर्परे विसर्जनीयः).

[219]Compare P.8.3.48 (कस्कादिषु च), and the SK (p. 32) on it for the examples. The *kaskādigaṇa* is also referred to in PS 279 below.

[220]This rule seems to combine P.8.2.66 (ससजुषो रुः) and P.8.3.15 (खरवसानयोर्विसर्जनीयः).

[221]Expand to *udāharaṇam.*

[222]Expand to *lopaḥ.*

[223]This practice is specifically mentioned in the RPR (2.31: ओष्ठ्ययोन्योर्भुग्नमनोष्ठ्ये वकारोऽत्रान्तरागमः). However, the RPR rules are structured in a reverse way. The RPR rule (2.25-28) say that *ai* and *au* are changed to *ā* before

१.१०.१)। 'इन्द् ओजिष्ठः' (ऋग्वेद ९.६६.१६)। भानौ औन्नत्यं भाना औन्नत्यम् । अभावोदाहरणे । 'इन्दविन्द्राय' (ऋग्वेद ९.६९.१०)। 'वायवा याहि' (ऋग्वेद १.२.१)। 'इन्दवेषाम्' (ऋग्वेद ९.५२.४) इति । **२६५. नाम्युपधस्य रेफः (च.आ. २.२.३)।** नाम्युपधस्याभिनिष्ठानस्य स्वरे रेफः स्यात् । उ° अग्निरेतु । विष्णुरायातु । दीर्घे तु नदीः चमूः मातॄः श्रीरिति । **२६६. घोषवति च (च.आ. २.२.४)।** नाम्युपधस्य रेफः । **२६७. अकारोपधस्योकारोऽकारे (च.आ. २.२.१४)।** अकारोपधस्य विसर्गस्य उकारो भवति अकारे परे । कृष्णः अर्भः इति पूर्वपरयोरेकादेशाद्विसर्गोपधस्योकारे जाते । एकारौकारान्तात्पदादेरकारस्य पूर्वरूप एकादेशात्कृष्णोऽर्भ इति । **२६८. क्वचित् प्रकृत्या (च.आ. ३.२.३१)।** देवो अत्र गच्छति । मेषे अर्कः । **२६९. आकारोपधस्य लोपः (च.आ. २.२.१६)।** अत्र विसर्गस्य लोपः स्यात् स्वरे परे । विप्रा आयाताः । **२७०. घोषवति च (च.आ. २.२.१४)।** अकारोपधस्य विसर्गस्य उकारो भवति । चकारादाकारोपधस्य लोपो भवति पुनश्चकारादुत्वं घोषान्तस्थाहकारेषु अत्रैवाकारोपधस्य लोपः लोको गच्छति । वीरो जयति देवो ददाति । भक्तो यजति । मनोरथः । चौरो वञ्चयति दुष्टो हसति । देवा यान्ति । भक्ता भजन्ति । चौरा रुदन्ति । धन्या हसन्ति इति । **२७१. एषस्यस व्यञ्जने (च.आ. २.२.१८, पाठान्तरम्)।** व्यञ्जने परे एषः स्यः सः एषां पदानां विसर्गलोपः । 'राजन् स चैष ते पुत्रः स्य बन्धुः स्य पिता तव' (source?)। **२७२. स्वरे यत्वं तल्लोपश्च (not found in CA)।** अकारे उकारः । 'सोऽहमेषोऽर्कतुल्यः स्यां स्योऽग्निवद्रिपुवृन्दधृक्' (source?)। **२७३. नञि व्यञ्जनेऽपि**[224] **(not found in CA)।** नञि समासे व्यञ्जनेऽप्युत्वम् । अनेषो गच्छति । **२७४.**

---

vowels, and *e* and *o* are changed to *a* before vowels. However, before non-labial vowels, there an insertion jof *v* after *a* and *ā* derived from labial sounds. Note that all the cited examples come from the RV, rather than from the AV. Also consider the examples वायं उक्थेभिः (RV 1.2.2), वायविन्द्रंश्च (RV 1.2.5-6), ऋतावृधावृतस्पृशा (RV 1.2.8), and तुविजाता उरुक्षया (RV 1.2.9).

[224]Compare P.6.1.132 (एतत्तदोः सुलोपोऽकोरनञ्समासे हलि).

शषसेषु विसर्गः (not found in CA)। असः शिवः । **२७५. न सस्य दीर्घः** (not found in CA)। सकारस्थानीयविसर्गलोपे पूर्वस्वरस्य दीर्घो न । उदा॰ **२७६. दीर्घायुत्वायादिषु च (च.आ. २.२.२०)। २७७. केवल उकारः स्वरपूर्वः (च.आ. ३.२.१३)।** 'एष उ स्यः' (ऋग्वेद ९.३.१०)। स उ एकाग्निः (?)। स्वरपूर्वः केवल उकारः स्वरूपेणैव तिष्ठते । **२७८. भोभगोअघोसां शषसेषु न विसर्गश्च लोपः**[225] (not found in CA)। **२७९. कस्कादीनां पुमो न**[226] (not found in CA)। अधीहि भोः सावित्रीम् । भोभगोसोर्बृहस्पतेः । वाचस्पतेस्तस्करस्य सकारस्तु निपातजः[227] । अथ सकारनिपाताः । **२८०. दुर उकारो दाशे परस्य मूर्धन्यः (च.आ. २.३.१)।** दुरोऽभिनिष्टानस्थाने उकारः दाशे परे परस्य दस्य डकारादेशः । दु उ डाशः सवर्णे दीर्घः दूडाशः । **२८१. दभधीनाशेषु च**[228] (not found in CA)। दूडभम् । दूढ्यम् । दूणाशम् । **२८२. शुनि तकारः (च.आ. २.३.२)।** दुरो विसर्गस्य तकारः शुनि परे । दुत् शुनः । परसस्थानत्वादुच्छुनः । **२८३. समासे सकारः कपयोरनन्तः सद्यःश्रेयश्छन्दसाम् (च.आ. २.३.३)।** तकारस्य स्थाने कपयोः परयोः अनन्तः पदमध्ये समासे सति सकारादेशः स्यात् । तत् करः तकारस्य सकारादेशे तस्करः । पे परे बृहत्पतिः । बृहस्पतिः । सद्यस्कालः । श्रेयस्कामः । छन्दस्पदम् । **२८४. निर्दुराविर्हविरसमासेऽपि (च.आ. २.३.४)।** एतानि पदानि असमासेऽपि विसर्गस्थाने सत्वं भजन्ते कपयोः परत्र । निष्कृतिः। निष्पत्रम् । दुष्कृतिः । आविष्कारः । हविष्पात्रम् । एषु विकल्पश्च[229] । षकारो नाम्युपधत्वात्[230] । **२८५.**

---

[225]Compare P.8.3.17 (भोभगोअघोअपूर्वस्य योऽशि).

[226]Compare P.8.3.48 (कस्कादिषु च) and P.8.3.6 (पुमः खय्यम्परे). Kṛṣṇadāsa's rule seems to be a combination of these two.

[227]For the forms *taskara* and *bṛhaspati*, see Vārttika : तद्बृहतोः करपत्योश्चोरदेवतयोः सुट् तलोपश्च on P.6.1.157.

[228] Compare the addendum quoted in the CAB on CA (2.3.1). Also compare the Vārttika (दुरो दाशनासदभध्येषु) on P.6.3.109. Also see the notes on CA (2.3.1).

[229]The CA rules do not seem to offer any option. However, I suspect that

सान्तेभ्यः कुप्वोः[231] (not found in CA)। यावत्सकारस्थानीयः विसर्गः अन्ते येषां तेभ्यः पदेभ्यः कवर्गपवर्गयोः सकारः । पयस्पानम् । 'द्विस्त्रिश्चतुरिति कृत्वोऽर्थे' (पा. ८.३.४३) इति पाणिनिः । **२८६. त्रिः** (च.आ. २.३.५)। **२८७. कुरुकरंकरत्कृणोतुकृतिकृधिष्वकर्णयोः** (च.आ. २.३.६)। **२८८. ततस्परौ ब्रह्मपरे** (च.आ. २.३.७)। **२८८. ततस्परि**[232] । **२८९. पञ्चम्याश्चाङ्गेभ्यः पर्यादिवर्जम्** (च.आ. २.३.८)। **२९०. दिवस्पदे** (not found in CA)। **२९१. दिवस्पृष्ठम्** (not found in CA)। **२९२. दिवस्पृथिव्यां सचतिवर्जम्** (च.आ. २.३.९)। **२९३. पृष्ठे च** (च.आ. २.३.१०)। पृथिव्यास्पृष्ठे[233] । **२९४. यः पतौ गवामस्याः परवर्जम्** (च.आ. २.३.११)। गोष्पदे । गोष्पतिः[234] । **२९५. षष्ठ्याश्चाशच्याः** (च.आ. २.३.१२)। **२९६. इडायास्पदे** (च.आ. २.३.१३)। **२९७. पितुः पितरि** (च.आ.

Kr̥ṣṇadāsa's notion that there is an option may have been derived from the Pāṇinian system. P.8.3.45 (नित्यं समासेऽनुत्तरपदस्थस्य) prescribes obligatory cerebralization in compounds, while P.8.3.44 (इसुसोः सामर्थ्ये) is traditionally interpreted in such a way that even when there is no compounding, there can be optional cerebralization, if there is semantic-syntactic connection between the constituents of an expression. See the SK on P.8.3.44 (p. 34): एतयोर्विसर्जनीयस्य षः स्याद्वा कुप्वोः । ... सामर्थ्यमिह व्यपेक्षा ।. It should also be noted that Kr̥ṣṇadāsa has offered only the examples of compounded expressions. The condition असमासेऽपि demands that one offer examples of uncompounded expressions as well. See the notes on CA (2.3.4).

230 This refers to CA (2.4.1: अत्र नाम्युपधस्य षकारः).

231 Compare P.8.3.38 (सोऽपदादौ).

232 The manuscript K smears this segment with yellow color, indicating that this is a rule. It may either be a corrupt repetition of the preceding, or perhaps an example of the preceding rule. See the CAB on CA (2.3.7) for the example *tatas pari*.

233 This cannot be an example of CA (2.3.10), unless it is taken out of its original context. See the CAB on CA (2.3.10).

234 The rule PS 294 (= CA 2.3.11) has something to do with the expression *yas patiḥ*, and nothing to do with the forms *goṣpade* and *goṣpatiḥ*. Kr̥ṣṇadāsa has evidently misunderstood the rule. See the notes on CA (2.3.11).

२.३.१४)। 'पितुष्पिता' (अ.वे. २.१.२) । पितुष्पुत्रः[235] । **२९८. द्यौश्च** (च.आ. २.३.१५)। 'द्यौष्पितः' (अ.वे. ६.४.३) । **२९९. आयुः प्रथमे** (च.आ. २.३.१६)। **३००. प्रे मुषिजीवपरे** (च.आ. २.३.१७)। **३०१. परिधिः पतातौ** (च.आ. २.३.१८)। **३०२. निवतस्पृणातौ** (च.आ. २.३.१९)। **३०३. मनस्पापे** (च.आ. २.३.२०)। **३०४. रायस्पोषादिषु च** (च.आ. २.३.२१)। अथ रेफान्तानि । **३०५. रेफप्रकृति घोषवत्स्वरेषु** (not found in CA)। रेफः प्रकृतिः पदान्तो यस्य तद् घोषवत्सु च स्वरेषु च रेफित्वेनैव तिष्ठते । हरिर्गच्छति । भानुरायातु[236] । अग्निवृत्तिः[237] । धूर्जटिः । धूःपतिः । धूष्पतिः । धूर्पतिः[238] । **३०५. अहरादीनां पत्यादेर्विभाषा**[239] (not found in CA)। अहःपतिः । अहर्पतिः । गीःपतिः । गीष्पतिः । गीर्पतिः । धूःसु । धूर्षु । **३०६. अव्ययानि च** (not found in CA)। **३०७. आवःकरकश्च विवरबिभरसर्वनाम्नः** (च.आ. २.२.५)। **३०८. द्वार्वारिति** (च.आ. २.२.६)। **३०९. अजह्यतेरहाः**[240] (च.आ. २.२.७,

---

[235]This expression cannot be an example of PS 297 (= CA 2.3.14). The *kaskādigaṇa* lists the expression *bhrātuṣputraḥ*. The example *pituḥputraḥ* as an *aluk*-compound, in the sense of पितुरन्तेवासी, is cited under P.6.3.23 (ऋतो विद्यायोनिसम्बन्धेभ्यः) in the KV.

[236]The examples हरिर्गच्छति and भानुरायातु cannot be treated as examples of a *rephaprakṛti* type.

[237]This looks like an unrelated intrusion.

[238]This example is cited in the SK (p. 37) under P.8.2.69 (रोऽसुपि) to illustrate the Vārttika (अहरादीनां पत्यादिषु वा रेफः).

[239]Compare the Vārttika (अहरादीनां पत्यादिषु वा रेफः) cited by the SK on P.8.2.69. It originates in the MB statement अहरादीनां पत्यादिषूपसंख्यानं कर्तव्यम् on P.8.2.70, which is not given as a Vārttika by Kielhorn, but is treated as such by the KV and the SK. The examples *aharpatiḥ* and *gīrpatiḥ* go back to the MB on P.8.2.70, and are found in the later commentaries. The example *dhūḥsu* / *dhūrṣu* is not related to this rule.

[240]This reading for CA (2.2.7) is found in a number of manuscripts, though the example *ajarghāḥ* has nothing to do with this rule. See the notes on CA (2.2.7).

पाठान्तरम्)। अजर्घाः । ३१०. **एकामन्त्रिते रौद्विवचनान्तस्य** (च.आ. २.२.८)। ३११. **अन्तःपुनःप्रातःसनुतःस्वरव्ययानाम्** (च.आ. २.२. ९)। ३१२. **स्वर्षाश्च** (च.आ. २.२.१०)। ३१३. **अहर्नपुंसकम्** (च.आ. २.२.११)। अहन् नपुंसकम् । तत्र प्रथमैकवचने रेफादेशः । अहरहः । अहर्गणः । कुप्वोर्वा रेफः । अहःपतिः । अहर्पतिरिति । ३१४. **न विभक्तिरूपरात्रिरथन्तरेषु** (च.आ. २.२.१२)। एतेषु परेषु अह्नो नकारस्य रेफादेशो न । किञ्च सकारादेशः स्यात् । घोषवति तस्योत्वं च । अहोभ्याम् अहोभिरिति अहोरात्रे । अहोरूपम् अहोरथन्तरम् । ३१५. **ऊधोऽम्नोभुवसाम्** (च.आ. २.२.१३)। ऊधः अम्नः भुवः एषां सान्तानां पदानां क्वचिद्रेफादेशोऽन्ते । 'अम्नरूधरवरित्युभयथा छन्दसि' (पा. ८.२.७०) इति पाणिनिः । ३१६. **भुवोमहसोर्लोके** (not found in CA)। लोके परे भुवोमहसोः सस्य रेफः । भुवर्लोकः । महर्लोकः । ३१७. **उषसो वसूयुबुधयोः** (not found in CA)। उषसो विसर्जनीयस्य सस्य रेफः वसूयुबुधयोः परयोः । 'उषर्वसूयवः' (ऋग्वेद १.४९. ४)। 'उषर्बुध आ वह' (ऋग्वेद १.४४.९)। लोप इत्यनुवृत्त्या ३१८. **रेफस्य रेफे** (च.आ. २.१.१९)। रेफधर्मिणः पदान्तस्य विसर्गस्य रेफे परे लोपः स्यात् । ३१९. **दीर्घः** (च.आ. ३.१.१, अंशः) ३२०. **आदिषु** (च.आ. ३.१.४, अंशः, or ३.१.१६, अंशः) इति अनुवृत्ते ३२१. **रलोपे** (च.आ. ३.१.२०)। रेफलोपे आदिषु समानाक्षरेषु दीर्घः स्यात् । प्रातः रत्नम् इत्यत्र प्रातरिति रेफिविसर्गलोपे पूर्वस्वरस्य दीर्घः । प्राता रत्नम् । हरी राजते । शंभू रमते । स्वसृ रक्षते । कवे राष्ट्रम् । उच्चै रौतीति । ३२२. **एषस व्यञ्जने** (च.आ. २.२.१८)। व्यञ्जनमात्रे वर्णे परे एषसयोर्विसर्गस्य लोपः स्यात् । असंपर्कयोः । स खनति । स चरति । एष छ(ा?)दयते । स्य फणी । स पविः । 'एष उ स्य वृषा रथः' (ऋग्वेद ९.३८.१)। असंपर्कयोः किम् । स्वार्थे कप्रत्ययेन अथ च नञ्समाससम्बन्धरहितयोः[241] । एषको रुद्रः । असः शिव इति । व्यञ्जने

[241]Compare P.6.1.132 (एतत्तदोः सुलोपोऽकोरनञ्समासे हलि), and the examples cited on this rule in the SK (p. 39).

इति किम् । तर्हि नामिषु यत्वम् अनामिनि उत्वम् । एष इन्द्रः । एषोऽर्कः । स एति । सोऽयम् । **३२३. न सस्य दीर्घः** (not found in CA)। सकारस्थानीयविसर्गलोपे पूर्वस्य दीर्घो न । उदाहरणं **३२४. दीर्घायुत्वादिषु च (च.आ. २.२.२०)।** अत्र विसर्गलोपः प्रातिज्ञ एव । न तु सौत्रः विसर्गलोपे न पुनः स्वरैः सन्धिः । दृश्यते च वैदिके पादपूरणे । 'सेमामविड्ढि' (ऋग्वेद २.२४.१)। 'सेदु राजा क्षयति' (ऋग्वेद १.३२.१५)। 'सोऽचि लोपे चेत्पादपूरणम्' (पा. ६.१.१३४) इति पाणिनिः । पादपूरणाभावे । 'स इत् क्षेति' (ऋग्वेद ४.५०.८) इत्युदाहृतिः । आर्षेष्वपि क्वचित् ।

सैष दाशरथी रामः सैष राजा युधिष्ठिरः ।
सैष कर्णो महात्यागी सैष भीमो महाबलः ।। इति ।।
इत्यादिपादपूरणार्थः सन्धिः ।
यदुक्तं लौकिकायेह तद्वेदे बहुलं भवेत् ।
सेमां भूम्याददे सोषामित्यादीनामदुष्टता ।।
क्वचित्प्रवृत्तिः क्वचिदप्रवृत्तिः क्वचिद्विभाषा क्वचिदन्यदेव ।
विधेर्विधानं बहुधा समीक्ष्य चतुर्विधं बाहुलकं वदन्ति ।।
वर्णागमो वर्णविपर्ययश्च द्वौ चापरौ वर्णविकारनाशौ ।
धातोस्तदर्थातिशयेन योगस्तदुच्यते पञ्चविधं निरुक्तम् ।।
वर्णागमो गवेन्द्रादौ सिंहे वर्णविपर्ययः ।
षोडशादौ विकारः स्याद्वर्णनाशः पृषोदरे ।।
वर्णे विकारनाशाभ्यां धातोरतिशयेन यः ।
योगः स उच्यते प्राज्ञैर्मयूरभ्रमरादिषु ।।[242]

---

[242] All these verses, beginning with सैष दाशरथी ... etc. are cited from the Sārasvata-Vyākaraṇa. They occur in the commentary on Sārasvata-Vyākaraṇa (1.118-9, pp. 17-8). I have corrected the text as given in the manuscript K by using the Sārasvata-Vyākaraṇa. Especially, note the corrupt reading सेमा भूम्पाददे which is now corrected to सेमां भूम्याददे. The expression *semām* refers to the irregular sandhi of *saḥ+imām*. The expression *bhūmy-ādade* refers to the irregular sandhi of *bhūmiḥ+ādade*. The expression *soṣām*

यदुक्तमाचार्येण । **३२५. चतुर्णां पदजातानां नामाख्यातोपसर्गनिपातानां सन्ध्यपद्यौ गुणौ प्रातिज्ञम्** (च.आ. १.१.२)। तत्र सन्ध्यो गुणः पञ्चविधो व्याख्यातः । पद्यो द्विविधः । सिद्धः साध्यश्च । तौ प्रसङ्गप्रकरणे[243] व्याचिख्यास्यामः ।

इति श्रीमदथर्वकौत्सव्याकरणे विसर्गसन्धिः पञ्चमः[244] ।

---

refers to the irregular sandhi of *saḥ+uṣām*. All these verses are explained at length in the commentary Candrakīrti on the Sārasvata-Vyākaraṇa, (part I, pp. 42-44).

[243]This is significant in that it indicates that Kṛṣṇadāsa had probably composed further sections of this work. However, I was not able to find any manuscripts of these portions.

[244]After this follows the final segment in red letters added by the copyist: संवत् १९२० । शके १७८५ । कार्तिकमासे शुक्लपक्षे तिथौ पञ्चम्यांया रविवासरे तद्दिणे इदं पुस्तकं तिवाडि इत्युपनाम आत्मारामेन लिखितं । शुभं भवतु । ॐ नमो भगवते वासुदेवाय नमः । श्रीरामचन्द्राय नमः । ग्रंथसंख्या । श्लोकसंख्या । ६०० । पत्रसंख्या ३६ । The manuscript was received by the Vaidika Saṃśodhana Maṇḍala, Pune, from the Gore family of Sangli in southern Maharashtra. However, it appears that the manuscript was copied most probably in Gujarat by a person named Ātmārāma Tivāḍi.

Bibliography & Abbreviations

Abhyankar, K.V. 1974. *Vedapadapāṭhacarcā*, with *Upalekhasūtra. Post Graduate and Research Department Series.* Pune: Bhandarkar Oriental Research Institute.

Abhyankar, K.V. and Shukla J.M. 1977. *A Dictionary of Sanskrit Grammar. Gaekwad's Oriental Series 134.* 1st edn. 1961. 2nd revised edition 1977. Baroda.

Abhyankar, S.R. 1984. "Introduction to the Commentary Prātiśākhya Jyotsnā." In *The Proceedings of the All-India Oriental Conference, 31st Session, University of Rajasthan, Jaipur, October 1982,* pp. 167-177. Pune: Bhandarkar Oriental Research Institute.

Aitareya Āraṇyaka. With parts of the *Śāṃkhāyana-Āraṇyaka.* Edited and translated by Arthur B. Keith. 1909. London: Oxford University Press.

Aitareyabrāhmaṇa (*AB*). *Ānandāśrama Sanskrit Series*, No. 31, Pts. I-II. 1896. Pune: Ānandāśrama.

Aithal, Paramesvara. 1991. *Vedalakṣaṇa: Vedic Ancillary Literature. A Descriptive Bibliography.* Stuttgart: Franz Steiner Verlag.

Akkole, Subhashchandra. 1968. *Prācīn Marāṭhī Jain Sāhitya* (in Marathi). Nagpur: Suvichar Prakashan Mandal.

Allen, W.S. 1953. *Phonetics in Ancient India. London Oriental Series*, Volume I. London: Oxford University Press.

----------. 1962. *Sandhi: The theoretical, phonetic, and historical bases of word-junction in Sanskrit.* The Hague: Mouton.

Amarakośa, by Amarasiṃha, with the commentary of Kṣīrasvāmin. Edited by H.D. Sharma. 1941. Pune: Oriental Book Agency.

Aniṅyam, ed. by V. Venkataram Sharma. 1932. Madras: Univ. of Madras.

Āpastambīyagr̥hyasūtra. Edited by M. Winternitz. Vienna, 1887.

Āpastambaśrautasūtra. Edited by Richard Garbe. *Bibliotheca Indica*, 3 volumes. Calcutta, 1882, 1885, 1892.

Āpiśaliśikṣā. In *Śikṣāsūtrāṇi, Āpiśali-Pāṇini-Candragomi-viracitāni.* Edited by Yudhishthira Mimamsaka. Ajmer, 2024 Saṃvat.

Āpiśaliśikṣā, edited by Raghu Vira. 1934. In *The Journal of Vedic Studies*, Vol.I, No. 2.

APR = *Atharvaprātiśākhya* (edited by Suryakanta).

Apte, V.M. 1940-41. "Non-Ṛgvedic Mantras rubricate in the Āśvalāyana-gṛhya-sūtra: Sources and Interpretation." In *New Indian Antiquary*. Vol. III, Nos. 2-7.

Aṣṭādaśa Upaniṣadaḥ. Edited by V.P. Limaye and R.D. Wadekar. 1958. Pune: Vaidika Saṃśodhana Maṇḍala.

Āśvalāyanagṛhyasūta. Edited by Adolf Friedrich Stenzler. Leipzig, 1864.

Āśvalāyanaśrautasūtra. Edited by Ramanarayana Vidyaratna. *Bibliotheca Indica*. Calcutta, 1874.

Ātharvaṇapariśiṣṭam. See: *Śikṣāsaṃgraha*, pp. 479-480.

Atharvapariśiṣṭāni. Ed. by Ram Kumar Rai. 1976. Banaras: Chowkhamba Orientalia.

Atharvapariśiṣtas. See: Bolling and Negelein (1910).

Atharvaprātiśākhya. (APR) Edited and translated by Surya Kanta, with critical introduction and notes. 1939. Lahore: Mehar Chand Lachhman Das. Reprinted from Delhi in 1968 by Mehar Chand Lachhman Das.

Atharvaprātiśākhya, edited by Vishva Bandhu Vidyarthi Shastri. 1923. Lahore: Punjab University.

Atharvaveda of the Paippalādas. Edited by Raghu Vira. 1979. Delhi: Arsha Sahitya Prachar Trust.

Atharvaveda (*Śaunakīya*), with Sāyaṇa's commentary. Edited by S.P. Pandit. Bombay, 1895-98.

Atharvaveda (*Śaunakīya*), with the *Padapāṭha* and the commentary by Sāyaṇa. Edited by Vishva Bandhu. In five parts. *Vishveshvarananda Indological Series,* Volumes 13-17. 1960-1964.

Atharvavedasaṃhitā (*Śaunakīya*). Edited by R. Roth and W.D. Whitney. 1856. Berlin: Ferd. Dümmler's Verlagsbuchhandlung.

AV = Atharvaveda.

Bare, James. 1980. *Phonetics and Phonology in Pāṇini, The System of Features implicit in the Aṣṭādhyāyī. Natural Language Studies*, No. 21. Ann Arbor: Department of Linguistics, The University of Michigan.

Basu, Subhra. 1978. "The phenomenon of *abhinidhāna* and its scope." In *The Proceedings of the All-India Oriental Conference, 28th Session, Karnataka University, Dharwar, November 1976*, pp. 443-450. Pune: All-India Oriental Conference, Bhandarkar Oriental Research Institute.

Baudhāyanaśrautasūtra. Edited by W. Caland. *Bibliotheca Indica*, No. 163, Vols. I-III. 1904, 1907, and 1913. Calcutta: Asiatic Society.

Bender, Earnest. 1992. *The Sālibhadra-Dhanna-Carita. American Oriental Series*, Vol. 73. New Haven: American Oriental Society.

Bhāradvājaśikṣā. Edited and translated into Latin by Aemilius Sieg. 1891. Berlin.

Bhāradvājaśikṣā, with Nāgeśvara's commentary. Edited by V.R. Ramachandra Dikshitar and P.S. Sundaram Ayyar. *Government Oriental Series*, Class A, No. 6. 1938. Pune: Bhandarkar Oriental Research Institute.

Bhāṣikasūtra, of Kātyāyana, with the commentaries of Mahāsvāmin and Anantabhaṭṭa. Critically edited by Braj Bihari Chaubey. Hoshiarpur: Vishveshvaranand Vishva Bandhu Institute of Sanskrit and Indological Studies, Punjab Univrsity, 1975.

Bloomfield, Maurice. 1899. *The Atharva Veda.* Reprinted by Asian Publication Services in 1978.

----------. 1906. *A Vedic Concordance. Harvard Oriental Series,* Vol. 10. Cambridge: Harvard University Press. Reprinted in Delhi: Motilal Banarsidass, 1964.

Böhtlingk, Otto. 1887. *Pāṇinis Grammatik.* Leipzig: Verlag von H. Haessel.

Bolling, George Melville, and Negelein, Julius von. (1910). *The Pariśiṣṭas of the Atharvaveda.* Vol.I., Part II. Leipzig: Otto Harrassowitz.

Bṛhacchabdenduśekhara, by Nāgeśabhaṭṭa, in three volumes. Edited by Sitaram Sastri. *Sarasvatī Bhavana Granthamālā*, No. 87. Banaras, 1960.

Bṛhaddevatā. Edited and translated by Arthur Anthony Macdonell. *Harvard Oriental Series*, Vols. V and VI, 1904. Reprint edition, Delhi: Motilal Banarsidass, 1965.

Bright, William. 1958. "A Note on Visarga." *Deccan College Bulletin,* XVIII, pp. 271-273.

Bronkhorst, Johannes. 1981. "The orthoepic diaskeuasis of the Ṛgveda and the date of Pāṇini." In *Indo-Iranian Journal,* Vol. 23, pp. 83-95.

----------. 1982. "The Ṛgveda-Prātiśākhya and its Śākhā." In *Studien zur Indologie und Iranistik*, Heft 8/9, pp. 77-95.

----------. 1982a. "Some observations on the Padapāṭha of the Ṛgveda." In *Indo-Iranian Journal*, Vol. 24, pp. 181-89.

----------. 1991. "Pāṇini and the Veda Reconsidered." In *Pāṇinian Studies, Professor S.D. Joshi Felicitation Volume*, pp. 75-121. Edited by Madhav M. Deshpande and Saroja Bhate. Ann Arbor: Center for South and Southeast Asian Studies, University of Michigan.

Burrow, Thomas. 1955. *The Sanskrit Language.* London: Faber and Faber.

CA = *Śaunakīyā Caturādhyāyikā*, as constituted in this edition.

CAB = *Caturādhyāyībhāṣya*, as constituted in this edition.

Cāndravyākaraṇa, by Candragomin, with the *Svopajñavṛtti*, in two volumes. Ed. by K.C. Chatterji. 1953, 1961. Pune: Deccan College.

Cardona, George. 1964. "The Formulation of Pāṇini 7.3.73." In *Journal of the Oriental Institute*, Baroda.

----------. 1969. *Studies in Indian Grammarians I, the Method of Description Reflected in the Śivasūtras. Transactions of the American Philosophical Society, New Series*, Vol. 59, Pt. I. Philadelphia: American Philosophical Society.

----------. 1980. "On the Āpiśaliśikṣā." In *A Corpus of Indian Studies, Essays in Honour of Professor Gaurinath Sastri*. Pp. 245-256. Calcutta: Sanskrit Pustak Bhandar.

----------. 1980-81. "On the Domain of Pāṇini's Metarule 1.3.10: *yathāsaṃkhyam anudeśaḥ samānām*." In *Adyar Library Bulletin, Brahmavidyā, Dr. K. Kunjunni Raja Felicitation Volume*, Vols. 44-45, pp. 394-409.

----------. 1983. "Phonetics and Phonological Rules in Grammars." In *Linguistic Analysis and Some Indian Traditions*, pp. 1-36. *Pandit Shripad Shastri Deodhar Memorial Lectures*. Pune: Bhandarkar Oriental Research Institute.

----------. 1983c. "On the Formulation of Aṣṭādhyāyī 8.3.4: anunāsikāt paro 'nusvāraḥ." In *Surabhi, Professor E.R. Sreekrishna Sarma Felicitation Volume*, pp. 199-205. Madras.

----------. 1986. "Phonology and Phonetics in Ancient Indian Works: The Case of Voiced and Voiceless Elements." In *South Asian Languages, Structure, Convergence and Diaglossia*. Edited by Bh. Krishnamurti, Colin P. Masica and Anjani K. Sinha. Delhi: Motilal Banarsidass.

----------. 1987. "Some Neglected Evidence Concerning the Development of Abhinihita Sandhi." In *Studien zur Indologie und Iranistik, Festschrift Wilhelm Rau*, Vols. 13-14, pp. 59-68.

----------. 1991. "On Pāṇini, Śākalya, Vedic Dialects and Vedic Exegetical Traditions." In *Pāṇinian Studies, Professor S.D. Joshi Felicitation Volume*, pp. 123-134. Edited by Madhav M. Deshpande and Saroja Bhate. Ann Arbor: Center for South and Southeast Asian Studies, The University of Michigan.

----------. 1996. "Āmreḍita compounds?" *Professor Paul Thieme Festschrift, Studien zur Indologie und Iranistik*, Vol. 20, pp. 67-72.

Chandra, Lokesh. 1981. (Ed.) *Sanskrit Texts on Phonetics: A Collection of Śikṣā Texts. Śatapiṭaka Series*, Vol. 282. Delhi: International Academy of Indian Culture.

Chatterji, K.C. 1948, 1964. *Technical Terms and Technique of Sanskrit Grammar*, University of Calcutta, Calcutta, 1948. Revised edition by Gaurinath Shastri, Calcutta, 1964.

Chaubey, B.B. 1976. "Authenticity of the Bhāṣika Sūtra." In *The Proceedings of the All-India Oriental Conference, 27th Session, Kurukṣetra University, Kurukṣetra,* pp. 215-226. 1976. Pune: All-India Oriental Conference, Bhandarkar Oriental Research Institute.

Citrācārya, Jagadīśa. 1969. *Śikṣāśāstram* (in Sanskrit). Bahraich, Uttar Pradesh, India: Bālārka Veda Mandira.

Dantyoṣṭhyavidhi, the fourth *Lakṣaṇa* treatise of the *Atharvaveda*. Edited by Ramagopala Sastri. *Dayananda Mahavidyalaya Sanskrit Series*, No. 4. Lahore, 1921.

Delbrück, Berthold. 1888. *Altindische Syntax, Syntactische Forschungen*. Vol. V. Halle: Verlag der Buchhandlung des Waisenhauses.

Deshpande, Madhav M. 1972. "Pāṇinian Procedure of Taparakaraṇa: A Histoical Investigation." In *Zeitschrift für vergleichende Sprachforschung,* Band 86, Heft 2, Göttingen, pp. 207-254.

----------. 1975. *Critical Studies in Indian Grammarians I: The Theory of Homogeneity [Sāvarṇya]. The Michigan Series in South and Southeast Asian Languages and Linguistics*, No. 2. Ann Arbor: Center for South and Southeast Asian Studies, The University of Michigan.

----------. 1975a. "Phonetics of V in Pāṇini." In *Annals of the Bhandarkar Oriental Research Institute*, vol. 56, pp. 45-65.

----------. 1975b. "Phonetics of Short A in Sanskrit." In *Indo-Iranian Journal* 17, pp. 195-209.

----------. 1976. "On the R̥kprātiśākhya 13.5-6." In *Indian Linguistics* 37, pp. 171-181.

----------. 1976a. "New Material on the Kautsa-Vyākaraṇa." In *Journal of the Oriental Institute*, Vol. XXVI, No. 2, pp. 131-144.

----------. 1978. "Pāṇinian Grammarians on Dialectal Variation." In *Adyar Library Bulletin, Brahmavidyā*, Vol. 42, pp. 61-114.

----------. 1979. "Genesis of R̥gvedic Retroflexion: A Historical and Sociolinguistic Investigation." In *Aryan and Non-Aryan in India. Michigan Papers on South and Southeast Asia*, 14. Ed. by Madhav M. Deshpande and Peter E. Hook. Pp. 235-315. Ann Arbor: Center for South and Southeast Asian Studies, The University of Michigan.

----------. 1979a. *Sociolinguistic Attitudes in India: An Historical Reconstruction. Linguistica Extrania, Studia 5*. Ann Arbor: Karoma Publishers, Inc.

----------. 1980-81. "Announcing a critical edition of the Śaunakīyā Caturadhyāyikā (alias Whitney's Atharvaveda Prātiśākhya)." In *Adyar Library Bulletin, Brahmavidyā,* Vols. 44-45, *Dr. K. Kunjunni Raja Felicitation Volume,* pp. 241-252.

----------. 1981. "Revisiting Pāṇini 7.3.73." In *Indian Linguistics*, Vol. 42, Nos. 1-4, pp. 58-64.

----------. 1982. "Linguistic Presuppositions of Pāṇini 8.3.26-27." In *The Proceedings of the International Seminar on Pāṇini*, pp. 23-42. Pune: Centre of Advanced Study in Sanskrit, University of Poona.

----------. 1983. "Pāṇini as a Frontier Grammarian." In *CLS 19, Papers from the 19nth Regional Meeting,* pp. 110-116. Chicago: Chicago Linguistic Society.

----------. 1985. *Ellipsis and Syntactic Overlapping: Current Issues in Pāṇinian Syntactic Theory. Pandit Shripad Shastri Deodhar Memorial Lectures, Second Series. Post-graduate and Research Department Series No. 24*. Pune: Bhandarkar Oriental Research Institute.

----------. 1992. *The Meaning of Nouns, Semantic Theory in Classical and Medieval India. Nāmārtha-nirṇaya of Kauṇḍabhaṭṭa, translated and annotated. Studies of Classical India 13*. Dordrecht: Kluwer Academic Publishers.

----------. 1993. *Sanskrit and Prakrit: Sociolinguistic Issues. MLBD Series in Linguistics*, Vol. 6. Delhi: Motilal Banarsidass.

----------. 1994. "Grammars and Grammar-Switching in Vedic Recitational Variations." *Brahmavidyā, the Adyar Library Bulletin,* Volume 58, pp. 41-63.

----------. 1994a. "Ancient Indian Phonetics." In *The Encyclopedia of Language and Linguistics, (Volume 6) History of Linguistics*, edited by Ronald E. Asher. Pp. 3053-3058. Oxford: Pergamon Press.

----------. 1994b. "Prācīn Bhāratīya Dhvaniśāstra" (In Marāṭhī). In *Vācaspatyam, Pt. Vaman Shastri Bhagawat Felicitation Volume*. Ed. by Saroja Bhate and Madhav Deshpande. Pp. 57-69. Pune: Vaidika Saṃśodhana Maṇḍaḷa.

----------. 1995. "The Notion of Distinctive Features in Sanskrit Phonetics." In *Śilpasaṃvit : Studies in Jaina Art and Iconography and Allied Subjects in Honour of Dr. U.P. Shah*. pp. 125-134. Edited by R.T. Vyas. Baroda: Oriental Institute.

----------. Forthcoming. "Pāṇini and the Distinctive Features." In *Bulletin of the Deccan College Post-Graduate and Research Institute, Sir William Jones' Bicentenary of Death Commemoration Volume*, 1996 (?), Pune.

----------. Forthcoming. "The AV Prātiśākhyas and the Transmission of the ŚAV." In the *Proceedings of the First International Conference on Vedas*, held in New York in July 1993, International Foundation for Vedic Education, Rahway, New Jersey.

Devasthali, G.V. 1978. "Vedic Section, Presidential Address." In *Proceedings of the All-India Oriental Conference, 28th Session, Karnataka University, Dharwar, November 1976*, pp. 9-18. Pune: All-India Oriental Conference, Bhandarkar Oriental Research Institute.

Emeneau, M.B. 1946. "The Nasal Phonemes of Sanskrit." In *Language*, Vol. XXII, pp. 86-93.

Fry, A.H. 1941. "A phonemic interpretation of visarga." In *Language*, XVII, pp. 194-200.

Ghatage, A.M. 1941. *Introduction to Ardhamāgadhī*. Kolhapur.

Ghosh, Manmohan. 1938. *Pāṇinīya-śikṣā, critically edited in all its five recensions*. With introduction, translation and notes. Calcutta: University of Calcutta.

Gobhilagṛhyasūtra. Edited by Friedrich Knauer. 1884. Leipzig.

Gonda, Jan. 1971. *Old Indian*. (= *Handbuch der Orientalistik*, Zweite Abteilung, *Indien*, Erster Band, *Die Indischen Sprachen*, Erster Abschnitt, *Old Indian*). Leiden: E.J. Brill.

Gopathabrāhmaṇa. Edited by Vijayapal Vidyavaridhi. 1980. Calcutta: Savitri Devi Bagadiya Trust.

Heffner, R-M. S. 1952. *General Phonetics*. Madison: The University of Wisconsin Press.

Hinüber, Oskar v. 1981. "Die Paiśācī und die Entstehung der Sakischen Orthographie." In *Studien zum Jainismus und Buddhismus : Gedankschrift für Ludwig Alsdorf*, edited by Klaus Bruhn and Albrecht Wezler. *Alt- und Neu- Indische Studien* 23. Wiesbaden: Franz Steiner Verlag.

----------. 1989. *Der Beginn der Schrift und frühe Schriftlichkeit in Indien*. Akademie der Wissenschaften und der Literatur, Mainz. *Abhandlungen der Geistes- und Sozialwissenschaftlichen Klasse*, Jahrgang 1989, Nr. 11. Stuttgart: Franz Steiner Verlag Wiesbaden.

Hock, H.H. 1992. "Were r̥ and l̥ Velar in Early Sanskrit." In *Vidyāvratin, Professor A.M. Ghatage Felicitation Volume,* pp. 69-94. Edited by V.N. Jha. Delhi: Sri Satguru Publiations.

Howard, Wayne. 1977. *Sāmavedic Chant.* New Haven and London: Yale University Press.

----------. 1986. *Veda Recitation in Vārāṇasī.* Delhi: Motilal Banarsidass.

Hueckstedt, Robert A. 1995. *Nearness and Respective Correlation: A History of the Interpretation of Aṣṭādhyāyī 6.1.77: iko yaṇ aci.* Wiesbaden: Otto Harrassowitz.

Jha, V.N. 1987. *The Studies in the Padapāṭha and Vedic Philology.* Delhi: Pratibha Prakashan.

Jaiminīyabrāhmaṇa. Edited by Raghu Vira and Lokesh Chandra. Sarasvati Vihar Series. 1954. Nagpur.

Jog, K.P. 1978. "Mādhava on some aspect of the Padapāṭha as a means of R̥gvedic interpretation." In *Proceedings of the All-India Oriental Conference, 28th Session, Karnataka University, Dharwar, November 1976*, pp. 227-231. Pune: All-India Oriental Conference, Bhandarkar Oriental Research Institute.

Joshi, S.D. 1967. *The Sphoṭanirṇaya of Kauṇḍabhaṭṭa.* Edited with introduction, translation, and critical and exegetical notes. Pune: Centre of Advanced Study in Sanskrit, University of Poona.

----------. 1968. *Patañjali's Vyākaraṇa-Mahābhāṣya, Samarthāhnika.* Edited and translated with Explanatory Notes by S.D. Joshi. *Publications of the Centre of Advanced Study in Sanskrit,* Class C, No. 3. Pune: University of Poona.

Kāśikāvr̥tti (KV), by Vāmana-Jayāditya, with the commentary *Nyāsa* by Jinendrabuddhi and *Padamañjarī* by Haradatta. Ed. by Dwarikadas Shastri and Kalika Prasad Shukla. In six volumes. *Prācya Bhāratī Series 2.* 1965-7. Banaras: Tara Publications.

Kātantrarūpamālāvyākaraṇa, by Bhāvasena Traividyadeva. Edited by Jivaram Shastri Rayakawal. 1895. Bombay: Nirnaya Sagara Press.

Kātantravyākaraṇa, by Śarvavarman, with the commentary of Durgasiṃha. Ed. by J. Eggeling. *Bibliotheca Indica.* Calcutta, 1874-8.

Kāṭhakasaṃhitā. Edited by Leopold v. Schroeder. Four volumes. Leipzig, 1900.

Katre, S.L. 1938. "Kautsa-Vyākaraṇa: A Detailed Notice; Recovery of Kautsa's authorship." In *New Indian Antiquary I*, Bombay.

Katre, S.M. 1987. *Aṣṭādhyāyī of Pāṇini.* Austin: University of Texas Press.

Kauhalīśikṣā, edited by Sadhu Ram. In *Journal of Vedic Studies*, Vol. 2, No. 1, April 1935, pp. 1-9.

Kielhorn, Franz. 1876. "Remarks of the Śikṣās." In *The Indian Antiquary*, Vol. 5. Bombay.

Kiparsky, Paul. 1979. *Pāṇini as a Variationist.* Jointly published by the MIT Press, Cambridge, and Universiy of Poona, Pune.

----------. 1982. *Some Theoretical Problems in Pāṇini's Grammar. Professor K.V. Abhyankar Memorial Lectures, Post Graduate and Research Department Series No. 16.* Pune: Bhandarkar Oriental Research Institute.

Kṣīrataraṅgiṇī, by Kṣīrasvāmin, a commentary on Pāṇini's *Dhātupāṭha.* Edited by Yudhishthira Mimamsaka. Saṃvat 2014. Amritsar: Ramlal Kapoor Trust.

KV = Kāśikāvṛtti.

Ladefoged, Peter. 1971. *Preliminaries to Linguistic Phonetics.* Chicago: University of Chicago Press.

----------. 1973. "The Features of the Larynx." In *Journal of Phonetics*, vol.I, pp. 73-83.

Laghuṛktantrasaṃgraha, and *Sāmasaptalakṣaṇa.* Edited by Surya Kanta. Originally published in 1940. Reprinted in 1982 by Meherchand Lachmandas. Delhi.

Laghuśabdenduśekhara, by Nāgeśabhaṭṭa, with six commentaries. Ed. by Guru Prasad Shastri. *Rājasthan Sanskrit College Series* 14. 1936. Banaras.

Laghusiddhāntakaumudī, of Varadarāja. Edited by Ramchandra Bhikudev Gunjikar and Lakshman Vasudev Panshikar. 12th Reprint. 1933. Bombay: Nirnaya Sagara Press.

Lüders, Heinrich. 1894. *Die Vyāsa-Śikṣā, besonders in ihrem Verhältnis zum Taittirīya-Prātiśākhya.* Göttingen.

Macdonell, A.A. 1916. *A Vedic Grammar for Students.* Oxford University Press, reprinted in 1971.

Mahābhāṣya, or *Vyākaraṇa-Mahābhāṣya (MB)*, by Patañjali, with the commentaries *Pradīpa* by Kaiyaṭa and *Uddyota* by Nāgeśabhaṭṭa. In three volumes. 1967. Delhi: Motilal Banarsidass.

Mahābhāṣya, or *Vyākaraṇa-Mahābhāṣya*, by Patañjali. Edited by F. Kielhorn. Revised edition by K.V. Abhyankar. Vol. I, 1962; vol. II, 1965; vol. III, 1972. Pune: Bhandarkar Oriental Research Institute.

Mahulkar, D.D. 1981. *The Prātiśākhya Tradition and Modern Linguistics.* Baroda: M.S. University of Baroda, Department of Linguistics.

Maitrāyaṇīsaṃhitā. Edited by Leopold v. Schröder. Two volumes in four parts. Leipzig, 1881, 1886.

Māṇḍūkīśikṣā. See: *Śikṣāsaṃgraha*, pp. 463-478.

Māṇḍūkīśikṣā, edited by Bhagavaddatta. 1921. *Dayananda Mahavidyalaya Sanskrit Series*, No. 5. Lahore: The Research Department, D.A.V College.

Mantrabrāhmaṇa. Edited by Satyavrat Samasrami. Calcutta, 1947.

Mātrālakṣaṇa. Edited by Wayne Howard. *Kalāmūlaśāstra Series*, No. 1. 1988. Delhi: Indira Gandhi National Centre for the Arts & Motilal Banarsidass.

Mayank, Manjul. 1990. "Pāṇini's acquaintance with the Atharvaveda." In *Pāṇini and the Veda*, pp. 32-45. Edited by Madhav M. Deshpande. Leiden: E.J. Brill.

MB = *Mahābhāṣya*.

Mehendale, M.A. 1963. "Upaniṣadic Etymology." In *Munshi Felicitation Volume*. Bombay: Bharatiya Vidya Bhavan.

Meillet, Antoine. 1913. "La prononciation de *e* en védique." *MSL*, 18, 377.

Mimamsaka, Yudhishthira. 1958. *Vaidika-Svara-Mīmāṃsā*. Amritsar: Ramlal Kapoor Trust.

Mishra, R.C. 1984. "The Extant AV Śākhās and their Area of Circulation." In *The Proceedings of the All-India Oriental Conference, 31st Session, University of Rajasthan, Jaipur, October 1982,* pp. 207-214. Pune: Bhandarkar Oriental Research Institute.

Modak, B.R. 1993. *The Ancillary Literature of the Atharva-Veda : A Study with Special Reference to the Pariśiṣṭas*. New Delhi: Rashtriya Veda Vidya Pratishthan in association with Munshiram Manoharlal.

MS = *Maitrāyaṇīsaṃhitā*.

Mugdhabodhavyākaraṇa, by Bopadeva, with commentaries by Durgādāsa Vidyāvāgīśa and Śrīrāma Tarkavāgīśa. Edited by Jībānanda Vidyasagara. 1902. Calcutta.

Nāradīyaśikṣā, with the commentary of Bhaṭṭa Śobhākara. Edited with Translation and Explanatory Notes in English by Usha R. Bhise. *Research Unit Series No. 8*. 1986. Pune: Bhandarkar Oriental Research Institute.

Nirukta. By Yāska, with the commentary by Durgācārya. Edited by V.K. Rajwade. *Ānandāśrama Sanskrit Series,* Vol. 88, Pts. I-II. Pune, 1921, 1926.

Nirukta, with the commentary of Skanda Maheśvara. Edited by Lakshman Sarup. Originally published in three volumes in 1928, 1931, and

1934. Reprinted in two volumes in 1982 by Meherchand Lachhmandas. Delhi.

NR = *Nirukta*.

Nyāsa on *Kāśikāvṛtti*, see: *Kāśikāvṛtti*.

Oldenberg, Hermann. 1890, 1962. *Ancient India, Its Language and Religions*. Originally published in *Deutsche Randschau*, Berlin, 1890; Indian English Edition, 1962, Calcutta: Punthi Pustak.

----------. 1905, 1973. *Vedic Research*. Originally published in 1905. Translated into English by V.G. Paranjpe. 1973. Pune: Āryasaṃskṛti Prakāśana.

P = *Pāṇinisūtra*.

Pandeya, Ramagya. 1965. *Vyākaraṇadarśanapīṭhikā*. *Sarasvatī Bhavana Adhyanamālā 12*. Banaras: Sampurnananda Sanskrit Vishvavidyalaya.

Pandeya, Vijay Shankar. 1987. *Vaidika Dhvani Vigyāna*. Allahabad: Akshayavat Prakashan.

Pāraskaragṛhyasūtra. With five commentaries. Edited by Mahadev Gangadhar Bakre. 1917. Bombay: The Gujarati Printing Press.

Paribhāṣenduśekhara, by Nāgeśabhaṭṭa, with the commentary *Tattvādarśa* by M. Vāsudeva Shastri Abhyankar. Ed. by K.V. Abhyankar. Revised edition, 1962. Pune: Bhandarkar Oriental Research Institute.

PAV = *Paippalāda Atharvaveda*.

Pertsch, Guilelmus. 1854. *Upalekha: De Kramapāṭha Libellus*. Sanskrit text, edited and translated into Latin, with annotations. Berlin.

Phatak, Madhukar. 1972. *Pāṇinīyaśikṣāyāḥ śikṣāntaraiḥ saha samīkṣā*. Banaras.

Phiṭsūtras, of Śāntanava. Edited with Introduction, Translation, and Critical and Exegetical Notes by G.V. Devasthali. *Publications of the Centre of Advanced Study in Snskrit*, Class C, No. 1. 1967. Pune: University of Poona.

Pike, Kenneth L. 1943. *Phonetics*. 12th Printing in 1969. Ann Arbor: University of Michigan Press.

Pischel, Richard, and Geldner, Karl F. 1892,1897, 1901. *Vedische Studien*. In three parts. Stuttgart: Druck und verlag von W. Kohlhammer.

Prakriyākaumudī, by Rāmacandra, with *Prasāda* commentary by Viṭṭhala. Edited by K.P. Trivedi. *Bombay Sanskrit and Prakrit Series*, LXXVII (Pt. I) and LXXXII (Pt. II), 1925 and 1931. Bombay.

Prakriyākaumudī, with the commentary *Prakāśa* by Śrīkṛṣṇa. Edited by Muralidhara Miśra. *Sarasvatī Bhavana Granthamālā*, Vol. 112. In 3 Parts. Banaras: Sampurnanda Sanskrit Vishvavidyalaya. 1977-1980.

Prātiśākhyapradīpaśikṣā. See: *Śikṣāsaṃgraha*, pp. 210-326.

Prauḍhamanoramā, by Bhaṭṭojī Dīkṣita, with the commentaries *Bṛhacchabdaratna* by Hari Dīkṣita and *Laghuśabdaratna* by Nāgeśabhaṭṭa, upto the *Avyayībhāva* section. Edited by Sitaram Shastri. *Nepal Rajya Hindu Viśvavidyālaya Series* 3. 1964. Banaras.

Rai, Ganga Sagar. 1972. "Śākhās of the AV." In *Purāṇa*, Vol. XIV.

Rastogi, M.L. 1957. "Śaunaka and the *abhinihita* sandhi in the Ṛgveda." In *Indian Linguistics, Bagchi Memorial Volume*, pp. 21-29.

Renou, Louis. 1942. *Terminologie Grammaticale du Sanskrit*. Paris.

Ṛgvarṇakramalakṣaṇa, of Narasiṃhasūri. Edited by V. Krishnamacharya. 1959. Madras: Adyar Library and Research Centre.

Ṛgvedānukramaṇī, of Mādhavabhaṭṭa. Edited by C. Kunhan Raja. *Madras University Sanskrit Series*, No. 2. Madras: University of Madras, 1932.

Ṛgvedaprātiśākhya. (RPR) Edited by Mangal Deva Shastri. Vol. I, Critical text of *RPR*, 1959, Vaidika Svadhyaya Mandira, Banaras; Vol. II, *RPR* with Uvaṭa's commentary, 1931, The Indian Press, Allahabad; Vol. III, *RPR* in English translation, *Punjab Oriental Series*, No 24, 1937, Lahore.

Ṛgvedaprātiśākhya. Edited and translated into German by Max Müller. 1869. Leipzig: F.A. Brockhaus.

Ṛgvedaprātiśākhya. Études sur la Grammaire Védique. With a French translation and notes by M. Reinaud. 1856-1858. *Journal Asiatique*, Serie 5. Vols. VII-XII

Ṛgvedasaṃhitā, with Sāyaṇa's commentary. Edited by N.S. Sonatakke and C.G. Kashikar. Five volumes. 1933-1951. Pune: Vaidika Saṃśodhana Maṇḍaḷ.

Ṛktantra, ascribed to Śākaṭāyana. Ed. by Surya Kanta. 1939. Lahore. Reprinted by Meherchand Lachhmandas, Delhi, 1971.

Ṛṅmantrāṇāṃ Ghanapāṭhaḥ. Edited by V.R. Antarkar. 1984. Bombay: V.R. Antarkar.

Roth, Rudolph. 1846. *Zur Literatur und Geschichte des Weda*. Stutgart: A. Liesching & Comp.

RPR = *Ṛgvedaprātiśākhya*.

RV = *Ṛgveda*.

Śabdakalpadruma, of Raja Radha Kanta Deva. In 5 volumes. Originally published from Calcutta, Śaka 1808. Reprinted as *Chowkhamba Sanskrit Series*, No. 93. 1967. Banaras: The Chowkhamba Sanskrit Series Office.

Śabdakaustubha, by Bhaṭṭojī Dīkṣita. Ed. by Nene and Puntamkar. *Chowkhamba Sanskrit Series* 2, Vol. I, fasc. 1-5. 1933. Banaras.

Ṣaḍviṃśabrāhmaṇa. Edited by H.E. Eelsingh. 1908. Leiden: E.J. Brill.

Śaisirīyaśikṣā, ed. by Tarapada Chowdhury. In*The Journal of Vedic Studies*, Vol. 2, No. 2, August 1935, pp. 1-18.

Śamānalakṣaṇam Upalekhasūtraṃ ca. Edited by K.S. Venkataram Sastri. 1967. Srirangam: Vani Vilas Press.

Śāṃkhāyana Āraṇyaka. See *Aitareya-Āraṇyaka*.

Sārasvatavyākaraṇa, by Anubhūtisvarūpācārya. Ed. by Narayana Rama Acharya. 7th edition. 1952. Bombay: Nirnaya Sagara Press.

Sarasvatīkaṇṭhābharaṇa, by Bhojadeva, with the commentary *Hṛdayahāriṇī* by Nārāyaṇa Daṇḍanātha. Pt. I., *Trivandrum Sanskrit Series* CXVII, 1935. Trivandrum.

Sarma, V. Venkatarama. 1935. *Critical Studies on Kātyāyana's Śuklayajurvedaprātiśākhya*. Madras: University of Madras.

Sārthapiṅgalachandaḥsūtra. Edited and translated into Marathi by Shivaram Shastri Shintre. *Vedāṅgārthacandrikā*, Part 3. 1935. Bombay.

Sarvasammata-Śikṣā. Edited and translated into German by A. Otto Franke. 1886. Göttingen: Dieterichschen Univ.-Buchdrucherei.

Śatapathabrāhmaṇa. Edited by Albrecht Weber. Berlin, 1849. Reprinted in Banaras: *Chowkhamba Sanskrit Series*, vol. 96, 1964.

Śaunakaśikṣā. Edited by K.N.M. Divakara Dvijendra. Tripunithura, 1962.

ŚAV = *Śaunakīya Atharvaveda*.

ŚB = *Śatapathabrāhmaṇa*.

Sharma, K.L. 1974. "Prātiśākhyas and the Padapāṭha (The Problem of Avagraha)." In *Charudeva Shastri Fel. Volume*, pp. 133-148. Delhi.

Shastri, M.D. 1926. *A Comparison of the Contents of the Ṛgveda, Vājasaneyi, Taittirīya and Atharva-Prātiśākhyas. Princess of Wales Sarasvati Bhavana Studies*, Vol. 5. Banaras.

Siddhāntakaumudī (SK), by Bhaṭṭojī Dīkṣita, with the commentary *Tattvabodhinī* by Jñānendra Sarasvatī. Edited by Śivadatta. 1959. Bombay: Venkateshvar Steam Press.

Śikṣāsaṃgraha. edited and annotated by Pandit Yugalkishor Vyas. 1893. *Banaras Sanskrit Series*. Banaras.

Śikṣāsūtrāṇi, Āpiśali-Pāṇini-Candragomi-viracitāni. Edited by Yudhishthira Mimamsaka. Saṃvat 2024. Ajmer: Bharatiya Prachyavidya Pratishthan.

SK = Siddhāntakaumudī.

Stautzebach, Ralf. 1994. *Pāriśikṣā und Sarvasammataśikṣā: Rechtlautlehren der Taittirīya-śākhā.* Stuttgart: Franz Steiner Verlag.

Strunk, Klaus. 1983. *Typische merkmale von Fragesätzen und die altindische Pluti. Philosophisch-Historische Klasse Sitzungsberichte,* Jahrgang 1983, Heft 8. München: Bayerische Akademie der Wissenschaften.

Śulkayajurvedīyakāṇvasaṃhitā. Edited by S.D. Satavlekar. Śaka-Saṃvat 1862. Aundh: Svādhyāya Maṇḍal.

Suryakanta. 1981. *A Practical Vedic Dictionary.* Delhi: Oxford University Press.

Svaramañjarī, of Srīnarasiṃhasūri. Edited by G.V. Devasthali. *Research Unit Series,* No. 6. 1985. Pune: Bhandarkar Oriental Research Series.

Svarasiddhāntacandrika, of Śrīnivāsayajvan. Edited by K.A. Shivaramakrishna Shastri. 1936. Annamalainagar: Annamalai University.

TA = Taittirīya Āraṇyaka.

Taittirīya Āraṇyaka (TA). Ānandāśrama Sanskrit Series, No. 36, Pts. I-II. 1867-69. Pune: Ānandāśrama.

Taittirīyabrāhmaṇa. Edited by Rajendralal Mitra. Three volumes in *Bibliotheca Indica.* Calcutta, 1855-1870.

Taittirīyaprātiśākhya, with the commentary *Tribhāṣyaratna.* Edited and translated by W.D. Whitney. New Haven, 1868.

Taittirīyaprātiśākhya, with the commentaries *Tribhāṣyaratna* and *Vaidikābharaṇa.* Edited by K. Rangacharya and R. Shama Sastri. *Government Oriental Library Series, Bibliotheca Sanskrita,* No. 33. Mysore, 1906.

Taittirīyaprātiśākhya, with the commentary *Padakramasadana* by Māhiṣeya. Edited by V. Venkatarama Sharma. *Madras University Sanskrit Series,* No. 1. 1930. Madras: University of Madras.

Taittirīyasaṃhitā. Edited by Albrecht Weber. Two volumes, *Indische Studien* XI and XII. Leipzig, 1871-1872.

Taittirīyasaṃhitā. Edited by Anant Yajñeśvar Dhupkar. 1957. Aundh: Svādhyāya Maṇḍal.

Taittirīyasaṃhitā, with the commentaries of Bhaṭṭabhāskara and Sāyaṇa. Edited by N.S. Sontakke and T.N. Dharmadhikari. Vol.I, Pts. I-II. 1970, 1972. Pune: Vaidika Saṃśodhana Maṇḍaḷa.

TB = *Taittirīyabrāhmaṇa*.

Thieme, Paul. 1935. *Pāṇini and the Veda*. Globe Press. Allahabad.

----------. 1937. "Pāṇini and the Ṛkprātiśākhya." In *Indian HIstorical Quarterly*, Vol. 13, pp. 329-343.

----------. 1937-38. "On the Identity of the Vārttikakāra." In *Indian Culture*, Vol. IV, No. 2, pp. 189-209.

----------. 1985. "The first verse of the *Triṣaptīyam* (*AV*, *Ś 1.1* ≈ *AV*, *P 1.6*) and the beginnings of Sanskrit linguistics." In *Journal of the American Oriental Society*, Vol. 105, no. 3, pp. 559-565.

TPR = *Taittirīyaprātiśākhya*.

Tripathi, Ramdev. 1977. *Bhāṣāvigyān kī Bhāratīya Paramparā aur Pāṇini*. Patna: Bihar Rashtrabhasha Parishad.

TS = *Taittirīyasaṃhitā*.

Turner, R.L. 1960. *Some Problems of Sound Change in Indo-Aryan. Professor P.D. Gune Memorial Lectures 1*. Pune: University of Poona.

Uhlenbeck, C.C. 1898. *A Manual of Sanskrit Phonetics*. Amsterdam. Reprinted in 1960. Delhi: Munshiram Manoharlal.

Unithiri, N.V.P. 1987. "Padapradīpikā - A newly discovered treatise on the Padapāṭha of the Kṛṣṇayajurveda-Taittirīya-Saṃhitā." In *The Proceedings of the All-India Oriental Conference, 32nd Session, University of Gujarat, Ahmedabad, November 1985*, pp. 197-202. Pune: All-India Oriental Conference, Bhandarkar Oriental Research Institute.

Upalekhasūtra. See K.V. Abhyankar, 1974.

Vadegaonkar, N.D. 1945-1964. Marathi translation of Bhaṭṭojī Dīkṣita's *Prauḍhamanoramā*, with the commentary *Śabdaratna*, in 7 parts. Nagpur.

Vaidikapadānukramakośa. Vols. 1-15a. Edited by Vishva Bandhu. 1942-1965. Hoshiarpur: Vishveshvaranand Vedic Research Institute (= VVRI).

Vājasaneyiprātiśākhya, with commentaries by Uvaṭa and Anantabhaṭṭa. University of Madras Sanskrit Series 5. Madras, 1934.

Vājasaneyisaṃhitā, (*VS*). Edited by Albrecht Weber. 1852. Berlin.

Vājasaneyisaṃhitā (Mādhyandina). Edited by S.D. Satavlekar. Saṃvat 1984. Aundh: Svādhyāya Maṇḍal.

Varma, Siddheshwar. 1929. *The Phonetic Observations of Indian Grammarians*. London 1929. Indian reprint edition, Delhi, 1961.

----------. 1953. *The Etymologies of Yāska. Vishveshvaranand Indological Series - 5.* Hoshiarpur: Vishveshvarananda Vedic Research Institute.

Varma, Virendra Kumar. 1972. *R̥gveda-Prātiśākhya: Ek Pariśīlan. Banaras Hindu University Sanskrit Series*, Vol. VII. Banaras: Banaras Hindu University.

Varṇapaṭala. See: Bolling and Negelein (1910).

Vedavikr̥tilakṣaṇasaṃgraha, a collection of twelve tracts on Vedavikr̥tis and allied topics, edited by K.V. Abhyankar and G.V. Devasthali. 1978. *Research Unit Publications*, No. 5. Pune: Bhandarkar Oriental Research Institute.

Veer, Yajan. 1979. *The Language of the Atharvaveda.* Delhi: Inter-India Publications.

Vishva Bandhu. 1923. See: *Atharva-Prātiśākhya*, edited by Vishva Bandhu Shastri.

----------. 1963. *A Grammatical Word-Index to Atharvaveda* (both recensions). Hoshiarpur: Vishveshvaranand Vedic Research Institute.

von Nooten, B.A. 1973. "The Structure of a Sanskrit Phonetic Treatise." In *Oriental Studies, Acta et Commentationes Universitatis Tartuensis*, Vol. II, No. 2, pp. 408-436. Tartu.

VPR = *Vājasaneyiprātiśākhya.*

VS = *Vājasaneyisaṃhitā.*

Vyāsaśikṣā, ed. by V. Venkataram Sarma. 1929. Madras: University of Madras.

Vyāsaśikṣā, with the commentary *Vedataijasa.* Edited by P.N. Pattabhirama Sastri. 1976. Banaras: Veda Mīmāṃsā Research Centre.

Wackernagel, J. and Debrunner, A. 1896-1954. *Altindische Grammatik*, Vols. I-III. Göttingen: Vandenhoeck und Ruprecht.

Walleser, Max. 1927. "Zur Aussprache von skr. *a*." *Zeitschrift für Indologie und Iranistik*, Band 5. Leipzig.

Weber, Albrecht. 1873. "Über den Padapāṭha der Taittirīya-Saṃhitā." In *Indische Studien,* Vol. 13, pp. 1-128. Leipzig: F.A. Brockhaus.

Whitney, W.D. 1856. "Contributions from the Atharvaveda to the theory of Sanskrit Verbal Accent." In *Journal of the American Oriental Society,* Vol. V, pp. 1-33.

----------. 1862. *Atharvaveda-Prātiśākhya* or *Śaunakīyā Caturādhyāyikā*, ed. and translated with notes. In *Journal of the American Oriental Society,* vol. 7. New Haven: American Oriental Society.

----------. 1871. "On the nature of designation of the accent in Sanskrit." In *Transactions of the American Philological Association for 1869-70*, pp. 20-45.

----------. 1880. "Collation of the Second Mss. of the Atharvaveda Prātiśākhya." In *Journal of the American Oriental Society*. Vol. 10, pp. 156-171.

----------. 1881. *Index Verborum to the Published Text of the Atharva-Veda*. In *Journal of the American Oriental Society*, Vol. XII. New Haven: American Oriental Society.

----------. 1884. "On Lepsius's Standard Alphabet: A Letter of Explanation from Prof. Lepsius with Notes by Whitney." In *Journal of the American Oriental Society*, Vol. 8.

----------. 1889. *Sanskrit Grammar*. 9th issue (1960) of the second edition (1889). Cambridge: Harvard University Press.

----------. 1893. "The Veda in Pāṇini." In *Giornale della Società Asiatica Italiana*, Vol. 7, pp. 243-54.

----------. 1905. *Atharvaveda Saṃhitā, translated, with a critical and exegetical commentary*. Revised and brought nearer to completion and edited by Charles Rockwell Lanman. *Harvard Oriental Series*, Vols. VII and VIII.

Witzel, Michael. 1974 (distributed, Feb. 1975). "On some unknown systems of marking the Vedic accents." *Vishveshvaranand Indological Journal*, XII, pp. 472-502.

----------. 1989. "Tracing the Vedic dialects." In *Dialectes dans les littératures indo-aryennes*. Edited by Colette Caillat. *Publications de l'Institut de Civilasation Indienne*, Fasc. 55, pp. 97-265. Paris: Institut de Civilisation Indienne.

Yājñavalkyaśikṣā, with the commentary *Śikṣāvallī*. Edited by Amarnath Shastri. 1962. Banaras: Dīkṣita Kr̥ṣṇacandra Śarmā.

Yogopaniṣadaḥ. *Adyar Library Series*, Vol. 6. 1920. Madras: Adyar Library.

Alphabetical Index of the Sūtras of the Śaunakīyā Caturādhyāyikā

[including Sūtras in the *PS* not found in the *CA*]

अᳵकᳵपौ जिह्वामूलीयोपध्मानीयौ, PS: 73; not found in CA.

अकारस्याभ्यासस्य बहुलम्, CA: 3.1.13; Whitney: 3.13.

अकारान्तादह्नः, CA: 3.4.3; Whitney: 3.77.

अकारोपधस्योकारोऽकारे, CA: 2.2.14; Whitney: 2.53; PS: 267.

अक्षरस्यैषा विधा न विद्यते यद् द्विस्वरीभावः, CA: 3.3.34; Whitney: p. 174.

अक्षादूहिन्यां वृद्धिः, PS: 145; not found in CA.

अग्नी३त्प्रेषणे, PS: 174; not found in CA.

अग्नेः स्तोमसोमयोः, CA: 2.4.16; Whitney: 2.96.

अघोषेषु, PS: 243; not found in CA.

अघोषेषु च, CA: 2.1.4; Whitney: 2.4; PS: 204.

अङ्गयुक्तं तिङाकाङ्क्षम्, PS: 178; not found in CA.

अजहातेरहाः, CA: 2.2.7; Whitney: 2.46; PS: 309.

अजिनाग्रयोर्विभाषेति नौधात्वोश्चार्धम्, PS: 123; not found in CA.

अच्छारमस्तंहस्तलांगूलं..., CA: 4.1.22; Whitney: p. 262.

अञ्चतिजरत्पर्वसु, CA: 4.2.7; Whitney: 4.53.

अतोऽन्यत्संयुक्तम्, CA: 1.2.9; Whitney: 1.49; PS: 82.

अत्र नाम्युपधस्य षकारः, CA: 2.4.1; Whitney: 2.81.

अथाङ्गिरसः, CA: 1.1.1; Whitney: not found.

अध त्यन्धीः परवर्जम्, CA: 3.1.25; Whitney: 3.25.

अधियोगे सप्तम्यर्थे द्वितीया, PS: 155, not found in CA.

अधिस्पर्शं च, CA: 1.1.11; Whitney: 1.9; PS: 18, 106.

अध्यभिभ्यां स्कन्देः, CA: 2.4.24; Whitney: 2.104.

अनतौ विसंभ्यां प्राणाख्या चेत्, CA: 4.1.61; Whitney: 4.39.

अनर्थककर्मप्रवचनीयान्ययुक्तैर्विग्रहोऽभिवितन्वादिषु, CA: 4.1.25; Whitney: 4.3.

अनाख्यातं कृदन्तम्, PS: 86; not found in CA.

अनिङ्गेन पूर्वेण, CA: 4.1.34; Whitney: 4.12.

अनिश्चये एवे च, PS: 141; not found in CA.

अनुदात्तपूर्वात्संयोगाद्यवान्तात्स्वरितं परमपूर्वं वा जात्यः, CA: 3.3.8; Whitney: 3.57.

अनुदात्तं प्रश्नान्ताभिपूजितयोः, PS: 182; not found in CA.

अनुदात्तेन चोदात्तं सभावो ..., CA: 4.1.10; Whitney: p. 261.

अनुदात्तो गतिः सर्वैः ..., CA: 4.1.18; Whitney: p. 262.

अनुदात्तो गतिर्मध्ये ..., CA: 4.1.11; Whitney: p. 262.

अनुनासिकदीर्घत्वं प्रयोजनम्, CA: 4.4.20; Whitney: 4.119.

अनुनासिकस्य च पूर्वेणैकादेशे, CA: 1.3.7; Whitney: 1.69.

अनुनासिकं च, CA: 1.2.13; Whitney: 1.53; PS: 42.

अनुनासिकः पूर्वश्च शुद्धः, CA: 4.4.22; Whitney: 4.121.

अनुनासिकानां मुखनासिकम्, CA: 1.1.27; Whitney: 1.27; PS: 12.

अनुनासिकोऽन्तःपदे ह्रस्वः, CA: 1.3.23; Whitney: 1.83; PS: 35, 164.

अन्ऌकारः स्वरः पद्यः, CA: 1.1.6; Whitney: 1.4.

अनेकोऽनुदात्तेनापि, CA: 4.1.24; Whitney: 4.2.

अन्तःपदेऽपि पञ्चपद्याम्, CA: 3.3.10; Whitney: 3.59.

अन्तःपुनःप्रातःसनुतःस्वरव्ययानाम्, CA: 2.2.9; Whitney: 2.48; PS: 311.

अन्तस्थापत्तावुदात्तस्यानुदात्ते क्षैप्रः, CA: 3.3.9; Whitney: 3.58.

अन्तस्थोष्मसु लोपः, CA: 2.1.32; Whitney: 2.32; PS: 228.

अन्त्यः स्वरः सोत्तरावयवष्टिः, PS: 69; not found in CA.

अन्यस्मन्व्यञ्जने चतुर्थमष्टमं वा, CA: 1.4.11; Whitney: 1.102; PS: 122.

अन्येनापि पर्वणा, CA: 4.3.5; Whitney: 4.77.

अपसव्याभ्यां च, CA: 2.4.15; Whitney: 2.95.

अभिनिहितः प्राश्लिष्टः ..., CA: 3.3.2; Whitney: p. 154.
अभिनिहितप्राश्लिष्टजात्यक्षैप्राणाम् ..., CA: 3.3.16; Whitney: 3.65.
अभिपूजिते, PS: 193; not found in CA.
अभि स्याम पृतन्यतः, CA: 2.4.27; Whitney: 2.107.
अभ्यासविनतानां च, CA: 4.3.10; Whitney: 4.82.
अभ्यासव्यवायेऽपि स्थः, CA: 2.4.13; Whitney: 2.93.
अभ्यासस्य परोक्षायाम्, CA: 4.3.12; Whitney: 4.84.
अभ्यासाच्च, CA: 2.4.11; Whitney: 2.91.
अमी बहुवचनम्, CA: 1.3.16; Whitney: 1.78; PS: 159.
अरमृवर्णे, CA: 3.2.23; Whitney: 3.46; PS: 133.
अर्धं ह्रस्वस्य पादो दीर्घस्येत्येके, CA: 3.3.32; Whitney: p. 174.
अवग्रहादृकारात्, CA: 3.4.16; Whitney: 3.85.
अवग्रहे च, CA: 3.3.20; Whitney: 3.69.
अवग्रहे च, CA: 3.3.24; Whitney: 3.73.
अवग्रहे सविधः, CA: 3.3.15; Whitney: 3.64.
अवर्णस्येवर्ण एकारः, CA: 3.2.21; Whitney: 3.44; PS: 130.
अवर्णान्तेनैकाक्षरेण प्रतिषिद्धेनाप्रयावादिवर्जम्, CA: 4.2.10; Whitney: 4.56.
अवशा आ बभूवाँ ३ इतीतावेकारोऽप्लुतः, CA: 1.4.6; Whitney: 1.97.
अवसानं विरामोऽन्तश्च, PS: 67; not found in CA.
अविभक्तिकं नाम प्रातिपदिकं च, PS: 84; not found in CA.
अव्ययानाम्, CA: 4.2.25; Whitney: 4.71.
अव्ययानि च, PS: 306; not found in CA.
अशूद्राधिकारे आशिषि, PS: 186; not found in CA.
अष्टपदयोगपक्षपर्णदंष्ट्रचक्रेषु, CA: 3.1.2; Whitney: 3.2.
असंवृताः स्वरा नामिनः, PS: 55; not found in CA.
असिद्धं बहिरङ्गमन्तरङ्गे, PS: 91; not found in CA.
अस्मे युष्मे त्वे मे इति चोदात्तः, CA: 1.3.15; Whitney: 1.77; PS: 158.
अस्वराणि व्यञ्जनानि, CA: 3.3.26; Whitney: p. 174; PS: 53.

अहरादीनां पत्यादेर्विभाषा, PS: 305; not found in CA.

अहर्नपुंसकम्, CA: 2.2.11; Whitney: 2.50; PS: 313.

अहोरात्रे, CA: 4.2.6; Whitney: 4.52.

आकारः केवलः प्रथमं पूर्वेण, CA: 3.2.15; Whitney: 3.38; PS: 127.

आकारोपधस्य लोपः, CA: 2.2.16; Whitney: 2.55; PS: 269.

आकारोपधस्याभिनिष्ठानस्य लोपः, PS: 256; not found in CA.

आकारोपधस्योपबद्धादीनां स्वरे, CA: 2.1.27; Whitney: 2.27; PS: 251.

आकारौकारादि पुनः, CA: 4.4.16; Whitney: 4.115.

आख्यातं यत्क्रियावाचि नाम ..., CA: 4.1.2; Whitney: p. 261.

आद्यन्तानि टवर्गकवर्गव्यञ्जनानि, PS: 90; not found in CA.

आद्युदात्ता दशैतेषामुच्चा ..., CA: 4.1.21; Whitney: p. 262.

आन्तर्येण वृत्तिः, CA: 1.4.4; Whitney: 1.95.

आमन्त्रितं चेतावनार्षे, CA: 1.3.19; Whitney: 1.81; PS: 162.

आम्रेडितं भर्त्सने, PS: 177; not found in CA.

आयुष्प्रथमे, CA: 2.3.16; Whitney: 2.75; PS: 299.

आर्त्नी इवादिष्विवादितिपरः, CA: 1.3.20; Whitney: 1.82; PS: 163.

आवःकरकश्च विवरबिभरसर्वनाम्नः, CA: 2.2.5; Whitney: 2.44; PS: 307.

आशा दिशि, CA: 4.2.26; Whitney: 4.72.

आशिषि, PS: 192; not found in CA.

आशीर्बभूवेति प्लुतस्वरस्य सिद्धत्वात्, CA: 4.1.28; Whitney: 4.6.

आस्थापितं च, CA: 1.2.8; Whitney: 1.48; PS: 81.

इकारयोः प्राश्लिष्टः, CA: 3.3.7; Whitney: 3.56.

इङ्ग्यवच्च, CA: 4.3.22; Whitney: no such rule.

इङ्ग्यानाम्, CA: 4.3.4; Whitney: 4.76.

इच्छायां च यकारादौ, CA: 3.1.18; Whitney: 3.18.

इडायास्पदे, CA: 2.3.13; Whitney: 2.72; PS: 296.

इतो लोपः, PS: 92, 117; not found in CA.

इदमूष्वादिषु त्रिपदत्वात्, CA: 4.3.27; Whitney: 4.98.

इवे च, CA: 4.1.63; Whitney: 4.41.

ईऊए द्विवचने प्रगृह्यम्, PS: 74; not found in CA.

ईकारोकारौ च सप्तम्यर्थे, CA: 1.3.12; Whitney: 1.74; PS: 154.

ईयसश्च, CA: 1.3.27; Whitney: 1.89.

ईषत्स्पृष्टमन्तस्थानाम्, CA: 1.1.30; Whitney: 1.30; PS: 21.

उकारः परिहार्य एव, CA: 4.4.17; Whitney: 4.116.

उकारस्य सर्वत्र, CA: 3.3.11; Whitney: 3.60.

उकारस्येतावपृक्तस्य, CA: 1.3.10; Whitney: 1.72; PS: 152.

उञ इदमूष्वादिषु, CA: 3.1.4; Whitney: 3.4; PS: 320.

उत्तमा अनुनासिकाः, CA: 1.1.13; Whitney: 1.11.

उत्तमा उत्तमेषु, CA: 2.1.5; Whitney: 2.5; PS: 202, 205.

उत्तररूपं शाङ्खमित्रिः, CA: 3.3.30; Whitney: p. 174.

उद हन्तिहरतिस्थास्तम्भिषु, CA: 4.2.16; Whitney: 4.62.

उदात्तस्तु निपातो यः ..., CA: 4.1.8; Whitney: p. 261.

उदात्तादनुदात्तं स्वर्यते, CA: 3.3.18; Whitney: 3.67.

उदात्तानुगतिर्यत्रानुदात्तं .., CA: 4.1.12; Whitney: p. 262.

उपजाते परेण, CA: 4.1.32; Whitney: 4.10.

उपरिष्टाद्बिन्दुरनुस्वारः, PS: 71; not found in CA.

उपरिस्विदासी३दिति च, PS: 184; not found in CA.

उपर्षन्त्यादिषु च, CA: 3.2.24; Whitney: 3.47.

उपसर्ग आख्यातेनोदात्तेन समस्यते, CA: 4.1.23; Whitney: 4.1.

उपसर्गस्य धात्वादावारम्, CA: 3.2.25; Whitney: 3.48; PS: 134.

उपसर्गस्य नामिनो दस्ति, CA: 3.1.11; Whitney: 3.11.

उपसर्गाद्धातोः, CA: 2.4.10; Whitney: 2.90.

उपसर्गाद्धातोर्नानापदेऽपि, CA: 3.4.5; Whitney: 3.79.

उपसर्गेणावकारे, CA: 4.1.59; Whitney: 4.37.

उभयाद् द्युभि, CA: 4.1.43; Whitney: 4.21.

उभयोर्लकारे लकारोऽनुनासिकः, CA: 2.1.35; Whitney: 2.35; PS: 233.

उरु, CA: 3.4.9; Whitney: no such rule.
उवर्ण ओकारः, CA: 3.2.22; Whitney: 3.45; PS: 132.
उषसो वसूयुबुधयोः, PS: 317; not found in CA.
ऊधोऽम्नोभुवसाम्, CA: 2.2.13; Whitney: 2.52; PS: 315.
उः पाकारे उपध्मा वा, PS: 246; not found in CA.
ऊष्मणां विवृतं च, CA: 1.1.31; Whitney: 1.31; PS: 22.
ऊष्मस्वेवान्तःपदे, CA: 2.1.33; Whitney: 2.33; PS: 231.
ऋकारान्तात्सदेः, CA: 2.4.19; Whitney: 2.99.
ऋगर्धर्चपदान्तावग्रहविवृत्तिषु मात्राकालः कालः, CA: 3.3.35; Whitney: p. 174; PS: 37.
ऋणवत्सतरकम्बलवसनदशानामृणे, PS: 135; not found in CA.
ऋतवृधवरीवानेषु, CA: 3.1.24; Whitney: 3.24.
ऋतूँरुत्सृजते वशीत्येवमादीनाम्, PS: 249, part of CA: 2.1.29; Whitney: 2.29.
ऋवर्णरेफषकारेभ्यः समानपदे नो णः, CA: 3.4.1; Whitney: 3.75; PS: 111.
ऋवर्णस्य रेफात्परं यत्, CA: 1.3.9; Whitney: 1.71.
ऋवर्णे वा, PS: 167; not found in CA.
एकमात्रो ह्रस्वः, CA: 1.2.19; Whitney: 1.59; PS: 38.
एकाक्षरा उदात्ता आद्युदात्ता ..., CA: 4.1.20; Whitney: p. 262; PS: 65.
एकादेश उदात्तेनोदात्तः, CA: 3.3.17; Whitney: 3.66.
एकादेशस्वरसन्धिदीर्घविनामाः प्रयोजनम्, CA: 4.4.15; Whitney: 4.114.
एकामन्त्रिते रोद्विवचनान्तस्य, CA: 2.2.8; Whitney: 2.47; PS: 310.
एकारश्च, CA: 1.3.14; Whitney: 1.76; PS: 157.
एकारैकारयोरैकारः, CA: 3.2.27; Whitney: 3.50; PS: 138.
एकारौकारयोर्विवृततमम्, CA: 1.1.34; Whitney: 1.34; PS: 25.
एकारौकारान्तात्पूर्वः पदादेरकारस्य, CA: 3.2.30; Whitney: 3.53; PS: 149
एकारौकारौ पदान्तौ परतोऽकारं सोऽभिनिहितः, CA: 3.3.6; Whitney: 3.55.
एकेऽस्पृष्टम्, CA: 1.1.33; Whitney: 1.33; PS: 24.

एना एहा आदयश्च, CA: 3.2.11; Whitney: 3.34.
एवमिहेति च, CA: 1.1.3; Whitney: 1.2.
एष स व्यञ्जने, CA: 2.2.18; Whitney: 2.57; PS: 271, 322.
ओकारान्तश्च, CA: 1.3.18; Whitney: 1.80; PS: 161.
ओकारौकारयोरौकारः, CA: 3.2.28; Whitney: 3.51; PS: 143.
ओष्योश्च, CA: 3.3.12; Whitney: 3.61.
ओत्वोष्ठयोः समासे वा, PS: 147; not found in CA.
ओमभ्यादाने, PS: 170; not found in CA.
ओमाङोश्च, PS: 148; not found in CA.
ओषधेरपञ्चपद्याम्, CA: 3.1.5; Whitney: 3.5.
ओष्ठ्यानामधरौष्ठ्यम्, CA: 1.1.25; Whitney: 1.25; PS: 10.
ऐकारौकारयोर्विवृततमम्, CA: 1.1.34; Whitney: 1.34.
कण्ठ्यानामधरकण्ठ्यः, CA: 1.1.19; Whitney: 1.19; PS: 3.
कस्कादीनां पुमो न, PS: 279; not found in CA.
काम्याम्रेडितयोः, CA: 4.1.62; Whitney: 4.40.
कारे सत्यसहवर्णोः (?), PS: 95; not found in CA.
कार्ये प्लुतः, PS: 128; not found in CA.
किं सन्धेः स्वरितम्, CA: 3.3.28; Whitney: p. 174.
किमक्षरस्य स्वर्यमाणस्य स्वर्यते, CA: 3.3.31; Whitney: p. 174.
कुरुकरंकरत्कृणोतुकृतिकृधिष्वकर्णयोः, CA: 2.3.6; Whitney: 2.65; PS: 287.
कृत्वे समासो वा नानापददर्शनात्, CA: 4.1.49; Whitney: 4.27.
कृपिरुपिरिषीणामनह्वानाम्, CA: 4.3.14; Whitney: 4.86.
कृपे रेफस्य लकारः, CA: 1.3.2; Whitney: 1.64.
के व्यञ्जनात्, CA: 4.1.47; Whitney: 4.25.
केवल उकारः स्वरपूर्वः, CA: 3.2.13; Whitney: 3.36; PS: 277.
क्रमाध्ययनं संहितापददार्ढ्यार्थम्, CA: 4.4.9; Whitney: 4.108.
क्रमे परेण विगृह्यात्, CA: 4.3.6; Whitney: 4.78.
क्रियायोगे गतिः पूर्वः समासो यावन्तो ..., CA: 4.1.5; Whitney: p.261.

क्वचित्प्रकृत्या, CA: 3.2.31; Whitney: 3.54; PS: 268.

क्वचिदप्लुतवत्, PS: 194; not found in CA.

क्षुभ्नादीनाम्, CA: 3.4.24; Whitney: 3.92.

खण्वखा ३ इ खैमखा ३ इत्याकारा ..., CA: 1.4.5; Whitney: 1.96.

खण्वखा ३ इ खैमखा ३ इ मध्ये तदुरीदं भूया ..., CA: 1.4.14; Whitney: 1.105; PS: 189, 190, 195

गविष्टौ गवेषण इति च, CA: 2.1.23; Whitney: 2.23.

गुर्वन्यत्, CA: 1.2.12; Whitney: 1.52; PS: 41.

गोरगर्धं पूर्णं च स्वहव्ये..., PS: 119; not found in CA.

गोसन्यादीनां च, CA: 2.4.23; Whitney: 2.103.

घोषवति च, CA: 2.2.4; Whitney: 2.43; PS: 266.

घोषवति च, CA: 2.2.14; Whitney: 2.54; PS: 270.

घोषवति परे, PS: 257; not found in CA.

ङणनानां हकारे, CA: 1.2.7; Whitney: 1.47; PS: 80.

ङणना ह्रस्वोपधाः स्वरे, CA: 3.2.2; Whitney: 3.27; PS: 222.

ङणनेभ्य ऊष्मसु प्रथमानां द्वितीया वा, PS: 210; not found in CA.

ङणनेभ्यः कटतैः शषसेषु, CA: 2.1.9; Whitney: 2.9; PS: 209.

चटतवर्गैश्च, CA: 3.4.26; Whitney: 3.94; PS: 113.

चटवर्गयोश्च, CA: 2.1.14; Whitney: 2.14; PS: 216.

चतुर्णां पदजातानां नामाख्यातोपसर्गनिपातानाम् ..., CA: 1.1.2; Whitney: 1.1; PS: 1, 325.

चतूरात्रोऽवग्रह एव, CA: 4.3.8; Whitney: 4.80.

चवर्गीये घोषवति, CA: 2.1.11; Whitney: 2.11; PS: 213.

चिदुपमार्थे, PS: 183; not found in CA.

च्यावयतेः कारितान्तस्य, CA: 4.3.19; Whitney: 4.91.

छकारस्य, CA: 3.2.4; Whitney: no such rule. PS: 223.

जातीयादिषु च, CA: 4.1.50; Whitney: 4.28.

जास्पत्यम्, CA: 4.2.18; Whitney: 4.64.

जिह्वामूलीयानां हनुमूलम्, CA: 1.1.20; Whitney: 1.20; PS: 4.
जीवन्तीमोषधीम्, CA: 3.1.6; Whitney: 3.6.
जीहीडाहम्, CA: 3.1.14; Whitney: 3.14.
टकारात्सकारे तकारेण, CA: 2.1.8; Whitney: 2.8; PS: 208.
टवर्गीये णकारः, CA: 2.1.12; Whitney: 2.12; PS: 214.
तकारस्य शकारलकारयोः परसस्थानः, CA: 2.1.13; Whitney: 2.13; PS: 215.
ततस्परौ ब्रह्मपरे, CA: 2.3.7; Whitney: 2.66; PS: 288.
ततोऽप्याकारस्य, CA: 1.1.35; Whitney: 1.35; PS: 26.
ततो मृदुतरः स्वारः ..., CA: 3.3.4; Whitney: p. 154.
तत्तानग्रादिषु, CA: 2.4.5; Whitney: 2.85.
तदेव स्फोटनः, CA: 1.4.12; Whitney: 1.103; PS: 188.
तद्धिते तकारादौ, CA: 2.4.3; Whitney: 2.83.
तद्धिते धा, CA: 4.1.35; Whitney: 4.13.
तरतमयोः, CA: 4.1.38; Whitney: 4.16.
तवर्गीयाच्छकारः शकारस्य, CA: 2.1.17; Whitney: 2.17; PS: 211, 219.
तस्य पुनरास्थापितं नाम, CA: 4.4.26; Whitney: 4.125.
तस्यान्तेन परस्य प्रसन्धानम्, CA: 4.4.12; Whitney: 4.111.
तातिलि, CA: 4.1.42; Whitney: 4.20.
ताभ्यां समानपदे तवर्गीयस्य पूर्वसस्थानः, CA: 2.1.15; Whitney: 2.15; PS: 217.
तालव्यानां मध्यजिह्वम्, CA: 1.1.21; Whitney: 1.21; PS: 5.
तुविष्टमः, CA: 3.4.28; Whitney: 3.96.
तृतीयान्तस्य, CA: 3.1.19; Whitney: 3.19.
तृतीयासमासे च, PS: 137; not found in CA.
तेनैवोपसृष्टेऽपि, CA: 4.1.58; Whitney: 4.36.
तेभ्यः पूर्वचतुर्थो हकारस्य, CA: 2.1.7; Whitney: 2.7; PS: 207.
तैरोव्यञ्जनपादवृत्तौ ..., CA: 3.3.5; Whitney: p. 154.
त्राकारान्ते, CA: 4.1.36; Whitney: 4.14.

त्रिः, CA: 2.3.5; Whitney: 2.64; PS: 286.

त्रिमात्रः प्लुतः, CA: 1.2.22; Whitney: 1.62; PS: 49.

त्रीणि पदान्यपृक्तमध्यानि, CA: 4.4.14; Whitney: 4.113.

त्रेधा, CA: 4.2.20; Whitney: 1.66.

त्र्यादिभ्यः, CA: 2.4.18; Whitney: 2.98.

त्वे चान्तोदात्ते, CA: 4.1.48; Whitney: 4.26.

थानेकाक्षरेण, CA: 4.1.37; Whitney: 4.15.

ददातौ तकारादौ, CA: 4.2.15; Whitney: 4.61.

दधातौ च हकारादौ, CA: 4.2.17; Whitney: 4.63.

दन्त्यानां जिह्वाग्रं प्रस्तीर्णम्, CA: 1.1.24; Whitney: 1.24; PS: 9.

दभधीनाशेषु च, PS: 281; not found in CA.

दिवस्पदे, PS: 290; not found in CA.

दिवस्पृथिव्यां सचतिवर्जम्, CA: 2.3.9; Whitney: 2.68; PS: 292.

दिवस्पृष्ठम्, PS: 291; not found in CA.

दीदायत्, CA: 4.3.17; Whitney: 4.89.

दीदायादीनां द्वितीयस्य, CA: 3.1.22; Whitney: 3.22.

दीर्घः प्रगृह्यश्च, CA: 1.3.11; Whitney: 1.73; PS: 153.

दीर्घप्लुतयोः पूर्वा मात्रा, CA: 1.1.38; Whitney: 1.38; PS: 29.

दीर्घप्लुतव्यवधाने च, PS: 131; not found in CA.

दीर्घस्य विरामे, CA: 4.3.7; Whitney: 4.79.

दीर्घायुत्वायादिषु च, CA: 2.2.20; Whitney: 2.59; PS: 276, 324.

दीर्घायुत्वायादीनां च, CA: 4.3.29; Whitney: 4.100.

दीर्घो नपुंसकबहुवचने, CA: 1.3.22; Whitney: 1.84; PS: 36.

दुर उकारो दाशे परस्य मूर्धन्यः, CA: 2.3.1; Whitney: 2.60; PS: 280.

दुर्णाम्नः, CA: 3.4.15; Whitney: 3.84.

दूरादाह्वाने गाने रोदने..., PS: 169; not found in CA.

दृशि सर्वनाम्नैकारान्तेन, CA: 4.2.23; Whitney: 4.69.

देवताद्वन्द्वे च, CA: 4.2.3; Whitney: 4.49.

द्यौश्च, CA: 2.3.15; Whitney: 2.74; PS: 298.
द्रव्यार्थादेशा धातवः, PS: 61; not found in CA.
द्वाभ्यामुकारः, CA: 4.4.19; Whitney: 4.118.
द्वार्वारिति, CA: 2.2.6; Whitney: 2.45; PS: 308.
द्वितीयचतुर्थाः सोष्माणः, CA: 1.1.12; Whitney: 1.10; PS: 19, 239.
द्वितीयाः शषसेषु, CA: 2.1.6; Whitney: 2.6; PS: 206.
द्विमात्रो दीर्घः, CA: 1.2.21; Whitney: 1.61; PS: 48.
द्विरुक्ते चावगृह्ये, CA: 4.1.66; Whitney: 4.44.
द्विवचनान्तौ, CA: 1.3.13; Whitney: 1.75; PS: 156.
द्वे पदे क्रमपदम्, CA: 4.4.11; Whitney: 4.110.
धातुस्थादयकारात्, CA: 3.4.8; Whitney: missing.
नकारमकारयोर्लोपे पूर्वस्यानुनासिकः, CA: 1.3.5; Whitney: 1.66; PS: 229.
नकारस्य च, CA: 2.1.34; Whitney: 2.34; PS: 232, 244.
नकारस्य चटतवर्गेषु, CA: 2.1.26; Whitney: 2.26; PS: 242.
नकारस्य शकारे ञकारः, CA: 2.1.10; Whitney: 2.10; PS: 212.
न कृपादीनाम्, CA: 1.3.3; Whitney: 1.65.
न घारिषां सुसहेत्येवमादीन्युदाहरेत् ..., CA: 4.1.9; Whitney: p. 261.
न चवर्गः, CA: 1.1.9; Whitney: 1.7; PS: 15.
नञि व्यञ्जनेऽपि, PS: 273; not found in CA.
न टवर्गस्य चवर्गे कालविप्रकर्षस्त्वत्र भवति ..., CA: 2.1.39; Whitney: 2.39; PS: 259.
न तकारसकाराभ्यां मत्वर्थे, CA: 4.2.1; Whitney: 4.47.
न दीर्घात्, CA: 4.1.55; Whitney: 4.33.
न दीर्घोपधे, PS: 139; not found in CA.
नभेः, CA: 3.4.18; Whitney: missing.
न मिनन्ति, CA: 3.4.17; Whitney: 3.86.
नमौ सन्ध्यौ, CA: 3.2.14; Whitney: 3.37; PS: 104 (न समौ सन्ध्यौ).
न युष्मदस्मदादेशा अनुदात्ताः ..., CA: 4.1.15; Whitney: p. 262.

नलोपेऽपि, CA: 2.4.9; Whitney: 2.89.
नवतेश्च, CA: 3.4.13; Whitney: 3.82.
न विभक्तिरूपरात्रिरथन्तरेषु, CA: 2.2.12; Whitney: 2.51; PS: 314.
न विसर्जनीयः, CA: 3.2.6; Whitney: 3.29.
नशेः षान्तस्य, CA: 3.4.22; Whitney: 3.90.
न समो राजतौ, CA: 2.1.36; Whitney: 2.36; PS: 234.
न समासे, PS: 166; not found in CA.
न समैरयन्तादीनाम्, CA: 2.1.30; Whitney: 2.30; PS: 250.
नसश्च, CA: 3.4.7; Whitney: missing.
न सस्पदीष्ट, CA: 2.2.19; Whitney: 2.58.
न सस्य दीर्घः, PS: 275, 323; not found in CA.
न सृपिसृजिस्पृशिस्फूर्जिस्वरतिस्मरतीनाम्, CA: 2.4.22; Whitney: 2.102.
नाकाराद्वकारस्य, CA: 2.1.22; Whitney: 2.22.
नाख्यातानि समस्यन्ते न चाख्यातं च ..., CA: 4.1.14; Whitney: p. 262.
नादो घोषवत्स्वरेषु, CA: 1.1.15; Whitney: 1.13.
नान्तगतं परेण, CA: 4.4.13; Whitney: 4.112.
नान्तःपदे सन्ध्ये तकारे च, PS: 245; not found in CA.
नाम नाम्नानुदात्तेन समस्तं ..., CA: 4.1.3; Whitney: p. 261.
नामानुदात्तं प्रकृतिस्वरो गतिरनुच्चो वा ..., CA: 4.1.4; Whitney: p. 261.
नामिकरेफात्प्रत्ययसकारस्य, CA: 2.4.7; Whitney: 2.87.
नामोपसर्गगतिभिः समस्यन्ते ..., CA: 4.1.17; Whitney: p. 262.
नाम्युपधस्य रेफः, CA: 2.2.3; Whitney: 2.42; PS: 248, 265.
नाम्युपधस्य रेफ ऋतूँरुत्सृजते ..., CA: 2.1.29; Whitney: 2.29; PS: 248-9.
नाम्युपधस्य सस्य षकारः, PS: 241; not found in CA.
नारकादीनाम्, CA: 4.3.18; Whitney: 4.90.
नारकादीनां प्रथमस्य, CA: 3.1.21; Whitney: 3.21.
नाष्टनः, CA: 4.3.23; Whitney: 4.95.
नासिक्यानां नासिका, CA: 1.1.26; Whitney: 1.26; PS: 11.

निगृह्यानुयोगे च, PS: 176; not found in CA.

निपातस्य स्वः, CA: 3.4.11; Whitney: missing.

निपातोऽपृक्तोऽनाकारः, CA: 1.3.17; Whitney: 1.79; PS: 34, 160.

निर्दुराविर्हविरसमासेऽपि, CA: 2.3.4; Whitney: 2.63; PS: 284.

निवतस्पृणातौ, CA: 2.3.19; Whitney: 2.78; PS: 302.

नोदात्तस्वरितपरम्, CA: 3.3.21; Whitney: 3.70.

नैकारौकारयोः स्थानविधौ, CA: 1.1.41; Whitney: 1.41; PS: 32, 58.

पञ्चजना लोकेषु, CA: 4.4.6; Whitney: 4.106.

पञ्चम्याश्चाङ्गेभ्यः पर्यादिवर्जम्, CA: 2.3.8; Whitney: 2.67; PS: 289.

पञ्चम्युत्तरस्य, PS: 88; not found in CA.

पदाध्ययनमन्तादिशब्दस्वरार्थज्ञानार्थम्, CA: 4.4.7; Whitney: 4.107.

पदान्तः पद्यः, CA: 1.1.5; Whitney: 1.3; PS: 63.

पदान्तविकृतानाम्, CA: 4.3.9; Whitney: 4.81.

पदान्तस्पर्शयुक्तस्य, CA: 3.4.21; Whitney: 3.89.

पदान्तानामनुत्तमानां तृतीया घोषवत्स्वरेषु, CA: 2.1.2; Whitney: 2.2; PS: 197, 198.

पदान्तावग्रहयोश्च, CA: 1.2.5; Whitney: 1.45; PS: 78.

पदान्ते च, CA: 1.2.14; Whitney: 1.54; PS: 43.

पदान्ते चाघोषाः, CA: 2.1.3; Whitney: 2.3; PS: 203.

पदान्ते व्यञ्जनं द्विः, CA: 3.2.1; Whitney: 3.26; PS: 100, 102, 221.

पदेनावर्जितेन, CA: 3.4.27; Whitney: 3.95.

पद्यं च, CA: 1.2.17; Whitney: 1.57; PS: 46.

परमेभ्योऽनापाके, CA: 2.4.14; Whitney: 2.94.

परस्य स्वरस्य व्यञ्जनानि, CA: 1.2.15; Whitney: 1.55; PS: 44.

परिधिष्पतातौ, CA: 2.3.18; Whitney: 2.77; PS: 301.

परेः स्तृणातेः, CA: 2.4.25; Whitney: 2.105.

परेर्हिनोतेः, CA: 3.4.20; Whitney: 3.88.

पार्श्वबिन्दुद्वयो विसर्गः, PS: 72; not found in CA.

पांसुमांसादीनाम्, CA: 1.3.23; Whitney: 1.85.

पितुष्पितरि, CA: 2.3.14; Whitney: 2.73; PS: 297.

पिप्पल्यादिषु पूर्वात्, CA: 3.2.5; Whitney: missing; PS: 224.

पीडितः सन्नतरो हीनश्वासनादः, CA: 1.2.3; Whitney: 1.43; PS: 33.

पुनर्णयामसि, CA: 3.4.12; Whitney: 3.81

पुमो मकारस्य स्पर्शेऽघोषेऽनूष्मपरे विसर्जनीयो..., CA: 2.1.25; Whitney: 2.25; PS: 237.

पुरुष आ बभूवाँ ३ इत्यवसाने, CA: 1.3.8; Whitney: 1.70.

पुंसश्च, CA: 1.3.29; Whitney: 1.91.

पूर्याणः, CA: 3.4.14; Whitney: 3.83.

पूर्वं तु भाषायाम्, PS: 180; not found in CA.

पूर्वपदनिमित्तानाम्, CA: 4.3.3; Whitney: 4.75.

पूर्वपदाद् द्रुघणादीनाम्, CA: 3.4.2; Whitney: 3.76.

पूर्वपरयोरेकः, CA: 3.2.18; Whitney: 3.41; PS: 124.

पूर्वरूपमित्यान्यतरेयः, CA: 3.3.29; Whitney: p. 174.

पूर्वरूपस्य मात्रार्धं समानकरणं परम्, CA: 1.2.10; Whitney: 1.50.

पूर्वस्यान्ते परस्यादौ, PS: 125; not found in CA.

पूर्वं रेफश्चेत्स ऊर्ध्वगः, PS: 97; not found in CA.

पूर्वस्वरं संयोगाविघातश्च, CA: 1.4.13; Whitney: 1.104; PS: 187.

पूर्वेणाभिविपश्याम्यादिषु, CA: 4.1.26; Whitney: 4.4.

पूर्वेणावग्रहः, CA: 4.1.29; Whitney: 4.7.

पृष्ठे च, CA: 2.3.10; Whitney: 2.69; PS: 293.

प्रकृतिदर्शनं समापत्तिः, CA: 4.3.1; Whitney: 4.73.

प्रकृत्या वा, PS: 150; not found in CA.

प्रगृह्यावगृह्यचर्चायां क्रमवदुत्तरस्मिन्नवग्रहः, CA: 4.4.24; Whitney: 4.124.

प्रगृह्यावगृह्यसमापाद्यान्तर्गतानां द्विर्वचनं ..., CA: 4.4.18; Whitney: 4.117.

प्रगृह्याश्च प्रकृत्या, CA: 3.2.10; Whitney: 3.33; PS: 151.

प्रतिश्रवणे चोदात्तम्, PS: 181; not found in CA.

प्रत्यये व्यञ्जनमित्, PS: 70, 116; not found in CA.

प्रथमान्तानि तृतीयान्तानीति शौनकस्य ..., CA: 1.1.10; Whitney: 1.8; PS: 14, 17, 105, 200-201.

प्रपणः पणतेरेव, CA: 4.3.26; Whitney: 4.97.

प्रपराभ्यामेनः, CA: 3.4.6; Whitney: 3.80.

प्रपराणिसमादुर्णिरवाधि ..., CA: 4.1.19; Whitney: p. 262; PS: 64.

प्रश्ने, PS: 191; not found in CA.

प्राणति प्राणन्ति, CA: 4.2.11; Whitney: 4.57.

प्रादूहोढयोर्वृद्धिः, PS: 146; not found in CA.

प्रेत्य ज्योतिष्ट्वं कामयमानस्य, CA: 4.4.2; Whitney: 4.102.

प्रे मुषिजीवपरे, CA: 2.3.17; Whitney: 2.76; PS: 300.

प्लुतश्चाप्लुतवत्, CA: 4.4.21; Whitney: 4.120.

बर्हिपथ्यप्सुदिविपृथिवीति च, CA: 2.4.20; Whitney: 2.100.

बहुलं मतौ, CA: 3.1.17; Whitney: 3.17.

बहुलं रात्रेः, CA: 3.1.8; Whitney: 3.8.

बोधप्रतीबोधौ केसरप्राबन्धाया ..., CA: 4.3.25; Whitney: 4.96.

ब्रह्मण्वत्यादीनाम्, CA: 3.4.10; Whitney: missing.

ब्रह्मण्वत्यादीनाम्, CA: 4.3.28; Whitney: 4.99.

ब्रू३हिप्रे३ष्यश्रौ३षड्..., PS: 173; not found in CA.

भानोश्च, CA: 3.4.19; Whitney: 3.87.

भिर्भ्याभ्यःसु, CA: 4.1.53; Whitney: 4.31.

भुवोमहसोर्लोके, PS: 316; not found in CA.

भूतकरणस्य च, CA: 3.2.26; Whitney: 3.49.

भोभगोअघोसां ..., PS: 278; not found in CA.

मकारस्य स्पर्शे परसस्थानः, CA: 2.1.31; Whitney: 2.31; 226.

मतौ, CA: 4.1.39; Whitney: 4.17.

मनस्पापे, CA: 2.3.20; Whitney: 2.79; PS: 303.

मनुष्यत्, CA: 4.2.19; Whitney: 4.65.

मयेऽसकारात्, CA: 4.1.46; Whitney: 4.24.
मात्रे च, CA: 4.1.44; Whitney: 4.22.
मामनुप्रतेप्रवामी ..., CA: 4.1.16; Whitney: p. 262.
मिथोऽवगृह्ययोर्मध्यमेन, CA: 4.1.64; Whitney: 4.42.
मुखे विशेषाः करणस्य, CA: 1.1.18; Whitney: 1.18; PS: 2.
मूर्धन्यानां जिह्वाग्रं प्रतिवेष्टितम्, CA: 1.1.22; Whitney: 1.22; PS: 6.
मोऽनुस्वारः, PS: 225; not found in CA.
यः पतौ गवामस्याः परवर्जम्, CA: 2.3.11; Whitney: 2.70; PS: 294.
यज्ञततिर्न पृथग्वेदेभ्यः, CA: 4.4.4; Whitney: 4.104.
यज्ञे पुनर्लोकाः प्रतिष्ठिताः, CA: 4.4.5; Whitney: 4.105.
यत्तदेतेभ्यो वतौ, CA: 4.2.2; Whitney: 4.48.
यत्रानेकोऽनुदात्तोऽस्ति परश्च ..., CA: 4.1.6; Whitney: p. 261.
यत्रोभे प्रकृतिस्वरे पूर्वं ..., CA: 4.1.13; Whitney: p. 262.
यथाशास्त्रं प्रसन्धानम्, CA: 4.4.23; Whitney: 4.122.
यरोष्मापत्तौ च, CA: 1.3.6; Whitney: 1.68.
यवलोपे, CA: 3.2.12; Whitney: 3.35; PS: 254, 264.
यस्य चोत्तरपदे दीर्घो व्यञ्जनादौ, CA: 4.2.4; Whitney: 4.50.
याज्ञिकैर्यथासमाम्नातम्, CA: 4.4.3; Whitney: 4.103.
याज्यान्तःप्रणवश्च, PS: 172; not found in CA.
यातुमावत्, CA: 4.1.30; Whitney: 4.8.
यादाविच्छायां स्वरात् कर्मनाम ..., CA: 4.1.51; Whitney: 4.29.
यावयतेराख्याते, CA: 4.3.20; Whitney: 4.92.
युष्मदादेशे तैस्त्वमादिवर्जम्, CA: 2.4.4; Whitney: 2.84.
ये३यजामहे, PS: 171; not found in CA.
योनावध्यैरयन्तादिषु च, CA: 4.1.27; Whitney: 4.5.
रलोपे, CA: 3.1.20; Whitney: 3.20; PS: 321.
रायस्पोषादिषु च, CA: 2.3.21; Whitney: 2.80; PS: 304.
रेफपरस्य च, CA: 2.4.26; Whitney: 2.106.

रेफप्रकृति घोषवत्स्वरेषु, PS: 305; not found in CA.

रेफसकारयोर्विसर्गः पदान्ते, PS: 262; not found in CA.

रेफस्य दन्तमूलानि, CA: 1.1.28; Whitney: 1.28; PS: 8

रेफस्य रेफे, CA: 2.1.19; Whitney: 2.19; PS: 318.

रेफहकारक्रमजं च, CA: 1.2.18; Whitney: 1.58; PS: 47.

रेफहकारौ परं ताभ्याम्, CA: 3.2.8; Whitney: 3.31; PS: 110.

रेफादूष्मणि स्वरपरे स्वरभक्तिरकारस्यार्ध ..., CA: 1.4.10; Whitney: 1.101; PS: 120-121.

लकारविसर्जनीयौ च, CA: 1.1.7; Whitney: 1.5.

लकारस्य रेफः पादमङ्गुरिमित्येवमा..., CA: 1.3.4; Whitney: 1.66; PS: 114.

लकारस्योष्मसु, CA: 1.2.6; Whitney: 1.46; PS: 79.

लेशवृत्तिरधिस्पर्शं शाकटायनस्य, CA: 2.1.24; Whitney: 2.24; PS: 108

लोप उदः स्थास्तम्भोः सकारस्य, CA: 2.1.18; Whitney: 2.18; PS: 220.

वकारादौ च, CA: 4.1.40; Whitney: 4.18.

वनियमिश्रथिग्लपीनाम्, CA: 4.3.21; Whitney: 4.93.

वर्गविपर्यये स्फोटनः पूर्वेण चेद्विरामः, CA: 2.1.38; Whitney: 2.38; PS: 236.

वर्णकार्यादर्शनं लोपः, PS: 75; not found in CA.

वर्णग्रहे सवर्णमात्रम्, PS: 94; not found in CA.

वर्णादन्त्यात्पूर्व उपधा, CA: 1.4.1; Whitney: 1.92; PS: 68.

वर्णैक्यं संहिता, PS: 57; not found in CA.

वर्तादिषु, CA: 3.1.12; Whitney: 3.12.

वसुधातरः सहस्रसातमेति वसुसहस्राभ्याम्, CA: 4.1.67; Whitney: 4.45.

वसौ ह्रस्वात्, CA: 4.1.57; Whitney: 4.35.

वस्वन्तस्य पञ्चपद्याम्, CA: 1.3.26; Whitney: 1.88.

वस्ववस्वप्नसुम्नसाधुभिर्या, CA: 4.1.52; Whitney: 4.30.

वाक्यस्य टेः प्लुतः, PS: 168; not found in CA.

वावृधानप्रभृतीनां च, CA: 4.3.13; Whitney: 4.85.

वा सुपि, PS: 136; not found in CA.

विकल्पो विभाषा, PS: 66; not found in CA.
विचार्यमाणानाम्, PS: 179; not found in CA.
विदेश्च, CA: 1.3.28; Whitney: 1.90.
विद्मादीनां शरादिषु, CA: 3.1.16; Whitney: 3.16; PS: 320.
विधायकस्य न, PS: 93, 118; not found in CA.
विनामे च, CA: 4.1.56; Whitney: 4.34.
विभक्त्यागमप्रातिपदिकान्तस्य, CA: 3.4.4; Whitney: 3.78.
विभाषा पृष्टप्रतिवचने हेः, PS: 175; not found in CA.
विभाषाप्राप्तं सागान्ये, CA: 1.1.4; Whitney: 1.2.
विवृततमा वृद्धिः, PS: 60; not found in CA.
विवृततरौ गुणः, PS: 59; not found in CA.
विवृत्तौ पादवृत्तः, CA: 3.3.14; Whitney: 3.63.
विश्पतिर्विश्पत्नी, CA: 4.2.14; Whitney: 4.60.
विश्वस्य नरवसुमित्रेषु, CA: 3.1.9; Whitney: 3.9.
विश्वाद्दानीमि, CA: 4.1.45; Whitney: 4.23.
विसर्गस्य स्वरे यकारः, PS: 252; not found in CA.
विसर्जनीयस्य परसस्थानोऽघोषे, CA: 2.2.1; Whitney: 2.40; PS: 260.
विसर्जनीयोऽभिनिष्ठानः, CA: 1.2.1; Whitney: 1.42; PS: 76.
वृक्षाँ वनानीति वकारे, CA: 2.1.28; Whitney: 2.28; PS: 255.
वृद्धेनैकाक्षरेण स्वरान्तेन, CA: 4.2.9; Whitney: 4.55.
वेदाध्ययनं धर्मः, CA: 4.4.1; Whitney: 4.101.
व्यञ्जनं परतः सन्धयेत्, PS: 109; not found in CA.
व्यञ्जनविधारणमभिनिधानः, CA: 1.2.2; Whitney: 1.43; PS: 77.
व्यञ्जनव्यवेतस्तैरोव्यञ्जनः, CA: 3.3.13; Whitney: 3.62.
व्यञ्जनानि च, CA: 1.2.20; Whitney: 1.60; PS: 39.
व्यञ्जनान्यव्यवेतानि स्वरैः संयोगः, CA: 1.4.7; Whitney: 1.98; PS: 54.
व्यधावप्रत्यये, CA: 3.1.3; Whitney: 3.3.
व्यधौ, CA: 4.2.22; Whitney: 4.68.

व्यवाये शषलैः, CA: 3.4.25; Whitney: 3.93; PS: 112.
व्यासेऽपि समानपदे, CA: 3.3.19; Whitney: 3.68.
व्यासेऽपि समानपदे, CA: 3.3.23; Whitney: 3.72.
शषसाः स्वरे, CA: 3.2.9; Whitney: 3.32.
शषसेषु विसर्गः, PS: 274; not found in CA.
शसि वीप्सायाम्, CA: 4.1.41; Whitney: 4.19.
शकल्येष्यादिषु पररूपम्, CA: 3.2.29; Whitney: 3.52; PS: 140.
शान्मान्दानाम्, CA: 1.3.25; Whitney: 1.87.
शुनः पदे, CA: 3.1.10; Whitney: 3.10.
शुनि तकारः, CA: 2.3.2; Whitney: 2.61; PS: 282.
शेपहर्षणीं वन्दनेव वृक्षम्, CA: 2.2.17; Whitney: 2.56.
श्वासोऽघोषेष्वनुप्रदानः, CA: 1.1.14; Whitney: 1.12.
षकारस्य द्रोणिका, CA: 1.1.23; Whitney: 1.23; PS: 7.
षकारान्नानापदेऽपि, CA: 2.1.16; Whitney: 2.16; PS: 218
षट्पुरसोरुकारोऽन्त्यस्य दशदाशयोरादेश्च मूर्धन्यः, CA: 1.3.1; Whitney: 1.63.
षडेव स्वरितजातानि ..., CA: 3.3.1; Whitney: p. 154.
षत्वणत्वोपाचारदीर्घ ..., CA: 4.3.2; Whitney: 4.74.
षष्ठ्याश्चाशच्याः, CA: 2.3.12; Whitney: 2.17; PS: 295.
षोडशी सन्देहात्, CA: 4.2.5; Whitney: 4.51.
स एकपदः परिहार्यश्च परिहार्यश्च, CA: 4.4.27; Whitney: 4.126.
संज्ञायाम्, CA: 4.2.21; Whitney: 4.67.
संपरिभ्यां सकारादौ करोतौ, CA: 4.2.12; Whitney: 4.127.
सप्तमी पूर्वस्य, PS: 89; not found in CA.
समन्तः पूरणे, CA: 4.1.60; Whitney: 4.38.
समानपदेऽनुत्तमात्स्पर्शादुत्तमे ..., CA: 1.4.8; Whitney: 1.99.
समानयमेऽक्षरमुच्चैरुदात्तं नीचै ..., CA: 1.1.16; Whitney: 1.14-16; PS: 50.
समानाक्षरस्य सवर्णे दीर्घः, CA: 3.2.19; Whitney: 3.42; PS: 126.
समापाद्यानामन्ते संहितावद्वचनम्, CA: 4.4.25; Whitney: 4.124.

समासयोश्च, CA: 4.1.65; Whitney: 4.43.

समासावग्रहविग्रहान्पदे ..., CA: 4.1.1; Whitney: p. 261.

समासे च, CA: 4.1.31; Whitney: 4.9.

समासे सकारः कपयोरनन्तः ..., CA: 2.3.3; Whitney: 2.62; PS: 238, 283.

समुद्रादिषु च, CA: 4.2.8; Whitney: 4.54.

सलकारम्ऌवर्णम्, CA: 1.1.39; Whitney: 1.39; PS: 30.

सस्थानकरणं सवर्णम्, PS: 56; not found in CA.

सस्थाने च, CA: 3.2.7; Whitney: 3.30.

सस्थाने लोपेऽनुनासिकः, PS: 258; not found in CA.

संधौ पदान्ते च, PS: 165; not found in CA.

संध्यक्षराणामयवायावः, CA: 3.2.17; Whitney: 3.40; PS: 115.

संध्यक्षराणि संस्पृष्टवर्णान्येक..., CA: 1.1.40; Whitney: 1.40; PS: 31.

संध्ये च वकारे, CA: 2.1.37; Whitney: 2.37; PS: 235

संपर्युपेभ्यः करोतौ च क्वचित्, PS: 240; not found in CA.

संयुक्ते स्वेन धर्मेण, PS: 261; not found in CA.

संयोगादि पूर्वस्य, CA: 1.2.16; Whitney: 1.56; PS: 45.

संयोगादि स्वरात्, CA: 3.2.3; Whitney: 3.28; PS: 101, 230.

संयोगे पूर्वं व्यञ्जनं पूर्वमुत्तरमुत्तरम्, PS: 96; not found in CA.

सर्वतीक्ष्णोऽभिनिहितः ..., CA: 3.3.3; Whitney: p. 154.

सर्वमिति शाङ्खमित्रिः, CA: 3.3.33; Whitney: p. 174.

सर्वस्मिन्नेवागमसकारादौ ..., CA: 4.2.13; Whitney: 4.59.

सर्वादीनि सर्वनाम, PS: 85; not found in CA.

संवृतोऽकारः, CA: 1.1.36; Whitney: 1.36; PS: 27.

संस्पृष्टरेफमृवर्णम्, CA: 1.1.37; Whitney: 1.37; PS: 28.

सहावाडन्ते, CA: 4.2.24; Whitney: 4.70.

सहावाडन्ते दीर्घः, CA: 3.1.1; Whitney: 3.1; PS: 319.

संहितादाढ्यार्थम्, CA: 4.4.8; Whitney: missing.

संहितायाम्, CA: 2.1.1; Whitney: 2.1; PS: 98, 196.

सहेः साड्भूतस्य, CA: 2.4.2; Whitney: 2.81.

साढः, CA: 3.1.7; Whitney: 3.7.

सात्रासाहादीनामुत्तरपदाद्यस्य, CA: 3.1.23; Whitney: 3.23.

साधकतमा विभक्तिः, PS: 62; not found in CA.

सान्तेभ्यः कुप्वोः, PS: 285; not found in CA.

साह्याम, CA: 3.1.15; Whitney: 3.15.

साह्याम, CA: 4.3.16; Whitney: 4.88.

सीमन्ते ह्रस्वः, CA: 3.2.22; Whitney: 3.43; PS: 129.

सुञः, CA: 2.4.17; Whitney: 2.94.

सुप्राव्या च, CA: 4.1.33; Whitney: 4.11.

सुभिषक्तमस्तमे, CA: 4.1.68; Whitney: 4.46.

सोपसर्गं तु यन्नीचैः ..., CA: 4.1.7; Whitney: p. 261.

सोष्मणि पूर्वस्यानूष्मा, CA: 1.4.3; Whitney: 1.94.

सौ च, CA: 1.4.54; Whitney: 4.32.

स्तृतस्वस्वपिषु, CA: 2.4.6; Whitney: 2.86.

स्त्रैषूयम्, CA: 2.4.8; Whitney: 2.88.

स्त्रैषूयं नार्षदेन दुष्टरं त्रैष्टुभं ..., CA: 4.3.11; Whitney: 4.83.

स्थानार्था षष्ठी, PS: 87; not found in CA.

स्थासहिसिचीनामकारव्यवायेऽपि, CA: 2.4.12; Whitney: 2.92.

स्पर्शस्य स्पर्शेऽभिनिधानः, CA: 1.2.4; Whitney: 1.44; PS: 78.

स्पर्शाः प्रथमोत्तमाः, CA: 1.1.8; Whitney: 1.6; PS: 13, 199.

स्पर्शादुत्तमादनुत्तमस्यानुत्तमे, CA: 2.1.20; Whitney: 2.20; PS: 107.

स्पर्शेषु सस्थानः स्ववर्गः, PS: 83; not found in CA.

स्पृष्टं स्पर्शानां करणम्, CA: 1.1.29; Whitney: 1.29; PS: 20.

स्वतवसः पायादेव, PS: 247; not found in CA.

स्वरलोपे हन्तेः, CA: 3.4.23; Whitney: 3.91.

स्वरवन्तीत्यान्यतरेयः, CA: 3.3.27; Whitney: p. 174.

स्वराणां च, CA: 1.1.32; Whitney: 1.32; PS: 23.

स्वराद्यवयोः पदान्तयोः, CA: 2.1.21; Whitney: 2.21; PS: 253.

स्वरितस्यादितो मात्रार्धमुदात्तम्, CA: 1.1.17; Whitney: 1.17; PS: 51.

स्वरितादनुदात्तमुदात्तश्रुतिः, CA: 3.3.22; Whitney: 3.71.

स्वरितोदात्तेऽनन्तरमनुदात्तम्, CA: 3.3.25; Whitney: 3.74.

स्वरे नामिनोऽन्तस्थाः, CA: 3.2.16; Whitney: 3.39; PS: 99.

स्वरे मकारः, PS: 227; not found in CA.

स्वरे यकारः, CA: 2.2.2; Whitney: 2.41; PS: 263.

स्वरे यत्वं तल्लोपश्च, PS: 272; not found in CA.

स्वरोऽक्षरम्, CA: 1.4.2; Whitney: 1.93; PS: 52.

स्वरोपजनश्चादृष्टः पदेषु संहितायां च, CA: 4.4.10; Whitney: 4.109.

स्वर्षाश्च, CA: 2.2.10; Whitney: 2.49; PS: 312.

स्वादीरेरिणोर्वृद्धिः, PS: 142; not found in CA.

हकारान्नासिक्येन, CA: 1.4.9; Whitney: 1.100.

हनिगम्योः सनि, CA: 1.3.24; Whitney: 1.86.

हिदिविभ्यामस्तेः, CA: 2.4.21; Whitney: 2.101.

हिनोतेः, CA: 4.3.24; Whitney: 4.95.

है३हेरामेति गुरोः स्वरादनृकाराच्चेति, PS: 185; not found in CA.

ह्रस्वं लघ्वसंयोगे, CA: 1.2.11; Whitney: 1.51; PS: 40.

Index of Sanskrit Terms

Note: This index exhaustively covers the vocabulary of the Sūtras of the CA. For the commentaries, only the technical terms are included.

a 33, 39, 45, 119, 121, 127-129, 149, 150, 155-157, 162, 164, 165, 170, 211, 226, 244, 255-257, 259, 294, 301, 309, 310, 320, 321, 348-353, 355, 359, 362, 367, 375, 379, 381, 382, 384, 391, 392, 410, 411, 413-421, 426, 427, 432, 436, 440, 453, 454, 472, 515, 551, 557, 569, 589, 624, 633, 636, 638, 640, 644-646, 651, 655-657, 659-661, 663, 664, 679, 681

á 45

à 45

ã 45

ã́ 45

ã̀ 45

aK 412, 654, 655, 658, 659

akaḥ 310, 311, 684

akāra 12, 40, 50, 78 , 93, 128, 141, 155, 156, 165, 255-257, 259, 320, 321, 359, 384, 420, 426, 427, 453, 454, 475, 515, 569, 589, 632, 638, 643, 644, 645, 655-660, 663, 681

akāravyavāya 359

akārādi 515, 644

akārānta 93, 453, 454, 569, 645

akārārdha 655

akārottara 658

akāropadha 320, 321, 681

akṣara 11, 33, 74, 75, 120, 121, 136, 162, 164, 165, 186, 188, 189, 192, 193, 197-199, 242-244, 250, 410, 412, 448, 450, 513, 514, 555-557, 618, 631, 635, 639, 641-644, 647, 648, 650, 654, 656, 658, 667, 668, 670-672, 675, 680, 685

akṣarasamāmnāya 35, 38, 49, 639

akṣarārtha 668

akṣarāśraya 644

agni 363

agra 132-136, 636

agrasta 34

aghoṣa 44, 58, 69, 73, 113, 114, 117, 119, 246, 265, 266, 288-291, 305, 306, 316, 639, 640, 669, 672, 676, 677, 679

aghoṣatā 58

aghoṣaśvāsānupradāna 640

aṅga 71, 185, 192-194, 196, 198, 244, 515, 666

aṅgayukta 666

aṅguri 205

aṅebhyaḥ pari 335, 336

aC 195, 197, 224, 225, 299, 395, 403, 404, 431, 454, 495, 623, 639, 641, 643, 646, 686

acsadr̥̥śa 395

ajanta 495

ajbhakti 658

añcati 553

aṬ 359, 451, 456, 474, 591
aḍvyavāya 359
aṆ 212, 278, 283, 410, 649, 650
aṇumātrā 437, 439
aT 453, 454, 472, 473, 663
ataḥ 182, 648
atantra 125
atiṄ 649
atiprasakta 616
ativivṛta 155
atiśaya 686
atiśāyana 515
atiṣṭhipam 601
atisaṃspṛṣṭaprayatna 147
atpūrvasya 472, 473
atra 239, 348, 679,
adanta 453, 454
adarśana 648
aduṣṭatā 686
adṛṣṭa 613
adha 392
adhara 76, 126-128, 130, 136, 137, 636
adharakaṇṭha 126-128
adharakaṇṭhya 126, 137, 636
adharahanumūla 130
adharauṣṭha 136, 137, 636
adharauṣṭhasparśana 137
adharauṣṭhya 136, 636
adhātu 454, 479, 648
adhi 370
adhika 259
adhikāra 263, 425, 442, 453, 467, 476, 637, 641, 656, 663, 666, 668, 674
adhikāranivṛtti 453
adhikṛta 263
adhisparśa 107-110, 112, 287, 288, 637, 651, 652
adhodantapaṅkti 156
adhobhāga 121, 128, 130, 135, 137
adhyayana 610-614
adhyāhāra 676
adhvaparimāṇa 655
anaC 395
anañpūrva 331
anañsamāsa 681, 685
anaṭka 590-592
anati 537, 559
anatiśāyana 515
anadhikāra 476
ananudarśana 88, 106
ananunāsika 106, 249, 641
ananta 682
anantara 182, 446, 447, 645
anantya 199, 641, 642
anabhihita 34
anarthaka 500, 501, 503, 647
anarthāntara 620
analvidhi 210, 651
anavagraha 550
anahva 590-592
anākāra 223-225, 617, 641, 664
anākhyāta 649
anāṄ 224, 225, 641, 647
anāpāka 361
anāmin 686
anāmnāta 629
anārṣa 68, 81, 227-229, 249, 621, 664, 665
anārṣānta 621
aniṅga 510, 598
aniṅgya 510, 511, 548, 579, 598
aniṅgyatva 579
aniyoga 661
anirasta 34
aniścaya 661

aniṣṭa 158
aniṣṭarūpa 158
aniṣṭarūpāpatti 158
anukaraṇa 496, 497
anugati 487
anucca 480, 481
anuttama 69, 139, 251, 253, 263-269, 283-285, 615, 652, 668, 670, 671
anuttarapadastha 683
anudarśana 88, 106
anudātta 11, 43, 75, 120-125, 173, 221, 247, 248, 425, 426, 428, 429-432, 434, 439, 441-447, 479, 480, 482, 484-487, 490, 491, 499, 500, 525, 611, 614, 641, 643, 644, 666
anudāttapūrva 429, 430
anudāttādi 611
anunāsika 40, 41, 106, 111, 113, 116, 125, 138-142, 189, 190, 207-214, 230-239, 249, 267, 297-300, 407, 408, 534, 622-624, 636, 641, 642, 665, 669, 672, 674, 675, 678, 679
anunāsikatā 190
anunāsikatva 214, 623
anunāsikadīrghatva 622
anunāsikasthāna 140
anunāsikasvara 674
anunāsikādeśa 211
anunāsya 663
anupasarga 361
anupradāna 43, 63, 102, 113-119, 252, 637, 640
anuyoga 666
anuvartana 653
anuvr̥tti 349, 651, 659, 663, 685
anusvāra 39, 40, 42, 113, 139, 140, 151, 183-185, 188-190, 193, 194, 230-232, 234-236, 292, 296-299, 301, 356, 408, 471, 472, 636, 638, 642, 648, 673, 674, 675
anusvāravyañjanayoga 183
anusvārādhikāra 674
anūṣman 73, 84, 244, 245, 288-290, 192, 291, 399, 670, 676
anūṣmapara 73, 288-290, 291, 676
anr̥kāra 666
anr̥t 642, 666
anl̥kāra 103, 412
aneka 499, 500, 513, 514, 632, 647
anekākṣara 513, 514
anekārtha 632, 647
anekārthaikaśabda 632
anoṣṭhya 680
anotpara 460
anaimittika 395
anta 68, 78, 88, 93, 99, 106, 136, 148, 171, 176, 177, 182, 183, 187-191, 193, 194, 198, 202, 208, 210, 212, 218, 219, 221, 226, 228, 235, 237, 238, 263-269, 285, 314, 349, 365, 366, 374, 376, 383, 388, 389, 395, 397, 399, 418, 426, 429, 430, 433, 450, 454-456, 470, 492, 504, 511, 513, 523, 530, 533, 536, 537, 542, 543, 555-557, 562, 569, 570, 585, 595-597, 610, 611, 614-617, 621, 624, 626, 637, 642, 644, 647-650, 656, 657, 660, 661, 663-666, 668-670, 672-676, 680, 682-684, 685

antaḥpada 172, 229-231, 296, 298, 299, 431, 432, 594, 641, 665, 675, 677
antaḥpātitva 177
antaḥpāda 168, 352, 420, 421, 663
antagata 616, 620, 621, 626
antajñāna 610
antar 146, 177, 594
antaraṅga 78, 646, 649
antaratama 144, 211, 246, 277
antarvartinī vibhaktiḥ 665
anta(ḥ)sthā 34, 35, 38, 39, 42, 73, 76, 119, 146, 147, 158, 182, 183, 246, 297, 410, 430-432, 434, 611, 618, 636, 638, 650, 651, 653, 671, 674, 681
anta(ḥ)sthāpatti 158, 430-432, 434, 611
antādivat 656
antādiśabdasvarārthajñāna 610
antodātta 432, 433, 492, 493, 504, 511, 523, 530, 536, 537, 614
antya 66, 68, 69, 73, 113, 128, 188, 199, 200, 241, 454, 520, 615, 639, 641, 642, 648, 657, 666
anya 182, 187, 257, 580, 642, 648, 655
anyatarasyām 269, 670, 671
anyayukta 500-503
anyayoga 620
anyayoganivr̥tti 620
anyāya 562
anyāyasamāsa 562
anyāśraya 644
anvaya 660
anvarthasaṃjñā 110
apa 362
apañcapadī 377, 432, 433
apada 533, 534, 618
apadādi 683
apadādhyāyin 611, 612
apadānta 177, 208, 210, 268, 349, 471, 675
apanodana 613
aparaparyāya 151
aparihārya 620
apavāda 572, 597, 646
api 279, 330, 331, 356, 357, 359, 360, 431, 432, 442, 443, 445, 446, 451, 453, 456, 468, 470, 474, 475, 482, 499, 500, 533-535, 591, 600, 614, 626, 636, 637, 639, 641, 644, 646, 653, 656, 658, 659, 661, 663, 667, 670, 672, 673, 675, 677, 679, 681, 682
apūrṇa 112
apūrva 429, 430, 682
apr̥kta 68, 214, 215, 223-225, 616-618, 623, 641, 663, 664
apr̥ktamadhya 616-618
apeta 645
apragr̥hya 164, 212
apratyaya 331, 375, 376, 454, 479, 648, 649
apratyayānta 376
aprathamā 378
aprayāvan 557, 558
apravr̥tti 686
aprasaṅga 395
aprāpta 369
aprāptavidhi 223
apluta 199, 248, 249, 259, 623-625, 667
aplutavat 11, 199, 248, 249, 259, 623-625, 667
aplutavadbhāva 249, 259

apsu 366
abibhar 310, 311, 684
abhāva 644, 648, 655, 657, 658, 672, 677, 681, 686
abhi 370
abhighāta 114, 667
abhidhāna 610
abhidheya 610
abhinidhāna 73, 167, 169-173, 175-183, 251, 648
abhinipāta 167, 171, 172
abhiniṣṭ(h)āna 11, 167-169, 183-186, 194, 259, 260, 648, 667, 678-681
abhiniṣṭānapara 259, 667
abhinihata 167
abhinihita 122, 167, 423, 424, 426, 437-440
abhipūjita 641, 666, 667
abhi vi tanu 500
abhi vi paśyāmi 502
abhi syāma pr̥tanyataḥ 372, 373
abhūṣaṇa 677
abheda 653
abhyaghāyanti 601
abhyantara 665, 675
abhyādāna 666
abhyāsa (study) 46
abhyāsa (reduplication) 67, 68, 71, 88, 358, 360, 384, 586, 588, 589, 627
abhyāsakr̥ta 627
abhyāsavinata 586
abhyāsavyavāya 360
aM 290
amanaḥprayoga 115
amāṅyoga 591
amātra 171, 172
amitākṣara 647
amī 222, 223, 664
amnaḥ 318, 319, 685
ampara 290, 677, 682
ay 285, 410, 411, 654, 680
ayakāra 460
ayasmayādi 193
ayāvādividhāna 654
ayoganivr̥tti 620
ayogavāha 49
ar 415, 416, 659, 660
arucibīja 657
artha 216, 217, 610, 634, 639, 647, 655, 664, 666, 667, 670, 674, 686
arthajñāna 610
arthabala 639, 670
arthadvaya 674
arthavat 454, 479, 648
arthātiśaya 686
arthādeśa 647
arthāntara 647, 664
arthāntaragamaka 647
ardha 70, 124, 125, 157, 164, 165, 168, 184, 185, 198, 212, 242, 255, 256, 449, 450, 506, 626, 642, 643, 655, 657, 679, 680
ardha akāra 655
ardhamātrā 43, 124, 157, 165, 198, 256, 642, 643, 657
ardharca 212, 450, 506, 616, 626
ardharcavirāma 212
ardharcādi 616
ardharcāntagata 616
ardhavisarga 168, 648, 679, 680
ardhavisargasadr̥śa 168, 648, 679
ardhavr̥ttadvayātmakalipi 680
ardhahrasva 76, 124, 125, 643
ardhākāravarṇa 256
aL 210, 241, 641

alakṣaṇa 205
alopa 540
alpaprāṇa 44
av 285, 410, 411, 654, 655, 680
ava 529
avakāra 533-535
avakr̥ṣṭa 172
avakr̥ṣṭatara 172
avagr̥hya 177, 540-542, 548, 556, 574, 576, 577, 579, 581, 583, 588, 613, 620, 621, 625, 626
avagr̥hyatva 577, 626
avagr̥hyapada 177, 556
avagr̥hyamāṇa 579, 598
avagraha 99, 123, 150, 176, 177, 201, 202, 230, 410, 436, 437, 443, 446, 450, 453, 466, 467, 478, 480, 499, 505-514, 517-537, 539-547, 550-559, 561-568, 570, 571, 577, 579-581, 584, 585, 598, 604, 605, 625, 626, 648
avagrahapada 177
avagrahasthāna 510
avaccheda 643
avati 509
avayava 648, 657
avarja 645
avarṇa 39, 50, 78, 128, 153, 162, 163, 226, 413-418, 557, 638, 659, 661, 662
avarṇakula 45, 50
avarṇavarja 645
avarṇānta 226, 417, 418, 557
avaśā 248, 249, 259, 667
avasanna 172, 173
avasannatara 172, 173
avasāna 78, 88, 106, 107, 145, 156, 176, 188, 194, 211-213, 265, 310, 314, 395, 396, 442, 443, 615, 621, 624, 637, 642, 648, 673, 680
avasānika 106
avikr̥ṣita 510
avighāta 258, 259
avibhakti 648
avibhaktika 221
avidhīyamāna 649, 650
avirāma 156
avivakṣaṇa 641
avivakṣita 641
aviśeṣa 533
avaidika 214
avyañjanamiśraśuddhakevalasvara 617
avyapara 663
avyaya 315, 319, 497, 570, 685
avyaveta 182, 249, 250
aŚ 285, 682
aśabda 115
aśuddhīkaraṇa 92
aśūdrādhikāra 666
aṣṭa 375, 599, 600
aṣṭama 257, 259, 655
asaṃyoga 111, 182, 185, 186, 642
asaṃśliṣṭa 641
asakāra 71, 522
asattva 479, 641
asandigdha 641
asandeha 151
asamartha 489
asamāsa 330, 331, 453, 456, 600, 682
asamparka 685
asampr̥kta 663
asarūpa 53
asarvanāman 310, 311, 684
asavarṇa 589

asaṃvr̥ta 645
asasthāna 84, 268
asahavarṇa 650
asāmarthya 489, 502
asāṃhitika 618
asiddha 78, 250, 281, 408, 471, 505, 649, 672
asiddhavat 250
asti 367
asthita 126
aspr̥ṣṭa 44, 147, 149, 150, 154, 638
asme 220, 221, 664
asyāḥ 338, 338
asvara 188, 447, 644, 652
ahan, ahar 317, 443, 444, 685
ahār 312, 313, 684
ahorātre 552, 553
ahrasva 392, 533, 534
ā 39, 45, 52, 73, 119, 121, 127, 128, 149, 152, 154-156, 170, 209, 210, 223-226, 241, 244, 246-248, 286, 292-294, 301, 309, 310, 321, 348-353, 355, 382, 408-410, 413-415, 417-419, 475, 525, 547, 556, 565, 583, 594, 610, 617-619, 624, 636, 638, 639, 647, 651, 664, 678-681
ā́ 45, 248, 307
ā̀ 45
ā̃ 45
ā̃́ 45
ā̃̀ 45
ā3 45, 119, 127, 128, 149, 164, 165
ā́3 45, 247, 248
ā̀3 45
ā̃3 45, 624
ā̃́3 45
ā̃̀3 45
ākāṅkṣā 666
ākāra 45, 50, 78, 78, 154, 155, 209, 223-225, 241, 247, 248, 286, 292, 293, 321, 408, 409, 507, 513, 565, 610, 617, 619, 638, 639, 641, 647, 656, 664, 678, 679, 681
ākārapraśleṣa 78, 639
ākāravarjita 475
ākārāgama 507
ākārānta 513
ākāropadha 241, 292, 293, 321, 678, 679, 681
ākr̥ti 33, 53, 361
ākr̥tigaṇa 361, 465
ākr̥tigrahaṇa 53
ākṣipta 12, 75, 120, 121, 643
ākṣepa 644, 658
ākhyā 302, 537
ākhyāta 98, 226, 227, 410, 478, 479, 482, 488, 489, 498, 500, 502, 594, 596, 597, 632, 634, 649, 687
ākhyāna 641
āgama 68, 181, 454, 456, 476, 560, 561, 562, 629, 646, 655, 659, 670, 680, 686
āgamanakāra 456
āgamavat 562
āgamasakāra 560
āgamasakārādi 560
āgamādeśakāla 651
āgamādeśabala 646
āṄ 224, 225, 408, 451, 474, 641, 647, 662, 664
ācamana 610
ācāryanāman 640

āṬ 374, 418, 570
āḍanta 374, 570
āT 164
ātmanebhāṣā 629
ātva 547
ādi 66, 74, 78, 99, 123, 145, 176, 177, 182, 192, 193, 198, 201, 205, 209, 230, 232, 233, 244, 294, 295, 319, 320, 335, 336, 350, 352, 361, 364, 365, 366, 369, 370, 376, 383, 386, 388, 390-392, 398, 399, 405, 416-419, 426, 452, 462, 473, 492, 503, 515, 517, 526, 533, 534, 536, 537, 547, 550, 552, 555, 557, 559, 560, 562, 564, 571, 573, 579, 580, 582, 585, 586, 590, 595, 603, 604, 610-612, 634, 636, 641, 642, 649, 651, 656, 659-661, 663, 665, 666, 673, 674, 677, 678, 681, 682, 685
ādigrahaṇa 205
āditaḥ 123-125, 643
ādibhūta 651
ādima 670
ādimadhyāntalupta 562
ādimākṣara 670
ādisaṃśaya 552
ādeśa 78, 176, 201, 210, 211, 221, 233, 285, 351, 352, 355, 357, 406, 426, 440, 455, 489, 617, 618, 646, 647, 653, 654, 656, 659, 661-663, 670, 676, 677, 679-682, 685
ādya 128, 391, 636, 658
ādyakṣara 648
ādyanta 649
ādyudātta 244, 481, 487, 488, 492, 493, 536, 537, 571
ādhikya 679
ān 290, 292, 573, 574
āṅ̊ 290
ānaṄ 549
ānunāsikya 45, 641
ānupūrvya 139, 408
āntaratamya 45, 55, 56, 120, 144, 246, 277, 640
āntaratamyaparīkṣā 640
āntarya 246, 277, 296, 305, 410
ānpada 573, 574
ānyabhāvya 41, 111
āpatti 158, 208-210, 430-432, 434
āpāka 367
ā babhūvã3 211-213, 248, 249, 259, 504, 667
ābhyantara 51, 76-78, 117, 118, 145, 146, 148, 635, 636, 639
ābhyantaprayatna 51, 76-78, 117, 118, 145, 146, 148, 635, 636
āmantrita 68, 227, 228, 313, 314, 479, 524, 664, 665, 685
āmnāta 493, 608, 629, 634
āmnāna 607, 608
āmnāya 35, 38, 49, 634, 639
āmreḍita 91, 329, 538, 539, 666
āmreḍitasamāsa 91, 329, 539
āy 285, 410, 411, 654, 680
āyāma 643
ār 416-418, 659, 660
ārtnī iva 229, 665
āryā 189
ārṣa 78, 227-229, 249, 621, 659, 664, 665, 686
āyuḥ 342, 343, 684
āv 285, 410, 411, 654, 680
āvar 310, 311, 684

āvarjita 475
āviḥ 330-332, 682
āśā 571
āśis 666, 667
āśī3ḥ 259, 504, 505, 667
āśīrvacana 665
āśraya 644, 653, 667
āsī3t 259
āsthāpita 180, 181, 627, 628, 648
āsya 51, 52, 70, 126, 140, 412, 635, 638, 645, 646
āsyaprayatna 51, 52, 70, 126, 140, 141, 146, 156, 276, 412, 635, 638, 645
āsyayatna 646
āhuḥ 303, 679
āhvāna 665
i 39, 83, 119, 121, 131, 132, 149, 150, 153, 162, 164, 165, 216, 223, 244, 247, 248, 255, 277, 305, 349, 359, 377, 378, 380, 409-414, 427-429, 440, 454, 524, 525, 533, 534, 569, 583, 585, 589, 618, 624, 636, 638, 640, 644, 646, 651, 657, 659, 663, 664
í 427-429, 430, 433, 440
ĩ 43
iK 377, 410, 431, 536
ikāra 132, 141, 165, 223, 247, 248, 427-429, 533, 534, 569, 618, 651, 657, 659, 663
ikārānta 569
iṅga 598
iṅgita 548
iṅgya 11, 541, 542, 579, 581, 598, 606
iṅgyamāna 579-581
iṅgyavat 598, 606
icchā 527, 528
iṬ 534
iḍāyāḥ 339, 683
iṆ 349, 355, 357, 359
it 78, 648, 654, 655
iT 164, 331
iti 11, 12, 55-57, 70, 72, 81, 100-102, 106, 111, 112, 116, 122-124, 132, 133, 139, 140, 144, 155, 156, 158-161, 163, 165, 166, 169, 171, 174, 185, 189, 192, 193, 198-200, 205-207, 209, 211, 212, 214-230, 232, 233, 238, 239, 247-250, 259, 260, 286, 289, 290-292, 294-296, 299-301, 303, 310-312, 317, 318, 326, 330, 332, 337, 339-346, 348, 350, 351, 359, 362, 363, 367, 369, 370, 375, 379, 381, 386, 392, 413, 428, 447-449, 452, 453, 458, 467, 476, 484, 489, 493, 504, 507, 509, 511, 514, 523, 526, 529, 533, 534, 536, 550, 553, 557, 558, 563, 566, 567, 571, 573-575, 577-579, 583-585, 587, 588, 590, 593, 601, 610, 617, 618, 620-627, 637-639, 642, 645-650, 653, 655-661, 663-665, 667, 668, 670, 676-678, 680, 681, 684, 685
itikaraṇa 217, 230, 249, 622
itikāra 230
itipara 229, 623, 665
itipūrva 624
itimadhya 620, 621
itva 524, 525
itvaN 524
idam ū ṣu 376, 603

idā3m 259, 667
iyaṄ 589
iyā3m 259, 667
iva 229, 230, 322, 323, 539, 540, 626, 646, 665
ivarṇa 50, 72, 74, 131, 153, 163, 412-414, 659
ivasU 534
iha 2, 62, 63, 72, 83, 100-102
ī 39, 119, 121, 131, 149, 216-218, 223, 244, 412, 413, 427-429, 433, 569, 638, 648, 656, 659, 661, 664
í 432, 433
ī̀ 440
ī3 119, 131, 149, 164, 659
īkāra 68, 69, 216-218, 569, 656, 661, 664
īkārānta 217, 569
īT 219, 223
īdanta 223
īyas 236
īyasUN 237
īṣatspṛṣṭa 44, 77, 78, 146-148, 151, 636, 638
īṣadvivṛta 44, 57, 147, 149, 151, 155, 638
īṣadvivṛtakaraṇa 149
u 33, 39, 56, 119, 121, 136, 137, 149, 150, 153, 162, 164, 165, 174, 201, 202, 214, 215, 224-227, 244, 255, 301, 320, 321, 326, 327, 349, 376, 377, 407, 410, 414, 433-435, 461, 534, 536, 574, 584, 589, 617-620, 623, 632, 636, 638, 640, 643, 644, 646, 653, 657, 659, 663, 664, 680-682
ú 429, 430, 433
ū̃ 43
ukāra 66, 68, 136, 137, 141, 165, 201, 214, 225, 320, 321, 326, 407, 433, 434, 617, 620, 622, 623, 632, 643, 653, 657, 663, 681, 682
ucca 480, 481, 492, 493
uccāra 124, 128, 132-136, 139, 156, 185, 194, 635, 636, 637, 642, 643, 679
uccārakāla 642
uccāraṇa 125, 130, 135, 139, 143, 197, 199, 200, 640, 648, 653-655, 679, 680
uccāraṇakāla 679
uccāraṇasāmarthya 654
uccāraṇasthāna 125, 130, 143
uccāraṇārtha 655
uccārasthāna 124, 128, 132
uccaiḥ 11, 74, 120, 121, 643
uñ 68, 225, 226, 376
uT 164, 331, 649
uttama 69, 72, 101, 104, 113, 139, 251, 253, 263-269, 283-285, 615, 636, 637, 652, 668-671
uttamatva 668
uttara 78, 122, 125, 127, 136, 164, 168, 181, 202, 251, 253, 263, 281, 282, 285, 286, 327, 355, 357, 358, 363, 364, 366, 367, 370, 371, 383, 391, 395, 422, 448, 451, 458, 466, 550, 583, 611, 625, 626, 648-650, 654, 657, 658, 670, 683
uttarakaṇṭha 127
uttarapada 168, 202, 327, 361, 364, 383, 391, 550, 583, 611, 683
uttarapadastha 361, 364, 683
uttarapadādi 202, 327

uttarapadādya 391
uttararūpa 448
uttarastha 362
uttarasthasakāra 362
uttarārdha 122, 125
uttarāvayava 648, 657
uttarottara 646
uttarauṣṭha 136
utva 174, 202, 327, 681, 685, 686
utsarga 63, 102
ud 282, 563, 564, 672
udaya 397, 437
udātta 11, 43, 75, 76, 120-125, 173, 200, 220, 221, 244, 247, 248, 410, 425, 426, 428, 429, 431-434, 437, 439-447, 479-488, 490-493, 498, 504, 505, 511, 519, 521, 523-525, 530, 536, 537, 571, 591, 611, 614, 641, 643, 644, 664, 666
udāttatara 123
udāttatā 124
udāttapara 444
udāttavat 482
udāttaśruti 445, 446, 611
udāttasvaritapara 173, 441, 444, 447
udāttasvaritodaya 437, 439, 611
udāttānta 611
udit 649
udghāṭita 156
upacāra 609
upajana 613
upajāta 507, 508, 554
upadiṣṭa 250
upadeśa 331, 456
upadhā 68, 69, 73, 74, 191, 241-243, 292-296, 308, 309, 320, 321, 326, 331, 348, 349, 352-354, 396, 397, 648, 658, 661, 669, 673, 677-679, 681, 682, 683
upadhmā 677, 678
upadhmānīya 39, 41, 42, 72, 74, 111, 117, 136, 137, 168, 169, 305, 307, 582, 636, 640, 648, 679, 680
upapada 294, 311, 372, 379, 481, 634
upapadavibhakti 634
upabaddha 292, 293, 678
upamā 666
upamārtha 666
upayoga 639
upariṣṭād binduḥ 648
uparṣanti 416, 417
upalakṣaṇa 186, 251
upasañcaya 111
upasaṃhāra 43, 128, 151
upasarga 64, 68, 98, 225, 226, 331, 356-361, 366, 382, 383, 410, 416, 417, 453, 456, 457, 459-461, 468, 470, 478, 479, 481-484, 486-490, 492-494, 497-505, 511, 533-535, 627, 628, 634, 647-649, 659, 660, 661, 675, 677, 678, 687
upasargapūrva 489, 502
upasargavr̥tti 481, 493, 494, 497, 499, 500
upasargasamāsa 533-535
upasargastha 357, 359, 360, 457
upasr̥ṣṭa 534, 535
upasthita 248, 249, 624
upāṃśu 114, 115
upācāra 572-574
upādāna 395
ubha 299, 300, 675

ubhaya 520, 521
ubhayathā 685
ubhayadharma 643
uras 43
urasya
uvaṄ 589
uvarṇa 78, 137, 153, 163, 320, 414, 434, 659
ū 39, 119, 121, 136, 149, 216-218, 244, 414, 433, 434, 584, 589, 638, 643, 648, 653, 656, 664
ū́ 433
ū̃ 214, 215, 225, 623, 663
ū3 119, 136, 149, 164, 643
ūkāla 197, 643
ūkāra 69, 216-218, 433, 434, 653, 656, 664
ūkārānta 217
ūṬH 662
ūT 219
ūdhaḥ 318, 319, 685
ūrdhvaga 650
ūrdhvadantāgra 137
ūrdhvabhāga 121, 137
ūṣman 34, 35, 38-42, 73, 77, 84, 110-112, 146-149, 151, 178, 179, 182, 188, 208-210, 244, 245, 255, 256, 288, 289, 291, 297-299, 399, 637, 638, 642, 648, 655, 670, 671, 674-676, 679, 680
ūṣmānta 188, 642
r̥ 33, 39, 56, 57, 73, 75, 76, 78, 102-104, 119, 121, 129, 130, 133, 144, 149, 150, 157, 158, 159, 203, 213, 214, 244, 255, 256, 349, 365, 366, 368, 410, 415-418, 451, 466, 467, 473, 638-640, 642, 644, 653, 656-658-660, 665-667, 677, 678
ərə 157, 213
ərə̊ 213
ərrə 157
r̥l̥varṇasāvarṇya 161
r̥kāra 52, 76, 133, 141, 256, 365, 366, 417, 418, 466, 467, 653, 656-658, 666, 667, 678
r̥kāravarjita 667
r̥kārasvarabhakti 256
r̥kārādi 417, 418
r̥kārānta 365, 366
r̥gardharca 450, 506
r̥T 417, 467, 549, 642
r̥ta 391, 392
r̥ti 256
r̥tū̃r ut sr̥jate vaśī 294, 295, 678
r̥l̥varṇayoḥ sāvarṇyam 653, 658
r̥varṇa 72, 78, 157-161, 203, 213, 256, 368, 415-417, 451, 639, 653, 659, 665
r̥varṇastharepha 203
r̥ṣiproktamantra 612
r̥̄ 39, 73, 119, 121, 129, 149, 157, 159, 160, 244, 415, 638, 656
r̥̄3 119, 129, 149, 157, 159
r̥̄kāra 656
l̥ 39, 56, 72, 73, 103, 119, 121, 129, 130, 135, 136, 149, 150, 160-162, 203, 244, 349, 410, 412, 413, 636, 638-641, 644, 653, 656, 658-660
ələ 160
əllə 160
l̥kāra 52, 78, 103, 121, 135, 161, 203, 656, 658-660
l̥tva 658

l̥varṇa 72, 129, 142, 160, 161, 639, 653
l̥̄ 39, 119, 123, 129, 149, 160, 161
l̥3 119, 149, 160-162
e 33, 39, 53, 71-74, 76, 119, 121, 127, 128, 131, 132, 142, 144, 149, 150, 152-155, 162-164, 166, 211, 219-221, 228, 244, 248, 249, 255, 277, 285, 305, 320, 349, 409, 411, 418, 420, 421, 426, 455, 521, 569, 610, 618, 636, 638, 639, 644, 646, 648, 654, 659, 661, 663, 664, 681
é 440
è 440
e3 119, 149
ẽ 43, 624
eka 54, 68, 112, 137, 159, 162, 163, 165, 196-198, 210-212, 233, 313, 314, 406, 411, 412, 414, 426, 440, 445, 453, 555-557, 562, 611, 613, 617, 618, 627, 639, 641, 642, 646, 647, 652, 655, 656, 661-663, 674, 679, 681, 685
ekakālāvaccheda 643
ekatva 112, 618
ekadeśa 562, 679
ekadeśalopa 562
ekadha 652
ekapada 541, 542, 613, 627, 628, 653
ekapadabhāva 542
ekapadāśraya 653
ekapadībhāva 541
ekamātra 159, 196-198, 642
ekamātrākāla 197, 198
ekamātrika 159, 198
ekamātroccāra 642
ekaya 652
ekavacana 212, 314, 685
ekavacanānta 212
ekavat 163, 225
ekavadbhāva 137
ekavadvr̥tti 225
ekavarṇavat 54, 162, 163, 165, 639
ekavibhakti 652
ekaśeṣa 639, 652, 655, 674
ekaśruti 445, 611
ekasvara 647
ekākṣara 492, 493, 555-557
ekāC 224, 641, 647
ekādeśa 78, 210, 211, 233, 406, 426, 440, 617, 618, 656, 661-663, 681
ekādhikārarūpa 656
ekāmantrita 313, 314, 685
ekāra 152, 162, 164-166, 199, 219, 221, 248, 249, 320, 413, 414, 418, 420, 426, 455, 569, 610, 618, 638, 639, 644, 647, 654, 659, 661, 663, 664, 681
ekārādi 644
ekārānta 569, 610, 663, 664, 681
ekāraukārānta 420, 426
ekārthānekaśabda 632
ekāL 224, 641
ekībhavana 646
eke 150, 255, 638, 655
eṄ 153, 163, 413, 661-663
eṅanta 663
eṅādi 661, 662
eC 164, 408, 410, 418, 419, 654
eT 70, 72
eta(d) 547
etāvattva 294, 311, 372, 379

etva 661
edyubhi 520
edyusUC 521
ena 457, 458
enā ehāḥ 405
eva 298, 299, 326, 337, 392, 422, 482, 487, 533-535, 550, 556, 571, 579, 584, 601, 620, 624-626, 637-640, 645, 649, 651, 653, 655, 656, 659, 661, 663, 667-670, 672, 674, 675, 677, 678, 680, 682, 684, 686
evam 2, 62, 63, 72, 83, 100-102, 205, 294, 678
eṣa 324, 681, 685
o 33, 39, 53, 71-74, 76, 119, 121, 127, 128, 132, 136, 142, 144, 149, 150, 152-155, 162-164, 166, 174, 224-228, 244, 285, 320, 349, 411, 414, 419, 420, 421, 426, 461, 619, 636, 638, 639, 644, 646, 647, 654-656, 659, 661, 663, 664, 680, 681
ó 440
ò 440
o3 119, 136, 149
õ 43
ŏ 156
okāra 72, 74, 78, 137, 152, 162, 164-166, 225, 226, 228, 320, 414, 419, 420, 426, 619, 638, 639, 647, 654-656, 659, 661, 663, 664, 681
okārānta 226, 228, 663, 664, 681
oṇyoḥ 435
oT 461
otva 174
odanā3ḥ 259, 667
om 631, 633, 662, 666
oṣadhi 377-379
oṣṭha 39, 43, 128, 132, 136, 137, 139, 141, 142, 144, 151, 156
oṣṭhanāsika 139, 141
oṣṭhasthāna 136, 141
oṣṭhya, 54, 55, 72, 74, 75, 136-138, 141, 636, 680
oṣṭhyayoni 680
oṣṭhyasvara 680
ai 33, 39, 53, 71, 74, 76, 119, 121, 127, 128, 131, 132, 142, 144, 149, 150, 152, 153, 155, 162-166, 244, 285, 349, 411, 418, 556, 636, 638, 639, 644, 646, 647, 654, 659, 661, 680
ai3 119, 149, 165
ā3i 165
aikāra 50, 152, 163, 164, 166, 418, 638, 639, 647, 654, 659, 661
aikya 646
aiC 153, 163, 164
aiT 70, 72, 74, 128
au 33, 39, 71, 74, 76, 119, 121, 127, 128, 132, 136, 142, 144, 149, 150, 152, 153, 155, 162-164-166, 244, 285, 349, 411, 414, 419, 556, 636, 638, 639, 644, 646, 647, 654, 661, 662, 664, 680
au3 119, 136, 149, 165
ā3u 165
aukāra 152, 163-166, 419, 638, 639, 647, 654, 661
auT 74, 128
aurasya 112, 636
aurasyahakāra 112, 636
auṣṭhya 636
ṃ 39, 40, 42, 49, 139, 638, 648
ꣳ 675

ḥ 39, 40, 42, 49, 90, 104, 127-130, 167, 169, 174, 210, 260, 288, 292, 305, 306, 308-310, 312, 314, 316-322, 324, 326-328, 330, 332, 334, 335, 337-346, 348, 401, 573, 574, 636, 638-640, 648
ḫ (*jihvāmūlīya*) 39, 41, 42, 49, 130, 169, 174, 305, 582, 636, 639, 640, 648, 677, 680
ḫ (*upadhmānīya*) 39, 41, 42, 49, 136, 137, 169, 174, 305, 582, 636, 639, 640, 648, 677
k 33, 39, 41, 42, 50, 56, 116, 117, 127, 129, 130, 138, 169, 251, 271, 273, 284, 301, 302, 305, 307, 328, 330, 332, 333, 349, 355, 418, 573, 574, 636, 640, 649, 655, 670, 671, 679, 682, 683
k̊ 138, 251, 254
ka 69, 76, 78, 84, 91, 104, 112, 117, 125, 129, 130, 145, 176, 181, 271, 272, 284, 306, 328, 348, 354, 355, 359, 636, 640, 649, 655, 670, 671, 679, 682, 683
ka (suffix) 522, 523
kakāra 50, 141, 655, 670
kaṇṭha 39, 43, 71, 75, 116, 121, 126-130, 132, 141, 142, 144, 153, 155, 156, 636, 640, 679
kaṇṭhatālavya 71, 74, 76, 144, 153
kaṇṭhatālu 132, 142, 144
kaṇṭhatālunāsika 142
kaṇṭhanāsika 141
kaṇṭhabila 128, 130
kaṇṭhasthāna 127
kaṇṭhoṣṭhaja 71, 74, 76, 144
kaṇṭhoṣṭhanāsika 142
kaṇṭhauṣṭha 132
kaṇṭhauṣṭhya 153
kaṇṭhya 74, 126-129, 137, 141, 636, 651, 679
kampa 123, 439
kar 310, 311, 684
karaṇa 43, 51, 54, 55, 63, 70, 75, 76, 77, 102, 114, 115, 125-127, 129, 131, 133-152, 154, 155, 184, 185, 635, 637, 638, 645, 646
karaṇamadhya 134, 148
karaṇavat 115
karat 332, 683
karam 332, 683
karoti 525, 559, 676, 677
karṇa 332, 683
kartṛ 103
karman 527, 528, 607, 608
karmanāman 527, 528
karmapravacanīya 360, 482, 486, 487, 500-503
karmaśeṣa 607
karṣaṇa 303, 679
kavarga 40, 50, 72, 78, 129, 148, 306, 355, 636, 649, 679, 683
kavi 437, 439
kaṣayoga 670
kādi 145, 176, 636
kāmayamāna 607, 608
kāmya 538, 539
kāmyaC 538, 539
kāraka 481, 634
kārakavibhakti 634
kāraṬ 640
kāraṇa 609
kārita 595-597
kāritānta 595-597

kārmanāmika 528
kārya 609, 646, 648-650, 653, 655, 656
kāryādarśana 648
kāryopacāra 609
kāla 43, 45, 185, 197, 199, 215, 217, 230, 303, 450, 467, 506, 577, 613, 621, 642, 643, 645, 679
kālaviprakarṣa 303, 679
Ki-KiN 71, 533, 534
kiñcidadhikaśvāsoccārasahita 637
kit 649
kU 129, 251, 349, 355, 357, 359, 451, 456, 474, 677, 679, 682, 685
kUK 271, 671
kutva 251
kuru 332, 683
kr̥ṇotu 332, 683
kr̥t 71, 454, 480, 481, 487, 523-525, 533, 534, 543, 649
kr̥tadīrgha 174
kr̥ti 86, 90, 332, 683
kr̥tva 66, 525, 526
kr̥tvas 66, 525, 526
kr̥danta 487, 543, 649
kr̥dhi 86, 90, 332, 683
kr̥pā 203, 204
kr̥pi 202, 203, 590, 591
kevala 192, 407-409, 574, 617, 636, 645, 650, 656, 682
keśaveṣṭa 413
kesaraprābandhāyāḥ 601
komala 423
krama 111, 112, 165, 195, 196, 212, 244, 249, 255, 311, 313, 315, 316, 319, 326, 394, 397, 403, 404, 429, 572-588, 590-592, 595, 596, 598-605, 612-623, 625-628, 635, 642, 654, 670, 675, 676
kramakāla 577, 613, 621, 626
kramaja 196, 255, 403, 642
kramapada 583, 584, 614-619, 625
kramaparihāra 626
kramapāṭha 212, 249, 311, 313, 315, 316, 319, 326, 429, 572-588, 590-592, 595, 596, 598-605, 612-623, 625-628, 635, 675, 676
kramavat 576, 577, 625, 626
kramādhyayana 612-614
kriyāpradhāna 479
kriyāyoga 481, 492, 497, 647, 648
kriyāvācin 479
klībatā 152
kvacit 421, 484, 667, 676, 677, 681, 686
KvasU 235, 236, 534
KvIP 376
kṣubhna 473
kṣaipra 122, 146, 423, 424, 429-435, 437, 439, 440, 509
kṣaiprasandhi 146
kh 39, 41, 42, 50, 56, 116, 117, 130, 169, 251, 289, 305, 307, 349, 355, 640, 670, 671, 676, 679
kh̐ 139, 251, 254
kha 111, 112, 117, 129, 130, 640, 670, 671, 679
khaṇvakhā3i khaimakhā3i 247, 248, 259, 667
khatva 670
khaY 290, 640, 682
khaR 266, 310, 314, 672, 680

g 39, 41, 50, 56, 116, 117, 245, 251, 284, 302, 349, 418, 640
g̊ 118, 119, 139, 251
ga 112, 119, 129, 130, 250, 251, 640
gakāra 250
gati 480-483, 486, 487, 489, 490, 492, 494, 496, 497, 501, 647, 648
gami 85, 234
gavām 338, 339
gaviṣṭi 286, 287
gāna 665
guṇa 40, 41, 45, 58, 98, 99, 111, 112, 418, 649, 687
guṇa (ref. *adeṅ guṇaḥ,* P.1.1.2) 203, 414, 646, 647, 662
guṇamātrā 112
guṇopasañcaya 111
guru 112, 172, 186-191, 198, 199, 231, 642, 658, 666
gurutā 172
gurutva 112, 189, 198, 658
gosani 369, 370
grah 203
graha 78, 650
grahaṇa 166, 177, 209, 223, 294, 311, 316, 372, 379, 649
glapi 597, 598
glah 203
gh 39, 41, 50, 53, 56, 116-118, 245, 251, 349, 640
gh̊ 118, 119, 139, 251
gha 111, 112, 119, 129, 130, 640
ghoṣa 34, 40-42, 44, 58, 59, 111, 113, 114, 116, 117, 119, 246, 263-266, 274, 275, 288-291, 305, 306, 309, 316, 321, 639, 640, 668, 669, 672, 676, 677, 679, 681, 684
ghoṣatā 58
ghoṣanādabhāgin 640
ghoṣavat 34, 40, 42, 44, 58, 69, 116, 118, 119, 263, 264, 274, 275, 309, 321, 668, 672, 679, 681, 684, 685
ghoṣin 40, 58, 111
ṅ 39, 73, 105, 113, 116, 138, 175, 179, 180, 182, 271, 273, 284, 296, 349, 396, 636, 640, 648, 670, 671, 673
ṅa 84, 104, 113, 119, 129, 130, 139, 179-181, 183, 251, 271, 272, 284, 396, 397, 636, 640, 648, 670, 673
ṅakāra 670
ṅatva 251
ṅaM 397
ṅaMUṬ 397
ṅit 664
ṅidanta 664
c 33, 39, 40, 41, 56, 105, 131, 274, 277, 278, 281, 289, 290, 301, 303, 305, 451, 474, 636, 637, 640, 653, 672, 677, 679
c̊ 253
ca 73, 76, 104, 105, 112, 117, 125, 131, 132, 145, 250, 274, 275, 277, 278, 290, 291, 303, 306, 451, 474, 636, 637, 640, 653, 672, 677, 679
ca ('and') 100, 104, 107, 147, 149, 176, 180, 189, 190, 194, 195, 198, 201, 208, 210, 215, 216, 219, 220, 225, 227, 236-238, 258, 265, 266, 277, 286, 299, 301, 309, 316, 321, 335,

337, 339, 341, 345, 358, 362, 366, 369, 371, 388, 399, 401, 404, 405, 416, 417, 423, 424, 435, 443, 446, 464, 469, 474, 482, 485, 487-489, 491, 503, 507, 508, 517, 521, 523, 526, 531, 532, 539, 541, 548, 550, 555, 562, 564, 586, 590, 605, 613, 623, 624, 628, 637, 638, 642, 648, 651, 654, 655, 659, 660-667, 669, 675-677, 681-686
cakra 375
catur 98
caturtha 41, 72, 99, 110-112, 116, 119, 245, 253, 255-257, 259, 269, 278, 615, 637, 655, 670, 671, 676
caturthavarṇa 670
caturthī 634
caturthyartha 634
caturmātra 199
catūrātra 584, 585
caY 269, 671
caR 203
carcā 249, 476, 573-577, 581, 582, 618, 620, 625, 626
carcāpada 574
cartva 672
cal 203
cavarga 40, 72, 74, 105, 131, 132, 250, 274, 275, 277, 278, 290, 291, 303, 306, 451, 474, 637, 653, 672, 677, 679
cavargīya 274, 275, 278, 672
cāritārthya 642
cu 250, 278, 636
cutva 250
cet 301, 302, 537
cyāvayati 595, 596
cch 281
ch 39, 40, 41, 56. 274, 280-282, 305, 399, 640, 671-673, 679
cȟ 254
cha 105, 111, 112, 117, 131, 132, 274, 280, 281, 327, 399, 640, 671-673, 679
cha (affix) 130
chakāra 11, 274, 280, 281, 327, 399, 671-673
chatravat 646
chandas 71, 189, 328, 329, 352, 384, 455, 467, 478, 524, 533, 534, 591, 629, 685
chaV 291, 677
chāndasa 524, 533, 534
j 39, 40, 41, 274, 640
j̊ 253
ja 105, 112, 119, 131, 132, 250, 640
jakāra 250
jaṭā 311, 577, 578, 615, 622, 627
jaṭāpāṭha 311, 577, 578, 615, 622, 627
jani 524
japana 171, 172
jara
jarat 553, 554
jaratparvan 553
jaŚ 264, 265
jahāti 312, 313, 684
jāgāra 601
jāta 98, 634, 649, 687
jāti 640, 658
jātīya 66, 526, 527
jātīyaR 527
jātīyādi 526, 527

jātya 122, 124, 423, 424, 429-431, 437-440
jātyasvara 430
jāspatya 564, 565, 587, 588
jihvā 39, 41-43, 57, 72, 129-135, 582, 636, 640, 640, 679
jihvāgra 76, 132-136, 636
jihvāpārśva 135
jihvāmadhyadeśa 132
jihvāmadhyabhāga 636
jihvāmūla 43, 72, 129, 130, 139, 305, 307, 582, 636, 640, 648, 679
jihvāmūlanāsika 139
jihvāmūlasthāna 129
jihvāmūlīya 39, 41, 42, 57, 72, 111, 117, 129, 130, 133, 168, 169, 305, 307, 582, 636, 640, 648, 679
jihvya 130, 131
jīva 343, 684
jīvantīm oṣadhīm 378, 379
jīhīḍāham 385, 593
jj 401
jñāna 610, 612
jñāpaka 112, 677
jyotis 608
jyotiṣṭva 607, 608
jh 39, 40, 41, 44, 118, 274, 281, 640
jha 105, 111, 112, 119, 131, 132, 640
jhaY 269, 670, 671
jhaR 672
jhaL 208, 264, 265, 299, 454, 470, 675
jhaŚ 264
ñ 39, 40, 41, 43, 49, 105, 113, 138, 175, 274, 280, 296, 636, 640, 671, 672
ña 104, 105, 113, 119, 131, 132, 139, 250, 274, 275, 636, 640, 671, 672
ñakāra 250, 274, 275, 671, 672
ñatva 250
ñch 272, 281
ṭ 33, 39, 40, 41, 56, 63, 270, 271, 273, 275, 277, 278, 284, 290, 301-303, 305, 451, 474, 636, 640, 649, 653, 670-672, 677, 679, 680
ṭ̊ 253
ṭa 73, 76, 104, 112, 117, 125, 133, 145, 181, 270-272, 275, 277, 278, 284, 290, 291, 303, 306, 326, 451, 474, 640, 649, 653, 670-672, 677, 679, 680
ṭakāra 76, 143, 270, 670
ṭavarga 40, 72, 73, 76, 78, 133, 148, 275, 277, 278, 290, 291, 303, 306, 326, 451, 474, 649, 653, 672, 677, 679
ṭavargīya 275, 326, 672
Ṭā 70, 84, 509
ṭi 212, 648, 656, 657, 665
ṭilopa 656, 657
ṭit 649
ṭU 63, 72, 74, 78, 99, 102, 278, 307, 327, 573, 574, 636
ṭUK 271, 671
ṭutva 99, 573, 574
ṭh 39, 40, 41, 56, 305, 640, 671, 680
ṭha 76, 111, 112, 117, 133, 640, 671, 680

ḍ 39, 40, 41, 56, 145, 201, 271, 276, 326, 418, 640, 653, 670, 682
ḍa 76, 112, 119, 133, 134, 145, 202, 640, 653, 670, 682
ḍakāra 653, 682
ḌatamaC 516
ḌataraC 516
ḍatva 202
ḍalayor abhedaḥ 653
ḌāvatU 547
ḍh 39, 40, 41, 44, 56, 99, 118, 145, 278, 279, 283, 639
ḍha 72, 76, 99, 111, 112, 119, 133, 134, 145, 278, 279, 283, 639
ḍhatva 99, 278, 639
ṇ 36, 39, 40, 41, 43, 50, 105, 113, 138, 175, 179, 180, 271, 273, 275, 284, 296, 316, 331, 396, 397, 451-454, 456-458, 460, 462, 463, 465-475, 546, 572-574, 581, 583, 600, 602-604, 634, 636, 640, 648, 653, 658, 670-673
ṇa 76, 84, 104, 113, 119, 133, 139, 179-181, 183, 271, 272, 275, 284, 331, 368, 396, 397, 451, 452, 454, 456-458, 466-468, 470-475, 572-574, 581, 634, 636, 640, 648, 653, 658, 670, 672, 673
ṇakāra 36, 275, 451, 452, 454, 456-458, 466, 468, 470-475, 670, 672
ṇatva 467, 471, 572-574, 581, 634, 653, 658
ṇatvavidhāna 658
ṆiC 596
ṇijanta 596
ṇopadeśa 331, 453, 456
t 33, 39, 40, 41, 56, 135, 181, 184, 251, 252, 269, 270-273, 276-280, 282, 284, 290, 295, 301, 302, 305, 327, 350, 351, 382, 399, 407, 451, 474, 546, 560-562, 574, 640, 653, 670-672, 677, 680, 682
t̐ 253
ta 76, 84, 104, 112, 117, 125, 135, 145, 181, 250, 270-272, 274, 276-281, 284, 290, 291, 296, 297, 306, 326-328, 350-352, 383, 451, 474, 546, 561, 562, 640, 653, 670-672, 677, 680, 682
takāra 68, 73, 74, 76, 93, 143, 270, 276, 277, 290, 327, 328, 350-352, 383, 546, 562, 670, 672, 677, 682
takārādi 350-352, 383, 562
takārānta 93
takārottara 670
tataḥ 154, 638
tatas pari 335, 683
tad 257, 258, 269, 278, 303, 352, 353, 402, 437, 439, 534, 535, 547, 615, 627, 652, 667, 670, 672, 679
taddhita 68, 74, 239, 350, 351, 454, 480, 512, 513, 517, 518, 524-526, 543, 556, 566
tanmānin 527, 528
tama 514-516, 525, 543, 544, 561, 644, 647, 654
tara 514-516, 525, 543, 644, 654
tarkabuddhi 629
talopa 561

tavarga 40, 73, 135, 148, 250, 274, 278-281, 291, 295, 297, 306, 326, 451, 474, 653, 672, 677
tavargīya 274, 278-281, 326, 672
tātiL 68, 519, 525
tāthābhāvya 123
tā3d 259, 667
tādi 350, 351
tān agre 352, 353
tāna 611
tānasvara 611
tālavya 71, 131, 132, 144, 277, 636
tālu 39, 43, 72, 128, 131, 132, 139, 141, 142, 144, 277, 303, 635, 636
tālunāsika 139, 141, 142
tālusthāna 131
tiṄ 482, 647, 649, 666
tiṅanta 219, 482, 647
tiṅākāṅkṣa 666
tirovirāma 122
tīkṣṇa 423, 424
tīvra 423
tU 278, 636
tUK 272, 399
tulya 126, 635, 638, 641, 644, 645
tulyatā
tulyaliṅga 112
tulyavr̥tti 425
tulyāsyaprayatna 70, 141, 146, 156, 276, 412, 635, 638, 645
tuviṣṭama 476, 560
tūṣṇīmbhāva 115
tr̥tīya 41, 69, 88, 93, 106, 108, 110-112, 119, 171, 245, 253, 263, 264, 266, 388, 389, 615, 637, 651, 668-670
tr̥tīyavarṇa 668, 669
tr̥tīyavarṇānta 668
tr̥tīyā 509, 660
tr̥tīyānta 88, 93, 106, 171, 266, 388, 389, 637, 651, 668
tr̥tīyāsamāsa 660
tairovirāma 435
tairovyañjana 122, 423-425, 428, 435-438, 441
tais tvam 351, 352
tt 401
tyam 392
trā 531
tri 86, 194, 199, 200, 332, 333, 402, 603, 604, 618, 642, 643, 656, 667
tridhātu 86, 332, 333
tripada 603, 604, 618, 619
tripadakrama 619
tripadamadhyāvayava 618
triprabhr̥ti 402
trimātra 199, 200, 642, 643, 656
trividha 667
trisaṃyoga 194
tredhā 566
traiṣṭubha 587
traisvarya 611
traihāyaṇa 587
tva 523, 524
tve 220, 664
ts 184, 282
th 39, 40, 41, 56, 184, 279, 280, 305, 640, 671, 672, 680
tḣ 253
tha 111, 112, 117, 135, 640, 671, 672, 680
thakāra 672
thā 513, 514

d 39, 40, 41, 201, 269, 302, 326, 569, 640, 653, 657, 669, 670, 682
da 112, 119, 135, 202, 250, 640, 653, 657, 669, 670, 682
daṃṣṭra 375
dakāra 250, 653, 669, 670
dakāranipātana 669, 670
datva 657
dadāti 383, 562
dadhāti 564
danta 43, 72, 135, 139, 142-144, 156, 425, 636, 646, 653
dantanāsika 139, 142
dantapaṅkti 156
dantamūla 43, 72, 75, 76, 135, 136, 142-144, 425, 636, 653
dantamūlasthāna 143
dantamūlasparśin 135, 136
dantamūlīya 57, 63, 72, 102, 135, 144
dantasthāna 135, 141
dantāgra 76, 137
dantoṣṭhanāsika 142
dantauṣṭhya 137, 138
dantya 55, 135, 136, 141, 276, 636, 636, 653
dantyo(/au)ṣṭhya 55, 75, 76, 78, 137, 636
dantoṣṭhyatā 137
darśana 525, 572, 573
daśa 201, 202
dā 382, 383
dādhāra 601
dān 85, 89, 234, 234
dānīm 521, 522
dārḍhya 612, 632
dāśa 201, 202
divaḥ 337, 683
divi 366, 367
diś 571
dīdāya 390, 594
dīrgha 43, 50, 63, 67, 68, 71, 72, 74, 75, 78, 88, 99, 102, 121, 124, 141, 158, 159, 160, 174, 186-188, 197-200, 214, 215, 231, 232, 233-239, 242-244, 278, 283, 326, 374-376, 378-382, 384-392, 412, 449, 531, 532, 538, 548-550, 449, 572-574, 584, 589, 594, 597, 617, 618, 622, 623, 629, 639, 641-643, 646, 653, 655-659, 661, 663, 667, 673, 681, 682, 685, 686
dīrghatā 214, 215, 233
dīrghatva 548-550, 572, 589, 594, 597, 618, 622, 623, 655, 658
dīrghatvasamāpatti 597
dīrghaplutavyavadhāna 659
dīrghasaṃśaya 538, 559
dīrghasvarita 124
dīrghābhāva 658
dīrghāyutva 324, 325, 605, 682, 686
dīrghībhāva 574
dīrghopadha 661
duḥ 326, 330, 682
duḥspr̥ṣṭa 162
durṇāman 466
duṣṭatā 686
duṣṭara 587
dūrād āhvāna 665
dūrāddhūta 665
dr̥ḍha 422, 423
dr̥ḍhatara 422
dr̥bdha 640
dr̥śi 569

devatā 548, 549
devatādvandva 548, 549
dairghya 653, 656, 663
dyubh(i) 520, 525
dyauḥ 341, 684
dravya 479, 647
dravyapradhāna 479
dravyārthādeśa 647
drāghita 215
drughaṇa 452
druta 46, 197
droṇikā 134, 135, 156, 636
dvandva 548-550
dvār 312, 684
dvi 39, 54, 56, 68, 111, 112, 128, 152, 153, 159, 194, 196, 198, 199, 218, 223, 250, 313, 314, 395, 403, 450, 613, 642, 643, 648, 651-653, 664, 665, 673, 685
dviḥ 394, 397-399, 401-403, 651-653, 672-674
dvitīya 41, 84, 110-112, 117, 245, 268, 390, 391, 615, 623, 626, 637, 652, 658, 669-671, 676
dvitīyavarṇa 669, 676
dvitīyā 232, 235, 253, 457, 634, 664
dvitva 111, 112, 196, 250, 651-653, 673, 676
dvitvavikalpa 652
dvitvaniṣedha 651
dvitvapratiṣedha 652
dvidha 652
dvidhā 675
dvipada 613
dvimātra 159, 198, 199, 642, 643, 658
dvimātraka 199
dvimātrika 159
dviya 652
dvirukta 541, 542
dvirukti 652
dvirbhāva 196
dvirvacana 395, 539, 577, 620, 621, 626, 628
dvirvacanavr̥tti 539
dvivacana 68, 218, 219, 223, 313, 314, 648, 664, 665, 685
dvivacanānta 68, 218, 219, 223, 313, 314, 664, 665, 685
dvivarṇa 39, 54, 56, 152, 153
dvivyañjanasandhi 111
dvisaṃyoga 194
dvisthāna 128
dvisvarībhāva 243, 450
dvailiṅgya 112
dvyakṣara 565
dh 39, 40, 41, 44, 56, 118, 245, 271, 640, 652
dh̐ 253
dha 111, 112, 119, 135, 640, 652
dhakāra 652
dharma 607, 609, 635, 641, 643, 644, 658, 680, 685
dharmaśeṣa 610
dharmin 685
dhā 512
dhātu 11, 68, 203, 204, 223, 234, 235, 250, 357, 358, 417, 418, 453, 456, 457, 460, 461, 463, 468, 470, 479, 533, 562, 647, 648, 659, 660-662, 675, 678, 686
dhātunakāra 457
dhāturūpa 675
dhātustha 460, 461, 463
dhātvanta 533

dhātvartha 647
dhātvartharañjaka 647
dhātvādi 417, 659, 660
dhātvekadeśalopa 562
dhīḥ 392
dhUṬ 271, 670
dhaivata 423
dhvani 114, 115
n 39, 40, 41, 43, 113, 138, 175, 179-182, 207-209, 252, 271-275, 280, 281, 284, 290-292, 295-297, 299, 300, 316, 356, 368, 396, 407, 408, 451-459, 461-466, 468-475, 534, 546, 572, 573, 581, 583, 600, 602, 604, 636, 640, 648, 653, 670-675, 677, 678
n^h 254
na 84, 104, 113, 119, 135, 139, 179, 180, 183, 207, 208, 210, 250, 251, 271, 272, 274, 275, 278, 284, 290, 291, 293-295, 297-300, 356, 357, 388, 396, 397, 407, 451, 452, 454, 456-458, 464, 466, 468, 470-475, 636, 640, 648, 653, 670-675, 677, 678
na (negation) 13, 34, 52, 57, 61, 63, 68, 71, 78, 86, 88, 91, 93, 102, 106, 107, 112, 146, 148, 149, 151, 154, 163, 165, 185, 186, 188, 189, 202-205, 209, 224, 236, 249, 250, 286, 287, 295, 300, 301, 303, 317, 318, 324, 325, 333, 368-371, 381, 382, 385, 387, 389, 395, 401-403, 444, 450, 462, 468, 470-475, 479, 488-490, 512, 514, 523, 531-536, 547, 548, 551-553, 556-559, 561-566, 568, 570, 571, 589, 591, 599, 600-605, 608, 610, 614, 616, 618, 620, 626, 627, 629, 637, 639-641, 645, 646, 649-661, 664, 665, 667, 668, 673, 675, 676-680, 682, 685, 686
nakāra 73, 93, 207, 208, 210, 250, 251, 274, 275, 278, 290, 291, 293-295, 297-300, 407, 451, 452, 454, 456-458, 464, 466, 468, 470-474, 653, 670-672, 674, 675, 677, 678
nakārānta 677, 678
nakṣatra 608
naÑ 244, 331, 681, 685
nañsamāsa 244, 685
nadī 432, 433
napara 674
napuṃsaka 78, 93, 231, 232, 299, 317, 454, 641, 659, 685
napuṃsakabahuvacana 641
napuṃsakaliṅga 232, 641
nara 381
nalopa 356
navati 464
naśi 471
nāda 44, 58, 59, 114, 116-120, 171-175, 264, 639, 640
nādadhvanisaṃsarga 114
nādaprayatnaka 174
nādabhāgin 640
nādānupradāna 119
nānāpada 65, 279, 453, 456, 457, 468, 470, 525, 583, 628, 672
nānāpadadarśana 525
nāman 98, 226, 466, 478-480, 482, 484, 488-490, 527, 528,

627, 632, 634, 640, 645, 648, 649, 656, 687
nāmasvarūpa 656
nāmākhyātopasarganipāta 634, 687
nāmikarepha 354
nāmin 69, 73, 74, 241, 246, 294, 295, 308, 309, 348-350, 352-355, 357, 359, 365, 382-384, 410, 432, 433, 618, 636, 645, 650, 651, 658, 677, 678, 681-683, 686
nāmisvara 636
nāmyanta
nāmyupadha 74, 241, 294, 295, 308, 309, 348-350, 352-354, 658, 677, 678, 681-683
nāraka 390, 595
nārṣada 587
nāśa 686
nāsikā 43, 55, 113, 125, 138-142, 254, 636
nāsikāsthāna 139, 141
nāsikya 42, 113, 125, 138-141, 254, 255, 636
niḥ 330, 682
nigama 221, 634
nigṛhya 666
nigṛhyānuyoga 666
nighāta 437, 439, 611, 614
nitya 163, 201, 202, 209, 226, 397, 428, 548, 623, 646, 683
nityatva 209
nityasaṃhita 163, 226
nidhana 609
nipāta 11, 64, 98, 223-226, 319, 462, 463, 478, 479, 484, 496, 497, 634, 639, 641, 647-649, 664, 678, 682, 687
nipātaja 682
nipātana 639, 653, 669, 670, 680
nipātavat 639
nipātādhikāra 641
nipātānta 226, 379, 521
nipātopasargavarjita 649
nimitta 112, 357, 359, 360, 395, 452, 454, 455, 457, 578, 579, 582, 627, 629
niyoga 661
nirāsa 651
nirdiṣṭa 649, 664
nirdeśa 476
nirvāpa 609
nirvikalpaka 632
nivatas pṛṇāti 344, 345, 684
nivāraṇa 111
nivṛtti 453, 620
niścaya 661
niṣāda 423
niṣiddha 177
niṣiddhāvagraha 177
niṣedha 549, 639, 646, 651
niṣṭhā 379
nīca 123
nīcaiḥ 11, 74, 120, 121, 483, 643
nUM 68, 299, 356, 357, 451, 454-456, 474
naimittika 627, 629
nts 282
nn 401
nyāya 432, 433
nś 272, 281
ns 282
p 33, 39, 42, 56, 169, 301, 305, 307, 328, 330, 331, 338, 342, 573, 574, 636, 640, 677, 679, 680, 682, 683
p̊ 253

pa 76, 91, 104, 112, 117, 125, 136, 137, 145, 307, 328, 348, 640, 677, 679, 680, 682, 683
pakṣa 375
pañca 615
pañcajana 609
pañcapadī 68, 69, 235-239, 378, 431-433
pañcama 111, 113, 119, 139, 253, 423, 636, 637, 668, 669, 674
pañcamavarṇa 668, 669
pañcamī 78, 335, 336, 649, 683
pañcavarga 112
paṇati 602
patāti 684
pathi 366
pada 33, 63, 69, 73, 98, 99, 102-108, 139, 146, 147, 163, 168, 172, 176, 177, 182, 183, 188, 190, 191, 193, 194, 198, 202, 208, 210, 212, 215-222, 226-231, 248-251, 253, 263-270, 277, 279, 282, 285, 286, 296-301, 310, 311, 314, 316, 319, 320, 322-329, 331, 339, 349, 353-356, 358, 360, 361, 364, 365, 368, 371, 374, 375, 378, 380, 382, 383, 386, 391, 393, 394, 396, 397, 399, 409, 410, 413-415, 419, 420, 426, 430, 431, 442, 443, 445, 446, 450-457, 462, 465-468, 470, 472, 475, 476, 478, 480-484, 486-490, 494, 495, 499, 502, 503, 505-507, 509-511, 514-521, 523-537, 539-543, 546-553, 556-558, 561-588, 590-596, 598-605, 610-616, 618, 619, 624-629, 631, 632, 634, 635, 641, 642, 644, 647-651, 653, 656, 657, 660, 661, 663, 665, 668, 669, 671-678, 680-683, 685, 687
padakāla 163, 215, 217, 230, 467, 577, 613, 626
padagrahaṇa 316
padajāta 98, 634, 649, 687
padatva 511, 515, 523-525, 533-535
padadvayapūrva 212
padapāṭha 37, 60, 65, 66, 67, 81, 82, 93, 98, 99, 177, 195, 201, 212, 215-222, 226-230, 248, 249, 263-266, 269, 270, 282, 286, 299, 300, 310, 311, 314, 316, 319, 322-329, 331, 349, 353-355, 358, 360, 361, 371, 374, 375, 378, 380, 382, 386, 391, 393, 396, 409, 413-415, 419, 430, 442, 443, 445, 446, 450, 452, 453, 455, 462, 465-467, 470, 476, 478, 480-484, 486-488, 490, 494, 495, 499, 503, 505-507, 509, 510, 514-521, 523-537, 539-543, 546-553, 556-558, 561-588, 590-592, 594-596, 598-602, 604, 605, 610-616, 618, 619, 624-628, 634, 635
padapūraṇa 647
padaprakṛti 37, 98, 634, 635
padamadhya 644, 677, 682
padavat 577
padavidhi 489, 502
padavibhāga 612
padavyavāya 475
padaśaḥ 611
padaśāstra 625

padasamāmnāya 634
padādi 73, 177, 182, 202, 250, 320, 327, 420, 426, 533, 534, 656, 661, 663, 681, 683
padādisparśa 177
padādya 391, 556
padādhyayana 610-612
padādhyāyin 611, 612
padānta 69, 73, 102, 106, 145, 146, 148, 158, 163, 172, 176, 177, 182, 183, 188, 190, 191, 193, 194, 198, 202, 208, 210, 263-269, 285, 349, 394, 397, 399, 426, 450, 470, 506, 585, 615, 642, 644, 647, 648, 650, 657, 660, 661, 663, 665, 668-676, 678, 680, 685
padāntagrahaṇa 177
padāntanakāra 678
padāntavikṛta 585, 615
padāntavirāma 146
padāntasandhi 163, 177, 193
padāntasparśa 177, 615
padāntābhāva 657
padāntya 102
padābhyantara 665, 675
padya 88, 94, 98, 99, 102-107, 109, 194, 198, 244, 278, 413, 418, 615, 637, 642, 647, 649, 687
panispadā 601
para 68-70, 72, 78, 99, 112, 139, 165, 172, 173, 177-180, 184-186, 188, 191-196, 198, 208, 210, 213, 217, 228, 229, 239, 255, 256, 259, 276-278, 288-291, 296, 305, 306, 316, 326, 327, 335, 343, 371, 372, 392, 402, 403, 408, 411-415, 419, 425, 428-431, 441, 443, 444, 446, 453, 454, 461, 471, 482-484, 486, 487, 489, 507-511, 524, 542, 547, 549, 582, 615, 616, 621, 624, 637, 642, 646, 650, 652-657, 659-663, 665, 667-682, 685
paracaturthatva 72, 99, 278
parataḥ 74, 176, 178, 180, 202, 210, 214, 234, 235, 245, 249, 253, 264, 268, 270, 272, 274, 275, 277, 283, 284, 296, 297, 300, 301, 308, 309, 318, 320, 321, 326, 328, 337-345, 350, 354, 374-376, 381-383, 386, 387, 392, 397-399, 410-412, 414, 415, 418, 426, 427, 432, 434, 445, 447, 511, 512, 517-519, 522, 523, 527, 529-533, 538, 540, 544, 563, 570, 596, 652, 660, 661, 675
paratva 661
parama 361
pararūpa 413, 415, 419, 657, 661, 662
paravarja 338, 392
parasannikarṣaṇa 646
parasaṃyoga 654
parasaṃyojana 653
parasavarṇa 276, 408, 471
parasasthāna 69, 73, 246, 276, 277, 296, 305, 306, 327, 672, 673, 679, 682
parasmaibhāṣā 629
parā 457, 458
parāṅga 198
parāśraya 644
pari 371, 470, 559
parigraha 621

paridhiṣ patāti 344, 684
paripāṭha 259, 667
paribhāṣaṇa 635
paribhāṣā 635, 640, 649, 650
pariveṣṭita 636
parihartavya 623, 624
parihāra 123, 212, 310, 311, 313, 316, 317, 319, 326, 476, 573-577, 581-583, 605, 616, 619-628
parihārakāla 623, 624
parihārya 620, 621, 622, 628, 629
parīkṣā 640
parokṣā 71, 588, 589
paroṣmāpatti 210
parṇa 375
paryudāsa 161, 395
parvan 508, 509, 541, 542, 553, 580, 581
pavarga 40, 136, 137, 307, 683
pāṃsu 232, 233
pākāra 677, 678
pākṣika 672
pāda 159, 189, 190, 242, 335, 352, 420, 421, 436-438, 449, 551, 610, 675, 676, 680, 686
pādapūraṇa 686
pādapūraṇābhāva 686
pādam aṅgurim 205-207, 653
pādamātrā 159, 680
pādamātrika 680
pādavivṛtta 436
pādavivṛtti 436
pādavṛtta 122, 423-425, 436-438, 441
pādavaivṛtta 436
pādānta 189, 190, 675, 676
pārśvabindudvaya 648
pitar 340, 341, 683
pibati 524
pīḍana 145
pīḍita 171-173, 640
pU 451, 456, 474, 636, 677, 682, 685
puṃliṅga 645
puṃśca 288-290, 676
puṃs 93, 146, 238, 239, 288, 289, 317, 676
punar 315, 609, 619, 627, 685
punargrahaṇa 209
punar ṇayāmasi 463
puras 201, 202
puruṣa ā babhūvā̃3 211-213
pūraṇa 536, 647
pūrṇa 112, 644, 655
pūrṇa akāra 655
pūrṇatvābhāva 655
pūrṇākṣara 644
pūryāṇa 565, 566
pūrva 68-70, 73, 78, 84, 112, 158, 159, 164, 165, 181, 184, 185, 192-196, 207-212, 241, 244, 245, 251, 253, 256-259, 269, 278, 279, 283, 297, 298, 301, 302, 320, 331, 356, 361, 364, 365, 397, 399, 403, 407-409, 411, 412, 414, 420, 422, 425, 428-430, 448, 452-455, 472, 473, 481, 483, 486, 487, 489, 502, 505, 507, 510-512, 524, 525, 533-535, 540, 543, 578, 579, 583, 611, 624, 637, 639, 642, 646, 648-650, 653, 656-659, 661, 663, 666, 670-675, 677, 678, 681, 682, 685, 686
pūrvacaturtha 269, 670, 671

pūrvapada 158, 202, 356, 361, 364, 365, 452-455, 540, 578, 579, 583, 611
pūrvapadanimitta 578, 579
pūrvapadaprakṛtisvaratva 540
pūrvapadastha 452, 454, 455
pūrvapadādhikāra 453
pūrvapadānta 158, 193, 202
pūrvapadāntavyañjana 193
pūrvapara 411, 412, 656, 661, 681
pūrvapūrvasvara 259
pūrvabādha 637
pūrvarūpa 70, 184, 185, 448, 663, 681
pūrvavat 653, 654, 672, 677
pūrvaśāstra 64, 629
pūrvasadṛśa 637
pūrvasasthāna 278, 279, 672
pūrvasasvara 256
pūrvasvara 194, 208, 258, 259, 666, 674, 685
pūrvākṣara 658
pūrvāṅga 185, 196, 244
pūrvārdha 121
pūrvottara 181
pṛkta 41, 111, 223-225, 616-618, 623, 641, 663, 664
pṛṇāti 684
pṛthak 112, 151, 168, 541, 542, 670
pṛthak-iṅgya-samāsa 541, 542
pṛthakkaraṇa 667
pṛthaktva 112, 151
pṛthakpada 168
pṛthaksattva 112
pṛṣodaratva 657
pṛṣṭaprativacana 666
pp 401
pra 343, 457, 458, 684
prakāra 205, 213, 379
prakṛti 68, 114, 116, 117, 296, 297, 404, 406, 407, 420, 421, 479-483, 486, 487, 540, 550, 572, 573, 581, 634, 635, 641, 663, 665, 667, 670, 680, 681, 684
prakṛtidarśana 572, 573
prakṛtipratyayasamudāya 670
prakṛtibhāva 641, 660, 663, 667
prakṛtibhūta 635
prakṛtisvara 64, 479, 480-483, 486, 487, 540
prakriyā 78, 638, 639, 645
prakriyākāla 645
prakriyādaśā 78, 638
pragṛhya 68, 164, 212, 214-218, 220-230, 404, 574, 575, 577, 613, 620-623, 625, 626, 641, 648, 663-665, 667
pragṛhyatā 229
pragṛhyatva 577, 626, 641, 663
pragṛhyaprakṛti 665
pragṛhyasandhi 663
pragṛhyāvagṛhya 577, 613, 626
pragṛhyāśraya 667
praṇava 633, 666
pratijñā 256, 438, 641, 668
pratijñāna 88, 93, 98, 99, 106, 107, 110, 266, 637, 668
pratijñānunāsikya 641
pratiyatna 676
prativeṣṭana 134
prativeṣṭita 76, 132-134
pratiśravaṇa 666
pratiṣiddha 557
pratiṣedha 204, 395, 405, 515, 549, 554, 616, 652
pratiṣṭhita

pratihata 423
pratyañcā3m 259, 667
pratyabhivāda 666
pratyaya 69, 70, 130, 168, 169, 185, 221, 224, 234, 235, 237, 354-357, 359, 376, 479, 512, 514, 514, 596, 640, 641, 646, 648, 654, 655, 670, 680, 685
pratyayavyañjana 654
pratyayasakāra 354-356, 359
pratyayānta 221, 235, 237
pratyāpati 572
pratyāhāra 51
prathama 41, 88, 93, 104, 106-108, 111-113, 117, 141, 171, 212, 245, 253, 263, 266, 390, 408, 409, 498, 592, 595, 637, 652, 656, 668-671
prathamapadya 94, 498
prathamavarṇa 669
prathamā 221, 232, 235, 378, 685
prathamānta 88, 93, 106, 171, 266, 637, 668
prathamaikavacana 212, 685
prathamaikavacanānta 212
pradeśa 655
prapaṇa 602
prabhṛti 388, 402, 590
pramāṇa 668
prayatna 43, 44, 51, 57, 58, 70, 76-78, 109, 112, 116, 117, 119, 125, 126, 133, 140, 141, 145-148, 150-152, 155, 156, 173, 174, 276, 285, 287, 412, 635-640, 645, 646, 652
prayatnabhda 57
prayoga 78, 203, 638, 659, 665
prayogārha 203
prayojana 83, 97, 102, 187, 217, 230, 241, 610, 617, 618, 622, 637, 642
pravṛtti 686
praśna 641, 665-667
praśnānta 641, 666
praśliṣṭa 153, 160, 163, 423, 424, 639
praśliṣṭāvarṇa 153, 163
praśleṣa 157, 429, 639
prasakta 616
prasaṅga 395, 687
prasajyapratiṣedha 395
prasandhāna 582, 615, 624, 625
prasāraṇa 535, 536
prastīrṇa 135, 636
prākṛtadhvani 46
prākśliṣṭa 122, 424, 427, 437
prāṇa 34, 36, 44, 637, 672
prāṇati, prāṇanti 558, 559
prātar 315, 685
prātijña 62, 72, 98-101, 649, 686, 687
prātipadika 68, 454-456, 479, 648, 649
prātipadikānta 454-456
prāpta 101, 102, 190, 221, 250, 533, 637, 651-654
prāpti 111, 651
prāśī3ḥ 259, 667
prāśliṣṭa 122, 423, 424, 427-429, 437-440
pretya 607
prepsu 527-529
preraṇa 666
preṣaṇa 666
pluta 10, 43, 75, 121, 124, 159, 161, 164, 165, 187, 188, 197, 199, 200, 212, 213, 244, 247-

249, 259, 260, 504, 505, 623-625, 629, 639, 641-643, 646, 656, 659, 663, 665, 667
plutakārya 656
plutatā 200
plutatva 212
plutavat 667
plutasandhi 663, 667
plutasvara 187, 504, 505
plutasvarita 124
plutānunāsika 213
pluti 11, 247, 259, 667
ph 39, 42, 56, 169, 305, 307, 640, 680
pha 111, 112, 117, 136, 137, 640, 680
phyakāra 194
b 39, 56, 138, 302, 640, 651
ba 112, 119, 136, 137, 640, 651
bakāra 651
babhūva 504, also see: *ā babhūvā̃3*
barhiḥ 366, 367
bala 34, 36, 37, 646, 655, 670
balavat 653
balābala 424
balīyas 646, 665
bahiraṅga 78, 649
bahula 71, 352, 380, 381, 382, 384, 386-389, 461, 533, 534, 567, 589, 591, 629, 677, 686
bahulagrahaṇa 380, 381
bahulādhikāra 677
bahuvacana 68, 76, 143, 221-223, 231, 232, 641, 664
bahuvacanagrahaṇa 223
bahuvacanānta 221, 223
bahusaṃyoga 198
bādha 637
bāhulaka 686
bāhyaprayatna 58, 78, 116-118, 120, 636, 639, 640
bindu 648
bodhana 641
bodhapratībodhau 601
brahma 335, 683
brahmaṇvat 604
brahmayajña 611
bh̥ 39, 56, 104, 118, 640, 651, 652
bh̊ 253
bha 111, 112, 119, 136, 137, 189, 640, 651, 652
bhakāra 189, 651, 652
bhatva 193
bhartsana 666
bhavati 330, 679
bhānu 469
bhāle puṇḍravat 646
bhāva 479, 647, 663, 667, 672, 677, 680, 681
bhāvapradhāna 479
bhāvya 122, 123
bhāvyamāna 649
bhāṣā 666
bhiḥ 530, 531
bhinnapadathatva 627, 629
bhugna 680
bhuvaḥ 318, 319, 685
bhūta 348, 417, 418, 533
bhūtakaraṇa 69, 417, 418
bhūyā3ḥ 259, 667
bhūvādi 647
bhūṣaṇa 677
bheda 639, 641, 644, 661, 662
bhedaka 45
bhyaḥ
bhyām 530, 531

m 39, 113, 138, 175, 207-209, 251, 252, 254, 288, 296-301, 322, 387, 407, 408, 507, 546, 633, 636, 637, 640, 669, 673-676
m^h 254
ma 76, 78, 104, 106, 113, 119, 136, 137, 139, 176, 188, 207, 208, 210, 241, 242, 246, 288, 289, 296-298, 300, 301, 407, 507, 633, 636, 637, 640, 669, 673-676
makāra 188, 207, 208, 210, 241, 246, 288, 289, 296-298, 300, 301, 407, 507, 633, 673-676
makāropadha 241
maṇḍala 423
mata 106
matabheda 106
matU 68, 71, 242, 387, 507, 517, 525, 526, 546, 669
matUP 71, 242, 507, 517, 525, 526, 546
matvartha 68, 238, 507, 546
madhya 76, 113, 116, 131, 132, 134, 143, 197, 244, 253, 486, 562, 616-618, 620, 636, 644, 651, 653, 677, 682
madhyajihva 131, 132, 636
madhyadeśa 76
madhyabhāva 618
madhyama 46, 540-542, 617
madhyasthāna 76, 143
madhyodātta 244
manas pāpa 345, 684
manuṣyat 565, 566
mantra 610, 611
mantraprayoga 611
mantrārthajñāna 610
mapara 674
maya 71, 522, 525, 526
mayaṬ 71, 522, 525, 526
mahāprāṇa 44, 111, 672
māṃsa 232, 233
māṄ 591
māṅyoga 591
mātṛkā 638
mātra 521
mātraC 521
mātrā 37, 70, 72, 74, 112, 124, 125, 128, 157, 159, 160, 165, 184, 185, 196-200, 256, 437, 439, 450, 506, 631, 639, 642, 643, 656-658, 679
mātrākāla 450, 506, 642
mātrādhikya 679
mātrārdha 70, 123, 124, 125, 184, 185, 643
matrāvibhāga 159
mātroccāra 643
mān 85, 89, 234, 235
mānta 673
māvasāna 145, 176, 637
māvasānānika 106
mIT 454
mitākṣara 647
mitra 381
mitravat 646
mithaḥ 540, 541
mināti 467, 468
miśra 617, 671
mīmāya 601
mukha 76, 113, 125, 133, 137, 140, 141, 148, 151, 635, 636
mukhanāsika 113, 125, 140, 141, 636
mukhanāsikāvacana 113
mukhaprāntādhobhāga 137

mukhaprāntordhvabhāga 137
mukhabila 133
mukhamudraṇa 151
mud 84, 268
muṣi 343, 684
mūrdhan 43, 72, 76, 133-135, 139, 142-144, 636, 653, 658, 682
mūrdhanāsika 139, 142
mūrdhanya 57, 63, 66, 72, 75, 76, 78, 102, 130, 132-135, 143, 201, 202, 326, 349, 369, 636, 653, 682
mūrdhanyalakāra 653
mūrdhanyasthāna 133
mūrdhaprānta 135
mūrdhasthāna 134, 143
mūla 64, 116, 636, 640, 648, 653, 679·
mūlakāraṇa 116
mūlaśāstra 64
muṣi 343
mṛdu 145, 147, 423, 424
mṛdutara 424
mṛduprayatna 145, 147
me 220-222
mradīyas 422
y 33, 39, 42, 43, 56, 108, 125, 146, 174, 209, 210, 214, 285, 287, 288, 292, 296, 297, 300, 308, 349, 359, 388, 406, 410, 429, 430, 432, 460, 527-529, 534, 565, 566, 585, 586, 636, 638, 640, 651, 652, 655, 674, 678, 680, 681
ỹ 42, 43, 296, 297, 300, 674
ya 11, 50, 72, 74, 107, 119, 131, 132, 142, 146, 174, 208-210, 285, 308, 321, 388, 406, 429, 430, 432, 460, 527-529, 565, 566, 585, 586, 636, 638, 640, 651, 652, 655, 674, 678, 680, 681
yakāra 11, 50, 107, 132, 142, 209, 210, 285, 308, 321, 388, 406, 460, 529, 565, 566, 651, 652, 655, 674, 678, 680
yakārarephoṣmāpatti 209
yakārādi 388, 529
yakārādeśa 652
yaṄ 589
yajña 607-609, 611, 633, 666
yajñāṅga 666
yajñatati 607-609
yaṆ 410, 431, 536
yaT 654, 655
yatna 636, 646
yatva 585, 586, 681, 686
yathā 251, 608, 625
yathāmnāta 493, 629
yathāmnātasvara 493
yathāśāstra 614, 624, 625
yathāsaṃkhya 55, 56, 128, 139, 141, 246, 251, 253, 271
yad 213, 547, 550
yama (nasalized stop-allophones) 42, 117-119, 128, 138, 139, 192, 193, 251-254, 272, 398, 637, 640
yama (register) 120, 121, 643
yama (dual sounds?) 121
yami 597, 598
yaY 408, 471
yaR 267, 395, 403, 407, 408, 669
yaroṣmāpatti 208
yavalapara 674
yavānta 429, 430
yas patiḥ 338, 683
yā 529

yājuṣa 675
yājñika 607, 608
yājyāntaḥ 666
yātumāvat 506
yāthātathya 663
yādi 527, 528
yāvayati 596
yukta 470, 472, 500-503, 666, 667
yugapadvacana 157
yuṣmad 351, 352, 524
yuṣmadasmadādeśa 489
yuṣmadādeśa 351, 352
yuṣme 220-222
yoga 172, 176, 177, 179, 180, 183, 225, 226, 250, 636, 653, 654, 657, 658, 664, 670, 676, 686
yonāv adhy airayanta 503
yoni 680
yy 401
r 33, 39, 42, 56, 133, 142, 144, 157-160, 174, 178, 196, 202-205, 207, 213, 214, 255-257, 276, 283, 290, 294, 295, 298, 300, 309-312, 314-319, 349, 368, 372, 389, 402-404, 410, 416, 418, 451, 452, 455, 456, 461, 473, 474, 603, 621, 636, 638, 640, 652, 653, 655, 656, 657, 675, 685
ra 75, 78, 102, 119, 133, 146, 157, 174, 195, 196, 208, 278, 283, 389, 403, 451, 452, 456, 471, 472, 475, 636, 638, 640, 653, 657, 675, 685
rakāra 657
rakāradvayayoga 657
rakta 215
rañjaka 647
rañjana 215
rathantara 317, 685
ralayoḥ sāvarṇyam 653
ralopa 389, 685
rahita 649
rājati 300, 675
rātri 317, 318, 685
rāyas poṣa 345, 346, 684
riphita 311, 621
riṣi 590, 591
rU 318, 533, 534, 677, 680
rutva 533, 534
ruvidhi 318
rupi 590, 591
rūḍhi 515
rūpa 53, 70, 148, 158, 172, 174, 184, 201, 202, 250, 379, 419, 448, 639, 652, 655, 657, 658, 661, 662, 663, 674, 675, 682
repha 12, 67, 69, 72, 73, 75, 76, 102, 142, 157-159, 161, 172, 195, 196, 202-205, 209, 213, 241, 255-257, 259, 283, 294, 295, 308, 309, 311, 312, 314-319, 354, 355, 359, 368, 371, 372, 402, 403, 425, 451, 636, 639, 642, 650, 653, 655, 656, 658, 660, 675, 676, 678, 680, 681, 684, 685
rephatva 658
rephatvābhāva 658
rephadharmin 685
rephapara 371, 372
rephaprakṛti 684
rephahakārakramaja 195, 255, 403, 642
rephādeśa 685
rephānta 684
rephitva 684

rephin 684, 685
rephivisargalopa 685
rephottara 658
rodana 665
rau 313, 314
raudvivacanānta 313, 314, 685
rh 403
l 33, 39, 42, 43, 56, 104, 135, 160, 178, 179, 202, 203, 205, 207, 214, 276, 296-299, 349, 410, 451, 473, 636, 638-640, 648, 653, 658, 672, 674, 675
l̃ 42, 43, 276, 296, 297, 299, 300, 674, 675
la 69, 119, 135, 146, 160, 161, 178, 179, 183, 202-205, 276, 277, 299, 300, 327, 451, 473, 636, 638-640, 648, 653, 658, 672, 674, 675
lakāra 12, 67, 69, 104, 135, 142, 160, 161, 178, 179, 183, 202-205, 276, 277, 299, 300, 327, 473, 639, 648, 658, 672, 675
lakṣaṇa 63, 83, 102, 122, 205, 510, 574, 614, 617, 629, 640, 641
laghu 109, 112, 145, 147, 173, 182, 185-189, 285, 642
laghuguruprayojanābhāva 187, 642
laghugurulakṣaṇa 642
laghuprayatnatara 109, 112, 125, 145-147, 173, 285, 287, 652
latva 203, 204
lākṣaṇa 422
liṅga 112, 146, 232, 629, 641
liṅgasāmānya 112
lIṬ 212
liṭprathamaikavacanānta 212
lipi 251
luk 589, 664
lupta 174, 562
lekhana 250, 648, 679, 680
leśavr̥tti 107-110, 287, 288, 652
loka 609
lopa 78, 81, 99, 207, 208, 210, 223, 241, 278, 282-287, 297-299, 321, 323, 325, 326, 356, 357, 389, 395, 397, 406, 472, 540, 552, 562, 565, 566, 573, 629, 645, 646, 648, 651-654, 656-658, 664, 672, 674, 675, 678-682, 685, 686
lopābhāva 672
laukika 562, 686
lh 179
ll 401
v 33, 39, 42, 43, 56, 108, 125, 137, 138, 146, 214, 285-288, 294, 297, 299-301, 349, 387, 406, 410, 429, 430, 507, 517, 518, 533-536, 548, 566, 636, 638, 640, 653, 669, 674, 675, 678, 680
ṽ 42, 43, 297, 300, 674
va 75, 119, 136, 137, 142, 146, 189, 210, 241, 242, 285-287, 294, 301, 406, 429, 430, 507, 517, 533-535, 548, 566, 636, 638, 640, 653, 669, 674, 675, 678, 680
vakāra 55, 76, 78, 107, 137, 142, 189, 285-287, 294, 301, 406, 507, 517, 533-535, 548, 566, 636, 653, 675, 678, 680
vakārādi 517, 548
vacana 113, 256, 626
vatu 68, 546, 547
vatUP 242, 546, 547

vatva 241
vadanti 437, 439
vani 597, 598
vandaneva vṛkṣam 322, 323
varī 391, 392
varga 40, 50, 53, 72, 106, 108, 111-113, 119, 128-133, 136, 137, 139, 141, 250, 257, 274, 275, 278-281, 296, 297, 301, 302, 306, 307, 326, 355, 474, 636, 637, 648, 668, 670-672, 675, 680
vargaprathama 668, 670
vargaprathamākṣara 668
vargaviparyaya 257, 301, 675
vargākṣara 670, 671
vargāntara 141
vargādi 141
vargāntya 119, 128
vargottama 139
vargīya 274, 275, 278, 280, 281, 672
varja 335-338, 351, 352, 392, 481, 557, 560, 645, 683
varjita 649, 667, 676
varṇa 3, 33, 37, 39, 40, 44, 46, 49, 50, 68, 69, 72-74, 76, 78, 102, 111, 113, 116, 117, 119, 124, 125, 127-129, 131, 133, 135, 136, 139-141, 143, 153, 156, 157-163, 165, 167, 168, 173, 201, 208, 209, 213, 226, 241, 243, 244, 251, 253, 256, 264, 276, 394, 395, 397, 404, 412-414, 416, 427, 451, 471, 552, 557, 629, 634-636, 638-641, 645, 646, 648-652, 654, 658, 659, 661, 663, 668-675, 685
varṇakāryādarśana 648
varṇakrama 244, 394, 397, 404
varṇaguṇa 41, 58, 111
varṇagraha 78, 650
varṇajāti 640
varṇadvayaja 163
varṇadharma 251, 253
varṇanāśa 686
varṇaprakṛti 116
varṇalopa 552
varṇavikāra 686
varṇaviparyaya 686
varṇasamāmnāya 49
varṇasāmānya 243, 634
varṇāgama 686
varṇānta 136, 557
varṇāntara 395
varṇābhāva 648
varṇoccāra 133, 635
varṇoccāraṇa 76, 125
varṇoccāraṇasthāna 125
varṇoccārasthāna 124
varṇaikya 646
varta 383
vartana 106
vaṃśakrama 618
vasantatilakā 189
vasu 381, 529, 542
vasU 68, 69, 235-238, 533-536
vasudhātaraḥ 542
vasvanta 68, 69, 235, 237, 238
vā 55, 69, 72, 75, 101, 107, 146, 149, 151, 173, 174, 193, 200, 207, 257, 259, 265, 267, 399, 407, 408, 429, 430, 480, 482, 483, 510, 525, 561, 652, 655, 660, 662, 663, 665, 667, 669, 671, 673, 677, 678, 680, 683, 685

vākya 505, 611, 629, 647, 661, 665, 676
vākyapūraṇa 647
vākyabheda 661, 662
vākyādhyāhāra 676
vāna 391, 392
vānta 654
vāyu 110
vār 312, 684
vāvṛdhāna 590
vi 537
vikampita 437-439
vikalpa 75, 83, 525, 637, 648, 652, 653, 655, 661, 662, 665, 679
vikāra 634, 635, 686
vikṛta 148, 173, 557, 585
vikṛṣita 510
vikrānta 187
vigṛhya 316, 582, 583
vigraha 478, 486, 487, 489, 500, 501-504, 525, 563, 564, 610
vighāta 258, 259
VIC 543
vicāryamāṇa 249, 666
VIṬ 543
vidi 237
vidma 386, 387
vidhā 243, 436, 437, 450
vidhāna 624, 658, 660, 686
vidhāyaka 649, 650, 654
vidhāraṇa 169-173, 648
vidhi 210, 223, 241, 318, 395, 489, 629, 639, 646, 680, 686
vidhīyamāna 649, 650
vinata 586
vināma 532, 617
vināśa 78, 649
vināśonmukha 78, 649
viniyoga 91
viparīta 302
viparyaya 257, 301, 302, 675, 686
viprakarṣa 303, 679
vipratiṣedha 653
vibhakta 611
vibhakti 68, 221, 317, 318, 378, 454-456, 511, 540, 629, 634, 641, 645, 647-649, 652, 664, 665
vibhaktinakāra 456
vibhaktirahita 649
vibhaktilopa 645, 664
vibhaktyanta 647
vibhaktyartha 511
vibhaktyalopa 540
vibhaktyāgamaprātipadikānta 454
vibhaktyādeśa 455
vibhāga 158, 159, 612
vibhāṣā 2, 62, 72, 83, 100-102, 205, 285, 526, 637, 640, 648, 654, 655, 660, 663, 666, 680, 684, 686
vibhāṣāprāpta 100-102, 637
virāma 146, 151, 152, 155, 156, 188, 191, 212, 249, 257, 301, 302, 435, 505, 584, 586, 648, 673, 675
vilambita 46, 198
vivakṣaṇa 641
vivakṣita 641
vi var 310-312, 684
vivaraṇa 148, 151
vivāra 120, 640
vivṛta 34, 43, 44, 52, 57, 77, 78, 116, 134, 147-156, 162, 636, 638, 645, 646, 654
vivṛtakaraṇa 149
vivṛtatama 44, 54, 56, 151-153, 155, 162, 638, 644, 647, 654

vivṛtatara 44, 54, 151-153, 155, 638, 644, 646, 647, 654
vivṛtatarāvarṇa 153
vivṛttasandhi 217, 218, 230
vivṛtti 436, 450, 506
viveka 635
viśeṣa 125, 126, 205, 510, 533, 635, 637, 646
viśeṣaṇa 152, 646
viśeṣapratipatti 205
viśpati 561, 562
viśpatnī 561, 562
viśrambha 644
viśva 381, 521, 522
viṣaya 647, 656
visarga 39, 42, 86, 90, 117, 128, 129, 146, 148, 158, 167-169, 172, 174, 185, 187, 188, 193, 194, 306, 329, 561, 638-640, 648, 678-682, 685, 686
visargalopa 681, 686
visargasandhi 146, 679
visargādeśa 679
visargopadha 681
visarjanīya 12, 73, 90, 104, 127-129, 167, 168, 184, 209, 246, 260, 285, 288, 289, 291-295, 305-312, 314, 316-328, 330-341-346, 356, 357, 401, 636, 638, 640, 648, 651, 658, 660, 676, 678-680, 683, 685
visarjanīyalopa 658
vīpsā 518
vUK 536
vṛkṣān vanāni 294
vṛtti 46, 54, 78, 88, 93, 98, 99, 106-110, 162, 163, 165, 197, 225, 246, 266, 287, 296, 305, 410, 438, 480, 481, 494, 539, 637, 639, 652, 668
vṛddha 555, 556
vṛddhi 408, 418, 419, 556, 557, 647, 661, 662
vṛddhimān 556
vṛddhisvarānta 556
veda 607-610
vedādhyayana 607-609
vaikṛta 676
vaikṛtadhvani 46
vaidika 659, 665, 686
vailiṅgya 112
vaivṛtta 436
vyañjaka 258
vyañjana 11, 34, 69, 72, 78, 111, 112, 117, 119, 120, 169-173, 179, 181-185, 187, 188, 191-194, 196, 198, 243, 249, 250, 256, 257, 259, 324, 392, 394, 435, 436, 438, 441, 447, 522, 523, 550, 617, 642, 645, 646, 648-652, 654, 655, 658, 667, 668, 672, 675, 677, 679, 681, 685
vyañjanacatuṣka 194
vyañjanatrayasaṃyoga 193
vyañjanatva 658
vyañjanapara 259, 667
vyañjanamiśra 617
vyañjanarūpa 172
vyañjanavidhāraṇa 169-173, 648
vyañjanavyaveta 435, 436
vyañjanasandhi 182, 668, 679
vyañjanādi 550
vyañjanānta 187, 188
vyatyaya 250, 512, 552, 629
vyadhi 376, 568
vyapekṣā 683

vyapeta 435
vyavadhāna 250, 253, 270, 272, 653, 659
vyavasthā 102
vyavasthita 83, 102, 205, 525, 526
vyavasthitavibhāṣā 205, 526
vyavāya 12, 69, 302, 356, 357, 359, 360, 451, 455, 473-475, 653
vyavāyin 302
vyaveta 182, 249, 250, 256, 435, 436
vyākhyāna 205
vyāvṛtti 221
vyāsa 442, 443, 445, 446
ś 33, 39, 41, 42, 56, 57, 90, 178, 268, 271-274, 276, 277, 280-282, 284, 305, 306, 334, 403, 451, 473, 636, 638, 640, 653, 669-672, 675, 679, 680, 682
śa 69, 72, 74, 84, 111, 117, 131, 132, 148, 172, 174, 179, 181, 193, 268, 271, 272, 274, 276, 277, 280, 281, 284, 327, 403, 451, 473, 636, 638, 640, 653, 669-672, 675, 679, 680, 682
śakalyeṣin 419, 420
śakāra 132, 192, 274, 276, 277, 280, 281, 327, 473, 671, 672, 680
saṅkā 651, 665
śaṅkānirāsa 651
śaṅkāpraśna 665
śacī 339, 683
śataudana 607
śatruvat 646
śatva 172
śabda 167, 194, 202, 205, 212, 213, 221, 223, 226, 228-230, 233, 239, 249, 279, 415, 509, 511, 515, 525, 529, 561, 565, 566, 571, 594, 610, 612, 632
śabdavidhi 112
śabdaśāstra 632
śabdasaṃjñā 167
śaR 269, 271, 356, 357, 404, 640, 671, 680
śara 386, 387
śarpara 680
śas 518, 519
śān 85, 89, 234, 235
śāstra 629, 637
śāstradṛṣṭi 629
śikṣā 37
śīghratara 637
śuddha 211, 617, 624
śuddhīkaraṇa 92
śun 327, 328, 382, 682
śūdrādhikāra 666
śepaharṣaṇīm 322, 323
śeṣa 610
śeṣatā 610
ścu 278
śp 561
śrathi 597, 598
śravaṇa 667, 672
śruti 40, 442, 445
śreyaḥ 328, 329
śvāsa 44, 58, 113, 114, 116, 117, 119, 171-175, 637, 639, 640, 679
śvāsadhvanisaṃsarga 114
śvāsaprayatnaka
śvāsānupradāna 117, 640
śvāsaikadeśa 679
ṣ 33, 36, 39, 41, 42, 56, 90, 134, 268, 271-273, 279, 280, 284, 305, 306, 316, 327, 333, 334,

341-343, 348-365, 367, 369-372, 403, 404, 451, 452, 456, 461, 473, 532, 572-574, 578-583, 586, 588, 590, 618, 627, 628, 636, 638, 640, 653, 658, 669-672, 675-677, 679, 680, 682, 683

ṣa 75, 78, 84, 102, 111, 117, 133-135, 148, 172, 174, 178, 181, 202, 268, 271, 272, 279, 284, 348, 350, 352-364, 366-372, 403, 451, 452, 456, 461, 471, 472, 473, 475, 572-574, 578-582, 586, 590, 627, 628, 636, 638, 640, 653, 658, 669-672, 675, 677, 679, 680, 682, 683

ṣakāra 36, 72, 74, 133-135, 279, 348, 350, 352-364, 366-372, 451, 461, 636, 653, 672, 677, 680, 682, 683

ṣakārānta 279

ṣaṭ 201, 202

ṣatva 172, 572-574, 578-582, 586, 590, 627, 628, 658

ṣatvaṇatvavidhāna 658

ṣatvavidhāna 658

ṣaṣṭha 615

ṣaṣṭhī 78, 542, 543, 649

ṣaṣṭhīsamāsa 543

ṣaṣṭhyanta 542

ṣānta 471

ṣoḍaśin 551, 552

ṣṭu 72, 99, 278, 307, 327, 354, 574

ṣṭutva 99, 278, 327

ṢyaÑ 612

ṣṣ 354

s 33, 39, 41, 42, 86, 90, 135, 184, 252, 268, 270, 271, 273, 279, 280, 282, 284, 291, 292, 305, 306, 316, 322, 328-330, 332-338, 340-346, 348-372, 403, 451, 473, 476, 522, 532, 546, 559-561, 572, 573, 581, 583, 588, 618, 636, 638, 640, 669-672, 675-677, 679, 680, 682, 685, 686

sa 69, 84, 86, 111, 117, 135, 148, 172, 174, 179, 181, 202, 268, 270-272, 282, 284, 307, 328-330, 332, 333, 336-346, 348, 350, 353-364, 366, 367, 369-372, 403, 451, 473, 476, 522, 546, 559, 560, 636, 638, 640, 669-672, 675-677, 679, 680, 682, 685, 686

saḥ 324, 681, 685

saṃkhyā 525

saṃjñā 501, 515, 621, 635, 641, 642, 644-646, 648, 649, 651, 654, 656, 658, 663, 667, 668

saṃyukta 70, 72, 170, 171, 182-185, 250, 648, 677, 680

saṃyoga 111, 112, 172, 179, 182, 183, 185-188, 192-194, 198, 245, 249, 250, 251, 256, 258, 259, 395, 397, 398, 402, 429, 642, 645, 647, 648, 650, 651, 655-658, 661, 662, 667, 668, 670, 674

saṃyogapara 198, 642

saṃyogādi 192, 193, 198, 398, 402, 642, 651, 674

saṃyogānta 395, 397

saṃyogābhighāta 667

saṃyogāvighāta 258, 259

saṃyojana 653, 655

saṃvr̥ta 44, 52, 78, 116, 150, 155-157, 421, 636, 638, 640, 645, 647
saṃvr̥takaraṇa 156
saṃśaya 510, 538, 552, 559, 610, 612
saṃśayaccheda 612
saṃśliṣṭa 641
saṃsarga 114
saṃsr̥ṣṭa 157, 165
saṃskāra 528
saṃspr̥ṣṭa 54, 147, 157-160, 162, 163, 165, 639
saṃspr̥ṣṭarepha 157, 159, 160, 639
saṃspr̥ṣṭavarṇa 54, 162, 163
saṃhita 226, 614
saṃhitā 11, 35, 36, 37, 80, 81, 91, 98, 99, 166, 212, 215, 216, 218, 220, 221, 227, 248, 249, 263, 265, 266, 282, 286-288, 299, 300, 310, 311, 313-317, 319, 322, 323, 325-327, 343, 349, 355, 371, 372, 374, 375, 380, 382, 386, 396, 406, 414, 419, 430, 442, 445, 450, 460-462, 467, 470, 476, 524, 528, 534, 561, 563, 580, 581, 583-588, 590-597, 599-602, 604, 605, 610-614, 621, 624, 626-628, 634, 635, 641, 646, 650, 668
saṃhitākāla 467, 626
saṃhitādārḍhya 612
saṃhitāpadadārḍhya 613
saṃhitāpāṭha 98, 99, 194, 212, 215, 216, 218, 220, 221, 227, 248, 249, 263, 265, 266, 282, 286-288, 299, 300, 310, 311, 313-317, 319, 322, 323, 325-327, 343, 349, 355, 371, 372, 374, 375, 380, 382, 386, 396, 406, 414, 419, 430, 442, 450, 460-462, 467, 470, 476, 524, 528, 534, 561, 563, 580, 581, 583-588, 590-597, 599-602, 604, 605, 610-614, 621, 624, 626-628, 634, 635
saṃhitāvat 626-627, 629
saṃhitāvadvacana 626, 627
sakāra 68, 69, 71, 74, 91, 135, 270, 282, 307, 328-330, 332, 336-346, 348, 350, 353-364, 366, 367, 369-373, 476, 522, 546, 559, 560, 672, 676, 677, 680, 682, 683, 685, 686
sakārasthānīyavisarga 682, 683, 686
sakārāgama 476
sakārādi 559
sakārādeśa 685
sacati 683
sajātīya 652
satva 86, 172, 333, 682
sattva 112, 479, 528, 641
sattvanāman 528
sattvapr̥thaktva 112
sattvapradhāna 479
sattvākhya 479
sadi 365-367
sadr̥śa 637, 679
sadyaḥ 328, 329
saN 85, 233-235
sanutar 315, 685
santāna 37
sandigdha 641
sandeha 66, 67, 201, 205, 328, 532, 538, 547, 551-553, 559, 612, 613

sandehāpanaya 612
sandehāpanodana 613
sandhāna 614, 615, 618, 624, 625
sandhānalakṣaṇa 625
sandhānavidhāna 624
sandhi 109, 111, 158, 162-165, 177, 182, 187, 216-218, 230, 249, 292, 299, 317, 323, 404, 406, 408, 409, 419, 420, 425, 428, 448, 538, 611, 617, 618, 625, 633, 635, 641, 644, 646, 650, 652, 654, 658, 663, 665, 667, 668, 675, 677, 679, 686
sandhija 428
sandhiyoga 658
sandhisādhana 635, 650
sandhistha 651, 675, 677
sandhisthānādeśīyavarṇa 651
sandhya 98, 99, 167, 278, 301-303, 407, 410, 418, 649, 651, 675, 677, 687
sandhyakṣara 39, 53, 54, 76, 121, 136, 143, 150, 154, 162-165, 410, 411, 644, 651, 654, 675, 680
sanna 172-174, 183, 441, 444, 447, 640
sannatara 170-174, 183, 441, 444, 447, 640
sannikarṣa 646
sannipāta 302
saptamī 68, 69, 78, 216, 217, 649, 664
saptamyartha 68, 69, 216, 217, 664
sabhāva 485
sam 300, 537, 559, 560, 675
sama 651
samanta 536
samartha 481, 489, 502
samasta 479, 480, 490, 557
samasyate 498, 524, 525, 544
samāna 39, 70, 74, 78, 121, 126, 139, 140, 150, 156, 184, 185, 251, 252, 259, 278, 279, 368, 442-446, 451, 452, 456, 471, 472, 475, 618, 637, 640, 641, 643, 644, 653, 656, 658, 659, 667, 672, 685
samānakaraṇa 70, 184, 185
samānatva 641
samānadharma 651
samānapada 139, 251, 253, 278, 279, 368, 442, 443, 445, 446, 451, 452, 456, 471, 472, 475, 626, 653, 672
samānayama 11, 120, 121, 643
samānākṣara 11, 68, 74, 259, 412, 618, 641, 656, 667, 685
samānākṣarapara 259, 667
samānāsyaprayatna 70, 140, 156, 412
samānasthānakaraṇāsyaprayatna 141, 646
samāmnāta 608, 634
samāmnāya 35, 38, 49, 634, 639
samāpatti 67, 201, 202, 462, 572, 573, 577-580, 582, 584-589, 590, 593-597, 599, 603-605
samāpādya 572, 574, 620, 621, 626, 627
samāsa 65, 66, 68, 91, 193, 328-331, 348, 453, 454, 478, 480-482, 499, 501, 507, 523, 525, 526, 533-535, 539-543, 562, 600, 657, 660, 662, 665, 676, 681-683, 685
samāsavat 539

samāsānyāya 562
samāhāra 153, 163, 643
samāhāravarṇa 153
samudāya 670
samudra 555
sam airayan ta 295, 296, 678
samparka 685
sampr̥kta 663
samprasāraṇa 536
sambaddhārtha 488, 489
sambandha 610, 678, 685
sambandhin 678
sambuddhi 81, 227, 229
sambodhana 645, 665
sayama 192, 193, 398
sarūpa 45, 53, 639, 652, 655, 674
sarva 560
sarvatīkṣṇa 424
sarvatra 433, 434
sarvanāman 221, 310, 311, 569, 649, 684
sarvavedapāriṣada 101
sarvādi 649
sarvānudātta 491
salakāra 160, 161, 639
savarga 51
savargīya
savarṇa 50-52, 68, 70, 71, 74, 78, 117, 126, 140, 141, 144, 146, 149, 153, 156, 276, 408, 412, 471, 589, 635, 638-640, 645, 646, 649, 650, 653, 655, 656, 659, 675, 682
savarṇagrahaṇa 51-53, 56, 141, 144, 649
savarṇadīrgha 412, 656, 682
savarṇadharma 635
savarṇamātra 650
savarṇavat 52
savikalpaka 632
savidha 436, 437
savya 362
savyañjana 192
sasavarṇa 650
sasthāna 40, 41, 69, 84, 111, 246, 268, 276, 278, 279, 296, 305, 306, 327, 401, 645, 648, 651, 653, 672-674, 679, 680, 682
sasthānakaraṇa 645
sasthānatva 653, 682
sasthānatvabala 651
sas padīṣṭa 324
sasvara 256
sahayoga 670
sahasra, sahasrasātama 542-544
sahi 348, 350, 359, 374, 379, 570, 594
sahita 670, 674
sāṃhitika 618
sāṭ 348-350
sāḍbhūta 348-350, 374
sāḍha 379, 380
sātrāsāha 391
sādr̥śya 648, 654, 679
sādhaka 641, 647
sādhakatama 635, 647
sādharmya 668
sādhu 529
sādhya 687
sānusvāra 188, 189, 642
sānta 683, 685
sāmagāyana 667
sāman 37
sāmarthya 489, 501, 502, 641, 660, 683
sāmānya 2, 62, 63, 72, 78, 100-102, 112, 155, 637, 646
sāmānyaśāstra 637

sāmīpya 143
sārūpya 652
sāvarṇya 57, 78, 116, 149, 161, 646, 653, 656, 658, 659
sāhyāma 386, 593, 594
sici 359, 628
siddha 223, 250, 281, 408, 471, 504, 505, 535, 634, 635, 649, 653-657, 659, 671, 672, 677, 678, 687
siddhatva 504, 505
sīmanta 413
su 531
sukhoccāra 644
sUṬ 210, 561, 677, 682
suÑ 68, 363, 364, 377
suP 219, 647, 660-662, 664
suptiṅanta 647
suprāvyā 508-510
subanta 219, 647
subdhātu 661, 662
subhiṣaktama 544
sumna 529, 530
suluk 664
sūtracāritārthya 642
sūtrabala 653, 655
sūtravidhānasāmarthya 660
sūtrasāmarthya 641
sūtrārambha 223
sṛji 368, 369
sṛpi 368, 369
sottarāvayava 648
sopapada 294, 311, 372
sopapadagrahaṇa 294, 311, 372, 379
sopasarga 483
soma 363
soṣmatā 111
soṣman 40, 41, 84, 110-112, 244, 245, 399, 637, 670, 676
sautra 659, 686
skandi 370, 371
st 184
stambh 282, 672
stambhi 563
stu 278
stṛṇāti 371
stṛta 353
stoma 363
strīpuṃsaliṅga 146
straiṣūya 355, 356, 587
sthā 282, 359-361, 563, 672
sthāna (point of articulation) 43, 51, 54, 63, 72, 75, 76, 78, 84, 102, 111, 114, 117, 121, 124, 125, 127-130, 132-137, 139-144, 151, 163, 164, 165, 172, 246, 268, 278, 279, 296, 305, 306, 327, 401, 635, 636, 639, 645, 646, 648, 672-674, 679, 680
sthāna (place) 144, 164, 165, 176, 211, 246, 281, 639, 640, 646, 649, 651-656, 659-662, 668, 670, 672, 674, 676-678, 680, 682
sthānakārya 640
sthānapradeśārtha 655
sthānaprayatnabala 646
sthānaprayatnaviveka 635, 640
sthānavidhāna 165
sthānavidhi 163-165, 639, 646
sthānaviveka 635
sthānārtha 649
sthānin 210, 281, 651
sthānivat 210, 281, 651
sthānivadbhāva 210, 281, 651

sthāniśaṅkānirāsa 651
sthāneyoga 144, 164, 176, 649
sthiti 111
sparśa 34, 35, 38, 39, 41, 43, 73, 76, 78, 88, 104-111, 113, 135, 137, 139, 145, 146, 175-177, 179, 182, 183, 239, 246, 251, 253, 283, 284, 287-289, 296, 470, 472, 636-638, 648, 651, 652, 668, 673, 674, 676
sparśana 128, 137, 151
sparśayukta 470, 472
sparśavarga 113
sparśasaṃyoga 179
sparśasama 253
sparśākṣara 651
sparśāntaḥsthasaṃyoga 183
spr̥śi 368, 369
spr̥ṣṭa 2, 44, 76, 78, 126, 132, 145-147, 150-152, 158, 636-638, 652
sphurati 369
sphulati 369
sphūrji 368, 369
sphoṭa 46
sphoṭana 257-259, 301-303, 667, 675
smarati 368, 369
sva 353, 354
svapi 354
svapna 529
svabhāva 163
svar 315, 316, 452
svara (accent) 37, 43, 45, 426, 430-432, 434-437, 447, 450, 479, 480-483, 486, 487, 493, 504, 505, 540, 610-613, 629, 635, 643
svara (vowel) 3, 11, 34, 69, 75, 77, 78, 103, 111, 116, 118-121, 128, 141, 145, 146, 149-151, 155, 157-159, 161, 173, 182, 184, 187, 188, 191, 192, 194-196, 199, 200, 208-211, 213, 217, 224, 230, 242-244, 246, 249, 250, 255-259, 263, 264, 285, 292, 293, 301, 308, 309, 321, 392, 396-399, 403, 404, 407, 408, 410-412, 416, 472, 504, 505, 515, 527, 528, 555-557, 611, 617, 618, 629, 635, 636, 638, 641, 642, 644-648, 650, 651, 653, 655, 656, 658, 660, 661, 663, 665-668, 672-674, 678, 680-682, 684-686
svarajñāna 612, 635
svarati 368, 369
svaratva 658
svaradharma 658
svarapara 255, 256, 259, 655, 667
svarapūrva 407, 660, 682
svarabhakti 255, 257-259, 301, 416, 655
svarabhāga 159, 161, 213, 655
svaramātrā 157
svaralopa 472
svaravant 447
svaravibhāga 158
svaravyañjanānta 187, 188, 642
svarasandhi 617, 618, 650, 663
svarasādhana 635
svarahīna 611, 642, 644, 645, 652
svarahīnamantradoṣa 611
svarādi 230, 392, 515
svarānta 555-557, 617
svarābhighāta 667

svarita 43, 75, 120-125, 173, 187, 188, 422-425, 427, 429-431, 433, 435-439, 441, 442, 444-447-449, 490, 491, 509, 611, 614, 641, 643, 644
svaritapara 444
svaritamaṇḍala 423
svaritabheda 122
svaritādi 490, 491
svarūpa 148, 682
svarodaya 397
svaropajana 613
svargakāmo aghāyatām 607
svaryate 441-444, 448, 449, 509, 644
svaryamāṇa 242, 448
svarṣāḥ 316, 685
svavarga 253, 648, 668
svavargatṛtīya 668
svasthānakaraṇa 127, 141
svasvara 437
svādi 645
svāra 424
svārabalābala 424
svārtha 259, 533, 667, 685
svāhākāra 609
h 33, 39, 41, 42, 56, 99, 112, 113, 118, 127-129, 138, 178-180, 196, 254, 255, 269, 278, 279, 349, 402, 403, 564, 636, 638-640, 642, 648, 651-653, 670, 671, 674, 675, 679, 681
ḣ 138, 254, 675
ha 116, 119, 129, 148, 179, 180, 183, 192, 195, 196, 254, 255, 269, 402, 403, 564, 636, 638-640, 642, 648, 651-653, 670, 671, 674, 675, 679, 681
hakāra 41, 44, 111-113, 116, 117, 128, 138, 179, 180, 195, 196, 254, 255, 269, 402, 403, 564, 636, 639, 642, 648, 651-653, 670, 679, 681
hakārasadṛśa 679
hakārādi 564
hani 85, 234, 472
haninakāra 472
hanu 76, 130, 133, 143, 636
hanumadhyadeśa 133
hanumūla 72, 130, 143, 636
hanti 472, 563
harati 563
haL 182, 639, 645, 646, 673, 685
haviḥ 330, 682
hasaṃyoga 183
hi 367, 368
hinoti 470, 600
hīna 172-174, 640
hīnaśvasanādaḥ 172-174, 640
hṛdaya 636
hrasva 43, 50, 74, 76, 78, 121, 124, 125, 141, 159, 165, 182, 185-187, 190, 191, 196, 197, 200, 230, 231, 239, 242, 243, 256, 296, 350, 351, 392, 396, 397, 413, 432, 433, 449, 533, 534, 550, 594, 629, 638, 641-644, 646, 656, 657, 665, 672, 673
hrasvagrahaṇa 125
hrasvanāmin 432, 433
hrasvapūrva 397
hrasvasvara 673
hrasvasvarita 124
hrasvābhāva 644
hrasvopadha 191, 296, 396, 397, 673

Index of Textual Sources and Authors

Abhyankar, K.V. 480, 539, 573, 591
Abhyankar, Sunanda R. 77
Ādināthapurāṇa 634
Agnipurāṇa 161
Āgniveśya 90, 306, 334
Aitareya-Āraṇyaka 34, 35, 36, 41, 111, 146
2.2.4: 33, 111
3.2.1: 33, 111, 146
3.2.6: 36
Aitareyabrāhmaṇa 114, 633
Aithal, Paramesvara 14
Akkole, Subhashchandra 634
Allen, W.S. 32, 43, 90, 109, 116, 118, 121, 123, 126-128, 131, 134, 135, 137, 138, 144, 146-148, 150, 157, 158, 162, 169, 171, 173, 181, 189, 190, 191, 197, 198, 199, 252, 254, 255, 257, 259, 301-303, 306, 307, 334, 342-344, 421
Anantabhaṭṭa 64
Anubhūtisvarūpācārya 13, 79
Anulomakalpa 191
Ānyatareya 447, 448
Āpastambaśrautasūtra 375
Āpiśali 660
Āpiśaliśikṣā 37, 114-117, 127, 129, 130, 134, 141, 152
APR, see: *Atharvaprātiśākhya*
Apte, V.M. 633
Āśvalāyanagṛhyasūtra 167, 633
Āśvalāyanaśrautasūtra 375, 465
Ātharvaṇapariśiṣṭa 3, 14, 70, 191, 425
Atharvaprātiśākhya (*APR*, ed. by Surya Kanta) 2, 14, 60, 79, 82-87, 89-91, 93, 94, 121, 124, 143, 179, 204, 209, 220-222, 228, 229, 232, 234, 265, 267, 268, 270, 272, 273, 275, 277, 283, 287, 293, 295, 296, 307, 311, 315, 317-319, 324, 325, 327, 329, 331, 333-346, 351-353, 361, 363-370, 373-375, 377, 378, 380, 383-393, 401, 404-407, 409, 413, 415, 416, 420-422, 427, 432-435, 440, 444, 456-458, 462, 465, 468-470, 472, 473, 482, 483, 487-489, 498, 501-504, 511, 516, 518, 519, 522-524, 526, 527, 529-532, 538, 550, 552-564, 566-569, 571, 572, 574, 580, 589, 592, 593, 595-597, 600-602, 604, 605, 625, 629
Atharvaveda, Paippalāda 80, 83, 87, 92, 175, 177, 178, 183, 185, 186, 192, 196, 203, 204, 206, 209, 210, 221, 226, 231, 236, 238, 239, 249, 398, 465, 494, 496, 512, 513, 551, 664, 665
1.10.1: 551
1.10.3: 551
1.41.3: 192
1.89.3: 183

Atharvaveda, Paippalāda (cont.)
2.31.2: 192, 398
2.55.5: 496
5.16.5: 203
5.21.4: 238, 239
5.34.2: 496
6.6.8: 664
7.5.8: 177
8.14.8: 186
9.4.9: 221, 222
9.8.1: 494
9.10.5: 414
10.9.7: 175
12.7.8: 183
14.2.13: 185
15.10.4: 665
15.18.6: 494
15.19.1-12: 494
16.2.9: 465
16.23.1: 210, 231
16.35.2: 105
16.127.1-5: 186
16.139.18: 206
16.151.7: 209
17.14.4: 186
17.20.2: 249
17.23.4: 226
17.36.4: 236
19.6.3: 512
19.41.5: 204
20.13.8: 196
20.58.6: 231
Atharvaveda, Śaunakīya 1-3, 14, 33, 35, 67, 74, 79, 80-94, (passim)
1.1.1: 33, 122, 339, 364, 480, 482, 498
1.1.2: 122, 224, 225, 480, 617
1.1.3: 122, 193, 229, 500, 665
1.1.4: 186, 197, 225, 241, 481, 507, 615
1.2.1: 227, 386, 507
1.2.2: 122
1.2.3: 158, 297, 357, 358, 368
1.2.4: 122, 186, 191, 192, 197, 225, 387
1.3.1: 104, 122, 188, 280, 352, 434, 480, 481, 573, 577, 578, 583
1.3.3: 298, 480
1.3.6: 172
1.3.8: 357
1.4.1: 388, 528
1.4.2: 122, 480
1.4.3: 188
1.4.4: 186, 266, 443, 531
1.5.1: 174, 191, 367, 582, 584
1.5.2: 122
1.5.3: 156
1.6.1: 174, 610
1.6.2: 156, 176, 188
1.6.4: 122, 168, 214, 444, 611
1.7.2: 498
1.7.3: 122, 174, 187, 191, 193
1.7.4: 156, 168, 183, 183, 191, 292, 398, 401
1.7.5: 199
1.7.7: 293
1.8.1: 194, 238, 239
1.8.2: 122, 191, 197, 225, 548
1.8.3: 501
1.8.4: 590
1.9.1: 188, 266, 401
1.9.3: 139, 208, 498
1.9.4: 346
1.10.1: 335
1.10.2: 105, 183, 186, 193
1.10.3: 122

Atharvaveda, *Śaunakīya* (cont.)
1.10.4: 101, 103, 267
1.11.1: 257, 259, 372, 491
1.11.2: 295
1.11.3: 183
1.12.1: 307, 513, 566
1.12.2: 257, 259, 480, 584
1.12.3: 187, 346
1.12.4: 172, 174, 185
1.13.1: 326
1.13.2: 306
1.14.2: 120, 124, 163, 226, 430
1.14.3: 199, 295
1.14.4: 306, 328
1.15.1: 122, 491, 500
1.15.2: 295, 409
1.15.3: 498
1.16.2: 191, 194, 198
1.16.3: 371, 385, 485
1.16.4: 194, 198
1.18.4: 365
1.19.1: 281, 568
1.19.3: 183, 186, 197, 293, 315
1.19.4: 139, 195, 255, 306, 402, 403, 557
1.20.2: 163, 596
1.20.3: 386, 596
1.20.4: 142, 391
1.22.2: 325, 570, 605
1.24.1: 399, 401, 556
1.24.4: 143, 283, 364, 376, 389, 500, 603, 618
1.24.8: 568
1.25.2: 419
1.25.3: 188
1.25.4: 520
1.26.4: 358, 586
1.27.1: 336
1.27.2: 187
1.27.3: 302, 384, 385
1.28.1: 488, 500, 551
1.28.3: 206
1.28.4: 183
1.29.1: 383, 385, 573
1.29.3: 195, 402, 403
1.29.6: 365, 391
1.30.3: 367, 378
1.31.1: 154, 571
1.31.4: 158
1.32.1: 226, 558, 579
1.32.3: 219
1.32.4: 383
1.33.2: 274, 275, 548-550, 574
1.33.4: 122, 434
1.34.1: 491
1.34.2: 103, 186, 192, 197, 198, 399
1.34.3: 517, 573, 578
1.34.4: 101, 267, 514, 516
1.34.5: 405
1.35.1: 105
1.35.4: 218, 352, 548
1.94.9: 326
1.100.16: 172
2.1.1: 264
2.1.2: 238, 303, 340, 533, 684
2.1.3: 174
2.1.4: 218, 361, 550
2.1.5: 168, 174, 503, 513
2.2.1: 174, 338, 532
2.2.2: 338
2.2.3: 172, 174
2.2.4: 174, 381
2.2.5: 168, 172, 174
2.3.1: 258, 302, 523
2.3.3: 168, 169, 307
2.3.4: 174
2.3.6: 174

Atharvaveda, Śaunakīya (cont.)
2.4.1: 582
2.4.5: 172, 174
2.4.6: 168
2.5.1: 172
2.5.2: 120, 122, 124, 172, 198, 315, 316, 431, 440, 444
2.5.3: 105, 148, 172, 350, 374, 385, 485, 570
2.5.4: 174, 409, 440, 617-619
2.5.5: 186, 192
2.5.6: 168, 172, 174
2.5.7: 388, 528
2.6.1: 172
2.6.2: 277
2.6.3: 558
2.6.4: 361
2.6.5: 172
2.7.2: 172, 328, 556, 573
2.7.5: 194
2.8.4: 174
2.8.5: 168
2.9.2: 122, 514, 544
2.9.4: 174
2.9.5: 172, 174
2.10.2: 378
2.10.4: 174
2.10.7: 313
2.10.8: 458
2.11.1: 237
2.11.2: 237, 368
2.11.3: 237
2.11.4: 237
2.11.5: 237
2.12.1: 186, 253, 443
2.12.2: 436, 442, 447
2.12.3: 436, 442, 447
2.12.4: 188, 550
2.12.5: 417
2.12.6: 210, 428, 429
2.12.7: 206, 390, 595
2.13.2: 143, 278, 560
2.13.3: 283, 389
2.15.1: 188, 199, 387
2.15.3: 401
2.15.5: 183, 188
2.20.1: 103
2.25.1: 311
2.26.1: 527
2.26.2: 535
2.27.3: 122
2.27.5: 176, 209, 540, 573
2.27.6: 191
2.28.2: 572
2.28.4: 172, 352
2.29.4: 122, 175
2.29.5: 177
2.30.1: 405
2.30.3: 179, 321-2
2.30.5: 156, 183
2.31.1: 102, 106, 176, 191, 194, 209, 394
2.31.2: 179, 181
2.32.1: 180, 397
2.32.3: 517
2.32.5: 611
2.33.1: 532
2.33.5: 531
2.33.6: 205, 531
2.34.2: 484
2.34.3: 353
2.34.4: 123, 172, 353, 508
2.34.5: 336
2.35.1: 511, 529
2.35.2: 296, 297
2.35.3: 250, 533
2.36.1: 103, 556
2.36.2: 121

Atharvaveda, *Śaunakīya* (cont.)
2.36.4: 324, 366
2.36.8: 298
2.55.5: 496
3.1.1: 324
3.1.2: 569
3.1.3: 274, 281, 388, 528
3.2.3: 397
3.3.2: 596
3.3.3: 148, 198
3.3.4: 188
3.4.1: 402
3.4.4: 548
3.5.1: 378, 557, 558
3.5.5: 519
3.5.7: 452
3.6.1: 140, 190, 231, 239, 298, 336
3.6.2: 472
3.6.4: 416, 590
3.6.8: 458
3.7.1: 206, 365
3.8.1: 203
3.8.3: 390, 594
3.8.5: 222, 307
3.8.6: 253
3.9.1: 341
3.9.2: 186
3.9.4: 528
3.9.6: 370
3.10.1: 546
3.10.4: 495, 532
3.10.5: 330
3.10.6: 339
3.10.8: 142, 183
3.10.10: 148, 158, 610, 611
3.10.11: 303
3.10.12: 123, 359, 360
3.11.3: 437
3.11.4: 193, 437
3.12.2: 387, 388, 546
3.12.6: 231
3.12.7: 372
3.12.9: 122
3.13.1: 432, 440
3.13.3: 264, 312
3.13.6: 312
3.13.7: 177, 308, 312
3.14.1: 298, 487
3.14.3: 419, 536
3.15.4: 460, 581, 602
3.15.5: 402, 602
3.16.1: 315, 570
3.16.4: 242
3.16.7: 387, 388, 390, 594
3.17.1: 322
3.17.5: 519
3.18.1: 185, 379
3.18.5: 590
3.18.6: 490
3.19.1: 210
3.19.4: 237
3.19.6: 206, 269-70, 496
3.20.2: 105, 494
3.20.6: 103, 218, 286, 405, 548-550
3.20.10: 370
3.21.1: 421
3.21.3: 590
3.21.5: 502
3.21.6: 437
3.21.9: 297
3.22.5: 547
3.22.6: 582
3.23.3: 238-9
3.23.4: 352
3.23.6: 342
3.24.2: 120, 124, 430

Atharvaveda, Śaunakīya (cont.)
3.24.6: 186, 544
3.24.7: 103
3.25.2: 179, 203
3.25.6: 187
3.26.1: 122, 440
3.26.4: 376
3.27.3: 553
3.27.5: 188
3.28.3: 532
3.28.4: 542, 543, 544
3.28.5: 300
3.29.1: 202, 264, 551
3.29.3: 300
3.29.6: 188, 199
3.30.3: 529
3.30.5: 298, 300
3.30.7: 556
3.31.4: 219
3.31.9: 559
4.1.1: 311, 370
4.1.3: 101, 267, 570
4.2.2: 559
4.2.4: 523
4.2.5: 188, 199, 218
4.2.7: 601
4.2.8: 179
4.3.1: 105, 560
4.3.2: 400, 401, 528, 560
4.3.4: 368
4.3.6: 512, 513, 546
4.4.1: 323, 326, 379, 573
4.4.8: 514, 515
4.5.4: 380
4.5.6: 561, 562
4.6.2: 360
4.6.3: 546, 591, 592
4.6.5: 362
4.6.8: 352
4.7.3: 328, 329, 353, 591, 592
4.7.5: 104, 168, 186, 384, 398, 401, 591
4.7.6: 352, 591
4.8.6: 222, 474
4.9.9: 336
4.10.1: 336
4.10.2: 503
4.10.4: 336, 337
4.11.1: 148, 194
4.11.3: 510, 511
4.11.4: 253
4.11.7: 361, 381
4.11.8: 547
4.11.9: 321
4.12.3: 400, 401
4.12.4: 232, 233
4.12.5: 206
4.13.2: 286
4.13.5: 553
4.13.6: 544
4.14.1: 156
4.14.2: 185, 338
4.14.5: 355
4.14.7: 530, 563
4.14.9: 532
4.15.5: 183, 195, 196, 403
4.15.11: 409, 440
4.15.15: 165, 166, 200, 247, 248, 259-261
4.16.1: 101, 267, 268, 490
4.16.2: 602
4.16.3: 163, 226
4.16.6: 220
4.17.2: 597
4.17.5: 297, 466, 556
4.18.3: 168, 234
4.18.6: 191, 205, 206, 225
4.19.1: 399

Atharvaveda, Śaunakīya (cont.)
4.19.2: 587, 588
4.19.5: 293
4.19.7: 180, 293
4.20.2: 304
4.20.5: 325, 330, 605
4.20.7: 495
4.21.1: 220, 221
4.21.4: 559
4.21.6: 206
4.22.4: 229
4.22.6: 534
4.20.7: 346
4.22.2: 353
4.23.1: 235, 535
4.23.3: 501
4.24.1: 472
4.24.5: 287
4.25.3: 228, 469
4.25.4: 330
4.25.5: 216, 217
4.25.6: 228, 411, 491
4.25.7: 189
4.26.1: 219, 220
4.27.1: 183, 390
4.27.4: 337
4.27.6: 569
4.28.1: 548
4.29.1: 517
4.29.2: 517
4.29.4: 145
4.29.5: 365, 567
4.29.6: 515, 516
4.29.7: 529
4.30.4: 122, 225, 497, 558
4.30.6: 509
4.31.3: 220, 221, 245, 523
4.31.4: 228
4.32.1: 386, 594, 663
4.32.3: 428
4.32.4: 365: 391
4.32.5: 314, 385, 593
4.32.6: 142, 208, 209, 228, 295
4.32.7: 211, 233
4.33.2: 511, 529, 530
4.33.3: 122, 192, 197
4.33.6: 336
4.34.1: 371
4.34.3: 415
4.34.5: 536
4.35.1: 455
4.35.2: 455
4.35.3: 455
4.35.4: 455
4.35.5: 455
4.35.6: 455
4.36.1: 272, 388
4.36.5: 296
4.37.1: 143, 174, 283, 389, 567
4.37.4: 567
4.38.3: 457
4.38.5: 300, 585
4.39.1: 418
4.39.2: 309, 342
4.39.4: 284, 309
4.39.9: 328, 495
4.40.8: 148
5.1.1: 101, 267
5.1.2: 232
5.1.3: 219, 221
5.1.5: 219, 364, 376, 385, 603
5.1.7: 253
5.2.1: 210
5.2.3: 220-222
5.2.5: 152
5.2.7: 403
5.2.8: 316
5.3.6: 168, 461

Atharvaveda, Śaunakīya (cont.)
5.3.8: 384, 591
5.3.9: 338
5.3.55: 515
5.3.57: 515
5.4.1: 409, 440
5.4.2: 336
5.4.3: 513
5.4.8: 397
5.4.10: 317, 330
5.5.3: 462, 604
5.5.4: 332, 333
5.5.6: 74, 350, 351
5.5.9: 358, 586, 626
5.6.4: 364, 376, 603
5.6.5: 430
5.6.9: 601
5.7.2: 498, 578
5.7.6: 218, 286, 405, 428
5.7.7: 320
5.7.8: 511, 529
5.8.2: 368
5.8.5: 498
5.8.7: 275
5.11.3: 601
5.11.5: 582
5.11.6: 327, 471, 472
5.11.7: 142, 208, 209, 295
5.11.8: 532
5.11.10: 122
5.12.2: 513
5.12.5: 445, 529
5.12.6: 358, 390, 550, 586, 594
5.12.8: 145, 566
5.12.11: 158
5.13.5: 228
5.13.6: 209, 309, 391
5.13.8: 446
5.13.9: 376, 568
5.14.4: 493, 494
5.14.7: 464
5.14.8: 374, 570
5.14.9: 568
5.14.11: 370
5.15.2: 140, 190, 208, 231, 298
5.15.3: 190, 231, 298
5.15.4: 140, 190, 231, 298
5.15.6: 279, 304
5.17.1: 420, 427
5.17.4: 328
5.17.5: 264
5.17.9: 120, 124, 431
5.17.11: 495
5.18.7: 297, 611, 614
5.18.11: 601
5.18.12: 322
5.19.1: 521
5.19.2: 306
5.19.3: 179, 303
5.19.4: 502
5.19.7: 375, 599
5.19.8: 328
5.19.10: 601
5.19.13: 204, 385, 588
5.20.1: 231
5.20.2: 517
5.20.4: 183
5.20.6: 337, 547, 579
5.20.8: 270
5.20.9: 470, 611
5.20.10: 329
5.20.11: 287, 350, 374, 570
5.21.8: 309, 398
5.22.1: 74, 351, 529
5.22.2: 341, 342
5.22.5: 179
5.22.6: 353
5.22.7: 306

Atharvaveda, Śaunakīya (cont.)
5.22.9: 178
5.22.14: 275
5.23.1: 241-2
5.23.4: 206
5.23.7: 258, 302, 523
5.23.8: 293
5.24.1: 317, 474
5.25.8: 370
5.25.9: 517
5.26.12: 258, 302
5.27.1: 123
5.27.6: 542
5.27.8: 358
5.27.9: 314
5.28.11: 553
5.28.14: 213, 277
5.29.2: 344, 514
5.29.3: 344
5.29.11: 205
5.29.12: 231
5.30.1: 105, 199
5.30.9: 380
5.30.10: 601
5.30.16: 601
5.31.10: 458
5.31.11: 205, 222
5.34.2: 496
6.1.1: 226
6.1.2: 368
6.1.3: 365
6.4.1: 157, 339, 353, 587
6.4.2: 187, 210, 231
6.4.3: 341, 342, 460, 684
6.6.4: 377
6.8.1: 405, 536, 537
6.8.2: 405
6.8.3: 405
6.9.1: 604
6.9.3: 386, 597
6.10.4: 335
6.11.1: 140, 190, 298
6.11.2: 239, 627
6.11.3: 160, 203, 356, 587, 591, 610
6.12.2: 546
6.14.1: 361
6.15.1: 293, 514
6.15.2: 293, 557, 558
6.16.2: 178
6.16.4: 611
6.17.1: 370
6.17.2: 370
6.17.3: 370
6.17.4: 370
6.18.2: 544
6.20.2: 378
6.21.3: 586
6.22.1: 186
6.22.3: 122, 345, 626
6.24.2: 544, 545
6.26.5: 254
6.27.3: 216
6.28.2: 475
6.29.1: 180
6.29.2: 557
6.30.2: 178, 179, 185
6.32.1: 315
6.33.1: 306
6.33.3: 476, 560
6.34.4: 502
6.35.3: 593
6.36.1: 392, 517
6.36.2: 209, 214, 295
6.36.3: 300
6.37.2: 583
6.39.1: 444, 519
6.39.3: 514

Atharvaveda, Śaunakīya (cont.)
6.40.1: 333
6.40.2: 333
6.40.3: 333
6.43.2: 563
6.45.1: 208, 294, 320, 345
6.46.3: 183, 185, 250, 354
6.47.3: 556
6.50.1: 611
6.50.2: 188
6.51.1: 273
6.53.1: 73
6.53.3: 333, 591, 592
6.54.3: 293, 558
6.56.1: 368
6.56.3: 301
6.60.1: 108, 286, 288, 406, 580, 581
6.60.2: 226
6.61.2: 295
6.62.1: 392
6.63.3: 103
6.63.4: 339, 340
6.64.3: 366, 485, 537
6.65.1: 567
6.67.2: 278
6.67.3: 419
6.68.1: 107, 228, 278, 286, 288, 406, 409, 440
6.68.3: 517
6.69.2: 293
6.70.1: 604
6.70.2: 339, 604
6.70.3: 604
6.71.1: 353, 444
6.72.2: 306, 588
6.73.3: 333
6.75.1: 556
6.76.4: 188, 196, 253, 455, 456
6.77.2: 101, 267, 391
6.78.3: 86, 332
6.79.3: 238
6.81.3: 310, 311
6.82.3: 519
6.83.1: 333
6.83.3: 494
6.85.3: 512
6.89.1: 307, 335, 336
6.91.1: 375, 599
6.91.2: 120, 122, 124, 198, 431
6.92.2: 383, 562
6.92.3: 428, 429
6.93.1: 235, 236, 535
6.100.3: 337
6.102.3: 267
6.103.2: 312, 313
6.103.3: 222, 312, 313
6.104.3: 333, 546
6.105.2: 443
6.106.1: 186, 284, 583
6.106.3: 86, 332
6.108.2: 105, 462, 546, 604
6.109.1: 399, 401
6.109.2: 401, 432, 440
6.109.3: 496
6.110.3: 467
6.111.1: 176, 443, 527, 588
6.112.2: 550
6.112.3: 367
6.113.3: 512
6.114.1: 416
6.115.1: 238
6.115.2: 192
6.116.1: 264
6.116.2: 385
6.117.1: 383, 562
6.117.3: 466
6.118.3: 585

Atharvaveda, Śaunakīya (cont.)
6.119.3: 571
6.121.1: 354
6.122.2: 152
6.125.1: 431
6.125.2: 337
6.126.1: 513
6.126.3: 122
6.127.1: 207
6.127.3: 206
6.128.2: 174
6.128.3: 318, 550, 553
6.129.1: 232
6.132.1: 257, 259
6.133.4: 416
6.134.3: 413
6.136.2: 210, 213
6.137.2: 346
6.137.3: 386, 597
6.139.1: 432
6.141.2: 333
6.141.3: 549, 550
7.1.1: 217
7.5.1: 278
7.6.1: 523, 524
7.6.2: 183, 376, 603
7.6.3: 578
7.6.4: 308
7.7.1: 73, 291
7.7.6: 484
7.9.1: 451
7.9.2: 571
7.9.3: 470, 471
7.9.4: 296, 297
7.10.1: 311
7.11.1: 183
7.14.1: 435
7.15.1: 181
7.17.1: 315, 339
7.17.2: 315
7.17.3: 315
7.18.1: 315, 428, 440, 457, 469
7.18.2: 457, 469
7.21.1: 474
7.26.3: 228
7.26.4: 233
7.26.7: 428, 429
7.28.1: 452
7.31.1: 324, 346
7.32.1: 333
7.33.1: 333
7.35.3: 508
7.38.3: 482, 500
7.38.5: 378
7.40.2: 236
7.43.2: 172
7.43.3: 172
7.45.1: 189, 335-337
7.46.2: 192, 193, 250, 365
7.46.3: 561
7.49.1: 306
7.49.2: 186, 188
7.50.1: 193
7.50.7: 531
7.50.9: 192
7.51.1: 333
7.52.2: 282
7.53.3: 313
7.55.1: 511, 529, 530
7.56.6: 435
7.57.1: 293
7.58.1: 548
7.60.2: 546
7.60.4: 507
7.60.6: 326
7.60.7: 237
7.62.7: 237
7.63.1: 455, 456

Atharvaveda, Śaunakīya (cont.)
7.64.1: 580
7.65.1: 293
7.66.1: 163, 582
7.67.1: 315
7.72.2: 224, 619
7.72.3: 443
7.73.4: 445
7.73.5: 490, 546
7.73.6: 102, 106, 148, 191, 194, 394
7.73.7: 122, 264
7.73.10: 346, 565, 588
7.73.11: 522
7.74.2: 399
7.74.3: 351
7.74.4: 245
7.79.2: 120, 124, 430, 440
7.81.1: 295
7.81.3: 211
7.81.4: 315, 536, 537
7.82.1: 430, 431
7.82.3: 354
7.83.3: 391, 597
7.83.4: 354
7.85.1: 364, 377
7.87.1: 186
7.91.1: 333
7.92.1: 203, 315, 570
7.93.1: 372, 373
7.94.1: 332
7.95.2: 601
7.97.3: 235, 236, 535
7.97.4: 406
7.97.6: 485, 510
7.99.1: 366, 371
7.115.2: 323
7.102.1: 493
7.104.1: 168, 473
7.107.1: 183
7.109.2: 232, 233
7.109.3: 253
7.109.6: 527
7.110.1: 544
7.115.2: 323
7.115.4: 580
7.117.1: 205
8.1.20: 464, 465, 495
8.2.6: 379, 485
8.2.17: 343
8.2.21: 193, 443
8.3.1: 193, 452, 472
8.3.7: 193
8.3.10: 532
8.3.14: 298
8.3.16: 458
8.3.26: 143, 283, 389
8.4.1: 298, 548
8.4.6: 229, 404, 470
8.4.8: 390, 595
8.4.10: 365, 368, 524, 525
8.4.18: 532
8.4.21: 568
8.4.23: 507
8.5.9: 436
8.5.11: 382
8.6.1: 466
8.6.2: 298
8.6.3: 582
8.6.4: 466
8.6.5: 523
8.6.9: 517
8.6.10: 188
8.6.11: 457
8.6.12: 300
8.6.13: 521
8.6.14: 361, 362
8.6.16: 557

Atharvaveda, Śaunakīya (cont.)
8.6.17: 202, 270, 419
8.6.18: 376, 568
8.6.19: 319
8.6.21: 179, 183
8.6.23: 517
8.6.26: 517, 518, 556
8.7.1: 253
8.7.2: 342
8.7.6: 379, 485
8.7.8: 464
8.7.20: 338, 346
8.8.4: 333
8.8.19: 452, 580
8.8.22: 202, 514, 514
8.8.23: 362
8.9.1: 185
8.9.2: 206
8.9.8: 102, 106, 191, 194, 264, 394
8.9.9: 220, 221, 270, 559
8.9.10: 302
8.9.12: 329
8.9.13: 188
8.9.14: 363, 365
8.9.15: 160, 203
8.9.16: 174, 304
8.9.17: 272
8.9.20: 102, 105, 106, 188, 191, 194, 267, 307, 394
8.9.21: 599, 600
8.9.22: 191
8.10.4: 415, 437
8.10.12: 319
8.10.21: 520
8.10.29: 556
8.10.33: 582
8.12.2: 254
9.1.1: 337
9.1.3: 67, 235
9.1.6: 187
9.1.9: 403
9.1.19: 293
9.2.5: 458, 490
9.2.7: 333
9.2.13: 597
9.2.25: 352, 532
9.3.1: 154
9.3.2: 470
9.3.10: 579
9.3.17: 103
9.3.21: 375, 599
9.3.22: 312
9.4.2: 333
9.4.4: 611
9.4.11: 415
9.4.13: 399
9.4.14: 563
9.4.17: 187, 199, 338
9.4.19: 406
9.4.23: 474
9.5.4: 314, 518
9.5.6: 336, 562
9.5.8: 232
9.5.10: 338
9.5.16: 455, 497
9.5.17: 389
9.5.19: 532
9.5.25: 253
9.5.26: 253
9.5.32: 542
9.5.33: 542
9.5.34: 542
9.5.35: 542
9.5.36: 542
9.5.37: 485, 510, 511
9.6.1: 231, 299, 357
9.6.2: 371, 451

Atharvaveda, *Śaunakīya* (cont.)
9.6.4: 457
9.6.5: 457
9.6.11: 541
9.6.12: 202
9.6.14: 211
9.6.15: 494
9.6.18: 188, 200, 259, 260
9.6.19: 563
9.6.22: 493, 496
9.6.24: 235
9.6.31: 174
9.6.40: 363
9.6.43: 317
9.6.46: 195, 255, 308, 402, 403, 454
9.6.53: 505
9.6.54: 482, 500, 505
9.7.1: 207
9.7.8: 206
9.7.19: 309
9.8.9: 323
9.8.14: 416
9.8.15: 416
9.8.16: 416
9.8.20: 207
9.9.2: 360, 361, 503
9.9.4: 120, 124, 197, 431, 546
9.9.10: 199, 386, 597
9.9.15: 340, 341, 462, 604
9.9.16: 518
9.9.20: 401
9.10.1: 302, 365, 523, 556, 587
9.10.10: 122
9.10.12: 434
9.10.14: 193
9.10.19: 360
9.10.21: 187, 536, 602
9.10.24: 267
9.10.25: 522
9.10.26: 103, 514
9.14.4: 122
9.14.4: 122
9.14.20: 399
10.1.2: 105, 462, 604
10.1.5: 468, 470, 600
10.1.8: 416
10.1.10: 420
10.1.13: 386, 596
10.1.14: 159
10.1.15: 406
10.1.16: 307
10.1.18: 245
10.1.25: 225
10.1.26: 388
10.1.29: 282
10.2.1: 179, 218, 405
10.2.3: 444
10.2.4: 168, 169, 185, 186, 193
10.2.8: 446
10.2.11: 298
10.2.13: 537, 538
10.2.20: 389
10.2.28: 142, 188, 200, 212, 213, 248, 249, 259-261, 504, 623
10.2.31: 375, 599
10.2.33: 178
10.3.2: 458
10.3.13: 284
10.3.14: 293
10.3.15: 293
10.4.2: 205, 206
10.4.5: 206, 434
10.4.8: 142, 368
10.4.16: 548
10.4.21: 511, 529
10.4.23: 377

Atharvaveda, Śaunakīya (cont.)
10.4.24: 299
10.4.25: 596
10.5.7: 309
10.5.22: 587
10.5.29: 571
10.5.32: 377
10.5.36: 359, 360
10.6.1: 309
10.6.2: 355
10.6.5: 538
10.6.19: 508
10.6.20: 309
10.6.31: 86, 245, 332, 334
10.6.35: 245
10.7.6: 219, 577, 626
10.7.15: 486
10.7.25: 336, 503
10.7.33: 464
10.7.42: 577, 626
10.7.43: 473
10.8.2: 559
10.8.10: 416, 418
10.8.13: 474
10.8.18: 250, 454
10.8.19: 559
10.8.24: 308
10.8.27: 103
10.8.39: 522
10.8.41: 447
10.8.43: 321
10.9.1: 437
10.9.3: 205
10.9.12: 367
10.10.6: 551
10.10.18: 123
10.10.19: 581
10.10.23: 129
10.10.25: 496
10.10.29: 512
11.1.1: 419, 611
11.1.2: 270
11.1.5: 176
11.1.6: 333
11.1.10: 485
11.1.12: 346
11.1.20: 474
11.1.22: 346
11.1.30: 122
11.1.34: 541
11.1.35: 559
11.1.36: 482, 483, 500, 506
11.2.2: 402
11.2.9: 65, 525, 526
11.2.12: 428, 440
11.2.13: 440
11.2.14: 548
11.2.25: 231
11.2.29: 460, 591, 592
11.3.1: 419
11.3.6: 493, 496
11.3.9: 192, 197, 250
11.3.18: 122
11.3.26: 259-261, 504, 505
11.3.27: 259, 260, 504, 505
11.3.28: 505
11.4.8: 559
11.4.9: 228
11.4.10: 558
11.4.14: 559
11.4.22: 375, 599
11.4.23: 444
11.5.2: 270
11.5.3: 120, 124, 183, 430, 491
11.5.11: 219
11.6.5: 318, 553
11.6.14: 231, 299, 357
11.6.19: 392

Atharvaveda, Śaunakīya (cont.)
11.6.21: 210
11.7.1: 277
11.7.3: 192, 206
11.7.5: 496
11.7.10: 329
11.7.11: 551, 584
11.7.13: 588
11.7.26: 582
11.8.1: 107, 285-6, 288, 406
11.8.4: 541
11.8.7: 514
11.8.22: 186
11.9.10: 382
11.9.14: 432, 440
11.9.15: 328, 446, 452, 581
11.9.22: 293
11.9.24: 293
11.10.8: 382
11.10.16: 309
11.10.19: 452
11.10.25: 493
11.10.26: 376, 568
12.1.1: 333
12.1.7: 557
12.1.22: 494
12.1.25: 239
12.1.26: 232
12.1.30: 308
12.1.31: 553
12.1.33: 482, 502, 547
12.1.38: 158
12.1.43: 333
12.1.47: 560
12.1.48: 456
12.1.51: 294, 596
12.1.54: 350, 374, 570
12.1.55: 523, 524
12.1.63: 314, 483
12.2.2: 541
12.2.3: 557
12.2.4: 367, 600
12.2.8: 470
12.2.9: 213
12.2.12: 338
12.2.16: 331
12.2.26: 446
12.2.29: 65, 525, 526
12.2.42: 331
12.2.45: 343, 344
12.2.51: 538
12.2.54: 179
12.3.10: 284
12.3.12: 93
12.3.14: 177
12.3.21: 298
12.3.26: 337
12.3.28: 523
12.3.30: 282
12.3.33: 405
12.3.35: 596
12.3.36: 563
12.3.37: 482, 500
12.3.39: 91, 329, 539
12.3.41: 473
12.3.43: 143, 283, 285, 389
12.3.52: 538
12.3.55: 619
12.4.11: 490
12.4.16: 587
12.4.18: 319
12.4.29: 233, 234, 330-332
12.4.30: 233, 234, 253
12.4.35: 535
12.4.36: 390, 595
12.4.42: 248, 249, 259, 260
12.5.7: 266
12.5.24: 581

Atharvaveda, Śaunakīya (cont.)
12.5.34: 563
12.5.44: 275
12.5.48: 473
12.5.50: 259, 260
12.5.64: 391
13.1.1: 580
13.1.4: 312, 313
13.1.5: 313
13.1.16: 185
13.1.19: 556
13.1.22: 372
13.1.25: 573
13.1.26: 336
13.1.34: 85, 120
13.1.35: 352
13.1.37: 219
13.1.46: 203
13.1.47: 219
13.1.52: 203
13.2.3: 218, 219, 503
13.2.5: 293
13.2.13: 223
13.2.14: 358, 528, 586
13.2.18: 293
13.2.20: 181, 397
13.2.21: 293
13.2.24: 188
13.2.26: 328
13.2.28: 174, 219
13.2.29: 188, 208, 293
13.2.33: 206
13.2.36: 570
13.2.37: 337
13.2.39: 188
13.2.46: 372, 469
13.3.3: 558, 559
13.3.11: 219
13.3.19: 512
13.4.1: 338
13.4.5: 108, 142, 286, 288, 406, 407, 620
13.4.10: 512
13.4.25: 440
13.4.28: 217
13.4.41: 407
13.4.44: 163
13.4.47: 339
13.7.7: 338
13.7.16: 199
14.1.1: 282, 563
14.1.3: 231, 533
14.1.8: 185
14.1.12: 522
14.1.18: 332
14.1.23: 295
14.1.27: 206
14.1.29: 174, 517, 547, 556, 579, 580
14.1.36: 359, 360
14.1.41: 332, 485
14.1.42: 556
14.1.43: 358, 587
14.1.44: 300, 434
14.1.45: 293
14.1.55: 293
14.1.57: 253
14.2.2: 338, 437
14.2.6: 487
14.2.9: 360, 361, 434
14.2.10: 293
14.2.12: 296, 475
14.2.14: 321
14.2.17: 296
14.2.20: 332
14.2.26: 434
14.2.33: 366
14.2.34: 285

Atharvaveda, *Śaunakīya* (cont.)
14.2.37: 219
14.3.43: 550
14.2.44: 296
14.2.48: 103
14.2.61: 277
14.2.63: 437
14.2.72: 388
14.2.73: 434
14.19.2: 366
15.1.8: 103
15.2.1: 174, 238, 289, 371, 491, 495
15.2.2: 495
15.2.3: 495
15.2.4: 495
15.2.6: 578
15.3.2: 420, 427
15.6.4: 484
15.6.7: 181, 194
15.8.1: 420, 427
15.10.2: 237
15.10.6: 622
15.10.7: 411, 622
15.11.2: 192, 197, 483
15.12.1: 501, 563
15.12.7: 490
15.13.1: 381
15.13.12: 403
15.14.7: 497
15.14.8: 496
15.15.7: 108, 286, 288, 406
15.18.3: 420, 427
15.18.4: 219
16.2.1: 491
16.3.5: 467
16.4.6: 308
16.6.6: 339
16.6.9: 582
16.7.6: 331
16.7.11: 317
16.9.1: 359
17.1.1: 237
17.1.2: 237
17.1.3: 237
17.1.4: 237
17.1.5: 237
17.1.9: 352
17.1.22: 494
17.1.25: 317
18.1.1: 188, 224, 225
18.1.3: 220, 221
18.1.4: 270
18.1.5: 405, 468
18.1.10: 380, 381
18.1.11: 188
18.1.16: 364, 377, 603, 604
18.1.20: 163, 446
18.1.21: 392
18.1.23: 307
18.1.24: 228
18.1.30: 401
18.1.31: 550, 665
18.1.32: 216, 217, 312
18.1.33: 281, 365, 368
18.1.37: 364, 377, 603
18.1.39: 216, 217
18.1.42: 220, 221
18.1.43: 421
18.1.45: 325, 605
18.1.46: 532
18.1.48: 346
18.1.49: 177, 235, 236, 535
18.1.51: 325, 367, 605
18.1.54: 465, 466
18.1.55: 318
18.1.61: 338
18.2.3: 343

Atharvaveda, Śaunakīya (cont.)
18.2.4: 208, 384, 592
18.2.6: 258, 302
18.2.12: 367
18.2.13: 293, 462
18.2.18: 293
18.2.23: 392
18.2.25: 296
18.2.28: 352
18.2.31: 387, 610
18.2.32: 319
18.2.34: 564
18.2.36: 270
18.2.46: 537
18.2.49: 340, 341
18.2.54: 501, 596
18.3.5: 401
18.3.7: 377, 604
18.3.14: 226
18.3.15: 188, 567
18.3.16: 381, 567
18.3.17: 393
18.3.21: 391, 392, 393, 514
18.3.23: 204
18.3.38: 229
18.3.44: 226, 227, 231, 299, 357, 363, 365
18.3.46: 340, 341
18.3.47: 177
18.3.50: 177
18.3.51: 177
18.3.55: 382
18.3.59: 340, 341
18.3.61: 517
18.3.63: 245, 381
18.3.67: 460
18.3.70: 314
18.3.71: 270
18.4.1: 467
18.4.2: 330, 404
18.4.5: 300
18.4.14: 400
18.4.17: 103
18.4.37: 400, 409, 440
18.4.40: 159, 470, 600
18.4.50: 482, 483, 500, 506
18.4.51: 157
18.4.54: 381
18.4.59: 204, 274, 280
18.4.60: 468
18.4.63: 465
18.4.64: 103
18.4.67: 366
18.4.78: 367, 582
18.4.89: 399, 401
19.2.1: 404, 495
19.2.3: 545
19.3.1: 337
19.6.5: 286
19.6.8: 293
19.6.14: 183
19.7.2: 206
19.9.12: 548, 549
19.9.14: 168
19.10.10: 168
19.13.1: 186
19.13.8: 293
19.17: 465
19.17.6: 377
19.18.6: 377
19.19: 465
19.20.2: 338
19.26.3: 293
19.32.7: 293, 365
19.36.4: 293
19.37.1: 195, 402, 403
19.38.4: 612
19.39.1: 336

Atharvaveda, Śaunakīya (cont.)
19.39.4: 382
19.39.5: 336
19.42.2: 564
19.44.3: 207
19.44.5: 338, 346
19.47.8: 308
19.50.4: 293
19.58.4: 467
19.59.2: 293
19.59.3: 122
19.60.2: 435
20.1.1: 616
20.4.1: 617
20.6.2: 619, 627
20.6.3: 627
20.11.1: 590
20.15.4: 578
20.18.3: 181
20.19.6: 590
20.31.2: 180
20.34.4: 142
20.35.2: 350
20.35.3: 172
20.35.5: 199
20.37.1: 596
20.38.5: 206
20.46.1: 236
20.48.4: 181
20.51.1: 195, 402, 403
20.53.1: 122, 174
20.53.3: 210
20.54.2: 172
20.57.11: 122
20.61.6: 142, 190
20.67.1: 583, 587
20.67.2: 588
20.67.6: 174
20.68.11: 583
20.73.6: 239, 589
20.88.1: 583
20.89.2: 596
20.95.2: 226
20.101.3: 678
20.113.2: 628
20.116.2: 188
20.117.1: 628
20.126.16: 206
20.126.22: 206
20.127.7: 293
20.127.9: 186, 192, 197, 198
20.128.4: 293
20.128.5: 293
20.129.7: 231
20.135.2: 104
20.135.3: 104
20.136.15: 293
Atharvavidhāna 3
Bare, James 43-45, 49, 141, 153
Bender, Ernest 276, 418
Bhagavadgītā 244, 427
Bhāgavatapurāṇa 632
Bhārgava-Bhāskara 13, 14, 75-77, 88, 92-94, (passim)
Bhartṛhari 46, 480
Bhāṣikasūtra 38
Bhaṭṭojī Dīkṣita 13, 14, 75, 77, 471, 639, 649, 657, 664, 669, 676-679
Bhāvasena Traividyadeva 634, 673
Bhoja 650
Böhtlingk, Otto 115, 165, 167, 289, 319, 400
Bolling, G.M. 131, 135, 141
Bopp, F. 290
Bṛhacchabdenduśekhara 57, 643
Bṛhaddevatā 497, 647
Bronkhorst, Johannes 33

Bühler, Georg 3
Burrow, Thomas 441, 442
CA, see: *Śaunakīyā Caturādhyāyikā*
CAB, see: *Caturādhyāyībhāṣya*
Candrakīrti (on *Sārasvata-vyākaraṇa*) 687
Cāndravyākaraṇa 652, 677
Cardona, George 44, 45, 49, 55, 58, 61, 81, 99, 116, 117, 119, 139, 228, 246, 264, 421, 524, 539, 608, 635, 657
Caturādhyāyībhāṣya (*CAB*) 13, 14, 26, 41, 42, 58, 62, 64, 65, 70-77, 79, 85-88, 90-94 (passim)
Chandaḥsūtra 187-189, 643, 658
Chāndogya-Upaniṣad 34, 111
2.22.2: 111
2.22.5: 34
Chatterji, K.C. 114, 633, 645, 646, 654
Chāya (on *Uddyota*) 2
Citrācārya, Jagadīśācārya 120
Dantyoṣṭhyavidhi 138, 631
Debrunner, Albert. 158, 247, 248, 255, 495
Delbrück, Berthold 247
Deshpande, Madhav M. 35, 40, 43-45, 50, 53, 55, 58, 61, 116, 118, 119, 126, 141, 144, 151, 153, 154, 246, 264, 402, 412, 451, 465, 479, 639, 640, 646, 649, 658-660, 674
Durga (on *Kātantra*) 660
Durga (on *NR*) 528
Fry, A.H. 90, 306, 334
Gaṇeś Bhaṭ Dādā 88
Gārgya 88, 106
Gāyatrībrāhmaṇa 206
Ghatage, A.M. 189, 395
Ghosh, Manomohan 161, 162
Gobhilagṛhyasūtra 167
Gopālayajvan 64, 66
Gopathabrāhmaṇa 98, 633
Grammont 134
Haridīkṣita 657
Heffner, R-M. S. 176, 184
Hock, H.H. 130
Hrasva Māṇḍūkeya 34, 35, 36, 146
Hueckstedt, Robert 45, 49, 55, 56, 246, 410
Jaiminīyabrāhmaṇa 318, 332
Jaṭāpāṭha 61
Jha, Vasishth Narayan 61, 65
Joshi, S.D. 46, 508
Kaiyaṭa 395, 405, 414
Kāṇvaśuklayajurvedasaṃhitā 186, 188, 195, 203, 206, 228, 665
Kāśikāvṛtti (*KV*) 14, 55, 70, 73, 74, 79, 91, 101, 143, 168, 169, 180, 183, 221-223, 226, 229, 242, 247, 265, 267, 272, 278, 280, 283, 285, 290, 291, 307, 320, 331, 351, 358, 366, 369, 375, 379, 383, 389, 395, 397, 402, 404, 407, 408, 411, 412-414, 417-420, 431, 452, 453, 455, 456, 461, 467, 472, 496, 501, 534, 641, 661, 664, 665, 676, 677, 684
Kātantrarūpamālāvyākaraṇa 634, 673
Kātantravyākaraṇa 634, 652, 660, 673
Kāṭhakabrāhmaṇasaṃkalana 206

Kāṭhakasaṃhitā 188, 203, 207, 279, 456
Kaṭhasaṃhitā 188, 203, 207
Katre, S.L. 4, 11
Katre, S.M. 168
Kātyāyana 46, 52, 53, 413-415, 480, 521, 540, 549, 572, 640, 658, 660, 671, 674
Kautsavyākaraṇa 4, 7, 8, 10, 13, 77, 79, 92, 210, 233, 422, 545, 630, 631 (passim)
Keśava Bhaṭ 88, 577
Kiparsky, Paul 49, 55, 265, 267
Kṛṣṇadāsa 75, 77, 92, 187, 320, 407, 631 (passim)
Kṣīrasvāmin 464
Kṣīrataraṅiṇī 464
Kuddala, Shivadatta 2
Kumārasambhava 657
KV, see: *Kāśikāvṛtti*
Ladefoged, Peter 118
Laghuśabdaratna 657, 680
Laghuśabdenduśekhara 643, 657, 670
Laghusiddhāntakaumudī 148
Lanman, C.R. 207, 260, 271, 307, 330, 394, 395, 465, 558
Macdonell, A. 269, 482
Mādhyandinaśuklayajurveda-saṃhitā 186, 188, 195, 203, 206, 566
Mahābhāṣya (*MB*) 2, 35, 46, 56, 61, 62, 80, 81, 101, 148, 149, 153, 161, 163, 199, 203, 204, 205, 207, 215, 216, 226, 244, 256, 376, 395, 405, 411, 413-415, 427, 479, 489, 508, 512, 540, 572, 574, 634, 649, 656, 658, 676, 684
Maitrāyaṇīsaṃhitā (*MS*) 115, 186, 188, 195, 203, 207, 247, 465
Mallinātha 657
Māṇḍūkīśikṣā 3, 14, 77, 79, 122, 123, 145, 147, 149, 424, 425, 572, 574
Mantrabrāhmaṇa 169
MB, see: *Mahābhāṣya*
Mehendale, M.A. 222
Mishra, R.C. 92
MS, see: *Maitrāyaṇīsaṃhitā*
Mugdhabodhavyakaraṇa 634
Müller, Max 100, 118, 252, 572
Muralīdharamiśra 657
Nāgeśabhaṭṭa 2, 46, 57, 643, 657, 670
Nāradaśikṣā 37, 138
Negelein, J. 131, 135, 141
Nighaṇṭu 397
Nirukta (*NR*) 31, 37, 98, 115, 226, 400, 455, 464, 479, 528, 562, 632, 647
  1.1: 528
  1.9: 647
  1.12: 226
  1.13: 528
  1.17: 37, 98
  2.1: 562
  2.13: 528
  3.1: 528
  3.19: 464
  5.4: 455
  9.5: 400
  7.10: 115
  10.34: 115
  13.13: 632
NR, see: *Nirukta*
Nyāsa (on *Kāśikāvṛtti*) 369, 467, 534

Nyāyasūtra 647
Oldenberg, Hermann 80
Padamañjarī (on *Kāśikāvṛtti*) 467
Padapāṭha 60, 61, 65-67, 81, 93, 98, 99, 102, (passim)
Pañcasandhi 7, 13, 75, 77-79
Pāṇḍeya, Rāmājñā 161, 638
Pandeya, Vijay Shankar 170
Pandit, S.P. 88, 92, 207, 275, 577
Pāṇini 2, 14, 37, 38, 46, 50-53, 55, 56-58, 62-81, 87, 89, 91, 93, 99, 100, (passim)
1.1.2: 647
1.1.6: 376
1.1.7: 182, 645
1.1.8: 141
1.1.9: 51, 70, 113, 126, 141, 146, 149, 156, 276, 412, 635, 636, 638, 639, 645
1.1.10: 2, 52, 57, 58, 78, 148, 149, 154, 639, 646
1.1.11: 68, 218, 405, 665
1.1.12: 222, 223
1.1.13: 221
1.1.14: 224, 225, 641, 647
1.1.16: 81, 227, 229, 665
1.1.17: 68, 215, 225
1.1.18: 215, 225
1.1.19: 68, 69, 216, 218, 664
1.1.27: 649
1.1.37: 319, 497
1.1.41: 224
1.1.43: 69
1.1.45: 536
1.1.46: 649
1.1.47: 454
1.1.49: 164, 176, 649
1.1.50: 55, 56, 211, 246, 277
1.1.51: 199
1.1.56: 210, 651
1.1.64: 657, 662
1.1.65: 68, 69, 241
1.1.66: 649
1.1.67: 649
1.1.68: 53
1.1.69: 51, 56, 574, 639, 649
1.1.70: 46, 51, 70
1.1.73: 556
1.2.17: 656
1.2.27: 197, 643
1.2.29: 75, 643
1.2.30: 75, 643
1.2.31: 75, 643
1.2.32: 76, 124, 125, 643
1.2.39: 445
1.2.40: 173, 441, 447
1.2.41: 214, 641
1.2.45: 454, 479, 648
1.2.46: 454, 479
1.2.64: 78, 652
1.3.1: 479, 647
1.3.2: 641
1.3.3: 78, 639
1.3.10: 55, 56, 251
1.3.13: 71
1.3.14: 91, 143, 283
1.4.2: 653
1.4.3: 433
1.4.9: 512
1.4.10: 642
1.4.11: 642
1.4.12: 642
1.4.14: 647
1.4.42: 635
1.4.56: 226
1.4.57: 479, 496
1.4.58: 226, 479
1.4.59: 226, 479, 492, 648

Pāṇini (cont.)
1.4.60: 481, 492, 495, 648
1.4.61: 481, 496
1.4.62: 481, 496
1.4.63: 481
1.4.64: 481, 494
1.4.65: 481, 497
1.4.66: 481
1.4.67: 481, 495
1.4.68: 481, 494
1.4.69: 481, 494
1.4.70: 481
1.4.71: 481, 495
1.4.72: 481
1.4.73: 481
1.4.74: 481, 495
1.4.75: 481
1.4.76: 481
1.4.77: 481, 494
1.4.78: 481
1.4.79: 481
1.4.84: 81
1.4.93: 501
1.4.96: 634
1.4.101: 113
1.4.104: 455
1.4.109: 46
2.1.1: 489, 502
2.1.2: 508
2.1.4: 508, 540
2.1.17: 414
2.1.58: 62, 101
2.4.2: 137
2.4.34: 457
2.4.40: 534
3.1.6: 67, 89, 234
3.1.9: 539
3.1.93: 71, 649
3.1.134: 653
3.2.3: 543
3.2.67: 543
3.2.74: 543
3.2.83
3.2.88: 71, 534
3.2.107: 236, 534
3.2.171: 71, 534,
3.2.174: 544
3.3.57: 464
3.4.101: 55
4.1.2: 70, 509
4.1.31: 380
4.1.45: 223
4.1.76: 68
4.4.128: 68
4.4.142: 68, 519
4.1.43: 519
4.4.143: 519
5.1.123: 612, 613
5.2.37: 521
5.2.39: 68, 547
5.2.94: 71, 517, 526
5.3.22: 521
5.3.37: 677
5.3.69: 66, 527
5.3.92: 516
5.3.93: 516
5.4.17: 65
5.4.21: 526
5.4.67: 496
5.4.129: 250
6.1.7: 71, 589
6.1.39: 676
6.1.65: 456
6.1.67: 68
6.1.68: 223
6.1.73: 399
6.1.74: 399
6.1.75: 399, 673

Pāṇini (cont.)
6.1.76: 399, 673
6.1.77: 56, 246, 247, 410, 431
6.1.78: 411, 654
6.1.79: 654, 655
6.1.84: 68, 412, 414, 453
6.1.85: 656
6.1.87: 414
6.1.88: 408, 418, 419, 661
6.1.89: 414, 660-662
6.1.90: 69, 418
6.1.91: 68, 417
6.1.92: 660
6.1.94: 413, 657, 661, 662
6.1.95: 408, 662
6.1.101: 68, 74, 412, 658
6.1.109: 663
6.1.115: 68, 420, 421, 663
6.1.122: 654, 663
6.1.123: 655
6.1.124: 655
6.1.125: 68. 623, 624
6.1.128: 415
6.1.129: 199, 248, 624, 667
6.1.132: 681, 685
6.1.133: 63, 102
6.1.134: 686
6.1.137: 676, 677
6.1.138: 677
6.1.157: 560, 682
6.1.193: 519
6.1.197: 68
6.1.223: 68
6.2.49: 481
6.2.139: 481
6.3.14: 62, 101
6.3.23: 684
6.3.25: 549
6.3.26: 549
6.3.67: 495
6.3.78: 654
6.3.90: 569
6.3.91: 547, 569
6.3.109: 327, 465, 682
6.3.110: 544
6.3.111: 72, 99, 278, 279, 283
6.3.112: 379
6.3.113: 379
6.3.116: 376
6.3.124: 383
6.3.125: 375
6.3.128:381
6.3.129: 381
6.3.130: 381
6.3.132: 378
6.3.134: 68, 377
6.4.4: 543
6.4.16: 234
6.4.64: 534
6.4.71: 591
6.4.74: 591
6.4.75: 591
6.4.78: 71, 589
6.4.88: 536
6.4.100: 534
6.4.132: 662
6.4.143: 516
6.4.148: 521
7.1.1: 641
7.1.36: 237, 238
7.1.37: 331
7.1.39: 216
7.1.72: 299, 454
7.2.7: 642
7.2.67: 534
7.3.55: 68
7.3.73: 55
7.3.103: 68

Pāṇini (cont.)
7.4.83: 71, 589
8.1.41: 574
8.1.71: 482
8.2.1: 408, 471, 505, 637, 639, 640, 648, 679
8.2.7: 666
8.2.9: 242, 387, 546
8.2.18: 67, 69, 161, 202-204, 207
8.2.23: 395, 397, 652
8.2.30: 250
8.2.31: 72, 99, 278
8.2.32: 245
8.2.39: 264, 265, 269
8.2.40: 72, 99, 278
8.2.41: 99, 307
8.2.66: 73, 242, 680
8.2.67: 530
8.2.68: 318
8.2.69: 684
8.2.70: 319, 320, 684, 685
8.2.71: 319, 320
8.2.82: 505, 665
8.2.83: 666
8.2.84: 665
8.2.85: 666
8.2.86: 161, 199, 642, 666, 667
8.2.88: 666
8.2.89: 666
8.2.91: 666
8.2.92: 666
8.2.93: 666
8.2.94: 666
8.2.95: 666
8.2.96: 666
8.2.97: 249, 504, 666
8.2.98: 666
8.2.99: 666
8.2.100: 641, 666
8.2.101: 666
8.2.102: 666
8.2.105: 164, 641
8.2.106: 164, 166
8.3.1: 68
8.3.2: 534
8.3.4: 189, 676
8.3.6: 289, 290, 676, 682
8.3.7: 74, 291, 534, 677
8.3.8: 534
8.3.10: 677
8.3.11: 678
8.3.13: 72, 99, 278, 279, 283
8.3.14: 158, 389, 653
8.3.15: 310, 314, 680
8.3.17: 682
8.3.18: 125, 146, 287, 652
8.3.19: 81, 285, 287, 652
8.3.23: 408, 673
8.3.24: 208, 471
8.3.26: 674
8.3.27: 674
8.3.28: 73, 181, 183, 271, 272, 671
8.3.29: 73, 181, 183, 272, 670
8.3.30: 73, 181, 183, 271, 272
8.3.31: 181, 272
8.3.32: 180, 397
8.3.34: 676
8.3.35: 680
8.3.36: 73, 183, 680
8.3.38: 169, 683
8.3.41: 331
8.3.43: 683
8.3.44: 683
8.3.45: 683
8.3.48: 680, 682
8.3.55: 349

Pāṇini (cont.)
8.3.56: 349, 374
8.3.57: 69, 349, 355, 357, 359
8.3.58: 356, 357
8.3.59: 256, 355, 357
8.3.63: 359
8.3.65: 358
8.3.73: 371
8.3.74: 371
8.3.75: 371
8.3.76: 369
8.3.82: 363
8.3.86: 167, 168, 169
8.3.88: 366
8.3.92: 362
8.3.97: 362
8.3.98: 366
8.3.99: 74
8.3.101: 350, 351
8.3.103: 352
8.3.106: 356, 364
8.3.107: 364
8.3.108: 369, 370
8.3.110: 368, 372
8.4.1: 451, 452, 456, 471, 472, 475
8.4.2: 69, 451, 456, 474, 475
8.4.3: 452
8.4.7: 453
8.4.11: 68, 454-456
8.4.14: 331, 453, 456, 600
8.4.15: 468, 600
8.4.16: 600
8.4.22: 472, 473
8.4.24: 675
8.4.26: 467
8.4.27: 459, 461, 463
8.4.28: 459-461
8.4.36: 472
8.4.37: 471
8.4.38: 475
8.4.39: 89, 473
8.4.40: 247, 250, 278
8.4.41: 72, 73, 278, 354
8.4.42: 280
8.4.45: 62, 72, 101, 267, 407, 408, 669, 670
8.4.46: 195, 196, 394, 403
8.4.47: 394-396
8.4.48: 269, 394, 671
8.4.49: 394, 404
8.4.50: 394, 402
8.4.51: 394, 396, 652
8.4.52: 394
8.4.53: 55, 264
8.4.55: 266
8.4.56: 69, 75, 107, 265
8.4.57: 212
8.4.58: 69, 408, 471
8.4.60: 276, 672
8.4.61: 282, 672
8.4.62: 269, 670, 671
8.4.68: 52, 156, 638
Pāṇinīyadhātupāṭha 148, 223, 250, 456, 464
Pāṇinīyaśikṣā 14, 37, 43, 50, 54, 71, 74, 75, 77, 79, 129, 131, 142, 144, 149, 152, 161, 197, 636, 638, 640, 642, 644
Pañjikā (on *Pāṇinīyaśikṣā*) 161
Pāraskaragṛhyasūtra 167
Paribhāṣenduśekhara 149, 634, 646
Pāriśikṣā 423
Patañjali 35, 46, 49, 50, 56, 57, 61, 80, 101, 116, 121, 149, 153, 163, 199, 203, 204, 207, 215, 244, 249, 256, 327, 376, 395,

405, 411, 413, 479, 480, 512, 540, 574, 640, 649, 662
Pauṣkarasādi 269, 671
PAV, see: *Atharvaveda, Paippalāda*
Pāyaguṇḍe, Vaidyanātha 2
Phiṭsūtra 64, 481
Pike, Kenneth 128
Piṅgala 187, 189, 643, 658
Pradīpa (on *Mahābhāṣya*) 376, 405
Prakāśa (on *Prakriyākaumudī*) 657, 660, 662, 676
Prakriyākaumudī 657, 660-663, 676
Pratiśākhya (generic ref.) 2, 3, 31, 38, 39, 47, 48, 50-52, 54, 59, 60, 62-66, 77, 80, 83, 84, (passim)
Prātiśākhyajyotsnā 77
Prātiśākhyapradīpaśikṣā 492
Prauḍhamanoramā 657, 670, 679
Puṇyarāja 634, 635
Rai, Ram Kumar 192
Rāmacandra Śeṣa 657
Raśmi (on *Prakāśa* on *Prakriyākaumudī*) 657
Ratate, Narayan Shastri 4
Ratnākara 657
Regnier, M. 252
Renou, Louis 167, 241, 455, 591
Ṛgveda (*RV*) 35, 38, 63, 74, 80, 87, 145, 162, 166, 169, 175, 177, 179, 186, 193, 195, 198, 200, 206, 213, 216, 217, 220, 221, 226, 228, 311, 319, 320, 328, 351, 354, 388, 404, 420, 464, 476, 482, 506, 509, 538, 545, 551, 559, 561, 565, 566, 568, 576, 592, 593, 602, 604, 632, 633, 653, 663-665, 678, 679, 681, 682, 685, 686
1.2.1: 665, 681
1.2.2: 681
1.2.5: 228, 681
1.2.6: 681
1.2.8: 681
1.2.9: 681
1.10.1: 681
1.12.3: 678
1.15.5: 678
1.18.2: 551
1.24.8: 568
1.27.1: 206
1.32.15: 686
1.34.4: 509
1.36.20: 506
1.38.3: 226
1.44.9: 685
1.46.6: 221
1.49.4: 685
1.60.1: 509
1.83.1: 509
1.85.7: 663
1.186.6: 561
1.116.21: 328
1.164.21: 602
2.13.6: 186
2.13.9: 509
2.24.1: 686
2.33.4: 545
2.39.2: 665
3.9.2: 175
3.19.1: 186
4.2.6: 678
4.9.2: 509
4.9.8: 653
4.25.6: 509
4.26.5: 509

Ṛgveda (cont.)
4.35.7: 311
4.49.4: 221
4.50.8: 686
4.51.5: 482
5.28.3: 565
5.29.13: 226
5.51.5: 228
5.62.5: 195
5.99.7: 228
6.28.1: 220
6.70.1: 664
6.75.4: 664
7.1.5: 506
7.55.3: 328
7.66.16: 193, 198
7.96.4: 388
7.104.6: 404
7.104.23: 506
8.1.20: 179
8.19.5: 633
8.33.9: 354
8.49.20: 506
8.56.4: 226
8.100.10: 632
9.3.10: 682
9.6.2: 665
9.12.3: 216, 217, 664
9.52.4: 681
9.66.16: 681
9.69.10: 681
9.83.1: 685
9.96.12: 166
9.100.11: 632
10.10.3: 220
10.10.14: 604
10.16.1: 592
10.17.8: 220
10.32.3: 74, 81, 351
10.34.11: 195
10.36.14: 177
10.50.4: 319, 320
10.83.5: 593
10.84.3: 220
10.97.15: 169
10.109.1: 420
10.110.8: 566
10.120.3: 220
10.125.2: 509
10.132.3: 679
10.146.1: 200, 213
10.161.5: 464
Ṛgvedakhilasūktas 142, 213
Ṛgvedaprātiśākhya (*RPR*) 2, 36-38, 40, 42, 58, 62, 71, 80, 83, 98-102, 104, 106, 107, 110, 111, 114, 116, 117, 123, 126, 136, 139, 151, 181, 184, 187, 191, 197, 213, 215, 217, 223, 246, 252, 258, 315, 319, 335, 395-397, 408, 416, 436, 437, 445, 461, 479, 492, 572, 574, 621, 634, 635, 637, 644, 680
Ṛktantra 38
Roth, R. 2, 7, 82, 115, 165, 167, 247, 274, 289, 308, 330, 400, 566
RPR, see: *Ṛgvedaprātiśākhya*
RV, see: *Ṛgveda*
Śabdakalpadruma 289, 609
Sadāśivabhaṭṭīya (on *Laghuśabdenduśekhara*) 657
Ṣaḍviṃśabrāhmaṇa 195
Śākalya 36-38, 61, 80, 81, 87, 90, 229, 287, 306, 334, 396, 556, 652
Śākaṭāyana 88, 89, 90, 94, 107, 108, 110, 287, 288, 306, 334,

402, 459, 460, 478, 495, 497, 530, 652
Śāṃkhamitri 243, 448-450
Śāṃkhāyana-Āraṇyaka 36, 633
Śāntanava 64
Sārasvatavyākaraṇa 13, 79, 637, 641, 642, 644-650, 662, 663, 673-675, 686, 687
Sarasvatīkaṇṭhābharaṇa 650
Sarvasammataśikṣā 157
Śarvavarman 634
Śatapathabrāhmaṇa (*ŚB*) 32, 38, 247, 551, 633
Śaunaka 38, 80, 81, 86-89, 93, 94, 99, 106-110, 161, 264, 266, 268, 269, 272, 498
Śaunakaśikṣā 144, 187
Śaunakīyā Caturādhyāyikā (*CA*)
1.1.1: 15, 97, 438
1.1.2: 2, 15, 72, 91, 98, 278, 279, 283, 418, 635, 649, 687
1.1.3: 2, 62, 63, 72, 83, 100, 267
1.1.4: 15, 62, 63, 83, 101, 637
1.1.5: 15, 102, 309, 615, 647
1.1.6: 15, 103, 413
1.1.7: 15, 104, 194
1.1.8: 15, 104, 105, 263, 265, 637, 668
1.1.9: 15, 105, 637
1.1.10: 15, 75, 87, 88, 93, 94, 98, 106, 108, 171, 264, 266, 460, 498, 530, 637, 651, 668
1.1.11: 15, 107, 108, 288, 637, 651
1.1.12: 15, 40, 41, 58, 110, 116, 288, 401, 637, 676
1.1.13: 15, 113
1.1.14: 15, 113, 539
1.1.15: 15, 118, 539
1.1.16: 15, 75, 85, 120, 242, 449, 643
1.1.17: 15, 76, 123, 431, 449, 643
1.1.18: 15, 76, 125, 479, 635
1.1.19: 15, 70, 72, 74, 126, 137, 138, 140, 636
1.1.20: 15, 72, 129, 636
1.1.21: 15, 72, 74, 131, 162, 636
1.1.22: 15, 72, 75, 76, 130, 132, 636
1.1.23: 15, 134, 636
1.1.24: 15, 130, 135, 636
1.1.25: 15, 72, 74-76, 127, 136, 138, 140, 162, 636
1.1.26: 15, 125, 138, 140, 254, 636
1.1.27: 15, 70, 113, 125, 140, 146, 156, 412, 636
1.1.28: 15, 72, 75, 76, 85, 128, 132, 133, 142, 425, 636
1.1.29: 15, 76, 145, 638, 645
1.1.30: 15, 77, 146, 638
1.1.31: 15, 77, 147, 151, 638
1.1.32: 15, 77, 129, 149, 638
1.1.33: 15, 150, 638
1.1.34: 16, 151, 152, 162, 638, 644, 647
1.1.35: 16, 154, 638, 647
1.1.36: 16, 150, 155, 638
1.1.37: 16, 157, 256, 639
1.1.38: 16, 159, 160, 639
1.1.39: 16, 160, 639
1.1.40: 16, 54, 162, 639
1.1.41: 16, 163, 248, 639, 646

Śaunakīyā Caturādhyāyikā (cont.)
1.2.1: 16, 167, 184, 648
1.2.2: 16, 169, 170, 250, 648
1.2.3: 16, 169, 170, 173, 640
1.2.4: 16, 87, 175, 648
1.2.5: 16, 176, 180, 648
1.2.6: 16, 178, 179, 648
1.2.7: 16, 179, 648
1.2.8: 16, 180, 648
1.2.9: 16, 73, 87, 171, 182, 250, 252, 268, 648
1.2.10: 16, 70, 170, 171, 184, 252
1.2.11: 16, 182, 185, 642
1.2.12: 16, 187, 190, 642, 643
1.2.13: 16, 189, 230, 642
1.2.14: 16, 190, 642
1.2.15: 16, 69, 191, 642
1.2.16: 16, 192, 642
1.2.17: 16, 194, 642
1.2.18: 16, 195, 255, 402, 403, 642
1.2.19: 16, 196, 642
1.2.20: 16, 198, 642
1.2.21: 16, 198, 643
1.2.22: 16, 165, 199, 643
1.3.1: 17, 201, 552
1.3.2: 17, 67, 69, 202
1.3.3: 17, 203
1.3.4: 17, 203, 205, 653
1.3.5: 17, 207, 297, 298, 356, 674, 679
1.3.6: 17, 113, 208, 210, 292
1.3.7: 17, 210, 211
1.3.8: 17, 113, 211, 624, 625
1.3.9: 17, 213, 624
1.3.10: 17, 68, 214, 617, 623, 663
1.3.11: 17, 215, 225, 623, 663
1.3.12: 17, 68, 69, 216, 218, 225, 664
1.3.13: 17, 68, 218, 219, 664
1.3.14: 17, 219, 664
1.3.15: 17, 87, 220, 664
1.3.16: 17, 68, 87, 222, 664
1.3.17: 17, 214, 223, 617, 641, 664
1.3.18: 17, 225, 363, 664
1.3.19: 17, 68, 227, 664
1.3.20: 17, 229, 665
1.3.21: 17, 230, 641, 665
1.3.22: 17, 231, 363, 641
1.3.23: 17, 232
1.3.24: 17, 85, 87, 233
1.3.25: 17, 67, 85, 87, 89, 234
1.3.26: 17, 68, 69, 85, 235, 237, 238
1.3.27: 17, 236, 237
1.3.28: 17, 237, 237
1.3.29: 17, 238
1.4.1: 18, 68, 69, 73, 241, 648
1.4.2: 18, 242, 644
1.4.3: 18, 84, 244, 399, 670
1.4.4: 18, 246, 277, 296, 305, 410
1.4.5: 18, 165, 166, 247, 261
1.4.6: 18, 199, 248
1.4.7: 18, 182, 249, 256, 645
1.4.8: 18, 139, 251, 272
1.4.9: 18, 138, 254
1.4.10: 18, 157, 255, 416, 655
1.4.11: 18, 157, 257, 259, 416, 655
1.4.12: 18, 257, 258, 301, 302, 523, 667
1.4.13: 18, 256, 258, 667
1.4.14: 18, 199, 248, 259, 260, 261, 504, 667

Śaunakīyā Caturādhyāyikā (cont.)
2.1.1: 18, 263, 396, 442, 650, 668
2.1.2: 18, 69, 87, 263, 419, 615, 668, 669
2.1.3: 18, 69, 265, 669
2.1.4: 18, 266, 669
2.1.5: 18, 62, 72, 101, 267, 408, 668, 669
2.1.6: 18, 83, 243, 268, 280, 355, 670
2.1.7: 18, 269, 670, 671
2.1.8: 18, 270, 670
2.1.9: 18, 83, 87, 180, 181, 271, 273, 275, 284, 670, 671
2.1.10: 19, 274, 280, 671
2.1.11: 19, 274, 672
2.1.12: 19, 87, 275, 672
2.1.13: 19, 276, 280, 672
2.1.14: 19, 73, 87, 277, 672
2.1.15: 19, 278, 283, 672
2.1.16: 19, 278, 279, 672
2.1.17: 19, 272, 274, 216, 278, 280, 399, 671, 672
2.1.18: 19, 282, 563, 672
2.1.19: 19, 87, 283, 685
2.1.20: 19, 283, 284, 652
2.1.21: 19, 210, 285, 292, 308, 406, 678
2.1.22: 19, 286
2.1.23: 19, 286
2.1.24: 19, 107, 108, 110, 287, 652
2.1.25: 19, 288, 676
2.1.26: 19, 73, 289, 290, 295, 408, 677
2.1.27: 19, 209, 290, 292, 678
2.1.28: 19, 208, 294, 678, 679
2.1.29: 19, 209, 290, 294, 678
2.1.30: 19, 295, 296, 678
2.1.31: 19, 69, 296, 297, 407, 408, 673
2.1.32: 19, 297, 674
2.1.33: 19, 298, 675
2.1.34: 19, 299, 356, 363, 675, 677
2.1.35: 19, 296, 297, 299, 300, 675
2.1.36: 19, 300, 675
2.1.37: 19, 298, 301, 675
2.1.38: 19, 257, 258, 301, 675
2.1.39: 19, 303, 679
2.2.1: 19, 87, 246, 305, 679
2.2.2: 19, 210, 285, 292, 294, 308, 321, 678, 680
2.2.3: 20, 73, 241, 283, 308, 681
2.2.4: 20, 283, 309, 681
2.2.5: 20, 310, 684
2.2.6: 20, 312, 684
2.2.7: 20, 312, 313, 684
2.2.8: 20, 87, 313, 315, 685
2.2.9: 20, 315, 685
2.2.10: 20, 310, 316, 685
2.2.11: 20, 87, 317, 685
2.2.12: 20, 87, 317, 685
2.2.13: 20, 87, 318, 327, 685
2.2.14: 20, 320, 681
2.2.15: 20, 321
2.2.16: 20, 241, 321, 679
2.2.17: 20, 322, 324, 327, 406
2.2.18: 20, 324, 681, 685
2.2.19: 20, 324
2.2.20: 20, 324, 605, 682, 686
2.3.1: 20, 326, 682
2.3.2: 20, 327, 539, 682

Śaunakīyā Caturādhyāyikā (cont.)
2.3.3: 20, 68, 91, 328, 329, 334, 348, 574, 676, 682
2.3.4: 20, 87, 330, 334, 348, 682, 683
2.3.5: 20, 332, 348, 683
2.3.6: 20, 86, 87, 90, 332, 334, 348, 683
2.3.7: 20, 335, 339, 683
2.3.8: 20, 87, 335, 683
2.3.9: 20, 337, 683
2.3.10: 20, 337, 683
2.3.11: 20, 338, 683
2.3.12: 20, 339, 683
2.3.13: 20, 339, 683
2.3.14: 21, 87, 340, 341, 348, 684
2.3.15: 21, 87, 341, 348, 684
2.3.16: 21, 87, 342, 343, 348, 684
2.3.17: 21, 87, 343, 348, 574, 684
2.3.18: 21, 344, 348, 684
2.3.19: 21, 344, 684
2.3.20: 21, 345, 684
2.3.21: 21, 335, 338, 345, 348, 684
2.4.1: 21, 348, 349, 683
2.4.2: 21, 348, 570
2.4.3: 21, 68, 74, 348, 350
2.4.4: 21, 348, 351
2.4.5: 21, 348, 352
2.4.6: 21, 87, 348, 353, 354
2.4.7: 21, 69, 354, 356-360
2.4.8: 21, 355, 357
2.4.9: 21, 356
2.4.10: 21, 68, 279, 356-358, 366
2.4.11: 21, 68, 358, 587
2.4.12: 21, 359
2.4.13: 21, 360
2.4.14: 21, 361, 362
2.4.15: 21, 362
2.4.16: 21, 363, 365
2.4.17: 21, 68, 363, 364
2.4.18: 21, 353, 363, 364, 366, 368
2.4.19: 21, 365
2.4.20: 21, 366
2.4.21: 21, 367
2.4.22: 21, 357, 366, 368, 371, 372, 451
2.4.23: 21, 357, 369, 370, 373
2.4.24: 22, 357, 370
2.4.25: 22, 357, 371
2.4.26: 22, 357, 368, 371
2.4.27: 22, 357, 372
3.1.1: 22, 374, 685
3.1.2: 22, 375, 599, 600
3.1.3: 22, 375, 568
3.1.4: 22, 68, 364, 376, 604, 685
3.1.5: 22, 87, 377
3.1.6: 22, 378
3.1.7: 22, 379
3.1.8: 22, 380
3.1.9: 22, 381
3.1.10: 22, 382
3.1.11: 22, 382
3.1.12: 22, 383, 678
3.1.13: 22, 384, 385, 390, 589, 682
3.1.14: 22, 385, 386, 593
3.1.15: 22, 386, 390
3.1.16: 22, 386, 685
3.1.17: 22, 378
3.1.18: 22, 388, 529
3.1.19: 22, 388, 389

Śaunakīyā Caturādhyāyikā (cont.)
3.1.20: 22, 87, 283, 389, 685
3.1.21: 22, 384, 386, 390, 411, 592, 595
3.1.22: 22, 390, 411, 594, 595
3.1.23: 22, 349, 391
3.1.24: 22, 391
3.1.25: 22 , 392
3.2.1: 23, 244, 394, 397, 651, 672
3.2.2: 23, 180, 396, 673
3.2.3: 23, 193, 196, 398, 651, 674
3.2.4: 23, 399, 673
3.2.5: 23, 112, 399, 673
3.2.6: 23, 401
3.2.7: 23, 401, 651
3.2.8: 23, 195, 196, 402, 652
3.2.9: 23, 403
3.2.10: 23, 68, 87, 404, 663
3.2.11: 23, 405
3.2.12: 23, 406, 411, 680
3.2.13: 23, 407
3.2.14: 23, 407, 651
3.2.15: 23, 408, 419, 617, 656
3.2.16: 23, 246, 410, 585, 618, 651, 653
3.2.17: 23, 285, 410, 654
3.2.18: 23, 68, 411, 453, 656
3.2.19: 23, 68, 74, 412, 656
3.2.20: 23, 413, 656
3.2.21: 23, 411, 413, 417, 659
3.2.22: 23, 320, 321, 414, 659
3.2.23: 23, 415, 417, 659
3.2.24: 23, 87, 416, 417
3.2.25: 23, 416, 417, 659
3.2.26: 23, 69, 417
3.2.27: 23, 276, 418, 661
3.2.28: 23, 419, 661
3.2.29: 23, 419, 661
3.2.30: 23, 320, 420, 426, 427, 663
3.2.31: 23, 87, 421
3.3.1: 24, 26, 242, 422, 425
3.3.2: 24, 26, 423, 426
3.3.3: 24, 26, 424
3.3.4: 24, 26, 424
3.3.5: 24, 26, 425-427, 429
3.3.6: 24, 424, 426, 440
3.3.7: 24, 424, 427, 429, 440
3.3.8: 24, 424, 429, 430
3.3.9: 24, 424, 430, 431, 611
3.3.10: 24, 424, 431
3.3.11: 24, 424, 433
3.3.12: 24, 424, 435
3.3.13: 24, 424, 429, 435, 441
3.3.14: 24, 424, 436, 441
3.3.15: 24, 436
3.3.16: 24, 437, 614
3.3.17: 24, 425-427, 440
3.3.18: 24, 435, 441, 447
3.3.19: 24, 435, 442, 446, 450, 506, 618
3.3.20: 24, 435, 443, 446
3.3.21: 24, 435, 441, 444, 447
3.3.22: 24, 441, 445, 447
3.3.23: 24, 445
3.3.24: 24, 436, 446
3.3.25: 24, 445, 446, 506
3.3.26: 24, 26, 447, 644, 645
3.3.27: 24, 26, 447, 645
3.3.28: 24, 26, 448
3.3.29: 24, 26, 448
3.3.30: 24, 26, 243, 448
3.3.31: 24, 26, 243, 448
3.3.32: 24, 26, 243, 449
3.3.33: 24, 26, 243, 449
3.3.34: 24, 26, 243, 450

Śaunakīyā Caturādhyāyikā (cont.)
3.3.35: 24, 26, 443, 450, 506, 642
3.4.1: 25, 368, 451, 474, 653
3.4.2: 25, 452, 456, 462, 469
3.4.3: 25, 453
3.4.4: 25, 68, 454
3.4.5: 25, 87, 452, 456, 459, 468-470, 473
3.4.6: 25, 87, 457, 459, 464, 466
3.4.7: 25, 459
3.4.8: 25, 459, 460, 463
3.4.9: 25, 459, 461, 463
3.4.10: 25, 459, 462, 471
3.4.11: 25, 459, 462
3.4.12: 25, 459, 463
3.4.13: 25, 464
3.4.14: 25, 465
3.4.15: 25, 466
3.4.16: 25, 466
3.4.17: 25, 467, 470
3.4.18: 25, 457, 468
3.4.19: 25, 469
3.4.20: 25, 468, 470
3.4.21: 25, 462, 470, 472, 604, 615
3.4.22: 25, 471
3.4.23: 25, 472
3.4.24: 25, 87, 88, 457, 473
3.4.25: 25, 69, 451, 473, 653
3.4.26: 25, 69, 451, 474, 653
3.4.27: 25, 475
3.4.28. : 25, 476, 561
4.1.1: 26, 28, 478
4.1.2: 26, 28, 478, 479
4.1.3: 26, 28, 478, 479
4.1.4: 26, 28, 478, 480
4.1.5: 26, 28, 478, 481, 499, 500
4.1.6: 26, 28, 478, 482, 499, 500
4.1.7: 26, 28, 478, 483, 509
4.1.8: 26, 28, 478, 484
4.1.9: 26, 28, 478, 484
4.1.10: 26, 28, 478, 485, 511
4.1.11: 26, 28, 478, 486
4.1.12: 26, 28, 478, 487
4.1.13: 26, 28, 478, 487
4.1.14: 26, 28, 478, 488
4.1.15: 26, 28, 478, 489
4.1.16: 26, 28, 478, 489
4.1.17: 26, 28, 478, 490
4.1.18: 26, 28, 478, 490
4.1.19: 26, 28, 478, 488, 491, 647
4.1.20: 26, 28, 478, 488, 492, 642
4.1.21: 26, 28, 478, 488, 492
4.1.22: 26, 28, 478, 481, 493, 499
4.1.23: 26, 410, 478, 504
4.1.24: 26, 482, 483, 499, 500
4.1.25: 27, 258, 500
4.1.26: 27, 502
4.1.27: 27, 503
4.1.28: 27, 261, 504
4.1.29: 27, 499, 500, 505, 507
4.1.30: 27, 505
4.1.31: 27, 507, 539
4.1.32: 27, 507, 540
4.1.33: 27, 70, 508
4.1.34: 27, 510, 512, 529, 540, 598
4.1.35: 27, 512, 566
4.1.36: 27, 513, 522
4.1.37: 27, 513, 522

Śaunakīyā Caturādhyāyikā (cont.)
4.1.38: 27, 71, 267, 514, 522, 543, 555
4.1.39: 27, 516, 526, 546
4.1.40: 27, 517, 518, 546-548
4.1.41: 27, 518
4.1.42: 27, 68, 519
4.1.43: 27, 520
4.1.44: 27, 521
4.1.45: 27, 521
4.1.46: 27, 71, 522, 526
4.1.47: 27, 522
4.1.48: 27, 71, 523
4.1.49: 27, 65, 66, 71, 519-522, 525
4.1.50: 27, 66, 526
4.1.51: 27, 526
4.1.52: 27, 107, 498, 510, 529
4.1.53: 27, 530, 531
4.1.54: 27, 531
4.1.55: 27, 531, 554
4.1.56: 27, 532
4.1.57: 27, 71, 533-535
4.1.58: 27, 534
4.1.59: 27, 534, 535
4.1.60: 27, 536
4.1.61: 27, 537, 559
4.1.62: 27, 329, 538
4.1.63: 27, 539
4.1.64: 28, 537, 540, 542
4.1.65: 28, 541
4.1.66: 28, 541
4.1.67: 28, 542
4.1.68. : 28, 544
4.2.1: 28, 68, 546, 555
4.2.2: 28, 68, 547, 555
4.2.3: 28, 548, 555
4.2.4: 28, 550, 553, 555
4.2.5: 28, 66, 201, 328, 532, 538, 547, 551, 553, 555, 559
4.2.6: 28, 66, 550, 552, 555
4.2.7: 28, 553, 555
4.2.8: 28, 516, 555, 564
4.2.9: 28, 555, 556
4.2.10: 28, 557, 558
4.2.11: 28, 538, 558
4.2.12: 28, 559
4.2.13: 28, 560
4.2.14: 28, 561, 562
4.2.15: 28, 562
4.2.16: 28, 87, 282, 563
4.2.17: 28, 564
4.2.18: 28, 564, 565, 588
4.2.19: 28, 565, 566
4.2.20: 29, 513, 566
4.2.21: 29, 87, 567
4.2.22: 29, 568
4.2.23: 29, 569
4.2.24: 29, 569
4.2.25: 29, 570
4.2.26: 29, 506, 571
4.3.1: 29, 572
4.3.2: 29, 322, 573, 579, 585, 605, 626
4.3.3: 29, 578-580, 583
4.3.4: 29, 579, 598
4.3.5: 29, 580
4.3.6: 29, 582
4.3.7: 29, 584, 586
4.3.8: 29, 584
4.3.9: 29, 585, 615
4.3.10: 29, 586
4.3.11: 29, 355, 565, 587, 588
4.3.12: 29, 71, 588, 593
4.3.13: 29, 87, 590
4.3.14: 29, 590, 592

Śaunakīyā Caturādhyāyikā (cont.)
4.3.15: 29, 593
4.3.16: 29, 593
4.3.17: 29, 594
4.3.18: 29, 595
4.3.19: 29, 595, 603
4.3.20: 29, 596
4.3.21: 29, 597, 598
4.3.22: 29, 598
4.3.23: 29, 599
4.3.24: 29, 468, 600
4.3.25: 29, 582, 601
4.3.26: 30, 602
4.3.27: 30, 364, 603
4.3.28: 30, 105, 462, 470, 604
4.3.29: 30, 325
4.4.1: 30, 607, 608
4.4.2: 30, 607
4.4.3: 30, 608
4.4.4: 30, 607, 608
4.4.5: 30, 609
4.4.6: 30, 609
4.4.7: 30, 610
4.4.8: 30, 612
4.4.9: 30, 612, 613
4.4.10: 30, 613
4.4.11: 30, 614
4.4.12: 30, 615, 624
4.4.13: 30, 616
4.4.14: 30, 214, 409, 616
4.4.15: 30, 409, 617
4.4.16: 30, 409, 619
4.4.17: 30, 619, 620
4.4.18: 30, 212, 574, 616
4.4.19: 30, 620, 622
4.4.20: 30, 622
4.4.21: 30, 199, 623, 625
4.4.22: 30, 624
4.4.23: 30, 614, 624, 625
4.4.24: 30, 574, 576, 577, 625
4.4.25: 30, 626
4.4.26: 30, 627
4.4.27: 30, 64, 628
ŚAV, see: *Atharvaveda, Śaunakīya*
Sāyaṇa 86, 87, 91-93, 115, 165, 216, 222, 268, 323, 329, 345, 376, 379, 465, 481, 482, 494, 496, 497, 512, 524, 525, 530, 543, 558, 568
ŚB, see: *Śatapathabrāhmaṇa*
Schröder, Otto 465
Shastri, M.D. 2, 83, 100
Shastri, Vishva Bandhu 3, 4, 82, 92, 175, 178
Shukla, J.M. 591
Siddhāntakaumudī (*SK*) 13, 14, 75, 77, 79, 125, 130, 180, 225, 250, 289, 379, 471, 544, 547, 635-642, 648, 649, 652-654, 657, 658, 660-665, 667, 669-673, 675-677, 679, 680, 683, 684
Śikṣā (generic ref.) 31, 37, 39, 47, 48, 50-52, 54, 63, 70
Śikṣāprakāśa (on *Pāṇinīyaśikṣā*) 161
Śikṣāsaṃgraha 3, 123, 138, 147, 424, 425, 492, 574, 646
*Śivasūtra*s 52, 53, 140, 161, 205, 572, 641
SK, see: *Siddhāntakaumudī*
Śrīkṛṣṇapaṇḍita 657, 676
Stautzebach, Ralf 59, 109, 171
Śūravīra Māṇḍūkeya 36
Surya Kanta 2-4, 14, 59, 60, 67, 79, 82-94, 107, 120, 143, 175, 183, 206, 209, 220, 234, 265, 267, 268, 270, 272, 273, 275-

277, 283, 287, 291, 293, 307, 315, 317-319, 327, 328, 331, 333, 334, 336, 337, 341-343, 354, 373, 375, 389-391, 393, 404, 410, 412, 416, 417, 421, 422, 432-434, 456-458, 469, 473, 502-504, 524, 527, 555, 558, 562-563, 567, 568, 580, 590
Taittirīya-Āraṇyaka 549
Taittirīyabrāhmaṇa (*TB*) 491, 559, 566
Taittirīyaprātiśākhya (*TPR*) 38, 50, 64, 99, 102-117, 123, 127, 128, 130, 134, 139, 148, 150, 151, 157, 190, 191, 214, 223, 282, 396, 397, 417, 427, 436, 445, 495
Taittirīyasaṃhitā (*TS*) 64, 115, 166, 169, 179, 185, 186, 188, 195, 206, 215, 230, 247, 253, 279, 307, 328, 427, 472, 495
Taittirīya-Upaniṣad 37
1.2: 37
Tāṇḍyamahābrāhmaṇa 188
Tattvabodhinī (on *SK*) 547, 640-642, 648
TB, see: *Taittirīyabrāhmaṇa*
Thieme, Paul 33, 34, 38
TPR, see: *Taittirīyaprātiśākhya*
Tribhāṣyaratna 115, 116
Tripathi, Ramadeva 2, 161
TS, see: *Taittirīyasaṃhitā*
Turner, R.L. 109, 110
Uddyota (on *MB*) 2, 46
Uṇādisūtra 223, 464, 524
Upalekhasūtra 572, 577, 621
Uvaṭa 2, 58, 62, 64, 83, 100, 101, 110, 217, 492, 562, 634, 637
Vaidikābharaṇa 64, 66, 123
Vājapyāyana 53
Vājasaneyiprātiśākhya (*VPR*) 38, 52, 54, 64, 77, 84, 99, 102, 104, 126, 141, 193, 214, 223, 241, 242, 246, 258, 268, 282, 303, 335, 377, 396, 417, 445, 459, 540, 552, 560, 562, 565, 574, 621, 638, 646
Vājasaneyīsaṃhitā (*VS*) 221, 328, 575, 576
Vākyapadīya 634
Vālmīki 90, 306, 334
Varāhopaiṣad 289
Varma, Siddheshwar 169, 171, 173, 178, 180, 189, 191, 403, 423, 455, 464
Varṇapaṭala 14, 70, 117, 119, 128, 129, 131, 135, 137, 139-141, 143, 160, 425
Varṇaratnapradīpikāśikṣā 646
Vārttika (*Vt.*, by Kātyāyana) 46, 52, 280, 318, 327, 395, 396, 405, 413, 414, 508, 521, 540, 547, 549, 572, 640, 655-658, 660-662, 671, 674, 676, 682, 684
Vātsapra 287
Veṅkaṇ Bhaṭjī 577
Veṅkaṭamādhava 216
VPR, see: *Vājasaneyiprātiśākhya*
VS, see: *Vājasaneyīsaṃhitā*
Vyāḍi 53
Vyāsaśikṣā 37, 150, 307
Wackernagel, Jakob 158, 214, 247, 248, 255, 495, 655
Wadegaonkar, N.D. 657
Weber, Albrecht 3, 4, 108-110

Whitney, W.D. 1-4, 6, 7, 9-32, 82-86, 89, 91, (passim)
Yājñavalkyaśikṣā 37
Yāska 455, 464, 479, 562, 632, 647
Yogopaniṣadaḥ 289